Contemporary Jewish Religious Thought

*Original Essays on Critical Concepts,
Movements, and Beliefs*

Contemporary Jewish Religious Thought

Original Essays on Critical Concepts, Movements, and Beliefs

Arthur A. Cohen and Paul Mendes-Flohr

EDITORS

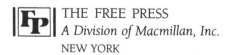 THE FREE PRESS
A Division of Macmillan, Inc.
NEW YORK

Collier Macmillan Publishers
LONDON

The Free Press
A Division of Macmillan, Inc.
866 Third Avenue, New York, N.Y. 10022

Collier Macmillan Canada, Inc.

First Free Press Paperback Edition 1988

Printed in the United States of America

printing number
3 4 5 6 7 8 9 10

Library of Congress Cataloging-in-Publication Data

Contemporary Jewish religious thought: original essays on critical
concepts, movements, and beliefs / Arthur A. Cohen and Paul Mendes
-Flohr, editors.
    p.   cm.
Includes bibliographies and index.
ISBN 0-02-906040-0 (pbk.)
   1. Judaism—Dictionaries. I. Cohen, Arthur Allen.
II. Mendes-Flohr, Paul R.
[BM50.C64 1988]
296'.03'21—dc19
                                     87-33595
                                         CIP

Contents

Preface to the Paperback Edition   xi
Introduction   xiii

AESTHETICS   *Steven S. Schwarzschild*   1
AGGADAH   *David Stern*   7
ANTI-JUDAISM AND ANTI-SEMITISM   *Hyam Maccoby*   13
APOCALYPSE   *Nahum N. Glatzer*   19
ATHEISM   *Gershon Weiler*   23
AUTHORITY   *Stephen Wald*   29
BIBLE CRITICISM   *Moshe Weinfeld*   35
CATASTROPHE   *Alan Mintz*   41
CHARITY   *David Hartman and Tzvi Marx*   47
CHOSEN PEOPLE   *Henri Atlan*   55
CHRISTIANITY   *David Flusser*   61
COMMANDMENTS   *Yeshayahu Leibowitz*   67
COMMUNITY   *Everett Gendler*   81
CONSCIENCE   *Steven S. Schwarzschild*   87
CONSERVATIVE JUDAISM   *Gerson D. Cohen*   91

CONVERT AND CONVERSION   *Johanan Wijnhoven*   101
COVENANT   *Arnold Eisen*   107
CREATION   *Alon Goshen-Gottstein*   113
CULTURE   *Paul Mendes-Flohr*   119
DEATH   *Henry Abramovitch*   131
DESTINY AND FATE   *Albert Friedlander*   137
DOGMA   *Menachem Kellner*   141
ECUMENISM   *Geoffrey Wigoder*   147
EDUCATION   *Janet Aviad*   155
EMANCIPATION   *Paula E. Hyman*   165
ENLIGHTENMENT   *Robert Seltzer*   171
EROS: SEX AND BODY   *David Biale*   177
ESCHATOLOGY   *Arthur A. Cohen*   183
ETERNITY AND TIME   *David Ellenson*   189
ETHICS   *Shalom Rosenberg*   195
EVIL   *Richard L. Rubenstein.*   203
EXEGESIS   *Moshe Greenberg*   211
EXILE   *Arnold Eisen*   219
EXISTENCE   *Richard L. Rubenstein*   227
FAITH   *Louis Jacobs*   233
FAMILY   *David Biale*   239
FEAR OF GOD   *Byron L. Sherwin*   245
FEMINISM   *Susannah Heschel*   255
FREEDOM   *Eugene Borowitz*   261
FREE WILL   *David Winston*   269
GESTURE AND SYMBOL   *Josef Stern*   275
GNOSIS   *Gedaliahu Guy Stroumsa*   285
GOD   *Louis Jacobs*   291
GRACE OR LOVING–KINDNESS   *Ze'ev Harvey*   299
GUILT   *Jacob Arlow*   305
HALAKHAH   *David Hartman*   309
ḤASIDISM   *Arthur Green*   317
HEBREW   *Lewis Glinert*   325
HELLENISM   *David Satran*   331
HERESY   *Ze'ev Gries*   339
HERMENEUTICS   *Michael Fishbane*   353
HEROISM   *Yeshayahu Leibowitz*   363
HISTORY   *Paul Mendes-Flohr*   371
HOLINESS   *Allen Grossman*   389
HOLOCAUST   *Emil Fackenheim*   399

HOLY SPIRIT   *Aaron Singer*   409
HOPE   *Charles Vernoff*   417
HUMANISM   *Ernst Akiva Simon*   423
HUMILITY   *Bernard Steinberg*   429
I AND THOU   *Maurice Friedman*   435
IDOLATRY   *Yeshayahu Leibowitz*   445
IMAGINATION   *Geoffrey Hartman*   451
IMAGO DEI   *Joseph Dan*   473
IMMORTALITY   *Alan Arkush*   479
INDIVIDUALITY   *Peter Ochs*   483
ISLAM   *Nissim Rejwan*   487
JERUSALEM   *Shemaryahu Talmon*   495
JUDAISM   *Gershom Scholem*   505
JURISPRUDENCE   *Ze'ev W. Falk*   509
JUSTICE   *Haim Cohen*   515
KINGDOM OF GOD   *Warren Zev Harvey*   521
KINGDOM OF PRIESTS   *Daniel Schwartz*   527
LAND OF ISRAEL   *Eliezer Schweid*   535
LANGUAGE   *Josef Stern*   543
LITURGY   *Eric Friedland*   553
LOVE   *Steven Harvey*   557
MEANING   *Jack Spiro*   565
MEDIEVAL JEWISH PHILOSOPHY   *Jacob Agus*   573
MEMORY   *David Roskies*   581
MENTSCH   *Moshe Waldoks*   587
MERCY   *David Blumenthal*   589
MESSIANISM   *R. J. Zwi Werblowsky*   597
METAPHYSICS   *Alan Udoff*   603
MIDRASH   *David Stern*   613
MIRACLE   *Alan Arkush*   621
MIZVEH   *Moshe Waldoks*   627
MODERN JEWISH PHILOSOPHY   *Steven S. Schwarzschild*   629
MUSIC   *Moshe Idel*   635
MYSTICISM   *Moshe Idel*   643
MYTH   *Galit Hasan-Rokem*   657
NATURAL LAW   *Jeffrey Macy*   663
ORAL LAW   *Jacob Neusner*   673
ORTHODOX JUDAISM   *Emmanuel Rackman*   679
PEACE   *Aviezer Ravitzky*   685
PEOPLE OF ISRAEL   *Alon Goshen-Gottstein*   703

POLITICAL THEORY   *Ella Belfer and Ilan Greilsammer*   715

PRAYER   *Michael Fishbane*   723

PROPHECY   *Peter Zaas*   731

PROVIDENCE   *Hillel Levine*   735

RABBI AND TEACHER   *David Ruderman*   741

REASON   *Eugene Borowitz*   749

RECONSTRUCTIONISM   *Harold Schulweis*   755

REDEMPTION   *Arthur A. Cohen*   761

REFORM JUDAISM   *Michael A. Meyer*   767

RELIGION AND STATE   *Aharon Lichtenstein*   773

REMNANT OF ISRAEL   *Nahum N. Glatzer*   779

REPENTANCE   *Ehud Luz*   785

REST   *Arthur Waskow*   795

RESURRECTION OF THE DEAD   *Arthur A. Cohen*   807

REVELATION   *Shalom Rosenberg*   815

REWARD AND PUNISHMENT   *Ephraim Rottenberg*   827

RIGHTEOUSNESS   *Joshua O. Haberman*   833

SACRED TEXT AND CANON   *David Stern*   841

SANCTIFICATION OF THE NAME   *Hyam Maccoby*   849

SCIENCE   *Hillel Levine*   855

SECULARISM   *Ben Halpern*   863

SERMON   *Marc Saperstein*   867

SILENCE   *Andre Neher*   873

SIN   *Adin Steinsalz*   881

SOUL   *Rachel Elior*   887

SOUL SEARCHING   *Adin Steinsaltz*   897

SPIRITUALITY   *Arthur Green*   903

STATE OF ISRAEL   *Michael Rosenak*   909

STRANGER   *Joseph Levi*   917

STUDY   *Aharon Lichtenstein*   931

SUFFERING   *David Hartman*   939

SURVIVAL   *Yossi Klein Halevi*   947

TALMUD   *Adin Steinsalz*   953

THEODICY   *Byron L. Sherwin*   959

THEOLOGY   *Arthur A. Cohen*   971

TIME   *William E. Kaufman*   981

TOLERANCE   *Alan Udoff*   987

TORAH   *James Kugel*   995

TRADITION   *Natan Rotenstreich*   1007

TRUTH   *Peter Ochs*   1017

UNITY   *Charles Vernoff*   1025
UTOPIA   *Lionel Kochan*   1033
WOMAN   *Blu Greenberg*   1039
WORK   *Abraham Shapira*   1055
ZIONISM   *Ben Halpern*   1069

Glossary   1077
List of Abbreviations   1097
List of Contributors   1101
Index   1117

Preface to the Paperback Edition

Arthur A. Cohen died on the 31st of October 1986. Although severely enfeebled by disease for nine months—a period coinciding with the last stage of this volume's preparation—he diligently saw the manuscript to press. A former publisher and a master editor, he attended to every detail with consummate care. A bound copy of the volume reached Arthur less than a week before his death.

Graced with a prodigious capacity for friendship, Arthur regarded this volume as principally an act of sharing—a sharing with the participants of the volume (whom he deemed to be his colleagues in the deepest sense) and in a special way, with me, his co-editor. With a gentle enthusiasm he introduced me to the joy and fantasy of publishing, of conceiving and creating a volume of such enormous dimensions. The actual process, of course, was often beset with tedious, vexing chores. Arthur taught me how to acknowledge frustration, and to bound back with renewed commitment. Through transcontinental post and occasional meetings—in New York City, Jerusalem and at "Los Tres Almendros," Arthur's summer retreat in Mallorca— he shared with me his seasoned strategies of editing, illuminating the art of reading critically and helping an author recast his or her thoughts to achieve conceptual precision without a sacrifice of elegance. Arthur was a sympathetic editor who appreciated exuberance and rhetorical flourish, but he insisted in maintaining a rigorous distinction between homily and intellectual passion, between sermon and theological reflection. He also insisted that we vigilantly guard against the confusion—which he held to be the bane of contemporary religious discourse—of theological apologetics masquerading as theological argument. A fastidious man of the most refined intellectual and artistic taste, Arthur did not suffer fools lightly. But he was no intellectual snob; as in his friendships, he did not relate to individuals and their work through the prism of their credentials. He listened to each sympathetically, prepared to delight in the discovery of new insight and understanding. This volume would thus be open to all who, regardless of rank and stature, had "something to say." As an editor—and as a human being—I grew under Arthur's affable tutelage.

Arthur also saw this book as sponsoring the type of intellectual sharing that quickens genuine spiritual fellowship between thinking individuals. It was Arthur's hope that by bringing Jews of diverse theological opinion together in a forum of shared reflection, the volume would highlight that the bonds that ultimately bind the Jews are drawn not only by the imperatives of communal solidarity, but also a universe of discourse grounded in a shared spiritual heritage and concern.

I thus regard this volume as Arthur's gift to me personally, and to all who wish to affirm Judaism as a spiritually and intellectually engaging discourse. May this volume serve to honor Arthur's blessed memory.

Erev .Rosh Ha-Shanah 5748
Jerusalem
Paul Mendes-Flohr

Introduction

Contemporary Jewish Religious Thought was conceived during the summer of 1982 while the editors, in defiance of the thunders of the north, strolled through the charmed gardens of the American Colony Hotel in East Jerusalem. Our convivial but random conversation eventually focused upon the subject of the alleged Jewish disinclination to engage in theology. We quickly dismissed as both simplistic and rhetorical the frequently rehearsed explanation that Jewish theological reticence is due to Christianity's historical preemption of "God talk". Nor did we regard as adequate the frequently advanced explanation that Judaism is a religion preeminently grounded in concrete religious acts and thus has no need for the ostensibly disembodied speculations associated with theological indulgence. What was clear to both of us was that theology is the discipline Jews eschew while nonetheless pursuing it with covert avidity. Virtually every concept that has occupied a position of significance within the discourse of world religions has its cognate or analogue in Jewish religious thought. *Theologumena* have, however, preoccupied Jews. Not as extraneous intrusions, but as an indigenous endeavor to illuminate their own experience. Indeed, insofar as the

Jewish people was convoked by the giving of the Torah at Mount Sinai, its life thereafter was devoted with considerable passion and intelligence to the issues raised by that holy convocation: Who is this God that calls us forth to be his own and what is the character of life under his dominion?

In the process of assessing the implications of an evident situation of paradox—that Jews elaborate and refine religious conceptions while disdaining to call their enterprise theology—we determined to undertake an invitational volume in which contemporary Jewish thinkers would be matched to terms and ideas that have otherwise engaged their reflections. The result, it was hoped, would fill a lacuna in the contemporary literature. Clearly, although Judaism may not acknowledge a formal theological tradition, it nonetheless possesses a rich and nuanced theological history. The model that we set ourselves was that of the *Stichwörterbuch,* or technical dictionary based on a thematic scheme. As a more specific exemplum for the enterprise we examined *A Handbook of Christian Theology,* co-edited by Arthur A. Cohen and Marvin Halverson in 1958, which brought together major figures in Protestant theology and historical research (with the exception of Cohen himself, who contributed the essays on Atheism and Judaism) to consider the state of reflection on the principal conceptions in Protestant theological discussion during the 1950s. Having determined that the design of *Contemporary Jewish Religious Thought* would be that of the definition-essay, we then identified the salient themes, concepts, and movements that animate Jewish religious thought.

As we began to draw up the list of possible candidates to write the various definition-essays, we were struck by the considerable number of individuals—rabbis, academics, and laypersons—currently engaged in a creative and genuinely reflective manner in the enterprise of Jewish religious thought, itself another indication that the time was ripe for the volume we had in mind. It was hoped that not only an illuminating portrait of Jewish religious thinking would emerge but that the project as well would stimulate its further development.

In assigning the essays—guided solely by the criteria of proven competence and thoughtfulness with regard to the respective topic—we became aware that contemporary interest in Jewish religious thought embraces virtually the full ideological spectrum of Jewish life: Orthodox, Conservative, Reform, Reconstructionist; Zionist, non-Zionist; secular Jews as well as Jews of religious sensibility who find it difficult to declare their denominational affiliation.

Contemporary Jewish Religious Thought does not reflect any ideological bias or preference. Rather it represents the plurality of Jewish life and projects the healthy and balanced self-assurance that presently characterizes Jewish thought. While none of the essays suffers from a self-enclosed parochiality, they all avoid the propensity of classical as well as nineteenth- and early-twentieth-century Jewish thought to assume an apologetic mode of discourse that had the deleterious effect of encouraging non-Jews (whether hostile or affectionate) to set the parameters, the terms of argument, and even the tone of Judaism's theological self-articulation.

As editors of this volume we have undertaken to facilitate the nonapologetic character of its inquiry by deliberately excluding from the list of topics such antinomic themes from the lexicon of Jewish apologetics as "law and grace," "particularity and universalism," "justice and love." Such dialectical antinomies are precisely that, dialectical foils for the elaboration of abstract stances and postures that neither illuminate the religious thinking of the Jews nor constitute an appropriate forum for ecumenical discourse. They are the vocabulary of triumphalist theologies—whether Jewish or non-Jewish—the triumphalism of whatever order speaks out of an old tradition of *odium theologicum* in which Jews have no share.

We are particularly delighted by the generous enthusiasm of the contributors whom we have invited to join with us. Very few invitees declined to participate, and from those who pleaded the immensity of prior obligations we received much encouragement in the pursuit of the enterprise. In assigning the essays our instructions were minimal. We indicated the desired word length and proposed the essay to be written neither as an encyclopedic discussion of the issue nor simply a rehearsal of the historical literature. What we sought rather was a historically-grounded reflection that would offer a new crystallization of the issue, an adumbration of fresh speculative possibilities, a proposal of nuance and direction for future discussion. The tone and emphasis were left to the judgment of the particular author. Hence, the essays tend to vary in their attention to historical and textual detail and in speculative thrust.

Nonetheless, despite the absence of methodological (and, as noted, ideological) uniformity, a pattern of four distinctive vectors is shared by virtually all the essays. With respect to those essays which consider the seminal ideas of classical Judaism, each regards the Hebrew Bible as the foundation of Jewish religious existence; each affirms talmudic-rabbinic teachings as decisive in the shaping of the Jews' understanding of God's word; each has recourse to the insights developed by the medieval philosophic and mystical tradition, with the enduring significance of Maimonides's magisterial contribution being particularly discernible; and finally, most of the essays indicate a refined awareness of the collapse of the ideational and institutional consensus that has marked the passage of Judaism into modernity.

In recognition of this indisputably troubling situation, many of the authors note that the consequent weakening, even abandonment, of classical Jewish religious norms and expressions can be reversed only if a new hermeneutic and interpretative language is developed in order to accommodate both the historical sensibilities and epistemological criteria of contemporary Jews. Moreover, many of the essays conclude with a peroration in reference to the devastating impact of the Holocaust on the structure and meaning of Jewish religious life. Many of these perorations stand as given since their interpretations are both original and evocative of the contributors' viewpoints; however, a number of others were excised by the editors since they were little more than a coda of personal despair and confusion. Such references were more an index of psychological desperation—an assertion that something had been wrought of such monumentality that it must have devastating impact upon Jewish religious life; but, at the same time, a confession that the writer had not yet mastered a method of assimilating or interpreting that impact.

It is no less clear to the editors that the emergence of a new hermeneutic and interpretative language is implicit in the essays of this volume. Such a hermeneutic, as the essays abundantly testify, has but one common language, namely Hebrew, and the shared literary sources of Jewish religious memory and community. In the absence of such a language, the essays implicitly propose, Jewish theology is vacuous, fruitless, and bound to wither. A shared language and literature has both a diachronic and synchronic dimension: diachronically it provides continuity with the past and synchronically it binds the disparate constituencies of Jewish life—both geographic and ideological—into a community of discourse out of which, if not a new consensus of practice will emerge, at least surely a consensus of focus and concern will become manifest. This commonality of enterprise is surely underscored by the fact that contributors to this volume are drawn from North America, Europe, and the State of Israel and that it has been necessary to translate many of the essays from Hebrew, French, and German into this principal language of the diaspora, English.

It is surely not appropriate for us as editors to interpret the implications of this volume, to provide an exegesis of its points of convergence and disagreement. There are striking observations that emerge, surprising intellectual immensities whose constant quotation and interpretation leave us with a gratifying sense that even if no theological tradition has defined the Jewish historical discourse, there are nonetheless Jewish thinkers whom every other contemporary researcher is obliged to consult. We have noted the continuing power of Maimonides as the indisputable center of medieval Jewish interpretation; to Maimonides may be added such twentieth-century luminaries as Franz Rosenzweig and Rav Joseph D. Soloveitchik, to whom many of the contributors refer as warrants of their own discussion.

It would appear then that a theological community is gathering, a discourse is underway, a conceptual reconstruction collectively engaged in by all the ideological tendencies of Jewry is being pursued. Such a benefice to Jewish life is palpable insofar as the editors share the profound conviction that in the face of the freezing of ideological and political commitments on the part of many Jews, the only meaningful option in the face of the immutable nature of halakhic orthodoxy and the dissent of other sectors of religious Jewry is that theological discourse and interpretation takes place in a pluralistic, open society where ideas, values, imagination, and experience are immensely fluid and protean. *Contemporary Jewish Religious Thought* is not a group of separate and disconnected essays, but in itself constitutes a theological document of major importance. We have in this volume nothing less than an accurate record of Jewish theological reasoning in the latter decades of the twentieth century, *post Auschwitz mortuum, post Israel natus.*

Editors' Notes: There are a number of specific observations on the apparatus and machinery of this volume to which attention must be drawn.

Theological Gender Language

Many of our most attentive readers will undoubtedly be women intent upon elaborating their own religious consciousness and sensibility. And yet in the main, with few exceptions, the contributors to this volume have been—if not consciously indifferent—for the most part unaware of the issue raised by women's groups regarding the ongoing masculinization of Jewish theological language. We have made no particular effort to eliminate this usage, accepting it rather as the stage of development to which we have come. We are aware, as the essays of David Biale, David Ruderman, and Susannah Heschel have shown, that there is a problem in Jewish tradition, but at the same time unable to edit out the masculine identification of God and to substitute for it some neutral or bisexual concoction. Neologism of such order neither advances nor compliments feminine sensibility. It serves to obscure the issue, which does not reside in the formal structure of language but rather in its substance. We will always have to refer to God as being a "something of sex," since English has no neuter form and is not quite certain what advantage would be wrought by making God sexless. Nor is it easy to replace in every context "human" and "humankind" for "man" and "mankind". Where possible—when the term "man" was overused—editorial good sense has driven us toward moderation but not to elimination. All that we can assure our readers of is the good sense and conviction of the editors that God is above and beyond sexual differentiation but that the conventions of language are not.

Bibliography

The bibliography that follows each essay is intended to point the reader toward the appropriate literature for further inquiry. It is in no way imagined that the three to five bibliographic citations usually given can possibly exhaust the literature. We nonetheless regarded these bibliographies—chosen with great care by the authors of the respective essays—however brief, to be both apposite and helpful.

Glossary and Abbreviations

The schedule of abbreviations has been adapted from that provided by *The Encyclopaedia Judaica* and our acknowledgment and thanks are extended to its publishers, Keter Publishing Company of Jerusalem. Moreover, we have adapted the system of general transliteration of Hebrew endorsed by *The Encyclopaedia Judaica*. In developing our glossary, we have been guided by the wish to supply basic information to the reader with respect to terms, authors, historical movements and events which appear at least twice in the essays that make up the volume. Where it is sufficient to identify a person or book by a relevant date, we have done so parenthetically, but in many cases rather than break the flow of the essay we have relegated the required information to a glossary. The glossary has been prepared by Edward Hanker, and the editors are deeply grateful for his enterprise and care.

Acknowledgments

The editors wish to thank Professor David Stern for his avid brainstorming in connection with the development of the thematics and prospective contributors to the volume. We also wish to express special gratitude to Dr.

Ze'ev Gries for his patient and unfailing assistance in matters of arcane and scholarly detail. Mr. Hayim Goldgraber has also been of inestimable help, and of great moral support. It is amazing how the mind passes over the obvious but is scrupulous about detail. It wasn't until the volume was nearly complete that the editors realized that they had omitted the idea of Rest (Shabbat) from consideration. Our gaffes would have been even more disastrous had not we had the patient cooperation of David Stern and many others who offered their proposals and reflections as the volume was developing.

We wish to acknowledge with gratitude the following translators who have rendered various essays into English: Carol Bosworth-Kutscher, Jeffrey M. Green, Deborah Grenimann, David Maisel, Arnold Schwartz, Jonathan Shipman, and Michael Swirsky.

We are also grateful to Mrs. Fania Scholem for allowing us to publish an edited text of the late Professor Gershom Scholem's discussion of Judaism which is culled from the transcript of his remarks at the Center for the Study of Democratic Institutions (Santa Barbara) in 1974. Our acknowledgment and thanks to the Center without whose permission the text could not appear.

Dr. Michael Rosenak wishes to express his thanks to the Oxford Centre for Post-Graduate Hebrew Studies for the hospitality and library services extended him during August, 1983, which enabled him to write his paper for this volume.

We also wish to express our thanks to Elizabeth Elston, Stephen Weinstein, and Laura Gross for their enthusiastic work on *Contemporary Jewish Religious Thought*.

One is always grateful to one's family for tolerating the excesses that arise with the making of books. To our various families and friends, to Rita Mendes-Flohr as well as Inbal and Itamar, to Elaine Lustig Cohen and to Tamar Judith, who stood to one side while the preoccupying detail of this volume was pursued, we are thankful.

ARTHUR A. COHEN and PAUL MENDES-FLOHR

Aesthetics

אסתטיקה

Steven S. Schwarzschild

A t first consideration the notion of Jewish aesthetics seems ludicrous. If something is beautiful, what does its putative Jewishness have to do with its beauty? Furthermore, what would make an art object Jewish: its so-called subject matter? But, if that is the case, what about a menorah made by a gentile craftsman? Or the religion of the artist? If so, what about a crucifixion scene painted by a Jew? Finally, it has been noted that, however creative Jews have been in such fields as religion, law, literature, science, and economics, until recent times—that is, until large numbers of Jews, and with them their artistic traditions, were assimilated into non-Jewish cultures—no Jewish art was produced, nor were there Jewish artists of any great significance. There can thus be no surprise that there has never been any body of Jewish literature on art or aesthetics. How then Jewish aesthetics—that is, a Jewish theory of art?

Nevertheless, the public and private collection of Jewish art began in the second half of the last century and has been rapidly increasing since then. A body of literature, though limited and almost invariably of a historical rather than of a theoretical, aesthetic character, has been produced. And art continues to be created that calls itself, and sometimes is indeed, Jewish.

Extant Jewish art consists almost totally of religious artifacts, such as spice boxes for the ceremony concluding the Sabbath, illuminations in Passover *Haggadot,* and synagogal architecture. All of these follow the rabbinic injunction to "beautify the service of God" (BT Shab. 133b, on Ex. 15:2). For the rest, what is generally accepted as Jewish art concerns itself with descriptions of one sort or another of the life of Jews, but this is not, as we have seen, necessarily Jewish art any more than, say, a Portuguese picture of a fourteenth-century Mexican Indian is Mayan art. There has always been a considerable amount of Jewish nongraphic art: certainly literature, including poetry of all sorts, as well as synagogal and other music (whose prehistory in classical as well as modern times is much debated). Taken together, the bulk of Jewish art is, thus, to this day in the realm of "arts and crafts," utilitarian rather than absolute—*"l'art pour l'art."*

Utilitarian Jewish art would then be the first class of objects with which Jewish aesthetics deals. This immediately raises the question of whether there are any implicit principles that can be shown to underlie such actual as well as acceptable Jewish art, and, if so, what they are. Thereupon other questions arise: for example, how do such Jewish aesthetic principles, if any, accord with other principles of Judaism (which are, in turn, always much controverted)?

What one would obtain, though, if one were able to answer these questions would be a theory, an aesthetic, of Jewish art, but not yet by any means a Jewish aesthetic of art in general. There are, nonetheless, compelling reasons for stipulating a universal Jewish aesthetic, and some basic specifications can be adduced with which to enflesh them.

To begin with, Judaism, and even Jewish law, has from the outset and to this day said a few but fundamental things about art in general, and not only about art by or for Jews. The best-known such statement is, of course, the so-called Second Commandment (Ex. 20:4, Deut. 4:16–18, 5:8), which prohibits making an "image" of everything on, above, or below the earth, most especially of God. This broad prohibition of idolatry is, in the Jewish view, enjoined on all human beings. It would seem, if taken literally, to leave little or no room for "images" and "representations." And this is, indeed, generally asserted to be the reason for the striking poverty of plastic and graphic arts in Jewish history.

In the development of rabbinic Judaism this *negativum,* the normative absence of representations or of attempted representations of the divine, was rightly taken to entail the perennial and important principle that, unlike physical nature, which is both capable of and allowed to be "imaged," spirit, however conceived—whether as metaphysical realities, or reason, or morality—is unsusceptible to representation. Hermann Cohen read the Second Commandment, therefore, as saying: "Thou shalt not make an image of the moral subject."[1] (Some contemporary scholars dispute at least the historical side of this claim, and have collected much material with which to contradict it. What their evidence should be taken to prove, however, is that (1) the principle here under discussion was, of course, interpreted and applied differently by different people in different situations, and (2) Jewish art, like Judaism in general, has been subject to many external influences from many quarters.) "Spirit" can be and is instantiated, not represented, preeminently in God and then in varying degrees in angels, human beings, and other sacred entities. To try to depict God or the spirit of other "inspirited" individuals is then worse than something that *should not* be done—it *cannot* be done (what some modern philosophers call a "category mistake"). It is a mistake, however, with the widest and most grievous consequences: The whole universe is misunderstood and, therefore, maltreated. It is a sin.

The operative Jewish legal code, the *Shulḥan Arukh,* offers a convenient summary of the legal applications to art, Jewish and non-Jewish, of the Jewish aesthetic doctrine that we have so far developed (Sh. Ar., YD, Hilkhot Avodat Kokhavim, ch. 141, "Din ha-Ẓelemim ve-ha-Ẓurot shel Avodat Kokhavim"). In the history of Jewish graphic art, the most interesting ramification of that doctrine has always been the permissibility of showing the absence of spirit in purely physical, because pictorial, representations of spiritual beings, particularly humans. The rabbis continually insisted that the only "ikon" of God was the presence, not the re-presentation, of a human being (e.g. Deut. R. 4:4; Rashi ad loc. Deut. 21:23). But how to depict an absence? Here what I have called "the theology of the slashed nose" comes into operation: The nose was slit to symbolize that what one could see did not really represent the inspirited object adumbrated. Rachel Wischnitzer has called it "the Jewish principle of incompleteness."[2] This is, as it happens, also one of the earliest components of the "modernist" revolution in art; what is usually called "distortion" is thus quintessential and aboriginal Jewish aesthetics. Kant and the German-Jewish impressionist Max Liebermann punned in calling such distortion *verzeichnen,* that is, "to note" as well as "to mis-draw." What might be called "Picasso's third eye," that is, the face as it looks not when artificially arrested but when humanly active, expresses the same conception in another fashion. The halakhic prohibition of three-dimensionality in naturalistic human sculpture is another example. The artistic effect of invisible light on the visual world and the resultant "elongation" from Velasquez to the bohemian Jew Modigliani are yet further specimens of "the theology of the slashed nose." "For Modigliani and by a modern paradox for most of us, only a mask wears the features of the soul . . . in a world of unremitting pain."[3]

Two further important inferences are to be drawn. The first might be thought to impose the obligation to image as much as possible and in one way or another to image the invisible "forms" of reality. For example, of the patriarch of modern art in Palestine/Israel, Mordecai Ardon, Avram Kampf says that he "makes visible what one does not see."[4] The second inference is that action, rather than being, is the ultimate purpose of art—either real action such as mobiles or art "events" or artistic invitations to action, as it were, such as depictions of productive human activities, projections of a world made better, or ironic-critical representations of the actual world of injustice and pain, as in "the ash-can school" of American painting, for example.

The modernist revolution broke decisively with the pervasive Greek principle of mimesis-imitation in favor of creativity, the production of something new not given by nature. (Creativity is, *nota bene,* the first and foremost attribute of God in the Bible, and man is in Judaism challenged to be his partner through *imitatio Dei,* that is, through moral action, not through what the Greeks called *poiesis,* "poetry" in the sense of artistic "making.") This revolution spawned abstract or abstracted painting and sculpture as well as Arnold Schoenberg's serial, quasi-mathematical music. Schoenberg's *magnum opus,* "Moses and Aaron," is both musically and textually an extended dramatization of Jewish iconoclasm, reaching its climax when Moses destroys the golden calf to the words (not sung!): "Perish, you embodiment of the impossibility of putting the Infinite in an image!"[5] So too did it generate nonlinear, modernist literature that produces its own new worlds in words *(davar/logos).* Calligraphic art has always commended itself for several obvious reasons,[6] among Moslems even more than among Jews; Susan Handelman has most usefully crystallized "the emergence of rabbinic interpretation in modern literary theory" in a recent study.[7] So one could go on.

Kant and Hermann Cohen stipulated that humor and irony be among the chief elements of art, inasmuch as these administer aesthetic-ethical criticism to the actual world for its evils: prophetic irony about the dumb idols—Solomon dedicating the Temple in Jerusalem with a prayer that declares a building's unsuitability to "house" the infinite God. Cohen even quotes Giotto's joke about Joseph in a "Holy Family" looking so sad "quite naturally, considering his relationship to the child."[8] Or consider Paul Tillich on Picasso's "Guernica" and, by extension, much of the nineteenth- and twentieth-century art of alienation: "He who can bear and express meaninglessness shows that he experiences meaning within the desert of meaninglessness."[9] In short, true aesthetics, Kantian and Jewish, subsumes art indirectly but decisively to ethics. "High art," like craft art, ultimately also serves God—not through ritual but through morality. The rabbis, therefore, punned about "the beauty (*yoffi*) of Japhet (Greece) in the tents of Shem (Israel)" (BT Meg. 9b on Gen. 9:27).

Kant's *Critique of Judgment* has laid a new foundation for art. Whatever Romanticism and Absolute Idealism made of it, Kant's third *Critique* analyzed art to precisely the effect here proposed—as the actualization of the ideal (otherwise a theoretical impossibility), as the asymptotic embodiment of human, rational, ethical values, and as the glory of the conception of infinity and the pain of human inadequacy to that conception under the judgment of "sublimity." Though Kant was generally not sympathetically disposed toward Judaism, he here erupts in apostrophes to Jewish and Moslem iconoclasm. And Kant's Jewish avatar, Hermann Cohen, went on to radicalize as well as to Judaize Kantian aesthetics throughout his oeuvre but most systematically in the *Aesthetics of Pure Feeling,* a study unique in Jewish history. The work ends with a paean to impressionism, then still a revolutionary force, for depicting proletarians rather than court personages. When, fourteen years later, the first great Hebrew journal of art was inaugurated, Rachel Wischnitzer opened it with a programmatic article, "The New Art and We,"[10] in which she formulated the Jewish divorce from "naturalism," "distanced from the world of reality," and the Jewish concern with the "inner face, the inside of things." With the rise of the Frankfurt School, composed essentially of self-consciously Jewish Hegelian neo-Marxists, the same theme was taken up again in the form of an aesthetic, especially in T. W. Adorno's writings on music, that struggles against idolatry and on behalf of ethicism: Art is action that envisions and suffers from the unattainability of Utopia; it is not a state of being. Throughout the work of the Frankfurt School, the conclusion of Goethe's *Faust* is quoted as a recurrent motto by such Jewish aestheticians: "The indescribable—here it is done." Or as Hermann Cohen had put it, art depicts the Messiah; that is, art is man's anticipatory construction of the world as it ought to be, as God wants it to be.[11]

On such an analysis it turns out that in the twentieth century art has finally begun, by divorcing itself from the pagan aesthetic of nature and from the Christian aesthetic of incarnation, to catch up with the aboriginal Jewish aesthetic (for Jews and Gentiles alike) of a phenomenal world in eternal pursuit of the ideal, divine, or at least messianic world. The devil had it right, as usual, when he had the Nazis identify modern art with degenerate Jewishness. In modernism, art is assimilating Judaism. Mark Rothko provided the occasion for the apt statement by the German scholar Werner Häftmann: "The amazing fact should become clear to historians . . . that Judaism, which for 2,000 years remained 'imageless,' has found in our century—with the help of the meditative process of modern art—a pictorial expression of its own, a Jewish art of its own."[12]

REFERENCES

1. Hermann Cohen, *Kants Begrundung der Ethik* (1877), 283.
2. Rachel Wischnitzer, *The Bird's Head Haggadah* (1967).
3. Edgar Levy, "Modigliani and the Art of Painting," in *The American Scholar* (Summer 1964), 405ff.
4. Avram Kampf, *Jewish Experience in the Art of the Twentieth Century* (1984), 192.
5. For a discussion of Jewish music in contrast with pagan/Platonic sensuousness, militarism, and socialist realism, cf. Boaz Cohen, "The Responsum of Maimonides Concerning Music," in *Law and Tradition in Judaism* (1959), 167ff.; Eric Werner, *A Voice Still Heard* (1976).
6. Cf. Kampf, *Jewish Experience in the Art of the Twentieth Century*, 30f., 44f., 161.
7. Susan Handelman, *The Slayers of Moses* (1982).
8. Hermann Cohen, *Aesthetik des reinen Gefühls, I (1908)*, 343.
9. Paul Tillich, "Protestantism and Artistic Style," in *Theology of Culture* (1959), 75.
10. *Rimon* 1, I (1922).
11. Hermann Cohen, *Der Begriff der Religion im System der Philosophie* (1915), 96.
12. Quoted in Kampf, *Jewish Experience in the Art of the Twentieth Century*, 201.

BIBLIOGRAPHY

Franz Landsberger, *A History of Jewish Art* (1973).
Ze'ev Levy, "The Values of Aesthetics and the Jewish Religious Tradition" (Hebrew), in *Jewish Culture in Our Time: Crisis or Renewal* (Hebrew), (1983).
Leo Art Mayer, *Bibliography of Jewish Art* (1967).
Leo Art Mayer, *Journal of Jewish Art*, annual since 1974, Center for Jewish Art at the Hebrew University, Jerusalem.
Clare Moore, *The Visual Dimension—Aspects of Jewish Art* (1982).
Steven S. Schwarzschild, "The Legal Foundation of Jewish Aesthetics," in *Journal of Aesthetic Education*, 9 (Jan. 1975).

Aggadah

אגדה

David Stern

Aggadah, or haggadah, is the generic title for the entire body of rabbinic tradition that falls outside the perimeters of the halakhah, the legal teachings of the rabbis. The term *aggadah* (pl., *aggadot*), literally "that which is told," tells us more about the manner of its transmission than about the content of what was transmitted. The rabbis themselves never define aggadah except to speak of its virtually irresistible and seductive attractiveness, which they liken in one place to the manna of the desert (Mekh. Vayassa 6) and in another to wine "which draws after it the heart of man" (Sif. Deut. 317). Although modern scholars have offered various definitions for aggadah—as "scientific mythology,"[1] "a tale implied or derived from Scripture,"[2] or "speculation with edification in view"[3]—the aggadah is in fact a widely heterogeneous body of materials that range from extra-biblical legends and tales about the rabbis to snippets of popular folklore and fully elaborated homilies.

The question of its genre (for this is what aggadah, with halakhah, primarily represents) can be clarified if one considers aggadah as an extension of the biblical genre of wisdom literature, a genre that also includes diverse literary forms such as narrative, poetry, proverbs, and allegory. Like wisdom literature, aggadah is intended to convey to its audience truths distilled from human experience in order to guide their better judgment. That such truths can be presented equally in the form of parables and sermons is irrelevant to the real point, which is the didactic purpose of the material. "If you wish to come to know Him who by His word created the world, study aggadah" (Sif. Deut. 49), the rabbis declared in what is one of the most celebrated of all their aggadic sayings. This statement underlines the functional character of the material as well as raising the problematic relationship of aggadah to rabbinic theology—a question to which we will return shortly.

Although aggadah is to be evaluated mainly in terms of its content and function, its form cannot be ignored; indeed, the question of form has special relevance to the separate issue of aggadah's relationship to theology. As its name suggests, much aggadah bears the special traits of traditional oral literature. It is thus common for an aggadah—an apothegm as well as a narrative—to exist in several versions or by-forms that differ significantly in details but maintain the same general shape. In rabbinic literature, aggadah has been preserved both in exegetical contexts, as in midrashim, and independently, in the form of tales or opinions cited associatively in the course of a talmudic discussion. In post-rabbinic medieval literature, collections of aggadot were presented as moral treatises or pseudo-historical accounts. As a result, the same aggadah is frequently found in several texts and contexts; in general, the material of aggadah is extremely plastic and easily adaptable, a fact that also makes it difficult to speak of the genesis or history of any specific aggadah. To be sure, some aggadot can be shown to be Judaized versions of myths or folk-motifs that must have circulated throughout the ancient world—for example, the use of the Pandora myth in Avot de Rabbi Nathan, ch. 1—while others originated in response to "problems" in Scripture, as part of midrashic exegesis. Even in such cases, however, once an aggadah was created, it could take on an independent existence and circulate freely, moving from one context to another, often changing its meaning in the course of its wanderings without substantially changing its form.

A striking example of such an odyssey is the famous aggadah about how God, before he gave the Torah to the children of Israel, offered it to the gentile nations, each of whom declined to accept it. This aggadah, as Joseph Heinemann has shown in a brilliant analysis of its development, first appears in the early Palestinian targumim, the Aramaic translations of the Pentateuch, in which it helped to explain the enigmatic description of God's revelation in Deut. 33:2. Following this exegetical beginning, this aggadah served various functions in other contexts: as an apologetic response to the hostile question why the Torah, if it was indeed the word of God, was possessed only by the Jews, as well as a polemical proof of the unworthiness of the gentile nations (Mekh. Baḥodesh 5); as a rationalization for God's justice in punishing Israel for disobeying his law (Ex. R. 27:9), and as the basis for Israel's complaint to God that he has treated her unworthily (Lam. R. 3:1). In each of these cases, the meaning of the aggadah is a direct function of its context. Viewed in isolation, the aggadah, strictly speaking, has no meaning of its own. On the other hand, a change in context can also lead to the misinterpretation of aggadah. The famous legend that God uprooted the mountain of Sinai and threatened to drop it upon the children of Israel if they did not agree to accept the Torah originated in Palestine as a playful interpretation of the phrase in Ex. 19:17 "And they took their places at the foot of the mountain." When this midrash reached Babylonia, however, the sages there understood it literally and objected on halakhic grounds that a contract like the Sinaitic covenant made under conditions of force could not be legally valid, and thus the Israelites could not be held punishable if they violated its conditions (BT Shab. 88a).

The case of this aggadah suggests the troubled reaction aggadah, especially midrash aggadah, has historically aroused. Although midrash and aggadah have always been considered part of sacred tradition, as part of the oral Law, in historical fact the two have been the neglected stepchildren of rabbinic literature, ignored and disparaged in favor of the more serious and practical rigors of the halakhah and the Talmud. Testimony to criticism midrash aggadah received for its excessive playfulness is preserved in midrashic literature itself. On the verse "And the frog (haẓefardea, singular) came up and covered the land of Egypt" (Ex. 8:2), Rabbi Akiva proposed an almost Kafkaesque interpretation: "There was only one frog, and it covered the whole land of Egypt." To which Rabbi Eleazar ben Azariah responded: "Akiva! What business have you with aggadah! Cut out such talk—and go back to the topics of plagues and pollutions of tents!" (Ex. R. 10:4). Rabbi Eleazar's own interpretation—that first a single frog came alone and then it called all its fellow frogs to follow—is not much more probable. But his attitude to Akiva's offering is echoed somewhat more clearly in the tenth-century saying attributed to Sherirah Gaon, "The derivations from verses of Scripture which are called midrash and aggadah are merely conjectures" (Sefer ha-Eshkol, ed. A. Auerbach, 1868, pt. II, 47). In the twelfth century, Maimonides described two kinds of readers aggadah had found: those who piously accepted its every interpretation as the literal meaning of Scripture, and those who dismissed all of it as ridiculous if not fraudulent. Maimonides himself proposed an allegorical method for reading aggadah, a path that was widely followed throughout the Middle Ages. While this philosophical approach did not help readers to understand aggadah on its own terms, it nonetheless firmly established aggadah as the basic source for the reconstruction of rabbinic theology.

As a theological source, midrash aggadah has posed two basic difficulties for its students. The first and more obvious one is the grossness of some aggadot when they are taken to be expressions of elevated spiritual or theological truths. The most famous examples of such problematic aggadot are the many anthropomorphic and anthropopathic descriptions of God that are found throughout rabbinic literature, passages that describe God wearing phylacteries (BT Ber. 6a), studying the Torah for three hours every day (BT Av. Zar. 3b), shedding tears and squeezing his legs beneath the Throne of Glory (BT Ber. 59a), and so on. Now, in fact, for many rabbis anthropomorphism clearly did not pose a serious theological difficulty. Though they warned simple Jews not to interpret biblical anthropomorphisms literally, the rabbis' own sayings are far freer in anthropomorphizing than the Bible ever is—undoubtedly because, on the one hand, the rabbis knew that no one in their time actually believed that God was humanlike, and, on the other, they recognized that to describe God intimately they had no recourse but to use anthropomorphic language. Indeed, it is a paradoxical fact that the rabbis' portrayals of God are far more psychologically nuanced than are their narratives about humans. The function of these descriptions is, furthermore, often transparently ideological: to extol the religious deed (and it is always a deed of religious or spiritual import) that God is depicted as performing. The theological significance of these passages lies, as it were, in the gesture behind them—whether it be ideological or an attempt to represent God as a familiar presence—rather than in their literal or figurative meaning. Even so, there are other rabbinic aggadot that cannot be explained this way, aggadot that seem to preserve mythological conceptions from much earlier periods of Israelite religion or that give birth to myth anew out of genuine religious needs the rabbis themselves experienced. These passages suggest that there may have existed within rabbinic thought a serious divide between mythological and monotheistic conceptions of God; this division calls into question the very possibility of constructing a unified theology out of the material of aggadah.

The second difficulty that stands in the way of using aggadah as a source for rabbinic theology has to do with its form and overall lack of system. This difficulty has been addressed in the past in several ways. Specific doctrines and ideas have been studied historically for their (even discontinuous) development, as in Ephraim E. Urbach's *The Sages;* other scholars have attempted to disentangle the apparent chaos of rabbinic ideas by isolating schools and dividing tendencies between them, as in the studies of A. Marmorstein. Of all such attempts, however, the most ambitious effort to come directly to terms with the unsystematic character of rabbinic thought was undertaken by Max Kadushin. Instead of viewing aggadah as a garbled or corrupted philosophical system, Kadushin stressed the fundamentally associative and alogical character of aggadic discourse, which he saw as an aggregate of "value-concepts"—as Kadushin called such ideas as charity, worship, and the election of Israel—which together formed a dynamically organic, or "organismic," whole. The ultimate goal of this whole was the achievement of "normal mysticism," a felicitous expression Kadushin invented to describe the awareness of God's presence throughout daily existence, the basis, according to Kadushin, of rabbinic theology.

The difficulty with Kadushin's approach is that it seeks to elevate the problem—the chaos of aggadah—to the level of a concept without ever seriously accounting for the problem. Rabbinic thought, according to Kadushin, is not a philosophy or a myth or even a theology so much as it is a way of thinking, a virtual psychology; indeed, the model for Kadushin's organicism was early Gestalt psychology. Yet this problem is not unique to Kadushin's work. It faces every attempt to traduce a theology from aggadah, to translate the latter's context-specific themes and formulations into discursive, abstract, and systematic concepts.

As we have seen, aggadah has often been compared, even opposed, to the halakhah. Historically, the latter has frequently been viewed as serious, the former as frivolous. More recently, the terms of the comparison have been reversed, and halakhah now tends to be depicted as the heavy yoke of the law, as the prescriptive and binding side of Judaism, while aggadah is portrayed as free and imaginative, expressing the spiritual, ever-searching heart of religion. In fact, the line between halakhah and aggadah is often blurred. Aggadah frequently extolls and elucidates halakhic practice, while halakhah occasionally extends to matters of dogma (like the belief in resurrection). Jewish creativity has always been expended on halakhah as much as on aggadah (perhaps even more). Although one need not agree with Hayyim Nachman Bialik's statement that "halakhah is the crystallization of aggadah, while aggadah is the refinement of halakhah,"[4] it is possible to suggest that their common creativity has resulted from the tension between the two disciplines, from the ways they have grown and fed upon each other. The possibility of a new aggadah freed from the fetters of the halakhah, which some modern thinkers have invoked as the basis for a

Judaism redivivus, is in fact unattractive: such an aggadah would be ground-less, soft, a kind of piety lacking the hard commitment and demand of law.

The genuine opposite to aggadah is not halakhah but dogmatic theology. Standing at the very origin of classical Judaism, aggadah presents the fundamental obstacle to every effort to fix Jewish thought in a static moment, to convert its didactic assertions into systematic discourse. The present-day theological significance of aggadah lies in the way its chaotic richness resists being organized into orderly discourse—in its open preference for homily over theology, for impassioned assertion over reasoned argument. Most playful and novel in form precisely when it is most commonplace in content, aggadah represents all that is quintessentially untheological about Judaism. As such, it is the point of discontinuity against which every theology of Judaism must take a stand in order to make its own beginning.

REFERENCES

1. Franz Rosenzweig, *On Jewish Learning*, ed. N. N. Glatzer (1955), 39. Note that Rosenzweig refers here to Midrashim, though he clearly means Midrash Aggadah.
2. Shalom Spiegel, Introduction to *Legends of the Bible*, by Lewis Ginzberg (1956), xiii.
3. Raphael Loewe, "The 'Plain' Meaning of Scripture in Early Jewish Exegesis," in *Papers of the Institute of Jewish Studies*, 1 1964), 153.
4. Ḥayyim Nachman Bialik, *Kitvei H. N. Bialik*, II (1925), 244.

BIBLIOGRAPHY

Ḥayyim Nachman Bialik, *Halachah and Aggadah*, tr. Leon Simon (1944).
Joseph Heinemann, *Aggadot ve-Toldoteihen* (1974).
Max Kadushin, *The Rabbinic Mind*, 2d ed. (1965).
M. Saperstein, *Decoding the Rabbis: A Thirteenth-Century Commentary on the Aggadah* (1980).
Shalom Spiegel, "Introduction" to Louis Ginzberg, *Legends of the Bible* (1956).

Anti-Judaism and Anti-Semitism

שנאת־ישראל, אנטישמיות

Hyam Maccoby

I t is generally agreed that the term *anti-Semitism* should be used not in its purported sense of "antagonism to Semites" but as the equivalent to "Judaeophobia" or "Jew hatred." The term *anti-Semitism* was coined in the nineteenth century as a would-be scientific attempt to give a rational justification for Jew hatred when theological explanations had come to seem out of date, but the alleged biological or racial reference and the implied extension of hatred to other Semites, for example, Arabs, were never taken very seriously even by anti-Semitic theorists. The term *anti-Semitism* is thus parallel to *Anglophobia* or *Francophobia,* and means a hatred of Jews at a paranoid level, that is, accompanied by an inclination to attribute a wide range of evils to the activities and influence of the Jews. The term *anti-Semitism,* therefore, can even be used to describe the attitude of ancient writers such as Apion or Seneca, who had no biological or racial theory about the Jews but regarded them as a pernicious people actuated by hatred of mankind and responsible for a wide range of harmful activities. Even the Jew hatred evinced in the present by

Arabs, themselves a Semitic people, is described correctly as anti-Semitism given the history of the term, though it is unfortunate that this usage has become so universally accepted.

The question to be discussed here is: How does Judaism fit into the anti-Semitic picture? Does anti-Semitism always entail anti-Judaism? If it does, the question arises: Is Judaism regarded as the cause or as the symptom of Jewish evil? Finally, the question must be asked: Does anti-Judaism necessarily entail anti-Semitism? This last question is of special significance in view of certain arguments that have been put forward to defend traditional Christian teaching from the charge of being anti-Semitic.

In almost all forms of anti-Semitism, Judaism also is the subject of adverse comment, although it is not always made clear whether the Jews are considered evil because they have an evil religion or vice versa. In Apion's anti-Semitic scheme, as reported by Josephus, the Jews were originally a band of outcast lepers who, on being ejected from Egypt, concocted a misanthropic religion; here, clearly, the despicable status of the Jews as a people is primary, the defects of their religion secondary. In modern times, Nazi anti-Semitism followed a similar pattern. The defect is located primarily in the Jews themselves, as constituting an inherently inferior racial group; Judaism is secondarily stigmatized as the kind of poisonous weltanschauung to be expected of such flawed beings. In Nazism, ideologies are merely the outward expression of the underlying reality, which is racial. In Karl Marx's thought, the underlying reality is not race, but economic class; and in his form of anti-Semitism, Judaism is merely the ideological expression of the economic position of the Jews as hucksters and middlemen, roles he considered representative of all that is wrong with capitalist society.

In one very significant variety of anti-Semitism in the ancient world, the relationship between the Jews and their religion is apparently reversed. In certain Gnostic sects contemporaneous with the birth of Christianity, the Jewish religion is regarded as the primary source of evil and the Jews are seen as its agents rather than its originators. This view arises from a fundamental dualism in which the universe is conceived as the arena of a conflict between a good Power and an evil Power. The evil Power created the earth and rules over it. He is the God worshiped by the Jews, who are his chosen people, and to whom he gave the evil revelation known as the Torah. The Jewish religion is thus a direct expression of evil, emanating from the source of all evil, and the Jews are the people chosen by the evil Power, or Demiurge, to act as his earthly representatives in the struggle against the Light. As against the Torah, it is alleged, there exists an alternative tradition of true knowledge (gnosis), transmitted from early times by non-Jewish sages such as Seth, Enoch, and Melchizedek, by which initiates may escape from thralldom to the Demiurge and join the good Power in the heavens.

This radical form of anti-Semitism gives the Jews a role of cosmic evil as the instruments of a demonic Power, and their religion thus also becomes the instrument of that Power, by which he consolidates his rule over the earth. However, it can hardly be said that modern forms of anti-Semitism are less demonizing in their effects than ancient Gnosticism. Though Nazism and Marxism invoke no cosmic principle, their concepts of an underlying reality of which peoples and religions are only the outward expression give rise to similar demonizing effects when a given community is identified with the retrograde forces of history. Indeed, allowing for the influence of humanism, which requires explanatory forces to be located in human history rather than in the seven heavens, the Nazi and Marxist presentations of the Jews as the people of evil can be regarded as not very different from that of Gnosticism.

It may be concluded from the above discussion that the more virulent forms of anti-Semitism do entail anti-Judaism. The more paranoid anti-Semitism becomes, that is, the more the Jews are assigned a role of wide-ranging evil import, the more Judaism is included as the program and ideology by which the Jews direct their evil activities. Without such a program, the Jews would be regarded as only a minor nuisance. On examination, many apparently trivial forms of anti-Semitism, by which the Jews are stigmatized as, for example, vulgar, money grubbing, or socially unacceptable, may turn out to have a hidden metaphysical basis in which the allegedly evil nature of the Jewish religion plays a role.

Undoubtedly, it is in Christianity, in which anti-Semitism is intertwined in a very complex way with anti-Judaism, that the most influential form of anti-Semitism historically is to be found. That Gnostic anti-Semitism, with its picture of the Jews as ordained enemies of the Light, lies in the background of the Christian portrayal of the Jews as predetermined enemies of the incarnate God is rendered probable by the Gnostic documents discovered at Nag Hammadi, which confirm the existence of a pre-Christian Gnosticism. But there are also important differences between Christian and Gnostic anti-Semitism. The dualism of Pauline Christianity does not extend to a denial of the creation of the world by a good God. Nor does Pauline Christianity deny the divine origin of the Torah. Consequently, the Jews cannot be portrayed as enemies of the Light in the same radical way as in Gnosticism. Yet for every element in Gnostic anti-Semitism, there is a corresponding element in Pauline Christianity, and there are certain elements in the latter that further darken the picture of the Jews, making them even more demonic than in Gnosticism.

Thus, instead of the creation of the world by an evil Demiurge, Pauline Christianity substitutes the domination of the world by Satan, who is the ruler, or "prince," of this world, though not its creator. Instead of the concept of the Torah as an evil revelation, Pauline Christianity has the concept of the Torah as a limited, temporary revelation (Paul even says that it was given by "angels," not by God), so that to continue to revere it after the coming of Christ is a betrayal of the Light. The Jews, in allegedly rejecting and killing Christ, thus become agents of Satan in his cosmic war against God, and, in continuing their loyalty to the Torah after God has declared it obsolete, they are furthering the purpose of Satan to nullify the soteriological mission of the Son of God.

These elements of the Christian myth, closely corresponding to the Gnostic anti-Semitic myth, are alone sufficient to set the stage for a considerable anti-Semitic formation in Pauline Christianity; but certain additional elements dramatize the role of the Jews as cosmic villains to a far greater extent. In Gnosticism, the Jews were not primarily portrayed as offering violence to bearers of the *gnosis,* but rather as being the bearers of a false, rival gnosis. If Gnostic documents do sometimes show the Jews as physically oppressing the teachers of the true *gnosis,* this is described as a diffused process of opposition to the Light, rather than as a climactic act of demonic violence. In Pauline Christianity, however, instead of a long succession of teachers of *gnosis* of equal status, there appears a unique figure on whom the salvation of all mankind depends at a unique point in human history. The betrayal and killing of this figure by the Jews thus focuses their role in a mythic drama in such a way as to brand them as the unique instrument of Satan and sets the stage for a form of anti-Semitism far more imbued with loathing and metaphysical disgust than anything in Gnosticism.

It should be noted that this extra element in the Christian anti-Semitic myth is derived from the mystery cults, which were themselves without any anti-Semitic orientation but provided the idea of salvation through the death and resurrection of a divine-human figure, and also even provided the idea of a dark, evil figure who brings about this necessary death (for example, Set, in Egyptian mythology; Mot, in Phoenician mythology; and Loki, in Scandinavian mythology). The Pauline-Christian anti-Semitic myth thus takes its tone from Gnosticism, but sharpens the drama of the evil Jewish role by adding the sacrificial motifs of the mystery cults.

The relationship between anti-Semitism and anti-Judaism in Pauline Christianity can thus be analyzed as follows. The Jewish religion is regarded as God-given, but its whole aim was to point to the coming of Christ and, consequently, to practice Judaism after his coming is to misconceive its nature and purpose and therefore to practice another religion that is not God-given. There is a tendency to say that the Jews, even before the coming of Christ, never understood their own religion and continually rebelled against its true meaning, and showed violence against all the prophets God sent to them, thus foreshadowing the treatment they would give to the Son of God. The prophets themselves, in this interpretation, are regarded not as Jews but as proto-Christians, so that, in this pre-Christian period, there is an anti-Semitism combined with a pro-Judaism: The Jews are conceived as having a religion that was too good for them. This pre-Christian Judaism pointing to Christianity is, however, conceded a certain validity even after the coming of Christ. Jews who practice Old Testament Judaism, even in a "blind" way, may come to see eventually that it points to the truth of Christianity; so Old Testament Judaism was given status as a licit religion, and it was expected that through its practice, the Jews' "blindness" would eventually be lifted, as Paul had prophesied in Romans 11:26. What could never be conceded, however, was that Judaism after the coming of Christ was a living, developing religion with its own vital principles. Consequently, post-Christian developments in Judaism, that is, the Mishnah, the Talmud, and later classics, were regarded as inadmissible and "heretical," since they were based on the premise that the Jewish rejection of the messiahship of Jesus was not an error. This explains the numerous attempts made by Christians in the Middle Ages and later to outlaw and obliterate the Talmud. This kind of anti-Judaism was thus closely linked to the Christian anti-Semitic myth, by which the Jews were stigmatized as the betrayers and murderers of Christ; the Talmud was regarded as an expression of the Jewish persistence in this role, and Jewish devotion to the Talmud as an obstinate refusal to show repentance.

Some modern writers have argued that Paul himself evinced anti-Judaism, but not anti-Semitism. Later his attitude was misconstrued and Christian anti-Semitism arose, casting the Jews in the role of the people of Satan and giving rise to popular legends about the Jews as child murderers, well poisoners, and desecrators of the Host. In this view, anti-Judaism does not necessarily lead to anti-Semitism. Paul, it is argued, was against Judaism only because he regarded it as an inadequate solution to the human dilemma, which could only be tackled by a radical salvationist doctrine. Judaism, in Paul's view, was too hopeful in thinking that the Torah could guide people into virtuous living. Human evil was too profound for such a pedagogical remedy and required a process of rebirth. The Torah gave a correct program, but one that could not be followed by fallen beings. Paul thus rejected Judaism not as an evil religion, but as too humanist and meliorist to cope with the true dimensions of the human crisis.

This interpretation of Paul glosses over certain passages in Paul's writings that emphasize the mythological role of the Jews in bringing about the sacrificial death of Jesus. Indeed, this whole approach errs in making Paul into a phenomenological thinker rather than a religious innovator, the creator of a new and powerful myth. However, this interpretative approach does at least point to the possibility of a kind of anti-Judaism that is not bound up with anti-Semitism, though this attitude seems essentially a product of the modern world, alien to the thought processes of both the ancient and the medieval worlds. Where Judaism is thought of as a philosophy of life— optimistic, rationalistic, and instructive—it may be rejected by certain types of thinkers as failing to come to grips with what is most problematic in human nature without the adoption of a paranoid view of the Jews as responsible for everything that has ever gone wrong.

As a matter of historical fact, however, anti-Judaism and anti-Semitism have been very closely associated with each other. Those who regard the Jews as an evil people, whether because of their racial defects, their economic situation, or their role in a mythological drama, have regarded the Jewish religion as the ideological expression of this innate personal evil. Those who have regarded the primary evil as lying in the pernicious doctrines of Judaism have regarded the Jews as conditioned to evil by the practice of an evil religion. There is at least in these attitudes a perception of the intimate relationship between Jews and Judaism: an understanding that the Jews as a people and a nation were formed and molded by the religion based on the Exodus from Egypt and the giving of the Law on Sinai.

BIBLIOGRAPHY

John G. Gager, *The Origins of Anti-Semitism* (1983).
Hyam Maccoby, *The Sacred Executioner* (1982).
Rosemary Ruether, *Faith and Fratricide* (1974).
E. P. Sanders, *Paul and Palestinian Judaism* (1977).
Joshua Trachtenberg, *The Devil and the Jews* (1966).

Apocalypse

תורת הקץ

Nahum N. Glatzer

pocalypse (from the Greek *apokalypsis*, literally, to uncover, reveal) refers to divine revelation, especially with regard to the future of Israel and the world. The literature of the apocalyptic visions originated with the cessation of biblical prophecy and is in many respects its continuation. Vision may start with an interpretation of past events (which the visionary knew) in order then to turn to the future, offering the visionary's own peculiar interpretation. In the Book of Daniel, for example, the author knows the history of Alexander the Great up to Antiochus Epiphanes (ch. 8), which story is followed by an apocalyptic prophecy (ch. 12). In a more precise sense, the visionary describes the miraculous End of Days and the new world, heaven and the netherworld, paradise and hell, angels and demons. The visionary or apocalyptic writer uses names out of the biblical past to give his words greater authority; he speaks in allegories, vague allusions, or dreams. The concrete announcements of the biblical prophets took on in the Apocalypse a mysterious connotation. The apocalyptic writer is troubled by unfulfilled biblical prophecies and expects a revelation that will disclose their "meaning."

The End of Days in particular presented ever-new problems. The fall of Persia was not the end of paganism; a new pagan kingdom (Greece) arose and kept Israel in bondage. Antiochus Epiphanes' aggression against the Judaic religion and Jerusalem called for an interpretation. The pious Jews of this dark period saw in it the End of Days and expected the coming of the Messiah. But neither the Hasmonaean kingdom nor the rebellion against the mighty Roman rule pointed in the direction of messianic fulfillment.

The Book of Daniel (especially chapters 2 and 7) may be considered a good example of apocalyptic literature in its first period, that is, the mid-second century B.C.E. The visionary is deeply convinced of divine providence, of God's hand as guiding history in all its details; he sees four world empires rising and succeeding each other yet forming a united "world history"; the end is clearly predetermined and the present generation is to be the last. We hear the visionary's protest at the enemy's rebellion against God and his people. But after the "four empires" comes the kingdom of God; it brings the pagan kingdoms to an end and endures in eternity (Dan. 2:37–45). In a parallel vision, four beasts rise from the great sea, the fourth being the most dreadful; it had ten horns and then grew a new little horn with a mouth, speaking "great things." Now follows the main point of the vision: "Thrones were set in place and the Ancient of Days took His seat . . . His throne was tongues of flame . . . A river of fire streamed forth from before Him . . . The court sat and the books were opened . . . The beast was killed as I looked on; its body was destroyed . . . One like a human being came with the clouds of heaven . . . He reached the Ancient of Days, . . . Dominion, glory, and kingship were given to him; all peoples and nations of every language must serve him. His dominion is an everlasting dominion that shall not pass away, and one that shall not be destroyed" (7:1–15).

The beasts came up from the sea—the lower, demonic realm—while the "one like a human being," who is man, "came with the clouds of heaven"—from the divine sphere. This "man" personifies the new epoch; from now on he is in charge of the world's dominion. Now Michael shall appear "the great prince . . . who stands beside the sons of your people . . . at that time your people will be rescued, all who are found inscribed in the book. Many of those that sleep in the dust of the earth will awake, some to eternal life, others to reproaches, to everlasting abhorrence" (Dan. 12:1–2). The seer who has seen (or heard) all this in a dream asks for an explanation, but is advised that "these words are secret and sealed to the end of time" (Dan. 12:9).

The text does not say who will merit the Resurrection: it is assumed that the visionary does not include the Israelite, but, in the first place, those who suffered martyrdom in the battles; those who will be doomed to reproaches and abhorrences must be those who oppressed the pious. The concept of a universal Resurrection is not evident.

The expectation of the messianic redemption is central in the apocryphal Psalms of Solomon, written (in Hebrew, but preserved in Greek) around the period of Pompey, who invaded the Holy Land in 63 B.C.E. The time was ripe for the coming of the Messiah. The author prays for the end of the enemies of the Lord and for the rise of his kingdom. "May God cleanse Israel against the day of mercy and blessing, against the day of choice when He bringeth back His anointed. Blessed shall they be that shall be in those days." Messiah, the anointed, "will direct every man in the works of righteousness by the fear of God"; he will "establish them all before the Lord . . . in the days of mercy" (18:6–8). In contradistinction to the Hasmonaean princes who had forsaken the way of the Lord, the pious expect a new king, "the son of David . . . that he may reign over Israel thy servant" (17.23f.).

Punishment of the wicked and the bliss of the righteous is thought to be eternal. The reward of the righteous takes place in this world. The reestablishment of the kingdom of God depends partly on human action, partly on the divine loving-kindness.

All apocalyptic visions culminate in the Ezra Apocalypse, also called IV Ezra or Second Ezdras, written by an anonymous seer shortly after the destruction of the Second Temple by Rome in 70 C.E. The seer is deeply troubled by the incongruity of the prosperity of wicked Rome and the enslavement of Israel. In a series of dream visions a resolution is granted: The first Adam's sin caused man to have a "wicked heart" (3:21). Still, the captive Israelites are better than the Babylonian (i.e., Roman) oppressors. The angel Uriel advances the view that these matters are beyond human comprehension. The seer insists that the Lord does apparently spare the ungodly and destroy his people—the problem of Job. He is told that the passage to the new, better world is a narrow and a difficult one (7:12). The apocalyptic visionary is informed about the resurrection of the dead, the Day of Judgment, and the messianic period. He asks, "O thou Adam, what hast thou done?" since the sin of Adam involved all his descendants (7:118). From the concern with individual man, the seer moves to the fate of Zion. He sees a mourning woman whom he tries to comfort. Suddenly she disappears and in her place he sees the picture of a beautiful city: a new Jerusalem (9–10). In another vision the seer beholds the conquering Messiah who destroys the hostile armies and calls the chosen people, including the "lost ten tribes" (13:1–13).

Other historically significant examples of apocalyptic writings are the

Sibyline Books and the Book of Enoch. The talmudic-midrashic literature displays a greatly reduced interest in eschatological themes, though without eliminating them completely. There are references to heaven and the netherworld, Satan, angels and demons, the Remnant, the Messiah and Elijah his herald, the End of Days and divine judgment. These writings helped to sustain Jewish hopes for better days to come and for the Redeemer to restore Zion and the world.

BIBLIOGRAPHY

Joshua Bloch, *On the Apocalyptic in Judaism* (1952).
Julius H. Greenstone, *The Messiah Idea in Jewish History* (1948).
Joseph Klausner, *The Messianic Idea in Israel* (1955).
Bernard McGinn, *Visions of the End* (1979).
Gershom Scholem, *The Messianic Idea in Judaism* (1971).

Atheism

אתיאיזם

Gershon Weiler

theism is an intellectual position derivative of and parasitic upon theism. Its exponents hold that the thesis "God exists" is false. Thus the varieties of atheism largely correspond to the kinds of theism professed and these, significantly, include the varieties of religions. The character of any version of atheism essentially depends on the kind of answer that its theistic rival gives to the question, What is meant by *God*? or put differently, Under what description is the term *God* to be understood?

God is a logically troublesome term, for it is not readily classifiable either as a proper name (like *Churchill*) or as a class-name (like *table*); the difficulties that follow from this circumstance are well highlighted in the doctrine of Maimonides about the negative nature of divine attributes. By reason of this ambiguity, various doctrines of theism and various religions fill the term *God* with different content and meaning; hence, the varieties of atheism. Against theists who hold that God is the creator, the atheist argues for the eternity of matter and the absurdity of thinking that something could come from nothing, with the consequence that creation ex nihilo cannot be a true account of the origin of anything. Against theistic attempts to explain away evil by asserting that it is only apparent and that, in truth, the world in its entirety is a manifestation of God's infinite wisdom and kindness, the atheist argues that evil in the world is real and that, therefore, it is impossible that there should exist a God who is infinitely good and infinitely powerful. Against the cosmological arguments of the theist, according to which God is the First Cause and the First Mover, the atheist points out that these alleged proofs for the existence of God rest upon obsolete Aristotelian physical theory. Against the teleological arguments allegedly supporting theism, the atheist follows David Hume's classic refutations in his *Dialogues Concerning Natural Religion* (1779) and holds, for example, that it is a mistake to think of the world-as-a-whole as if it were an artifact, and thus exhibits design by an intelligent being, since artifacts are no more inherently intelligible than the production of organisms by biological generation. The atheist will also adopt Hume's observation that the world bears no more witness to the existence of a creator than it does to a committee of designers.

Of particular philosophical interest is the atheistic proof for the nonexistence of God invented by John Findlay. This consists of an inside-out version of the ontological proof for the existence of God, itself the most impressive of all proofs for God's existence. Findlay's disproof, in brief, is this: The theist is right in holding that only a God whose existence is necessary could be a worthy object of worship; however, since all existence is factual and contingent and thus nothing satisfies the theistic requirements, it is therefore impossible for God to exist.[1]

Atheism is often sharply distinguished from agnosticism; however, both positions overlap to a considerable extent. The agnostic claims not to know whether it is true or not that God exists, but this position can be understood in two different ways. The agnostic can be taken to mean that he is aware of considerations for and against the truth of God's existence and that he cannot make up his mind. But he can also be taken to mean that while he has no proof to offer that "God exists" is false, yet he has no reason either for believing it to be true. This second interpretation is but a variety of atheism. To elucidate, consider the following: "There is a little green man somewhere in the Himalayas who exercises telepathic influence over the doings of all mankind." Now, the truth of this assertion is neither entailed nor contradicted by all we know, and indeed, it can be made consistent with all we know. Yet most people would not say that they are agnostics with respect to the existence of the little green man, but rather would flatly deny that there is any such thing, meaning thereby that they have not the slightest reason for holding that he exists. It is perfectly rational, and thus quite common, to take the same attitude toward the God of established religion and hold that there is no more reason for supposing that there exists, for example, a God under the description of an all-benevolent, all-powerful creator who takes a special interest in the behavior of the Jews than there is for believing in the existence of any of the personages of classical mythology. A person who subscribed to such a view would be straddling agnosticism and atheism.

Historically, atheism is usually taken to mean the denial of the existence of God described in Judeo-Christian Scripture. Hence, the atheist typically denies the divine origin of these Scriptures. Since for many centuries all social order has been taken to rest not only upon the truth of those Scriptures but also upon the rules of conduct they endorsed, an atheist was regarded as a socially dangerous person. For this reason the history of atheism is also the record of persecution of atheists. Plato in his *Laws* subjects some of them to "one death . . . or two,"[2] while Thomas Aquinas no less than Moses Maimonides directs that they be done away with.[3] Even the great advocate of religious toleration, John Locke, in his *A Letter Concerning Toleration* specifically excepts atheism together with Catholicism from the range of views to be tolerated. In 1964, however, Pope Paul VI, in his *Ecclesiam Suam,* acknowledged that some atheists have been undoubtedly inspired by "great-hearted dreams of justice and progress."[4]

The thinker who most readily comes to mind in this context is Baruch Spinoza. He was certainly an atheist in the sense indicated here since he pioneered the view that Scripture bears all the marks of a human product given that it abounds with textual corruption, grammatical errors, downright forgeries, and even mistakes in arithmetic. He once told a secret agent of the Inquisition, whose report survives, that he believed in God "only philosophically," that is, only under the description of "the sum-total of the laws of nature."[5] He was, therefore, not only an atheist in the general sense but also one within the meaning of Judaism, since the chosenness of the Jews is inconsistent with the uniformity of the laws of nature.

In the context of Judaism, the most articulate specification of the concept of atheism is to be found in Maimonides. The issue is complicated by the fact that his term *kofer* (literally, he who denies) does not possess the same built-in neutrality as does the English term *nonbeliever*. A *kofer*, (pl. *kofrim*) is one who denies the true conviction, arrived at after due study and consideration, that "the object is exactly as apprehended" (*Guide* 1, 50). Maimonides takes God's existence to be a demonstrable truth and thus the *kofer* is wrong in precisely the same way as someone who denies that the sum of the angles in a triangle is equal to two right angles. The very term *kofer* suggests that it is truth itself that is being denied.

Actually, Maimonides carefully distinguishes between two kinds of denial. The *kofer* just mentioned is *kofer be'ikkar,* since the existence of God is the *ikkar,* that is, the first principle "that all depends on it" (MT Yesodei ha-Torah 1:6). The "all" includes the Torah. Yet Maimonides is chiefly concerned to denounce as *kofrim* not simply those who deny God's existence but also those who hold wrong views about God, for example, that God is not one in the sense he specifies, or that God is corporeal (*Guide* 1, 36). This makes very good sense, since "existence" as such is empty unless filled with content.

Against the *kofrim be'ikkar,* Maimonides sets the *kofrim ba-Torah,* who deny the Torah (MT Teshuvah 3:8). Maimonides does not distinguish with sufficient clarity this latter type of *kofrim* from *apikorsim,* whose name derives from the philosopher Epicurus. Indeed, in the locus indicated, he treats them together. The *kofer ba-Torah* denies that the Torah as we have it, both written and oral, originates from God in its totality. The *apikores* denies, among other things, the very possibility of prophecy in general and the veracity of Moses' prophecy in particular. It is easy to see, then, that both the *kofer ba-Torah* and the *apikores* are engaged in discrediting the institutional authority of the Torah and of its authoritative interpreters. Accordingly, in the introduction to Maimonides' chapter *Helek* of the *Mishneh Torah,* the term *apikores* is taken to refer also to someone who "denigrates the Sages, or even an individual scholar *(talmid ḥakham)."* A far cry from denying God's existence, this qualification is nonetheless a natural extension of the concept of atheism in the context of the Jewish religion.

An atheist, finally, can deny God under one or more descriptions. Thus a deist, for example, would be an atheist under descriptions specific to Christianity or Judaism, but not necessarily in every sense. Spinoza was certainly both a *kofer be'ikkar* and a *kofer ba-Torah* in the sense of Maimonides, yet he surely possessed his own notion of God. Hence, the problem and the unease of recognition granted by monotheistic religions to believers in other such religions. Maimonides' own high rating of Islam versus his low rating of Christianity is very much in point. For the believer in the God of one religion may well be an atheist under a description adopted by another. Therefore, no less important than the question, What is meant by *atheism?* is the question, What kind of atheism is intended?

REFERENCES

1. John N. Findlay, "Can God's Existence Be Disproved?" in *New Essays in Philosophical Theology*, ed. Antony Flew and Alisdair MacIntyre (1955), 47–56.
2. Plato, *Laws*, Book 10, especially 908ff.
3. Thomas Aquinas, *Summa Theologiae*, I.Q 9, Art. 3.
4. Pope Paul VI, *Ecclesiam Suam* (1968).
5. Baruch Spinoza, *Tractatus Theologico-Politicus*, ch. 8–10.

BIBLIOGRAPHY

Paul Edwards, "Atheism," in *The Encyclopedia of Philosophy*, I (1967).

Antony Flew and Alisdair MacIntyre, eds., *New Essays in Philosophical Theology* (1955).

Fritz Mauthner, *Der Atheismus und-seine Geschichte im Abendlande*, 4 vols. (1920–1923).

Richard Robinson, *An Atheist's Values* (1964).

Authority

סמכות

Stephen Wald

The question of religious authority divides into two parts: first, Who possesses religious authority? and second, What is the source of its power to obligate? Maimonides, in his *Mishneh Torah,* answers unambiguously that the rabbinic High Court in the Temple in Jerusalem possesses the ultimate religious authority in Judaism:

> The High Court in Jerusalem is the root of the Oral Law and the pillars of instruction and from them law and judgment go out to all Israel, and in them the Torah trusted saying: "According to the Torah which they will instruct you"—this is a positive commandment; and everyone who accepts Moses our Master and his Torah is obligated to determine religious acts in accordance with them and to rely upon them.
>
> (MT Mamrim 1:2).

This authority derives from the Torah itself. The authority of Moses and the revelation at Sinai stand behind rabbinic authority. But on this point Maimonides is ambiguous: everyone who accepts (or believes in) the Torah is obligated to accept rabbinic authority. Only if this first acceptance is itself obligatory will the consequent acceptance of rabbinic authority be, strictly speaking, obligatory. For if the initial acceptance of Moses' Torah is a matter of choice, then so is the rabbinic authority that depends upon it. But precisely on this crucial point Maimonides is silent. How does one come to accept Moses and his Torah? Is it a free act of will? Is it somehow necessary and binding? On this point rests the entire question of the obligatory character of Jewish law as it has been transmitted through the generations. We will concentrate on this point and examine it from the differing perspectives of three medieval interpreters of rabbinic thought, Maimonides, Naḥmanides, and the *Zohar*.

The rabbis of the Mishnah asked why the Ten Commandments began with the words, "I am the Lord your God." As a simple statement of fact, indeed an obvious one to anyone who had experienced the Exodus from Egypt, it seems superfluous. Why did not the Ten Commandments simply commence with the first "command," that is, the prohibition of idol worship? The rabbis responded with a parable:

> It is comparable to a king of flesh and blood who entered a city. His servants said to him: Impose decrees upon them. He said to them: No! When they accept my kingship, I will impose decrees upon them, for if they will not accept my kingship, how should they accept my decrees?
>
> (Mekh. Yitro 6).

First the fact must be established that there is a king. Only afterward will his decrees be binding. This recognition of God's authority to impose decrees on his subjects is called by the rabbis accepting the kingdom of heaven. This acceptance is the necessary prerequisite for any authoritative command. This fact is reflected in the order of the paragraphs in the recitation of Shema. The tanna Rabbi Yehoshua ben Korḥa justified the order by claiming that "one should accept upon himself the kingdom of heaven first, and only afterwards accept upon himself the yoke of the commandments" (BT Ber. 2:2).

We have identified this concept in its classic rabbinic formulation. But, as this formula—accepting the kingdom of heaven—is expressed in terms of the parable quoted above, we must still ask: What reality is represented by the parable? How does one in fact come to recognize God's authority to command? What is the nature of this recognition, and what are its implications vis-à-vis the nature of religious authority?

When Maimonides comes to justify the order of the paragraphs of the

Shema, he substitutes for the rabbinic phrase "accepting the kingdom of heaven" a phrase of his own that illuminates his interpretation of the rabbinic phrase:

> One recites the paragraph of Shema first because it has in it the unity of God and the love of him and his study which is the great principle upon which all is dependent.
>
> (MT Shema 1:2).

This defines the content of "accepting the kingdom of heaven" as knowledge of God and his unity and the love of God, which Maimonides holds to be necessarily consequent upon true knowledge (MT *Yesodei Torah* 1:1– 2:2). The love of God and the burning desire to be close to him provide the only adequate motivation for the fulfillment of his will (MT Teshuvah 10), and therefore it is in them alone that the authority of his commandments is to be found.

But how does one come to such knowledge? Maimonides' answer is as unequivocal as it is controversial. He claims that one reaches the recognition of God and the desire to fulfill his will not through revelation but through independent investigation and reflection upon the world order. That faith in divine revelation should be grounded in the Aristotelian tradition of physics and metaphysics has seemed to not a few Jewish thinkers strange and indeed outrageous. But Maimonides' intent is clear and his reasoning sound. Authority that possesses no verifiable ground is at best doubtful. One that has no objective ground at all, but rather is constituted solely by the subjective act of acceptance, is arbitrary. If someone should reflect upon the fact that this authority is binding upon him only by his own subjective and arbitrary act of will, he must realize that this very act of unconditional will can just as easily release tomorrow what it bound today. An unconditional acceptance of authority cannot provide the true conviction necessary to found a life of faith within an authoritative framework. Paradoxically, in order for the commandments to be truly authoritative, they must ground themselves in a reality that precedes the act of acceptance and is therefore not dependent on the act of acceptance itself. This is the significance that Maimonides sees in the rabbis' observation that the first "commandment" could not be a simple command, to be accepted only on authority. Rather it had to be a statement of fact, an independently ascertainable truth, which, precisely by its independence and verifiability, could serve as a foundation for an acceptance of authority that would not immediately collapse under the weight of its own internal contradictions. It was this internal theological demand, and not any external apologetic pressure, that prompted Maimonides to look beyond the boundaries of authoritative tradition for the ground of its own authority. Even those who reject the specific content of Aristotelian metaphysics must contend with the power of this theological analysis: If authority wishes to absolutize itself by grounding itself in objective knowledge, it may have to relativize its specific content by admitting an external standard of truth. But if it wishes to absolutize its content by rejecting all external standards of truth, it must relativize its authority by making it wholly dependent upon the arbitrary and subjective will of the believer.

Nahmanides, the thirteenth-century talmudist and kabbalist, disagreed with Maimonides' notion of "accepting the kingdom of heaven." We cannot examine here Nahmanides' thought in detail, for it is neither simple nor unambiguous. Two elements of it, however, are fairly clear. First, Nahmanides felt that metaphysical proofs for the existence of God fail to demonstrate precisely those aspects of the traditional view of God upon which Jewish piety is based, namely, that God knows our deeds and rewards and punishes us accordingly. In Nahmanides' view all piety must be based upon fear of punishment for transgressing God's will and anticipation of reward for fulfilling it. Second, he claimed that historical knowledge as preserved faithfully in Jewish tradition forms the starting point for Jewish knowledge of God. Only through knowledge of the Exodus from Egypt can the Jew be certain that God knows and acts in history to save the righteous and punish the wicked, as he states in his introduction to his commentary on Job and comment on Exodus 20:2.

The certitude of historical knowledge and its ability to ground religious faith was and is a highly controversial issue. However, it is Nahmanides' first point that is of immediate interest to us, that is, that the foundation of true piety must be fear of divine retribution. It is the knowledge of this theological truth attained through history that, for Nahmanides, constitutes "accepting the kingdom of heaven."

The most striking criticism of Nahmanides' position is not to be found among the Jewish philosophers, but in the words of the *Zohar,* the central work of Spanish kabbalah. The *Zohar* agrees that the first commandment must be conceived as "fear of God," but qualifies the meaning of the term:

Fear may be divided into three types, two of which lack the proper root of fear and one of which has the root of true fear. Some fear God so that their children will live and not die, or he fears punishment of his body or loss of his money . . . Some fear God because they fear the punishment of the next world and the punishment of Gehinnom. These two are not the root of fear nor the core of it. The fear which is the root, is that one should fear his Lord because he is the master and ruler, root and core of all worlds, and all else is insignificant before Him.

(*Zohar* Gen. 11b).

This is a classic restatement of the famous assertion in *Pirkei Avot* (*Ethics of the Fathers*):

Do not be as servants who serve the master in order to receive a reward; rather be as servants who serve the master not in order to receive a reward; and let the fear of heaven be upon you.

(*Pirkei Avot* 1:3).

The *Zohar* seems to have understood the final words to mean "*only* then will the fear of heaven be upon you," for it goes on to make the radical claim that

one who fears because of punishment . . . the fear of God that is called the fear of the living God does not rest upon him.

(*Zohar* Gen. 11b).

Moreover, if one does not have this true fear, his service of God is meaningless:

One who observes "fear" observes all the rest; if he does not observe "fear" he does not observe the commandments of the Torah for it (fear) is the gateway to all the rest.

(*Zohar* Gen. 11b).

The *Zohar* does not doubt that God does reward and punish in this world. But it is precisely this divine justice that brings with it a mortal danger: perhaps people will fulfill God's will not as an act of devotion to him, but rather out of fear of punishment. Yet it is only the act of devotion, the inner truth of the act, that grants the act religious value. An act performed out of fear of punishment is irreconcilable with an attitude of devotion to and love of God. But this attitude, "accepting the kingdom of heaven," is the prerequisite for any truly religious act, for any real commandment. The fact that the punishment comes from God does nothing to alter the basic nature of the act. A cowering act of fearful submission does not, according to the *Zohar,* acquire any additional religious significance simply because the overpowering and threatening figure is divine and not human. From this it would be safe to infer that certainly no religious significance can be ascribed to acts compelled by social pressure or political coercion, even if those who compel are duly constituted religious authorities.

In summary, not all authority exercised in the name of religion, whether by human or divine agents, can strictly speaking be termed religious authority. Much authority exercised by religious figures in this manner may even be considered antireligious. True religious authority, which is grounded in true fear of heaven, must be an authority that elicits, that "compels," a religious act, an act of devotion to and love of God. As argued above, this kind of authority can derive only from the independent authority of some objective standard of truth, whether philosophical, historical, or mystical.

BIBLIOGRAPHY

David Hartman, *Maimonides: Torah and Philosophic Quest* (1976).
Gershom Scholem, *On the Kabbalah and Its Symbolism: Authority and Mysticism* (1965).
Efraim Urbach, *The Sages: Their Concepts and Beliefs* (1975).

Bible Criticism

ביקורת המקרא

Moshe Weinfeld

Critical questions concerning the composition of biblical literary creations, and especially the Pentateuch, were raised as early as medieval times. Joseph Ibn Kaspi, the fourteenth-century Provençal Jewish philosopher and exegete, paid special attention to the differentiation of divine names in the Torah: Tetragrammaton on the one hand and Elohim (God) on the other. It is true that Ibn Kaspi never entertained the idea that because of the interchange of divine names there might be two sources represented in the Pentateuch. However, his attempts to account for the different names of God in the Torah may be considered a forerunner of the modern approaches to the same problem.[1]

The pioneer of biblical source criticism was the eighteenth-century Parisian physician Jean Astruc, who laid the foundations for the distinction of sources in the Pentateuch on the basis of the different divine names used in the various pericopes of the book of Genesis.[2] Another pioneer of the modern study of the Bible, Johann Gottfried Eichhorn, elaborated Astruc's thesis, grounding it on literary and ideational considerations.[3] It was only through the writings of Hermann Hupfeld, however, that the now famous

thesis that still dominates biblical scholarship regarding the four constitutive documents of the Bible—J (Jahwist), E (Elohist), P (Priestly Source),
and D (Deuteronomy)—was firmly established.[4]

J and E (Jahwist and Elohist) are most readily separable in the book of
Genesis, where the division into sources is based on the striking external
feature of J's use of *YHWH* for God as opposed to E's use of *Elohim*. These
sources are more difficult to differentiate in the subsequent books of the
Torah, because after the revelation of the burning bush the name YHWH is
used by E as well. For this reason, it is customary to speak of JE, thereby
avoiding the problem of uncertain division. The differentiation between J
and E in Genesis helps to explain such contradictions and repetitions as the
two flights of Hagar (Gen. 16, 21:9–21); the two abductions of Sarah (Gen.
12:10–20, 20); Jacob's wealth, acquired by his own cunning on the one
hand (Gen. 30:25–43) and by the advice of an angel in a dream on the
other (Gen. 31:9, 11ff.); Reuben's rescue of Joseph through causing him to
be thrown into a pit and pulled out by the Midianites on the one hand (Gen.
37:20–24, 28a, 29–30) and Joseph's being saved by virtue of Judah's selling
him to the Ishmaelites on the other (Gen 37:25–27, 28b), and Reuben's
offering surety for Benjamin (Gen. 42:37) against Judah's identical offer
(Gen 43:9). The division into sources is supported by both the varying use
of divine epithets and the employment of different names for Jacob (Jacob
as opposed to Israel). Similarly, the two sources can be recognized by their
different religious ideologies. While J represents direct contact between
God and the patriarchs, E tends to soften and refine this contact by introducing a dream or an angel as an intermediary (see, for example, Gen.
20:3ff., 28:12, 21:11–13), even though this difference is not to be viewed
as absolute and decisive. The difficulties encountered in separating the
sources stem from the fact that the redactor who combined them attempted
to smooth out rough spots and create uniformity, creating the impression
that we are dealing not with two independent sources but with only one
(J), which was simply supplemented by a later source (E).

The Priestly Source (P) is marked by a systematic religious and ideological
outlook not found in JE. It is P who explicitly states the idea that God did
not reveal himself in his true name prior to Moses (Ex. 6ff.), and according
to this source the God of Israel designated the tabernacle erected by Moses
as his abode, the only place where sacrifices could be offered (cf. Lev. 17).
In accordance with this view the priestly source describes the patriarchal
period as devoid of divine worship through sacrifice. Circumcision and the
Sabbath occupy significant positions in this source (Gen. 1; Ex. 12:44, 48,
16:12–17, 35:1–3). It is only natural that priestly circles should be highly

concerned about these matters, which give external-physical expression to Israel's uniqueness. Furthermore, circumcision and the Sabbath, along with the rainbow (Gen. 9:1–17), are, according to the Priestly Source, parts of the complex of signs symbolizing the covenants made by God with mankind and with the Israelite forefathers. The priestly material in Genesis has the sole purpose of serving the priestly-sacred tendency that emphasizes the element of holiness in Israel and its institutions—the purpose served also by the priestly passages in Exodus, Leviticus, and Numbers.

Central to the world of the Priestly Source is the Temple and all that it entails. The Temple is so important in the priestly work that it supersedes even such a crucial event as the Sinaitic covenant. In contrast to JE and D, the priestly source says nothing about the revelation of the giving of the law at Sinai. It describes instead a theophany at the time of the dedication of the tabernacle, when fire comes forth from before YHWH and consumes the burnt offering and the fats on the altar (Lev. 9:24), symbolizing the establishment of the divine Presence in Israel.

The material in the priestly source deals primarily with matters of holiness and cult such as sacrifices (Lev. 1–10), impurity and purity (Lev. 11–16), abstinence for the sake of holiness pertaining to the Israelites (Lev. 18, 20) and the priests (Lev. 21, 22), holy seasons (Lev. 23; Num. 28–29), and sabbatical and jubilee years as the land's observance of the Sabbath of the Lord (Lev. 25). Even when recounting a past event—the creation (Gen. 1:1–2, 3), the covenants with Noah and Abraham (Gen. 9:1–17, 17), or the Exodus from Egypt—interest is still centered upon sacred institutions of Israel like the Sabbath, circumcision, the prohibition against eating blood, or the paschal offering.

Another source, contained in one book of the Pentateuch and literally an organic composition, is Deuteronomy (D). It is fashioned as a farewell address of Moses delivered in the plains of Moab, is written in an autobiographical fashion (Deut. 1–31), and is characterized by a unique style and expression. Both by its ideas and by its linguistic peculiarities it influenced the redactor of the books of the early prophets, especially the editor of Kings, and also the book of Jeremiah.

This book was fundamental for the determination of the dates of the pentateuchal sources in general. De Wette established the still-accepted premise that Deuteronomy reflects, in both content and form, the period of Hezekiah-Josiah.[5] Thus he paved the way for the historical-chronological sequence of the pentateuchal sources whose actual existence was already recognized in the eighteenth century. De Wette looked for a historical anchor for the formation of the Pentateuch and found it in the account of the discovery of a book of the law in 622 B.C.E. (II Kings 22–23). The story of the book's discovery, the description of its contents, and the activity that it stimulated indicate that the book that was found was the book of Deuteronomy.

The most important proof of Deuteronomy's date is the centralization of the cult in Jerusalem: according to the information in the book of Kings, the first king to unify the cult in Jerusalem was Hezekiah in the eighth century B.C.E. (II Kings 18:3); before De Wette this idea had occurred to no one. We also know that in the Pentateuch the only law that demands unity of worship is found in Deuteronomy.[6] We can therefore assume that this law started to develop in the time of Hezekiah and was already fully formed and had achieved literary expression in the days of Josiah. The criterion of cult unification in dating D is supplemented by two other criteria: (1) a style of a sort that does not appear before Josiah's time, but afterward spread rapidly and dominated biblical literature, namely, Kings, Jeremiah, and the books of the later prophets; (2) the book of Deuteronomy, which is structured along the lines of a covenantal document, beginning with a historical introduction in chapters 1–11, followed by stipulations in 12:1–26 and 15 and commitments in 26:16–19 and 27: 9–10, and concluding with blessings and curses in chapter 28, contains a wealth of literary forms and modes of expression known to us from contemporary Assyrian literature of the eighth and seventh centuries B.C.E., especially from treaties between the Assyrian kings and their vassals.[7]

The date of the book of Deuteronomy serves as a point of departure for determining the dates of the remaining pentateuchal sources. Those assuming the existence of noncentralized worship, such as Exodus 20:21–23, clearly belong to the pre-Hezekiah-Josianic age, while those demanding centralized worship come from a later period. Accordingly, it is clear that JE is earlier than D; as for P, however, there is still debate. In the view of the German scholar Julius Wellhausen, P was written during the Babylonian Exile and therefore takes unification of the cult for granted.[8] The Israeli scholar Yehezkel Kaufmann, by contrast, refutes Wellhausen's claims and convincingly proves that P does not assume unification of the cult, but rather that the priestly laws reflect a stage prior to centralization.[9] The decisive factors in dating P are the time of the cultic institutions described and the style of the source. Wellhausen's claims do not stand up to either of these tests. Documents from the ancient Near East show us over and over again that institutions such as those found in P were known throughout the ancient Near East centuries before Israel even entered its land.[10] On the other hand, the priestly style has no features that would indicate lateness.[11]

Source criticism was based on the conception that each source has its author who lived in a certain period and worked under defined historico-social circumstances. This supposition was undermined by the discovery of texts of the ancient Near East that made clear that the ancient authors did not create works out of their own mind—as do modern ones—but rather collected ancient traditions, oral or written, and imparted to them a framework. It was Hermann Gunkel and Hugo Gressmann who stressed the necessity of going beyond the sources and isolating the traditions that lie behind the sources. These traditions belong to different circles and to different periods. Moreover, these traditions fulfilled a function in the life of the nation and as such were built around a certain fixed pattern. Through revealing the pattern of a tradition one is able to define its role or place in life (Sitz im Leben) and to identify its bearers, as, for example, priests, elders, prophets, or members of the court.

This new approach proved itself efficient, especially when applied to the traditional themes and cycles embodied in the Pentateuch, such as the Exodus cycle in Exodus 1–15, the Sinai cycle in Exodus 19–24, and the conquest cycle in Numbers 20–35. Exodus 1–14, for example, was seen by Johannes Pedersen as an independent literary cycle originating in the Passover drama.[12] The Sinaitic cycle, on the other hand, has been seen by Gerhard von Rad[13] as the outcome of the covenant festival, or Pentecost.[14] The conquest cycle, which is linked to the Gilgal traditions in Joshua, has been seen as rooted in a ceremony performed annually in the sanctuary of Gilgal.

The form-critical or traditional approach did not see itself as replacing the source-critical approach, but only as supplementing it by looking into the material incorporated into the sources. One must admit, however, that positing the existence of literary traditional cycles is not without problems for the source-critical approach.[15]

The existence of independent traditions makes it difficult to distinguish the connections between one tradition and the other, and therefore the integrity of the large cycle of traditions looks defective. In spite of this, however, one must admit that the cycle of traditions, that is, the source, constitutes a continuous story in which events evolve one from the other and thus form one plot.

REFERENCES

1. Cf. B. Herring, *Joseph ibn Kaspi's Gevia' Kesef: A Study in Medieval Jewish Philosophic Bible Commentary* (1982), 77–79.

2. Jean Astruc, *Conjectures sur les mémoires dont il paroît que Moyse s'est servi pour composer le livre de la Gênese* (1973).
3. Johann Gottfried Eichhorn, *Einleitung in das Alte Testament*, 3 vols. (1780–1783).
4. Hermann Hupfeld, *Die Quellen der Genesis und die Art ihrer Zusammensetzung* (1853).
5. W. M. L. De Wette, *Dissertatio critico-exegetica, qua Deuteronium a prioribus Pentateuchi libris diversum, alius cuiusdam recentioris auctoris opus esse monstratur* (1805).
6. Cf. Deut. 12 and other laws presented there, based on the idea of centralization.
7. Cf. Moshe Weinfeld, *Deuteronomy and the Deuteronomic School* (1972).
8. Julius Wellhausen, *Prolegomena to the History of Ancient Israel* (1957).
9. Yehezkel Kaufmann, *The Religion of Israel*, tr. and abridged by Moshe Greenberg (1960).
10. Cf. Moshe Weinfeld, "Cultic and Social Institutions in the Priestly Source Against Their Ancient Near Eastern Background," in *Eighth World Congress of Jewish Studies* (1983), 95–129.
11. Cf. A. Hurvitz, *A Linguistic Study of the Relationship Between the Priestly Source and the Book of Ezekiel* (1982).
12. Johannes Pedersen, "Passahfest und Passahlegende," in *Zeitschrift für die alttestamentliche Wissenschaft* 33 (1934), 161ff.
13. Gerhard von Rad, *Das formgeschichtliche Problem des Hexateuch* (1938).
14. Cf. Moshe Weinfeld, "Pentecost as a Festival of the Giving of the Law," in *Immanuel (Bulletin of Religious Thought and Research in Israel)* 8 (Spring 1978).
15. Rolf Rendtorff, *Das Überbeferungsgeschichtliche Problem des Pentateuch* (1977); Hans Heinrich Schmid, *Der sogennante Jahwist* (1976).

BIBLIOGRAPHY

Yehezkel Kaufmann, *The Religion of Israel*, tr. and abridged by Moshe Greenberg (1960).

Gerhard von Rad, *The Problem of the Hexateuch and Other Essays*, tr. by E. W. T. Dicken (1966).

Moshe Weinfeld, *Deuteronomy and the Deuteronomic School* (1972).

Julius Wellhausen, *Die Composition des Hexateuchs und der historischen Bucher des Alten Testaments*, 4th ed. (1963).

Julius Wellhausen, *Prolegomena to the History of Ancient Israel*, tr. by Black and Menzies (1957).

Catastrophe

חורבן

Alan Mintz

atastrophe may be defined as a national calamity that undermines the received paradigms of meaning concerning the relationship between God and Israel. The national, collective nature of catastrophe distinguishes it from the related but separate problem of evil, the theme of Job and the Wisdom Literature, which pertains to the justification of individual suffering detached from historical events. The catastrophic potential in historical events can be gauged not by the quantum of pain, death, and material destruction but rather by the degree of damage to the cognitive, theological frameworks that bind the people to their God. In its historical aspect, the problem of catastrophe involves the study of how in different periods of Jewish history these frameworks of explanation were reconstructed or transformed.

In biblical and midrashic literature the explanation for catastrophe is rooted in the conception of the covenant developed by the Deuteronomist and later focused by the classical prophets. The provisions of the covenant attempted to anticipate and defuse the grave theological dangers triggered by the temptation to interpret massive political-military reversals in one of several ways: as an eclipse of God's power in the world arenas, as a permanent and willful abandonment of the people, or as an insufficiently motivated act of anger. The idea of the covenant, by contrast, required that historical destruction be understood as a deserved and necessary punishment for sins committed, and one carried out by means strictly controlled by God. Catastrophe therefore constituted a corrective moment in an on going relationship; it signaled the perseverance of divine concern rather than its withdrawal. If Israel would accept catastrophe as punishment and return to God, then the surviving remnant would serve as the basis for renewed national fortune.

When the destruction occurred in fact in 587–586 B.C.E., this covenantal paradigm was submitted to extraordinary stress. The stunned anguish recorded in the Book of Lamentations reveals how tenuous was the hold of the prophetic theology on the people and on the cultic establishment. For it was widely believed that God's commitment to the Davidic succession of the monarchy and to the inviolability of the Jerusalem Temple was absolute. With the wiping out of these institutions came severe disorientation: What sins could have been so heinous, it was asked, to have warranted the visitation of so massive a destruction? The poets of Lamentations strive to defuse such questions by attending to the literary representation of suffering and by working toward a newly felt connection between suffering and sin. The dimensions of this theological crisis are indicated by the nature of the text of Second Isaiah. Isaiah preached a message of imminent restoration to the exiles of the Destruction based upon God's appointment of Cyrus as the nemesis of the Neo-Babylonian Empire. The main burden of Isaiah's prophecy, however, is more fundamental. The very faculty of belief had atrophied. Through strategies of rhetorical brilliance, the prophet labors to restore the predisposition to accept God as capable once again of directing history and renewing the covenant.

When it comes to the destruction of the Second Temple, it is impossible to separate the issue of the rabbis' complex attitudes to the Jerusalem cult from the formation of the entire edifice of rabbinic Judaism. Although such institutions as the system of *mizvot*, the role of the sage, and the doctrine of the afterlife all developed before the Destruction, they can be interpreted as anticipatory responses to that loss and as functional compensations in its aftermath. In a more strictly theological framework, the explanation of the catastrophe offered by the rabbis was roughly of a piece with the covenantal paradigm of the prophets—with the exception that the rabbis deferred the moment of restoration and redemption to a messianic era after the end of history. Although the paradigm was the same, the means available of reconfirming it were very different. In the Bible, God speaks to the prophets and reveals his intentions to them; for the rabbis, God's will is manifest only in the texts of the Bible and recoverable only through the work of exegesis. As the central biblical text concerning destruction, Lamentations required interpretation. Yet at the same time it was an exceedingly difficult text to assimilate into the covenant paradigm: the depiction of God's victimization of his people is gruesome, Israel's consciousness of wrongdoing is dim, and in the face of repeated entreaties there is no offer of consolation, only God's silence.

The considerable exegetical ingenuity of the rabbis is applied to these challenges. They discover in the text of Lamentations hints of extreme transgression, which "justify" the enormity of the Destruction, and they introduce the theme of divine pathos, in which God is depicted as a mourning father stricken with sorrow over the fate of his children. A teaching of consolation is made possible by the rabbis' belief in Scripture as a total system of divine signs. The severity of Lamentations could therefore be mitigated by juxtaposing it with visions of redemption from other stations in the universe of Scripture, such as the prophecies of Second Isaiah. The one biblical theme that remains unsusceptible to rabbinic reinterpretation is the shame of Israel before the nations. Reasons can be given for the sufferings of Israel on account of its sins; however, that the nations would prosper and jeer at Israel in its expiatory ordeals constituted a humiliation too painful to be assuaged.

In the Middle Ages the theological responses to catastrophe must be tracked in the separate spheres of Ashkenaz and Sephard. The writings of Maimonides on the Almohade persecutions and those of the exiled historians on the Spanish Expulsion strive to explicate the fluctuations of Jewish history in ways that could account for recent distresses and thereby offer consolation for these tribulations. Although their means are different, the goal of these arguments is continuous with the biblical-rabbinic effort to rationalize catastrophe within the drama of covenantal history.

In the sphere of Ashkenazi Jewry, however, the received paradigm was transformed altogether. Catastrophe as punishment, the central component of the biblical-rabbinic view, was no longer experienced as applicable to explaining what took place in the Rhineland Jewish communities during the Crusader massacres in the eleventh and twelfth centuries. The correlation between the massive visitation of destruction and the massive commission of transgression was an admission that the self-perception of the Jews of Mainz, Speyer, and Worms could not authorize. Their confidence in the righteousness and strength of their scholarship and piety was so secure that an alternative means of explanation had to be found. The solution was to adopt the concept of "afflictions from love," a minor rabbinic explanation for suffering, akin to the idea of the trial in the Bible, which had hitherto been applied to cases of anomalous individual misfortune but not to collective destruction. Rehabilitated and reinforced, this conception held that suffering is an opportunity awarded by God to the most worthy for the display of righteousness and for the garnering of otherworldly rewards. Destruction was thus divorced from sin; the singling out of the generation's leaders for suffering became a spiritual compliment.

The ritual suicides and homicides with which some Jews met the Crusader demands for conversion were unprecedented acts, indeed acts unmandated by Jewish law. In the treatment given these events in the liturgical poetry of the next generation, the historical circumstances recede before the symbolic concentration on the sacrificial acts themselves. In the imagination of the *payyetanim* (the liturgical poets) these contemporary martyrdoms become assimilated to the drama of the sacrificial cult of the ancient Jerusalem Temple. The self-willed, ritually perfect human offering of the martyr not only collapsed the exilic distance between himself and the lost Temple but also transcended the ancient cult's restriction to animal sacrifice.

The act of martyrdom now moves to the center of the literary responses to catastrophe. In the Midrash, the portrayal of individual suffering functioned merely to underscore the pathos of the Destruction and to convey the covenantal meaning of the event. Nowhere is the moment and manner of dying dilated upon as it is in medieval Ashkenaz. Martyrdom was a spiritual arrival that conferred distinction not only upon the martyr but also upon his descendants, who could use his example as an argument to God for averting future persecutions, or, if it came to that, as a model for doing their duty. The sense of shame before the nations, which is prominent in the midrashic and Sephardic responses, is absent in Ashkenaz. Feelings about the Gentiles are projected outward in the form of contempt and malediction; the role played by the victimizer is secondary to the inner Jewish drama of the martyr's consummation.

The persecutions and depredations that followed the Crusader period—especially at the time of the Black Death in 1348 and the Chmielnicki Uprising in 1648—took place under varying constellations of religious and political forces. Each crisis confronted the Jews with a different set of demands and choices, and the actions taken in response were not uniform. In absolute terms of material destruction and loss of life, moreover, the Crusader massacres were less devastating than later misfortunes. Yet at the level of the iconographic imagination, especially as expressed in the traditions of synagogue poetry, the martyrological norm set in the Crusader period remained dominant.

With the exception of a figure like Naḥman Krochmal, the engagement with the issue of catastrophe in the nineteenth and early twentieth centuries is displaced from theological writing to a variety of secular discourses: Hebrew literature (Ḥayyim Naḥman Bialik, Uri Zevi Greenberg), the writing of history (Heinrich Graetz, Simon Dubnow), and ideology (Zionism, Socialism). The destruction of European Jewry provided the sad occasion for the resumption of theological debate.

BIBLIOGRAPHY

Sidra DeKoven Ezrahi, *By Words Alone: The Holocaust in Literature* (1980).

Ivan G. Marcus, "From Politics to Martyrdom: Shifting Paradigms in the Hebrew Narratives of the 1096 Crusade Riots," in *Prooftexts* 2:1 (January 1982).

Alan Mintz, *Ḥurban: Responses to Catastrophe in Hebrew Literature* (1984).

David G. Roskies, *Against the Apocalypse: Responses to Catastrophe in Modern Jewish Culture* (1984).

Shalom Spiegel, *The Last Trial,* Judah Goldin, tr. (1967).

Charity

צדקה

David Hartman and Tzvi Marx

The concept of *zedakah* (charity), a word that is etymologically related to *zedek* (justice), involves a person's response to the needs of other human beings. According to the Talmud and Maimonides, the disposition to be responsive to human beings in need is a *conditio sine qua non* of membership in the covenantal community of Israel.

Belief, in Judaism, is related to self-transcendence. It involves not only dogma and doctrine but also the psychological ability to acknowledge and respond to that which is other than oneself. A person who is imprisoned within his private needs and interests may be characterized as a nonbeliever insofar as his life lacks the dimension of transcendence. A person may utter the words "I believe," yet if he is unresponsive to others and generally unmoved by the world beyond his private domain, he fails to demonstrate belief in a transcendent God.

Through personal moral training in the very specific issues involved in *zedakah*, Maimonides and the fourteenth-century halakhic authority Jacob ben Asher (known as the Tur) suggest that the foundation is laid for the reformation of society in its juridical and political dimensions. Efforts to solve the dilemmas and frustrations in the microcosm of charity are expected to bear fruit in the macrocosm of righteousness. The particularity of the problem tackled by *zedakah* does not detract from the magnitude of the value achieved. On the contrary, its ripple effect is felt on the broader levels of society. Thus Maimonides can claim, on the authority of Rabbi Assi (BT BB 9a), that "we are duty bound to observe the *mizvah* of *zedakah* more than all other *mizvot 'aseh'* (positive commandments)" (MT Hil. Matenot Aniyyim 10:1). It is because of the overreaching effect that *zedakah* works upon the character of man that such a claim can be made. The value meaning of the achievement of *zedakah* lies at the heart and soul of all the *mizvot*, and for this reason it is seen as the standard bearer of the seed of Abraham.

There is an interesting midrashic comment on one of the biblical verses dealing with assisting those in need. The verse reads:

> And if your brother become poor and his means fail him with you, then you shall strengthen him, be he a stranger or a settler, he shall live with you.
>
> (Lev. 25:35).

Rashi's commentary on this verse (paraphrasing the midrash in *Torat Kohanim, Behar,* 5:1) focuses on the clause "you shall strengthen him":

> Do not let him slip down until he falls completely, for then it will be difficult to raise him; rather strengthen him as he begins to fall. To what is this comparable? To a burden upon an ass: while it is still on the ass, one person can hold it and set it in place; if it falls to the earth, even five people cannot set it back.

One can understand this midrash as making a commonplace point about the difficulty of assisting a person who has fallen into total poverty. The midrash tells the reader: "Don't wait for him to fall completely." Perhaps the psychological insight underlying this midrash is that people often prefer responding to the needs of others where there is total helplessness rather than where the dependency is not so obvious. It is particularly difficult to respond to a dependency situation when we are not certain that the recipient will be fully aware and appreciative of our help and concern. One may refer to the case cited by Rashi as *preventive zedakah:* anticipating the needs of others and responding in a manner that forestalls total failure and helplessness. Preventive *zedakah* may lack the drama and glamor of crisis *zedakah*, yet because of this it ranks as a high and refined level of *zedakah*.

The most subtle expression of *zedakah* involves one's response to a person one cannot adequately help.

If a poor man requests money from you and you have nothing to give him, speak to him consolingly. It is forbidden to upbraid a poor person or to shout at him because his heart is broken and contrite, as it is said, "A broken and contrite heart, O God, You will not despise" [Ps. 51:19], and it is written, "To revive the spirit of the humble, and to revive the heart of the contrite" [Isa. 57:15]. Woe to him who shames a poor man. Rather one should be as a father to the poor man, in both compassion and speech, as it is said, "I am a father to the poor"[Job 29:16].

(MT Hil. Matenot Aniyyim 10:5).

Maimonides is addressing himself to the problem of the hostility we may feel toward a person we are unable to help. Our inability to respond adequately to such a person's needs exposes our inadequacies and, therefore, we may transfer the anger we feel toward ourselves onto the needy person.

Zedakah is not only measured by concrete, efficacious action. It also involves the subjective response of sympathy—listening and sharing in the pain of the person in need irrespective of one's ability to solve or ameliorate the problematic condition at hand. *Zedakah* involves not only *"naton titten"* ("give to him readily") (Deut. 15:10), but also *"lo teammetz et levavkha"* ("do not harden your heart") (Deut. 15:7), irrespective of the feasibility of effective action.

Dealing with the sense of inadequacy of the benefactor, individually and/or communally, is one of the considerations that enter into the formulation of specific guidelines in the halakhic approach. Guidelines, or *halakhot,* help to defuse the tendency toward all-or-nothing reactions when people are faced with seemingly insoluble problems. They are a bridge between the sought-after dream and the commitment to the possible. The prophets dreamed in metaphors of turbulent streams of righteousness, as in "Let justice well up like water, Righteousness (*zedakah*) like an unfailing stream" (Amos 5:24). Rabbinic halakhah translated these visions into the possible. The Mishnah, at Pe'ah 8:7, recommends that "one must not give the wandering poor man less than a loaf worth a *pondion* [Roman coin equal to a half zuz or two issars] at a time when four se'ahs of wheat cost one sela [nine selah equal four pondions; four se'ahs equal 24 kabs]." In this way the scriptural "mighty stream of righteousness" was converted into the talmudic "half a kab or 12 eggs volume of bread."

How are needs rated in terms of urgency and intensity? Do economic categories alone suffice to evaluate human needs? Some insight into the treatment of this problem can be seen from the discussion of the respective marital needs of the *yatom* and *yetomah* (boy and girl orphans). In the halakhic framework, marital needs are placed on a par with economic needs (parnassah). In the competition to satisfy this social and emotional need, the community is enjoined to apply the principle of greater neediness. In this case, the *yetomah* (orphan girl) and her needs take precedence over the *yatom*. "If an orphan boy and an orphan girl applied for a marriage grant, the girl orphan is to be enabled to marry first and the boy orphan is married afterwards, because the loss of self-esteem *(bushah)* of a woman is greater than that of a man" (BT Ket. 67b). In connection with this halakhah, we are also told in the same talmudic passage that "our Rabbis taught: If an orphan applied for assistance to marry, a house must be rented for him, a bed must be prepared for him and he must also be supplied with all household objects required for his use, and then he is given a wife in marriage . . ." (BT Ket. 67a).

In view of the orphan boy's apparently greater economic pressure insofar as he has to be provided with housing and furniture as well as wedding expenses, one may well ask, why does the orphan girl take precedence? The Talmud here expands the notion of helplessness to include the loss of self-esteem at being unmarried. *Bushah* is experienced by both the single man and the single woman who have reached marriageable age, but the woman's *bushah* is markedly greater, and this warrants extending assistance to her first. Whether the reality of losing face is understood in sociopsychological terms as reflecting social values during the Talmudic period or in existential terms as a permanent feature of the feminine personality is not the issue in this discussion. What is pertinent is that a noneconomic variable of deprivation is taken seriously in determining *zedakah* priorities. The sensitivity inherent in such an inclusion again emphasizes the complexity of the *zedakah* response. Economic deprivation does not exhaust the need considerations to which the system responds.

To feel the obligation of *zedakah* is to realize that each person belongs to others as others belong to him or her. It is to experience the emotion of communal identity. To be a Jew in light of the *mizvah* of *zedakah* is to meet another human being face to face. To be sensitive to an individual's needs makes a difference not only to that person but also to one's own self-understanding. One cannot ignore the human traffic that crosses the threshold of sympathy. One must extend one's identity and concern to encompass the other, in an awareness that one's "I" is impoverished if it cannot bridge this moral space. "If I am only for myself what am I?" (M. Avot 2:14).

The Talmud states in the name of Rabbi Ḥiyya bar Abba: "Rabbi Johanan pointed out that it is written (Prov. 11:4) . . . 'but righteousness *(zedakah)* delivers from death' . . . what kind of charity delivers a man from an unnatural death? When a man gives without knowing to whom he gives and the beggar receives without knowing from whom he receives" (BT BB 10a).

The halakhah, however, classifies the poor into distinct groups for purposes of assistance and recognizes distinguishing features that cut through the fog of total anonymity. The *yetomah* suffering with respect to her specific feminine anguish of *bushah* compels one to think of the poor in two classes, male and female. Even so, when one helps the *yetomah* first, it is not necessarily "her" specific need that one is trying to satisfy, but "her" need as a typical *yetomah*.

One senses here a dilemma of specificity. The halakhah wants us to meet the person in his or her human condition. How else can we be responsive? It is the human in the recipient of *zedakah* that arouses the human in us. Our identification is all the more pronounced to the degree that we can make out the particularity of the person in need. At the same time, the pauper's dependency on charity threatens his dignity and makes his claim to anonymity convincing.

The following story involving Hillel is very revealing.

> Our rabbis taught [commenting on Deut. 15:8] *"sufficient for his need"* [implies] you are commanded to maintain him, but you are not commanded to make him rich; *"in that which he wanteth"* [includes] even a horse to ride upon and a slave to run before him. It was related about Hillel the elder that he bought for a certain poor man who was of a good family a horse to ride upon and a slave to run before him. On one occasion he could not find a slave to run before him, so he himself ran before him for three miles.
>
> (BT Ket. 67b).

Hillel fulfilled the norm of *zedakah* by acting as a chauffeur for a poor person who had previously been wealthy. According to Hillel, *zedakah* requires that one give a person what that person lacks.

How far ought the particularization of the pauper's needs go? Does the ideal of *zedakah* direct one to respond to the idiosyncratic person in "his" poverty, with all the particularization that this entails? If that is so, his unique idiosyncratic needs are legitimate claims upon us that are limited only by our resources. On the other hand, one can claim that the pauper has a responsibility to formulate his needs within average and normal bounds. The state of poverty deprives him of his right to demand the luxury of particular satisfactions to which his particular way of life might have accustomed him, even though his deprivations in this regard constitute very real suffering. The thirteenth-century talmudic commentator Me'iri of Perpignan, for example, takes a narrow approach to the particular needs of the poor. He interprets the talmudic discussion that is supportive of those very special needs to apply only to situations that are acute (*Beit ha-Behirah*, ad loc. BT Ket. 67ff.).

We thus have two models of *zedakah* that relate to the issue of particularity. One defines the ideal *zedakah* response in terms of the individual qua individual: each pauper is a special case defined by his own history, temperament, and habits. The other meets the pauper as a member of a class and relegates his individual needs to the needs of the subclass of those paupers who share that need: the pauper's need is perceived as reflecting a more general mode of needs. In the latter view, the benefactor can remain indifferent to needs that are unique to the claimant. It was suggested that *duhka de zibura*—the burden to the community—can be the differentiating factor between these views. It should be apparent, however, that even those supporting the approach based on particularity do not demand responses that are completely beyond the resources of the community (cf. BT Ket. 67b).

Perhaps another issue lies behind this disagreement. The Me'iri's approach might be an argument to exclude responses to individual particularity even where resources are unlimited. By restricting particularity of need to class limitations, his ideal welfare structure makes it impossible for the pauper to work out and express his entire and legitimate style of life within the framework of welfare dependency. To know that his most personal mode of living can never be fulfilled within a welfare structure is an incentive to leave that structure and to relate to it as a transient. This built-in feature of frustration serves to prevent the poor person from organizing his life around his helplessness.

Charity and welfare programs all too often foster permanent helplessness and dependency. The Jewish tradition's understanding of the various forms of *zedakah* reveals a sensitive appreciation of this problem.

> There are eight degrees of charity, one higher than the other. The highest degree, exceeded by none, is that of the person who assists a poor Jew by providing him with a gift or a loan or by accepting him into a business partnership or by helping him find employment—in a word, by putting him where he can dispense with other people's aid. With reference to such aid, it is said, "You shall strengthen him, be he a stranger or a settler, he shall live with you" (Lev. 25:35), which means strengthen him in such a manner that his falling into want is prevented.
>
> (MT Hil. Matenot Aniyyim 10:7).

The highest level of *zedakah* is providing a person with the opportunity to work for a living so that he can alleviate his suffering and satisfy his needs by his own efforts and initiative. This aspect of *zedakah* focuses on the universal need for a person to become responsible for coping with the problems of his life through his own efforts. The norm of *zedakah* directs us to provide the needy with conditions wherein they can experience the dignity of self-help and personal adequacy. This, however, is not easily accomplished. "Charity," with all its paternalistic connotations, causes the poor to lose faith in themselves and empties people of the self-respect necessary for independence and self-reliance.

It is not necessary for the poor to express their needs in *zedakah* categories in order to qualify for *zedakah*. The benefactor should try to comprehend unspoken needs and respond to them, thereby maintaining the poor person's sense of dignity. Therefore, when possible, *zedakah* ought to be dispensed as a loan to maintain the façade of the destitute individual's self-sufficiency, even though in fact repayment will not be demanded (BT Ket. 67b): form determines content. And as previously mentioned, *zedakah,* to the degree possible, is to be dispensed anonymously (BT BB 9b). What is perhaps most radical in the talmudic consideration of the poor is the indulgence of the pauper in some degree of conspicuous consumption to help maintain his façade of self-sufficiency (BT Ket. 67b). We do not expect the unfortunate pauper to parade his indigence. At the same time, the Talmud avoids the romanticization of the pauper by soberly acknowledging that he may seek to exploit the sensitive responses of sympathetic people.

Zedakah forces one to see oneself at one's worst as well as at one's best. The benefactor discovers the temptation to ignore others, to be indifferent to their fates, and to rationalize his indifference in respectable terms. "R. Eleazar said, 'Come let us be grateful to rogues for were it not for them, we would have been sinning every day' [in that we do not give charity to our capacity]" (BT Ket. 68a). That there are those who take advantage of our benevolent inclination, the Talmud emphasizes, serves as an irresistible rationalization to curb our generosity in all events. The rogue "out there" helps to conceal the rogue within ourselves.

The pauper discovers the tragic meaning of his dependency upon his fellow man in having to swallow his pride and conceal his real personality in asserting very limited claims. His need for *zedakah* reveals his temptation to deceive in exploiting the guilt and sympathy of his benefactor.

According to the Talmud, belief in God shatters egocentricity. Inflated self-centeredness precludes the living expression of belief in the God of the covenant. The norm of *zedakah* in the Jewish tradition indicates the way in which transcendence becomes manifest in a person's responsiveness to the needs of another. In this sense, Isaiah's national prayer and prophecy that "Zion shall be redeemed with justice and they that return to her through *zedakah*" (Isa. 1:27) reflects the very same optimism that characterizes the individual who, having heard the cry of the weak and helpless, believes that he can rally the forces of his own redemption for the redemption of the other.

BIBLIOGRAPHY

David Hartman and Tzvi Marx, *The Dynamics of Tzedakah* (1983).
Tzvi Marx, "Priorities in Tzedakah and Their Implications," in *Judaism* 28 (1979).

Chosen People

עם סגולה

Henri Atlan

The prime source of the biblical concept of a chosen people is Exodus 19:5, where the God of Israel refers to the children of Israel as "my treasured possession among all the peoples [li segulah mikol ha-amim]" (cf. Deut. 7:6). Employing the verbal meaning of the root of the term *segulah* as elaborated in medieval, postrabbinic literature (viz. *segel,* to adapt, to adjust), one may homiletically interpret this passage as suggesting that there was a perfect match or harmony between Israel and its god. Indeed, one may speak of the chosen-people concept as pointing to a mutual adaptation between a particular people—a tribe of freed slaves whose existence as a people was inaugurated by the experience of liberation—and its god, who was revealed and defined only in that experience of liberation.[1] This perfect match, this mutual adaptation between a people and its god, had, of course, the immediate effect of differentiating that people from other peoples, separating it through the very act that established and defined it.

From the very outset this perfect match was expressed in the form of a covenant or constitution that, at the same time, identified the people with a plan, namely, "You shall be to me a kingdom of priests and a holy nation" (Ex. 19:6). The consequences of this plan could, however, be as unfortunate and catastrophic as they could be a blessing, depending upon the path taken by the people in its inner organization as well as in the behavior of its members, upon the function of its families and social mores, and its relations with surrounding peoples.

An almost immediate consequence of the definition and constitution of this people by its plan, by its social organization, and by the way family structures are preserved within the tribal organization led it to be conscious of a certain isolation even while its national and territorial fulfillment were but a promise. The election of a people by its god, with the separation that this implies, is not at all exceptional in the polytheistic context of myths describing the origins of ancient peoples. The Bible must be read, at least initially, as the myth of the origin of the people of Israel. Every people plays a central role in the cosmogony its culture teaches. The election of the Hebrews by their god, as described in the Bible, must first be understood in the context of myths of origin, in which each people considers itself the center of the universe.

In the Jewish tradition two currents of thought that emphasize different and apparently contradictory aspects of the content of election can be discerned. One of those currents emphasizes the universality of the biblical message. Election does not imply superiority or inherent sanctity, since the correct reading of the Bible in fact implies conditional chosenness. The election is one of duty, not of rights or attributes. Superiority and sanctity do not belong to historical Israel, to concrete individuals, but to a mythical Israel, held up as a model and ideal, defined by submission to God's commandments and respect for the covenant. Thus superiority and sanctity are not simply conferred, but are promised as a consequence of respect for the covenant and observance of the law, whereas transgression automatically entails inferiority and consequent decline. Maimonides is a major proponent of this view; his halakhic authority assures its centrality in the tradition. Nevertheless, the concept of election through duty and the covenant, through obedience to the law, merely relegates the problem to another level, because the character of the privileged relationship is not eliminated.

That is why, at the same time, one may not ignore the other current, represented by such thinkers as Judah Halevi, the Maharal of Prague, certain streams of Ḥasidic thought, and Abraham Isaac Kook. There is an important kabbalistic tradition taken up by the Ḥasidim and the Sephardim concerning the particular qualities of "Jewish souls" (which can also inhabit non-Jews). They hold that the keeping of the commandments is a pedagogical path to build those souls through generations, and that, vice versa, the particularJewish soul predisposes Israel to keep the commandments. Undeniably these notions are quite dangerous, as are other kabbalistic notions, if they are taken literally and applied directly to the concrete reality of individuals. The Maimonidean current takes account of these dangers and serves to guard against mad idolatry based on the people, the land of Israel, myth, or folklore.

Whatever line of thought informs the concept of a chosen people, our uneasiness with regard to election must be viewed largely as a result of a Western semantic bias. The Greco-Roman Christian West has imposed its languages—scientific, theological, and philosophical—on most other cultures. It is the text and the context of those languages that make election questionable, in that they have now become "objective" vehicles of thought that claim to be universal and to describe reality "as it is," seen by a "rational" observer without subjectivity, without arbitrariness, and without passion. Christianity and Islam have, in effect, taken up the plan of the God of Israel, while at the same time separating it from the historical and social context of the Jews, which was its place and origin, and extending it to the Roman Empire or to the Arab world.

These two civilizations have adopted the God of Israel but have taken him, if one may dare say so, too literally, regarding him as the only legitimate god of the entire planet. To achieve this universality, Christianity and Islam, monotheistic religions of universalist vocation, regarded election as an individual reality (and thus potentially universal, but also completely arbitrary), obtained by grace of baptism or the act of faith.

In terms of the interiorization of the message and the creation of a means of communication among people of different cultures, that step doubtless represents a degree of progress. The Jewish masters of the Talmud, and then the rabbis of the Middle Ages, including the Aristotelian Maimonides, took care not to ignore it. But in their case the starting point for opening up to an inner and potentially universal discourse was the particular experience of the law and of an identity that was deepened from within. That identity sought to relinquish nothing of its particular humanity, thus achieving rapport with others and true universality by taking differences into account. In contrast to the Jewish view, the two universal monotheistic religions, Christianity and Islam, hold that election has become the election of believers—of individuals, so that the community is defined as one of believers—by a unique God—no longer by a tribal god or even by a god who is "greater than the others," but by the only one.

This implies a theology where all others are relegated to the nonexistence of those who are not saved. The meaning of history is also changed in such a way as to exclude the majority of real human beings. It becomes the doctrine of the fulfilled promise, of the end of history, and of the general history of humanity viewed as the history of its redemption, which now passes along privileged pathways. History has been fulfilled, terminating in Christianity, and later again in Islam: The Messiah or the last prophet has already arrived. After that, other people have no choice but to convert voluntarily or to be converted by force, or to disappear. It is this doctrine, laicized, that has been taken up, after Hegel, by totalitarian ideologies of the meaning of history.

That development is the reason for the scandal of the election of Israel, which is scandalous only in the context of the two monotheistic cultures derived from Judaism—cultures that, unlike the religion of their paternity, lay claim to a universal vocation, and which happen to be the cultures where the dispersed Jewish people lived out its exile. These two monotheisms each claimed election by the God of Israel for itself, distorting its image so much that they became the only two sociocultures that claimed universality by divine right, justifying and sanctifying everyone's conversion by fire and sword.

Judaism avoided being drawn into a universalistic, proselytizing monotheism through its interpretation of election as a duty, the particular relation between a people and its god, in its social and historical reality. The mortal danger, from the point of view of Jewish monotheism itself, is confusion of the two levels: the infinite and the finite, the theological and the existential, the theoretical and the lived. For what is truly at stake is this: Given the irreducible particularism and egocentrism of every individual, of every family, of every nation, how can we facilitate reciprocal relations among individuals, families, and people? The idea of a unique god, uniting all the families, can be helpful if it is not a prerequisite for the existence of any one of them. Given the reality of human diversity and particularity, it is probably more realistic and humane to manage relations by taking account of that which each individual and family is called upon to do by its own god, who is different from the others, and to put off the unification of the gods until a messianic era that has yet to arrive. "In that day [the eschatological future], there shall be one Lord [YHWH] with one name" (Zech. 14:9).

REFERENCES

1. Henri Atlan, *Entre le cristal et la fumée* (1979), ch. 11.

BIBLIOGRAPHY

Henri Atlan. The present article is a condensed version of an essay previously published in French under the title "Un peuple qu'on dit elu," in *Le genre humain*, No. 3–4 (1982).

Arnold Eisen, *The Chosen People in America* (1983), ch.1.

R. J. Zwi Werblowsky, "Universal Religion and Universalist Religion," in *International Journal for Philosophy of Religion*, 2 (Spring 1971).

Christianity

נצרות

David Flusser

One of the principal tenets of the Jewish religion, together with its universalistic and monotheistic outlook, is the concept of the election of Israel by God. Christianity accepted monotheism; its God is identical with the God in whom Jews believe. The election of Israel, however, remains problematic. While some Christians today no longer hold that the election of Israel was abolished by the emergence of the Church, election still means something different to them than it does to the Jews. In the view of most such Christians, Israel remains God's people de jure, but it will again become the elect people de facto only when the whole of Israel accepts the Christian truth.

The roots of this kind of Christian theology of Judaism go back as far as chapter eleven of Paul's Epistle to the Romans, but it reached full development in some Christian groups only after the Reformation. Several fundamentalist groups have maintained the hope that in the eschatological future the time of the Gentiles will come to an end and the Jewish people, converted, will be the principal herald of Christianity. This approach picked up strength particularly after the Six Day War in June 1967, which seemed to witness the partial fulfillment of God's promises to Israel. Even according to such an ideology, however, Israel is not an end unto itself but a means. That is to say, those Christians who do not regard the post-Christian existence of Israel as an ontological impossibility view the post-Christian Jewish people, like ancient Israel, as an object of the Christian faith rather than as an autonomous spiritual reality.

In the Jewish religion, the existence of Christianity (and Islam) can be understood as the fulfillment of God's promises to Abraham to make him the father of many peoples, and Jews (like Moslems) are consequently less prone to occupy themselves with the theological meaning of the existence of Christianity than Christians are to speculate on the theological meaning of Judaism. The Jews, moreover, can view Christians (and Moslems) as "God fearers," Gentile descendants of Noah who have rejected paganism and will be saved if they behave in an ethical way. Christians can be admitted to this category even if they believe in the Holy Trinity and adore the saints, for the Jewish definition of the God fearers dwells only upon what is forbidden to them and not upon positive obligations. Several Jewish authorities were thus in agreement as early as the Middle Ages that religious syncretism is not forbidden to Noachites. Only the Jews are obliged to fulfill the law, while others can be saved without Jewish religious precepts. For Christian theologians, on the other hand, the Jewish people and its survival constitute a theologoumenon inherent to the very structure of Christian belief. It is almost impossible for them to believe that one who does not accept the Christian faith can be saved. Moreover, Christianity saw Judaism as its point of departure and claimed to be its heir. Judaism thus poses a more essential question to Christianity than does Islam, which came into being only later.

The Christian faith on the one hand knows no national boundaries, and on the other hand we have seen that it is not particularly open minded toward those who would not embrace Christianity—this in marked contrast to the rabbinic doctrine acknowledging the "righteous Gentiles." The Church's attitude, as several medieval Jewish thinkers already understood and accepted, need not prevent the building of spiritual and even theological bridges between Judaism and Christianity. There is a further issue involved, however, and it is one that has largely been neglected by Jewish participants in the Jewish–Christian dialogue. The Christian religion is not only highly exclusive; it is also, by its very nature, Christocentric. The central religious experience of the overwhelming majority of Christian believers is not theological or ethical but rather that of their personal redemption through the vicarious offering of Christ on the cross and Christ's subsequent resurrection. Even Christianity's belief in the divine nature of Christ is not as important for the living Christian faith as is the violent death and resurrection of Jesus Christ. Yet, surprisingly, this dimension of the Christian experience is muted in the synoptic gospels. This requires explanation. The Gospels of Matthew, Mark, and Luke are our main historical sources for information about the sayings and deeds of Jesus and the events of his life. The expiating function of Jesus' death is mentioned explicitly in these Gospels only in two verses from Mark: 10:45 (which influenced Matthew 20:28) and 14:24 (which influenced Matthew 26:28). Jesus' expiatory death is not even mentioned in the Lukan parallel (22:27) to Mark 10:45; it is easy to show, moreover, that the verse in Luke is the more original and that the parallel in Mark is a secondary formulation. As for the Lukan parallel to Mark 14:24, which is Luke 22:20 (cf. Luke 22:19b), the whole passage in which it appears (Luke 22:19b–20) is lacking in one of the best manuscripts of Luke and is considered by many important scholars to be part of a later interpolation from I Corinthians 11:23–25. Philological analysis thus shows that there is no evidence that the motif of the expiatory death of Jesus appeared in the most ancient sources. The notion was introduced some time before Paul, who became its principal exponent.

The belief in expiation through the death of martyrs is Jewish and antedates Christianity. In Christianity, however, the vicarious force of martyrdom is restricted only to Christ on the cross —the death of ordinary Christian martyrs is never understood as expiating the sins of the believers. The redemptive force of Christ's death and the belief in his resurrection had become a part of the Christian metahistorical drama extending from the creation of the world through Christ, his incarnation, his expiatory death and resurrection, his return to his heavenly father, and his eschatological return to the world. As we have said, this redemptive function of the cross and of Christ's resurrection—and not the Jewish teaching of Jesus and his historical activities among his people—constitutes the principal religious experience of the overwhelming majority of Christians. It is precisely the teachings of Jesus—and not Christology, in both its broader and its more restricted senses—that are the area in which Jews and Christians can most easily meet, help one another, and learn from one another. For many Christians, however, such a clarification does not directly touch their main Christian experience and interest, even though it may prove helpful and strengthen their own belief. Knowledge of the "historical," Jewish Jesus is but a necessary frame for the core of their belief, namely, the metahistorical drama of Christianity.

In a famous fragment, Gotthold Ephraim Lessing distinguished between the religion of Christ (that is, Jesus) and the Christian religion. The religion of Christ, he wrote, is "clearly depicted" in the Gospels, but it is impossible on this basis alone to arrive at a consensus regarding the content of the Christian religion.[1] My own studies have shown, moreover, that the main Christological passages regarding Christ's expiatory death in the synoptic Gospels mostly originate in only one of the three, and that they were first conceived in Greek. They are thus evidently secondary redactional changes or interpolations impressed upon the original sources of the Gospels, which were probably translated into Greek from Hebrew. The best available explanation for this would be that the primary source—or sources—of the synoptic Gospels is to be sought in the circles of those of Jesus' disciples who were interested primarily in the doctrines and miraculous deeds of their master and at least partially in his self-awareness, and less so in the Christological, metahistorical drama of Christ. The Gospels themselves, however, were composed some years or decades later by early Christians who, believing to various degrees in Christ as a redemptive figure, needed to know his history and teaching in order to base their faith upon a historical and ethical formulation. To this end they edited and partially reshaped a source or sources whose origin lay in the Jewish Palestinian circles of Jesus' disciples, who had been more interested in Jesus' faith than in faith in Christ. Even in the present redacted form of the synoptic Gospels, however, Jesus never asks his followers to believe in him.

This scholarly digression has been necessary in order for us to arrive at an understanding of the dual nature of the Christian religion, which comprises both Jesus' faith and faith in Jesus. The first aspect, that of Jesus' faith, consists of the tenets of Christian love and ethics. These were a special development of the new Jewish ethical sensitivity that developed in the period of the Second Commonwealth, and while this aspect of Christian behavior and feeling stems primarily from Jesus' own preaching, it was also influenced by contemporary Jewish ethics and theology. The latter aspect of the Christian religion centers around what is known as the charisma of Christ. The primary motifs of Christian messianism and Christology are also derived mainly from Judaism, and I would venture that their point of departure lay in the acute self-awareness of Jesus himself. As already stated, this latter belief in the metahistorical drama of Christ and especially in the idea of redemption through Christ's death and resurrection became the cornerstone of Christian religious experience and until very recently was a kind of *conditio sine qua non* for calling oneself a Christian. This does not necessarily mean, however, that the aspect that we have described as Jesus' faith was more or less neglected. Especially in the pre-Constantine period, Christians saw themselves mainly as humble peacemakers who prayed for their persecutors. Later on, as the dogmatic belief in Christ prevailed in both the Orient and the Occident, it often happened that the precepts of love and of

Jesus' ethical and religious message sank into oblivion or were seen as commandments applying mainly to the perfect ones, the monks. Even in the Middle Ages, however, there emerged individuals and communities for whom Jesus' Jewish message of love was a decisive element. From the time of the Reformation, return to Jesus and his first community of disciples became the aim of various groups and sects such as the Bohemian brothers, the Mennonites, and the Quakers. This return to Jesus as teacher found its echo among the Catholics as well, for example, in the doctrines of Erasmus of Rotterdam. The humane side of Christianity as represented by Jesus' ethical teaching was especially stressed in the period of the Enlightenment, which saw a general weakening of the Christological aspect of Christian belief. Our own time is characterized by a complexity of views, but neither the most militant fundamentalists nor those who prefer the Pauline Christ over the historical Jesus can today deny the human and social meaning of Christianity. In the wake of the Second World War, moreover, many Catholic theologians have argued for the importance of returning to Jesus' social message of love.

We have affirmed that both aspects of the Christian religion grew from Jewish roots. The teachings of Jesus can, indeed, easily be understood as an expression of the Jewish religion. More difficult for a Jew to understand is the Christian belief in Christ and all that is bound up with it. Because of the Jew's own religious feeling, he is virtually unable to comprehend the central Christian experience of the redemptive power of Jesus' death and resurrection—unless, of course, he experiences a conversion to Christianity. This does not mean that similar or parallel trends and ideas have not existed and do not exist today within Judaism, even if they have not created developed dogmatic systems like that of Christianity. Never within Judaism (with the exception of the adherents of Shabbetai Zevi and Jacob Frank) has acceptance of a metahistorical drama centered on a specific, more than simply human person involved the consequent rejection of the rest of Jewry. And although movements of believers in a Jewish superhuman savior (or saviors) have, to be sure, arisen, the very nature of Judaism has prevented their acceptance by the Jewish people as a whole. They were ephemeral, as can indeed be seen from the history of Jewish Christianity in antiquity.

For Jewish thought, Christian philosophy and its understanding of God and one's fellow man may have a particular significance. If Judaism has frequently been able to enrich its own spiritual heritage through confrontation with foreign ideas, how much more ought it to be open minded toward Christian motifs and theological and ethical ideas that are of Jewish origin? Jewish thinkers may also learn from Christianity and its development of concepts immanent in its originally Jewish impulses More importantly, Jewish thinkers can grow by accepting the Jewish outlook of Jesus as a part of the Jewish heritage. No Jew, naturally, is obliged to consent to all of Jesus' religious and ethical interpretations of the Jewish faith—just as he is not obliged to accept uncritically the opinions of Hillel, Shammai, Rabbi Akiva, Maimonides, and other Jewish thinkers. Nothing should hinder us from pondering Jesus' ideas with the same seriousness that we do those of other important Jewish creative personalities of the past and the present. While we must take into account that the synoptic Gospels are an incomplete and sometimes distorted testimony to Jesus' weltanschauung, an attentive reading will nevertheless make us aware that Jesus proposed interesting solutions to certain Jewish ethical and theological problems within the framework of the Hillelite trend of his time. His solutions and his humane understanding of man, God, and the Torah have a potentially positive message for Judaism today. Study of Jesus' doctrines as a part of ancient Judaism can also help us uncover other hidden forces in our glorious past which, to our own detriment, have been forgotten or neglected.

Let us return, in closing, to the beginning of this essay. Even the most benevolent Christian approach to the election of Israel is not identical with Jewish self-awareness. Throughout the ages, moreover, Christianity has proved a wellspring of anti-Jewish ideologies and movements. The Christian attitude toward Judaism and Jews is and has always been ambivalent, for the existence of a post-Christian Judaism and of non-Christian Jews continues to pose a serious problem for Christianity. The authentic Christian interpretation of itself is that it is the true religion of Israel and that without faith in Christ no one can be redeemed (there are, to be sure, exceptions to this rule: even among Catholics there are those who believe that a Jew can be saved without professing faith in Christ). We must acknowledge, then, that it is extremely difficult for a good Christian to set the Jews on the same level as other Christians. By its very nature, moreover, Christianity cannot really renounce offering its salvation to all. Judaism is thus more pluralistic than Christianity, for it has room for the view that Christians, being non-Jewish "Noachites," are eligible for salvation. Christianity, however, must run against its own nature to exempt the Jews from the bliss of its missionary zeal. Jewish readers must bear this in mind; nevertheless, Judaism and Christianity share the same root and also, as we have seen, the same hope.

REFERENCES

1. H. Chadwick, ed. & tr., *Lessing's Theological Writings* (1956), 106.

Commandments

מצוות

Yeshayahu Leibowitz

The *mizvot*, or ritual commandments, enjoined by the Torah are to be regarded first and foremost as religious praxis. As such the *mizvot* are the ground of the living religious reality known as Judaism. The *mizvot* are thus to be understood not in terms of their so-called philosophical "reasons" but rather as the matrix of Judaism as one lives it and is capable of living it in the here and now, in the everyday life of the believing Jew who has bound his life to the rule of God's Torah. As a religion of *mizvot* Judaism is an institutional religion: its institutions, viz., the *mizvot*—not its dogmas and values—define its spiritual content. Accordingly, Judaism is not an abstract or confessional faith, but is rather an emphatically concrete faith grounded in a complex of well-defined religious deeds and ritual practices.

To be sure, there is a vital interdependence between the institutional reality of religion and its values and beliefs. The nature of this relationship often depends, however, on the spiritual disposition of the individual. Thus there are religious individuals for whom faith is prior to their religious praxis and others for whom religious praxis is prior to their faith. There are individuals who from a world of abstract values—dogmas and feelings of obligation—seek the realization of these values in a specific form of life; and there are others who come to a world of values through having accepted a specific form of life and religious praxis—the yoke of institutional religion, which, in turn, also leads them to faith. Whoever has a basically religious temperament will attain religious values and faith only through institutional religion. Hence, it may be said that a Jew is one who attains religious values and faith by virtue of the *miẓvot,* which bear not only Judaism's values but also its categories of religious knowledge and feeling.

The primary features of Judaism qua a religion of *miẓvot* is that it is primarily a religion of the ordinary, unexceptional individual who is not necessarily blessed with a spiritual disposition. In consonance with this fact, Judaism is also a realistic religion: It apprehends the individual in his concrete, everyday existence and regards him in light of this reality, and not in terms of a "vision" of an ideal reality. Judaism is concerned with the individual's tasks, obligations, and responsibilities in his concrete, mundane existence, and renders it impossible for him to evade his responsibilities through the deception of attaining a different, "higher" reality. Indeed, halakhic religion considers the person strictly from the standpoint of his trivial, quotidian reality. *Miẓvot* are norms for this humdrum existence, the real and constant reality of man: Halakhic religion is not enthusiastic about the ecstatic, unusual episodes of one's spiritual life, the "holiday" moments of life, so transient and momentary; *miẓvot* relate essentially to the general and constant, not the exceptional, which is by definition only occasional and ephemeral. Grounded in *miẓvot,* Judaism renders religion the prose of life, a religion of mundanity. This is the very strength of Judaism. There is no intention here to denigrate the poetry of life, the episodic occasions when an individual rises above his or her daily existence, achieving blissful moments of ecstasy and enthusiasm; on the contrary, it may well be that ordinary existence pales in significance beside those episodes; nonetheless, the basis and continuity of human existence are not those moments of rare poetic elevation, but rather the even keel of prose. At the age of forty or more, Monsieur Jourdain of Molière's *Le bourgeois gentilhomme* suddenly discovered that all along he had been speaking prose. Had Monsieur Jourdain been a poet, he would never have sung his verse unawares; a person recites poetry only intentionally, in extraordinary moments of his life. A religion that primarily seeks to promote spiritual exaltation and even ecstasy is a religion of poetry, a religion that is principally an ornament to life. The religion of *miẓvot* is the religion of life itself.

It is in the nature of halakhic Judaism to be antirhetorical, antipathetic, antivisionary, and, above all, to oppose all self-deception: It does not permit one to believe that reality is different from what it actually is and it prevents him from trying to escape from his responsibilities and obligations in this terrestrial world to an imaginary, ideal world that is all good, beautiful, and sublime. It is not by chance that a very large portion of the *miẓvot* have to do with a person's body—conception and birth, eating and drinking, sexual intercourse, illness and death. The largest division in the basic formulation of the halakhah, the Mishnah, is the tractate *Taharot* (Purity), which deals with all the "filthy" aspects of one's biological existence, from which there is no escape.

The most characteristic quality of the life of *miẓvot* is its nonpathetic nature. The life of *miẓvot* does not rely upon the awakening of religious feelings and does not grant importance to a special spiritual impulse prompting unusual experience and actions. It constantly strives to establish the religious act—even in its more sublime manifestations—as a fixed pattern of fulfilled obligation: "Greater is he who is commanded and does, than he who is not commanded and does" (BT Kid. 31a). And precisely this very nonpathetic tendency manifests a tremendous pathos. How vain and empty is the vaunted antithesis between the intense religious experience and the formalism of *miẓvot,* an antithesis often advanced by opponents of traditional Judaism.

Hence, in contrast to Judaism, directed to human existence as it is, there are religions that seek to redeem man from his mundane existence and transpose him spiritually to another order of existence in which utterly different tasks and obligations obtain. Christianity is clearly a religion of the latter type. The Christian who accepts that Jesus Christ died for his sins is said to be redeemed; that is to say, the basis of his spiritual existence is ontologically changed—among other things, he is free from the *miẓvot*. Needless to say, halakhic Judaism does not recognize such redemption. The obligation it places on a person is permanent and eternal, and no religious achievement can be deemed as so absolute that one acquires a dispensation from any further obligation. The fulfillment of the Torah and its *miẓvot* is only a preparation to continue to fulfill the Torah and *miẓvot*. The existential stance of the Jew and the tasks that follow from it are not changed one iota through any external religious event or internal religious achievement.

A symbolic exemplification of this is to be found in the great moment of the conclusion of the Yom Kippur service. After this day of atonement, prayer, and fasting, through which Jews are "purified"—"and before

Whom do they purify themselves and Who purifies them?" as Rabbi Akiva rhetorically asks in the very last sentence of the Mishnah *Yoma*—there comes the *Neilah,* the closing prayer of the service in which the Shema is recited by the entire congregation and the *shofar* is awesomely sounded. But this is immediately followed by the opening prayer from the daily evening liturgy: "And He the merciful One will forgive our sins." That is to say, the situation of the individual at the conclusion of the Yom Kippur service is exactly as it was before the afternoon prayer of the day before Yom Kippur. His achievement is no more than just his religious effort on that great day, and he must begin forthwith to prepare for the next Yom Kippur, a process that repeats itself until the end of his days. Similarly, devotion to the study of Torah is not a means to attain a specific goal but a toil that is a goal unto itself. As Maimonides comments, "Until when must one learn? Until the days of one's death" (MT Hil. Talmud Torah 1:10).

As a religion that opposes all forms of self-deception, halakhic Judaism surely does not delight a person envisioning religious life as the attainment of a goal. The life of *mizvot,* which obligates a person from earliest maturity to death, is not affected whatsoever by any spiritual achievement one may attain. The fulfillment of the *mizvot* is the way leading a person toward his God, an infinite way whose goal is never attained and is, in fact, unattainable. Indeed, it is incumbent upon the Jew to realize that the way is eternal. He embarks on this way and is always at the same point. The realization that the religious task placed on one is infinite and that one can never reach the goal—this is the religious faith realized in the fixity, continuity, and permanence of the *mizvot.* The circle of the *mizvot* always returns to its beginning: "Every day should be as new in your eyes" (Rashi, ad loc., Ex. 19:1), because after every performance of the *mizvot* one's position remains as it had been before. A person cannot attain the goal of nearness to God, who is infinitely removed from Him: "For God is in heaven and you are on earth" (Ecc. 5:1). And yet the meaning of the *mizvot* lies precisely in the very effort one expends in reaching the paradoxically unattainable goal.

Mizvot as a way of life, as a fixed and permanent form of human existence, preserve religion as a goal in itself and prevent it from turning into a means for attaining a goal. Indeed, most of the *mizvot* have no sense unless we regard them in this manner, as an expression of selfless divine service. Most of the *mizvot* have no instrumental or utilitarian value and cannot be construed as helping a person fulfill his earthly or spiritual needs. A person would not undertake this way of life unless he sees divine service as a goal in itself, not as a means to achieve any other purpose. Therefore, the halakhah directs its attention to one's duties and not to one's feelings.

If *mizvot* are service to God and not service to man, they do not have to be intended or directed to man's needs. Every reason given for the *mizvot* that bases itself on human needs—be they intellectual, ethical, social, or national—voids the *mizvot* of all religious meaning. For if the *mizvot* are the expression of philosophic knowledge, or if they have any ethical content, or if they are meant to benefit society, or if they are meant to maintain the Jewish people, then he who performs them serves not God but himself, his society, or his people. He does not serve God but uses the Torah of God for human benefit and as a means to satisfy human needs.

Therefore, the so-called "reasons for the *mizvot*" *(taamei ha-mizvot)* are a theological construct and not a fact of religious faith. The only genuine reason for the *mizvot* is the worship of God, and not the satisfaction of a human need or interest. If, for example, the meaning of the Sabbath were social or national, it would be completely superfluous: The secretary of the labor union takes care of the workers' need for rest. The divine Presence did not descend upon Mount Sinai to fulfill that function. If the Sabbath does not have the meaning of holiness—and holiness is a concept utterly devoid of humanistic and anthropocentric meaning—then it has no meaning at all.

The same evaluation can be applied to the ethical meaning that the secularists seek to attribute to the Torah and its *mizvot*. Ethics as an intrinsic value is indubitably an atheistic category. Accordingly, only he who sees man as an end unto himself and as a supreme value—that is to say, puts man in the place of God—can be an ethical person. He who looks upon man as one creature within creation and recalls the verse "I am ever mindful of the Lord's presence" (Ps. 16:8) cannot accept ethics so conceived as the criterion and touchstone of his behavior before God. Ethics has only one of two meanings: (1) directing a person's will according to his rational recognition of the truths of nature—namely, the ethics of Socrates, Plato, Aristotle, the Epicureans, and the Stoics (especially the latter), and in modern philosophy Spinoza; or (2) directing a person's will according to his recognition of rational, ergo human, obligation —namely, the ethics promoted by Kant and German idealism. In contradistinction to both these conceptions of ethics, the Shema declares, "So that you do not follow your heart and eyes" (Num. 15:39), "do not follow your heart," in effect a negation of Kant's concept of ethical autonomy; "do not follow your eyes" is the negation of Socrates' conception of ethics. The Torah gives us immediately the reason for this double negation: "I the Lord am your God" (Num. 15:41). The Torah does not recognize ethical commandments whose source is in the recognition of natural reality or the recognition of man's obligation to man; it recognizes only *miẓvot*. The Torah and the prophets never appeal to man's conscience, for such an appeal is always suspect as a possible expression of idolatry. In fact, the term *conscience* is not to be found in the Hebrew Bible. The guidance of conscience is an atheistic, indeed, an idolatrous concept; "the god in one's heart" whose standard is raised by humanistic ethical teachers is a foreign god. The halakhah as a religious instruction does not tolerate the concept of ethics, and needless to say it does not tolerate any utilitarian criteria for behavior, whether the benefit is to accrue to the individual, nation, or society. "Love your neighbor as yourself" (Lev. 19:18) is the great principle of the Torah not because it is an idea beyond the formalism of the law and above the specifications of the *miẓvot,* but precisely because it is one of the 613 *miẓvot.* The principle to "love your neighbor as yourself" is not unique to Judaism; similar teachings were propounded by sages and thinkers who were not at all influenced by Judaism and never heard of it, the sages of China, India, and Greece. Moreover, the verse "You shall love your neighbor as yourself," as it is generally cited, does not exist in the Torah: the biblical verse actually reads: "You shall love your neighbor as yourself—I am the Lord" (Lev. 19:18). The duty of loving one's neighbor does not derive from the status of a person as a person but from his status before God. "You shall . . . ," without the conclusion "I am the Lord" is, in fact, the great principle of the atheist Immanuel Kant. The novelty and greatness of this noble principle in the Torah is in its position within the framework of the *miẓvot,* namely in its inclusion in the long list of *miẓvot* in the portion of the Hebrew Bible known as *Kedoshim* (lit., "sanctified actions"; Lev. 19–20) along with such *miẓvot* as reverence for father and mother; the Sabbath; prohibition of idolatry; rules of sacrificial offerings; the prohibition against reaping the edges and gleanings of one's fields (which must be left for the poor to gather); the prohibition of theft, fraud, false oath, and the delay in paying for a worker's labor; the prohibition of mixed seeds and garments of linen and wool; the law of an indentured female servant; the prohibition of eating from a fruit tree during its first three years. In this context, "You shall love . . . " ceases to be merely good advice, a pious wish, a noble striving and sublime ideal, and becomes something real, a law to which a person must relate seriously and solemnly, like the laws of a state. Let not the laws of the state be regarded contemptuously, for it was the talmudic sage Rabbi Johanan ben Zakkai who addressed his pupils before his death: "May it be God's will that the fear of God be as real for you as the fear of a human being" (BT Ber. 28b). Similar to the misleading effect of the partial citation of "You shall love . . . " is the falsifying quotation "And you shall do the good and the upright," for the verse states, "Do what is right and good in the sight of the Lord" (Deut. 6:18).

What does the religious person attain from the fulfillment of the *mizvot*? This is clarified by the last of the biblical prophets: "And you shall come to see the difference between . . . him who has served the Lord and him who has not served Him" (Mal. 3:18). The *mizvot* are means by which one serves God, and only through them can one actually assume the yoke of the kingdom of heaven. For as long as one's religious life expresses only one's personal understanding, conscience, ethics, and values, one's religious acts are merely self-serving, and hence tantamount to rebellion against the kingdom of heaven. There is an absolute opposition between service to God through the Torah and its *mizvot* and the service of "the God in the heart" or "the conscience" of humanistic religion, which ultimately can be nothing but service to man. This latter form of religion is the idolatry referred to in the verse "so that you do not follow your heart" (Num. 15:39). Every action through which one satisfies his own needs, whether physical or spiritual, is a service to himself and not service to God. If one attributes to such an action a religious meaning, it means in the final analysis that one makes one's god a means and an instrument for oneself. One serves God only when one takes it upon oneself to fulfill *mizvot* that are an expression of God's will and not a means to satisfy one's physical or spiritual needs. Therefore, in Judaism an expression of genuine service to God is, for example, the donning of *tefillin* (phylacteries) in accordance with all the detailed requirements of the Torah. There is absolutely no instrumental incentive for undertaking this act, nor can there be any other incentive except to do the will of God, who commanded this rite of donning the *tefillin*. Similarly, the observance of the Sabbath with all its strange laws—laws that have no discernible significance for man's physiological, social, or psychological life— is service to God. Sabbath-prohibited work is not in the least determined by the amount of energy invested in particular types of prohibited labor or the toil this labor may entail, but rather by the very principles of halakhah itself. The only genuine meaning of the Sabbath is its holiness—to submit a seventh of one's life to the rule of a special regimen, not stemming from one's nature, inclinations, and needs but only from one's decision to accept the yoke of the kingdom of heaven and concomitantly to submit to a way of life that is diametrically different from the natural way of life. Indeed, the very laws of the Sabbath emphasize and highlight this difference: "It shall be a sign for all time between Me and the people of Israel" (Ex. 31:17). Hence, the Sabbath loses all its pristine religious meaning should its laws be adjusted to human inclination and convenience. Similarly, the laws of

family purity or the dietary laws, which contrary to some "modern" interpretations have no physiological reason, are meant only to subdue human
nature of the service of the divine creator.

Having no physiological, philosophical, or sociological reasons and being
required neither by man's reason nor by his feelings, *mizvot* are to be understood in the light of the problem of freedom. For of the person who takes
upon himself Torah and *mizvot,* it may be asked whether he has forfeited
his autonomy. It is well known that many argue—and many are the arguments—that a person who has assumed the yoke of Torah and *mizvot* has
enslaved himself. Both the concept of enslavement and that of freedom,
however, require careful semantic analysis. "The world pursues its natural
course" (BT Av. Zar. 54b). That is to say, there is a lawfulness to the world
of natural happenings; there are fixed functional connections between
events. The very recognition of this fixed, lawful pattern in accordance with
which man must live and act is of great religious significance, and, moreover, is the basis upon which the life of halakhah is structured—in contradistinction to a faith in repeated interventions from above. If there is a fixed
pattern and lawfulness in the world, man is a part of it and is necessarily
subject to the whole system of natural reality that includes not only his body
but also his soul. Man is subject to the natural order both physiologically
and psychologically. (Although it is of concern to metaphysics, the purported division of body and soul is irrelevant and superfluous from the
standpoint of religious faith. From a religious point of view, the dividing line
is not between "matter" and "spirit" but between the creator and the created, that is, between God and the world. Creation—the world, nature—
includes everything material and spiritual apprehended by man.) From this
perspective, freedom is then the acceptance of a way of life that does not
stem from man's nature. To be sure, there are many definitions of human
freedom. Philosophically, the most profound conception is that of Spinoza,
who holds that freedom is acting from the necessity of one's own nature.
Does man, however, truly have his own nature? As a natural being he is only
a part of nature as a whole, and his nature is only a link in a causal chain
of inanimate nature and biological reality that acts on and through him.
Further, human psychology is only an expression of these forces. Where,
then, is man's vaunted autonomy? Man activated by his "own" nature is
actually only a puppet activated by the forces of nature, just like an animal
pasturing in the field, which is also free of Torah and *mizvot,* that is to say,
from every law externally imposed. In the Talmud, Rava says, "All bodies
are sheaths, happy is he who has been privileged to be a sheath for the
Torah" (BT Sanh. 99b). A person is never completely of "his own"; he is

always a receptacle for something not "his own." To be sure, he may regard himself as being free from every external command, acting according to a Spinozistic freedom, guided by his nature alone, but his nature is an expression of all the blind forces of nature in general, as well as man's psychological nature—his wishes, inclinations, and desires. From a religious point of view there is no place for the threefold division of nature–spirit–God. There are, as noted, really only two basic entities: nature, which includes man's spiritual aspects, and God. There is only one way man may liberate himself from subjugation to the forces of nature, namely by attachment to God. Concretely, this means doing God's will and not that of man, since man's will is intrinsically a fact of nature.

Contrary to the modern atheistic perversion of the Hebrew Bible, it is necessary to emphasize that it does not recognize man's spirit as antithetical to matter. The famous verse, so often distorted and falsified by modern commentators, does not set human spirit against matter but rather against the spirit of God: "Not by might nor by power, but with My spirit" (Zech. 4:6)—the spirit of man belongs to "might" and "strength." Hence, there is no freedom from the chains of nature except through accepting the yoke of the Torah and *mizvot,* a yoke not imposed by nature. This is the meaning of the rabbinic saying, "The only free person is he who is concerned with Torah" (M. Avot 6:2). Such an individual is free from enslavement to nature, precisely because he lives a life contrary to nature. Therefore, there is no need—from either a religious or a philosophic perspective—to submit the world of *mizvot* to the world of human concepts and interests; in the very "strangeness" of the *mizvot* lies hidden their strength. Attempts to rationalize the *mizvot* and to delineate their "reasons" are religiously and philosophically meaningless and have but trivial theological or psychological interest.

Genuine human freedom is thus attained only through the religion of *mizvot.* Yet some have criticized this religion as being mechanical, for by the very testimony of the Hebrew Scripture itself such a religion is the "commandment of men learned by rote" (Isa. 29:13). After all, the critics argue, even the rabbis realized that "the Merciful One demands the heart" (Sanh. 106b) and that every deed should be determined by the heart's intention. Therefore, the critics ask, what is the value of a religion whose main theme is a way of life attained by habitual practice till it becomes second nature? However, the "commandment of men learned by rote" is not necessarily a flaw in religious behavior, just as it is not a flaw in obedient citizenship. Only a very small minority of people actually determine their conduct of life upon the basis of a conscious decision, and even such individuals determine their conduct on the basis of conscious, intentional decisions only in special moments of life—the moments of poetic exaltation, which occasionally punctuate the overwhelmingly dominant prosaic flow of one's life. In the prose of life one acts according to habit, upon the basis of practices and conventions to which one is accustomed and which direct one's conduct quite unawares. Let us not hold such habitual action, "the commandment of men," in contempt, for it—and not the rare personal decision and intention—is the main shield against barbarism. If certain human societies attained a social order in which there was a basic minimum of human decency and civility and became societies of law-abiding citizens, they did not attain this because their citizens struggled with all the perplexities considered by the imprisoned Socrates until like him they recognized that a person must obey the laws of his state even if they run counter to his personal interests, but simply because as citizens they had become habituated to civilized behavior. "It is not the practice of our place" (Gen. 29:26)—this is the classic expression of the "commandment of men." The contempt poured upon "social superstitions," "meaningless habitual behavior," "empty conventions"—this contempt loosens the social bonds, removes the restraining reins, and lets loose dark, violent forces that had been controlled only by "commandments."

Our generation more than any previous one has with untold pain learned that most people are incapable of living as human beings on the basis of their own "autonomous" decisions and personal responsibility. The same principle applies to the sphere of religion: Only the prophet Isaiah, whose eyes saw the king, lord of hosts, was permitted to despise the "commandment of men learned by rote" and to deem it as religiously inadequate. As for us ordinary mortals, would that we be privileged to stamp upon our lives the seal of a bond to God through the habitual and disciplined norms of *miẓvot*. After we have been privileged to attain the religious level of life of the "commandments of men," inculcated by the regimen delineated in the *Shulhan Arukh* that the proponents of purified religion so despise, we will strive to advance further toward a religious existence in full consonance with the proper intentionality and spiritual awareness. The champions of spiritual spontaneity who scorn religion that restrains experience with laws and disciplined mores and concomitantly celebrate the unbounded expression of experience have often been the cause of the greatest atrocities. How powerful was the religious feeling and how mighty the religious experience of the idolators who sacrificed their sons to Molech and surrendered their daughters to the sacred prostitution of Ashtoreth (cf. Lev. 18:21; 20:3–5). The Torah, however, utterly rejects such free, spontaneous, and natural reli-

giosity, which it deems tantamount to idolatry. The Torah unabashedly confines one in the "prison" of *miẓvot* and is not at all daunted by the danger
of becoming a religion of commandments "learned by rote."

The molding of one's life on the basis of divine commandments means
creating a sphere of deeds endowed with holiness. In Judaism, holiness—
which in the religious sense of the term is to be clearly distinguished from
its intemperate secular uses—is achieved only by the performance of the
miẓvot, those precepts specifically intended as service to God. Every other
type of action, whether it is deemed good or bad, that a person does for his
pleasure or to satisfy a physical or spiritual need is in the last analysis service to himself and as such is intrinsically secular. The distinction between
the sacred and the secular is a primary religious category; moreover, it is a
basic feature of institutional religion, the religion of *miẓvot.* To conceive of
the sacred as an immanent quality of specific things—be they persons,
places, institutions, objects, events—is a fundamentally mystical, even
magical view, and smacks of idolatry. There is no holiness except in the
divine sphere—that is, the realm of human deed formed not by human values but through the *miẓvot* of God, in which man acts for the sake of God
alone: "The Holy One, blessed be He, possesses in His world only the four
cubits of halakhah" (BT Ber. 8a). There is nothing in the world that is
intrinsically holy, there is only that which is "holy *to* God," that is, deeds
sanctified to God through the specific purpose of service to God. Halakhic
Judaism knows only this concept of holiness. Indeed, the biblical declaration "You shall be holy" (Lev. 19:2) introduces a passage dealing largely
with specific *miẓvot,* and the words "for you are a holy nation" (Deut. 7:1)
prefaces a passage devoted exclusively to specific *miẓvot.*

One of the shrewdest stratagems of anthropocentric secularism, which
hides behind the mask of pure religion, is to proclaim the cancellation of
the separation between the holy and the profane and to spread a mantle of
holiness over natural functions and human values. If holiness is present in
the elements of natural reality in and of itself, or if the forces and drives of
man himself are holy, there is no place for "the Holy God" transcendent to
natural reality, for this reality itself is divinity and man himself is God. The
abolition of the specific category of religious holiness and the enthronement
of human functions and psychic drives as holy is a most dangerous phenomenon, not only from a religious point of view but also from a communal,
educational, and ethical perspective. Our generation—more than all preceding generations—has been witness to what has been done for the sake
of and in the name of the homeland, the nation, honor, freedom, equality,
and every human value rendered holy as a consequence of man's having

forgotten the basic truth that holiness exists only in a world beyond human values. In the light of the grievous confounding of the holy and the profane, we might better appreciate the extraordinary educational importance of the *mizvot*. Grounded in the transcendent sphere of holiness, the *mizvot* constitute by their very existence a constant demonstration and announcement that everything outside their framework is not holy and cannot be authentically exalted as holy—and, alas, there is nothing that our generation needs to be daily reminded of more than this.

It may be asked whether the creation of a sphere of holiness through the *mizvot* is indeed the goal of religion. One must reply both yes and no. On the one hand, there is no doubt that the religious goal that the prophets call "knowledge of God" and the psalmist "closeness to God" is not merely a matter of one's conduct. As Maimonides observed, "Man's perfection is not found in actions or ethical qualities but in knowledge" (*Guide*, 3:52). The goal of religious life is then spiritual perfection, spiritual knowledge, and worthiness. Accordingly, Maimonides, it would seem, places the *mizvot* not in the realm of perfection but in the realm of the preparatory and the educational. In this sense the *mizvot* are not the religious goal itself, but only a means and method.

However, in the profound dialectic of Maimonides' philosophic outlook, the preparatory position of the *mizvot* is transformed into the goal of the religion: "Know that all the practices of the worship, such as reading the Torah, prayer and the performance of the other *mizvot*, have only the end of training you to occupy yourself with His *mizvot*, may He be exalted, rather than with matters pertaining to this world; you should act as if you were occupied with Him and not with that which is other than He" (*Guide*, 3:51). So we find, after nine chapters (26–34) that deal with the "intention of the Torah," that is, the intention of its *mizvot*, in general, and fifteen chapters (35–49) of specific reasons for *mizvot*, emphasizing their usefulness in improving man and society, that Maimonides reveals to us the secret that the performance of the *mizvot*, which is nominally presented to us as an educational means, has as its goal to train a person to recognize that the knowledge of God and drawing close to him are these very same *mizvot*. And this is also the meaning of his summarizing remarks in his Commentary on the Mishnah (Intro. to Sanh. 10:1, ch. *"Ḥelek"*): "The purpose of truth is only to know that it is true; and the Torah is true, and the purpose of knowing it—to fulfill it."

On the other hand, religious perfection can never be actually realized; it always remains as an eternal guidepost, pointing toward the right direction as an infinite road. A person cannot fulfill the Torah perfectly—because it is divine, not human. Even the perfect individual cannot cling to God, because, as Maimonides puts it, he can never remove the last barrier separating him—"being an intelligence grounded in matter"—from God (Commentary on the Mishnah, Shmoneh Perakim, ch. 7). Therefore, the act of "fulfilling the Torah" can be only the eternal striving to fulfill it.

The eternal striving toward the religious goal that is never attained is embodied in the performance of the *mizvot*. This performance is never completed, the extent of the task is never diminished no matter how much effort is invested in it, and the goal draws no closer despite the amount of ground the person has covered in moving toward it. Every morning a person has to arise to the service of the creator, that very service that he performed yesterday, and at the conclusion of the Yom Kippur service—after the great realization of *teshuvah* (return) and forgiveness—there begins again the yearly cycle of the daily *mizvot* toward the coming Yom Kippur, and so on eternally. It turns out, therefore, that the *mizvot,* even though they are only a means toward an intrinsically unattainable goal of religious perfection, are from man's standpoint the final goal of religious perfection that he is able to attain.

Gotthold Ephraim Lessing, a leading spokesman of the Enlightenment, said that if God were to give him the choice between the pure truth and the eternal search after the truth he would choose the latter, "for the pure truth is for God alone."[1] A great Jewish leader of the socialist movement, Eduard Bernstein, expressed himself in a similar vein: "The movement itself is everything, the goal is nothing."[2] So, too, will a proponent of the "religion of *mizvot*" say to a proponent of "pure religion": "The eternal striving toward the religious goal through the constant performance of religious acts—that is the true goal of religion for man." Or in the concluding words of Ecclesiastes (12:13): "The sum of the matter when all is said and done; Revere God and observe His *mizvot!* For this applies to all mankind." The final goal is one of God's secrets. And so we find Abraham Isaac Kook saying: "If man is always liable to go astray . . . this does not spoil his perfection, for the essential basis of this perfection is the striving and fixed desire to attain perfection" (*Orot ha-Teshuvah,* ch. 5). One of his pupils, Yaakov Moshe Harlap, expands on these remarks in the actual language of Lessing—whose work he certainly did not know, and of whose statement he surely never heard: "The endeavor is more than the actual attainment, and particularly according to Maimonides' explanation that there is no goal in the world other than God alone, so that the essence of the endeavor is only the striving for the goal. . . . We must give precedence to the search for wisdom over the attainment of wisdom" (*Mei Marom*, ch. 7).

REFERENCES

1. Gotthold Ephraim Lessing, "Eine Duplik, " in *Werke*, Fritz Fischer, ed., 6 (1965), 297.
2. Eduard Bernstein, *Evolutionary Socialism: A Criticism and Affirmation*, Edith C. Harvey, tr. (1970), 202.

BIBLIOGRAPHY

Eduard Bernstein, *Evolutionary Socialism: A Criticism and Affirmation*, Edith C. Harvey, tr. (1970).

Yitzhak Heinemann, *Taamei ha-Mizvot be-Sifrut Yisrael*, 2 vols. (1942–1957).

Gotthold Ephraim Lessing, "Eine Duplik," in *Werke*, Fritz Fischer, ed., 6 (1965).

Joseph B. Soloveitchik, *Halakhic Man*, Lawrence Kaplan, tr. (1983).

Efraim E. Urbach, *The Sages: Their Concepts and Beliefs*, Israel Abrahams, tr., 1 (1979), chs. 1 and 2.

Community

קהילה

Everett E. Gendler

*K*ehillah (community) refers to the organized communal units of Jewish existence. Widely used in the Bible, its root designates the act of convoking an assembly. Such an assembly might be especially summoned for a specific purpose: for religious matters such as fasting, feasting, worshiping, or hearing the words of the Torah, or for civic matters such as rebellion or war. Such an assembly might, on the other hand, stand as an organized body or congregation; in this latter usage the term usually refers to the entire community of Israel.[1]

Closely related to the concept of *kehillah* in the biblical schema are *mishpaha* (clan or family), *bet av* (the father's house), and *am* (people). The presupposition of family is the union of man and woman, a union on which, at the time of creation, "was laid the blessing to which later generations owe their existence."[2] Family, deriving from this union, implies common ancestry and kinship; at the same time it has a fluid boundary: "The family extends as far as the feeling of unity makes itself felt . . . wherever there is a whole bearing the impress of a common character."[3] Connecting the household with the tribe, family thus makes possible the further formation of a community, a people.

Like family, community is at first defined by blood: "Every community is a community of kinsmen with a common ancestor."[4] Yet two separate communities may become one by virtue of joining, living together, and coming to share common characteristics. Thus the foundation is laid for the inclusion of others, for the development of a community whose basis of unity transcends the biological.

From the biblical perspective, community is also the essential background for the individual. "When we look at the soul, we always see a community rising behind it. What it is, it is by virtue of others . . . it must live in community, because it is its nature to communicate itself to others, to share blessing with them."[5]

This profound reading of the biblical evidence helps in understanding the dynamics of *kehillah* as organic or organized Jewish communal units. There is also an essential theological dimension to the historical persistence of Jewish community in a wide variety of forms and settings.

Theologically, human community may be characterized as the divinely initiated counterpoise to solitude, both for human beings and for the Divine. For humans, this is evident already in the emphasis on companionability found in the J account of creation: "The Lord God said: 'It is not good for man to be alone; I will make him a fitting helper for him'" (Gen. 2:18).

That the human community in turn provides companionship, as it were, for the Divine is supported by both biblical and classical rabbinic tradition. The language of the creation account in Genesis 1 suggests that a new quality informs the world with the advent of human beings. All previous creations came about by solitary divine fiat: "And God said"; "And God made"; "And God saw"; "And God blessed." With human beings the language shifts to the plural: "And God said, 'Let *us* make man in *our* image, after *our* likeness.'"

The classical rabbinic tradition asked: "With whom did God consult?" Several answers were proposed: "With the prior works of heaven and earth"; "with the prior works of each day"; "with Himself"; "with the angels." Most remarkable, however, was that which asserted divine consultation with human beings: "With the souls of the righteous He consulted" (Gen. R. 8:3–4, 6).

The motivation for divine–human communality in creation is expounded in another midrash: "From the first day of creation the Holy One, blessed be He, longed to enter into partnership with the terrestrial world, to dwell with His creatures within the terrestrial world" (Num. R. 13:6).[6]

It is by virtue of this divine involvement that Jewish community, biblically understood, comes into existence. The common ancestor, Abram (along with Sarai), is called by God (Gen. 12) and, become Abraham (along with Sarah), enters into covenant with God (Gen. 17). Their descendants, already in Egypt designated an *am,* a people (Ex. 1:9), are soon to become that special community that shall make visible to all God's active involvement in and concern for human beings in history. "And the Egyptians shall know that I am the Lord, when I stretch out My hand over Egypt, and bring out the Israelites from their midst" (Ex. 7:5).

At Sinai the word is proclaimed that, contingent upon the keeping of the covenant, "you shall be to Me a kingdom of priests and a holy nation" (Ex. 19:5–6), thus reaffirming, at Israel's most solemn moment of encounter with the Divine, the communal dimension of this covenant. In fact, the specific content of the decalogue itself has been persuasively interpreted by Buber as addressing, in three parts, "the *God* of the community . . . the *time,* the one-after-the-other of the community . . . the *space,* the one-with-the-other of the community."[7]

The Abrahamic covenant, the Exodus, and Sinai intertwined to form a cord both strong and elastic. On the one hand, its strength was sufficient to link the Divine in history with the fate of the Jewish community while at the same time shaping and unifying that people, and its elasticity was sufficient to permit the community to assume, through the centuries and throughout the world, diverse yet functionally comparable forms. This is evidenced in the numerous agencies and institutions each community developed to afford its members religious, educational, judicial, financial, and social welfare services that reflected the sense of covenant as expressed in halakhah.

In the self-contained patterns of Diaspora Jewish living, individual community structures became all the more important as the authority of Palestinian patriarchs and Babylonian exilarchs receded with the passage of time and the further dispersion of the people. "Jewish autonomous life became ever more decentralized in favor of the basic unit, the community."[8]

Until the French Revolution, Jewish communal life continued largely self-contained; its morale was maintained by an ever-renewed sense of covenant and sacred history transmitted by the structures and practices of the community. "The small-town Jewish community of Eastern Europe—the shtetl—traces its line of march directly back to Creation. The Exodus from Egypt, the giving of the Law on Mount Sinai, are seen as steps along the way, historical events no less real than the Spanish Inquisition or the Russian Revolution."[9] Thus personal identity was "supported, reaffirmed, 'nurtured' in interactions with others" while "the overall framework of meaning within which the individual can make sense of his life" was provided.[10]

As a result of emancipation and the Jewish entrance into modernity, both the identity- and the meaning-functions of community were seriously affected. As individual Jews related directly to the surrounding culture and state rather than through the established *kehillah,* Jewish community lost these long-standing functions. A further reduction in community cohesion has resulted from such technical developments as the automobile, highways, and rapid surface transportation. These have made possible the dispersion of population, with the consequent reduction in the number and strength of once distinctive, tradition-sustaining, and identity-nurturing Jewish neighborhoods.

A further development in the Western democracies, whose full implications are yet to be assessed, is the increase in intermarriage. On the one hand, the given biological or kinship basis of community is weakened by intermarriage; on the other hand, as non-Jews choose to become Jews, the covenantal and commitment factors may become increasingly determinative of Jewish life among the identified.

Two other developments, both especially evident in the United States, should be mentioned. One is the quest for styles of community leadership that will facilitate communal self-direction and growth. Drawing from Mordecai M. Kaplan's definition of Judaism as an "evolving religious civilization" and most visible in the *havurah* movement, participants seek small-group intimacy and active involvement as equals in religious and social expression.

Often combined with this quest is the reassertion of the feminine in Jewish life today. Socially, women are assuming new leadership roles, a development both validated and advanced by the fact that the Reform, Reconstructionist, and Conservative seminaries now accept women as candidates for rabbinic ordination. Theologically, searching questions are being asked concerning the possible overmasculinization of God in traditional Jewish portrayals of the Divine, a likely consequence of which will be considerable revision of the former "overall framework of meaning."

Simultaneously, for Jewish communities throughout the world, the "overall framework of meaning within which the individual can make sense of his life"[11] has suffered severe challenges in the modern age, perhaps exceeding the earlier theological questions raised by Spinoza, the textual questions propounded by Bible critics, and the weltanschauung issues posed by modern science. In this century, fundamental questions concerning God's relation to history and to the Jewish community have been painfully intensified by two world wars, by the use and further development of nuclear weapons, and, especially for the Jewish psyche, by the Holocaust.

Problematic also for the world Jewish community, though not widely recognized as such, is the modern State of Israel, a cause for rejoicing among most Jews and a focus of Jewish concern everywhere. Apart from thorny issues of defining the relation of the Diaspora to Israel, it is also unclear how the ideal of Zion, embodied in a modern power political unit, the nation-state, can escape secularization, "normalization," a disturbing reenactment of certain elements of the earlier conquest of the land, and reduction to becoming "like all the nations" (cf. I Sam. 8). Such a reduction would effectively nullify the redemptive function of the Jewish people and the injunctions that stand both at this community's inception—"and you shall be a blessing . . . the families of the earth shall bless themselves by you" (Gen. 12:2–3)—and at one of its prophetic peaks:

I the Lord have called you in righteousness,
And I have grasped you by the hand.
I created you, and appointed you
A covenant-people, a light of nations.

(Isa. 42:6).

To reintegrate the covenantal with the organic and to reaffirm universality with particularity may well be the central challenges to Jewish communal existence today.

REFERENCES

1. Cf. Frances Brown, S. R. Driver, and Charles Briggs, *Hebrew and English Lexicon of the Old Testament* (1962); Ludwig Koehler and Walter Baumgartner, *Lexicon in Veteris Testamenti Libros* (1948).
2. Johannes Pedersen, *Israel, Its Life and Culture,* 1 (1959), 61.
3. Ibid., 48–49.
4. Ibid., 54.
5. Ibid., 263.
6. In Abraham Joshua Heschel, *Between God and Man* (1965), 140–45.
7. Martin Buber, "The Words on the Tablets," in *Moses* (1958), 195.
8. Salo Baron, *A Social and Religious History of the Jews,* 2 (1952), 200.
9. Mark Zborowski and Elizabeth Herzog, *Life Is With People* (1952), 29.
10. Brigitte Berger and Peter L. Berger, *The War Over the Family,* 147, 165.
11. Ibid.

BIBLIOGRAPHY

Nahum N. Glatzer, ed., *Franz Rosenzweig: His Life and Thought* (1953).
Will Herberg, ed., *The Writings of Martin Buber* (1956).

Abraham Joshua Heschel, *Between God and Man,* Fritz A. Rothschild, ed. (1965).

Johannes Pedersen, *Israel, Its Life and Culture,* 4 vols. in 2 (1959). (See entries on "community".)

Sharon Strassfeld and Michael Strassfeld, eds., *The Third Jewish Catalog: Creating Community* (1980).

Conscience

מצפון

Steven S. Schwarzschild

Human beings generally insist on some morality. The question immediately arises: Whence do we obtain it? One initial and plausible source is pre-existing human ideas of morality and their institutionalizations. But it is simultaneously clear that there are many human notions of morality that are invidious: "The heart is more perverse than anything else, because it is human; who can fully understand it?" (Jer. 17:9). Therefore, a higher court of appeals is sought for morality.

At this point some sort of "natural law" seems to commend itself. Proverbs 6:6ff., for example, represents the ant as a model for human behavior. But Jews, like other men, experienced evil in nonhuman nature—death, disease, drought, and so on—much too often, as classically depicted in the biblical figure of Job,[1] to be satisfied with a facile resort to nature. Compare, for example, Isaac Watt's "busy little bee" and Lewis Carroll's retort in terms of "the little crocodile [that] welcomes little fishes in . . . his claws."[2] Indeed, Spinoza would not have needed to excoriate biblical and rabbinic Judaism in order to earn his excommunication from the synagogue: the passage in his *Theologico-Political Tractate* in which he, quite consistently, declares that the big fish swallow up the little fish by the might, which is synonymous with the right, of nature, which in turn is God, should have sufficiently outraged historical Jewish sensibility.

Now what option is left? God can be turned to for reliable ethical standards. But, of course, men have always had many gods and their respective, conflicting moralities. Even when the only God is acclaimed and his revealed commands are laid down, humans have to interpret his expressed will and apply it to present moral problems. We seem to be pushed back to our earlier quandary and still bereft of ultimately authoritative "sources of morality," to use Henri Bergson's phrase.

Finally, then, something called *conscience* may be invoked. However fuzzy the notion, it is generally taken to entail some sort of innateness, universality, and trustworthiness.[3] Historians and anthropologists, if not philosophers, tend, on the contrary, to observe that conscience varies widely with society, culture, and history, as well as with individual propensities.

It has often been pointed out that neither in the Bible nor in rabbinic Judaism is there a proper term for conscience. Only in medieval Jewish philosophical writings does such a term develop, slowly and vaguely.[4] But the absence of a specific term does not, of course, necessarily imply the lack of a notion roughly corresponding to conscience. David Daube, for example, refers to the biblical passages Genesis 39:8ff. and I Kings 2:44 to illustrate personal moral certainty.[5] The rabbis speak of "matters left to the heart."[6] But what these and similar sources document is that in Jewish culture, as elsewhere, men have commonly been believed to "know the right in their hearts"; they do not necessarily stipulate how men have come to this knowledge—and this is the problem broached by the notion of conscience.

Here now the historical absence of conscience in Jewish culture can be used instructively: If there were such a thing as conscience, what need of the law? As against this, can the law, moral and/or positive, cover all possible and necessary problems? Indeed, does the law not itself often appeal to something like conscience, for example, all the commandments that are classified as "duties of the heart" and the obligations that fall on "the other side of the line of the law *(lifnim me-shurat ha-din)*"? In other words, we seem to stand in need of moral knowledge both from within ourselves and from without—in Kant's terminology, autonomously and heteronomously. The very etymology of the term *conscience (con-scientia)*, and its variants in the modern languages, may then be taken to convey some such sense: "two knowledges in one."[7]

Kant (philosophically) and Hermann Cohen (philosophically as well as in Jewish terms), basing their thought on the entirety of human cultures—including philosophical and practical ethics—extricated themselves from this predicament by crystallizing "pure" reason as the norm of the universal instrument that, as religion puts it, we have, or ought to have, in common with God and by means of which we can and ought to formulate ever more fully the "oughts," "commands," and "imperatives" of morality.[8] These imperatives we do and ought to strive to "internalize," so that increasingly they become an inner, natural voice of "conscience." When Kant and Cohen then speak of "the primacy of practical/ethical reason" they are only putting in modern philosophical language what Judaism has classically proclaimed as the ultimacy of the God of morality.[9]

Put differently, ethics logically comes to us by virtue of reason, and as we become increasingly "virtuous" we hear the voice of inner conscience more and more from within ourselves. When that inner voice has grown identical with God's voice, then the law will no longer be chiseled on tablets of stone but, as the prophet said, written as "the new covenant" on the tablets of the human heart, and the kingdom of God will have been established on earth.

REFERENCES

1. Cf. BT Er. 100b, where Job is adduced together with the passage from Prov. 6:6.
2. Martin Gardner, *The Annotated Alice* (1970).
3. Cf. Charles Baylin, *Encyclopedia of Philosophy,* s.v. "Conscience."
4. Cf. Jakob Klatzkin, *Thesaurus Philosophicus,* s.v. *"maẓpun"* ("the hidden [voice]").
5. Cf. David Daube, *Interpreter's Dictionary of the Bible,* s.v. "Conscience"; David Daube, *Ancient Jewish Law—Three Inaugural Lectures* (1981), 64ff., 126–29.
6. Cf. Maxwell Silver, *The Ethics of Judaism* (1938), index under "conscience."
7. Cf. R. J. Zwi Werblowsky, "The Concept of Conscience in Jewish Perspective," in *Conscience* (1970), 83ff.
8. Cf. Immanuel Kant, *The Metaphysical Principles of Virtue,* J. Ellington, tr. (1964), 57–61; Hermann Cohen, *Religion of Reason out of the Sources of Judaism* (1972), 186, 202f.
9. For a good survey of historical, though not philosophical, Jewish evidence to the effect that reason is treated as "the heart" and as "conscience," see Werblowsky, "The Concept of Conscience in Jewish Perspective," 94, 102. Werblowsky concludes that "truth does not come *out* of the heart, though it should enter *into* the heart." Ibid., 88 (emphasis in original).

BIBLIOGRAPHY

Menachem Marc Kellner, *Contemporary Jewish Ethics* (1978).
Moritz Lazarus, *The Ethics of Judaism,* 2 vols. (1900–1901).
R. J. Zwi Werblowsky, "The Concept of Conscience in Jewish Perspective," in *Conscience,* Curitorium of the J. C. Jung Institute (1970).

Conservative Judaism

יהדות מסורתית

Gerson D. Cohen

Conservative Judaism, the largest of the three major Jewish religious classifications in the United States and Canada, is most accurately described as a number of organizational affiliations of rabbis and congregations as well as laity who identify themselves and who are identified by others as Conservative. While the name embraces a variety of theological orientations and norms of religious usage, Conservative Judaism bears certain identifying marks and professes certain standards that set it apart from all other contemporary Jewish religious groups.

Despite the impressive increase in recent years of Conservative Jewish institutions and congregations in Israel and in many countries—particularly in Latin America and Europe—Conservative Judaism is primarily an American movement whose religious orientation has been determined by the institution that continues to be its chief academic and ideological center, the Jewish Theological Seminary of America. Established in New York in 1886 by Rabbi Sabato Morais of Philadelphia as a traditionalist but modern rabbinical school, the Seminary was reorganized in 1902 under the academic and religious leadership of Solomon Schechter. He mobilized a young but impressive faculty, all of whom were endowed with formidable training in rabbinics—indeed, in all of classical Hebrew literature—and all of whom possessed doctorates in Hebrew and classical studies earned in secular universities. Simultaneously, the lay leadership of the Seminary placed at its disposal a small but highly impressive library that, in time, has grown into the largest collection of rare Judaica and Hebrew manuscripts ever assembled under one roof in all of Jewish history.

Early in the history of the reorganized Seminary the name *Conservative* was adopted by its faculty and lay leadership in order to reinforce recognition of its total commitment to traditional rabbinic Judaism and to the reformulation of that tradition in modern terms and forms. The best summary of the mission that the Seminary saw itself fulfilling was given by Solomon Schechter in his *Seminary Addresses and Other Papers,* which, despite occasional polemic and apologetics, remains the most lucid affirmation of the traditionalist but modern Judaism that the founding fathers of the Seminary upheld. Nevertheless, while the name *Conservative* was meant to set the Seminary and its scholarship apart from the contemporary Orthodox world, with its antimodernist postures in learning and custom, the two currents the new Seminary was most concerned to stem were Reform Judaism and nineteenth-century Protestant Christian scholarship in the Bible and rabbinics. The Reform movement had renounced three of the basic pillars of Judaism: halakhah, the hope for national deliverance, and the de facto centrality of Hebrew in the synagogue service. Although it insisted on maintaining the commitment to a discrete Jewish people and faith, it focused its emphasis on "prophetic ethics" and dismissed the ritual usage that constituted the framework of rabbinic Judaism.

As for nineteenth-century Protestant biblical and rabbinic critical scholarship, Schechter and his colleagues opposed it vehemently because of the "higher anti-Semitism" that pervaded so much of it. In nineteenth-century Protestant thought, Hebrew monotheism was seen to have developed relatively late in the biblical period and soon thereafter to have become incurably corrupted by the relegation of prophetic monotheism to a place far below that of priestly ritual. By the days of the Second Temple, according to this perception, Judaism had become so intensely nationalistic and so Temple-centered that its pristine message could be restored only by the ideological and behavioral revolts of Jesus, Paul, and their disciples. It was sensitivity to this animus that underlay the decision of the new rabbinical Seminary to omit higher biblical criticism, especially of the Pentateuch, and, indeed, to omit even the study of much apocryphal and apocalyptic literature from its curriculum, and to encourage, albeit discreetly, such eminent non-Jewish scholars as George Foot Moore to correct the generally distorted Christian reading of Jewish materials then commonplace.

The urgent desire to develop a form of traditional Judaism that was responsive to a post–Enlightenment world and at the same time to rescue Jewish history from the scrap heap of Western culture had led, in Germany and Central Europe in the nineteenth century, to the development of a movement called *Wissenschaft des Judentums* (Science of Judaism). Outside of Eastern Europe no religious group in modern Jewish history was so directly oriented toward the study of its basic texts and religious practices as the advocates of *Wissenschaft des Judentums*. The scholars of this movement were obsessed with the necessity of convincing themselves and the rest of the world that at no stage in its development had Judaism ever been just a faith, but that at every stage it had been—and still was—a culture, one that was properly understood and defined only when examined in light of the contemporary Jewish and secular historical moment.

These men dedicated themselves to the elucidation of texts and forms that had been ignored by Jews and Christians alike during the days of the Enlightenment: the casuistry of the Babylonian Talmud, the medieval poets, and medieval Jewish philosophy, to name but three fields of the many to which they devoted themselves. From their research they came to believe— as Conservative Judaism continues to believe—that just as Jews have carried their Torah with them wherever they have gone, so they have also carried with them the mandate to make their tradition—law, liturgy, midrash, and theology—relevant and meaningful to every generation.

In the twentieth century Solomon Schechter and his colleagues dedicated themselves to the continuation of this work. It is not fortuitous that Conservative Judaism has made its schools of learning—the Seminary itself, the University of Judaism in Los Angeles, and Neve Schechter in Jerusalem— its spiritual centers. The centrality of these institutions to the Conservative movement and the academic foundation they give it are reflected in the veneration that the movement has accorded its scholars, not only those who were its founding fathers—Israel Davidson, Israel Friedlaender, Louis Ginzberg, Alexander Marx, Solomon Schechter—but also the next generation of scholars, such as Louis Finkelstein, H. L. Ginsberg, Robert Gordis, Abraham Joshua Heschel, Saul Lieberman, Shalom Spiegel, and Moses Zucker. Each of these men has radically extended and deepened our contemporary understanding of the Jewish religious and cultural heritage.

Indeed, if there is anything Conservative Judaism has accomplished in the last hundred years, it has been the total transformation of the concept of Jewish history and culture; its scholarship has been the basis of the development of a cultural self-understanding that is profoundly new. The students and scholars in the Conservative movement do not confine their study of Torah to Bible and Talmud; for them the study of Torah embraces the religious literature of every age. Ideally, every Jew should become aware of the great variety of Jewish religious expression that has been produced over the centuries, because its existence is witness to a religious experience that has been far more multifaceted and multicolored than anything understood heretofore. At the Seminary a knowledge of midrash, philosophy, liturgy, medieval poetry, modern theology, and modern Hebrew literature is considered to be indispensable both to the rabbi and to the learned Jewish layman.

Nevertheless, the unquestioning affirmation of historic Jewish doctrines and the unquestioning acceptance of traditional Jewish practices that were characteristic of Conservative Judaism in its first two decades began to show some internal weakening by 1910. Although the small group of scholars who stood at the academic and religious helm of the seminary at that time were giants in the field of twentieth-century Jewish scholarship, a younger member of the faculty, Mordecai M. Kaplan, began to take issue with his colleagues' policy of encouraging theological, philological, and textual debate while resisting any consideration of change with respect to traditional concepts and practices. Kaplan was impatient with a system that coupled dispassionate scholarship with theological immobility and that was receptive to novelty in exegesis but impervious to the need of the ordinary American Jew for guidance in responding to the challenges of modernity and citizenship. Although at first Kaplan confined his dissident views to the Seminary and his pulpit, it was clear that a vigorous attack on Conservative Judaism was germinating within the highest ranks of the movement itself. Nor, despite an initial attempt to dissuade Kaplan from continuing to speak out, did Schechter ever consider more punitive steps against a member of the Seminary faculty.

Kaplan's monumental work *Judaism as a Civilization* (1934) contained, among other themes, nothing less than a complete repudiation of traditional Conservative Judaism as it had been expressed up to that point. The critical examination of classical Jewish texts had demonstrated to Kaplan, as it had to so many others, that the history of the Jewish tradition was a history of constant development and renewal. But to him it was also immediately evident that Judaism was once more in urgent need of rejuvenation. He felt a vacuum in the Jewish life he saw around him—especially in Conservative Jewish life—that led him to question the continued relevance of the traditional authority, faith, and practice that Schechter and his faculty had defended so vigorously. Even though Kaplan's plea for halakhic reconstruction and his continued devotion to the concept of the centrality of the Jewish people, to the renewal of Hebrew as a spoken language and as a literature, indeed his continued observance of Jewish rituals, and to the reestablishment of a strong Jewish presence in Palestine set him clearly apart from Reform Judaism, he was, nonetheless, fierce in his polemic against traditional Conservative Judaism. He was dismayed, for instance, by the refusal of the faculty to confront the fact not only that most American Jews were failing to observe the practices considered by the traditionalists to be essential, but that they were not even committed to these practices in theory.

To be sure, even Schechter and his disciples had not been insensitive to the problems articulated by Kaplan. He himself had been inspired by Zacharias Frankel's view that Judaism was the product of a positive historical development and had suggested that what had governed the process of development within the tradition was the consensus of *Kelal Yisrael,* a phrase he translated as "catholic Israel." What *Kelal Yisrael* said and did represented the manifestation at that particular moment of divine inspiration, that is, of the development of Torah in theory and practice at that point. Of course, the concept of catholic Israel did not include those who had renounced the obligations and demands of their faith. To be counted in the consensus one had to be knowledgeable in the traditional literature and to have set oneself to live by the results of the exegesis and reasoning that formed the tradition.

For Schechter, however, the process of religious development had been slow and quietly effective; whatever changes had been introduced into the tradition had not challenged the basic foundations of faith. Not that Judaism had escaped controversy. The impact of Saadiah Gaon and Moses Maimonides on their generations belies the perception by both Jews and non-Jews of a monolithic Jewish community. Still, in the final analysis the work of these men had challenged existing institutions, not the unquestioned validity of rabbinic authority. Kaplan, on the other hand, insisted—and others came to agree with him—that since scholarship had illuminated the actual dynamics of change, that is, since it had revealed to us the laws and mechanisms within Judaism and the halakhah that had permitted the continuous evolution of Jewish culture, it could now be used more actively—even aggressively—to modify law, practice, and even canons of belief.

Although Conservative Judaism has largely rejected Kaplan's theology (Kaplan's followers have established a new Reconstructionist movement and theological seminary), his vocabulary and fundamental idiom permeated the religious approach of virtually every member of the Rabbinical Assembly (the official organization of Conservative rabbis) and generated a new temper among the Conservative laity. In 1948 the Committee on Jewish Law and Standards of the Rabbinical Assembly was reorganized and began, albeit slowly, to break with many of the traditional attitudes toward faith and ritual held by the majority of the Jewish Theological Seminary faculty. Thanks to the influence of Kaplan's perception of religion, the standards of Jewish behavior could no longer be determined exclusively by the hitherto acknowledged supreme halakhic authorities of Conservative Judaism. In truth, the ideas of Mordecai Kaplan caused such a basic reorientation within Conservative Judaism that its posture today is at variance with that which obtained in the years following its birth.

While retaining the basic principles of traditional faith and practice, the rabbinate and laity of Conservative Judaism are today increasingly reflective, if unconsciously, of the insights derived from the critical study of Jewish sources, and consciously open to the possibilities of new exegesis. The primary desire of Conservative Judaism's leaders and scholars is to translate law and usage into renewed expressions of an ancient tradition—to employ all the knowledge they have gained of the development of the Jewish tradition, as well as their contemporary moral perceptions, in order to come to halakhic decisions that will be acceptable to the learned believer in the modern world. They are committed to promulgating fresh formulations of the components of a totally authentic, yet modern, Jewish life—formulations that will rearticulate the fundamental principles of normative Judaism as interpreted in the light of the latest advances in technology, sociopolitical organization, and modern moral values. These extra-legal considerations are vital because if the yardsticks for religious validity or for change are restricted to the traditional halakhic ones, the Jews of the modern world are then caught in a web of precedents established in different settings and in different ages with vastly different conceptions of morality and conscience. There are two questions Conservative Judaism asks in gauging the authenticity of any halakhic decision: (1) Is it grounded in the history and wording of the law itself? and (2) Will it result in the enhancement of Torah as a whole? If the Committee on Jewish Law and Standards of the Rabbinical Assembly permits the modification of a talmudic norm regarding the Sabbath, it is because it is believed that the modification will result in increased observance.

The most widely known departures of Conservative Judaism from established practice have been in the decisions of the committee to permit riding to the nearest synagogue on the Sabbath, to count women as legitimate members of a minyan, and most recently—and most resoundingly—the decision of a majority of the Seminary faculty to admit women to the rabbinical school as candidates for ordination. After reading the report of a commission appointed by the chancellor that had traveled throughout the country to sound out the opinions of large numbers of Conservative Jews to establish a consensus of the movement on this matter, and after reading numerous halakhic opinions submitted by faculty members, the faculty put the question to a vote. Those who voted in favor of the motion did so, first, because they believed that it was halakhically sound, that there was nothing in rabbinic Judaism to inhibit women from functioning as rabbis; and, second, because they believed that since it was halakhically sound, it was religiously imperative, in the context of the Conservative Jewish community, to move on the issue at that time. They believed that to continue to deny admission to the rabbinical school to women who are committed to halakhah and dedicated to God, the service of Torah, and Israel would fail to be responsive to the felt desire of the greater part of the community and of Conservative Judaism altogether. Instead they, and through them the Conservative movement, have opened the gates of Jewish leadership to new sources of vitality, dedication, and talent.

It should be obvious—although frequently it seems not to be—that this faculty decision obligated no one and no congregation. It merely meant that—as the Conservative movement interpreted the halakhah with respect to this issue—there is a choice. It recognized—as has the tradition since the rabbinic age—that there may be more than one acceptable opinion about the application of a particular law to a particular set of circumstances. In the past thirty-seven years the Committee on Jewish Law and Standards has consistently circulated both majority and minority opinions, leaving the final decision to the individual rabbi and congregation. Indeed, the vitality of Conservative Judaism will depend, for the foreseeable future, not only on the authenticity and wisdom of its interpretations of halakhah, but also on the recognition of all concerned of the validity even of legitimate interpretations with which they may disagree.

Flexibility can engender fear. Many require a religious movement to be unequivocal in its ideology and to advocate, at least in theory, a unitary form of ritual practice. But the leadership of the Conservative movement functions on the principle that competent authorities can reach a variety of authentic answers to the complex issues of faith and life. In fact, it is when seen from this perspective that the Conservative movement can be said to be quasi-congregationalist in its organization, each congregational unit (rabbi and synagogue membership) deciding for itself which of the positions deemed acceptable by the Committee on Jewish Law and Standards it wishes to adopt.

Nevertheless, although Conservative Judaism endorses a pluralistic approach in matters of doctrine and observance, it insists, at the same time, upon the acceptance of certain basic categories of faith and worship. All Conservative congregations affirm the binding obligation of halakhah, the Sabbath, the festivals, *kashrut,* circumcision, daily prayer, marriage, divorce, and conversion according to Jewish law, and the centrality of Hebrew in the synagogue service. And all affirm the spiritual centrality of the land of Israel and the people of Israel. It is important to emphasize here, however, that whereas the word *Israel* in this formulation means Israel in its transtemporal and transgeographic sense, the fact is that the State of Israel and its Jewish population bear a spiritual importance that transcends their local existence. Moreover, it is also important to emphasize in regard to the concept of the people of Israel that just as the Conservative movement tolerates diversity within its own camp, it tolerates diversity outside itself as well. In other words, Conservative Judaism has always insisted on the solidarity of the Jewish people as a whole, in all its myriad forms and orientations. From the Conservative perspective the secular Jew is as much a Jew as the observant Jew, and the destiny and welfare of the non-Conservative as much the concern of the movement as the destiny and welfare of those within its fold.

Conservative Judaism is not monolithic. As it takes root in different parts of the world, it will express itself in each case in a dialect that is appropriate to each particular situation. Nevertheless, wherever Conservative Judaism will be found, it will be found to be dedicated to fostering a life of Torah— in the synagogue, in the home, in the school, and in the community. The Jewish people has acquired the ability to reinterpret its Torah, linguistically and conceptually, in every generation. This is what Conservative Judaism is trying to do for the contemporary generation of Conservative Jews both within the United States and outside it. For unless each generation of Jews, no matter where they may find themselves, can master this process of reinterpretation, the Jewish tradition will lose its hold in that place. Conservative Judaism is not a halfway point between Orthodoxy and secularism. On the contrary, for the past century, combining the critical study of Jewish texts and Jewish history with an unalterable commitment to the Jewish tradition, Conservative Judaism has offered a fresh and authentic approach to the modern world.

BIBLIOGRAPHY

Max Kadushin, *Worship and Ethics: A Study in Rabbinic Judaism* (1964).
Mordecai M. Kaplan, *Judaism as a Civilization* (1934).
Solomon Schechter, *Some Aspects of Rabbinic Theology* (1909).
Marshall Sklare, *Conservative Judaism* (1955).

Convert and Conversion

גר, גיור

Jochanan H. A. Wijnhoven

Hebrew scriptures use the concept of conversion to denote the fundamental decision by which the total human being responds to God's call. It is the human attitude that corresponds to the divine action of election. Election calls for conversion, and conversion is experienced as an election. The radical change, or conversion, of one's inner orientation has been described as a true enlightenment, as a rebirth, and in the Hebrew Scriptures as *teshuvah*, both in the meaning of "answer" and "return." The Jewish convert is the *baal teshuvah*, or the person who has "answered the inner appeal," and who has "truly returned." This conversion is a conversion from the periphery to the center, and is the most basic choice man is offered in life. While the Hebrew Scriptures stress this as the deepest sense of Israel's relationship to God, this "conversion" has universal human applicability. All men are called to turn to God. It is the conversion that Jonah preached to Nineveh, reluctantly, for initially he considered conversion an affair between God and the Hebrew people. The Jonah story reaffirms the concept of God's covenant with man. The inner content of conversion, justice, is the moral of the Noah story in Genesis 6–

9. The Scriptures present the Mosaic covenant as a covenant within the universal covenant with Adam and Noah, and consequently Judaism is committed to the conversion of man to God, as well as the conversion of the Jew to "Jewishness."

There is another meaning attached to conversion, which denotes not the movement from the periphery to the center but "from the outside to the inside." This is the "change of religion" most commonly associated with the concept of the convert and conversion. The two meanings are not mutually exclusive. In fact, a conversion to the specificity of Judaism, if this is the form chosen for converting to God, is a maximum goal to be desired from the Jewish perspective. Historical Judaism, however, has seen conversion to Judaism as a free association with various degrees of intensity.

The Jewish term for convert is *proselyte,* which in its Greek meaning (*proselytos*) emphasizes the voluntary act of joining. Jewish theology always stressed the optional nature of "coming to" the Jewish people, whereas it saw conversion to God as a universal, divine imperative. Ruth the Moabite is the scriptural model of the volunteer who joins the specificity of Israel's way of life and belief: "Wherever you lodge, I will lodge; your people shall be my people, and your God, my God" (Ruth 1:16). Ironically, proselytism received the pejorative connotation of aggressive, undesired conversion activity, while its Christian counterpart, the mission, which sees conversion from the perspective of the converter (missionary) rather than that of the convert, escaped the bad taste that proselytism implies. It is only recently, when indifference to religious views is seen as true tolerance and any religious view is considered frivolous, that the concept of mission has been given the historical verdict of proselytism.

Except for a brief episode under the Hasmonaean kings (142–63 B.C.E.), when Judaism was forced upon Edomites and Samaritans, Judaism has upheld an openness of association. The Hebrew term for proselyte is *ger* (literally, stranger or sojourner), which is similar to our notion of alien resident. The land of Israel has always been multinational, or polyethnic. The Hebrew Scriptures, therefore, deal frequently with the relationship of Jew and non-Jew in the same land. While alien enemies, such as Philistines, have to be dealt with militarily, the peaceful alien who has cast his lot with Israel is to be accepted; he is to be loved, protected, and assisted in the same way the Torah cares for Israel's poor, widows, and orphans. "When a stranger resides with you in your land, you shall not wrong him. The stranger who resides with you shall be to you as one of your citizens; you shall love him as yourself, for you were strangers in the land of Egypt: I am the Lord your God" (Lev. 19:33–34).

The conviction that the God of Israel, the God of the Fathers, possessed a universal truth as ruler of the world and all the nations grew during and after the Babylonian exile. Israel's perspective on history, its "end vision," was that "the Lord shall be king over all the earth; in that day there shall be one Lord, with one name" (Zech. 14:9). With the translation of the Scriptures into Greek and the spread of the Jewish Diaspora in the Hellenistic world, we can observe a number of non-Jews confessing the God of Israel and desiring to join the community of Jews. Next to the earlier *ger toshav*, the loyal resident alien, we now have newcomers, *proselytoi*, associate Jews, to whom the "equal rights" notion previously attached to the resident alien is extended. The technical term for the sincere convert to Judaism, the outsider who now has his dwelling in righteousness, is *ger ẓedek* or *ger emet*: true proselyte. Besides the resident alien and the true proselyte, the complex term *ger* absorbed historically a third category, that of semi-proselytes. These are also referred to as the "God fearers," non-Jews who worship the one and only God and lead an upright moral life. They are *ḥasidei umot olam*, pious Gentiles. Such a pious Gentile is called *ger shaar*, a proselyte of the gate or a son of Noah.

After the rise of Christianity the rabbis were by virtue of canon law prohibited from and hence less enthusiastic about accepting proselytes into the synagogue; instead they developed further the notion of the Noachites, the members of God's universal covenant with man. While keeping open the possibility for true proselytes who, like Abraham, would leave family and nation to join the covenant of circumcision and become full-fledged-- Jews, the primary outreach to the world to join Israel in worshiping the true Lord was as sons of Noah. The Talmud sets forth the seven commandments of the Noachite covenant as follows: not to worship idols, not to abuse God's name, to avoid bloodshed, to refrain from adultery, to refrain from theft, to obey law courts, and "not to cut flesh from living animals" (that is, to refrain from cruel exploitation of animals) (BT Sanh. 56a ff.). Reverence for God, life, family, private property, and social order, as well as kindness to fellow creatures, characterizes a just man, a son of Noah.

Maimonides viewed both Christendom and Islam as semi-proselytes, confessing Israel's God and stressing upright moral life. The concept that proselytes "come to dwell under the wings of the divine Presence *(Shekhinah)*" gave him occasion to discuss the various degrees and different categories of proselytes. The Jewish theologian and synthetizer Joseph Albo saw in the Noachite commandments the nucleus of natural, that is, rational law. While the Mosaic covenant was seen as the specific covenant for the Jews, Gentiles living in accordance with natural law were seen as having covenanted with God according to Noah's covenant. Seventeenth-century gentile thinkers such as Hugo Grotius, John Selden, and John Toland in turn drew on the rabbinical concept of the Noachites in explaining natural law and natural religion. It became a matter of controversy whether Noachism implied merely ethical Deism, or also a belief in revelation. For some, upright moral life was sufficient to belong to God's covenant. Nineteenth-century Reform thinkers were generous in extending the universal covenant to general humanistic beliefs in natural rectitude as the underlying principles of the Western civilized world. Noachism thus became a religion to which most of its members did not know they belonged. In the nineteenth century, an Italian Jewish theologian, Elijah Benamozegh, revived the notion of the Noachite covenant in close association with Judaism. For him the righteous Gentile was a meaningful and conscious associate of the Jew in the Lord's universal kingdom. The Scriptures, rather than natural law, were the basis upon which to unify men in the Lord's service. Aimé Pallière, a follower of Benamozegh, demonstrated his belonging to Judaism by learning Hebrew, praying in the synagogue, and defending Jews and Jewish causes without "conversion" to Judaism; he still remained a Catholic.

Conversion to Judaism in the strictest sense signifies the process by which a non-Jew confesses to become, and to be, a Jew. Jewish tradition offers appropriate rituals for this event. They vary in different historical periods and among the different movements (for example, Orthodox, Conservative, Reform). Male converts should become circumcised, and female converts, except in Reform practice, should undergo ritual immersion *(tevilah)*. Application for conversion and preparatory demands vary greatly in practice and strictness. Since conversion to Judaism is existentially joining a community defined as a people, which acts as a body politic rather than a congregation of believers, conversion in the context of marriage has the preponderant attention and pastoral interest of rabbis. The voluntary nature of committing oneself to Jewish specificity (acquiring Jewishness) as the expression of one's commitment to God's law places the initiative to "Judaize" with the proselyte rather than with the community or the rabbis. At all times there has been a minority of spiritual pilgrims who found their way to Judaism as their unique source of spiritual life. The Jewish community has welcomed them as true sons of Abraham, as full Jews. Proselytism is the beautiful and sensitive way by which non-Jews unite with Jews, first of all from the periphery to the center in the essence of conversion. Then there are those who integrate their life's interests with those of the Jewish people without becoming technically Jews. Such a one can be called a present-day *ger toshav*. The central category is that of the sincere convert, who takes on Jewish specificity as the human expression of religious life. This is the *ger ẓedek*, or true proselyte. Finally, one can speak of the "associates in the Lord's kingdom, or His coming kingdom." They are the different religious specificities of the Noachite covenant, of which a member can be considered a *ger shaar*. In all various degrees and nuances the process of aggregation *(proseluteuo)* is to be a drawing near to the Jewish community. As Judaism cannot exist without Jews, love for Judaism cannot coexist with dislike for Jews. This primary solidarity with the Jewish community is absent if the concept of the convert were to include all the para-communities or rival claimants to the Jewish heritage. Para-communities in the past were Samaritans and Karaites; nowadays they are more likely to be Seventh Day Adventists, the Church of Jesus Christ of Latter Day Saints, and those forms of Christianity that believe in God's rejection of the Jews and a displacement of the divine covenant. Creating a copy of what one may (sincerely) believe to be the Israel intended by God and seeing the Jewish community as straying or apostate from God's intended commonwealth is to segregate from rather than aggregate to the Jewish phenomenon of Judaism.

A parallel experience of the Jew and of the proselyte/foreigner is stressed in the Hebrew Scriptures. Like the proselyte, the Israelite also knows what it is to be a stranger, a *ger*. "I also established My covenant with them, to give them the land of Canaan, in which they lived as sojourners" (Ex. 6:4); "For like all my forebears I am an alien, resident with you" (Ps. 39:12, 119:19). Jacob fled to Haran and died in Egypt. Moses was exiled in Midian and died at the threshold of the land. Israel was oppressed in Egypt and wandered through the desert. A proselyte who joins the Jewish people affirms an identity of the experience of uprooting, estrangement, and hope of return. In harking to God's call from Sinai, where the historic community of Israel "constituted itself," a proselyte joins a community that cherishes as its "end vision" the times of which Isaiah says that "also the sons of the foreigner join themselves to the Lord to serve Him and to love His name, to be his servants, everyone observing the sabbath, and taking hold of the covenant . . . even them, the foreigners, will I bring, says the Lord, in my house of prayer. Their offerings and sacrifices will be accepted on my altar, for my house shall be called a house of prayer for all peoples" (Isa. 56:6ff.).

BIBLIOGRAPHY

Bernard J. Bamberger, *Proselytism in the Talmudic Period* (1968).
William G. Braude, *Jewish Proselytizing in the First Five Centuries of the Common Era: The Age of the Tannaim and Amoraim* (1940).
David M. Eichhorn, ed., *Conversion to Judaism: A History and Analysis* (1965).
Jacob Katz, *Exclusiveness and Tolerance: Studies in Jewish-Gentile Relations in Medieval and Modern Times* (1962).
Joseph R. Rosenbloom, *Conversion to Judaism: From the Biblical Period to the Present* (1978).

Covenant

ברית

Arnold Eisen

By appropriating the political lexicon of the ancient Near East to describe an unprecedented relation between a people and its God, the Bible accomplished far more than the awesomely significant "transference of suzerainty from a flesh and blood emperor to a supreme and unique deity."[1] It bequeathed to the world a way of conceiving the inconceivable—a metaphor that, among Jews, has proven remarkably flexible and enduring. The concept of God's *brit* (covenant) with Israel survived the destruction of his dwelling place and helped to contain the tragedy of exile. More recently, it has emerged from the twin onslaughts of modernity and the Holocaust to preside over the gropings of contemporary Jewish theology toward authentic Jewish faith. Like the very wounding of flesh which most symbolizes it, covenant has continued to hold Jews—seizing them, in large part, through the power of their own ambivalence.

The monarchs of the biblical period, we learn from recent scholarship, entered into several sorts of covenant (*biritu* in Akkadian) with their peers and subjects. In one type, generally known as the suzerainty treaty, the king bound his vassals to a set of obligations, which he defined. In return, the sovereign promised nothing, except—implicitly—his own protection, conferred in return for the subjects' loyalty and trust. Parity treaties, by contrast, stipulated the mutual obligations undertaken by two equal parties. A third sort of pact, the promissory grant, presumed the inequality of the parties, but nonetheless bound the sovereign unilaterally. Out of sheer beneficence, he agreed to the performance of stipulated acts on behalf of his inferiors.

At Sinai, the suzerainty model is borrowed (cf. Ex. 19–20). If Israel will "obey Me faithfully, and keep My covenant," it shall become God's chosen "kingdom of priests and holy nation" (Ex. 19:5), uniquely enjoying his presence and protection. The *brit,* initiated by God, binds Israel to him—and, equally significant, to each other. Deuteronomy's reiteration of the covenant follows the parity form precisely, adopting even the standard six-part structure: preamble, historical prologue, detailed stipulations, provision for deposit and/or reading of the text, invocation of divine witnesses (in this case, heaven and earth), and, finally, the recitation of blessings and curses. By contrast Noah (Gen. 9:8), Abraham (Gen. 15:18; 17:4), and David (II Sam. 7) are the privileged recipients of promissory covenants. God binds himself to be their patron and benefactor. Like a lover, he accepts the partner just as he is—David even in his sinfulness, the whole of humanity despite a nature that is evil from its youth.

Here lies the terror of the *brit*—and its comfort. The awesome creator of mankind is brought into the human camp, demanding a degree of ethical and ritual purity that mere mortals are hard pressed to achieve. Yet the *mysterium tremendum* is thereby rendered accessible and, to a degree, comprehensible. Israel cannot penetrate the fire and cloud of God's presence, but the people can know what God wants of them. Even more remarkably, they can rest confident that God will submit to the seeming indignity of human conversation. He will negotiate, with Abraham, over the destruction of Sodom, and agree, after the pleading of Moses, to pardon the transgressions of Israel.

God, it seems, has no choice. This is the true daring of the covenant idea: God, who inscrutably commands Abraham to bind his son, no less inscrutably binds himself to his own children through cords of immutable obligation. A moral God who seeks a moral world, he has created humanity free to disobey. Perforce a moralist, he is compelled to bargain. Suppose there are fifty righteous men in Sodom, Abraham asks hesitantly—then, more boldly, what if there are forty, thirty, twenty, ten? Israel, too, alternately trembles before the father's wrath, appeals to his love, and presumes upon the net of historical facticity into which he has cast his lot. Certainly we deserve destruction, the people concede—but what would the Egyptians say?

When Israel's repeated failure to fulfill its part of the bargain led to expulsion from the land where God's presence especially dwelled—so the prophets saw the exile—the people were comforted by a series of "lawsuit addresses" that called it to account for breach of promise, but refused to decree divorce. The covenant, after all, was written upon their flesh. Israel's failure to mark it in Sabbaths or confirm it through social justice (cf. Isa. 58) would not result in the covenant's unilateral cancellation. Yet the terror of the covenant was thereby reinforced as well. God would permit the destruction of Jerusalem, and the loss of all but a remnant. His merciful refusal to punish, tit for tat, only highlighted Israel's inability to contain him in terms narrow enough for human understanding.

The rabbis, in the wake of a second exile (this time not followed by return), could only articulate the biblical paradoxes surrounding the covenant, not resolve them. On the one hand, Israel had freely accepted God's Torah, when all the other nations of the world, put off by the covenant's demands, had politely declined. On the other hand, Israel had been forced into the "yoke of commandment" against its will. God had held Sinai over them like a barrel, saying, "If you accept my Torah, well and good, but if not, this shall be your burial ground." (BT Shab. 88b). Parity had its advantages when it came to coping with rejection. "He has made me singled out, and I have made him singled out,"[2] goes a sing-song passage in the *Mekhilta* which expresses reciprocity—and so reassurance—in its very rhythm. Did God not owe something to the only people willing to deal with him? A bold midrash in *Lamentations Rabba* (3:1) has a queen protest her exile from the palace on the charge of insolence by reminding the king that "I am the only wife you received." No one else had been willing to take God's Torah. Suzerainty too had its comforts: Could Israel be blamed for failure to obey terms that it had had no voice whatever in framing? The covenant would continue, then, even if Israel had not been entirely faithful. What could not be explained could be expressed, and even rehearsed. A fate beyond comprehension could nonetheless be endured.

This achievement of the rabbinic imagination protected God's covenant from the destruction that befell his holy land and Temple and permitted the process of covenantal revision, that is, halakhah, that has continued down to our own day. It also, however, made the rabbis unwitting accomplices in the more thorough attempt at revision of the covenant undertaken in the last century and a half, through which liberal Jewish thinkers have sought to cope with the jolts of modernity. The direct stimulus for this latter revision was Immanuel Kant, who insisted that moral action could emerge only from the "autonomous" undertaking of an individual to obey the law dictated to his or her reason. An event such as Sinai, Kant argued, could secure only heteronomous compliance—the mountain suspended over Israel like a barrel—but not a freely given "we will do and obey." The demands of such a covenant, even if authentic (which Kant of course doubted) were ethically illegitimate. Modern Jews for whom personal dignity is inextricably bound up in the sense of freedom have proved sensitive to Kant's challenge, even as they have continued to seek grounding in an obligation and an identity which cannot be escaped. Hence the special appeal of the covenant idea for Jewish thought in the modern period, and its intractable difficulty.

Hermann Cohen, seeking to circumvent Kant's objections to the Sinaitic *brit*, detached "God's covenant with us" from any specific event or codified content. Leo Baeck, in a similar move, placed the initiative for the covenant between Israel and God squarely on the shoulders of the former. Israel was elect because "it elects itself." Martin Buber significantly omitted the concept entirely from his writings on Jewish spirituality, employing it elsewhere only to stress that Israel, more than any other people, had always inextricably linked its faith and its nationhood. Among contemporary thinkers, Emil Fackenheim has made use of the idea to express the paradox of a "Divine Commanding Presence" that at once "destroys and addresses human freedom" (*pace* Kant). The *brit*, he adds, binds individual Jews to the fate of the Jewish people whether they are obedient to its stipulations or not. Eugene Borowitz, for whom the concept is most central, has likewise adopted the formulation that the covenant's terms are created by Israel (and hence autonomous) but emerge out of a "covenantal relation" with God (and so are heteronomous). The revisions of each generation must be appropriate to its particular situation, Borowitz writes, but true to the nature of the pact as well. In the recent debate over the theological significance of the Holocaust, several thinkers have urged and described a new "voluntary covenant" joining Israel to God, "voluntary" because God failed to fulfill his part of the bargain—protection of his people.

For an Orthodox thinker such as Joseph Soloveitchik, such equivocation on the matter of the covenant's authorship, and such theological conclusions from the Holocaust, are unacceptable. Soloveitchik has distinguished between two covenants: that of fate, or "Egypt," which binds individual Jews inescapably to the shared history, suffering, and responsibility of their people; and the covenant of destiny, or "Sinai"—a freely chosen attempt to realize the "historic being" of the Jew via the shared and directed way of life that we know as halakhah. In a midrash Soloveitchik discerns two very different personas of Adam in the Garden of Eden and in each of us. As Adam I, we seek majesty or dignity: knowledge, creativity, control of our world. As Adam II, we enter into a "covenantal community" in which we find friendship with and responsibility to our fellows, as well as obligation to and colloquy with our God. While attentive to the wish for autonomy (the covenant of destiny must be undertaken freely) and responsive to the primacy accorded peoplehood in much of modern Jewish thought, Soloveitchik nonetheless makes such considerations subservient to the binding covenant of Sinai.

It is no coincidence, surely, that the biblical elements of suzerainty and parity figure so crucially in this modern debate, the first now draped in the forms of halakhah, transcendence, heteronomy, and fate; the second appearing as ethical obligation, immanence, autonomy, and destiny. Distance and relation are, as Buber has taught us, the polar coordinates of all encounter with a Thou, and Israel's troubled relationship with the "Eternal Thou" has, as we have seen, been no exception. One suspects, however, that the terms of contemporary discussion owe less to the tradition's mandate than to the peculiar situation of modern Jews and Judaism. The faith of self-conscious (and self-preoccupied) Adam I, engaged in the scientific ordering of the universe, cannot but cavil at a concept of covenant that seems to threaten the degree of freedom so essential to our modern selves. "Covenantal community," by contrast, is an idea made even more appealing by the retreat of much of Jewish faith to the fortress of Jewish community—that is, to an identification with a unique people, through which transcendent meaning of a sort can still be located even in our day.

Israel's covenant with God, then, has been retained and awarded prominence in the modern period, but its traditional force has been neutralized. Whether the *brit* can long survive such subversion only time will tell. One may imagine, however, that this broken myth, like others, will not persist indefinitely in the absence of the larger healing awaited by Jewish faith and the Jewish people. In the meantime, theology that invokes the *brit* while refusing to supply it with any content runs the risk of becoming cant. It assumes, on the one hand, a rabbinic vocabulary in order to legitimate a rejection of divine sovereignty and, on the other hand, asserts a parity between man and God that the ancient rabbis would have found unacceptable.

Theologians driven by the death of the 6 million to pronounce the covenant shattered seem no less unfaithful to Jewish tradition, which has always been far too subtle to permit such a black-and-white reading of the covenant text. Those in search of the contemporary significance of covenant in a time such as ours may well find theology unavailing and be forced to affirm in faith more than they can manage reasonably and persuasively to believe.

REFERENCES

1. E. E. Mendenhall, "Covenant," in *The Interpreters Dictionary of the Bible,* 1 (1962), 719.
2. Mekh. 366, M. Friedmann, ed. (1870).

BIBLIOGRAPHY

E. E. Mendenhall, "Covenant," in *The Interpreters Dictionary of the Bible,* I (1962).
Joseph Soloveitchik, "Lonely Man of Faith," in *Tradition,* 7 (Summer 1965).

Creation

בריאה

Alon Goshen-Gottstein

Revelation begins with creation, and its position at the outset of the biblical narrative may be taken to indicate that all that follows—history, law, and religious experience—derives its meaning from a thought-pattern arrived at by pondering the fact and story of creation. When we speak of creation, we are not, essentially, in the realm of physics, ancient or modern. We are making a statement of religious thought, which affords answers to questions about the meaning, purpose, and direction of life. Nor do we view creation merely as the first link in a chain of historical events. It is, rather, an event whose meaning transcends the historical process. What is of salient importance is the structure of creation, which manifests itself in the historical process as in other dimensions of existence.

The term *creation* refers not only to the result of a process, but also to the process itself. As process, creation is ever-regenerating, its outcome ever-changing. However, the relationship between creation and creator and the aspect of existence that creation demonstrates remain constant. It is to the constant, as it illuminates the meaning of all created life, that we shall address ourselves.

We take it almost for granted that certain attributes ascribed to God—his existence, omnipotence, and goodness, his will and his knowledge of and involvement with each and every created being—belong within the context of a Jewish doctrine of creation. But God's unity, the most central feature of Jewish theology, is often thought irrelevant to a discussion of creation. It is precisely this tenet of the Jewish faith that we will make our point of departure, for it is this aspect of divine life that is least discernible within creation, while, regarding this tenet, creation may be said to have effected the greatest change.

The Midrash teaches us that "Before the world was created, the Holy One, blessed be He, with His name alone existed" (Pd Re [ed. Friedlander], 10). We learn from this that before the world's creation the unity of God entailed more than merely the nonexistence of other, higher powers. It meant that God was the only reality and therefore all of reality was One. The creation of a reality that could view itself as being separate from God—though it might not ultimately be so—signaled a transformation in reality as it had been up to that point. It was no longer a unity; multiplicity had been introduced as a mode of existence. The traditional emphasis that God was alone and unaided in his work of creation further heightens the tension between the idea of the unity of the creator and that of the multiplicity of his works. Thus, if we understand God's unity as the ultimate unity of all existence, we must view creation as that process through which fragmentation and multiplicity enter a hitherto unified reality.

We may illustrate this understanding of the process of creation from several traditional sources. Following the rabbis' explanation of why the creation story begins with the second letter of the Hebrew alphabet (the *bet* of *Bereshit*), we may say that not only are there two worlds, but creation itself introduces duality and thus multiplicity into reality. Multiplicity is the hallmark of creation. The biblical narrative's odd way of counting the days of the creation: "one," "second," "third," and so on, highlights the distinction between unified reality, to which the idea of number does not apply, and created reality, which brings numeration and multiplicity in its wake. creation's birth in a number of stages, rather than through a single act, is not merely a teaching regarding process but a statement about the manifold nature of creation.

One of the central processes through which creation comes to be, as we are taught in the first chapters of Genesis, is that of separation. A hitherto undifferentiated reality is separated into two distinct realities. The separation of light and darkness, upper and lower waters, land and sea are clear examples of such a process. This process continues, we may further suggest, with plant and animal life coming into their own, and culminates with the separation of woman from man. Rabbinic speculation enlarges the category of the pairs of opposites that come into play in creation. Two polar divine modes of creation, thought and action, and two polar divine forces, justice and mercy, are involved. The work of creation itself is compounded of the basic dyad of heaven and earth. Later generations, moreover, have observed that the fundamental duality of good and evil is itself an outcome of the duality of God and creation. The departure from the original oneness in God's will is the point whence evil, and therefore sin as well, arises.

One may represent all that has been suggested through any number of antinomies. Any theoretical frame of understanding will yield further categories through which the multiplicity of creation may be presented. That is to say, one may develop further series of interdependent pairs of opposites to capture the full range of diversity within creation. Thus, the door is open for current and future generations to elaborate upon the composite nature of creation, as upon the modes of rediscovering unity, which must be the outcome of the recognition of the antinomies inherent in creation.

Judaism's recognition of the manifold nature of creation and the move away from unity that it represents has not led it to view creation as a negative, unreal, or illusory phenomenon. Judaism's affirmation of the goodness of God's nature, from which creation springs, leaves no room for the emergence of a radical, Gnostic attitude. The Jewish sources reflect a recognition of the goodness of creation and an aspiration to discover unity within the created order. The antinomies that are manifest in the creative process, and which govern life, ought not to be perceived then as hopelessly in conflict. They may be polarized, but in fact they complement one another and find their resolution in a higher order.

The ultimate unity of created life may be stated theologically, in relation to God, and also symbolically, in relation to man. It is precisely Judaism's affirmation of God's unity that necessitates its understanding that unity is manifested through and beyond the diversity of creation. The divine attribute of goodness, as a factor motivating the creative process, may be suggested as a unifying principle evident throughout creation.

In a more picturesque manner, the relation between unity and diversity within creation may be portrayed through the following rabbinic midrash. The rabbis tell us that several entities were created even before the world (Ber. Rab. 1:4). However, such a statement should not be regarded as historical, but rather as symbolic. The meaning of the midrashic proposition that, inter alia, the Torah (representing spiritual being and discipline), the People of Israel qua spiritual center, the Temple in the dimension of space, and *teshuvah*—penitence or return—as spiritual practice are premundane can be understood as follows: these are realities that transcend the duality of later creation. They are an anchor, within the created order, for a higher, unified order; they are center-points through which the diversity of creation can reconnect with a plane of unity as well as apprehend that self-same unity within the created order. The Sabbath, too, poses a unifying principle to balance the preceding six distinct stages of the manifestation of creation. It introduces the principles of rest, integration, and unity into the pattern of diversity, serving as a point of transfer to a different order of reality through which an ultimate perspective on created works may be attained. The quest to discover a plane of unity also underlies religious activity. Any *mizvah*—any religious action or gesture—constitutes a move from diversity to unity and, conversely, a means by which unity may become known within the field of diversity. This process is at work in a long-range, evolutionary sense as well. The rabbis taught that the name of the Messiah was among the entities created before the world. Stage by stage, we move toward a recognition of the primordial unity within creation—a process that can be consummated only in the messianic end. The strong historical bent of Jewish thinking thus addresses the ontology of creation.

At this point we may venture to address the question of the reason and purpose of creation. The ultimate answer to this lies beyond the scope of human knowledge; one can only refer to God's will, the source of which is hidden from us. However, our knowledge of God's revealed will and of the structure of creation may suggest an approach to the question.

Existence as a whole has two aspects, that of God/unity and that of creation/plurality, and perfection applies to and encompasses both. Or, to put it differently, we may express the range of the modes of existence by saying that "being" moves into "becoming." Perfection thus has a dynamic, active aspect to it, which comes to light in the multiple works of creation. But what is gained by the move into "becoming," that is, into plurality?

One standard answer within Jewish thought is that God created in order to share his goodness and bounty with a world that, as some would emphasize, is otherwise imperfect. This view seems to lead to a perception of creation as the means through which God's ability to give can be realized. God's dependence upon and need for creation, according to such a view, would lead to an emphasis upon his innate qualities of goodness and generosity as the ground for creation. In any event, it is through its distinctness from God that creation can receive of his goodness.

Another classic answer views creation as a way for God to realize aspects of himself that could not otherwise be realized. Creation is the arena through which his glory, greatness, and kingship can be made known. The aim of the creative process is thus the recognition of God. Who is it that recognizes God? Again, it may be creation as distinct from God. But a further possibility emerges here: one may suggest a continuum between God and creation; creation is an extension of God's inner life, which turns back in order to face and recognize him. Creation's purpose would then be, as some have suggested, for God to realize and bring to expression aspects of himself that could not otherwise be known and made manifest.

The traditional answer discussed above may be integrated into a wider perspective in which the relationship between God and creation may be described in yet more far-reaching terms. It is a commonplace of Jewish thought that man is a microcosm, containing within himself in miniature the forces that manifest themselves throughout creation. It is therefore legitimate, traditionally speaking, to try to induce from man to creation as a whole. Human reality is a soul that, for the purpose of its evolution, has assumed a body in order to be able to operate on a physical plane. There it experiences, learns, and grows through the various opportunities that life, in its diverse forms, affords. Creation, ranging in scope from minute detail to the vast regions of the universe, may be understood along the same lines. Physical creation is the body through which the divine operates. We may conjecture that evolution is the motivating drive behind this process, originating in God's will and therefore substantively unknown to us. It follows that the spiritual development of creation is of consequence to the life of him whose body it constitutes.

There are rabbinic statements to the effect that the world was created on behalf of man, on behalf of Israel, or on behalf of the righteous. Precisely man, who has the conscious capacity to do right and wrong, has the responsibility to further the development of creation by raising it to its spiritual ideal. Spiritual perfection, which serves the very purpose of creation, is Israel's collective goal; and it is the righteous, individually, who attain it. As elaborated above, the essence of this spiritual perfection is the discovery of unity within the diversity of creation. It is a return to the original unity, the source of creation, from the diversity of physical phenomena. That is why many of the symbolic expressions for unity within creation that are described above referred not to creation per se but to man and his spiritual ideals. For man reflects the wider cosmic process in miniature, encompassing spirit and body, unity and diversity within his person. He therefore holds a special position within creation. He is perfectible in spirit; it is he who has the ability to discover unity and so further the evolution and purpose of creation.

Judaism sees creation as both perfect and imperfect. When we consider the perfect God who made it in his goodness and proclaimed it to be good, when we recall that unity is the ultimate order of God's self-expression in creation, we must acknowledge its perfection. But when we consider the evolutionary aspect of life, always striving to greater perfection, we must call it imperfect. The common perception of reality as governed by multiplicity, which necessitates man's role in the elevation of creation, bars us from making an unequivocal statement regarding the perfection of creation.

Judaism's attitude toward creation is thus one of positive affirmation, qualified by a sober appreciation of the complexity of the powers involved. It is a compound attitude, taking into account the whole as well as the parts, ontology as well as process. Creation, though perfect, must always strive toward a higher reality that transcends its antinomies. Its ultimate significance, while realized within creation, must enter from without. This striving must be an integral part of any Jewish conception of creation—a conception that allots to man the responsibility for furthering the evolution of creation and bringing to completion the works of God. Someday we will be able to affirm unequivocally the perfection of creation. This is Judaism's messianic vision: "On that day God will be One and His Name will be One" (Zach. 14:9).

BIBLIOGRAPHY

R. Naḥman of Bratslav, *Likkutei Moharan, Section 51*
Eugene Mihaly, *Song of Creation. A Dialogue With a Text*, (1975)

Culture

תרבות

Paul Mendes-Flohr

"**P**eoples of the past," Franz Rosenzweig once whimsically remarked, "did not know whether they were living in the fifth or fourth century B.C."[1] In contrast to the ancients, the denizens of the modern world are often painfully aware of their place in time and in the ever-unfolding drama of human history. The modern historical consciousness is deepened still further by an appreciation of the varied tapestry of human "cultures," past and present, and the concomitant realization that one's culture is but one possible pattern of human spiritual and social organization. Indeed, the term *culture* as denoting the particular intellectual and material qualities of different peoples and societies is distinctive of the self-conciousness of moderns. As a denotation of a given society's or people's specific way of life, the term *culture* crystallized in late-eighteenth- and early-nineteenth-century Europe,[2] undoubtedly under the impact of the discovery of the Americas, the Asian continent, and other civilizations beyond Europe.[3]

Already by the seventeenth century, travelogues and reports by missionaries had inspired Gottfried Wilhelm von Leibniz to celebrate the neo-Confucian wisdom of China[4] and Voltaire to pen the first universal history of man's diverse customs and intellectual life.[5] The irreverent philosophe in particular scandalized Christian Europe by seeking intellectual and moral virtue well beyond the acknowledged Hebrew and Greek origins of occidental civilization.

In the writings of Johann Gottfried Herder, where the term in its modern usage first attains prominence, *culture* is pointedly not confined to European Christianity.[6] In an imaginary exchange (written in 1802) between a Hindu sage and a European, Herder included the following query:

> "Tell me, have you still not lost the habit of trying to convert to your faith people whose property you steal, whom you rob, enslave, murder, deprive of their land and their state, to whom your customs seem revolting? Supposing that one of them came to your country, and with an insolent air pronounced absurd all that is most sacred to you—your laws, your religion, your wisdom, your instruction, and so on, what would you do to such a man?" "Oh, but that is quite a different matter," replied the European, "we have power, we have ships, money, cannon, *culture* [italics added]."[7]

With occasional irony and relentless scholarship, Herder presented a vast panorama of cultures, each with its "singular and wonderful"[8] spirit. The spirit of each people, its *Volksgeist,* Herder insisted, is thus incommensurable and intelligible only in its own terms.

Herder was, however, also aware that already in his day the term *culture* had taken on many hues and become notoriously vague, as witnessed by a confounding of anthropological with elitist usages of the term.[9] Clearly the multivalence and ambiguity of the term were indicative of the perplexity entailed in the realization of the diversity of human cultures. Few of Herder's contemporaries were prepared to draw the relativistic conclusions that he had, and, accordingly, they tended to speak of "high" culture or to reserve *culture* as a badge of prestige to be associated with the intellectual and aesthetic attainments of Europe.[10] Hence, Herder's cultural relativism, or rather pluralism, was at odds with the Enlightenment's tendency to view the cultures of the world as part of an integral historical process leading inexorably and "progressively" toward a universal "high" culture and "elevated" humanity.

This defense of the ultimate supremacy of European culture was, of course, most forcefully enunciated in the early nineteenth century by Georg Wilhelm Friedrich Hegel in his notion of world history (*Weltgeschichte*), whose essential movement is crowned by the "unfolding" of the European, and specifically the German, "spirit." European high culture, he taught, is heir to the preceding cultures of the world; Europe has absorbed and dialectically elevated the "antecedent" and hence lower expressions of culture. Refracted through the mind of the enlightened European, the cultures of the world are "sublated" *(aufgehoben)* and freed of the dross of their specificity and "primitive" trappings. The European is thus an embodiment of the finest elements of the cultures of the world. In a similar vein, Goethe coined the concept of world literature *(Weltliteratur)*, by which he sought to establish not only the curriculum of the cultivated European but also his task: By laying claim to the "literary treasures" of all the "historically accessible periods and [cultural] zones," the European would fulfill his destiny as a "world citizen."[11]

This dialectical and ambiguous linkage in the imagination of the West of the anthropological, with its pluralistic presuppositions, and the elitist conception of culture[12] would confound the Jews in their efforts to find a place for themselves and their ancestral culture in the modern world. Indeed, the Jews first sought entrance into modern European life and letters precisely at the time when this dual conception of culture was beginning to crystallize. In fact, the terms of their political emancipation were often perceived as requiring their acquisition of "high" culture. Thus, it is not fortuitous that the first Jewish periodical published in German, *Sulamith*, founded in 1806, bore a subtitle that also served as a gentle admonition: *Eine Zeitschrift zur Beförderung der Kultur und Humanität unter der jüdischen Nation* (A Journal for the Promotion of Culture and Humanity Among the Jewish Nation). By *culture*, of course, the journal unambiguously had in mind high culture, which it sought to encourage Jews to attain as an integral part of the struggle for emancipation, or as one of its founding editors, David Frankel, put it, "the people of Abraham, fighting against obstacles of all kinds, . . . working their way upwards to humanity."[13] In conjunction with *Bildung*, education—the cultivation of reason and aesthetic sensibility—"culture" would make it possible for the Jews to "embrace Europe."

Reflecting a similar conception of culture and its role in furthering Jewish emancipation, an eager group of Jewish students at the University of Berlin established in 1819 a society to sponsor the scholarly study of Judaism and the Jews, and appropriately called it the *Verein für Cultur* [sic] *und Wissenschaft der Juden* (Society for the Culture and Science of the Jews). The society also formulated a conception of "Jewish culture," which would be the subject of Jewish scholarship. Jewish culture was comprehensively defined by Immanuel Wolf, one of the Society's founders, as "the essence of all the circumstances, characteristics, and achievements of the Jews in relation to religion, philosophy, history, law, literature in general, civil life, and all the affairs of man.''[14] The Society called upon the educated European—Jew and non-Jew alike—to appreciate the rich and nuanced reality of Jewish culture. Furthermore, the educated European was encouraged to recognize Judaism as an essential part of his own heritage, not just as a remote background to nascent Christianity. Jewish culture, it was held, continued to flourish beyond the period of its biblical glory and contributed in a multifarious and decisive fashion to the shaping of Europe's most refined intellectual and spiritual sensibilities. The Jews—so was the implied but clarion message—thus participate in modern European culture and lay claim to the attendant political rights not as interlopers but by entitlement. Jewish culture is not to be viewed as setting the Jews apart from Europe, and its affirmation need not separate the Jews from humanity. Indeed, Jewish cultural consciousness was to be an intrinsic part of one's elevated humanity and identity as a European.

In his inaugural address, Eduard Gans, the founding president of the Society, who was also a famed disciple of Hegel, articulated this vision in anticipatedly dialectical terms:

> Today's Europe, in our view, is not the work or the outcome of chance which could have been different, . . . but the inevitable result of the effort made, through many millennia, by the Spirit of Reason which manifests itself in world history. The meaning of this process, abstractly speaking, lies within the plurality whose unity can only be found in the whole. . . . As we behold the particular structure of today's Europe, we shall discern it mainly in the blossoming wealth of its manylimbed organism. . . . Let us now consider the Jews and the Jewish life. If one defines Europe as the plurality whose unity can only be found in the whole, one may now define the Jews as follows: they are the unity which has not yet become a plurality. . . . Kept apart, and keeping themselves apart, the Jews lived their own history side by side with world history, held together by the artful convergence of their domestic, political, and religious life on the one hand and by the disunion of the other classes of society on the other. . . . In recent times, however, Jewish particularity has become problematic. . . . [For] the demand of present-day Europe is: the Jews must completely incorporate themselves into [the social and cultural fabric of Europe]. . . . This demand, the logical consequence of the principle of Europe, must be put to the Jews. Europe would be untrue to itself and to its essential nature if it did not put forth this demand.[15]

But Gans clearly had difficulty in explaining how Jewish culture was to be maintained in the context of European high culture. How was it to be expressed, and what would be its abiding manifestations? It would seem that for Gans Jewish cultural consciousness would be confined to a literary and contemplative appreciation of Israel's past contributions to world history and to the unfolding of a universal culture. With the manifest emer-

gence and crystallization of this culture, Jewish culture would shed its specific identity and merge with Europe. But, being the incorrigible Hegelian
that he was, Gans insisted that "to merge does not mean to perish." For it
is "the consoling lesson of history properly understood that everything
passes without perishing; it persists, although it may have long since been
consigned to the past." This is why, Gans concluded, "neither the Jews will
perish nor Judaism dissolve; in the larger movement of the whole they will
seem to have disappeared, and yet they will live on as the river lives on in
the ocean." Gans regarded this expression of Jewish cultural affirmation as
a genuine alternative both to Jewish self-denial and to any attempt to detach
Judaism from Europe and humanity. The advocates of these polar positions,
he contended, indicate that "they have neither understood the age nor the
question at hand."[16]

To be sure, Gans' dialectical gyrations obfuscate more than they illuminate, for he hardly explains how Judaism bereft of an independent reality
could continue to be culturally relevant. Yet his understanding of the challenge posed by modern European or Western culture is perspicacious. For
it would, indeed, be a serious misreading of the modern world, certainly as
experienced by the vast majority of Jews, not to acknowledge the nature of
its high culture—of what we might define here as its syncretistic pluralism.[17]
To deny this would be myopic. For better or worse, modern Jews—as moderns, in general—participate in a culture made of an eclectic skein. Ever
open to the rush and influence of diverse cultural experiences—ideas, values, worldviews—that flow into his life from untold tributaries, the Jew as
a modern is perforce culturally syncretistic. Gans was thus right that it
would be fatuous to deny this situation, even if one did not recognize it as
a blessing. A syncretistic pluralism is the regnant and irrefragable cultural
reality of the modern world.

The sociologist Peter Berger has appropriately characterized the "modern
situation" as one that bids us to cultural "heresy"—to radical choices, as
the Greek origin of the term *heresy* suggests.[18] In contrast to the prescriptive
norms of traditional society, the modern world confronts us with an unprecedented abundance of choices: We are exposed to an array of beliefs,
values, and worldviews from which we may and do choose. Our libraries—
our choice of reading—open before us a veritable panoply of cognitive possibilities. In the same afternoon we may traverse any number of cultures,
moving from Zen haiku poetry to Shakespeare's sonnets, then pursuing
Wittgenstein's *Philosophical Investigations,* and following up with meditations on rabbinic *midrashim.* If we read—make our voyage into these
various, cognitively distinct realms—with intellectual and spiritual earnest-

ness, we of necessity open ourselves to the epistemological and axiological claims of each. Correspondingly, modern man increasingly lives in multiple communities, each perhaps supporting a distinctive culture; our residential, professional, recreational, ideological, and religious communities need not be coterminous. As Berger puts it, "modernity pluralizes."[19]

The abounding pluralism of the modern world is, then, not just a growing appreciation of cultural diversity; in its essential thrust this pluralism is in the mind of the individual—the boundaries between one culture and another intersecting and often blurring. The modern individual resides in many cultures. In light of this cognitive situation, it may be asked whether Judaism can maintain its commanding hold on the mind of the Jew. This question has, in fact, engaged Jews since the time of Moses Mendelssohn and their first flirtations with modern European culture. The question is more than theoretical, of course. The adoption of European culture entailed often far-reaching acculturation and a concomitant attrition of traditional Jewish culture. Specifically, European culture was obtained through the acquisition of a knowledge of the relevant languages, and not infrequently with an attendant neglect of—and loss of competence in—Hebrew, the principal medium of traditional Jewish culture. The dramatic integration of the Jews into European culture was hence paralleled by an equally dramatic decline of Jewish literacy. The eclipse of Hebrew and Jewish learning also tended to strengthen the secularity seemingly demanded by the modern cultural disposition. Moreover, the fact that Jewish culture was an intricate weave of religious and national values meant, as the late Israeli literary critic Baruch Kurzweil observed, that "any surrender of its religious culture [was tantamount] to surrendering *all* [emphasis in original] its national values."[20] One may dispute Kurzweil's emphatic *all*, but it is indisputable that the loss of Jewish literacy implied a decisive estrangement from the sources of high Jewish culture. Hence, acculturation was characteristically accompanied by secularization and, to varying degrees, a loss of religious faith. Accordingly, for a secular Jew whose primary language—and hence cultural references— is, say, French, a meaningful Jewish cultural identity is no longer self-evident.

Martin Buber recognized this situation when he noted that the modern Jew typically "suffers" a disjunction between his "community of substance"—ethnic origin—and his "objective" community of language, landscape, and mores *(Lebensformen)*.[21] Because language "colors [one's] thinking," and landscape determines one's historical associations, and the "way of life" in which one shares "shapes one's actions," the modern Jew "does not see his substance [i.e., his Jewishness] unfold before him in his environment; it has been banished into a deep loneliness, and is embodied for him in only one aspect: his origin."[22]

Deracinated and severed from the sources of traditional Jewish culture, many of these Jews Buber describes have nonetheless maintained in varying degrees a sense of attachment to the Jewish people and its heritage, and what with uniquely modern inflections is called Jewish identity. Clearly, these Jews of modernity could not endorse Saadiah Gaon's famous dictum that "the Jews are a people solely by virtue of its Torah."[23] But surely to be considered a culture, as Buber underscored, Judaism would have to be more than a mere sediment of memory and sentiment. Indeed, to be more than a matter of ethnic pride and solidarity, Judaism would have to be what Clifford Geertz calls a "cultural system"—a body of shared "conceptions embodied in symbolic forms" and "structures of meaning" by means of which "men communicate, perpetuate, and develop their knowledge about and attitudes toward life."[24] Bereft of such "semiotic significance," culture will surely cease to be intellectually and existentially compelling. Culture, as Umberto Eco pithily puts it, must have "a semiotic profile."[25] The question is thus whether Judaism can serve the modern Jew as a "vehicle of signs" guiding his reflexes of imagination and intellect, and facilitating a meaningful organization of his passions and the ongoing experiences of life, or at least significant aspects of life.

To be sure, Judaism as a culture can be delimited to the organization of the communal life of Jews—to maintain certain patterns of kinship, communal celebrations and commemoration, birth, marriage, and mourning. In the context of national autonomy, such as that enjoyed by the State of Israel, the Jewish cultural heritage can be distilled as a broadly conceived "civil religion."[26] Indeed, the cultivation of Judaism as "a kind of national or ethnic folklore," as R. J. Zwi Werblowsky has observed, has characterized much of modern Judaism, a tendency manifestly prompted by considerations of its value in "safeguarding a sense of historic continuity." Drawing attention to similar efforts in modern German Protestantism, Werblowsky further comments:

> It has been said of nineteenth-century *Kulturprotestantismus* that what it cultivates is not Protestantism but a pious reverence for Protestantism's past. A similar quip could be made, *mutatis mutandis,* with reference to modern Judaism. The name of Aḥad Ha'am is the first to spring to mind when mention is made of modern, secular "culture-Judaism," but that of Mordecai M. Kaplan is no less significant from a sociological point of view. Kaplan's "Reconstructionism" which considers Judaism as a cultural social totality is perhaps not a major formative influence, but it is surely a symptomatic expression of much contemporary Jewish life. In

fact, it could be argued that much of what is called Judaism both in Israel and in the Diaspora is a series of variations on the Kaplanian theme, often coupled with a determined effort to dissimulate this fact.[27]

As an ethnic or national heritage, Jewish culture could conceivably relegate other salient areas of life to the domain of other culture systems. Reflection (ontological and existential), art, and politics, for example, would then be dealt with by cultural systems other than Judaism. This, however, would constitute a serious constriction of the cultural purview of traditional Judaism, which, as Saadiah Gaon implied, was conceived as a comprehensive or at least self-sufficient cultural system.

Certainly, traditional Judaism made serious ontological and existential claims pertaining to the ultimate meaning of existence. Should the modern Jew, even he who maintains a religious commitment and allegiance to the traditional teachings of Judaism, seek to identify with these claims, he could not do so by excluding the claims of other culture systems without, as we have noted, forfeiting the challenge and, indeed, prerogatives of modern high culture. To be sure, boundaries may be self-imposed; certain values, moral judgments, symbolic, and aesthetic criteria may be anathematized as non-Jewish. It would seem, however, that ultimately such boundaries of Jewish cultural "legitimacy"—be they based on an appeal to the integrity of Jewish identity, ethnic pride, or national interests—cannot but be intellectually arbitrary and dogmatic.

However, aside from extreme forms of Jewish nationalism and orthodoxy, this type of cultural autism has not guided the various strategies devised to secure Judaism as a culture under the conditions of modernity. Often boldly imaginative, these strategies range from the Neo-Orthodox affirmations of Samson Raphael Hirsch—who promoted traditional Jewry's acceptance of modern humanistic culture by appealing to the Mishnaic maxim *torah im derekh erez* ("Torah with the way of the world"; M. Avot 2:2)—to Abraham Geiger's endeavor to "re-form" Judaism as a largely confessional religion that would make few claims on the Jew's cultural affiliations; and from Chaim Zhitlowsky's conception of Yiddish as the focus of an autonomous Jewish workers' culture in the Diaspora to Eliezer ben Yehudah's vision of the "rebirth" of Hebrew as the basis of a comprehensive secular Jewish culture to arise in the land of Israel. A review of the full medley of alternative strategies would resonate much of what is most passionate, intense, and creative in modern Jewish thought. In consonance with the resplendent diversity of ideological and religious opinion characteristic of this thought, the positions regarding Jewish culture, to say the least, diverge enormously. What the advocates of these positions share, however, is a conviction perhaps best captured by Martin Buber. Noting that the modern Jew perforce dwells in several cultures, Buber voiced the view that it would be chimerical if not simply asinine to try and "expel, relinquish or overcome the one or the other; it would be senseless . . . to try to shed the culture of the world about us, a culture that, in the final analysis, has been assimilated by [our] innermost forces . . . and has become an integral part of ourselves. We need to be conscious of the fact that we are a cultural admixture, in a more poignant sense than any other people." And Buber quickly adds: "We do not, however, want to be the slaves of this admixture, but its masters."[28]

Indeed, it is the primordial destiny of the Jewish people, according to Rosenzweig, to embody—and master—an ensemble of cultures. Abraham, the father of the Hebrew nation, Rosenzweig pointed out, was born in Mesopotamia—or as the Hebrew Bible has it, *Naharaim*—"a land of two rivers" (Gen. 24:10): the Euphrates and the Tigris. Remaining true to their origins in *Naharaim*—which Rosenzweig rendered in his and Buber's German translation of the Hebrew scriptures as *Zweistromland*—the Jews are sustained by a confluence of sources, an ever-replenishing inflow of diverse cultural "streams." Thus, Rosenzweig titled a volume of his writings on both general and Jewish themes—which he deliberately did not separate— *Zweistromland*.[29] The Jew resides on the banks of two cultures, that of the world and that of Judaism. For Rosenzweig, however, Judaism is ultimately metacultural.

Although Judaism is a culture—or rather has a culture—it is eminently more than a culture. Indeed, Rosenzweig found it theologically insidious to equate Judaism with its culture alone (or with any culture, for that matter), even if that culture were to be celebrated as a "religious" culture. For, he exclaimed, "God created the world, not religion."[30] After all, culture— including religion as a specific form of culture—is a fact of man; in contrast to religion, religious faith provides one a transcendent perspective whence one is to recognize the mundane limitations of all human endeavors, even the most sublime. In the reality of his experience of faith the pious Jew, Rosenzweig taught, stands upon the threshold of the eternal—the true source of human existence—and therein knows that all culture, no matter how refined and noble, is but part of a finite, therefore contingent, "unredeemed" realm.

"Faith," as Joseph B. Soloveitchik reflects, "is experienced not . . . as something which has been brought into existence by man's creative cultural gesture, but rather something which was given to man when the latter was overpowered by God." Indeed, he continues, "faith is born of the intrusion of eternity upon temporality. . . . [And] its prime goal is redemption from the inadequacies of finitude and, mainly, from the flux of temporality." The man of faith, however, is not to look askance at the man of culture, and sequester himself in the bosom of the eternal. There must be, Soloveitchik implores, a continuous dialogue between the man of faith and the man of culture. "The man of faith must bring to the attention of the man of culture the *kerygma* of original faith in all its singularity and pristine purity in spite of the incompatibility of this message with the fundamental credo" of the man of culture, especially of modern secular society. "How staggering this incompatibility is! This unique message speaks of defeat instead of success, of accepting a higher will instead of commanding, of giving instead of conquering, of retreating instead of advancing." Through this dialogue the man of culture—who ideally is also to be a man of faith—realizes that all cultural endeavors, notwithstanding their potentially "majestic," blessed quality, are bound to a finite, evanescent reality.[31]

The faith experience may thus be said to desacralize culture. It engenders, as the Protestant scholar Herbert N. Schneidau has remarked in a nuanced study of the Hebrew Scriptures, an "ambivalence with culture and its works."[32] What the Bible, particularly as refracted through the voice of the prophets, "offers culture is neither an ecclesiastical structure nor a moral code, but an unceasing critique of itself," a critique that emerged from a "painfully intense experience of alienation: as the prophet's sense of Yahweh weighs him down, he sees man as dust, man's strivings as futility."[33]

Yet it is this very "mistrust of culture" that, as Schneidau notes, paradoxically makes for a culture that is truly dynamic—critical of itself, and thus forever "restless and unfulfilled."[34] It is this "sacred discontent" that quickens the self-transcendence that is the fulcrum of all genuine creativity and inspired human endeavor.

REFERENCES

1. Franz Rosenzweig, unpublished diary, 29 February 1929, Archives of the Leo Baeck Institute, New York.
2. A. L. Kroeber and Clyde Kluckhohn, *Culture: A Critical Review of Concepts and Definitions* (1952).
3. As a critical opposition, the terms *East* and *West* are also distinctive to the modern period. Cf. Johan Huizinga, "Osten und Westen als Kulturgeschichtlicher Gegensatz," in J. Huizinga, *Wenn die Waffen Schweigen,* tr. from the Dutch by W. Hirsch (1945), 34–60.
4. Cf. David E. Mungello, *Leibniz and Confucianism: The Search for Accord* (1977).

5. Voltaire, *Essai sur les moeurs et l'espirit des nations* (1769). The term *culture* itself, however, was not available to Voltaire. Cf. Huizinga, "Die Sprachbegriff Kultur," op.cit., 20.

6. Cf. "Is there a people upon earth totally uncultivated? and how contracted must the scheme of Providence be, if every individual of the human species were to be formed to what we call cultivation [*Kultur*], for which refined weakness would often be a more appropriate term? Nothing can be more vague, than the term itself; nothing more apt to lead astray, than the application of it to whole nations and ages. . . . " J. G. Herder, *Outline of a Philosophy of the History of Man [Ideen zur Philosophie der Geschichte der Menschheit]*, T. Churchill, tr. (1800, reprinted 1966), v.

7. Cited in Isaiah Berlin, *Vico and Herder* (1976), 161. Herder insisted that there is no *"Favoritvolk"* (favored people): "There must be no order of rank; . . . the negro [*sic*] is as much entitled to think the white a degenerate, as the white man is to think of the negro as a black beast" (ibid., 163, n. 3).

8. Ibid., 214.

9. See Norbert Elias, *The Civilizing Process: The History of Manners*, Edmund Jephcott, tr. (1978), 3–10.

10. This is true of all Western European languages. Cf. Huizinga, "Die Sprachbegriff Kultur," op. cit., 23ff.

11. Friedrich Gundolf, *Goethe* (1930), 681.

12. This tension is not unique to German thought. For a discussion of the concept of culture in English literature, see Raymond Williams, *Culture and Society: 1780–1950* (1960).

13. Cited in George L. Mosse, *German Jews Beyond Judaism* (1985), 3.

14. Cited in Hans G. Reissner, *Eduard Gans: Ein Leben im Vormaerz* (1965), 64ff.

15. Eduard Gans, "A Society to Further Jewish Integration," in P. Mendes-Flohr and J. Reinharz, eds., *The Jew in the Modern World* (1980), 190ff.

16. Ibid., 193.

17. Cf. Kurt Rudolph, "Synkretismus: Vom theologischen Scheltwort zum religionswissenschaftlichen Begriff," in *Humanitas Religiosa: Festschrift für Haralds Biezais* (1979).

18. Peter Berger, *The Heretical Imperative* (1979), 1–31.

19. Ibid., 17.

20. Baruch Kurzweil, *Sifrutenu he-Ḥadashah: Hemshekh o Mahapakhah?* (1971), 31.

21. Martin Buber, "Judaism and Jews" (1909), in Buber, *On Judaism*, N. N. Glatzer, ed. (1967), 16ff.

22. Ibid., 17.

23. Saadiah Gaon, *Emunot ve-Deot*, Yosef Kapach, tr. (1970), third treatise, ch. 7, 132. The translator notes that the last term in Saadiah Gaon's original Arabic may be rendered as either *torot* (meaning the written and oral Torah) or *mizvot* (the commandments).

24. Clifford Geertz, *The Interpretation of Cultures* (1973), 89.

25. Umberto Eco, *A Theory of Semiotics* (1976), 28.

26. Cf. Charles S. Liebman and Eliezar Don-Yihiya, *Civil Religion in Israel* (1983).

27. R. J. Zwi Werblowsky, *Beyond Tradition and Modernity* (1976), 50.

28. Buber, "Judaism and Jews," op. cit., 19.

29. Rosenzweig, *Zweistromland: Kleinere Schriften zu Religion und Philosophie* (1926). Cf. editors' foreword to the second edition of this volume, in *Franz Rosenzweig: Der Mensch und sein Werk. Gesammelte Schriften*, Reinhold and Annemarie Mayer, eds., 3 (1984), xi–xxii.
30. Rosenzweig, *Briefe*, Edith Rosenzweig, ed. (1935), 430.
31. Joseph B. Soloveitchik, "The Lonely Man of Faith," in *Tradition*, 7 (Spring 1965), 62–65.
32. Herbert N. Schneidau, *Sacred Discontent: The Bible and Western Tradition* (1976), 115.
33. Ibid., 16ff.
34. Ibid., 39.

BIBLIOGRAPHY

Shmuel Hugo Bergman, *"Tarbut ve-Emunah,"* in Bergman, *Anashim ve-Derakhim* (1967).
Arthur A. Cohen, *The Natural and Supernatural Jew* (1962).
Christopher Dawson, *Religion and Culture* (1949).
Nathan Rotenstreich, *Tradition and Reality* (1972).

Death

מות

Henry Abramovitch

J ewish attitudes toward death are paradoxical. On the one hand, there is a profound acceptance of the fact of mortality: death as part of a natural process marks the inevitable end to life in this world and is a fate common to all God's creatures. On the other hand, death is seen as punishment for sin, as expressed in the rabbinic phrase, "there is no death without sin." This theologizing of death is poignantly expressed in a beautiful midrash cited in the *Zohar,* which states that Adam, the First Man, appears before each dying man. When the dying person sees this vision, he cries out, "It is because of you that I must die!" The First Man answers this angry accusation by saying, "It is true that I once sinned, a sin for which I was severely punished. But you, my son, how many sins have you committed?" A list of the dying man's misdeeds is revealed, ending with the phrase, "there is no death without sin."[1]

The dialectic between the recognition of death as a biological reality and a theological conception of death is expressed in the rabbinic notion of a distinctive fate for the body as contrasted with that of the soul. The body, after death, returns to the dust, fulfilling the observation of Genesis 3:19, "for dust you are, and to dust you shall return"; whereas the soul, often identified as the divine spark, finds its way back to the divine creator, as in the saying, which forms part of the funeral service, "The Lord has given and the Lord has taken away, blessed be the Name of the Lord" (Job 1:21). Both body and soul return to their original source.

The return of the soul to the divine carried with it an implicit assumption of some ultimate judgment. Mainstream Judaism, however, avoided dwelling on or elaborating explicit notions of the afterlife, although such notions do exist in the various Jewish folk religions. Rabbinical authorities preferred to use theologically neutral terms such as *olam haba* (the World to Come) or *olam emet* (the World of Truth); but even these terms clearly suggested that activity in this world was only a preparation for life in the World to Come. Belief in an afterlife or in an ultimate resurrection is not explicitly mentioned in Hebrew Scripture, but these notions became normative in rabbinic Judaism and were ultimately enshrined in Maimonides' Thirteen Articles of Faith. Orthodox Judaism still clings staunchly to such notions, but other strands of modern Jewish thought are uncomfortable with the notion of an afterlife.

The Jewish orientation toward death and its meaning was not elaborated either in formal doctrine or in theological treatises, but rather was developed in detailed discussions of the specific ritual and halakhic context of mourning. This "ritualized theology in action" provided not only an implicit strategy for dealing with death but also an understanding of it based on a subtle dialectic of "realism, halakhah, community and God."[2] Following the spirit of the rabbinic tradition, we will focus on Jewish ritual practice as the pragmatic and philosophical key to the Jewish conception of death.

Jewish religious teaching tends not to stress death and the role of the dead, in consonance with Moses' admonition, toward the end of his life, "I have put before you life and death, blessing and curse. Choose life" (Deut. 30:19). Such an affirmation of life militated against martyrdom, except in the most extreme cases, and provided an ideological rejection of both suicide and cultic veneration of the dead. One of the reasons given for the anonymous burial of Moses, who is the "patron saint" of the Jewish Burial Society, known as the Ḥevra Kadisha (literally, holy fellowship), was to prevent the development of a cult of the personality, which his shrine might engender.

Jewish burial practice, since the fourth century C.E. rabbinic reforms, places great emphasis on speed, simplicity, and an explicit confrontation with the facts of finitude. Ideally, a person should be buried, garbed in white, before nightfall, certainly within the compass of a day's twenty-four hours. The funeral service, aside from local custom, is remarkably uniform for men and women, rich and poor, scholar and unlettered, so that no material expression of social standing is permitted. A dying man is urged to confess: "Many have confessed and not died; many have died and not confessed."[3] Nothing active may be done that might, even inadvertently, hasten death. Once death has occurred, the honor due to the dead requires that the deceased be handled with care, watched over and treated always with respect. In this regard, the body is compared to an invalid Torah scroll, which, although no longer fit for ritual use, must be accorded due respect and ultimately buried. Likewise, the dead, who are called "poor" because of their lost ability to perform religious commandments, remain holy vessels. During the vigil, it is forbidden to perform any religious commandments in the immediate vicinity of the deceased, lest the doer be accused of "mocking the poor."

Everything undertaken prior to the funeral is done to honor the deceased (and in traditional rabbinic Judaism, this includes forbidding an autopsy), while almost everything performed after burial is done for the sake of the mourners. In the disorienting period between death and burial, the immediate relatives are in a deeply liminal state of mourning, known as *aninut,* during which they are formally excused from all positive commandments except for the obligation to arrange for the funeral. In practice, however, this obligation is taken over by the fraternal society of Hevra Kadisha, which takes responsibility for the cleansing, ritual purification, and final preparation of the body.

The funeral begins with a ritual rending of garments on the part of the mourners, the breaking of a shard on the lintel of the deceased's abode, and the recitation of the saying of Akavyah Ben Mahalalel, a first-century C.E. sage:

> Look upon three things and you shall not come unto sin: From where have you come? To where are you going? And before Whom are you destined to give judgment and reckoning?
>
> (M. Avot 3:1).

After further prayers, the chief male mourner recites the *Kaddish* (literally, holy) prayer, in what is clearly the dramatic high point of the ritual. Since this prayer, a declaration of faith and sanctification of God's name, is traditionally recited in Aramaic, few mourners understand the text they are obliged to recite. Nonetheless, the *Kaddish* does serve as a marker of an initial public acceptance of the death while reaffirming faith in divine justice.

Forgiveness is then petitioned for the soul of the deceased by the leader of the *Hevra Kadisha,* who then releases the deceased from all obligation or any associations to which he or she may have belonged. The burial of the corpse thus corresponds with the demise of the "social person," although it is customary for parents to leave not only provisions for their estate but also ethical wills. At the graveside, prayers for divine mercy are repeated along with the *Kaddish.* Those in attendance are encouraged to give charity both for the sake of the soul of the deceased and to save themselves from an untimely death, since "charity saves from death." The leader of the *Hevra Kadisha* goes on to urge the soul to find eternal rest in paradise and to be bound up in the everlasting "bond of life" *(tzror ha-hayyim).* In this manner, the funeral ritual completes a cycle of an eternal return to the Garden of Eden, which began personally with the birth of the individual and mythically with the expulsion from paradise.

At the end of the graveside service, the mourners pass through two lines of male nonmourners who comfort them with the ritual phrase, "May you be comforted within the community of mourners of Zion and Jerusalem." The mourners then continue home where they begin the *shivah,* the seven-day mourning period. Judaism provides further obligatory periods, in the case of the death of parents, during which the bereaved may gradually adjust to their loss under the nurturing eyes of the community.

The collective image of a "bad death" is that of a corpse left unburied. An unburied corpse is the archetypal source of ritual uncleanness *(tumah),* and passes on its taint not only through direct contact but even to those who only come within the shadow of its enclosure. The honor due to the dead requires that the corpse undergo ritual purification so that the soul may be in an internal state of purity to meet its divine maker. Only those slain by bloodshed do not undergo purification. Even after the corpse is pronounced pure *(tahor),* any who come into contact with it will still be polluted.

Only through contact with the earth is it possible to overcome the irradiating pollution of the corpse. The necessity for the body to decompose in a natural way led to burial as the exclusive means of disposal of bodily remains and to the strong preference for burial in the land of Israel. Many communities symbolize this desire and their attachment to the land of Israel by placing a handful of holy earth taken from Jerusalem's Mount of Olives in the grave with the deceased at the time of burial.

The event of death is often attributed to an "angel of death," but a "good death" is compared to a kiss by the divine spirit or, more simply, to the ease with which a hair may be plucked from a bowl of milk.

Jewish attitudes concerning death may be summed up in the phrase "repent one day before your death" (M. Avot 2:9). Since man does not know the time of his death, he ought to treat each day as if it were to be his last. This awareness of the imminence and inevitability of death, far from demoralizing Jews, brings them all the more into life and its divinely conceived moral dimension.

REFERENCES

1. *The Zohar,* H. Sperling and M. Simon, trs. (1949), 576.
2. Jack Riemer, ed., *Jewish Reflections on Death* (1974), 13.
3. Naḥmanides, in Y. M. Tukachinsky, *Gesher ha-Ḥayyim* (1960), 34.

BIBLIOGRAPHY

Leopold Greenwald, *Kol Bo al Avelut* (1973).
Maurice Lamm, *The Jewish Way in Death and Mourning* (1969).
Jack Riemer, ed., *Jewish Reflections on Death* (1974).
Nosson Scherman, *The Kaddish Prayer: A New Translation with a Commentary Anthologized from Talmudic, Midrashic and Rabbinic Sources* (1980).
Y. M. Tukachinsky, *Gesher ha-Ḥayyim,* 3 vols. (1960).

Destiny and Fate

יעוד וגורל

Albert H. Friedlander

D estiny and fate are best understood as existential self-expressions of a particular religious tradition and a particular people. In Judaism, they are the internal structure of a people bound by revelation and by its own capacities and needs to become "a kingdom of priests and a holy nation" (Ex. 19:6). Such an internal structure leads Israel to the obligation of concrete action to which no limits are set beforehand, but which manifests both limitations and divine grace in the action itself.

Martin Buber has proposed that "man has been appointed to this world as an originator of events, as a real partner in the real dialogue with God."[1] It is human destiny that is the issue here, the insistence upon a religious life that is totally concrete and irreducible. This is how Judaism understands creation: it is God's plan in which the human being enters upon a path of freedom. In that kingdom of freedom, destiny is realized. A Ḥasidic master once gave a paradoxical interpretation of the first word in Genesis: "'In the beginning'—that means: for the sake of the beginning did God create heaven and earth. For the sake of man beginning, that there might be one who would and should begin the direction towards God.'"[2]

The created world imposes its laws upon humanity, a set fate that must be accepted. Awareness of uncaring nature and its forces often led the rabbis to deterministic statements: "Ben Azzai taught: by your destined names will men call you and in your appointed place will they place you and give you what is intended for you. No man can take what is prepared for his fellow man and no kingdom can touch its neighbor even by a hair's breadth" (BT Yoma 38b–39a). Against this, Akiva taught: "Everything is foreseen, but freedom of choice is given" (M. Avot 3:15); and we find: "Everything is in the hand of heaven, except the fear of heaven" (BT Ber. 33b; BT Meg. 25a; BT Nid. 16b). There is consequently a dialectical interrelation between destiny and fate: on the one hand, there is a free movement toward God engendered within the individual, a destiny of dialogue in which a single person or a people reaches toward partnership with God in the kingdom of freedom; on the other hand, the world of nature, with its immutable laws, restricts this forward movement within the person or the people achieving their destiny. Fate intervenes, but cannot destroy those who live in freedom—a single moment can bring eternal freedom.

It is Israel's destiny to move toward God as a people, struggling against the imposition of a pattern beyond its control. One must accept the fate imposed by nature, containing all of the particularities of a human being tied to his physical surroundings, of a flawed Jacob-people limping along darkened mountain paths. But Jacob is also Israel. Freedom of action, a share in the divine task of creation, brings the Jews toward a destiny in which isolation and despair are way stations where vision and integrity rise above the flawed fate that has been given. Israel moves toward others, and such encounters shatter its isolation. It is part of human fate that individuals become part of a collective, attached to a community that may remove major choices from their volition. This process can be a numbing, soul-destroying experience—a robotlike fate imposed by a society in which individual capacities are numbed, destroyed, or turned away from the task of creation. The function of the Jew is to fight against that darkness, to transcend his natural dimensions and to discover the "supernatural Jew"[3] who returns to that destiny where freedom is still possible.

The parameters of destiny are time and space. We take too much upon ourselves when we consider ourselves as ruling these dimensions, when our conceptual use of cosmological time freezes all time into a structure in which we move at will through past and future. Even when we stand in the anthropological time of actual, conscious human will that cannot know the future, that can only explore the past as an aspect of cosmological time— even then we cannot move beyond the space we occupy. The past is past, and the future is dependent upon decisions that have not yet taken place. Buber underscores this truth: "Within the boundaries of the human world which is given in the problems of human being there is no certainty of the future. The time which Hegel introduced into the groundwork of his image of the universe, cosmological time, is not actual human time but a time in terms of thought. It lies in the power of human thought but not of living human imagination to incorporate perfection in the reality of what is; it is something which can be thought, but not lived."[4]

Perfection stands beyond creation; it is the end and it is the beginning. Any people striving to achieve its destiny must move toward that perfection; messianism in Jewish tradition is clearly a necessary concomitant of the world of freedom. It brings a dimension of hope into a world where grace comes from beyond, but dynamic human action is not only commanded but engendered by the very nature of the human condition, which can expect the Messiah at any given moment. Paths diverge. Most religions attempt to calculate the exact moment when perfection will enter the world. Placed into a definition of human fate in which man is helpless— where the separation between the divine and human spheres is absolute and movement comes only from above through divine grace—the human role is reduced to hoping and waiting. Judaism also waits and hopes. But Israel's destiny as a people is seen precisely in the role of moving forward, of accepting human limitations and frailty which cannot bring perfection on its own but can move humanity closer to the kingdom of God. At times, self-definition has taken the Jew outside of history, has seen Israel as waiting with God for the rest of humanity. Seen as the eternal people, its destiny assured, it created a "between," the end of the beginning, the beginning of the end. The eternal people "already lives its own life as if it were all the world and the world were finished. In its Sabbaths it celebrates the sabbatical completion of the world and makes it the completion and starting point of its existence."[5]

Enclaves of Jewish life and tradition exist where this self-definition can still be maintained. Yet too many boundaries have been removed, too many walls have shattered. In the world after Auschwitz, few would define Jewish destiny as the life of a teacher-people with a mission to bring rational understanding of ethical standards to their neighbors until all humanity has been taught to live in a world of reason where perfection can be achieved. Rationalism died in the twentieth century, in the trenches of World War I no less than in the death camps—that *tremendum* beyond all reason and beyond much of faith. Today, self-definition for the Jew begins with the rejection of imposed concepts of Jewish destiny that view Israel as the vicarious atonement, as a lamb of God or a suffering messiah figure. The *tremendum* that overtook the Jew in our time may never be defined as Jewish destiny.

The Jew is in dialogue with all humanity and with God. Responses must be given in a world where there can be a turning away from God and a return to God. Self-definition rests not only with the internal structure, but also in the totality of human existence. Leo Baeck, after he emerged from a concentration camp, saw every people as a question asked by God which had to be answered. And he saw Israel's destiny as existing solely within the freedom that reached beyond all other freedoms, and which heard the world rising out of the Mystery, the commandment—"I am He-Who-Is, thy God, who brought you out of the land of Egypt, out of the house of bondage [Ex. 20:2]."[6]

It is Israel's destiny to be the people of God. In dark times, it is also its fate. In past, present, and future it is also its freedom. Baeck concluded *This People Israel* with that assertion of confidence expressed in Exodus 15:13: "Once they sang unto Him-Who-Is; so will they yet sing unto Him-Who-Is."[7]

REFERENCES

1. Martin Buber, *Mamre* (1946), 7.
2. Ibid., 8.
3. Cf. Arthur A. Cohen, *The Natural and the Supernatural Jew* (1962).
4. Martin Buber, *Between Man and Man* (1955), 141.
5. Franz Rosenzweig, *Star of Redemption* (1964), 420.
6. Leo Baeck, *This People Israel* (1965), 402.
7. Ibid., 403.

BIBLIOGRAPHY

Leo Baeck, *This People Israel* (1965).
Martin Buber, *Between Man and Man* (1955).
Martin Buber, *Mamre* (1946).
Martin Buber, *Pointing the Way* (1957).
Arthur A. Cohen, *The Natural and the Supernatural Jew* (1962).
Arthur A. Cohen, *The Tremendum* (1981).

Dogma

עִיקְרִים

Menachem Kellner

If we understand dogma to mean selected beliefs or teachings
set down by competent authority as the *sine qua non* of Jewish
faith and thereby distinguished from and valued as more
important than other beliefs and teachings of Judaism, it must be concluded
that biblical and talmudic Judaism, with the possible exception of Sanhedrin 10:1, have no dogmas. Indeed, according to this definition it may be
asserted that the first statement of dogmas in mainstream rabbinic Judaism
was that of Moses Maimonides. This is not to say that biblical and rabbinic
literature do not teach specific beliefs; they do, but none of the beliefs cited
is singled out as enjoying special status. To claim that Maimonides was the
first Jew to posit dogmas in Judaism is also not to maintain that no Jewish
thinkers before Maimonides discussed specific beliefs of Judaism. They did,
as, for example, in Saadiah Gaon's *Sefer Emunot ve-Deot (Book of Beliefs and
Opinions)*, Baḥya ibn Paquda's *Ḥovot ha-Levavot (Duties of the Heart)*, and
Judah Halevi's *Kuzari*; however, none of these authors singled out any
beliefs as having a status—salvational, logical, or pedagogical—more fundamental than that accorded to other beliefs.

The absence of dogma in traditional Judaism ought not to be surprising. There is nothing in the nature of monotheistic faith that necessitates its being presented in creedal form. Judaism, as expressed in biblical and rabbinic texts, does not specify some beliefs as dogmas. Rather it emphasizes practice—the fulfillment of the *miẓvot*—over theology—which might include, for example, determining who a Jew is and how one achieves a portion in the World to Come with little explicit reference to beliefs—and it defines the term *faith* less in terms of specific propositions that are to be accepted or rejected (beliefs) than in terms of trust and reliance. In other words, one may say, for example, that biblical and rabbinic Judaism demands belief *in* God rather than belief *that* God exists. In this regard it is instructive to compare Ecclesiastes 12:13 with Romans 10:9.

Both early Islam and Karaite Judaism adopted the tools of Greek philosophy and logic, which defined belief (in Greek, *pistis*) in explicitly propositional terms.[1] Such religious movements could not be ignored by the Judaism of that era, and in their attempt to expound and defend Judaism in this context, medieval Jewish thinkers began to conceive of the nature of belief in propositional terms. It is hardly surprising, therefore, that the first systematic exposition of Jewish beliefs was undertaken by Saadiah Gaon, in light of his exposure to the latest currents of Moslem thought in tenth-century Baghdad and his involvement in the struggle against Karaism. Once the term *belief* was defined in terms of specific propositions to be accepted or rejected, as opposed to an attitude of trust and reliance upon God and acceptance of his Torah, it was only a question of time until an attempt would be made to codify in creedal fashion the most important beliefs of Judaism. That two hundred years were still to elapse between the provocations of Saadiah's day and the enterprise of Maimonides is a tribute to the conservative nature of the Jewish tradition. That Maimonides undertook the project at all is a tribute to his boldness.

In 1168 Maimonides completed his first major work, the commentary on the Mishnah. In the course of this work Maimonides commented on Mishnah Sanhedrin 10:1, which reads as follows:

> All Israelites have a share in the world to come, as it is written, "Thy people also shall be all righteous, they shall inherit the land forever; the branch of my planting, the work of my hands, wherein I glory" (Isa. 60:21). But the following do not have a share in the world to come: he who says that resurrection is not taught in the Torah, he who says that the Torah was not divinely revealed, and the *epikoros* . . .

By way of interpreting this text Maimonides composed a lengthy essay in which, among other things, he defines the various terms occurring in the mishnah under discussion.[2] It was apparently by way of defining the term *Israelites* in this mishnah that Maimonides listed those thirteen beliefs that, in his estimation, every Jew qua Jew had to accept. These beliefs, known as the Thirteen Principles, may be summarized as follows: (1) that God exists; (2) that God is one; (3) that God is incorporeal; (4) that God is ontologically prior to the world; (5) that God alone is a fit object of worship; (6) that prophecy occurs; (7) that the prophecy of Moses is superior to that of all other prophets; (8) that the Torah was revealed from heaven; (9) that the Torah will never be uprooted or altered; (10) that God knows the acts of human beings; (11) that God rewards the righteous and punishes the wicked; (12) that the Messiah will come; and (13) that the dead will be resurrected.

Maimonides concludes his discussion with the following peroration:

> When all these foundations [of the Torah] are perfectly understood and believed in by a person he enters the community of Israel and one is obligated to love and pity him and to act towards him all the ways in which the Creator has commanded that one should act towards his brother, with love and fraternity. Even were he to commit every possible transgression, because of lust and because of being overpowered by the evil inclination, he will be punished according to his rebelliousness, but he has a portion [in the World to Come]; he is one of the sinners of Israel. But if a man doubts any of these foundations, he leaves the community [of Israel], denies the fundamental, and is called sectarian, *epikoros,* and one "who cuts among the plantings." One is required to hate and destroy him. About such a person it was said, "Do I not hate them, O Lord, who hate Thee?" [Ps. 139:21].

Maimonides here defines dogmas as beliefs that are set down by the Torah and are both necessary and sufficient conditions for being a Jew and for earning a portion in the World to Come.[3] Maimonides reiterated this list with little change in Chapter 3 of *Hilkhot Teshuvah* ("Laws of Repentance"), referred to it in later writings, and even reworked portions of it toward the end of his life. Moreover, he unflinchingly accepts the halakhic implications of his position, excluding heretics from the Jewish community (see MT Hil. Avodat Zarah 2:5; Hil. Edut 11:10; Hil. Sheḥitah 4:14, and especially Hil. Rozeaḥ 4:10).

Maimonides' teachings here include the following revolutionary claims: Judaism has dogmas and accepting the dogmas of Judaism without doubt and hesitation is a necessary and sufficient condition for being considered a Jew and for achieving a portion in the World to Come; although one may transgress commandments out of weakness or inadvertence *(ba-shogeg)* without excluding oneself from the community of Israel and the World to

Come, disbelief in any one of the thirteen dogmas for any reason is heresy and costs one his membership in the community of Israel and his portion in the World to Come. Heresy is heresy, whether it is intended as such or not.

In the two hundred years following the death of Maimonides almost no attention was paid to the question of dogma in Judaism. This may be a consequence of the fact that Maimonides' spiritual legacy split after his death. Whereas Maimonides had sought to amalgamate two paths to human felicity—that of rational cognition and that of observance of the *mizvot*—his followers emphasized one or the other of the two paths. Those who were halakhists had no reason to be interested in purely theological questions, while the philosophers were aloof to what they regarded as narrow theological issues and, therefore, neither group took up the question of dogma.

In fifteenth-century Spain, however, we find that although Jewish philosophers as such had all but disappeared, in the face of a renewed theological attack by the Church upon Judaism—expressed in polemics, disputations, and forced attendance at conversionary sermons—and in the wake of the profound problems presented by forced converts (the Marranos), the Jewish communal and halakhic leadership was forced to take up the theological exposition and defense of Judaism and to deal with the principles of Jewish adhesion. Given that the terms of the dispute were more or less dictated by Christianity and given the example of Maimonides, it was only natural that many fifteenth-century Spanish Jewish thinkers once again emphasized the issue of dogma.

The fifteenth century witnessed a plethora of competing systems of dogmatics. Ḥasdai Crescas, Joseph Albo, and Isaac Abrabanel each composed complete books on the subject (the only such works written by Jews until the nineteenth century). In addition, Simeon ben Ẓemaḥ Duran, Abraham Bibago, and Isaac Arama all devoted systematic and extensive attention to the question of dogma in Judaism. The issue is also treated briefly in the writings of Abraham Shalom, Joseph Jabeẓ, Yom Tov Lippman Muelhausen, Elijah del Medigo, and David ben Judah Messer Leon.

A number of interesting points emerge from the study of these writings. First, each of these authors defines dogma differently. Crescas, for example, regards dogmas as those beliefs that cannot consistently be denied if one believes in revelation; Albo defines Judaism in geometric terms and sees the dogmas of Judaism as its axioms; Arama understands the dogmas of Judaism to be those beliefs (coupled, in his view, with associated observances) that distinguish Judaism from other religions on the one hand and from philosophy on the other.

Second, despite the abundance of competing dogmatic systems, we do not find the rise of schismatic sects within fifteenth-century Judaism, as opposed to Christianity, in which creedal differences have been associated with sectarianism. This may be an indication that attention to dogma was understood to be more of an intellectual exercise and response to the specific needs of the time than an actual attempt once and for all time to indite the essential nature of Judaism.

Third, of all the thinkers who devoted serious attention to the question of dogma in Judaism after Maimonides, only two, Bibago and Abrabanel, explicitly allied themselves with Maimonides' claim that inadvertent heresy (ba-shogeg) was actually heresy. All the other authors seem to adopt the traditional rabbinic conception that ignorance of the law and inadvertence are exculpatory factors.

Finally, only one thinker raised the question, does Judaism indeed have dogmas? This was Isaac Abrabanel in his *Rosh Amanah,* in which he answered the question in the negative, insisting that all the beliefs and teachings of Judaism are equivalent. In effect he raised every teaching of Judaism to the level of dogma, requiring absolute doctrinal orthodoxy from every Jew on every issue.

With the passing of the generation of the Expulsion of the Jews from Spain, the issue of dogma disappeared from the agenda of Jewish intellectuals. The intellectual energies once devoted to philosophy and theology were turned to kabbalah, and the halakhic/communal leadership, no longer faced with the conversionary pressure of the Church militant and the pressing problem of defining Jews and Judaism vis-à-vis the Marranos, reverted to its traditional noninvolvement with theological issues.

During the three centuries following the Spanish Expulsion, no works of or about Jewish dogma were composed. The Thirteen Principles of Maimonides gradually assumed semicanonical status, and two of the scores of poems based upon his creed (*Ani Ma'amin* and *Yigdal*) were incorporated into the liturgy of Ashkenazi Jewry.

Classical Reform Judaism defined itself in creedal terms, and in the nineteenth century dozens of attempts were made to summarize that creed.[4] With the passing of what may be called the "orthodox" stage of Reform Judaism, interest in dogma qua dogma diminished.[5]

Today, for all intents and purposes, the question of dogma qua dogma in Judaism is a dead issue. Orthodox, Conservative, and Reconstructionist Judaism all emphasize, each in its own way, practice over dogma, and even Reform Judaism, despite its repeated attempts to define itself in quasi-dogmatic terms, basically appears to operate within the same framework.

REFERENCES

1. See Aristotle, *Topics* 100a30–100b21; Harry A. Wolfson, *The Philosophy of the Church Fathers,* 3d rev. ed. (1970), 113, 115.
2. The essay is most easily available in I. Twersky, ed., *A Maimonides Reader* (1972).
3. Compare Maimonides' commentaries on M. Sanh. 10:2 and 11:3, which confirm this interpretation of the passage quoted in the text.
4. See Jacob Petuchowsky, "Manuals and Catechisms of the Jewish Religion in the Early Period of the Emancipation," in Alexander Altmann, ed., *Studies in Nineteenth Century Jewish Intellectual History* (1964).
5. Compare, for example, the Pittsburgh Platform of 1885 with the Centenary Perspective of 1976. See also Eugene B. Borowitz, *Reform Judaism Today,* 3 vols. (1978).

BIBLIOGRAPHY

Isaac Abrabanel, *Principles of Faith (Rosh Amanah),* translated, with introduction and notes, by Menachem M. Kellner (1982).

Arthur Hyman, "Maimonides's 'Thirteen Principles,'" in Alexander Altmann, ed., *Jewish Medieval & Renaissance Studies* (1967).

Louis Jacobs, *Principles of the Jewish Faith: An Analytic Study* (1964).

Menachem Kellner, "Dogma in Medieval Jewish Thought: A Bibliographical Survey," in *Studies in Bibliography and Booklore,* 15 (1984).

Solomon Schechter, "The Dogmas of Judaism," in *Studies in Judaism,* 1st Series (1986).

Ecumenism

אקומניזם

Geoffrey Wigoder

Whereas the revision of Christian attitudes toward Jews and Judaism dates back only to the end of World War II, the Jews' reconsideration of Christianity has been proceeding for two centuries, sparked by the emancipation, when Jews for the first time could examine Christianity in an atmosphere of free inquiry unimpeded by the artificial external pressures previously exerted. To be sure, Jews continued to respond to an internal pressure to demonstrate to the emancipated Jew the superiority of Judaism, with the consequence that most enlightened Jewish thinkers of the nineteenth century were still largely concerned with polemic, albeit of a refined nature, in their attitudes toward Christianity.

New positions were being taken, however. Echoing Maimonides' statement that Jesus and Mohammed helped to prepare the way for the Messiah (MT Hil. Melakhim 9, 4), Samuel Hirsch stated that Christianity had brought ethics and monotheism to the pagan world,[1] and Solomon Formstecher characterized Christianity and Islam as "the northern and southern missions of Judaism to the pagan world."[2] The main center of this new thinking was to be found in Protestant environments, especially Germany, where Hermann Cohen found a deep affinity between Judaism and Christianity and where later, in the twentieth century, Franz Rosenzweig and Martin Buber sought to construct a new relationship without polemic. Rosenzweig and Buber felt that Judaism should recognize in Christianity a path to God, while demanding a reciprocal recognition from Christianity.

New Christian perceptions emerged only after World War II. The first step came with the realization that the traditional Christian teaching of contempt had created the atmosphere in which a Holocaust was possible. This led to a critical reexamination of doctrines and attitudes toward Jews and Judaism.

Generalizations about "Christian" or "Jewish" views are misleading because of the pluralistic composition of both communities. Within Christendom the centristic structure of the Catholic church has facilitated the development of a comparatively unified position regarding Judaism and the Jews, initially expressed in the *Nostra Aetate* Declaration (Declaration on the Relation of the Church to Non-Christian Religions) issued at the end of the Second Vatican Council in 1965 and elaborated in the interpretative guidelines published in 1975. Abandoning the traditional teaching concerning the continuing responsibility of the entire Jewish people for the death of Jesus, the Catholic church has undertaken the expunging of anti-Jewish sentiments and stereotypes from Catholic prayers, catechetical instruction, and textbooks; the cessation of direct missions to Jews; the condemnation of anti-Semitism; and the growth of more constructive Jewish-Catholic relations throughout the world. The late Israeli historian Uriel Tal has even suggested that the Catholic church's renewed confrontation with mankind's terrestrial condition has opened up common grounds of complementarity with the Jewish concepts of Torah and halakhah.[3]

A third Vatican document, entitled "Notes on the Correct Way to Present the Jews and Judaism in Preaching and Catechesis in the Roman Catholic Church," was issued in 1985. While stressing the Jewishness of Jesus, the Jewish roots of Christianity, and the positive contributions of the Pharisees, it retained many of the church teachings that have proved objectionable to Jews down the ages. Although quoting with approval John Paul II's statement calling Jews "the people of God of the Old Covenant which has never been revoked," the document affirms that Judaism cannot be seen as a way to salvation (which is reached only through Jesus), that the Jews were chosen to prepare the coming of Christ, and that the Hebrew Bible should be interpreted through typology, that is, that its events and personalities are to be seen in the light of the New Testament ("The Exodus, for example, represents an experience of salvation and liberation that is not complete in itself but . . . accomplished in Christ"). Thus, despite the progress made in historical understanding and existential relations, this reassertion of the Catholic church's basic triumphalism pointed up the problematics of theological dialogue.

In a series of statements since the Holocaust, all major Protestant churches have taken stands opposing anti-Semitism and declaring their readiness to be active in combating its manifestations. The existence of residual theological anti-Semitism, however, remains a matter of contention. Strong expression is still given in certain Protestant circles to the belief in the displacement of the Jews and the discontinuity of their role in the divine scheme as a result of their rejection of Jesus' messiahship. A further source of tension is the continuance of missionary activity in many Protestant churches. Although several of the Protestant churches have renounced this activity, those who maintain it insist that "ultimate truth" cannot be excluded, even in a dialogue situation. And where traditional mission has been modified, many Jews continue to suspect a "hidden agenda." At the same time it must be noted that a small but growing body of Christian thinkers are acknowledging the theological validity of the Jewish way to God.[4]

Interfaith exchange with fundamentalist Christian groups has been theologically restricted because fundamentalism entails exclusivity; moreover, the explicit missionary objectives of evangelical Christians have naturally militated against extensive theological dialogue between them and Jews. In addition, dialogical encounter with the Orthodox churches has hitherto been almost entirely nonexistent.

The new Christian attitudes have required an appropriate Jewish response. There is, however, an asymmetry in the relationship and an imbalance of expectations. For the Jews, Christianity does not pose a theological problem, and Jewish participation in the dialogue does not have the same level of theological motivation as among the Christians. For the Christians involved, their very Christianity grows out of Judaism and indeed depends on it; for the Jews there is no relationship of dependency or causality. The Jew is motivated more by historical and pragmatic considerations, based on the conviction that mutual understanding is the key to coexistence.

Among the Jews, too, there is no unanimity regarding the dialogue with Christians and Christianity. Opposition has been centered in Orthodox circles. Eliezer Berkovits has found that dialogue yields no significant results and fails to tackle what he sees as the root question—the meaning of the Jewish experience in the midst of Christendom throughout history and "the truth of Christian historical criminality against the Jewish people."[5] Most influential has been Joseph B. Soloveitchik, who opposes any attempt to engage in interfaith dialogue. His contention that the inner life of faith must not be exposed to interreligious encounters and that the search for common denominators of faith is futile has been endorsed by many, especially in the Orthodox community. However, Soloveitchik approves of dialogue directed to humanitarian and common cultural concerns. He finds no contradiction in coordinating social and cultural activities with members of another faith community while respecting in silence the integrity of their faith. His conditions for such cooperation include the realization that the act of faith of one community is incomprehensible to another; that each retains its independence and must beware of speaking of any "common trend," except in a historico-cultural context; and that it is not up to Jews to suggest to Christians what they should change.[6]

On the other hand, Abraham Joshua Heschel has stressed that common concern for the world has replaced the mutual isolation of the respective faith communities. The supreme issue today is not the more parochial questions of halakhah or church but a commitment to the world as a divine reality. The prerequisite of interfaith dialogue is faith, and the choice in today's world is between such faith and nihilism. Accordingly, Heschel stresses that interdependence between all persons of faith is crucial.[7]

For Jews, interreligious dialogue can pose the problem of entry into alien modalities. This begins with the very language Jews are obliged to use, be it terms that are strange to Judaism, such as *secularism* and *witness,* or terms that are used in a completely different sense by Christians, such as *faith, law,* and even *religion.*

A major issue in the Jewish–Christian encounter is the State of Israel. For the Jews, conveying an understanding of the essentiality of Israel to Jewish self-understanding is a high priority in the dialogue. For Catholics, attitudes can still be governed by theological residues (for example, the belief that Jewish exile was a divine punishment for the rejection of Jesus), while political and pragmatic considerations have played a negative role. While the Vatican's 1985 document recognizes the Jewish religious attachment to the land, it warns against seeing this attachment in any Christian religious perspective (in other words, God's promise of the land to the Jews has lost its validity). Israel is also frequently a barrier in the development of the relationship with mainline Protestant churches. Their umbrella body, the World Council of Churches, has representation of the Russian Orthodox church and the Middle East Arab churches, all hostile to Israel, and is deeply involved with the Third World. The Council's political statements, which tend to reflect Third World viewpoints, including anti-Israeli sentiments, have caused resentment in Jewish circles. Jews were disillusioned by the indifference and lack of understanding on the part of many Christian partners in dialogue when the Jewish state was perceived to be endangered in 1967 and 1973. This led Jews to serious reassessment of the nature and content of interfaith encounter and a renewed determination to affirm unambiguously the meaning of Israel for the Jew. An appreciation of Jewish perceptions and sensibilities is more often evinced among Christians at a grass-roots level than among ecclesiastical hierarchies. Concomitantly, the pragmatic welcome afforded by Jews to the enthusiastic support of the evangelical churches for the State of Israel is mitigated by the knowledge that here the agenda is far from hidden; the continuing existence of the State of Israel is seen as an indispensable prerequisite to the Second Coming of Jesus—at which time the Jews will be brought to a belief in Jesus as the Messiah.

Ideally, interfaith efforts in the Western world should be conceived not as a dialogue but as a trialogue among Jew, Christian, and Moslem, and a number of tentative efforts have been made in this direction. The obvious laboratory for such a development should be Israel, but attempts to develop a meaningful trialogue there have been frustrated by the conflicts and tensions of the region. Even elsewhere, encounters with Moslems have proved problematical, both because of the very nature of Islam and because of the integral role of the State of Israel for the Jewish participants.

Although only a few decades old, Jewish–Christian dialogue has staked out its basic theological paradigms. Most encouraging is the fact that the two sides involved no longer look at each other as objects. Jewish, Catholic, and Protestant thinkers of vision have delineated outlines that require to be filled in and to reach more widespread acceptance, but it is doubtful whether the boundaries can be extended any further without compromising the nature of the respective faith communities. Accordingly, Christian–Jewish rapprochement, from the Jewish side, is founded on the recognition that the ultimate barriers are not to be overcome, coupled with an awareness of the pitfalls of syncretism. There is also the realization that Jews enter dialogue with different premises from the Christians and with a differing agenda. In the words of Henry Siegman, former executive director of the Synagogue Council of America, the Jews are motivated "by history rather than theology."[8] High on the Jews' priorities is the hope for Christian recognition that anti-Semitism is not integral to Christianity but is a discardable accretion—despite the view of the Christian writer Rosemary Ruether that anti-Judaism is too deeply embedded in the foundations of Christianity to be rooted out without destroying the whole structure[9] (cf. the statement of Eliezer Berkovits that the New Testament is the most dangerous anti-Semitic tract in human history).[10] Many scholars, Christian as well as Jewish, now recognize crucial sections of the New Testament to be anti-Jewish polemics, but nonetheless even the most liberal Christians will not dare tamper with the text, although they acknowledge it as promoting, by its very nature, anti-Semitic sentiments. Furthermore, and despite new attitudes, the triumphalism of the church, as already noted, has been but partly muted, while on the other hand the Jewish experience of religious pluralism, together with new-found national independence, has introduced a note of countertriumphalism in certain Jewish sectors. These trends have inevitably vitiated some of the impact of the dialogue. Nonetheless, dialogue has clearly helped in the delineation of theological paradigms and a mapping of the irreconcilable areas.

Dialogue can thus discover but not reconcile fundamental theological differences. Judaism will continue to deny the Christological fulfillment asserted by Christianity. The Christian salvational concept constitutes an insuperable obstacle, even if postponed to an eschatological era. Jews can never accept the assumption, explicit or implicit, that ultimately they can be redeemed only through Jesus Christ; as Arthur A. Cohen has pointed out, Israel must be regarded not as the object of salvation but as its agent.

The continuing differences have put into question the concept, popular in the Western world, of "the Judeo-Christian tradition." For Paul Tillich this was a historical and present reality with Jews and Christians united by the unique series of events recorded in the Hebrew Bible as revelatory.[11] However, the Bible, the ground of Jewish–Christian commonality, divides no less than it unites. The common area, called by Christians the Old Testament—in itself a pejorative term to Jews—is perceived in a contradictory manner by Jews who view it through the perspective of rabbinic teaching and Christians who view it through the prism of the New Testament.

Jews and Christians have indeed come to share a certain culture by virtue of their common background in the Western world. This, however, is relevant only for the Ashkenazi sector of Jewry; the Sephardim, and especially the so-called Oriental Jews, lack this shared culture and at the same time have escaped the historical tensions. Indeed, the focus of continuing anti-Christian attitudes among Jews is within the Ashkenazi world, the result of centuries of defensive conditioning and reaction to anti-Jewish traumas in addition to the continuing feeling of superiority inbred in religious traditions, especially those of a fundamentalist nature.

While we should not expect, or desire, that the theological barriers be eliminated, we can work for mutual understanding. Quasi-theological commitments that are the result of historical considerations, however, can be modified on either side, leading to rapprochement, that is, an approach to each other that stops short of any attempt at fusion or identification. One potentially promising area of interfaith understanding is in social action. Social ethics have always been basic to Judaism, but recently the churches have become more militant on these issues and more aware of the prophetic insistence on man's role in the improvement of society. In the Jewish–Christian context, this new-found fellowship was most graphically symbolized in the picture of the black civil rights leader, Martin Luther King, Jr., and Abraham Joshua Heschel linked arm-in-arm in pursuit of human rights.

In the contemporary world, Christianity has joined Judaism in the role of a minority. Faced with the growth of other faiths in Asia and Africa and of Marxism, atheism, and nonbelief in the Western world, Christianity now is fighting an uphill battle. Compared with each other, the differences between Christianity and Judaism are obvious, but in world perspective, the two are on the same side of the fence. Those committed to dialogue point to the many positive entries in the ledger—and recall that not so long ago there was not even a ledger.

REFERENCES

1. Samuel Hirsch, *Die Religionsphilosophie der Juden* (1842), 832ff.
2. Solomon Formstecher, *Die Religion des Geistes* (1841), 411.
3. Uriel Tal, *Ha-Nusah he-Hadash ba-Siah she-ben Yehudim ve-Nozrim* (1969).
4. Cf. Paul Van Buren, *A Christian Theology of the People Israel* (1983).
5. Eliezer Berkovits, *Faith After the Holocaust* (1973), 37–66.
6. Cf. Joseph B. Soloveitchik, "Confrontation," in *Tradition* 6:2 (Spring–Summer 1964).
7. Abraham Joshua Heschel, "No Religion Is an Island," in *Union Seminary Quarterly Review* 21 (January 1966), 117–24.
8. Unpublished lecture, 1975, at a meeting of the Vatican Commission for Religious Relations with the Jews and the International Jewish Committee for Inter-religious Consultations.
9. Rosemary Ruether, *Faith and Fratricide* (1974), 227ff.
10. Eliezer Berkovits, "Facing the Truth," in *Judaism* 27 (1978), 324.
11. Paul Tillich, "Is There a Judeo-Christian Tradition?" in *Judaism* 1 (1952), 106–109.

BIBLIOGRAPHY

Walter Jacob, *Christianity Through Jewish Eyes* (1974).

Leon Klenicki and Geoffrey Wigoder, eds., *A Dictionary of the Jewish–Christian Dialogue* (1984).

Helga Kroner and Leon Klenicki, eds., *Issues in the Jewish–Christian Dialogue* (1979).

Frank E. Talmage, ed., *Disputation and Dialogue* (1975).

Education

חינוך

Janet Aviad

In his seminal work on the history of Greek culture and education, Werner Jaeger stated that "since the basis of education is a general consciousness of the values which govern human life, its history is affected by changes current within the community. When these are stable, education is firmly based; when they are displaced or destroyed, the educational process is weakened until it becomes inoperative. This occurs whenever tradition is violently overthrown or suffers internal collapse."[1] Jewish education today reflects the internal and external upheavals that have occurred within Jewish society during the past three centuries. Emancipation, secularization, the Holocaust, and the building of new Jewish communities in Israel and in the Diaspora are events and processes that have changed and mirror changes in every aspect of Jewish life. Specifically, Jewish education flounders today, attempting to respond to the challenges of life in a modern open society where formations of Jewish culture and identity are constantly emerging and changing.

Every community seeks to preserve and transmit its fundamental values through education, thereby ensuring its own continuity. Biblical society consciously emphasized the critical role of education. Knowledge of the covenant experience and the ritual and ethical obligations deriving from it, upon which the unity of the Hebrew tribes was based, had to be conveyed from generation to generation. Therefore, fathers were commanded to teach the divine law to their children (Deut. 6:7), and family and communal rituals were the occasion for instruction in sacred history (Ex. 12:26–27; Lev. 23:43).

Following the destruction of the First Temple and the exile to Babylonia in 586 B.C.E., however, educational functions were quickened and deepened in a way peculiar to Jewish society. The conditions of exilic life forced the Jews to organize themselves as a religious community and to depend upon education for their very survival. It was at this time that the disparate oral traditions recording the relationship of God and his people were gathered and canonized. This sanctified Torah became the foundation of Jewish life everywhere, according meaning to the events that befell the chosen people and defining a ritual framework that both ordered the life of the exiles and preserved their distinct identity.

Only through intense loyalty to the ritual framework and to the religious ideas that gave it significance could exilic life be maintained. Instruction in the Torah, therefore, was indispensable, and study, *talmud torah,* necessarily assumed the highest place in the hierarchy of Jewish values. An educational system developed whose purpose was the transmission of those truths, perceived as absolute, that defined the vocation of the individual and the community in exile. Further, the educational system provided the structure of initiation and training in the law incumbent upon members of a minority group determined to maintain boundaries between itself and the surrounding culture. Education in the proscriptions and prescriptions of the Torah culture was the key to whatever social control the Jewish community exercised over its members.

Talmud torah became a distinct and powerful form of religious experience for the Jews. Study was more than a search for knowledge—it was an act of devotion and a form of prayer. The sanctity of God's presence was said to reside among those who studied together (M. Avot 3:3). Indeed, study was a form of *imitatio Dei,* and those who exemplified the ideal of total dedication to study were accorded the highest status in Jewish society. The sage was Judaism's religious virtuoso, the model of intellectual, ethical, and spiritual excellence. Men of the Torah, engaged in study as a way of drawing near to God, represented the central religious experience of Judaism, and constituted an intellectual elite upon whose authority and charisma traditional Jewish society rested.

The study hall itself, the *bet midrash,* was viewed as a sacred space. Prayer and study were interwoven: either the study hall was located contiguous to a synagogue or the same space served both activities. All male adults were obligated to spend some time in study. Universal elementary education was established from the first century C.E. Any settlement where twenty-five children lived was required to provide a teacher and supervision over the education of the children (BT BB 21a). The elementary school was designed to convey the fundamental traditions of Jewish culture through the study of the Pentateuch and its most widely accepted commentary, that of Rashi. This basic knowledge, together with education in ritual life and customs received from the family and synagogue from the earliest age, encapsulated the child in a compact and total culture, regarded as true and absolute. The solidity of the whole was seen as resting upon the education of children from the youngest age.

The situation in which culture, society, and Torah were totally interwoven, creating a nexus of religious certainty and a context of religious-ethnic unity, broke down under the force of Emancipation and Enlightenment in the eighteenth century in western Europe and, later, in eastern Europe. The encounter with the processes of modernization in western Europe may be taken as paradigmatic, in its main contours, for Jewish communities throughout the world. Two polar responses to the processes of secularization emerged: one, a whole-hearted rejection of Western culture and a determination to remain outside Western society; the other, a whole-hearted aspiration to participate in Western culture, to appropriate Western forms, and to assimilate fully within Western society. Between these polar extremes a variety of compromise postures and ideologies emerged, which attempted to integrate Jewish and Western culture and society. All such compromises and accommodations were based upon a positive evaluation of the secularization of aspects of Jewish life and a concomitant resistance to the elimination of Jewish distinctiveness, religious or ethnic. All faced the inherent problem of compromise—the tendency to lose content and force.

In Judaism's struggle to survive in the modern world, in whatever form, education has not only remained a central value and framework but has been a critical arena for the working out of paths of Jewish adjustment and adaptation. Conflicts over the goals and patterns of Jewish education are symptomatic of the social and ideological problems of modern Jewry. Changes in education represent the concrete embodiment of alternative resolutions to these problems.

The reevaluation of values and its impact upon education can be seen most clearly during the period of the Enlightenment in western Europe. Jews embraced rationalism as an intellectual orientation, offering a new framework of meaning in which scientific explanations replaced or challenged religious ones. Judaism ceased to provide an overall cognitive or spiritual order, and sacred institutions, grounded upon the traditional world view, lost their hold. Enlightenment, however, was more than an intellectual orientation for the Jew. It was a social ideal—the promise of a new society, founded upon liberal, humanistic, and rational principles to which Jews would have full access. Entry and acceptance within enlightened society was seen to depend upon acculturation to European ways and upon the rejection of traditional patterns deemed irrational, retrograde, and divisive.

Education was understood by Jewish thinkers of the Enlightenment to be the major vehicle for realizing the changes in Jewish society they projected. Advocates of Enlightenment, therefore, dedicated great efforts to refashioning Jewish education. Treatises were written designing new curricula, and innovative schools were founded.

The enlightened Jew underwent a shift in his own intellectual interests. Learning might still be at the center of his existence, but it was learning in new modes, through new methods, and channeled towards new sources of truth. Religious learning was dislodged. The principle innovation called for by the Jewish Enlightenment mirrored these changes. Humanistic studies and science were viewed as valuable in themselves, as requisite in the process of acculturation, and as not only legitimate but also primary in the educational process. They were to become the mainstay of the curriculum. Further, Jewish education was to be practical, oriented toward meeting the new social and economic aspirations of the Jews within the general society and providing skills appropriate to new roles.

Jewish proponents of Enlightenment offered a variety of alternatives regarding sacred learning, depending upon their own relationship to the Jewish tradition. Religious studies might be displaced altogether, or might remain, supplemental to secular content, and reduced in scope and intensity. The classical Jewish Enlightenment treatise on education, defining the place and role of both religious and secular studies, is *Divrei Shalom ve-Emet* (Words of Peace and Truth) by Naphtali Herz Wessely, which was published in Hebrew in 1782. Wessely, while insisting that knowledge of God and revelation are essential in the education of every Jewish child, proposed that "human knowledge" precede the study of "divine knowledge." By reversing the traditional order, and placing the secular before the religious, his proposal reflects Enlightenment preferences and priorities.

Other educators of the same period, more radical than Wessely, limited the number of hours of religious studies in the curriculum and changed the character of what was taught. Talmud was generally eliminated. Sections of the Bible that expressed universal truths and ethical norms were retained. Moses Mendelssohn's German translation and commentary upon the Pentateuch replaced Rashi's commentary, so that rabbinic values and attitudes transmitted implicitly by Rashi were no longer taught. Paralleling the philanthropists' approach to Christianity in the German public schools, advocates of the Enlightenment proposed that Judaism be presented as a rational system of universal truths, in which morality was stressed and ritual ignored.

The program of Enlightenment and reform aroused a sharp reaction from defenders of tradition. Orthodoxy as an ideology developed in several forms, establishing new institutions and reinforcing old ones. The most resilient educational expression of the traditional resistance to change in Judaism is the yeshivah. This institution, an academy of advanced study in which students dedicate themselves fully and for an unlimited period of time to mastering sacred texts, has existed throughout the centuries of exile. It has been in the past two hundred years, however, that the yeshivah has become the symbol of resistance to secularization and the source of traditional values in the modern age.

In a letter sent to Jewish communities throughout the world announcing the founding of a new yeshivah and pleading for support, Rabbi Ḥayyim of Volozhin presented this institution as a counter to the phenomenon of the decline in religious study, the denigration of the status of the Torah in the Jewish world, and the pervasive decline in the number of students and scholars. "Brothers, perhaps the hour has come to repair the break in the fence, to return to uphold the Torah with all our strength, some to be teachers, some to be students, and some to support the Torah through material means."[2]

The growth of the yeshivah in eastern Europe during the late nineteenth and early twentieth centuries, and its transplantation following World War II, mainly to Israel but also to Diaspora communities, is an objective representation of orthodoxy's ability to respond to the crisis of modernity. Closed and total, the yeshivah defends and embodies the traditional order, rejecting attempts at accommodation with Western culture. Yeshivah study is more than an act of piety and more than the pursuit of religious truth; it is a symbolic act: a militant assertion of the exclusive, absolute truth and authority of traditional Judaism in an age of challenge and threat.

Powerful historic models call to those prepared for the path of semiwithdrawal from secular culture, restoration of a total integrated Jewish community, and self-contained frameworks of education. Neotraditionalism, however, cannot be a solution for the large sections of the Jewish population who live outside traditional structures, even for those whose discontent with secular culture leads them to seek alternatives to it. The majority of contemporary Jews live in a secular world, in which a variety of cognitive, spiritual, political, and communal orientations, structures, and authorities compete for loyalty. In this world the texture of consciousness, modes of experience, perspective on the world, and basic values differ fundamentally from those of traditional Jewish society.

Jewish learning must be appropriate to the ways of Jewish existence in the modern world. It cannot be based upon a negation of modernity and a nostalgic return to the traditional. It must be founded upon openness to general culture and a desire to speak to those Jews among whom no Jewish consensus on any idea or norm exists. Indeed, attempts have been made in education to respond to the needs and aspirations of the secular majority. New formulations of content, new structures of behavior, and new educational paths have emerged during a period when catastrophic and redemptive events have caused constant rethinking and rebuilding.

The educational forms that have emerged to meet the needs of those Jews intent on integrating into secular society reflect reduced religious interest and commitment. Secondary in every sense to secular learning in the eyes of those who attend them, these institutions have produced minimal results in transmitting the content of Jewish culture. And yet, in the current encounter of Judaism with modernity, educational institutions have emerged that demonstrate vitality and sustenance and are neither defensive nor reactionary. These institutions are grounded upon a revival of interest in Jewish culture and a concomitant recognition that secular culture is insufficient. They are a response to a need to reaffirm communal roots and to find spiritual meaning beyond secular culture.

Paradigmatic and most significant is the adult education movement begun in pre–World War II Germany and continued today in many countries. The originator of this undertaking was Franz Rosenzweig, who, in the decade following World War I, identified the problem of his generation as that of becoming a Jewish person. His contemporaries, he said, were distant from Jewish sources, found Jewish values foreign to themselves, and were removed from Jewish living. The law, the home, and the synagogue had ceased to be authoritative for those whom he described as having migrated spiritually and intellectually to the West.

In Rosenzweig's view, the key to the renewal of Jewish life was the renewal of Jewish learning. He pointed to a new learning, distinct from the traditional structures that assumed a world view and community framework from which the modern Jew was estranged. "We draw strength from the very circumstance that seemed to deal the death blow to 'learning'; from the desertion of our scholars to the realm of alien knowledge of the 'outside books,' from the transformation of the erstwhile *talmidei ḥakhamim* into the instructors and professors of modern European universities. A new learning is about to be born—rather, it has been born."[3]

The Freies Juedisches Lehrhaus (Free Jewish House of Learning) in Frankfort was founded by Rabbi Nehemiah Nobel in 1920. Rosenzweig directed the institution according to his conception of the new Jewish learning, hoping to create through it a renewal of study of a new Jewish intelligentsia that would be at home in both the Jewish and general worlds. The same analytic tools would be used in both. The *Lehrhaus* was to be a modern *bet midrash* where sacred sources, recognized as sacred, were to be studied scientifically and approached openly. Yet Rosenzweig did not dedicate himself to the *Lehrhaus* simply to arouse and satisfy intellectual curiosity or to create a Jewish equivalent of a university. The *Lehrhaus* was a framework of return. As Rosenzweig envisioned it, the process of return began with the decision to study. In the course of study, one moved closer to Judaism and eventually to the observance of Jewish law.

The *Lehrhaus* was established for Jews rooted in secular culture whose return to Judaism would not and could not involve an abandonment of that culture. Rosenzweig built upon the autonomy and rationality of the educated German Jew. He did not suggest that commitment to Judaism be constructed upon a fallen secular world or upon the negation of the individual's secular interests and involvements. "All of us to whom Judaism, to whom being a Jew, has again become the pivot of our lives—and I know that in saying this here I am not speaking for myself alone—we all know that in being Jews we must not give up anything, not renounce anything, but lead everything back to Judaism. From the periphery back to the center; from the outside, in."[4]

Rosenzweig's vision of the new Jewish learning was directed to all Jews. In its fullness, however, it speaks to those open to religious interpretation and commitment. As a guide for his generation, Rosenzweig's explicit goal was to achieve return, meaning that Judaism would become a spiritual power in the lives of his students and that this power would lead to religious practice. He desired that students study the prayerbook, not only as a primary source of spiritual life but as a vehicle of participation in the Jewish community. "Therefore, the transmission of literary documents will never suffice; the classroom must remain the anteroom leading to the synagogue and participation in its service. An understanding of public worship and participation in its expression will make possible what is necessary for the construction of Judaism: a Jewish world."[5]

Rosenzweig's vision of the new learning was a response to the religious-cultural needs of Jews at home in the Diaspora, for whom the national dimension of Judaism was not salient, and for whom the secular cultural definition was insufficient. In the State of Israel different responses, emerging from the situation of the Jewish collective seeking to shape its present and future in relationship to its past, have led to other forms of new Jewish learning. The poignant and much-debated question has been how to treat Jewish subjects in public schools—a question that touches upon the basic ideological and spiritual commitments of each citizen as well as upon the collective vision of the state.

As long as Israel defines itself as a Jewish state, Judaism must be constitutive of its identity and must provide its fundamental cultural symbols and meanings. It is recognized by Israeli thinkers and educators, tacitly or openly, that Judaism must be taught as a source of living content and values. Torah must remain Torah. The problem lies, however, in developing an educational approach to the vast religious-cultural heritage of the past that will make it possible to derive humanist content from that heritage without distorting its authentic religious meaning.

This necessitates breaking through the secular-religious dichotomy or living rationally with the tension it creates and attempting to make the cumulative tradition of Judaism available to the Israeli child in a critical but open way. Throughout the last decade, attempts have been made by Israeli educators from all ideological streams to meet this challenge. The climate within which such attempts are made is reflected in a statement from a pamphlet published in 1974 by the Association for Humanistic-Jewish Education in Israel. "No true humanistic education needs to dissociate itself from religious creativity and its outlook and ways; it can grapple with it as well, for the religious heritage as a philosophical, emotional, and practical answer to the question of the meaning of human existence touches on every man, fertilizing his thought and behavior, even when he does not accept this answer in whole or even in part."[6]

The extremely difficult task of translating this resolution into practice has been assumed by the Israeli public school system, which seeks to transmit Jewish culture in order to build a distinctive collective identity. While the objective national framework provides certain supports for Jewish education—as in the case of language—it does not guarantee continuity of values or ideas. Continuity and creativity within Jewish culture depend upon the strength of values, symbols, and ideas that remain meaningful and compelling within the context of a pluralistic Jewish society responding constantly to the Eastern and Western cultural influences of the environment.

The task of Jewish education in Israel and in the Diaspora is to present Jews with an appreciation of the spiritual reality of Judaism. Education must consist of an intellectually challenging inquiry into tradition, which bears witness to values and dimensions of existence other than those of scientific or humanistic education. Jewish education must rival secular education while not isolating itself from it. It must represent the vitality of Jewish culture in a secular world, secure in its role of rendering the world intelligible to the mind and spirit.

REFERENCES

1. Werner Jaeger, *Paidea* (1939), xiv.
2. Immanuel Etkis, "Shitato u-Poalo shel R' Hayyim me-Volozyin ke-Teguvat ha-Hevra ha-'Mitnagdit' la-Hasidut," in *Proceedings of the American Academy for Jewish Research* 40 (1972), 17.
3. Nahum Glatzer, ed., *Franz Rosenzweig: His Life and Thought* (1953), 230.
4. Ibid., 231.
5. Franz Rosenzweig, *On Jewish Learning*, ed. Nahum Glatzer (1955), 30.
6. J. Schoneveld, *The Bible in Israeli Education* (1976), 144.

BIBLIOGRAPHY

Mordecai Eliav, *Ha-Hinukh ha-Yehudi ba-Germania be-Yamei ha-Haskalah ve-ha-Emanzipaziah* (1960).
Immanuel Etkis, "Shitato u-Poalo shel R' Hayyim me-Volozyin ke-Teguvat ha-Hevra ha-'Mitnagdit' la-Hasidut," in *Proceedings of the American Academy for Jewish Research* 17 (1972).
Nahum Glatzer, ed., *Franz Rosenzweig: His Life and Thought* (1953).
Franz Rosenzweig, *On Jewish Learning*, Nahum Glatzer, ed. (1955).
J. Schoneveld, *The Bible in Israeli Education* (1976).

Emancipation

אימנציפציה

Paula E. Hyman

Emancipation was a political event with far-reaching theological implications for modern Judaism. In its narrowest definition, emancipation simply brought Jews into the body politic by proclaiming them citizens of their native lands. However, the political act of emancipation was grounded in the expectation of profound transformations in the culture, socioeconomic behavior, and mentality of the Jews. Attending the politics of emancipation was an ideology that declared that, in the absence of persecution and enforced segregation, Jews and Judaism would assimilate to the prevailing social and cultural norms of the environment. Indeed, in granting equal civic rights to Jews, proponents of emancipation sought the elimination of virtually all Jewish particularity.

Jewish emancipation was linked to liberal concepts of state and society that diffused gradually throughout the West. Indeed, the process of emancipation in Europe and America extended over more than a century—from the first act in 1790 during the French Revolution to the final curtain in 1917 during the Russian Revolution. Because the drama was accompanied by a lively public debate, emancipation made demands, both explicit and implicit, upon Jews with regard to their self-definition, religious organization, and theology.

When Enlightenment writers placed the naturalization of the Jews upon the political agenda of the day, they did not use the term *emancipation*. Rather, they spoke, in the words of Christian Wilhelm Dohm, of the "civic amelioration" of the Jews, or, in the terminology of the French philosophes, of making the Jews "happier and more useful." Improvement of the Jews' status was to be accompanied by self-improvement on the part of the Jews themselves. As Jacob Katz has pointed out, only in the aftermath of the successful Catholic struggle for political equality in Great Britain in 1829 was the term *emancipation* applied to the Jewish campaign for equal rights.

While a fine example of pointed political rhetoric, the slogan *emancipation* created a distorted perception of the historic process of Jewish political and social integration in Europe and America. It implied redemption of Jews from slavery and degradation, whereas, as Salo Baron has argued, in reality the Jews merely passed from one set of rights and obligations to another. In comparison to the disenfranchised masses, the Jews were by no means in an inferior position, and their corporate right of self-rule, while unacceptable in the light of modern concepts of state and society, was a potent guarantor of cultural self-determination.

Prior to emancipation, Jews and Gentiles shared basic assumptions about Jewish rights and responsibilities. They agreed that Jews were living in exile in punishment for their sins and awaiting (mistakenly, the Christians felt) their restoration to the land of Israel through messianic redemption. As a community apart, as a corporate group in societies comprised of many such groups, the Jews enjoyed the right of self-government according to Jewish law and the right to enforce the law among all members of the community, that is, among all Jews by birth who had not formally renounced their religion in favor of another faith. Gentile authorities, both Christian and Moslem, upheld these powers.

Emancipation shattered these assumptions. By conferring rights of citizenship upon Jews as individuals, it restricted the power of the organized Jewish community to compel membership and to govern Jews according to Jewish law. Communal affiliation and adherence to Jewish law became voluntary. As early as 1783, the German Jewish philosopher Moses Mendelssohn had anticipated and promoted this consequence of emancipation. Adopting the values of the Enlightenment and applying them to the contemporary Jewish scene, he persuasively argued in *Jerusalem,* his magnum opus, for the separation of church and state and for the necessary restriction of Jewish communal autonomy, thus paving the way for the acceptance of

Jews as citizens. For Mendelssohn, religion lay entirely within the realm of opinion, which could not be coerced by either the gentile state or the Jewish community.

The entry of Jews into the general body politic and the transformation of the Jewish community from a self-governing corporate body with police powers to a voluntary religious association challenged the very nature of Jewish self-understanding. Increasingly, Jews were seen, and defined themselves, as adherents of a religious faith rather than as members of a religio-ethnic polity, a people-faith. Their rabbis became religious functionaries—preachers and spiritual counselors—rather than judges and interpreters of the law.

This transformation of Judaism and of the Jewish community facilitated the emergence of denominations within Judaism, particularly in America, where the voluntary nature of the Jewish community was most fully realized. Any group of Jews who could muster the requisite financial and human resources to establish a synagogue, school, or journal were free to do so and thereby to disseminate their conception of Judaism. The modern Jewish community became ideologically and institutionally pluralist, as different interpretations of Judaism, all cognizant of the changed conditions of modernity, competed for adherents. Because emancipation made possible the integration of Jews within their countries of residence, modern interpretations of Judaism were also colored by the particular and diverse ideological trends and social conditions that prevailed in different nations. Emancipation thus brought to a close the hegemony of rabbinic Judaism, which had depended not only upon a consensus of belief in the authority of the rabbis but also upon the existence of a self-governing autonomous Jewish community and upon a rabbinic elite whose training and contacts transcended national boundaries.

Emancipation affected Jewish concepts and practice as well as communal institutions. As citizens, Jews found it increasingly difficult to maintain the immediacy and relevance of the theological concept of *galut* (exile). Indeed, the debate surrounding Jewish emancipation had made it clear that Jews had to display undivided loyalty to their European and American homelands. Their emancipation was predicated upon their presumed ability to renounce religious observances and dogma that would impede the fulfillment of their obligations as citizens.

Weary of the trials of *galut* and eager for the benefits of citizenship, the Jews embraced emancipation and thereby disavowed the passive waiting for the Messiah that had characterized much of Jewish life and thought since the destruction of the Second Temple. Internalizing the values of the

Enlightenment, Jewish leaders accommodated Jewish ritual practice and religious tenets to the new conditions of modernity. Beginning in the early nineteenth century, modernizers in Germany, the United States, England, France, and Hungary revised worship in the synagogue to reflect the aesthetic standards and values of the European and American bourgeoisie, to whose ranks Jews now aspired. They emphasized the necessity of decorum, sermons in the vernacular, and the translation and abbreviation of much of the liturgy in order to foster the spiritual edification modern Jews expected in their religious devotions. Often, they drew upon modern scholarship to legitimate changes in ritual practice and custom.

Seeking to adapt Judaism to the spirit of the age, which they themselves cherished, leaders of the Reform movement rejected the obligatory authority of the halakhah (Jewish law) because the halakhic process, which valued the opinion of the earlier rabbinic authorities over their successors, denied progress and came into conflict with the newly revealed insights of reason. Jewish tradition became a resource to be mined selectively for its wisdom, not an authoritative guide to daily living. Reluctant to jettison the halakhah, Zacharias Frankel's Positive-Historical School, the central European forerunner of Conservative Judaism, argued for the developmental nature of Jewish law and sought a basis for adaptation in the interplay of rabbinic authority and popular consensus. Most significantly, the Reform movement introduced important changes in theology. It eliminated prayers referring to the restoration to Zion and denied that emancipated Jews were in *galut*. Indeed, it universalized the concepts of *galut* and messianic redemption, stripping them of their connectedness to the lived experience of historic Jewish reality. *Galut* came to signify the imperfection of the world and messianic redemption its perfectibility (with or without a personal messiah). Even Neo-Orthodoxy, the branch of modern Orthodoxy that accepted emancipation while continuing to espouse the validity of halakhah, deemphasized *galut* and messianic hopes.

With the erosion of the centrality of *galut* for understanding Jewish fate and the meaning of Jewish existence, emancipated Jews developed a new concept—the mission theory—to endow Judaism with a divinely ordained purpose. Traditional Judaism had seen exile as a punishment for the sins of the Jewish people. Much of post-emancipation Judaism saw the dispersion of the Jews in a positive light, as God's way to bring his message in its purest form, embodied in a living religious community, to the nations of the world. The mission concept thus legitimated the Diaspora and provided Jews with a rationale for survival as a distinct religious group even after their emancipation. Indeed, by bringing them closer to the peoples among whom they lived, emancipation facilitated the mission of the Jews. If autonomy and self-segregation had been necessary to preserve the divine message in pre-modern times, when the Gentiles were not ready to hear it, in the modern age the integration of Jews in their respective societies, as they fashioned a model religious community, would serve to propagate God's teachings of ethical monotheism to a more receptive audience. The mission concept transcended denominational lines within Judaism, for it was espoused by figures as diverse as the Reform rabbi Abraham Geiger, the Neo-Orthodox rabbi Samson Raphael Hirsch, the proto-Zionist socialist Moses Hess, and the secular Zionist Aḥad Ha'Am. Curiously, newly emancipated Jews saw no contradiction between their expressed need to adapt Judaism to modern standards and their expressed conviction that Judaism was the bearer of God's truth in its most pristine form. They continued to uphold the chosen-people concept, even though it aroused hostility among the gentile population.

That tension between the need to restate Judaism in a modern idiom and the need to proclaim its superiority to ensure the continued loyalty of generations of Jews acculturated to Western values has characterized much of modern Jewish thought. Emancipation and its accompanying ideology stimulated Jewish intellectuals to extract the universal from Judaism and disseminate it both to Jews and to their gentile fellow citizens. Thus, the *maskilim,* the thinkers of the Jewish Enlightenment, stressed the centrality of the Bible, rather than the Talmud, in Jewish tradition. The Reform movement preached the message of ethical monotheism and the ideals of the prophetic traditon. Modern Jewish philosophers from Hermann Cohen to Martin Buber and Mordecai Kaplan likewise reinterpreted Judaism through the prisms of Kantianism, existentialism, and pragmatism.

The emphasis upon the universal within Judaism, upon the common ground that Judaism shared with other religions or intellectual traditions, legitimated Judaism for emancipated Jews shaped by the values of modernity. Yet all post-emancipation interpretations of Judaism have had to strike a balance between the universal and the particular. For if the universal within Judaism were readily available elsewhere—within secular rationalism, revolutionary socialism, or Christianity—then there would be little reason to remain Jewish and suffer the stigma of minority status and deviation from the cultural norm. Thus, virtually every modern variety of Judaism has ultimately accepted a form of Jewish particularity—be it the mission theory, the chosen-people concept, or the presentation of Judaism as the noblest version of monotheism.

Although most Jews in the past two centuries have welcomed emancipation and its benefits and recast their Judaism accordingly, they have rejected the most radical presumptions of the proponents of emancipation. Most were unwilling to renounce the last vestiges of particularism and assimilate fully within the larger society, even though many had lost their faith in the tenets of traditional Judaism. Whatever the theoretical redefinition of Judaism as a creed, Jews also retained a sense of ethnic solidarity that has led nonbelievers to continue to avow their Jewishness. In our own century, the impact of Zionism and the Holocaust has led to the strengthening of the concept of peoplehood within all branches of modern Judaism. The legacy of emancipation, however, looms large, as does its challenge: to prove the religious, intellectual, and social viability of Judaism within an open, modern society.

BIBLIOGRAPHY

Salo Baron, "Ghetto and Emancipation," in *Menorah Journal* 14 (June 1928).
Salo Baron, "Newer Approaches to Jewish Emancipation," in *Diogenes* 29 (Spring 1960).
Jacob Katz, "The Term 'Jewish Emancipation': Its Origin and Historical Impact," in Alexander Altmann, ed., *Studies in Nineteenth-Century Jewish Intellectual History* (1964).
Jacob Katz, *Out of the Ghetto* (1973).
Michael Meyer, *The Origins of the Modern Jew* (1967).
Reinhard Rürup, "Jewish Emancipation and Bourgeois Society," in *Leo Baeck Institute Yearbook* 14 (1969).

Enlightenment

השכלה

Robert M. Seltzer

In recent Jewish history *Haskalah* designates the movement that appeared in central and eastern Europe from the 1780s to the 1880s advocating rapid and deliberate Jewish cultural modernization. The *Haskalah* movement, in its first (Berlin or Mendelssohnian) phase, was primarily infuenced by the French and German Enlightenment of the eighteenth century, so that *Haskalah* in this context is usually translated Enlightenment. (Other European intellectual movements penetrated the *Haskalah* in the nineteenth century.) Proponents of *Haskalah* became known as *maskilim* (singular, *maskil*). Somewhat like the eighteenth-century philosophes, the *maskilim* were a loose, informal corps of critics and writers impatient with the conservatism and isolation of traditional Jews and Judaism. To rectify the alleged backwardness of Jewry and eliminate the supposed irrational features of Judaism at that time, the *maskilim* advocated energetic reforms of Jewish education, livelihood, and religious practice. These reforms were deemed necessary if Judaism was to shine forth as a purified, rational religion, and were also considered essential as preparation for political emancipation. During most of the history of the *Haskalah*, the *maskilim* were a self-confident minority of westernized or partly western-ized men who stood in righteous confrontation with a rabbinic leadership often fearful of innovation and progress. The *maskilim* felt a special rapport with liberally inclined non-Jewish intellectuals whose expressions of benev-olent toleration they viewed as harbingers of the happy future of Jewish–Gentile relations. The *maskilim* also tended to lavish praise on certain European absolutistic rulers who supported reforms of Jewish education; the Jewish masses, on the other hand, considered the *maskilim* misled as to the true intentions of these rulers toward the Jews.

In modern Jewish history, the *Haskalah* movement makes its presence felt on three levels. First, inasmuch as almost all *Haskalah* books and jour-nals were written in Hebrew (a few were written in Yiddish, which most *maskilim* despised as a barbaric jargon), the *Haskalah* was an important force in the modernization of the Hebrew language and literature. Second, the *Haskalah* was an identifiable style in the emergence of new forms of Jewish identity during the transition from tradition to modernity: the *maskil* was a recognized type in speech, dress, and secular culture until the time when the majority of Jews were similarly transformed. Third, even though the *Haskalah* was not per se a movement for Jewish spiritual renewal, as an ideology of self-criticism and conscious adaptation to new circumstances it had profound consequences for Jewish religiosity.

The *Haskalah* inevitably underwent decisive changes in location and character during the century of its flourishing. The year 1783 can be des-ignated the formal inception of the movement, with the establishment in Königsburg (East Prussia) of the Society of the Friends of the Hebrew Lan-guage. This society published the first successful modern Hebrew literary periodical, *Ha-Meassef (The Gatherer);* transferred to Berlin in 1787, *Ha-Meassef* appeared with increasing gaps until 1811. The intellectual hero of the *meassefim* (the *maskilim* who wrote for *Ha-Meassef*) was Moses Men-delssohn. Mendelssohn was a prime model for having been the first Jewish intellectual to gain a reputation for literary criticism and popular philosophy in advanced European circles, for his writings on Judaism (even when his definition of Judaism as natural religion and revealed law was later rejected), and for his contribution to the first Jewish translation of the Torah into German and for the Hebrew commentary to it (the *Biur*), to which many of the early *maskilim* contributed. The *meassefim* praised reason, tol-erance, and human perfectibility; they insisted on the centrality of the moral law in religion and the importance of secular learning, especially the natural sciences. They lauded the beauty of pure biblical Hebrew and affirmed the need to know contemporary European languages. During the early years of the French Revolution they became somewhat deistic and more daring in their criticism of traditional Judaism. The practical program of *Ha-Meassef* concentrated on the value of "productive labor" (agriculture and crafts) rather than Jewish overconcentration in commerce, and on a new educational curriculum devoting less time to Talmud and more time to secular subjects and Jewish ethics. By the early nineteenth century, there had appeared a network of schools for Jewish youth in the larger cities of central and then of eastern European Jewry where *maskilim* served as teachers and administrators.

By the end of the Napoleonic period, the center of *Haskalah* had shifted to the Hapsburg empire. In Germany the *Haskalah* impulse, more narrowly focused on religious ritual and theology, was carried on in the German language by the Reform movement. In the 1820s, the Galician *Haskalah* (Galicia was the Polish province of the Austrian empire) had begun openly to attack the "benighted superstition" and "medieval fanaticism" of the Hasidim, directly and in literary satire. A new cycle of *Haskalah* journals appeared (*Bikkurei ha-Ittim, Kerem Hemed, He-Halutz*) in which *maskilim* developed a modern Jewish historical scholarship in Hebrew, parallel to that emerging as the *Wissenschaft des Judentums* (Science of Judaism) in Germany. Among the contributors to this undertaking, outstanding was the Galician *maskil* Nahman Krochmal, who drew on German absolute idealism in his seminal philosophy of Jewish history. From Galicia the *Haskalah* spread to southwestern Russia, where Isaac Baer Levinsohn called for reform of Jewish education and occupations in the 1820s and 1830s and sought to defend the Talmud against anti-Semitic accusations. A second center of the Russian *Haskalah* developed in the northwest at this time. Strongly influenced by Romanticism, the Lithuanian *Haskalah* of the 1830s and 1840s produced the first original modern lyric poetry and the first novels in Hebrew—expressions of the heightened individuality and yearning for Jewish spontaneity outside the confines of a life lived according to the rabbinic rules.

The zenith of the Russian phase of the *Haskalah* occurred between the late 1850s and the 1870s, with the rise of a regular eastern European Jewish newspaper press and the inroads of positivistic social and literary criticism. The younger generation of *maskilim* became more explicit and bold in criticizing the narrowness of the rabbinate, the hermeticism of talmudic learning, the need for sweeping religious reform—and the illusions and uselessness of the *Haskalah* itself. After the pogroms of 1881–1882, however, the *Haskalah* suffered a fate similar to that which the *maskilim* had sought to inflict on traditional Judaism. Reduced to stereotyped formulas and attitudes held inimical to Jewish survival, the *Haskalah* was treated as a straw man in the ideologies of new, more vibrant movements. According to the spokesmen for Ḥibbat Zion (an early phase of the Zionist movement) and other forms of collective Jewish activism, *Haskalah* was deficient in cultural integrity and legitimate self-assertion. The *Haskalah* had held that the main obstacles to Jewish advancement were stubborn, obscurantist adherence to tradition and the world's ignorance of the true character of Judaism; the successor movements blamed Jewish self-denial and rampant anti-Semitism. Legal emancipation was no longer considered the utopian solution to Jewish alienhood, and cultural modernization was no longer a matter of special controversy, since both had unleashed new dangers requiring courageous new solutions.

The *Haskalah* was one response to social and intellectual changes that were found in almost every Jewish community at the onset of modernity, although a specifically Jewish Enlightenment did not take root in each of these Jewries. Emerging during the incipient acculturation of a European Jewry still thoroughly familiar with the Hebrew language, the classic texts, and the old religious way of life, the *Haskalah* was a symptom of a crisis of Jewish disorientation and reorientation. All received truth for the *maskilim* was to be evaluated by the light of universal reason and the discoveries of the sciences. Welcoming the principle that human beings had inalienable rights in the liberal society that was to emerge from the dismantlement of the ancien régime, the *Haskalah* sought to remold Jewry with an eye to the justice of its inclusion in the new family of citizens where every individual could expect to be treated with dignity and respect as equal in the eyes of the law of the state. What would happen to Ashkenazi Judaism when it no longer could rely on communal autonomy, the juridical authority of the rabbinate, and intensive talmudic education to inculcate Jewish values and halakhic practice? In the new dispensation the Jewish individual would awaken to a fully autonomous personhood in matters of religious belief and action. At its bravest and most sincere, the *Haskalah* adhered to Kant's famous dictum that "Enlightenment is man's emergence from his self-imposed tutelage. . . . Dare to know! Have courage and strength to use your own intellect!"[1] Post-*Haskalah* Judaism presupposed this freedom, even when defending Jewish particularity and the nonrational nature of Jewishness. And the critical spirit created a more complex, nuanced, distanced relation between the enlightened individual and his tradition, which posed a new range of problems for a truly modern Jewish religiosity.

A central paradox of the *Haskalah* was that its critical, sometimes aggressive stance to the tradition blinded it to certain assumptions of which *Has-*

kalah itself rested. The *Haskalah* drew on an Enlightenment that brooked no claim on behalf of particular heritages (least of all Judaism); as a result, the *Haskalah* called for reforms in a tradition while offering no ongoing legitimation for its continuance, and it excoriated self-isolation without defining the parameters of minority survival in a premessianic world. (Only in the philosophy of Krochmal did these themes receive the attention they deserved.) Indeed, the *Haskalah* faced a dilemma inherent in the Enlightenment as a whole: However inevitable the liberation accomplished by critical and scientific reason, can this reason, prohibited from concern with *telos* and ultimacy, generate moral imperatives and the ultimate ground of meaning? Or do values and reason remain, in more than a historical sense, fruits of that faith in which the particular heritages (in this case Judaism) are rooted?

In its century of development, the *Haskalah* remained loyal to an eighteenth-century view of progress as a benign, linear process in which the light of truth, pitted against the darkness of ignorance, shines forth in all its brilliance at the end. The *Haskalah* lacked a vision that creative advance proceeds by negation and conflict as much as, if not more than, by the steady accumulation and application of secular knowledge. In actuality, however, the *Haskalah* was a moment in the dialectic of modern Jewish thought, having shaped, through opposition to venerable, unquestioned Jewish attitudes, a radically changed context for even more modern modes of Jewish spirituality.

REFERENCES

1. Immanuel Kant, "What Is Enlightenment?" in *On History*, Lewis White Beck, ed. (1963), 3.

BIBLIOGRAPHY

Jacob Katz, *Tradition and Crisis: Jewish Society at the End of the Middle Ages* (1961), 23–24.
Shalom Spiegel, *Hebrew Reborn* (1930).
Israel Zinberg, *A History of Jewish Literature*, vols. 8–12 (1976–1978).

Eros: Sex and Body

ארוס : מין וגוף

David Biale

J ewish thought unreservedly accepts sexuality as a necessary part of procreation and continuation of the species. Even if eroticism is typically associated with the evil impulse (*yeẓer ha-ra*), its role is considered dialectically justified, as the midrash asserts: "Were it not for the evil impulse, no man would build a house, take a wife, beget a child, or engage in business" (Gen. R. 9:9). Where eros becomes much more problematic is when it is separated from procreative purpose. On the one hand, the halakhah is explicit in permitting sexual relations for pleasure independent of procreation. Thus, sex with a pregnant wife or one who is in any other way incapable of conception is both permitted and commanded. But, on the other hand, within the framework of the law there remain a variety of ambivalent attitudes toward sex and the body.

The Bible itself reflects some of these contradictory positions on sexuality. Sexuality has its proper place within marriage and is condemned only when it deviates from marital norms. Indeed, sexual intercourse was the primary means for acquiring a wife. The implicit eroticism of the Song of

Songs was entirely legitimate in the biblical view, since the book describes a courtship ritual in which sex would constitute the very act of marriage. Theologically, the frequent use by the prophets of erotic metaphors to describe the relationship between God and Israel also has its locus in the proprieties of courtship. The prophets chastise Israel for violating the covenantal marriage with God by "whoring" after other gods; by implication, the proper relationship between God and Israel is one of sexual exclusivity, as in a human marriage. The later argument by Rabbi Akiva that the Song of Songs is not about love between two human beings, but is rather an allegory of the love between God and Israel, falls squarely into this prophetic tradition. To allegorize the Song of Songs in this fashion certainly transposed eros into another realm, but it did not purge the sexual element from the book.

On the other hand, the second creation account in Genesis 2 and 3 suggests a less positive attitude toward sexuality. By eating the fruit of the tree of knowledge of good and evil, the man and woman discover their nakedness (ervah), a term whose root is the same as improper sexuality. By acquiring this sexual knowledge, the man and woman "become like gods." While the later rabbinic tradition did not regard this "original sin" as sexuality per se, as did many Christian writers, what seems clear from the text itself is that sexual knowledge causes human beings improperly to imitate God.

The postbiblical rabbinic texts (Talmud and Midrash) expand on this dual attitude toward sexuality. The rabbis viewed sexuality with great suspicion, even if they recognized it as necessary for procreation. The body itself could be a source of sin. Masturbation is summarily condemned: "In the case of a man, the hand that reaches below the navel should be chopped off" (BT Nid. 13a). As a source of sexual arousal, women were seen as the greatest cause of temptation to sin: "When woman was created, Satan was created with her" (Gen. R. 17:9). The antidote to the dangers of sexuality is early marriage. Thus, Rav Ḥisda is quoted as saying, "I am better than my fellows since I married at sixteen; and had I married at fourteen, I would have said to Satan: 'An arrow in your eye!'" (BT Kid. 29b–30a). Conversely, "He who is twenty years of age and is not married spends all his days in sin" (ibid.). But even within marriage, the rabbis tried to curb sexuality, arguing that a man should not be "like a rooster" with his wife (BT Ber. 22a) and that "man has a small member [the penis]—when he starves it, it is satisfied, [but] when he satisfies it, it becomes hungry" (BT Suk. 52b). The rabbis altered the biblical equation of sexual intercourse with marriage by ruling that it is improper to marry by intercourse alone. Instead, they added two other methods ("money" and "deed"), which are not to be found in the

Bible. Despite these measures and strictures, there were those who still regarded marriage as incapable of assuaging sexual passion. Thus, Rav Isaac is quoted as saying, "Since the destruction of the Temple, sexual pleasure has been taken [from those who practice it properly] and given to sinners . . . " (BT Sanh. 75a).

On the other hand, these ascetic tendencies never found expression in an ideal of chastity or in any reticence about discussing sexuality. While public behavior must be modest, the rabbis permitted great latitude in private. Sexual intercourse must be undertaken without any clothing, and a man who vows that he will not sleep with his wife unless both wear their clothes must divorce her and pay her the full sum of her marriage contract (BT Ket. 47b–48a). Similarly, all sexual positions are allowed (BT Ned. 20a–b). The rabbis recognized and legitimated sexual pleasure, as a midrash in the name of King David testifies: "Did father Jesse really intend to bring me into the world? Why, he had only his own pleasure in mind. . . . As soon as they had satisfied their desires, he turned his face to one side and she turned her face to the other side. It was You who then led every drop [of semen] to its proper place." Man is motivated by sexual pleasure and it is left to God to direct procreation.

If the rabbinical attitude toward male erotic pleasure was ambivalent, it was far more unreservedly positive toward female sexuality. The rabbis understood women as highly sexual (cf. Rashi's commentary on Gen. 3:16: "Your urge shall be for your husband . . .") but unable to initiate sex. Thus, their husbands are commanded to satisfy them sexually on a regular basis (these are the laws of *onah*). Women are allowed to request sex whenever they so desire, provided they do so modestly.

The various attitudes found in the rabbinic texts served as the basis for the many positions on sexuality that appear in posttalmudic writings. There were those among both the halakhists and the philosophers who took ascetic attitudes to an extreme. Thus, Joseph Caro, the author of the sixteenth-century law code the *Shulhan Arukh*, wrote: "Even when he is with her, let him not intend [sexual relations] for his own pleasure. . . . It would be better for him to put off his passion and subdue it" (OH 240a). Saadiah Gaon, the tenth-century philosopher, denounced both sexuality and erotic love in his *Sefer Emunot ve-Deot (Book of Beliefs and Opinions)*. Those who are motivated by a desire for sexual pleasure not only cause themselves physiological damage, but also degenerate into antisocial behavior and eventually adultery. Only the goal of procreation justifies sexuality (ibid., 10:6). Love has similar deleterious effects and has its place within marriage only "for the sake of maintenance of the world [i.e., procreation]" (ibid.,

10:10). A similar attitude can be found in the writings of the twelfth-century philosopher Moses Maimonides. In his *Guide of the Perplexed* (3:49) he quotes Aristotle to the effect that the sense of touch, which leads to sexual intercourse, is not to be viewed positively. All of the sexual prohibitions in Jewish law are designed to "make sexual intercourse rare and to instill disgust for it so that it should be sought only very seldom." In his code of Jewish law, the *Mishneh Torah,* Maimonides was compelled to transmit the rabbinic decision that a man may have intercourse with his wife in any way he chooses, but he added that "it is an attribute of piety that a man should not act in this manner with levity. . . . A man should not turn aside from the normal way of the world and its proper procedure, since the true design of intercourse is fruitfulness and multiplication of progeny" (Hil. Issurei Bi'ah, 21:9).

Against such ascetic attitudes, one can find many medieval writers who celebrated eroticism. Perhaps one of the most notable texts is the *Iggeret ha-Kodesh (Letter of Holiness),* written in the thirteenth century by Moses Naḥmanides or one of his later disciples. The unusually positive attitude toward sexuality in this text and others of the period may have been due to the Spanish influence, which also played a role in the development of the often frankly erotic poetry of the Spanish Jewish poets from the eleventh century onward. The author of the letter explicitly rejected Maimonides' position on the sense of touch. Since God created the body, as he did everything else, to denounce intercourse as repulsive is blasphemous: "All organs of the body are neutral; the use made of them determines whether they are holy or unholy. . . . Therefore marital intercourse, under proper circumstances, is an exalted matter. . . . Now you can understand what our Rabbis meant when they declared [in BT Sot. 17a] that when a husband unites with his wife in holiness, the divine presence abides with them." The Bible calls intercourse "knowing" *(da'at)* and therefore endows sexuality with special holiness.

The author of the *Iggeret ha-Kodesh* was a kabbalist, and many of the terms he uses reflect the influence of the mystical theory of eroticism. For the mystics, God himself is composed of male and female *sefirot* (emanations; sing., *sefirah*), which are in a perpetual state of intercourse with each other. Some of the major texts of the kabbalah, notably the *Zohar,* describe this divine sexuality with such detail as to be almost pornographic. The divine intercourse is sustained by proper acts of intercourse by righteous human beings. Improper intercourse causes the male and female elements in God to mate instead with the forces of evil. The term *knowing* referred to in the *Iggeret ha-Kodesh* is none other than the *sefirah* produced by the intercourse of the divine father (*ḥokhmah*) and mother (*binah*). The divine Presence (*Shekhinah*) is the tenth *sefirah* and is the element of God that mediates between the upper realms and our world. Thus, proper intercourse between human beings causes these divine elements to function properly and to ensure the stability and harmony of the lower worlds. Here, then, is an erotic theology that exalts human sexuality as indispensable to God himself.

To be sure, the kabbalah was not free from the ambiguity that characterized the Jewish attitude toward eros in other sources. The dangers of improper sexual actions or even thoughts were magnified by the influence human eroticism had on the divine. For example, nocturnal emissions, which carry no prohibitions in Jewish law, were regarded with the utmost horror by the kabbalists. In an ascetic kabbalistic movement like eighteenth-century eastern European Ḥasidism, these tendencies frequently overwhelmed the more positive attitude toward eros in the earlier mystical sources. For example, Elimelech of Lyzhansk understood the term for carnal knowledge (*da'at*) as pejorative rather than holy. Adam "knew" his wife in the sense that he had lascivious thoughts about her during the act of intercourse. The evil Cain was the result of this sin. A man must not even think about his wife physically during sex. If he does so, he causes a disruption in the *sefirot* (cf. *Noam Elimelech* ad loc. Gen. 2b).

On the other hand, the erotic hints in the kabbalah could be taken to nihilistic extremes in antinomian movements. The more radical offshoots of the mystical-messianic Sabbatean movement such as the Polish Frankists of the eighteenth century translated theological abstractions into explicit sexual acts. Their messianic theology, based on a dualistic godhead and an antinomian attitude toward Jewish law, became the rationale for sexual perversions and even orgies.

Thus, a range of attitudes can be discerned in the tradition. While some writers sanctioned sexuality only for procreative purposes, others, following the majority view of the halakhah, viewed eroticism positively even when it is motivated solely by the desire for pleasure. What characterizes all of the various attitudes is that there was never a suggestion that eroticism might be renounced altogether. In its attention to the nonprocreative and pleasurable dimension of sexuality, then, the tradition has much in common with contemporary sexual mores. But in its insistence on the sanctity of marriage and its strict disapproval of any public display of sexuality, traditional Judaism remains far from modern. If the modern world has broken down the distinctions between public and private, it is this very difference that the normative Jewish tradition upholds.

BIBLIOGRAPHY

Rachel Biale, *Women and Jewish Law: An Exploration of Women's Issues in Halakhic Sources* (1984).
Louis Epstein, *Sex Laws and Customs in Judaism* (1948).
David Feldman, *Birth Control in Jewish Law* (1968).
Raphael Patai, *Sex and Family in the Bible and the Middle East* (1959).
Gershom Scholem, *Major Trends in Jewish Mysticism*, 3d ed. (1961).

Eschatology

תורת אחרית הימים

Arthur A. Cohen

Eschatology signifies the doctrine of the last and final events that will consummate the life of man and the cosmos and usher in the "day of the Lord." Such a definition, broad and general as it is, encompasses a considerable variety of classic Jewish belief and undergirds the language of the prayer book insofar as these convey teachings regarding the life that succeeds death, the coming of the Messiah, and the establishment of God's kingdom. Eschatology reflects a constellation of Jewish hopes and expectations for God's working the miracle of the end as he wrought the miracle of the beginning. Eschatological speech, as it appears in the traditional prayer book from the numerous formulations of the *Amidah* to the declaration of the *Aleinu* to the recitation of Maimonides' Thirteen Principles, reflects a coherent movement of Jewish conviction and elicits a credal reflex that, as often as it is obediently delivered, remains nonetheless obscure.

There is a thoroughgoing Jewish eschatology, but there is certainly no normative clarity as to the meaning or intention of its formulas. The language of eschatology—promising the gifts of eternal life, the transformation of history, the bringing of the nations to the worship of the God of Israel, the emergence of the messianic personage, the apocalyptic end of time and nature, the promulgation of divine kingship and sovereignty, the ransoming of the dead and their restoration to physical and spiritual vitality—all these represent elements of eschatological teaching. However, as the formulae of eschatology become elaborate and replete with allusions to biblical sources, apocryphal and apocalyptic emphases, Gnostic byways, rabbinic elucidations and metaphors, medieval speculation and modern reformulation, it becomes ever more explicit that despite the insistence of the tradition that there is a core of dogmatic affirmation that constitutes the Jew's dream of promise fulfilled and expectation gratified, the eschatological teaching is a muddle. There is profound disagreement with regard to the interpretation and reception of the belief in life beyond death. Some thinkers speak of two resurrections, some of spiritual resurrection alone without need for bodily vivification, and yet others formulate a naive and gross teaching of bodily transfiguration and paradisal gratification. No less is the disagreement over the doctrine of the Messiah, who is seen by some as entailing only a political ransoming of the Jews from subjection to the nations (with the malign consequence that often contemporary Jews believe that the establishment of the State of Israel coincides with the beginning of messianic restoration), while others continue to maintain that the Messiah is a person specially endowed by God and anointed to leadership of his people, and yet others hold that the Messiah is not a person at all but a mood of universal ethical regeneration. The apocalyptic end of time and history, the great mystical orgy of ruin and consummation, the triumphant emergence of the avenging God succeeded by the God of victorious compassion is—even more than the preceding notions—fraught with difficulties and stubborn unclarity.

What does it all mean? What need is there for an eschatological doctrine? Why is it indubitably a portion of the teaching of historical Judaism? And how may its tenets be submitted to judgment and refinement so that its essential intentions may be clarified and set straight? Rather than analyze the specific eschatological thought of Israel, this essay addresses the question: Why eschatology? Why teachings regarding the End of Days and fulfillment beyond our years and the implication of such a rich working of the theological imagination?

Eschatological teaching, grounded in the hope that God will ransom, redeem, and reward the faithful while bringing evil under final judgment at the End of Days, clearly implies ethical resolutions as these are entailed by the doctrines of providence and reward and punishment. Since it is taught that the Jew should not do the will of his creator out of crass desire for reward, there can be little conviction that doing the will of God and observing the Torah with a clean heart and an obedient spirit will be rewarded. Moreover, what reward could God give to obedience in this life, in the midst of living, when the task is not yet done nor the full course of life completed? God does not reward in the midst of life; indeed, it is surely questionable whether God rewards contingent service and its finite human performer at all. (The evil surely prosper and the holy and obedient are still brought low with suffering.) However much the simple believer may wish to espouse a belief in meticulous reward and punishment, the evidence of this world is hardly conclusive. Murderers too often die of old age and their victims remain dissolved in the lime pits of concealment. The belief in some kind of accurate distribution of rewards and punishments (moral accuracy on the part of God being a critical aspect of such distribution) is hardly possible. There is always disequilibrium and imbalance in God's administration of rewards and punishments, with the consequence that we take refuge once again in a noetic fog where God's intentions remain impenetrably hidden. Unfortunately, then, providential compensations and divine settlements do not help us much in understanding the source for the development of eschatological teaching.

At the core of most interpretive definitions of the ethics of eschatology is a sense of the universe as a mathematical composition in which the analogues of the human condition are devised out of systems of rectification and mathematical models of restored equilibrium and balance. God's equation is expected to work: divine promises are expected to be honored; however, if they cannot be honored under conditions where freedom and voluntary choice obtain, they are reserved by God until this life (and this world) have come to an end. In the age that succeeds our own, then, in the era beyond human life when freedom has ceased to be an ontological obstruction, God is able to exercise the power that during the days of man he was obliged to check. In other words, the displacement of divine compensation from the time of this world to the World to Come is a subtle revindication of a divine omnipotence necessarily challenged by the demanding reality of freedom and a reassertion that in the time of the *eschaton* (which is beyond time) God is once again alone and all-powerful. The content of eschatological teaching is formally a repostulation of a divine fiat that acknowledges no human opposition or human contrast; it reaffirms at the end what was present before the beginning of creation.

How do we know the promises of eschatology? By what combination of divine and human potencies are the teachings of eschatology woven together as a skein of hope laid over the disappointments of unrequited longing and unrewarded service? This is the hardest of difficulties. It would have been sufficient had there been a divine mechanism for acknowledging in the midst of life or even at its end that a person's work was remembered and loved by God—if only God had reserved a miracle of self-disclosure to each of those who had lived and prepared to die. But there is no machinery of approbation and appraisal. No man dies knowing for certain the worth of his days. Into the silence of God man puts forth a suite of hopes that ratify and confirm the workings of a life, the faith that history will be clarified, that good works will be rewarded, that life will be restored, that the just will live into eternity in the presence of God.

And yet it must be asked if these hopes for salvation beyond the days of our life are truly what we project them to be. Without a sure continuity of consciousness between the living and the dead revived, there is no real resurrection. Without the certain knowledge that the self regenerated by divine love remembers and is identical with the self that has died, the reward to self is chimerical. Without a sure persuasion that the cruel and unmerciful are actually damned to a torment of absence from the living God, there is no punishment that has any theological vivacity or appropriateness. Even then the Messiah—he who comes to restore the Jewish people and establish the conditions for reforming the human stock in preparation for the kingship and reign of God—is thin hope except insofar as this hope lives upon the passion for an ultimate vindication of millennial suffering and depletion. The Messiah is believed in wholeheartedly, since without the promise of his advent how can we justify the unparalleled suffering of the Jewish people? The coming of the Messiah is proof then not of the victory of God (which takes place between time and eternity), but of the faithfulness of Israel, who has been given every reason to defect and did not.

To deal with questions such as these (and there is a vast structure of questions, each holding itself intact and erect by implying its dependence upon other elements of the structure), it becomes necessary to probe beneath the questions rather than to inquire about their objective coherence and consistency. Any eschatological doctrine can be made coherent and self-sufficient; however, without a curiosity about the nature of human trust and hope that is the nonrational presupposition out of which such doctrine emerges and from which it derives its self-conscious authenticity, it is hardly possible to make such doctrine both true and believable. Even eschatology must stand upon the foundations of the fundamental inquiry into the ground of the self and its placement before the presentness of God.

Theological argument in this century has pursued several lines. One line of argument has undertaken to ground the initial movement toward faith, that is, the first urging to go beyond the sufficiencies of the empirically self-grounding self toward a rock that lies outside the self, upon the acknowledged fact of man's terror of death and the inability of philosophy to remove the sting from dying. Other theological explorations have made the discovery that every interaction between human beings is ontologically defective unless the presence of an eternal Other or an eternal Thou is set down in its midst. Still another line of argument has undertaken a critique of the idealist tradition, arguing that reasonableness and the schemas of reason at best organize programs of abstraction that have little efficacy in ordering and containing the outbursts of unreason that periodically inundate human life. In each argument an epistemological insufficiency is made the occasion for an ontological corrective: A failure of human knowledge is overcome by a preliminary intuition of another order of being that addresses, compensates, and completes the epistemological defect.

The opening of awareness to an ontological source outside the self through which the self secures its ground becomes the starting point for the quest to God. God first appears to faith not as promiser or savior, but as source of life, the God who creates and sustains. As such God is set against the reality of man's dying, and however utter the reality of death, death does not lose its power to command into life, to shape life not by the putative evil of dying (for death is no evil), but by the simple fact that death is an ontological surd, a simple zero, a negativity that passes no judgment. Death stops life, nothing more. The various ascents of the self confirmed out of God toward the incorporation of the eternal Thou in human interaction or the turning of God toward a critique of human knowledge (or any of the other methodological starting points for faith) are interruptions that compel the attentive to stop and scrutinize, to think deeply, to put into question settled assumptions, to open ways of incertitude, to formulate a metaphysics of finitude, and so forth, all with the intention of opening the being of the self to being itself, and beyond even being itself to the holy ground of being who is called God.

Eschatology originates in the very beginnings of belief in God. Indeed, it is argued that the constellation of hopes that makes up eschatological teaching is given as the first gift of faith, given at the same instant that belief takes itself beyond the self-grounding of the self to a grounding that has its source beyond the self. The only risk of faith is the first. Everything afterward is a consequential unraveling of the self and the enravelment of God into the self, a dialectic that is mandated by the opening of the self to the ultimate Other and the authenticating movement of the Other from mysteriousness, hiddenness, and abscondite distance to presentness. Indeed, it is perhaps here in the personal intimacy of the divine–human encounter that the divine indifference to history (which leaves it vulnerable to such uncontainable cruelty as we have experienced in this century) may be located.

God begins working at the beginning, and the response of man out of his equally mysterious—but imponderably finite freedom—is to go forth out of finite being toward being itself, toward encompassment, toward expansion of the minute kingdom of the self grounded now by the Other, toward visionary hopes for a universe grounded by the Other, toward fundamental reordering of empirical being, toward a redemption that turns and actively reorients creation. It is this procedure that is the drama of eschatological hope. It is no mere psychological projection, but an ontological dream that grows forth from the ground of man's first beginnings in belief. All eschatological teaching is directed toward an enhancement and confirmation that the finite being that gives itself to being and to God is justified, solaced, even rewarded, surely ransomed from history, indubitably redeemed into being, and given the sureties of divine presentness and eternity.

BIBLIOGRAPHY

Robert Henry Charles, *Eschatology: The Doctrine of a Future Life in Israel, Judaism, and Christianity* (1963).

Hans-Georg Gadamer, "On the Origin of Philosophical Hermeneutics," in *Philosophical Apprenticeships* (1985).

Thomas Francis Glasson, *Greek Influence in Jewish Eschatology* (1961).

George Foot Moore, *Judaism in the First Centuries of the Christian Era*, 3 vols. (1946).

Franz Rosenzweig, *The Star of Redemption* (1970).

Eternity and Time

נצח וזמן

David Ellenson

R eflecting on the attempt to define the relationship between the eternal and the time bound, T. S. Eliot observed, "To apprehend/The point of intersection of the timeless/With time is an occupation for the saint."[1] To grasp the point in which eternity and time meet is also a task for the theologian. Philosophy, however, poses serious problems to this task, for it has classically regarded the realm of time as one of endless flux and succession, as a series of irreversible moments marked by coordinates of "before" and "after." Transitoriness is the fate of all things existent in time. Eternity, in contrast, is seen as impervious to succession and passage. It does not signify an infinite succession of times. Rather, it points to a transcendence above and, by extension, an immutability beyond all existence in time. The Bible itself reveals this conceptual division between what exists in time and what is eternal; in the words of the Psalmist: "Of old You established the earth; the heavens are the work of Your hands./They shall perish, but You shall endure; they shall wear out like garments; You change them like clothing and they pass away./ But You are the same, and Your years never end" (Ps. 102:26–28).

The distinction between the temporal and the eternal has posed a number of problems for theologians. Central among them has been the issue of how God, who is eternal, unchanging, and therefore seemingly removed from passage, can relate to the temporal and act, as the Bible and rabbinic literature assert God does, in history. Jewish theologians in the Middle Ages wrestled laboriously with this dilemma of how a transcendental God for whom time does not exist could call into existence a world of matter, creating it within the limits of space and time, and, in addition, reveal himself in that world without thereby subjecting himself to the limitations and mutations inherent in the nature of the universe itself. Maimonides, for example, attempted to resolve the problem by positing an incorporeal God who possessed an eternal will unbound by natural laws. Depending upon an Aristotelian definition of time, he asserted that time possessed no independent reality and was, instead, a product of the motion of the heavenly bodies. Time came into existence with the creation of the world. Prior to creation, God existed alone in a timeless eternity. As God is incorporeal, God has no relation to motion and, consequently, none to time. Maimonides thus claimed to view God's creation of the world in time as a miracle, an extraordinary and unique event produced by the will of God. It is on account of this "belief in the creation of the world in time" that "all miracles become possible and the law [that is, God's revelation in space and time] becomes possible" (*Guide* 2, 25). Timelessness thereby remains an attribute of the creating and revealing God who simultaneously dwells in an eternity beyond time and space.

In recent generations, Abraham Isaac Kook and Abraham Joshua Heschel altered the boundaries of the medieval discussion concerning time and eternity by abandoning the focus on the philosophical problem of the relationship between time/space and eternity. Rather, they centered their discussion of time around the traditional Jewish issue of how time could be hallowed, that is, how the sanctity and holiness of the transcendent God could be made immanent in the activities of this world. In his prayerbook commentary on the Maimonidean hymn *Yigdal,* Kook wrote that time exists only for humanity, not for God. Reflecting a Kantian notion of time as a human construct of apperception, Kook argued that human existence is bound up with time and that time appears as a flow from which persons cannot escape. However, Kook posited that there is an existence—a true existence that is the source of human and material existence—beyond the ravages of time, beyond the natural processes of generation and decay. The absolute, unlimited God is not coeval with the world and the human beings God has created. Indeed, it is on this basis that Kook attacks the Christian doctrine of incarnation for its notion of the consubstantiality of God with humanity. Instead, Kook posits that Judaism teaches a *unio mystica,* the ultimate unity of all being—the eternal with the transient. The religious spirit of Judaism allows the Jew, through the observance of God's commandments, to experience the eternal in time. Thus, the daily activities of humanity can be infused with transcendental purpose, meaning, and reality. Similarly, Heschel defined time as a human construct, "a measuring device rather than a realm in which humanity abides."[2] For Heschel, Judaism is transformed into a religion of timelessness: "To men with God time is eternity in disguise."[3] The Jew, by observing *mizvot,* comes to encounter God and, in so doing, sanctifies time and enters into a holy dimension that partakes of eternity. Jewish tradition thus instructs humanity on "how to experience the taste of eternity or eternal life within time."[4]

This transformation of the discussion concerning the relationship between time and eternity from a medieval struggle with the philosophical issues to a modern quest for experiencing the eternal within time can be found, with variations on the themes introduced by Kook and Heschel, in the work of Franz Rosenzweig. Like Heschel and Kook, Rosenzweig saw time as having no validity when applied to God. Instead, Rosenzweig taught that God, to whom he ascribed the attribute of creation, related to his temporally bound handiwork through the act of revelation. God is thus conceived as an eternal indwelling personality who relates to humanity in an act of revelation, which the non-Orthodox Rosenzweig saw as a continuous dialogue between the ever-revealing God and the individual whose soul is born in the moment of revelation. As Rosenzweig asserts, "For man was created as man in revelation."[5] That is, humanity, through the phenomenon of revelation, moves out of the realm of the temporal to bask in the rays of the eternal. Revelation, for Rosenzweig, represents a "timeless" region where the human encounters the eternal. It is without definable content and occurs between the past of creation and the future of redemption.

Rosenzweig's views led him to a rather Hegelian idealist focus on the calendar and liturgy as the "essence" of Judaism. The Sabbath liturgy, with its themes of creation, revelation, and redemption, allowed Rosenzweig to see Judaism as in, but not of, history and time. Instead, the Jew observes a cyclical repetition of holidays and liturgy that permits the recognition and celebration of the existence of eternity within historical time. In so viewing the rhythm of Jewish religious life, Rosenzweig sees the Jew as living in an "eternal present" that is a "vigil of the Day of Redemption."[6] Judaism is thus removed from the flux of history through its response to an atemporal revelation, and the Jewish people, for Rosenzweig as for the ancient rabbis, alone experiences the "taste of eternity in time."

By analyzing the relationship between time and eternity in this manner and by removing the Jew from the domain of history, Rosenzweig laid himself open to such critiques as that of Emil Fackenheim in the present time. In an era that has witnessed the Nazi onslaught against the Jews and the rebirth of the State of Israel, theologies such as Rosenzweig's, which center on the issue of revelation and how it mediates between time-bound humanity and the eternal God, are seen by Fackenheim as inadequate and erroneous. Relying upon the views of the German philosopher Martin Heidegger, Fackenheim notes that the question that must now be asked is: "What is the fate of eternity in our time?"[7] That is, is the Eternal manifest? Can it be perceived in this time? Heidegger, Fackenheim reminds the modern Jew, states that true being *(Sein)* can become so only in temporally conditioned ways. Rosenzweig's views on time and eternity are thus irrelevant precisely because they remove the Jew from history, that is, from a connection with those temporally conditioned moments in which the *Sein,* eternal being, might reveal itself. For "an absolute transcendence of time," as suggested by Rosenzweig, "is not attainable in our time."[8] Contemporary Jewish existence indicates that transcendence can be realized and eternity experienced only in fragmentary, precarious moments—and even those occur not in the realm of the synagogue, but in individual acts of spiritual courage that point to a transcendence of time toward eternity. Fackenheim ultimately shares the emphasis of those he criticizes on the way in which the eternal becomes manifest in time, that is, how holiness appears in history. Unlike the others, however, he displays no optimism that the Eternal is present in time in an ongoing, significant way.

As Jewish theologians continue to ponder the relationship between time and eternity, it seems clear that most will follow the direction indicated by Fackenheim. Jewish theological reflections upon the issue of time and eternity are not likely to be centered upon abstract theological systems apart from the reality of the Jewish community. Rather, they will probably focus upon what individual Jewish religious thinkers perceive as the continuing realities of Jewish existence in confrontation with God. The question of how the historical and temporal relates to the transhistorical and eternal therefore promises to remain a vexing theological issue.

REFERENCES

1. T. S. Eliot, "The Dry Salvages."
2. Abraham Joshua Heschel, *The Sabbath* (1951), 96.
3. Ibid., 100.

4. Ibid., 74.
5. Franz Rosenzweig, *The Star of Redemption* (1964), 420.
6. In Emil Fackenheim, *To Mend the World* (1982), 93.
7. Ibid., 320.
8. Ibid., 324.

BIBLIOGRAPHY

Emil Fackenheim, *To Mend the World* (1982).
Abraham Joshua Heschel, *The Sabbath* (1951).
Louis Jacobs, *A Jewish Theology* (1973).
Nathan Rotenstreich, *Jewish Philosophy in Modern Times* (1968).

Ethics

מוסר

Shalom Rosenberg

My purpose is to attempt to apply certain modern categories to the study of classical Jewish ethics. This is a dangerous enterprise, because we are entering the minefield of anachronism. Nevertheless, I think it can produce fruitful results. I would like to show first of all that in classical Jewish philosophy there are several different ethical theories, four of which will be discussed here, namely, the deontological, teleological, and anthropological ethical theories, and ethics conceived as imitatio.

Let us begin with a general description of the first type, which may be called the deontological theory. It is based on the premise that we cannot reduce moral value to natural goodness, happiness, and sufferance. Rather, there are considerations that render an action right or wrong other than the goodness and badness of its consequences. The reasons for ethical conduct involve neither convenience nor utility. This type of theory presents us with a moral code that applies to human actions. The code is generally defined by a system of positive and negative commandments, as in Moses Maimonides' *Sefer ha-Mizvot (Book of the Commandments)*.

We find two different but complementary explanations of the deontological theory of ethics. The basis of the theory is above all halakhah, which has its roots in the biblical commandments. But in Jewish philosophy in different periods and among different thinkers there are philosophical explanations of these commandments that are based on an intuitive grasp of moral values, of right and wrong. This type of theory is manifest in Saadiah Gaon's *Sefer Emunot ve-Deot* (*Book of Beliefs and Opinions*), a work influenced by stoic ideas transmitted via the Mutazilite version of the Kalam. Kalam.

Moral precepts may be considered as rational precepts, that is, as having their roots in a rational intuition. We can speak, therefore, of the first type of ethical theory as that of natural law. Religious ethics are natural ethics, because they may be learned not only from revelation but also through the discoveries and intuitions of unaided human reason.

At this point we must be careful to distinguish between this kind of rational intuition and what we might call emotive theories. Medieval Aristotelians spoke of moral values as *mefursamot,* that is, as almost universally accepted propositions that fail, however, to convey rational meaning. These *mefursamot* exhibit an emotive quality that is irrelevant from a rational and scientific point of view. The *mefursamot* do not represent a normative theory but rather a descriptive theory of ethics and, indeed, of aesthetic values as well.

As is generally known, Maimonides accepts the theory of the *mefursamot* and expresses it through his interpretation of the Tree of the Knowledge of Good and Evil in the Garden of Eden. Maimonides explains that when Adam ate the forbidden fruit he had an immediate comprehension of this kind. As a result he became subject and subjugated to these emotions. According to Maimonides, although we are bound to some kind of moral conduct, as was Adam, the emotive component of our conduct is a burden that was imposed upon us as a result of the original sin. In other words, human beings exhibit moral values that have an emotional base. They react emotionally to actions and events. These reactions are almost universal. We must, however, emphasize the word *almost,* as there are societies and, of course, individuals whose scales of values are totally different. Sexual mores represent the prime example of this type of relative value system.

The *mefursamot* therefore represent a philosophical descriptive theory. The theory describes a situation that is always emotional, mostly useful, but at times harmful to society and to individual development. As we shall see, this interpretation of the source of ethical values does not prevent Maimonides from attempting to present a normative theory of morality. Even so,

Maimonides sometimes utilizes the descriptive theory as if it had normative import.

It should be emphasized that Maimonides distinguishes carefully between what one may call values and norms, or, more specifically, between descriptive values and prescriptive norms. In Book 1, Chapter 2, of the *Guide of the Perplexed* we read that man "in his most perfect and excellent state" possessed intellectual cognitions, but had no faculty to grasp the *mefursamot,* the generally accepted notions—even the most manifestly evil, namely, nudity. Later, in Book 3, Chapter 8, Maimonides asserts that our values must be changed. He writes that "The disapproval of the uncovering of the private parts is a generally accepted opinion," while drunkenness, which ruins the intellect and the body, is a vice according to reason. Beyond the *mefursamot* a different realm of ethics—rational ethics—exists.

The second type of ethical theory can be characterized as teleological or, more specifically, utilitarian. This theory appears throughout Maimonides' *Guide* as well as in his halakhic works. We find it expressed in other medieval thinkers as well, for instance in the writings of Abraham ibn Daud and Judah Halevi. We can describe this type of morality as a set of minimal conditions needed to sustain any human society. According to a medieval philosophical commonplace, even a gang of thieves must have a minimal ethical code in order to survive. This theory presents us with a second type of natural law. Ethics represent a necessary condition for the existence of society. Since society is a product of nature, it follows that ethics have a natural base. Some philosophers have even said that legislators' actions must be viewed as a kind of natural phenomenon through which nature (that is, the active intellect) attempts to improve society. For Maimonides, however, society does not constitute an aim in and of itself, but rather comprises the foundation that enables individual existence. The correct system of law is therefore the one that not only assures social stability but also encourages true individual freedom: freedom from misery and from compulsion as well as freedom from idolatry and from false and deceiving ideals.

A third type of theory exists that may be designated an anthropological conception of ethics. Actually, we could consider it teleological, albeit a particular kind of teleology, one that refers to a change in the internal rather than the external world.

In order to clarify the differences between the three types of morality I have outlined above, I will compare them to three approaches to the theatre. According to one view, the theatre represents the realization of a script, and the author constitutes the source of activity. According to a second view, the theatre is above all an attempt by the director to bring about a specific situation. The third approach sees the theatre as a mere psycho-drama; real drama takes place not in the external realm but in the internal world. Applying these distinctions to the realm of ethics, we see that the first, the deontological theory, regards ethics as the realization of a divine command or of a rational norm. The utilitarian theory sees the center of ethics as that which will occur on the stage, that is, as the perfection of society. Finally, the anthropological theory sees the true aim of ethics as a psychodrama, that is, as the perfection of the individual human soul.

Maimonides refers to two different aims evident in the Torah, namely, the perfection of the body, that is, of society, and the perfection of the soul, a concept that must be understood as referring to the perfection of the individual. The central document for our analysis of this third theory is Mai-monides' introduction to *Pirkei Avot (The Sayings of the Fathers)*, his well-known *Shmoneh Perakim (Eight Chapters)*. I would characterize Maimonides' theory as presented in this introduction as a theory of self-realization or self-actualization, but I hasten to add a cautionary note. Maimonides presents a concept of self-actualization within the framework of a theory that asserts that all human beings share a common essence. In medieval terminology, all individuals strive to actualize their full potential. The aim of self-realiza-tion is therefore not particular to the individual. Rather, it is shared by the entire human race, albeit it is achieved by only a few individuals.

The tension between the social and the anthropological conceptions of morality has existed throughout the ages. In medieval philosophy it is reflected in the intellectual conflict between two of Maimonides' philosoph-ical mentors: the Muslim thinkers al-Farabi and Avenpace (ibn Bajja). Refer-ring approvingly to the hermit's regimen, the latter believed in the possi-bility of achieving the height of individual perfection outside human society. Al-Farabi, in contrast, did not believe in the possibility of a metaintellectual experience, as implied in ibn Bajja's theories. For him the peak of human activity, of philosophical endeavor, is political philosophy—salvation not of the individual, but of society.

Maimonides' conception falls somewhere between these two extremes. Maimonides believed in the possibility of attaining individual perfection, but only on the condition that social perfection be achieved. Hence Mai-monides' ethical theory represents a combination of the utilitarian and anthropological conceptions, a synthesis of the second and third types of ethical theories delineated above.

Al-Farabi came to his conclusion about politics after despairing of the possibility of what can be called individual metaintellectual experience. According to al-Farabi, the only door that remains open for man is that of political action. Al-Farabi's case is unusual. In the history of philosophy the contrary trend is more frequently found: a spiritual movement that in its early stages devotes its efforts to changing the social structure eventually loses faith in the feasibility of this aim and finally restricts itself to the sole aim of changing the individual. That is, it passes from the second type of model to the third type. A similar phenomenon occurred with medieval Ashkenazi Ḥasidism and in modern times in the Musar movement. Even without attempting to trace the Musar movement's historical development, we can see how the anthropological theory figures in it. Some proponents of the Musar movement eventually came to reject the possibility of changing the world, even to the point of maintaining a severe and strong fatalism. According to their view, man is only a spectator in a tragic drama, bound by forces stronger than himself. Despite this, our ethical efforts are indeed meaningful, but only as a kind of psychodrama.

We can easily detect in the Musar movement the profound influence of Maimonides' *Eight Chapters.* However, a deep difference is also evident. In the Musar movement the Aristotelian aim of self-actualization is not to be found. Rather, we find a theory that elucidates the repercussions human actions have on the soul. Accordingly, the prohibition against stealing exists neither because it represents the product of a rational intuition nor because stealing is harmful to society. Rather, it stands because a wrong action stains the soul, even when that action is not explicitly forbidden and even when it presents no harmful consequences for the external world.

This type of theory represents a full crystallization of an idea implicit in those commandments that concern covert intention, and above all in the Tenth Commandment, "Thou shalt not covet." Jewish thinkers from the talmudic period on—the tannaitic rabbis, Philo, Maimonides, and modern authorities—have held that this prohibition refers not only to external action (as the halakhic interpretation holds) but also to the internal emotion of desire. In the Musar movement, even concerning those commandments that pertain to overt action, *kavanah*—the right motivation in the worship of God—became of utmost importance. In the words of a disciple of a Musar yeshivah, which I remember hearing some years ago: "The road to hell is paved by good *deeds.*"

What we have said up to this point may throw light on Maimonides' discussion, in Chapter 6 of the *Eight Chapters,* of the difference between the *ḥasid* (the saintly person) and the person who exercises self-restraint *(ha-kovesh et yiẓro).* Maimonides writes in opposition to "our later sages, who were infected with the illness of the *mutakallimun,*" who regarded as "rational laws" the commandments against those things "which all people commonly agree are evil, such as the shedding of blood, theft, robbery, fraud, injury to one who has done no harm, ingratitude, contempt for parents and the like." In contrast, Maimonides himself holds that such moral commandments are not rational laws and therefore have no special status from the standpoint of the deontological theory. Nevertheless, they have a very special status within religious law, from the standpoint of the anthropological theory. Nature is the basis of ethical theory not as an efficient cause but as a final one. The aim of religious philosophical ethics is the shaping of the human personality in accordance with its true nature through ethical commandments. Ethical law is natural law, insofar as it is built upon the telos of human activity. Ethics is not the final telos, but it is a necessary one. This is most true with respect to religious laws in general. Regarding ceremonial precepts a person can say, "I wish to transgress this law, but I must not, for my Father in heaven has forbidden it." This claim cannot be made regarding ethical values. In other words, our nature must be built in accordance with our moral values. Ideally, we should not even desire to commit moral transgressions. This represents the aim of ethical education.

I have thus far briefly described three types of ethical theories, but we have not yet reached the end of the itinerary. For in classical Jewish thought, philosophical ethics is but an introduction to metaphysics. The final stages are intellectual perfection, prophecy, and, in certain rare cases, "death by a kiss," the final conjunction with the upper worlds. According to Maimonides, there are four types of achievement that may be deemed perfection: possessions, bodily constitution, moral virtues, and rational attainments. Only the last, rational attainments, is truly ours. Of rational virtues it is said, "They will be yours alone" (Prov. 5:17). The anthropological ethical theory that sees ethics as the way to self-realization is an ultrarefined type of philosophical egoism. It can even become ethical solipsism, at which point the ethical relationship is no longer twosided but rather is reflexive. According to this view, even if one is a solipsist, even if the world does not exist and everything exists only in one's imagination, ethics have meaning. The utmost expression of this ethical idea is not external, but the transformation of human internal reality. The "ought" should be transformed into the "is." God should be revered with both instincts: the *yezer ha-tov* and the *yezer ha-ra,* the good and evil instincts.

At this point we encounter yet another paradox. For having finally arrived at the summit of intellectual perfection, we discover that there is yet a higher stage of morality. Maimonides reads the following verses in Jeremiah 9:22–23 as symbolizing man's destiny: "Thus said the Lord: Let not the wise man glory in his wisdom; Let not the strong man glory in his strength;

Let not the rich man glory in his riches. But only in this should he glory, that he understands and knows me." The apprehension of God thus represents man's noblest end. But Jeremiah's statement does not stop here. Knowledge of God means imitation of God, and the actions that ought to be known and imitated are lovingkindness, judgment, and righteousness—*ḥesed, mishpat,* and *ẓedakah (Guide* 3:54).

A fourth ethical theory is now apparent, ethics as *imitatio Dei,* which represents the ideal type of religious morality. After the highest expression of egoism, we find the highest expression of altruism, of grace, of self-abnegation. The creation of the world represents an act of *ḥesed,* of lovingkindness, and the highest type of morality requires imitation of God's *ḥesed.* Man's imitation of God is expressed above all in his role as leader. True *ḥesed, mishpat,* and *ẓedakah* come into being through the imitation of God. Indeed, one of the central commandments in Judaism is the imitation of God: "and you shall walk in His ways" (Deut. 28:9).

The imitation of God, the walking in his ways, is thus the highest norm determining the Jew's actions. More precisely, it is a meta-ethical principle from which religious statutes or *halakhot*—literally, ways of walking—are derived. Here *the way* is emphasized. In another sense, the imitation of God is seen not as a commandment, but as a goal and a promise. A resemblance to God is promised as a state to be attained in the End of Days and as the goal of personal salvation. This meaning of the notion is found in Plato's *Theaetetus* (176a–b) and later in Philo (*De specialibus legibus* 4:188). Through *ẓedakah* (righteousness), an individual comes to resemble God and attains immortality. This notion was also expressed by the rabbis:

> Rabbi Levi ben Ḥama said: "If one worships idols he becomes like unto them" [Ps. 115:8]; should then not one who worships God all the more become like unto Him. And whence do we know that this is so? Because it is written, Blessed is the man that trusteth in the Lord and whose trust the Lord is [Jer. 17:7].
>
> (Deut. R. 1:12)

There is an interesting parallel to this teaching in Philo, who employed the notion of *imitatio Dei* to ridicule idol worshipers. One outstanding example of the idea, among many, is the statement of Rabbi Eleazar about the *ẓaddik,* an individual who accomplished the imitation of God and reached the spiritual level designated as holiness: "Rabbi Eleazar said: 'There will come a time when "Holy" will be said before the righteous as it is said before the Holy One, blessed be He; for it is said: 'And those who remain in Zion and are left in Jerusalem . . . shall be called Holy' [Isa. 4:3]" (BT BB 75b).

A cognate though not identical idea to *imitatio Dei* is that of the creation of man in the image of God. Here the resemblance is not a command but a fact, not a goal but the point of departure for human development. Moral behavior thus has two sources. As a subject man must so direct his actions that his ways be the ways of God. But man is also an object, and as such he possesses rights, which determine realms and set the boundaries of his activities, in that he is a creature fashioned in the image of God. This idea appears in a number of variations. Another development, similar in principle to this, regards mankind as a whole, rather than the individual, as that which is in the image of God. However, both variants emphasize the value of man, the subject of human action.

A living morality is not assessed as a system of values but, as Martin Buber has observed, in the way it determines an ought, and an ought not only in the here and now. Accordingly, the tension between halakhah and ethics does not originate in an extra-halakhic category but is prominent within the halakhah itself. This tension comes to the fore when concrete *halakhot* are formulated. As in any ethical system, however, the move from the ethical principles animating halakhah to the determination of concrete norms is difficult and complex. This is an issue that is touched upon in a telling way in the following classic instance: "Rabbi Naḥman answered in the name of Rabbah ben Avuha: 'Scripture said, "But thou shalt love thy neighbor as thyself," choose for him an easy death'" (BT Ket. 37b).

Presumably, the death penalty signifies the total failure of moral principles. Nonetheless, the general moral principle, "love your neighbor as yourself," applies to this halakhic determination—the death penalty—as well. It may happen that one must perform actions that appear morally repugnant, but then, too, one is guided by moral principles that point out the way one must follow.

BIBLIOGRAPHY

S. Daniel Breslauer, *Contemporary Jewish Ethics: A Bibliographical Survey* (1985).
Marvin Fox, ed., *Modern Jewish Ethics* (1975).
Menachem Marc Kellner, *Contemporary Jewish Ethics* (1978).
Raphael Lowe, ed., *Studies in Rationalism, Judaism and Universalism* (1966).
Daniel J. Silver, ed., *Judaism and Ethics* (1970).
Shubert Spiro, *Morality, Halakha and the Jewish Tradition* (1963).

Evil

עֵר

Richard L. Rubenstein

The term *evil* (in Hebrew, *ra*) is defined by the Oxford English Dictionary as "the most comprehensive adjectival expression of disapproval, dislike, or disparagement." As such, the term means the opposite of good. There is no significant difference between the English and the Hebrew usage of the term to denote a negative state, condition, or phenomenon. There are, however, differences in the religious use of the term.

Although the term *ra* was used frequently in both biblical and rabbinic sources, these sources contain little if any systematic reflection on the related questions of the nature and source of evil and the problem of God and evil. There was, of course, considerable concern with both issues, as evidenced, for example, by the Book of Job.

Systematic reflection on the question of evil developed during the Middle Ages. Because of his preeminent authority as a master of both the philosophical and the rabbinic traditions, the opinions of Moses Maimonides are especially important. According to Maimonides, three kinds of evil can befall man: (1) Evils that are a consequence of the "coming to be" and the "passing away" of that which is endowed with matter. These include natural phenomena that negatively affect human beings, such as earthquakes, floods, and birth deformities. Since all material bodies are subject to generation and corruption, such evils are necessary for the perpetuation of the species. (2) Social evils that men inflict upon one other, such as war and violent crime. (3) Those evils that an individual inflicts upon himself as a consequence of vice and bodily overindulgence (*Guide* 3,12).

In view of the normative Jewish belief that the cosmos is the creation of an omnipotent, omniscient, benevolent deity, the question of God's involvement in the three kinds of evil is inescapable. Maimonides insisted that the misfortunes that befall individual men are without exception the divinely inflicted punishments they deserve (*Guide* 3,17). At one level, the attitude of normative Judaism toward the question of God's involvement in the existence of evil had been settled by Deutero-Isaiah (author of chs. 40–66 of the Book of Isaiah). Living in the time of Cyrus, king of Persia, Deutero-Isaiah rejected the dualistic mitigation of the problem, declaring:

> I am the Lord and there is none else
> I form light and create darkness
> I make weal and create woe [ra]—
> I the Lord do all these things.

> (Isa. 45:6–7)

Although dualism (the belief that the cosmos is governed by two conflicting powers) did not entirely disappear from Jewish sectarian circles for many centuries, after Deutero-Isaiah the problem of evil in normative Judaism was increasingly dealt with within the context of an uncompromising monotheism.

In his response to the problem of evil, Maimonides emphasized that he did not rely upon philosophical speculation but upon "what has clearly appeared as the intention of the Book of God and the books of the prophets" (ibid.). Asserting as a "fundamental principle of the Law of Moses our Master" that man has "the ability to do whatever he wills or chooses among the things concerning which he has the ability to act" and that "it is in no way possible that He [God] . . . should be unjust," Maimonides affirmed unconditionally that "all the calamities . . . and all the good things that come to men, be it a single individual or a group, are all of them determined according to the deserts of man . . . in which there is no injustice whatsoever" (ibid.). Maimonides went so far as to insist that no feeling of pain or pleasure, no matter how minute, can be other than a divinely inflicted punishment or reward. Maimonides was so insistent upon seeing misfortune as punitive that he quoted with approval Rabbi Ammi's dictum that "there is no death without sin, and no sufferings without transgression" (BT Shab. 55a).

With this citation Maimonides linked his response to the problem with the biblical account of the fall of Adam. Rabbi Ammi's statement is followed immediately by a tradition in which the ministering angels are depicted as asking the Holy One, "Why didst Thou impose the penalty of death upon Adam?" God is depicted as replying, "I gave him an easy commandment, yet he violated it" (BT Shab. 55b). The rabbinic view, reaffirmed by Maimonides, that mortality is punitive rather than natural is consistent with the biblical notion that death was the penalty inflicted upon Adam for his primal disobedience (Gen. 2:17). Thus, there is a tradition within Judaism's religious mainstream, extending from the ancient Yahwist epic through the rabbis to Maimonides and beyond, that the natural and social evils that befall man are inherently punitive in character. This opinion is consistent with the view that there is nothing intrinsically evil about God's creation. If creation were intrinsically evil or if the cosmos contained a suprahuman power capable of inciting men to evil, men could not be regarded as wholly responsible before God for their disobedience, as they are in biblical and rabbinic Judaism. Fundamental to the experience of evil in classical Judaism is the idea of the freely chosen disobedience of man.

The notion of the punitive, divinely inflicted character of evil is in turn dependent upon the distinctive view of the relationship between God and man that pervades Scripture, according to which the divine–human relationship and, most especially, the relationship between God and Israel, was defined for all time by a structure known as the *brit* or covenant. This institution resembled a treaty form used by the Hittite rulers in the ancient Near East in the fourteenth and thirteenth centuries B.C.E. to define the relationship between a royal suzerain and the vassals who ruled his client states. Both the biblical and the Hittite treaties were asymmetrical in that the superior partner (the king in Hittite documents and God in Scripture) stipulated the terms of the relationship and spelled out the dire misfortunes entailed in any act of rebellion or disobedience. Typically, in both the biblical and Hittite covenants, the vassal responded by taking a solemn oath, that is, a conditional self-curse, calling upon his God or gods to visit terrible punishments upon him should he fail to abide by the terms of the covenant.

According to biblical tradition, Israel became a community by virtue of entering into a covenant with God at Sinai. As in the Hittite covenants, the superior party in the Sinai covenant is depicted as recounting his past benefits to the inferior party: "I the Lord am your God who brought you out of the land of Egypt, out of the house of bondage" (Ex. 20:2). The superior party then prohibits the inferior from loyalty to any rival power (Ex. 20:3–5) and stipulates both the benefits that will accrue from fidelity to the covenant and the dire penalties that will follow from infidelity (Ex. 3:6). This is followed by the solemn acceptance of the covenant by the inferior party: "All the things that the Lord has commanded we will do" (Ex. 24:3, cf. Ex. 19:8). Of special importance to the covenant relationship is the conviction that God exercises his power in a manner that is both ethical and rational. Put differently, there was thought to be a predictable and dependable relationship between Israel's conduct and the manner in which God exercised his power over his people.

Scripture recounts that the covenant relationship between God and Israel was reaffirmed at Shechem when, under the leadership of Joshua, "all the tribes of Israel" pledged themselves to abide by the solemn pact (Josh. 24:1–28). The author of this biblical narrative stressed that the tribes of Israel freely chose to enter into the covenant with full knowledge of the dire consequences of infidelity. Thus, Joshua is depicted as warning the people:

> You will not be able to serve the Lord, for He is a holy God; He is a jealous God; He will not forgive your transgressions and your sins. If you forsake the Lord and serve alien gods, He will turn and deal harshly with you and make an end of you.
>
> (Josh. 24:19–20)

When we turn to the prophets, we note that they frequently depicted God as addressing Israel as if he were the plaintiff in a lawsuit against his people (Isa. 1:2ff.; Jer. 2:4ff; Micah 6:1ff). The image of the sovereign and majestic creator of heaven and earth taking upon himself the role of a plaintiff makes sense only if his complaint is that Israel has broken the terms of its sworn pact with God. The prophet served as God's mouthpiece to remind Israel of the broken covenant and to seek its restoration to wholeness.

It can thus be seen that any attempt to understand the problem of evil within Judaism must start with the absolute and enduring primacy of the covenant in defining the divine–human relationship. Even the relationship between God and Adam can be seen as a modified covenant in which God as the superior party stipulates both the conditions of his protection and the cost of disobedience (Gen. 2:17). Similarly, God is explicitly depicted as establishing a covenant with Noah and his descendants (Gen. 9:1–17). These covenants anticipate the covenantal relationship between God and Israel. In the light of that primacy, there can be in normative Judaism only one definition of the evil men do, namely, rebellion against or transgression of God's covenant. There is no autonomous realm of the ethical in covenantal religion. All offenses are ultimately made against the Lord of the covenant, as is evident from the biblical account of the covenant at Sinai. The relationships between man and man, such as the honor due to parents and prohibitions against murder, adultery, theft, and false witness, are not portrayed as expressions of an independent ethical or legal realm. Instead, they are depicted as covenantal injunctions, as, indeed, are all of the Torah's norms. The covenant and it alone legitimates the corpus of behavioral norms in Scripture.

In the light of the definition of human evil in biblical and rabbinic Judaism as breach of the covenant, natural and social misfortunes, such as plague, famine, and war, are, as noted, interpreted as God's just and appropriate response. The justice of even the worst misfortunes meted out to those who break the covenant follows from the fact that the conditions of the relationship were spelled out explicitly in the original pact. The unremitting ethical rationalism of this system is also manifest in the fact that neither at Sinai nor at Shechem do we find even a hint of a suprahuman power, such as Satan, moving Israel to disobedience. Israel's disobedience is seen as freely chosen. By rejecting the dualism inherent in affirming a source of evil other than God, Deutero-Isaiah preserved the unremitting ethical rationalism of the system. The volitional element in both compliance and deviation and, hence, the offender's responsibility for the results of his conduct are stressed in Deuteronomy:

> I call heaven and earth to witness against you this day: I have put before you life and death, blessing and curse: Choose life if you and your offspring would live.
>
> (Deut. 30:19; cf. Jer. 21:8)

Obedience to the terms of the covenant is the path of life; rejection of the covenant is ipso facto the individual's election of misfortune, unhappiness, and death. The latter cannot be seen as evil insofar as they are the just response of the offended deity. Similarly, in the case of communal disasters, the community's sufferings were understood to be misfortunes Israel called down upon itself when, at Sinai and Shechem, it bound itself by an oath to the covenant, calling upon God to punish it were it ever to prove unfaithful. As can be seen from the twenty-eighth chapter of Deuteronomy, no matter how bitter are the misfortunes visited by God upon the offender, they are regarded as no more than the offender's just deserts.

Obviously, such a system invites attempts at mitigation. The figures of the serpent and Satan represent such attempts. If there is a supernatural force tempting men to evil and rebellion, then disobedience need no longer be regarded as wholly a matter of free choice, and misfortune need no longer be seen as an expression of divine justice. The Book of Job is another such attempt. Its strategy of mitigation replaces the stern ethical rationalism of covenant theology with an understandable retreat into mystery. This has been a perennial strategy throughout Jewish history in the face of great communal disaster. Instead of answering the question of why evil afflicts the innocent, Job ends with the assertion of the radical incommensurability of the ways of God and the ways of man (Job 38:1–42:6). By contrast, in strict covenant theology there can be no innocent sufferers.

Other strategies of mitigation included the interpretation of affliction as a "chastisement of love" inflicted upon the individual to increase his future reward in the World to Come. This view was given expression by Rabbi Eleazar ben Zadok:

> God imposes suffering on the righteous in this world that they may inherit the world to come. . . . God gives the wicked abundant good in this world, to drive them down into, and cause them to inherit, the lower depths of hell.
>
> (BT Kid. 40b)

Whenever overwhelming historical catastrophe overcame Israel, the problem of evil confronted the community with special urgency. Normally, the view prevailed that misfortune was God's just punishment for Israel's failure to keep the covenant. Put differently, misfortune was regarded as the fulfillment of the terrible curses promised in Deuteronomy 28:1–68, such as:

> And as the Lord once delighted in making you prosperous and many, so will the Lord delight in causing you to perish and in wiping you out.
>
> (Deut. 28:63)

Thus, when Nebuchadnezzar conquered Judea and destroyed Jerusalem's sanctuary, Jeremiah depicted God as declaring, "Assuredly, . . . I am delivering this city into the hands of the Chaldeans and of King Nebuchadnezzar of Babylon" (Jer. 32:28). Jeremiah further depicted God as declaring that the offense for which Israel and Judah were to be punished was breach of the covenant (Jer. 32:30–35). Similarly, when Jerusalem fell to the Romans at the end of the long and bloody Judaeo-Roman war of 66–70 C.E., that defeat, with its terrible loss of life, was interpreted by the rabbis as God's further punishment against his elect community. Among the abundant sources that give expression to this view is the midrash on Lamentations, *Ekah Rabbah,* which was traditionally studied on Tishah be-Av, the Ninth of Av, the day which in Jewish tradition commemorated both the first and second destructions of Jerusalem.

The religious problem of evil gained unprecedented urgency for Jewish religious thought in the aftermath of the worst communal disaster ever experienced in all of Jewish history, the extermination of the European Jews during World War II. From the perspective of the normative theology of covenant and election, the Holocaust could be understood only as God's just and righteous punishment of Israel for her failure to abide by her ancient and immutable covenant. Nevertheless, even among the most stringently Orthodox, few thinkers were able to interpret the Holocaust as Jeremiah had interpreted the first fall of Jerusalem and Rabbi Johanan ben Zakkai had interpreted the second. Once again, Jewish religious thinkers attempted to mitigate the harsh and uncompromising ethical rationalism of covenant theology. In general, the mitigations sought to reaffirm the abiding validity and credibility of God's relation to Israel, while rejecting the punitive interpretation of the Holocaust. Thinkers such as Arthur A. Cohen and Eliezer Berkovits have limited God's role to that of teacher of essentially free human agents and identified the Holocaust as the work of human beings who have rejected the teachings of the teacher. Emil L. Fackenheim has adopted a different approach, rejecting the ethical rationalism of covenant theology when literally understood while metaphorically reaffirming God's presence in Jewish history. Still another strategy of mitigation has been advanced by Ignaz Maybaum, who has reaffirmed the literal meaning of the covenant while identifying the Holocaust victims as vicarious sacrificial offerings for the redemption of humanity rather than the objects of divine punitive justice.

This writer, alone among modern theologians, has insisted that, if the covenant as traditionally understood within the Jewish religious mainstream is to be reaffirmed in the aftermath of the Holocaust, none of the mitigating strategies will prove to be of enduring credibility. This writer has further argued that after Auschwitz, Jewish religious belief has been thrust on the horns of an exceedingly bitter dilemma: One can affirm either the abiding validity of Israel's covenant with God or the nonpunitive character of the Holocaust—but not both. If God is taken to be the all-powerful author of the covenant, the biblical and rabbinic interpretation of the first and second destructions of Jerusalem must be seen as the model for the Jewish religious interpretation of the Holocaust. If it is no longer possible to interpret Israel's history in accordance with this model, the traditional view that God acts justly in Israel's history loses much of its residual credibility.

Thus, in the aftermath of the Holocaust, the religious problem of evil raises questions that go to the very heart of Israel's perennial understanding of its relation to God and indeed of the viability of Judaism as a religious tradition. It may be that the metaphor for the understanding of Israel's relationship with God that arose out of the international politics of the ancient Near East in the fourteenth and thirteenth centuries B.C.E. must give way to an as yet unformulated new metaphor.

BIBLIOGRAPHY

Eliezer Berkovits, *Faith After the Holocaust* (1973).
Arthur A. Cohen, *The Tremendum: A Theological Interpretation of the Holocaust* (1981).
Delbert R. Hillers, *Covenant: The History of a Biblical Idea* (1969).
Moses Maimonides, *The Guide of the Perplexed,* Shlomo Pines, tr. (1963), Part 3.
Ignaz Maybaum, *The Face of God After Auschwitz* (1965).
George E. Mendenhall, *The Tenth Generation: The Origins of the Biblical Tradition* (1973).
Richard L. Rubenstein, *After Auschwitz* (1966).
Richard L. Rubenstein, *The Religious Imagination* (1968).

Exegesis

פרשנות

Moshe Greenberg

Jewish exegesis works with a canon, or a set of inspired books, subject to the following conditions: (1) the number and the text of these books are fixed and may not be added to or brought up to date; (2) the books are authoritative—that is, they bind the Jews to a certain worldview and way of life; (3) they are perceived as a harmonious whole, conveying a coherent divine message for the guidance of the individual and the community. Since the Jews have clung to this canon through the ages and amid the most diverse circumstances, an unbridgeable gap in understanding and perceived relevance might well have interposed between them and these books were it not for the succession of exegetes whose ever-renewing interpretation of the Bible maintained its vitality for the faith community. The continuing sacred status of the Bible among the Jews is due entirely to their faithful work.

The concerns of Jewish Bible exegesis arise from the aforesaid conditions; they include (1) how to enlarge the content of the closed canon so as to apply it to new topics; (2) how to render the fixed text pliable and subject to change in accord with arising cultural and intellectual needs; (3) how to relate to the original sense of Scripture after exegesis had departed from it; and (4) in modern times, how to maintain the sacred (or at least the special) status of the canonical literature in the face of scientific and historical challenges to the traditional conceptions of its truth and validity.

Among the earliest aims of exegesis was the application of prophecy to current events. In the mid-second century B.C.E., when the canon of the Prophets had long been closed, the Seleucid persecution of pious Jews in Judea awakened interest in the ancient prophecies of consolation. Daniel 9 records the solution of a contemporary visionary to the riddle of the delayed fulfillment of God's promise revealed to Jeremiah (in the sixth century B.C.E.) to restore Jerusalem's glory in seventy years: seventy sabbaths of years—that is, 490—were meant. The sectarians of the Qumran commune in the Judean desert read into the ancient prophecies allusions to their situation in the second or first centuries B.C.E. Thus, their commentary to Habakkuk 2:15 reads: "Its interpretation concerns the Wicked Priest [the archenemy of the sect] who pursued the Righteous Teacher [the inspired leader of the sect], to destroy him . . . in his exile abode, and at the appointed time of the rest-day of atonement appeared to them to destroy them and make them stumble [= err] on the sabbath-day fast of their rest."

Legal exegesis derived new laws from the old scriptural ones, and connected traditional and innovated unwritten laws to biblical verses. For example, Hillel, in the first century B.C.E., once used three modes of interpretation in order to decide that the paschal sacrifice might be slaughtered even if it fell due on the sabbath, when ordinary slaughter is forbidden. These were (1) analogy alone: since the regular daily offering is a public sacrifice and so is the paschal offering, the latter overrides sabbath prohibitions, as does the former; (2) argument *a fortiori*: if the regular daily offering, for whose omission there is no penalty of excision, overrides the sabbath prohibitions, the paschal offering, for whose omission that penalty is exacted, surely overrides it; and (3) argument from identical phrases: in both offerings the expression "in its appointed time" appears, hence rules governing the time of each are the same. Seven hermeneutical principles or modes (*middot*) are ascribed to Hillel; Rabbi Ishmael, a second-century C.E. sage, is purported to be the author of an expanded list of thirteen.[1] Reference to these modes is surprisingly infrequent in talmudic literature; in effect the constructive work of the legists proceeded very freely.

During this age of exuberant creativity, a period extending from the second century B.C.E. to the sixth century C.E., no preference was given to the plain (contextual) sense of the text over any other sense derived from or based on it, however fancifully. Indeed, it was a cardinal talmudic principle that every biblical utterance was polysemous: alongside its contextual sense it might yield many others when taken in isolation. The principle was "heard" in a prophetic passage, itself treated as polysemous: "Behold, My word is like fire—declares the Lord—and like a hammer that shatters rock" (Jer. 23:29). Contextually, this means that overwhelming power and penetrating impact characterize genuine, as opposed to spurious, prophecy; isolated and interpreted as expressing an exegetical axiom, the passage is heard to say, "As a hammer[stroke] scatters many slivers (or sparks) so a single Scriptural passage yields many senses" (BT Sanh. 34a). A psalm text displaying a commonplace parallelistic number pattern (x / x + 1) when taken by itself serves as another proof-text for this axiom: "'One thing God has spoken; two things have I heard' (Ps. 62:12)—a single Scriptural passage yields several senses, but one and the same sense cannot be derived from several passages" (Ibid.). This axiom lies at the heart of the proliferation of talmudic midrash, that searching (darash) of Scripture for its latent meanings, its suggestions and associations.

The danger to recognition of the plain sense posed by the prevalence of midrash is reflected in the warning principle: "The plain sense of a Scriptural passage is never superseded." An example of its operation is the following (BT Shab. 63a): Rabbi Eliezer ruled that a sword was an ornamental part of male attire, and hence might be worn on the sabbath without violating the sabbath ban on carriage, on the basis of the verse, "Gird your sword upon your thigh, O hero, in your splendor and your glory" (Ps. 45:4). Another sage protested: it was common knowledge that the verse had been interpreted allegorically, "sword" being Torah learning (and "hero" being the talmudic sage; hence the verse could not serve to decide the status of a real sword). To this came the reply, "The plain sense of a Scriptural passage is never superseded"; that is, midrashic, "second" meanings—here the allegory—add to the primary one but never annul it (hence the Psalm verse may be invoked to prove that a sword is an ornament for a man). This assertion of the permanent validity of the primary, contextual sense, despite all hermeneutical reinterpretation, was repeatedly resorted to during the Middle Ages to defend the plain (historical) sense against subversion by Christian spiritualization and allegorization.

The luxuriance of talmudic-midrashic exegesis turned the Bible into a treasury of meaning that has proven to be inexhaustible. Jewish interpreters through the ages have been shaped by it—some adopting it or continuing to create in imitation of it, some opposing its whimsicality in favor of a single, true sense of Scripture, and some simply revelling noncommittally and eclectically in its wealth.

Methodic Jewish Bible interpretation arose during the conflict between talmudic Judaism and its adversaries during the early centuries of Islam, the seventh to tenth centuries C.E. Jews participated in the cultural ferment caused by the challenge of an Islam that was soon fortified by the best minds and philosophies of the age and that posed a threat to all traditional faiths and authorities. The most serious manifestation of dissolution among Jewry was the Karaite schism, inaugurated by Anan ben David during the eighth century; rejecting talmudism in the name of rationalism and individualism, it sought legitimation by an independent and often capricious interpretation of Scripture. For example, Anan rejected the talmudic ban on eating meat with milk products by interpreting the proof-text, "You shall not boil a kid (gedi) in its mother's milk" (Ex. 23:19)—so greatly extended by the Tal-mud—to mean "Do not cause fruit (meged) to ripen by [daubing it with] sap of its tree."[2] By boldly metaphorizing the verb and the prepositional phrase, Anan obtained a meaning that related the clause to what precedes it, namely, the admonition to bring first fruits to the temple. Furthermore, freethinkers both inside and outside of Jewry subjected all revealed Scrip-ture to rationalistic criticism, ridiculing their anthropomorphism, their fab-ulous tales, and such theological scandals as sacrificial worship. Talmudism, at first helpless, eventually found its champion in Saadiah ben Joseph, Gaon of Sura (ninth–tenth centuries), who met these challenges by devising a methodic exegesis. The need, as Saadiah saw it, was to define the conditions in which the language of Scripture could or must be metaphorized, so that, on the one hand, the caprices of the Karaites might be controlled and, on the other, objections to the literal sense of Scripture might be parried. Saa-diah formulated the following grand rule: the common, prevalent sense of words must determine the meaning of a passage, except when it would yield a meaning that conflicted with one of the four sources of knowledge: (1) the senses (that Eve was "the mother of all the living" [Gen. 3:20] cannot be taken literally); (2) reason ("the Lord your God is a consuming fire" [Deut. 4:24] cannot be taken literally, for while fire is a created thing, reason dictates that God is not); (3) a clear passage ("Do not try the Lord your God" [Deut. 6:16] is a clear passage that requires giving some kind of a figurative interpretation to Mal. 3:10, "Bring the full tithe . . . and thus put me to the test"); (4) the oral (talmudic) tradition ("You shall not boil a kid in its mother's milk" must be metaphorized so as to signify a ban on eating meat with milk). In other words, as revealed truth, the Bible must be recon-cilable with the highest attainments of the human mind. The equation of the truths of reason and revelation asserted by Saadiah remained a govern-ing principle of Jewish exegesis until its overthrow in the seventeenth century by Baruch Spinoza, who insisted that the meaning of Scripture could not be prejudged by the antecedent conviction that it was equivalent to the truth as determined through reason.

Subsequent Jewish exegesis is characterized by (1) its incorporation of the advances of Judeo-Spanish Hebrew philology—for example, the discovery of the triconsonantal nature of Hebrew roots, making possible a scientific grammar, etymology, and lexicography; utilization of Arabic, Aramaic, and postbiblical Hebrew to clarify obscurities in biblical Hebrew; (2) ever-increasing skill in, and preference for, ascertaining the plain sense—based on context and on parallel and analogous passages—and an awareness of the invalidity of midrashic interpretations as an exegetical resource (most impressive strides toward emancipation from midrash were made in the school of Rashi, eleventh–twelfth centuries); (3) a growing interest—particularly in reaction to Christian spiritualizing exegesis—in the historical context of prophecies, curbing Christological reference by setting the prophecies in a specific time frame (for example, David Kimhi).

From the vantage point of an exegete whose aim is to ascertain the primary sense of Scripture, premodern Jewish exegesis suffers from two disabilities. First, in matters legal and normative for religious practice, it submits to the authority of the Talmud, interpreting the Bible according to the pertinent talmudic view (including the dogma of the supremacy of Moses' prophecy, which necessitated conforming all the rest of the Bible to it). This submission was, first of all, a response to Karaism, and then a reflection of the role of law as the bond of the Diaspora—the guarantor of unity and survival despite scattering and the temptations of heresy, apostasy, and free-thinking. Its effect on the interpretation of biblical passages having legal implications is harmonizing and often enough distorting. It is the unusual commentator—for example, Samuel ben Meir, a grandson of Rashi—who shows independence of talmudic authority in interpreting legal texts, although it is not clear, in most such cases, what motivates this merely academic exercise. On the other hand, in treating matter that has no normative implications, the outstanding commentators, such as Rashi, ibn Ezra, Nahmanides, and Abrabanel, have no compunctions about differing from the Talmud among themselves. From time to time, in an entirely sporadic manner, a nontalmudic interpretation of a legal topic may occur in the writings of one of these commentators, but its rarity only proves the rule.

The second disability of premodern exegesis is that in identifying the teaching of Scripture with the best current thought, most exegetes interpreted passages of ethical and theological import in accord with their favorite philosophical or mystical system. An example of the consequences is the particularly powerful effect of Bahya's *Hovot ha-Levavot* (*Duties of the Heart*) and Maimonides' *Guide of the Perplexed* on the exegesis of Psalms and the wisdom books (Proverbs, Ecclesiastes), markedly diminishing the medieval Jewish contribution to the understanding of the plain sense of these biblical books.

The issues of modern exegesis were posed by Baruch Spinoza in his *Theological Political Tractate,* published in 1670, in which he sought to dethrone Scripture and its traditional interpreters by separating the question of meaning from truth. Judgment of the truth content of the Bible, Spinoza declared, must follow upon the determination of what it means. That determination can rest only on a philological method analogous to the method of natural science: collection of data, classification, and, finally, generalization. In no way may information from outside the text of the Bible be imported into the determination of what its words mean. Knowledge of the historical context of the various books and their authors is also needed for ascertaining their sense. Since the intended audience of the prophets consisted of sinners and common folk, it was wrong to suppose that any sort of philosophic sophistication was requisite for understanding their message. On the contrary, Scripture addresses the imagination and the passions rather than reason; much of it is "unintelligible," that is, irrational. (The Jewish medieval commentators would not have disagreed with Spinoza about the method of ascertaining the plain sense of Scripture; they would have insisted, however, that it is but a cloak for higher ideas.)

With the advance of empirical sciences, modern exegesis did in fact relinquish the medieval claim that the Bible was a source of scientific and philosophic knowledge. Instead, it came to be appreciated for other virtues. In the eighteenth century, the aesthetic and poetic qualities of the Scriptures were discovered and carefully delineated by gentile and Jewish scholars such as Robert Lowth, Johann Gottfried Herder, Moses Hayyim Luzzatto, and Moses Mendelssohn in his *Biur*. The ethical and moral excellence of the law and the prophets was stressed by Samuel David Luzzatto in the nineteenth century.

As biblical criticism broke down the integrity of the books of the Bible, assigning their composition to various hands and times, and as comparative data revealed more and more similarities between it and the literatures of neighboring peoples from which the Israelites most likely borrowed, Jewish exegesis of the twentieth century has developed along the following lines: (1) The Bible is approached as a "special" book whose divine origin is reflected in the spiritual riches it yields to the careful, reverent reader. While not assuming that the received text is perfect, the exegete, aware of the trail of discredited emendations of suspected corruptions made by earlier critics, is wary of adding to them by making further conjectural emendations of his own. And while not denying the genetic heterogeneity of any given book, he is chiefly concerned with its finally redacted, canonical form—whether because that alone is a fact of historical import, or because, with Franz Rosenzweig, he resolves the critical siglum R (for redactor) as *rabbenu* (our teacher), "For whoever he was and whatever material he had at his disposal, he is our Teacher, his theology, our Teaching."[3] Modern Jewish exegetes such as Benno Jacob, Franz Rosenzweig, Martin Buber, and Moses David Cassuto have concentrated their efforts on showing the design in the composition of biblical books and the leading motifs, key words, and ideas that link complexes into unities. In the wake of these efforts, a new appreciation of the art of storytelling and poetry is being gained, as in the work of Meir Weiss. Talmudic-midrashic literature is receiving new attention for the light it sheds on the principles of biblical composition (for example, association of ideas) and its illustration of exegetical processes that can be discerned as already present within the Bible itself (later texts building on earlier ones). (2) The comparative resources of ancient Near Eastern culture are exploited for showing not only what Israel held in common with its neighbors, but wherein it differed from them. This need not be (though it often is) motivated by apologetics, but by a sincere, scholarly pursuit of the individual character of biblical creativity.

Thus, the modern substitute for finding in Scripture the highest and best truths is to find in it design that bespeaks subtle intelligence, and an artful observation of and reflection on a reality that can still speak to the contemporary reader. Furthermore, the peculiarly Israelite character of the Bible, demonstrable by comparison, enables us to discern in it the origin of the ethos and the values comprising the Jewish expression through the ages. Jewish exegesis thus continues to serve the faith community by providing it access to its basic document that both edifies the community and enables it to retain its identity through continuity with its past.

REFERENCES

1. See W. S. Towner, "Hermeneutical Systems of Hillel and the Tannaim: A Fresh Look," in *Hebrew Union College Annual* 53 (1982).
2. A. Harkavy, *Aus den ältesten Käraischen Gesetzbüchern* (1903), 151–52.
3. Franz Rosenzweig, "Die Einheit der Bibel," in Martin Buber and Franz Rosenzweig, *Die Schrift und ihre Verdeutschung* (1936), 47.

BIBLIOGRAPHY

Salo Baron, *A Social and Religious History of the Jews* 6 (1958), 253–313.
"Bible Exegesis," in *Jewish Encyclopaedia* 3 (1902).
Moshe Greenberg, ed., *Parshanut ha-Mikra ha-Yehudit: Pirkei Mavo* (1983). Contains extensive bibliography.
Simon Rawidowicz, "On Interpretation," in Nahum N. Glatzer, ed., *Studies in Jewish Thought,* (1974).
E. I. J. Rosenthal, "The Study of the Bible in Medieval Judaism," in G. W. H. Lampe, ed., *The Cambridge History of the Bible* 2 (1969), 252–79.
Franz Rosenzweig, "Die Einheit der Bibel," in Martin Buber and Franz Rosenzweig, *Die Schrift und ihre Verdeutschung* (1936), 46–54.
W. S. Towner, "Hermeneutical Systems of Hillel and the Tannaim: A Fresh Look," in *Hebrew Union College Annual* 53 (1982).
Geza Vermes, *The Dead Sea Scrolls in English* (1962), 214–47.
Meir Weiss, *The Bible from Within* (1984).

Exile

גלות

Arnold Eisen

The banishment of Adam and Eve at the very beginning of Genesis introduces a theme that stamps all the Five Books of Moses. From Abraham's departures for Canaan and beyond, through the Israelites' extended wanderings in the wilderness, to the marvelous promise of home conveyed near the end of Deuteronomy and promptly overwhelmed by the threat of renewed homelessness, the Torah is preoccupied with exile as it never could be with Paradise. So it is with the rest of the Bible, and so it has been with Jewish reflection ever since. One senses in this attention to the themes of loss and estrangement a desire to exorcise the terrors of dispersion by giving them a name; certainly there is comfort in knowing that one's own fate has been shared by one's ancestors, and there is even—given the rich legacy of narratives that we shall survey briefly here—a modicum of explanation. That tradition of reflection, unbroken since Genesis, has not lost its hold even today, when part of the Jewish people has returned to its promised land: the burden of history is too strong and the Jews are too well-schooled in the meanings of human exile to call the place of their return by the simple—but messianic—name *home*.

The two primary meanings or dimensions of *galut* (exile) appear at the outset of Genesis' account of human history, and have been intertwined in Jewish reflection ever after. Exile is, first, the metaphysical or existential condition of human beings upon God's earth. Adam and Eve, exiled from the Garden, become strangers to both innocence and perfection. They are outcasts from God's presence as well, destined to seek (and hide from) their creator. They stand at one remove from all other creatures—including each other. Finally, the earth from which they have come, and to which they shall return in death—the very *adamah* from which humanity (*adam*) gets its name—is cursed because of their sin, and their relationship to it is eternally disrupted. Henceforth they will "till the ground from which [humanity] was taken" by the sweat of their brow (Gen. 3:17–20), the word *taken* reverberating in the triple sense of birth, alienation, and banishment.

The second punishment in biblical history, the second exile, both extends the first and introduces the other primary dimension of *galut*: the political. Cain (Gen. 4:11–16) shall be "more cursed than the ground" originally cursed by the sin of his parents, Adam and Eve. They were condemned to struggle for daily bread; Cain is told that his labors will prove futile. They were banished from Eden; he is cast out from everywhere, a ceaseless wanderer. The punishment is indeed "too great to bear." As if metaphysical exile "from off the face of the earth" as well as from "God's face" were not enough, Cain will suffer the fate of the alien denied the protection of his clan. "Anyone who meets me may kill me." God must therefore become Cain's sole protector—an eerie foreshadowing of the destiny of God's people Israel. They too will be made strangers, by God's will, in strange lands, and safeguarded only because God's blessing proves a shelter as well as a curse.

When Isaac digs the wells dug by his father Abraham, reenacting in the third of Genesis' "wife-sister" stories the pattern of his father's relations with the local powers that be, his demonstrable blessedness excites the envy of his hosts, who therefore harass and finally expel him (Gen. 18–21). "Why have you come to me," Isaac demands when the Philistine king appears with the chief of his army, "seeing that you have been hostile to me and have driven me away from you?" Their answer is equally blunt. "We now see plainly that the Lord has been with you and we thought: Let there be a sworn treaty between our two parties . . . that you will do us no harm. . . . From now on, be you blessed of the Lord!" (Gen. 26:27–29). Their hatred is overcome by his usefulness—a lesson learned to great advantage by the original court Jew, Joseph, and pondered by later generations who saw in these stories of the ancestors a "sign for the children"

(Nahmanides, *Commentary on the Torah,* ad loc. Gen. 12:6). Joseph is forced to serve his earthly lord, the Pharaoh (and in the process, to exploit that lord's subject population), because his heavenly Lord has sent him into exile in order to work his own mysterious purposes with Israel. Only in death does Joseph return home to his native soil—precisely like the first man of whom Genesis tells us. Don Isaac Abrabanel—adviser to Spanish kings, and then exiled ignominiously with the rest of his people in 1492—could not but identify with Joseph. He understood his own rise and fall all too well (*Commentary on the Torah,* ad loc. Gen. 41:45, 47:21).

These founding narratives set a pattern for Jewish reflection that has continued until our own day. The commentators found in these stories of ancient Israelites invaluable lessons concerning the estate of humanity as a whole. The homelessness of the ancient ones furnished a model of the rigors facing political aliens in any time and place as well as a reproof of those who mistakenly believed that they were or could be at home upon the earth, which in truth belongs to God. Home, for Jews, would always mean far more than conquest, which in any event could never establish absolute ownership. It is rather a state of being, which land makes possible but cannot in and of itself establish; it is a sacred order of commandment in which the curses pronounced in the Garden of Eden are in large measure reversed. The quintessential description of homecoming in Chapter 26 of Deuteronomy (later made the centerpiece of the Passover Haggadah) speaks in the future perfect tense of blessings made palpable, promises fulfilled, covenantal relations of justice and harmony with one's fellows, and a renewed intimacy with God and the land. At home upon God's earth, the Israelite can pray, and his prayer is that the order he has been privileged to know should continue, not that it be established against all expectation. The language, like the land, is full to overflowing. But it is all too good to be true. The threat of renewed exile follows at once (Deut. 28:15–68), and that threat just as quickly turns to prophecy (Deut. 30:1, 31:16–20). Exile proves to be the rule, not the exception. Genesis is not a mere prologue, but the main act of the human drama. Home remains an affair of the imagination, located in the future perfect tense.

The prophets expounded these lessons imparted in the shadow of Genesis by the Deuteronomist. They also introduced the terms by which Israel's destiny was henceforth defined: *golah,* the exiled population, and *galut,* the act of expulsion and later the condition of exile, both political and metaphysical. Israel had been banished as punishment for its disobedience, just like the original exiles from the Garden. But there was comfort in this chastisement: the wilderness of Babylonia could prove a testing ground preliminary to homecoming, just as had the wilderness of Sinai, provided Israel purified its heart through suffering and determined to cleave to the covenant. The people could return from exile to inherit the land conquered but not properly lived in the first time. And when these prophecies of return had also come to fruition, and Israel had been replanted in its land—only to lose it again when history proved recalcitrant and the sacred order elusive—the Torah's double vision of failure and perfection, curse and blessings, proved more important than ever before. God's sanctuary lay in ruins and his people were decimated, but their exile was not without precedent and, therefore, not without hope. God's Messiah would come, in time, and in the meantime his presence would join his people in exile from the land.

It is clear from the Mishnah—redacted several generations after the Destruction in 70 C.E. and formulated in part amidst the chaos that preceded and attended it—that exile for the rabbis was coextensive with the earth. No place in the world lay outside its domain, the land of Israel included. The task that the rabbis faced and, to a degree, accomplished was enormous: carving out, in the midst of idolatrous time and space, an order in which life could nevertheless be lived according to God's command. The land of Israel remained the focus of that labor. It retained unique sanctity despite the pollution that had utterly overrun its borders. But the condition of the land was not essentially different from that of all those lands to which God's presence, with his people, had been exiled. The Palestinian and Babylonian Talmuds, along with contemporary collections of midrash, elaborate further on the exilic construction of sacred order—at home and abroad, in better times and worse, in anger or resignation. In the space between destruction and redemption that the rabbis called *ha-zeman ha-zeh,* "the present time," life could be properly lived in no other way. Meaning would not exist unless they put it there: "From the day the Temple was destroyed, the Holy One Blessed be He has in His world only the four cubits of the halakhah" (BT Ber. 8a). Homelessness, comprehended through the inherited categories, had to be resisted; homecoming, initiated by God's Messiah, could only be awaited. Even the world to come was imagined in terms of return to the land: "All Israelites have a share in the world to come, for it is written [Isa. 60:21]: 'Thy people also shall be all righteous, they shall inherit the land for ever'" (M. Sanh. 10:1).

Exile was variously borne and perceived, of course. Moses Maimonides, like Jeremiah, counseled patience, and discouraged calculation of the "end-time" that would terminate exile. Judah Halevi, by contrast, chastised his people in *The Kuzari* for not trying with every means at their disposal to return to the land instead of permitting both it and themselves to languish.

The commentators regularly interpreted events of their day as fulfillments of biblical tales read as prophecy or foreshadowing: "signs for the children" to be pondered for their implications and embraced for their consolation. Two developments in the wake of the Expulsion from Spain merit special attention. The first, emphasized by historian Haim Hillel Ben Sasson, finds in works such as Solomon Ibn Verga's *Shevet Yehudah* and in contemporary homiletic literature the beginnings of political awareness. Reasons of state figure as a cause of the latest banishment alongside divine displeasure. The second, drawn to our attention by the research of Gershom Scholem, was the daring interpretation given *galut* by the kabbalah of Isaac Luria, who took the rabbinic notion of God's presence in exile one giant step further. In Luria's view of things the entire cosmos, including God, was "shattered," fragmented, out of place. "Seen from this vantage point, the existence and destiny of Israel, with all their terrible reality, with all their intricate drama of ever-renewed calling and ever-renewed guilt, are fundamentally a symbol of the true state of all being."[1] Israel could return home only when the *tik-kun* or repair of all creation had been completed.

Baruch Spinoza and Moses Mendelssohn, who inaugurated modern Jewish thought by respectively challenging and redefining the purpose of Jewish existence, wrought three further changes in the classical understanding of exile. First, homelessness, like the land, was demystified, stripped of the layers of imagery and significance in which it had been draped for centuries. Second, the meaning of exile and return was universalized. Jerusalem came to connote the state of perfection centered there in the imagination of the prophets; it could rise "in England's green and pleasant land" or anywhere else. Exile indicated the human condition short of that perfection, and so, in the minds of many Jewish thinkers in the West, bore no relation to the real land of Israel, where Jews no longer lived. Dispersion was in fact a blessing and not a curse: the ground on which God's word would be planted and come to fruition. Third, the concepts of homelessness and homecoming were further translated into strictly political terms. Exile signified a lack of rights or equality to be remedied in the countries where Jews were at present aliens, but in the future would be citizens. Redemption would come with emancipation rather than ingathering—until the founders of modern Zionism despaired of both this and the traditional conception of homecoming, and determined to bring the Jews back to their real home, the original home, by secular political means of which the classical sources could not have conceived, let alone approved.

Zionist historiography is nearly unanimous in regarding this return as the only option available to Jews in the modern period. Ben Sasson applauded the dawning political awareness he discerned. Scholem contrasted the "return to history," the "modern Jewish readiness for irrevocable action in the concrete realm," with the "life lived in deferment" of the exile, "in which nothing can be done definitively."[2] Yehezkel Kaufmann, in the most profound meditation to date on the experience of *galut* (*Golah ve-Nekhar,* 1929–32), demanded that his generation strive with all its might for *geulah* or redemption—understood in the political sense exclusively: sovereignty, territory, a real holding in the world. Indeed, Zionist thought as a whole can usefully be classified according to the emphasis upon one or the other dimension of exile that thinkers of every variety "negated." Ahad Ha'am's "spiritual Zionism," transmitted by Martin Buber and A. D. Gordon, emphasized the metaphysical. Theodor Herzl and his disciples (for example, Kaufmann, Jacob Klatzkin, and Vladimir Jabotinsky) stressed the political. Religious Zionists, and preeminently Abraham Isaac Kook, sought synthesis. Only they for whom return from exile meant "the beginning of the flowering of our redemption" dared claim that the political and metaphysical dimensions sundered at the Destruction might soon be reunited. Other religious thinkers were profoundly skeptical, whether Orthodox Jews, for whom the return was an unlawful "hastening of the End," or Franz Rosenzweig, whose magisterial quest for eternity in *The Star of Redemption* is premised on the divorce of the Jewish people from the accoutrements of historical normality: land, language, the laws of the state.

The split between the political and the metaphysical also characterizes contemporary debate between Israel and the Diaspora. Thinkers in the former, for whom *galut* remains a concept of central importance, insist that homecoming has now been accomplished, or at least initiated, and that America, like all previous way stations of Jewish wandering, is exile. American thinkers, for whom *galut* is at best of marginal concern, tend to argue that in political terms America is different from exiles past, while reminding the Israelis that in the metaphysical sense every place on earth is exile until the redemption—even the land of Israel. Both parties draw on the same tradition, but emphasize different strands; they are alike, too, in that for both (and indeed for contemporary non-Jewish religious thought) the significance of the return from exile is predominantly mythic, conceived in the terms we have surveyed. Deserts bloom; life emerges from the ashes of the Holocaust; faith, for once, is rewarded; power is alternately contained and inflated by the vestments of the sacred; normality is mitigated or even transcended. Much of the power of the Zionist vision over the past century has lain in non-Jewish refractions of the biblical–rabbinic vision that have been pressed back into Jewish service. Prophetic jeremiads resounded in the young Marx's theory of alienation and figured crucially, from Moses Hess onward, in socialist Zionism. The image of a world adrift, cast off from the anchor of faith and meaning, became in Friedrich Nietzsche the distinctive mark of modernity—and in Martin Buber that which organic Jewish communities in the land would rectify. Zion attracted young Zionists, in other words, because it was *home* as well as "the land"; exile repelled them because it was not only *galut* but the universal human condition of homelessness—which might now be overcome.

The reborn Jewish state, then, remains captive to the tradition if not the reality of exile. So long as its two dimensions dominate Jewish historical memory—so long, that is, as Jews witness to the awareness of being somewhere else than where God is and humanity should be—normalization will seem an impossible aspiration. For all the world is exile, even if some times and places are more exilic than others. Life either is "lived in deferment" to a significant degree, awaiting the messianic homecoming, or it is not the life for which Abraham commenced his people's wanderings "to the land that I will show you" (Gen. 12:1).

REFERENCES

1. Gershom Scholem, "Kabbalah and Myth," in *On the Kabbalah and Its Symbolism* (1969), 116.
2. Gershom Scholem, *The Messianic Idea in Judaism* (1971), 35.

BIBLIOGRAPHY

Haim Hillel Ben Sasson, "Golei Sefarad al Azmo," in *Zion* 26 (1961).
Arnold Eisen, *Galut: Modern Jewish Reflection on Homelessness and Homecoming* (1986).
Yehezkel Kaufmann, *Golah ve-Nekhar* (1962).
Jacob Neusner, *Method and Meaning in Ancient Judaism* (1979).
Gershom Scholem, "Kabbalah and Myth," in *On the Kabbalah and Its Symbolism* (1969).

Existence

קיום

Richard L. Rubenstein

Etymologically, the term *existence* derives from the Latin verb *ex(s)istere,* "to stand out," that is, to be perceptible and hence to have a place in the domain of reality. The related term *being* has as its principal meaning "existence, the fact of belonging to the universe of things material or immaterial."[1] By virtue of its character as that which stands out, existence is often thought to be that which stands out of nonbeing, nothingness, or the divine ground of being.[2] In mystical theology, the divine ground of being is often regarded as the originating nothingness *(Ein Sof)* out of which that which exists stands.[3] Whereas things in the world of actuality are divisible and limited, the divine ground is beyond both limit and division. Consequently, the divine ground is not a thing and can properly be said to be nothing. An important corollary of this type of religious thought is the assertion that God cannot be said to exist, for existence can be affirmed only of finite entities that come into being and pass away.[4] The paradoxical implications of this insight have often been softened by ascribing to God alone necessary existence, which is identical with his essence. God's existence is, so to speak, thus absolutely, qualitatively distinct from the contingent existence of finite entities (*Guide* 1:57). Of course, when the divine nothingness is contrasted with contingent, finite existence, God alone is thought to be truly real, albeit in an ineffable sense. All else partakes of privation and imperfection.[5]

There are basically two views within Judaism of how the cosmos came into existence, the mystical and the biblical.[6] In spite of all attempts at reconciling them, the two perspectives remain fundamentally in conflict. The mystical view is epitomized by the affirmation that "all proceeds from the One and returns to the One."[7] Creation is thought of as an act of divine emanation (Solomon ibn Gabirol), self-limitation, or self-estrangement (Isaac Luria). Originally, God was the perfectly self-contained, seamlessly undivided unity of all that is. Somehow, the divine ground overflowed, divided, or estranged itself, the overflowed or estranged component eventually becoming the basis of the created order. Insofar as there is an eschatological element in these views, the ultimate goal of existence is to return to the undivided unity of the primordial divine ground. For mystical theology, existence is divinity in alienation or otherness.

For those who affirm a mystical view, existence is likely to have an enchanted character insofar as some elements of divinity continue to inhere in the separated ingredients of what was originally a single, primordial divine ground. Within the mystical cosmos, the human agent will be unable to deal with the objective world solely by means of the rational calculation of ends and means. Instead, he or she will feel constrained to seek the favor of the mysterious forces within things. Alternatively, he or she will seek ways of liberating the divine sparks from the malevolent forces that hold them in thrall.

Moreover, the mystical view of creation is not inconsistent with practical polytheism. Insofar as divine sparks subsist within the domain of finite existence, some are likely to assume the character of minor divinities coexisting with a high god. Finding favor with them will tend to become as important as the rational calculation of ends and means. In any event, within the mystic's universe the boundaries between the human, the natural, and the divine are relative rather than absolute and are destined to be obliterated when all existence returns to its originating divine ground.

A radically different view of existence is to be found in the biblical world. There does not appear to be a biblical word whose usage corresponds to *existence* as denoting all that has a place in the domain of reality. Nor is there anything corresponding to systematic philosophic reflection on such concepts as essence, necessary existence, and contingent existence. Instead, one finds references to the act of creation (Gen. 1:1; 1:27; 2:3;

Deut. 4:32; Isa. 40:26) and to that which is created. Fundamental to the biblical view, which is accepted by the rabbinic mainstream, is the notion that existence constitutes a created order wholly dependent upon the unique, sovereign, and transcendent creator of the universe. Although the creation stories in the first and second chapters of Genesis did not originally imply the idea of creation *ex nihilo,* the logic of this teaching became almost irresistible even in biblical times (II Maccabees 7:28). Insofar as creation came to be regarded as the effortless fruit of the free will of the creator, it became difficult to regard any domain of reality as opaque to divine intention. Moreover, divine residues and subordinate or rival deities are wholly absent from the Genesis creation stories. The Babylonian goddess Tiamat has been reduced to a spiritless aqueous mass known as *tehom* (Gen. 1:2). The great sea monsters are no longer participants in a primeval mythic combat between the creator god and a sea monster personifying the forces of chaos. Instead, the monsters are depicted as created by and dependent upon God (Gen. 1:20). The absence of divinities or deified powers other than God is also implied in Psalm 33:6:

> By the word of the Lord the heavens were made,
> by the breath of His mouth, all their host.

Thus, in the biblical perspective existence has only the dependent potency assigned to it by its creator.

The biblical understanding of the created and dependent character of existence was an expression of one of the most influential revolutions in consciousness human beings have ever experienced. That revolution has been characterized by the German sociologist Max Weber as the "disenchantment of the world." Disenchantment of the world occurs when existence comes to be regarded as utterly devoid of mysterious forces and is thought of as a domain in which all things can be mastered by the rational calculation of ends and means. As noted, such a view is impossible wherever divinities or divine residues are thought to inhere in things. By contrast, disenchantment is logically irresistible when the cosmos is regarded as the work of a sovereign, transcendent creator who excludes all rivals and is wholly outside the created order. When the author of Genesis wrote, "In the beginning God created heaven and earth" (Gen. 1:1), he gave expression to that revolution in consciousness. No longer did men have to contend with powers immanent in the natural or political orders. Moreover, the relation between God and man was conceived in such a way as further to foster the rationalization of every domain of human existence. God's favor could be won neither by personal magic nor by means of a charismatic mediator. It could be won only by a life of disciplined obedience to the divine will as expressed in the covenant.

Disenchantment of the world can also be understood as the process of radical desacralization. When the believer declared concerning God that "Thou alone art holy," it followed that nothing else in the created order was intrinsically sacred. The biblical tradition of God's revelation to Moses out of the burning bush exemplifies this desacralizing consciousness. No rival spirit is present. There is nothing sacred per se about the bush. It is only the freely elected presence of God that makes it possible for him to say to Moses, "The place on which you stand is holy ground" (Ex. 3:5). Inasmuch as the modern mind has been shaped by the biblical understanding of existence as God's creation, woods, mountains, streams, and caves are taken to be simply natural objects devoid of any spiritual potency. When, for example, pine forests are today methodically cut down and replanted by paper-manufacturing corporations, the trees are regarded as commodities rather than the abode of woodland spirits. There is no longer anything inherently sacred in the trees as there was for the pagan Saxons in the time of Charlemagne. Nor is this transformation in consciousness limited to the natural order. Wherever civilization was based upon the value system of biblical monotheism, the political order also tended to become desacralized. The tendency toward sociopolitical desacralization can be seen in the vehement opposition of the prophets of Israel to the ancient Near Eastern institution of divine kingship.

It is sometimes thought that the related processes of disenchantment, desacralization, and secularization were the consequence of the ongoing rational analysis of traditional religious beliefs and institutions. However, it is highly unlikely that the disenchanted consciousness could have taken hold as a mass cultural phenomenon on the basis of intellectual criticism alone. If, for example, a person is taught by parents from earliest childhood that trees are the dwelling place of sacred spirits that must be appeased lest they do harm, it is hardly likely that a course in biology or philosophy taken as a young adult could alter such opinions. Only faith in a unique, absolutely sovereign creator could have brought about the revolution in consciousness necessary for an entire civilization to negate a worldview accepted by men and women from time immemorial. If one wishes to find the origin of the modern view of existence as a desacralized, disenchanted realm lying at hand for rational human mastery, one must turn to biblical monotheism. Moreover, the influence of the biblical view has become so pervasive in the modern Western world that many men and women who are unable to believe in the biblical creator tend to accept without reflective analysis the biblical view of existence as a realm of actuality devoid of mysterious powers or spirits.

In view of the abiding importance of the biblical view of creation it is hardly surprising that Jewish religious thinkers, from Philo Judaeus in ancient times to Moses Maimonides in the Middle Ages to Franz Rosenzweig in modern times, have tended to reject the view that there was an eternally preexistent domain of existence before God created the world. Every significant thinker within the Jewish mainstream has insisted on the affirmation of some version of creation *ex nihilo*. Thus, Maimonides took issue with Aristotle and the Aristotelians, who affirmed the preexistence of an eternal material substratum before creation, although he acknowledged that creation *ex nihilo* was a matter of faith rather than rational proof (*Guide* 2:25). Franz Rosenzweig interpreted the idea expressed in the traditional prayer book that God "renews daily the work of creation" to mean that existence is wholly dependent upon God rather than upon an autonomous realm.[8] Even the mystics felt compelled to affirm creation *ex nihilo,* although they insisted that the nothingness out of which the world was created was the primordial divine ground itself. Within Judaism it is impossible to speak of existence without at the same time speaking of creation.

There is, however, extraordinary irony in the view of existence as creation. Faith in the transcendent creator can lead to its own negation. The doctrine of creation became inextricably bound up with the disenchantment of the world and the desacralization of the natural and political orders. This in turn has tended to intensify the perception of the self-contained worldliness of the world. A further consequence has been that for many men and women only creation and not the utterly remote creator appears to be actual. In place of the self-contained, originating ground of being or the transcendent creator effortlessly calling existence into being, all that remains for them is wholly immanent, self-contained, spiritless existence.

REFERENCES

1. *Oxford English Dictionary,* s.v. "Being."
2. Paul Tillich, *Systematic Theology,* 2 (1957), 20–21.
3. Gershom Scholem, *Major Trends in Jewish Mysticism* (1946), 25.
4. Paul Tillich, loc. cit.
5. David ben Abraham ha-Laban, *Masoret ha-Brit,* cited in Gershom Scholem, loc. cit.; Johannes Scotus Erigena, *De Divisione Naturae,* 3: 19–23.
6. Julius Guttmann, *Philosophies of Judaism* (1964), 3–17.

7. Gershom Scholem, *Sabbatai Sevi: The Mystical Messiah* (1973), 16.
8. Franz Rosenzweig, *The Star of Redemption* (1971), 118–22.

BIBLIOGRAPHY

Peter Berger, *The Sacred Canopy* (1967), 105–25.
Julius Guttmann, *Philosophies of Judaism* (1964), 3–17.
Moses Maimonides, *The Guide of the Perplexed,* Shlomo Pines, tr. (1963), pt. 1.
Franz Rosenzweig, *The Star of Redemption,* William W. Hallo, tr. (1971), 112–55.
Gershom Scholem, *Major Trends in Jewish Mysticism* (1946).
Gershom Scholem, *Sabbatai Sevi: The Mystical Messiah* (1973).
Paul Tillich, *Systematic Theology,* 2 (1957), 20–21.

Faith

אמונה

Louis Jacobs

A theological discussion of faith should begin with a brief account of its history in Judaism. When the Bible and rabbinic literature use the word *emunah* (faith) for man's relationship to God, it always denotes not belief but trust in God. It never signifies belief that God exists. It is an emotional and responsive term rather than a cognitive one. Faith is synonymous with *bittaḥon* (trust), rather than with God's reality or existence. Hardly anyone in biblical and rabbinic times doubted that God (or the gods) existed. Theoretical atheism was virtually unknown. All the tensions in the matter of faith were with regard to man's relationship with God, that is, whether man conducts himself adequately in the presence of the Being who makes moral and religious demands upon him. The believer acts in such a manner that God is real to him. It is no accident that *emunah* is applied to other human beings,[1] as well as to God. It makes no sense to speak of belief in the existence of one's neighbor. Except by a pseudo-sophistication foreign to ancient thought, it is impossible to deny that the neighbor exists. But it does not follow necessarily from the neighbor's existence that he is trustworthy.

It was not until the Middle Ages, when the atheistic challenge was presented, that Jewish thinkers, defending theism, resorted to the term *emunah*
to convey the idea of belief that there is a God. The medieval work *Sefer ha-
Emunah ve-ha-Bittahon*,[2] attributed to Nahmanides, gives a typical demonstration of the change in meaning. *Emunah* and *bittahon* are no longer the
same thing. From this period, trust in God has henceforth to be preceded
by rational demonstration that there really is a God in whom trust can be
placed. This is not to suggest that cognitive beliefs were unknown to the
biblical authors and the rabbis. To trust in a nonexistent deity is an absurdity, as is obedience to the Torah as God's word if revelation never occurred.
Cognitive affirmations were undoubtedly implied, but they were taken for
granted. For the biblical writers God was ever-present and assumed. As G.
K. Chesterton rightly observed, God is not the chief character in the Bible;
He is its only character. The same is true for the rabbis. A very revealing
formulation of the Mishnah (M. Sanh. 10:1) states that among those who
have no share in the World to Come is the one who *says (ha-omer)* there is
no Torah from heaven. Significantly, the denial that the Torah is from
heaven is cast in the form of a verbal declaration. "One who does not
believe that the Torah is from heaven" is an impossible formulation for the
rabbis, implying, as it does, a formal, propositional structure. It is not so
much that the unbeliever alluded to in this mishnah has achieved his unbelief through intellectual argument. It is rather that he refuses to accept the
doctrine of a revealed Torah and to place his reliance upon the Torah. Nor
do the rabbis who castigate him for his heresy do so by reasoned argument.
They rather state categorically that the doctrine "The Torah is from heaven"
is so essential to Judaism that anyone who does not share it is to be excised
from the community of believers. The debate here between the believers
and the nonbelievers is of a totally different order than the debates between
the School of Hillel and the School of Shammai. There, arguments and
counterarguments occur; here, only rejection and denunciation. It is far less
a matter of the mind than of the moral will and purpose.

In the Middle Ages, when the problem of reconciling faith and reason
loomed large, faith was never actually equated with reason, but the need to
justify faith at the bar of reason came to be strongly felt. Of the traditional,
philosophical proofs for the existence of God, the ontological argument is
not found at all, and the teleological argument only occasionally; the cosmological argument is the one most generally preferred by medieval Jewish
theologians. Modern thinkers, however, conscious of David Hume's treatment of cause and effect in general and of the Kantian critique of every
argument from the world to God, have become suspicious of the whole

medieval exercise of proving God's existence. Consequently, many Jewish thinkers have come to prefer Søren Kierkegaard's "leap of faith," looking upon all attempts at a demonstration of God's existence as irrelevant to faith in the living God. Kierkegaard's formulation is telling: What can be more impertinent than to interrupt an audience with the enthroned king to debate the king's existence?

Jewish believers who have embraced the existentialist approach to faith have sometimes found encouragement for their stance in the claim that it is a return to the biblical and rabbinic faith in which trust matters far more than reason—that, in fact, the existentialist approach is more authentically Jewish than the exaggerated claims for reason made by the medieval tradition. The medieval thinkers, it is suggested, were fooling themselves; their proofs convinced only those who already believed in God, for whom no proofs were necessary. Reasoning toward faith cannot, however, be so easily dismissed. The classical proofs may have been dealt a deathblow by modern philosophical criticism, but the energy and ingenuity they consumed are powerful indicators that life makes more sense with reasoned belief than without it. Once atheism becomes a live option, the theist must try to persuade himself and others that his faith is reasonably held. In the final analysis, it is probably true that the leap of faith is constantly demanded, but to scrutinize before one leaps remains sound advice. If to believe that God exists without trust in him is no more than mere assent to a bare proposition, it is equally the case that maintaining trust in God without really believing in his existence is magical and ridiculous.

Cognitive faith may be further specified by distinguishing between interpretive beliefs and factual beliefs. Belief in God's existence is interpretive insofar as it involves one's whole philosophy of existence. It does not purport to explain this or that particular fact, but is a way of looking at the universe as a whole and the role man plays in the fulfillment of the divine purpose. Logical positivists may assert that any interpretation capable of accommodating all the facts is logically meaningless, incapable as it is of either verification or denial. Few religious believers, however, are disturbed by the suggestion that their belief makes no difference to their lives. There is no need to invoke the notion of an eschatological verification, that is, that everything will be clarified one way or the other in the hereafter; rather the believer affirms in the here and now that his philosophy of life affects the whole tenor and quality of his conduct. Examples of interpretive beliefs in Judaism are that the Torah is God's word (however the scope of Torah is conceived); that the Jewish people has a special role to play in God's plan (no matter how many qualifications the idea of the chosen people receives), and that the way man lives on earth has eternal significance, determining his capacity to enjoy God forever. These beliefs involve assertions about the nature of human existence and about the truths by which men live.

Factual beliefs require the acceptance that certain particular events, said to have taken place in the past, really did take place in the precise manner the tradition states they did—for example, that God gave to Moses the whole of the Pentateuch during the forty-year journey through the wilderness or that the world was created less than six thousand years ago in six days. It is not difficult to see that, once tried methods of literary and historical research have convinced the believer that the factual beliefs are far less plausible than they could have appeared to be in the precritical age, he cannot fall back on faith in this area if he is to preserve his intellectual integrity.

The distinction between these two types of belief becomes clearer when the different responses to the challenges presented to them are considered. Belief in the goodness of God is a basic interpretive belief in Judaism. The believer in God's goodness, when his belief is challenged by the evil in the universe, does not deny that evil is real. He proceeds by faith, believing that somehow evil is a condition necessary for the good. He may seek to explore the idea of a limited God, or he may favor the free-will defense (that evil is necessary if the universe is to be an arena in which man's freedom to do good is unaborted), or he may hold that it is not given to the finite mind of man to grasp the mysterious ways in which God works. The believing Jew who still maintains his belief in God's goodness despite the Holocaust does not feel compelled to deny that there was a Holocaust.

With regard to factual beliefs—for instance, that the whole of the Pentateuch was given to Moses—the question at issue is the nature of the facts. Here criticism suggests that the Pentateuch is a composite work, edited, at the very least, long after Moses. The believer can, of course, reject such untraditional theories because he finds them unconvincing. He may deny that the evidence points to the critical conclusions, but if this is what he does he is himself engaging in criticism by surveying the facts objectively. What he must not do, if he is to be intellectually honest, is to reject theories that seem to him plausible because faith has decided otherwise. To invoke faith in order to reject highly circumstantial evidence comes perilously close to belief in a God who plants false clues. It is to send back to heaven the angel who, in Abraham ibn Ezra's felicitous phrase, is the human mind. To identify learning with heresy is to equate orthodoxy with obscurantism.

If the above distinction is sound, it follows that the Jewish man of faith need not—indeed, should not—accept purely on faith every assertion in the Jewish tradition regarding what transpired in the past. The discovery or attempted discovery of what happened in Jewish and world history is a matter for scholarship, not for faith; for historians, philologists, literary critics, and anthropologists, not for theologians qua theologians. A sound Jewish theology cannot afford to fly in the teeth of the evidence. The believing Jew will give due weight to his tradition, preferring this to other interpretations of the facts until the application of tried methods of investigation renders the traditional account implausible. He will allow critical inquiry a voice in determining which traditional formulations about historical events are true to the facts and which fictitious, mythical, or speculative.

The distinction between interpretive and factual beliefs is valid, but creates problems of its own since the two types of belief are interlinked. If it be granted that the factual beliefs are open to doubt, does not such an admission shake the foundations of the whole traditional structure, including those affirmed as interpretive beliefs? The answer involves a frank recognition that no belief can rest solely on the ground that it is traditional. Surely the believing Jew is not an ancestor worshiper. He constantly buttresses the beliefs that have come down to him by their credibility under reasoned scrutiny. When, for instance, tradition informs the believer that God exists, only the first step toward the acknowledgment of the truth has been asserted. Consciously or unconsciously, the believer applies tests of coherence and intelligibility.

There is always an ebb and flow in the life of faith, a lengthy, agonizing process in which despair yields gradually to confidence, doubt to certainty. Moreover, historical investigation has succeeded in demonstrating the extent to which, in every age, the response of faith has been conditioned, to some degree, by social and cultural circumstances. Moses Maimonides' special emphasis, for example, on the essentiality of his thirteen principles of faith was made not because he had been vouchsafed a divine revelation that it was so (nor did he ever make such a claim), but rather because these, more than any others, were critical principles for Jews living in an Islamic environment in the twelfth century. To be sure, Maimonides was able to quote chapter and verse for each of his contentions, but obviously criticism and reflection came first and scriptural and other proofs were seen to lend their support. In other ages and against a different cultural background a different attempt is required at understanding the basic principles of Judaism. The possibility of openness to new knowledge and the reinterpretation of essential beliefs is no illusion since, historically considered, the basic principles themselves are the product of a God-seeking people reflecting on their destiny and their role in the divine scheme—a people trying to find

God and being found by him. The speculative, interpretive element is itself basic to Jewish faith.

The either/or notion of faith—adopted both by the simple believer who refuses to surrender the smallest detail of the tradition because, for him, to reject any part is to reject the whole, and by the unbeliever who wraps it all up in the same uncomplicated bundle—is untrue to the history of the Jewish faith and its dynamism. The Jewish man of faith knows only too well of its confusions and uncertainties. His is a questing faith, in which to seek is already to have found.

REFERENCES

1. E.g., Ex. 14:31; I Sam. 27:12; II Chron. 20:20.
2. *Kitvei Moshe ben Naḥman,* H. D. Chavel, ed., 2 (1964) 341–448.

BIBLIOGRAPHY

Louis Jacobs, *Faith* (1968).
Louis Jacobs, *Principles of the Jewish Faith* (1964).
Aaron Roth, *Shomer Emunim* (1959).
Solomon Schechter, "The Dogmas of Judaism," in *Studies in Judaism* (1945).
Milton Steinberg, *Anatomy of Faith,* Arthur A. Cohen, ed. (1960).

Family

מ**שפחה**

David Biale

The family is one of the main pillars of Jewish life, not only historically and sociologically but also religiously. The opening chapters of Genesis culminate with the creation of the first family and thus propose a myth of marriage and procreation that gives divine sanction to family life. Indeed, the rabbis understood the fertility blessing of Genesis 1:28 ("be fertile and increase, fill the earth and master it") as the first commandment (*miẓvah*). To marry and have children thus became a cardinal religious duty incumbent on all Jewish men; women were excluded from this commandment, although the biblical verse seems clearly directed at both sexes.

Yet marriage is not solely a union for purposes of procreation. Since woman was created from man's rib (Gen. 2:21–24), the unification of their bodies in marriage is a result of a natural tendency to make complete that which was originally sundered apart. This notion of companionship as the reason for marriage receives a theological dimension in Genesis 1:27. Man and woman were both created in the image of God. Only their reunification can, implicitly, re-create the divine image. In a passage reminiscent of Plato's *Symposium,* the midrash *Genesis Rabbah* speaks of the original human being as an androgyne who was then separated into two halves (Gen. R. 8:1). Marriage is the reconstitution of this original Adam.

These notions of marriage and procreation are rendered more ambiguous in chapters 2 and 3 of Genesis (the second account of creation). In Genesis 3:5 and 3:22, God asserts that by acquiring sexual knowledge, the specific consequence of eating from the tree of knowledge of good and evil, Adam and Eve became like God. Their godlike characteristic must be that they, too, can now create life *ex nihilo.* God then banishes them from the garden in order to prevent them from also eating of the tree of life and thereby acquiring immortality. Yet had they eaten from the tree of life first, they would have had no need for sexual knowledge, since immortality would exclude the biological need for a family; immortality having been lost, however, procreation became the answer to the death of the individual. In this account, the basis for the family is a transgression and a curse rather than a blessing.

The implicit equality of man and woman in Genesis 1 is also undermined in the second creation story. The woman is cursed with the pain of childbirth and is told that "your urge shall be for your husband, and he shall rule you" (Gen. 3:16). The sexual nature of woman is taken as the justification for the inequality between men and women in the family, an inequality that characterizes the patriarchal family of biblical times.

Much of the later biblical and rabbinic law can be understood as an attempt to respond to the problems raised by Genesis 2–3. In recognition of the inferior status of women in the family, laws were promulgated to protect the rights of women (see, for example, Ex. 21:10–11). The *ketubah* (marriage contract) of rabbinic times extended these rights. Women were never made equal in the family, but their status was protected.

In addition, the institution of marriage can be seen as an answer to the problem of sexuality raised in Genesis 2–3. When Adam and Eve discover their sexuality, they see themselves as "naked" *(erom)*. In Levitical law (Lev. 18 and 20), all forbidden sexual relations are called by a term derived from the same root: "uncovering of nakedness" *(gilui arayot)*. On the other hand, marriage is referred to as "covering the nakedness" *(kisuay ervah:* cf. Hos. 2:11; Ezek. 16:8). Thus, properly constituted marriage is the correct response to the original sexual knowledge, for it creates a divinely sanctioned sphere for sexuality. At the conclusion of the list of offenses against the family in Leviticus 20, God says: "You shall be holy *[kedoshim]* to Me, for I the Lord am holy *[kadosh],* and I have set you apart from other peoples to be Mine" (Lev. 20:26). The proper maintenance of the family not only prevents the sin of "nakedness" but also renders the Israelite sacred and therefore like God. If Genesis 3 condemned Adam and Eve for using their sexual knowledge to become like God, the Levitical laws respond that such *imitatio Dei* is indeed legitimate in the proper marital framework.

The intimate involvement of God in the family affairs of his nation is particularly evident in the stories of the patriarchs and matriarchs in Genesis. Common to the three generations of Abraham, Isaac, and Jacob is the problem of their wives' fertility. In each case, God miraculously causes the barren woman to conceive. Thus, the future of the nation is ensured by propitious divine intervention. These fertility stories are connected with the original human family of Genesis 1 in the repetition of the blessing "Be fertile and increase," a blessing always associated in the patriarchal materials with the divine name *El Shaddai*.

A further indication of God's involvement in the continuation of the family through procreation is the ceremony of circumcision *(brit milah)*, first mentioned in Genesis 17:10–14, immediately following one of the Genesis fertility blessings. In Exodus 4:24–26 there is the suggestion that Moses' failure to circumcise his son—subsequently mitigated by his wife, Zipporah, who performed the operation—was a serious infraction against God. In this enigmatic text, circumcision may be an expression of gratitude (in the form of a substitute sacrifice) for the gift of fertility. In all these biblical contexts, procreation is unthinkable without divine involvement; God becomes quite literally the godfather of all families.

In the rabbinical materials, the biblical emphasis on marriage and family is made even more explicit. Various reasons are adduced for marriage: "Rabbi Tanḥum stated in the name of Rabbi Hanilai: Any man who has no wife lives without joy, without blessing, and without goodness. . . . In the West [that is, Palestine] it was stated: Without Torah and without a [protecting] wall" (BT Yev. 62b). Marriage not only confers necessary companionship but also guards against sexual temptation. Proper study of Torah requires the protection of the married state. One rabbi, Ben Azzai, who did not marry claimed that "my soul is in love with the Torah" (BT Yev. 63b), but the rabbis regarded him as an aberration.

Procreation, too, is regarded as a commandment and is given a theological rationale: "Rabbi Jacob said: [He who does not engage in procreation is] as though he has diminished the divine image, since it is said, 'for in the image of God he made human beings' [Gen. 9:6] and, immediately after, 'be fertile and increase' [Gen. 9:7]" (BT Yev. 63b). Here the rabbis make explicit the biblical message that procreation fulfills the divine image in which human beings were created. And further along in the same passage:

"[If] any person has not engaged in the propagation of the race, does he not thereby cause the divine Presence [*Shekhinah*] to depart from Israel?" (ibid.). The *Shekhinah,* which was originally considered that part of God which dwelt within the Temple, was thought by the rabbis to have accompanied the Jews into exile following the destruction of the Temple. Thus, not to create a family banishes God from amongst the Jews; conversely, proper family life strengthens the divine Presence.

The notion of the influence of private family life upon theology reached its most developed expression in the kabbalah, medieval Jewish mysticism. In its system of divine emanations (*sefirot*), the kabbalah portrayed God as consisting of male and female parts, comprising a divine family. These male and female elements are arrayed in two generations: the divine "father" and "mother" (*hokhmah* and *binah*), and the divine "son" and "daughter" (*tiferet* and *malkhut*). Under ideal conditions, these emanations are engaged in perpetual intercourse (ironically, the relationship between the latter two is clearly incestuous).

The maintenance of the harmony within this divine family is a result of the actions of Jews within their own families. The classic texts of thirteenth-century kabbalah, most notably the *Zohar,* speak of the proper intercourse of husband and wife as causing a flow of energy into the divine sphere, which in turn causes the intercourse of the male and female *sefirot.* If human sexual relations are carried on correctly, then the action of the *sefirot* leads to the emanation of a righteous soul that is then implanted in a human body at birth. If, however, there is something improper in human sexual relations, whether a violation of the family laws or even licentious thoughts, the divine harmony is disrupted and an evil soul is produced. This description of the mutual influence between the human and divine families thus considerably expanded the original biblical notion of God's intimate role in the creation of the family and its progeny.

Although marriage and family life are central to every human culture, the religious insistence on marriage and procreation in the classical Jewish texts probably led to a relatively higher rate of marriage among Jews than among their neighbors. There was no ideal of chastity or bachelorhood for any class in Jewish society, and social institutions such as that of the *shadkhan* (marriage broker) ensured that religious values would be preserved. The age of marriage was also quite young in most Jewish communities, again as a result of religious injunctions (cf. BT Kid. 29b; BT Yev. 62b; *Shulḥan Arukh, Even ha-Ezer* 1:1). Only in the modern period, starting in the seventeenth and eighteenth centuries in western Europe, the nineteenth century in eastern Europe, and the twentieth century in the Middle East, did traditional control of marriage and family diminish, with a consequent rise in the age of marriage, an increase in the percentage of those who did not marry at all, and a change in the structure of the family. Although secular factors such as emigration and urbanization have contributed to changes in the Jewish family, the decline of religious traditionalism has played a central role in transforming the sacrament of marriage into a matter of sentiment. Marriage and family increasingly have been taken out of the public sphere of the sacred and have become fundamentally private.

BIBLIOGRAPHY

Rachel Biale, *Women and Jewish Law: An Exploration of Women's Issues in Halakhic Sources* (1984).
Roland de Vaux, *Ancient Israel* (1961).
David Feldman, *Birth Control in Jewish Law* (1968).
Jacob Katz, *Tradition and Crisis* (1961).
Raphael Patai, *Sex and Family in the Bible and the Middle East* (1959).

Fear of God

ירְאַת הַשֵּׁם

Byron L. Sherwin

T he Torah is of no use to an individual but for *yirat shamayim* (lit., fear or awe of heaven, that is, of God), for it [*yirat shamayim*] is the very peg upon which everything hangs."[1] This observation in the medieval ethical treatise *Orḥoṭ Ẓaddikim* reaffirms the perspective of Hebrew Scripture that considers *yirat shamayim* to be the essential attitude that characterizes the religious personality. The term *yire shamayim* is used in Hebrew, as the term *God-fearing* is used in English, to refer to a person of religious faith and moral virtue. In Judaism the religious person is not characterized primarily as a believer who assents to a given creed, as in other religions. Rather, the religious person is depicted as one who has *yirat shamayim* or *yirat ha-Shem*, fear and awe of God. Indeed, for Judaism, *yirat shamayim* is almost a synonym for *religion*.

While Scripture considers love as the primary attitude of God vis-à-vis human beings, *yirah* is Scripture's primary attitudinal requirement for human beings in their relationship with God. The obligation for one to have *yirah* of God is stated many more times in Hebrew Scripture than is the requirement for one to love God.

Scripture identifies *yirah* of God with religious commitment. For example, when Jonah states that he is a "Hebrew," he explains that to mean that he is one who has "*yirah* of the God of Heaven" (Jonah 1:9). The opening verse of the Book of Job describes Job as "blameless and upright; he had *yirah* of God and shunned evil" (Job 1:1; see also Gen. 22:12, 42:18). The Book of Proverbs characterizes the righteous as those who have *yirah* of God (Prov. 10:27, 14:27, 19:23).

Yirah of God is inextricably related by Scripture to moral action. *Yirah* of God is considered by Scripture to be the essential ingredient for a life of happiness and of virtue (see, for example, Ps. 112:1; Prov. 19:23). Indeed, *yirah* of God engenders moral and even courageous behavior (see Ex. 1:21). *Yirah* of God also serves as the ultimate justification for moral behavior: one should treat one's fellow in a particular manner because one has *yirah* of God (see Gen. 42:18; Lev. 19:14, 32, 25:17, 36, 43). Conversely, *yirah* of God is described as a necessary and sufficient means of dissuading immoral behavior (see Gen. 20:11; Ex. 20:17; Mal. 3:5; Prov. 8:13, 14:27, 16:6; Neh. 5:15). Implicit in these texts is the expectation that fear of God's punishment and awe of his majesty provide fundamental motivation for a life of moral rectitude. Other texts explicitly regard longevity as a reward that can be anticipated by those who live a life motivated by *yirah* of God. Finally, for Scripture, *yirah* of God ensures not only moral rectitude but also wisdom (Job 28:28; see also Isa. 11:3; Ps. 111:10; Prov. 2:5–9, 9:10, 15:33).

The term *yirat shamayim* is of rabbinic, not biblical, origin. The Hebrew Bible uses direct terms such as *yirat elohim* or *yirat adonai* to denote fear or awe of God. In biblical Hebrew, the term *yirah* denotes fright or fear, and awe or reverence.[2] It can also denote anxiety, as in Genesis 26:24, which may be translated, "Do not be anxious, for I [God] am with you" (see also, for example, Gen. 15:1; Isa. 41:10; Jer. 1:8). In rabbinic Hebrew and in rabbinic literature, the semantic and conceptual features of *yirah* of God were expanded and clarified.

Discussion of *yirah* of God in rabbinic literature focuses on two issues: the distinction between fear and awe of God and the relationship between *yirah* of God and love of God. These two issues also provide much of the agenda for medieval Jewish literature's further analysis and amplification of the notion of *yirah* of God.

While Scripture does not distinguish between fear of God and awe of God, both denoted by *yirah*, rabbinic literature initiates a discussion that attempts to differentiate between these two distinct attitudes, denoted by the identical word. Furthermore, while Scripture clearly subordinates love of God to *yirah* of God, rabbinic literature resists considering the matter a closed one.

These two issues are implicitly raised in the following early rabbinic statement of Antigonus of Sokho, in which the term *fear of heaven* (here *mora shamayim*) is used for the first time: "Be not like servants that minister to the master for the sake of receiving reward . . . and let the fear of heaven be upon you" (*M. Avot* 1:3). The implication here is that a servant who serves without expectation of reward serves out of love of the master, that is, of God. In this view, love and *yirah* of God are inextricably intertwined (compare Ben Sira 2:16). Furthermore, Antigonus of Sokho's characterization of *mora shamayim* as being properly separated from the expectation of reward for virtue and, by implication, from the expectation of punishment for sin establishes the basis for later, explicit distinctions in medieval Jewish literature between two disparate connotations of *yirah* of God: fear of God, that is, of God's punishment for sin, and awe and reverence for God's majesty.

The term *yirat ḥeit,* or fear of (punishment for) sin, makes its first appearance in rabbinic literature and seems to indicate the beginning of an implicit distinction between fear of God and awe of God. According to rabbinic theology, *yirah* of God, understood as fear of punishment, was clearly an undesirable, though not completely unacceptable, attitude. As a prophylactic measure to prevent sin, fear of God served a function (see BT Ned. 20a). However, as a basis for religious life, fear of God could not be deemed preferable either to awe or to love of God.

It may well be that the association of *yirah* of God with the principle of divine reward and retribution encouraged some rabbinic authorities to elevate love of God over *yirah* of God, in a blatant reversal of the biblical view that considered *yirah* of God to be supreme. It is therefore ironic that the rabbis, while elevating love over *yirah,* link reward both to love and to *yirah.* For example, *Sifrei on Deuteronomy* (ed. Finkelstein, 1969, 54) states, "Act out of love, for the Torah distinguishes between one who acts out of love and one who acts out of *yirah.* In the former case reward is doubled and redoubled."[3]

Whether the motivation for serving God is the promise of reward or selfless devotion, the rabbis clearly opt for love over *yirah.* The representative rabbinic view is epitomized by the statement of Rabbi Simeon ben Eleazar: "Greater is he who acts from love than he who acts from *yirah*" (BT Sot. 31a). Summarizing the rabbinic consensus, Solomon Schechter observed, "It is known that the rabbis always elevated actions motivated by love over actions motivated by *yirah.*"[4]

Implicit within the aforementioned statement of Antigonus of Sokho is the understanding that *yirah* of God and love of God are inseparable. Later rabbinic sources make this notion explicit by affirming that authentic *yirah* of God has love of God at its source (see Tos. Sot. 6:1; BT Sot. 31a in the name of Rabbi Meir). The distinction between *yirah* as fear and *yirah* as awe that begins to emerge in rabbinic literature becomes clear and explicit in medieval Jewish literature. The debate as to whether *yirah* or love of God is granted priority reverberates throughout Jewish medieval philosophical, legal, mystical, and ethical literature.

Among medieval Jewish philosophers, Baḥya Ibn Paqudah, Abraham Ibn Daud, Moses Maimonides, and Joseph Albo speculated about the meaning of *yirah* of God.

For Baḥya Ibn Paqudah, *yirah* is the necessary prerequisite for and the proper conduit to love of God. Baḥya distinguishes between a lower and a higher form of *yirah*. The lower form is not fear of God per se, but fear of God's punishment for sin. The higher form is reverence and awe of God, and of God exclusively. It is this variety of *yirah* that inevitably transmutes into love of God (*The Book of Direction to the Duties of the Heart,* tr. M. Mansoor, 1973, 432–37).

The twelfth-century Jewish philosopher Abraham Ibn Daud distinguishes between two varieties of *yirah*: "awe of greatness" and "fear of harm." For Ibn Daud, the former is clearly the more desirable of the two varieties. Ibn Daud defines "awe of greatness" as an attitude that makes one aware of "one's deficiencies in relation to the object of one's awe, i.e., God." Like other medieval authors, Ibn Daud relates *yirah* to a feeling of "embarrassment" before God (*Emunah Ramah,* 1852, 100).

In his *Guide of the Perplexed,* Moses Maimonides clearly endorses awe of God as a necessary but insufficient expression of divine worship. For Maimonides, awe of God insures right action and moral perfection, which constitute the necessary prelude to the more desirable attitude of love of God. Love of God leads to right thinking and to the higher level of intellectual perfection (Guide 3:52; see also MT H.I., Yesodei ha-Torah 2:1).

In his earlier *Commentary to the Mishnah* (ad. loc. Avot 1:3) and *Book of the Commandments* ("Positive Commandment" no. 4), Maimonides posits value to fear of God when it serves as a means of stimulating religious observance. However, in his subsequent legal code, *Mishneh Torah,* Maimonides denigrates fear of God in the form of fear of God's punishment for sin as an "improper manner of serving God. One who serves in this manner serves from fear. This is not the standard set by the prophets and the sages." For Maimonides, only if service from fear becomes a conduit for service from love can it retroactively claim any validity (MT H.I. Teshuvah 10:1,2,5).

Maimonides' discussion of the well-known talmudic statement, "Everything is in the hands of heaven, except *yirat shamayim*" (BT Ber. 33b), also bears mention. In one of his responsa, Maimonides interprets this statement to mean that the term *everything* refers to the natural order of things, but not to human deeds. Moral choice remains the province of human beings (*Responsa* no. 345, ed. A. Freimann, 1934, 309–10; see also BT Nid. 16b).

The discussion of *yirah* of God in Joseph Albo's fifteenth-century philosophical work *Sefer ha-Ikkarim* (ed. I. Husik, 1946, 3, 31–33) is more reminiscent of Ibn Daud than of Maimonides. Like Ibn Daud, Albo clearly distinguishes between *yirah* as fear of harm and *yirah* as awareness of human deficiency when standing in awe of God's sublimity. Unlike Maimonides, Albo does not condemn fear of punishment, but considers it a necessary first step toward awe of God. For Albo, fear of God aims at the physical nature of human beings, while awe of God relates to the higher spiritual aspects of the human personality. Following scriptural precedent, though in opposition to Maimonides, Albo finds *yirah* of God, rather than love of God, to be the conduit to wisdom.

Besides Maimonides, other medieval halakhists discussed *yirah* of God. For example, the thirteenth-century *Sefer ha-Ḥinukh*, ascribed to Aaron ha-Levi of Barcelona, defines *yirah* of God primarily in terms of fear of God's punishment. As did Maimonides' earlier writings, this work stresses the value of fear of God as a catalyst for religious observance and counts fear of God among the 613 commandments of the Torah (*Sefer ha-Ḥinukh* no. 432).[5] This text also observes that fear of God, like love of God, is one of a severely limited number of the commandments that must be practiced at all times by everyone.

The fourteenth-century code of Jacob ben Asher and Moses Isserles' glosses to the sixteenth-century code *Shulḥan Arukh* begin by stressing *yirah* of God, not love of God, as the primary religious attitude upon which divine worship and observance of Jewish law rest. These codes further insist that only *yirah* of God, not social pressure, is a viable reason for religious observance (*Tur Oraḥ Ḥayyim* 1:1; Sh. Ar. OḤ 1:1). The reluctance of the legal writers to affirm the supremacy of the love of God, as indicated by the fact that the codes open with a discussion of *yirah* of God, is shared by some ethical and kabbalistic writers.

Yirah of God is a subject widely discussed in medieval Jewish pietica and ethical literature. *Yirah* of God is often described in such texts as being essential to the quest for piety. For example, the *Sefer Ḥasidim* of Judah ben

Samuel he-Ḥasid directly claims that "the root of piety is *yirah*." The *Sefer Ḥasidim* further defines *yirah* of God as an attitude that leads one to suppress one's natural appetites and desires. The ability to withstand a trial of faith is proof that an individual has *yirah*. The more severe the trial, the greater the *yirah*. More than fear of punishment, *yirah* of God is characterized as the fear of not being able to withstand God's trials; it is fear of not loving God adequately (*Sefer Ḥasidim*, ed. R. Margaliot, 1960, nos. 12, 13). For Eleazar of Worms, love of God is an essential aspect of *yirah* of God, rather than the opposite, as many of the talmudic rabbis would have it (Eleazar of Worms, *Sefer Raziel*, 1701).

In the section on *yirah* in Baḥya ben Asher's thirteenth-century ethical-homiletical treatise *Kad ha-Kemaḥ*, *yirah* of God is characterized as "the foundation of the entire Torah . . . the root of all the commandments." Like Ibn Daud and Albo, Baḥya ben Asher holds that fear of God's punishment inevitably leads to the awareness of God's majesty. Nevertheless, following talmudic precedent, Baḥya ben Asher insists that *yirah* itself is insufficient unless it includes love of God. Love is clearly the supreme desideratum in divine worship (sec. "love of God").

In opposition to Maimonides and like Albo, Baḥya ben Asher identifies true wisdom with *yirah* of God, rather than with love of God. A similar approach is also taken in the anonymously written medieval ethical tract *Orḥot Ẓaddikim* ("*Yirat Shamayim*," 590–629). Following talmudic precedent, *Orḥot Ẓaddikim* finds scholarship uninformed by *yirah* of God to be a crippled variety of knowledge—intellectual attainment devoid of wisdom (see *BT Shab.* 31a–b; *BT Yom.* 72b, *BT Pes.* 22b, *Ex. R.* 30:14).

Orḥot Ẓaddikim also distinguishes among three varieties of *yirah*: fear of social disapproval, fear of punishment, that is, fear of harm to oneself, and awe of God's greatness. Because awe is rare and difficult to achieve, the author, like a number of aforementioned sources, considers fear of punishment to be a halakhically acceptable, though theologically undesirable, motivation for divine worship. Despite the significance attached to *yirah* of God by this author, he nevertheless follows earlier precedents by describing *yirah* as a rung on the ladder of ascent toward the higher rung of love of God (*ahavah*, "Love of God," 121). Indeed, the highest variety of *yirah* is actually intertwined with love: "'Serve the Lord with *yirah*' [Ps. 2:11], that is, fear losing His love. . . . Thus, this fear is really love" (129).

The *Sefer ha-Yashar*, an ethical treatise traditionally ascribed to Jacob ben Meir, known as Rabbenu Tam, and probably written in the thirteenth century, sees *yirah* as the necessary by-product of love of God but considers fear of God in itself inadequate, "not the service of the truly pious, but of the wicked or of the nations of the world" (ed. and tr. S. Cohen, 1973, 32–39).

Extensive discussion of *yirah* of God is found in Moses Ḥayyim Luzzatto's eighteenth-century ethical tract *Mesillat Yesharim* (*The Path of the Upright*, tr. M. M. Kaplan, 1936, 12, 310–16, 422–43). Luzzatto distinguishes between two varieties of *yirah* of God: fear of punishment and a sense of awe. Fear of punishment, a universal trait, is easily attainable and is rooted in self-interest. A sense of awe, though difficult to attain, evidences both moral perfection and the acquisition of wisdom. Fear of punishment can be experienced at all times and is characteristic of the masses, while awe of God is a rare commodity, characteristic of the saintly scholar.

The medieval Jewish mystical tradition reaches no consensus as to whether *yirah* or love of God is the higher spiritual trait. The *Zohar*, in opposition to many earlier Jewish philosophical and kabbalistic sources, identifies religious consciousness with *yirah* of God. While identifying both *yirah* and love with various pairs of the divine emanations (*sefirot*), the *Zohar* consistently equates *yirah* with the higher emanation.[6]

The *Zohar* distinguishes among three varieties of *yirah* (1:11b–12a), only one of which is deemed true and proper. The first variety is fear of physical punishment in this world for oneself and for one's family. The second is fear of punishment in the World to Come. Neither is considered genuine *yirah* of God. These are "evil fears" as opposed to the third variety, which is "holy fear." This third valid variety of *yirah* is characterized by awe of God's majesty, and it inevitably intertwines with selfless love of God. Thus, for the *Zohar*, love is a by-product of true *yirah*. Indeed, *yirah* is the foundation not only of love of God, but also of faith and of all of creation.[7]

In his kabbalistic-ethical writings, the sixteenth-century writer Judah Loew of Prague rejects the view of the *Zohar* that elevates *yirah* over love of God. Loew returns to a position that considers awe of God to be inferior to love of God. For Loew, awe is a necessary step in preparing the individual for communion with the divine, which is the result of love of God. Awe guarantees the prerequisite wisdom and the prerequisite self-abnegation that are the premises upon which love of and communion with God are predicated (*Netivot Olam*, 2:20–37).

The most comprehensive analysis of *yirah* of God in Jewish literature is found in *"Shaar ha-Yirah,"* the opening section, consisting of fifteen chapters, of Elijah de Vidas's sixteenth-century mystical-ethical treatise *Reshit Hokhmah*. Like Loew, de Vidas considers *yirah* to be the necessary prerequisite for the higher attitude of love of God.

De Vidas expands upon earlier distinctions between fear of sin and awe of God. Developing earlier kabbalistic notions of sin, de Vidas places considerable significance on fear of sin, since sin affects not only the human self but the godhead as well. For de Vidas, fear of sin is motivated not simply by a fear of self-harm but by a fear of causing a flaw in all of the "worlds" that are placed between us and the divine. Indeed, for de Vidas, fear of sin entails fear of disrupting the flow of divine grace to our world, of disturbing the balance of the *sefirot*, and of causing injury to the *Shekhinah*. For de Vidas, as for Luzzatto, fear of sin is a necessary spur directed at the coarser features of the human personality. The coarser the person, the more fear of sin is required. Like Luzzatto, de Vidas reserves the higher *yirah*, awe of God, for the saintly and for the wise. In the course of his discussion, de Vidas transmits a manuscript on the tortures of hell *(Massekhet Gehinnom)* that contains typical medieval descriptions of the tortures of hell reserved for those who were devoid of fear of sin during their lifetimes.

Though the earlier distinction between fear and awe was perpetuated by the Musar movement that arose in nineteenth-century Lithuania, this movement strongly emphasized fear of punishment as the primary means to human self-development and as a necessary prophylactic measure against improper behavior.[8]

In eighteenth- and nineteenth-century Hasidic thought, fear of punishment for sin is deemphasized and fear of punishment in hell is absent. Hasidic literature perpetuates the distinction between a lower and a higher variety of *yirah* of God. Levi Isaac ben Meir of Berdichev, for example, considers the "lower" to be both a prelude for and a conduit to the "higher." For Levi Isaac, echoing Judah Loew, awe of God means the surrender of self-awareness in response to the majesty of God (*Kedushat Levi,* "Ekev," 1962, 876–86).

The first Hasidic author, Jacob Joseph of Polonnoye, identifies the "lower" *yirah* with outward expression and the "higher" *yirah* with the inwardness of the soul. He proceeds to address the longstanding problem of the reconciliation of *yirah* and love of God by asserting that at a high level of inwardness, *yirah* and love of God coalesce into one and become inseparable and indistinguishable, thus obviating a need to give priority to one over the other (*Toledot Yaakov Yosef,* "Ekev," 2, 1961, 628–32).

Despite the considerable discussion of *yirah* in classical Jewish literature, modern Jewish thinkers have largely ignored the notion of *yirah* of God. An exception is Morris Joseph, who, in *Judaism as Creed and Life* (1903), stresses fear of God as a concept with modern relevance in that it may still serve as a powerful motive for engendering responsible moral behavior (112–26). Abraham Joshua Heschel offers a short phenomenological analysis of *yirah* in *God in Search of Man* (1955, 73–79). Heschel stresses the role of awe as a prerequisite for faith and discusses the interrelationship between awe and wisdom. Louis Jacobs offers informative and erudite analytical essays on *yirah* of God in *Jewish Values* (31–50) and in *A Jewish Theology* (174–82). Jacobs correctly observes that religion devoid of *yirat shamayim* tends to become reduced to comfortable sentimentality.

Despite the relatively sparse attention given the notion of awe of God by modern Jewish theologians, *yirah* persists as an omnipresent theme throughout the Jewish liturgy, particularly the High Holiday liturgy. What has been evaded by contemporary theologians in their writings is nevertheless continuously articulated and affirmed by Jews in their prayers. For example, in the "Prayer for a New Month," the liturgy, refusing to relegate the attainment of *yirat shamayim* to human effort alone, requests the enlistment of divine grace in its attainment. Further, the High Holiday liturgy perpetuates the hope that the *yirah* of God might stimulate all creatures to acknowledge God and to unite in a single fellowship in the performance of his will. In the final analysis, it is not the speculation of theologians that determines the features of faith. Rather, one must "go and see what the people do" (BT Er. 14b). Though neglected by many Jewish theologians, *yirat shamayim* is not neglected either by Jewish prayer or by Jews at prayer.

REFERENCES

1. *Orḥot Ẓaddikim,* ed. and tr. S. Cohen (1969), 590.
2. See, for example, Franciscus Semkowski Zorell, *Lexicon Hebraicum et Aramaicum Veteris Testamenti* (1968), s.v. *yirah.*
3. See also *Seder Eliyahu Rabbah,* ed. Friedman, n.d., ch. 28, 140–41.
4. Solomon Schechter, *Abot de Rabbi Natan* (1967), 26, n. 11. Compare text and n. 10 on page 26. See also Adolf Büchler, *Studies in Sin and Atonement in the Rabbinic Literature of the First Century* (1928), 118–75; Efraim Urbach, *The Sages: Their Concepts and Beliefs* 1 (1975), 400–19.
5. For precedents for this view see, for example, Rashi, ad loc. BT Meg. 25b; Midrash Tenaim, ed. Z. Hoffmann (1908), 260.
6. See I. Tishbi, *Mishnat ha-Zohar* 2 (1961), 293–95.
7. See also Eccl. R. 3:14, para. 1.
8. See, for example, the views of Isaac Blazer in Dov Katz, *Tenuat ha-Musar* 2 (1973), 260–73.

BIBLIOGRAPHY

Bernard Bamberger, "Fear and Love of God in the Old Testament," in *Hebrew Union College Annual* 6 (1929).

Adolf Büchler, *Studies in Sin and Atonement in the Rabbinic Literature of the First Century* (1928), 119–75.

Louis Jacobs, *A Jewish Theology* (1973), 174–83.

Louis Jacobs, *Jewish Values* (1960), 31–50.

Efraim Urbach, *The Sages: Their Concepts and Beliefs* 1 (1975), 400–19.

Feminism

פמיניזם

Susannah Heschel

Jewish feminism focuses on three issues: attaining complete religious involvement for Jewish women; giving Jewish expression to women's experiences and self-understanding; and highlighting the imagery, language, and rituals already present within Jewish tradition that center around the feminine and women. These efforts involve changing or eliminating aspects of Jewish law, customs, and teachings that prevent or discourage women from developing positions of equality to men within Judaism as well as bringing new interpretations to bear on the tradition. The implications of the proposed radical reevaluations go to the heart of Jewish beliefs concerning God, revelation, and Torah. For example, if the Torah holds women in positions of subservience or contempt, contradicting women's self-understanding, then, feminism concludes, either the God who has revealed the Torah is a malevolent deity or the Torah is not God's revelation, but merely the projection of a patriarchal society intent on preserving its status quo.

Such conclusions lead some feminists away from Jewish theology to a secularized revision of Jewish beliefs and community completely outside the framework of Torah. Another conclusion contends that the Torah's claim to revelation must be understood to allow interpretations of its content in consonance with feminist values and principles. This option seeks to place feminism in the context of other major revisions in Judaism, such as the shift from sacrificial to liturgical worship after the destruction of the Temple.

Making feminist goals comparable in magnitude to those achieved after the destruction of the Temple raises broad implications that have only recently begun to be recognized. During the last two decades most Jewish feminist writings called for specific, concrete changes in Jewish observance and maintained a tone of optimism. Feminism and Judaism were not in the least contradictory, many argued, and equality of women and men was for the good of the entire community. Such optimism grew from a theological position that emphasized the intentionality of Jewish sources. According to this position, equality of women and men was honestly intended by Judaism's prophetic teachings of justice and by the devotion to God underlying talmudic law. The intention had not been realized during the course of Jewish history for sociological, not theological, reasons.

Cynthia Ozick has articulated this position by arguing that Torah itself, while lacking a commandment stating "Thou shalt not lessen the humanity of women," nonetheless contains the basis for eliminating its own diminution of women's humanity in its proclamation of justice as an absolute requirement.[1] Yet her argument fails to address the problem of how a teaching that claims to be divinely revealed can legislate practices that are in opposition to its self-proclaimed goal of justice. If Torah is the revealed word of God, how can it be other than just and right in all its aspects? Moreover, how can we even claim knowledge of what is just and right without that divine source of knowledge? Finally, Ozick's argument shares with those of other Jewish theologians the seemingly insoluble quandary of determining what constitutes the revealed, immutable essence of Judaism and what should be viewed as merely a temporal, human invention.

In recent years, Jewish feminists have sought new approaches to Judaism by attempting to redefine both feminism and Judaism. The starting point for this newly emerging Jewish feminism is the application of the classic formulations of feminist thought to Jewish texts, beliefs, and practices. Feminist writers such as Mary Daly and Simone de Beauvoir define patriarchy as the situation in which men's experiences and expressions of those experiences are equated with normative human nature and behavior. Women stand as Other to those norms and are denied the opportunity to define themselves except in relation to men. De Beauvoir writes, "Thus humanity is male and man defines woman not in herself but as relative to him; she is not regarded as an autonomous being. . . . She is defined and differentiated with reference to man and not he with reference to her; she is the incidental, the inessential as opposed to the essential. He is the Subject, he is the Absolute, she is the Other."[2]

Turning to Judaism, feminists discover a structure in which women are viewed as Other not only in the synagogue or within the Orthodox community but also within basic Jewish teachings, symbols, and language. Women stand as Other while men are the Subjects in the liturgy, in halakhah, and even in Judaism's theological formulations of God as father and king. Woman as Other is expressed, for example, by Judaism's "purity" laws, in which women convey impurity not to themselves or to other women but only to the men with whom they come into contact. Women enter into the discussions of Judaism's law codes only insofar as the codes affect men's lives and, with only rare exceptions, women have historically been banned from writing and studying Jewish texts. As Judith Plaskow writes, "Men are the actors in religious and communal life because they are the normative Jews. Women are 'other than' the norm; we are less than fully human."[3]

The significance of the Otherness of women within Judaism has received different evaluations. Most Jewish feminists today agree with de Beauvoir's definition of woman as Other, but differ as to whether and how women's status can be shifted from Other to Subject. Increasing numbers of feminists insist that the incorporation of female language, particularly about God, is the most important and perhaps the only way this shift can be brought about. As long as God is described and addressed solely in male language and imagery, they argue, women will remain identified as Other. Only when God is addressed as She or as Goddess will women become subjects in the monotheistic religious framework. A key problem for feminists is what should be the source of this language and imagery. Naomi Goldenberg, Rita Gross, and others draw mainly from personal, inner symbols and experiences in their description of the Goddess and urge that these sources be brought into a Jewish context.[4] Simply employing female imagery is not enough, they argue; it is the type of imagery that matters. They reject as patriarchal the imagery already present within the kabbalistic tradition, which views the feminine aspect of the godhead as passive and receptive. Instead, feminists suggest strong, dynamic, creative, and active images of the female.

Addressing God as She or as Goddess raises the question whether Jewish feminists are giving a new name to the traditional God of Jewish patriarchy or evoking a Goddess of the ancient world, worshiped, according to the Bible, by many ancient Israelites. Feminists such as Savina Teubal and Jane Litman argue that biblical and talmudic sources hint at a vibrant tradition of women's religiosity eventually excluded from the mainstream of Jewish religion.[5] Those traditions of prior generations of Jewish women that can be reconstructed from the scanty sources are being urged as the basis for a new, feminist Judaism. Such reconstructions would include the celebration of the New Moon as a woman's holiday and the fifteenth day of the month of Av as a day for women to dance and rejoice.[6]

Other feminists, such as Lynn Gottlieb and Arthur Waskow, argue that the ways women have traditionally been viewed—for example, as sensitive, accommodating, gentle, intuitive—have been denigrated by patriarchal society. Rather than such attributes being rejected in favor of traditionally masculine values, they require recognition as significant human values for men as well as women.[7] Waskow argues that the status of women as Other within Judaism and the denigration of women's attributes are not accidental, but are intrinsic to a masculine way of thinking characterized by dualism and projection. According to Waskow, by eliminating the dominance of masculine thinking and encouraging the adoption by men and women of traditionally feminine modes of thinking not only will women become equal with men, but Judaism will achieve its own goal of redeeming the world. A feminist Judaism, in this vision, will emphasize God's immanence rather than transcendence. Equality would not be achieved simply by women performing the Jewish rituals heretofore limited to men. Rather, this group of feminists urges a renewal of customs traditionally limited to women, such as immersion in the mikveh, hallah baking, and praying separately. Not only will the values that emerge from women's experiences be strengthened, but so will the sense of identity with the historical experience of Jewish women.[8]

At issue in all the approaches are both the relationships of women to Jewish history and tradition and feminism as a mode of reinterpreting Judaism. In trying to maintain a link to the historical experiences of Jewish women, some feminists fear they may simply perpetuate the view of women created by patriarchal culture. Yet in breaking with traditional women's roles and identities feminists also risk the danger of making maleness the goal for women. The broader theological implications of feminism are shared by all interpreters of texts, history, and symbols. A central point is whether feminists are explicating the deeper meaning of Jewish tradition or grafting onto it their own, new concerns. The more radical feminists question whether aspects of Judaism that have functioned during history to keep women in a position of Other can today be made meaningful through reinterpretation. Most Jewish feminists try to remain within Judaism's framework, viewing their efforts as a new stage in a continually developing Judaism. But they are faced with the problem of trying to justify the continued relevance of traditions and beliefs they want to retain. Once the laws and teachings regarding women are viewed as an outgrowth of a particular historical period, we need a theological justification for the relevance of all traditions and texts that we might wish to observe and study, from the Sabbath to the Talmud. This last problem, which has only recently come to be articulated by feminists, joins women with other Jewish theologians and places feminism at the forefront of current theological discussion.

REFERENCES

1. Cynthia Ozick, "Notes Toward Finding the Right Question," in *On Being a Jewish Feminist,* ed. Susannah Heschel (1983), 120–51. See also Blu Greenberg, *Women and Judaism: A View from Tradition* (1982).
2. Simone de Beauvoir, *The Second Sex,* ed. and tr. H. M. Parshley (1953), 16.
3. Judith Plaskow, "The Right Question Is Theological," in *On Being a Jewish Feminist,* 224.
4. Naomi Goldenberg, *The Changing of the Gods* (1979); Rita M. Gross, "Steps Toward Feminine Imagery of Deity in Jewish Theology," in *On Being a Jewish Feminist,* 234–47.
5. Savina J. Teubal, *Sarah the Priestess: The First Matriarch of Genesis* (1984); Jane Litman, "How to Get What We Want by the Year 2000," in *Lilith: The Jewish Women's Magazine* 7 (1980), 21–22.
6. Arlene Agus, "This Month Is for You: Observing Rosh Hodesh as a Woman's Holiday," in *The Jewish Woman: New Perspectives,* ed. Elizabeth Koltun (1976).
7. Arthur Waskow, "Feminist Judaism: Restoration of the Moon"; Lynn Gottlieb, "The Secret Jew: An Oral Tradition of Women" and "Spring Cleaning Ritual on the Eve of Full Moon Nisan," in *On Being a Jewish Feminist,* 261–80.
8.. Rachel Adler, "Tum'ah and Toharah," in *Response: A Contemporary Jewish Review* 18 (Summer 1973), 117–24.

BIBLIOGRAPHY

Rachel Biale, *Women and Jewish Law* (1984).
Bernadette Brooten, *Women Leaders in the Ancient Synagogue* (1982).
Carol Christ and Judith Plaskow, *Womanspirit Rising: A Feminist Reader in Religion* (1979).
Naomi Goldenberg, *The Changing of the Gods* (1979).
Blu Greenberg, *On Women and Judaism: A View from Tradition* (1982).
Susannah Heschel, *On Being a Jewish Feminist: A Reader* (1983).
Elizabeth Koltun, *The Jewish Woman: New Perspectives* (1976).
Roslyn Lacks, *Women and Judaism: Myth, History and Struggle* (1980).
Moshe Meiselman, *Jewish Woman in Jewish Law* (1978).
Savina Teubal, *Sarah the Priestess* (1984).

Freedom

חירות

Eugene B. Borowitz

The unique contours of the contemporary discussion about freedom appear most clearly against the background of classic Jewish views.

The Bible contains little direct reference to freedom. The fewer than two dozen direct references in it mainly concern the release of a slave or otherwise legally encumbered person. National freedom receives scant mention. By contrast, much of the Bible's legislation and literary allusion speak of slavery, personal and ethnic. While no sure inferences can be drawn from the writers' essentially negative attitude toward nonfreedom, the pervasiveness and significance of this attitude shape the later development of the issue.

This concern with freedom coheres well with the root reality of Hebraic religious experience, that the one and only God brought the people of Israel out of Egyptian slavery and gave them his own instruction. Torah, the foundation of all other biblical values, placed its greatest emphasis on law and commandment. Remember and do, it continually exhorts; do not go after your own heart and eyes. In such a worldview, Torah delineates appropriate freedom, giving it proper scope and worth.

Both the economic and political aspects of freedom receive considerable adumbration in rabbinic literature. While accepting the institutions of slavery and temporary bondage, the rabbis increased responsibilities for owners and benefits for those in bondage. A number of teachers explicitly derogate a social status that inhibits the initiative they believe Jews ought ideally to bring to the observance of God's Torah. The same reasoning applies to the people of Israel as a whole. "Subjugation to the nations," a widely used rabbinic theological term, impedes the service the people of Israel owe God. For the rabbis, this punishment that has come upon their people is the equivalent of their ancestors' slavery in Egypt, and they fervently look forward to their own exodus and redemption. Personally and nationally, the continuity of the rabbis with the biblical writers stands out. Freedom remains an instrumental value, cherished as a condition for fulfilling Torah.

This fundamental notion takes another form in the Middle Ages. While the rabbis' concerns manifest themselves in the succeeding centuries—with the issue of personal status declining in interest—the focus of medieval Jewish thinkers becomes ontological. Since God knows everything, thus determining what is, how can one have free will with which to respond to the Torah's behests?

The question agitated medieval Jewish philosophers because it brings into contradiction two fundamental beliefs of Judaism (as of the religions derived from it): God's sovereignty and human responsibility. The former now required that God know everything, hence the future as well as the past. The Torah calls Jews to obedience to God's instruction, regularly exhorting them about the major consequences of their response. But if what they do is not a matter of their volition, the entire scheme seems irrational, particularly the retribution that so strongly characterizes it.

Almost all the major medieval Jewish thinkers refused to compromise on the reality of human initiative. Some argued that the problem lies beyond human capacity, whereas others preferred to conceptualize causation so as to allow for the free exercise of will. Only an occasional thinker found himself required to affirm some variety of determinism. The Jewish mystics, however, who often utilized philosophic notions, had little difficulty with this issue. They regularly reconciled paradoxes through the employment of an elaborate symbol system that could be manipulated in endless ways on multiple levels.

With the modern period, a revolutionary change occurred in Jewish status, both personal and ethnic. The term used to describe this shift, *emancipation*, literally means the formal process of freeing a slave. With the birth of democratic states and their new notion of citizenship, the term could be applied metaphorically to the granting of civil rights to those previously disenfranchised. On the human level, the results, though slow in coming and marred by a new anti-Semitism, were monumentally beneficial to the Jews. This extraordinary social progress permeated the modern Jewish consciousness and fundamentally shaped the contemporary Jewish discussion of freedom.

Theoretically, the modern democratic state derives from the idea of the dignity of each individual, a concept that emerged gradually after the late Middle Ages. Several major points in that development shape the modern Jewish version of the problem of freedom: Descartes's insistence on the individual's right to doubt all ideas until he could make them clear and convincing to himself; Rousseau's argument that this human capacity to think could be reconciled with government only if people were self-governing; and, above all, Kant's extension of this idea to the moral realm, that only an autonomous ethics is worthy of a rational person.

Though this Kantian notion of the modern person as self-legislating has dominated the agenda of modern Jewish thought, the fate of the problem of freedom of the will deserves some mention. When scientific determinism exercised considerable hold on thinkers, the problem did receive some general attention. But, as in the Middle Ages, life (if not intellect) seemed to refute the denial of freedom. Though research continues to unveil ever-further determinants of human nature, the general discounting of science's omniscience and the record of unpredictable human responses to the extraordinary (and sometimes ordinary) circumstances of this century have kept determinism at the outer periphery of intellectual concern.

Autonomy, however, strikes at the very heart of classic Jewish faith: God, not the self, gives law. If, then, modernity instructs the Jew to contravene what the sages of our day declare to be Torah, then the observant Jew will reject the blandishments of the philosophy of autonomy. For a minority of Jews, freedom within Torah remains the only way one can continue to be faithful to the covenant. The overwhelming majority of Jews, convinced by the spiritual benefits of emancipation, have sought some way of accommodating to it and thus to its emphasis on freedom.

The problem assumed its classic form when, for the sake of stemming conversion to Christianity, laymen started breaching accepted Jewish law so as to modernize the synagogue service and Jewish life. When thinkers began validating this process, they utilized the newly developed critical notion of history as continual change. To this they later added the scientific metaphor of evolution. For much of modern Jewry, historical development became the ideological validation for breaking with Jewish law or radically catalyzing its development. This ideology continues to function well wherever people can still believe that the onward march of events itself can, in some fashion, indicate where Jewish tradition needs to be maintained or modified.

Jewish thinkers who desired to give this notion philosophical respectability had Hegel and the Christian Hegelians available for their theorizing, but despite some efforts in this direction, no full-scale Jewish Hegelianism ever received much attention. Not the least reason for this was, by contrast to Kant, the highly limited place of ethics and thus human initiative in unreconstructed Hegelianism.

The first great modern Jewish philosophy, that of Hermann Cohen, makes ethics, and therefore human freedom, primary to the entire system. To Cohen as to Kant, human nature is identified with rationality, which, in turn, defined in terms of ethics, science, and aesthetics, is so self-evident as to require no justification. One cannot then deny human freedom without rejecting what makes us persons, not beasts. To be modern and rational, then, meant for Cohen to be autonomous and to legislate for oneself such laws of conduct as reason, so carefully defined by him, might dictate.

Cohen's notion of freedom goes one extraordinary step further, for he closely identifies reason with creativity. For him, the mind does not exist as such and then begin to think when energized by thinkers; rather, at our rational best, we create the apparatus by which the work of thinking proceeds—or somewhat less fundamentally, we originate an idea by which we will then rationally construct reality (in interaction with what we encounter, to be sure, but meeting that, of course, which our foundational idea allows to enter our experience). Creativity out of nothing, so to speak, is the apex of Cohen's rationalism. Thus for him freedom has as good as infinite worth.

In a Kantian, regulative sense, Cohen believed that his comprehensive, ethical worldview lay at the heart of Judaism, with the prophets providing its clearest articulation. With considerable polemic vigor, he argued that Judaism, of all historic religions, came closest to exemplifying his concept of a religion of reason. He realized that this theory only validated universal ethics as Jewish duty; proud Jew that he was, Cohen sought to provide a broader mandate to enable Judaism to survive. He did this by delineating the particular role remaining for religion once philosophy had done its work, and became more particular only when he occasionally argued that by its origination of the idea of ethical monotheism (in his sense) Judaism retained unique insight into it.

From Cohen's time on, a major focus of modern Jewish thought has been the proper limits of self-legislation. Two developments have raised this issue to critical importance. On the human level, explorations of ethical freedom have revealed not only new dimensions of personhood but also ethical proposals that radically contradict much prior ethical teaching. In the realm of Jewish experience, the strong rational validation of universal ethics makes the rest of Jewish practice seem optional in a time when Jewish ties badly need strengthening. No subsequent liberal solution to these problems has succeeded in winning a substantial number of adherents. How rationally to mandate an ethical system and how to justify group authority against individual autonomy remain utterly troublesome philosophic issues. Until this general problem of human authority is philosophically resolved, rationalistic theories of Jewish freedom are unlikely to return to liberal Jewish popularity.

As with regard to other traditions in America at large, liberalism's loss of its prior self-evident correctness and its continuing inability to transcend its weakened cultural props have made possible a revival of Jewish orthodoxy. Human freedom having shown itself unreliable if not destructive, God's gracious gift of Torah once again manifests its virtue as the only proper way for Jews. In modern Orthodoxy, much space can be made for the exercise of individual freedom and participation in contemporary culture.

Thus far, no systematic discussion of the proper role of personal freedom in Orthodoxy has yet appeared. In his essay *Halakhic Man,* Rabbi Joseph B. Soloveitchik demonstrated how rationality functions in the life utterly grounded in the law. That paper clearly lays out the Orthodox Jewish analogue of Hermann Cohen's rationality. But neither there nor elsewhere in his published works has Rabbi Soloveitchik given us an extensive analysis of the individual Jew's legitimate exercise of self-determination. He has, on occasion, made reference to possible tensions that might arise between the individual will and God's dictates. These he treats as the existential equivalent of sacrifices, with faithful Jews offering up their freedom at God's behest.

For all the fresh appeal of Orthodoxy, most modernized Jews have not been willing to accept it; they prefer the notion of tradition to that of Torah as discipline. At its best, this response acknowledges that, for all their failings, modernity and its central notion of autonomy must find a place in Judaism. The immediate issues that have forced this question upon the community have been women's rights in Judaism and the place of democracy. On both counts, there seems a fundamental clash between what much of the community believes to be ultimately right and what the overwhelming majority of sages declare to be halakhically binding.

National freedom has similarly been thoroughly recast in modern times. The human initiative asserted on the personal level gave rise to the notion of ethnic self-determination, most notably manifest in nineteenth-century nationalism. Among Jews this produced Zionism, despite the accepted understanding of the Torah that God alone, through the Messiah, should reestablish Jewish political sovereignty—a difficulty still manifest in the continuing ambivalence toward Zionism of the most observant sector of the Jewish community.

The establishment and positive accomplishments of the State of Israel have won it the support and admiration of almost all of world Jewry. But the continuing confrontation with perilous circumstances has aborted the occasional efforts to turn Zionist thought from ideology to systematic analysis. In particular, the problem of what limits there should be to the exercise of Jewish national freedom has received little theoretical discussion. In part this has been due to the intense community opposition to any public discussion of Diaspora Jewish concern with particular policies of given Israeli administrations. In equal part, at least, the problem also arises from the difficulty of establishing standards, certainly from a secular point of view, by which to make such judgments.

I have sought to approach these issues by adumbrating a theory of Judaism in terms of the particular relationship in which the autonomous Jewish self stands. In my personalist understanding of the covenant, Kant's secular autonomy has been radically transformed. Rather than reason guiding the self, the individual stands in intimate relationship to God, and from that— or from the tradition that or the teachers who authentically articulate the consequences of this relationship—the individual discovers what must be done.

That is true universally; all mankind shares in the Noachide covenant. The Jewish self, however, does not stand in isolated relationship with God but shares in the people of Israel's historic covenant. Jewish duty derives from this and is, therefore, as ineluctably particular as it is universal, social as it is personal. Yet it must ultimately be individually appropriated and projected. For all that the Jewish self comes before God as one of the Jewish people, the Jew remains a self with the personal right to determine what God now demands of the people of Israel and of any particular member of it.

Often this personalist approach to Jewish duty will lead to acknowledging the lasting value of classic Jewish teaching and thus to simple obedience. But it may also require modification or abandonment of an old practice or the creation of a new form adequate to the continuing reality of an ancient relationship. Discipline has thus been internalized, but the consequent subjectivity has been contained by defining the self in terms of its relationship with God and the Jewish people. Were there enough Diaspora Jewish "selves" who lived by this standard, communal norms of Jewish duty might once again arise, though in forms different from those created when Jewish discipline was essentially objectified.

This covenantal understanding applies equally to the State of Israel as to individual Jews. Here, too, freedom becomes responsible only in the service of God in continuation of the Jewish people's millennial relationship with God.

BIBLIOGRAPHY

Eugene B. Borowitz, "The Autonomous Jewish Self," in *Modern Judaism* 4, 1 (February 1984).

Eugene B. Borowtiz, "The Autonomous Self and the Commanding Community," in *Theological Studies* 45, 1 (March 1984).

Hermann Cohen, *Religion of Reason out of the Sources of Judaism* (1972).

Hillel Halkin, *Letters to an American Jewish Friend* (1977).

Joseph B. Soloveitchik, *Halakhic Man* (1983).

Free Will

בחירה חופשית

David Winston

Biblical monotheism, which tended to subordinate the entire natural world to the sovereign power of YHWH, was ineluctably driven to attribute even the human psychological sphere to the all-determining divine action. "There was no other way of expressing the uncanny, overpowering, 'demonic' character of the power of sin, than by seeing this too as a work of Yahweh, even if one executed in anger."[1] We thus find a series of human events explicated by Scripture through the notion of psychic invasion. God directly intervenes in Pharaoh's inner deliberations, "hardening his heart" in order to demonstrate his divine might (Ex. 10:1). God also hardens the heart of Sihon, king of the Amorites (Deut. 2:30), and applies the same divine strategy to the Canaanites (Josh. 11:20). Conversely, God does not permit Abimelech, king of Gerar, to sin with Abraham's wife Sarah (Gen. 20:6). In an encounter with Saul, David suggests that it may have been the Lord who has incited Saul against him (I Sam. 26:19), and when the Lord's anger is kindled against Israel, we are told that he incites David to number Israel and Judah (II Sam. 24:1). On the other hand, the Deuteronomist emphasizes the crucial significance of human choice and its consequent culpability when it has gone astray (Deut. 30:19–20). Nonetheless, Scripture makes no attempt to harmonize the moral freedom of the individual with God's effective action in all things, but remains content to affirm both.

In light of the scriptural emphasis on divine intervention, it is not difficult to see how Jewish wisdom and apocalyptic writings came to emphasize the decisive importance of God's prior gift of wisdom for the determination of human character. What baffles the reader of this ancient literature, however, is the easy coexistence in it of two apparently contradictory strands of thought, namely, an emphasis on God's ultimate determination of all human action coupled with an equally emphatic conviction that the human will is the arbiter of its own moral destiny. The Apocryphal writer Ben Sira thus asserts that God has predetermined human character from birth and has divided humanity into two antithetical groups, the godly and the sinners (Ecclus. 1:14–15, 33:10–15). Yet at the same time he teaches that we are free to choose our individual life paths and must not blame God for our transgressions (Ecclus. 15:11–17). A similar dilemma confronts us in the Qumran Scrolls. The author of the *Hodayot* scroll, for example, is acutely aware of God's overwhelming and all-regulating power (1QH 15:20–21). Yet alongside the inevitability of the divine plan with its prior determination of every human psyche for all time, we find a recurrent emphasis on human voluntaristic action (1QS 6:13; 5:1).

The solution to the apparent contradiction confronting us is to be found in the realization that the freedom which the ancients generally ascribed to humanity was of a relative rather than of an absolute kind. The Stoic view serves as a good illustration of a relative free will theory of the causal type. The Stoics believed unflinchingly in a universal causal chain called *Heimarmenē*. That which is apparently uncaused is so only from the point of view of our limited range of knowledge. Man's entire deliberative process is therefore also subject to the causal nexus. But an important distinction is then drawn between *Heimarmenē*, which constitutes the proximate cause of human action, and our inner psyche, which constitutes the principal cause of such action. This distinction emphasizes our relative autonomy. Ultimately, all the factors in the process of human deliberation are determined, but the Stoic joyfully and enthusiastically embraces his destiny, content with the capacity consciously to share in the processes that initiate action. In short, within the framework of a theory of relative freedom (or "soft determinism," in the phrase of William James), the concepts of determinism and predestination may freely coexist with that of voluntarism. God can be envisaged as predetermining human nature to include the power of deliberative choice, though as human nature's sovereign author he also determines its mode of operation and consequently all that results from it. It did not particularly bother most ancient writers, however, that God was thus ultimately responsible for human moral delinquency and the punishments that followed it. They simply accepted this hard reality as part of the divine mystery. It was only under the impact of extraordinary catastrophes that their concepts of freedom and predestination became unglued and required new and more subtle interpretations to put them together again.

Having outlined the ancient perspective on human freedom, we may now readily ascertain the rabbinic view. Following in the footsteps of Mosaic Scripture, the rabbis wished only to emphasize human moral responsibility without compromising the all-determining power of divine Providence. To this end they taught a doctrine of freedom roughly equivalent to the relative free will theory found in ancient Greek philosophy. They were fully alert to the ultimate divine determination of human character, and they did not attempt to diminish its essential mystery. A late midrash, for example, put the following critique into the mouth of Cain: "Master of the world, if I have killed him [Abel], it is thou who hast created in me the Evil Yezer [drive] . . . It is Thou who has killed him" (Tanḥ. Gen. 9b). In a more pointed attempt to locate the source of human motivations in God, the rabbis pleaded in favor of the brothers of Joseph, "When Thou didst choose, Thou didst make them love; when Thou didst choose Thou didst make them hate" (BR 84–18, Theodor Albeck, ed., 1022). Elijah, too, spoke insolently toward Heaven, saying to God, "Thou hast turned their heart back again," and God later confessed that Elijah was right (BT Ber. 31b; cf. BR 34.10, Theodor Albeck, ed., 320). A similar critique is voiced with almost consistent monotony by the author of IV Ezra: "This is my first and last word; better had it been that the earth had not produced Adam, or else, having once produced him, [for Thee] to have restrained him from sinning" (IV Ezra 7:116; cf. Apoc. Abr. 23:14).

Although the statement of Rabbi Ḥanina ben Ḥama, a first-generation Palestinian *amora,* that "everything is in the hand of Heaven except the fear of Heaven" (BT Ber. 33b; cf. BT Nid. 16b) has sometimes been taken to imply an absolute free will doctrine, it is most unlikely that this interpretation is correct. Rabbi Ḥanina probably only meant to imply that whereas God's providence in every other aspect of human life involves direct guidance and at times even intervention, this does not apply to human moral deliberations, which ultimately depend upon the spiritual endowments initially bestowed on a person by God. Moreover, the famous paradox of Rabbi Akiva that asserts that "everything is foreseen [by God], yet man has the capacity to choose freely" (M. Avot 3:15)—or as Josephus put it, "to act rightly or otherwise rests for the most part with man, but in each action Fate cooperates" (*Wars* 2, 162–63)—is undoubtedly a Jewish version of the well-known Stoic paradox that although everything is in accordance with *Heimarmenē,* yet human action is within our power (in Greek, *eph hēmin*) (cf. Mikh. Pisḥ a, Lauterbach ed., 1:134).

The situation is not very different in the writings of the Jewish religious philosophers. Philo's position, as I have demonstrated elsewhere,[2] is that insofar as we share in God's Logos, we share to some extent in God's freedom. That this is only a relative freedom is emphasized by him when he says that God gave man such a portion of his freedom as he was capable of receiving, and that he was liberated as far as might be (*Deus* 47–48). In another passage he states more bluntly that "we are the instruments, now tensed now slackened, through which particular actions take place, and it is the Artificer who effects the percussion of both our bodily and psychic powers, he by whom all things are moved" (Cher. 128). Turning to medieval thinkers, it would seem at first blush that Saadiah insisted on God's omniscient foreknowledge coupled with a doctrine of absolute free will (Saadiah, *Sefer Emunot ve-Deot,* 4:3). Saadiah, however, nowhere speaks of an uncaused volitional action and all he seems to claim is that God's foreknowledge of human action does not preclude the choice process. Only if God had arbitrarily determined human action by bypassing the deliberative process could we speak of acting out of compulsion rather than freely. When Saadiah speaks, for example, of those biblical verses that "describe God's work in shaping man's basic nature," and which are "erroneously believed by some to be tantamount to usurping and influencing man's will" (ibid., 4:6), he is simply denying that there is any divine irruption that interferes with human deliberation, for, as he puts it, "what God foreknows is the final denouement of man's activity as it turns out after all his planning, anticipations, and delays" (ibid., 4:4). Similarly, Isaac Husik's objection that Judah Halevi's exposition of the free will problem (*Kuzari* 5, 20ff.) involves a contradiction misses the mark. According to Husik, the contradiction arises because Halevi "admits that the will is caused by higher causes ending ultimately in the will of God, and yet maintains in the same breath that the will is not determined";[3] however, Halevi's teaching, like Saadiah's, does not require him to say that the human will is uncaused. As for Maimonides, Shlomo Pines has correctly pointed out that his esoteric theory teaches nothing beyond a relative free will doctrine, for Maimonides indicates that just as God determines through secondary causes the volition of animals, so is he the ultimate cause of the so-called free choices of rational beings.[4]

The relative nature of the freedom of the human will was fully spelled out in medieval Jewish thought only by Ḥasdai Crescas. Our will, he says, has the possibility of choosing between alternatives, but the causes operating on it determine its choices. If two men were equal in every way, their choices would be identical under the same conditions.[5] But having openly acknowledged that God is the ultimate cause of all human action, how could Crescas justify divine reward and punishment? To this he gave two answers. First, the purpose of divine retribution lies not in itself, but in its power to deter or reinforce human behavior, thus serving as an aid to strengthen the righteous and lead them to bliss. Second, reward and punishment are only the necessary concomitants of virtuous or vicious behavior and therefore do not impugn the divine justice in any way. Finally, to ward off any possible criticism, Crescas took the precaution of indicating that if his formulation of this issue should prove to be contradictory to Scripture, it would have to be abandoned.[6]

In modern Jewish thought, the only indication of the possibility of absolute free will is to be found in the writings of Abraham Heschel, though he confines it to a very limited sphere. Freedom, he says, is not a principle of uncertainty, the ability to act without a motive; nor is it identical to an act of choice. Rather, it is the ability to react to the unique and the novel. It is liberation from the tyranny of the self-centered ego, an event that occurs in rare creative moments of self-transcendence as an act of spiritual ecstasy. Its nature is a mystery, but without it there is no meaning to the moral life.[7]

In sum, Jewish religious thought has generally been content with a relative free will theory, although this has rarely been spelled out with any precision even in the medieval and modern periods. A striking exception in the modern period is the nineteenth-century Jewish mystic Mordecai Joseph Leiner of Izbica, who wrote that the signal characteristic of the future world is that in it the illusion of free choice will vanish, and that acts will no longer be ascribed to their human agents but to God, their true author.[8] Hence the attempt of some modern Jewish theologians to solve the problem of radical human evil, which has become especially acute since the Holocaust, by rooting such evil in the divine gift of human freedom has proved a failure, since the concept of relative freedom found in classical Jewish sources fully acknowledges that all free human action is ultimately attributable to the efficacy of the divine causality.

REFERENCES

1. J. Köberle, *Sünde und Gnade im religiösen Leben des Volkes Israel bis auf Christum* (1905), 51 ff., cited in Walter Eichrodt, *Theology of the Old Testament* 2 (1967), 180.
2. David Winston, "Freedom and Determinism in Philo of Alexandria," in *Studia Philonica* 3 (1974–75).
3. Isaac Husik, *A History of Medieval Jewish Philosophy* (1948), 171–73.
4. Guide 2, 48; Shlomo Pines, "Abu'l-Barakat's Poetics and Metaphysics," in *Scripta Hierosolymitana* 6, Excursus (1960), 195–98.
5. Ḥasdai Crescas, *Or Adonai,* Ferrara ed., 2.5.2, 46a.
6. Ibid., 2.5.3, 48ab.
7. Abraham Joshua Heschel, *God in Search of Man* (1955), 410–11.
8. Mordecai Joseph Leiner, *Mei ha-Shiloah,* 1, 14b.

BIBLIOGRAPHY

Alexander Altmann, "The Religion of the Thinkers: Free Will and Predestination in Saadia, Bahya, and Maimonides," in S. D. Goitein, ed., *Religion in a Religious Age* (1974).
David Winston, *The Wisdom of Solomon,* Anchor Bible 43 (1979), 46–58.
David Winston, "Freedom and Determinism in Philo of Alexandria," in *Studia Philonica* 3 (1974–75).

Gesture and Symbol

תנועה וסמל

Josef Stern

G estures—a term that can be used for both nonverbal objects and bodily movements—are among the most distinctive elements of Jewish ritual. Only a few have a practical purpose, for example, covering the eyes with the hand in order to concentrate while reciting the first verse of the *Shema*. Most are said to symbolize themes or feelings or to refer to historical events or eschatological experiences. Yet while the gestures are familiar and the claim that they are symbols oft repeated, it remains to be explained how they function as symbols or vehicles of reference—reserving these two general terms to cover all ways of bearing semanticlike relations to objects, events, and states of affairs. That is, in what ways—assuming that there are multiple modes of symbolization—do gestures in Jewish rituals symbolize or refer to themes or things? To take some first steps toward answering this question, I will construct a taxonomy of symbolic gestures in Jewish rites, drawing on various categories of reference first distinguished by Nelson Goodman and since elaborated by Israel Scheffler.

Central to this approach is a distinction between the medium of the symbol and its mode of symbolization. Gestures in all mediums—olfactory, auditory, visual, and verbal—serve as symbols in the rituals of Judaism, but in each of these mediums there also function alternative modes of symbolization, different ways in which the gestures in that medium relate to what they purport to symbolize or stand for. Three modes prove especially prominent within Jewish ritual: representation or denotation, exemplification, and expression. A few gestures symbolize by just one of these modes, but what is characteristic of ritual gestures is that they are multiply symbolic: they simultaneously refer to different things according to distinct modes of symbolization, some through simple, single-mode referential relations, others through complex chains of reference that involve different mediums as well as different modes. Indeed, a distinctive feature of Jewish ritual is a type of multimedium symbolizing that combines the symbolic interpretation of a gesture with the figurative exegesis of a scriptural text.

To analyze their symbolic functioning, we can abstract ritual gestures from the religious, historical, and social contexts in which they originated and in which they are now employed, and from the various ways in which their symbolic meaning has changed over time. Important as these issues of genesis and transformation are, the concern here will be entirely with the structure of the gestures' symbolic meaning.

The first of the modes of symbolization is gestural denotation or representation, which is the same mode of reference as that employed by names that denote their bearers and pictures that represent their subjects (I will assume that the notions of verbal denotation and pictorial representation are sufficiently clear for the purposes of this discussion, however difficult it may be to analyze them precisely). However, while pictorial representation and verbal denotation both comprise one mode of reference, that is not to deny all differences between pictures and words; some gestures portray or depict their referents after the manner of pictures or dramatic mime, while others describe or designate them like linguistic expressions.

The many ritual gestures said to commemorate significant events, individuals, or objects in the history of Israel utilize a mode of symbolization that is almost always denotation or representation. Some gestures, for example, circumcision, which commemorates God's covenant with Abraham, seem to denote their referents simply by virtue of the fact that the Torah decrees, in the manner of a linguistic stipulation, what they symbolize. Others secure their denotation by depicting one or more of its features, for example, the *ḥaroset* (a mixture of mashed fruits and nuts eaten at the Passover feast) denotes the mortar the Israelites made in Egypt by depicting its color, and the *shofar* (ram's horn blown at the High Holidays) denotes what was heard at Mt. Sinai by making a like sound. And some dramatically portray what they represent, for example, the Sephardic custom for the master of the *seder* (Passover feast) to lay the wrapped *afikoman* (the "dessert" *mazah*) on his shoulder, take a few steps, and say: "This is in memory of our forefathers, who left Egypt bearing their kneading troughs wrapped in their clothes upon their shoulders." Finally, yet other gestures denote figuratively or metonymically, for example, the (prohibited) sinew of the thigh, which commemorates Jacob's struggle with the Angel, or the ram's horn used for the *shofar,* which commemorates the binding of Isaac. Literal or figurative, all such commemoration is generally symbolization by denotation.

A second mode of symbolization is exemplification: reference by a gesture to a selected feature of which it is a sample. When is a gesture a sample of a feature? First, it is necessary, but not sufficient, that the gesture possess the feature. The tailor's swatch of cloth is typically a sample of—or exemplifies—its color or weave but not its size or shape, though it equally possesses all of these features. Those it exemplifies are those it both possesses and refers to, but what it refers to will vary from occasion to occasion with the purpose and context of the performance.

For example, Israel is commanded to bring as a thanksgiving offering "some of every first fruit of the soil" (Deut. 26:2), though the rabbis legislate that it is necessary to bring the first fruit only of the seven species mentioned in Deuteronomy 8:8. Nevertheless, in the typical context of performance the seven species used in the ritual will exemplify all the fruit of the soil. However, a performance of that same ritual may sometimes also serve to demonstrate to others the type of ritual of which it is a performance. For how people in fact learn a ritual generally is not by mastering rules or through explicit teaching but by observing actual performances, which thereby function as samples of their type of rite. For that purpose the above gesture must exemplify only those seven species, and no others, on pain of misrepresenting the ritual.

While denotation is the preponderant mode of reference for verbal languages and exemplification is more central to the arts, the two generally function in tandem in ritual gestures. Thus, the flame lit during the *havdalah* ceremony (marking the conclusion of the Sabbath) represents, and thereby commemorates, the first fire, said to have been created by Adam with divine assistance on the night following the Sabbath of Creation (cf. BT Pes. 54a); at the same time, because it is also the first thing the individual produces by his own efforts after resting on the Sabbath, it also exemplifies human creative activity. Here, moreover, these two symbolic relations interact with each other and the halakhah, engendering still more symbolism. Among the many accounts and myths found throughout ancient literature in which the creation of fire is used to exemplify human creativity, the talmudic version of Adam's act, aided by God and commemorated with a blessing, (BT Ber. 5) is unique, especially, as the late Saul Lieberman observed, in contrast to the Prometheus myth, in which man steals the original fire from Zeus and is punished for his act. For in making a blessing over the flame he brings into being, the individual acknowledges that the product of his own apparently free, creative action is ultimately due to God. Furthermore, once this blessing has been introduced, it brings in its train additional halakhically motivated gestures. Because such a blessing of enjoyment cannot be recited unless there is actual benefit from the object blessed, the light over which the blessing is made must serve some immediate good. Hence, the practitioner folds the palm of one hand, turns its back to the light, and opens it again, using the light to distinguish the tissue of the nail from the flesh and light from shadow. Although this last gesture is possibly the most unusual in the ritual, it is, ironically, the only one that is primarily practical—though it, too, comes to symbolize the distinction between the sacred and the profane, illustrating how symbolic meanings tend to be read into gestures in context even where the gestures would never have had these meanings in themselves.

Exemplification is not, however, limited to features the symbolic object literally possesses. A third mode by which ritual gestures symbolize is metaphorical exemplification or expression. A symbolic gesture expresses a feature if it metaphorically rather than literally possesses the feature and exemplifies it. Thus, a painting that is said to express solemnity is not literally, but only metaphorically, solemn. Similarly, many ritual gestures exemplify features, such as feelings or attitudes, that can be ascribed to them only metaphorically; consequently, in this sense, they are also expressed. Thus, bowing during the *Amidah* (the eighteen benedictions recited while standing) expresses respect for God and submission to his will; beating one's breast while confessing one's sins expresses regret and contrition; and kissing the Torah or *ẓiẓit* (knotted fringe of the prayer shawl) or touching one's *tefillin* while praying, express feelings of love and affection for all *miẓvot*, which are as a whole literally exemplified by the individual articles.

In each instance of exemplification and expression, it should be emphasized, what is symbolized is always a feature related to the symbolic gesture itself, not to its performer or his state. When a person bows during the *Amidah*, it is his gesture that expresses humility in the presence of God regardless of what he happens to feel or intend at that moment. Not that there is no connection between the features or feelings symbolized by the gesture and those felt or had by its performer. On the contrary, the point of ritual—here possibly in contrast to works of art—is to affect its performer by making him have certain feelings and by inspiring him with certain values. But the relation between the feelings and attitudes of the performer and those his gesture symbolizes is also more subtle than identity. Frequently the feeling excited in the performer is caused by, but quite different from, that expressed by the gesture. Thus Rabbi Moses Isserles, the Rama, cites the custom of the very observant to sway while reading or studying the Torah "after the example of the Torah which was given [at Sinai] with terror and shaking" (Sh. Ar. 48). But if the act of swaying is meant to express those feelings, that is not to say that the person studying Torah should himself be seized with terror and shaking—a state in which all productive study is obviously impossible. Rather, the point of the ritual is achieved when its performer appreciates what the gesture symbolizes and is thereby led to regard his study of the Torah with the appropriate seriousness. Moreover, this suggests a broader moral: the feeling aroused in the performer is never simply the effect of the performance per se, but of his understanding of its significance, his reflection on its meaning, and his performance of the ritual out of a realization of what it symbolizes.

Now, with these three basic modes of symbolization—denotation, exemplification, and expression—in hand, let us turn to gestures where they function not only concurrently but in combination, linked together in chains of reference. Consider the Passover *zeroa,* or shankbone, which is said to be "in remembrance of the Paschal sacrifice." According to the earliest reference to this symbol, which is found in Babylonian tractate Pesaḥim 114a, the mode by which it commemorates the historical sacrifice is entirely unrelated to its being a shankbone. Why, then, the *zeroa?* Because that limb is said to symbolize the "outstretched arm" *(zeroa netuyah)* with which God is described as having punished the Egyptians and redeemed Israel (Deut. 26:8). The object on the seder plate exemplifies the feature of being a shankbone, the name for which *(zeroa),* when applied to God in the Torah, metaphorically denotes his might and power: thus, the shankbone symbolizes God's might, but only through the mediation of the textual verse. A chain of reference extends here from the symbolic object to an exemplified feature, from there, in turn, to a scriptural use of the term for that feature and, finally, to the metaphorical denotation of the term in its scriptural context.

In this example, the figurative interpretation of the scriptural term determines but is not itself determined by the symbolic meaning of the gesture.

In other cases, though, text and gesture are so closely connected that the symbolic interpretation of each is derived from the other. One further example of a ritual chain with a scriptural link will illustrate this.

Three aspects of the *lulav* (palm frond) ritual on *Sukkot* are given symbolic interpretations: the waving itself, that it accompanies the recital of certain verses in the *Hallel* (a selection of Psalms 113–18) and not others, and that the *lulav* is pointed and waved in all four directions as well as upward and downward. To explain the first two of these, Rabbi Asher ben Yeḥiel (Commentary on BT Suk. 3, par. 26) cites a midrash according to which the nation of Israel received the *lulav* on *Sukkot* as a sign of celebration to hold aloft and thereby proclaim publicly that, among all the nations of the world who came before God to be judged on Rosh Hashanah and Yom Kippur, it had been judged innocent. While the palm may have been generally regarded at that time as a symbol of innocence or victory, certainly in this midrash the gesture, like waving a banner, expresses Israel's victorious elation. Further, by contrasting Israel with the nations, the midrash also makes the *lulav* into a national emblem. However, Rabbi Asher hints at still other symbolic interpretations for the gesture, linked to the verse "then shall all the trees of the forest shout for joy at the presence of the Lord, for He is coming to rule the earth" (I Chron. 16:33), which he cites as a proof-text of the midrash. Just as forest trees swaying in the wind can be seen as dancing in joy, so the motion of the *lulav* can be taken to depict a dance of rejoicing. And seeing the *lulav* as a sample of nature, the gesture might also exemplify the figurative meaning of the verse and, indeed, of much of the surrounding Chronicles chapter, which describes how the entire natural universe praises God. Rabbi Asher himself, though, connects the verse to the gesture differently. He figuratively reinterprets the verse to yield a description of the rabbinically defined ritual of *lulav*. The verse, in his account, is really elliptic. What it actually means, remembering the midrash, is that with "the trees of the forest"—standing for, and exemplified by, the tree-shaped *lulav*—Israel "shall rejoice before the Lord" after he has come to judge the world, that is, after the High Holidays. Moreover, because the two subsequent verses in Chronicles, 16:34–35, parallel almost verbatim the *Hallel* passages, Ps. 118:1–4, 25, accompanying which the *lulav* is waved, Rabbi Asher interprets those verses as literally exemplifying—as a sample of—the very words in the *Hallel* Israel is to recite while waving the *lulav*. Thus, in the one direction, the scriptural passage figuratively refers to the ritual of *lulav* in all its rabbinic detail; in the other direction, the gesture symbolizes the natural, the joyous, the victorious—the literal and figurative meanings of the verse. Both gesture and verse concurrently function as symbols, each complementing and commenting on the multiple interpretations of the other.

Finally, the *lulav* is waved in all directions. To explain its symbolism, the Talmud quotes a discussion of the same gesture employed in another ritual: the Temple rite of waving the altar loaves, also in all directions, on *Shavuot*. Two explanations are given. According to Rabbi Yoḥanan, the gesture symbolizes—in our terminology, expresses—homage to "he who is master of the four directions and the Heavens above and the Earth below"; according to the Palestinian rabbis in the name of Rabbi Yose bar Ḥaninah, it serves to expel or avert evil spirits, a quasi-magical function reminiscent of, and perhaps in opposition to, pagan harvest rituals in which wind deities were summoned from all directions to bless the harvest (BT Suk. 37; cf. also BT Men. 61a).

Now, apart from the details of these explanations, this discussion also suggests yet a fifth mode of symbolization that holds between the two rituals themselves. By appealing to the *Shavuot* ritual to explain the style and symbolism of the otherwise unrelated *Sukkot* ritual, the rabbis establish a symbolic link between the two; the one is patterned after the other and thereby indirectly refers to it. Rabbi Yossi's opinion suggests a similar, though possibly even more indirect, way in which the common gesture in the two Jewish rituals refers to the antecedent pagan rite they were instituted to counteract. This mode of indirect reference from one gesture to another is not denotation, representation, exemplification, or expression. Instead, let us say that the one alludes to the other. Allusion is one among several referential relations that hold between parallel gestures that are performances of the same or different rituals. Although intersymbolic relations like allusion are often effected through intermediate features—for example, the *Sukkot* ritual alludes to the *Shavuot* rite by virtue of the same exemplified pattern of waving—if we arranged all referential relations in a hierarchy, the ultimate terms between which relations like allusion hold would all be located on one symbolic level.

Probably the most familiar intergestural symbolic relation is reenactment. One gesture reenacts another only if the two are replicas of one another, that is, only if they are performances of the same type of ritual. However, reenactment is not merely a matter of performing another replica repeating past performances. One reeenacts a ritual only if one also performs it aware that one's gesture is a replica of past performances, that the given performance belongs to a succession of parallel performances, and, with this historical perspective, that it falls within a tradition. In this specific sense of the term reenactment should not, then, be confused with commemoration.

A gestural symbol, like any other singular thing, can be denoted—and thus commemorated—by another symbol, but what a given ritual performance reenacts is its replicas qua fellow performances of the same ritual type. Thus, a typical performance of the Sabbath ritual commemorates, by denoting, the creation, but it reenacts past performances of the Sabbath ritual itself. Yet what is also characteristic of many rituals in Judaism is that, as they have historically evolved, they have explicitly incorporated within the very structure of later performances of a given ritual denotative references to earlier performances of the same ritual, performances that the present one reenacts. By thus combining commemorative denotation with reenactment, Jewish ritual achieves the sense of constantly—and quite literally—performing the old anew.

An example is the act of prostration performed as part of the recital of the *Avodah,* the description of the sacrificial service conducted in the ancient Temple, during the *Musaf* (additional) service of Yom Kippur. Three times during this narration, we tell how the congregation in the Temple court "fell upon their knees, prostrated themselves, and worshipped" when they heard "God's glorious and revered name clearly expressed by the High Priest"; and at exactly those moments it is now customary for present congregants to fall upon their faces, prostrating themselves. At least three different modes of symbolization are at work in this gesture. First, the narration as a whole commemorates—by descriptive denotation—the ancient Temple service; and the act of prostration, acting out one element in this narrative, depicts the historical gesture. However, our present prostration is not just a matter of denoting ancestral acts. Certainly a central aim of the intense poetic account is for present congregants, listening to the reader describe how the high priest pronounced the name of God, to imagine that the reader has now himself called out God's name and spontaneously, overcome with awe and emotion, prostrate themselves. The gesture, then, further expresses a feeling in its own right, though of the same type as that expressed by the historical gesture it denotes. And, finally, inasmuch as the present prostration replicates past performances of the same ritual, it also reenacts them. Like the recitation of the *Avodah,* which also parallels the actual sacrificial service (cf. Rashi, Commentary on BT Yomah 36b, 56b), our gesture of prostration parallels, and thus indirectly refers to, all past performances of the same type. And both reenacting and historically commemorating the same ritual also creates a community with all past performers spanning Jewish history. The creation of such a community conscious of its own tradition in its present practices is a central aim of much ritual.

BIBLIOGRAPHY

Erwin R. Goodenough, *Jewish Symbols in the Greco-Roman Period* (especially vol. 4) (1954).

Nelson Goodman, *Languages of Art,* 2d ed. (1976).

Louis Jacobs, *Hasidic Prayer* (especially ch. 5) (1973).

Israel Scheffler, "Ritual and Reference," in *Synthèse* 46 (March 1981).

Gerschom Scholem, "Tradition and New Creation in the Ritual of the Kabbalists," in *On the Kabbalah and Its Symbolism* (1965).

Gnosis

גנוזים

Gedaliahu G. Stroumsa

Since the nineteenth century, a great deal has been written on the relationships between Gnosticism and Judaism, and in particular on the existence and nature of Jewish Gnosticism. Due to the lack of sources, however, much remains speculation. It is only in recent years that the publication of the Coptic Gnostic texts found at Nag-Hammadi (Upper Egypt) in 1945 has enabled scholars to map more precisely those trends in late-antique religion commonly referred to as Gnosticism and to establish with greater care their relationships with various religions in the eastern Mediterranean in the first centuries of the Christian era.

Gnosticism appears as a cluster of rather loosely related syncretistic attitudes and mythologies. Despite the new discoveries, evidence is still too scarce to permit even a vague sociological description of the milieus in which Gnosticism emerged and developed. Yet a few features common to most texts and traditions may be described. It is, first of all, a dualistic, anticosmic movement, stemming from a monistic background against which it revolts. Another aspect of Gnosticism lies in its esoteric character.

Gnosis (Greek for knowledge) is revealed only to the members of the Gnostic community. Its nature is clearly soteriological: without this secret knowledge, no one can be saved. In Gnostic mythologies, humanity is clearly
divided along a dualistic pattern to which corresponds a dualistic anthropology. The body, made by the creator of the world, or demiurge, is material
and hence evil. Only the soul, or rather its spiritual apex, the *pneuma*
(spirit), belongs to the divine world and can be saved.

Blooming in the second and third centuries C.E., Gnosticism developed
into one of the most significant spiritual trends of late antiquity. It is in the
course of their fierce argument with the Gnostics that the Church Fathers
first articulated the main themes of Christian theological discourse. Infil-
trating Plotinus' students, the Gnostics forced the Neo-Platonic philosopher
into masterful polemics against them. Last but not least, Manichaeism, the
new religion that became for a while a most serious threat to Christianity
and succeeded in surviving ferocious persecution, from eastern Asia to
north Africa, for about a thousand years, emerged out of Gnostic trends in
third-century Mesopotamia.

Heinrich Graetz, the great nineteenth-century historian of Judaism, was
the first to inquire into the relationships between Judaism and Gnosticism,
baffled as he was by the fact that Judaism, alone among the religions of late
antiquity, had apparently remained immune to Gnostic influence. Recent
research, however, has tended to emphasize that Judaism, rather than Persia, was a major origin of Gnosticism. Indeed, it appears increasingly evident that many of the newly published Gnostic texts were written in a context from which Jews were not absent. In some cases, indeed, a violent
rejection of the Jewish God, or of Judaism, seems to stand at the basis of
these texts.

Within the compass of this discussion, we shall address ourselves first—
in a most cursory way—to Jewish factors in the emergence of Gnosticism,
and then to possible Gnostic influences on later trends in Jewish spirituality, as well as to the question of Jewish Gnosticism as such.

Prima facie, various trends in Jewish thought and literature of the Second
Commonwealth appear to have been potential factors in Gnostic origins.
Wisdom literature comes first to mind in such a context. Sophia, the major
heroine of Gnostic mythology, is evolved from the figure of *ḥokhmah* (wisdom). Indeed, she often betrays her Hebrew origins when called *Sophia
achamot,* a pun between *ḥokhmaot* (plural of *ḥokhmah*) and the Hebrew
word for death, *mavet, mot,* that is preserved in the Gnostic texts. Jewish
speculation on *ḥokhmah's* crucial role in cosmogony is here picked up and
transformed. Philo, too, has been mentioned as being often close to Gnostic

ways of thought, although no specific points of direct contact have been singled out. On closer examination, however, it is mainly Philo's Platonic frame of mind, emphasizing the duality between sensate and spiritual realities, that is responsible for his Gnostic affinities. Indeed, Gnosticism was marked by popular philosophy—mainly in its Platonic mode—to the extent that it has been called "a Platonism run wild" (A. D. Nock).

More precise parallels to Gnosticism are reflected in the Dead Sea Scrolls, which refer to the salvific teaching of the sect as *daat* (knowledge), which is a gnosis of sorts. Like the Gnostics, the Qumran conventicle set itself in opposition to the rest of mankind, who are incapable of achieving salvation: they are the "sons of light" in a world of darkness. In Qumran's case, one can plausibly speak of a proto-Gnosticism; however, here, too, crucial linking evidence is missing and one remains in the field of speculation.

Apocalyptic literature is now recognized as the main stream in Jewish thought to have had a major role in the formation of Gnostic mythology. Jewish apocryphal and pseudepigraphical literature, written in the first centuries B.C.E., reflects remythologizing trends in Judaism, with a marked interest in revelatory discourse, heavenly ascents, and speculation about the origin and the end of time. This speculation emphasizes the opposition between this world (*olam;* the Greek equivalent, *aion,* in English *aeon,* is a central concept in Gnostic myths) and the heavenly reality. The Christian heresiologists tell us that some Gnostics were fond of apocryphal literature. The Nag-Hammadi texts reveal much more clearly the extent to which major elements in this literature were reinterpreted and transformed to stand at the core of Gnostic mythology. The story of Adam and Eve, their creation and their eating the fruit from the tree of knowledge, was as crucial for the Gnostics as it had been in apocalyptic circles. The Gnostics thought themselves to be sons of Seth, issued from "another seed" (Gen. 4:25), while non-Gnostic humanity was identified as sons of Cain, stemming from Eve's impure relationship with the snake or Satan himself, who was often identified with the evil demiurge. To take another example, the "sons of gods" who had copulated with the daughters of men (Gen. 6:4) underwent a Gnostic transformation and appeared in a new garb as mythological figures in some of the Nag-Hammadi texts.

These few examples are enough to testify about the Gnostics' deep interest in the Hebrew Bible, in particular the book of Genesis. One could also show in detail how this interest was fostered by rather developed exegetical methods. The extent to which Jews actually participated in the final redaction of the Gnostic texts remains unclear. Yet a detailed analysis of some passages shows at least a clear knowledge of Hebrew exegetical traditions, which could hardly have been transmitted and reinterpreted by non-Jews. The paradoxical interest expressed in the Scripture of a condemned religion cannot be understood only as an activistic phenomenon or in the light of the audiences addressed by the Gnostic texts, who often had some kind of exposure to the Bible through Christianity.

The once-fashionable theory that Gnosticism emerged out of disillusioned Jewish messianic hopes after the destruction of the Temple in 70 C.E. still remains to be buttressed by conclusive evidence. Yet it seems probable that both Christianity and Gnosticism stem from the explosive nature of first-century Judaism, both in Palestine and in the Diaspora. In this respect, the role of early Jewish Christians in the crystallization and propagation of Gnostic ideas has yet to be more precisely analyzed.

Although the possible Jewish sources of Gnosticism have recently received much scholarly interest, it is the Gnostic influence on Judaism that Jewish scholars have most sought to probe since the nineteenth century. The heretics of rabbinic literature are often thought to have challenged the rabbis through their dualistic—or gnosticizing—patterns of thought. A caveat is here in order: while the Christian heresiologists first expounded the doctrines of their opponents in order to refute them, the rabbis preferred to "kill their enemies by silence." Therefore, very little is actually known of the *minim* (a generic term referring to various kinds of heresies) and their teachings.

There is no denying that some Jews broke out of rabbinic circles and adopted dualistic, gnosticizing ideas. Elisha ben Avuyah, a second-century rabbi, is a case in point. Meditation on the problem of evil brought him to apostasy through denial of divine providence and justice. According to talmudic sources, Elisha believed that there were "two powers"—rather than only one—in heaven. The exact meaning of the phrase is difficult to ascertain, and may have referred to two hierarchical, not necessarily opposed, powers. The idea of the two powers grew out of speculation about the nature of Metatron, the archangel seated beside God in heaven and bearing his name. Here again, one should point out that similar patterns of thought appear in early Christianity, where Christ replaces Metatron.

Much has been written recently on *Merkavah* literature, a body of texts dealing with the chariot of Ezekiel, a symbol of mystical life. In particular, the *Heikhalot* texts, which offer lavish descriptions of the mystic's ascent to the heavenly palaces, have been identified as instances of "Jewish Gnosticism." This, however, is an illegitimate use of the term. Gnosticism is not only an esoteric movement of mystical ascent but essentially emphasizes cosmic and anthropological dualism. There is no Gnosticism without estrangement from the world, considered to be the creation of the ignorant and/or evil demiurge. Of such dualism there is no trace in the *Heikhalot* tractates, where the demiurge, the *Yozer Bereshit* (literally, the primeval creator), is always praised.

Indeed, there can be no Gnosticism without a revolt against the Jewish God. As a syncretistic phenomenon, Gnosticism appears to have flourished at the expense of existing religious structures in the ancient world. It is no mere chance that Gnostic ideas proved to be much more of a challenge for the Church Fathers than for the rabbis. In Christianity, monotheism was less rigidly defined than in Judaism and, therefore, the allure of radical doctrines seeking a resolution of such complex issues as the relationship between the two Testaments or material and spiritual realities has continued throughout the ages.

Various trends in later Judaism, however, have preserved traces of Gnostic ideas or myths. It has long been noted that the first text of medieval kabbalah, the *Sefer ha-Bahir,* edited in late-twelfth-century Provence, retains some old Gnostic mythologoumena. These seem to have traveled underground through the centuries, although the channels through which they were transmitted cannot be ascertained more precisely than can those that transmitted dualistic lore and patterns of thought to the medieval Cathars, a Christian heretical sect active in Provence in the twelfth century.

The complex theory of emanation and contraction of the divinity, and in particular the idea of the divine sparks *(nizozot),* elaborated by the sixteenth-century Palestinian mystic Isaac Luria, shows some striking phenomenological parallels with Manichaean cosmological mythology. Here, however, no direct historical link has yet been detected. According to the views concocted by Shabbetai Zevi, the seventeenth-century false messiah, and his disciple Nathan of Gaza, the God of Israel had a higher status than the Master of the Universe. This has been referred to as an "inverted Gnosis," which might actually prove to be the peculiar way through which the Gnostic "virus" can attack the structure of Jewish theology.

The theological anti-Semitism of Gnosticism does not preclude its Jewish origins or the centrality of the Jewish factor in its formation. One need only refer to a modern example of Jewish theological *Selbsthass* (self-hate) in order to ascertain this point: the French philosopher Simone Weil developed a theory close to that of the second-century Marcion, with its virulent opposition between the Jewish warrior God and Jesus Christ, the symbol of love.

Any living theological tradition is likely to recognize the complexity and the fundamental ambivalence of most issues in religious life. Temptations are bound to appear at any time in such a tradition to reject this ambivalence and this complexity. In Judaism, the overreaching tension is between universalist message and national consciousness. Thus, contemporary Jewry's affirmation of the national dimension brings with it not only the danger of nationalism, but also the temptation of an "inverted Gnosis" similar to Shabbetai Zevi's, in which more respect is paid to the God of Israel than to the creator.

BIBLIOGRAPHY

Ithamar Gruenwald, "Aspects of the Jewish-Gnostic Controversy," in Bentley Layton, ed., *The Rediscovery of Gnosticism,* 2 (1981), 713–23.

Kurt Rudolph, *Gnosis: The Origins and Development of a World Religion* (1983).

Gershom Scholem, *Jewish Gnosticism, Merkabah Mysticism and Talmudic Tradition* (1960).

Allan E. Segal, *Two Powers in Heaven: Early Rabbinic Reports About Christianity and Gnosticism* (1977).

Gedaliahu G. Stroumsa, "Aḥer: A Gnostic," in Bentley Layton, ed., *The Rediscovery of Gnosticism,* 2 (1981), 808–18.

Gedaliahu G. Stroumsa, *Another Seed: Studies in Gnostic Mythology* (1984).

God

אלוהים

Louis Jacobs

Whether belief in God erupted spontaneously in ancient Israel or whether there can be traced in the biblical record a gradual evolution from polytheism through henotheism to pure monotheism, it is certain that, from the sixth century B.C.E. at the latest, God was conceived of as the One Supreme Being, Creator and Controller of heaven and earth. Maimonides opens his great digest of Judaism, the Mishneh Torah, with: "The foundation of all foundations and the pillar of all sciences is to know that there exists a Prime Being who has brought all things into existence. All creatures in heaven and earth and in between enjoy existence only because He really exists" (MT Hil. Yesodei ha-Torah 1:1). Maimonides' thought-patterns and language are those of medieval Jewish philosophy, but his basic credo would have been shared by virtually all believing Jews until modern times.

Since, by definition, belief in God is belief in a unique Being totally different from any of his creations, the problem for Jewish as for all theists has always been how to give expression in language to the nature of that deity. The popular distinction between the comprehension and the apprehension of God—the former impossible for humans—is generally shared by Jewish theologians, although the linguistic problem remains: how to identify the divine Subject that is apprehended. Judah Halevi observes that humans can dwell on God's works but must refrain from describing his nature, "For if we were able to grasp it, this would be a defect in Him" (*Kuzari*, 5, 21). Joseph Albo tells of the sage who, when invited to describe God's essence, replied: "If I knew Him I would be He" (*Sefer ha-Ikkarim* 2, 30). Consequently, throughout the history of Jewish thought there has been considerable tension in the matter of God-talk. To say too much, without qualification, is to fall into the trap of gross anthropomorphism. To say too little is to court the opposite risk of having so many reservations that the whole concept suffers, in Anthony Flew's pungent phrase, "the death of a thousand qualifications."[1] Between these extremes Jewish thinkers can be divided into those who passionately declare that, for all the tremendous divide between God and man, God can still be spoken of, within limits, in human terms, and those who prefer the negative path, seeing the sheer wondrousness of God in that he is utterly beyond all human conceptualization. These latter echo the words of the psalmist (in the usual rendering of the verse): "For Thee silence is praise, O God" (Ps. 62:2), though they are often as inconsistent in pursuing the way of negation as the psalmist himself in this very psalm. In this area, if not in others, Solomon Schechter was right in contending that the best theology is not consistent.

The Bible abounds in descriptions of God in human terms. He has an eye and a hand; he is good, compassionate, and merciful; his wrath is kindled against evildoers; he occasionally changes his mind and yet elsewhere it is stated that he is not a human being who can change his mind. This type of description is partly due to the concrete nature of classical Hebrew, which is deficient in abstract terms, and, especially in biblical poetry, has its origins in ancient mythological conceptions regarding the nature and activity of the pagan gods. In any event, anthropomorphism presented no problem to the biblical authors. Nor was it much of a problem to the rabbis of the Talmud and Midrash, who were in no way averse to inventing new anthropomorphisms of their own while qualifying the bolder, not to say outrageous, of these by the word *kivyakhol* (as it were). The nonphilosophically-minded Jews of Germany and France in the Middle Ages were quite content to follow the biblical and rabbinic precedents, though few were evidently prepared to go all the way with the learned thirteenth-century German talmudist Moses of Tachav, who in *Ketav Tamim* held that it is necessary for a Jew to believe that God really does sit on a throne in heaven surrounded by his angels or, at least, that he does so when he reveals himself to his prophets. A century earlier, Abraham ben David of Posquieres (known as Rabad), in his stricture on Maimonides' round declaration, probably aimed at the Christian doctrine of the incarnation, that anyone who states that God has a corporeal form is a heretic, retorted: "How can he call such a person a heretic? Many greater and wiser than he have followed this line of thought because of what they had seen in Scripture and even more so because of what they had seen in certain [rabbinic] *aggadot* which bring about perverse opinions" (Comm. to Mishneh Torah, ad loc. Hil. Teshuvah 3:7).

The more theologically sophisticated Jews of medieval Spain and other lands similarly influenced by Greek philosophy felt themselves obliged to reject all anthropomorphism and reinterpreted the Bible and rabbinic literature to accord with their attitude. Maimonides is the most persistent advocate of this school, maintaining that one can only say with regard to God's essence what it is not, never what it really is (*Guide* 1, 51–60). One can, however, speak of God's actions in a positive way provided it is recognized that, for instance, when God is described as good it is to claim no more than that certain actions, if performed by a human being, would be attributed to the goodness of that person's nature.

The kabbalists, impressed by the philosophers' case for negation and yet hungry for the living God of religion, tried to solve the problem by postulating two aspects of deity. God as he is in himself is unknown and unknowable. This aspect of deity is called *Ein Sof* ("That which is without limit"). From *Ein Sof* ten powers or potencies—the *sefirot*—emanate, and it is God as manifested in these *sefirot* who is the God of religion, the God whom human beings can know and worship. The godhead of the kabbalists is conceived of as a dynamic organism; each of the *sefirot* carries out its own function and has its own role to play in the control and government of the universe. *Ein Sof* is completely beyond all human thought, and is not even referred to in the Bible except by a faint allusion here and there. The kabbalists, however, do allow—indeed they advocate—the use of positive descriptions of God as manifest in the *sefirot*. Such a doctrine can easily lend itself to a thoroughgoing dualistic interpretation. Moreover, critics of the kabbalah have argued that the doctrine comes perilously close to decatheism, a belief in ten persons in the godhead, "worse," the critics maintained, "than the Christian doctrine of the Trinity" (Isaac ben Sheshet Perfet, *Responsa,* ed. I. H. Daiches, no. 157). The kabbalists spring to the defense of their doctrine by using various metaphors to convey the idea of complete unity between the *sefirot* and the *Ein Sof* manifested in them—as in the image of clear, transparent water poured into bottles of different hues, which partakes temporarily of the color of the particular bottle into which it is poured (Moses Cordovero, *Pardes Rimmonim,* 4, 4, 17d). These metaphors are remarkably reminiscent of Christian attempts at describing how the three persons of the Trinity can yet be one within the godhead, and like them are as unconvincing to the nonkabbalist.

The kabbalistic system developed by Isaac Luria in sixteenth-century Safed grappled with the questions: How can the Infinite have produced the finite? How can the universe containing multiplicity, error, and naked evil have emerged from an all-wise and veracious God? Indeed, it may be asked, if God is All, how can there be any universe? According to Lurianic kabbalah, the primordial act of *Ein Sof* was "to withdraw from Himself into Himself" so as to leave an "empty space" into which the *sefirot* could be emanated and, through the *sefirot,* all lower worlds, until there eventually emerged the world of space and time as we encounter it (Ḥayyim Vital, *Eẓ Ḥayyim* 1, i, 2, 22). This process involves the constant emergence and subsequent withdrawal of the light of *Ein Sof.* Such gradual beaming forth of light followed by its recoil represents God constantly allowing that which is other than God to enjoy existence, balancing at every stage in the process how much light creatures require for their existence and how much of it needs to be recalled into infinity so that creatures might not dissolve in its effulgence.

In the thought of the Ḥasidic movement, which matured in Eastern Europe during the eighteenth century, Lurianic ideas were developed to produce what amounts to a complete transformation of the traditional view of the relationship between God and the world. Although it is only in the *Ḥabad* branch of Ḥasidism, founded by Shneur Zalman of Lyady, that the new doctrine is conveyed in a systematic way, it is nonetheless typical of Ḥasidism as a whole. In the view of Shneur Zalman, *ẓimẓum,* the primordial act of withdrawal, does not really take place but represents that screening of the divine light by means of which creatures can have independent existence. As the *Ḥabad* thinkers are fond of putting it, the finite world and the creatures that inhabit it enjoy existence only "from our point of view." From "God's point of view" there is no universe and there are no creatures to enjoy any existence independent of and apart from God. This Ḥasidic idea is best described as panentheism ("all is in God"), differing from Spinoza's pantheism ("all is God") in a number of important respects but chiefly in that for Spinoza God is the name given to the totality of things, whereas in Ḥasidic panentheism the universe enjoys no existence whatsoever in any absolute sense. The statement in the Shema that God is One is now understood to mean that, despite appearances, there is only the One and nothing else. Just as the kabbalists grappled with the problem of how

Ein Sof and the *sefirot* can form a unity, the Ḥabad theorists grapple with the even more acute problem of how it can be said that God is All since the evidence of the senses shows that there is a finite universe. The tendency is to deny that this problem can ever be solved. It is described as *pele*, a "marvel," the astonishing miracle beside which all other miracles pale into insignificance—the mystery of mysteries.

The common strand in all these varieties of Jewish theism is that God is viewed as a person, though this term itself is unknown in Jewish theology. A personal God is understood to mean a real Being and not merely a name given to some aspect of the universe or to the universe as a whole. Even when the kabbalists speak of *Ein Sof* as ineffable, as wholly other, they never suggest even remotely that they are hinting at the nonexistence of the impersonal Ground of Being. The reluctance to ascribe gender to God as he is in himself is not to imply that the Ground of Being is an "It" but rather that, in the words of William Temple, God is more than "He." An "It" is less than a "He," a mere thing, totally inferior to humans endowed with personality, whereas a more-than-He who has brought into existence intelligent persons, with a moral sense and a capacity to create and reach out for beauty, can be an object of worship infinitely higher than they. To worship an "It" as God is a form of idolatry. Idolatry is not the worship of false gods (for such do not exist), but the worship of a figment of the human imagination. In the later passages of the Bible the gods are *elilim*, "nonentities."

It is the many and varied challenges presented to traditional theism by modern thought that seemed to many to demand this radical transformation in the idea of God. Indeed, the very notion of the God-idea, as opposed to the objective reality of the living God, has arisen as a result of these challenges. The Kantian critique of the traditional arguments for the existence of God, while unsuccessful in demolishing them as pointers, has rendered them unconvincing as proofs. More recently, speculation on the nature of God has, like all such metaphysical exploration, been treated with suspicion by the linguistic philosophers on the grounds of its incoherence, and by the existentialists on the grounds that, as cosmic talk, it is irrelevant to the human situation. The emergence, growth, and success of scientific method has made a mechanistic explanation of the universe more plausible so that there is no longer any need for the God-hypothesis in order to explain how and why things are as they are. Biblical criticism has called into question the traditional view of biblical infallibility. The acknowledgment of a human element in revelation has tended to encourage an attitude of mind in which biblical statements about God are seen as human reflection on God rather than as divine communications. Both the Marxist view of religion as the product of man's social needs and strivings and the Freudian view of religion as an illusion have eroded still further the belief in the reality of God. The problem of evil has always been a stumbling block to believers in a supremely beneficent Being, and the problem is acute when even one child is born hideously deformed or dies a horrible death. In this sense the problem is as old as the belief in God. Yet, after the Holocaust, many Jewish thinkers have found themselves psychologically incapable of accepting the traditional solutions that evil is a means to a glorious end. Some Jews, overwhelmed by such challenges, have abandoned any belief in God and, if they have wished to retain some allegiance to the ancestral faith, have embraced a secular Judaism in which whatever ancient rituals have been retained are made to serve not the God of Israel but the peoplehood of Israel. Many Jewish thinkers, on the other hand, still declare that they believe in God, though not in the God of traditional Jewish theism.

The most seemingly plausible (though hardly the most popular) of the modernist reinterpretations is to understand God as Person but as limited to some extent by the given, that is, by that over which God has no control. This idea, first advanced by John Stuart Mill in the last century, has antecedents in the thought of the fourteenth-century philosopher Levi ben Gershom, known as Gersonides, who held that God's power does not extend over the contingent precisely because it is contingent. Hence, while God knows all the choices open to an individual he does not know beforehand how that individual will, in fact, choose; otherwise such human choice would be meaningless (Milḥamot ha-Shem 3, 6). This way of looking at the problem undoubtedly has considerable power. It can be argued, as Gersonides does, that God as he appears in the Bible and the rabbinic literature is limited by the contingent. Yet it is hard to see how such a view fails to result in a kind of dualism—God and that which imposes the limits of the "given." If, as proponents of such views maintain, there are "dysteleological surds," what is one to make of the whole idea of a divine telos? When Isaac Husik remarks of Gersonides' view "we might almost say it is a theological monstrosity,"[2] he may be too sweeping, but similar qualifications of the doctrine of divine omnipotence do present very severe difficulties, for which, to date, no adequate solutions have been offered.

In spite of the popularity of religious existentialism among Jewish theologians in this century, and the absurdity of regarding it as a form of atheism, it is nonetheless hard to see how any affirmation that the objective reality of God is irrelevant to religious commitment can avoid the danger of a reverent agnosticism shading off eventually into an agnosticism reminiscent of T. H. Huxley's metaphysical incertitude regarding God's existence. The Kierkegaardian leap of faith, moreover, has been overworked in much of contemporary Jewish theology.

The naturalistic understanding of God, favored by some Jewish thinkers reluctant to abandon completely a concept of such significance, conceives of God not as a supernatural Person but rather as the power in the universe that makes for salvation. That is to say, the universe is so constituted that righteousness will eventually win out. What is required is not to jettison the God-idea but to read new meaning into the concept—in Mordecai Kaplan's words, to pour new wine into the old bottles. In reality, many of the Jewish "Death of God" theologians claim, something of the kind has always been implicit in the Jewish tradition; even when our ancestors addressed God as a person and worshiped him as such, their subconscious motivation was to draw on the impersonal force that their experience and that of their people had convinced them was at work and could be drawn upon for the spiritual enrichment of their lives. If God is thought of in this way, the mechanistic picture, supposedly demanded by science, can be accepted in its totality: nature operating by its own laws without any need for intervention by a supernatural power. The problem of evil is no problem for believers in a naturalistic God, since for them the old dilemma—either God can prevent evil and does not choose to do so or he wishes to prevent evil but cannot do so—is meaningless. A God who can choose or wish simply does not exist.

The new scientific picture does require a fresh understanding of divine providence. Many events hitherto seen as evidence of direct, miraculous, divine intervention can now be explained adequately in purely naturalistic terms. They can even be accurately forecast. It is now essential to reexamine such elements of traditional faith as miracles and petitionary prayer. But none of this is cause for absolute rejection of supernaturalism. It does not follow at all from investigation into the natural order that there is no beyond, no Being by whose fiat that order came into existence and by whose power it continues. The new methods are themselves the product of creative thinking, impossible to explain unless there is Mind in and beyond the universe.

Moreover, the naturalistic understanding of God is logically incoherent in a way in which the personalist/supernaturalist understanding is not. Once the belief in a personal God is surrendered, how can what remains offer the worshiper a guarantee that righteousness will triumph? To call "the winning-out process" God is an abuse of language. By attempting to read this new meaning into the old word *God* the naturalist has, in fact, so changed the whole concept that he is really saying to the atheist: If you believe, in faith, that the universe is so constituted that righteousness will eventually triumph you believe in God. The atheist might well retort that he refuses to be converted by a definition.

Difficulties with ideas about the nature of God have always been with us. They are inescapable. A god whose nature could be grasped with our finite intelligence would not be God at all. That is why the distinction was made between God as he is in himself and God in the variety of his manifestation. When all is said and done, it is impossible to know God. But it is possible to know that there is a god.

REFERENCES

1. Anthony Flew and Alisdair MacIntyre, eds., *New Essays in Philosophical Theology* (1955), 97.
2. Isaac Husik, *A History of Mediaeval Jewish Philosophy* (1958), 346.

BIBLIOGRAPHY

Louis Jacobs, *A Jewish Theology* (1973).
Israel Konovitz, *Ha-Elohut* (1908).
Arthur Marmorstein, *The Old Rabbinic Doctrine of God* (1968).
Gershom Scholem, *Major Trends in Jewish Mysticism* (1955).
Milton Steinberg, *Anatomy of Faith,* Arthur A. Cohen, ed. (1960).

Grace or Loving-Kindness

חסד

Warren Zev Harvey

"The world," said the Psalmist, "is built on *ḥesed*" (Ps. 89:3). According to a Mishnaic teaching, *gemilut ḥasadim*—doing acts of *ḥesed*—is (together with the Torah and the Temple service) one of the three things by which the world is sustained (M. Avot 1:2). The Hebrew *ḥesed* (plural: *ḥasadim*) is usually translated as "grace" or "loving-kindness," but sometimes also as "mercy" or "love." An act of *ḥesed* is an act of kindness done neither to repay a debt nor for the sake of gain, but freely and purely out of love. All being, Moses Maimonides taught, is an act of divine *ḥesed*, for the universe has come into existence only by virtue of God's abundant grace or loving-kindness, and not because of any claim it could possibly have had upon him (*Guide* 3, 53).

That God governs the world in *ḥesed* is, according to one rabbinic view, the first and last message of the Torah:

> Taught Rabbi Simlai: "The beginning of the Torah is *gemilut ḥasadim* and its end is *gemilut ḥasadim*. Its beginning is *gemilut ḥasadim*— as it is written, 'And the Lord God made for Adam and for his wife garments of skin, and clothed them'

[Gen. 3:21]. And its end is *gemilut ḥasadim*—as it is written, 'And He buried [Moses] in the valley' [Deut. 34:6]."

(BT Soṭ. 14a; cf. Tanḥ. Va-yera 1; Eccles. R. 7:2)

Moreover, according to another rabbinic view human beings are enjoined by Scripture to imitate God's acts of *ḥesed:*

> Said Rabbi Hama bar Hanina: "What is the meaning of the text, 'After the Lord thy God ye shall walk' [Deut. 13:5]? Is it possible for a man to walk after the Divine Presence? Has it not been said, 'The Lord thy God is a devouring fire' [Deut. 4:24]?! Rather, walk after the *attributes* of the Holy One, blessed be He. As he clothes the naked—as it is written, 'And the Lord God made for Adam and for his wife garments of skin, and clothed them' [Gen. 3:21]; so you clothe the naked! The Holy One, blessed be He, visited the sick—as it is written, 'And the Lord appeared unto [Abraham, who was recovering from his circumcision] by the terebinths of Mamre' [Gen. 18:1]; so you visit the sick! The Holy One, blessed be He, comforted mourners—as it is written, 'And it came to pass after the death of Abraham, that God blessed Isaac his son' [Gen. 25:11]; so you comfort mourners! The Holy One, blessed be He, buried the dead—as it is written, 'And He buried [Moses] in the valley' [Deut. 34:6]; so you bury the dead!"

(BT Soṭ. 14a; cf. Gen. R. 8:13)

This moral *imitatio Dei* is an ethics based on compassion, but also one based on strength. Far from the slave morality despised by Friedrich Nietzsche, it is a God morality. The moral act derives not from weakness or bondage, but from power and freedom. As the omnipotent Creator sustains his creation in grace and loving-kindness, so we—with our mortal strength—are to emulate him and to do acts of grace and loving-kindness for those who may be disadvantaged, such as the naked, the sick, the mourner, the dead. Burying the dead was seen as the paradigmatic act of *ḥesed,* since the dead person is devoid of all strength, unable to help himself or to repay those who care for his needs (cf. Gen. R. 96:5 and parallels; Rashi, Commentary on Gen. 47:29).

The bold anthropopathisms in the statements of Rabbis Simlai and Hama bar Hanina are at root statements about man. They are more anthropology than theology. Above all else, they teach that in doing acts of grace or loving-kindness man is able to imitate the divine *ḥesed* manifest throughout nature.

It was in particular in the biblical stories about Abraham that the rabbis, with keen midrashic insight, found their most vivid illustrations of *gemilut ḥasadim* as moral *imitatio Dei*. The Bible, for example, relates that God appeared to Abraham in the terebinths of Mamre, but does not state the purpose or content of this revelation (Gen. 18:1; but cf. Rashbam, ad loc.). Rabbi Hama bar Hanina taught that God appeared to Abraham for the purpose of visiting the sick, since Abraham had been ailing following his circumcision (BT BM 866; Tanh. Ki Tissa 15; cf. Gen. 17:23–27). Abraham, the Bible continues, suddenly broke off his communion with God, and ran out to welcome three unidentified desert wayfarers (Gen. 18:2). Just as God had performed an act of *ḥesed* (visiting the sick) by appearing to Abraham, so Abraham now broke off his communion with God, and—despite his ailment—ran out in order to imitate God by doing an act of *ḥesed* (hospitality). Abraham preferred to do an act of *ḥesed* for other human beings than to receive an act of *ḥesed* from God. The lesson that emerges from this midrashic exegesis is clear: moral *imitatio Dei* should take precedence even over the enjoyment of divine revelation; ethics, one might say, takes precedence over mysticism; "the act of hospitality is greater than the act of receiving the Divine Presence" (BT Shab. 127a; BT Shevu. 35b). Yet there is a further lesson to be learned from Abraham's breaking off his communion with God in order to do an act of *ḥesed*. Maimonides (*Guide* 1, 54; 3, 54) and Baruch Spinoza after him (*Ethics* IV, 37, sch. 1) held that true religion expresses itself in the acts of loving-kindness that result directly from man's highest knowledge of God. Abraham's welcoming the wayfarers would thus be understood as the direct result of his communion with God: seeing God enables one to see other human beings.[1]

From the midrashic elaborations on the Abraham stories, we learn also that an act of grace or love is an act of divine service no less than prayer in a temple or sacrifice upon an altar. Thus, the Bible records that "Abraham planted a tamarisk at Beer-sheba, and invoked there the name of the Lord, the Everlasting God" (Gen. 21:33). The text is surprising. What does planting a tamarisk have to do with calling on the name of the Lord? Did not the religion of Abraham reject the cult of trees and idols? What sort of divine worship is indicated by Abraham's curious tamarisk? A splendid answer is found in the Midrash (BT Sot. 10a and Rashi *ad loc.*; Gen R. 54:6). The Hebrew word for "tamarisk," *eshel* (spelled with the letters *alef, shin, lamed*), is interpreted by the Midrash as an acronym for three words: *akhilah* (eating), *shetiyyah* (drinking), and *linah* (sleeping) or—according to another version—*levayah* (accompanying). Abraham did not merely plant a tree. He opened an inn. There he would welcome wayfarers, offering them food, drink, and bed, or, according to the other version, escort. In other words, Abraham "invoked the name of the Lord" *by means of doing acts of loving-kindness*. The notion that *gemilut ḥasadim* is a form of divine service is underscored by a statement of Rabban Johanan ben Zakkai to Rabbi Joshua, when they beheld the Temple in ruins: "My son, be not grieved. We have another atonement as effective as [the Temple]. . . . It is acts of loving-kindness, as it is said, 'For I desire ḥesed, not sacrifice' [Hos. 6:6]" (ARN [Version A], 1955, 13, 34).

Not only did Abraham do acts of ḥesed, but he commanded his descendants and followers to do likewise. According to a statement of Rabbi Judah bar Nahamani (BT Ket. 8b), gemilut ḥasadim is the distinguishing characteristic of the children of Israel, who hold to the covenant of Abraham. Rabbi Judah cites God's words regarding Abraham: "For I have singled him out, that he may instruct his children and his posterity, to keep the way of the Lord, by doing what is just and right" (Gen. 18:19). It would thus seem that the very purpose of the covenant of Abraham is gemilut ḥasadim, which is "the way of the Lord"; that is, the purpose of the covenant is moral imitatio Dei (cf. MT Deot 1:6–7). In his first words to Abraham, God had promised to make him a "great nation" and a "blessing" to all the families of the earth (Gen. 12:1–3): the promised strength of Abraham's children would enable them to do acts of ḥesed near and far. In fact, social service and philanthropy have traditionally characterized the Jewish community.

Gemilut ḥasadim is a heroic ethics: an ethics that begins not with my rights, but with the other's needs; not with the other's power to coerce, but with my power to love. Nowhere is the heroic nature of gemilut ḥasadim more dramatically asserted than in the audacious kabbalistic doctrine that God needs human acts of ḥesed. According to this doctrine, the passage from Deut. 33:26, God is "riding the heavens to help you," is to be read as God is "riding the heavens with your help" (Sefer ha-Bahir 185, ed. R. Margaliot, 1951, 83). God built his universe on ḥesed, but whether the universe is at any moment a true arena of grace and loving-kindness depends ultimately on the free deeds of man. Having created man free, God is now at man's mercy. By acts of cruelty toward others, we cause him anguish. By acts of ḥesed toward others, we give him cause to rejoice, thereby helping him to "ride upon the heavens." In other words, we do an act of ḥesed for God. This kabbalistic doctrine is in a sense the opposite of the Christian doctrine of Original Sin: after Adam, God is in need of human grace.

"All commandments between a man and his fellow," wrote Maimonides, "are comprised in gemilut ḥasadim" (Commentary on the Mishnah, Pe'ah 1:1). This statement is perhaps another way of saying what the prophet had already said: "He has told you, O man, what is good, and what the Lord requires of you. Only to do justice and to love ḥesed, and to walk modestly with your God" (Micah 6:8). If God is a God of grace and loving-kindness, what surer way could there be to imitate him or to worship him than by doing acts of grace and loving-kindness?

REFERENCES

1. Cf. Nahum N. Glatzer, *Franz Rosenzweig: His Life and Thought* (1953), 247.

BIBLIOGRAPHY

Louis Ginzberg, *The Legends of the Jews*, 7 vols. (1909–1938).
Warren Zev Harvey, "Love: The Beginning and the End of the Torah," in *Tradition*, 15, 4 (1976).
Nehama Leibowitz, *Studies in the Book of Genesis* (1972), 158–63.
George Foot Moore, *Judaism in the First Centuries of the Christian Era*, 3 vols. (1927–1930).
Solomon Schechter, *Aspects of Rabbinic Theology* (1961).

Guilt

אשמה

Jacob A. Arlow

Guilt is an unpleasant affective state in which a person condemns himself or is dissatisfied with himself for having done wrong or for having failed to live up to certain standards or ideals. The commitment to do right and to conform to ideals develops primarily from childhood experiences, from wanting to be sure of parental love and protection and to avoid parental displeasure and punishment. Norms of conduct and ideals develop from identifications with persons who serve as models, but this is not the only source of such identifications. Moral values and ideal character traits are culturally determined and transmitted by tradition. In large measure, moral concepts and ideal character traits represent how a society or community has integrated the lessons of its history. They articulate those principles that have proved useful and valued in the course of experience. Education and religious training underscore the significance of such values.

The principal instrument for transmitting moral values and for shaping character in keeping with these values is the family. Reward and punishment, frustration and gratification, loving and withholding love are the pressures used to influence the development of the child. From the vicissitudes of these conflicts, each individual develops concepts of right and wrong, a sense of conscience. Ultimately the individual tries to be in the good graces of his conscience, as earlier he had wished to be on good terms with his parents and other educators. When he feels he has failed to do so, what he experiences is guilt. Thus, development of conscience represents a transformation of a set of interpersonal relationships into an internal, that is, an intrapsychic, experience.

To a greater or lesser extent, each person incorporates into his moral code the values and ideals of the community. This becomes part of his self-image. Concomitantly, each society, through its child-rearing practices, encourages certain preferred modes of conflict resolution, and through its educational procedures and religious teaching aspires to establish in the succeeding generation character structures consonant with the ideals and values that it cherishes. Conscience, regulated by guilt, becomes the internalized guardian of the values of the society. It serves to regulate relations among individuals and to strengthen group identity, thereby assuring continuity.

To the extent that the individual identifies his standards with the teachings of his religion, to that degree will religion influence the conditions under which guilt is experienced, as well as the means by which guilt can be exculpated. Different religions vary considerably in this respect. Certain distinctive features of Judaism serve to enhance the development of conscience in the individual. First is the strict monotheistic concept of an indivisible, noncorporeal God, who is everywhere, who cannot be seen, and who, at least since the Diaspora, has no special abode. God is not identifiable in any way as a person; no plastic representation is permitted. In addition, there is no intermediary between God and man. Accordingly, moral judgments become personal, individual, intrapsychic responsibilities. The will of God, which in Judaism articulates the standards of morality, now separated from identification with any human figure, is impersonally incorporated into the voice of conscience. The moral imperative, having been internalized, like God becomes ubiquitous. There is no escaping it. The fear of punishment and disapproval from without is replaced by disapproval from within, by the individual himself. This psychological transition marks the beginning of true conscience.

In religions in which the concept of God is concretely personalized a wide range of specific measures, measures appropriate to interpersonal relations, may be used to overcome guilt. Confession to a priest, begging forgiveness of an icon, and giving gifts to ecclesiastical institutions represent institutionalized modes of overcoming remorse and lowered self-esteem. In addition, an extreme, though by no means uncommon, way of dealing with guilt is to inflict physical pain and humiliation on oneself, so that compassion for the suffering experienced will bring about forgiveness from God and a loving reconciliation with him. Psychologically, this represents a denigration of morality into a more physical, erotic, interpersonal form of masochism.

In Judaism, on the other hand, the relationship to God is less concrete, and morality is regulated primarily intrapsychically. Accordingly, the range of appropriate, personalized, expiatory practices tends to be comparatively limited. For years, obsessive observance of ritualistic details seems to have met the corresponding needs for many observant Jews. In addition, the distinctive features of Judaism mentioned above may have contributed to the predominance among Jews of moral masochism, as opposed to physical masochism, although in certain periods of history and in certain places the latter was far from unknown.

The notion that the Jews are God's chosen people may be an additional element in intensifying guilt and fostering moral masochism. According to Scripture, the selection of the Jews is predicated on God's love and Israel's obedience. The situation of the favorite child who falls out of grace is indeed a painful one. Since, in Judaism, God represents the essence of perfection, there can be no injustice in his ways. Thus, the vicissitudes of Israel's painful history of defeat and suffering stimulate not rebelliousness but intensified guilt. This, indeed, was the interpretation of history that the prophets gave and that the talmudic teachers reaffirmed. Because of their sins, the Jews have had to endure defeat, Diaspora, and suffering. Every misfortune was further proof of their culpability. The counterpart in the individual of this propensity toward guilt may be seen in the common clinical phenomenon of persons who experience feelings of guilt most intensely following misfortune. With the secularization of Jewish identity into nationality, this attitude has changed. In Zionist circles, especially those of a more nationalistic inclination, national misfortune often fails to stimulate soul searching and guilt, but rather elicits anger and the desire for retaliation.

The return to Zion is an aspiration of both religious Jews and nationalists. For the devout, the notion of hastening the return by direct action represents a guilt-laden, sinful pursuit, one in opposition to an attitude of passively awaiting redemption by the Messiah, the agent of God's love and forgiveness. For the Zionists, on the other hand, such an attitude represents weakness, submission, and even cowardice.

In keeping with the goals they pursue and the values they prize, each of these communities draws from history and tradition images of ideal person-ages, mythic heroes whose deeds and character may serve as a standard for the younger generation. Out of the Roman wars, for example, the pious Jews glorified the figure of Rabbi Johanan ben Zakkai. He came to epitomize the qualities of devotion to tradition by submission to temporal authority, by renunciation of force as a solution for national problems, and by surren-dering aspirations for a political state in favor of idealizing learning and religious observance. The incorporation of ben Zakkai's idealized character traits into the personality structure of generations of Jews may have helped to preserve national identity in the unfavorable historical circumstances of living in dispersion, powerless and unprotected.

Out of the same historical experience, on the other hand, the Zionists, with a different, nonreligious vision of the solution for the Jewish problem, sought out and mythologized the heroes of Masada. The zealots of Masada have become the central, ideal figures of a new mythology, a mythology that serves to create a psychological climate fostering character structure con-sonant with new ideals and with changed political objectives.

These last considerations illustrate how, from the historical point of view, the morality of the group reflects and articulates the morality of the individ-ual members of the group. Once established, however, the moral code of the group influences how members of succeeding generations are treated and what standards and ideals are held up to them—essentially under what conditions they are expected to feel the unpleasant affect of guilt.

BIBLIOGRAPHY

Jacob A. Arlow, "Ego Psychology and the Study of Mythology," in *Journal of the American Psychoanalytic Association,* 9 (1961), 371–93.

Aḥad Ha-Am (Asher Ginzberg), "Two Masters" and "Priests and Prophets," in *Selected Essays* (1912).

Mortimer Ostow, *Judaism and Psychoanalysis* (1982).

Halakhah

הלכה

David B. Hartman

Halakhic Judaism is often characterized as an extensive and detailed code of norms. As the name of the celebrated codification of Jewish law, the *Shulḥan Arukh* (Set Table) suggests, Judaism is seen as a way of life that is completely worked out and prepared. All that is required of a person is the willingness to sit at the table and to partake of the meal, that is, to follow the prescribed rules and regulations.

The *Shulḥan Arukh* seems to simplify human life by reducing the complexity of alternatives to one straightforward choice: to obey or not to obey. Doubt, confusion, uncertainty, agonizing deliberation in the face of complexity all seem alien to the experience of one committed to halakhah (traditional Jewish law and the way of life defined by it). A person within the comprehensive framework of halakhah may think he knows exactly what to do from the moment he wakes to the moment he goes to sleep, "from the cradle to the grave." Nothing in human existence is unregulated; there is a correct way of responding to each and every event in one's life.

This identification of Judaism with behavioral conformity to the detailed norms of the halakhah reveals a limited vision of the tradition and of halakhah itself. Halakhah revolves around two poles: the legal, that is, specified and detailed rules of behavior, and the relational, that is, the yearning to give expression to the intimate covenantal relationship between God and Israel. Both these poles have shaped halakhic thought and practice. The legal pole, the tendency to fix formulations for conduct, may reflect the yearning and need of human beings for order and predictability in relationships. The way is given. The task of the covenantal Jew is merely to respond. On the other hand, the covenantal pole emphasizes that halakhah is not only a formal system concerned with rules of procedure but also an expressive system grounded in the love relationship symbolized by God's invitation to Israel to become his covenantal community. The understanding of halakhah as a covenantal relational experience guards against the mistaken notion that a dynamic living relationship with God can be structured exclusively by fixed and permanent rules. The need for order must not be at the expense of spontaneity, personal passion, novelty, and surprise. One committed to the halakhic system can meet God in new ways. The perennial problem that one faces in living by halakhah is how to prevent the covenantal relational pole from being obscured by the massive, seemingly self-sufficient legal framework.

Halakhic norms are ultimately grounded in shared historical memories. The Ten Commandments, which were perceived by the tradition as the foundational framework for all of halakhah, begin with the statement, "I the Lord am your God who brought you out of the land of Egypt, the house of bondage" (Ex. 20:2). The historical memory of a living relationship between God and the community forms the foundation for the way one is to hear the strong and demanding statement of "you shall" and "you shall not." Events create a bond between Israel and God, which in turn forms the basis of the covenant of *mizvah* between God and Israel.

> When, in time to come, your son asks you, "What mean the exhortations, laws, and norms which the Lord our God has enjoined upon you?" you shall say to your son, "We were slaves to Pharaoh in Egypt and the Lord freed us from Egypt with a mighty hand."
>
> (Deut. 6:20–21)

Postbiblical Judaism could not point to dramatic historical events like those described in the Bible and was often compelled to explain God's silence rather than exalt his saving presence (Mekh. Shirata 8). Halakhic Judaism, however, instituted structures to preserve the interrelationship of historical events and the normative system. Of inestimable importance in this regard was the structured re-creation of events of the sacred past by dramatic rituals, public readings, and prayer. What was often absent in daily reality was thus discovered through reenactment and remembering. Through structures of symbolic sacred time, halakhic Judaism incorporated memory and history into the normative experience of the Jew.

Kant believed that an analysis of moral norms would reveal certain formal conditions by virtue of which rules became normative for human beings. Moral autonomy was the fundamental condition for moral action. In the case of halakhah, however, the covenantal relationship between God and Israel constitutes the ground of the normative consciousness of halakhic man. To say that one's identity, which is defined by one's relationship to God, entails a commitment to a particular normative system does not mean, however, that one must negate the force of many of these self-same norms outside of that relational context. One's relationship to God may be a sufficient condition for one's commitment to certain norms and not a necessary and sufficient condition, that is, the relationship need not presuppose that ethical norms lack normative force unless grounded in divine will.

The relational feature of halakhic norms accounts for the central place different images of God have for halakhic practice. As a relational framework, halakhah seeks to bind the individual to God. When the relational pole is enhanced, God appears not only in the guise of legislative authority, but as one whom we seek to identify with and to imitate. Those drawn to halakhic practice by love of God understand that what God requires of man cannot be exhausted by means of a precise, delimited structure of norms. They are drawn to a God who inspires action not only on the basis of his authoritative will but also by his goodness and perfection.

In Maimonides' description of the law of the heathen slave (MT Hilkhot Avadim 9:8), there is a marked difference between action based on the legislative authority of God (din) and action stemming from imitation of the God of creation. If an individual were to conduct himself on the basis of the strict requirements of the law, he would refrain from treating harshly only a Hebrew slave. Ethical responsibility toward a non-Jewish slave results from understanding God's relationship to all of creation. The legal category of din channels one's perception of God within the particular juridical relationship of God to Israel. When the boundaries of man's perception of God are expanded, he discovers that the very existence of all men reflects God's compassion. The boundaries of his ethical obligations, therefore, change also; he then finds himself unable to restrict his ethical responsibilities only to individuals who are members of the halakhic community.

The halakhic category of *din*—law that defines the line of strict legal requirement—can be understood as reflecting the behavior of one who cannot transcend the legislative pole of halakhah. The halakhic category of *lifnim mi-shurat ha-din* (law that is beyond the line of legal requirement), by contrast, reflects the behavior of one who has integrated the legal and relational frameworks into his halakhic practice.

For Naḥmanides also, compliance with the explicit norms of halakhah does not exhaust the full scope of Judaism. In fact, one's conduct may be judged sinful and reprehensible even if one has not violated any explicit rule. In his commentary on the Torah to the verse "You shall be holy, for I the Lord your God am holy," he develops the notion that a person may even become a "degenerate within the framework of the Torah" (Naḥmanides, Commentary on Lev. 19:2).

Halakhah is a system of laws prescribing actions that every member of the community must carry out. The obligatory character of the system is based upon the acceptance by Jews of the legislative authority of God and of those human authorities who are recognized as his legitimate agents. Nonetheless, obligations based on the legal authority of God do not exhaust the scope of the halakhah. Statements like "Let all thy deeds be for the sake of heaven" (M. Avot 2:17) and "I have set the Lord before me continuously" (Ps. 16:8) are not formulae that yield precise legal norms of behavior. Their comprehensiveness reflects the aspiration of one who desires to sanctify every aspect of human conduct. They express the aspiring movement of the covenantal Jew to God, as opposed to the legislative movement from God to the community.

Besides the poles of legality and relationship in halakhah, there is also a polarity within halakhic practice between the individual and the community.

Religion is often regarded as essentially an activity of the individual. The movement of the "alone to the Alone" or "what one does with one's aloneness" are plausible definitions insofar as they focus on the common belief that ultimately the religious experience is personal and individual. Such definitions, however, are inaccurate when applied to Judaism. The covenant is made between God and the people of Israel. In a revealing midrashic account of Moses' forty-day encounter with God on the secluded heights of Mount Sinai, God "notices" the people's perversion around the golden calf and straightaway interrupts Moses with the order: "Go down! All the greatness that I have given you is for the sake of Israel! And now that they have sinned, what need do I have of you?" (Ber. 32a). Revelation in Judaism is first and foremost the giving of the Torah to the people of Israel. "That I may be sanctified in the midst of the Israelite people" (Lev. 22:32).

The primacy of community accounts for the characteristic uniformity and standardization of halakhic practice. The centrality of community in halakhah dictates what Joseph Soloveitchik refers to as the democratization of the spiritual. The concern for developing a community of action explains the tradition's legitimization of minimal standards of practice, however impure the motives:

> One who says: "This *selah* is for charity so that my son will recover from sickness or so that I shall enter the world to come," behold this person is a perfectly righteous person.
>
> (BT Pes. 8a, b)

Halakhah praises such deeds because the act benefits another. The beneficial consequences of the act, whatever the agent's reasons for performing it, are what inform the halakhic judgment.

The halakhic principle "*mizvot* do not require *kavannah* [intention]," as formulated by Rava in the Talmud (RH 28a), leads to the puzzling case where one who had been forced to eat *mazah* during Passover is regarded as having fulfilled the commandment of eating unleavened bread. The absence of the intention to fulfill a religious norm and the presence of coercion notwithstanding, the mere swallowing of *mazah* on Passover fulfills the legal norm. Prima facie this ruling appears puzzling. It would appear as if Judaism lacked any concern with the internal religious feelings of its members. But willingness to validate acts resulting from imperfect motives reflects a deep-seated rabbinic belief that action in conformity with the halakhah, irrespective of its motive, can lead a person to higher forms of spiritual motivation. The rabbis even went so far as to encourage halakhic practice without proper belief in God.

> Rabbi Huna and Rabbi Jeremiah said in the name of Rabbi Hiyya b. Abba: It is written, They have forsaken me and have not kept My law [Jer. 16:11]—i.e., Would that they had forsaken Me but kept My law, since by occupying themselves therewith, the light which it contains would have led them back to the right path. R. Huna said: Study Torah even if it be not for its own sake, since even if not for its own sake at first, it will eventually be for its own sake.
>
> (PdRK 15:5)

Besides the pedagogic reason for validating actions performed without proper intention, these rulings may be explained in relation to the primacy of community in halakhic practice. In contrast to many philosophers, who evaluate action exclusively in terms of the motive of the subject, halakhic teachers apparently were prepared to evaluate acts by the perception of the community. That is to say, the community affirms that the individual is a part of the religious community not through an investigation of his motives but through observation of his practice. In acting in accord with the *mizvot* the individual appropriates the spiritual language of the community. The community's perception and not only the individual's motives then becomes constitutive for defining the quality of the individual's act as a *mizvah* performance.

Another situation that reveals the centrality of community in halakhah is that of prayer. On one level, halakhah includes statements affirming the spontaneous features of prayer: "Make not thy prayer a fixed routine but let it be beseeching and entreaty before God" (M. Avot 2:13). On another level halakhah instituted fixed times and text and, hence, formalized the "service of the heart." For Maimonides as well as for Soloveitchik, the overriding constraint of community welfare led to the formulation of a fixed language of prayer; the philosopher, the poet, and the simple inarticulate Jew are bidden to stand before God at the same time and to address God with the same words. Were community not central to Jewish spirituality, prayer would have remained the spontaneous outpouring of each individual Jew, with its length, form, and time differing according to the needs and abilities of every individual.

Legitimizing an action without *kavannah,* providing a fixed language and time for worship, allowing a people to begin a spiritual process, and not demanding purity of motive as the sole criterion for action reflect the communal pole of halakhah. The individual stands before God in the midst of community. The collective drama of Israel is the framework through which an individual is to hear the *mizvot.* Only as a member of Israel does one become a commanded one. He who separates himself from the community has no share in the God of Israel. The heretic in the tradition is one who does not feel solidarity and empathy with the joys and suffering of his community. One who seeks to embrace Judaism must be taught historic solidarity with the people of Israel before he or she embraces the covenant of *mizvot.* One begins the spiritual pilgrimage as a Jew by identifying with a slave community in Egypt. The Jewish religious consciousness must become historic and communal before it can appropriate the covenantal invitation of God at Sinai. However, this communal pole, which is a vital constitutive force shaping halakhic thinking and practice, must not blind us to the enormous effort of many Jewish thinkers to elaborate an approach to halakhah that affirms the significance of the individual in Jewish spirituality.

Maimonides' *Guide of the Perplexed* reflects the individualistic pole of his spiritual thinking. He devoted as much effort to it as to the *Mishneh Torah,* his formal legal code. Maimonides' effort to bring the philosophical pathos into halakhah can be understood not only as an attempt to integrate revelation with Aristotle but above all as the building of a philosophy of community that does not crush the religious passion of singular individuals. Similarly, Soloveitchik brings existentialist themes concerning the uniqueness of the individual into his appreciation of halakhah.

The midrash portrays the God of Sinai as a teacher. As a teacher, God invites each member of the community to hear *mizvah* as a personal address meant to be appropriated by each person according to his own individual temperament.

> The Divine Word spoke to each and every person according to his particular capacity. And do not wonder at this. For when manna came down for Israel, each and every person tasted it in keeping with his own capacity—infants in keeping with their capacity, young men in keeping with their capacity, and old men in keeping with their capacity. . . . Now if each and every person was enabled to taste the manna according to his particular capacity, how much more and more was each and every person enabled according to his particular capacity to hear the Divine Word.
>
> (PdRK 12:25)

This is not to deny that there are many other midrashim in which the God of Sinai is portrayed in his role as monarch and supreme legal authority. Halakhah from the monarchical-legislative perspective mediates authority, order, and stability. Yet there are other midrashim in which the metaphor of God as lover and teacher is used to explain the moment of Sinai. The tension between these two metaphors must be retained if justice is to be done to the complexity of the halakhic experience. The covenant invites an appreciation of halakhah both as an ordered political system and equally as a framework for the individual to respond to God's invitation to a personal love relationship. Halakhah as an expressive framework allows the individual to find his personal mode of covenantal love for God outside of explicit rules. Halakhah as a legal framework requires obedience. As an expressive system, it requires knowledge. Halakhah as law is concerned with Israel as a political national unit. The building of a shared spiritual language for the community is its essential telos. Halakhah as an expressive system allows different individuals within the community to appropriate the communal framework of halakhah in ways that encourage each to say, "This is my God and I will adore Him."

BIBLIOGRAPHY

David B. Hartman, *A Living Covenant* (1985).
David B. Hartman, "The Joy of Torah," in *Joy and Responsibility* (1978).
Abraham Joshua Heschel, *God in Search of Man* (1955), 320–60.
Joseph B. Soloveitchik, *Halakhic Man* (1983).

Ḥasidism

חסידות

Arthur Green

asidism, the mystical revival movement that swept through eastern Europe in the latter half of the eighteenth century, is a major and largely untapped source of theological language and ideas. While there are many presentations of Ḥasidism for the modern reader, most such treatments avoid the intricacies of Ḥasidic theology. The few historians who have examined these matters have not discussed their viability for a contemporary theology of Judaism. The discussion here will suggest two areas in which Ḥasidic thought merits further consideration: the unity of God, including questions of monism or panentheism, and the drama of spiritual ascent and descent in "the redeeming of sparks." These topics by no means exhaust the valuable theological materials to be found scattered through Ḥasidic literature; the treatment of them will, it is hoped, provide a model for the reexamination of others as well. These include extensive reflections on mystical notions of revelation, religious language, prophecy and charisma, and leadership and community.

The *fons et origo* of Ḥasidism lies in the overwhelming experience of the all-pervasive presence of God. The founding personality of Ḥasidism, Israel Ba'al Shem Tov, and his immediate circle never tired of insisting that the divine is everywhere, even—and perhaps especially—where we least expect to find it. This insight, received and conveyed in ecstatic form by the first Ḥasidic generation, converted such earlier immanentist formulations as "the whole earth is full of His glory" or "there is no place devoid of Him" into enthusiastic watchwords. The brief aphorisms characteristic of early Ḥasidic thought constantly drive this point home: there is no place, no hour, no person or object that does not serve to garb God's presence. Perhaps the most radical expression of this reality, stripped of all traditionalist niceties, is the claim—made by a disciple of Dov Baer of Lubavich some four generations into the movement's history—that *alts iz got,* "all is God." This formulation, culled from a private letter not intended for publication, is what lies behind more typical and guarded expressions such as "the life of God is garbed in all things," or the reading of such innocently theistic phrases as "there is none beside Him" to mean "there is *nothing* beside Him."

This monism, first applied to devotional and mental states, emerged from the Ba'al Shem Tov's insistence that there is no thought in the human mind that is not a thought of God. In relieving the burden of guilt his followers felt for having "wayward" or distracting thoughts, especially when at prayer, he stood firm in teaching that there are no distractions, since the very thought that distracts is itself a thought of God, no less holy in potential than pious concentration on the words of prayer. When stripped of its corporeal or even debased garments, the distraction may lead to yet higher prayer than would have been possible without it.

In the school of Mezhirech, the center of Ḥasidism in the generation following the death of the Ba'al Shem Tov, this devotional insight is developed into a mystical metaphysic; nonduality becomes a claim about the universe as well as about the mind. Dov Baer of Mezhirech used earlier kabbalistic terminology to construct a theology out of his own master's enthusiastic but fragmentary teachings. The *sefirot,* stages in the emanation of divinity and way stations in the mystical ascent to God, are used by Dov Baer in a new way. The first of the ten *sefirot,* by the Ḥasidic ordering, is *ḥokhmah,* or divine wisdom. This beginning or primal point contains virtually all reality that is ever to exist as completely unformed prime "matter." As such, *ḥokhmah* is called by the kabbalists *ayin* (nothing), for it contains no definition. The last of the ten *sefirot* is *malkhut* (kingdom), or *Shekhinah* (God's presence). Unlike any prior kabbalist, Dov Baer fully identifies *Shekhinah* with the presence of divinity in this world, recovering the older prekabbalistic usage of that term. *Shekhinah* is the fullness that plays opposite the primal emptiness of *ḥokhmah;* it is the realized world, the divine energy fully extended into all its worldly garb, a garb that is in no way separable from the divine "body" itself. Thus *Shekhinah* may appropriately be called *yesh* (that which is), for it is identical with all of being as it is.

This primal pair—potential and actual, or nothingness *(ayin)* and being *(yesh)*—is the essential dyad of Ḥasidic mysticism. The realization of their oneness—the realization that *yesh* is *ayin* and *ayin* is *yesh*—is the essential goal of mystical awareness. The two are held together by the eight other *sefirot,* the mediating stages in the process of emanation. For Dov Baer, however, these mediating stages are essentially psychologized; they are the human qualities employed in the realization that *ḥokhmah* and *malkhut* are one, or in the pursuit of the religious life that emerges from that insight. Sometimes these stages are epitomized by the single quality of *da'at* (knowledge or awareness, encompassing also the biblical sense of intimate knowledge), as that which joins together the two poles and reveals their oneness. By the power of unifying awareness, the "empty" and "full" stages in the progressive self-manifestation of divinity are revealed to be aspects of a single one.

This highly abstract panentheism seems to leave little room for the personal religious metaphors that so characterize traditional Jewish theology. What is the place of "Father" or "King" if the religious task is one of cultivating a mystical awareness of the ultimate identity of being and nothingness? Paradoxically, Ḥasidism provides room for the most highly theistic religious language, often expressed in terms of intimate endearment, to exist side by side with these rather nontheistic formulations. While occasional hints, here as in earlier kabbalah, suggest that such personal imagery is human projection onto the universe, the paradox remains mostly unresolved; the devotee is offered the option of returning from abstraction to seek consolation in the warm and familiar figures of a safer and better-known Jewish theology. The personalistic imagery of Jewish devotion was deeply ingrained in the folk mentality of Jewry long before Ḥasidism—or even kabbalah or philosophy—came onto the scene. Surely Ḥasidism, in its attempt to appeal to the popular imagination, was hardly interested in fighting religious philosophy's ancient battles against the anthropomorphic deity, even if its own mystical elite did by far outgrow such thinking.

It is in Ḥabad (an acronym derived from the names of the three highest *sefirot*) Ḥasidism, particularly in the teachings of its founder, Shneur Zalman of Lyady, and his disciple Aaron of Starosielce, that the acosmic implications of the Mezhirech doctrine are most fully drawn forth. Ḥabad is a theological system in which God alone has real existence and all else is illusion. For Dov Baer truth lay in the meeting of *ḥokhmah* and *malkhut;* it is not certain whether he thought that the world as it is should be viewed as illusion or whether both partners in the primal pair represent equally valid manifestations of reality. His disciples vary in their reports of this all-important issue. Shneur Zalman falls clearly within the former camp, demanding of his own followers that they see through the falsehood of this world in order to realize the single divine truth. Here another kabbalistic term is reused, in this case the Lurianic idea of *zimzum,* that is, the self-contraction of the infinite God that preceded the creation of "primal" space.

Zimzum in Lurianic kabbalah had been used to explain how the non-God, and especially evil, could come to exist in a divinely ordained universe. As God absents himself from primal space, allowing for the creation of the other, the primal roots of the demonic take hold in the vacuum brought about by the divine withdrawal. The Ḥasidic authors, however, viewed the problem of God's all-pervasive presence and the existence of the non-God again in purely psychological terms: how can the human mind with its individual self-consciousness exist in the world where "all is God"? *Zimzum,* they thus teach, is that gift of illusion by which we are permitted to view ourselves as individuals. It is only from our human point of view that there has been a *zimzum,* a reduction of the divine presence within creation so that the non-God might exist. From God's point of view there has been no *zimzum,* there can be no non-God, and the existence of the world is illusory. The task here is the systematic training of the human mind to see the world as God does, to become aware that none exists but the One itself.

The presence of this nontheistic religious language at the heart of a traditional Jewish piety has yet to be taken seriously in modern Jewish thought. The influence of existentialism on the theology of the earlier twentieth century made personalistic language seem attractive even when taken to the extreme. Even such figures as Martin Buber and Abraham Joshua Heschel, so steeped in the study of Ḥasidism, mostly ignored its abstract theological language, favoring the biblical metaphors of personal relationship between God and Israel (now universalized as "man"). Only since the mid-twentieth century have the historical researches of Israeli scholars begun to render Ḥasidic materials accessible, and the influence of mysticism, especially that of contemplative Buddhist and Hindu origin, on the intellectual life of the West has created an atmosphere in which such nonpersonalistic terminology is of increased interest. The "death-of-God" movement, although short-lived, served to underscore the fact that God as "Father" or "King"—the essential personal metaphors preserved in later

Jewish theology—describes a religious reality no longer known by many contemporary seekers. In the 1970s the feminist critique of religious language also pointed up the inadequacy of these terms, not only because they are masculine in gender but because they represent a patronizing authority that no longer seems acceptable.

The language of mystical or panentheistic abstraction is attractive in a number of ways. It allows one to view religious awareness as an added or deepened perception of the world, one that complements rather than contradicts ordinary and profane perception. It seems to be nurtured by an openness to a more profound rung of human consciousness, rather than calling for the "leap of faith" requisite for theism. The theology that would emerge from such a reappropriated Ḥasidism could be characterized as belonging to religious "naturalism" in that it entails no literal belief in a deity that is willful or active in human affairs. On the other hand, this is a naturalism deeply tempered by a sense of the supernatural, an openness to the profundities of inner experience, and a humility about the limits of human knowledge.

As in traditional Ḥasidism, there should be room for such mystical abstraction to coexist with the more ancient religious language of Judaism. Our modern awareness of the strong projection element in our personal metaphors for God should not be incapacitating: our need to call out as humans to the infinite may at times require that we picture it as human. At the same time, God as King takes its place as one metaphor among many, each called forth by varying needs within that most complex of human activities, the stretching out toward the mystery both within and beyond.

The motif of *yeridah ẓorekh aliyah* (descent for the sake of ascent) provides the essential dramatic rubric for the Ḥasidic vision of the spiritual life. It is derived from the Lurianic myth of the breaking of the vessels, according to which the intensity of divine light given in creation was too great for the lower worlds to bear and the vessels containing that light were smashed in transit. The human task (expanding "Israel" to "humanity") is to descend in search of these scattered bits of light and to ascend with them, restoring them to their source in God. This notion, too, has undergone drastic revision in Ḥasidism.

For the kabbalist, the retrieval of divine sparks was an active participation in the ongoing drama of cosmic redemption. Gershom Scholem has shown how Lurianic kabbalah shifted the focus of mystical attention to the messianic and how the Sabbatean movement was its direct outgrowth. In Sabbateanism the need to descend into the depths for the sake of redemption became a truly central motif, used first to explain the periodic bleak moods of the would-be messiah, Shabbetai Ẓevi, and later to defend acts of intentional sin and even apostasy on the part of his disciples as well.

Born in circles quite close to those that produced Polish Sabbateanism, Ḥasidism was both at pains to dissociate itself from the hated heresy and attracted to certain of its spiritual values. The sense of the *ẓaddik* (literally, "the righteous one," the leader of a Ḥasidic community) as one who holds fast to both upper and lower worlds, himself serving as a channel through which matter is transformed into spirit, is a legacy from earlier Judaism by way of Sabbateanism. The preachers who were the first intellectuals of the Ḥasidic revival, themselves struggling to uplift and transform their audiences by words of inspiration, were much attracted to the paradoxical rhythm of descent for ascent's sake. Purifying the notion of any taint of intentional sin, they used it to explain how it is that the *ẓaddik* undergoes even a thought of temptation, or why he has to associate with sinners, even in the role of preacher. Ultimately it was used to justify the role of the Ḥasidic master: the mystic who comes forth and raises up the fallen spirits of those around him is greater than the one who remains closeted even with the most profound of mysteries.

As the movement developed, the motif of descent and ascent was used in a more extended metaphoric way. Just as night precedes day in the order of creation, or as the long night of exile precedes the dawn of Israel's redemption, so do times of darkness alternate with those of light in the life of each individual, "for light is greater when it proceeds from the dark." Each person must go through periods of inner darkness (depression, doubt, temptation) in order to increase the light that emerges in the triumph over them. This is the closest Ḥasidism comes to offering a theodicy: the task of transforming suffering and evil into "light"—the joy of God's service—is left in human hands. The more profound the sufferings given to an individual, the higher the sparks that lie within that person's grasp to redeem, if the strength can but be found to effect that transformation. Ultimately there is nothing in the universe so irremediably evil, since all comes from God, that it cannot be recovered for the holy. The Ḥasidic masters admit, however, that there are certain types of sparks, including those found in forbidden foods, for example, that may be uplifted only at the end of time.

Going yet a step further in the transformation of the Lurianic idea, Ḥasidism emphasized the notion of particular sparks that belong to each individual person. The tools that come into a person's hands, the food one eats, the places one travels are all assigned by the grace of heaven, as each contains some special spark that the individual soul alone can and must redeem. Here we see Ḥasidism as a movement that straddles the late-medieval and modern periods in the history of Judaism; it reads a medieval mythic motif so as to give expression to the strikingly modern idea of the unique religious task of each individual. In a broader sense as well it may be said that the Ḥasidic adaptation of the sparks motif is a bridge to modernity. For the kabbalists the idea was a deeply theurgic one: when only specific ritual acts, accompanied by prescribed formulas for meditation, effect redemption, we are in the quasi-magical world of medieval esotericism. When Ḥasidism declares that wholeness of heart rather than esoteric knowledge allows the sparks to be redeemed, personal piety has taken the place of occultism. When we read this claim as expressing the transforming power of concentrated divine/human energy to effect healing in a damaged cosmos, we find ourselves surprisingly close to certain contemporary trends in psychology and medicine.

Implicit in this entire complex of images is the notion that God has need for human help in the ongoing redemption of the universe, which is also the redemption and fulfillment of the divine self. The sacrifice of omnipotence in such a concept, long troubling to kabbalah's Jewish critics, should pose little difficulty to moderns who, especially in the face of the Holocaust, see little evidence of omnipotence as a divine attribute. On the contrary, a sense of human partnership with God in the redemption that both require should be an exciting model for contemporary theology. In this partnership, as we would read it today, humans are needed to take a fully active role, for only they can act on the material plane. God is the source of inspiration and the ever-renewing center of strength for this ongoing struggle. In fact, the separation between that which is human action and that which is the handiwork of God through human agency seems to be an artificial one. Even though only humanity is active in the uplifting of sparks, we are not alone in our labors.

BIBLIOGRAPHY

Martin Buber, *Hasidism and Modern Man* (1966).
Martin Buber, *Tales of the Hasidim*, 2 vols. (1947).
Arthur Green, "Hasidism: Discovery and Retreat," in Peter Berger, ed., *The Other Side of God* (1981).
Arthur Green and Barry W. Holtz, eds., *Your Word Is Fire: The Hasidic Masters on Contemplative Prayer* (1977).
Gershom Scholem, *Sabbatai Sevi* (1973).

Hebrew

עברית

Lewis Glinert

Hebrew lies at the heart of traditional Judaism, its principal medium and in some ways an actual mode of behavior. That the written law, the study of which stands out among other personal responsibilities, was revealed in Hebrew (Gen. R. 31:8) self-evidently makes Hebrew pivotal: no language is an adequate translation of another, and although the law was to be "explained" to mankind, "it is told that five elders wrote the Torah in Greek for King Ptolemy, and that day was as hard for Israel as the day the golden calf was made, for the Torah could not be adequately translated" (Sof. 1:7).

But more than this, Hebrew itself is deemed sacred—and not merely as texts for study, prayer, *tefillin* (phylacteries), or *mezuzah* (the parchment scroll fixed to the doorpost), let alone as a text in time momentarily sanctified like Mount Sinai itself—but as an organic and developing language in the fullest sense of a *langue*, a language system, as well as a *parole*, a body of utterances. In what sense this sanctity is due to the Torah, as its medium, or instead transcends the Torah has preoccupied Jewish thought and halakhah.

The Bible appears to take the role of Hebrew for granted until its existence is threatened, at which point Nehemiah 13:24 condemns mixed marriages and their issue who know no *yehudit* (Hebrew). Merely as a distinguishing mark, Hebrew is singled out by the midrash as one of the four redeeming virtues of the Jews in Egypt (Mekh. Bo 5), though by a perennial dialectic the nation itself *(ivri, yehudi)* is viewed as a religious entity (Gen. R. 42:8). And to his own generation at the turn of the second century C.E., when spoken Hebrew was succumbing to Aramaic, Rabbi Judah ha-Nasi (the Prince) insisted on a combination of Greek and Hebrew for the holy land and demonstrated the point by editing the entire Mishnah in Hebrew. Rabbi Judah Loew of Prague expresses this notion in more general terms: "Just as speech constitutes the form of Man, so language is considered the form of nations; when it perishes, the nation has lost its form."

Postbiblically, Hebrew is invariably called *leshon ha-kodesh,* the "language of holiness," indicating that Hebrew is intrinsically holy (at least as the language underlying the Scriptures) rather than a mere natural language elevated by revelation: "Just as the Torah was given in *leshon ha-kodesh,* so the world was created with *leshon ha-kodesh*" (Gen. R. 18:4, commenting on Gen. 3:23, "To this shall be called woman *(isha)* for she was taken from man *(ish)*"). This midrash, taken in the sense that the true semantics of existence is a Hebrew semantics, can be related to Genesis Rabbah 1:1: "God looked into the Torah and created the World," Torah being seen as a statement of what is as well as what should be. This semantics, indeed epistemology, of existence relates also to higher worlds: "Said God to Moses: 'speak in Hebrew like an angel'" (Mekh. de Rabbi Shimon, Shemo 1), or as articulated in kabbalah: "All material things have their likeness and root on high; there dwells the essential Hebrew name of that thing, e.g., fire: its essential feature on high is the quality of *Gevurah,* . . . and material fire is called thus by a transmuted name, not a 'metaphorical name' of the usual kind but the letters above descended by the downchaining of worlds from the Ten Utterances and are invested in all earthly things."[1] Unlike natural language, Hebrew has meaning, metaphysically, in its consonants, as classified phonetically by the *Sefer Yeẓirah,* in the number of units and the numerical value of letters, and in the shapes of its letters: "Open *mem* and closed *mem:* an open teaching and a closed [esoteric] teaching" (BT Shab. 104a). "The letter *Daled* is a holy letter and the letter *Resh* belongs to the evil side. Behold the differences between their forms is that the letter *Yud* is added on to the back of the letter *Daled.* The letter *Yud* reflects self-nullification."[2] (By contrast, the distinct pre-exilic Hebrew script, which may have been used in the Revelation at Sinai, as suggested in BT Sanhedrin 21b, has no rabbinic sanctity.) Such meanings also inhere in postbiblical prayers composed under the influence of the "holy spirit."

Even greater linguistic abstraction is found in, for example, Abraham Abulafia's medieval "Doctrine of combinations": "Combination, separation, and reunion of letters reveal profound mysteries to the kabbalist, and unravel to him the secret of the relation of all languages to the Holy Tongue."[3] Vowel sounds and the scriptural chant are similarly considered a Sinaitic (oral) tradition.

Occasionally, a more aesthetic note is sounded: "It is an intrinsically pleasant language . . . even better, it conveys meaning concisely, as our sages taught: 'One should always teach one's disciple concisely.'"[4]

The effect of speaking Hebrew is to "purify the soul."[5] As a practical matter, this purifying effect has been noted, for example, in the distinction between "you, feminine" (at) and "you, masculine" (atah): "One quickly senses, while listening outside, if someone is talking alone with a woman or a man, and it is called The Holy Tongue because it protects Jews from immorality."[6] Maimonides, too, had explained the term holy tongue as meaning the absence of sexual nouns save euphemisms (Guide 3, 8).

As a natural language, Hebrew was held by some sages to have been vouchsafed to Adam and in general use until Babel, perhaps at least as a lingua franca.[7] Judah Halevi stated: "The language created by God, which he taught Adam and placed on his tongue and in his heart, is without any doubt the most perfect and most fitted to express the things specified" (Kuzari, IV:25). In a similar vein, the Zohar asks, "Why was their language confounded? Because they all spoke the Holy Tongue, and this was of help to them." Thenceforth, Hebrew was possibly a sacred register special to Abraham and his lineage (Kuzari, II:68) or perhaps the general Canaanite tongue[8] used in counterpoint for the divine, becoming the national Hebrew tongue and the medium of revelation.

Leshon ha-kodesh functions in several modes: (1) study of the law; (2) performing certain mizvot, particularly addressing God, and (3) communicating with others.

With regard to studying the law, halakhah, unlike the Mishnah (M. Meg. 1:8) insists that biblical scrolls be in Hebrew. Nevertheless, halakhah does not forbid translations in book form if essential. The Aramaic Targum (translation of the Bible), for example, is thus authoritative in content but not in form. Forget Hebrew and the Torah will be forgotten (cf. Neh. 13). Despite the demise of vernacular Hebrew, the Mishnah was edited in this language; the Aramaic of the Talmud, while in some sense a capitulation to foreign influences, still ensured a passive knowledge of Hebrew (BT Pes. 87a). This knowledge is expected of everyone: "May all of us, children, women, and servants, be able to understand and study Hebrew, and thus understand the Torah laws."[9] The midrash even insists that parents speak Hebrew to their children as part of the biblical duty to teach (Sif. Deut. Ekev), as do some moderns;[10] however, neither the Talmud nor halakhah in general require this. Grammatical analysis, too, if sometimes branded as heresy, has been widely commended as an aid to study, creative writing, and correct recital of Scripture and Prayer—but specifically biblical grammar, although Judah Halevi also praised Mishnaic Hebrew (Kuzari, III:67). "The Judeans, who were [grammatically] scrupulous with their language, held on to the Torah. The Galileans, who were not, did not" (BT Er. 53a). Grammar yields new insights into the literal sense of the Torah, although not impugning traditional ones; indeed, some grammarians stressed that the tradition lacked any interpretation for some words. But underlying the literal study of Scripture is drash, the nonliteral interpretation often based on stylistically marked variations in grammar or vocabulary, or on redundancy. As articulated in the oft-quoted motto employed by Rabbi Akiva: "The Torah did not use ordinary language [in such language, redundancy is normal]."

With regard to the performance of mizvot, we may note that whereas certain mizvot involving written or spoken texts must be in Hebrew, notably tefillin and mezuzah (M. Meg. 1:8) and the priestly blessing (M. Sot. 7:2), others, in principle, need not, notably the Shema and public prayer. In practice, however, particularly since the Enlightenment, the transcendental qualities of Hebrew as speech act have been emphasized over its natural semantic qualities: Hebrew is a mode of behavior. Thus, on the basis that the postexilic Hebrew prayers were composed for a public that itself was not at home in Hebrew, Rabbi Moses Sofer argued that the metaphysical power of untranslatable ideas and numerical allusions, the psychological power of "speaking to the King in the King's own tongue," and the national value of maintaining Hebrew on all fronts meant that even those who did not know Hebrew should pray in it. Logic dictates that all prayer be in Hebrew (Sh. Ar. 185:3). The Zohar even depicts the Babel generation as unlocking some special potential through Hebrew: "For in the utterance of prayer, it is Hebrew words which fully express the purpose of the heart, and thus help to the attainment of the desired goal; hence their tongue was confounded in order that they might not be able to express their desires in the Holy Tongue."

Finally, we may consider the role of Hebrew in communication with others. From the study of Torah in Hebrew (typically in groups) and the recital of prayer in Hebrew (often quite privately), it is but a short step to conversing with others in Hebrew on the Sabbath when pious thoughts reign, although this has usually been a kabbalistic-Ḥasidic rather than a general practice. "One will thus remember that it is Sabbath and refrain from work and business."[11] Indeed, the kabbalist Moses Cordovero bade his disciples: "Speak Hebrew with your fellows at all times,"[12] and followers of Ḥasidism have been similarly enjoined in recent times. If Hebrew and the Sabbath are well suited for one another, so too are Hebrew and the Land of Israel: "As it is under direct divine supervision, its population should talk the Holy Tongue employed by God."[13]

Hebrew can also be employed for everyday, though not frivolous, matters, even to call for some soap in the bath (BT Shab. 41a). Some authorities, therefore, deny it intrinsic sanctity;[14] many others differ, even permitting the reading of secular letters or history on the Sabbath "if they are written in Hebrew, for the language itself has sanctity and one learns from it words of Torah" (Isserles, ad loc.). The holiness of the script itself adds further sanctity.[15] Thus, Hebrew would seem to have at least potential sanctity.

The attitude to other languages is ambiguous. One talmudic tradition appears to forbid them (JT Shab. 1:4); Aramaic is particularly scorned. However, the creation of Jewish forms of Aramaic and German, and other languages, written in Hebrew script and rich in hebraisms seems to have satisfied the midrashic value of "not changing one's tongue." Indeed, Naḥman of Bratzlav stated: "Rabbi Shimon bar Yohai so sanctified Aramaic [in the *Zohar*] that even other things written in it are liable to promote the service of God." Kabbalah teaches the value of speaking other tongues: "Some words from the Torah survive in all the World's languages, vivifying them, and Israel was exiled so as to recover the Torah letters, raising the words to their 'source.'"[16] For example, *totafot* (head phylacteries) involves two foreign words for *two*, throwbacks to pre-Babel Hebrew.[17]

The rebirth of native Hebrew in this century has quickened an age-old process of development that was generally approved of, in practice at least. The Gemara frequently contrasts Torah Hebrew and rabbinic Hebrew, yet the holiness of the whole is indivisible. Maimonides, commenting on the Mishnaic coinage *taram* (give priestly tithe), stated: "As the basis of any language is what speakers say, and these Mishnaic authors were doubtless Hebrews . . . and they used *taram,* it proves that it is acceptable in the language."[18] To Franz Rosenzweig it was here, too, the uniqueness of Hebrew lies: "Whatever has accrued integrally to Hebrew through the ages is never lost. This is not the growth of an organism but the accumulation of a treasury."[19]

REFERENCES

1. *Sefer ha-Likkutim,* invoking Moses Cordovero's *Pardes Rimonim.*
2. Joseph Schneersohn, *Bosi L'Gani* 5710, commenting on the *Zohar.*
3. Gershom Scholem, *Major Trends in Jewish Mysticism* (1941), 132.
4. Moses Ḥayyim Luzzatto, *Leshon Limmudim,* introduction to Part 2.
5. Cf. *Korban ha-Edah* on JT Shekalim 13a.
6. Cf. Y. Eibeschutz, *Yaarot Dvash* 2.
7. Baruch Halevi Epstein, *Torah Temimah,* commenting on Gen. 11:1.
8. Naḥmanides, commenting on Gen. 45:12, Ex. 30:13.
9. Saadiah Gaon, Introduction to *Agron.*
10. Baruch Halevi Epstein, *Torah Temimah,* commenting on Deut. 11:19.
11. I. Lampronto, *Paḥad Yiẓḥak, Leshon Kodesh.*
12. Horodetzky, ed., *Torot ha-Kabbalah,* 1920, 279.
13. Moses Sofer, *Torot Moshe, Naso.*
14. See, for example, Taz, commenting on Sh. Ar., *Orah Hayyim,* 307.
15. Z. Chayes, *Responsa* 12.
16. De Rossi, *Me'or Einayim.*
17. Horowitz, *Shelah,* 409b.
18. Moses Maimonides, Commentary on Terumah 1:1.
19. Franz Rosenzweig, *Zweistromland: Kleinere Schriften zur Religion und Philosophie* (1926), 114.

BIBLIOGRAPHY

William Chomsky, *Hebrew: The Eternal Language* (1957).
Shimon Federbush, *Ha-Lashon ha-Ivrit be-Yisrael u-va-Amim* (1967).
Abraham S. Halkin, "The Medieval Jewish Attitude Toward Hebrew," in Alexander Altmann, ed., *Biblical and Other Studies* (1963).
Eduard Y. Kutscher, *A History of the Hebrew Language* (1982).
Chaim Rabin, *A Short History of the Hebrew Language* (1973).

Hellenism

יוונות

David Satran

A constant feature of the Jewish intellectual tradition is the attempt to draw boundaries, to distinguish between that wisdom which is essential to the nation and that which remains "foreign." Already in the book of Deuteronomy (4:6) we find an attempt to define that knowledge which sets Israel apart from her neighbors—"Observe them [the statutes and ordinances] faithfully, for that will be proof of your wisdom and discernment to other peoples." This recurrent attempt to distinguish between divine and human wisdom and to identify the former as the exclusive provenance of Israel was never more than partially successful. The Bible itself provides vivid witness to the inroads made by the wisdom literature and traditions of ancient Israel's neighbors. Indeed, the history of Jewish thought, from its biblical origins through its modern expressions, is an unceasing reflection of external influences on the developing cultural tradition of Israel. Even during those periods in which the spiritual life of the individual and community seemed most immune to the broader geographical and cultural contexts in which they existed, there was an element (perhaps unconscious, generally unacknowledged) of response to these surroundings. The history of foreign influences on the Jewish intellectual tradition, then, parallels the history of Jewish thought itself.

At certain junctures in the development of the tradition, however, one encounters a heightened sensitivity to this process. The influence of "foreign wisdom" is then perceived as a potent, often problematic, factor in the religious life of certain sectors of the community. It can become the essential criterion by which certain individuals, a group, or the majority define themselves vis-à-vis one another. This sensitized perception of "foreign wisdom" as a challenge to the cultural tradition can be, of course, the result of a significant increase in the degree or nature of such external influence. It is equally possible, though, that other, less clearly related factors have brought this issue to the fore. The threat of religious or cultural persecution, sectarian dissension within a community, a forceful challenge to established practices or beliefs—each of these circumstances can be perceived as a crisis whose roots lie in the threat posed by "foreign wisdom."

The classic expression of this awareness arose from the confrontation between Judaism and Greek culture. In the wake of the campaigns of Alexander the Great, both Greece and the civilizations of the Near East were faced with a constellation of beliefs and practices, patterns of thought and action alien to their own. The lasting result of this sudden meeting, the gradual development of the intellectual and spiritual energies thus unleashed, is the phenomenon known as Hellenism. The Jewish communities of the area—whether in Egypt, Palestine, or Asia Minor—were exposed as well to this cultural upheaval.

The first overtures would appear to have come from the Greeks themselves during an initial stage of fascination with the wisdom and piety of the Orient. Hecateus of Abdera, an intellectual at the court of Ptolemy I of Egypt (323–285 B.C.E.), described sympathetically the history of the Jews and their political constitution within the tradition of Greek historiography. Theophrastus and Clearchus (ca. 300 B.C.E.), both students of Aristotle, depicted the Jews as a race of philosophers; the latter described a (probably fictitious) meeting between his master and a Jewish sage, who was "Greek not only in his language, but in his very soul" (Josephus, *Against Apion* 1, 177–81). These writings reflect an early attempt on the part of the Greeks to come to terms with the other, the foreigner, but almost completely within their own cultural frame of reference as a curiously exotic extension of themselves.

Jewish experience within the Hellenistic world could be equally one-sided. Popular tradition, as expressed, for example, in the *Letter of Aristeas,* presented the translation of the Pentateuch into Greek, the Septuagint, as a genuine expression of cultural intercourse, namely the magnanimous response of the high priest in Jerusalem to a request from Ptolemy II (285–248 B.C.E.) on behalf of the famed library of Alexandria. It is far more likely, however, that the translation, a generally faithful attempt to preserve the quality of the original Hebrew text, arose from the internal needs of the Greek-speaking Jewish community. Gradually, more daring attempts were made to understand the Bible and its injunctions in terms of the intellectual concepts and categories common in the Hellenistic world. Aristobulus, an Alexandrian Jew of the second century B.C.E., is the earliest known philosophical exegete of the Scriptures and employs techniques of allegorical exegesis—similar to those devised by the Stoics in their treatment of Homer—as a means of purging the Bible of its embarrassing tendency toward anthropomorphic descriptions of the deity. Yet Aristobulus too was intensely self-conscious about his adoption of this method and its results. Accordingly, he prefaces his exposition with the astonishingly bold claim that the fathers of Greek philosophy—Pythagoras, Plato, Aristotle—were directly dependent upon the teachings of Moses, and that their doctrines reveal the clear influence of the Jewish Scriptures. Thus, in a single anachronistic stroke, the first thoroughly Hellenized Jewish thinker attempted to neutralize the problem of "foreign wisdom": the use of philosophy, the wisdom of the Greeks, is nothing other than the recovery of authentic Jewish tradition. This claim was to reverberate through the centuries, in both Jewish and Christian sources. It was a dangerously two-edged argument, however, and could be adopted by the opponents of religious rationalism (see, for example, Judah Halevi, *Kuzari* 1:63; 2:66) in their attack on the nobility of the philosophical tradition.

The acme of Jewish Hellenism lies in the voluminous writings of Philo of Alexandria, who lived from approximately 20 B.C.E. to 40 C.E. Primarily concerned with an exacting commentary on the Pentateuch, his works reveal a first-hand knowledge of current philosophical themes that places him squarely within the Middle Platonist tradition. So thoroughgoing is his integration of biblical source material and Greek structures of thought and analysis that scholars have long pursued the (probably fruitless) debate whether he is primarily a Jewish exegete or a Hellenistic philosopher. Indeed, it is precisely the lack of inner tension in Philo's writings that marks them as the quintessential expression of the Jewish-Hellenistic synthesis.

This meeting between cultures, however, could have aspects neither harmonious nor desirable. The Hasmonaean revolt in 169–165 B.C.E. has been recorded in Jewish history as the paradigmatic statement of spiritual opposition to the intrusion of foreign practices on traditional beliefs and worship. It is significant that a localized political struggle whose underlying motives were in part economic and social should be perceived in the popular and scholarly imagination as a purely ideological confrontation between Jewish and Greek values. This perception is already well established in the Book of Second Maccabees—an epitome of the lost volumes of Jason of Cyrene—where we first encounter the terms *Judaism* (2:21, 8:1, 14:38) and *Hellenism* (4:13) representing opposing spiritual forces. Yet the same author, when he comes to narrate the heroic resistance of the aged and pious Eleazar (6:18–31), skillfully employs the literary model of Socrates' adamant refusal to compromise himself before the citizens of Athens. The greatest irony, though, lies in the history of the period itself: the successful outcome of the Hasmonaean revolt brought about the establishment of a Jewish kingdom whose own Hellenizing tendencies grew ever more pronounced. This was not the last time that the intrusion of "foreign wisdom" was to prove surprisingly resilient.

Hellenistic Judaism was ultimately to suffer a double measure of misfortune. As a vibrant community, it disappears from the stage of history in the mystifying, though apparently violent, series of events that followed the destruction of the Second Temple in Jerusalem in 70 C.E. No less severe was the treatment of its memory in later Jewish tradition. Rabbinic sources preserve almost no record of the cultural achievement that abounded in Alexandria over a period of centuries; no trace survives of the formidable attempt to create poetry, drama, historiography, and philosophy from the narratives of the Bible. In fact, were it not for the Christian preservation and transmission of this literature, an entire phase of Jewish intellectual history would have been lost. The ambivalence of the rabbinic attitude to the Jewish-Hellenistic endeavor is well illustrated by the opposing traditions regarding the translation of the Scriptures into Greek. The Septuagint could be objectively studied and even praised (BT Meg. 9a), yet other sources could speak of the day of its completion—a festival among the Jewish community of Alexandria—as "a day as tragic for Israel as that in which the Golden Calf was fashioned" (M. Sof. 1:7). Most striking, perhaps, is the fate of Philo of Alexandria: for a period of fifteen hundred years, he virtually disappeared from the arena of Jewish intellectual history, until the sixteenth century when that remarkable product of the Renaissance, Azariah Rossi, restored his memory and rightful position.

This cultivated neglect of Jewish-Hellenistic thought by the rabbis should be understood within the context of their own attitudes toward the persistent problem of "foreign wisdom." Recent scholarship has demonstrated

with great aplomb the extent to which Palestinian rabbis were knowledgeable about Greek language, customs, administrative organization, and legal
terminology. The influence of the Greco-Roman world is discernible on
almost every level of tannaitic and amoraic literature, yet nowhere is this
more striking than in the formulation of principles of biblical exegesis. The
secrets of Scripture were subjected to a variety of Hellenistic techniques
commonly applied to the interpretation of dreams and visions. The achievement of the rabbis in the area of natural science also bears witness to the
breadth of their learning. Their knowledge of botany, medicine, and astronomy often paralleled that of contemporary non-Jewish circles. So developed
was the study of astronomy, in particular, that the above-cited verse regarding "your wisdom and discernment to other peoples" [Deut. 4:6] could be
interpreted as a reference to rabbinic accomplishments in celestial observation and prediction (BT Shab. 75b).

It would be a mistake, however, to exaggerate the nature or the extent of
the rabbis' interest in Hellenistic culture. Nowhere do we find an attempt
to come to terms with the Greek intellectual heritage in its most fundamental expressions—drama, philosophy, historiography—as we do among the
Jewish-Hellenistic community. Indeed, Saul Lieberman has argued convincingly that there is not a single representation of Greek philosophical
terminology in the vast extent of rabbinic literature. This failure to confront
Greek thought and to contend with its most basic premises stands in sharp
contrast to the attempts of Christian intellectuals of that period (one thinks
especially of Clement and Origen in Alexandria or of the Cappadocians in
Asia Minor) to address the challenge that philosophical rationalism posed
for religious tradition. The ultimate intensity of this confrontation in medieval Jewish thought, and the passions it aroused, may be in some measure
the result of a meeting so long delayed or, perhaps, avoided. It is in light of
these self-imposed restrictions that the well-known rabbinic phrase *hokh-
mat yavanit* (BT Sof. 49b; BT Men. 99b) must be understood. It is neither
so narrow as to denote only *Greek language* nor so broad as to include all of
Greek wisdom, but rather refers to a proficiency or aptitude for things
Greek—for those skills or sciences whose practical application contributes
to the explication of the law and the welfare of the community. Through
the de facto establishment of this enlightened yet rigorously utilitarian standard, the rabbis shaped an attitude toward "foreign wisdom" that has determined the complexion of traditional Judaism to this day.

During the long period of Islamic rule in North Africa and Spain, the Jewish intellectual tradition was once more exposed to significant external
influences. The challenge of Greek thought appeared once again, this time

through the mediation of Arabic translation and an independent tradition of Islamic philosophical inquiry. Over the centuries a broad range of expression evolved in the response to this renewed acquaintance with Greek philosophy by thinkers as varied as Saadiah Gaon, Ibn Gabirol, and Judah Halevi, yet the issue of "foreign wisdom" remained problematic and largely unresolved. During the twelfth century, however, the emergence of Maimonides as the preeminent Jewish spokesman for religious rationalism was decisive. His unequivocal demand—"Accept the truth from whomever it may come" (Comm. on Mishnah, *Shemonah Perakim,* intro.)—not only affords a bold approach to the problem of "foreign wisdom," but informs his mature philosophical inquiry *(Guide of the Perplexed)* as well as his achievement in legal codification *(Mishneh Torah)*. Still more daring was Maimonides' attempt to restructure the very nature of traditional Jewish learning. The rabbinic injunction that the individual divide his time between the study of Bible, Mishnah, and Talmud (BT Kid. 30a) had become an established standard for defining acceptable areas of inquiry. Maimonides enjoins a subtly altered tripartite division—Bible, oral law, Talmud (MT Talmud Torah 1:11-12)—whose hidden implications are enormous. Talmud, in this context, as Isadore Twersky has pointed out, is no longer identical with the rabbinic category of Gemara (discussions on the Mishnah by the amoraim), but has come to include the study of the principles underlying the law and even philosophical inquiry. Thus, through the recasting of the very core of the Jewish intellectual tradition, Maimonides strove to secure a central position for that wisdom which long had been regarded as "foreign."

Under the influence of Maimonides and his writings, religious rationalism became an essential stream of later medieval Jewish thought. Its legitimacy was constantly challenged, though, particularly with regard to the question of the infiltration of foreign doctrines and methods. The most direct challenge came from rabbinical authorities and community leaders who perceived the pursuit of philosophy as potentially undermining the literal veracity of Scripture and the absolute centrality of halakhah. There arose as well a powerful movement of mystical speculation that addressed a number of issues not unlike those taken up by the rationalist thinkers, yet claiming ancient Jewish tradition (for example, Simeon bar Yoḥai) as the exclusive source of its wisdom. In fact, many of the opponents of philosophical inquiry were blissfully unaware of how deeply they themselves had absorbed language, imagery, and concepts that were the products of external influence. Another form of the antirationalist reaction lay in the carefully restricted participation in those sciences (mathematics, pre-Copernican astronomy) whose implications for Jewish belief and practice were minimal. In the sixteenth century, Judah Loew (the Maharal) of Prague provides a fascinating example of an intellectual and community leader who is both a man of science and an ardent opponent of philosophical rationalism. Common to all of these reactions is a deeply rooted commitment to the essential opposition—an opposition Maimonides had labored so arduously to erase—between human and divine wisdom.

With the emancipation of European Jewry, the problem of "foreign wisdom" is radically transformed. It is no longer an external influence, an alien knowledge, which confronts the individual or community; rather, the modern Jew shares the intellectual and cultural tradition of the larger society of which he has become a member. Thus, in contrast to earlier periods in which Jewish thinkers had drunk deeply of a wisdom clearly foreign to their own, modern Jewish intellectuals have often been involved in the very creation of such nontraditional wisdom (sociology, psychology, physical science, et al.). The most significant development in postemancipation Judaism, the Zionist movement, furnishes eloquent witness to this modern tension, for it is nourished by the logic and passion of both traditional belief (longing for Zion) and modern European wisdom (the ethic of national liberation). The State of Israel, often torn between the values of Jewish tradition and those of Western democracy, continues to seek a resolution of this tension.

In a certain sense, the problem of "foreign wisdom" has lost its traditional meaning. Franz Rosenzweig, the German-Jewish theologian of the beginning of this century, provides a fascinating counterexample to that of Maimonides, considered earlier. The medieval Jewish philosopher had struggled valiantly to find a place for the wisdom of the Greeks within Jewish tradition. The modern Jewish intellectual, thoroughly immersed in the European cultural sensibility, must struggle no less heroically to secure a niche for the lost wisdom of his people. This remarkable metamorphosis of the relationship between Jewish tradition and what once could securely be called "foreign wisdom" is best expressed, perhaps, by Rosenzweig's own defiant turn of a famed Latin epigram: "Nothing Jewish is foreign to me."

BIBLIOGRAPHY

Saul Lieberman, *Greek in Jewish Palestine* (1942).
Saul Lieberman, *Hellenism in Jewish Palestine*, 2d ed. (1962).

Saul Lieberman, "How Much Greek in Jewish Palestine?" in Alexander Altmann, ed., *Biblical and Other Studies* (1963).

Arnaldo Momigliano, *Alien Wisdom: The Limits of Hellenization* (1975), 74–122.

Avigdor Tcherikover, *Hellenistic Civilization and the Jews* (1959).

Isadore Twersky, *Introduction to the Code of Maimonides (Mishneh Torah)* (1980), 356–514.

Heresy

כפירה

Ze'ev Gries

There are three commonly used terms for heresy in Jewish literature: *minut, kefirah ba-ikkar,* and *epikorsut.* Moreover, the word *heresy* itself, which comes from the Greek *hairesis,* made its way into Hebrew literature in the Middle Ages through conflation with the Hebrew word *harisah,* which has a similar sound and whose root, *h-r-s,* in biblical usage already included the realm of meaning attached to the word *heresy.* The Greek *hairesis,* the source of the English word, originally meant "taking" in the sense of "taking away" a part of the principal body, that is to say, the division of a body to form a religious sect. The Hebrew word *harisah* used as a synonym for sectarianism (*minut*) appears in a chapter heading of an anonymous kabbalistic work, *Ma'arekhet ha-Elohut,* printed in Mantua in 1558 (113a): *"Shaar ha-harisah bo yitbaer inyan kizzuz ha-netiot she-hu ha-minut ve-ha-epikorsut"* ("The chapter on heresy, in which the matter of the 'cutting of the plants,' which refers to *minut* and *epikorsut,* will be explained").

Nor was it coincidental that the author based his explanation, in the opening lines of this chapter, on Exodus 19:24: "But let not the priests or the people break through [*yeharesu*] to come up unto the Lord," for the word *yeharesu* here literally means "to break through a boundary or framework," which is indeed how it is interpreted by the famous traditional Bible commentators Abraham ibn Ezra and David Kimḥi.[1] Moreover, it must certainly have been cognizance of the Greek term that underlay the interpretations of Onkelos and of Midrash Tanhuma Yashan, at the end of the section on Korah, to Numbers 16:1: "And Korah . . . took men"; this "taking," they explained, referred to the sectarian split with the people of Israel as a whole that was initiated by Korah and his men.[2]

Let us now look at the three more common terms for heresy in Jewish literature. As we shall see, an analysis of the sources of their denotations reflects upon our understanding of the worldviews of those who used them.

The term *minut* is apparently derived from the Hebrew word *min*, which denotes a type or species to be distinguished from others to which it may be closely related. It came to be used as a term for such heretics against the Jewish faith as the groups of Jewish Christians active toward the end of the Second Temple period and after, during the first years of Christianity.[3] Some say that the word *min* itself was originally simply an acronym for the words *maaminei Yeshu* [*ha-*]*nozri* ("believers in Jesus of Nazareth"); this was Rashi's interpretation, though it was censored out of his commentaries.[4] *Min* was also used to refer to Gentiles in general, and thence to anyone who adopted the ways of the Gentiles.[5]

The term *kefirah ba-ikkar* is a combination of two words: *k-f-r*, which existed in ancient Hebrew but was first used by the Sages in the sense of "deny," and *ikkar*, which comes from an Aramaic term meaning "root" and, in this context, refers to God. Note, however, that the meaning of the term was not the same in different periods; as used by the tannaim and amoraim it referred not to denial of the existence of God but rather to denial of the unity, providence, and omnipotence of the God of Israel.[6] In the Middle Ages, on the other hand, it was used primarily to signify the denial of some dogma or principle of the faith.[7]

The word *epikorsut* is apparently derived from the name of the Greek philosopher Epicurus, who opposed the prevalent Greek belief that the gods were provident and were not indifferent to the world and rejected the view that the soul continued to exist after death.[8] Note, however, the definition of Moses Maimonides in his commentary to Mishnah Sanhedrin 10:1, in which he understands *epikoros* to be an Aramaic word derived from the root *p-k-r*, meaning heresy:

"Epikoros" is an Aramaic word that refers to scorning or making light of the Torah or of scholars of the Torah, and it is thus used derivatively to refer to anyone who does not believe the basic principles of the Torah or who shows contempt for the Sages, or some scholar, or his own teacher.[9]

A look at the rabbinic statements on the issue and at those of the medieval scholars shows that there was some disagreement as to the boundaries of the halakhic definition of the heretic. Some used the terms *min, kefirah ba-ikkar,* and *epikoros* interchangeably, while others made distinctions among them. Maimonides attempted a precise and separate definition of each (MT Hil. Teshuvah 3:7–8), but his system also had its opponents.[10]

The later biblical literature contains some evidence of inner struggle over questions of faith—in the books of Ecclesiastes and Job, for example—but it does not clearly testify to any battle against heretics and heresy, which would have manifested itself in the literature in a legal definition of heresy and a list of the punishments designated for offenders.

With the spread of the Greek empire and its Hellenistic culture (particularly during the fourth century B.C.E. and after), however, the Sages were increasingly exposed to controversies over the faith and beliefs as well as customs and laws of Judaism. Significant numbers of Jews, drawn to the alien culture, adopted some of its beliefs and abandoned or violated the commandments imposed upon them by the halakhah. The Sages were now impelled to define just who would have no part in the World to Come (M. Sanh., ch. 10): "Anyone who says that there will be no revival of the dead or that the Torah is not of divine origin, and the *epikoros.*" (Rabbi Akiva and some of the other Sages go on to list several more sins that deny one a part in that world.)

Examination of the development of antiheretical legal measures will show, however, that they occupied an extremely marginal place in Jewish history.[11] Up to the modern period, in fact, the unity of the people was marred by only a very few sectarian divisions: those of the Sadducees, the Boethusians, and the Judean Desert Sect, and those of the Karaites and the Sabbateans. One of the indicators most aptly demonstrating this fact is the use of the *herem* (ban), which was a principal means of law enforcement in Jewish communities applied to those who rebelled against the religious authorities or violated the halakhah. It is no accident that the twenty-four cases in which the *herem* could be used[12] do not include slips of faith, but only scorn or insult for the principal bearers of the faith—the scholars. Indeed, the history of the *herem* shows that throughout most of Jewish history it was not exercised against heretics. An examination of the *Pinkas Va'ad Arba Arazot* (Record Book of the Council of the Lands), for example, shows that in the eighteenth century the *herem* was used mostly in cases of business or trade infractions and disputes over copyright. Even the explosion of Sabbateanism did not create a situation in which the *herem* was threatened or declared primarily in order to deal with spiritual offenses or with heresy, as in the controversial case of Rabbi Jonathan Eybeschuetz. For many years the rabbi, who was regarded as a great preacher by his disciples, was investigated for alleged Sabbatean formulae and even for being a secret Christian. The exceptional cases of the famous bans in the seventeenth century against Baruch Spinoza and Uriel Da Costa testify only to the fact that in certain political contexts the *herem* could be used to punish and to remove from the Jewish community persons whose beliefs and opinions were considered to be in heretical violation of the basic principles of the faith, the best-known formulation of which is the thirteen principles of the faith articulated by Maimonides (Comm. to M. Sanh., ch. 10). It is of interest to note that the wording of these bans nonetheless adhered to the traditional formulation in which contempt for the law was condemned as the offending act.[13]

The explanation for this phenomenon lies in the fact that the Jewish religion, as it developed, came to be based primarily on the *mizvot ma'asiot*—the commandments regarding specific actions or abstentions to which its adherents are obligated. The halakhah is the legal apparatus for determining how these commandments are to be kept and for ensuring that they are indeed fulfilled properly. By its very nature, halakhah was not designed as a means for investigating or overseeing the quality of one's faith. The prevailing assumption, rather, as expressed in the sixteenth-century work *Sefer ha-Hinukh,* was that a man's motivations are determined by his actions; that is, if children and adults kept to and were continually educated toward a rigorous day-to-day observance, the unity and omnipotence of God would naturally become fixed in their consciousness. The Jewish Sages believed that this experience of unwavering observance maintained a state of affairs in which there was no need for tiresome and useless inquiry into the essential nature of faith and how to instill it.

Public sensitivity to heretical activity grew especially great whenever there arose a movement or group that not only expressed certain opinions but also vented them publicly and translated them into an active deviance from the traditional mode of observing the commandments, so that the authority of the sages who led the community, the halakhah they taught, and the community's accepted customs were undermined. This will become obvious to anyone who inspects the system of sanctions laid down by the halakhah, which clearly sets a high priority on punishing actions or failures of observance that concern or influence the community at large.

The great majority of Jewish heretics left no systematic corpus of writing for those who came after them, and we know of their opinions only from their being intentionally (and tendentiously) paraphrased in the writings of the Jewish sages who opposed them. With the famous exception of Baruch Spinoza, who did leave us writings of his own, the spiritual biographies of these heretics thus reach us not at firsthand, but from what their opponents had to say about them. We have no idea, for example, how the sectarians at the end of the Second Temple period went about studying halakhic issues, for we have no firsthand written record of their scholarly debates.

We learn from this that even though there were very few Jewish heretics, there was a concerted educational effort to wipe out all trace of their doctrines. What was true in the early Christian period was certainly no less so in the case of such heretics as Hiwi al-Balkhi in the second half of the ninth century, of whose arguments we would have no knowledge at all had they not been preserved in the responsa written to combat them, primarily by Saadiah Gaon.[14]

The main struggle to be waged against heresy was always viewed by the Sages as that which took place within the community against those who had been brought up on the commandments and literature of Judaism and had rejected them (see Tosef. Shab. 13:5). This recognition of the importance of the educational process undergone by the individual is especially prominent in the writings of Maimonides, who as a halakhic authority, commentator, and teacher of philosophy and medicine wielded great influence over both his own generation and those that followed.

Maimonides addressed his writings on the subject both to the individual and to the leaders of the community who were responsible for its education, the rabbis and legal masters. As he saw it, the development of heretical ideas in an individual had its source in a particular spiritual quality characteristic of the heretic. Thus it was the responsibility of the rabbi to be extremely precise in his interpretation of the texts and traditions he taught his pupils, so that no support should be found in them for heretical views.[15]

Maimonides was cognizant of man's duty to be aware of his own qualities and to nurture them, so that he might achieve spiritual balance and develop his spiritual nature to the utmost (see MT Hil. Teshuvah 7:3). Concern about the possible development of heretical beliefs in those who did not have the capacity to confront and withstand their own misleading tendencies led him to state in his teachings for the general public that "we are cautioned not even to raise the slightest thought which might cause a person to reject any of the principles of the Torah" (MT Hil. Avodat Kokhavim 4:3). The careful reader will discern in what he has to say, however, that those individuals who do have the capacity to study these dangerous topics may nonetheless do so. His teaching for the general public was formulated out of concern for the *epikorsim* (MT Hil. Avodat Kokhavim, ch. 5), whose basic character was unalterable and might lead them to heresy.

Furthermore, Maimonides felt that the basic essence of heretical belief matched the spiritual nature of those who held it, for heresy was primarily characterized by quarrelsomeness and divisiveness, and these were also the qualities of its adherents (see his Commentary to M. Avot 1:3). The true faith, on the other hand, united its believers and held them together. Every real heresy had founded itself on the true religion. The heretics would cunningly lay hold of the borders of the truth—that is to say, they would recognize and acknowledge some part of the true faith so that they could make their voice heard in the community and so that they could then go on to reject the principal path and obligations of that faith, the oral law, its study and its instructions, which set the pattern of the Jewish way of life (Commentary to M. Avot 1:3; cf. *Teshuvot ha-Rambam,* ed. Joshua Blau, 1960, 501–502). Maimonides saw this kind of danger to the true faith as issuing not only from within but also from without, from the Islamic faith, under whose dominion he lived. As he acknowledged, the Muslims were not idolatrous, and there was an element of truth to their faith in that it was monotheistic. The principal danger presented by another monotheistic religion that rejected the superiority and unique truth of the faith of Israel was, however, again not external but internal in nature; it was that the Jewish sages would shut their eyes to that element of Islam which was true, which would impede their own understanding and their attitudes toward others and toward converts to their own faith (see Maimonides' responsum to Ovadia the convert, *Teshuvot ha-Rambam,* 726–28).

On the other hand, Maimonides knew that the mere establishment of a fine educational system was in and of itself insufficient to preserve the true faith. And even if the sages and the most gifted exponents of the Torah were to serve as instructors in the schools and academies, it would not suffice to secure the integrity of the true faith among Israel. That this was the case was proven by historical events. The patriarch Abraham, who arrived at the true faith through his own understanding, sought to further it by establishing schools for its instruction, an effort that was continued by his immediate descendants. Faith was nevertheless almost completely forgotten, and it would have perished utterly during the Exile in Egypt had it not been kept up by the tribe of Levi. If the true faith was to persist and flourish over the course of time, it had to be instilled in the consciousness of those who were brought up to it, not only through academic study but also in their way of life. That was what Moses accomplished when he set before the people the system of divine commandments, which taught them "how to serve Him, and what would be the punishment of idolatry and of those who strayed after it" (MT Hil. Avodat Kokhavim 1:3).

At the same time, Maimonides was the chief scholar to impress upon the consciousness of the people the need for capable and talented individuals to study such secular subjects as philosophy and medicine. Such study might well have seemed to threaten traditional attitudes toward the Jewish sages and to violate the basic principles of the faith, for the true philosopher had no need, in order to perfect his philosophical attainments, of adhering exclusively to the faith of Israel, and the same was true of the expert doctor. The guardians of the faith had reason, then, to distrust Maimonides' pupils and their followers, fearing that they would be unable, unlike their master, to walk the fine line separating strict observance of Jewish law and its commandments and the heretical violation of them. It was this fear that lay at the bottom of the thirteenth-century controversy over Maimonides and the bans issued at the time against philosophical study. However, a careful reading of the wording of these bans, whose most prominent signatory was Rabbi Solomon ben Abraham Adret, reveals that philosophical study was not utterly forbidden, but rather limited to persons over the age of twenty-five. Moreover, the prohibition against studying philosophy or any other Greek science until the age of twenty-five did not apply to the study of medicine.[16]

The kabbalah, the new Jewish mysticism that arose toward the end of the twelfth century, aroused grave concern that it might undermine the foundations of the monotheistic faith. Instead of letting suffice the one God who reveals himself through history, it posed ten or sometimes thirteen divine potencies or hypostases constituting different manifestations or emanations of the one hidden God, whose unity was meant thus to be preserved. The very real suspicions of its opponents found their most acute expression in an epistle of Rabbi Meir ben Simeon Ha-Me'ili that attacked mysticism, its understanding of the divinity, and how that understanding was translated into its conception of the commandments that the Jew was obligated to fulfill.[17]

The history of the kabbalah does include the growth, in the seventeenth and eighteenth centuries, of the heretical movement of Sabbatean messianism. Most Jewish mystics, however, whether they lived before or after the emergence in the sixteenth century of the messianic kabbalah of Isaac Luria, considered the halakhah sacred and studied and practiced it diligently. If we are to judge the extent and character of their divergence from traditional Judaism and their heretical ideas by the degree to which they adhered to the halakhah and the accepted Jewish way of life, we will find that they were not, nor did they ever pretend to be, "new Jews" with a new halakhah or a new path different from that of their forefathers. Never did the kabbalists—or even the Sabbateans—seek to create an alternative to the entire body of halakhah, and most certainly not to its criminal and civil law. Moreover, they created no new kind of educational framework or institutions for themselves or for their offspring such as might have constituted the foundation for a new community with a different way of life and self-definition. If the kabbalists did introduce new customs into Judaism, most of these were changes in or additions to its ritual or prayers, realms in which custom has always been allowed a broad range for alteration and innovation, particularly in the synagogue service for the Sabbath and festivals.

It is true, to be sure, that Sabbateanism is founded upon the kabbalah in general, and in particular upon the Lurianic kabbalah with its messianic doctrine, according to which man's task on earth is to redeem the divine sparks scattered throughout creation, whose ingathering will bring about his redemption together with that of the cosmos as a whole. It was only a tiny minority of the adherents of the Sabbatean heresy, however, who took the ultimate, drastic step of converting, like their "Messiah," Shabbetai Ẓevi, to Islam—or, like another heretical leader, Jacob Frank, to Christianity. The vast majority of those who had put their faith in this new messianism never reached the stage of abrogating the halakhah or radically altering it. It is doubtful, then, that we can say with any degree of conviction that the kabbalah by its very nature impelled people in the direction of heresy or of abandoning their faith. Messianic yearnings and hopes for redemption existed among Jews before the advent of the kabbalah, alongside it, and even within it without necessarily having recourse to its doctrine, and it was in the wake of these messianic waves that there were incidents of deviation and of heresy. One did not have to be a mystic in order to be a heretic.

Jewish existence and the Jewish experience from the end of ancient times and throughout the Middle Ages were characterized, for the Jew, by a way of life that was Jewish in every respect. Religion was universally central to life, but particularly so for the Jew. If heretics did rise against the faith, from within it or from without, they did not turn to a secular way of life (which, of course, at the time was not an existing option); they took on another faith, a different image of God or of the gods, and different beliefs.

This situation changed with the onset of the modern era. With the emancipation of the Jews in Western and Central Europe, the holistic framework of Jewish life became undermined and broke down. What happened among the Jews was part of a tremendous process of change that was taking place within the Christian peoples. The tide of Protestantism, Enlightenment, and national consciousness that swept through Europe brought with it the ascendancy of secular values and vision, and the symbols of material success increasingly took the place of religious hopes and yearnings.

For the first time ever, a huge number of Jews who identified themselves as Jews sought, in the process of formulating their identity, to justify freeing themselves of a part of the traditional Jewish way of life and of the commandments and customs that were inseparably tied to it. As the doctrines of Orthodoxy and Reform took shape in the nineteenth century, they would seem to have been totally antithetical in this regard. In Western Europe, the Neo-Orthodox, whose chief spokesmen were Samson Raphael Hirsch and Isaac Breuer, emphasized the continuity of Jewish law and the need to maintain a strict adherence to it. Their Reform opponents, on the other hand, represented by Abraham Geiger and his circle, demanded the adaptation of the law to the changing circumstances of the people and emphasized the importance of religious feeling. The spiritual, noninstitutionalized aspect of the "reform" trend reached its most radical expression in the thought of Martin Buber, who sought to encourage a Jewish spiritual renewal that would be entirely independent of ritual observance. A polarization thus emerged between those seeking to maintain an unbending fidelity to halakhah and those committed to a renewal of Judaism on the basis of a cultural and spiritual revivification—that is to say, with translating and reformulating parts of the Jewish literary heritage so that it might serve the Jewish person in his attempt to understand himself and to construct an identity as a modern Jew. It was for this purpose that Buber set about reshaping and transmitting the literature of the Ḥasidic followers of the Baal Shem Tov, which he saw as containing a powerful impulse for religious renewal, and it was for the same reason that he undertook, with his friend Franz Rosenzweig, a new translation of the Bible into German.[18]

The polarization between the two groups was, however, not what it appeared, as Max Weiner so finely discerned:

> But whatever the designations of these different factions, whether they called themselves observant or traditionalist, Liberal or Reform, what they all had in common from the point of view of holistic Judaism is that, counter to the cultural homogeneity that had prevailed in the period before the Emancipation, they

sought a religiosity that could be maintained within the context of a universal cultural framework that imposed itself upon the Jew as well, demanding that he live within its domain.[19]

This bursting of the bonds of holistic Jewish life was acidly described, with more than a touch of self-hate and self-pity, by the German Jewish satirist Sammy Gronemann. The battle between the followers of Samson Raphael Hirsch, the father of German Jewish Orthodoxy, and those of Abraham Geiger, the father of the Reform movement in Germany, he wrote,

> was waged on the field of assimilation. Both parties were united on one point, namely, that Judaism was but a religious faith, and the Jewish people no longer existed; that the Jew was in fact a German, differing from other Germans solely with respect to his faith. . . . They refused to understand that the lowliest street urchin had a surer eye for the physiognomy of those who "professed the Mosaic faith" than the scholar who studied the race.[20]

This refusal on the part of the emancipated generation to understand its new circumstances led to a situation in which, as Gronemann wrote, the most radical reformers were no more than

> heretics who had gathered under the banner of Reform, . . . [for] that very dogma of [Hirsch's] Neo-Orthodoxy that held that there was no Jewish people left them no choice but either to deny their Jewishness or to associate themselves for show with a religious sect that was no more to them than an empty, futile cover.[21]

The Orthodox, on the other hand,

> often reduced the Torah and the rigid observances to a farce . . . and there was more and more of a tendency, as they pursued their superficial worship of forms, to become oblivious to any inner significance. Women in these circles covered their hair with wigs "in order not to be attractive to other men," not as the Jewish women in Poland, for example, had done, but with all manner of glamorous creations, styled according to all the nuances of Paris fashion, which fit so well with the accepted cut of the décolletage. Then there were the yeshivah students who, strictly refraining from the use of money on the Sabbath, arranged to be served on credit on that day in brothels . . . that is to say, the holy one was turned right and left into the profanest of the profane.[22]

Attitudes toward heresy and heretics developed differently in Eastern Europe. Until the rise of Zionism toward the end of the nineteenth century, the influence of the Enlightenment and its adherents did not succeed in diminishing the consciousness of the Eastern European Jews or their sense of commitment to a total Jewish life. The example of Nachman Krochmal is not atypical in this respect. A leading representative of the Jewish Enlightenment in Poland, he was careful to make apologies for his connections with a Karaite scholar (the Karaite sect broke away from mainstream Judaism in the tenth century), emphasizing that he himself was known to be strictly observant and to have continually studied the Torah.[23]

The great threat to the strictly observant Judaism of Eastern Europe appeared in the shape of the Zionist "devil," which took the traditional national hopes for an ingathering of the exiles, the renewal of Jewish sovereignty over the land of Israel, and a revival of Jewish cultural life and imbued them with a powerfully heretical coloration. Among the foremost spokesmen for Zionism were radicals such as Joseph Ḥayyim Brenner, who emphasized over and over that the new national Jew was to be freed of the "hunchback" of his religion; his new Jewish culture would be the product of his own physical labors and of a mind loosed of its ancient immersion in talmudic study and of the limitations and minute observances that had sustained so many generations of parasitic religious functionaries and distorted the spirit and backbone of the Jewish people. In order to bring about this Jewish renewal, the Jew must become a Zionist and go to live in the land of Israel; he must bring about the realization of his Jewish political sovereignty in order to become sovereign over his experience and way of life as a Jew.[24]

Nevertheless, in the early years of Zionism not all the religious leaders of Eastern European Jewry rejected out of hand the possibility of cooperating with the "heretics" for the sake of redeeming the Jews from their plight in exile. An awareness of their national distress had permeated the consciousness of all of Eastern Europe's Jews. There were those among the faithful who wholeheartedly believed that the resettlement of the ancient homeland would ultimately lead to the growth of an integral and sovereign Judaism, one that could not, by its nature, take anything but the traditional religious form; it would dominate the lives of the Jews in the land, and the religion and its institutions would naturally reign supreme.[25] The notion that resettling the land in cooperation with the heretics would bring about a flourishing of holiness, so that the heretical trend would diminish and ultimately disappear, was among the guiding principles of the thought of Abraham Isaac Kook.[26]

The second generation of Kook's followers made the settlement of the land their most sacred principle and formed a popular movement, *Gush Emunim* (lit., Bloc of the Faithful), to promote it. The prominent Israeli thinker Yeshayahu Leibowitz has called this movement a pseudomessianism, Sabbatean in character. It forces messianic strivings upon reality in utter disregard for Jewish tradition, which has always sought to moderate and regulate any activity toward realizing the messianic hope. In Leibowitz's view, such a movement cannot but lead to disillusion, heresy, and abandonment of the land.[27]

A new phenomenon has arisen in the State of Israel, that of the existence, for the last three generations, of a large Jewish population—comprising the majority of the state's Jews—that identifies itself as Jewish and is identified as such by Jewish law, but is largely not brought up to observe the strictures of the Torah and receives no traditional education. From a halakhic point of view, a person who has never had a chance to experience the Torah and to live by it is not considered a heretic. Whatever he may say against Judaism, his status is that of a "babe taken captive"; he is viewed, in other words, as one who has from infancy been an involuntary prisoner in another culture. Nevertheless, the language of our time—both written and spoken—calls anyone who decides to reject the nonreligious way of life to which he was brought up in order to embrace the faith a *hozer bi-teshuvah* ("one who returns in repentance"), as though he had been a heretic and now changed his ways.

This erroneous use of the term, so frequently heard, is no mere slip of the tongue; it reflects the consciousness of those who use it. Israeli Orthodoxy seems to find it particularly convenient to perpetuate the old struggle. The Jews of Israel and the Diaspora are to be viewed, as it were, as though they were still a homogeneous unit sharing the same consciousness and self-definition; if some of its members have unfortunately gone astray and deserted the true path, they must be brought back to it, to the bosom of "total" Judaism, which is no mere image but a reality.

As a result of the peculiar wiles of the coalition politics prevailing in the State of Israel, secular politicians have made far-reaching concessions to religious political parties, ironically obliging the secularists to accept Orthodoxy's conception of "wayward" Jews as the implicit basis of both the state's internal policy on Jewish matters and its external policy toward the large Conservative and Reform movements of the Diaspora, whose adherents find it extremely difficult to be absorbed and to conduct their communal activities in the State of Israel. Moreover, the possibilities for non-Orthodox Jews living in Israel—who make up the majority of the population—to conduct Jewish lives on an individual and communal basis along non-Orthodox lines are extremely limited.

Most of Israel's politicians have the simplistic idea that they ought to pursue "larger" matters such as peace with the state's Arab neighbors, and that their concessions on such "smaller" matters will do the people no harm. As the former prime minister, Shimon Peres, put it: "Nothing will happen to you if you don't eat pork, but things will be very bad if we don't renew the peace process" (Ha-Arez, 8 September 1985, 7). What the politicians and the public at large that stands behind them do not understand is that there is a direct connection between the character of the inner life of the Jews of Israel and the character and quality of the peace they seek—and may attain—with their Arab neighbors. They fail to see that their "small" concessions in such realms as observance of the Sabbath and dietary laws are really a large concession on the cultural level; in making these concessions, they relinquish their attempt to arrive at their own independent evaluation of their identity as Jews and to extrapolate the implications of that evaluation in terms of their individual and political behavior. Moreover, by surrendering to such erroneous usages, artificially taken over from the age-old struggle against heresy, the politicians and the public at large evade the pressing demand upon them to reevaluate and deal with the situation of the Jews in the modern world, both in Israel and in the Diaspora. The consequences of that surrender may well prove extremely harmful to the State of Israel and the Jewish people at large.

REFERENCES

1. See also the discussion by Samuel ibn Tibbon in his appendix, Perush ha-Millim ha-Zarot, to his translation of Maimonides' Guide of the Perplexed, published separately by J. Even Shemu'el (1946), 48.
2. See the lengthy discussion in Y. Liebes, "Mazmiah Keren Yeshu'a," in Mehkarei Yerushalayim be-Mahshevet Yisra'el, 3 (1984), 346–47, n. 81.
3. See Ha-Arukh ha-Shalem, 2nd ed., 5 (1926), s.v. "min."
4. See Y. Avineri, Heikhal Rashi, Pt. 2 (1985), 623–25.
5. See Samuel Krauss, Griechische und lateinische Lehnwörter im Talmud Midrash und Turgum (1898), xv, n. 2; Saul Liebermann, Yevanit ve-Yavnut be-Erez Yisrael (1962), 109, n. 196.
6. See Efraim E. Urbach, The Sages: Their Concepts and Beliefs (1975), 21.
7. See A. Holz, Be-Olam ha-Mahshavah shel Hazal (1978–1979), 69–71.
8. See Ha-Arukh ha-Shalem 1, s.v. "Epikoros"; Urbach, op. cit., 23–24.
9. Cf. Jacob Levy, Wörterbuch über die Talmuden und Midrashim, 4 (1924), s.v. "p-k-r."
10. See Enzyklopediah Talmudit, 5th ed. (1979), s.v. "Epikoros."
11. See the detailed entry on heresy in the Jewish Encyclopedia (1904).
12. See MT Hil. TT 6:14.

13. For the text of Spinoza's ban see P. Mendes-Flohr and J. Reinharz, eds., *The Jew in the Modern World* (1980), 50.
14. See Samuel Abraham Poznanski, "Hivi ha-Balkhi," in *Ha-Goren*, 7 (1908); Israel Davidson, *Saadia's Polemic Against Hiwi al-Balkhi* (1915).
15. See Maimonides, Commentary to M. Avot 1:3 and 1:11. The same interpretation of his views is presented by his successor Menaḥem ben Shelomo ha-Meiri in *Ḥibbur ha-Teshuvah* (1950), 106.
16. See A. S. Halkin, "Ha-Ḥerem al Limmud ha-Pilosofia," in *Perakim*, 1 (1967–1968), 35–55.
17. See Gershom Scholem, "Teudah Ḥadashah le-Toledot Reshit ha-Kabbalah," in *Sefer Bialik* (1934), 148–50.
18. See A. E. Simon, "Martin Buber ve-Emunat Yisrael," in *Iyyun*, 9 (1958), 13–50.
19. Max Weiner, *Ha-Dat ha-Yehudit be-Tekufat ha-Emanzipaziah* (1974), 40.
20. Sammy Gronemann, *Zikhronot shel Yekke* (1946), 27.
21. Ibid., 29 (emphasis added).
22. Ibid. (emphasis added).
23. See S. Ravidovitch, ed., *Kitvei Ranak*, 2d ed. (1961), 413–16.
24. See J. H. Brenner, "Le-Ha'arakhat Azmenu be-Sheloshet ha-Kerakhim," in *Kol Kitvei Brenner*, 3 (1967), 57, and "Ba-Ḥayyim u-va-Sifrut," in *Kol Kitvei Brenner*, 2 (1960), 59.
25. See E. Luz, *Makbilim Nifgashim* (1985), 79–85.
26. Ibid., 15–16, 378–79.
27. See Yeshayahu Leibowitz, *Yahadut, Am Yisrael u-Medinat Yisrael* (1975), 412–14, and *Emunah, Historiah ve-Arakhim* (1982), 218–19.

BIBLIOGRAPHY

Enzyklopediah Talmudit, 5th ed. (1979), s.v. "Epikoros."
Julius Gutmann, *Philosophies of Judaism* (1964), 184ff., 244–47.
Gershom Scholem, "Redemption Through Sin," in Gershom Scholem, *The Messianic Idea in Judaism*, Michael Meyer et al., tr. (1971).
Efraim E. Urbach, *The Sages: Their Concepts and Beliefs* (1975), 26–30.

Hermeneutics

הרמנויטיקה

Michael Fishbane

Hermeneutics refers to the principles, the presuppositions, and, in some cases, also to the rules that govern or condition the act of interpretation. As a philosophical area of inquiry, it is focused largely on texts; but in modern discussions the term *hermeneutics* is also used more broadly in connection with art, music, and even existence itself. When applied to texts, a distinction may be made between *explicatio,* whose avowed task is to explain the philological or historical content of an earlier document in its presumed historical setting, and *interpretatio,* which always involves a more far-reaching retrieval of the document by and for later generations. Ideally, both *explicatio* and *interpretatio* presuppose that a temporal, linguistic, and ideational distance between a reader and a text can be closed; however, *explicatio* is principally intent upon circumscribing the text within a specific historical horizon, whereas for *interpretatio* the horizon of the text is not temporally fixed, and it is read as a living document. Naturally enough, readers do not always perceive this distinction, and explicators often believe that their explications reveal the enduring meaning of the text, just as interpreters sometimes presume that their interpretations also disclose the original historical meaning of the text. The distinction is, nevertheless, of fundamental significance and reveals fundamentally different textual attitudes and presuppositions.

In brief, the process of *explicatio* tends to lock a text into one historical period, to consider the linguistic content as something that can be understood once and for all given the right philological-historical tools, and to confine itself to a derivative ministering to a creative work. In contrast, *interpretatio* delivers the text from its original historical context, treating its linguistic content as powerfully multivalent—and so, in principle, resistant to reductive or final readings—while treating its own work of interpretation as a fundamental moment in the creative life of the text. Text-cultures are not free of either *explicatio* or *interpretatio,* and, in fact, some of their greatest readers purport to practice both. Nevertheless, it can be said that text-cultures are such primarily because of the *interpretatio* that animates them and which, aside from the meanest paraphrase or linguistic annotation, quickly conquers *explicatio* and transforms it into its own image. This is true especially of religious text-cultures and of Judaism in particular.

From its earliest classical periods, and to some extent even within the formative biblical period, Judaism has developed rules for interpreting the biblical text and thereby deriving from it not merely philological explications but legal rulings (halakhah) and theological-moral significations (Haggadah). These rules developed in scholastic contexts and proliferated under different teachers, with succeeding generations focusing on different concerns. For example, certain tannaitic sages were concerned to establish their rulings in relation to the biblical text; many amoraic sages tried to show how certain mishnaic rulings are derived or derivable from Scripture. With time, the complexity and concerns of the hermeneutical enterprise developed and became specialized in a variety of areas. Incisive canons of practical legal reasoning and deduction emerged, along with theoretical exercises in hermeneutical pyrotechnics *(pilpul).*

In other domains of Jewish life a wide range of allegorical, philosophical, and mystical modes of interpretation proliferated. To be sure, the nature of textual argument in the latter cases may occasionally have derived from Greek or Arabic rhetoric and logic, or have been keyed to a closed system of symbolic theosophy. Nevertheless, it would be correct to say that the explicit and implicit roots of all these interpretive systems lie in the Bible and that the starting point for understanding the nature of traditional Jewish hermeneutics in its vastness and detail is the realization that there is nothing, when all is said and done, that can be deemed—in principle and in fact—alien or alienable from Scripture, God's instruction.

A Jewish hermeneutics of Scripture starts with the presupposition of its revealed, divine origin (in some sense)—this being the written Torah—and its necessary and hence paradoxical coordination with a religious tradition that clarifies, expands, and even delimits it—this being the oral Torah, or interpretive tradition. The relationship between these two categories has been fundamental to Judaism since classical times, although the precise nature of this relationship has varied considerably, each variation having a decisive bearing on what constitutes the hermeneutical task and the measures of its freedom and responsibility.

To better understand the nature of this relationship, we may pose the issue as alternative possibilities. Are revelation and tradition fundamentally two categories, so that the former is one and immutable and the latter many and mutable and not exegetically derived from it (the Sadducean position)? Or, alternatively, are revelation and tradition fundamentally one category, so that the former is immutably one and the latter mutably many and exegetically derived from it (the Pharisaic position)? This second alternative developed with mixed and confused musings even among its own practitioners and propagandists, but gradually the position that "all the words" that God spoke on Sinai (cf. Ex. 20:1) were nothing less than the entirety of the written Torah as well as the totality of all oral traditions for all future generations became a fundamental tenet of Judaism. For good measure, the early Pharisees even provided a genealogy of the chain of transmission of the oral tradition that extended from Moses to their contemporary colleagues, and which was further updated by Abraham ibn Daud and Moses Maimonides.

The point of all this is, of course, that tradition had no independent authority, since it was dependently part of revelation, and, more paradoxically, that revelation had no independent status, since it could be interpreted only according to the exegetical teachings or principles given simultaneously with it. There is, then, no *sola scriptura*, no Scripture that is only Scripture and whatever meanings one might independently derive from it. There was only scriptural revelation as hermeneutically filtered through the tradition of this or that authoritative community. No wonder, then, that ancient and medieval polemics among Jewish groups, or between different religious communities, challenged the legitimate authority of their adversaries' exegeses, and not the shared text, Scripture, which was profoundly mute before the oral interpretations.

This profound rabbinic dignification of interpretation, which actually gives it the privileged position of divine revelation even as it requires the participation of the human sage for its actualization, survived the yet more profound mythologization found in the later kabbalah. According to the kabbalah, the Torah received at the Sinaitic revelation, in its overt (written) and covert (oral) dimensions, is itself the divinely filtered oral expression of a more deeply hidden written Torah, esoterically inscribed, as it were, in the supernal depths of the godhead. In this view, the exalted hermeneutical task is nothing less than a mystical return to the theosophical ground of all Being where divinity eternally reveals itself within itself.

One does not have to take this last kabbalistic step, or the many intervening allegorical and philosophical ones, to realize that already for the ancient rabbis—and here we come to the corollary presupposition of Jewish hermeneutics—Scripture is a unique communication and, in the most basic sense, unlike human speech. For the divine revelation, the written Torah, communicates directly and indirectly: its direct communication is its plain linguistic sense, its surface discourse, and its continuously unfolding historical episodes and divine instructions; its indirect communication, in a supplementary way, puts all this into question.

Through the means established by rabbinic hermeneutics, Scripture is not restricted to its surface discourse, not even to the received sequence of its letters, words, and paragraphs. Rather, starting from the assumption of the autonomy of its divinely communicated parts within one organically interactive matrix, the totality of Scripture, the ancient rabbis proceeded to connect words from vastly different contexts; at the same time, starting from the assumption that nothing in Scripture is superfluous, the rabbis projected differentiations into apparently synonymous lines and harmonizations into apparently contradictory teachings, and starting from the assumption that God's word is eternal, although given to one audience at one historical time, the rabbis found their own history and much of the future embedded in the ancient text. The Bible, then, was perceived by the sages as a complex code—even very like a dream, as they said[1]—that must be decoded by hermeneutical techniques uniquely suited to it. Turn it this way, trope it that way: all is in it, as is meet for the divine word.

The singularity of the textual artifact did not delimit, then, the plurality of its complexly derivable senses, but rather was dialectically related to it. God's speech is not like other speech: it is a flowing fountain of eternal life, believed the sages, and the visible sign of and guide to Israel's eternity. Allegorical interpretations were thus one more sign of the divine wisdom and spiritual guidance hidden within the surface sense of Scripture for those who would be so instructed. For such disciples of wisdom, Maimonides provided, at the beginning of his *Guide of the Perplexed,* a dictionary of key biblical terms together with their philosophical-allegorical meanings. Properly read, then, and so in its deepest constitution, Scripture was nothing less than a divine guide to philosophical beatitude, to a contemplative love of divine wisdom. Or alternatively, it was this and much more, since for the mystic, as intimated earlier, Scripture as divine speech was not so much communicable meaning, in any sense, as it was a spiritual principle of the universe, communicating symbolically the reality of the infinite, even unmanifested, One. Scripture, so seen, was in truth a mystical inscription of the reality of God, in all its complex and dynamic living combinations. "Woe to him," says the *Zohar*, who "looks upon the Torah as merely presenting narratives and everyday matters." This is simply the "outer garment"—"but we, we are bound to penetrate beyond" (III.152a). From ancient rabbinic assertions that "all is in it," then, to philosophical-allegorical notions of the deep sense *(hyponoia)* of hidden meaning *(batin)* of Scripture, even to mystical testimonies that the Torah is the "secret" or "root principle of all," the idea that God's word is a unique communication has pervaded the length and breadth of Jewish hermeneutics.

It is thus a constituent factor of Jewish hermeneutics that the meaning and efficacy of Scripture as a unique communication is not restricted to its original historical, linguistic, and theological or legal contexts. Ancient Israelite Scripture has decisively shaped the sacred cultural patterns (halakhah) and the ideas and imagination (haggadah) of every generation of Jewry up to the present. Indeed, the textual context of Scripture has been the decisive factor in the formation and reformation of the moral and spiritual destiny of Jews and Judaism during two millennia of differing historical contexts. To be sure, each different historical context sponsored its own understandings of what was meaningful and valuable, delimited its own horizon of expectations as to what was conceivable or plausible, and conditioned its own patterns of piety and perfectibility. But the remarkable fact was that all of this was "found" in Scripture, through one form of hermeneutical justification or another, so that it would be fair to say—and just this is the power of *interpretatio*—that Scripture created Israel so that Israel could ever recreate itself scripturally.

The traditional hermeneutics of Jewish *interpretatio* is thus less witness to every generation's alienation from its formative sources than it is the creative retrieval of meaningfulness in terms of, and, indeed, in the terms of, its sources. And so what modern hermeneutics considers a complex philosophical problem, namely, the entry of a latter-day reader into the circle of intelligibility of an older text, would have rung a false note to every traditional Jewish reader: there was no problematic entry into Scripture as an alien horizon of meaning, for one had never left it; its horizons were, through traditional hermeneutical techniques, always and ever more one's own. All history collapsed into the scriptural world, whose words were the pure mirror onto which the changing face of interpreted Scripture was projected.

From this perspective, Jewish hermeneutics has always been, profoundly, a cultural and individual self-creation and a re-creation of the image of God in the person. And, if the haggadahic depiction of God studying the *interpretatio* of Israel be taken for the serious theological image it is, then Jewish hermeneutics has also always been the re-creation of the image of God by the person. God's act of learning Israel's teachings thus expresses the profound Jewish realization that hermeneutics is not a desperate act of spiritual alienation, but the essential dialectic of religious existence: God is, paradoxically, not ultimately autonomous, but realizes on earth the infinity of its potentiality in and through the engaged responses of persons to his being—which is to say, for the Jew, through interpreters of his word.

As a fixed, special communication, derived from the plenitude of God, Scripture sponsors, correlatively, a plenitude of interpretations. These are traditionally fixed in form by the authorized hermeneutical rules and in content by the judgment of a majority of sages with respect to halakhah or by the consensus of plausibility or authenticity with respect to theological matters. Nevertheless, to underscore this point of scriptural plenitude, classical rabbinical books are invariably anthological, preserving majority and minority legal decisions, diverse haggadahic speculations, and contradictory lexical explications and theological interpretations all in the same context.

But the same truth is also dramatized from precisely its polar opposite: the Torah is read aloud weekly without simultaneous commentary—even though it is not Jewish Scripture except through those commentaries—so as to proclaim, as it were, the eternity and centrality of the divine word and the necessary mutability of its reception and filtering. Here, too, is a profound aspect of Jewish hermeneutics: the remarkable assertion that the divine voice, while unique and authoritative, is always an unstable and changing voice filtered diversely in the human community. It is, moreover, following the Targum's reversal of the meaning of Deuteronomy 5:19, a "mighty and unceasing voice," whose bounty is limited only by the human religious imagination. "For it is not an empty thing for you," says Scripture, and Rabbi Akiva comments that "if it is an empty thing, it is because of you—for you do not know how to interpret [Scripture]" (Gen. R. 1:14). From early haggadahic levels to mature mystical reflections, Sinai is not simply one historical event among other unique and unrepeatable moments in time. It is, rather, an ever-present mythical moment in the imagination and the soul, a moment when one is hermeneutically present to the divine voice once and eternally given from that mountain.

But what is heard? Since it is a special communication, everything is heard from Scripture, but not all at once and not everything by all persons. What is heard depends on historical interest (*peshat*, or plain sense), ritual-legal interest (halakhic *derush* or exposition), theological and spiritual interest (haggadahic *derush* and *raz*, or philosophical allegory), and theosophical and contemplative capacity (*sod*, or mystical-symbolic meaning). God speaks, and one hears in accordance with one's life task and spiritual level or need.

To be sure, the proponents of each level hierarchize the whole, or even delimit it, relative to their privileged sphere; above all else, the ritual-legal dimension of the hermeneutical enterprise would at least be acknowledged by the proponents of all levels, for without it the concrete basis of a religious community would be lacking. There is, moreover, a complex simultaneity among these hermeneutical levels, worked out in different ways by different generations, so that mystical interpretations may penetrate halakhic ones, or moral elements may infuse the theosophical understanding of the secret life of the godhead. But, at the same time, and especially from a mystical point of view, the hermeneutical levels of Scripture constitute, even when no one of them is abandoned, a spiritual journey into God.

Indeed, it is just here, in the end, that one may perceive a profound paradox and reversal of the entire hermeneutical enterprise. For if it is true that Scripture starts with a response to the living divine presence as voice and instruction, that context of religious immediacy is gradually succeeded by more mediate layers of *interpretatio*, whose daring power and purpose is to keep that presence and instruction alive in the community. Increasingly, however, the presence of God perceived as proclamation is replaced by an interpreted proclamation that stands surety for this presence—now often a textual memory. It is, therefore, the driving force of the mystical quest, which sees in Scripture the symbols of divine reality and presence, that reverses the trend and reestablishes the primacy of the living divine context or milieu. Hereby, Scripture as the mediated presence of God becomes the means for recontextualizing one's existence as part of the immediacy of God's infinite Being. The task of hermeneutics is thus not to forge another link in the chain of tradition deriving from God's living presence, but to encounter God in fact. So viewed, God's speech in Scripture is his very Being. And so it is Scripture that teaches, beyond any specific content of its text, the truth that the divine life crystallizes in the symbolic expressions of human existence but is also infinitely more than that.

What, now, of our present historical situation—when Scripture is displaced from its authoritative cultural preeminence; when traditional hermeneutics, even when known, often provides only one of several competing hermeneutical models whose interrelationships are often conflicting and in no permanent hierarchical arrangement, and when Scripture is no longer, or not uniquely, a special text—different in kind and spiritual resourcefulness from other texts, be they even poems, or novels, or political manifestos—and so requiring a special hermeneutics for its study? What now, when the call is for an objective religious-political history of ancient Israel; when natural and empirical models have widespread plausibility; when the illusions of a distanced and distancing *explicatio* hold sway? To all latter-day Spinozists, enamored of these methods and possibilities, one can hardly advocate a simple return to older hermeneutical models, if only because there is a little "Spinoza" in every modern Jew, and because the possibility of a monolithic communal or intellectual life has been shattered, possibly beyond repair, by the competing options of the modern age.

The two tablets handed down by tradition—Scripture and interpretation—have been broken before the new images constructed in the absence of their plausibility as absolute religious truth. But, according to a talmudic legend, these very fragments were preserved and put into the ark alongside their new copy. Both accompanied Israel in its wanderings, and both served as the testimony of an instructing divine presence in the holy sanctuary. And just this may give us pause—and hermeneutical hope.

The fragments of Torah and tradition may thus be retrieved, if not as truths then as the truthfulness of ancient wisdom to instruct us partially or in the new combinations each person must assemble over and over again. The cultural and theological imperative of preserving the fragments for retrieval is that although not all Torah and tradition may belong to us now, at this hour, we belong to all of it, now and always. Here, then, is the basic presupposition of a renewed hermeneutics. Faith in Torah and its fragments is, ultimately, faith in the power of the divine presence and the fragments of tradition to provide instruction. In this way we may reclaim the Torah as a teaching for life, a *Torat Ḥayyim,* from a living God for a religious community.

Every retrieval is an *interpretatio,* and indeed so is every purported textual explication that projects models of modern competence upon the text and then claims to understand it in its own terms. There is no simple "in its own terms"; the Torah fragments are empty in proportion to the emptiness

of our hermeneutical models and spiritual life. Each must be nurtured separately and reciprocally and brought to bear on the Torah in our midst. This
is the second presupposition, then, of a renewed Jewish hermeneutics. All
our human resources must be utilized to hear a renewed plenitude of scriptural meanings. In this way each person may find, singly and through the
other, something of the plenitude of divinity that transcends all textuality
and something of the enduring power of divinity to instruct in and through
a text. Torah may no longer be our only text, but it is our shared text; and
so in this sharing of Torah, and the interpretations derived from it, lies the
possibility of the renewed religious community.

REFERENCES

1. Margulies, ed., *Midrash ha-gadol, Genesis,* 39.

BIBLIOGRAPHY

Michael Fishbane, *Biblical Interpretation in Ancient Israel* (1985).
Isaak Heinemann, *Darkei ha-Aggadah,* 2d ed. (1954).
Simon Rawidowicz, "On Interpretation," in *Studies in Jewish Thought* (1974).
Gershom Scholem, "The Meaning of the Torah in Jewish Mysticism," in *On the Kab-
balah and Its Symbolism* (1965).
Gershom Scholem, "Revelation and Tradition as Religious Categories in Judaism,"
in *The Messianic Idea in Judaism* (1971).

Heroism

גבורה

Yeshayahu Leibowitz

The first words of the *Shulḥan Arukh* (OH 1:1) are: "One should pull oneself together" (lit., "overcome oneself," *le-hitgaber,* from the root *g-b-r*). Heroism (*geburah,* from the same root) is one of the most significant terms relating to man's consciousness, will, and behavior. It is very difficult to define formally. We may say, though, that conceptually heroism is always linked with the struggle between a man's choice of values, which is conscious and which he decides to exercise, and an urge arising from his nature and operating within him without his knowledge and even against his will. If in such a struggle the individual stands his ground in keeping with his decision and against the promptings of his nature, that is heroism; it is the meaning of the sage's words: "What is a hero? He who overcomes his urges" (M. Avot 4:1).

All heroism is the resistance of temptation. For this reason, heroism may be embodied in a person's behavior in every sphere of existence in which his nature impels him to strive for gain, pleasure, or achievement, when between them and him is interposed an imperative or principle that he considers a binding value. If this sense of obligation is not imposed upon him from without but arises from his own consciousness, and if for this consciousness the person must pay by forfeiting gain, pleasure, or achievement, that is heroism—the devotion of self to a value that does not "give" one anything (in any objective sense) but rather demands something of him.

Such is the overcoming of the urge for possessions when the attainment of wealth entails the employment of means that a person's sense of values rejects. The same is true of the urge for honors and power or for sexual pleasure, all of which may operate within an individual without his knowledge. If he rejects these urges with all the might of his conscious will, then he is aware that the means of attaining them under the circumstances are unacceptable. In contrast to the moral prohibitions are those obligations that are not imposed on one by any necessity of nature, existence, society, or psychology, but which the individual takes upon himself even in opposition to objective factors, against his own interests. Such, for example, is one's loyalty to his people or country at a time when abandoning them would seem to promise one greater rewards. The same is true of the "acceptance of the yoke of the Kingdom of Heaven and the yoke of the Law and the commandments," the heroism to which the *Shulḥan Arukh* refers.

A greater urge, greater perhaps than that for possessions, honors, or power, and even greater than the sexual urge, is the urge for physical existence, one's clinging to life, fear of death, and recoiling from mortal danger. Values are measured in terms of what a person is willing to pay for them. The price may be life itself, as in *kiddush ha-Shem,* the sacrifice of an individual's life for the sake of others, for his country, for liberty, justice, or honor (or what one perceives as liberty, justice, or honor). That heroism, consisting of risking one's life, even to the point of sacrificing it for the sake of something that is acknowledged to be a supreme value, may be found in every aspect of life. Consider the person who enters a burning building to rescue a baby trapped inside, or who leaps into a raging river to save a drowning man. Yet the prevailing opinion in most nations and cultures links the concept of heroic death with death in battle. This linkage, prevalent in the State of Israel today, has excited a great deal of study and discussion.

What has the soldier's death in common with the other forms of heroism? From the standpoint of the meaning and value of heroism, there would seem to be no difference between the heroism of the person who risks or sacrifices his life in order to save another human life and the heroism of the soldier who risks or sacrifices his life for his people or his country. Furthermore, in ordinary life, even without the risk or sacrifice of one's life there may arise situations that require spiritual heroism that is in no way inferior to that required in sacrificing one's life in war. Nonetheless, there is something special about fighting, for in all the other acts of heroism, the individual battles with himself ("conquers his urge"), and if he finds that he must sacrifice his life, he sacrifices only his own life. By contrast, in war the individual battles with another, and alongside his willingness to sacrifice his own life he also, and even primarily, intends to deprive the other individual of his life. Yet it is precisely this form of heroism that makes the deepest impression on the common man.

Without attempting any axiological-philosophical analysis of the concept of heroism or a critique of its various manifestations, it can be determined that military heroism is the least worthy kind of heroism. For it is the only one that is to be found among the masses and in every people and culture in every period in history regardless of the spiritual, moral, or social level of those who possess it. This is certainly not the case with regard to the heroism of controlling the natural urges, for it has always been rare in every time and place. Nor have we found, either in history or in present-day life, that the good and the spiritually and morally superior have a monopoly on military heroism. Rather, it occurs with the same frequency among the inferior. Hence it is easier for the average person heroically to stand the test of risking his life in battle than to stand the test in daily life in the battle against the temptations of the urge for possessions or power, sexual pleasure, and so on. Heroism in battle is no indication of a person's stature as a human being. If one is a hero in the military sense (an excellent soldier), it is no guarantee that he is a superior person, either in terms of wisdom and intelligence or in honesty and integrity. On the other hand, a person who has heroically withstood urges arising from envy, hatred, or lust is certainly one of the elite few.

Hence we must discuss the meaning and evaluation of war in the world of Judaism. In human awareness as a whole, there are two extreme views on war. The first is the absolute rejection of war. According to this view, nothing can justify resorting to arms and killing human beings, nor does anything obligate a person to be killed by resorting to arms. Human life, the life of the human individual, can never be replaced. Thus the preservation of human life is the supreme task of the laws of human behavior and of what is worthy of the name of morals, and no end can justify any deviation from this principle. Everything human—society, nation, and state—must be sacrificed for the preservation of human life, and whatever is generally considered to be a value must be waived for the sake of this supreme value. This position, the thoroughgoing pacifist stand, has had very few exponents in the history of civilization. In recent times, its representatives have included Tolstoy and perhaps also Gandhi, although I am not certain whether the latter's pacifism was truly the product of profound moral consciousness or merely a clever political tactic in his struggle against British rule. Tolstoy, though, unquestionably represents pacifism, and the same may have been true of the man who lived two millennia ago and about whom we know nothing certain, but who was regarded as the Messiah (Christ) by the Gentiles.

The diametrically opposed view considers war and fighting to be the supreme moments of human existence, heroism on the battlefield the highest manifestation of humanity, and death in battle the supreme human achievement. This conception was and still is represented not only by certain human collectives (Sparta and perhaps the Roman Republic have been the quintessential examples of this view in history), but also by great personages in the philosophy and civilization of various societies.

There are, of course, positions between these two extremes: the rejection of war as a value at the same time that it is recognized as necessary in certain circumstances; the view that war is justified and even necessary for the attainment of certain ends that are more exalted than the existence of the individual or even of many individuals, or for the prevention of a fate worse than death, for the preservation of values without which life is not worth living. Hence also the differing valuations of the warlike qualities of man and of heroism in battle.

Judaism, as represented in its literary sources and in the existential civilization of scores of generations from ancient Israel up to, but not including, the generation of the mid-twentieth century, rejects war, yet is not pacifistic. From Judaism's sources and history it is not possible to derive the pacifist position in the sense we have given above. Judaism recognizes war as a fact of human life because mankind, to which the Jewish people belongs, exists in an imperfect world. This is the realism, at times even the brutal realism, of Jewish religious law (halakhah), which relates to the world as it is and not as it should be according to the messianic vision. The perfect world, the world of peace that is perfection ("the name of the Holy One, blessed be He!"), is a vision of a hypothetical utopian world. But the actual concern of the religious law in which the Torah is embodied is the world as it is, imperfect and "unredeemed."

It would be fair to say that war belongs to the level of the collective filth of human existence. Just as man's biological existence is not ideal, so, too, his collective existence in the world as it is is not ideal.

At this point, we may draw an analogy from the halakhic attitude toward the problems of the individual to the problems of all mankind. The largest of the six tractates of the Mishnah—at least in terms of its scope, its fun-

damental and thorough crystallization of halakhic Judaism—is the tractate
Taharot (Purities). It deals with the amnion and the umbilical cord, the
blood of childbirth, menstrual blood, diseases, discharges, the impurity of
the dead body—in short, with the biological filth of human existence. All
of these halakhah treats at length because they are the reality of human life.
Of course, we would not go so far as the preacher who says, "for this is the
whole of man" (Ecc. 12:14), but this *is* man. To be sure, there are higher
levels in him than this, but the one beginning with the umbilical cord and
ending with the corpse is the level of human existence, and halakhah, which
encompasses all of human existence within the framework of divine worship, deals at length and matter of factly with this level.

The history of the independent Jewish people is rife with wars. In every
period in which the Jewish people was capable of waging war it has been
involved in wars. This is not the place to discuss the question of whether
the Jews or their enemies started these wars. The point is that the Jews
fought, and neither the prophets in First Temple times nor the Sages of the
Second Temple period rebuked them for it.

However, a most important fact now emerges. The war that had the greatest impact on Jewish history was unquestionably the conquest of Canaan,
for the war of Joshua the son of Nun with the thirty-one Canaanite kings
marks the beginning of the history of the Jewish people as a fully constituted
people in its own land. It was also a holy war. And yet this war, with its
immortal victories, is not commemorated by any day of remembrance, festival, thanksgiving day, or day of prayer, despite the fact that it was waged
at God's behest by a servant of the Lord.

Furthermore, David's conquest of Jerusalem some four hundred years
later and his transformation of the Jebusite town into Jerusalem the eternal,
"an eternal dwelling," the site of the Temple, has no day of remembrance
or festival in its honor in the Jewish calendar. Or again, two centuries later,
when Israel's king Jeroboam, the son of Joash, one of Israel's greatest warriors, "restored the territory of Israel from Lebo-hamath to the sea of the
Arabah . . . he recovered Damascus and Hamath for Judah in Israel" (II
Kings 14:25, 28), these great victories and conquests were "buried" in
three verses in II Kings 14 and are barely mentioned in the living historical
tradition of modern Judaism.

Only in memory of the war and victory of the Maccabees in a comparatively late period, centuries after the "closing" of the canonical Old Testament, did the people of the law decide to appoint an eight-day festival,
Ḥanukah, during which the *Hallel* prayer of thanksgiving and joy (Ps. 113–
18) is offered. Even the Passover festival is only seven days long, and the

Hallel is not recited during it. How, then, did the Maccabees' war differ from all the other wars? The answer is that this was a war for the sake of the law, and this is the reason for its sacred aura. Even Joshua's conquest of Canaan as commanded by the Lord was not accorded such an aura. Thus, no war is holy unless it be for the sake of the law. When the Jewish people conquered Canaan under Joshua it did not do so purely because of any religious commandment, but sought to conquer the land that was meant for it. And in fact, as soon as the Jews had settled in Canaan, they began to worship idols. Similarly, King David conquered Jerusalem so that it should serve as his capital and the capital of the kingdom of Israel. These other wars and conquests were never sanctified by a religious aura, and on this point Judaism reveals its own special attitude toward war, heroism in battle, and victory. Here is no sweeping pacifistic approach that brands every war unacceptable since nothing can justify the taking of human life. On the contrary, according to the Pentateuch, there is one thing for which human life may be sacrificed, and that is the preservation of the Torah itself. A "nationalist" war, on the other hand, has no religious significance. Even King David realized that he was disqualified from building the Temple because of all the blood he had shed in the course of his wars, which had been merely wars of the Jewish people.

Let us not forget a fact that is commonly obscured in present-day education in the State of Israel, namely, that the war of the Maccabees was not primarily a war of national revival but rather a civil war between those who observed the law and the Hellenized Jews. Mattathias began it by killing a Jew who had sacrificed to a pagan god, and his son Simon ended it twenty-five years later with the conquest of the citadel of Jerusalem. From whom did Simon conquer the citadel? From other Jews. Greek rule had come to an end twenty-two years before; Jerusalem remained the stronghold of the Hellenized Jews. The political independence achieved by this twenty-five-year war was a mere by-product, not the goal of the war. This war of the Maccabees, the war for the law, was the only Jewish war in whose memory a Jewish festival was appointed. Yet in modern times, those who are considered the spokesmen of religious Judaism, the chief rabbis of the State of Israel, who are appointed by secular Jewish authorities, have designated a religious festival on the 28th of Iyyar (circa May–June) to mark the conquest of the Temple Mount and the Old City of Jerusalem by the Israeli Defense Force in 1967. Whether owing to a misunderstanding or by design, they ignored the crucial fact that, in this case, the Temple Mount had not been conquered by Jews fighting for the law but by the Hellenized Jews of today, the fighters on behalf of nationalism and a secular government, who despise or are at least indifferent to the Jewish law.

As for military heroism, it may be stated categorically that there is no reverence for it in the Jewish tradition. This is not because of any pacifist approach that rejects it. We have stressed that Judaism recognizes war as a fact of human existence, which may be justified in certain circumstances and under certain conditions. Hence the fighter's role requires him to display heroism. But nowhere in Jewish sources is there any of the reverence for the heroism of the fighter that is so prevalent in many non-Jewish cultures, even the most enlightened. Nor on Ḥanukah would we recite the added prayer "Al ha-Nissim" (lit., for the miracles) for the Maccabees if they had not fought the Lord's war and saved the holy law. Their heroism in battle is not mentioned at all; it is taken for granted.

In the event of war, it is the soldier's duty to be a good soldier, just as it is the farmer's duty to be a good farmer, the plumber's to be a good plumber, or the physician's to be a good physician. Judaism does not marvel particularly at military heroism. Yet at present in Israel, the reverence for a man principally because of his excellence as a soldier is rampant, and bravery on the battlefield is thought to atone for serious character defects, and even for intellectual or moral inferiority.

The Siddur, the Jewish prayer book, contains a memorial prayer for "the holy communities which gave their lives for the sanctification of God's Name (kiddush ha-Shem)," and in the elevated language of the Bible they are described as "swifter than eagles, stronger than the lion" (II Sam. 1:23). This is the way the prayer book characterizes Jews who never held a weapon, but "went like sheep to the slaughter," as Israelis are accustomed to say. For in Israel it is considered a shameful thing to go like sheep to the slaughter. It is felt to be the result of "Diaspora meekness," as opposed to the heroism of the ancient Jewish people of the Bible and our own heroism as fighting Israelis. However, the expression "like sheep to the slaughter" did not originate in Diaspora life but in the Book of Isaiah the Prophet, a man of biblical Israel. The prophet describes what he considers the highest human type, the servant of the Lord: "He was maltreated, yet he was submissive, He did not open his mouth; Like a sheep being led to slaughter, Like a ewe, dumb before those who shear her, He did not open his mouth" (Isa. 53:7). We do not live in Isaiah's spiritual world, nor do we think that the ultimate perfection of man is to be a servant of the Lord such as the prophet describes. But no one would refer to biblical heroism in order to bolster his claim that in the State of Israel we have returned to the sources of Judaism and overcome the defects of Diaspora life. "Original Judaism" surely includes Isaiah, not necessarily the generation of David Ben-Gurion or Ariel Sharon.

Violence, the veneration of heroism in battle, and contempt for human life are all interconnected. In this context we should mention one other thing that is evidence of our barbarization and the penetration of the spirit of violence into the very heart and fiber of Jewish consciousness in Israeli society. We are all familiar with the words of the memorial prayer recited at the Jewish funeral service: "among the souls of those holy and pure." The wish is that the soul of the departed may take its place among these souls. There is no expression more lofty than this. Yet again, there are those who, speaking in the name of the Jewish religion and considered to be its representatives, the chief rabbis, have dared to add a word to this prayer when it is recited at the funeral of a soldier who has fallen in one of Israel's wars in recent times: "among the souls of those holy and pure and *heroic*."

It is not necessarily praise to say that a person is a war hero, although an act of military heroism is not a sign of inferiority either. There have been righteous war heroes—but there have also been wicked ones, pure as well as impure ones. Thus again we say that the addition to the funeral prayer *"El Maaleh Raḥamim"* (lit., God, full of compassion) is nothing but an expression of that spirit of violence that has penetrated into the heart of modern religious Judaism. How much graver, then, is the elevation of heroism in battle to a religious value and the representation of arms as an instrument of holiness? As Ezekiel said 2,580 years ago:

> O mortal, those who live in these ruins in the land of Israel argue, "Abraham was but one man, yet he was granted possession of the land. We are many; surely, the land has been given as a possession to us." Therefore say to them: Thus said the Lord God: You eat with the blood, you raise your eyes to your fetishes, and you shed blood—yet you expect to possess the land!

> (Ezek. 33:24–25)

History

היסטוריה

Paul Mendes-Flohr

The eve of the concluding day of the Passover feast is marked by an ancient custom. The community gathers in the synagogue and chants the hymn of thanksgiving—*shirat ha-yam*—sung by Moses and the Israelites upon the miraculous crossing of the Red Sea:

> I will sing to the Lord, for He has triumphed gloriously;
> Horse and driver he has hurled into the sea.
> The Lord is my strength and might;
> He has become my salvation.
>
> (Ex. 15.1–18)

In contemporary Jerusalem the Ḥasidim of Reb Areleh[1]—*ha-ḥevrah shomrei emunim* ("the society of the faithful")—elaborate the recitation of *shirat ha-yam* with a special ritual. For hours prior to the ceremony the synagogue—a bare hall emptied of all seats—fills with an endless stream of humanity. At a point when it seems that the walls begin to bulge to accommodate the masses of Reb Areleh's Ḥasidim the ceremony begins with a soft humming of *shirat ha-yam*. Suddenly, in the middle of the tightly packed throng, there is a "parting," through which the rebbe, currently Reb Avraham Yiẓḥak Kahan, a patriarchal figure now in his eighties, slowly dances. Amid the undulations of his swaying, chanting Ḥasidim, the parting rhythmically opens and closes, and the aged rebbe dances to and fro—seemingly for hours. The chanting of *shirat ha-yam*, steadily growing stronger, is interspersed with a melodious rendition of Psalm 114, "When Israel went forth from Egypt."

In this ritual reenactment of "the parting of the sea," the rebbe becomes Moses and his Ḥasidim become the children of Israel. As their song and dance meld with the cadences of a trance, they experience God's deliverance anew. For Reb Areleh and his Ḥasidim—and other congregations that have similar rites—the Passover is no mere exercise in historical recollection.[2] Nor is it simply an imaginative leap across time. The ceremony of *shirat ha-yam* brings to a height the Passover experience of sacred time, the retrieval of the primordial—and thus eternal—moment of Israel's redemption.

In its traditional mode, Jewish historical memory, as Franz Rosenzweig observed, is thus not a "measure of time." For Israel, "the memory of its history does not form a point fixed in the past, a point which year after year becomes increasingly past. It is a memory which is really not past at all, but eternally present."[3] What is recollected is not a serial, diachronic past, but an enduring past—or rather an eternal reality that first became manifest in the historical past. Nurtured principally by Israel's liturgical calendar and its cycle of ritualized commemorations, this recalled past shapes the individual Jew's contemporary spiritual reality. As the Passover Haggadah declares, "In each and every generation let each person regard himself as though he had come forth out of Egypt" (cf. M. Pes. 10:5).[4] Periodically requickened by ritual and liturgical recitations, Jewish memory is thus preeminently a mode of numinous consciousness in which the Jew experiences the eternal and gracious presence of God. Indicatively, the Jewish calendar as it finally evolved does not measure historical time but dates from the year of creation, the point when the Eternal first touched the temporal.[5] In fact, chronology, a defining feature of the diachronic conception of history,[6] is hardly of significance to the Jewish historical imagination. Thus the rabbis could claim that "there is no late and early in the Torah" (BT Pes. 6b). The sacred history (and teachings) of the Torah are eternal and not bound by the sequential or linear progression of profane time.

To be sure, the God of the Torah—of the Bible—is also the God of profane history. As the sovereign and benevolent God of creation, Yahweh exercises providential lordship not only over nature but also over the temporal sphere allotted to man. Indeed, the transitory *pragmata*, that is, the events that come about through the moral and political action of men, are of profound concern to God. And in his capacity as "the king of the universe" (BT Ket. 7b), he judges man's moral and political deeds according to his revealed law that sets as its ultimate criterion the expectation of justice, love, and compassion: "Learn to do good. Devote yourself to justice. Aid the wronged" (Isa. 1:17). The Hebrew Bible thus places history in the ambit of good and evil, truth and falsehood. As judge, God also punishes disobedience and transgression and rewards fidelity and righteousness: "If, then, you agree and give heed, You will eat the good things of the earth; But if you refuse and disobey, You will be devoured by the sword" (Isa. 1:19–20; cf. Ex. 32:34).

The historical narratives of the Bible serve to illustrate God's lordship. Thus in bold contrast to the contemporary chronicles of the ancient Near East, written exclusively to glorify an earthly king and his exploits, Hebrew scriptures tell of the folly, betrayal, and sin—and the attendant punishment—of the children of Israel and their leaders (cf., for example, II Kings 3ff.). But the God of Israel is also a shepherd, lovingly devoted to his "chosen people," and comforting them in their sorrow and despair—"the Lord is my shepherd, I lack nothing. He makes me lie down in green pastures" (Ps. 23:1–2). God supplements this comfort with a promise of redemption, of a future free of folly and sin, of a future blessed with everlasting peace. This future, which in postbiblical Jewish literature was to be associated with the person of the Messiah, is projected as an alternative future: It is not to be a repeat of yesterday or today, but a genuine tomorrow, a qualitative historical—perhaps ontological—departure:

> And I will put a new spirit within you.
>
> (Ezek. 11:19)

> A babe shall play
> Over a viper's hole,
> And an infant pass his hand
> Over an adder's den.
> In all of My sacred mount
> Nothing evil or vile shall be done.
>
> (Isa. 11:8–9)

The promised future, however, is not oracular; it cannot be foretold or calculated. In the words of Rabbi Zera, a talmudic sage of the third century: "Three things come unawares: the Messiah, a found article, and a scorpion" (BT Sanh. 97a). As God's ultimate act of grace, redemption is emphatically beyond history—at least as we know it—and thus not the result of human endeavor. The assignment of redemption to the advent of God's anointed servant, the Messiah, merely underscores its miraculous, metahistorical nature. Accordingly, as Walter Benjamin once observed:

> We know that the Jews were prohibited from investigating the future. The Torah and the prayers instruct them in remembrance, however. This stripped the future of its magic, to which all those succumb who turn to the soothsayers for enlightenment. This does not imply, however, that for the Jews the future turned into homogeneous, empty time. For every second of time was the strait gate through which the Messiah might enter.[7]

Awaiting the miraculous redemption, the prophets nevertheless also focused on the actions of man within the bounds of history, suggesting that the future is paradoxically both a divine promise and a human responsibility.

The Hebrew affirmation of history undoubtedly struck other denizens of the ancient world as ludicrous. Although having a far richer and more nuanced conception of historiography, the Greeks regarded the historical *pragmata* of men—transitory and contingent as they were—as utterly devoid of meaning. Only that which reflected the eternal order of the Logos, according to the sages of Hellas, could have meaning. For them, as Karl Loewith has pointed out, "it was inconceivable that the Logos of the eternal cosmos could enter into the transitory *pragmata* of the history of mortal men."[8] Similar sentiments were later echoed by Shakespeare's Macbeth: "To-morrow, and to-morrow, and to-morrow, creeps in this petty pace from day to day, to the last syllable of recorded time. . . : It is a tale told by an idiot, full of sound and fury; signifying nothing" (*Macbeth,* act 5, scene 5, lines 19–21, 26–28). And the great German poet Goethe was no less mordant when he declared history to be "the most absurd of things" and a veritable "web of nonsense."[9] In the same spirit Friedrich Nietzsche ridiculed the historical optimism of the Jews and their Christian votaries, considering it to be not only incorrigibly naive but a cruel lie: "To regard nature as if it were proof of the goodness and care of God, and to interpret history as enduring testimony to the moral order and ultimate purpose of the world—such a view is no longer tenable: it has conscience against it."[10]

Although Nietzsche's fulminations may have been in order with respect to the bourgeois optimism of the nineteenth century, he was flagrantly mistaken in associating that optimism with biblical faith. The meaning attributed by the Bible to nature and history is not an immanent quality discernable to the naked eye. It is rather a revealed meaning beheld by the eye of faith. Accordingly, it has been observed that "optimism is a natural vice, and hope a supernatural virtue."[11] Hope is a divine gift, an eschatological promise that the future bears a "new beginning." From the perspective of the eschatological future, affirmed in faith, the meaning of history becomes manifest.

This obstinate confidence that history has a "future" and thus moral and spiritual meaning constitutes, according to the philosopher Hermann Cohen, Judaism's most precious gift to humanity:

> The concept of history is a creation of the prophetic idea. . . . What the Greek intellect could not achieve, monotheism succeeded in carrying out. History is in the Greek consciousness identical with knowledge simply. Thus, history for the Greek is and remains directed only toward the past. In opposition, the prophet is the seer, not the scholar. To see, however, is to gaze. . . . The prophets are the idealists of history. Their vision begot the concept of history as the being [essentially] of the future. . . . They turn their gaze away from the actuality of their own people, as well as from the actuality of other peoples, in order to direct it only to the future. Thereby originates their new concept of history, namely, that of world history.[12]

Emerging from the prophetic conception of history, as Hermann Cohen emphasizes, is a compelling sense of obligation to live in history. The Hebrew prophets thus urge us to be alert to injustice and the anguish of others. And it is crucial, as the rabbis indefatigably taught, that compassion be linked to justice.[13] For—as the kabbalists were later to elaborate with such enchanting detail—when these two divine attributes, midat ha-din (justice) and midat ha-rahamim (mercy), are in imbalance, catastrophe, both cosmic and historic, is sure to follow.[14] It is this insistence on coupling mercy and justice that gives the prophetic imagination its historical, indeed political thrust. Hermann Cohen contrasted the prophets' appreciation of the urgencies of history to the teachings of Stoicism enjoining ataraxia, the ideal of tranquillity to be attained by freeing oneself from emotional concerns and anxiety:

> How could the misfortune of the righteous be reconciled with God's justice? Should one perhaps find a way out of this by declaring that misfortune is irrele-

vant? Should the religious consciousness perhaps adopt the wisdom of stoicism? The [prophetic] religious consciousness was protected against this ambiguity by its natural connection with the political and purely moral. Even if the individual were able and were permitted to train himself successfully and with good reason to disregard his own well-being and woe, he is not permitted to disregard the woe of the other fellow. He might perhaps even disregard the well-being of the evil one, but he is not permitted to disregard the woe of the good one.[15]

The prophetic sensibility points to a possible dialectic between sacred and profane history, between the experience of cyclical and linear time. To be sure, in anthropology and the study of religion it has become fashionable to regard these two modes of time consciousness as mutually exclusive. But, as Paul Ricoeur has argued, this conception reflects a methodological confusion, namely, a tendency to isolate and sever typological analysis of religious experience from the phenomenological and historical reality of religion. This reality, Ricoeur avers, in fact vividly shows that both modes of time consciousness are expressed in greatly varied forms, "and, more interestingly, [display] numerous overlappings and mixed forms." The experience of sacred, cyclical time, Ricoeur observes, thus need not exclude "a return to the historical field of action," that is, it need not preclude a religious involvement in profane time. With specific reference to the Hebrew Scriptures, Ricoeur suggests that "the Jewish conception of time" be cast as an "experience of nowness or presentness." In contrast to "the isolated punctual instant," which marks a break in the continuity of time and has no experiential duration, "nowness designates the lived present intentionally directed toward the past through memory and toward the future through expectation." The ritual experience of nowness possesses a temporal "thickness" allowing it to integrate secular time into the Jew's religious consciousness. Secular time is experienced under the dual sign of the remembered and anticipated redemption.[16]

One may thus also question Mircea Eliade's observation that cyclical time—freeing as it does, one from "the terror of history," the realm of irreversible and ruthlessly contingent change—perforce "annihilates" the significance of secular, linear time.[17] Moreover, seeking shelter in the primordial experiences of cyclical time may not be the only way to fend off the terror of history; directing history to a goal—the vision of a just and compassionate world—may be viewed as an equally dignified "attempt to tame its terror."[18] On the other hand, it would be amiss, indeed blatantly anachronistic, to regard the prophetic affirmation of history as comparable to the modern historical consciousness, especially as primed by the belief in ineluctable progress. For the prophets, as virtually all the biblical and later

Jewish authors, there is a radical disjunction between history and redemption. Marking a sudden eruption of transcendence into history—like "a beam of light" penetrating the darkness—the Messiah will arrive at God's appointed hour.[19] And more often than not, in light of the messianic promise, the prophets—and later the rabbis—urge spiritual repentance, and not historical action per se.[20] The dialectics of biblical futurism may also engender a certain quietism; one may passively wait for God, the celestial custodian of the promised future, to redeem one from history. A detachment from history is especially manifest when messianism is wedded to apocalyptic expectations of an imminent advent of redemption, the intense concentration upon the ultimate moment inducing an "indifference toward intermediate stages of worldly happenings."[21]

The sources of the apocalyptic mood are complex; among its more significant tributaries was undoubtedly a despair in the historical present, in the existent social and political order. Crystallizing during the anguished, desperate years of the Second Temple, apocalyptic messianism was to accompany the tragic vicissitudes of Jewish history and, as Gershom Scholem has shown, to become one of the most tenacious, albeit often suppressed, motifs of Jewish thought.[22] Indeed, apocalyptic messianism—which may be distinguished from prophetic messianism, which displays a greater attention to the here and now of history—had a particularly powerful resonance in *Galut* (Exile).[23] Banished from their ancestral home, dispersed and subject in varying measure to the humiliations of a despised minority, the Jews of *Galut* were, so to speak, secluded from history—from the instruments of social and political power that provide a people with a sense that they can shape history. It is thus said that in *Galut* the Jews had no history; as the nineteenth-century Jewish historian Leopold Zunz put it: "A nation *in partibus* [a nation "scattered" and in exile] performs no acts."[24] Accordingly, Zunz and others have concluded that the Jews of *Galut* lost their historical consciousness, their conviction that history is meaningful.[25] Indicative of the purported loss of interest in history, it is held, is the Jews' lack of interest in their own history—as is evident in the almost total absence, aside from a brief flowering in the sixteenth century, of Jewish works of history until the Enlightenment and Jewish emancipation.[26] This charge, however, is again somewhat anachronistic, for in Europe the historian's craft and a concomitant public interest in his labors only began to come of age with the Renaissance. To be sure, the Middle Ages produced some noteworthy historical writings, but they were sporadic, did not conform to scholarly procedures, and hardly reflected a widespread interest in a critical understanding of the past. For, as George Peabody Gooch has observed, "The influence of Augustine weighed with almost physical pressure on the mind of Europe for a thousand years, diverting attention from secular history and its problems. In view of the constant interposition of Providence, the search for natural causation became needless and impertinent." For the medieval Christian, history was at most "a sermon, not a science, an exercise in Christian evidences, not a disinterested attempt to trace and explain the course of civilization."[27] Mutatis mutandis, the same could be said for the Jews in this period.

Furthermore, historiography—with its critical interest in the details of the past—is not the only expression of historical consciousness. Tradition, which is grounded in the past and in the successive transmission of the generations, is manifestly an alternative form of historical consciousness, albeit with a distinctive epistemological and ontological basis.[28] Prayer and ritual, as we have seen, are also profound repositories of Jewish memory. Legends and folktales may also be viewed as distinct modes of relating to the past.[29] Neither does the absence of historiography necessarily imply an indifference to the historical here and now. A perusal, for instance, of rabbinic responsa literature, recording the day-to-day questions, quandaries, and concerns of Jews addressed to the custodians of Torah and halakhah, will indicate that the Jews were not totally detached, either religiously or morally, from the mundane political and social reality of their lives.[30]

In the minds of the rabbis and other guardians of Jewish consciousness, the Jews of *Galut* remained a *corpus historicum*— a historical people bound to the concrete world flush with mundane concerns and responsibilities. But as a historical people the Jews were specifically a nation born under the sign of a covenant, enjoying a special relationship with God. Thus, the abiding historical reality of the Jews perforce had a religious significance, their profane history mirroring their relationship with God. R. J. Zwi Werblowsky has aptly remarked that "Judaism is the religion of a people—not in the sense of being a religion that happens to have been adopted by a certain people, but an essential dimension of its national identity, and destiny."[31] *Galut,* the overarching historical fact of postbiblical Jewish existence, accordingly, was perceived to be preeminently a theological issue. Why, it was queried of God, do the wicked nations of the world prosper and the chosen people dwell in humiliation? "Have the deeds of Babylon been better than those of Zion? Have any other nation known Thee besides Zion? . . . If the world has indeed been created for our sake, why do we not enter into possession of our world? How long shall this endure?" (IV Ezra 4:23–25). This plaintive cry of an author writing some twenty-five years after the destruction of the Second Temple was to echo ever anew throughout Israel's sojourn in *Galut:* "And His people what did they do to Him that he exiled them from their land?" (ARN[2] 1:4). The tenth-century rabbinic scholar and philosopher Saadiah Gaon sought to comfort Israel by explaining that it is inconceivable that God "is not aware of our situation or that He does not deal fairly with us or that He is not compassionate . . . nor . . . that He has forsaken us and cast us off" (*Beliefs and Opinions,* treatise 8).

Indeed, *Galut* was one of the central preoccupations of the Jewish imagination, a near obsession that pervaded virtually every genre of Jewish literature.[32] Jewish historical consciousness remained lively and acute; it simply was conflated with theology. Israel's protracted torment as a people of exile was not a matter for historians to explain; it was rather a question of theodicy, of understanding God's benevolent rule in the face of seemingly inexplicable suffering. It is significant that the Jews did not blame Titus, who commanded the Roman siege of Jerusalem—or any other historical agent—for the calamity of *Galut,* but alternately regarded it as a divine punishment, a test of faith, or a mission.[33]

The secular details of history were, needless to say, deemed unedifying; war and politics were considered the frivolous affairs of the Gentiles. This does not mean that for postbiblical Judaism history was devoid of meaning. Its meaning, however, was to be sought not at the level of history itself. History, the kabbalists taught, is but a symbol—a dim reflection of the deepest mysteries of being. Israel's anguished peregrinations through time mirror events occurring in the very formation of the cosmos, indeed of the godhead itself and the theogonic process as it "overflows" into creation and the history of the world. The destiny of the Jews thus only appears to be subject to the whims of historical contingencies; Jewish history, as the arcane wisdom of the kabbalah discloses, marks a trajectory from creation to redemption—marks, that is, the eternal God's reconciliation with time and finite being.[34]

Hence, as the "children of the covenant" (M. BK 1:2), the Jews were no mere *corpus historicum* but also a *corpus mysticum*—a community evincing a religious mystery. The bridge between both these dimensions of Jewish existence was the halakhah, providing, as it were, an arch of holiness between the sacred and the profane. The halakhah binds Israel's everyday, historical reality with its metahistorical vocation to be God's "holy people" (Isa. 62:12). As the interface of these homologous realities, halakhah had the effect of both removing the Jews from the imperious claims of history and pari passu endowing them with an effective instrument for redeeming history. In conjunction with prayer and *talmud torah,* halakhah "from the rabbis' perspective embodied more powerful instruments than any other for the achievement of a better age for which Jews longed."[35]

The metapolitical quality of the halakhah attained explicit and powerful expression in the Lurianic kabbalah of the sixteenth century. If performed with the requisite intent *(kavvanah),* ritual and liturgical deed, according to Luria's mystical teachings, have the power of restoring the world—and the godhead—to its primordial wholeness; leading God back from "exile," Israel decisively contributes not only to its own redemption but also to the redemption of the entire cosmic order: "To Luria the coming of the Messiah [thus] means no more than the signature under a document that we ourselves write."[36]

The messianic activism inspired by Isaac Luria ended—seemingly inexorably—in the debacle of Shabbetai Zevi. To the eyes of many modern observers, this attempt to rush the messianic future and overcome the terror of history brought to a head the inherent tragedy of dealing with history in metahistorical terms. "The magnitude of the Messianic idea," Gershom Scholem exclaims in a magisterial essay on messianism and its effect on the Jewish "outlook" on history, "corresponds to the endless powerlessness in Jewish history during all the centuries of exile, when it was unprepared to come forward on the plane of world history."[37] Regarding history from the metahistorical perspective of messianism, Scholem avers, had prevented the Jew from coming to a realistic understanding of history, his ability to act rationally in history pinioned by an otherworldly hope: "There is something grand about living in hope, but at the same time there is something profoundly unreal about it."

At the conclusion of his famous lecture of 1922, "Science as a Vocation," Max Weber also referred to the messianic hope of the Jews as something unreal, as a sad delusion that sober, rational men eager to be historically effective should eschew:

> [F]or many who today tarry for new prophets and saviors, the situation is the same as resounds in the beautiful Edomite watchmen's song of the period of exile that has been included among Isaiah's oracles: "He calleth to me out of Seir, Watchman, what of the night? The watchman said, The morning cometh, and also the night: if ye will enquire, enquire ye: return, come."—The people to whom this was said has enquired and tarried for more than two millennia, and we are all shaken when we realize its fate. From this we want to draw the lesson that nothing is gained by yearning and tarrying alone.[39]

The perceived historical passivity of traditional Jewry was particularly scorned by modern, secular Jews eager to lead their people back to the arena of real history, in which this formerly humbled people would stand erect and act to master their fate. The Hebrew writer Ḥayyim Hazaz, in purposefully hyperbolic strokes, portrayed the Zionist position in an angry sermon denouncing Jewish history, at least as experienced in the *Galut:*

> "I have no respect for Jewish history!" Yudka repeated the same refrain. "'Respect' is really not the word, but what I said before: 'I am opposed to it.' . . . I want to explain why. Just be patient a little while. . . . First, I will begin with the fact that we have no history at all. That's a fact. And that's the *zagvozdka*—I don't know how to say it in Hebrew. . . . In other words, that's where the shoe pinches. Because we didn't make our own history, the *goyim* made it for us. Just as they used to put out our candles on Sabbath, milk our cows and light our ovens on Sabbath, so they made our history for us to suit themselves, and we took it from them as it came. But it's not ours, it's not ours at all! Because we didn't make it, we would have made it differently. . . . In that sense, and in every other sense, I tell you, in every other sense, we have no history of our own."[40]

In addition to Zionism various other secular Jewish ideologies sought to return the Jews to history, to propel them to be sovereign actors once again in history. Indubitably, Zionism has remained the most creative of these ideologies sponsoring the Jews' reemergence as a historical people. But Zionism's path has not been untroubled—not the least because it has not been able to put a brake on messianic passion. For Scholem, this was a fateful question:

> The blazing landscape of redemption (as if it were a point of focus) has concentrated in itself the historical outlook of Judaism. Little wonder that overtones of Messianism have accompanied the modern Jewish readiness for irrevocable action in the concrete realm, when it set out on the utopian return to Zion. It is a readiness which no longer allows itself to be fed on hopes. Born out of the horror and destruction that was Jewish history in our generation, it is bound to history itself and not to meta-history; it has not given itself up totally to Messianism. Whether or not Jewish history will be able to endure this entry into the concrete realm without perishing in the crisis of Messianic claims which has virtually been conjured up—that is the question which out of this great and dangerous past the Jew of this age poses to his present and to his future.[41]

Scholem is perhaps emblematic of the modern Jew's paradoxical attitude toward history. On the one hand, he consciously and vigorously attempted to break with the regnant patterns of the Jewish past—and not only with respect to its historical outlook; on the other hand, as a great historian of Judaism, he sought to hold fast to the past, indeed, to retrieve it before it receded into oblivion. But, as Scholem was well aware, the endeavor to retrieve the past— to maintain a continuity with it—is fraught with, as the

Hegelians would say, inner contradictions. The modern historian—a child of the last two hundred and fifty years in the West—is obliged by his calling to posit, at least methodologically, a break with the past. While appropriating knowledge of the past, the historian sets himself at a critical distance from the past. Indeed, as J. H. Plumb has succinctly put it, "History . . . is not the past."[42] All societies have a sense of the past and their continuity with it—each drawing upon the past to explain its origins and purposes. A society turns to the "past" as a source of moral, religious, and ideological legitimation and edification. In contradistinction, Plumb suggests, "history" is borne by a quest for truth: "The historian's growing purpose has been to see things as they really were, and from this study to attempt to formulate processes of social [and intellectual] change which are acceptable on historical grounds and none other."[43] Because of his critical sensibility, Plumb argues, the historian has sounded the death knell for the "past." Hence the baffling paradox that despite modern man's unprecedented knowledge of the past, in ever-increasing measure it ceases to live for him. Surely, as Hans Meyeroff notes, "Previous generations knew much less about the past than we do, but perhaps felt a much greater sense of identity and continuity with it."[44]

Yet, as Claude Lévi-Strauss—and Nietzsche before him—observed, a fear of discontinuity pervades modern society, and it turns to the historian, beseeching him to furnish the lost sense of continuity with the past.[45] It does so in seeming refusal to acknowledge that the very premise of the historian is that we are "to understand the past as a time different than our own."[46] This divergence between the actual horizons of the historian's craft and the expectations of his public is all the more manifest when one turns to the historian for a sense of continuity with a religious past. For the historian, of course, also applies what Paul Ricoeur has called the "hermeneutics of suspicion" to the study of religion and its institutions, and subjects religion to the historicist presupposition, as Herder put it, "that we live in a world we ourselves create."[47] Through the prism of the historian's labors the authority of the past—and the religious teachings transmitted by the past—are thus no longer self-evident.[48]

From its very beginnings in early-nineteenth-century Germany, modern Jewish studies—the so-called *Wissenschaft des Judentums* (lit., Science of Judaism)—accepted the presuppositions of critical historical scholarship. In 1818, in his inaugural essay as a scholar, "On Rabbinic Literature," Leopold Zunz—the dominant figure of the first generation of *Wissenschaft des Judentums*—made two crucial methodological stipulations that, in his judgment, would assure that the fledgling discipline would indeed be a *Wissen-*

schaft, a "science." The study of Judaism, Zunz argued, should be pursued in an emotionally detached, objective fashion. Within the context of this study "it is not at all our concern whether [rabbinic literature] should, or could, also be the norm of our own judgments."[49] Further, Zunz held, the time is particularly propitious for such a study, since "rabbinic literature" is being carried to "its grave." Zunz and his colleagues, accordingly, assumed that Judaism was an object of the past to be assessed objectively and without prejudice, thereby preparing for Judaism, in the words of another illustrious pioneer of *Wissenschaft des Judentums,* Moritz Stein-schneider, "a decent burial."[50]

Though certainly not all the practitioners of *Wissenschaft des Judentums* regarded themselves as morticians of Judaism, most were undoubtedly caught in the bind of historicism. Already in the 1830s, the Galician sage Nachman Krochmal deemed historicism to be the single greatest challenge to Judaism as a living faith. How does one, he asked, affirm God's eternal Torah while at the same time accepting the insights of historical scholarship, pointing, as they do, to the reality of change and assembling unassailable evidence of historical, that is, human influence in the shaping of sacred writings and teachings? One could ignore the challenge of historicism, Krochmal warned, only at the peril of alienating the generation of Jews who have embraced modern culture and its historical attitudes.[51]

Implicitly following Ernst Troeltsch's famous dictum of "overcoming history through history,"[52] Scholem articulated a dialectic that he felt could lead beyond the impasse of historicism.[53] He viewed the historian as potentially a revolutionary. In opposition to what he regarded as the heteronomous and stultifying rule of the rabbinic tradition, Scholem assigned the historian the task of opening up the past anew, of tapping the rich and varied array of Judaism's forgotten and often suppressed experiences, imaginings, and teachings, rendering them accessible to the present generation. As such, the historian's calling is neither that of a mortician nor that of a curator, in Nietzsche's sarcastic phrase, of "picture galleries of the past" that serve merely to cater to the sentimentality of a self-satisfied clientele.[54]

The historian's retrieval of the past, Scholem seems to suggest, is not simply an exercise of anamnesis, of recollection and reminiscence. Rather, as an act of memory it is what Greek dramatists called anagnorisis—a critical recognition or discovery, especially as it precedes a peripeteia, a reversal or change of one's actions, thought, or perceptions. Scholem's dear friend and closest intellectual companion, Walter Benjamin, held that the genuine historian does not seek to preserve, but to cleanse and unsettle:

To articulate the past historically does not mean to recognize it "the way it really was" (Ranke). It means to seize hold of a memory as it flashes up at a moment of danger. . . . In every era the attempt must be made anew to wrest tradition away from a conformism that is about to overpower it. The Messiah comes not only as the redeemer, he comes as the subduer of Antichrist. Only that historian will have the gift of fanning the spark of hope in the past who is firmly convinced that even the dead will not be safe from the enemy if he [the enemy] wins.[55]

The true, the revolutionary historian, Benjamin insisted, is wary of being "drained by the whore called 'Once upon a time' in historicism's bordello." He seeks "to blast open the continuum of history," transforming the present with "chips of Messianic time."[56]

The messianic motif thus reappears. Benjamin was torn between a competing commitment to Judaism as a context of messianic anagnorisis and historical materialism as the best strategy for realizing the messianic future, eventually yielding to the latter. His contemporary, Franz Rosenzweig, attributed to historical scholarship, both general and Jewish, the twin role of binding one to tradition and messianic commitment:

For "the turning of the hearts of the fathers to the children" is, according to the Prophet Malachi, a final preparation for the last day. Without scholarship each generation would run away from the preceding one, and history would seem to be a discontinuous series (as in fact it really is) and not (as it ought to appear) the parable of a single point, a *nunc stans*—as history really is at the final [eschatological] moment, but thanks to scholarship . . . appears to be already in advance, here and now.[57]

REFERENCES

1. Rabbi Aaron Roth (1894–1944) of Szatmar, who toward the end of his life settled in Jerusalem.
2. This rite, which is shared by both Ḥasidic and non-Ḥasidic congregations in Jerusalem, apparently reaches back to the kabbalistic circle of Isaac Luria of sixteenth-century Safed. For a description, presented as a dream, of this ritual practice, including a diagram of the dance, see the report by Luria's disciple Ḥayyim Vital, *Sefer ha-Ḥezyanot,* Aaron Aescoly, ed. (1954), 123. I wish to thank Dr. Ze'ev Gries and Professor Moshe Idel for bringing this volume to my attention.
3. Franz Rosenzweig, *The Star of Redemption,* William W. Hallo, tr. (1970), 304.
4. On the phenomenology of Jewish ritual, with some suggestive remarks regarding the difference between kabbalistic and rabbinic rite, cf. Gershom Scholem, "Tradition and Creation in the Ritual of the Kabbalists" in *On the Kabbalah and Its Symbolism,* Ralph Mannheim, tr. (1965), 118–57, esp. 121ff. For a brief but

incisive comment on Scholem's reflections, cf. Yosef Ḥayim Yerushalmi, *Zakhor: Jewish History and Jewish Memory* (1982), 117, n. 26.

5. Until the sixteenth century, Jews had in addition to the *anno mundi,* which organized their religious life, two "historical" calendars. Cf. Yerushalmi, op. cit., 41.

6. Cf. "There is no history without dates. . . . Dates may not be the whole of history, nor what is most interesting about it, but they are its sine qua non, for history's entire originality and distinctive nature lie in apprehending the relation between *before* and *after,* which would perforce dissolve if its terms could not, at least in principle, be dated." Claude Lévi-Strauss, *The Savage Mind* (1962), 258.

7. "Theses on the Philosophy of History," in Walter Benjamin, *Illuminations,* Harry Zohn, tr., Hannah Arendt, ed. (1969), 264.

8. "The Quest for the Meaning of History," in Karl Loewith, *Nature, History and Existentialism* (1966), 135.

9. Cited in Karl Loewith, *Meaning in History* (1949), 53.

10. Friedrich Nietzsche, "Die froehliche Wissenschaft," in *Werke* 3 (1926), par. 357, 283f.

11. This epigram, making oblique reference to Thomas Aquinas' distinction between "natural" and "theological" virtues, was coined by my colleague R. J. Zwi Werblowsky, and communicated orally.

12. Hermann Cohen, *Religion of Reason,* Simon Kaplan, tr. (1972), 261ff. The Jews' affirmation of the meaning of history does not necessarily imply that the here and now was devoid of meaning for them. The life of halakhah, God's law, endowed the everyday with all its mundane details with sacred, and thus with an eminently meaningful quality. Cf. Aharon Lichtenstein, "Tahalikh ve-Sium be-Historiah," in Yehezkel Cohen, ed., *Ḥevrah ve-Historiah* (1980), 245–58.

13. Cf. Efraim E. Urbach, *The Sages: Their Concepts and Beliefs,* (1979), 448–61.

14. Scholem, *Kabbalah* (1974), 106ff., 130–33.

15. Cohen, *Religion of Reason,* 132.

16. Paul Ricoeur,"The History of Religions and the Phenomenology of Time Consciousness," in *The History of Religions: Retrospect and Prospect,* Joseph M. Kitagawa, ed. (1985), 19, 24, 28.

17. Mircea Eliade, *Cosmos and History: The Myth of the Eternal Return,* Willard R. Trask, tr. (1959), 36ff., 141–47.

18. R. J. Zwi Werblowsky, "In nostre tempore," in *Die Mitte der Welt: Aufsätze zu Mircea Eliade,* Hans Peter Duerr, ed. (1984), 131. Eliade regards biblical futurism as fundamentally "an antihistoric attitude." For "the Hebrew tolerates [history] in the hope that it will finally end, at some more or less distant future moment." Eliade, op. cit., 111.

19. "Toward an Understanding of the Messianic Idea in Judaism," in Scholem, *The Messianic Idea in Judaism,* Michael A. Meyer, tr. (1971), 10ff.

20. Cf. "History in the light of revelation is a confession of sin." H. Richard Niebuhr, *The Meaning of Revelation* (1952), 114.

21. Loewith, *Meaning in History,* 198.

22. Scholem, "Toward an Understanding of the Messianic Idea in Judaism," loc. cit., 6–12.

23. With respect to apocalyptic messianism, "it should be emphasized that in the history of Judaism its influence has been exercised almost exclusively under the conditions of the exile as a primary reality of Jewish life." Scholem, "Toward an Understanding of the Messianic Idea in Judaism," loc. cit., 2.

24. Leopold Zunz, *Literaturgeschichte der synagogalen Poesie* (1865), 1, cited in Lionel Kochan, *The Jew and His History* (1977), 3.

25. Cf. "After the destruction of the Second Temple, historical consciousness utterly ceased in Israel." Simon Bernfeld, "Dorshei Reshumot," in *Ha-Shiloah*, 2 (April–Sept. 1899), 193, cited in Kochan, op. cit., 120, n. 12.

26. Jewish historiography prior to the modern period is perceptively discussed in both Kochan and Yerushalmi, op. cit. A convenient and judicious annotated anthology of Jewish historical writings throughout the ages is Michael A. Meyer, *Ideas of Jewish History* (1974).

27. George Peabody Gooch, *History and Historians in the Nineteenth Century* (1959), 1.

28. Cf. Nathan Rotenstreich, *Tradition and Reality: The Impact of History on Modern Jewish Thought* (1972), 7–11; Eduard Shils, "Tradition," in *Comparative Studies in Society and History*, 13 (1976), 122–59.

29. On the Midrash as a form of "creative historiography," see Yitzhak Heinemann, *Darkei ha-Aggadah* (1950). See also Jacob Neusner, "History and Midrash," in J. Neusner, *History and Torah: Essays on Jewish Learning* (1965), 17–29; Paul Ricoeur, *Time and Narrative*, K. McLaughlin and D. Pellauer, trs. (1985).

30. Responsa literature is among the primary sources of Jacob Katz's various studies of traditional Jewish society's response to social and political change in the period of transition to modernity. Cf. J. Katz, *Tradition and Crisis: Jewish Society at the End of the Middle Ages* (1961).

31. R. J. Zwi Werblowsky, *Beyond Tradition and Modernity: Changing Religions in a Changing World* (1976), 51.

32. Cf. Yitzhak F. Baer, *Galut,* Robert Warshow, tr. (1947); Hayyim Ben-Sasson, *Encyclopedia Judaica,* s.v. *"Galut."*

33. Cf. Ben Halpern, "Galut," in *Jewish Frontier,* 21 (April 1954), 6–9; Ben-Sasson, op. cit.

34. Cf. Scholem, "The Messianic Idea in Kabbalism," in Scholem, *The Messianic Idea in Judaism,* 37–48.

35. Jacob Neusner, "Religious Uses of History," in *History and Theory* 2(1966), 170.

36. Scholem, "Kabbalah and Myth," in *On the Kabbalah and Its Symbolism,* 117.

37. Scholem, "Toward an Understanding of the Messianic Idea," loc. cit., 35.

38. Ibid.

39. "Science as a Vocation," in *From Max Weber: Essays in Sociology,* tr., ed., and introd. by H. H. Gerth and C. Wright Mills (1946), 156.

40. "The Sermon," Ben Halpern, tr., in *Israeli Stories,* Joel Blocker, ed. (1965), 68–70.

41. Scholem, "Toward an Understanding of the Messianic Idea," loc. cit., 35ff.

42. J. H. Plumb, *The Death of the Past* (1970), 17.

43. *From Max . . . .*

44. Hans Meyeroff, *Time and Literature* (1955), 109.

45. Lévi-Strauss, op. cit., 256ff.

46. Plumb, op. cit., 21.

47. Ricoeur, "The Critique of Religion," in *Union Seminary Quarterly Review,* 28 (1973), 206ff.; Herder, as cited in Isaiah Berlin, *Vico and Herder* (1976), 204.

48. Cf. Van Harvey, *The Historian and the Believer: The Morality of Historical Knowledge and Christian Belief* (1966), passim.

49. Leopold Zunz, "On Rabbinic Literature," in Paul Mendes-Flohr and Jehuda Reinharz, *The Jew in the Modern World: A Documentary History* (1980), 197.

50. Moritz Steinschneider, "Die Zukunft der jüdischen Wissenschaft," in *Hebräische Bibliographie,* 9 (1869), 76. Cf. Scholem, "The Science of Judaism—Then and Now," in *The Messianic Idea in Judaism,* 307.

51. Nachman Krochmal, *Moreh Nevukhei ha-Zman,* originally edited and published posthumously by Zunz in 1851. Excerpts are translated in Meyer, op. cit., 189–216.

52. Ernst Troeltsch, *Der Historismus und seine Probleme* (1922), in *Gesammelte Schriften* 3 (1925), 772.

53. On Scholem's "historiographical dialectic" and his relationship to Troeltsch, see Werblowsky, "Gedenkrede auf Gershom Scholem (1897–1982)," in *Berliner theologische Zeitschrift,* 1 (1984), 97–106, esp. 103ff.

54. Nietzsche, *The Use and Abuse of History,* Adrian Collins, tr. (1949), 13.

55. Benjamin, "Theses on the Philosophy of History," op. cit., 255.

56. Ibid., 262, 263.

57. Letter from Franz Rosenzweig to Eugen Rosenstock-Huessy, undated, in *Judaism Despite Christianity: The "Letters on Christianity and Judaism" Between Eugen Rosenstock-Huessy and Franz Rosenzweig,* E. Rosenstock-Huessy, ed.;, Dorothy Emmet, tr. (1971), 168.

BIBLIOGRAPHY

Lionel Kochan, *The Jew and His History* (1977).

Michael A. Meyer, *Ideas of Jewish History* (1974).

Nathan Rotenstreich, *Tradition and Reality: The Impact of History on Modern Jewish Thought* (1972).

Yosef Hayim Yerushalmi, *Zakhor: Jewish History and Jewish Memory* (1982).

Holiness

קדושה

Allen Grossman

Holiness, in Hebrew, *kodesh*, indicates the highest value, or —more precisely—what can be said by men (or angels) when God comes immediately to mind, as in Isaiah 6:3: "Holy, holy, holy is the Lord of hosts." Holiness is the word by which men describe God and therefore the ultimate doxological predicate, because it is the word by which God describes himself. "You shall be holy, for I, the Lord your God am holy" (Lev. 19:2). Hence, *holiness* is the abstract term taught man by God to mark God's difference and the nature of everything that comes to be included (obedient to the absolute imperative implicit in the idea of "highest value") within his difference.

The vital life of holiness in the human world is primarily transactive. The root of the word *holiness* (*k-d-sh*) occurs most often in the Bible as an adjective, the result of an ascription (for example, "holy ground," "holy nation," "holy name," "holy spirit," "holy mountain," "the Holy One of Israel"), or as a verb that commands or accomplishes the inclusion of something within the category of holiness (as in the sanctification of the Sabbath, or of Aaron and his sons, or of anything consecrated to the Lord, such as a beast or a house or a field). In this latter sense, words formed from the root of *holiness* are related in function to words meaning to sacrifice, and especially to the root *ḥ-r-m,* which is found in relation both to cult and also to God-commanded warfare, as in Lev. 27, 28:1. "Every proscribed thing is consecrated to the Lord" [*kol ḥerem kedosh kedoshim*] and Joshua 6:16–17: "For the Lord has given you the city. The city and everything in it are to be proscribed [*ḥerem*] for the Lord." The transactions of holiness, by which anything is included in its category, of which God is a member, may be violent in proportion as the difference between God and his world as established in the creation is severe. The pacification of the transaction of holiness depends on the right use of freedom.

More generally, the supreme human work (man's service and creativity) is the voluntary performance of the transactions of holiness, which reciprocate and complete God's creation of the world by restoring it day by day, fact by scattered fact, to his nature. The specification of such work, as in the 613 *miẓvot* or commandments, defines a culture of holiness, a system of transactions by which through the mediation of holiness man and God come to be included within the precinct of the same term. The Jew affirms this each time he recites the blessing that accompanies the performance of a commandment: "Blessed are you, O Lord our God . . . who has sanctified us by your commandments. . . ." As Philo remarked: "That which is blessed and that which is holy are closely connected to one another."[1] Holiness therefore specifies the coincidence of the wills of man and God and defines the freedom of both. That freedom expresses itself as the voluntary, continuous, cooperative maintenance of the world—sanctification, *kedusha.*

The "highest value," which holiness indicates and which the transactions of holiness produce, is not in its fundamental nature ethical value, because the actions of holiness are performed in the relationship of man and God and not the relationship of man and man, which is the plane where ethical meanings occur. Indeed, inclusion in the category of holiness erases the intrinsic nature of a thing and returns it, as in the restoration of the literal meaning of a text from the alien intentionality of interpretation, to the source of all being where it has in itself (intrinsically) no nature at all except its freedom. From the standpoint of human experience, therefore (the point of view of language), *holy* is not in the ordinary sense a predicate, a word that asserts something about a term, but the sign of the withdrawal of all reference into its source, a determinator of the radical disablement of metaphor and the absolute preemption of the truth of discourse at the supremely privileged moment of reference to reality. Hence, when the Lord is in his holy temple (*be-heikhal kadsho*) all earth must be silent (Hab. 2:20), because the order of sacred structure has superseded all other order; the meaning of all terms has been preempted by the Holy One—nothing has a name of its own to say.

As in the sacrifice of the productions of earth in cult, the predication of *holy* effects a rotation of the significance of words toward the origin of significance in God, who is outside of experience and therefore outside language. As he is aniconic—without image because perfectly free—so also he is antimetaphoric—a "man of war" who defeats comparison. "Who is like you, majestic in holiness?" (Ex. 15:11). That which enters the class of things of which he is a member ("holiness") loses its provenance in nature and history at the moment it is restored to the precinct of divinity. Hence, the rationality of martyrdom in Judaism is expressed as "the sanctification of the Name" *(Kiddush ha-Shem)*. This is the case because martyrdom, as the willed assimilation or sacrifice of the person to the category of the holy, repeats in a radical form the structure of all acts performed in response to the divine commandment to sanctify the world and therefore the self, even the keeping of the Sabbath. And, indeed, all such acts have in the course of history become the occasion of martyrdom. "Why art thou brought out to be killed?" "Because I have performed the rite of circumcision upon my son." "Why art thou to be stoned to death?" "Because I have observed the Sabbath." "Why art thou led out to die by fire?" "Because I have studied the Law."[2] As God is the immaterial source of material life and the nonnarratable source of narrative, so also is he the nonethical source of the ethical. Hence Maimonides, in *The Guide of the Perplexed,* is free to explain the human utility of the *mizvot* only after first demonstrating that no term that can be predicated of anything else can be predicated of God—that is to say, after having first ensured that the meaning of the *mizvot* as transactions of holiness cannot lie in human use.

The most common name for God in rabbinic usage (derived, it would seem, from Second Isaiah and Jeremiah) is the Holy One of Israel *(yhvh kedosh yisrael)*. The Holy One, who, as we have seen, repels all metaphoric amplification, expresses his power as a man of war by his holiness, the determinator that defeats all the facts of the world. Holy war is the semantic war of holiness upon the world of pagan and secular reference—a war of mutually exclusive legitimacies.[3] In this sense, the "holy people" (e.g., Deut. 7:6, 26:19, 28:9) contradict, by the logic of their transcendental legitimacy, all the nations of the world. By that same logic, the Book of which the holy people are custodians disqualifies the legitimacy and changes the meaning of all other books. The warfare of Scripture as holy text on all other texts takes the form of dispossession of reference, as the warfare of the holy people in Joshua takes the form of the dispossession of peoples by reason of prior right—holiness, the power of priority. Reciprocally, the absolute prior legitimacy of holiness by which the holy people are empowered to dispossess requires, by the reflexive implication of the severe logic of holiness, that the holy people also be dispossessed, alienated from God as wanderers whose home is always elsewhere. Hence, we may say that holiness is the uninterpretable a priori literal fact of being, the source of interpretation (precisely as the Holy One is the source of the world) in which interpretation, as the trace of autonomous human purpose, seeks to extinguish itself. In this sense, holiness makes war against culture—the making or imaging of anything that is not itself; and the Holy One, the Lord of Hosts, makes war as a master of a prior dispensation, the sacred order of existence absolutely self-canonizing, intolerant of "discontent" that produces the one real world as its only artifact.

However, when God made the world, as Genesis reports, he did not call it *holy*—he called it *good*. The word *good* is as characteristic of Genesis, in which the transaction of holiness is invoked on the single occasion of the institution of the Sabbath, as the word *holy* is characteristic of Exodus. The rabbis accordingly derive only three of the 613 actions of holiness (*mizvot*) from Genesis. The culture of holiness begins (with the single exception noted) in the precinct of the burning bush—"the place on which you stand is holy ground" (Ex. 3:5)—which is the occasion of the commissioning of Moses and the annunciation of the tetragrammaton (*yhvh*), the name of God as a form of the verb *to be* (*h-y-h*). The transactions of holiness in Exodus mark the beginning of religion, by contrast to the heroic relation to God prior to religion that is the principle of transaction in Genesis. The historical moment of the alienation of humankind from unmediated relationship to reality—the Egyptian servitude and consequent multiplication of the people—requires the reconstruction of that relationship within a system of mediation toward a God whose name is being itself. That system is the culture of holiness, including cult and the later displacement of cult to language and prayer.

The bush (*ha-sneh*) which burns but does not burn up manifests the repeal of natural causality in the same way that the liberation from Egypt accomplishes escape from the domination of immanent generative process, the autonomy of the world not holy. In Genesis the threat to human generativity came from God and the power of generativity, the continuity of life through time, was supplied by him directly. In the Egyptian servitude to nature's laws, the tribe multiplied, but without the principle of order that refers the meaning and therefore the life of all things immediately to their source in God. That principle of order is supplied by the flame and precinct of the bush at the commissioning of the master of the new culture of holiness, which will function like a language with only one word—the sacred name—into which must be translated all the terms of experience. The wanderings in the wilderness under the guidance of Moses' God enact, once again, the necessary concession of the autonomy of the human community to the one creative will, and the turning of the transcendental imperatives of Torah, the text received on Sinai, that supersedes the countertext of nature, against the totality of merely human interests represented by the calf of gold.

In Genesis the Sabbath was announced by the voice of God, blessed, and sanctified *(vayekadesh oto)*. It was not called *good*. In the repose of God, the autonomy of the world was displayed, not as a consequence of its inherent structure, but of its identity with source. The root *k-d-sh* introduced at the institution of the Sabbath in Genesis reappears at Horeb where it defines the precinct of the burning bush. The Jew invokes the power of *k-d-sh* weekly as a privilege of the human will (the two texts joined) in the creational announcement of the *kiddush,* which memorializes both the creation of the world and the liberation from Egypt. As God, not nature, produces the bread and the wine, so God creates the freedom *(yeziat mizraim,* the liberation from Egypt) that the culture of holiness indicates, not in the *goodness* of immediacy, but in the rigorous transactions of distance that history compels.

By contrast to the Genesis relationship to God experienced in hearing and wrestling and dreaming, the Exodus relationship to God is presented as sacred writing *(kodesh* as the sign of absence); the priest Aaron bears on his forehead "the engraving of a signet: holiness to God *[kodesh le-yhvh]* that he may bear the iniquity of holy things *[avon ha-kedoshim]*" (Ex. 29:36, 38). The iniquity of holy things is thus managed by the perpetual restatement, as in writing, of the principle of difference by which the world is created and in the light of which it must be maintained. The decline of the world from the goodness ascribed to it at the moment after creation is the chief event of history, indeed the process of history itself insofar as history entails captivity to the logic of narrative, which by its nature contradicts the nonnarratable freedom of God as source. Just as the function of the code of holiness is to extinguish history by subsuming its narrative within the sacred story of obedience to legislation, so too the work addressed by the prayers of holiness—the *kedusha* and the *kaddish*—is nothing less than the repair of the creation under the sign of absence, the reconstruction of goodness as holiness after the loss of holiness as the primordial goodness of oneness with source.

The Talmud attests the world-maintaining function of prayer and study: "Since the destruction of the Temple, every day is more cursed than the preceding one; and the existence of the world is assured only by the kedusha . . . and the words spoken after the study of Torah."[4] Since the kedusha incorporates the salute to God by the angels in Isaiah 3 ("Holy, holy, holy is the Lord of hosts"), the repetition of the kedusha became equivalent to Torah study enjoined on every Jew as a daily obligation (the eleventh miz-vah of Maimonides' Sefer ha-Mizvot); and Torah study was equivalent to the sanctification of the name—kiddush ha-Shem—by which language about the world is restored to its true reference in God whose name as announced in Exodus 3 subsumes the name of all things and thereby secures their reality. Thus the kedusha performs the continuous exchange of experience for holiness by which the world is maintained: the voluntary concession of the meaning of the world to its source obligatory upon the Jew, as the trans-active reciprocation of the creation and as responsive to the free act of God by which the Jew was "chosen from among the peoples." The performance of this exchange—the symbolic repetition of the akedah, the binding of Isaac—constitutes the culture of holiness, which conserves the value of the person and his world precisely at the point of the disavowal of autonomous right.

In prayer, as in Torah study, the Jew acts out a relationship to all source and therefore to his own reality. The structure of this performance consti-tutes the rationality of the Jewish religion. But the narrative of Jewish history in the Bible and beyond is an account of the failure of this culture of holi-ness. The right functioning of the culture of holiness as in the akedah, its mighty archetype, returns the world it wills to be slain back to the worshiper in the scale of human use and enjoyment—an exchange of all claims by humanity to autonomous continuity in return for the appropriate, and there-fore holy, part. But the severity of the claims of the culture of holiness— experienced as the appalling moment between the sacrificing of all and the return of the human part—exacts a confrontation with the horror of loss (in effect, the experience of history) greater than the terms of exchange can be imagined to compensate in the world of prayer, the empty realm of lan-guage that is the last temple of sacrifice. By its nature the culture of holi-ness—addressed to the world of fact it founds—is inimical to the partial exchanges and ethical rationalities that are the consolations of interpreta-tion, as the Book of Job compels us to recognize. Hence, death, which is a negative restatement of holiness as absolute loss—insofar as death is a crisis of consolatory rationality—is the primal antagonist of the culture of holiness, and the chief source of pollution in Judaism. It is for this reason that Joseph Soloveitchik remarks that "death and holiness constitute two contradictory verses, as it were, and the third harmonizing verse has yet to make its appearance."[5]

The mourners' *kaddish,* which begins, "Magnified and sanctified be his great name in the world which he has created according to his will," repeats as an act of the congregational person God's paradigmatic self-reference in Ezekiel 38:23: "I will magnify and sanctify myself . . ." (cf. Ezek. 36:23), and thereby affirms God's knowledge of himself in the language in which he states it. As a marker of the division of the service and as a song that both defines and negotiates the space, as it were, between God and his knowledge of himself, the *kaddish* functions to effect the restoration of the created world after its diminishing by death by reestablishing and also overcoming the difference between God and man as in the creation. But the *kaddish* also aggregates death to the severe rationality of the sanctification of the name ("sanctified be his great name") that is at once holiness—the right order of the world—and martyrdom, the gathering of all being into the one sign, the name, which is the shadow of his wings.

The *kaddish,* as also the *kedusha,* is an act of ridding the pollution of death from the world of the living. In this context, the pollution of death is understood to be the disease of the will that can no longer praise the Name, that can no longer by words of sanctification on its own behalf return the world to its maker. "What is to be gained from my death, from my descent into the pit? Can the dust praise You? Can it declare Your faithfulness?" (Ps. 30:9). The intention accomplished by these central doxological prayers is the alignment of all wills with the one will, which is existence itself (*yhvh*) and of which death would otherwise be a diminishment. The peace that is prayed for at the end of the *kaddish* ("May the maker of peace above also make peace among us") is the order of the world restored, as in the moment before creation, to its original unity, of which holiness is the sign.

All cultures function to produce the human world—space, time, objects, and persons—by negotiating differences within and against the background of primary fact. The success of this negotiation—economic in character, as are covenants in general—is the order of the world experienced as at peace. But the nature of the Hebrew culture of holiness—in accord with the strict monotheism that founds it—is peculiarly severe, admitting, as in the *kaddish,* no affirmation less than total even in the face of death. The refusal of the will to accept God's description of the one world is the refusal of being.

There is no space, as in Greek culture, for example, for the valorization of the oppositional self, and therefore, in the modern sense of things, no space for the self. Again, it may be said that all systems of order, all cultures, are both constructive and destructive. The culture of holiness, however, being legitimated by an absolute conception of order—creation as the radical difference between nothing and something—is in its central nature absolutely destructive of the long and precious inventory of human concerns that are not itself. Such, for example, are the Amalekites, whom it is a *mizvah* to abolish. As we have noted, only insofar as the laws of relationship between man and God are ethical can the culture of holiness be called ethical. But the nature of God affirmed in the acts of holiness demands that the difference between man and God (obedient to the paradigm of the creation) be maintained as absolute, at the same time that the good of both, an inference from the nature not of man but of God, is asserted to be identical. Insofar as Judaism as a religion is characterized by the requirements of holiness, the problem of holiness structures the problem of religion for the Jews.

On the other hand, holiness is an aspect of the divine nature, appropriation of which is commanded by God—a tree of life given and not withheld. The injunction to sanctify the name of God (Maimonides' ninth positive commandment, perhaps the highest in Israel) implies the obligation and also the privilege of expressing the totality of things as one word, the name of the Other and the destiny of each self. This injunction is inferred from Leviticus 22:32–33, where the transaction between God and man mediated by holiness—the praxis of covenant—is associated with the liberation from Egypt, exemption from nature as cause, the re-creation of the world by God: "You shall not profane My holy name, that I may be sanctified in the midst of the Israelite people. I the Lord who sanctify you (*mekadshkhem*), I who brought you out of the land of Egypt to be your God (*yhvh*), I the Lord." The substance of the liberation accomplished by the Holy One of Israel, of which the culture of holiness is the trace—a liberation that validates the honor of all the facts of the world in themselves—is expressed concretely in Maimonides' eighth principle of faith:

> [We are to believe] that the Torah has been received from heaven. . . . Thus no distinction is to be made between such verses as, *And the sons of Ham: Cush and Mizraim, And his wife's name was Mehetabel, And Timna was concubine,* and such verses as, *I am the Lord thy God* and *Hear, O Israel*—all equally having been received from the almighty, and all alike constituting the Law of the Lord, which is perfect, pure, sacred, and true.[6]

Just as there is no trivial writing of God, so holiness gives us the authenticity of the facts of the world, including ourselves and all persons, without distinction. Both "And Timna was concubine" and "Hear, O Israel" are "perfect, pure, sacred, and true." We are inexchangeable for any other thing, uninterpretable except in the light of holiness in which we find our place in the order of the one world, if we are to find our place at all. Holiness, then, presents us with our freedom as an inference from our existence, not as an enigma (there is no mystery) but as a problem—the inaugural problem of culture altogether. It neither consoles nor promises, but sets the terms of the work.

REFERENCES

1. Philo, On the Allegories of the Sacred Laws, I, 7.
2. For these and other examples, see Kaufmann Kohler, The Jewish Encyclopedia, s.v. "Kiddush ha-Shem." Kohler cites Mekh., Yitro 6, and Mid. Teh. to Ps. 12:5.
3. Cf. the phrase kadshu milhama ("consecrate for battle") in Jer. 6:4 and Joel 3:9.
4. BT Sot. 49a, cited in Elie Munk, The World of Prayer 1 (1961), 182.
5. Joseph B. Soloveitchik, Halakhic Man (1983), 36.
6. "Concerning the Torah Being Received from Heaven," in C. B. Chavel, The Commandments, 1, 277.

BIBLIOGRAPHY

Mary Douglas, Purity and Danger (1966).
James Hastings et al., Encyclopedia of Religion and Ethics, s.v. "Holiness."
Elie Munk, The World of Prayer, 2 vols. (1961).
Rudolf Otto, The Idea of the Holy (1910).
Joseph B. Soloveitchik, Halakhic Man, tr. Lawrence Kaplan (1983).

Holocaust

שואה

Emil L. Fackenheim

*H*olocaust is the term currently most widely employed for the persecution of the Jewish people by Nazi Germany from 1933 to 1945, first in Germany itself and subsequently in Nazi-occupied Europe, culminating in "extermination" camps and resulting in the murder of nearly six million Jews. However, the Hebrew term *Shoah* (total destruction) would be more fitting, since *Holocaust* also connotes "burnt sacrifice." It is true that, like ancient Moloch worshipers, German Nazis and their non-German henchmen at Auschwitz threw children into the flames alive. These were not, however, their own children, thrown in acts of sacrifice, but those of Jews, thrown in acts of murder.

Is the Holocaust unique? The concept *unprecedented* is preferable, as it refers to the same facts but avoids not only well-known difficulties about the concept of *uniqueness* but also the temptation of taking the event out of history and thus mystifying it.[1] To be sure, Auschwitz was "like another planet," in the words of "Katzetnik 135683," the pen name of the novelist Yechiel Dinur, that is, a world of its own, with laws, modes of behavior, and even a language of its own. Even so, as *unprecedented,* rather than *unique,* it is placed firmly into history. Historians are obliged, so far as possible, to search for precedents; and thoughtful people, by no means historians only, are obliged to ask if the Holocaust itself may become a precedent for future processes, whether as yet only possible or already actual. Manès Sperber, for example, has written: "Encouraged by the way Hitler had practiced genocide without encountering resistance, the Arabs [in 1948] surged in upon the nascent Israeli nation to exterminate it and make themselves its immediate heirs."[2]

The most obvious recent precedent of the Holocaust is the Turkish genocide of the Armenians in World War I. Like the Nazi genocide of the Jews in World War II, this was an attempt to destroy a whole people, carried out under the cover of a war with maximum secrecy, and with the victims being deported to isolated places prior to their murder, all of which provoked few countermeasures or even verbal protests on the part of the civilized world. Doubtless the Nazis both learned from, and were encouraged by, the Armenian precedent.

But unlike the Armenian genocide, the Holocaust was intended, planned, and executed as the "final solution" of a "problem." Thus, whereas, for example, the roundup of Armenians in Istanbul, the very heart of the Turkish empire, was discontinued after a while, Nazi Germany, had it won the war or even managed to prolong it, would have succeeded in murdering every Jew. North American Indians have survived in reservations; Jewish reservations in a victorious Nazi Empire are inconceivable. Thus the Holocaust may be said to belong, with other catastrophes, to the species *genocide.* Within the species, defined as intended, planned, and largely executed extermination, it is without precedent and, thus far at least, without sequel. It is—here the term really must be employed—unique.

Equally unique are the means without which this project could not have been planned or carried out. These include: a scholastically precise definition of the victims; juridical procedures, enlisting the finest minds of the legal profession, aimed at the total elimination of the victims' rights; a technical apparatus, including murder trains and gas chambers, and, most importantly, a veritable army not only of actual murderers but also of witting and unwitting accomplices—clerks, lawyers, journalists, bank managers, army officers, railway conductors, entrepreneurs, and an endless list of others.

All these means and accomplices were required for the *how* of the "Final Solution." Its *why* required an army of historians, philosophers, and theologians. The historians rewrote history. The philosophers refuted the idea that mankind is human before it is Aryan or non-Aryan. And the theologians were divided into Christians who made Jesus into an Aryan and neo-pagans who rejected Christianity itself as non-Aryan. (Their differences were slight compared to their shared commitments.) Such were the shock troops of this army. Equally necessary, however, were its remaining troops: historians, philosophers, and theologians who knew differently but betrayed their calling by holding their peace.

What was the *why* of the Holocaust? Even the shock troops never quite faced it, although they had no reason or excuse for not doing so. As early as 1936 Julius Streicher was on record to the effect that "who fights the Jew fights the devil," and "who masters the devil conquers heaven."[3] Streicher was only expressing more succinctly Hitler's assertion in *Mein Kampf* that "if the Jew will be victorious" in his cosmic struggle with mankind, his "crown" will be the "funeral wreath of humanity, and this planet will, as it did millions of years ago, move through the ether devoid of human beings."[4]

Planet Auschwitz was as good as Streicher's word. When the Third Reich was at the height of its power, the conquest of heaven seemed to lie in the apotheosis of the master race; even then, however, the mastery of the Jewish devil was a necessary condition of the conquest. When the Third Reich collapsed and the apocalypse was at hand, Planet Auschwitz continued to operate until the end, and Hitler's last will and testament made the fight against the Jewish people mandatory for future generations. The mastery of the Jewish devil, it seems, had become the sufficient condition for the "conquest of heaven," if indeed not identical with it.

To be sure, this advent of salvation in the Auschwitz gas chambers was but for relatively few eyes to see. What could be heard by all, however, was the promise of it years earlier, when the streets of Germany resounded to the stormtroopers' hymn: "When Jewish blood spurts from our knives, our well-being will redouble."

Never before in history had a state attempted to make a whole country— indeed, as in this case, a whole continent—*rein* (free) of every member of a whole people, man, woman, and child. Never have attempts resembling the Holocaust been pursued with methods so thorough and with such unswerving goal-directedness. It is difficult to imagine, and impossible to believe that, this having happened, world history can ever be the same. The Holocaust is not only an unprecedented event. It is also of an unfathomable magnitude. It is world historical.

As a world-historical event, the Holocaust poses new problems for philosophical thought. To begin with reflections on historiography, if, by near-common philosophical consent, to explain an event historically is to show

how it was possible, then, to the philosopher, the Holocaust historian emerges sooner or later as asserting the possibility of the Holocaust solely because it was actual. He thus exposes the historian's explanation as being, in fact, circular. This impasse, to be sure, is often evaded, most obviously when, as in many histories of World War II, the Holocaust is relegated to a few footnotes. An impasse is even explicitly denied when, as in Marxist ideological history, Nazism-equals-fascism-equals-the-last-stage-of-capitalism, or when, as in liberalistic ideological history, the Holocaust is flattened out into man's-inhumanity-to-man-especially-in-wartime. (Arnold Toynbee, for example, considered that "what the Nazis did was nothing peculiar."[5]) The philosopher, however, must penetrate beyond these evasions and ideological distortions. And when such a philosopher finds a solid historian who states, correctly enough, that "the extermination grew out of the biologistic insanity of Nazi ideology, and for that reason is completely unlike the terrors of revolutions and wars of the past,"[6] he must ponder whether "biologistic insanity" has explanatory force or is rather a metaphor whose chief significance is that explanation has come to an end. As he ponders this, he may well be led to wonder "whether even in a thousand years people will understand Hitler, Auschwitz, Maidanek, and Treblinka better than we do now. . . . Posterity may understand it even less than we do."[7]

Such questions turn philosophical thought from methodological to substantive issues, and above all to the subject of man. Premodern philosophy was prepared to posit a permanent human nature that was unaffected by historical change. More deeply immersed in the varieties and vicissitudes of history, modern philosophy generally has perceived, in abstraction from historical change, only a human condition, which was considered permanent only insofar as beyond it was the humanly impossible. At Auschwitz, however, "more was real than is possible,"[8] and the impossible was done by some and suffered by others. Thus, prior to the Holocaust, the human condition, while including the necessity of dying, was seen as also including at least one inalienable freedom—that of each individual's dying his own death.[9] "With the administrative murder of millions" in the death camps, however, "death has become something that was never to be feared in this way before. . . . The individual is robbed of the last and poorest that until then still remained his own. In the camps it was no longer the individual that died; he was made into a specimen."[10]

As well as a new way of dying, the Auschwitz administrators also manufactured a new way of living. Prior to the Holocaust no aspect of the human condition could make so strong a claim to permanency as the distinction between life and death, between still-being-here and being-no-more. The

Holocaust, however, produced the *Muselmann* (Muslim; pl., *Muselmän-ner*)—camp slang for a prisoner near death—the skin-and-bone walking corpse, or living dead, the vast "anonymous mass, continuously renewed and always identical, of non-men who march and labor in silence, the divine spark dead within them, already too empty really to suffer. One hesitates to call them living. One hesitates to call their death death."[11] The *Muselmann* may be called the most truly original contribution of the Third Reich to civilization.

From these new ways of being human—those of the victims—philosophical thought is turned to another new way of being human, that of the victimizers. Philosophy has all along been acquainted with the quasi-evil of sadism (a mere sickness), the semievil of moral weakness, the superficial evil of ignorance, and even—hardest to understand and, therefore, often ignored or denied—the radical or demonic evil that is done and celebrated for its own sake. Prior to the Holocaust, however, it was unacquainted with the "banality of evil"[12] practiced by numberless individuals who, having been ordinary or even respected citizens, committed at Auschwitz crimes on a scale previously unimaginable, only to become, in the Holocaust's aftermath, ordinary and respectable once more—without showing signs of any moral anguish.

The evil is banal by dint not of the nature of the crimes but of the people who committed them: these, it is said, were made to do what they did by the system. This, however, is only half a philosophical thought, for who made the system—conceived, planned, created, perpetuated, and escalated it—if not such as Himmler and Eichmann, Stangl and Hoess, to say nothing of the unknown-soldier-become-S.S.-murderer? Already having difficulty with radical or demonic evil, philosophical thought is driven by the "banal" evil of the Holocaust from the operators to the system, and from the system back to the operators. In this circular movement, to be sure, banal evil, except for ceasing to be banal, does not become intelligible. Yet the effort to understand is not without result, for from it the Holocaust emerges as a world or, rather, as the antiworld par excellence. The human condition does not dwell in a vacuum. It "always-already-is" within a world, that is, within a structured whole that exists at all because it is geared to life and that is structured because it is governed by laws of life. Innocent so long as they obey the law, the inhabitants of a world have a right to life, and forfeit it, if at all, only by an act of will—the breach of the law. The Holocaust antiworld, while structured, is governed by a law of death. For some—Jews—existence itself was a capital crime (a hitherto unheard-of proposition) and the sole raison d'être of the others was to mete out their punishment. In this world, the degradation, torture, and eventual murder of some human beings at the hands of others was not a by-product of, or means to, some higher, more ultimate purpose. They were its whole essence.

Modern philosophers, we have said previously, were able to conceive of a human condition because not all things were considered humanly possible. Even so, some of their number, possibly with modern history in mind, have not hesitated to ascribe to man a "perfectibility" that is infinite. Auschwitz exacts a new concession from future philosophy: whether or not man is infinitely perfectible, he is in any case infinitely depravable. The Holocaust is not only a world-historical event. It is also a "watershed,"[13] or "caesura,"[14] or "rupture"[15] in man's history on earth.

Is the Holocaust a rupture in the sight of theology? This question requires a separate inquiry. Theology, to be sure, at least if it is Jewish or Christian, is bound up with history. But it can be, and has been, argued that this is a *Heilgeschichte* immune to all merely secular historical events. Thus, for Franz Rosenzweig nothing crucial could happen for Jews between Sinai and the Messianic days. And for Karl Barth it was "always Good Friday *after* Easter," the implication being that the crucial saving event of Christianity has already occurred and is unassailable ever after.

Is the Holocaust a rupture for Christianity? German Christians, and possibly Christians as a whole, "can no longer speak evangelically to Jews."[16] They cannot "get behind" Auschwitz; they can get "beyond it" if at all only "in company with the victims," and this latter only if they identify with the State of Israel as being a Jewish "house against death" and the "last Jewish refuge."[17] Christians must relate "positively" to Jews, not "despite" Jewish nonacceptance of the Christ but "because" of it.[18] Even to go only this far and no further with their theologians (it seems fitting here to cite only German theologians) is for Christians to recognize a post-Holocaust rupture in their faith, for the step demanded—renunciation of Christian missions to the Jews, as such and in principle—is, within Christian history, unprecedented. (Of the Christian theologians who find it necessary to go much further A. Roy Eckardt is, perhaps, the most theologically oriented.) To refuse even this one step, that is, for Christians to stay with the idea of mission to the Jews in principle, even if suspending it altogether in practice, is either to ignore the Holocaust, or else sooner or later to reach some such view as that mission to the Jews "is the sole possibility of a genuine and meaningful restitution (*Wiedergutmachung*) on the part of German Christendom."[19] Can Christians view such a stance as other than a theological obscenity? The Jewish stance toward Christian missionizing attempts directed at them, in any case, cannot be what it once was. Prior to the Holocaust, Jews could respect such attempts, although of course considering them misguided. After the Holocaust, they can only view them as trying in one way what Hitler undertook in another.

It would seem, then, that for Christians Good Friday can no longer be *always* after Easter. As for Jews, was the Holocaust a crucial event, occurring though it did between Sinai and the Messianic days? Franz Rosenzweig's Jewish truth, it emerges in our time, was a truth not of Judaism but of *Galut* (exile) Judaism only, albeit its most profound modern statement. *Galut* Judaism, however, has ceased to be tenable.

Galut Judaism may be characterized as follows:

(1) A Jew can appease or bribe, hide or flee from an enemy and, having succeeded, can thank God for having been saved.

(2) When *in extremis* such salvation is impossible, when death can be averted only through apostasy, he can still choose death, thus becoming a martyr; and then he is secure in the knowledge that, while no Jew should seek death, *kiddush ha-Shem* (sanctifying God's name by dying for it) is the highest stage of which he can be worthy.[20]

(3) Exile, though painful, is bearable, for it is meaningful, whether its meaning consists in punishment for Jewish sins, vicarious suffering for the sins of others, or whether it is simply inscrutable, a meaning known only to God.

(4) *Galut* will not last forever. If not he himself or even his children's children, at any rate some Jews' distant offspring will live to see the Messianic end.

These are the chief conditions and commitments of *Galut* Judaism. Existing in the conditions and armed by the commitments, a Jew in past centuries was able to survive the poverty of the eastern European ghetto; the slander, ideologically embellished and embroidered, of anti-Semitism in modern Germany and France; the medieval expulsions; the Roman Emperor Hadrian's attempt once and for all to extirpate the Jewish faith; and, of course, the fateful destruction of the Jerusalem Temple in 70 C.E., to which *Galut* Judaism was the normative and epoch-making response. All these *Galut* Judaism was able to survive. The Holocaust, however, already shown by us to be unprecedented simply as an historical event, is unprecedented also as a threat to the Jewish faith, and *Galut* Judaism is unable to meet it.

(1) The Holocaust was not a gigantic pogrom from which one could hide until the visitation of the drunken Cossacks had passed. This enemy was

coldly sober, systematic rather than haphazard; except for the lucky few, there was no hiding.

(2) The Holocaust was not a vast expulsion, causing to arise the necessity, but also the possibility, of once again resorting to wandering, with the Torah as "portable fatherland."[21] Even when the Third Reich was still satisfied with expelling Jews there was, except for the fortunate or prescient, no place to go; and when the Reich became dissatisfied with mere expulsions, a place of refuge, had such been available, would have been beyond reach.

(3) The Holocaust was not an assault calling for bribing or appeasing the enemy. This enemy was an "idealist" who could not be bribed, and he remained unappeasable until the last Jew's death.

(4) The Holocaust was not a challenge to Jewish martyrdom but, on the contrary, an attempt to destroy martyrdom forever. Hadrian had decreed death for the crime of practicing Judaism and thereby inspired the martyrdom of such as Rabbi Akiva, which in turn inspired countless Jewish generations. Hitler, like Hadrian, sought to destroy Jews but, unlike Hadrian, was too cunning to repeat the ancient emperor's folly. He decreed death for Jews, not for doing or even believing, but rather for being—for the crime of possessing Jewish ancestors. Thus, Jewish martyrdom was made irrelevant. Moreover, no effort was spared to make martyrdom impossible as well, and the supreme effort in this direction was the manufacture of *Muselmänner*. A martyr chooses to die; as regards the *Muselmänner*, "one hesitates to call them living; one hesitates to call their death death."[22]

It cannot be stressed enough that, despite these unprecedented, superhuman efforts to murder Jewish martyrdom, countless, nameless Akivas managed to sanctify God's name by choosing how to die, even though robbed of the choice of whether to die; their memory must have a special sacredness to God and man. Such memory is abused, however, if it is used to blot out, minimize, or even divert attention from the death of the children as yet unable to choose and the death of the *Muselmänner* who could choose no more.

That these four *nova* have made *Galut* Judaism untenable has found admirable expression in an ancient midrash that was originally intended to expound the then-new form of Judaism. In this midrash God, at the beginning of the great exile initiated by the destruction of the Temple in 70 C.E., exacts three oaths, one from the Gentiles and two from the Jews. The Gentiles are made to swear not to persecute the Jews, now stateless and helpless, excessively. The Jews are made to swear not to resist their persecutors, and not to "climb the wall," that is, prematurely to return to Jerusalem.

But what, one must ask, if not Auschwitz, is "excessive persecution"? In response, some have said that the Jews broke their oath by climbing the wall, that is, by committing the sin of Zionism, and that in consequence God at Auschwitz released the Gentiles from obligation. Any such attempt to save *Galut* Judaism, however, reflects mere desperation, for it lapses into two blasphemies: toward the innocent children and the guiltless *Muselmänner,* and toward a God who is pictured as deliberately, callously, consigning them to their fate. There remains, therefore, only a bold and forthright taking leave from *Galut* Judaism. It was the Gentiles at Auschwitz who broke their oath, and the Jews in consequence are now released from theirs.

A "post-*Galut* Judaism" Judaism is, unmistakably, in the making in our time. Its most obvious aspects are that "resisting" the persecutors and "climbing the wall" have become not only rights but also ineluctable duties. After the Holocaust, Jews owe anti-Semites, as well as, of course, their own children, the duty of not encouraging murderous instincts by their own powerlessness. And after the absolute homelessness of the twelve Nazi years that were equal to a thousand, they owe the whole world, as well as, of course, their own children, the duty to say no to Jewish wandering, to return home, to rebuild a Jewish state.

These aspects of the Judaism in the making are moral and political. Their inner source is spiritual and religious. In the Warsaw ghetto Rabbi Isaac Nissenbaum, a famous and respected orthodox rabbi, made the statement—much quoted by Jews of all persuasions in their desperate efforts to defend, preserve, and hallow Jewish life against an enemy sworn to destroy it all—that this was a time not for *kiddush ha-Shem* (martyrdom) but rather for *kiddush ha-ḥayyim* (the sanctification of life). It is a time for *kiddush ha-ḥayyim* still. The Jewish people have passed through the Nazi antiworld of death; thereafter, by any standard, religious or secular, Jewish life ranks higher than Jewish death, even if it is for the sake of the divine name. The Jewish people have experienced exile in a form more horrendous than ever dreamt of by the apocalyptic imagination; thereafter, to have ended exile bespeaks a fidelity and a will to live that, taken together, give a new dimension to piety. The product of this fidelity—the Jewish state—is fragile still, and embattled wherever the world is hostile or does not understand. Yet Jews both religious and secular know in their hearts that Israel—the renewed people, the reborn language, the replanted land, the rebuilt city, the state itself—is a new and unique celebration of life. There are many reasons why Israel has become the center of the Jewish people in our time; not least is that it is indispensable to a future Judaism. If a Jewish state had

not arisen in the wake of the Holocaust, it would be a religious necessity—
although, one fears, a political near-impossibility—to create it now.

REFERENCES

1. See the warnings voiced by Yehuda Bauer.
2. . . . *Than a Tear in the Sea* (1967), xiii.
3. Quoted in *The Yellow Spot: The Extermination of the Jews in Germany* (1936), 47.
4. Hitler, *Mein Kampf,* tr. R. Manheim (1943), 60.
5. In a debate with Yaacov Herzog. See Yaacov Herzog, *A People That Dwells Alone* (1975), 31.
6. K. D. Bracher, *The German Dictatorship* (1971), 430.
7. Isaac Deutscher, *The Non-Jewish Jew* (1968), 163 ff.
8. A statement by Hans Jonas, made to Ernst Simon as reported in the latter's "Revisionist History of the Jewish Catastrophe," *Judaism,* vol. 12, no. 4 (Summer 1963), 395.
9. See especially Martin Heidegger's *Sein und Zeit* (1935), section II, chapter 1.
10. Theodor Adorno, *Negative Dialektik* (1966), 354 ff.
11. Primo Levi, *Survival in Auschwitz,* tr. Stuart Woolf (1959), 82.
12. See, e.g., Hannah Arendt, *Eichmann in Jerusalem: A Report on the Banality of Evil* (1977), passim.
13. Franklin Littell, *The Crucifixion of the Jews* (1975), passim.
14. Arthur A. Cohen, *The Tremendum* (1981), passim.
15. Emil L. Fackenheim, *To Mend the World: Foundations of Future Jewish Thought* (1982), passim.
16. Dietrich Bonhoeffer as quoted in *The German Church Struggle and the Holocaust,* Franklin H. Littell and Hubert G. Locke, eds. (1974), 288.
17. Johann Baptist Metz in *Gott Nach Auschwitz* (1979), 124 ff., 139 ff.
18. H. H. Henrix, F. M. Marquardt, M. Stoehr, all in personal conversation with this writer. The formulation is Henrix's.
19. The German Lutheran theologian Martin Wittenberg, as quoted in *Auschwitz als Herausforderung für Juden und Christen,* G. B. Ginzel, ed. (1980), 566.
20. See Maimonides in his *Responsum on Martyrdom.*
21. A celebrated and much-quoted dictum by the German Jewish poet Heinrich Heine.
22. See above, note 11.

BIBLIOGRAPHY

Eliezer Berkovits, *Faith After the Holocaust* (1973).
Arthur A. Cohen, *The Tremendum* (1981).
A. Roy Eckardt, with Alice Eckardt, *Long Night's Journey into Day* (1982).
Emil L. Fackenheim, *To Mend the World: Foundations of Future Jewish Thought* (1982).
Richard L. Rubenstein, *After Auschwitz* (1966).

Holy Spirit

רוח־הקודש

Aaron Singer

The holy spirit is the conventional translation of the Hebrew term *ruah ha-kodesh*. Since this rendering has obfuscated the divergent development of the concept in rabbinic and Christian theology, the Hebrew designation has been retained in the present discussion of the rabbinic concept.

Although different shades of meaning emerge from a study of the term, *ruah ha-kodesh* turns on the axis of God's self-revelation to man. Whatever the philological origins, *ruah ha-kodesh* has come to signify a prophetic spirit that graces an individual or community. The bearer experiences a clairvoyance that enables him to discern an event or human encounter in the continuum of time and space, illuminate a text of the Torah, be inspired to transcribe a book of Scripture, and, in some cases, perform supernatural feats. *Ruah ha-kodesh* also manifests itself as a personification of the holy writ or as a divine epithet. In this capacity, *ruah ha-kodesh* quotes Scripture to admonish, comfort, and guide Israel. The Holy Spirit in the dogma of the early church becomes a coeternal hypostasis in the doctrine of the Trinity.

Ruah ha-kodesh, on the other hand, is a didactic dramatization of God's immediacy and not a substantive intermediary between God and man.

In rabbinic literature, *ruah ha-kodesh* plays an active role in the haggadahic narrative of the Bible. The prophetic spirit supplies Adam with names to give the creatures God has created; appears in the courts of Shem, Samuel, and Solomon; advises Sarah; enlightens Jacob as to the future of his sons; flees from Moses due to the unworthiness of the Israel that worshiped the golden calf, and inspires David and Solomon to compose the books of Psalms and Ecclesiastes, respectively. *Ruah ha-kodesh* was attributed to forty-eight men and seven women of the Bible, and it was taught that *ruah ha-kodesh* was abundant in Israel before the disappearance of Elijah. The rabbinic sages report that the prophetic spirit rested on such colleagues as Rabbis Akiva, Simeon bar Yohai, Meir, Gamliel, and Phinehas ben Jair, and they continue to employ personifications of *ruah ha-kodesh* in their teachings.

Although the term *ruah ha-kodesh* covers all degrees of prophecy, the nature and function of this low-keyed prophetic spirit must be distinguished from biblical prophecy. As a king is compared to the statue promulgated in his likeness, so is biblical prophecy to all other, diminished, forms of prophecy. The prophet is compelled to admonish Israel for its sins and call for repentance before it is too late. He is often caught between the fire of his divine mission and his love of Israel. When tragedy and despair overwhelm Israel, he comforts it with messianic visions of better days. In contrast, the nonbiblical *ruah ha-kodesh* falls like a gentle rain, rather than a cataclysmic whirlwind, on its recipient. There is no radical reordering of one's life, no compelling vocation to speak the word of the Lord; merely an experience of illumination, a feeling of exaltation. Like other forms of theophany in rabbinic teaching, *ruah ha-kodesh* is associated with man's religious and moral behavior. *Ruah ha-kodesh* is a gift, not a burden, that is linked to performing a *mizvah* (religious precept) or living an exemplary life. Further, the experience of *ruah ha-kodesh* enables the righteous to enlarge the circle of his righteousness. Through the good offices of *ruah ha-kodesh,* for example, Rabbi Meir was able to mend a serious breach in the marriage of one of his disciples.

Some of the characteristic behavior that is associated with *ruah ha-kodesh* may be found in one who teaches Torah publicly, studies Torah in order to put it into practice, performs deeds of loving-kindness, is joyful of heart, sighs for the honor of God and Israel and pines for Jerusalem, and sacrifices self for the people of Israel. Equally instructive are the acts that drive *ruah ha-kodesh* away, such as arrogance, insensitivity to the anguish of others, living outside of the land of Israel, being a member of an unworthy generation, or committing one of the cardinal sins of shedding innocent blood or practicing immorality or idolatry.

As a poetic personification of holy writ or a divine epithet, *ruaḥ ha-kodesh* poignantly expresses God's pathos for his people. He cries for those who suffer injustice, mourns for those who choose to die rather than transgress his commandment, delights in those who recite the Shema with religious fervor, and comforts those who are conscience-stricken over their inadvertent violation of the Day of Atonement. Personification of *ruaḥ ha-kodesh* most clearly approximates biblical prophecy. However, the subject of divine concern as dramatized in such personifications usually relates to a specific situation or people, and rarely projects the divine pathos on the cosmic screen of biblical prophecy.

Even a brief survey of the concept of *ruaḥ ha-kodesh* must include the opposition of many sages who were wary of the effect that the free play of new revelations might have on the rule of Torah. Some denied its continued presence. "With the death of Haggai, Zechariah, and Malachi *ruaḥ ha-kodesh* ceased in Israel" (Tosefta Sotah 13.2). Others agreed that there was indeed a cessation, but attributed it to the unworthiness of the generation. Still others dealt with the issue by merging prophecy with the teaching of the rabbis. "Since the destruction of the temple, prophecy was taken away from the prophets and given to the sages" (BT BB 12a). The overriding concern of this school of thought is to contain the independent movement of prophecy, biblical or otherwise. Accordingly, they attribute no innovative laws to the prophets. The fact that some laws are indeed identified with the prophets gives rise to an ingenious exercise of casuistry. Either the law was given to Moses when he stood together, as the midrash portrays it, with the sages at Mount Sinai, and the prophet was simply reiterating what was heard at a later time, or the prophet authenticated the law by deducing it through his use of the accepted modes of rabbinic interpretation. A second school of thought, however, not only attributes laws to the prophets but recognizes the influence and inspiration of *ruaḥ ha-kodesh* in and behind the interpretations of the rabbis.

Despite the divergence of theory, one can trace the attempt of even those who affirm the presence of extra-legal revelation to normalize *ruaḥ ha-kodesh*, to legislate its boundaries and, through a process of internalization, to incorporate it into the body of the law. The process is discernible when we note that *ruaḥ ha-kodesh* is experienced almost exclusively by the rabbis and that the teachings linked with *ruaḥ ha-kodesh* come to reinforce the dictates of the rabbis.

Revelations, whether in the form of *ruah ha-kodesh*, the *Shekhinah* (divine Presence), or a heavenly voice *(bat kol)*, all have their respected place within tradition as long as they do not interfere with the rulings of the sages. When a heavenly voice concurs with the opinion of an individual sage in opposition to the majority, it is duly admonished and banished from the deliberations of the court. *Ruah ha-kodesh* becomes, even for its advocates, a handmaiden to rabbinic authority. An undisciplined outburst of revelation is seen as a threat to the foundations of a tradition, no less than to those who act as its guardian and interpreter. The tradition preserves not only the primary divine relationship, but insures continuity and stability to a dispersed and conglomerate people. For the rabbis to leave private revelations unattended was to court spiritual anarchy, which, to their mind, would pave the way for new prophets and new dispensations.

The imposed limitation of the sages notwithstanding, the recognition of the reality of *ruah ha-kodesh* gave the institutions and deliberations of the rabbis an immediate and vibrant sense of God's presence. "If there are no prophets, there is no *ruah ha-kodesh*. If there is no *ruah ha-kodesh* there are no synagogues or houses of study" (JT Sanh., ch. 10, hal. bet.).

The unsystematic, paratactic, and contradictory nature of rabbinic texts renders theological statements tenuous and arbitrary. Rabbinic teaching can be compared to the proverbial cave by the sea: the sea fills the cave, but suffers no loss. The following extrapolations are, therefore, offered as theological trends or tendencies that make no pretention of exhausting the subject of *ruah ha-kodesh*.

One of the striking features of *ruah ha-kodesh* is its accessibility. The aristocracy of learning epitomized by the *talmid hakham* (scholar-teacher-judge) is restricted to the intellectual elite and the religious virtuosi. The aspirant to nonbiblical *ruah ha-kodesh* can be one of more modest talent and express qualities of another kind. Unlike biblical prophecy, *ruah ha-kodesh* is an outgrowth of the religious and moral life that does not rest on one specific quality or talent.

As outlined above, the paths to *ruah ha-kodesh* are many and varied. Deeds of loving-kindness, study for the sake of practice, the joyful spirit are but a few. One sage opens wide the door to experiencing *ruah ha-kodesh* when he invites the individual to choose his own particular way. "Fulfill one commandment with wholehearted faith" (Mekh. Bashalach 14). However, two qualifying comments are in order. First, there are sages who take the long and thorny path to *ruah ha-kodesh*. The following prescription can be taken only by the most hardy ascetic willing to assume a monastic existence to reach the goal of *ruah ha-kodesh*:

The Torah leads to carefulness, carefulness to diligence, diligence to cleanliness, cleanliness to abstemiousness, abstemiousness to purity, purity to piety, piety to humility, humility to fear of sin, fear of sin to holiness, holiness to the *ruah ha-kodesh.* . . .

(M. Sot. 9:15)

There are sages who qualify the doctrine of accessibility from another vantage point. They contend that the attainment of *ruah ha-kodesh* is dependent not only on the merit of the individual, but also on the worthiness of the generation. The connection between the individual and society is critical. Just as the act of an individual can tip the balance of the world, so the collective acts of the world can obscure the deeds of an individual.

A second theological implication is the element of universality implicit in the concept of *ruah ha-kodesh*. Although rabbinic teaching directs itself primarily to the people of Israel and the individual Jew, one can discern inchoate elements that stretch the conventional conception. We note that Balaam, Rahab, Elipaz, and other non-Jews were blessed with a prophetic spirit. Here, too, there are detractors who explain that the quality of prophecy of non-Jews is inferior to that of Jews. However, it is to the credit of rabbinic teaching that, despite the religious and cultural insularity of their environment, and the sad and often tragic experience of Jews in the pagan world, the rabbis were still capable at moments of transcending experience and environment to achieve a more universal vision, expressed with such simple eloquence in the midrashic text: "I bring heaven and earth to witness that *ruah ha-kodesh* rests on a non-Jew as well as upon a Jew, upon woman as well as upon a man, upon maidservant as well as manservant. All depends on the deeds of the individual" (Tana Debe Eliyahu Rabba 9).

The most obtrusive and perhaps the least controversial implication of the concept of *ruah ha-kodesh* is the palpable presence of God in the world. The transcendent rule of the Torah has superseded prophecy. God's revelation is now the responsibility of the sage, the religious virtuoso, to preserve and interpret. The manifestation of *ruah ha-kodesh,* however, is evidence of the active involvement within and without the framework of halakhah. The concept demonstrates a consciousness of God's nearness and uninterrupted concern for his creatures. The possibility of experiencing *ruah ha-kodesh* helps redress the imbalance of a tradition that stresses the aristocracy of learning and the all-embracing authority of halakhah. The assertion of God's immanence together with his transcendence in rabbinic teaching reflects, concretizes, and completes the worldview of the Bible. "I dwell on high, in holiness, yet with the contrite and the lowly in spirit—reviving the spirits of the lowly, reviving the hearts of the contrite" (Isa. 57:5).

A final implication that can be drawn from the material at hand is its embodiment of a holistic approach to theological issues. The controversy between the sages who acknowledge and capitalize on the continuing activity of *ruah ha-kodesh* and those who either deny its reality or who insist on absorbing it in toto into the body of the law is a case in point. Both views are presented in rabbinic sources and remain intact together with rabbinic attempts to incorporate them into one comprehensive whole. It is to the credit of the editors of the oral tradition that these disparate lines of thought are preserved side by side with no need to force a resolution. Although individual sages do not exhibit or espouse anything that approaches the modern formulation of a holistic theology, an overview of the rabbinic gestalt does. Studying the text, we become party to an unconscious dialectic of the natural and necessary tension that exists between law and the prophetic spirit, between the claims of divine transcendence and divine immanence, between the consensus and continuity of tradition and the spontaneity and individuality of intuition and inspiration. This dialectic points to a deeper theological synthesis that is conscious and explicit in modern philosophy, but as Gershom Scholem observes, "Classical Judaism expressed itself, it did not reflect upon itself."[1] To abandon one in favor of the other would be to distort a greater reality that encompasses both views without compromising either. Each is essential to avoid the abuses and distortions that result from an excessive emphasis on one at the expense of the other. Each is needed to maintain an exquisite tension that eschews a one-dimensional dogmatism.

Law uninformed by a prophetic spirit becomes rote, self-serving, a means that becomes a dead end. A prophetic spirit unrelated to a structure of law becomes an unsubstantiated abstraction, an easy prey to irresponsible subjectivism. The indivisible polarity of law and prophecy that intuitively points to a holistic theology is characteristic of other inseparable polarities in early rabbinic thought—for example, learning and deed, this world and the World to Come, omniscience and freedom of will, particularism and universalism, God's justice and compassion, and, in our context, divine transcendence and divine immanence. What Morris Raphael Cohen wrote about individual and collective responsibility is true of the polarities of Jewish theology: "In the presence of obvious conflict between the principle of individual responsibility and that of the collective responsibility, the philosopher is tempted to decide for one or the other of these principles. But humanity continues to prefer both and to disregard both whenever necessary. . . . In the face of the complicated situation before us we cannot unqualifiedly accept either . . . nor absolutely deny either."[2]

REFERENCES

1. Gershom Scholem, *Major Trends in Mysticism* (1954), 23.
2. Morris Raphael Cohen, *Reason and Nature* (1931), 393–94.

BIBLIOGRAPHY

Joshua Abelson, *The Immanence of God in Rabbinic Literature* (1969), ch. 14–21.
Nahum N. Glatzer, "The Talmudic Interpretation of Prophecy," in *Review of Religion*, 18 (1946).
Efraim Urbach, "Halakhah ave-Nevuah," in *Tarbiẓ*, 17 (1943).
Efraim Urbach, *The Sages: Their Concepts and Beliefs* (1979).

Hope

תקוה

Charles Elliott Vernoff

H ope as a Judaic spiritual attitude has its basis in the covenant relation between God and Israel. The covenant originates as a reciprocal bond between God and Abraham directed toward the shared goal of producing a people dedicated to the divine service. What binds this original covenant of coresponsibility for the future is the faithful performance of actions—God's faithful leading, Abraham's faithful following. From such demonstrated mutual faithfulness grows the human disposition of simple and open trust (emunah) in God that seals the covenantal bond. This primordial condition of the covenant was bound to be disrupted, however, by virtue of the fundamental inequality of its two parties: God's transcendent knowledge would at some point require divine action beyond the comprehension of human wisdom. Such action would necessarily jeopardize covenant mutuality in seeming to violate the perceived faithfulness of divine responses in human situations. Human infidelities would eventually also threaten trust. Confronted with cognitive limitation by transcendence, first marked by the binding of Isaac, direct covenant trust accordingly had to extend itself toward deeper underpinnings in the reciprocal spiritual dispositions of faith *(bittaḥon)* and hope *(tik-vah)*. Only in relation to faith, therefore, may hope be understood.

Reciprocity constitutes a core principle of covenant itself: the fundamental biblical and Judaic notion that humanity is a partner with God in responsibility for completing the creation. Humanly initiated actions are indispensable contributions, along with divine initiatives, to redeeming the world. Humans must therefore maintain their own active intentionality toward redemption, alongside of and coordinated with the divine intent. From this autonomous covenantal dignity of human beings within Judaism derive the coefficient attitudes of faith and hope. Each is an expectant volition toward a cognitively obscure future, but whereas faith indirectly affirms transcendent divine intentionality, hope directly exercises mundane human intentionality. Faith is transrational and abstract, hope rational and concrete. Faith is the conviction, rooted in primal trust, that God remains actively intent upon bringing the redemption or some redeeming good despite any appearances to the contrary, and thus embodies an indirect volition toward that future goal. Hope, on the other hand, is a self-concerned, direct, and often specific volition toward a redeeming good, engendered by humans out of their pressing concrete needs. The two complement each other in balanced tension.

Faith holds fast to its conviction, regardless of how irrational circumstances become and how difficult it is to imagine their ultimate divine integration. Hope deepens in urgency through rational assessment of the extent of an immediate human problem, such as the suffering arising from Babylonian conquest and exile. Faith awaits some unanticipatable divine initiative toward long-range solution of mundane discord, which present difficulties may epitomize. Hope may expressly anticipate some divinely granted opportunity that human initiative might actively seize to help provide a short-range contribution to that objective. Thus faith asserts, "I am confident God will eventually deliver us, according to his unknowable plan." Hope contrapuntally declares, "I fervently wish God might deliver us soon, possibly through means of our own acts under propitious circumstances that we should be knowingly alert to discern." In the hour of his testing, at the binding of Isaac, Abraham gave birth to faith by affirming, in effect, "I believe with perfect faith that God will fulfill his promise to me." He likewise, no doubt, gave birth to hope with the thought, "Yet I hope with endless yearning that the fulfillment's preparation does not require me to harm Isaac."

Faith and hope support one another, in keeping with the covenant's dialectical correlation of divine and human initiatives. Faith inclines toward patient and passive waiting, hope toward urgent and active expectancy. Faith abides in the awareness that only God's act is decisive; hope recognizes that humans, too, must act responsibly with God's help to afford God the raw materials for him to dispose providentially. When faith and hope are in proper balance, they mutually sustain trust—a reliance on God that at the same time acknowledges human responsibility ever to initiate constructive action. Such trust finds quintessential expression in true prayer, through which humans take active initiative in petitioning God to redeem them in their patient waiting for him.

But faith and hope may lose their reciprocal equilibrium. Either, excluded from the counterbalancing influence of the other, may be carried to excess and so court disaster. Faith when improperly absolutized may degenerate to passive waiting for the divine initiative, neglecting human covenant responsibility to protect life through any available direct means. Hope when overly zealous can generate impetuous and ill-advised action apart from any consideration of divine providential intent, thus relying entirely on human initiative in disregard of divine covenant coresponsibility for the historical future. In their excess of faith, many Jews in Hitler's European Diaspora may have waited too long before attempting to leave; in their bold excess of hope, many Jews in the Diaspora of Rabbi Akiva's day prematurely flocked to a messianic banner raised by Bar Kokhba. As these examples make clear, faith must never "lose hope" and hope must always be "hope in the Lord," as implied by the root *yaḥal* (waiting with hope).

Hope, such as the hope for rescue from particular dire circumstances, outer or inner, thus depends squarely upon faith that God generally intends to redeem his faithful from their troubles. Only hope that looks in secure faith toward the Lord of history can therefore be real and valid hope. On the other hand, faith devoid of living hope for God's concrete help in particular circumstances must shrivel to an empty, sterile, and even covertly cynical gesture. Therefore true faith depends reciprocally on hope. It is precisely because the two are so inextricably interdependent that they become so easily confused. Their common and sustaining ground is a full acceptance of reality as envisioned by Judaism: God and humanity, each bearing genuine responsibility, interacting through particular events to advance the concrete world wherein they meet toward the general goal of complete eschatological harmony. In that advance, all is foreseen by God, yet to humans responsible free will is granted; but the movements of human freedom are precisely what God foresees and incorporates into his teleological design of redemption. Thus faith, embracing divine forevision, avows, "Thy will shall be accomplished," while hope, enacting humanity's mandated freedom, ventures, "May this be thy will." And only these together delineate the path of the one who trusts the Lord in all his ways.

Trust was originally occasioned by simple perception of God's faithfulness to perform covenanted actions. Faith and hope in turn arose out of a biblical need to unearth the groundwork of trust when events nearly failed to meet covenant expectations. When postbiblical occurrences demolished covenant expectations completely, faith and hope themselves had to be extended to their bedrock foundations in order to survive. With the total breakdown of any apparent correspondence between divine commitments and actions, God's faithfulness itself was inescapably at issue. This crisis, anticipated in the Book of Job, was fully precipitated by the Roman destruction of the Second Commonwealth. At just that time, the people of Israel seemed finally to have learned, by dint of much suffering, how to maintain the basic faithfulness in action that constituted its side of the covenant. For an indeterminate number of Jews, the calamitous and unintelligible divine response, which spared not even the Temple, therefore proved beyond endurance: "Since the Temple was destroyed, men of faith have ceased" (M. Sot. 9:12). Their faith having turned to bitterness and hope to despair, disillusioned Jews sometimes rejected outright Judaism's God of faithful historical action in favor of accepting a degree of dualism between God and the historical world—whether moderate, through Christianity, or radical, in the form of Gnosticism.

Although trust was rooted in an apprehension of God's faithfulness to shape historical events according to his promise, it could therefore now be salvaged—paradoxically—only through insulation from the impact of a history that had collapsed into total unintelligibility. The bedrock of faith and hope upon which trust rests would have to be located beyond history itself. If divine faithfulness could no longer be confirmed through God's perceived historical actions, it could yet be glimpsed through God's teaching word. Thus Torah became the sole arena within which postbiblical Judaism could seek grounding for continued trust in the God of its biblical fathers. Accordingly, the effort of faith to affirm causal order in history shifted to the quest for logical order in Torah. Israel, after all, had long ago been warned of history's mysterious opacity even as it had been encouraged to search out the mysteries of Torah. If the Torah has a perfectly logical inner order that study might search out, it must be of divine origin; if of divine origin, its historical promises must hold good even if their unfolding has proved humanly incomprehensible. On the other hand, if the teachings of the Torah could yet be humanly enacted to produce pockets of sacred order within a still often chaotic world, rational hope existed that divine authority might one day be extended throughout concrete reality.

In its rabbinic transformation, Judaism thus severed its attachment to historical immediacy in order to maintain a continuity of biblical faithfulness to historical ultimacy. The immovable bedrock of faith was discovered in learning Torah, an ongoing search for and contemplation of reality's divine logical order. The unshakable foundation for hope appeared in the doing of Torah, which ever confirms the possibility of human initiative operating under divine mandate to shape concrete reality toward God's eschatological design. As this preserving of faith allowed Judaism to endure the supreme historical trial of the Holocaust, so the root of hope maintained down the centuries through committal action has once again sent up a direct, historically dynamic shoot that, since the Holocaust, continues more than any reality in contemporary Judaism to embody and preserve the hope of Israel.

BIBLIOGRAPHY

Eliezer Berkovits, *Faith After the Holocaust* (1973).
Martin Buber, *Two Types of Faith* (1961).
Abraham Joshua Heschel, *Israel: An Echo of Eternity* (1969).

Humanism

הומניזם

Ernst Akiva Simon

Religious humanism comprises the boundless fullness of human life; as such, it is grounded in the freedom of man. Furthermore, like its secular analogue, religious humanism seeks to cultivate interhuman relations in the spirit of tolerance among individuals as well as between nations. Yet as religious humanism it judges the fullness of human life and deeds by the supreme criteria of moral good and evil, right and wrong, truth and falsehood. Finally, religious humanism establishes man's freedom on the rock of his peculiar dignity in being created in the image of God.

This doctrine may be elucidated with illustrations from the varied sources of traditional Judaism, including not only the Bible, which has become the common book of mankind, but also the oral tradition of legend, law, midrashic tales, and talmudic folklore, all of which have remained specifically Jewish. Central to all these strands of Jewish tradition is the concept of *imago Dei*. This ancient concept admits of two interpretations, one in the direction of man toward God, the other in the opposite direction, from God to man. The former was and remains the basis of all paganism from antiquity to our own times. Its essence was first formulated by the Hellenistic philosopher Euhemerus of Messene, who in the third century B.C.E. suggested that man created his god in his own image. The modern way of suspecting ideas as ideologies by regarding every idea as the mere reflection of either warring instincts or the forces of production is nothing but Euhemerism. This does not diminish the value of the necessary and useful labor devoted to the critical task of unmasking special intellectual or economic forces that appear in the camouflage of ideological superstructures. With the peculiar *horror vacui* of the human soul, Euhemerism in its modern form often leads to an undesirable result. Man, thus cut off from absolute values, cannot endure such a vacuum, which he fills with new, vital air by turning relative values, such as state, soil, labor, or race, into absolute ones. These values are legitimate within their sphere, but their elevation to absolute height as deified idols annihilates them. Once raised to power they are bound to make man, who exalted them, their first victim. In this plight man seeks a last refuge in his own idolized image.

Such thoughts are simply and convincingly expressed in a talmudic legend. According to the Bible, Abraham was the father of the faithful, the first man who knew the one and only God. His father, Terah, is described by Jewish tradition as a dealer in idols. Once, we are told (Gen. R 38:13), being prevented from looking after his shop, he put his son Abraham in charge. There entered an old woman who demanded an idol in the shape of an old woman, a lame man who asked for a lame idol, a hunchback who would be content with nothing but a hunchback, and so forth. Thus, Abraham realized that man had created the idols in his own image. He seized a stick, smashed all the rest of his wares, left the shop in a hurry, and began to worship the formless God, who had, paradoxically, created man in his invisible image. The very absence of shape, form, and utterable name renders possible the creation in his image not of the individual but of Adam, the prototype of mankind. In this way the absence of pictorial representation, figures, and names comprises all the myriad human pictures, figures, and names. This is the fundamental position of religious humanism in contradistinction to the modern worship of man's own mirrored image. Thus, the patriarch Jacob fails to wrest from the angel the divine name; instead, his own name undergoes a theomorphic change: he is henceforth called Israel, which signifies "He who fought with God."

Beholden to the image of God, man now realizes that his fullness as a human being recurrently requires a call for moral decision. Religious humanism acknowledges and underscores this call as absolute and unequivocal, and herein distinguishes itself from all other variants of humanism. In a somewhat dialectical fashion, the distinctiveness of religious humanism may be illustrated by a famous example from the classical tradition: The small Aegean island of Melos, as Thucydides reports in his *History of the Peloponnesian War* (V, 84–117), was engaged in a war for the defense of its freedom against the superior forces of Athens. According to the great Greek historian, Melos was first politically terrorized, then defeated in battle, and finally most cruelly punished. In his account of these events, Thucydides reveals a model of ancient *Realpolitik,* indeed, of a cynical Greek Machiavellianism. To the dismay of some contemporary readers, Thucydides does not utter a single word of disapproval. The philo-Hellenic humanist will, however, find fault not with Thucydides, but rather with those who would take exception to so callous a report, branding them philistines and unhistorical sentimentalists.

The religious humanist is prepared to face such a reproach. He is supported by his conviction that man has always been God's creature, even at the time when the Olympians still held unchallenged sway. The suffering of tiny Melos will move him, and its fate, always returning and constantly suffered afresh, will take away something from the aesthetic joy felt over Thucydides' superb language. Although his humanism includes aesthetic values, he does not subscribe to their absolute significance. When the Emperor Nero set fire to Rome, the burning city doubtless offered a gorgeous spectacle. Still, having to choose between the aesthetic and the ethical values, the religious humanist invariably decides against the former and in favor of the latter, and he knows only too well that at times such a decision must be made. He also realizes that this need for a decision may imply his renunciation of aesthetic values, so that he may lose in fullness what he gains in moral integrity.

This is the meaning of the call for decision that the religious humanist affirms. Closely linked with this call is the demand for wholeness. This means, as Martin Buber has indefatigably pointed out, that religion is not a reservation; it is no festive room set aside for the life of the soul, but rather it either pervades all of life or is not existent at all.

The separation between action and contemplation may sometimes be a moral act, but it can never be religious. Only nonreligious humanism is able to separate neatly the sphere of action from that of contemplation, politics from poetry, work from leisure. Religious humanism is forbidden to do so.

Man's life comprises relationships among individuals and groups. The legal treatise dealing with the ritual to be observed on the most solemn day of the Jewish year states in its conclusion: "The Day of Atonement expiates the sins of man committed by man against God. It does not expiate the wrongs committed by man against his fellow man, unless the pardon of the injured party has been obtained first" (M. Yoma 8:9). This applies to the relationship among individuals. Neither does the Day of Atonement overlook the relationship between groups, and it appeals to the principle of toleration that characterizes religious humanism.

This principle is different, however, from the enlightened toleration promulgated in the eighteenth century by Gotthold Ephraim Lessing. In Lessing's *Nathan the Wise,* the three rings representing the three monotheistic religions are exchangeable and equal, because the genuine ring is assumed to be lost. No such weak though noble attitude toward faith can rouse the enthusiasm of the members of a living religion for the idea of toleration. A living religion esteems as worthy of comparison not the substitutes for truth but rather the different paths leading toward the real truth. In the synagogues on the eve of the Day of Atonement the philosophical poem "The Kingly Crown" *(Keter Malkhut)* by the poet-philosopher Solomon ibn Gabirol is recited. The long hymn reads in its opening part: "Thou art the God of gods. All creatures are Thine witnesses . . . and Thine honor is not diminished by the worshipers of other gods, for it is the intention of all to reach Thee."

To toleration, freedom must be added. The two are interdependent. It is written in Exodus:

> When you acquire a Hebrew slave, he shall serve six years; in the seventh year he shall go free, without payment. . . . But if the slave declares, "I love my master, and my wife and children. I do not wish to go free," his master shall take him before God. He shall be brought to the door or the doorpost, and his master shall pierce his ear with an awl; and he shall then remain his slave for life.
>
> (Ex. 21:2–6)

An ancient sage raised the question why, of all the body's members, the ear was selected to bear the sign of permanent bondage that alone establishes full slavery. The answer runs: "The ear which has heard at the foot of Mount Sinai the words: 'For the children of Israel are mine servants and not the servants of servants' [Lev. 25:25]. But he went and took upon himself another Lord. His ear shall be pierced with an awl" (BT Kid. 22b).

This is the dilemma of human freedom within the philosophy of believing humanism, a term ultimately preferable to *religious humanism.* Man is confronted with the free choices of being either the servant of God and truly free, or the servant of man and a slave. This option of freely choosing to serve God constitutes the peculiar source of human dignity.

However, man's dignity, too, is faced with its own dilemma. Man may destroy it, for instance, through his own failings, which may make him liable even to suffering the penalty of death. But then, his execution not only deprives him of his own life. It also imperils the dignity of his executioner's soul—one of the strongest arguments against capital punishment. The Talmud, at any rate, hints at this contradiction in its comment on the prohibition pronounced in Deuteronomy (21:22–23):

> If a man have committed a sin worthy of death and he be to be put to death, and thou hang him on a tree, his body shall not remain all night on a tree, but thou shalt in any wise bury him that day; for he that is hanged is a curse to God.

Rabbi Meir elucidates that passage by a parable (BT Sanh. 41b):

> Once upon a time there lived in a city a pair of twin brothers. One was made king, the other became a highwayman. So the king ordered his execution. The passers-by who saw him hang would thereupon exclaim: "Here hangs the king!" and so the king gave order to take him down.

Man who is created in the image of God takes away from God's dignity by losing his own. This leads believing humanism to the notion of the fundamental equality of all men, hence to the conception of peace as the highest and final goal. An old Jewish tradition says (M. Sanh. 4:5):

> Man [Adam] was created an individual in order to teach that when a person destroys one single soul, the Scripture considers him as having destroyed an entire world; yet when a person saves a single soul, the Scripture considers him as having saved an entire world. A further reason is the promotion of peace among men, lest a man say to his neighbor: "My ancestor is greater than yours"; . . . finally, in order to testify to the glory of God, for when man impresses several coins with the same stamp, the coins turn out all alike; the King of Kings, however, the Holy One whose name be blessed, impresses each man with the stamp of the first and yet they all turn out different. Hence, each man ought to say: "For my sake the world has been created!"

Thus, the idea of man as created in the image of God, of unique individuality, of freedom and dignity, links up with the idea of peace and of man's responsibility for the world. As the Talmud has it: "Man should always regard himself as if his amount of sins neatly balanced his amount of merits. Blessed is he who has observed a commandment, for he has thereby tipped the scale of his merits; woe to him if he has committed a sin, for thereby he has tipped the scale of his sins." Thereupon Rabbi Eleazar, son of Rabbi

Simon, comments: "The world is judged by its majority and so is the individual. Blessed is he who has observed a commandment, for he has tipped the scale of merits in his *and* in the world's favor; woe to him if he has sinned, for he has tipped the scale of sins to his *and* [Eleazar's emphases] the world's detriment" (BT Kid. 40b).

According to this pedagogic conception, it is the individual who decides whether the verdict pronounced about the world is to be "It is damned" or "It is saved," for his decision may be made at a critical moment in the trial of the world and thereby affect its whole course.

With religious humanism, where it stresses action and cooperation of man with God, as in the case of Judaism, human deeds are not, as Goethe in *Iphigenie* would have it, the "manly daring" of one's autonomous nature, but rather the fulfillment of duties imposed by God. And the helping "arms of the gods" are not, as Goethe also avers, implicitly "invoked" by human deeds. Rather, man stretches his hands out toward God, whose decisions are ultimately free, though he may hope that God's grace will not reject his endeavor.

BIBLIOGRAPHY

Samuel Hugo Bergman, "The Humanism of the Covenant," in *The Quality of Faith: Essays on Judaism and Morality* (1970).
Martin Buber, "Hebrew Humanism," in *Israel and the World* (1963).
Martin Buber, "Biblical Humanism," in *On the Bible* (1980).

Humility

עֲנָוָה

Bernard Steinberg

To contemporary ears, the term *humility* strikes a discordant note. To minds shaped by the writings of Karl Marx, Sigmund Freud, or Friedrich Schleiermacher, humility connotes social paralysis, infantile dependency, and obsequious obedience. Educated within a tradition of humanist, liberal thought, the modern Jew may regard humility as a threat to some of his most cherished values: the dignity of man, freedom, and human efficacy. Many Jews, sensitive to psychological nuance, share Friedrich Nietzsche's view that the Christian ethos of the humble is but an insidious ruse of the weak-minded to gain power, a symptom of *ressentiment*. During moments of apologetic polemic, the modern Jew may even brand humility a specifically "Christian virtue," an alien and alienating relic not to be mistaken for an authentic life-enhancing Jewish value. Humility, it is argued, is the logical offspring of a Christian faith that, defined by *agape* (unmerited love), presupposes human depravity, engenders psychological passivity, and implies social quietism. Judaism, on the other hand, is imbued with an ethical activism demanded by a conception of *din* (justice/law), assumes human adequacy, and entails responsible action in the world. Apologetics aside, however, the fact remains that the concept of humility contains a worldview, an ethos of interpersonal relations, and a psychology, profoundly Jewish, that may prove seminal for contemporary religious thought.

The focus of our discussion will be an analysis of Moses Maimonides' examination of humility. Maimonides can serve as a useful paradigm, not only because of his preeminent position in Jewish thought as philosopher and halakhist, but also in a more specific sense: in Maimonides' teachings the virtue of humility becomes a touchstone of Jewish faith; humility becomes precisely that virtue which unites theological worldview and ethical action and, at the same time, distinguishes Judaism from Aristotelian thought. Humility becomes then a Jewish teaching par excellence. In this vein, the Maimonidean formulation enters modern Jewish thought through the writings of Nachman Krochmal and Hermann Cohen and emerges in our own century as a central theme in the writings of Joseph B. Soloveitchik, Franz Rosenzweig, Martin Buber, and Abraham Joshua Heschel. Despite revolutionary changes in the intellectual climate, the motif of humility serves as a thread of continuity, however slender, from the Bible to the present.

Humility is at once both a halakhic prescription (norm of behavior) and an anthropological description of the religious personality. Maimonides codifies the norm of humility in *Hilkhot Deot,* which appears in the *Book of Knowledge* of the *Mishneh Torah.* The first two chapters of *Hilkhot Deot* are based upon Aristotle's *Nicomachean Ethics* and hence formulate ethical norms in terms of the doctrine of the "middle path," the mean between extremes of behavior. In Maimonides' formulation, however, the virtue of humility constitutes an exception to the rule of the mean: "There are some traits to which it is forbidden merely to keep to the middle path. They should be shunned to the extreme. Such a disposition is pride. It is not enough that a man be simply modest: He should be utterly humble and unassuming. It is therefore written, concerning Moses, 'very modest' [Num. 12:3] and not just 'modest'. For this reason do the Rabbis of Blessed Memory advise 'Be very, very humble'" (MT Hil. Deot 2:3).

Two points must be emphasized in this unusual formulation. First, the exception of humility is a normative principle, as opposed to a therapeutic technique. In other contexts, Maimonides (and Aristotle) counsel extreme behavior in order to compensate for and to cure temperamental deficiencies. For example, the sexually indulgent are counseled to adopt an ascetic regimen and to abstain from sexual relations in order to curb sexual appetite and to introduce harmony within an imbalanced personality. Nevertheless, asceticism and sexual abstinence are not considered the ethical norm, but rather are considered necessary and temporary correctives. In the case of humility, however, the norm itself is extreme.

Second, the norm of humility is absolute. Commenting on the Mishnaic dictum, "Be exceedingly humble" (Pirkei Avot 4:4), Maimonides rejects the opinion of the talmudic sage Rava, who posits an extreme norm, and upholds the view of Rabbi Naḥman bar Yiẓḥak, who posits an absolute standard. In other words, the norm of humility differs in quality, not quantity, from the scale of the mean. This difference of kind hinges on the epistemological basis, the very rational ground, of the respective normative standards. The doctrine of the mean according to Aristotle is based on a description of those people known to be "big-souled." The mean is, in other words, a standard of social convention. Given this standard, Aristotle rules out the virtue of humility. For the "big-souled person" is, objectively speaking (that is, relative to other men), superior. Humility would therefore signal false modesty and would be—in Aristotle's words—"small-minded" and "slavish" (Nichomachean Ethics, Book 4:3). The standard of objectivity is social. It is this standard per se that Maimonides rejects.

To Maimonides, man does not measure himself against other men, but perceives himself in relation to God. Humility does not signify a neurotic self-image or a distortion of self-worth, but a quest for truthful self-knowledge. And the source of such self-knowledge is God. As codified in Hilkhot Deot, the norm of humility is an instance of the task of imitatio Dei. In turn, imitatio Dei presupposes a certain, indeed a seminal, religious consciousness, which is the subject of Hilkhot Yesodei ha-Torah, the preceding section of the Book of Knowledge: love and fear of God, which constitute the theological foundations of Maimonides' system. God's ways, the model of ethical activity, are known through contemplation of the world order: "How does one love and fear Him? When man inquires into His miraculous and wondrous deeds and creations and sees in them God's infinite and inestimable wisdom, then he will immediately love, praise, exalt and desire to know the Great God as David writes in 'My soul thirsts for the living God' [Ps. 42:3]. And the more man delves into these things he will immediately become humbled and afraid and realize that he is a lowly negligible creature, with no understanding at all as David writes: 'When I behold Your heavens, the work of Your fingers . . . [I think] what is man that You have been mindful of him?' [Ps. 8: 4–5]" (MT Hil. Yesodei ha-Torah 2:2).

Through contemplation of the natural world order, man loves and fears God. Love and fear of God, however juridically and abstractly formulated, signify states of human consciousness, perceptions of the world and of self.

Put differently, love and fear signal an inner, dynamic activity, a lifelong process of self-discovery.

By locating himself in the cosmic context of creation—the matrix of contemplation—man discovers his human identity in relation to God. Simply put, in the quest for the creator man discovers himself as creature. Such creature-consciousness becomes the source and substance of humility: through love of God, the creature senses his very life as gift. Creation implies a free act of God; the world and human existence did not have to be. Hence man regards the world as an expression of *ḥesed,* an outpouring of divine love. Aroused by this wondrous disclosure, the creature yearns, passionately and unceasingly, for the creator. In this sense, love becomes an expansive, outward movement of the self to embrace the world and the infinite source of its existence.

Yet the expansive dynamic of love toward the infinite entails the delimiting reflex of fear. In his very drive toward the creator, the creature exhausts his intellectual and emotional resources, and thereby discovers his spiritual borders, the outer limit of his selfhood. He is thrust backward reflexively into himself and discovers that, in spite of an infinite longing, he is but a finite creature. He thereby confronts the awful abyss that separates creature and creator. Paradoxically, the very awareness of the unbridgeable gap becomes the link between man and God. God enables man to know, ever more profoundly, that he cannot know God. The consciousness of love and fear is thus dialectic, and the source of man's humble self-knowledge. Man is humble, not in the eyes of other men, but in the presence of God.

If the norm of humility presupposes a religious weltanschauung, such a worldview finds expression in interpersonal terms. In other words, the theology of humility entails an ethic of humility. Moreover, this ethic is not one of rules *(din)* but of spontaneous self-expression *(lifnim mishurat ha-din).* The ethic of humility therefore presupposes not only a worldview, but a certain psychology; humility points not to a set of fixed prescriptions, but to a description of a humble personality.

To Maimonides, the consciousness of *ḥesed*—the recognition that life is a wondrous gift—once internalized, may subsequently be translated into actions of human love. Hence emerges the religious personality of the *ḥasid* who "graciously accepts his fellow-man," who "absorbs insult but does not insult others," "respects even those who curse him," and in general, whose force of personality "evokes a loving emulation" by the community (MT Hil. Yesodei ha-Torah 5:11). In a psychological sense, the *ḥasid* is able to accept others because he knows and fully accepts himself as creature. For this reason, the *ḥasid* considers his fellow to be related in a definitive sense:

Both he and his fellow are the mutual recipients of the gift of life and both stand together, in awe and trembling, on the far side of the abyss that divides the creature from the creator. Fellow creatures are thus united in an essential way. In the cosmic context, differences of biological strength, social stature, economic power, and cultural achievement are reduced to secondary importance. These differences are marginal to the authentic center of human identity. Moreover, aware of the essential limitation of his finitude, the hasid knows, objectively speaking, that he is no more worthy than his neighbor. The standard of objectivity is not social convention but relation to God.

Maimonides' concept of humility thus synthesizes the realms of theology, ethics, and psychology into an organic whole. Although the medieval discourse of rational metaphysics has long been discarded in Jewish thought, modern Jewish thinkers, whether in the language of idealism (Nachman Krochmal and Hermann Cohen) or existentialism (Franz Rosenzweig, Martin Buber, Joseph Soloveitchik), struggle to give expression to a root biblical awareness: "He has told you, O man, what is good, and what the Lord requires of you: only to do justice and to love goodness [hesed] and to walk humbly with your God" (Micah 6:8). Humility is clearly a sine qua non of Jewish religiosity, of trust in God's world and of faith in man's capacity for just dealings and loving-kindness.

BIBLIOGRAPHY

Hermann Cohen, *Religion of Reason* (1972), ch. 18.
Emil Fackenheim, *Encounters Between Judaism and Modern Philosophy* (1973), ch. 2.
Franz Rosenzweig, *The Star of Redemption* (1970), pt. 2, bk. 2, "Revelation, or the Ever-Renewed Birth of the Soul."
Joseph B. Soloveitchik, "The Lonely Man of Faith," in *Tradition* 7:2 (1965).
Joseph B. Soloveitchik, "Majesty and Humility," in *Tradition* 17:2 (1978).

I and Thou

אני ואתה

Maurice Friedman

I *and Thou* is the title of the English translation of Martin Buber's
classic religio-philosophical work *Ich und Du*. It is also a
pointer to that relationship of openness, presentness, immediacy, and mutuality that Martin Buber called the "I-Thou relationship"
(Ich-Du Beziehung) as opposed to the "I-It relation" *(Ich-Es Verhältnis)*.

I and Thou is already present in the friendship of David and Jonathan
and in the Song of Songs: "Set me for a seal upon thy heart, for love is
stronger than death" (8:6), as well as in the eighth and ninth books of Aristotle's *Nicomachean Ethics,* in which true friendship is seen as existing simply for the sake of the friend and not for the benefits one can derive from
the friend. As Buber remarked, in all ages the centrality of this relationship
to the individual human being has undoubtedly been glimpsed. In his "History of the Dialogical Principle" Buber points to such glimpses by the eighteenth-century German philosophers Friedrich Heinrich Jacobi and Johann
Gottlieb Fichte. It is the German philosopher Ludwig Feuerbach, however,
who first laid a broad philosophical groundwork for I and Thou, in the mid-
nineteenth century. Attacking the idealist philosophy of his predecessors

with its postulate of the identity of thinking and being, Feuerbach points to "the mystery of the need of the I for the Thou," which makes the union between man and man "the supreme and ultimate principle of philosophy." "The individual human being by himself does not contain the essence of man within himself, either as a moral or as a thinking being." This essence is found only in the unity of man with his fellow man, a unity that "rests only on the reality of the distinctness of I and Thou."[1] Buber criticizes Feuerbach because, instead of concluding that the unity of I and Thou is man in the true sense, Feuerbach oversteps this anthropological insight in the direction of "a pseudo-mystical construction" that substitutes an anthropological ersatz God for the transcendent God that Feuerbach renounces: "Man for himself is man (in the usual sense)—man with man— the unity of I and Thou is God."[2] The nineteenth-century Danish theologian Søren Kierkegaard, in contrast, preserves the transcendence of the divine Thou while making the I-Thou relation between person and person secondary and derivative. The "knight of faith" is God's friend and says Thou to God, Kierkegaard declares in *Fear and Trembling,* while warning in *Point of View* that one must be chary of having to do with one's neighbor. "The human Thou in Kierkegaard's existential thought is never transparent into the divine, the bounded never into the boundless."[3] The American philosopher-psychologist William James also touches on the theme of the divine Thou.

The neo-Kantian German philosopher Hermann Cohen takes up I and Thou in his *The Religion of Reason Out of the Sources of Judaism,* written toward the end of World War I and published posthumously in 1919. Cohen pointed toward the double I-Thou of man and man and man and God that was to be the foundation of all Martin Buber's work. However, Cohen neither discovered the Thou nor influenced Buber's *I and Thou.* Buber, unlike Cohen, does not content himself with correlating the dialogue between man and man and that between man and God in such fashion that one precedes or follows the other. For Buber, we can meet the eternal Thou, the eternally Thou, in the meeting with every concrete, unique, finite Thou, and above all that found in genuine interhuman dialogue.

In his philosophical masterpiece *The Star of Redemption* Franz Rosenzweig goes decisively beyond Cohen's correlation in the understanding of the Thou as a spoken one, fired by the solid concreteness of the philosophy of speech. Buber singles out as Rosenzweig's most significant theological contribution to I and Thou the link between God's call to Adam, "Where art Thou?" and the existence of "an independent Thou, freely standing over against the hiding God, a Thou to whom he can reveal himself as I." God calls us by name and thus shows himself "as the originator and opener of this whole dialogue between him and the soul."[4]

The Austrian Catholic school teacher Ferdinand Ebner also deserves mention here. Ebner sees the solitude of the I as resulting from its closedness to the Thou. The overcoming of this solitude, for him, was essentially the I-Thou relationship to God: "In the last ground of our spiritual life God is the true Thou of the true I in man. Man's I 'concretizes' itself in his relation to God." Like Rosenzweig, Ebner holds that God created man in speaking to him. Man was not the "first" person but the "second": "the first was and is God." At the same time Ebner speaks of the grace of God as "the trust of the I in the Thou that comes to meet it."[5] It is the personal relation to God that prevents God from being a mere ideal. Unable himself to find the Thou in man, Ebner is in the end, in Buber's words, "acosmic" and "ananthropic": "Where it is a question of the authenticity of existence, every other Thou disappears for him before that of God."[6]

In *I and Thou* Buber gave the I-Thou relation its classical form. Buber clarified the difference between the I-Thou and I-It relations and worked out the implications of this distinction in a thoroughgoing fashion. "As I become I, I say Thou." The "I" of man comes into being in the act of speaking one or the other of the two primary words—Thou or It. "The primary word I-Thou can only be spoken with the whole being. The primary word I-It can never be spoken with the whole being."[7] The real determinant of the primary word in which a person takes his stand is not the object that is over against him but the way in which he relates himself to that object. I-Thou, the primary word of relation and togetherness, is characterized by mutuality, directness, presentness, intensity, and ineffability. I-It, the primary word of experiencing and using, takes place within a person and not between him and the world. Whether in knowing, feeling, or acting, it is the typical subject-object relation.

To Buber, I-Thou and I-It alternate with each other in integral relation. The Thou must continually become It, and the It may again become a Thou; but it will not be able to remain one, and it need not become Thou at all. Man can live continuously and securely in the world of It, but he can only actualize his humanity if he interpenetrates this world with the relation to the Thou. Real communication, likewise, is a fruitful alternation between I-Thou and I-It. The word may be identified with subject-object, or I-It, knowledge while it remains indirect and symbolic, but it is itself the channel and expression of the direct and reciprocal knowing of I-Thou when it is taken up into real dialogue. This applies equally to the religious word and the religious symbol, which may point us back to a dialogue between us and

God when taken up into real meeting, but may obstruct that dialogue when taken as a reality in itself.

The presence of the Thou, according to Buber, moves over the world of It like the spirit upon the face of the waters. This does not imply any dualism between spiritual ideal and material reality, but rather the continuing task of drawing the line of demarcation according to the uniqueness of each concrete situation. What matters is that the spirit that says Thou, that responds, is bound to life and reality and not made into an independent realm. The spirit is effective in life only in relation to the world, permeating and transforming the world of It into Thou. I and Thou is not a teaching of compromise but of spiritual realism: it is the concrete question of what is possible and desirable at this moment and in this situation.

In *I and Thou* Buber speaks of the eternal Thou, which is reached through the finite Thous of nature, one's fellow man, and art. The eternal Thou is not just another up-to-date way of reintroducing the God of the philosopher and the theologians—the God whose existence could be proved and whose nature and attributes could be described as he is in himself apart from our relation to him. It is the reality of the "between," of the meeting itself; there and nowhere else does Buber find the unconditional, which no fathoming of the self or soaring into metaphysical heights could reveal. For this reason, what matters is not a creed or belief but one's life-stance.

Buber's concept of God as the eternal Thou who cannot become It has redirected the approach to philosophy of religion from the objective—concern with questions as to the existence and nature of God—and the subjective—questions as to the pragmatic effects and psychological or emotional accompaniment of religious belief—to the dialogical—the relation between man and God. Man knows God in relation and only in relation. The true God can never be an object of our thought, not even the Absolute object from which all others derive. God, to Buber, is "the Being that is directly, most nearly, and lastingly over against us, that may properly only be addressed, not expressed."[8] The eternal Thou is not a symbol of God but of our relation with God. God is not a person, but he becomes one in order to know and be known, to love and be loved by man. Man cannot discover God through philosophical speculation, but he can meet the eternal Thou in his direct, reciprocal meeting with man and nature. Man becomes aware of the address of God in every meeting with the concrete and the everyday, if he remains open to that address and ready to respond with his whole being. God is always present, says Buber. It is only we who are absent. Evil for Buber is not I-It, accordingly, but the predominance of the I-It relation that prevents the turning to the Thou. Good is not pure I-Thou, but the permeation of the world of It by the I-Thou relationship.

Rosenzweig criticized *I and Thou* because he felt it did not do justice to the It, a criticism that has been underscored by scholars such as Rivka Horwitz and Bernhard Casper as well as by Ernst Simon, a disciple of both Buber and Rosenzweig. Comparing Buber's and Rosenzweig's philosophy of dialogue, Horwitz quite rightly says that Rosenzweig's philosophy begins with "a leap of faith," a biblical faith without which one cannot philosophize on Rosenzweig's terms. Buber, in contrast, places philosophical anthropology and not theology at the center of his philosophy. Critics like Horwitz and Casper, who imagine some mythically pure I-Thou unmixed with It. end by seeing Buber as an idealist philosopher or even a Platonist who denies God's direct relation to nature. Buber's It, however, is not nature, but rather man's concepts and categories about nature. Buber's I-It relation is identical with Kant's approach to knowledge. But his I-Thou relationship breaks through all philosophical idealism to the impact of an otherness that can never be incorporated into the It.

Because Rosenzweig uses dialogue as speech only, as opposed to the address of all things, as Buber uses it, he has no actual place for the I-Thou relationship with nature. Therefore the It that he defends as prephilosophical, the It that can be spoken with the whole being, is actually Buber's Thou with nature, the directly comprehended, related to, concrete unique, though seen theologically through the eyes of God (He-It) rather than man. Rosenzweig starts with a theological presupposition that enables him to speak of God's relation to creation as if from God's point of view. Buber starts with the existentially given I-Thou relationship from which the I-It relation necessarily comes, because of the abstraction involved in our knowledge. Buber does not see either the It or the past as mere deficiency, as Casper claims, and he does not regard speaking about as an evil. This includes even the speaking about God that is necessary, although in this latter case one must recognize that this is a metaphor and can never be other than a metaphor. In the I-Thou relationship the Thou is not a metaphor, not a pronoun that stands for a name. Rather the spoken name takes on its ring of authority precisely through the fact that I know that when you call my name, you really mean me in my uniqueness, are really addressing me as Thou. Thus for Buber the meeting with the Thou, rather than the fact of the name, was the ultimate touchstone of reality, as it could not be for Rosenzweig. The difference here is between an emphasis upon the nature of what one meets—whether it is a person or a thing—and an emphasis on what kind of relation one has to what one meets—I-Thou or I-It. Buber's two primary words do indeed yield a twofold world and a twofold I, but these derive from the relation, rather than the relation deriving from the nature of what is related to.

Largely through the influence of Buber on such key Protestant theologians as Emil Brunner, Karl Barth, Reinhold Niebuhr, H. Richard Niebuhr, Paul Tillich, John MacMurray, John Baillie, Herbert H. Farmer, Friedrich Gogarten, Karl Heim, and J. H. Oldham, the "I-Thou" philosophy has become, in Tillich's words, "a common good of the Protestant world."[9] It has also penetrated deeply into the thought of such Catholic thinkers as Erich Przywara, Ernst Michel, Romano Guardini, Theodore Steinbüchel, and M. C. D'Arcy, as well as (independently of Buber) Ebner and Gabriel Marcel, and into that of the Russian Orthodox existentialist Nicholas Berdyaev. There are many Christian interpretations of the I-Thou philosophy, some of which see Christ as Thou (Gogarten), some as I (Guardini, Barth), some as both (J. E. Fison). Many of the Protestant Neo-Orthodox thinkers and theologians who have adopted the I-Thou philosophy have recast it, in contrast to Buber, in the form of a radical dualism between I-Thou, understood as good, and I-It, understood as evil. Writers like Gogarten, Brunner, and Barth, in varying degrees, equate I-It with man's sinful nature and I-Thou with the grace and divine love that are only present in their purity in Jesus Christ. The consequences of this dualism are often a deemphasis of the possibility and significance of ethical action and an emphasis upon the primacy of grace, the belief that God is always the addresser (I) and man always the addressed (Thou), and a view of ethical choices as between I or Thou.

In contrast to the philosophies of Plato, Aristotle, Kant, and Dewey that have been used to interpret Judaism down through the ages, the I-Thou philosophy may fairly claim to be based on Judaism as well as applied to it. It is no accident that Buber, who more than any others applied the I-Thou philosophy to Judaism, worked to translate the Hebrew Bible into German in such a way as to preserve the original spoken quality of the text. "Do we mean a book?" he asked. "No, we mean the Voice."[10] The "overagainstness" of the I-Thou relationship has meant, from Jeremiah and Job to Levi Yitzhak of Berdichev, Buber, and Elie Wiesel, that there is nothing man may not say to God so long as he remains within the dialogue.

The categories of creation, revelation, and redemption that Rosenzweig placed at the center of his interpretation of Judaism are bound up in the closest fashion with his I-Thou philosophy. The relationship between God and man in revelation is that of the I to the Thou; it is the relation to the person loved by God in his unique and particular existence. In a note on his translation of Judah Halevi's poetry, Rosenzweig wrote: "What matters is that, near or remote, whatever is uttered, is uttered before God with the 'Thou'. . . . that never turns away."[11] The imperative of love never leaves the circle of I and Thou, never becomes a third-personal He, She, or It addressing the individual merely as a part of some totality. Through the love of the next one (Nebenmensch), the love of the I for a Thou, we prepare for the "We" of redemption.[12]

Buber designated as the center of his life work "the one basic insight that has led me not only to the study of the Bible, as to the study of Hasidism, but also to an independent philosophical presentation: that the I-Thou relation to God and the I-Thou relation to one's fellow men are at bottom related to each other."[13] In "The Dialogue between Heaven and Earth" Buber writes: "The basic teaching that fills the Hebrew Bible is that our life is a dialogue between the above and the below. . . . In the infinite language of events and situations, eternally changing, but plain to the truly attentive, transcendence speaks to our hearts at the essential moments of personal life."[14] In the postscript to I and Thou, in strikingly similar language, Buber writes: "Happening upon happening, situation upon situation, are enabled and empowered by the personal speech of God to demand of the human person that he take his stand and make his decision."[15]

Although Abraham Joshua Heschel rarely uses the language of I and Thou, his writings too are filled with the partnership between God and man. Religious consciousness is characterized by ultimate commitment and ultimate reciprocity. The essence of Judaism is the partnership of man and God in unifying the world. Piety, to Heschel, is relation to the divine beyond oneself—a relation of openness, responsiveness, reciprocal giving, the answer to a call.

Although the I-Thou relationship is a common good not only of Judaism and Christianity, but of all human existence and all religions, especially the devotional religions, it is in Judaism and in contemporary Jewish thought that it finds its fullest expression. Here we can see the emphasis on the I-Thou as openness, mutuality, presentness, immediacy. Here we can see the dialogue between God and man in which God places an address and a claim on man, through all the events and happenings of nature and history, but in which also man is the full partner in response to that claim and may say anything to God as long as it remains within the dialogue, including even the lamentations of Jeremiah and the contending of Job, Levi Yitzhak of Berdichev, and Elie Wiesel, the "Job of Auschwitz." Revelation, as Rosenzweig said, never leaves the circle of I and Thou. Prophecy is a partnership of God and man in revelation, and even redemption is a completion of the dialogue between God and man. Because this is a full reciprocity between mortal man and "eternal Thou" it cannot be true in Judaism, as many Christian theologians and even the Jewish theologian Will Herberg have held, that God is always the I and man is always the Thou. There is no original sin in Judaism that abrogates the immediacy between God and man and makes man dependent upon the unmerited grace of God before he is able to say Thou to God. As with God's "Adam, where art Thou?" even guilt is a calling to account that draws man out of the ruptured dialogue with God back into the situation of calling and response. The true meaning of existential trust is not Paul Tillich's "courage to be" rooted in the paradoxical acceptance through the grace of Christ of the human beings who are unacceptable. It is rather "the courage to address and the courage to respond."[16]

REFERENCES

1. Ludwig Feuerbach, "Basic Principles of the Philosophy of the Future," Numbers 59, 60, and 73, tr. Leonie Sachs, in The Worlds of Existentialism: A Critical Reader, ed. Maurice Friedman (1973), 54.
2. Martin Buber, Between Man and Man, tr. Maurice Friedman (1985), 211.
3. Ibid., 212.
4. Ibid., 213.
5. Ferdinand Ebner, "The Word and Spiritual Realities," Maurice Friedman, tr., in The Worlds of Existentialism, ed. Maurice Friedman, 93.
6. Buber, op. cit., 213.
7. Martin Buber, I and Thou, tr. Ronald Gregor Smith (1958), 11 ff.
8. Ibid., 80.
9. Paul Tillich, "Jewish Influences on Contemporary Christian Theology," in Cross Currents II (1952), 38.
10. Martin Buber, Werke, II, Schriften zur Bibel (1964), 869.
11. Franz Rosenzweig: His Life and Thought, ed. Nahum N. Glatzer (1953), 281.
12. Franz Rosenzweig, The Star of Redemption, William W. Hallo, tr., in The Worlds of Existentialism, ed. Maurice Friedman (1973) 328.
13. Philosophical Interrogations, ed. Sydney and Beatrice Rome (1970), Interrogation of Martin Buber, conducted by Maurice Friedman, 99.
14. Martin Buber, On Judaism, ed. Nahum N. Glatzer (1967), 216.
15. Buber, I and Thou, 136ff.
16. Maurice Friedman, Touchstones of Reality: Existential Trust in the Community of Peace (1972), 318–31.

BIBLIOGRAPHY

Martin Buber, *Between Man and Man,* tr. Ronald Gregor Smith with an intro. by Maurice Friedman (1965).

Martin Buber, *I and Thou,* 2d ed., tr. Ronald Gregor Smith, with "Afterword: History of the Dialogical Principle" (1958).

Martin Buber, *On Judaism,* ed. Nahum N. Glatzer (1967).

Maurice Friedman, *Martin Buber and the Eternal* (1986).

Maurice Friedman, *Martin Buber's Life and Work: The Early Years—1878–1923* (1982); *The Middle Years—1923–1945* (1983); *The Later Years—1945–1965* (1984).

Maurice Friedman, *Martin Buber: The Life of Dialogue,* 3d ed. (1976).

Maurice Friedman, *Touchstones of Reality: Existential Trust and the Community of Peace* (1972).

Abraham Joshua Heschel, *Man Is Not Alone: A Philosophy of Religion* (1951).

Abraham Joshua Heschel, *The Prophets* (1962).

Franz Rosenzweig, *The Star of Redemption,* tr. William W. Hallo (1971).

Idolatry

עבודה זרה

Yeshayahu Leibowitz

lthough one who repudiates idolatry may not yet have acknowledged the Torah, in a way he has already done so. While his subjective acknowledgment of the Torah may have still to crystallize, he is regarded by the rabbinic sages as though he had already fully affirmed the God of Israel: "Anyone who repudiates idolatry is viewed as though he had acknowledged the entire Torah" (BT Kid. 40a). Hence, while he has not yet formally become a Jew, in a way he is already worthy of being so designated: "Anyone who repudiates idolatry is called a Jew" (Meg. 13a). This is already implicit in the Ten Commandments, the fundament of Jewish belief. The first verse of the Decalogue— "I am the Lord your God" (Ex. 20:2)—literally concerns the giver of the commandments, but the more far-reaching meaning of the verse is derived from the one that follows: "You shall have no other gods besides Me" (Ex. 20:3). Thus Maimonides, observing that the first positive commandment addressed to the Jew is "I am the Lord your God," explains it on the basis of the first negative commandment, "You shall have no other gods besides Me." Accordingly, he notes that God "cautioned us against believing in any other deity apart from him" (*Sefer ha-Miẓvot*, "*miẓvot lo ta'aseh*," a). The meaning of the "faith" implied here is further clarified as an injunction not to serve any other one "apart from Him" (*Sefer ha-Miẓvot*, "*miẓvot lo ta'aseh*," b).

From one point of view, the simple repudiation of idolatry is the first stage in the fulfillment of the commandment to believe in God. From another, however, it is the final stage, reached by the believer only after he has worked long and hard to purify his faith. Not everyone who sees himself as a believer in the one God is able to achieve this stage. While the word *idolatry* might, on the face of it, seem to refer to the making of "a sculptured image, or any [other] likeness" (Ex. 20:4), that is, to the worship of actual, concrete idols, its meaning is immeasurably augmented by the immediately preceding verse: "You shall have no other gods besides Me." Maimonides, though he knows full well that the deities of "the Sabians, the Chasdeans, and the Chaldeans . . . the Egyptians and the Canaanites" have passed from the world, also knows that man's devotion to idolatry in all of its sundry and peculiar forms is nowhere near vanishing, and that its power over his soul continues to be enormous. To this very day, even the most pious of the faithful are still not immune to it: "Consider how perfidious was he who originated this opinion and how he perpetuated it through this imagining, so that its trace was not effaced though the Law has opposed it for thousands of years" (*Guide*, 3:37).

Though the midrash in Yoma 69b may relate that the members of the Great Assembly succeeded in wiping out the Jewish people's idolatrous urge, this is mere legend. The Jewish world is and has always been the scene of a desperate, unceasing struggle between its monotheistic faith and the natural attraction of man—and Jews are no different from others in this respect—to the worship of idols, which may even appear in the guise of monotheism. How difficult it is for man to accept the distinction between the holy and the profane, between the creator, who alone is "truly real" (MT Hil. Yesodei ha-Torah 1:1) and utterly holy, and his own status in God's world, which is contingent and profane. It takes an enormous effort of faith on man's part to recognize that the world and all that is in it—including man himself—are subsidiary to God. This idea is expressed succinctly in the liturgical hymn *Adon Olam*: "Before the world was created—You were He, and now that the world has been created—You are He." Only when man has come to realize that the transcendent God is not in the world, while he himself is but a part of it, does man become aware of the task incumbent upon him: Only by his own efforts, through service to God—that is, by keeping his commandments—can man create a link between himself and God; and if such efforts on his part are lacking, the link will not be forged. It was Maimonides' belief that divine Providence requires man's awareness of God (Guide, 3:52). Such faith demands great spiritual strength, as expressed symbolically in the first words of the *Shulhan Arukh* (The Prepared Table): "One must overcome."

Far easier for man is mysticism—which is another name for idolatry—for it obfuscates the distinction between the holy and the profane by maintaining that the link between man and God is a given, the existence of that link stemming as a matter of course from the nature of the divine creation. Mysticism assumes, consciously or not, that God is in the world and that he is an aspect of the world. Man is thus assured of God's Providence—stern or gracious, as the case may be. In classical idolatry the gods belong to the natural world; in the covert idolatry of Christianity, God takes the form of man. In the kabbalah, the worlds are made up of, or at least thoroughly imbued with, spheres and configurations that are aspects of the divine, to the extent, as the *Zohar* puts it, that "there is no place devoid of Him" (*Tikkunei ha-Zohar*, Margoliot ed., *tikkunim* 70, 122b)—a paraphrase of the saying of a famous idolator, Thales of Miletus, "Everything is filled with gods." This idea directly contradicts the scriptural view of God, as expressed in the verse "The whole earth is full of His glory" (Isa. 6:3), the Bible's question being, "Where is the site of His glory?" The mystical conception turns monotheism into pantheism. Keeping the Torah and its commandments thus ceases to constitute service of God, the purpose of man, and becomes instead a system of magical functions that are somehow needed on high. Man and his world have become primary; God is merely activated on their behalf, and the commandments themselves have been turned into theurgic idolatrous acts.

One expression of the transformation of faith into idolatry is to be found in the distortion of the concept of holiness. The recognition that holiness is an attribute of God and is specific to him means that the word cannot be used as an essential description of anything else. To see holiness as the essence of some object existing in the world of nature or of history is to raise that thing to the level of the divine—and that is idolatry. In the world of faith, the term *holiness* as used in connection with particular entities is not a matter of their essence but rather of their being directed—or of the directedness of the subject—to the service of God; it is understood, that is, in a functional sense rather than as an immanent quality, and once the function has been completed the adjective is no longer relevant. That is how the word is used in such signal phrases as the prayer from the daily liturgy "Who has sanctified us with His commandments" and scriptural passages such as "Remember the Sabbath day and keep it holy" (Ex. 20:8); "Thus you shall be reminded to observe all My commandments and to be holy to your God" (Num. 15:40); "You shall be holy" (Lev. 19:2)—and not, it should be noted, "you are holy." So, too, we read in the Mishnah: "The land of Israel is the holiest land. And in what does its holiness consist? In that the omer and the first-fruits and the twin loaves are taken from it" (Kel. 1:6). It is not because the land is intrinsically holy that these things are taken from it. Rather the land is sanctified by virtue of the very fact that the omer and the first fruits are taken from it. This is the sense in which the term *holy* is consistently used in all the traditional texts of Judaism.

Holiness consists of doing God's command and can be ascribed neither to the subject who performs it nor to the objects that are the focus of its performance. The latter in and of themselves—like everything else in the world—are indifferent from a religious point of view. To raise them to the level of holiness is to make them divine, and that is as idolatrous as worship of the golden calf, itself a staggering religious phenomenon: an entire people in search of a god ("This is your God, O Israel" [Ex. 32:4]). Nor does the calf necessarily have to be of gold: It can be of stone; it can be a place, a country, or a people, or even an idea (for example, messianic redemption) or a particular personality.

The commandment to wear ritual fringes is accompanied by the commandment to seek holiness—indeed, holiness is made conditional upon Israel's fulfillment of this mighty requirement (Num. 15:37–40). Immediately following this passage the Torah—just four verses later—relates the central declaration of the rebel Korah: "All the community are holy" (Num. 16:3), that is, holiness is an immanent quality of the people of Israel. These two views of holiness illumine the distinction between faith in God and idolatry.

Korah's idolatrous utterance—that of the divinization of the people of Israel—has been taken up by numerous others in the history of traditional Judaism, from Judah Halevi in the *Kuzari* (as opposed to his penitent and devotional poems, which are sublime documents of a pure faith) through the Maharal of Prague and on to certain streams within Hasidism to Abraham Kook, whose way of thinking transformed the real Jewish people into "the soul of the nation," which is the same as *knesset Yisrael* (lit., congregation of Israel) of the Midrash and the *Shekhinah* (divine Presence) of the mystics, identified with the divine *sefirah* of *malkhut* (lit., kingdom). Anything that takes place within the Jewish people is thus a process occurring within the godhead itself; religious reality here becomes an idolatrous myth, and faith is transformed into idolatry—the consequences of which become ever more evident in the first and second generations of Kook's disciples.

The difference between the monotheistic and the idolatrous senses in which the concept of holiness may be understood is well put in a passage written by one of the great traditional thinkers of the end of the nineteenth and beginning of the twentieth centuries, Meir Simḥah ha-Kohen of Dvinsk. Commenting on Exodus 30:11–34:35 in his book *Meshekh Ḥokhmah,* written in 1927, ha-Kohen had the following to say in connection with Moses' breaking of the tablets:

> Everything that is holy—the Land of Israel, Jerusalem, etc.—is no more than an aspect of the Torah, and it is sanctified by the holiness of the Torah. . . . Do not imagine that the Temple and the Sanctuary are holy in and of themselves, God forbid! God dwells amongst His people, and if they transgress His covenant, they [the Temple and the Sanctuary] are bereft of their holiness and become as profane objects. . . . The tablets, bearing the writing of God, are also not holy in and of themselves; it is only for you that they are holy, and when the bride goes whoring from her canopy they become no more than pieces of clay; they are not holy in and of themselves, but only for you, if you keep [the commandments engraved upon] them. . . . In sum, there is nothing holy in the world. . . . Only God is holy, and it is Him who is befitting of praise and worship. . . . Holiness inheres in no created thing, except insofar as the people of Israel keeps the Torah in accordance with the will of the Creator.

The most dangerous use of all of the term *holiness* is in the phrase "the holiness of the people of Israel." If this term is to be saved from transformation into an object of idol worship, we would do well to heed the pithy declaration of Abraham Ibn Ezra in his commentary on the Torah. Commenting on the verse "The Lord will establish you as His holy people" (Deut. 28:9) he wrote: "And holiness lies in keeping the commandments."

BIBLIOGRAPHY

Hermann Cohen, *Religion of Reason out of the Sources of Judaism,* Simon Kaplan, tr. (1972), ch. 2.

Maimonides, *Guide of the Perplexed,* Shlomo Pines, tr. (1964), Book 1, ch. 36.

Ephraim E. Urbach, "The Rabbinic Laws of Idolatry in the Second and Third Centuries in the Light of Archaeological and Historical Evidence," in *Israel Exploration Journal,* no. 3 (1959–1960), 149ff; no. 4 (1959–1960), 229ff.

Imagination

דימיון

Geoffrey H. Hartman

There is no imagination without distrust of imagination. This interdependence is especially obvious when a powerful religion attempts to subsume imaginative activity. The relation between religion and fantasy must be intimate, even complicit, since religion is orbic as well as orphic, wishing to embrace the totality of human life.

When we study how a religion seeks to regulate imagination we also perceive the imaginative character of that religion itself. The Hebrew Bible has no word for imagination: *Yeẓer*, more correctly translated as *inclination* or *impulse*, is the term used in such famous passages as Genesis 6:6 ("every imagination of the thoughts of [man's] heart is evil from his youth"). A special word is needed only when the relation between the divine and the human sphere has become uncertain. Then imaginative representation supplements, even fills in for, presence; and though the Bible is already a representation, its force consists precisely in making us receive not only stories in which God is a participant but stories that suggest that there was another epoch, when the divine Presence was direct.[1] That epoch of "open vision" is over by the time of Samuel, yet prophets continue to stand in a direct relation to the Word of God. Imagination, according to medieval Jewish philosophy, is the faculty that, when perfect, both receives and communicates this much of the divine influence.

The imagination had ambivalent status, however. Maimonides, following Aristotle, said that it was limited to sense impressions and their combination. It could not raise itself to truly abstract or immaterial conceptions, that is, to philosophy; it produced, when it tried this, such fictions and phantasms as the corporeality of God. Yet without imagination there is no prophecy. The divine influence, after passing through the active intellect and the reason, was received by an imagination that the higher animals shared with man. The ambivalence surrounding imagination centered on this contrast between its low position in the hierarchy of faculties and its sublime function in prophecy. Prophecy is therefore defined by Maimonides as "the most perfect development" of the imaginative faculty, and includes vision and dream (which the rabbis called "the unripe fruit of prophecy") as its two principal modes. What was to be done with a gift that could go so wrong, yet on which prophecy depends?

Maimonides in effect moots the higher function of imagination by legislating prophecy out of existence until the messianic era, yet imagination continued to trouble both philosophy and theology. It might be denounced, but could it be regulated, since it was not (by the philosophers' and theologians' own account) distinctively human? When prophetic it was so not through the intellect that mankind shared, to a degree, with God; and when ordinary it was something common also to beasts.

But for its prophetic potential, imagination would not have been an issue. To clarify the nature of imagination was to resolve a question of authority. Who speaks "for" God in an era of uncertain vision? It has been argued that the very formulation of the mishnaic code by the rabbis involved a daring transfer of authority: The Mishnah became Scripture, not just an exilic elaboration on Scripture.[2] Imagination may always involve a question as to who speaks for God, or what authority such representations have.

In the Pentateuch the authority of God is declaratively set down in the First and Second Commandments. The most explicit biblical statement on imagination, in fact, is the Second Commandment's prohibition against graven images (Ex. 20:4–5), formulated in the context of religions with animal and astral gods. The prohibition did not suppress all figural representation, however. Bezalel is authorized in Exodus 31:4 (cf. II Chron. 2:6) to "devise skillful works . . . in gold, and in silver, and in brass, and in cutting of stone" for the sanctuary in the wilderness.[3] Excavations have uncovered the frescoes of the Dura-Europos synagogue (third century C.E.), unusual for its depictions of even the human form, while the decorative arts flourished in the period of the Second Temple. Yet when such work might induce idol worship *(avodah zarah)* it was curtailed, and certainly after the establishment of Christianity the visual arts did not develop as they did in Christian circles. Jewish craftsmanship was invested in ceremonial objects. If iconicity leads to idolatry, then the encouragement of a pictorial and iconic art by Christianity could have imposed a stricter application of the Second Commandment prohibition.

The productive side of that prohibition may, however, have channeled imaginative energies into writing, into graphic rather than graven forms. Whether the anti-iconic commandment stimulated aniconic forms of fantasy remains an open question: We still understand too little about the operation of a specifically verbal imagery.[4] There is, in any case, no glorification of the "human form divine" in Jewish thought, no sustained mythology that mingles, as in Greek polytheism, divine presences, nature spirits, and mankind by representing all beings under the species of an aesthetic anchored in the human body.

Yet nature as the physical world is not disparaged. While nature imagery in the payyetanic tradition remains emblematic (Eleazar Kallir's "Dew" with its strong rhyme and repetitions is a case in point), the presence in the canon of a moralized Song of Songs inspired a mode of expression blending sacred and secular imagery. For Judah Halevi the Song magnetized—eroticized—other biblical passages and justified, as it were, his use of Arabic poetics. Even if Halevi is celebrating a sacred marriage of the *Shekhinah,* it is by way of an Oriental and opulent, not an ascetic, technique. Moreover, though power rather than beauty is the focus of many Psalms, it is from them that later tradition takes its sense of the sublimity of nature.

The anti-iconic rule was formulated in the special context of representing the divine, so that Judaism came to be characterized by a defensive attitude toward anthropomorphism rather than toward nature. Yet Judaism, before the Enlightenment *(Haskalah),* did keep its distance from natural philosophy. The exceptions often show a Greek or Islamic influence: Ibn Gabirol's cosmological poetry in *Keter Malkhut* in the eleventh century C.E., or the conceit in the *Wisdom of Solomon,* compiled around 100 B.C.E. and taken up by Philo Judaeus, that the High Priest's robe described in Exodus 28 imaged the cosmos (the Greek allows a punning connection between *kosmos* as ornament and *kosmos* as world). As Nikolay Berdyayev has said, the Jews are concerned with history, the Greeks with the cosmos.

Consider the angels that link Judaism with folklore and pagan legend.

They have no independent existence, and as in the Jacob/Jabbok episode (Gen. 32:23–33) are purged of their character as nature spirits.[5] A probable reason is, again, avoidance of idolatry. The Hebrews lived among nations whose gods were totems connected by webs of correspondence with the heavens above and the earth below. Accordingly, when the Bible dealt with nature it was on the basis either of regulation (laws on land use, animals, consumption) or of a sublime imagery that clearly subordinated nature to God and reflected the triumph rather than the agon of Hebrew monotheism.

An unusual moment, such as Deuteronomy 31:28 and 32:1, in which heaven and earth are invoked as witnesses (as at the opening of Aeschylus' *Prometheus Bound*) is decisive in its very difference. Heaven and earth were eternal, were "gods" for the Greeks as for Near Eastern cults; if Moses calls on them at this crucial point to confirm the covenant and witness "against" the people, it is to imply that breaking the covenant may mean that earth and heaven will pass away, that they are eternal only as part of a contractual history beginning with God's promise after the Flood.

Pagan myth was full of rival deities associated with nature or its elements. Folklore, both Christian and Jewish, transformed them into good or evil spirits. Their dwelling place was generally the natural world that in its familiar beauty or unfamiliar and uncanny aspects could become a fatal distraction. One wonders what sort of imaginative compromise is found in the *Shulḥan Arukh,* which incorporates a strong, apotropaic belief in evil spirits. Starting at dawn, we are instructed to guard against them by cleansing rituals, which extend to the mouth—the accumulation of blessings and laudations in Jewish prayer. Does this not acknowledge the "other side" of God, or that the soul, restored to the body at dawn, may have fallen prey during the night to estranging (impure) influences? Midrash had transmitted a host of legends about the animosity of the angels to man, legends that may echo the Manichaean or polytheistic theme of a war in heaven—the very basis of pagan epics and even of such belated bards as Milton and Blake. "He who makes peace in His heavens, may He in His mercy make peace among us and all Israel" *(Kaddish)*. Though the Bible contains fewer of what Gunkel names "faded myths" than postbiblical literature does, traces of titans and cosmic deities remain.[6]

The powerful clichés contrasting Hebraism and Hellenism after Hegel's philosophy of history takes hold, and which attribute to Judaism a forbidding attitude toward nature and a severe scruple concerning all forms of animism not framed by an emphasis on divine mastery, make sense in one respect. Central to Jewish religion, insofar as it has a dogma, is the Shema: the confession of God's unity. Any contamination of this unity by an idea of reconcilement that seeks to join to God a form of body or any shape from nature *(demut guf)* is rejected. Here one does glimpse the convergence of a principle of faith and a trait of imagination, which allowed Hegel to emphasize the inherently alien character of the Hebrew God. God's unity, according to Hegel, was a nonunion, mere empty transcendence, mere antagonism to everything, including the creation itself. Hegel's view of Judaism is highly polemical, for he admires a very different kind of unity, the aesthetic balance of body and spirit in Hellenistic art, and the more intimate Christian mystery of the incarnation. Yet Hegel's portrait of Abraham may be unsurpassed in the clarity with which it highlights an uncompromising quest:

> The first act by which Abraham becomes the founding father of a nation is a separation, which severs the bond of communal being and love. . . . The very spirit that carried Abraham from his kin guided him throughout his encounters with foreign peoples for the rest of his life; this was the spirit of keeping himself rigorously antithetical to everything, having raised his thought [*das Gedachte*] to form a unity dominating an infinite and hostile nature. . . . He was a stranger on earth, a stranger to the soil and to men alike. . . . The whole world Abraham regarded as simply his opposite: if not a nullity, it was sustained by the God who was alien to it.[7]

The most searching affirmation of God's unity, or critique of the anthropomorphic imagination, remains that of Maimonides, whose *Guide of the Perplexed* has made us forever conscious of the difficulty of metaphoric expression in religious thought. For any likeness, any comparison of the divine to the human, is bound to introduce an anthropomorphic element. The Bible is full of anthropomorphisms, though it is rarely theriomorphic; and since the God of Judaism continues to act in human history, the Maimonidean scruple heightens the difficulty of any God talk (theology) that is not focused on the necessity of purifying imagination of metaphorical error.

It remains a possibility that, on the contrary, this scruple also helped to provoke Jewish mysticism, which in the form of the *Zohar* began the most dazzling phase of its career toward the end of the thirteenth century. For if metaphor cannot be avoided and allegorical interpretation is always called for, then to the *via negativa* prescribed by Maimonides' method of reading there may be joined a *via eminentia* aiming at the same goal through hyperbolic modes of exegesis.

With the kabbalah, cosmic fantasy and demonology, though not absent from rabbinic legend or Haggadah, broke forth and flourished anew. They are fueled, moreover, by the emphasis on writing, by a name and letter mysticism that elicits magnificent hypostases. Both the *maaseh bereshit* (lit., works of creation) and the *maaseh merkabah* (lit., works of the [divine] chariot)—according to the Talmud and Maimonides, mysteries for initiates only—become the very center of speculative fantasy. A community of spheres of being is envisaged, sustained by the Torah, the measure of all things: "The Torah it was that created the angels and created all the worlds and through Torah are all sustained."[8]

The anti-iconic rule may have played in the Jewish imagination a role similar to the antitheatrical prejudice in Protestant Christianity.[9] The Yiddish theater as well as other kinds of Jewish spectacular and pictorial art developed after the Enlightenment. It was not circus or theatre but Temple (or Palace) that haunted Jewish memory. The rabbinic imagination continued to evoke a memory temple and preserve in detail every aspect of ancient ceremonial and ritual law. Nonacceptance of the Diaspora and love of Israel as the holy land to which body as well as spirit would eventually return also kept Jews from letting imagination dwell on other places. There might be a covert or unconscious assimilation of the art forms and imaginative habits of those nations amid which Jews were to live, but there was also a dissimilation that made these forms something of a camouflage or protective coloring for Westerners whose hearts, like Judah Halevy's, remained in the East.

How can we sing our songs in a foreign land? That has been the question since the Babylonian exile. The Jewish imagination, like any other, must exert itself and risk profanation or fall silent and risk atrophy. Even if imagination is by nature always in exile, the tension in Jewish life between assimilation and dissimilation has been more continuous, because of the dispersion, and more intense, because of the anti-iconic rule.

Despite exile, Judaism never became a mystery religion. The Lurianic kabbalah skirted that possibility, yet even there one feels the persistence of a popular and earthbound element. Moreover, both the rabbinic and the kabbalistic imagination use gematria and similar "keys" mainly to intensify memory's cleaving to the written word, rather than to predict its obsolescence in fulfillment. As Walter Benjamin said of Judaism's conception of hope: It is not future oriented but paradoxically "hope in the past." That past was nothing but ruins, yet the very shards and broken vessels contained a liberating spark.

A permanent bequest of the kabbalah to the Jewish imagination was its expansion out of sparse talmudic sources of the concept of the *Shekhinah*. This is a female figure related to popular wisdom, and fulfills an integrating earthly function. Though bride or companion of the kabbalistic sphere of kingship *(malkhut),* the *Shekhinah* is no fatal or mysterious lady. Accompanying the religious person as partner or guardian spirit, she is often imagined as combining two presences: the divine Presence during man's or God's exile, and the wife's (or mother's) presence when the wanderer is away from home. For a contemporary feminist critique of the Jewish imagination, the *Shekhinah* is crucial. Suggested is not only a redemption *of* but also a redemption *through* the womanly element. A stratum wells up that seeks to penetrate and expand the covenant.

The kabbalah as a redemption narrative dares to draw even God into the area of the passions. God too may be in exile. There is, however, little emphasis on the radical other, or an alien, terrifying, and rejecting mystery—the *mysterium tremendum*.[10] Nor is there emphasis on the radical dualism, rather than duplicity, of the world of appearances. Despite gnosis—the methodized suspicion that God is not one, but split in his essence, and that the creator God of the Bible may be a mere demiurge or even satanic adversary, weaver of the illusions that seduce us into worldliness—despite traces of such a belief, otherworldliness does not triumph and does not cancel the Torah's worldly subject matter. As a story of redemption, kabbalah draws the "lower crowns" or demonic energies into the upper spheres; it is an attempt at restoration or restitution *(tikkun)* that respects the nonapocalyptic tenor of Deuteronomy 30:11-14:

[T]his instruction which I enjoin you this day is not too baffling for you, nor is it beyond reach. It is not in the heavens, that you should say "Who among us can go up to the heavens, and impart it to us, that we may observe it? . . . No, the thing is very close to you, in your mouth, and in your heart, to observe it."

The anti-iconic bias, which could have led to mystery, was also modified by a principle of accommodation. Resting chiefly on Genesis 1:27, "And God created man in his own image," this principle evokes the likeness of man to God: There is a measure of analogy or symmetry between a transcendent creator and his creation. The importance of story and parable in Jewish tradition, and anthropomorphic expressions generally, reinforces this aspect of analogy, but so do the Bible's more intimate details, since God himself (and not an angel) walks with Enoch and talks directly with Adam, Noah, and Abraham. He even contradicts Sarah in a surprising moment (Gen. 18:15).

The principle of accommodation was recognized by the talmudic rabbis who said that in the Bible God adjusts himself to the human intellect: "The Torah speaks in the language of man." The kabbalah, interested in expanding the analogical imagination, expresses the contrary aspects of divine transcendence and human likeness with an intensity that marks the Jewish imagination as a whole. "The world could not endure the Torah, if she had not garbed herself in garments of this world."[11]

Given these factors that modify the otherness or unlikeness of God—on the part of historical and secular Jewry, a protective if precarious assimilation, and, on the part of God, a deliberate accommodation—can we insist that there is a single unified type of imagination that could be identified as Jewish?

As we try to define the imagination through Jewish sources an additional problem arises, which characterizes modernity yet remains linked to the historicizing tendencies mentioned. Most scholars in the contemporary world stand both inside and outside Jewish tradition: We know the Bible in the context of other mythic narratives; we know the interaction, later, of Hellenism and Judaism; we continue to explore the reciprocities found in Judeo-Spanish culture before the Expulsion, and in Judeo-Italian culture from the later fifteenth century on. To this must be added the efflorescence of Yiddish, sensitive to its surroundings, from the Ḥasidic sages to the Holocaust; the philosophical and fictional productions of German Jewry; the reconstruction of Hebrew as a modern idiom; and the contemporary scene with its bewildering mixture of creative and scholarly writing in America, in Israel, and, increasingly, in France. As we explore this interaction between historicizing factors and the imagination—as Jewish religion, in its biblical, rabbinic, or extended form connects with literature—comparisons leap to mind that again cast doubt on essentialist perspectives that propose a uniquely Jewish or Hebraic factor.

We know, for instance, that the *mashal* (story simile), an important vehicle of accommodation that makes the ways of God intelligible, is also a crucial feature of New Testament parables.[12] Here, as in the case of the mystical poetry of John of the Cross, inspired by the Song of Songs, or in the case of William Blake's *Four Zoas* with their remarkable re-envisioning of the *maaseh merkabah,* common sources may have played their part. The clothes philosophy of the kabbalah finds a curious elaboration in Thomas Carlyle's *Sartor Resartus,* itself based on German Romantic speculations about the power and necessity of mediating symbols. In a poet like Dante (as close as one can get to the era that saw the rise of the *Zohar*) the Catholic imagination shapes a writer who unified the analogical sphere of likeness and the anagogical sphere of mystery and unlikeness. How deep do these similarities go, and how indebted are they to shared texts or modes of reading?

Rather than losing myself in a methodological account of the difficulties that beset the project of definition, I would like to propose a number of heuristic theses. Even when obvious they warrant repetition and scrutiny.

First, the Jewish imagination has been dominated by a turn to the written word and has developed within the orbit of the Hebrew Bible. The Jews are a people of the Book, and their mind is text dependent, even when it rebels against the text. They keep the word, not only the faith. Yet the Bible is an "encyclopedic form," to use Northrop Frye's useful designation: It is generically impure in that it mixes legends, poetry, legal prescriptions, proverbs (wisdom literature), and historical narrative. This impurity contrasts with the spirit of Aristotle's *Poetics,* which establishes separate genres, with the increasing acceptance in the West of those genres, and also with a modern tendency toward specialized knowledge that insulates fields of inquiry from one another.

The emphasis on genre, though it has not affected our esteem for the Bible (which is then simply viewed as a source book for all genres), may influence in a negative way the reception of satellite compilations, such as Talmud, Midrash, and kabbalah, as well as chronicles that record the life and death of Jewish communities—the *Memorbücher* and *Yizker* books. The Jewish prayer book, the *siddur,* also shows an accreted as well as stratified quality. It contains psalms and verbatim extracts from the Bible, sometimes modified by midrashic interpretation; liturgical poems or *piyyutim* that skillfully form a pastiche of Bible phrases; Maimonidean philosophy in the form of the *Yigdal* (Maimonides' thirteen articles of faith); and many composite prayers that plead with God in God's own words. These interlaced biblical words and formulas, petitionary or confessional, create a mosaic that treats the parent text synchronically, and whose historical and sequential elaboration—often motivated by forgotten or faded heresies—is hard to reconstruct. To an outsider this *siddur* or "order" is more like chaos: What is reenacted, what functions as the orientation point or dromenon—the original Temple ceremonies—is less visible here than in Catholic or Protestant worship.

The famous story (BT Hag. 14b) of the four who entered *pardes* (lit., garden, meaning paradise) reminds us that the Talmud is even more confusing than the Bible. Everyone may enter, but not everyone emerges sound in spirit. There are, of course, genres within this contiguous writing, some of which may still be unrecognized. Just as, for instance, Milton could depict the Song of Songs as a pastoral and the Book of Job as a "brief epic," just as Bishop Lowth could analyze the psalms as a species of "sublime" verse, so form criticism is beginning to penetrate the Talmud. We dimly discern formulaic blocks, put together by an oral method of recitation before being fixed as script. In the *Gemara* and the midrashic parts of the Talmud one often seems to overhear the table talk of the rabbis—the *Shulḥan Arukh* (The Prepared Table) was clearly an important occasion, a point of assembly that might escape suspicion and could serve political as well as theological purposes. A story recorded in the Haggadah about Rabbi Akiva and others, who conversed all night and almost forgot to recite the morning prayer, points in that direction.

The text dependency of the Jewish imagination means, already in the Bible itself, a respect for variant traditions and so a tension between book and order. God is one, but mankind or the Jewish people are not; and even though there must be a decision concerning the law, the Talmud records divergent and adversary opinions. There is a reluctance, moreover, to speak except in the name of older authorities, as if any interruption of the chain of transmission could prove fatal.[13] This anxiety about discontinuity is accompanied, especially in the Talmud, by an associative way of going from topic to topic that mixes law and lore and produces astounding feats of memorization. It lacks, however, that hypotactic unity of form or field characteristic of learned treatises in the West, and which Maimonides began to impose in his *Mishneh Torah,* by distinguishing between code and commentary. And though the closing of the biblical canon, as of the Talmud, was important for orthodox practice, in a sense neither of these *biblia* becomes esoteric because their study is formally enjoined. The difference between margin text (commentary) and main text (Talmud/Torah) is preserved, yet the margin continues to grow, and the commentary process was recognized as founded on Sinai, where God, it is said, gave Moses the oral law (commentary) as well as the written law (the fixed code of the Torah).

In sum, Jewish writing is liberated by the broad, encyclopedic form of biblical literature and a commentary process that circumvents such categorical distinctions as *scholarly* and *creative;* yet it is also hemmed in by an exemplary tradition that attributes everything to a divine source, referring it back to the Bible or to the chain of authority.

As a second thesis let it be noted that while apologetic works like Halevy's *Kuzari* can venture forth in the name of their author, imaginative and speculative works like the *Zohar* remain pseudepigraphic. A crucial part of the *Zohar* claims to be an ancient midrash and speaks in the person of Simeon ben Yohai, a talmudic sage of the second century C.E. Comparing Dante's *Commedia* to the *Zohar,* we see that both transform learning into a highly allusive form of art. Yet in Dante the exegetical frame falls away, burnt off like mist by the genius of a writer who enters his poem in propria persona, who is as historical as the people he describes. There is no incog-

nito. The *Zohar,* however, continues to use exegesis as a supremely imaginative device on which, as on the Torah, everything depends. It expands
the realm of analogy and explores "spheres" of being as intensively as
Dante, yet refuses to shed its pseudepigraphic cover and become recogniz-
ably historical.

Even in contemporary Jewish writing the pseudepigraphic impulse persists. So Edmond Jabès, in his *Book of Questions,* plays not only on the *responsa* form of medieval advisories, but also on the Jewish tendency to
depict everything as a saying of the fathers. (The talmudic rabbis gave a hint
by inventing Ben BagBag.) Modern Jewish literature arises as an involuntary
or insubordinate midrash: We do not find free-standing works of art but the
retold tale, the recycled motif, a sense of time that plays with the illusion
of time, and a style composed of both explicit and inner quotations.

The imagination can feel tradition as a suffocating burden. Some writers
welcome the personifying power of the pseudepigraphic style; others resent
becoming pseudepigraphic against their will. Hence Micha Josef Berdyczewski's complaint: "Our egos are not our own, our dreams and our
thoughts are not our own, our will is not the one implanted in us; everything
we were taught long ago, everything has been handed down to us."[14] That
similar expressions about the burden of tradition are found in other modern
literatures should not blind us to the acute nature of that problem in Judaism, where forgetfulness is sinfulness and where Bible and Talmud have
taught us to respect every word of their condensed, unschematic style.
Ḥayyim Naḥman Bialik, who called for a Hebrew dictionary whose purpose
would go beyond antiquarian collecting because philology should "bring the
language to bud and bloom, to grow in strength; it must be a sort of mid-
wifery," also foresaw the necessity of a selection from the past equivalent
to the *Ḥatimah* (canonical closure) that created Bible, Mishnah, and Talmud. The secular writer is caught between a poetics of quotation imitative
of midrash and so remaining in the field of force of these canonical texts,
and the need to make room for a supplementary modern scripture—still,
perhaps, an "écriture du désastre" (Maurice Blanchot) yet based on a rean-
imated and circulating language that seeks to purge itself of inflated or
sacred phraseology.

A more historical way of putting this is to say that the modern Jewish
imagination had to pass at once through Renaissance and Enlightenment
phases. It had to develop a distinctively secular idiom—of thought as well
as speech—by raiding its own traditions; and so it could not escape (except
by contrafacture or parody methods) the very medievalism it wished to
overcome. S. Y. Agnon's fiction is a well-known example; but even in such

Yiddish writers as Isaac Bashevis Singer (more indebted to the Russian novella's intimate realism), learning stimulates as well as burdens creative writing. We find veiled covenantal emblems, overt reminiscences of older storytellers, multilingual resonances, and—above all—the use of "keys." Compare the role of the "lost key" in Agnon's *Gates of Heaven* with the same theme in Singer's "A Friend of Kafka" and "The Key." Kafka himself, whose problem as a writer has to do with composing in an alien tongue, differs from both Agnon and Singer in creating a fictional world that seems deprived of "keys" that could open it to tradition or even to its own meaning. Kafka is important for both Jewish and world literature because his fictions are either antiparables (we cannot find the key to the *bet midrash* [house of study] that would open them to a trained exegetical understanding) or allegorical in Walter Benjamin's sense: without an exit into meaning, into some "keyed" form of understanding.[15]

A third thesis is that, though Christianity attempted to set the spirit against the letter by treating the Bible as a transcended Book of Laws, or stories blind to what they prophesied, for Jews this split between letter and spirit did not occur, or else was repaired by inventive exegetical methods that kept the law portion and the story portion as a single, inalienable donation. Here was God's plenty indeed. The driest list of names, as of the chiefs of Edom in Genesis, was potentially as crucial for interpretation as the Ten Commandments. Yet what legitimacy, in that case, might there be for the free rather than bound imagination, for what we now call secular art? By its very nature, commentary (or literature masked as commentary) was aware that its *nomos* lay in the Bible, that it had no autonomy, that it must strive to win the blessing of a patriarchal text.

Jewish fantasy is thus always shadowed by profanation. The fear of profanation becomes explicit when Hebrew is revived as a modern idiom; it hovers over most attempts at creative writing from Bialik to Yehuda Amichai. The view that extends this anxiety to earlier periods—for classical Judaism's adherence to the received text could hide revisionist aims—suggests that the transformation of Hebrew from a sacred into a secular tongue repeats what is always the case. The Jewish imagination fears not only *hillul ha-Shem,* profanation in the legal and ritual sense, but a less deliberate abuse: one that accompanies use and is inherent in literature itself as it broadcasts—scatters—the words of Scripture by giving them new or extended referents.

The fear of profaning Scripture, of using its words to "uncover one's face," is not confined to modern writers. There are moving stories about the early rabbis' relation to the Bible as a sacred and prophetic document.

Homer they punned into *ḥamor* (ass). But the Bible had to be inserted into the daily and often catastrophic life of the community. To legitimate writing, even in the form of commentary, was therefore to view it as an original repetition of Scripture.

Pagan myth, Jane Harrison showed, and Thomas Mann recalled in "Freud and the Future," was based on persons merging with an archetypal role or story, so that the individual life became a sacred drama.[16] This kind of repetition, dangerously imitative and fulfilling, and closely linked to theatre, is almost entirely absent from Judaism. There writing is lived through—worked through—as writing, and does not cancel itself by a mythic or messianic sort of incarnation. We see, in fact, an inversion of that pattern: The repetition performed by Jewish writers leads from world to Torah by the art of quotation already mentioned, or a virtuoso technique of verbal transformation and interpolation that journeys from one proof text to another. There is no name in tradition for that pattern, which is anti-incarnationist or countertypological. But many sayings typify it: that God looked into the Torah before creating the world, or, to quote Jabès:

> Writing is . . . a scrupulously Jewish act, for it consists in taking up a pen in that place where God withdrew Himself from his words; it consists indefinitely in pursuing a utopian work in the manner of God who was the Totality of the Text of which nothing subsists.[17]

From this perspective, all words are *zimzumim* (contractions). Or, what may be the same, writing as commentary is the expression of a postprophetic age, where even the *bat kol* (heavenly voice) is questioned, so that every author stands potentially under the accusation of being a false messiah or of counterfeiting the Word.

The catastrophes suffered by the Jews only intensified the danger of profanation—of blasphemy ("Curse God and die"), or of liquidating the burden of tradition. The severest disaster since the destruction of the Second Temple, the Holocaust, has led some to question the very possibility of avoiding profanation, except by dint of keeping silent. "A bloody dew clings to the flowers of speech," Karl Kraus remarked about the brutality of Nazi expressions. It is not the ineffable but the unspeakable that weighs on Paul Celan, who strangles lyric eloquence, who does not accuse the Bible but rather the language of the murderers, in which he continues to write. Others who have rejected silence, like Elie Wiesel, reanimate an eloquence that has become doubtful yet is inspired by the Ḥasidic masters or even by Scripture; by Job, for example, who rejects false comfort and cries to God, contending, arguing, calling him to witness, refusing to cover up.

Fourthly, we must cite the remarkable humor of the Jews. Jewish jokes may be the one genre their imagination has specifically contributed. Their humor bypasses silence and assuages the anguish of profanation. Jokes, Freud saw, escape the censor: They are often (when Jewish) self-deprecating; they reconcile disparities, as in matchmaker stories that put the best face (or legs) on everything, yet they skirt blasphemy, since anything can be their target. They are brief, moreover, and so resemble the sayings important to Jewish life and its storytellers. Even when as lengthy as Agnon's "Forevermore" they seem to be brief, twisting and turning ironically. They can mock the exquisite *pilpul* of talmudic commentary while celebrating, or reducing to absurdity, the wary ingenuity of the oppressed, as in Freud's Pinsk/Minsk joke. Above all, they share with midrash its unusual habit of inventing dialogues of the most colloquial sort—dialogues that are intimate even in sacred contexts. Martin Buber's fundamental words "I" and "Thou," which institute a relation of dialogue between God and man, or man and man, may grow out of this tradition, although its secular source is in German Romanticism and its more sublime source is Job's "Call Thou, and I will answer; or let me speak, and answer Thou me." For Rabbi Naḥman of Bratslav such a dialogue can take place whatever the distance between generations: It is of the very essence of commentary.

> For one person may raise a question, and the other who is far away in time or space may comment on it or ask a question that answers it. So they converse, but no one knows it save God, who hears, records and brings together all the words of men, as it is written [Mal. 3:16]: "They who serve the Lord speak to one another, and the Lord hears them and records their words in His book."

There is almost always something pithy and humorous in the midrashic or Ḥasidic anecdote: an unexpected detour, a sly consequence. Compare a comment from Va-Yikra Rabbah that develops Jacob's dream at Luz of angels ascending and descending, with a story about the Ba'al Shem Tov. In the midrash God suggests to Jacob that he should ascend the ladder with the angels, but Jacob is wary or fearful: Could he sustain being angelic; would he not have to descend again? So, despite God's reassurance, Jacob does not go up, and God tells him that had he believed and gone up, he would never have come down, but now his descendants are destined to be enslaved to the "Four Kingdoms." Jacob asks: Will this endure forever? God answers him that it will not: Ultimately Israel will be redeemed (so Jacob gains something after all). About the Ba'al Shem Tov it is related that he was the only person to ascend to heaven while still alive, and that God offered to let him stay. But he refused the offer, saying: If I stay here, and do not return to earth, I lose my chance of going to Israel.

These anecdotes suggest as another thesis a further characteristic of the Jewish imagination. There is a reticence within its ascendental or messianic fervor. This holding back can appear as a lack of faith (so in Jacob's response, perhaps; so in the accusation of the Church against Israel). It can also be a justifiable wariness of false promises or prophets, or more profoundly a knowledge that God is not above "testing" his servants. It may express itself as lack of interest in personal salvation: What matters is the covenant, the return of the entire community to Israel. He who gives up heaven for *erez Yisrael* shows an *ahavat Zion* (love of Zion) that is surely redemptive.

The reticence I mention contrasts vividly with the relation between word and promise, or Scripture and fulfillment, in Christianity. I suggested that difference when describing the repetitious yet unmystical nature of Jewish thought. To "fill the figure" was the technical expression for the interpretive method of Christian typology. So the words of Christ are said to subsume and complete the "Old" Testament, which contains but shadows and types of a truth now fully disclosed.[18] Moreover, the words of Christ are subsumed and completed by himself, by the incarnation, which failed to bring time to an end but identified Christ as the Savior and inaugurated the messianic age (*Annus Domini*).

Though Judaism is not devoid of speculation about First and Last Things—Gershom Scholem has shown that "normative" Jewish thought coexisted with a powerful current of messianic expectation—there is no doctrine that fixes itself in detailed pictures of heaven or hell, or otherworldly time. This restraint cuts two ways, however. The repression of eschatological yearnings may have been greater in Judaism than in Christianity, precisely because the latter allowed them a shared and authorized system of symbols. Scholem uses the catastrophic episode of Shabbetai Zevi to suggest that the acceptance of secular history by rabbinic Judaism was more precarious than previous scholarship had envisaged.[19] Yet the anti-iconic rule also strengthened an antiapocalyptic tendency. In this, a great pictorial artist like Rembrandt is peculiarly Jewish. He may contrast an opulent costume or golden helmet or other highlight with the ordinary, material, and domestic world, yet what is represented remains stable and evokes a world of such highlights and shadows rather than a drive for transfiguration. And, as Erich Auerbach has pointed out, biblical stories like the sacrifice of Isaac create a hermeneutic rather than iconic—pictorially clarified—space.[20]

Even if, as one recent critic, Frank Kermode, has said, we are all "fulfill-ment men," and even if the insistence in Judaism on the binding of spirit to place (the land of Israel) is as messianic a form of imagination as any other, the Church saw correctly that the patriarchs were always striving "with God and with men," that the promise or blessing was never bestowed fully on the single one. Contact with God, in fact, is so demanding that no individual, not even Moses, can perfect Israel's mission. The covenant is with the community as a whole, and every leader proves fallible. Indeed, so circumspect is the Bible's attitude toward human authority that Moses is deprived of grave and cult place. Though "never again did there arise in Israel a prophet like Moses — whom the Lord singled out, face to face" (Deut. 34:10)— "no one knows his burial place to this day" (Deut 34:6). We learn, likewise, very little about the great rabbis of the classical period, except through their sayings and anecdotes. While Christian tradition abounds in the lives of saints and meditations on the life of Jesus, in Judaism no sacred biography exists.[21] Philo's *Life of Moses* is the Hellenistic excep-tion. Not until recent years, when the issue of political leadership has become crucial once more, have Aḥad Ha-Am, Martin Buber, and others begun a modern meditation on Moses, while historical novels by such writ-ers as Sholem Asch and Lion Feuchtwanger have become popular. Even Freud once called his *Moses and Monotheism* a historical novel.

Finally, there is something incongruous in ascribing reticence to the Jew-ish imagination. Reticence? Are the prophets reticent, when they give Israel an imaginative foretaste of the worst and the best, the blessing and the curse, so that it might "choose life"? Is Isaiah reticent when he envisions the labor pains of the messianic age as well as the peace to follow: "The wolf and the lamb shall graze together. . . . In all My sacred mount nothing evil or vile shall be done—said the Lord" (Isa. 65:25)? Those who speak in the name of the Lord cannot be called reticent, even when his words are felt to be a consuming fire (Jeremiah) or a burden they shun (Jonah). Chris-tian messianism is, after all, explicitly based on Hebrew anticipations.

It is here that we reach an impasse, for to define the Jewish imagination is seen to involve the religious imagination generally, at least in the mono-theistic West. What does it mean to imagine God? Not a god, but God who is one and is clearly more—by the time the Hebrew Bible reaches us—than a victor, tyrant, or usurper who has triumphed over other tribal or national gods, now reduced to idols. Comparative religion may restore that tribal perspective; Hegel may indict (as well as admire) the abstractness of the Hebraic conception; the Enlightenment, culminating in Feuerbach's view, may see all such forms as enthusiastic figments and phantasms produced by the human spirit, which libels and alienates its own powers, and which gives itself over into the hands of priests, of established religion—the fact remains that the Jewish imagination gave us the God of the Bible as the Bible of God.

That communicative bond, strengthened by a hermeneutic tradition of over two thousand years, may be the determining feature rather than a mysterious reticence. We cannot say that a Jewish imagination existed prior to the Hebrew Bible, where nothing quite as gorgeous or fantastic as the Apocalypse of St. John is found. The Hebrew canon ends with two books of Chronicles (a turbulent history that looks to the restoration of the First Temple), not with cosmic cycles of destruction and a vision of the Last Things. In Isaiah the anticipation of redemption focuses on God, on what he will do, and what the community covenanted to him must do, not on a redeemer figure, the "suffering servant," who remains shadowy. That redemption will issue from the line of Jesse and David is a living tradition, but the imaginative center in Judaism is not the person of the redeemer. When the Messiah comes, he may come incognito, and time will not end necessarily. Judaism's rejection of Christ may have reinforced this anti-apocalyptic strain, but it also confirms the Hebrew Bible's attitude toward human and fallible mediators.

Even the "strong hand" of systematic theology is thus resisted in Judaism. There is no other hand like that which brought the Jews out of bondage and wrote what it wrought. Story and testimony prevail, and when, close to our time, the impulse to theological discourse revives, it tries to underwrite rather than codify, to restate the qualities found in the tradition. So Franz Rosenzweig's *Star of Redemption* wishes to free religious thought from "the tic of a timeless coming-to-knowledge" that has influenced both philosophy and theology. He aims to disturb even the dialectic—always resolved, always progressive—of the German idealist tradition by proposing a type of discourse he names *Sprechdenken* (speech thought).[22]

Rosenzweig's praise of *Sprechdenken*—that it is time haunted, that it does not know in advance what will appear, that its key words are given it by others (audience, dialogue partners, tradition), that it is, in sum, temporal rather than totalizing—recalls, surely, the aphoristic and anecdotal mode of Hillel, Yoḥanan ben Zakai, and other rabbis who met the challenge of being authorities in a postprophetic age. Feeling the pressure of history on time, they improvised in a way that gave time to time (Rabbi Tarphon). Other types of response are acknowledged by them—faith healing, wonder working, and even attempts to provoke the Messiah, because these too were of that time. Yet they continue to be interpreters rather than founders.

The rabbis did not know, and we do not know, what will come about. According to Rosenzweig, modern philosophy is mistaken on two counts: As a science of history it presumes it can find out exactly what happened, and so entertains the thought that objective knowledge may help to make the past forgettably past; and as a philosophy of (replacing) religion it seeks despite itself a uniquely fulfilling moment in and beyond time. Rosenzweig suggests that for its pet term *eigentlich* (verily, really, authentically) we should substitute the inconspicuous word *and*. This *and*, he writes, "was the first deriving from experience; so it must return among the last of truth." The *and* signifies relation and drives us back from thought to experience: "God and world and man." Yet this *and*, like the Hebrew *ve*, is a connective that links episodes paratactically rather than hypotactically, and subverts any last word: not *end* but *and*. Rosenzweig posits, moreover, an *and* that allows a passing over of the book into what he punningly defines as dailiness and total day (*All-tag*). A redemptive rather than apocalyptic appropriation of time is evoked, a "door" leading out of books into a *Nichtmehrbuch* (no-longer-book), or the direct seeing of "the likeness of the world in God's face" (*Weltgleichnis im Gottesantlitz*).

Rosenzweig's program, like that of the kabbalah, exalts the analogical imagination. As such it is potentially transgressive and triggers a strangely figurative language, almost as thick as Heidegger's. The "stepping" of the book toward this border vision, Rosenzweig writes, is a sin that can be purged only by its ceasing to be a book: "*Aufhören des Buchs.*" The word *Aufhören* is an undeveloped pun suggesting a passing from the closeted act of writing to an excursive and ecstatic hearing (*auf-hören*).

Any discussion of the Jewish imagination's relation to time has to mention the Sabbath, not only because there is so much surrounding mystical lore, so much ritual adornment and safeguarding of that day, but also because the institution of the Sabbath is itself an invention of the highest imaginative order. It exemplifies the way halakhah (law) grows out of or interacts with a more fluid Haggadah (lore). Bialik wrote: "Living and energetic halakhah is aggadah in its past and future state, and vice-versa. What are all the 613 commandments of the Torah but the last result, the synthesis upon synthesis of mythic words, of aggadah and immemorial customs?"[23] Halakhah, though a piecemeal historical mosaic, is as concentrated a work as the great medieval cathedrals of Cologne, Milan, and Paris. "The children of Israel have their own magnificent creation, a *day* holy and sublime, the 'Sabbath Queen.' "[24] It is the result, Bialik claims, of a spiritual labor at once pedantic and gigantic, to which generations of individual thinkers have collectively contributed. Every halakhic objection, every fence or limitation, is but a new ornament and picturesque addition to the Sabbath. As the laborious fruit of halakhic discussion, the Sabbath is Haggadah through and through.

There have been other, more speculative studies of such holidays, or of rituals associated with them, by Mircea Eliade, Theodor Gaster, and Theodor Reik.[25] Such studies involve large assumptions about the mind's relation to itself and prehistory: what originary event is being commemorated, how much history or reality (always catastrophic) we can bear, the role of memory and memory effacement, and what psychic structures have developed, obsessional or life enhancing.

What is certain is that how a people orders its time, how it keeps its calendar, is a way of regulating and directing the imagination. The reasons given in the Bible for remembering the Sabbath are clear enough: They combine an episode in God's own "life" (that he rested from the work of creation on the seventh day) with an episode in Israel's history (the liberation from Egypt). The two converging reasons form a very strong bond. The historical commemoration realistically counterpoints any mystical tendency to brood on the "life" of God, and it suggests that unending labor, or its anxious effect on the mind, is slavery. In short, it authorizes a limited "time out" for imagination. The diviner reason for the Sabbath is also essential: It introduces monotheism into the calendar, it subordinates the week to a creator who not only is unafraid to rest but consecrates that pause. There is almost no trace of a conflict in heaven or of the possibility that the weekdays may have had a theophoric linkage. The originality of this account, as of the Bible generally, has less to do with its priority in history than with its success in displacing or even effacing mythic names that comparative religion and linguistic research have never quite restored. Revelation includes a radical act of imagination of this kind, so inventive that it gives the impression of being a creation ex nihilo.

REFERENCES

1. Words denoting mental action are notoriously difficult to translate. For each language, or literary corpus, the semantic field may be differently constituted. So *mashal* and *hashav*, or words formed on the root *d-m-h*, may also approximate in the Bible what we mean by imaginative activity. (Buber solves the problem of *yezer* in his German translation of the Bible by the complex periphrasis *"Gebild der Planungen seines Herzens,"* that is, "imagery pertaining to the plans in man's heart.") This is the place to indicate that "no open vision" (see below) may mean "infrequent vision"; there is clearly, however, the sense of punc-

tuated time, of a period. Unmediated vision is in doubt. Now there must arise a reflection, positive or negative, on the relation of vision to imagination. Writing about mysticism, Gershom Scholem also presupposes a "first stage" world in which divine presence(s) can be experienced without recourse to intermediaries or ecstatic meditation. "There is no room for mysticism as long as the abyss between Man and God has not become a fact of the inner consciousness." See Gershom Scholem, *Major Trends in Jewish Mysticism,* 3d ed. (1961), First Lecture.

2. See Geza Vermes, *Scripture and Tradition in Judaism,* 2d ed. (1973), and Jacob Neusner's development and revision of that problematic.

3. The apparent contradiction between Exodus 20:4–5 and such passages as Exodus 25:2–31 or Exodus 31 prompted much commentary. Nehama Leibowitz brings together Don Isaac Abrabanel, Shemot Rabbah, and Midrash Aggadah Teruma in her *Studies in the Weekly Sidra* (1st Series), "Teruma."

4. Even literary analysis has not contributed much to this question. The unresolved issue, always falling back from theory into case study, is the relation of states of mind—collective or individual—with structures of representation. Hegel's intricate dialectic in *The Phenomenology of Mind* can suggest the difficulty of cultural typing within a historical schematism. There are, of course, interesting hints bearing on writers who seem to have developed an iconoclastic (or onomatoclastic) technique. Coleridge remarks on Milton's allegory of Sin and Death in *Paradise Lost,* Book 2: "The grandest efforts of poetry are where the imagination is called forth, not to produce a distinct form, but a strong working of the mind, still offering what is still repelled, and again creating what is again rejected; the result being what the poet wishes to impress, namely, the substitution of the unimaginable for a mere image." (The role of music, in this regard, and its relation to biblical or other liturgical texts might be of interest here.) See also, on Milton's "half-interdicted images" and his conception of verbal action that may lead back to Philo of Alexandria's *logos tomaeus,* Sanford Budick, *The Dividing Muse: Images of Sacred Disjunction in Milton's Poetry* (1985).

5. Cf. Nahum Sarna, *Understanding Genesis* (1966).

6. Hermann Gunkel, *The Legends of Genesis: The Biblical Saga and History,* William Foxwell Albright, introd.; William Herbert Carruth, tr. (1970). See also Mid. Tehillim 8:2 and *Mimekor Yisrael,* M. S. Bin Gorion, ed.; I. M. Lasky, tr. (1976). For an interesting hypothesis on the angels' enmity to Adam's creation, see "The Gnostic Background of the Rabbinic Adam Legends," in Alexander Altmann, *Essays in Jewish Intellectual History* (1981).

7. Georg Wilhelm Friedrich Hegel, *Early Theological Writings,* T. M. Knox, tr. (1971). Compare Hegel's emphasis with Maimonides' powerful rendition of the normative picture, as he describes the weaning of Abraham ("this spiritual giant") from idolatry, in MT Hil. Avodah Zarah.

8. "The Hidden Meaning of the Torah," in *Zohar: The Book of Splendor,* Gershom Scholem, ed. (1963).

9. The best account of that trend is Jonas Barish's *The Antitheatrical Prejudice* (1981).

10. For the concept, see Rudolf Otto, *The Idea of the Holy* (1923). For a strong counterstatement to the position taken by Otto, and on the very ground of pro-

phetic religion, see Abraham J. Heschel, "The Theology of Pathos," in *The Prophets* (1962).

11. "The Hidden Meaning of the Torah," in *Zohar: The Book of Splendor,* op. cit.

12. Few parables, however, are proportionate similes in narrative form. They are, most of the time, richer and more devious. For the Christian tradition, see Frank Kermode, *The Genesis of Secrecy* (1979), and J. Hillis Miller, "Parable and Performative in the Gospels and in Modern Literature," in *Humanizing America's Iconic Book,* Gene M. Tucker and Douglas A. Knight, eds. (1982).

13. Cf. the opening statement of *Pirkei Avot* and Halevy's Rabbi who asserts in the *Kuzari* that "uninterrupted tradition" is equal to the personal experience of revelation.

14. Cited in Simon Halkin, *Modern Hebrew Literature: Trends and Values* (1950), 93.

15. From "The Hebrew Book," in *Dibre Sifrut.*

16. Jane Ellen Harrison, *Themis* (1912) and most concisely *Ancient Art and Ritual* (1913). Thomas Mann, "Freud and the Future," in *Essays of Three Decades,* H. T. Lowe-Porter, tr. (1948).

17. Edmond Jabès, *The Book of Questions,* R. Waldrop, tr. (1973–1984). For an excellent presentation of Jabès see *The Sin of the Book,* Eric Gould, ed. (1985).

18. The best treatment of Christian typology remains Erich Auerbach's "Figura" essay, now available in *Scenes from the Drama of European Literature* (1984).

19. Gershom Scholem, *Sabbatai Sevi: The Mystical Messiah, 1626–1676* (1973).

20. "The Scar of Odysseus," in *Mimesis: Representation of Reality in Western Literature,* Willard Trask, tr. (1953).

21. Cf. Daniel Jeremy Silver, *Images of Moses* (1982), and Gershom Scholem's *Major Trends in Jewish Mysticism* (1961), 15–16.

22. See "Das Neue Denken," a series of supplementary remarks to *The Star of Redemption,* in Franz Rosenzweig, *Kleinere Schriften* (1937), 373–98.

23. "Halakha and Haggada," in *Dibre Sifrut.* I have benefited from Gershom Scholem's eloquent German translation in H. N. Bialik, *Essays,* Viktor Kellner ed., (1925).

24. Theodor Reik, *Ritual: Psycho-Analytical Studies* (1931).

25. Theodor Herzl Gaster, *Thespis: Ritual, Myth and Drama in the Ancient Near East* (1950); Mircea Eliade, *Cosmos and History: The Myth of the Eternal Return,* Willard Trask, tr. (1959).

BIBLIOGRAPHY

S. Y. Agnon, *Kol Sipurav* (1966).

Ḥayyim Nahman Bialik, *Essays,* V. Kellner, tr. (1925).

Martin Buber, *I and Thou* (1970).

Mircea Eliade, *Cosmos and History: The Myth of the Eternal Return.* Willard Trask, tr. (1959).

Sigmund Freud, *Moses and Monotheism: Three Essays* (1939), in *The Standard Edition of the Complete Psychological Works of Sigmund Freud,* James Strachey, tr. and ed., vol. 23 (1964).

Theodor Gaster, *Thespis: Ritual, Myth and Drama in the Ancient Near East* (1950).

Judah Halevy, *Book of Kuzari,* Hartwig Hirschfeld, tr. (1946).

Simon Halkin, *Modern Hebrew Literature: Trends and Values* (1950).

Irwin Haul, *The Talmud as Law or Literature: An Analysis of David W. Halivni's Mekorot Umasorot, 1* (1982).

Jane Ellen Harrison, *Ancient Art and Ritual* (1969).

Georg Wilhelm Friedrich Hegel, *Early Theological Writings,* T. M. Knox, tr. (1971).

Edmond Jabès, *The Book of Questions,* Rosmarie Waldrop, tr. (1983).

Moses Maimonides, *Guide of the Perplexed,,* tr. and with an intro. by Shlomo Pines (1963).

Theodor Reik, *Ritual: Psycho-analytical Studies,* Douglas Bryan, tr. (1976).

Franz Rosenzweig, *The Star of Redemption,* W. Hallo, tr. (1971).

Franz Rosenzweig, "Das Neue Denken," in *Kleinere Shriften* (1937).

Gershom Scholem, *Sabbatai Sevi: The Mystical Messiah* (1973).

Isaac Bashevis Singer, *A Friend of Kafka and Other Stories* (1975).

Zohar: The Book of Splendor, Gershom Scholem, ed. (1963).

Imago Dei

צלם־אלוהים

Joseph Dan

"And God said: 'Let us make man in our image, after our likeness . . . '" (Gen. 1:26). This verse is one of the most perplexing in the Hebrew Bible; Jewish commentators, from ancient times to the present, did their best to resolve the theological problems it presented. At the same time, it is difficult to find in the Bible a verse more pregnant with profound meaning, serving philosophers, mystics, and theologians as an ancient authority and source for their ideas. The uniqueness of this verse is the result of the unusual way in which it defines the relationship between God and man. It does not deal with a certain group of men or with any religious context dependent on man's deeds; its subject is man in the most general terms, referring to humanity more as a potential than as an actual existence. On the one hand it is vague, and the relationship described in it cannot be precisely defined; on the other hand it is sufficiently clear to denote an absolute intimacy between man and God, to a degree not usually expected in a religious context. Therefore, one is not surprised to find that this verse served as the basis for Jewish understanding of the nature of God and his relationship to man in a variety of ways, reflecting the deepest spiritual drives and religious sensibility of countless generations of Jewish thinkers.

This essay will deal primarily with one aspect of this verse, an aspect that has been central to the development of Jewish concepts of man and God: the transformation of the problem of anthropomorphic descriptions of God into the source of Jewish mystical symbolism concerning the nature of the godhead itself and the impact of this transformation on human religious behavior.

In ancient Hebrew rabbinic texts the main problem discussed concerning Genesis 1:26 is the plural language that God used when referring to the creation of man. Most of the sayings that tradition has preserved for us from this period are intended to defend Jewish monotheism from any doubt that may spring from the plural usage of the passage, "Let us create man in our image." Yet there are indications that the anthropomorphic consequences of the literal understanding of this verse were clear to the ancient rabbis, who apparently were not disturbed by them. It seems that ancient Judaism was able to accept an image of God that bore resemblance to the image of man without its basic theological monism being threatened. One may even suspect that this verse facilitated the development of anthropomorphic interpretations of other verses, even when the literal meaning of the biblical passages did not demand it.

The most outstanding example of such a process can be found in a second-century phenomenon that first appeared, in all probability, in the school of Rabbi Akiva: the understanding of the descriptions of the Lover in the Song of Songs as a divine self-portrait. From this school we have the first observations that disclose that the author of this biblical book was not King Solomon (Shlomo) but rather "The King of Peace" (Shalom), God himself; that the Song of Songs is the holiest book in the Bible; and that it was not "written" but "given" to the people of Israel in the same way that the Torah was "given," either when they miraculously crossed the Red Sea or as a part of the theophany on Mount Sinai. This attitude does not appear to be directly connected to the later allegorization of the Song of Songs as the story of the relationship between God and knesset Yisrael; rather, it should be understood as a stage in the development of the Shiur Komah, a mystical text of the talmudic period, and the central part of the ancient Heikhalot mysticism.

The Shiur Komah (literally, the measurement of the Height of the Creator, although actually it means imago Dei) was regarded in the Middle Ages as the worst and most embarrassing example of ancient Jewish anthropomorphism. Jewish philosophers did everything they could to cast doubt on its authenticity or to explain away its anthropomorphism. Yet if we examine this text in its historical background, it represents a denial of the literal meaning of *imago Dei* and the beginning of the process that turned this concept into a central one in the mystical structure of the relationship between man and God.

The text of the *Shiur Komah* is based on verses 5:10–16 of the Song of Songs, which describe the physical appearance of the Lover. It includes a list of the divine limbs, a list of their names, which are a long series of Hebrew letters, most of them completely unpronounceable and unintelligible, and a third list detailing the measurements of each limb. These measurements are given in units of tens of millions of *parasangs*, with a *parasang* explained as consisting of 18,000 *zeratot* (little fingers) of the creator, each as long as the whole world from one end to another. The limbs mentioned are human—eyes, neck, knees, arms, fingers—but their names and their measurements transcend human conception and imagination, and therefore literal anthropomorphism is denied. It is possible that this text is in fact a polemical answer to those who, following the new exegesis of the Song of Songs as the self-portrait of God, understood the physical descriptions of the Lover literally. The author of the *Shiur Komah* answers them by stating: Though God has a neck and arms, they are astronomical in their size—billions of times the length of the earth—and their essence is hinted in bizarre, unpronounceable names. Crude anthropomorphism is thus replaced by a sense of mystical awe toward the creator, who, though he is so radically different from anything resembling human physique, can still be described by the use of the names of human limbs.

Jewish mysticism prior to the Middle Ages, as far as we know it today, did not define the meaning of this resemblance between man and God in terms applicable to religious life. The early medieval thinkers were more interested in defending rabbinic Judaism from Karaitic charges of anthropomorphic superstition. They explained the *imago Dei* verse as well as the *Shiur Komah* as relating to a created angel, a lower divine being, or as an allegory concerning the relationship between man and the world, positing two levels of divine image—one found in the creation of the cosmos, the macrocosmic image, and one found in man—the microcosmic image. Nevertheless, during the early Middle Ages Jewish mystical speculation concerning the *Shiur Komah* and the mystical connection between the divine and human images persisted, to be revealed again in full force in the early works of the medieval kabbalists in the late twelfth and early thirteenth centuries.

In the earliest work of the kabbalah, *Sefer ha-Bahir*, the divine image is presented in symbolical anthropomorphic terms that advanced beyond the *Shiur Komah:* The limbs of this divine image denote not only parts of the image but also its different functions. The fingers of the divine left hand, for example, bring punishment to the wicked and evil of the world, while the right arm is the origin of divine deliverance and redemption. The main contribution of the kabbalah—up to and including its central work, the *Zohar,* written in Christian Spain at the end of the thirteenth century—to the concept of *imago Dei* in Judaism is the sincere belief in the symbolical connection between human limbs and the elements that constitute the fullness of the divine realm. There is a double layer of symbolism implicit in this connection. Not only is the relationship itself symbolical, but the celestial counterpart to the human image can be known only by its symbols, the full meaning of which remains completely beyond human knowledge and understanding. This double layer of symbolism prevented any anthropomorphic, and thus heretical, use of the *imago Dei* idea by Jewish mystics. Indeed, by the late thirteenth century Jewish mystics became so used to this symbolism that the human element in expressions like "God's beard" or "his heart" was almost completely lost and forgotten; in kabbalistic literature these symbolical terms referred first and foremost to the divine world.

The *Zohar* and other thirteenth- and fourteenth-century kabbalistic works introduced a dynamic element into the idea of *imago Dei* on two levels. One, begun by the *Sefer ha-Bahir,* was the equation of the limbs with the divine functions of providence with respect to creation; the second was the dynamic symbolism describing the interrelationship among the divine powers themselves: a vast treasury of symbols detailing the sexual relationship between the masculine and feminine parts of the divine world, between God and the *malkhut* (kingdom) or *Shekhinah* (divine Presence), as the female element in the hierarchy of divine emanations was often called. Another group of symbols described the mythological struggle between the elements of good and evil in the divine realm, after that realm had been conceived of in dualistic terms by Rabbi Isaac ben Jacob ha-Kohen in the second half of the thirteenth century. Both the beneficent divine powers and the evil ones were structured according to the same anthropomorphic image, consisting of ten descending emanations corresponding to human limbs.

The most intricate and imaginative Jewish description of the divine figure in anthropomorphic terms is to be found in the *Zohar,* which made use of all the images and symbols introduced by previous Jewish mystics and added to it the author's own creative mystical visions. Gershom Scholem dedicated to this portion of the *Zohar,* known as the *Idrot,* a major part of his penetrating essay on the idea of the *Shiur Komah* in Jewish mysticism.[1] As Scholem pointed out, the metaphysical element in these descriptions of the various limbs of the divine figure is interwoven and sometimes even overpowers the mythical one. The *imago Dei* tradition was used by the author of the *Zohar* in order to introduce his mystical conceptions of the processes operating within the godhead, directing the development in the mystical realm and influencing the divine providence of the lower worlds. Since the fourteenth century, when the *Zohar* increasingly became a dominant power in shaping Jewish ideas and symbols, the *Shiur Komah* image of the godhead became an accepted part of Jewish thought; the most orthodox sections of Jewish society used it more often and more profoundly than others.

Later kabbalistic schools, including the Lurianic kabbalah, which appeared in Safed in the last third of the sixteenth century, and the Sabbatean heresy of the seventeenth and eighteenth centuries used this symbolism in a most central manner. The image of *Adam Kadmon* (Primordial Man) became almost identical with the concept of the godhead. The *Shiur Komah* anthropomorphic structure was found by Jewish mystics not only in the image of the divine realm as a whole, but also in the inner structure of every part of that realm. The founder of Ḥasidism, Israel Ba'al Shem Tov, is reported by his disciples to have said that every letter of the Jewish prayers consists of *komah shelemah,* that is, an integrally whole *imago Dei* figure. This mystical figure became the building-block of every sacred particle of the divine and earthly realms.

The danger of anthropomorphism in a mystical-mythical concept of *imago Dei* can be overcome in one of two ways. It is possible either to downgrade it—that is, to claim, as did Saadiah Gaon and most of the Jewish philosophic tradition, that the anthropomorphic descriptions are related to a lower, relatively unimportant spiritual or even material figure, or to uplift it to such mythical heights that the fact that man also has the same physical structure becomes a minor point. The process of the development of this idea in Jewish mysticism, which began in the ancient text of the *Shiur Komah* related to the Song of Songs, is a perfect example of the second way. *Imago Dei* in Jewish mysticism is truly the image of God; it represents in a symbolical way the perfect structure of the godhead and hides within it the secrets of the inner dynamic life of God. The same divine image is reflected in God's creation, both in the divine emanations and the created, physical beings. Man is but one example of the appearance of this perfect structure outside of the divine realm.

Yet Jewish mysticism did not forsake the element of closeness between man and God that is inherent in the *imago Dei* symbolism. The parallel structure of both the human and divine realms enables man, in his religious and ethical deeds, to influence and even shape the divine processes. The *imago Dei* symbolism reflects not only the original structure of the body of Adam, but a continuous, permanent interdependence between God and his creatures. Thus, *imago Dei* in Jewish mysticism became a major force in enabling man to shape history as well as his own personal fate. Some of the divine powers represented in the transcendent *Shiur Komah* reside within man's own humble physical body. Jewish mysticism and the ethical literature that the kabbalah inspired directed man how to use these powers in order to assist God in achieving his mystical purpose in creating the universe.

REFERENCES

1. Gershom Scholem, "Die mystische Gestalt der Gottheit in der Kabbala," in *Eranos Jahrbuch* 29 (1960), 139–82.

BIBLIOGRAPHY

Alexander Altmann, "*Homo Imago Dei* in Jewish and Christian Theology," in *The Journal of Religion*, 48 (1968).
Joseph Dan, "The Concept of Knowledge in the *Shiur Komah*," in *Studies in Jewish Religious and Intellectual History in Honor of Alexander Altmann*, Siegfried Stein and Raphael Loew, eds. (1979).

Immortality

הישארות הנפש

Allan Arkush

The doctrine of immortality normally refers to the immortality of the soul—in contrast to the mortality of the body. This doctrine, as has often been pointed out, is not Jewish in origin but Greek. Judaism at first conceived of the life after death not as a liberation of the soul from the body, but as the "reunion of soul and body to live again in the completeness of man's nature."[1] In the End of Days, it was believed, the dead would be brought back to life. The righteous would then enjoy the rewards they had earned through their conduct in the course of their lives, and the wicked would receive appropriate punishments.

The Talmud, to be sure, includes some statements reflecting belief in the immortality of the disembodied soul, but these, as Julius Guttman has observed,[2] are curiously undeveloped—probably as a result of the competing concept of resurrection. Only in the Middle Ages does the idea of immortality begin to assume preeminence. In the teaching of Moses Maimonides, the resurrection of the dead is only a temporary, intermediate stage in the soul's journey. It is followed by a second death, after which those who have lived properly enjoy forever, as bodiless souls, "blissful delight in their attainment of knowledge of the truly essential nature of God the Creator." The wicked, on the other hand, are "cut off"; their souls perish.[3]

These divergent posthumous prospects should not, according to Maimonides, be the foremost things in a man's mind. One ought to study the Torah and perform its commandments for their own sake, and not ask "What will I get out of it?" But, Maimonides wrote, our sages knew that this is an exceedingly difficult thing to do. "Therefore, in order that the multitude stay faithful and do the commandments, it was permitted to tell them that they might hope for a reward and to warn them against transgressions out of fear of punishment."[4] In time, perhaps, they might awaken to the truth and serve God out of love.

For Maimonides and the other medieval Jewish philosophers, immortality is not an inherent property of the human soul but a consequence of virtuous behavior. They do not speak of *niẓhiyut ha-nefesh* (the eternality of the soul) but of *hisharut ha-nefesh* (the survival of the soul). For them it was important to affirm that the soul could outlast the body but presumptuous to argue that it was deathless. God could not be denied the power to destroy something he had created.

Not until modern times did a Jewish philosopher, Moses Mendelssohn, choose to speak of *niẓhiyut ha-nefesh,* in his work *Sefer ha-Nefesh,* and to argue that all human souls exist everlastingly. Unlike his medieval predecessors, Mendelssohn held that the human soul is by nature indestructible. He also maintained that every human soul is ultimately destined to taste of the felicity Maimonides had reserved for the virtuous alone. Granted, the wicked would receive some well-deserved punishments on their posthumous path to perfection, but these would be purely correctional and limited in duration. In the end, every individual is destined to attain a certain degree of happiness. Nothing else would be consistent with the infinite wisdom and goodness of God.

Mendelssohn, no less than Maimonides, stressed the superiority of virtuous acts performed because they are seen as desirable in themselves, and not for the sake of receiving a reward. He belittled what he called the "popular moral teaching," based as it was on threats and promises concerning the afterlife. Still, he did not try to uproot these popular ideas. "The common heap," he believed, are often incapable of understanding a better teaching, and it would be inexcusable to deprive them of their only incentive to live virtuously.

Mendelssohn was the last major Jewish thinker to argue that the existence of an afterlife was rationally demonstrable. He was the last, in fact, for whom the doctrine of a life after death was a consolation and not a source of some embarrassment. The new attitude toward this question on the part of later Jewish philosophers can be directly traced to the influence of the man Mendelssohn counted as a friend but described as the "all-destroyer"—Immanuel Kant. Kant demolished Mendelssohn's as well as everyone else's proofs of the soul's immortality, and although he himself still adhered to the doctrine, identifying it as a postulate of practical reason, his moral teaching taken as a whole discouraged even his most ardent Jewish disciples from following him on this matter. The great neo-Kantian Hermann Cohen strongly regretted Kant's failure to expunge this remnant of heteronomous morality from his system, and was careful not to repeat the same error in his own philosophy of Judaism.

Cohen did not altogether repudiate the idea of the immortality of the soul, but radically transformed it. He maintained that certain biblical expressions for death—"And thou shalt go to thy fathers," "He is gathered to his people"—reflect the biblical conception of immortality as "the historical living on of the individual in the historical continuity of the people."[5] In the later, more profoundly moral and universalistic perspective of messianism, the individual's frame of reference is necessarily broadened, and it becomes clear that "only in the infinite development of the human race toward the ideal spirit of holiness can the individual soul actualize its immortality."[6] Ideally, the individual's hopes are not to be focused on his own fate after death, or even on the ongoing life of the nation to which he belongs, but on the progress of mankind as a whole.

Cohen's interpretation of particular biblical expressions may be forced and tendentious, but there can be little doubt that he was closer to the viewpoint of the Bible than was postbiblical Judaism. But in eliminating the prospect of the individual soul's survival after death as itself, in full possession of its former identity, Cohen and other modern Jewish philosophers have once again placed Judaism face to face with the dilemma that the concept of a compensatory afterlife was originally meant to resolve. How can one account for what the rabbis called the "ṣaddik ve-ra lo" (the righteous man for whom things go badly)?

In the decades since Cohen wrote, the Jewish people has had to confront this question on an unprecedentedly massive scale, largely as a result of events initiated by the people Hermann Cohen lived among and believed to be important contributors to the progress of mankind. How could a just God have permitted the slaughter of millions of Jews, ṣaddikim (righteous individuals) and lesser men alike? No one can be satisfied by the thought that the victims live on, in some sense, in the rest of the human race. But without resorting to the ancient belief that they themselves live on beyond the range of our senses or will come back to life when God wills it, what else can we say? It is no wonder that contemporary theologians, deprived of this belief, have responded to the Holocaust with little more than confessions of incomprehension, nihilistic pseudo-theologies, and silence.

Apart from depriving it of a satisfactory theodicy, the abandonment of the idea of a compensatory afterlife has had another, less palpable consequence for Judaism: it has lessened its efficacy as a moral force. Maimonides or Mendelssohn would have noticed this problem immediately, but modern Jews are generally oblivious of it. We think too little of morality based on religious authority to regret its decline. And unlike Maimonides and Mendelssohn, we see no reason why everyone should not practice autonomous moral virtue.

Our need for a doctrine of immortality may, then, be as great as that of earlier generations. But we cannot adopt one simply because we need it, even if we were inclined to do so. And we are not so inclined. On the whole, we are suspicious of religious teachings that console us and receptive to those that challenge our security. We do not want to close our eyes to the harshness of life in this world, but neither are we at peace with a God who would have created nothing beyond it. We are, in short, at an impasse, and there is no way out in sight.

REFERENCES

1. George Foot Moore, *Judaism in the First Centuries of the Christian Era*, 2 (1971), 295.
2. Julius Guttmann, "Die Normierung des Glaubensinhalts im Judentum," in MGWD 27 (1927), 244.
3. Isadore Twersky, ed., *A Maimonides Reader* (1972), 412.
4. "Introduction to Helek," *Commentary on the Mishnah*, Sanh. ch. 10, quoted in Isadore Twersky, ed., *A Maimonides Reader* (1972), 406.
5. Hermann Cohen, *Religion of Reason out of the Sources of Judaism* (1971), 301.
6. Ibid., 308.

BIBLIOGRAPHY

Hermann Cohen, *Religion of Reason out of the Sources of Judaism* (1971), 296–338.
George Foot Moore, *Judaism in the First Centuries of the Christian Era*, 2 (1971), 287–322.
Isadore Twersky, ed., *A Maimonides Reader* (1972), 401–23.

Individuality

יחידיות

Peter Ochs

The concept of individuality refers to an event and a movement rather than to some enduring thing in the world. For Israel's sages, God alone endures, while the things of this world pass away, acquiring individuality only as instruments of God's purposes. Only idol-worshipers place their trust in mere things. For those not sharing the perspective of Israel's sages, however, concern to overcome worldly idolatries may also breed disrespect for our worldly limitations. Impatient with the things of this world, they try to possess eternity through their ideas of God or of another world. In place of eternity, however, they are left only with themselves, individual collections of ideas, desires, and fancies, cut off from this world and from the God who created it. The meaning and value of individuality depends on its source: creator or creature.

For biblical and rabbinic Judaism, the creator is the source of individuality: God is pure subjectivity, creating this world and then acting on it, through his spoken word (dibbur). The spoken word is the source of purposes in the world, in relation to which this world is a collection of possible agents. When God speaks, he designates certain objects in the world as agents of his purposes, making possible agents actual ones. Individuality is the quality of having been designated as such an agent. Something in the world becomes an individual as the effect of having been selected by God. A bush is an individual bush when God appears by way of it. A human being is an individual human being when God calls that being out of the world in which it normally operates, as, for example, God called to Abraham, "*Lekh Lekha!*" ("Go forth!") (Gen. 12:1).

For classical Judaism, individuality is a passing thing. Something is individual only while serving a purpose. Once the purpose is fulfilled, or aborted, the individuality evaporates, or is remembered not as an individuality but as an exemplary instrument of action. When he "went forth," Abraham was an individual; when he is remembered as Abraham *avinu* (our father), he is a model for the selection of other individuals.

The power of memory makes human beings both remarkable and troublesome instruments of God's purposes. For the most part, these purposes are implanted in the human soul as preconscious rules of behavior, products of biology and of childhood socialization. Acting in the world, humans select individual instruments of these purposes, like Adam naming the animals he might rule over. Remembering which individuals were more helpful agents than others, humans may enact their purposes most efficiently. In memory, however, individuals lose their evanescent character, becoming ideas or images of possible rather than actual individuals. With sufficient memory, humans may collect small worlds of such ideas, worlds that may interest them more than the one God created. Mistaking ideas for individuals, humans may try to enact their purposes in idea only, leaving the created world unchanged and their purposes unfulfilled. This is the source of what the rabbis call Adam's evil inclination: love of his private world, which breeds inattention to the created one.

For many modern Jews, Adam's evil inclination is a source of respite from a world they have grown to mistrust. Israel's suffering in Europe has made the created world appear an unsatisfactory arena for enacting God's purposes. In its place, they choose worlds of their own making, suggesting that the creature and not the creator is the source of individuality. For the secular disciples of the Enlightenment and the emancipation, the creature is an individual human being, made individual as agent of its own purposes. This human being is subjectivity and individual in one. Self-governing and thus self-individuating, it rules over a private world of speculation, fancy, and satisfaction. For the extreme orthodox, the creature is an individual community within the people Israel. This community first acquired its individuality through a history of shared suffering, understood as a shared experience of God's justice and mercy. It now preserves its separateness through an act of will. Replacing history with memory, the community now lives through shared ideas about its past, rather than through shared experiences of its present.

Mistrusting the one created world that we all share, modern individualists, secular or orthodox, place their trust in private worlds of ideas, or ideologies. Withdrawn from the one world that mediates among them, these ideologies appear isolated from one another. If it fostered Israel's suffering, *galut* (exile) also offered Israel's ideologues room for this kind of isolation. The land of Israel, however, is not so spacious. At the same time that it promises to negate the sufferings brought on by *galut,* the people Israel's return to its land has brought Israel's once isolated ideologues into immediate contact and, therefore, conflict. The land has thus, in our lifetime, offered a new setting for Israel's perennial conflict between service to the creator and service to the creature.

The land is itself that created thing par excellence through which God has revealed his purposes to Israel and in service to which Israel has achieved its individuality. We would hope that a return to the land would renew Israel's trust in the created world and shared commitment to the purposes that are revealed through it. Habits bred by so many years of suffering and fear are, however, not quickly overcome. The various ideologues of modern Israel lose touch with the land as a created thing and seek to possess it, instead, as if it were a mere idea, defined in different ways by their different and conflicting ideologies. We must assume that these ideologies will eventually display their irrelevance to the immediate conditions of life in the land. Until that time, however, we cannot expect Israel to be at peace with itself. And, until that time, we cannot expect Israel to recover the individuality it achieves only as an instrument of God's will.

BIBLIOGRAPHY

Ahad Haam, *Essays, Letters, Memoirs,* Leon Simon, ed. (1946).
David Hartman, *Joy and Responsibility* (1978).
Max Kadushin, *The Rabbinic Mind,* 2d ed. (1965).
Max Kadushin, *Worship and Ethics* (1963).
Mordecai M. Kaplan, *The Meaning of God in Modern Jewish Religion* (1962).

Islam

אסלם

Nissim Rejwan

Islam, a monotheistic religion founded by Muhammad in the seventh century, is the system of beliefs and rituals based on the Koran. The term *Islam* is derived from the Arabic verb *aslama* (submit), denoting the attitude of the Muslim to God. Although the creed in its barest outline consists of the declaration "There is no god but God (*Allah*) and Muhammad is his prophet," Islam is a religion of both faith and works, faith being but one of the five pillars (*arkan*, singular, *rukn*) that a believer should observe. In addition to faith, or *iman*, which consists of a recital of the creed, are *salat*, divine worship five times a day; *zakat*, payment of the legal alms; *sawm*, the month-long fast of Ramadan, and *hajj*, pilgrimage to Mecca.

Like Judaism, Islam stresses the unity of God, and the Koran specifically rejects the concept of the Christian Trinity. God has revealed himself to man through prophets, starting with Adam and including Noah, Abraham, and others; but he has given books only to three of them—the Law (*tawrat*) to Moses, the Gospel (*injil*) to Jesus, and the Koran to Muhammad. Muhammad, however, is the last of the prophets, the chosen instrument by which God sent the eternal message in its last and definitive form.

The Jewish and Christian presence in Arabia, where Muhammad was born and grew up, and his travels, first with the uncle who raised him after he was orphaned and then on behalf of his wife Khadija, are generally considered the most crucial influences on Muhammad's life and on his mission. At the age of about forty, in the year 610, Muhammad received a divine call through the archangel Gabriel commanding him to assume the role of prophet, bearing a new message embodied in an Arabic Scripture. But the notables of Mecca, where he resided, looked askance at the man and his message, while the following he had managed to command there was too small to fulfill his expectations. The turning point, however, came in 622, when Muhammad accepted an invitation to come to Yathrib (later to be known as Medina). He arrived there with a number of followers, and this migration (hijra) marks the beginning of the Islamic era and the first year in the Muslim calendar. Establishing himself in Yathrib as a political as well as a spiritual leader, Muhammad soon became master of the situation, extending his control to Mecca itself, which he purged of idols and "infidels." Jewish and Christian tribes in and around Medina were brought under tribute and delegations from Arab tribes came to declare allegiance and pay zakat. Indeed, at the time of his death in 632, Muhammad was the undisputed ruler of all Arabia.

At the time of Muhammad's appearance a great number of Jews lived in Arabia; large-scale commercial relations between Arabia and Palestine had existed already in the days of Solomon. The Hebrew Bible contains a number of references to the close relationship between Arabs and Jews, and the Books of Job and Proverbs contain many Arabic words. Moreover, some paragraphs in the Mishnah refer specifically to the Jews of the Arabian Peninsula. While considering himself the Messenger of God and "the Seal of all the Prophets," Muhammad did not intend to establish Islam as a new religion. Rather, he regarded himself as sent by Allah to confirm the Scriptures. His basic contention was that God could not have omitted the Arabs from the revelations with which he had favored the Jews and the Christians, and subsequently he accused the Jews of deliberately deleting from their Bible predictions of his advent.

Relations between Islam and Judaism can be dealt with under two main headings: Islam's indebtedness to Judaism and Muslim attitudes to Jews living in the realm of Islam. Concerning Judaic influences in Islam, there is a wealth of evidence to show the extent to which these have been deep and lasting. The very name for Islam's Scripture, Koran, while it may be a genuine Arabic word meaning "reading" or "reciting," is thought to be borrowed from the Hebrew or Aramaic *mikra,* used by the rabbis to designate the Scripture or Torah. Muhammad's principal Jewish source, however, was not the Bible but the later Haggadah, which was communicated to him by word of mouth. This is especially apparent in the numerous references in the Koran to "prophets" preceding Moses. Noteworthy among these is the exceptional position allotted to Abraham. Abraham is "the friend of God"; he is neither Jew nor Christian but, as a true believer in one God, is considered to be the first Muslim, the first to have submitted unquestioningly to the will of Allah. According to Erwin Rosenthal, Muhammad saw his mission as consisting of restoring the pure religion of Abraham. This change took place in Medina, and the exaltation of Abraham was the direct result of Muhammad's alienation from the Jews.

The Koran is the Holy Book of Islam in exactly the same way as the Hebrew Bible is the Holy Book of Judaism. In the same fashion, however, as Judaism created an enormous exegetic literature after the conclusion of the biblical period, so Islam after the death of Muhammad created an exhaustive literature based on its own Scriptures. While Judaism is a religion of halakhah, Islam is a religion of *shari'a,* both words denoting the same thing, namely, a God-given law minutely regulating all aspects of a believer's life: law, worship, ethics, social behavior. Halakhah and *shari'a* are both grounded upon oral tradition, called in Arabic *hadith* and in Hebrew *torah she-be-al peh.* As S. D. Goitein has observed, these authoritatively interpret and supplement the written law—*kitab* in Arabic and *torah she-bikhtav* in Hebrew, which are again similar terms. In Muslim and in Jewish literature the oral tradition falls into two parts, one legal and the other moral, and in both cases they assume the same form of loosely connected maxims and short anecdotes. Again, the logical reasoning applied to the development of the religious law is largely identical in Islam and Judaism, and this is seen by Goitein not as mere coincidence inherent in the nature of things but, as the similar terms used in both traditions show, the result of direct contact. Finally, in both religions the study of even purely legal matters is regarded as worship, the holy men of Islam and Judaism being not priests or monks but students of the divinely revealed law. Scholars have also remarked on the fact that Muslim religious law developed mainly in Iraq, which at the time was the leading center of rabbinic learning.

One of the manifestations of this close interaction between Islam and Judaism is the laws governing *taharah,* ritual purity and cleanliness, which are the same in both religions, as is the term itself. These laws concern forbidden food and drink, touching the sexual organs, bodily discharge, and contact with a corpse or a carcass—all of which cause ritual impurity and bar the affected from fulfilling religious duties such as prayer, presence in a place of worship, and recitation of Scripture. Prayer is another shared feature of these sister faiths: in Islam the first essential in prayer is *niyya,* intent, literally corresponding to the Jewish *kavvanah,* without which prayer is incomplete. According to Rosenthal, *taharah* and *niyya* are obviously imitations of the conditions for Jewish prayer as laid down in the talmudic treatise Berakhot. As far as dietary laws are concerned, while Muhammad came to reject most of these (which he considered a punishment for the Jews), he retained the prohibition against eating pig, blood, and carcasses, and decreed ritual slaughtering of all animals permitted for human consumption. Of social obligations and duties—which in both Islam and Judaism are considered religious duties incumbent upon every believer—*zakat* in Islam corresponds to *ẓedakah* (the giving of charity) in Judaism. The care of widows and orphans is also a religious duty in both religions, and visiting the sick is commended in Islam in terms identical to haggadahic recommendations.

The main point to be made about Islam's attitude to Jews and Judaism is that, as "People of the Book," Jews are not regarded as nonbelievers, since they share with Muslims the belief in the one and only God. Jews, however, are not regarded as true believers because they have failed to believe in the Koran and the mission of Muhammad. Consequently these "scripturaries" *(ahl el-kitab),* while allowed to live in the Islamic state unmolested, were granted this right on condition that they pay a poll tax, *jizya,* and accept the status defined in treaties and charters concluded with the Muslim community. As a protected minority, however, the Jews, along with the Christians and other "people of the covenant" *(dhimmis),* were exempted from payment of *zakat,* the alms tax imposed on Muslims as a religious precept. In this way the imposition of the *jizya* may be seen not as a penalty for religious nonconformity but as a kind of substitute for *zakat.* No less important was the fact that the tolerated non-Muslims were supposed to pay this special tax also as a levy on their exemption from taking part in the wars of the Muslims.

The rules and regulations governing relations between the Muslims and *ahl el-kitab* derive from the Koran, the oral tradition, and to a certain extent from local traditions and practices. These regulations included a number of disabilities, but practice differed considerably from the jurist's exposition of the law, the degree of tolerance depending largely on the whims of the rulers and their officials. Both sides, at times, tended to ignore and even violate the law with regard to the employment of non-Muslims in government, the payment of *jizya,* and the building of synagogues and churches. Jews and Christians were granted a large measure of self-rule, and each community was left to be governed by its own religious head, who was responsible to the Muslim ruler of the day.

As the power of Islam spread, and as it began to come in contact with more peoples and civilizations, the degree of its religious tolerance became more pronounced. During the Abbasid period, from the eighth to the thirteenth centuries, Jews and Christians held important financial, clerical, and professional positions. In 985, the Arab chronicler Al-Maqdisi found that most of the money changers and bankers in Syria were Jews, while most of the clerks and physicians were Christians. Under several caliphs we read of more than one Jew in the capital of the caliphate and the provinces assuming responsible state positions. In Baghdad, the capital, the Jews maintained a large, prosperous community. Rabbi Benjamin of Tudela, who visited the city in 1169, found the community in possession of ten rabbinical schools and twenty-three synagogues; he depicts in glowing colors the high esteem in which the head of the Babylonian Jews was held as a descendant of David and as Prince of the Exile, *Ras el-Jalut* (in rabbinic Aramaic, *Resh Galuta*).

There is a good deal of ambiguity about Islam's attitude to non-Muslims. S. D. Goitein points out that the Koran contains two diametrically opposed views on adherents of other faiths, as it does on several other vital matters, a fact that can be explained by the spiritual and political history of Muhammad and his young community:

> Unlike Christianity, which originated in opposition to its mother religion and therefore negated its right of existence, Islam came into being in defiance of paganism and through self-identification with the People of the Book, that is, Jews and Christians. This is the root of that primitive universalism—the belief that monotheistic religions were essentially one—which pervades the early parts of the Quran, and as a consequence of which Islamic law recognized in principle the right of existence of other monotheistic religions.[1]

Subsequently, however, Muhammad discovered that he could not maintain his claim to prophethood without establishing a church of his own, demanding for itself exclusive authority just as the synagogue and the various Christian denominations had done before. Moreover, Muhammad obtained by military and political means what he had failed to obtain by his powers of persuasion, with the result that the last ten years of his life were marked by incessant warfare. As the larger part of the Koran originated during this latter period, the imprint left on the character of Islam by these events is such that toward the end of his life Muhammad was exhorting his followers: "Fight until religion everywhere belongs to God," that is, fight until all of the world worships the one true God of Islam. Consequently, Islamic law divided the world into two domains—*dar al-Islam* and *dar al-harb,* the domains of Islam and of war, respectively. Thus, in theory, no Islamic state can make peace with a non-Muslim power; the most that is religiously permissible is an armistice of short duration. As far as Christians and Jews living in the domain of Islam are concerned, they have to pay the *jizya* and are to be kept in submission in order to demonstrate that Islam is the true and dominant religion. However, while Muslim scholars and law-makers laid down a long list of discriminatory laws to give expression to submission, the actual application of these laws differed from time to time and place to place depending on the existing socio-economic and religious situation.

Under Ottoman Islam, which by the beginning of the sixteenth century dominated Syria and Egypt, the conditions under which the Jews were per-mitted to live contrasted so strikingly with those imposed on their coreli-gionists in the various parts of Christendom that the fifteenth century wit-nessed a large influx of European Jews into the sultan's domain. The measures taken against the Jews in Spain, culminating in their expulsion in 1492, gave the greatest momentum to this migration. Istanbul soon came to host the largest Jewish community in the whole of Europe, while Salonika became a predominantly Jewish city. The degree of the Jews' integration into the life of Ottoman Islam was such that H. A. R. Gibb and Harold Bowen, two notable students of modern Islam, find that there has been "something sympathetic to the Jewish nature in the culture of Islam," since

> from the rise of the Caliphate till the abolition of the ghettos in Europe the most flourishing centers of Jewish life were to be found in Muslim countries—in Iraq during the Abbasid period, in Spain throughout the period of Moorish domination, and thereafter in the Ottoman Empire.[2]

In this connection it is of interest to note that, as far as Palestine is con-cerned, the right of Jews to "return" to live as a religious community in this strip of land was accepted by all the successive Muslim rulers from the Mus-lim conquest right to the end of the nineteenth century, when Zionist set-tlement, entangled as it was in European *Weltpolitik,* was viewed as a threat to the integrity of the Ottoman empire.

REFERENCES

1. Shlomo Dov Goitein, *Interfaith Relations in Medieval Islam,* the Yaacov Herzog Memorial Lecture (1973), 28–29.
2. H. A. R. Gibb and Harold Bowen, *Islamic Society and the West,* 1 (1950), 218.

BIBLIOGRAPHY

Barakat Ahmad, *Muhammad and the Jews: A Re-Examination* (1979).
Amnon Cohen, *Jewish Life Under Islam: Jerusalem in the Sixteenth Century* (1984).
H. A. R. Gibb and Harold Bowen, *Islamic Society and the West,* 2 vols. (1950–1957).
Shlomo Dov Goitein, *Jews and Arabs: Their Contacts Through the Ages,* 3d ed. (1974).
Abraham I. Katsch, *Judaism in Islam,* 3d ed. (1980).
Bernard Lewis, *The Jews of Islam* (1984).
Bernard Lewis, *Islam and the Arab World: Faith, People, Culture, Texts* (1976).
Erwin I. J. Rosenthal, *Judaism and Islam* (1961).

Jerusalem

ירושלים

Shemaryahu Talmon

In Hebrew Scripture the very name *Jerusalem* indicates that the city was built as a "foundation [for the deity] Salem," who can be identified with Shalmon or Shulmanu, a deity known to us from Assyrian sources. In view of the theophoric character of the name *Jerusalem*, that is, its being based on the divine appellation of Salem, it may be considered as highly probable that the *nomen locus* Salem mentioned in Genesis 14, in the well-known tradition connected with the patriarch Abraham, can also be identified with what was destined to become the Holy City of Israel—Jerusalem, Zion. Indeed, a tripartite equivalence of Salem, Jerusalem, and Zion is taken for granted in biblical literature, as may be deduced from the employment of Salem and Zion as synonyms in Psalm 76:3: "Salem became His abode; Zion, His den." By means of a popular etymology, the theophoric component Salem in Jeru-Salem was equated with the Hebrew word *shalom* (peace). This paved the way for the elevation of Jerusalem to the proverbial City of Peace, a concept that found its most stirring expression in Psalm 122: "Pray for the well-being of Jerusalem! . . . may those who love you be at peace." Even more expressly, Salem and *shalom* are identified in the New Testament, where in the Epistle to the Hebrews (7:1–2) the aforementioned passage from Genesis 14, in which Abraham meets Melchizedek, is paraphrased: "For this Melchizedek, King of Salem, priest of God Most High, went to meet Abraham, who was on his way after defeating the kings, and blessed him; to whom also Abraham gave a tenth of all he had; by the interpretation of his name, he is first 'King of righteousness,' and also King of Salem, that is, 'King of Peace.'"

Alas, this popular etymology, which, indeed, has clearly discernible roots already in Hebrew Scriptures, cannot be considered to have either a philological or a historical basis. In actual history Jerusalem seldom ceased being a city of bloodshed and war. In II Kings 21:16, for instance, it is noted that "Menasseh put so many innocent persons to death that he filled Jerusalem with blood from end to end." And in Matthew 23:29–30, we read, "Woe unto you, scribes and Pharisees, hypocrites! for you built the sepulchres of the prophets and garnish the tombs of the righteous, saying, had we lived in the days of our fathers, we would not have been joined with them in shedding the blood of the prophets." There is no need to enumerate the many references to wars about and around Jerusalem from the days of her conquest by David (II Sam. 5:4–9) to the battles in which it is to be embroiled according to late eschatological vision (for example, Zech. 14).

The pre-Israelite temple-city Jerusalem that had been ruled by the priest-king Melchizedek, who officiated at the shrine of El Elyon, God Most High, was Hebraized, as it were, by locating the *hieros logos* of Isaac's sacrifice by his father, Abraham (Gen. 22), on Mount Moriah, which from days of old was associated with Jerusalem. It may further be assumed that the above two traditions, which linked Abraham with Salem/Jerusalem, like many other patriarchal traditions, in fact reflect concepts of monarchic times that were retrojected into the days of the forefathers. Thus Abraham is portrayed exclusively dealing with none but kings and rulers. And it can hardly be a coincidence that the two main cities in which he appears, Jerusalem and Hebron (Gen. 23), would in the future serve King David, each in succession, as the metropolis of his realm (II Sam. 5:1–5).

The twofold association of Abraham with Jerusalem—one set in a political context arising out of the war against the five foreign kings who had invaded Canaanite territory to fight against the kings of Sodom and Gomorrah and their associates (Gen. 14), the other illustrating the religious character of the city where the patriarch had built an altar on Mount Moriah (Gen. 22)—projects the twofold significance of Jerusalem in the days of David. Initially inhabited by indigenous Canaanites, as we know from the Tel el Amarna letters of the fourteenth century B.C.E. and from chapter 10 of the Book of Joshua, Jerusalem was later ruled by another ethnic group, the Jebusites, as we learn from Judges 19:10–12. In both periods, there was probably a foreign cult center on the site (Gen. 14; II Sam. 24:18–25); only after its conquest by David did the city become the religious and political center of Israel. Jerusalem had no previous affiliation with any of the Israelite tribes David had set out to weld into one nation, and by transforming the city into the metropolis of his empire, he created a new unifying political focus for Israel. By building in Jerusalem the Temple dedicated to Israel's God or, to be more precise, by laying the foundations for the building operations to be carried out by his son Solomon, as described in I Kings 6–8, David also made Jerusalem the cornerstone for the religious and cultic unification of Israel.

Thus Jerusalem became the symbol and the most significant exponent of the transition from "peoplehood" to "nationhood" and "statehood." But it was never exclusively subjugated to or identified with the new sociopolitical phenomenon: when the state ceased to exist, Jerusalem did not lose its focal importance and symbolic meaning for the Jewish people. The meaning of the city that in antiquity had experienced one decisive transformation could be redefined in consonance with new and different historical situations. In fact, Jerusalem has been so redefined for hundreds of years without losing the prestige and symbolic value it has held since the days of David.

In capturing Jerusalem, David and the Davidic house apparently also took over the old emblems of sovereignty and the royal epithets of Melchizedek, the former priest-king of Jerusalem, as can be inferred, for example, from the text in Psalm 110:4, which, however, cannot be accurately translated. The Psalmist addresses himself to a prototypical king of the Davidic dynasty: "The Lord has sworn and will not relent, 'You are a priest [sanctified] forever, after the manner of Melchizedek.'" In the short period of unity under David and Solomon, Israel experienced an unprecedented and never again attained state of political glory, economic achievement, and cultic splendor. It is for this reason that the capital of the realm, Jerusalem, became a beacon of well-being and success for future generations. Late biblical and postbiblical Judaism made the idealized image of that historical Jerusalem the cornerstone of its hopes for a national and religious renaissance, and ultimately perceived in it the prototype of the New Jerusalem, the focus of its eschatological aspirations.

The idealized image of the real, historical Jerusalem was blended with the ancient Near Eastern mythic motif of the City on the Mountain, of which not only literary but also pictorial representations have come to us. The geographical elevation of the city whose acropolis is occupied by a sanctuary clearly symbolizes its closeness to heaven and gives rise to the claim to divine status. The ever-recurring emphasis on the mountainous character of Jerusalem and its surroundings, which, indeed, is anchored in geographical reality, is obviously meant to relate some of the notions inherent in the City on the Mountain motif by means of historicizing a myth. The description of the Temple as standing on the highest mountain in the area, and being the tallest building in the city, which later tradition will not allow to be topped by any other building, further illuminates the similarity with Canaanite, especially Ugaritic, and Mesopotamian themes. These mythic elements become exceedingly prominent in prophetic and psalmodic literature. In Psalm 68:16–17, for instance, we have a report, as it were, of a controversy between the mountains that had previously been chosen by God and now are superseded by Mount Zion:

> O majestic mountain, Mount Bashan,
> O jagged mountain, Mount Bashan,
> Why so hostile, O jagged mountain
> Toward the mountain God desired as His dwelling?
> The Lord shall abide there forever.

Mount Sinai is not mentioned in these verses, but we find an explicit reference to it in the verse to follow, where the Hebrew text should be corrected to read: "The Lord has come *from* Sinai in holiness" (*Adonai ba misinai ba-kodesh*). This may be taken to imply that Mount Sinai is also included among the mountains supplanted by Mount Zion.

In these nonhistoriographical strata of the biblical literature, national-religious imagination often soars high, leaving behind any consideration of reality. This phenomenon, which can repeatedly be observed in the Book of Psalms, may be seen as a process of mythologization of history. It appears that this dehistoricization will serve later generations as a launching pad for the ideological transfer of terrestrial Jerusalem to the celestial plane, *Yerushalayim shel ma'lah,* celestial Jerusalem, being an exalted and sublimated likeness of *Yerushalayim shel matah,* terrestrial Jerusalem. The celestial Jerusalem is envisioned as a radiant, infinitely refined version that bears only a remote resemblance to the terrestrial city. The idea of the celestial Jerusalem, however, as it was perceived by later Jewish thinkers, even by mystic fancy, never lost touch with down-to-earth reality. A definite strand of this-worldliness, which permeates mainstream Judaism in all its ramifications, effectively checked the tendencies that emerged among Jewish fringe groups and in Christian mysticism to paint a picture of a celestial Jerusalem that is untrammeled by the image of the historical city. Mainstream Judaism was less concerned with the metahistorical "heavenly Jerusalem" than with a future historical "New Jerusalem," which a restorative eschatology portrayed as an improved edition of its historical prototype.

The historical Jerusalem of the Hebrew Scriptures symbolizes the orderly civilized life of Israel. Her postconquest city organization is the opposite pole of the preconquest desert culture. Its monarchic regime is set off favorably against the democratic anarchism of the period of the Judges. As we have seen, Mount Zion in many respects is opposed to Mount Sinai. Though Mount Sinai represents the beginning of Israel's freedom, it also retains as yet the flavor of serfdom in Egyptian bondage, religiously, morally, and politically. Mount Zion and the covenant that God established there with David signify Israel's sovereignty in its full bloom, in civil and in sacred life. Since Jerusalem symbolizes orderly civilized life, her destruction spells anarchy. This thesis is borne out by biblical literature. The prophets invariably present the destruction of Jerusalem as the onset of a new chaos and a society in complete disintegration (for example, Isa. 3).

The basic realism of the biblical concept of Jerusalem is further illustrated by the recording of historical circumstances that less fact-minded writers might well have suppressed. Tradition freely admits that Jerusalem was not an Israelite city originally, that it was inhabited by foreigners even at the height of its occupation by the Israelites, and that it originally had served as a sanctuary of foreign cults and continued to serve as such even under many Israelite rulers. One is almost inclined to suspect that the biblical historiographers put special emphasis on the fact that Jerusalem always had a mixed population, knit into one social network, without making light of individual or group identities. We are told, for example, that Jebusites, from whom David had captured the city, continued to live in it unmolested side by side with the Israelites. Our sources also report at great length that the royal court literally was ridden with foreign warriors—Keretites, Pelethites, Hittites—and advisers, some of whom rose to prominence in the administrative hierarchy of the realm, as for example some of David's and Solomon's ministers. These foreign elements apparently were economically and socially fully integrated and in fact became a main pillar of support of the Davidic dynasty.

The resulting melting-pot situation was enhanced by an apparently liberal attitude regarding the admissibility of individuals and groups of foreign ethnic extraction into Jerusalem society. The manifold connections of the tribe of Judah, and especially of the Davidic dynasty, with originally non-Israelite elements is frequently mentioned in biblical traditions. Suffice it here to mention Tamar the Canaanite, who bore two sons to Judah, the eponym of the tribe (Gen. 38), Ruth the Moabite, great-grandmother of David (Ruth 4), and Absalom's mother, Maacah, a princess of Geshur in Transjordan (II Sam. 3).

On the other hand, we find especially in prophetic literature a recurring insistence on a future purge of Jerusalem of all foreign elements who have brought pollution into the city. In the days to come, Jerusalem will be inhabited exclusively by people of pure Israelite stock. They will worship in its Temple the one God, the God of Israel. This trend also makes itself strongly felt in postexilic historiography, and it would appear that it is intended to balance the opposite trend, which had prevailed in preexilic Israel, as exemplified in early biblical historiography.

In both instances a realistic historical concern seems to be at work, namely, the endeavor to cope with the actual situation and the problems inherent in it. Monarchic Israel, represented by the metropolis Jerusalem, settled with a numerous minority of foreigners, could conceive of no better way of handling the resulting situation than by absorbing those foreigners into Israelite society. The postexilic community of returnees from the Exile, a mere remnant of the once vigorous nation of early monarchic times, out-numbered many times over by the local population they encountered there, felt forced to segregate themselves from "the peoples of the land" in order to maintain their identity. Jerusalem, purified and holy, thus became the quintessence of a recessionist ideology, which shrank from any contact with those who had not gone through the purifying smelting furnace of the Exile.

Preexilic prophecy, indeed, had castigated Jerusalem, its kings, and its inhabitants, because "they abound in customs of the aliens" (Isa. 2:6). Alliance with foreigners, and with foreign rulers, spelled catastrophe (Isa. 7:4–9). Dissociation from other nations was considered the only way of preserving the metropolis and the nation of Israel from disaster. At the same time, prophecy viewed Jerusalem as the future center of an organized worldwide assembly of nations. In the days to come, Mount Zion, standing for Jerusalem as a whole, will become the goal of pilgrims from all nations: "At that time, they shall call Jerusalem 'Throne of the Lord,' and all nations shall assemble there, in the name of the Lord, at Jerusalem" (Jer. 3:17; cf. Isa. 2:2; 60; Micah 4:2). Punishment will be meted out to all peoples on earth that will not go up to Jerusalem to worship the King, Lord of Hosts (Zech. 14:17).

One is inclined to find here an expression of the significance of Jerusalem at its very peak: the city being raised from the status of the capital of the Israelite kingdom to that of the metropolis of the inhabited *ecumene*. The vision of Jerusalem as metropolis of the world included, indeed, a portrayal of the future fate of all nations. But first and foremost, it presents Jerusalem as holding promise for every Jew, whether inhabitant of the land of Israel or exiled in a foreign country. The city is expected to become a place of worship for every individual human being, Jew and non-Jew alike. The gloriously humanistic role to be played by the future Jerusalem fired the imagination of early Christian writers who perceived in it the apex of the spiritual development of Israel, crystallized in this noble image of the holy city.

Nonetheless, even in this ethereal portrait of the latter-day Jerusalem, biblical ideology remains earthbound. Late prophets, such as Jeremiah, do not fail to present that ideal Jerusalem in an almost disturbingly realistic fashion: "See, a time is coming—declares the Lord—when the city shall be rebuilt for the Lord from the Tower of Hananel to the Corner Gate; and the measuring line shall go straight out to the Gareb Hill, and then turn to Goah. And the entire Valley of the Corpses and Ashes, and all the fields as far as the Wadi of Kidron, and the corner of the Horse Gate on the east, shall be holy to the Lord. They shall never again be uprooted or overthrown" (Jer. 31:38–40). This vision of the future Jerusalem certainly was written by an author who knew the historical Jerusalem and could wish for nothing better than to have it restored in future to its one-time measurements.

Jeremiah's words throw some light upon yet another factor that has been decisive for the significance that attaches to the city of Jerusalem in Jewish tradition to this very day: it is the entire circumference of the city that is, and will be held, holy. Unlike other religions, which have pinned their pious reverence for Jerusalem on select localities within it that are connected with specific events in their own scriptural historiography, Judaism has sanctified the city as such, and in doing so has kept alive the biblical tradition.

In keeping with the historical realistic overtones that echo in the description of the future Jerusalem, the renewal of the covenant there will be preceded by great tribulations. Just as in historical Jerusalem war and bloodshed were always precursors of peace, so also the eschatological picture of the ultimate and final peace cannot unfold without a preceding catastrophe. The aeon of eternal peace to be inaugurated in Jerusalem will come after tumultuous wars, fought out against the nations, whom God decreed must perish in the valley of Jehoshaphat, the valley of his judgment (Joel 4:1ff). It is then that Jerusalem will again become the capital of the realm into which will be gathered the dispersed of Israel, who will find solace and comfort there (Joel 3:16). At that time, if righteousness should prevail in Jerusalem, "then through the gates of this palace shall enter kings of David's line who sit upon his throne, riding horse-drawn chariots, with their courtiers and their subjects" (Jer. 17:25; 22:4). Even this latter-day picture includes an actual king with his entourage: the vision remains earthbound.

The fervent hope for a future restoration of Jerusalem, which signifies the glorious revival of the nation, also became a common cause of Jewry after the destruction of the Second Temple. This is strikingly illustrated by a discovery in the temple area of Jerusalem of an inscription in square Hebrew characters incised into one of the huge dressed stones of the Western Wall, in a layer that until recently was hidden under the rubble that had accumulated over the centuries. It consists of the first part of Isaiah 66:14, exactly as it is preserved in the Masoretic text, which also reflects the major ancient versions: "You shall see and your heart shall rejoice, your limbs shall flourish like grass." The text refers back to the preceding verse, which ends on the promise: "And you shall find comfort in Jerusalem." It is obvious that the ancient mason or masons who had been at work reconstructing the temple wall, or re-dressing its stones, in their piety had conceived of their labor as a sign of the impending fulfillment of Isaiah's vision.

The stratum in which the inscription was discovered has been dated by archaeologists to the fourth century C.E., in the days of Julian the Apostate, famous for his liberal attitude toward non-Christian religions and for his zeal in restoring places of non-Christian worship. In this context the Temple of Jerusalem was given a new lease on life, although only for a very short period. The newly discovered inscription, in spite of its pitiful brevity, reveals the sentiment of Jewry at that time. It stands to reason that the inscription could not have been incised at the whim of some obscure worker; we may safely assume that it was sanctioned by some Jewish authority. More than the Bible-based emanations of future hopes in rabbinic literature, the solitary inscription on the wall of the defunct temple gives evidence of the continuing hope for an imminent restoration of Jerusalem as a renewed center of national worship and a source of rejoicing and well-being.

It is highly significant that Jews of Julian's day could find no more adequate means of expressing this complex hope, both historical and metahistorical, than by quoting a catch-phrase coined by a biblical prophet of the postexilic restoration period. In the Book of Isaiah, the phrase is preceded by a vivid description of the restored Jerusalem that will again become a metropolis in the truest sense of the word: a mother to the cities and villages surrounding it and to the people living within its confines: "Rejoice with Jerusalem and be glad for her, all you who love her . . . For thus said the Lord: I will extend to her Prosperity like a stream, the wealth of nations like a wadi in flood. And you shall drink of it. . . . As a mother comforts her son, you shall find comfort in Jerusalem" (Isa. 66:10–13).

BIBLIOGRAPHY

M. Burrows, "Jerusalem," in *Interpreter's Dictionary of the Bible*, 2 (1962).

Roderick A. F. MacKenzie, "The City [Jerusalem] and Israelite Religion," in *Catholic Biblical Quarterly* 25 (1963).

Norman W. Porteous, "Jerusalem-Zion: The Growth of a Symbol," in *Festschrift W. Rudolph* (1961).

M. Tsevat, "Yerushalayim," [*j^erusalem/j^erusalajim*], *Theologisches Wörterbuch zum AT* 3 (1982).

Yigael Yadin, ed., *Jerusalem Revealed: Archeology in the Holy City 1968–1974* (1976).

Judaism

יהדות

Gershom Scholem

Judaism cannot be defined according to its essence, since it has no essence. Judaism cannot therefore be regarded as a closed historical phenomenon whose development and essence came into focus by a finite sequence of historical, philosophical, doctrinal, or dogmatic judgments and statements. Judaism is rather a living entity which for some reason has survived as the religion of a chosen people. Indeed, for such a people to have endured for three thousand years as a recognizable entity, a phenomenal fact for which nobody has any truly sufficient explanation, is itself an enigma. The continued survival of the Jewish people seems to suggest that the Jews have in fact been chosen by someone for something.

The enigma of Jewish survival has intrigued generations. Why are the Jews there? What are they up to? Who are they? Are they simply a "fossil," as Arnold Toynbee opined? If not, what are they?

Judaism, however, cannot be defined by or with any authority, or in any clear way, simply because it is a living entity, having transformed itself at various stages in its history and having made real choices, discarding many phenomena that at one time were very much alive in the Jewish world. And having discarded these phenomena, Judaism bequeathes to us the question of whether that which was historically discarded is also to be discarded by present-day Jews or by the future Jew who wishes to identify himself with the past, present, and future of his people.

If Judaism cannot be defined in any dogmatic way, then we may not assume that it possesses any a priori qualities that are intrinsic to it or might emerge in it; indeed, as an enduring and evolving historic force, Judaism undergoes continuous transformations. Nevertheless, although Judaism is manifestly a dynamic, historical phenomenon, it has evolved under the shadow, so to speak, of a great idea, namely, monotheism—the idea of one unique God, the creator of the universe. Yet, it is clearly impermissible to understand this idea in such a manner that whatever follows or does not follow from it must necessarily be referred to the halakhah. To be sure, the halakhah is certainly an overwhelmingly important aspect of Judaism as a historical phenomenon, but it is not at all identical with the phenomenon of Judaism per se. Judaism has taken on many varied forms, and to think of it as only a legislative body of precepts seems to me as a historian and as a historian of ideas to be utter nonsense.

If I say that Judaism has no essence, this means two things. First, I do not accept as valid the all-embracing, Orthodox, or what I prefer to call fundamentalist definition of Judaism as a given law in which there are no differences between essential and unessential points—which, of course, is the point of view of strictly Orthodox halakhic Jews. Neither am I a partisan of the school that defines the "essence" of Judaism by reducing it to some essential spiritual statements such as those made by Moritz Lazarus, Hermann Cohen, Leo Baeck, Martin Buber, and many others during the last hundred and fifty years. Under a dominant Protestant influence, this tendency of modern Jewish thought has regarded Judaism as a purely spiritual phenomenon. But it is incorrect to consider Judaism in spiritual terms alone. Judaism certainly is a spiritual phenomenon, but it is a spiritual phenomenon that has been bound to a historical phenomenon, namely, to the Jewish people and the Jewish nation. To try to disassociate one from the other has proved impossible, as evidenced by the unsuccessful attempt made by Reform or Liberal Judaism to denationalize Judaism.

Similarly, Zionism's reaffirmation of Jewish nationality would be ill-advised to attempt severing its link with the spiritual dimension of Judaism. In fact, Zionism does not attempt to do this; it merely seeks to sponsor the return of the Jewish people and its spiritual life to history. When the halakhah governed their life, the Jews were not masters of their own destiny. This is one of the most problematic aspects of the halakhah, paradoxically, since the halakhah did play a very positive role in preserving the Jewish people. Yet it is nonetheless true that the halakhah as a body of laws and way of life ultimately relinquished responsibility for the historic destiny of the Jewish people.

One cannot, of course, anticipate what will become of Judaism as it reenters history, as the Jews become newly responsible for their own history. It has been said that the very success of Zionism—meaning the dialectical success it manifests in its historical founding of a state—constitutes a betrayal of the mission of Judaism. But this theory of mission, "to be a light unto the nations," which over the last hundred and fifty years was accepted by a large part of Jewry, was invented ad hoc by a people who were aware of their historical impotence, that is, their lack of vital resolve to live as a people. It was invented as a kind of spiritual recompense, a lame justification for the existence of Judaism in the Diaspora. The mission theory is one of the most dialectical (in some ways praiseworthy, in some ways shameful) aspects of Jewish experience since the emancipation. Thus, Zionism may indeed be a betrayal of the mission of the Jews invented by German, French, and Italian Jewry a hundred and fifty years ago. That it is a betrayal of the real mission of the Jews, namely, to face history in a social way as a people seeking to order their affairs, I disagree. To be sure, the return to Zion could be construed as the Jews' betrayal of their vocation to be a transcendent people—to be a people that is not a people, to quote Heine, a *Volksgespenst* (lit., phantom people), a people whose essence it is to disappear. That the essence of the Jewish people is to cease to be a people is, in my judgment, a highly perverse proposition.

Zionism, whimsically defined as a movement against the excessive inclination of the Jews to travel, is the utopian return of the Jews to their own history. The fathers of Zionism simply dreamt of bringing order into their own world as Jews, and of doing so under the shadow of some great ethical ideas such as socialism or other humanistic and religious ideas of elevated character. This is all that Zionism sought. Parenthetically, Zionism is not to be regarded as a species of messianism: I consider it the pride of Zionism that it is not a messianic movement. It is a great error, therefore—for which Zionism may have to pay dearly—if the movement attributes to itself messianic significance. Messianic movements are apt to fail. Zionism is rather a movement within the mundane, immanent process of history; Zionism does not seek the end of history, but takes responsibility within the history of an unredeemed and unmessianic world. To be sure, as an attempt to build a new life for the Jewish people in an unredeemed world, Zionism may have to confront certain messianic overtones that manifestly inhere in the idea of the return of the Jewish people to Zion.

As regards Judaism in the State of Israel, it is the living force of the people of Israel. As such it does not recognize an essence. There will be forms of Judaism devolving from the whole whirlpool, as it were, of Jewish history, from the struggle to create a just society and all that is implied by this struggle. Jewish theology may hence undergo radical changes in the State of Israel because secularism is a powerful reality, the meaning of which has to be lived out and confronted squarely. This confrontation will be between transcendental values and secular, that is, relative, values—essentially and principally relative values. It will be a fruitful confrontation because it will not be confined to a spiritual, abstract realm, but will occur within a living society of a people struggling for its liberation. Halakhah may emerge as one of the presuppositions of a future theology of Judaism to evolve in Israel, but it will be only one of many; *haggadah* will not remain any less creative and enduring. Furthermore, as noted earlier, those phenomena of Jewish history that were discarded by Diaspora Judaism from the talmudic period cannot be assumed to have been lost forever to Judaism.

It will be necessary to rethink Judaism in broader terms, and in much broader terms than those of halakhic Judaism. We have to face the question: How will a Judaism that evolves in a society of Jews work without taking refuge in traditional forms of ritual or of theology? I am not a prophet, but I welcome the struggle. I am not sure of its outcome. It might be deadly for the Jews. There is no guarantee that the State of Israel is or will be a full success in any sense, but I welcome the struggle because it will call forth the productive powers—whatever they are—of Jews. These productive powers will be dedicated to their own progenitors and will, if there is anything to radiate, radiate beyond them. We are not obliged to justify our existence by working for the world. Nobody, no other nation, has ever been put under such an obligation, and some of us see it as scandalous that unlike everyone else, we have to justify being Jews by serving some further purpose. No one asks a Frenchman why he is there. Everyone asks a Jew why he is there; no one would be content with the statement, I am just a Jew. Yet the Jew has every right to be just a Jew and to contribute to what he is by being just what he is. We are always asked to be something exceptional, something supreme, something ultimate. Maybe that very expectation will come to fruition one day, and perhaps then even the enigma of being the chosen people, which is not so easily discarded, will be resolved.

BIBLIOGRAPHY

Gershom Scholem, *On Jews and Judaism in Crisis: Selected Essays* (1976).

Jurisprudence

תורת־המשפט

Ze'ev W. Falk

J urisprudence is the delineation of the governing principles and methods of positive law, that is, the law established by political authority. This discussion will undertake to identify Jewish jurisprudence not only in terms of Judaism's formal legal system but also with respect to other normative aspects of Jewish tradition.

Many passages in the Bible and rabbinic literature have a legal structure. Among the terms describing the divine message, there are a number of legal concepts, such as *hukim* (statutes), *mishpatim* (ordinances), *mizvot* (commandments), and *pikudim* (precepts) (cf. Ps. 119). There are other terms, however, that point to the pedagogic rather than the legal character of the divine message, such as *torot* (teachings) and *derekh* (path). These terms refer to the religious and moral dimensions of Judaism, which must be observed together with legal norms.

Rabbinical terminology distinguishes between *halakhot*—rules that pertain to ritual and cultic as well as formal legal practices—and *aggadot*—stories, homilies, and commentaries that were evoked to teach religious and moral values. Thus rabbinical Judaism includes a legal code but is never only a legal system.

It was Spinoza who first undertook to interpret Judaism as a mere collection of laws.[1] He advanced this view in support of his thesis that the Jewish religion was but a legal superstructure of the Jewish state, and that this religion became essentially defunct with the destruction of the state it was designed to serve. The religious tradition of Israel, however, preceded the settlement of the people of Israel in the land of Canaan and the establishment of the Jewish state; moreover, the religion of Israel occasionally developed in conflict with the kings of Israel and the state's institutions. The teachings of the prophets, scribes, and rabbis often reflect their opposition to the temporal powers. Indeed, talmudic law emerged as a reaction of Judaism against what was regarded as arbitrary political power. Judaism cannot therefore be regarded as essentially a legal system no different from those formulated by writers of jurisprudence.

Indeed, should we employ a utilitarian concept of law such as that proposed by the eighteenth-century philosopher of jurisprudence Jeremy Bentham, which sets among its criteria for adjudging the validity of a legal code its utility, it would be difficult to understand halakhah (rabbinic law) as a genuine legal system, because very often a halakhic decision is made on a conceptual basis without regard for its consequences. According to the rabbis, a person should fulfill his duties for their own sake and not for extraneous motives (M. Avot 2:2, 12; 6:1). God's commandments were not intended to promote happiness (BT Er. 31a), which is the object of law according to the utilitarian school of jurisprudence.

A similar difficulty arises if we consider halakhah according to the imperative theory of law developed in the nineteenth century by John Austin, who regarded the rightful purview of law to be the commands of a human sovereign to his subjects, with appropriate sanctions against lawbreakers. Halakhah certainly cannot be understood in these terms. The closest system of jurisprudence admitting the legal character of halakhah is perhaps that of Eugen Ehrlich, who is associated with the so-called sociological school of jurisprudence. According to this view, law is contingent upon popular acceptance rather than upon legislation or adjudication. This legal theory regards the state as less essential for the definition of law than society. Such a theory would thus hold that halakhah could gain legal validation through its acceptance on the part of the Jewish people. But Jewish law also challenges the conduct of people, as in the case of the apostasy of a city or a tribe in Israel, and the prophets often reproached the people for deviating from God's will. Furthermore, rabbinic halakhah includes rules that are purely theoretical; the great majority of the people never followed, for instance, the rules of purity and tithing. According to Ehrlich's sociological conception, these aspects of the halakhah are not properly law.

At present halakhah has lost its hold on most Jews and is merely a private discipline of those individuals who regard themselves as bound by it. Mordecai Kaplan therefore declared the halakhah to be defunct and concluded that the Jewish people were in need of a new social contract. Meanwhile, the State of Israel has restored a binding legal status to at least some aspects of the halakhah.

In any event, Jewish law makes no sense without its complementary religious and moral teachings. Besides the aforementioned legal concepts, biblical theology speaks of *emunah*, which is best translated as faith in or faithfulness toward God. Rabbinical thought, as noted, is contained in aggadah, homilies and commentaries, as well as halakhah. As Naḥmanides observed, the norms of Judaism cannot be divorced from its extensive religious context:

> Belief in the existence of God, which has been transmitted to us by signs, miracles, and the revelation of the divine presence, is the root from which all the commandments grow. . . . Therefore the rabbis distinguished in the Shema between the submission to the Kingdom [of God] and the submission of the divine commandments.[2]

Rabbinical tradition also mentions *derekh erez* (lit., "the way of the earth"), which may be rendered as "ethics." The Midrash places *derekh erez* prior to the Torah (Lev. R. 40:3), as an obligatory preparation for the law and as its necessary complement. Ancillary aspects of this part of the rabbinic teaching are *middot* and *deot* (M. Avot 5:11). The former, *middot,* are the "measures" of one's moral character to be developed or subdued. The latter, *deot,* are one's "opinions" regarding the cognitive discourse of ethics and the subjective dimension of ethical statements.

While halakhah tends to make authoritative decisions, the other elements of Judaism are open-ended. Different opinions and beliefs in matters of religious doctrine and ethics can exist side by side. These variant positions may represent a mere divergence of fundamentally similar views or indicate differences that are beyond resolution. Everyone is therefore entitled to choose from among the various positions of the rabbis that which he deems correct, and, accordingly, the tradition maintains that no one is entitled "to impose upon others a particular belief or ethical statement."[3]

The basic norm implicit in all of Jewish law is the doctrine of divine revelation and the corresponding teaching that the Jew establishes his relationship to God through obedience to God's revealed word. Specifically, through obedience to the law, the Jew should regard himself as submitting to the kingdom of God. The rabbis formulated the religious intention involved in obedience to the law in the benediction to be recited upon the performance of a divine commandment or precept: "Blessed be You, Lord our God, King of the Universe, who has sanctified us by His commandments" (BT Shab. 23a). The corollary of this concept is to regard oneself as a servant of God, like Moses, Job, or the servant in the later chapters of Isaiah. Accordingly, no rule or aspect of Jewish law can be an end in itself. Every dimension and facet of Jewish law should be an expression of the love of God (Ex. 20:6; Deut. 6:5; Isa. 41:8), leading the observant Jew to saintliness (Num. 15:40) and *imitatio Dei* (Lev. 19:2). The prophets, therefore, severely criticized those who regarded obedience to God's law as a mere matter of external propriety and legalism (Amos 8:5; Isa. 29:13, 58:3), judging such behavior to be based on a fundamental misconception of the law as well as of religion and morality.

It is in light of the above discussion that one can appreciate the fact that some of the basic principles of Jewish theology are cast as legal concepts. The election of Israel by God takes the form of a covenant, to which the people are bound (Ex. 24:3,7; BT Shab. 88a). Similarly, the validity of the commandments is reaffirmed by the daily ritual submission of the individual to the covenant and the kingdom of God (M. Ber. 2:2). The Bible also describes God as playing various legal roles in his relationship to Israel. For example, God is said to be a king to whom obedience is due; he frees the Hebrew slaves from Egyptian bondage; he is the husband who may or may not divorce his wife for her misconduct. God, moreover, is concerned with justice and dispenses rewards and punishments, as well as demonstrating mercy and compassion.

Man, according to the rabbis, should aspire to be a *ẓaddik,* that is, to be righteous before the divine Judge, his righteousness to be adjudged according to whether he has met his obligations to God and his fellow men. Indeed, the religious tradition of Abraham is grounded in following God's way by pursuing equity and justice. This world-orientation of Judaism has resulted in a sustained religious concern for justice, a judicious allocation of ethical duties, and an equitable resolution of conflicts.

REFERENCES

1. Cf. Baruch Spinoza, *Theological-Political Tractate* (1670).
2. Naḥmanides, *Commentary to Maimonides' Book of the Commandments,* 1. Cf. Abraham Joshua Heschel, *God in Search of Man* (1959), 320–60.

3. *Responsa of the Geonim,* ed. Harkavy, 380; *Responsa of the Geonim,* "Sha'arei Teshuveh," 23; Shmuel ha-Nagid, *Mevo le-Talmud,* conclusion; Maimonides, Commentary to Mi.h Sot. 3:5; BT Sanh. 10:3; BT Shev. 1:4.

BIBLIOGRAPHY

Haim H. Cohn, *Jewish Law in Ancient and Modern Israel* (1971).
Ze'ev W. Falk, *Law and Religion: The Jewish Experience* (1981).
Moshe Silberg, *Talmudic Law and the Modern State* (1973).

Justice

צדק

Haim H. Cohn

Justice, the attribute of an omnipotent God, was "first of all man's assurance that God will not use His almighty power over His creatures without regard to right."[1] The assurance that God was just was a necessary complement to the tenet that he was omnipotent and omniscient: the pagan gods had always been believed to have no restraints whatever in their dealings with man, and one of the main attractions of monotheism was to be that there was now one God whose omnipotence would be exercised with the restraint flowing from a divine and paramount morality. It is true that even this fundamental notion could not hold out against threats of unbridled divine revenge and cruelty, when the wrath of God waxed hot (for example, Ex. 22:24), or of heavenly punishments out of all proportion to the measure of the crime, when his patience was at an end (for example, Lev. 26:21–39; Deut. 28:15–68). These threats were apparently believed to be necessary for purposes of general deterrence. Apart from these deviations, however, divine justice operated on the fundamental principle of measure for measure: God renders to every man according to his deeds (Ps. 62:13), rewarding all those who love and obey him and punishing all those who reject and defy him (Deut. 7:9–10). This amounts to the most straightforward kind of justice: *justitia commutativa* (commutative justice) at its purest. And as the divine criterion of justice was held imitable by man, it was elevated to normative rank: the *lex talionis,* the law of retaliation, of an eye for an eye (Ex. 21:24, Lev. 24:20, Deut. 19:21) reflected pure and perfect justice, easily appreciable even by the uneducated.

The most striking phenomenon in the evolution of the Judaic concept of justice is the recognition of the injustice inherent in both divine and human justice. As far as divine justice was concerned, it was not only the implacability of God's wrath and the inescapability of his judgment, but in large part the irrelevance of human peculiarities and idiosyncrasies that gave acts of divine retaliation the semblance of injustice. With regard to human justice, the justice of the talion was apparent rather than real, semantic rather than substantive: the natural inequality of the respective eyes of the victim and of the wrongdoer, or the impossibility of extracting an eye without endangering life (BT BK 83b–84a), were cogent enough indications of blatant injustice. While it was certainly not beyond God's power to determine exact measures for exact requitals, the human determination of any such measure could not possibly avoid risks of error and inexactitude; and when the measure is exceeded, measure-for-measure justice is *ipso facto* frustrated. Something drastic thus had to be done to rescue justice from well-nigh self-destructive tendencies.

It was by processes of relativization and individualization that the "rescue" of divine and human justice was sought. As for God, the attribute of justice was tied to the attribute of mercy, justice *(middat ha-din)* and mercy *(middat ha-raḥamim)* being pictured as competing with each other for ultimate predominance in the divine discretion. While justice is a standard applicable to all, mercy is an attitude to a particular agent; while justice denotes detachment, mercy reflects attachment, according to Abraham J. Heschel.[2] But then justice and mercy were held by some to be so in conflict with each other as to be mutually exclusive: whereas normally God must do justice, it was said, he may, if and when he so chooses, forsake justice and exercise mercy instead; but he cannot, in the nature of things, reveal both these attributes at one and the same time upon one and the same object. This dichotomy is reflected in the tradition that where Scripture speaks of God as Elohim, it refers to him in his capacity as dispenser of justice, and where his name is given as YHWH, mercy and grace are being imputed to him. Efforts were later made to abandon the division between justice attributed to Elohim and mercy attributed to YHWH, not least because of apprehension lest the Jewish deity be suspected of having two heads: there is only one God, with one will, and with one hand, which is "mighty" (Deut. 3:24) enough to give mercy predominance over justice. One homilist went so far as to picture God indulging in prayer to himself: "Oh, that I would always let my mercy prevail over my justice" (BT Ber. 7a). That divine justice eventually entered Jewish theology blended and impregnated with divine mercy is attested to by an abundance of verses and dicta in which the just and the merciful God is juxtaposed and made synonymous. The concept of divine justice is no longer purely objective or precisely definable; its subjectivity appears to be conditioned not only on the merits or demerits of the recipient, the victim of justice and the beneficiary of mercy, but no less on the unfathomable and unaccountable will of the omnipotent dispenser of justice and of mercy. The divine mixture of the personal and the general, of dispensing and receiving lines, of strict measure and overflowing generosity, in what is comprehensively entitled divine justice, defies all attempts at detailed parsing.

Whether it was because of the desirability of *imitatio Dei*—"As He is merciful, so be thou merciful" (BT Shab. 133b)—or because of a recognition of the merits of having objective standards blended with subjective needs, human justice came to be modeled on the divine pattern. Exceptions to general rules of law and the equality of mankind appear in Scripture in order to accommodate particular needs: widows, orphans, strangers, the poor, and the needy are singled out for special consideration and treatment, not only as the most vulnerable members of society and the easiest prey to oppression and exploitation, but also as special favorites of God (for example, Ex. 22:23, 26; Deut. 10:18), who is said to nourish a "bias in favor of the poor."[3] Not only does this preferment of the underprivileged not derogate from justice, it is one of its most important and characteristic elements; in addition, it demonstrates that justice and equality are not necessarily coextensive. It is true that explicit scriptural commandments to pursue justice such as those in Leviticus 19:15 and Deuteronomy 16:20 were interpreted as prescribing absolute equality of all persons before the courts of justice, without any show of favor to either the poor or the mighty (Deut. 1:17). But standards of judicial administration are not necessarily indicative of the kind of substantive justice to be pursued, nor is the equality before the courts of all litigants indicative of the merits of their respective causes. Indeed, the equalization of substantive as distinguished from procedural justice must ultimately produce injustice, in the sense of *summum ius summa iniuria* (extreme law is the greatest injury).

In a theocratic system of law, doing justice must at first sight be synonymous with obeying the law: God's law must by definition be just, the incarnation of justice, or else it would not be divine. There could not conceivably be anything that human ingenuity could add to improve upon divine law (cf. Deut. 4:2). It becomes axiomatic that there cannot be any justice other than "justice according to law,"[4] a legalistic justice for which the Pharisees came to be so undeservedly maligned. In fact, however, the divinity of the law did not protect it from scrutiny; human inquisitiveness is such that even the justice of divine law will have to be tested and measured against one's own sense of natural justice. Where on such a test a law is found to be manifestly unjust, one's own concept of natural justice may be dismissed out of hand, and one may, as Maimonides held, resign oneself unquestioningly to what must be the superior and hence conclusive, albeit incomprehensible, divine justice, or, following Spinoza, one may regard the manifest injustice of the law as sufficient refutation of its divinity; or again, one may try to interpret and mold the divine law in such a manner that injustice will be avoided and natural justice vindicated.

The propounders of the oral law pursued the third alternative, seeking, whenever possible, to bring the written law into line with what they conceived to be the requirements of natural, that is, human justice. Only where Scripture was so unambiguous that no hermeneutical efforts could get around it would they acquiesce in God's law without apprehending its justice. Any such acquiescence, however, was confined to laws governing relations between God and man; insofar as interhuman relations were concerned, the opinion was strong and widespread that common notions of justice should be paramount, even to the extent of disregarding or ousting positive law. Such biblical exhortations as to do "the good and the right" (Deut. 12:28) or to "follow the way of the good and keep the paths of the just" (Prov. 2:20) were invoked to extol justice contrary to law. People were admonished not to insist on their legal rights but to act "inside the line of the law" (lifnim me-shurat ha-din) with generosity and forbearance. And if earthly judges would, by administering the law as they found it, cause any injustice, there was a court in heaven that would, in due course of celestial justice, hold them to account for their pertinacity and iniquity. It has been said that it was the prevalence of law over justice that caused the destruction and downfall of ancient Jerusalem.

It came to this, then, that God was made the ultimate arbiter and vindicator of an eminently human justice. The divine justice inherent in his revealed laws was allowed—and required—to recede before the natural justice in interhuman relations. It now became the province and function of divine justice to watch over human justice so that it might thrive and rule. The humanization of divine justice seemed to have come full circle.

The lesson of the destruction of Jerusalem, however, has not really been learned. Positive law, or halakhah, was allowed to supersede all other values: the dogmatic assertion of its divinity and hence the unquestioning observance of its norms have for centuries been the distinctive characteristic of authoritative Jewish doctrine. That with the change of times and conditions new ideas of justice have sprung up of which the divine—but ancient—law could not have taken notice was held wholly irrelevant, as if God had no hand at all in such change. The primordial feat of diagnosing the injustice of justice (including divine justice) and of valiantly remedying inequity, has—at least with the orthodox—become a matter either of ancient history or of prejudicial or misinformed idealization.

Every system of justice bears within itself the germ of its own perversion. It is not only that injustice will result in the particular cases in which prima facie justice is carried to excess, but that propositions of justice generally are apt to turn into propositions smacking of injustice, whenever they are allowed to petrify out of consonance with contemporaneous and developing notions of justice, or whenever it is attempted to enforce them for a purpose or in a manner extraneous to their true and original nature. Both these dangers are especially acute in relation to divine justice. As for petrification, where concepts of divine justice are derived from divine law, which is asserted to be eternal and immutable, they will, in the nature of things, be infected with that immutability, too—the more so as the revelation of a change of the divine mind cannot ever reasonably be expected. The elevation of ancient law to sacrosanct and eternally and unconditionally binding status necessarily implies the continuous validity of the underlying conceptions of justice, however incompatible they may appear to be with currently acceptable ideas of justice. Take, for instance, the marital laws. They are based upon, and result in, a discrimination between the sexes that reflects notions of justice common in ancient patriarchal society but entirely out of tune with present-day concepts and standards. Still, the same sacrosanct validity that remains attached to the laws remains attached to the notion of the justice of unequal treatment of men and women, however preposterous and anachronistic such unequal treatment may appear to a contemporary observer. The second danger, however, is even graver. It lies in the notions of justice said to underlie the divine law, or a particular divine law, and invoked to attain purposes for which neither the laws nor their underlying notions of justice have ever been conceived. The divinity of that "justice" furnishes an unassailable argument to people pretending to carry out the will of God in pursuing their own political objectives. This kind of "divine justice" is, more often than not, incompatible not only with ideas of natural justice but also with the positive albeit secular law. Champions of "divine justice," however, are not normally deterred or deterrable from their crusades by either the injustice or the illegality of their action. The fact that for such perversions of divine justice medieval and modern precedents can be found in other religions is neither a consolation nor an excuse for the recurrence of such phenomena within Judaism.

Might it be that true divinity, of justice as of all else, is a description of quality rather than of origin? That God in his wisdom instilled in every human being a sense of justice and a sense of injustice to serve as the test to which all justice and injustice must be put? And that it is its deliberate orientation on changing human standards and human needs that makes for the divinity of divine justice?

REFERENCES

1. George Foot Moore, *Judaism in the First Centuries of the Christian Era*, 1 (1971), 387.
2. Abraham Joshua Heschel, *The Prophets* (1962), 220, n. 34.
3. Reinhold Niebuhr, *Pious and Secular America* (1958), 92.
4. Roscoe Pound, *Introduction to the Philosophy of Law* (1959), 48ff.

BIBLIOGRAPHY

Israel Abrahams, ed., *Hebrew Ethical Wills*, 2 vols. (1926).
Hermann Cohen, "Liebe und Gerechtigkeit in den Begriffen Gott und Mensch," in *Jahrbuch für Jüdische Geschichte und Literatur* (1900).
Alfred Dünner, *Die Gerechtigkeit nach dem Alten Testament* (1963).
Zeev W. Falk, *Legal Values and Judaism: Towards a Philosophy of Halakhah* (1980).
Hirsch Baer Fassell, *Die mosaisch-rabbinische Tugend- und Rechtslehre*, 2d ed. (1862, reprinted 1981).
Simon Federbusch, *Ha-Mussar ve-ha-Mishpat be-Yisrael* (1979).
I. Herzog, *Judaism: Law and Ethics* (1974).
Abraham Joshua Heschel, *The Prophets* (1962).
George Foot Moore, *Judaism in the First Centuries of the Christian Era*, 2 vols. (1971).
Hans Heinrich Schmid, *Gerechtigkeit als Weltordnung: Hintergrund und Geschichte des alttestamentlichen Gerechtigkeitsbegriffs* (1968).

Kingdom of God

מלכות שמים

Warren Zev Harvey

While God's kingship is a basic concept in the Bible, the usual Hebrew term for the "kingdom of God"—*malkhut shamayim* (lit., kingdom of heaven)—is first found in rabbinic literature. The kingdom of God, in Jewish thought, has two distinct yet intertwined meanings: one literal and political, the other metaphoric and metaphysical.

In its literal political sense, the kingdom of God refers to the government of the political community by God. In particular, it refers to the form of government that existed in ancient Israel until the coronation of Saul, when the Israelites—desirous of being "like all the nations"—rejected God in favor of a flesh-and-blood king (I Sam. 8:5–7, 19–20; 10:19; cf. Deut. 17:14). The kingdom of God, in this sense, is sometimes called *theocracy*,[1] but only when that term is carefully distinguished from *hierocracy*, the rule of priests or clerics; for the kingdom of God, in its political sense, means wholly literally that God alone is sovereign, and thus there can be no mortal ruler or rulers in his kingdom. That God's kingship precludes human sovereignty underlies the words of Gideon when he rejected the people's request that he be their king: "I will not rule over you myself, nor shall my son rule over you; the Lord alone shall rule over you" (Judges 8:23). In its rejection of all human sovereignty and in its consequent radical egalitarianism, the political kingdom of God is identical to anarchy, yet in truth the rule of the Almighty—though an invisible rule—is the very opposite of no rule at all. The question of how God the king makes his edicts known to his human subjects has been given many different answers, ranging from the supernatural (for example, continual prophetic revelations) to the wholly rational (for example, equating the word of God with reason). The kingdom of God, in its literal political sense, has been discussed by several Jewish and non-Jewish philosophers, including Isaac Abrabanel,[2] Thomas Hobbes,[3] Baruch Spinoza,[4] Moses Mendelssohn,[5] and Martin Buber.[6]

In its metaphysical sense, the kingdom of God refers to divine "rule" over the totality of existence. Hebrew benedictions, for example, begin with the well-known formula, "Blessed art Thou, O Lord our God, King of the universe." Here God's kingship is a metaphor for the ontological relationship of creator to creation. Sometimes, as in the opening line of the old synagogal hymn *Adon Olam* (Eternal Lord), God is said to have "reigned" as king even "*before* any created thing was created." Thus stretched, the kingship metaphor seems no longer to designate a relationship: either God's kingdom is independent of his creation, or his kingship is independent of his kingdom. To be sure, neither the Bible nor the rabbis spoke about the ontological relationship of creator to creation, but they did speak about God's oneness. In rabbinic usage, the phrase "to accept the yoke of the kingdom of heaven" means to proclaim God's oneness by reciting the Shema: "Hear [*shema*] O Israel, the Lord our God the Lord is One!" (Deut. 6:4). By proclaiming the Shema, one acknowledges God's kingship over all existence, and thus commits oneself to fulfill the king's commandments (M. Ber. 2:2).

Quite clearly, the political concept of the kingdom of God has metaphysical presuppositions, while the metaphysical concept has political ramifications. A political community would hardly accept God as its king unless its members had as individuals first taken upon themselves the "yoke of the kingdom of heaven"; at the same time, a political community whose members had as individuals taken upon themselves the "yoke of the kingdom of heaven" might well have no need or desire to submit itself to any rule other than God's.

An integration of metaphysical and political motifs is evident in many rabbinic texts concerning the kingdom of God. For example, an exegesis of Deuteronomy 6:4 interprets the repetition of "the Lord" ("the Lord our God the Lord is One") as referring to Israel and the nations: the Lord is *our*

God, and the Lord is—or will be—the *One* God of all humanity (Sif. Deut. 31). Support for this exegesis is found in Zechariah 14:9: "And the Lord shall be king over all the earth; in that day there shall the Lord be *One*, with one name." In this exegesis, the metaphysical concept of God's kingship as oneness serves as the base for a political vision in which God is king over all the earth.

A similar theme is enunciated in the introduction to the *Malkhuyyot* (kingship) section of the *Musaf* or Additional Service for the New Year. Owing to its theological importance, this introduction, known by its first word as the *Alenu* ("It is incumbent upon us" [to praise God]), was subsequently adopted as the concluding prayer of every daily service. The *Alenu* is divided into two paragraphs. In the first, praise is given to "the Lord of all . . . the Former of creation . . . the King of kings, the Holy One, blessed be He . . . our God . . . our King." In the second paragraph, hope is voiced that soon God will be not only our King, but also the king of all peoples; that is, the world will be perfected "under the Kingdom of the Almighty [*Malkhut Shaddai*], and all the inhabitants of the world will accept the yoke of [His] Kingdom." In the continuation of the *Malkhuyyot* section of the New Year liturgy, ten kingship texts are cited from the Bible: Exodus 15:18; Numbers 23:21; Deuteronomy 33:5; Psalms 22:29, 93:1, and 24:7–10; Isaiah 44:6; Obadiah 1:21, and, climactically, Zechariah 14:9 and Deuteronomy 6:4.

Metaphysical and political motifs are also integrated in the talmudic account of the martyrdom of Rabbi Akiva, where allegiance to the metaphysical *malkhut* of God enjoins resistance to the tyrannical *malkhut* of Rome. The Roman government (*malkhut*) had prohibited the study of Torah, but Rabbi Akiva continued teaching and was imprisoned and sentenced to death by torture. "In the hour they took Rabbi Akiva out for execution," reports the Talmud, "it was the time for the recital of the Shema, and while they were combing his flesh with iron combs, he accepted upon himself the yoke of the Kingdom of Heaven [that is, he recited Deuteronomy 6:4]. . . . He prolonged [the word] *ehad* ["One"], and his soul went out at [the word] *ehad*" (BT Ber. 61b). Proclaiming in extremis the divine oneness, Rabbi Akiva affirmed his absolute allegiance to the kingdom of God while defying the imperial oppressors.

God's kingship is associated with his oneness, but it is also associated with the oneness of man. Deuteronomy 33:5 reads: "Then He became King in Jeshurun, when the heads of the people assembled the tribes of Israel together." This verse was interpreted in the Midrash as follows: when the people are one, living together in peace, then God is their King; but when there is strife or dissension among them, he is not (Rashi, *ad loc.;* cf. Sif. Deut. 346). God's kingship in Israel depends on the togetherness of the community of Israel; or to put it more generally, God's oneness depends on man's oneness. We crown God king when we live in peace with our neighbors. If the coupling of Deuteronomy 6:4 and Zechariah 14:9 teaches that God is one to the extent that human beings recognize him as their king, then Deuteronomy 33:5 teaches that human beings recognize God as their king to the extent that they are able to live together as one.

Martin Buber assigned great significance to Deuteronomy 33:5, considering it to state a general definition of the Torah of Moses. Deuteronomy 33:4, he explained, tells us that "Moses commanded us a Torah," and Deuteronomy 33:5 goes on to define this Torah as the teaching that God is king in Jeshurun. The kingship of God, accordingly, is the essence of the Torah, the essence of Judaism.[7]

Moreover, Buber insisted, the kingship of God is also the essence of Zionism. When in 1957 David Ben-Gurion said that with the establishment of the State of Israel Zionism had achieved its goal and had thus become anachronistic, Buber replied that the vision Zion is not yet realized. Political independence, he argued, can be no more than a means toward realizing that vision; the State of Israel is at best "a step on the way." True Zionism, he said, is the desire to establish Zion as "the city of the great King" (Ps. 48:3), and Zionism in this sense lives and endures.[8]

In his speeches and writings on Judaism and Zionism, Buber advocated the kingdom of God here and now. He called for communities governed not by mortal rulers with their coercive institutions, but by the voluntary acknowledgment of the King. He was deeply impressed by the free, egalitarian, socialistic community of the kibbutz, which he saw as inspired by the biblical model of the kingdom of God.[9]

Calling for the kingship of God here and now, Buber may have been naive. In doing so, however, he stood in a good Jewish tradition. When the children of Israel crossed the Red Sea, leaving the bondage of Egypt behind them, they proclaimed as newly free men: "The Lord shall be King for ever and ever!" (Ex. 15:18). They wasted no time in proclaiming the kingship of God in place of the kingship of Pharaoh. Yet even this alacrity did not satisfy Rabbi Yose the Galilean. Disturbed by their verb tense, he taught: "Had Israel at the sea said 'The Lord *is* King for ever and ever,' no nation or kingdom would ever have ruled over them; but they said 'The Lord *shall be* King for ever and ever'" (Mekh. Shirata 10). For Rabbi Yose the Galileean and for Buber, the kingdom of God is deferred only at the price of human freedom.

Buber, of course, was not the only religious thinker to perceive modern Zionism in terms of the biblical concept of the kingdom of God. The prayer for the State of Israel, composed by S. Y. Agnon on behalf of the Chief Rabbinate of the State, concludes with the following passage, borrowed from the aforementioned *Malkhuyyot* section of the Additional Service for the New Year: "Shine forth [O Lord] . . . over all the inhabitants of Thy world . . . that every creature understand that Thou hast created it, and that all with the breath of life in his nostrils shall say 'The Lord, the God of Israel, is King, and His kingship ruleth over all.'" The new political independence of the Jewish state points beyond itself to Zechariah's old universalistic dream of the kingdom of God over all the earth.

REFERENCES

1. Cf. Josephus, *Against Apion,* 2:16.
2. See selections in Ralph Lerner and Muhsin Mahdi, *Medieval Political Philosophy* (1963), 254–70.
3. Thomas Hobbes, *Leviathan,* bk. 3.
4. Baruch Spinoza, *Theologico-Political Treatise,* ch. 17.
5. Moses Mendelssohn, *Jerusalem,* tr. A. Arkush (1983), 128–32.
6. Martin Buber, *Kingship of God* (1967); Martin Buber *Moses* (1946).
7. Martin Buber, *Moses* (1946), 107.
8. Martin Buber, *Israel and the World* (1948), 261–62.
9. Cf. Martin Buber, *Paths in Utopia* (1950), 139–49.

BIBLIOGRAPHY

Gerald J. Blidstein, "The Monarchic Imperative in Rabbinic Perspective," in *AJS Review,* 7–8 (1982–1983).
George Foot Moore, *Judaism in the First Centuries of the Christian Era,* 3 vols. (1927–1930).
Solomon Schechter, *Aspects of Rabbinic Theology* (1967).
Efraim E. Urbach, *The Sages* (1975).

Kingdom of Priests

ממלכת כוהנים

Daniel R. Schwartz

Kingdom of priests, a phrase borrowed from Exodus 19:6, is typically taken as the slogan of the ideal variously summarized as *universal priesthood, egalitarian access to the sacred,* or the like. It is, in brief, seen as contradicting the usual biblical norm of priesthood limited to those of a particular (Aaronite) descent. This article will discuss both the biblical passage whence the idea is derived and the idea itself, for the idea may have a role in Jewish theological discourse even if, as we shall suggest, it is not necessarily implied by the biblical source of its formulation.

Exodus 19, the prelude to the Ten Commandments, is the solemn initiation of the divine covenant with Israel. The chapter's twenty-five verses are divided among three sections: introduction (1–3a), negotiation of the covenant (3b–9), and preparation for the coming theophany (10–25). Our phrase appears in the crucial middle section:

(3) The Lord called to him from the mountain, saying, "Thus shall you say to the house of Jacob and declare to the children of Israel: (4) 'You have seen what I did

to the Egyptians, how I bore you on eagles' wings and brought you to Me. (5) Now then, if you will obey Me faithfully and keep My covenant, you shall be My treasured possession among all the peoples. Indeed, all the earth is Mine, (6) but you shall be to Me a kingdom of priests and a holy nation.' These are the words that you shall speak to the children of Israel."

Regarding these verses, two main questions arise. First, is "you shall be" in verse 6 indicative, or imperative? And second, what is meant by "a kingdom of priests"? If "you shall be" were an imperative, the implication would be that all Israelites (v. 3), even non-Aaronites, are capable of becoming priests. This virtually entails the further conclusion that *kingdom of priests* and *holy nation* are synonymous, the intervening copula being only a figment of biblical parallelism. Thus, it is not surprising that Abraham Geiger, one of the foremost Jewish spokesmen of the view that this phrase implies a universal priesthood, translated the verb as an imperative and added an adverb to clarify that both terms refer to the whole people: "You should all together *(Ihr sollt mir allesamt)* be unto Me a kingdom of priests and a holy people."[1]

The immediate context, lexicographic considerations, and other relevant biblical material militate against the Geiger interpretation and suggest another. First, verse 5b seems already to begin God's side of the covenant; it would be strange if verse 6 reverted to the Israelites' obligations. Second, while *tiheyu,* as "you shall," may serve as an imperative (despite its basically indicative sense), only a few verses later, in verse 15, we find the true imperative *heyu* used when needed; one would expect, therefore, that *tiheyu* in verse 6 is meant in its basic, indicative sense. Finally, note that this chapter goes on, in verses 21–24, to distinguish between two estates, "the priests" and "the people," unambiguously defining the priests as "those who come near the Lord" (v. 22). It would be surprising if verse 6 suggested otherwise.

As for lexicography, philologists have become increasingly convinced that *mamlakhah* (kingdom) does not refer to the realm, the subjects of the king, but rather means *king* or *royalty*[2]; this is especially the case when, as here, it is paired with *goy* (people)[3].

Combination of these brief inquiries into context and lexicography yields the following interpretation of verse 6: God promises the Israelites that fulfillment of their covenantal obligations will entitle them to be his royalty of priests and holy people, meaning either a monarchy ruled by priests and a holy people subject to them or a monarchy ruling over priests and holy people. The first interpretation links *priests* alone to *kingdom,* thus preserving the apparent parallelism of the verse but only by taking *priests* as an attribute ("priestly monarchy"); the second interpretation leaves *priests* as is but ignores the apparent parallelism by linking both *priests* and *holy people* to *kingdom*. There appears to be no definitive way of deciding between these alternatives, but the first seems preferable because the second implies the existence of a third factor, nonpriestly monarchs, which is otherwise strikingly absent.

Be that as it may, other biblical passages confirm the assumption, common to both interpretations, that *priests* as used here is different from *nation*. For everywhere, or almost everywhere, in the Hebrew Bible, *priests* are Aaronite priests. This is so obvious that it hardly needs demonstration, and we will restrict ourselves to a few exceptions that prove the rule. Melchizedek, "priest of the God Most High" (Gen. 14:18), was not an Aaronite, but neither was he Jewish; if Psalm 110 contemplated any role for him in the priesthood, it specified that this is an exceptional "order of Melchizedek." When Korah and his followers complained against Moses and Aaron, saying "You have gone too far! For all the community are holy, all of them, and the Lord is in their midst" [all of which is encompassed by the term *holy nation* in Ex. 19:6]; why then do you raise yourselves above the Lord's congregation?" (Num. 16:3), they are unambiguously condemned. When the rebellious Jeroboam "appointed priests from the ranks of the people, who were not of Levite descent" (I Kings 12:31), the very phrasing of this report, as well as the whole biblical attitude toward Jeroboam and his kingdom, indicates condemnation, which is expressed most specifically in II Chronicles 13:9–12. Or, for a final example, if II Samuel 8:18, in a list of court officials, laconically states "And David's sons were priests," the parallel in I Chronicles 18:17 eliminates this perplexing reference to non-Aaronite priests by making them "first ministers of the king."

We have seen, on the one hand, that the Bible draws a sharp line between priests and nonpriests. The ramifications of this could be elaborated at great length; suffice it to say that, as Exodus 19:22 puts it, priests are considered those who may approach God, while all others are frequently warned that any nonpriest who approaches shall be put to death (e.g., Num. 1:51; 3:10).

On the other hand, we have also encountered the biblical claim that the people is, or will be, a holy people; here, too, biblical parallels could be multiplied at will. To cite only one striking example, note that Leviticus 19, in the midst of that most priestly of all biblical books, begins with the admonition that the whole Israelite community shall be holy.

There is necessarily a tension between these two biblical positions, one that must have been especially obvious in antiquity, when the Temple stood in Jerusalem and differences between Aaronites and others with regard to access to the sacred were real and tangible. From the point of view of the nonpriest, this tension was expressed by the following question: Does not the difference between priests and others mean that, whatever our efforts, we others are doomed forever, by our low birth, to remain at a level that may be termed *holy* but is really less than that of which humans are capable?

One approach to this predicament is to hope for its disappearance; thus Isaiah, for example, promised that those who were willing to wait for "a year of the Lord's favor" or the creation of "the new heavens and the new earth" would then, at long last, indeed achieve priesthood (Isa. 61:1–6; 66:20–22). Those who were not willing to wait could deal with the tension in one of two ways. They might, most obviously, accept the functional priestly definition of sanctity, viz., the privilege to approach and administer the sacred sphere, and claim that since all are holy all may do so. This was the claim attributed to Korah and dramatically condemned, according to Numbers 16, by divine judgment: Korah and his followers were given the opportunity to offer incense in the sanctuary and God, in his ensuing wrath, destroyed them. Whatever the truth of this story, and whoever may have been interested in preserving it, it may in any case be stated that the norm of exclusive Aaronite priesthood remained virtually unchallenged until long after the destruction of the Second Temple. The only real exception of which we know, if it indeed was an exception, was Menelaus, the Hellenizing high priest of the days of Antiochus Epiphanes; according to II Maccabees 3:4 read together with 4:23 he was a Benjaminite. The text may be in disorder, but even if it is retained, we may note that Menelaus was condemned by Jewish tradition and his successor was received with enthusiasm as "a priest of the seed of Aaron" (I Macc. 7:14).

The converse way of resolving the tension between the concepts of priesthood and holy people is to define holiness as a spiritual ideal that is not limited to, or particularized in, any physical framework such as the Temple or Aaronite seed. It is thus possible to strive for holiness without claiming priesthood, and all Israelites may strive to be holy by fulfilling their divine obligations without intimating that they all have the same obligations or functions. This attitude, which makes the holiness of the priesthood a creation of the law rather than an innate trait, appears to have been most characteristic of the Pharisees, the major nonpriestly party of the late Second Temple period. An especially sharp statement of this view, which also expresses something of the antipriestly polemic that often accompanies it, is the following comment on the priestly blessing:

Do not say, "This priest, who is incestuous and a murderer, is to bless us?!" For the Holy One, blessed be He, says, "Who blesses you? Am not I the one who blesses you, as it is written: 'And they shall place My name on the children of Israel, and I shall bless them' [Num. 6:27]?"

(JT Git. 47b)

That is, priests are to do what God, the source of holiness, demands of them in his law; they are not themselves presumed to be sources of holiness.

Between these two opposing methods of resolving the tension there developed something of a synthesis, with most important implications for the slogan *kingdom of priests.* The attitude associated with the Pharisees, which we have just described, is predicated on the existence of a spiritual ideal of holiness. This allowed for sidestepping the priesthood, for, in the absence of an exclusive relationship between priesthood and holiness, the ordinary Israelite could strive for the latter without claiming the former. This attitude was especially natural in the context of Hebrew and Aramaic, where the word for priest *(kohen)* does not have any obvious etymology and therefore does not readily turn into a symbol. But in the Hellenistic-Roman world, where Jews were increasingly influenced by spiritualistic modes of thought in general, and by the derivation of the terms for priests *(hiereus, sacerdos)* from *holy (hieros, sacer)* in particular, it became easier to make non-Aaronites not only holy, but also *priests,* for priests, as the Temple itself, could now be defined without necessary connection to the real Temple in Jerusalem.

According to this approach, priests are priests because they symbolize or embody holiness, so all who are holy are priests, just as the Temple is the Temple because it symbolizes God's presence in the world: wherever God is present is a temple. Thus, while rabbis might claim that living in accordance to the law is, or is conducive to, *holiness,* Philo, the Alexandrian Jewish thinker, wrote that "a life led in conformity with the laws necessarily confer[s] priesthood or rather high priesthood in the judgment of truth."[4] Similarly, in connection with the allusion of Psalm 46:5 to the "city of God," Philo points out that there are two such cities: the world, and "the soul of the Sage, in which God is said to walk as in a city. For 'I will walk in you' He says, and 'will be your God' [Lev. 26:12]."[5] Philo clearly prefers the latter:

Therefore, do not seek for the city of the Existent among the regions of the earth, since it is not wrought of wood or stone, but in a soul.[6]

Philo did not, however, abandon the real institutions of the Temple and Aaronite priesthood. On the contrary, his trump argument against extreme spiritualization, which values the symbolism of the law but not its observance, is:

> Why, we shall be ignoring the sanctity of the Temple and a thousand other things, if we are going to pay heed to nothing except what is shown us by the inner meaning of things. Nay, we should look on all these outward observances as resembling the body, and their inner meaning as resembling the soul.[7]

It was left, therefore, to other, more radical, Hellenistic Jews to take the final step: retaining only the symbolism of the law, including Temple and priesthood, but rejecting the law itself as a "pedagogue" that is no longer needed (Gal. 3:24–25). Although Philo, just before the last-cited passage from *On the Migration of Abraham,* tells us that there were some in his own day who took this step, the only ones we can document are, as the above allusion to Paul hints, Christians. And among them spiritualization is, indeed, widespread; to limit ourselves to only some of the New Testament evidence, we may note Stephen, termed a *Hellenist,* who, combining prophetic moralism and Jewish Hellenism, makes a systematic attack on the sanctity of the holy land and the Temple, culminating in the attack of Isaiah (66:1–2), as well as Philo, on the earthly Temple, for God is omnipresent (Acts 7). Paul, a Jew from Tarsus, who identifies the individual Christian (I Cor. 6:19) and the Christian community (I Cor. 3:16–17; II Cor. 6:16, quoting, as did Philo, Lev. 26:12) as temples; and I Peter 2, which, as part of a general spiritualization of the temple cult, characterizes believers as a "holy priesthood" and a "royal priesthood," the latter being a literal quotation of the Septuagint version of Exodus 19:6. These developments of Hellenistic Jewish thought, however, bring us beyond the borders of Judaism.

Reverting to Jewish sources, the development of the concept of a kingdom of priests may be summarized quite briefly. If the Pharisaic approach outlined above sidestepped the priesthood and obviated the need to use *kingdom of priests* as a justification for claiming its privileges, the destruction of the Second Temple, which essentially brought an end to the real significance of the priesthood, left its preferential status even less a matter of interest. As scholars have noted, the phrase was the object of only minimal and marginal attention in rabbinic literature, and what comment there is offers virtually no opening for its use as an indication of universal priesthood. Thus, the Aramaic *targumin* (translations of the Bible) interpret Exodus 19:6 as referring to three separate estates—monarchy, priesthood, people. As to the three most popular medieval commentators, Rashi merely points out that *priests* here means *high officials* (as with David's sons in II Sam. 8:18); Nahmanides views the verse as a promise that the claim "you shall be holy" of Leviticus 19 will indeed be fulfilled, but makes no comment on the use of *priests*, and Abraham ibn Ezra, like Rashi, translates *priests* as *servants*, making no comment as to the relationship of these servants to the Aaronite priests. If, therefore, liberal Jews, especially since Abraham Geiger in nineteenth-century Germany, have frequently used the phrase as a weapon in their struggle against the Orthodox establishment, which claims sole authority to fix Jewish law and practice, comparable to the ancient priests' monopoly on access to the sacred, this was not an outgrowth of the Jewish interpretive tradition but rather an imitation of the Protestant Reformation, which had in that same Germany so successfully used the same slogan, a few centuries earlier, against the Catholic establishment.[8]

While we have dealt only with the typical (Protestant) interpretation of this slogan, which focuses on the comparative status of members of the given religion, one should note that *kingdom of priests* has often been used by Jews to claim that Jews are the priests of mankind; just as priests worship on behalf of the people, so the Jews worship on behalf of mankind (Philo) or have a divine mission to bring true religion to the rest of mankind (thus, for example, Obadiah ben Jacob Sforno, in his commentary to Exodus 19:6, compares it to Isaiah's promises that "you shall be called priests of the Lord" (61:6) and "for instruction [*torah*] shall come forth from Zion" (2:3).

This essay does not deal with this interpretation, except to the extent that it is excluded by the arguments against seeing in this verse the ideal of a universal priesthood of all Israelites, for the following reasons. First, the meaning usually ascribed to *a kingdom of priests* is that regarding internal relationships. Second, the most usual biblical slogan for this mission of Israel to the nations is not *kingdom of priests* but rather *light unto the nations* (Isa. 49:6). Third, inspection of Isaiah 61 will show that here, where the idea of the Israelites being priests in the future "favorable year" is brought into explicit connection with Gentiles, the point is not that the Israelites have a mission to perform on behalf of the Gentiles, but rather that they will fare better than the Gentiles.

In light of the evidence, it seems that the phrase *a kingdom of priests* should have no place in Jewish theological parlance today. The meaning usually attributed to it is foreign to the original meaning of the verse and, by and large, to the Jewish interpretive tradition; correspondingly, those branches of Judaism that did see it as a slogan of universal priesthood were either those in antiquity whose lasting significance was for the rise of Christianity or modern polemicists imitating Christian reformers.

The idea of universal holiness is, however, very much at home in Judaism. Those looking for formulas to replace *a kingdom of priests* might, indeed, try the former phrase or a sociological analogue such as *egalitarian access to the sacred* or the biblical injunction, "You shall be holy."

REFERENCES

1. Abraham Geiger, *Jüdische Zeitschrift für Wissenschaft und Leben* 2 (1863), 210.
2. See W. L. Moran, "A Kingdom of Priests," in John L. McKenzie, ed., *The Bible in Current Catholic Thought* (1962).
3. For another example of the pairing of *mamlakhah* and *goy*, see Isa. 60:11–12.
4. *The Special Laws* 2, 164, in Hans Lewy, "Philo," in *Three Jewish Philosophers* (1972), 101.
5. *On Dreams* 2, 248–51 in Hans Lewy, *op. cit.,* 81.
6. Ibid.
7. *On the Migration of Abraham* 89–93, in Lewy, *op. cit.,* 41.
8. See Charles Cyril Eastwood, *The Priesthood of All Believers: An Examination of the Doctrine from the Reformation to the Present Day* (1962).

BIBLIOGRAPHY

Aelred Cody, *A History of Old Testament Priesthood* (1969).
Charles Cyril Eastwood, *The Royal Priesthood of the Faithful: An Investigation of the Doctrine from Biblical Times to the Reformation* (1963).
Charles Cyril Eastwood, *The Priesthood of All Believers: An Examination of the Doctrine from the Reformation to the Present Day* (1962).
W. L. Moran, "A Kingdom of Priests," in John L. McKenzie, ed., *The Bible in Current Catholic Thought* (1962).
Daniel R. Schwartz, "Historia ve-Historiografia—'Mamlekhet Kohanim' ke-Sisma Perushit," in *Zion* 45 (1979/1980).
Daniel R. Schwartz, "Teshuvah le-He'arah," in *Zion* 46 (1980-1981) (exchange with Michael Meyer).
Max Wiener, "The Conception of Mission in Traditional and Modern Judaism," in *YIVO Annual of Jewish Social Science* 2-3 (1947-1948).

Land of Israel

ארץ ישראל

Eliezer Schweid

The land of Israel, as national heritage and holy land, has played a singular and central role in the history of the Jewish people and in the formation of its culture and religion. The special relationship to the land expressed in the covenant between God and his people, the unique interrelationship between national and religious elements, and the peculiar destiny of a nation that for most of its history was either en route to its land or in exile from it are all embodied in the ways the nation has envisioned the land and in the attitudes of the nation toward its land.

The point of departure for an understanding of this matter is that the Israelite tribes were united as a nation, on the basis of the Torah's covenant, prior to their arrival in the land. In the Bible the land is less often called the land of Israel than it is named after the Canaanites and the other peoples dispossessed by the Israelites. The land of Israel is perceived as the promised land, the acquisition of which involves a moral and religious problem and to the possession of which a moral condition applies. The previous inhabitants of the land lost their right to it because of their sins, and the

Israelite tribes will continue to reside in the land only if they will be just. As a consequence of the problem and condition attached to the acquisition and possession of the land, it acquired a special role and assumed a special character. Even as the basis of the nation's material existence, it symbolizes a religious destiny. It is the holy land, and only in it will the nation achieve a worthiness such that the Lord will dwell in its midst. The land of Israel is thus the land that was promised as a national homeland, the basis of the nation's economic weal and state power, but at the same time it symbolizes the Torah's universal moral and religious meaning. These two faces of the land were meant to be complementary, but in the course of the nation's history they were often in contention.

Among the main expressions of the dual character of the relationship to the land are the commandments that "depend on the land," that is, that can be observed only in the land: the laws of the sabbatical and jubilee years, the tithes and offerings to the priests, and the laws of the harvest that guaranteed that shares be left over for the poor. These commandments depend on the land not only in that they apply to the nation when the nation is in its land, but also because they are concrete applications of the moral and religious condition on which possession of the land depends. The idea underlying these commandments is that the nation is not the absolute owner of its land. The land is God's, who created it. God makes the land available to the people so that they may live there justly, without powerful individuals or groups becoming masters of it, lording over all. The land is sanctified by moral possession of it.

In addition to these commandments, there are ritual commandments specific to the land of Israel and Jerusalem. God may be worshiped by bringing sacrifices only to the Temple, which is the symbol that God dwells among his people. God reigns over his people in his land and is their leader; therefore, when the Temple is destroyed and the nation is not in its land, God cannot be worshiped in full nor can there be Jewish kingship. A fanatically exclusive attitude was shaped as a result: a legitimate Jewish kingdom is possible only in the land of Israel and only when the Temple exists in Jerusalem, and only there and then is it possible to live a fully realized Jewish way of life in keeping with the Torah. For that reason it is said of a Jew who lives among the Gentiles that "he is like one who has no God" (BT Ket. 110b).

What is there about this land in particular for it to be made the homeland of the chosen people? The Bible sings the praises of the land's abundance and its beauty, but there is nothing religious in that. A theological dimension appears in Deuteronomy, where a point is made about the difference between Egypt, which drinks river water, and the land of Israel, which drinks rainwater. Rainfall is a symbol of divine providence. Furthermore, according to the biblical stories, in the great riverine countries a nation's sense of ownership of its land and mastery of its destiny is reinforced, leading to the development of tyrannical regimes and slavery. In lands that drink rainwater, on the other hand, man constantly senses his dependence on God and for that reason such a land will sustain a regime of justice free of subjugation. Rainfall is perceived in the Bible as a means for the edification of the people. This is most pronounced in the early prophets, and above all in the story of Elijah and the prophets of Baal. We learn from that story that the dependence on rain is a form of trial. There is a great temptation to use pagan magic to ensure that rain falls, but that defiles the land and it then vomits up its inhabitants; it was, in fact, the source of the Canaanites' sin. The people of Israel must learn that only by observing God's commandments can they dwell in their land and enjoy its bounty.

In the later prophets we find a somewhat different variant of this theme. The land is located between the great river powers (Egypt, Babylonia) and between the desert and the sea. It is a middle land. It attracts all nations and is a pawn in the hands of the powers who fight for world dominion. Those who live in the land are tempted to take part in the struggle between the powers as a way to aggrandize power for themselves. But the only way to live in the land peacefully and to bring a vision of peace to the world is by refraining from participation in those pagan power struggles and by living a life of justice and truth in accordance with the Torah. In a word, then, the nature and status of this land embodies the conditions of the covenant made between the nation and God as expressed in the Torah.

In referring to the land of Israel in religious law and legend, the sages repeat the biblical themes, tending to exaggerate and idealize them. This tendency reflects a new problem in the relationship between the nation and its land, which is rooted in the tension between homeland and exile. From the point of view of the Bible, exile is punishment for the nation's sins. This understanding, however, was undermined by the voluntary residence in the Babylonian exile of many Jews after the return to Zion had in fact occurred, and by the formation of an extensive Diaspora in the lands of Hellenistic conquest as a result of Jewish emigration to them. Initially, the tension was between personal preferences: Where should a Jew live? Subsequently, tension also developed between the centers of Torah learning in Palestine and elsewhere in the Diaspora. Later, after the failure of the Bar Kokhba revolt, there began a movement away from the land, and the sages were then faced with a dual task: to keep the land from being abandoned entirely and to create tools to enable the Jewish people to live in exile, to preserve its religious distinctiveness and not be completely cut off from its land. The result was a view that perceives exile as a temporary state of affairs. The Jews can live in exile as the people of the Torah so long as exile is recognized for what it is and seen as intrinsically incomplete both "nationally politically" and "religiously ritually." Thus ritual patterns were created that perpetuated the memory of the land of Israel and endowed it with supreme symbolic significance.

The idealization of the land culminated in its absolute spiritualization. The process gained momentum as the Jewish community in the land crumbled and Christian and Muslim rulers who succeeded one another there made every effort to erase signs of the Jewish presence and sought to give their presence as successor religions concrete cultural expression by building churches and mosques on the sites that had been sanctified in Jewish tradition. An exilic situation was created in the land of Israel more intense than that obtaining in the lands of the Diaspora. The physical distance between the lands of exile and the land of Israel also grew as the dispersion itself became more extensive and the difficulties of travel increased. Only a few Jews visited the country. For most of the people, the land of Israel became an imagined place that was the focus of emotion, speculation, and ritual. Even the memories of the land from the time the nation dwelt there underwent mythologization and became displaced by messianic and apocalyptic hopes and dreams.

This development is reflected in medieval Jewish thought, in which there are two major directions, one exemplified by Judah Halevi and the other by Maimonides. Halevi based his view on the poetic and narrative motifs of the Bible and of the legends of the sages. He held that the land has the special status of a reality on the border between the material and the spiritual. It is the geographical center of the universe and the point of contact between the spiritual and the material spheres. Creation began at the heart of the land of Israel—in Jerusalem, and therefore Jerusalem and the land around it are the beginning point of space and time, which began along with creation. Time and space have their measure in the land of Israel, and the Sabbath, the time of holiness, occurs there first and above all. There, too, is the grand highway between the earth and the heavens, which is precisely why prophecy is possible only there, and why indeed only in the land does prayer reach its address. The land has then a sanctity of its own, and it is designated for the people devoted to prophecy; only when that nation dwells in that land does the land reveal its special character and the nation discover its special destiny.

Maimonides followed the halakhic sources, and his approach is closer to that of the later prophets. In his view, the land of Israel in and of itself is like all lands. It was sanctified by the commandments, and its special status is a halakhic determination that has political and legal significance. True, according to this determination, sacrificial worship and Jewish sovereignty will exist only in the land of Israel and Jerusalem, and the authority of the courts in the exile is derived from that of the Great Sanhedrin, which had existed in Jerusalem. But the reason for the distinctiveness accorded by halakhah is historical: the land was made sacred for the people by events and acts such as the binding of Isaac, the exploits of Joshua, and the deeds of the prophets and the kings.

Judah Halevi reached a practical conclusion from his conception of the land of Israel, namely, that every Jew must make every effort to return to the land of Israel, live there, and observe the commandments there. Though not a halakhic requirement, it is demanded by true piety. There were others who, sharing his views, came to the country and maintained a small Jewish community there almost without interruption. Maimonides, by contrast, passed through the land of Israel on his way to Egypt and lived his entire life in the Diaspora. In his view, the commandment to live in the land applies to all Jews only when there is Jewish sovereignty.

The tendency to spiritualize the character of the land of Israel influenced most Jews to accept a temporary existence in *galut* (exile), while retaining a ritual tie to the memory of the land and to the messianic hope to be redeemed in it by divine grace. Such a view is prominent in kabbalistic literature, which developed the spiritualist motif to its utmost. In the kabbalah the land is one of the ten *sefirot* (sing. *sefirah*, emanation), the emanation of *malkhut* (kingdom), and since *Knesset Yisrael* (Congregation of Israel) is also identified with the *sefirah*, it was possible to arrive at the idea that Israel, the Torah, and God are one, and to include the land of Israel in that equation. This spiritual and symbolic unity of nation and land facilitated acceptance of the people's physical separation until the time of the end. However, all that remained of the fusion of earthly homeland and holy land was holy land.

In the modern period the Jewish people reached an important juncture in its attitude toward both exile and the land of Israel. The substantial community of those who opted for emancipation ceased looking upon exile as a temporary situation and, indeed, ceased regarding it as exile at all. The countries that granted the Jews citizenship were regarded as fatherland. Those Jews took Zion to be a symbol of a vision of universal redemption, and they rejected the idea of a reestablishment of Jewish sovereignty. The

Orthodox minority that totally rejected emancipation continued to adhere to the medieval view: acceptance of exile until the advent of the Messiah and a spiritual relationship to the land as the holy land. The Zionist view favored the idea of the Jews' equality and emancipation, but wanted to realize it within an independent Jewish framework. A radical Zionist rejection of Jewish existence in exile followed inexorably. In the Zionists' view it was necessary to return to the land of Israel as to a physical national homeland.

A battle of ideas began to be waged over the people's relationship to its land and over the nature and significance of the land. The battle took the form of sharp controversy over basic principles and a variety of practical problems, and can be summarized by the following questions:

First, is it permissible from a religious point of view to initiate the nation's return to its land instead of waiting for divine initiative? This question occupied religious Zionism in its debate with anti-Zionist Orthodoxy, which viewed Zionist activism as a rebellion against God. Beyond the dogmatic question there was, of course, the question of the acceptability of using secular tools and modes of action in order to establish a national homeland in the land of Israel on the model of European secular nationalist movements. The initiative of self-redemption thus symbolized the internalization of secular symbols that would lead to total estrangement from the religious tradition that had formed over the generations in exile. Secular Zionism wanted such a revolution; Orthodoxy regarded it as heresy, and religious Zionism sought a middle way that would bridge the gap between the two.

Second, why specifically the land of Israel? That question engaged, in particular, the secular Zionists in their debate with the territorialists, who sought a Jewish homeland in any available territory. Beyond this question, too, was another more basic question: would Zionism, given its revolutionary character, be able to preserve the continuity of the nation's cultural and historical consciousness? For the Zionists, the land of Israel and the Hebrew language symbolized historical continuity and faithfulness to a distinctive heritage that is related to the land of Israel. To go to some other territory would mean to create a new nation.

Third, what right does the Jewish people have to return to its land after having been physically separated from it for generations? This question arose as a result of Zionism's confrontation with Arab opposition, but it very soon became a focus of a debate between different approaches within Zionism over the kind of right it was entitled to claim—natural right, historic right, moral right, or religious right. That debate had implications for the conception of the scope of Zionism's realization and the nature of its political institutionalization (national home or state, Jewish state or binational state, all of the land of Israel or partition) as well as for the determination of the moral principles that are to guide the process of settling the land—how lands are to be acquired, the form of settlement, the kind of defense to be employed against Arab attackers. Such questions brought to the fore once again some of the motifs permeating biblical thought about the conditions that attach to possession of the land.

Fourth, what will be the cultural character of the nation in its land in terms of society, kind of state, symbols, and way of life? This question is the focus of the debate over the meaning of the term *Jewish state,* the outcome of which will determine how the nation will look upon the land—as homeland of a secular people or a homeland that is also a spiritual symbol, a holy land.

Fifth, what will be the relation to its land of that part of the nation that remains in the Diaspora? A number of possibilities have taken shape: a view of the land as a spiritual center, a view of the land as a center equal in value to centers in the Diaspora, total disavowal of all relation to the land, or a conception of the land as the only national home to which the nation must return, even if in and through an extended historical process.

It would be simplistic and wrong to say that Zionism responded to the spiritualization of the land with an opposite conception—a physical, concrete, national homeland of an ordinary people. The questions and debates that have arisen within Zionism indicate that the tension between the two ways of conceiving of the nation's relationship to its land still exists. Only if the Zionist undertaking is able to give a new concrete meaning to the relationship between the two kinds of perceptions of the land—as homeland and as appointed land—will it be able to complete its work to redeem the nation in its land and sustain it there over time.

BIBLIOGRAPHY

Martin Buber, *Israel and Palestine: The History of an Idea* (1952).
Abraham Halkin, ed., *Zion in Jewish Literature* (1961).
Eliezer Schweid, *The Land of Israel: National Home or Land of Destiny,* tr. Deborah Greniman (1985).

Language

שפה

Josef Stern

anguage, as it first appears in Genesis, is divine. The first spoken words—"Let there be light" (Gen. 1:3)—are God's, and they not only announce the creation of light, but literally bring it into existence. Extending this role of language to all of creation, Rabbi Johanan states, "With ten utterances the world was created" (BT RH 32a), and the rabbis describe God as "He who spoke and the world was created" (BT Sanh. 19a). Each of the first three creations, moreover, is completed by an act of naming: light is called *day*, the firmaments *heavens*, and so on. Linguistic acts, then, frame each of these creations, and, through this literary device, the Torah comments on the nature of language as much as on the world that is created. Reality before creation is depicted as an amorphous lump, earth "unformed and void" (Gen. 1:2), in itself lacking articulation into objects and ontological categories; creation is their emergence through separation and division. But by integrating acts of speech and naming into the sequence of creation, the Torah suggests that how the world presents itself, divided into objects and structured according to kinds, is also inseparable from language. A name is not simply a label pinned to an object, identifiable independently of language. It is, rather, the expression of criteria of individuation and identity, without which there would be nothing to be named. The names God bestows determine as well as describe the essences of the objects to which they apply. If God is the creator, language is his blueprint.

A similar conception, according to various rabbinic statements, underlies the story of Adam naming the animals, the scriptural account of the genesis of human language. Adam's names are said to be "suitable" for the species (Gen. R. 17:4), that is, in accord with their essences. Naḥmanides explains: "God brought each wild beast and every bird before Adam and he recognized their natures and gave them names, that is, the names fitting for them according to their nature, and by the names it became clear [to the animals] who was fitting to be whose mate" (*Peirushei ha-Torah, ad loc. Gen.* 2:20). Adam's names, like God's, do not merely tag their objects for purposes of communication but fit them according to his knowledge of their nature, knowledge he possesses either through a divinely endowed faculty of naming or through revelation. Adamic language is thus formed in the image of the language of God. And in giving Adam the capacity and authority to name other creatures, God gives him power within the created world analogous to his own as its creator.

Underlying these opening chapters of Genesis and their rabbinic interpretation there is, then, a sustained conception of language, one we will call essentialist. In this view, words, especially proper and common names, do not arbitrarily refer or apply to individual things or categories; they refer to them by virtue of expressing their natures or essences. The essences of the things, wedded to their names, are the meanings of the names; the names, as it were, abbreviate descriptions of the essences of their bearers. Hence, the speaker of a language, who knows the meanings of its names as part of his linguistic competence, ipso facto knows the natures or essences of all the objects or kinds of things to which he can refer or about which he can speak.

The significance of language in this view is not simply its social use or instrumental role in communication. Language is primarily a source of knowledge about the world; indeed in Genesis, where it is originally attributed to God, language is not merely descriptive but constructive of reality, outside rather than within nature, aligned with the creator rather than the created.

This essentialist view is not the only conception of language within Jewish tradition, nor does it reflect the diverse concerns with language found in that tradition. In this century, for example, Buber and Rosenzweig have emphasized the use of language in speech—specifically the relation of dialogue or what Rosenzweig called "speech thinking" *(Sprachdenken)*, whose concrete temporal character and assumption of the presence of a second person (a "Thou") confronting the speaker (the "I") distinguishes it from purely abstract conceptual thought—in interpreting the experience of Judaism. And more recent theologians have explored what they believe are the radical consequences of the Holocaust for the language of religion. But by focusing on the philosophical history of the essentialist view, we may illustrate some of the many contexts within Judaism in which issues of language arise and one problem central to Jewish thinking about language which this conception raises.

At one extreme, perhaps the most elaborate formulation of the essentialist conception of language is the esoteric interpretation of creation and revelation in what Gershom Scholem calls the linguistic mysticism of the kabbalah. Within that tradition the essential role of human language also is not communicative. Although it is used in ordinary speech to refer to natural entities, its true significance lies in an inner meaning by which it symbolizes what the kabbalists call the language of God, a symbolic structure parallel to the system of divine emanations or *sefirot*. The symbols of language—names, words, letters—are taken as visible configurations of divine forces just as elsewhere in the kabbalah symbols of spheres of light or attributes symbolize the dynamic being of the divine realm. And just as the entire natural world symbolizes the divine process of creation, so every character of human language, especially in the Torah, the document of revelation, symbolizes the divine language and, thereby, God. The mystic discovers that divine essence through his esoteric interpretation of the language of the Torah, an idea the kabbalists expressed by saying that the entire Torah is the name or names of God. Moreover, because the divine essences symbolized by these names are also taken to be laws that map out the order of creation, language here also assumes a creative role with God. For some kabbalists, letters or names are "atoms" through whose combination he creates the world; for others language is his instrument in creation. But, in either case, the significance of a word is an essence, though in this kabbalistic version of the essentialist conception the essences are divine rather than natural.

A different form of the essentialist conception emerged among medieval Jewish philosophers, in part in the course of resolving an apparent contradiction they perceived between the existence of multiple, dissimilar human languages and the scriptural claim that mankind is descended from Adam. To demonstrate the veracity of Scripture, many simply appealed to the third scriptural episode concerned with the origin of language, the Tower of Babel, to explain why people are now "scattered . . . and their languages [are] different despite . . . their all having had one language . . . the consequence of being the children of a single individual" (*Guide* 3, 50). But others, most notably Judah Halevi, attempted to show not merely that Scripture is consistent with the present multiplicity of human languages, but that certain characteristics of language, for example, its grammatical structure, which bears marks of rational design, can be accounted for only if language had an originator, an Adam (Kuzari 1, 54). Halevi's argument, as Wolfson has demonstrated, is formulated in terminology borrowed from the ancient controversy over whether language originated in *convention* or in *nature*. Following Plato, Halevi holds that language is *conventional*, but in a sense of that term that implies that it is also *natural*: language was invented by someone who designated his terms to apply to things in virtue of their satisfying his knowledge of their nature. He denies, in other words, both Epicurus's view that language randomly emerged from the natural cries of animals and Aristotle's view that it is a man-made artifact that arbitrarily refers to objects without any relation to their nature. Halevi's view of language is thus a Platonic variant of the essentialist conception already encountered in the rabbinic interpretations of Genesis.

But Halevi also recognizes difficulties with the Platonic account, problems that point to more general tensions in essentialist conceptions of language. Despite the evidence of rational design, he finds it almost inconceivable that any one human within a multitudinous society could have so "contrived a language" (Kuzari 1, 55), probably because he finds it implausible that any one member could have simply forced his language on the others or perhaps because any social agreement among individuals adopting a language would itself require a language in which the agreement was expressed. The only explanation, he thinks, is the scriptural account that distinguishes two stages in the history of language. At the first stage, language is invented— but by God, who then teaches it to man, thus circumventing the practical difficulties involved in the conventionalist hypothesis that language is humanly contrived. Moreover, this divine-Adamic language—Hebrew—is also natural in that each creature named by Adam "deserved such name which fitted and characterized it"; indeed, its essentialist perfection is also the reason, Halevi suggests, why Hebrew is called "the Holy Language" (Kuzari 4, 25).

Yet Halevi also apparently believes that only Hebrew in "its *original* form" (emphasis added) truly satisfies the essentialist conception; later Hebrew "shared the fate of its bearers, degenerating and dwindling with them" (Kuzari 2, 68). Its present corrupted state, as well as the existence of multiple dissimilar languages among the nations, he seems to ascribe to Babel, the second stage in the history of language. Thus, Halevi's model of language remains the essentialist conception, but he also seems to acknowledge that it fits only a Hebrew now lost to us and that all other languages, that is, all languages we now actually possess, fall short of its ideal of a true language.

This tension between the idealized essentialist conception and the actual languages mankind uses, implicit in Halevi, becomes explicit in Maimonides, the first part of whose *Guide of the Perplexed* addresses the central question of religious language: whether and how human language can refer to, describe, or make predications about God. This question is especially problematic given the epistemological assumption of the essentialist view that we must, and therefore can, know the essence of whatever we can name or describe. Contemporary philosophers have criticized related views about names because they require the ordinary speaker to be omniscient with respect to natural things and kinds to which he can refer. The medieval Jewish philosophers, however, were mainly concerned with the metaphysical knowledge this view would require the human speaker to possess. How, they questioned, can man refer to metaphysical entities and, in particular, God, whose essence (it was widely believed) it is impossible for him to know? Furthermore, given what is known about God—that he is incorporeal and indivisible—how are we to understand the various names, descriptions, and predicates the Torah employs, which are literally false?

Answers to these questions fall into two groups. The first, exemplified by Halevi, interprets all scriptural descriptions of God symbolically—signifying what is "sought by inspiration, imagination, and feeling"—and claims further that reference to God can be had only through nonrational visionary modes of prophecy (Kuzari 4, 3). The second approach is that of Maimonides. Maimonides rejects the view that language should be interpreted symbolically and emotively, and emphasizes that, according to its literal "external" sense, human language, especially as found in the Torah, is a source of beliefs (for example, in God's corporeality and multiplicity) that are not merely false but idolatrous. To correct these misconceptions he therefore undertakes one of the boldest projects in the tradition of scriptural exegesis, identifying alternative interpretations for all anthropomorphic and anthropopathic descriptions of God (cf. *Guide* 1, 1–49) and reinterpreting affirmative divine predicates either as actions or as equivocal negative attributes (cf. *Guide* 1, 50–70).

Several general motifs run through this intricate and subtle program. As suggested, Maimonides vigorously and repeatedly undermines the primacy of the literal text and instead gives interpretation the central place. But because a tradition is often identified with its sacred texts, Maimonides must also show that his advocacy of nonliteral interpretation does not lead, at least openly, to substantive deviations in particular beliefs and is itself legislated by the tradition as the proper approach to its texts. Hence he marshals rabbinic precedent to illustrate how "the sages themselves interpreted Scriptural passages . . . as to educe their inner meaning from literal sense, correctly considering these passages to be figures of speech" ("Introduction to Helek," Comm. Mish., Sanh. 10). At the same time, Maimonides imposes no absolute constraints on the interpretation of texts, no matter how far they depart from their literal meaning. So his (at least overt) belief in creation, he insists, is "not due to a text. . . . For we could interpret [it] as figurative, as we have done when denying His corporeality. Perhaps this would even be easier to do . . . " (*Guide* 2, 25). One need only reread the first verses of Genesis to appreciate just how much freedom this statement grants to figurative interpretation.

Maimonides' focus on philosophically informed interpretation over literal meaning is not, however, due to a disregard for language so much as to concern for its deeper features—for its grammatically obscured logical or semantic significance as opposed to its superficial form. He clearly expresses this concern by distinguishing between what is uttered and what is "represented in the soul [or mind]"; only the latter, he emphasizes, is the object of belief and, therefore, his concern. This distinction is not between language and something nonlinguistic but between two types of language. For these "representations in the mind," though contrasted with "verbal language that is uttered and spoken with the lips," nonetheless have all the features of language. They, not verbal statements, are the proper bearers of truth and falsity (*Guide* 1, 50). And unlike "customary words" whose "bounds of expression in all languages are very narrow" and can express subtle notions only "loosely," they precisely conform to the Aristotelian rules governing logical judgment and represent "notions according to their true reality," as the intellect apprehends them. Like the artificial languages contemporary logicians study, Maimonides' mental representations constitute a "logically perfect" language whose "outward" grammatical form expresses its "inner" semantic content with a transparency unachieved in spoken language (cf. *Guide* 1, 57). Moreover, unlike verbal expressions, each representation in the mind refers, as the essentialist conception of names dictates, to the unique thing, existent or not, whose essence is given by its meaning. For example, Maimonides argues that whoever believes that

God possesses affirmative attributes does not "fall short of apprehending Him, . . . he has abolished his belief in the existence of the deity without being aware of it"; that is, he does not have a false apprehension about God, he has no belief about God at all. For if the essence the speaker associates with the name determines to what it refers, then if he believes that attributes can subsist within God's essence "he is ignorant of the being of the entity" and, despite what he imagines, "applies this term to absolute nonexistence." Although he uses the name *God,* that speaker has referred not to God but to a nonexistent being of his own "invention" (*Guide* 1, 60; see 2, 30).

Maimonides thus distinguishes two types of language: one that is used in vulgar human speech, the other in which philosophically justified beliefs are represented. This distinction is, in turn, paralleled by others: for example, between the exoteric, or external, literal meaning and the esoteric, or inner, figurative interpretation of sacred texts. Maimonides' critique of spoken language or the external meaning of a text is not, moreover, global but specific to contexts where it serves to represent true beliefs. He recognizes that spoken language may best serve other purposes. For example, although only the "internal meaning" of a parable "contains wisdom that is useful for beliefs concerned with the truth as it is," its external meaning "contains wisdom that is useful in many respects, among which is the welfare of human societies" (*Guide,* Intro.).

Maimonides' view of human language is best expressed, perhaps, through his inventive use of the tanna Rabbi Ishmael's principle "The Torah speaks in the language of the sons of men," which he cites to support his own exegetical practices (*Guide* 1, 26). In its original context (Sif. Num. 112; BT Yev. 71a), Rabbi Ishmael states this principle in response to Rabbi Akiva, who exploits every instance of repetition in the Torah for halakhic exegesis. According to Rabbi Ishmael, these repetitions are merely a stylistic device for emphasis, frequently found in human speech, and therefore should not be employed for special halakhic inferences (Rashi, ad loc 3a). Here, then, Rabbi Ishmael's principle prescribes a conservative approach to primarily legal exegesis.

Maimonides' use of the principle reverses this original intent. He appropriates the statement primarily for haggadahic or nonlegal interpretation, and uses it both to explain why the Torah uses anthropomorphic language—despite its falsity—to describe God and to motivate his own radical program of scriptural reinterpretation. Interpreting the phrase "the language of the sons of men" as the language specifically of the "multitudes, I mean the generality as distinguished from the elite" (*Guide* 1, 14), Maimonides takes Rabbi Ishmael to be explaining why the Torah adopts the language of the multitudes, for example, anthropomorphisms. Because it is meant to educate the entire nation of Israel, it adopts their mode of speech and aims at their level of comprehension (*Guide* 1, 33). The multitudes can conceive only of entities that are bodies, so the Torah describes God as a body. And despite the evils of affirmative predications of God, attributes were inserted into the canon of prayer out of "the necessity to address men in such terms as would make them achieve some representation" of God's perfection (*Guide* 1, 59). By the same token, however, this interpretation of Rabbi Ishmael's statement also implies that those whose intellectual apprehension enables them to grasp the truth as it really is need not, and therefore should not, interpret the Torah literally according to the "language of the sons of men." For this philosophical elite Rabbi Ishmael's principle serves, then, to authorize interpretation beyond, and contrary to, the literal meaning of the text, and, hence, to justify Maimonides' own liberal policy for scriptural reinterpretation. Indeed, the way Maimonides reinterprets Rabbi Ishmael's statement, reversing its talmudic meaning, exemplifies the very kind of reinterpretation he uses it in turn to motivate.

Yet, while the representations in the mind that express the correct interpretation of the Torah are theoretically superior to the verbal language in which it is written, Maimonides gives neither of them metaphysical or supranatural status. Among the anthropomorphisms denied of God he includes all terms signifying language, including representations "impressed" on the soul. And in light of his naturalistic theory of prophecy, he also emphasizes that the linguistic document of the Torah and "all speech that is ascribed to Him is created"; hence language, like all creation, is within rather than outside nature. In complete contrast to the rabbinic and kabbalistic accounts that make language God's virtual partner in Genesis, Maimonides denies speech any such role. "In all cases in which he said . . . occurs in the Account of the Beginning, it means He willed or wanted" (*Guide* 1, 65). Here the term *said* is not only stripped of the corporeal aspects of voice and sounds. Because its interpretation, the term *will*, is itself equivocal when applied to God, there is simply no saying what its content is. What is certain is that if language is created, neither it, nor anything resembling it, carries over to the creator.

Finally, because these "representations in the mind" are, as much as speech, created or natural entities, the question remains whether, and how, it is possible for man to use them to refer to God. If their referential use also requires knowledge of the essences of their referents, then man will also be limited to that which falls within the scope of his knowledge—hence, excluding God. This, in turn, is difficult to reconcile with some of Maimonides' other views. As an alternative to verbal prayer, Maimonides advocates silence as the only true praise of God. Here silence means, however, not an attitude emptied of all content but intellectual apprehension, which the individual simply restrains himself from verbalizing in spoken language (*Guide* 1, 59). Yet, what can even such an abstract apprehension of God be when we lack knowledge of his essence, as the essentialist conception demands? The extent to which negative attributes give us not simply knowledge but knowledge of God is controversial. Only the Tetragrammaton, Maimonides writes, "gives a clear unequivocal indication of His essence," yet he also concedes that, with our poor knowledge of Hebrew, we do not absolutely know what that essence is (*Guide* 1, 61). Thus, Maimonides' account leaves us with the following predicament: The essentialist conception of language requires knowledge that man lacks. Furthermore, in this view all human languages—spoken or thought—are created; hence, the essentialist predicament cannot be buttressed by linking an original Adamic human language with that of an omniscient God. Therefore, how is it possible for man to refer to God?

BIBLIOGRAPHY

Gershom Scholem, "The Meaning of the Torah in Jewish Mysticism," in *On the Kabbalah and Its Symbolism* (1965).

Gershom Scholem, "The Name of God and the Linguistic Theory of the Kabbalah," in *Diogenes,* no. 79–80 (1972), 57–80, 164–94.

Harry Austryn Wolfson, *Studies in the History of Philosophy and Religion,* 2 vols. (1973 and 1977).

Harry Austryn Wolfson, "The Veracity of Scripture from Philo to Spinoza," in *Religious Philosophy: A Group of Essays* (1961).

Liturgy

סדר תפילות

Eric L. Friedland

Not unlike the Hebrew Bible before its rescension, the Jewish liturgy—Israel's millennial creation of the spirit—mirrors the people's evolving self-conception in relation to God, humankind, and the world. As in the formation of Scripture and its canonization by stages, so in the crystallization of the Jewish "Book of Common Prayer," the siddur, steady accumulation is counterpoised by constant sifting and sorting out. Paralleling the Psalms, the hymnal of the Second Temple, which came to form an integral part of the biblical corpus, the siddur can be said to be, in a larger sense, an essential component in a prodigal oral tradition that has yet to stop. Inescapably, the global experiences of a folk dispersed everywhere and still very much on the move have left their imprint on the psyche and worship of the Jews.

The rabbinic sages of the Mishnah and Talmud were also responsible for drawing upon older and contemporary models, biblical and postbiblical, in their creation of the fundament of the liturgy: the formula of the benediction (berakhah), namely, "Blessed art Thou, O Lord our God, king of the universe"; and the core network of benedictions surrounding the climactic

Shema—"Hear, O Israel: the Lord our God, the Lord is one"—and its succeeding paragraphs from Deuteronomy 6:4–9, 11:13–21; and Numbers 15:37–41, all of which constitute not only an affirmation of faith but, significantly, a reading from Scripture as well. These benedictions salute God as nature's creator, as giver of the Torah, and as redeemer, and lead up to the prayer (tefillah) par excellence—the Amidah (lit., standing prayer). Hewing to the aforesaid pattern, the morning (shaharit) and evening (ma'ariv) services—as well as the afternoon (minhah) service which, however, basically comprises only the tefillah—formed a verbal sublimation and surrogate for a sacrificial cult in a Temple that no longer existed. The reading from Scripture (the Torah, the Prophets, and the Five Megillot [scrolls]) with its developing lectionary was to occupy on specified occasions a preeminent position in Jewish worship.

Although the ancient rabbis put us in their debt by shaping and fixing the contours of the liturgy in the way they did and as we still have it today, the discoveries in the genizah (storeroom) of an early-medieval Cairo synagogue revealed that much variation in the wording of liturgical texts existed during that period. And this, it might be stressed, all the while the rabbis' thematic outline in benedictory cast was faithfully adhered to. From time to time, to be sure, efforts were made to prevent textual and even, periodically, structural latitudinarianism from taking over or, worse, degenerating into a kind of liturgical free-for-all. Rites such as those introduced by Amram Gaon, Saadiah Gaon, and Moses Maimonides were specifically aimed at protecting the rabbinic imprint on the liturgy. Yet, alongside these attempts at an imposition of order (siddur is derived from the word seder, meaning arrangement or ordering) in worship, hardly a decade passed without new poetical creations, or piyyutim, being inserted into the normative service, largely for the sake of lending it variety and depth, contemporaneity and immediacy. The synagogue was privileged to derive spiritual replenishment from the literary-devotional outpourings by a host of religious songsmiths, paytanim, ranging from Yosé ben Yosé in the sixth century C.E. and Eleazar Kallir in the seventh century C.E. to Solomon ibn Gabirol and Judah Halevi in the eleventh century.

The mystical tradition, the kabbalah, followed another direction by concurrently maintaining the sacrosanct character of the liturgical text, even to the letter and its numerical value, and intromitting an elaborate theosophical system with theurgic aspects. Meditations, or kavvanot, before the recitation of a berakhah or the execution of a ritual act made the kabbalah's esoteric doctrines fairly explicit and efficacious for the worshiper. Lineal heirs to the medieval mystical tradition, the Hasidim forged ahead by trimming off some of its metaphysical excesses, adopting the rite of Isaac Luria of Safed, a partial fusion of the Ashkenazi and the Sephardic prayerbooks, and allowing for extra-synagogal devotions, the extraordinary output by Rabbi Naḥman of Bratslav perhaps being today the best known and most quoted of these efforts.

The daily, Sabbath, and festival siddur has not preempted the prayer life of the Jewish people. No less cherished over the centuries have been, among others, the *tehinnot* (lit., supplications; personal, private devotion for a wide variety of purposes), *seliḥot* (penitential prayers on different occasions and not just the High Holy Day season), *kinot* (elegies), and *sefer ha-ḥayyim* (lit., book of life; containing prayers that pertain to death, burial, mourning, and memorializing the departed). The piety, spiritual sophistication, psychological wisdom, and profound learning permeating these works are of an order that has probably yet to be surpassed. Not to be forgotten, of course, is the Passover Haggadah, which, with its countless transmutations, possesses an abiding universal appeal. The Passover manual and ceremonial meal are ineluctably bound up with the Jewish people's continually reenacted release from bondage to freedom, extending from pharaonic times to the present, in contexts and on levels religious, social, political, psychological, sexual, and ethnic. Each context and each level serves as one more touchstone for furthering and refining the Jew's self-understanding and self-authentication.

Among the primary endeavors of Reform, Conservative, and Reconstructionist Judaism as these movements emerged in response to emancipation, first in Europe and then in America, was prayerbook revision, to signal where each movement stood in the theological, liturgical, and attitudinal spectrum. Since 1818, when the first full-fledged Reform temple opened its doors, in Hamburg, the process has continued unabated. The desire to come to terms with the zeitgeist has often been accompanied by a reexamination and even reappropriation of overlooked classic sources. Nor were religious liberals the only ones to take up the challenge of modernity. Changing tastes and sensibilities were felt among Orthodox circles as well, as attested to by the meticulous historical-textual studies of Eliezer Landshuth and Seligmann Isaac Baer, the aestheticism of Michael Sachs, the Anglophile "sweetness and light" of Joseph H. Hertz and David de Sola Pool, and the innovations in the Israeli siddurim put out by the country's chief rabbinate. Nor has the old been neglected in liberal circles. A small indication of how the old is appreciated anew among the liberal prayerbook editors may be found in the use of Psalm 104, a paean to nature and its author, in settings other than merely the Sabbath afternoon service, where it is bypassed by most, and in the resuscitation of Psalm 122, a stirring ode to Jerusalem, in non-Orthodox prayerbooks that for a time opposed out of sincere conviction and religious principle the idea of the Jewish people's returning all together to Zion. A similar change of fortunes has affected the fast-day of Tishah be-Av, long omitted in most Reform/Liberal prayerbooks and now by and large reinstated, owing to the mature realization that, premessianically, tragedy, or in traditional parlance *galut* (exile), remains an immutable fact of Jewish life and the state of the world.

The Jewish liturgy continues to grow apace, as Jews learn of their past, from their fellow Jews the world over, and from the societies around them. The liturgical adage *haverim kol yisrael* ("Israel united in one fellowship") holds, across both ideological and ritual differences (such as the autonomous versus the heteronomous stance toward the Torah, or the theist versus the nontheist position, and across time and space). The soul of the Jewish people in contemplation, communion, prayer, and song is writ large in the siddur.

BIBLIOGRAPHY

Seligmann Baer, *Seder Avodat Yisrael* (1868).
Ismar Elbogen, *Der jüdische Gottesdienst* in *seiner geschichtlichen Entwicklung* (1913).
Nahum N. Glatzer, *The Language of Faith* (1967).
Joseph Heinemann, *Ha-Tefillah bi-Tekufat ha-Tannaim ve-ha-Amoraim* (1964).
Jakob J. Petuchowski, *Prayerbook Reform in Europe* (1968).

Love

אהבה

Steven Harvey

Judaism commands love *(ahavah)*. The Torah contains three distinct positive commandments to love: to love God, to love our neighbor, and to love the stranger.[1] In addition, Judaism also teaches other proper objects of love, which may or may not be included in the commandments of the Torah; for example, love of self, love of spouse, love of family, love of the land of Israel, love of the Torah, and love of wisdom. Although the meaning of love (or, at least, a meaning of love) as an affection or passion is generally recognized, the Torah's commandments to love are not as unambiguous as we might assume, and their proper performance is often effected in purely mechanical and dispassionate ways. Such dispassion should not be surprising. Indeed, love as passion cannot be commanded, because commandments involve will while love as passion is independent of the will. To understand the meaning of love in Judaism, we ought first to examine the three biblical commandments to love and discern clearly what the Torah is commanding with its directive to love.

The commandment to love one's neighbor is found in Leviticus 19:18: "Love your neighbor as yourself." Many of the traditional biblical commentators were struck by the literal implication of this verse that a person can somehow be expected to love other people, possibly all other people, as he loves himself. In perhaps the most influential commentary on this verse, Naḥmanides explains that it cannot be understood literally because "the heart of man is unable to accept the command to love his fellow as he loves himself."[2] Naḥmanides rather understands the verse to mean that a person should desire the well being of his fellow, that is, his acquisition of wealth, property, honor, knowledge, and wisdom, to the same extent that he desires his own well being. In this interpretation Naḥmanides is reflecting the glosses of earlier commentators like Ibn Ezra, who interprets the verse to mean that "a person should love the good for his fellow as he does for himself."[3] Interestingly, the standard medieval commentaries, unlike, in this respect, those of later thinkers like Naphtoli Herz Wessely and Malbim (Meir Loeb ben Jehiel Michael), are not concerned here about the problem of commanding love, and their solutions to the difficulties of the verse focus upon interpreting or restricting the object of love or limiting the application of love quantitatively—that is, that you should love your fellow with the same kind of love with which you love yourself, but not necessarily to the same degree. The commandment to love one's neighbor is accordingly still directed to the passions and not to the will.

There is good reason for viewing the above expression of the commandment to love one's neighbor as an ideal, and to seek fulfillment of the commandment in specific deeds rather than in emotions. The Talmud, for example, directs its followers to a number of actions on the basis of "Love your neighbor as yourself." On the authority of Leviticus 19:18, a swift and humane execution is prescribed for the condemned (BT Sanh. 45a, 52a–b); a son is permitted, if necessary, to let blood for his father (BT Sanh. 84b); a man is prohibited from betrothing a woman before he sees her (BT Kid. 41a); and a husband is forbidden to have sexual relations with his wife during the day (BT Nid. 17a). Similarly, while Maimonides describes the commandment in terms of the ideal, he also provides specific actions through which one can dispassionately fulfill it. In the *Book of Commandments* he presents the ideal:

> The 206th commandment is to love one another as we love ourselves, that my compassion and love for my coreligionist will be like my love and compassion for myself with regard to his property and self and everything that he has and that he desires. Whatever I wish for myself, I will wish the like for him.

But earlier in the same work[4] he enumerates specific commandments of action contained in the commandment to love one's neighbor. This list is expanded in the *Mishneh Torah* (MT Hil. Evel 14, 1) to include visiting the sick, comforting the mourners, joining the funeral procession, causing the bride to enter under the marriage canopy, escorting departing guests, engaging oneself in all the needs of the burial, carrying the dead on one's shoulder, giving a eulogy, digging the grave, burying the dead, and making the bride and bridegroom rejoice and providing them with all their needs. This list is, of course, only representative and suggestive of the ways in which the commandment to love one's neighbor is performed.[5] Maimonides concludes this list of deeds entailed by the commandment to love with the following epitomization of the commandment: "All the things that you would want others to do for you, do them for your brother in the Torah and the commandments." This formulation of the commandment is one to which the will can respond.

The commandment to love one's neighbor aims at an ideal to which all Jews should strive—a sincere and unbounded desire and concern for the well-being of others. But this sort of love cannot be commanded, although one can be commanded to endeavor to attain it. What can be commanded is the performance of acts of love, of treating others as one would if one truly cared about their well-being. This is the practical meaning of the commandment, and it underscores the practical application of Leviticus 19:18 in the four talmudic loci referred to above. Moreover, the praxis of love is the surest path to the ideal.[6] Thus, insofar as the performance of acts of love may well lead to feelings of love (see the formulation of this in the anonymous *Orḥot Ẓaddikim,* 5) when one fulfills the commandment through deeds, he at the same time fulfills it by striving to attain the ideal.

The commandment to love the stranger is found in Deuteronomy 10:19: "You shall love [*ahavah*] the stranger, for you were strangers in the land of Egypt." The meaning of this commandment may be illumined by the verse preceding it, which states that God "loves the stranger, giving him food and dress." Jews are thus commanded to love the stranger, that is, to provide him with his needs, as God does, especially since as past strangers they can appreciate his plight. This interpretation is supported by a similar statement of the commandment in Leviticus 19:34: "The stranger who resides with you shall be to you as one of your citizens; you shall love him as yourself, for you were strangers in the land of Egypt." Following our interpretation of "love your neighbor as yourself," this verse would command loving the stranger through acts of love, that is, in the way the Jews would have liked to have been treated when they were strangers in Egypt. Once again, Israel is commanded to strive for the ideal, for true love, the sincere caring for the well-being of the stranger, and once again, the performance of unemotional acts of love is halakhically sufficient. In the formulation of the popular fourteenth-century *Sefer ha-Ḥinnukh (Book of Education)*: "We are commanded to love the strangers, that is, we are urged not to cause them any sorrow, but to do good things for them and to deal kindly with them according to what is proper and within our ability" (n. 431).

It must be noted that much of the discussion of this commandment focuses upon the meaning of stranger (*ger*) and the relation of this commandment to the commandment to love one's neighbor. If *neighbor (rea)* connotes all men, then why the need for the specific commandment regarding the stranger, whatever its meaning? If *neighbor* refers to a coreligionist, then the purpose of the commandment is clear, unless *stranger* refers specifically to the righteous proselyte (*ger ẓedek*) (see Maimonides, *Book of Commandments,* n. 207). The meaning of *stranger* and *neighbor* (according to some, "like yourself") in these two commandments is for many reasons very important and has been argued, heatedly and dogmatically, by the greatest Jewish thinkers, but there is no *consensus omnium*. For our present purpose, there is no need to resolve the debate. We may speak of these commandments in their broader meaning, following, for example, Joseph Albo (*Sefer ha-Ikkarim,* 3, 25), keeping in mind that even those who understand the commandments in a more restrictive sense may interpret them as applicable universally (see, for example, *Sefer ha-Ḥinnukh* n. 431). What is at stake here is not the essence of the meaning of love, but rather the specific objects of that love.

The commandment to love God is stated explicitly in Deuteronomy 6:5: "You shall love the Lord your God with all your heart and with all your soul and with all your might." Once again the practical meaning of this commandment is not clear. An early halakhic midrash explains that one can learn how to love God and thus fulfill this commandment from the verse that follows, "And these words which I command you today shall be upon your heart," because if we put these words upon our heart, we will recognize God and cling to his ways (Sif. Deut., *ad loc.*). In other words, contemplation of God's words, of his Torah, leads to knowledge of God and to the observance of his commandments. Now contemplation of the Torah can certainly be commanded, but is either this contemplation or its desired result—the knowledge of God and the observance of his commandments—the intention of the commandment to love God? The thirteenth-century exegete Baḥya ben Asher combined this midrash with a preceding midrash in *Sifrei* and explained: "The meaning of love of God is that man reflect upon His Torah and His commandments and through them apprehend God and through this apprehension delight exceedingly. . . . He will make righteous the many", (*Commentary on the Torah* ad loc.). Baḥya later writes that the result of this apprehension of God and the accompanying delight is the leading of the many to the righteous life and the bringing of the love of God into their hearts (Kad ha-Kemaḥ, "Ahavah"). One loves God by reflecting upon his Torah, coming to apprehend him, delighting in him, and ultimately leading others to do likewise.

Bahya's understanding of the commandment to love God is, for the most part, representative of the normative Jewish interpretation of the commandment and its most well-known midrash. Insofar as Bahya borrowed greatly from Maimonides' exposition of this commandment, it is significant to observe where he departs from him. Maimonides explains that the commandment to love God is "to reflect upon and contemplate His commandments, His orders, and His acts in order to apprehend Him and through this apprehension to delight exceedingly" (Book of Commandments, no. 3). Bahya (unlike, for example, the Sefer ha-Ḥinnukh, n. 418), omits "and His acts," perhaps in his desire to stick more closely to text and midrash. The distinction is indeed significant. For Maimonides and the rationalist tradition of which he was a part, one comes to apprehend and love God from contemplation not only of his Torah and commandments, but also of his acts. The study of his acts, his works (that is, the study of natural science) becomes a religious obligation, an act of love. Indeed, Maimonides instructs the reader of his Mishneh Torah that the way to fulfill the commandment to love God is by "reflecting upon his great and wondrous works and creatures" from which he will see God's infinite wisdom and immediately come to love him (MT Yesodei ha-Torah 2, 2; cf. MT Teshuvah 10, 6). The midrash in Sifrei is again cited, but references to the contemplation of the commandments are conspicuously omitted. This manifestly inappropriate use of the midrash cannot, of course, be interpreted to imply that Maimonides may not have believed that contemplation of the Torah leads to love of God. It does, however, strongly suggest that study of God's works by itself can lead to love of God and on a certain level may be the proper way to perform the commandment.

There are other explanations of the commandment to love God. The Talmud teaches that the commandment means that "the Divine Name may be beloved through you" (BT Yoma 26a). It provides the illustration of the man who studies the Bible and Mishnah and deals honestly and speaks gently with people. Such a man reflects well on his religion and makes God beloved of man, not through preaching as in the midrash in Sifrei Deuteronomy, but through example. Nahmanides gives another explanation of love of God in his commentary on Exodus 20:6, where he explains it to mean worshiping and praising God alone and denying all other gods.

All of the above interpretations offer practical acts through which one can fulfill the commandment to love God. Unlike the two previous commandments to love, most of these acts are not acts of love, but acts that lead to love. Once again, most can be performed, at least initially, without passion, and once again the goal of the commandment is an ideal. Judaism commands its followers to love in the sense that it commands them to act as they would act if they loved and to act in ways that should lead them to love. What is not commanded, because it cannot be commanded, is the intended goal of these commandments, namely, that Jews indeed love.

The rabbis taught that every love that is dependent on some cause will come to an end when that cause disappears, but the love that is not dependent on a specific cause will never pass away (M. Avot 5:16; cf. Plato, Symposium 183e; Aristotle, *Nicomachean Ethics* 8, 3; 9, 1 and 3). A number of commentators on this teaching, such as Joseph Albo, Isaac Abrabanel, and Moses Almosnino, have sought to clarify it in terms of Aristotle's well-known division of the objects of love into the pleasant, the useful, and the good (*Nicomachean Ethics* 8, 2). Love that is dependent on some cause is the love of the pleasant and the useful, the love of something solely because of the pleasure or utility that may be derived from it, as if, in Abrabanel's words, "love were an instrument to attain this pleasure or this utility" (Comm. on *Naḥalot Avot,* ad loc.). Such, the rabbis tell us, was the infamous love of Amnon for Tamar described in II Samuel 13, which was as fleeting as it was lustful and selfish. Love for beauty, wealth, or position lasts no longer than beauty, wealth, or position, and often not even that long. This is not the love intended by the commandments of the Torah. Love that is not dependent on any cause is the true and desired love; it is the love of the good. It is love for no cause other than the beloved alone. As Abrabanel explains in a splendid exegesis on "Love your neighbor as yourself," just as you love yourself not for pleasure or benefit, so should you have no ulterior motive for loving your neighbor. The rabbis illustrate this binding and unselfish love with the paradigmatic, almost ethereal, love between David and Jonathan.

True love is thus the ardent caring for the beloved without any exterior motive or cause. This understanding of love extends beyond human love and resounds in the chambers of Jewish theology and halakhah with catchwords such as *torah li-shemah* (Torah for its own sake) and *oved me-ahavah* (worship out of love). Jews are directed to study Torah, to learn, not to become rich or famous, but simply for its own sake; they are urged to serve God, that is, to worship him and to observe his commandments, not out of fear of punishment or desire for reward, but purely out of love of God. Such love can no more be commanded than can love of man, and here too Judaism can only ask that its adherents perform acts of love in the hope that these acts might lead to love (see BT Pes. 50b).

But what is this true love of God? It is the complete and singleminded devotion of oneself to God alone; it is, in Maimonides' oft-quoted simile, like the exceedingly intense love of the lovesick, where the mind can think of nothing else save the beloved, only this love is even greater (MT Teshuvah 10, 3). According to the explicit statements of the greatest rabbis and philosophers throughout the ages, this ultimate love of God is the telos of man. They debate the meaning of this love, but agree on its supreme importance. For Maimonides and his followers, the love of God is directly related to the knowledge of him: "According to the knowledge will be the love" (MT Teshuvah 10, 6; Guide 3, 51). Others like Ḥasdai Crescas argue that "love is something other than intellectual cognition" (Or Adonai, bk. 2, Part 6, Chapter 1). Yet regardless of how this ultimate love of God is defined, it is difficult to appreciate it as a final end and to desire to achieve it above all else. Our passions, our love for this world, are simply too powerful for such an all-consuming transcendent love. We cannot truly love God because we love his works too much. Yet we cannot come to love God apart from his works.

The ultimate purpose and highest happiness of man lies in love; not surprisingly, as we have seen, the means to this end is love. Judaism commands love, for its goal is to teach man to love.

REFERENCES

1. See, for example, Maimonides, Book of Commandments, nos. 3, 206, 207.
2. Commentary on the torch, ad loc.
3. Ibid.
4. Maimonides, Book of Commandments, Introduction, Second Principle.
5. See further MT Hil Mattenot Aniyyim 8, 10.
6. See Immanuel Kant, Metaphysische Anfangsgründe der Tugendlehre, Introduction, xii.

BIBLIOGRAPHY

Leone Ebreo, The Philosophy of Love, tr. F. Friedeberg-Seeley and J. H. Barnes (1937).
Georges Vajda, L'amour de Dieu dans la théologie juive du moyen âge (1957).

Meaning

משמעות

Jack D. Spiro

eaning is the central problem of human existence. Does life make sense? Does it amount to anything? Is there any purpose or value in the human enterprise or in the individual's personal quest? Many writers answer these questions in the negative. Koheleth, the elderly sage who wrote the Book of Ecclesiastes, considered everything vanity. He concluded that life is nothing more than a breath of air, and he based his conclusion on the observation that everything passes away, that everyone eventually goes to the same place: All are composed of dust and return to dust. Just as we come forth from the womb, naked shall we return. No one has the power to retain the breath of life; there is one final event for all.

Koheleth's message is echoed in the musings of Shakespeare's Macbeth: "Life's but a walking shadow, a poor player that struts and frets his hour upon the stage and then is heard no more. It is a tale told by an idiot, full of sound and fury, signifying nothing" (Act 5, scene V, lines 24–28).

This same sense of meaninglessness overcame Arthur Schopenhauer, who wrote: "Time is that in which all things pass away. . . . Time which has been exists no more; it exists as little as that which has *never* been. . . . that which in the next moment exists no more, and vanishes utterly, like a dream, can never be worth a serious effort. . . . existence has no real value in itself."[1]

Even some biblical passages appear to support a negative response to the meaning of life: "Man, his days are like those of grass; he blooms like a flower of the field; a wind passes by and it is no more; its own place no longer knows it" (Ps. 103:15–16). "Man is like a breath, his days are like a passing shadow" (Ps. 144:4).

If, as all these writers suggest, death is the ultimate power, we may conclude with C. H. D. Clark that "if we are asked to believe that all our striving is without final consequence," then "life is meaningless and it scarcely matters how we live if all will end in the dust of death."[2] The question about the meaning of life becomes the fundamental problem of our existence as human beings.

The Jewish response to the question does not agree with the consensus reached by these writers. Viewing the vast panorama of Jewish tradition, we see that Koheleth and the psalmist are in fact a small minority. Neither other biblical writers nor the rabbis and theologians are so negative. They are, in contrast, convinced that life does have meaning, which is derived both from a special relationship between God and man and from a promise of immortality.

The biblical writers did recognize the minuteness of man compared to the magnitude of the universe and the eternity of time: "When I behold Your [God's] heavens, the work of Your fingers, the moon and the stars that You set in place, what is man . . . ?" (Ps. 8:3–5). But, despite the infinite immensity of space and time, the psalmist also believed that God made man "little less than divine, and adorned him with glory and majesty" (Ps. 8:5). Whereas Koheleth perceived no difference between human being and beast, other biblical writers believed that man was a moral and spiritual reflection of the creator: "God created man in His image, in the image of God He created him; male and female He created them" (Gen. 1:27). According to the Bible the meaning of human life derives from this special relationship between God and man.

The purpose of the relationship, the reason for creation, is for man to glorify God (Isa. 43:7). The glorification and sanctification of God can be expressed through worship, the offering of sacrifices, and the observance of the Sabbath and festivals. But most important, God is glorified and his ways are reflected by proper conduct: "The Lord of hosts is exalted by judgment, the Holy God proved holy by retribution" (Isa. 5:16).

The conviction that man lives in a unique and special relationship with God is only a partial answer to the question of meaning and to Koheleth's challenge that life is meaningless. How do other biblical figures deal with the psalmist's assertion that man's "days are like a passing shadow"? The idea of absolute oblivion—that "one fate comes to all"—was challenged, primarily in the latter part of the biblical period. It was not sufficient to believe that the covenantal relationship between God and man guaranteed a long life. If that were all, the length of one's days might be extended by obedience to God's will, but when life ended, meaning would end. Life would be meaningless, as Clark asserted, if "all our striving is without consequence." Isaiah, however, held out the promise that God "will destroy death forever" (Isa. 25:8) and the further hope that "your dead revive, their corpses arise" (Isa. 26:19).

But we must go beyond the Bible to note how the rabbis and other Jewish thinkers extended this positive perception of life's meaning as it is found in the relationship between God and man and in the promise of eternal life.

The fundamental premise of Judaism in response to the question of meaning was stated generally by Ludwig Wittgenstein: "To believe in God means to understand the question about the meaning of life. To believe in God means to see that the facts of the world are not the end of the matter. To believe in God means to see that life has a meaning."[3] In Martin Buber's words, the existence of God is the "inexpressible confirmation of meaning. It is guaranteed. Nothing, nothing can henceforth be meaningless."[4] When we seek answers to the question of life's meaning, our questions come to an end when we reach the point of affirming the existence of God. While the meaning of life, according to Albert Camus, "is the most urgent of questions,"[5] Judaism says that the question is answered with belief in God. We need not look further: God is the last word.

Yet we cannot stop here. Believing in God would not satisfy the search for meaning. From the study of a multitude of Jewish sources, it is obvious that our lives must matter to God; it is essential that he care for us. Because he does care, he created us in his image. Because he cares, he "takes man seriously" and "enters a direct relationship with man, namely, a covenant to which not only man but also God is committed."[6] There is meaning because our existence is directly and intimately involved in the fulfillment of divine purpose. For that fulfillment, God created the covenantal relationship with man. The existence of divinity does not give meaning to life without a personal meeting, a caring relationship, a purposeful dialogue between divinity and humanity.

Therefore, the primary, but not exclusive, source of meaning in human life is the covenant through which God and man enter into partnership: "Man is a partner of the Holy One, blessed be He" (BT Shab. 10a, 119b). Through the covenant, we are assured that God is interested in us, that we are significant members of the cosmos, although we may well remain infinitesimal specks in the immense concatenation of atoms.

This significant covenantal meeting, however, is contingent, as is every contract. God will care for us and protect us if we do his will. The divine will is expressed through the *mizvot,* the 613 commandments of the Torah, those laws and rules "by the pursuit of which man shall live" (Lev. 18:5). The commanding nature of God, the divine as *mezaveh,* is always present in and through the *mizvot,* which are the quotidian way of life for the Jew. The Torah is "not a trifling thing for you; it is your very life" (Deut. 32:47). The meaning of life is experienced through the divine Presence, a presence that is continuously manifest in the *mizvot.* If the *mizvot* are performed, Jewish life is blessed with meaning; if they are not performed, the Jew becomes estranged from the divine Presence, which is the source and core of meaning: "If a person obeys the Torah and does the will of his Father in heaven, behold he is like the creatures above [who live forever]. . . . But if he does not obey the Torah and performs not the will of his Father in heaven, he is like the creatures below [who die]" (Sif. Deut. 132a). Divine law guides man to the meaning of life as long as he performs the *mizvot* of the *mezaveh,* the commanding God. The *mizvot* affirm the special relationship between God and man.

The *mizvot* also affirm man's uniqueness and cosmic stature. As Saadiah Gaon wrote, "If one imagines that the highest degree of excellence is given to some being other than man, let him show us such excellence or a similar one in any other being. . . . Our belief in man's superiority is not a mere delusion. . . . it is something demonstrably true and perfectly correct." Agreeing with other theologians, Saadiah goes on to explain, "The reason why God in His wisdom endowed man with this excellence can only be to make him the recipient of commandments and prohibitions."[7] Following these commandments makes our existence more than "sound and fury, signifying nothing." The *mizvot* answer the questions: Why am I here? What is the purpose and point of my life? What is the meaning of it all? The answer is to acknowledge God and to walk in his ways.

Other explanations are given in the rabbinic literature for the *mizvot,* known as *taamei ha-mizvot* or "reasons for the commandments." However varied they may be, they all point to the idea that the meaning of human life derives from obedience to the divine will expressed in *mizvot*. Yet there were several commandments that caused the rabbis and philosophers some vexation, those that seemed too trivial or irrelevant to harmonize with God's intention that human life should be meaningful. If certain *mizvot* appeared to lack intrinsic worth or merit, deserving of divine authorship, how could they be justified as meaningful?

The conclusive answer of traditional Judaism was formulated by Moses Maimonides. No *mizvah* should be considered trivial simply because we do not understand its basic reasons: "[T]here is a reason for every precept, although there are *mizvot* the reason for which is unknown to us and in which the ways of God's wisdom are incomprehensible. . . . Every one of the 613 commandments serves to inculcate some truth."[8]

The covenant, the special relationship between God and man expressed in the giving and doing of *mizvot,* is the primary source of meaning for our lives on earth. But what if that were all? Suppose we glorified God and fulfilled the divine will completely and then there was nothing else? Suppose all our striving to be faithful and obedient still ended with the grave? Many people believe that only an afterlife can make sense of this life, which was expressed no more poignantly than by Leo Tolstoy, who asked, "Is there any meaning in my life that will not be destroyed by my inevitably approaching death?"[9]

The Jewish answer to Tolstoy might be that death would indeed destroy all meaning, but death is not the end. The Reform prayer book of 1940, reflecting this fundamental position of Judaism, states that "our life would be altogether vanity, were it not for the soul which, fashioned in Thine [God's] image, gives us assurance of our higher destiny and imparts to our fleeting days an abiding value."[10]

The *mizvot* provide this value and lead us to the second source of meaning—immortality. Joseph Albo, in fact, offers one of the most important reasons for the *mizvot* in relation to the meaning of our existence: They guide humanity "to true happiness, which is spiritual happiness and immortality."[11] Through obedience to the words of Torah, "man acquired for himself life in the world to come" (M. Avot 2:8).

The meaning of our existence is, then, affirmed through the permanence of existence, a permanence contingent on faithfulness to God and the performance of the *mizvot*: "In the hour of a person's death, neither silver nor gold nor precious stones nor pearls accompany him, but only Torah and good works" (M. Avot 6:9). A life of meaning is a life of permanent survival, and we use the brief time we have in this life to make us worthy of permanence: "This world is the entrance hall of the world to come. Prepare yourself in the entrance hall so that you may be allowed to enter the banquet hall" (M. Avot 4:16). For those who believe that an afterlife alone can make sense of this life, Judaism provides the answer that man, beyond death, can "behold the presence of the *Shekhinah*" eternally (Mid. Ps. 51b–52a). The incompleteness of life is resolved, and meaning is therefore assured forever.

Being thus assured, we are free to deepen our temporal lives with meaning. Many activities and efforts can help us enrich life, particularly our relationships with other people. As one talmudic sage put it, "Give me companionship or give me death!" (BT Ta'an. 23a). People matter to each other, and human fellowship is a profound source of meaning.

Above all, we experience meaning in our lives when daily events, activities, and aspirations are woven into a general pattern of life, when there is a life plan that motivates us in our work and our relationships. If the details of our lives can be integrated within a larger picture, then every detail acquires greater meaning than if it were isolated. The individual pieces of a mosaic bear meaning only when they are joined to form a complete design. Judaism provides a complete picture, a life plan, a total design through living by the *mizvot*. The separate *mizvot* become meaningful when they fit into the total design of the covenantal relationship between God and man. The covenant is a "tree of life to those who grasp it, and whoever holds on to it is happy" (Prov. 3:18).

REFERENCES

1. Arthur Schopenhauer, *The Will to Live: Selected Writings* (1967), 229–32.
2. Quoted in Paul Edwards, *The Encyclopedia of Philosophy*, s.v. "Meaning and Value of Life."
3. Ludwig Wittgenstein, *Notebooks: 1914–1916* (1961), 74.
4. Martin Buber, *I And Thou* (1970), 158–59.
5. Albert Camus, *The Myth of Sisyphus and Other Essays* (1955), 4.
6. Abraham J. Heschel, *Who Is Man?* (1965), 75.
7. Saadiah Gaon, *Sefer Emunot ve-De'ot* (1948), tr. 4, ch. 1.
8. Moses Maimonides, *The Guide of the Perplexed* 3:26, 31.
9. Leo Tolstoy, *Confession* (1983), 35.
10. *Union Prayer Book*, 1:101.
11. Joseph Albo, *Sefer ha-Ikkarim,* 1 (1929), 79.

BIBLIOGRAPHY

R. C. Chalmers and John A. Irving, eds., *The Meaning of Life in Five Great Religions* (1965).

Viktor Frankl, *Man's Search for Meaning* (1977).

Abraham J. Heschel, *Who Is Man?* (1965).

Gershom Scholem, *Encyclopedia Judaica,* s.v. "Commandments, Reasons for."

Medieval Jewish Philosophy

פילוסופיה יהודית בימי־הבינים

Jacob B. Agus

Medieval Jewish philosophy reflects the entire gamut of speculative religious thought in the West. It falls into one of three categories—rationalistic, romantic, or mystical. We should bear in mind, however, that great thinkers rarely fall into distinct categories. There are romantic and mystical elements in the thought of Maimonides and a reverence for the dictates of reason in the work of Judah Halevi. Moreover, pietists, like Baḥya ibn Paquda, are sometimes described as mystics, sometimes as rationalists.

The first great Jewish philosopher in the medieval era was Saadiah ben Joseph (Al Fayumi), known as Saadiah Gaon, who lived in the first half of the tenth century C.E. His work *Sefer Emunot ve-Deot (Book of Beliefs and Opinions)* was epoch-making, not alone by virtue of its logical persuasiveness, but principally because Saadiah was a *Gaon,* that is, head of the academy of Sura in Babylonia, at a time when the decisions of the Gaonate were still considered authoritative and binding.

Saadiah was principally influenced by the Mutazilite school of the Islamic Kalam, which stressed the unity and justice of God and the freedom of will of mankind. He asserted that rational reflection, pursued resolutely and systematically, justified and validated the revelation of God's will in holy Scripture and in the talmudic tradition. But the Torah, written and oral, states as unconditional imperatives the inferences that thinkers discover only after a long and painful process of cogitation. The injunctions of Torah, according to Saadiah, are expressions of divine grace, since those who reason things out for themselves with due care and perseverance are few and far between. On the other hand, scriptural passages that appear to contradict the dictates of reason must be interpreted not literally but figuratively.

Saadiah conceived of God as an eternal Being who transcends the categories of space and time. God's existence, he contended, is logically demonstrated by the circumstance that all things in our experience are constantly changing—hence, their existence is not ultimate reality. Accordingly, a Supreme Being must be postulated who, unchangeable in himself, brings all things into being anew moment by moment.

The verses in Torah and Scripture that refer to divine manifestations—God's word, his hand, his ascent and descent, his appearance in a "pillar of cloud"—refer to a "created light" (or nivra), which the Torah designates as "His Glory" (kavodo). This "created light," more commonly known as Shekhinah, accompanies verbal communication between God and his chosen prophets. Its purpose is to authenticate the messages given to the prophet. The cherubim in the vision of Ezekiel (Ezek. 1 and 10) are parts of the chariot (merkavah), which in turn is a manifestation of this "created light."

Saadiah assumed that the human soul is free either to obey or to disobey the will of God. "We affirmed that the soul is a pure rational substance, purer than the substance of the stars and the spheres. . . . After this, it became clear to me that as the soul acquires merit, it becomes still purer and more luminous . . . and that as its sins accumulate, it becomes opaque and dark . . ." (Sefer Emunot ve-Deot 5, 1). However, even the worst sinner remains free to repent, and the Lord is ever ready to wipe sins away as if they had never been committed.

Saadiah explained in great detail the belief in immortality, bodily resurrection of the righteous in the messianic era, and the wonders of "the world to come." It is noteworthy that in spite of his faith in the glories of the messianic age he described the human soul as longing, at all times, to rise above this physical reality and to attain its predestined heavenly place among the angels and the ethereal spheres (Sefer Emunot ve-Deot 9, 1). Saadiah's impact was felt not only in the rationalistic schools of Jewish thought but also in proto-kabbalistic circles, where his speculations concerned the "created light" were elaborated and carried forward.

Bahya ibn Paquda dedicated his work *Hovot ha-Levavot (Duties of the Heart)*, written toward the end of the eleventh century, to a detailed exposition of the emotional dimension of Jewish piety. To Saadiah's argument for the existence of God from the contingency of all creatures as against the one creator, he added the argument from design. And he articulated philosophical reflections in striking metaphors. "Do you not see that if a person spills ink suddenly on blank paper, it is impossible that the splotch assume the pattern of ordered writing and readable lines . . ." (*Duties of the Heart, 1, 6*).

Bahya stressed the open horizons of genuine piety, man's endeavor to purify his soul by the love of God. "Thus it was said of some pietists that they were always penitent, for as they grew in the cognition of God, they were constantly made aware of the insufficiency of their prior service . . ." (*Duties of the Heart* 3, 3). Both rationalism and pietism attained their highest peaks in the writings of Moses Maimonides. We are here concerned chiefly with his *Guide of the Perplexed*, written in 1200.

Maimonides examined every issue both as a philosopher and as a rabbinic sage. He pursued the pathway of reasoned reflection most rigorously, but he pointed out the limits of reason. Reason cannot decide the question of whether the cosmos was created or whether it was eternal; it can only determine that the scales are equally balanced. The Torah, a product of prophecy and the Holy Spirit, must be allowed to tip the scale in favor of creationism. In a created universe, we may assume that certain miraculous events were built into the causal sequence of phenomena. Furthermore, the only true being, self-existent, is that of the creator. Hence, the pietist is encouraged to channel his love directly to the creator, who is ultimate reality, instead of scattering his energies in temporal, secular concerns. The Fall of Man in the Garden of Eden consisted in the human couple failing to focus on the polarity of true and false and concerning themselves with the attractions of that which is conventionally good and pleasant (*Guide* 1, 2).

Man attains his highest level neither as a saint nor as a philosopher, but in the various degrees of prophecy, a synthetic product of both piety and rationality. The prophet is first a speculative philosopher, a master of intellectual disciplines; second, a morally sensitive person; third, he is the recipient of a flow of grace and guidance from God, through the mediation of the active intellect, and fourth, the prophet is the bearer of moral and intellectual energy, which God supplies to human groups with the object of impelling them to advance in all the dimensions of spiritual greatness.

The prophet thus is both a mystic and a statesman. He shares the quest of unity with God's will, as does a mystic, but he is not content with the experience of divine ecstasy. As a recipient of divine energy, he becomes a spiritual statesman and is driven to undertake formidable projects of social and educational improvement (*Guide* 3, 52–54). This blend of rationality and intuition explains the requirement that the prophet be perfect or complete, extraordinary in his imaginative abilities as well as in his intellectual faculties.

The prophet is an agent of "divine cunning" in leading mankind toward the goal of messianic perfection. Therefore the laws of the Torah must be understood in terms of their utility as steps toward personal growth and the promotion of a more perfect society. Laws that seem to be irrational or of dubious utility were probably designed to challenge and to overcome pagan ways of thinking and to encourage the various facets of monotheistic piety (*Guide* 3, 32).

Furthermore, certain ideas were tolerated, or even sanctioned, not because they were true in a literal sense but because they were necessary for the stability of the ideal society and conducive to its unity (*Guide* 3, 28). Beliefs that seem to be the essence of religion, such as the axiom that God hears our prayers, are true only in a borrowed or metaphorical sense. Yet the philosophical elite must accept such beliefs as stabilizing elements, interpreting them in accord with their own understanding and thereby helping to maintain a unified society.

Maimonides' image of five classes of persons seeking to come close to God does not set any dogmatic barriers save belief in God and in his unity. The philosopher-saints of other faiths may come closer to God than the "Talmudists" (*Guide* 3, 51), for the good God does not refrain from granting prophetic tasks to those who qualify, whatever their race or ethnic origin may be. Indeed, God used both Jesus and Muhammad as instruments for the dissemination of his ethical principles and the ideals of holy Scriptures, thus helping to prepare the world for the messianic era.

Maimonides interpreted the messianic hope as an era that will gradually emerge in the course of history, not as a sudden transformation of physical reality (MT Hil. Melakhim 10). He sought to guard against eruptions of pseudo-messianic frenzy, outbursts of mass hysteria that might be expected in times of great turbulence.

Judah Halevi, whose major work, *Sefer ha-Kuzari* (*The Kuzari*), was written in the first half of the twelfth century C.E., a generation or so before Maimonides' *Guide*, represented the romantic trend in Jewish thought. He championed the integrity of spiritual intuition generally and the religious insights of the Jewish people particularly. To the so-called God of Aristotle he counterposed the God of Abraham, Isaac, and Jacob. The former is a product of sheer thought, while the latter is a heart-gripping reality (*The*

Kuzari 4, 16). Saints and prophets find themselves drawn to him with bonds of "fear, love, and joy." This is why the Sabbath, cultivating this blend of emotions, is so central in Jewish observance.

Halevi asserted that Jewish people possessed a special intuition for the divine presence. They are endowed from birth with this capacity to sense the reality of the divine influence *(inyan Elohi)*. But this endowment needs to be developed. It was manifested clearly in biblical times, when the Israelites lived in the holy land and brought animal offerings to the holy Temple in Jerusalem. At that time, the *Shekhinah* was visible from time to time. Even in the Second Commonwealth, a "divine voice" would direct the deliberations of priests and sages. When the Israelites were scattered in many lands, their intuition for the divine influence was weakened, indeed nearly extinguished. However, should Jewish people disregard material necessities and return to the holy land, their metaphysical intuition would be revived. The union of the holy people with the holy land, in keeping with the holy Torah, will reawaken the authentic spirituality of the Jewish people, bringing about a new era of moral greatness for all mankind, for "Israel among the nations is like the heart among the limbs" (*The Kuzari* 4, 16). Yet while he extolled the virtues of the Jewish people, Halevi did not forget the prophetic ideal of the unification of all mankind in the service of God.

The philosophers Joseph Albo, Ḥasdai Crescas, Isaac Arama, and others explored the theological area between the two massive landmarks set up by Halevi and Maimonides, inclining now in one direction, now in the other. Albo's work is particularly interesting, since he was one of the representatives of the Jewish faith chosen for the disputation at Tortosa, Spain, in 1413. He admitted that some Torah laws may be changed in the course of time. "It is proper for the faith to be modified in accord with the manner in which the receptivity of the people observing it is altered by the change of circumstances" (*Sefer ha-Ikkarim,* 3, 14).

Ḥasdai Crescas (1340–1410) was also a frequent debater at the interfaith disputations. He dared to question the Aristotelian principle that there can be no infinity of space or time in reality. Torah learning is a surer guide to reality than philosophical speculation. "The gates of speculation are closed to us" (*Or Adonai* 2, 1, 1). The Jewish people as a whole form a missionary society, dedicated to the proclamation of divine truth. They are subject to a special providence over and above the concern of God with mankind generally. The antirationalist note in Crescas was intensified and generalized by the popular preacher Isaac Arama, who was one of the exiles from Spain in 1492. He lays it down as a rule that "philosophical speculation must not stir its hand or its foot, save with the permission of the inner logic of the Torah and the prophets" (*Ḥazut Kashot*, 8).

Living in a catastrophic age, Jewish philosophers could hardly maintain an intellectual posture of serene objectivity. Their abstract principles and their rigid logic could offer only cold comfort to people who were daily proving their readiness for martyrdom. Little by little, the philosophers yielded to the seduction of kabbalah, which claimed to be a sacred mystery offering reassurance that the Jewish people are, indeed, the primary concern of the God of the universe, and that the rituals of Judaism are freighted with cosmic consequences that the human imagination can hardly conceive.

In about 1280, the classic text of kabbalah, the *Zohar*, largely authored by Rabbi Moses de Leon, was published. In form a collection of commentaries on the Torah, it was in substance a counterphilosophical declaration, asserting that the world perceived by our senses is as unreal as it is transitory. The key to reality is the web of ancient legends, supplemented by the visions of contemporary mystics. Mystical knowledge yields power. Saints manipulating the names of the Supreme Being can affect "the miraculous Providence," which operates side by side with the so-called laws of nature (Naḥmanides, *Commentary on the Torah*, 17, 1; 46, 1).

Naḥmanides was instrumental in securing popular acceptance of the kabbalistic axiom that the secret mysteries of the Torah (*sitrei Torah*) constitute its real import and that these mysteries are revealed only by means of face-to-face instruction (*Commentary on the Torah*, Introduction).

While the realms of the open (*nigleh*) and the hidden (*nistar*) must be kept apart, the author of the *Shulḥan Arukh* (*The Prepared Table*), Rabbi Joseph Caro (1488–1575) was a living channel of kabbalistic revelation. A heavenly mentor (*maggid*) would speak to him while he was in a mystical trance and bring him tidings from the "world of truth." His great authority among Ashkenazi Jews as well as among the Sephardim helped to establish the kabbalah as the hidden wisdom of Israel.

The influence of kabbalah was intensified in the fifteenth and sixteenth centuries. Under its guidance, Jewish religious thinkers became steadily more subjective, withdrawing emotionally from the emergent era of freedom and rationalism that was then struggling to be born. A popular kabbalist writing on the threshold of the sixteenth century summed up the rejection of a rational faith:

> Jewish reason is different from the reason of other nations, even as the Jew is different in the possession of a different soul, as is known to the wise, and Jewish reason is perfected through the study of Torah, its mysteries and secrets, and

through the dialectics of the true wisdom, which is far above the wisdom that is derived from experience. (Meir ibn Gabbai, *Avodat ha-kodesh* 3, 17)

BIBLIOGRAPHY

Jacob B. Agus, *The Evolution of Jewish Thought* (1959).
Julius Guttmann, *Philosophies of Judaism,* (1964).
Isaac Husik, *A History of Medieval Jewish Philosophy* (1916).
Gershom Scholem, *Major Trends in Jewish Mysticism* (1946).

Memory

זכרון

David G. Roskies

In Judaism, memory is a collective mandate, both in terms of what is recalled and how it is recalled. From the Deuteronomic injunctions to "remember the days of old" (32:7) and to "remember what Amalek did to you " (25:17) to the persistent theme of remembering "that you were slaves in Egypt," the content of Jewish memory has been the collective saga as first recorded in Scripture and as later recalled in collective, ritual settings. Central to the meaning of the biblical past is the covenant, Israel's guarantee that history will follow a divine plan. Thus, the tremors that register most clearly are the breaches of covenant that Israel has been guilty of: "Remember, never forget, how you provoked the Lord your God to anger in the wilderness" (Deut. 9:7). The destructions of the Temple in Jerusalem, the exile from the land, and natural and national catastrophes are all seen as the consequence of God's retribution for the backslidings of his chosen people. This theme of guilt, retribution, and exile is most forcefully articulated in the two Tokheḥah (lit., reproof) sections of Scripture, Leviticus 26 and Deuteronomy 28, which later generations invariably returned to in times of unprecedented disaster.

After the destruction of Solomon's Temple (ḥurban ha-bayit) in 586 B.C.E., the biblical Book of Lamentations and prophetic consolation provided new forms of collective memory. The Book of Lamentations orchestrated a documentary account of Jerusalem's siege and destruction into individual and choral voices ideally suited for ritual mourning, while the prophets of the exile, notably Ezekiel and Second Isaiah, viewed the exile archetypally, in terms of visionary battles (Gog and Magog), resurrection (the Valley of the Dry Bones), a new Temple, and a new Exodus. This visionary impulse was carried further by Jewish apocalyptic writers who flourished in Palestine from about 200 B.C.E. to 100 C.E. Through their pseudepigraphic approach, the apocalyptic writers projected a vision of the imminent End of Days as shaped by an esoteric and highly mythic reading of biblical prophecy.

With the destruction of Herod's Temple in 70 C.E. and the subsequent failure of the Bar Kokhba revolt, the rabbis of Jabneh and Usha (the tannaim) triumphed as the sole arbiters of Jewish memory. Most of the apocalyptic writings were excluded from the biblical canon. Even the straightforward chronicles of the Maccabees were consigned to oblivion. Instead the rabbis proclaimed Scripture as the blueprint of history—past, present, and future. Through public fasts that celebrated God's historical intervention in nature; through public sermons that sought to link Scripture with the concrete life of the everyday; through the creation of public rituals to commemorate the salvations and destructions of the biblical past, the rabbis were able to canonize, codify, and ritualize historical memory for all generations to come.

The rabbinic approach was to implode history, to cut it down to manageable size. Events were disassembled and reassembled according to biblical archetypes: the Flood, Sodom and Gomorrah, the Akedah (binding of Isaac), the Exodus, Sinai, the breaking of the tablets, the destruction of the Temple, the Exile, the restoration of Zion. The rabbis selected, combined, and arranged events to fit them on a continuum. Thus, the separate destructions of both Temples (in 586 B.C.E. and 70 C.E.) were telescoped together, combined with the capture of Bethar (in 135 C.E.) and the ploughing up of Jerusalem (ca. 130 C.E.), and all four calamities were then linked to the original day of treason in the wilderness, described in Numbers 14 and identified as the ninth day of Av in all cases (BT Ta'an. 4:6).

As part of the selection process, the rabbis never treated the individual as worthy of memorialization. There was no place for heroes either in the commemoration of the Exodus on Passover or in the three-week period leading up to the ninth of Av. This collective focus remained in force throughout the Middle Ages, even in Christian Europe with its plethora of saints' days. Rabbi Akiva was remembered simply as one of the Ten *Harugei Malkhut,* the rabbinic martyrs during the Hadrianic persecution. This legendary construct was in turn refashioned sometime in the Byzantine period into a mythic tale with biblical antecedents (the selling of Joseph by his brothers), eventually to become part of the Yom Kippur liturgy (in the commemoration of the Ten Martyrs).

Indeed, it was liturgy that became the central repository of group memory in the Middle Ages. A number of historical chronicles were written in the wake of the Crusades, and the Expulsion from Spain was the major catalyst for the first serious attempts at postbiblical Jewish historiography, yet both national calamities were commemorated mainly in synagogue ritual: in memorial prayers for the dead, in penitential poems, in additions to the liturgy for the ninth of Av. Fasting and feasting remained the essential ways of recalling local events of special significance such as expulsions, plagues, or deliverance from danger.

Thanks to a system of dating events and of choosing representative places, it was now possible to create new linkages and historical clusters. Thus, the Cossack uprising of 1648/49 was followed by sixteen years of foreign invasion, but in Jewish memory, only *Taḥ vetat* (1648–1649), the period of pogroms, was recalled, while the destruction of Nemirov (May 1648) became the stand-in for the ruin of Jewish Poland. The anniversary of Nemirov's destruction, the twentieth of the Hebrew month of Sivan, became a commemorative fast day, linked by date to *gezeirat tatkla,* the martyrdom of the Jews of Blois in 1171. As always, it was the subjective reality, not the verifiable facts of destruction, that set the norm and gave rise to new responses. What was remembered and recorded was not the factual data but the meaning of the desecration.

This meaning, in turn, was shaped and expressed by analogies with earlier archetypes. The Hadrianic persecutions had given rise to the archetype of *kiddush ha-Shem,* defined in the Talmud as the public act of sanctifying God's name in times of persecution (BT Sanh. 74). *Kiddush ha-Shem* emerged after the Crusades in combination with two other archetypes. The Akedah and the Temple sacrifice were enlisted by the survivors of the First and Second Crusades in order to view as vicarious atonement the voluntary death of those who had resisted forced conversion. Similarly, the Marrano experience in sixteenth-century Spain and Portugal was legitimated in terms of Esther hiding her identity—a pun on Esther-*hester* (Hebrew for "hiding")—from King Ahasuerus. With the spread of kabbalah in the seventeenth century and its enormous impact on Ḥasidism in the eighteenth and nineteenth centuries, the spiritualization of history and the search for archetypal structures were revived just when the modern, critical study of history began to take hold among western European Jews.

Scholars are divided as to the continued viability of Jewish group memory in the modern era. Some, pointing to the fragmentation of art and consciousness in the high culture of western Europe, conclude that group memory suffered an irreversible blow with emancipation. Others, drawing on the folklore, literature, art, and politics of Jewish eastern Europe, argue that group memory was transformed and revitalized in a secular mode. The anti-traditionalist revolt, launched in eastern Europe by such intellectuals as S. Y. Abramowitsch (Mendele Mokher Seforim) and Ḥayyim Naḥman Bialik, rejected the theological premise of sin and retribution as the guiding principle of history, but continued nonetheless to disassemble the czarist pogroms, the expulsions, and the mass exodus in terms of the ancient archetypes. An apocalyptic mode of response gained momentum during and after World War I and the Bolshevik revolution, especially among cosmopolitan writers drawn to radical politics. These latter-day apocalyptic writers revived the mythic approach to history, reclaiming Jesus, Shabbetai Zevi, and Solomon Molcho as prophets of the millennium.[1] Events deliberately suppressed by the rabbis, such as the siege and defeat of Masada, took on mythic significance in this period of revolutionary upheaval.[2]

At the same time, a neoclassical trend also took hold among those writers and political thinkers who focused on the fate of the Jews. The normative past yielded material for a spate of historical novels and family sagas, enormously popular in the interbellum period, while new meanings were discovered for the collective archetypes of *Kiddush ha-Shem* and the *Kehillah Kedoshah* (the holy congregation). Even when used ironically, as in the work of S. Y. Agnon, these archetypes rendered the immediate crisis of European Jewry transtemporal.

Both the apocalyptic and neoclassical modes of response came together in the Nazi ghettos. Here, Yiddish, Hebrew, and, to some extent, Polish writers drew upon modern and classical Jewish texts alike in an effort to withstand the Nazi terror. Jews of all ages and political persuasions recognized the ghetto, the yellow star, the *Judenrat* (Jewish Council, appointed by German occupying authority), and the myriad acts of sacrilege as something already experienced, and this pervasive sense of déjà vu strengthened the search for archetypes. The more brutal and unprecedented the violence became, however, the more the ghetto poets, songwriters, and chroniclers subjected the familiar modes of response to parody. As the full extent of the Nazis' genocidal plan became known, secular writers such as Itzhak Katznelson and Abraham Sutzkever lent their voices to the cause of armed resistance while, paradoxically, they also revived the covenantal dialogue with God.

In the postwar era, to the extent that Jews have regrouped in large numbers, they have reshaped contemporary events into new archetypal patterns: *hurban* has given way to *Shoah* (Holocaust); the rebirth of the State of Israel has provided a concretized image of the ingathering of the exiles and of the return to Zion. More recently, the national reawakening of Soviet Jews is viewed as a latter-day exodus. Each of these three archetypes is celebrated with new communal rituals (public gatherings, parades, demonstrations), while the literary sources read at such occasions begin to take on liturgical significance. In particular, the phenomenon of *yizker-bikher*—memorial volumes to the destroyed communities of Europe—attests to the renewed vitality of group memory among the survivors of the Holocaust. In contrast to this traditional, collective focus, the exploits of individual heroes are celebrated in Israel by the issuing of memorial volumes to the fallen soldiers, in addition to legends that are told about Joseph Trumpeldor and other Zionist leaders.

The use of visual iconography—in painting, sculpture, and photography—is a new vehicle of group memory in modern times. Images of exile and martyrdom, revolt and rebirth, have made the archetypes accessible to an audience increasingly cut off from written Jewish sources. But given the eclectic nature of modern art and the dearth of icons in Judaism, borrowings from non-Jewish culture are inevitable. Chagall's Crucifixion Series (1938–1944) exemplifies the strengths and weaknesses of using Jesus as an emblem of Jewish suffering.[3]

And so while the link between memory and covenant has been irrevocably broken, while individual actions are now celebrated along with those of the collective, while old archetypes are displaced by new ones, and while visual images supplant the written word, it would seem that group memory and archetypal thinking are still a viable form of Jewish self-expression.

REFERENCES

1. See, for example, the early poetry of Uri Zevi Greenberg.
2. See Isaac Lamdan's expressionist poem "Masada."
3. Cf. David G. Roskies, *Against the Apocalypse: Responses to Catastrophe in Modern Jewish Culture* (1984).

BIBLIOGRAPHY

Jack Kugelmass and Jonathan Boyarin, eds., *From a Ruined Garden: The Memorial Books of Polish Jewry* (1983).

David G. Roskies, *Against the Apocalypse: Responses to Catastrophe in Modern Jewish Culture* (1984).

Yosef Hayyim Yerushalmi, *Zakhor: Jewish History and Jewish Memory* (1982).

Mentsh

אַ מענטש

Moshe Waldoks

Two folk witticisms exemplify the dual dimensionality of the word *mentsh* in Yiddish usage. The first, *mentsh trakht un got lakht* (man proposes and God disposes), aside from employing rhyme to achieve humorous effect,[1] provides a definition of *mentsh* that is closer to the German *mensch* (man), from which it is derived. A *mentsh* is thus a man, a human being. The second witticism, *a mentsh heyst a mentsh vayl er mentsht zikh* (a man is called man because he struggles), contains a clever word pun where "the German component is paired with a limited Slavic component *mentshen* (struggle) . . . [thus] 'man is called man because he struggles.'"[2] The former usage sees man as frail and existentially awkward, an advanced biological phenomenon, but seriously limited, while in the latter usage *mentsh* emerges as a description of a process of moral engagement in both interpersonal and intersocial spheres.

In Yiddish (and in what can be termed Yinglish, or Yiddish-American) usage *mentsh* bears a strong connotation of moral excellence and social rectitude. Indeed, the central contribution of the Yiddish usage of *mentsh* is the distinction it stresses between what human beings are and what they should be. One wishes that a child of either gender *zol vaksn a mentsh* (grow up to be a person). This sense of personhood is understood both as maturity and responsibility, and thus becomes a valued honorific. *Mentsh* is further expanded to *mentshlich* (humane) and *mentshlichkeyt* (humanity), as opposed to *mentshheyt* (mankind). *Mentsh* has in recent years made its way into American-English usage. Here the Yiddish connotation of the word is paramount. "He is a *mentshy* person" describes an unusually decent and considerate individual.

One can also fall from the state of being a *mentsh* and become *oysmentsh,* that is, to suffer either physical or psychological debilitation, or a combination of the two. In this usage it seems that dependency militates against remaining a *mentsh.* It should be mentioned that the Yiddish verb for pulling oneself together, or taking courage, is also derived from *mentsh (tsu mentshn zikh).*

These usages help us understand the gravity attached to being a *mentsh.* It includes not only maturity and responsibility in the social realm, but also independence of spirit and conviction. It is only a human being qua *mentsh* who can enter into a meaningful dialogue with the Almighty. Only in the *mentshlichkeyt* (humanity) of *mentshheyt* (humankind) can God's work be accomplished in the world.

REFERENCES

1. Max Weinreich, *The History of the Yiddish Language,* tr. S. Noble (1980), 236.
2. Ibid., 649.

BIBLIOGRAPHY

Max Weinreich, *The History of the Yiddish Language,* tr. S. Noble (1980).

Mercy

רחמים

David R. Blumenthal

The Hebrew language is rich in words describing mercy. A large number of roots (*rahem, hus, hamol, hitrazeh, hit-payyes, hanon, hesed, erekh apayim*) occur in many forms—as beseeching verbs, as evocative adjectives, and as powerful nouns—in the Bible as well as in the liturgy. These roots imply others (*hoshi'a, hazel, ga'al, azor, zakhor*) that mean, respectively, to save, to rescue, to redeem, to help, and to remember. There are many more. God's mercy is described as the mercy of a parent toward a child (Ps. 103:13). He is called *ha-Rahaman* and *Rahamana* (the merciful One) and *Av ha-rahamim* (the father of mercy). His people, when they practice mercy, are called *rahamanim benei rahamanim* (merciful ones, the children of merciful ones).[1]

What are the types of mercy found in the tradition? On what bases does the Jew appeal to God for mercy, and what are its limits? In the post-Holocaust world, how adequate is the concept of mercy? The Jewish appeal to God's mercy is twofold: the appeal from covenantal justice, which itself has two dimensions, and the appeal from helplessness.

The tradition teaches that in the very beginning there was God in his aloneness. In the mystery of his being there welled up in him a desire to create, to have children, and so he chose to form the world and to create humankind. Bringing humanity into existence, however, was not enough; God found that, because of his love, he had to give guidance to humankind. And so he chose humankind again and made a covenant with Adam, and then a covenant with Noah, and then a covenant with Abraham. Finally, God gave the Jews the Torah, together with the obligation to interpret it. He was pleased because some made the effort to mold themselves to his revealed image, and displeased that many did not.

God's love, then, is of two kinds. From part of his heart overflows a boundless unconditional love for his creatures. From another part of his heart flows a love engaged in human existence, a love devoted to guiding humanity. The former is called *ḥesed,* grace; the latter *raḥamim,* engaged love. The former was, and is, easy; it is of the immutable essence of God. The latter was, and is, hard; it requires patience, understanding, and forgiveness.

Ḥesed motivated creation. It brought the world into being. *Raḥamim* motivated revelation. Moved by it, God gave standards of action and measures of inner piety, and set forth his expectations of the Jewish people, together with his obligations to them; the result is a two-way street, a covenant between two parties. Generations would quarrel about the details and emphases, but the basic terms would abide: the Jewish people would not be alone. The Jewish people would always know what God wanted of them. And they could depend upon his engaged love to take into account their strivings and failings. *Justice* and *righteous judgment* would be the bywords of their relationship.

Within this covenantal understanding, the key metaphor is "our Father, our King"—the fair Father, the just King. He can say, "It has been told you, O man, what is good, and what the Lord requires of you" (Micah 6:8), and the Jew can ask, "Shall not the Judge of all the earth deal justly?" (Gen. 18:25). God can command, "Choose life" (Deut. 30:19), and the Jew can pray, "Grant us justice according to the law" (daily liturgy, *Amidah,* J. Hertz, *Authorised Daily Prayerbook,* rev. ed., 143). The final judgment, as C. S. Lewis has remarked, is to be a moment of joy and triumph, for then our devotion to God and his love for us will be justified.[2]

Were it not for this covenant, the Jew would not know how to address God. The Jew would be conscious of God's holiness, of his sublimity; would know his beauty and his power; would experience awe, reverence, and fear. But how would he approach God? What would be the protocol, the etiquette? What would be the expectations by which the Jew could come into God's presence and talk to him? Even kings of flesh and blood have procedures; even earthly fathers have standards on which relationships are based. Knowing God's expectations, the Jew stands in relation to him, with all the rights and responsibilities pertaining thereto.

This is the way of covenantal justice. The Jew appeals to God's mercy, *rahamim,* on the basis of the expectations of the Jewish people that God has set forth and the rights that that expression gives the Jewish people to justified recognition of their efforts. The Jew appeals to God's *rahamim,* mercy, on the basis of his *rahamim,* his engaged love for the Jewish people: "Our Father, our King, act for the sake of Your great *rahamim*" (daily liturgy, *Avinu Malkenu,* Hertz, 166). "If we have no righteousness or good deeds, remember for our sake the covenant with our fathers" (daily liturgy, *Tahanun,* Hertz, 178). "For You, God, are truth and Your Word is truth, valid forever" (New Year liturgy, *Amidah,* Hertz, 854).

It should be noted that the appeal to mercy on the basis of covenantal justice is not limited to the just reward of an individual's own fulfillment of God's expectations. The revelation was for all generations and the just reward is for all generations. The evil of one generation is not, however, transferable for any length of time. The collectivity of the reward is the "merit of the fathers" and it, too, is part of the appeal to mercy from covenantal justice.

It is also the case that covenantal justice demands that Jews be merciful just as, and because, God is merciful (BT Shab. 133b; Luke 6:36).

This mutual responsibility between God and the Jewish people for justice with love is difficult for some individuals to accept today. There is a peculiar romance to claiming "I am but dust and ashes; I revel in my creatureliness," and then escaping the true sense of demand that revelation imposes on the individual. All too often the individual resists the idea and the imagery of command and hence the need to respond with true commitment. Yet covenantal justice does proclaim God's demand, just as it guarantees the Jewish people's right to principled defense. Mercy in this sense is within justice.

There is another dimension to the Jewish appeal to God's mercy, still from within the covenant. There are moments when sin overcomes the individual, when he feels despair at returning to God, when hope for his own self-correction fades. In such times, the individual knows that he deserves the punishment that God metes out. The individual admits his failures and acknowledges the justness of God's claims against him. He has no defense and he knows it. "Those sins which are revealed, we have mentioned before

You; and those which are not revealed to us are known and revealed to You. . . . My God, before I was formed, I was not worthy, and now that I have been formed, it is as if I had not been formed. I am dust in my life, the more so in my death. I stand before You as a vessel filled with shame and remorse" (Day of Atonement liturgy, *Amidah,* Hertz, 920).

Even at such moments, however, the Jew recognizes that God wants him to return. God wants him to live within the covenant. "And You, in Your great engaged love, have mercy upon us for You do not wish the destruction of the world. . . . You want the return of the wicked and do not desire their death, as it says . . . 'Do I desire the death of the wicked person? Rather, that the wicked return from his ways and live'" (Day of Atonement liturgy, *Ne'ilah,* Hertz, 932–34, quoting Ezek. 33:11). And so the Jewish people appeal to God to suspend his justice; to have mercy on them, compulsive sinners though they are. They appeal from their grief and desolation to his love. This is the appeal to merciful forgiveness. It is mercy beyond due, but it is still within God's justice and his covenant.

The Jew may make another appeal to God's mercy, the appeal from helplessness. As firm as he is in his faith in the covenant, in God's commitment to justice based upon his revelation, the Jew cannot escape the fact that there is an unfathomable dimension to life. There is a realization that all human deeds, no matter how righteous, are nothing, that all his efforts do not protect the individual from the harshness of reality, that part of his fate is simply not in his hands, that some aspects of life are seemingly not within the covenant. The irrational presses in. Even pain and suffering close in, sometimes in extremes, beyond the wildest terrors. It is then that the individual realizes how truly helpless he is. It is then that he becomes aware of how severe are his limits in grasping God's ways. In these moments, he casts himself completely on God's mercy.

This is the way of pleading, propitiating, pacifying. "As the eyes of slaves follow their master's hand, as the eyes of a slave-girl follow the hand of her mistress, so are our eyes toward the Lord our God awaiting His mercy" (Ps. 123:2). "O Lord, deliver us! O Lord, let us prosper!" (Ps. 118:25). "He Who is propitiated by mercy and He Who is pacified by pleading, be propitiated and be pacified toward us for there is no other help" (daily liturgy, *Taḥanun,* Hertz, 184). "Even if a sharpened sword is touching one's neck, one should not inhibit oneself from asking mercy, as it says, 'Yea, though He kill me, I shall yearn for Him'" (BT Ber. 10a, quoting Job 13:15).

Total dependency upon God's mercy is one of the most difficult aspects of religion for some modern people to accept. To beg for mercy offends against the modern sense of self-determination, of personal liberty. To beg for mercy is the furthest humans can get from that delicate web of secure human relations that defines their world. It is the lowest rung on the ladder of self-respect; perhaps it is worse than death itself.

Grudgingly, the individual concedes that God has the right to make demands upon him and that, since he can also make demands upon God, there is validity to the appeal to God's mercy from covenantal justice. But the individual resists both the idea and the imagery of utter helplessness and, hence, of his need to cast himself upon divine mercy. Gladly, the individual accepts God's unfettered grace. But he resists the logic that he cannot bind that grace to him when fate goes against him. He accepts the possibility of atheism but rebels against the possibility of God's disavowing his promises to the Jewish people. Yet the power of his own experience of helplessness and the logic of the doctrine of grace impel him to recognize and to admit that God does not have to have mercy on him and that there are moments when he can only beseech it. Mercy, in this sense, is beyond justice.

Human existence confronts this interpretation of God's mercy and raises an important question. God does not always act mercifully. He does not always adhere to covenantal justice, nor does he always exercise merciful forgiveness. Sometimes he does not act out of mercy rooted even beyond justice. Logically and experientially these appeals contradict reality. One cannot logically assert both God's unbounded love for creation and his non-covenantal disregard of it. One cannot logically assert both God's judgment grounded upon revelation and his apparent indifference to it. Experientially, one becomes aware of God's grace and feels that one can rely upon it. One experiences God's providence and is reassured that his power is circumscribed by it. God is the Jewish people's rock, their fortress, their refuge, notwithstanding he acts in ways that deny this supposition.

At no time in Jewish existence has this problem been more forcefully in Jewish consciousness than in the aftermath of the Holocaust. The reality of that event both seals and oppresses faith. For in it God did not grant covenantal justice, nor did he show merciful forgiveness to the sinners and the sinless. Nor was he propitiated by mercy or pacified by pleading. "Yet You have rejected and disgraced us; . . . You make us retreat before our foe; and our enemies plunder us at will. You let them devour us like sheep; You disperse us among the nations. You sell Your people for no fortune. . . . It is for Your sake that we are slain all day long, that we are regarded as sheep to be slaughtered" (Ps. 44:10–23).

How can the Jew hold within him the tension between God's mercy and the reality of human existence? The answer of the tradition is complex. It should be noted first that protest is a part of the tradition. The Jew does not shrink from stating the injustice of God's acts. He does not refrain from putting forth his case under the covenant. "All this has come upon us, yet we have not forgotten You, or been false to Your covenant. Our hearts have not gone astray, nor have our feet swerved from Your path, though You cast us, crushed, to where the sea monster is, and covered us over with deepest darkness. If we forgot the name of our God and spread forth our hands to a foreign god, God would surely search it out, for He knows the secrets of the heart" (Ps. 44:18–22).

Second, the Jew prays. He turns yet again to God's mercy. The Jew calls upon God's mercy that is rightfully his due under the terms of God's own covenant. "Rouse Yourself; why do You sleep O Lord? Awaken, do not reject us forever! Why do You hide Your face, ignoring our affliction and distress? We lie prostrate in the dust; our body clings to the ground" (Ps. 44:24–26). And the Jew invokes God's act of merciful forgiveness: "Arise and help us, redeem us, as befits Your faithfulness" (Ps. 44:27). "We have sinned against You, Master; forgive us, according to the abundance of Your mercy, God" (daily liturgy, *Taḥanun,* Hertz, 186). And he pleads, propitiates, pacifies: "See our affliction for our pain and the oppression in our hearts have become great. Have mercy upon us in the land of our captivity. Do not pour out Your anger against us. . . . If not for our sake, act for Your own sake. Do not destroy the memory of our remnant" (daily liturgy, *Taḥanun,* Hertz, 178).

Finally, in this matter as in so many others in religion, God and the tradition intend people to think and to feel sequentially, that is, to let one's feelings and thoughts succeed one another without denying or suppressing those that may be in contradiction with one another. Anyone who has ever been on trial in a human court of justice knows that the defendant is confident, frightened, reassured, and despairing in turn. So it is on the Day of Judgment, which is every day. The Jew moves to and fro in his relationship to God. Rationalists, too, are cast about by the waves of life, though they appear to struggle a bit more to keep their balance. Faith in God's grace and his covenant sustains the Jewish people. Awareness of God's unbounded grace and his engaged love supports the Jewish people; the Jew must always return to the sense of his presence. With it, the Jew may suffer in his soul; without it, he is nothing. The Jew must know his helplessness, but he must also feel God's might. God's mercy encompasses all.

REFERENCES

1. Cf. Emil Hirsch, *Jewish Encyclopedia*, s.v. *compassion*; L. Silberman, *Encyclopedia Judaica*, s.v. *compassion*; Z. Szubin, *Encyclopedia Judaica*, s.v. *mercy*.
2. C. S. Lewis, *Reflections on Psalms* (1958), 9–19.

BIBLIOGRAPHY

C. S. Lewis, *Reflections on Psalms* (1958).
Joseph B. Soloveitchik, *On Repentance* (1984).

Messianism

משיחיות

R. J. Zwi Werblowsky

The notion of Jewish messianism is in itself far from simple or monolithic. In fact, it is a motley coat of many colors, and its historical evolution is complex. Its specific position on the diachronic scale of Jewish history, in both its ancient, medieval, and premodern and modern and secularized phases, is partly the result of immanent dynamisms and pressures and partly the result of the messianic (that is, Christological) character of a dominant daughter religion that succeeded in creating a situation in which Judaism, exposed to new pressures of humiliation, persecution, polemics, and self-definition, was forced to focus unduly on messianic themes such as, Who is the promised son of David, Messiah and Savior? Has he come? How are the relevant scriptural passages and proof-texts to be read and interpreted?

The difficulty of the undertaking is, moreover, compounded by a further array of semantic considerations, all of them, to be sure, the result of historical factors. The word *messiah,* derived from the Hebrew *mashaḥ* (anoint), denotes a person with a special mission from God who is not infrequently initiated into this mission either in actual fact or metaphorically—of necessity metaphorically if anointed by God himself, unless in a dream, as, for example, in the case of Shabbetai Zevi—by an act of anointing with oil at the hands of a priest or prophet who may himself, in other circumstances, require anointing. Hence in a broader and metaphorical sense the term can signify any man or office bearer divinely charged with a special task or function. And because the "Lord's Anointed" came, in due course, to mean the messiah par excellence, the ultimate redeemer, the expected king of the Davidic line who would deliver Israel from foreign bondage and restore the glories of its golden age, the term also gradually acquired an eschatological reference unlike, for example, the pre-Davidic and premessianic ad hoc savior in times of need known as *moshi'a*. Hence messianism has been, and is, used in a broad and at times very loose sense to refer to beliefs or theories regarding an eschatological or at least very radical and decisive improvement of the state of man, society, and the world (or the cosmos as a whole), or even of a final consummation of history.

Basic to messianism is a certain relationship to the dimension of time. The temporal process is expected to lead to a major change or even to a final consummation, as a result of which a happier, better, or perfect state of things will take the place of the imperfect present. Intrinsic to messianism is the negative evaluation of the present. If the present is satisfactory and right, it need not be fulfilled and transcended, but rather perpetuated or renewed and rejuvenated in accordance with a pattern set by myth and ritual. Because the present is viewed as unsatisfactory and blighted by suffering, oppression, exile, illness, death, sin, angst, *la nausée,* alienation, or other evils, it has to be changed and superseded by a new age or dispensation. The new age may be conceived as something utterly new—a utopia—or as a return to a past golden age—the Paradise lost–Paradise regained syndrome.

Clearly Judaism was, to begin with, not a messianic religion. The tribes that settled in Canaan surely felt themselves bearers of and witnesses to the fulfillment of a promise (though definitely not in the sense of "realized eschatology") rather than representatives of a messianic vocation. To the extent that God is gracious and grants salvation, it is—as the Psalms amply demonstrate—in his capacity to be an ever-present ad hoc help and rock of refuge. In him the Psalmist puts his trust, for God is a refuge in times of distress, the source and object of confident hope, a savior and redeemer whenever a saving intervention becomes necessary, for example, in times of sickness bringing the pious into the shadow of death, persecution, the triumph and taunts of the wicked, the oppressive sense of sin and guilt. "O Lord, deliver us! O Lord, let us prosper!" (Ps. 118:25) is precisely such an appeal for a permanent saving presence. The ancient litanies that belong to the earliest strata of the liturgy of the Jewish prayerbook contain many references to the acts of succor and salvation wrought by God, who "answered the prayers" of the patriarchs, biblical and postbiblical heroes, prophets and saintly men of old when they cried unto him in times of need. On the collective level it was the Exodus from Egypt that provided the paradigm of spectacular saving intervention, and this point is emphasized twice daily, in the morning and evening prayers. But precisely because the Exodus was not only paradigmatic but also constitutive of Jewish history, it could serve equally well as a paradigm of the messianic *eschaton* (ultimate fulfillment at the End of Days)—a kind of strictly historical *Urzeit,* primordial, original time (parallel to the cosmogonic one) undergirding the *Endzeit* (End of Time)—once eschatological concepts and perspectives had begun to develop. Deutero-Isaiah provides a good example of precisely this type of messianism.

Of course, there is no denying that the messianic complex moved from marginality to centrality, and at certain periods even into the very center of Judaism. But this movement of the messianic idea to a place of centrality and prominence has to be seen in proper perspective. For one thing it proves that no matter how nonmessianic Judaism was at its beginnings and remained in some of its aspects, it also possessed sufficient seminal potential to produce, in the fullness of time, a full-blown messianism strong enough to enable the Jewish people to survive with strength, steadfast faith and hope, dignity, and integrity the kind of suffering, persecution, humiliation, and oppression that would, in other circumstances, have led to disintegration. The messianic hope balanced the deficit in the present. But the present is not sheer *privatio boni,* deficiency, and expectation concentrated on the future. It had its own *summa bona* and immanent validity in its no less important nonmessianic dimensions, namely, the dimensions of Torah and halakhah. It is not without reason that kabbalistic messianism, in contrast to kabbalistic halakhism and even supernomianism, evinced such an ambivalent attitude to the halakhah, perhaps precisely because the latter is meant not so much to hasten the advent of the Messiah as, in what might be described in good scriptural manner, to assure the right, just, God-willed and God-pleasing order and life of both the sacred community and the individuals forming part of it. After all, Abraham was called not in order to be "saved," let alone bring salvation, but to be a model and paradigm of the righteous and blessed life, to be a paradigm of blessing (and not a source of blessing: this is a much later homiletical interpretation that, to be sure, is of the greatest interest to the historian of religion), and in order "that he may instruct his children and his posterity to keep the way of the Lord by doing what is right and just" (Gen. 18:19). This basic structure is continued in the teachings of the prophets recalling Israel to their obligations under the covenant, although, of course, for the prophets, preaching in a situation of disasters (actual or impending) and corruption, the recapture of God's promised blessing could not but assume a redemptive and at times near-eschatological character.

This structure is even more marked in the halakhic system of the rabbis. For although repentance (cf. Isa. 59:20) and the proper observance of the law might help to bring about or hasten the advent of redemption, the main purpose of Torah and halakhah was not redemption, let alone the frenzied pursuit of "justification," but the joyous and faithful living with God in accordance with his revealed will. Halakhah, as the most characteristic feature of historical (the so-called normative) Judaism as developed and bequeathed to later generations by the ancient rabbis, thus preserves the unique tension between its original quality of a manner of life in its own right and with its inherent religious values, on the one hand, and some kind of almost instrumental messianic-salvational reference, on the other.

If Jewish history produced messianic doctrines and expectations, these were rooted not in angst or *nausée* but in the concrete experiences of suffering and exile, not to speak of pogroms and constant humiliation. Hence the content of these hopes was essentially a *restitutio in integrum* (restitution to original perfection) of the lost boons of the (actual or idealized and imaginary) past. For Jeremiah—still blithely unaware of a personal messiah—the glorious future is simply a matter of Israel's faithfulness to God's law: "For if you fulfill this command, then through the gates of this palace shall enter kings [note the plural] of David's line who sit upon his throne, riding horse-drawn chariots, with their courtiers and their subjects" (Jer. 22:4). In other words, the "messianic" Jerusalem is a this-worldly city, teeming and bustling with life. But Jeremiah also knew of such realities as the new, that is, the reaffirmed and reestablished covenant, just as Ezekiel knew about the "new" heart which, of course, is no supernatural heart but a very human heart of flesh instead of the present heart of stone, so that with this new heart "they may follow My laws and faithfully observe My rules" (Ezek. 11:19–20).

The messianic perspectives thus widened with the passage of time. According to most textbooks on the phenomenology of religions, mysticism, because of its "Platonic," suprahistorical, and supratemporal stance, seeking eternity or the "everlasting now" rather than time, is held to allow little room for messianic preoccupations. Jewish messianism, however, at one of its most decisive stages became a thoroughly messianic mysticism—with all the implicit dangers thereof, as Gershom Scholem has shown. There are, interestingly enough, two such forms of mystical messianism. One is messianic in its impulses and psychological motivations but not in its internal doctrinal structure; this would seem to be the case with the kabbalah of Moses Cordovero and his circle. The other is explosively messianic in its doctrinal thrust and structure; this is the case with the Lurianic kabbalah. But even the mystical and spiritualized versions of Jewish messianism never lost touch with the realities of history, society and—*honi soit qui mal y pense*—politics.

This basic stratum of the messianic vision—the end of exile, ingathering of the dispersed, that is, territorial reconcentration of the scattered people regardless of those who think of building Jerusalem in every green and pleasant land, and renewed sovereignty under a Davidic king—thus never lost its primacy and was never spiritualized away. Jewish messianism, for the greater part of its history, retained its national, social, and historical basis whatever the universal, cosmic, or inner and spiritual meanings accompanying it. One may, perhaps, speak of a spiritual deepening of the messianic idea in the course of the history of Jewish thought, but these allegedly more "spiritual" elements never replaced the concrete, historical messianism; they were added to it. Jewish apologists tended to view Christian accusations of a "carnal" understanding of messianic deliverance as a compliment. To them it seemed that a certain type of "spirituality" was but an escape into a realm where one was safe from the challenges of historical reality whose tests one deftly evaded. "Humankind cannot bear very much reality" (T. S. Eliot, *The Four Quartets*)—and this may also be the key to certain types of theology. If messianic redemption has a spiritual dimension, then according to the Jewish thinkers and kabbalists it must be the inner side of a process that manifests itself in the "outer" sphere of historical facts and social realities.

Perhaps Jewish messianism should be compared to a multistoried structure. More and more spiritual, universal, and even cosmic, mystical, and theosophical levels were added, each transforming also the underlying levels on which it rested, but the later never minimizing, let alone abolishing, the earlier. On the other hand the growth, like the rings of a tree, of messianic ideas and doctrines, in both their restorative and utopian versions, prevented Judaism from permanently continuing to identify messianism with certain of its initial elements only. Contemporary Jewry has learned—and learned the hard way—that even if all Jews were to leave the Diaspora and settle in Israel, and even if Israel should one day move closer to the desired realization of its utopian dream of peace with its neighbors, the world and the realities of Israel would still be very far from "messianic." The dialectics of Jewish existence and Jewish messianism exhibit moments of messianization as well as of demessianization. There are forms of demessianization that are not simply on the order of "retreat from eschatology" (well known to all historians of religion) but the result of a more sober and serious assessment of the meaning of messianism.

Thus, before long Jews may begin to question the theological validity of the liturgical formula, sanctioned by the Israeli Chief Rabbinate and in use in many synagogues, describing the establishment of the State of Israel in an incredibly primitive dispensationalist reformulation of biblical terminology as the "beginning of the sprouting of our redemption." It is needless to point out that this foolish phrase (hardly offensive because so essentially primitive and naive) is a symptom of Zionist enthusiasm and theological immaturity rather than evidence of mature reflection and theological understanding. Precisely the messianic élan that contributed so decisively to the not inconsiderable achievements of Zionism, now revealing themselves more and more in all their ambiguity, may demand, in terms of its own messianic dialectic and of the shifting horizons on which messianic ideas and expectations are being projected, a careful and deliberate demessianization. History, including messianic history, is open ended. It contains multiple options, and also multiple surprises.

BIBLIOGRAPHY

Joseph Klausner, *The Messianic Idea in Israel, from Its Beginnings to the Completion of the Mishnah* (1955).
Abba Hillel Silver, *A History of Messianic Speculation in Israel* (1959).
Gershom Scholem, *The Messianic Idea in Judaism and Other Essays* (1971).
R. J. Zwi Werblowsky, "Messianism in Jewish History," in H. H. Ben-Sasson and S. Ettinger, eds., *Jewish Society Through the Ages* (1971).

Metaphysics

מטאפיסיקה

Alan Udoff

The question of metaphysics, which is in actuality the question of philosophy itself, shares the origins of the latter as well as its fate. Of its origins, Diogenes reminds us that "it was from the Greeks that philosophy took its rise: its very name refuses to be translated into foreign speech."[1] Similarly, no "foreign speech" has supplanted metaphysics, a term that is derived from the expression *ta meta ta physika* (lit., what comes after the physical) and names the inner essence of philosophy itself.[2] The ambiguities of this expression, particularly in relation to Aristotle's eponymous treatise, are well known: "what comes after" (*ta meta*) may refer to the things that come after the physical things in the hierarchy of being, that is, the supersensible realities that comprise the objects of metaphysical study, or to the corpus of texts that, in accordance with the editorial decision of Andronicus of Rhodes, was placed after the *Physics* in what would become the canon of Aristotle's writings.[3] The first view, of course, reflects the tradition of learning down to modern times, as well as suggesting the once common motivation behind that learning. The responsibility for the second view, which rejects by implication the dignity and authority traditionally vouchsafed metaphysics and renders it "as doctrinally meaningless as the heading 'appendices' over a nondescript group of documents unable to be absorbed into the regular sequence of a book,"[4] lies with Johann Gottlieb Buhle.[5] Notwithstanding its lack of supporting evidence and the compelling arguments that may be marshaled against it, Buhle's thesis continues to find acceptance.[6]

The lexical question thus helps bring into view—although at the same time keeping at a distance—the philosophical question of the origins of metaphysics. In raising this question, it is best then to set to one side the lexical issue and concentrate instead on the deeper, or fateful, issue of the decline of metaphysics, an issue to which Buhle's thesis stands as a mere symptom—and by no means the most revealing one.

The origin or source of metaphysics lies in the originative and persisting wonder that Plato identifies (Theat. 155D) as the *arché* or source of philosophy itself. The fate of philosophy is linked to this beginning. The medieval Arabic philosopher al-Farabi, in assessing the unique significance of Plato and Aristotle, mentions—as if in passing—the contours of this fate: "Both have given us an account of philosophy, but not without giving us also an account of the ways to it and of the ways to re-establish it when it becomes confused or extinct."[7]

The situation to which al-Farabi refers, the loss of the true and highest wisdom and the means of its recovery, cannot be understood so long as the threats to wisdom are not grasped in their difference and distinctiveness: the threat of persecution arising from without[8] and the forms of self-forgetfulness to which the philosophical vision, or life, are peculiarly susceptible from within. Each of these threats illuminates the nature or condition of philosophy's place in the world. In the case of persecution, that nature is revealed in terms of an understanding that remains prephilosophical or nonphilosophical—that remains an attempt to understand the higher in terms of the lower. No such understanding can prove adequate, however, for an exploration of the relationship of theology, or Jewish theology, to metaphysics.

In raising this question, however, it is necessary to bear in mind that the object of inquiry is also threatened from within; metaphysical thought may become "confused or extinct" ("self-forgetful," in Strauss's translation of al-Farabi) for reasons connected wholly with the nature of its own radical activity and intention. There is, then, no certainty that the course of this question has not already been predetermined by a way of thinking that goes by the name of philosophy and yet is closed to metaphysics; that the question has not been reduced already to a mere "mechanical repetition"[9] or "verbal formula,"[10] behind which the real question of being lies covered and obscure.

Nor may it be assumed that the means of dis-covery are simply ready at hand in the academic departments where questions of philosophy are ordinarily or customarily taken up. Rather, "the misinterpretations with which philosophy is perpetually beset are prompted most by . . . professors of philosophy . . . [whose] customary business . . . [is] to transmit a certain knowledge of the philosophy of the past, as part of a general education."[11] It should go without saying that in such an atmosphere, where philosophy has been reduced "at best . . . to the technique of philosophy,"[12] the writings of Plato and Aristotle will equally suffer misinterpretation. With the way back into philosophy thus sealed off, as it were, the only recourse is to attempt to clear an opening through the act of questioning being itself, ever mindful of and attuned to what this questioning reveals and requires.

Although "each one of us is grazed at least once, perhaps more than once, by the hidden power of this question,"[13] its full power cannot be released in this way. These moods of despair, rejoicing, and boredom which Heidegger cites may set at a distance the "commonplace"[14] and the hold it normally exercises on us; they do not, however, constitute that "leap through which man thrusts away all the previous security, whether real or imagined, of his life."[15] This is, moreover, no mere metaphor, as Heidegger is careful to stress: "The question is asked only in this leap; it *is* the leap; without it there is no asking."[16] It is in this attempted asking, then, where "the content and the object of the question react inevitably on the act of questioning,"[17] that philosophy occurs.[18] To situate that occurrence even more precisely, philosophy occurs where, in relation to being, we "push our questioning to the very end."[19]

The absoluteness of this endpoint and the questioning that actualizes it are, for Heidegger, authentically philosophy's own. The language through which this actualization is achieved is, however, subject to the inauthenticity of other frames of inquiry. That the language may remain the same in either case permits the lines of inquiry to be crossed under the cover of a repetition that dulls the edge of difference—as Heidegger correctly observes: "It can never be objectively determined whether anyone, whether we, really ask this question, that is whether we make the leap, or never get beyond a verbal formula."[20]

By way of illustration Heidegger restates a position he first argued at greater length in the Tübingen lecture of 1927, "Phenomenology and Theology":

Anyone for whom the Bible is divine revelation and truth has the answer to the question "Why are there essents rather than nothing?" even before it is asked: everything that is, except God himself, has been created by Him. One who holds to such faith can in a way participate in the asking of our question, but he can not really question without ceasing to be a believer and taking all the consequences of such a step. He will only be able to act "as if."[21]

Through this text Heidegger raises, at the deepest level, the question of the relationship of theology to metaphysics—by which name one understands philosophy as well. Having secured, or at least indicated what is involved in securing, this question, it is now possible to raise it anew as a theme for Jewish theological reflection. In initiating the turn to this reflection, the writings of Maimonides must be accorded a privileged position, for, as al-Farabi writes with regard to Plato and Aristotle, they "have given us an account of . . . [theology], but not without giving us also an account of *the ways to it and of the ways to re-establish it* when it becomes confused or extinct."[22] It is precisely in terms of the emphasized phrase that Maimonides' significance lies for the discussion that follows.

The situation to which al-Farabi refers recalls two texts, whose relationship must figure in any final reading of Maimonides' works: the introductory statements concerning the genesis of the *Mishneh Torah* (2b, 3b, and 4b) and the *itinerarium* in The Guide of the Perplexed (3:51). The significance of Chapter 51 in particular is indicated by Maimonides at the very outset: It stands as a "kind of conclusion" to the explanation of the true worship "which is the end of man" (*Guide* 3:51). The chapter itself is introduced by a simile that portrays the human condition through the relation of subjects to a ruler in a palace. The dispersion of these subjects, which, apparently, has nothing to do with persecution or other historical contingencies, ranges from the remotest regions (where theoretical wisdom is wholly extinct) to the proximity of the one individual (the shift to the singular at this point should be noted) who, having mastered this wisdom, "has come to be with the ruler in the inner part of the habitation" (*Guide* 3:51). The ranking that Maimonides establishes is based, thus, on the degree of demonstrable knowledge achieved "in divine matters, to the extent that that is possible" (*Guide* 3:51), that is, on the degree of metaphysical wisdom.

Metaphysical wisdom for Maimonides belongs to the life of contemplation. The sense of duration implied here is fundamental. What is required is a sustained contemplation of God. Even such speculative instruments of analysis as the *via negativa,* which now typically comprise no more than a single unit in philosophy courses, required for Maimonides years of systematic employment (*Guide* 1:59) before their end might be realized properly. The difference between these two kinds of regimen of instruction, the academic and the genuinely contemplative, corresponds to the difference between the correct yet "mechanical repetition" of a metaphysical formula and a way of seeing that in-forms the awareness of the speaker and sets him apart. The actual discourses spoken may not reveal this difference of awareness, but the difference nonetheless obtains (*Guide* 3:51). In what, then, does this seeing consist? What is called for here is something both more and less than the theory of intellects and emanations that explains the mechanism of theoretical insight and the metaphysical ground of its possibility. What must be recovered is the seeing itself. The text in which Maimonides comes closest to this appears in the *Mishneh Torah* (Hil. Yesodei ha-Torah 2:2).

> And what is the way that will lead to the love of Him and the fear of Him? When a person contemplates His great and wondrous works and creatures and from them obtains a glimpse of His wisdom which is incomparable and infinite, he will straightway love Him, praise Him, glorify Him, and long with an exceeding longing to know His great Name; even as David said "My soul thirsteth for God, for the living God" (Ps. 42:3). And when he ponders these matters, he will recoil affrighted, and realize that he is a small creature, lowly and obscure, endowed with slight and slender intelligence, standing in the presence of Him who is perfect in knowledge. And so David said, "When I consider Thy heavens, the work of Thy fingers—what is man that Thou art mindful of Him?" (Ps. 8:4–5).

The text at hand is preceded by others that establish the existence, oneness, and immateriality of God. The obligation to love and fear God, which Maimonides now considers, makes explicit the sense of divine majesty and awe that accompanied, at different levels of implication, the proofs in Chapter 1. The weight of these proofs does not rest, then, on this passage but rather supports it.

Maimonides' intention is to indicate the way in which the commandments to love and fear God are to be fulfilled. The way Maimonides chooses is, of course, not the only way. God's actions in history could also have been adduced as the basis of this obligation. Nor is the way Maimonides chooses free of obstacles or doubts, as is evident from his account of the origins of idolatry (MT Hil. Avodah Kokhavim 1:1). These glosses notwithstanding, there are compelling reasons that argue on behalf of Maimonides' strategy.[23]

The reader is, then, directed to the contemplation of nature. The evidence of divine wisdom he discovers immediately instills in him the love of God, the desire to "praise Him, glorify Him, and long with an exceeding longing to know His great Name." The movement from contemplation to love is presented here as immediate, as a natural movement; it is, in effect, a reflex of meditative association. The soul, therefore, is so constituted by its nature as to turn to God upon contemplating the works of His hands, that is, the order of nature in general and the wonder of its creations. The effect of this turn is to reveal, before the fullness of God's creation, the emptiness of the soul without God. Hence the citation of Psalm 42:3: "My soul thirsts for God, for the living God."

The fulfillment of the obligation to fear God follows, but only at a temporally significant distance from this point.[24] That significance may be stated precisely: The love of God is discovered through the direct contemplation of his works; the fear of God results from a thinking that situates the contemplative act itself over against the horizon of God's works, and "ponders" them together. Implicit in the longing of the soul for God is the awareness of the want or lack constitutive of (the) desire (for the good). When the measure of that want has as its referential good the wisdom of God, that desire becomes boundless—"exceedingly longing." In the act of contemplative love, however, where the face is turned toward God and the longing is saturated by his Presence—or the traces of his Presence—the condition of the soul's own impoverishment is not yet revealed. The fear of God arises at that moment of revelation. The fear of God, then, derives not from the recognition of what may be done to man through God's power, but from the recognition of the greatness of God measured, at last, against the utter lowliness of man;[25] it arises through the mediating image of man's longing for God and the recognition of the true being of man, as entailed by that longing, within the order of being itself.

In the preceding discussion Maimonides' writings could be cited only briefly and, to be sure, read only provisionally. Nevertheless, even in their simple repetition, the power of his thinking, the afferent force that has drawn the most thoughtful of Jewish readers to him, is present. The source of that power, the heart of its attraction, lies in the way in which the deepest concerns and highest aspirations of thought itself are actualized. As such, Maimonides' writings stand apart from those efforts that dominate the foreground of later Jewish thinking—in particular, its contemporary versions. The measure of the distance between them is the extent to which Maimonides understands faith and philosophy and their relationship to each other; one way of expressing that distance is to observe the place held by metaphysics in Maimonides' thought and the place it is currently allowed.

For Maimonides, the part (in this case, the human way of being) cannot be understood outside the context of the whole (being itself) or, more exactly, the truth of the whole. It is necessary only to reflect briefly on this statement and then consider what is implied in the uncritically accepted substitution of history for being and opinion for truth to grasp the seriousness of the change that has transpired.

The true greatness of Maimonides' work lies, then, in the way in which the life of faith, reflectively taken up and recast through the theological experience, is situated over against its philosophical counterpoint. Testamentary to the nature of the insight that drives this work forward is the way in which its reading allows for the realization of the equiprimordiality of these two lines of inquiry and the exclusiveness of their claims to pursue the truth of the whole—in Leo Strauss's formulation:

> When we attempt to return to the roots of Western civilization, we observe soon that Western civilization has two roots which are in conflict with each other, the biblical and the Greek philosophic, and this is to begin with a very disconcerting observation. Yet this realization has also something reassuring and comforting. The very life of Western civilization is the life between two codes, a fundamental tension. There is therefore no reason inherent in Western civilization itself, in its fundamental constitution, why it should give up life. But this comforting thought is justified only if we live that life, if we live that conflict, that is. No one can be both a philosopher and a theologian or, for that matter, a third which is beyond the conflict between philosophy and theology, or a synthesis of both. But every one of us can be and ought to be either the one or the other, the philosopher open to the challenge of theology or the theologian open to the challenge of philosophy.[26]

Through this formulation a single but all-important circuit of thought is completed. Against the one-sidedness of Heidegger's claim that "a faith that does not perpetually expose itself to the possibility of unfaith is no faith,"[27] there arises the question of the self-limitation of philosophy's unwillingness to be engaged by faith. With the writings of Heidegger and Maimonides as guides, it is possible to preserve philosophy and theology against the self-forgetfulness that would render this question "confused," if not "extinct."[28] In the scale of judgment, then, the question of metaphysics, and all that it entails, the question of Athens and Jerusalem itself, hangs in a precarious and fateful balance. There is no shame in not knowing the answer to this question; for the unexamined life that fails or refuses to ask it, there is little else.

REFERENCES

1. Diogenes Laertius, *Lives of Eminent Philosophers*, 1:5.
2. "Metaphysics is a name for the pivotal point and core of all philosophy." Martin Heidegger, *An Introduction to Metaphysics* (1959), 17.
3. Cf. Joseph Owens, *An Elementary Christian Metaphysics* (1963), 1–14.
4. Owens, op. cit., 3.
5. See Johann Gottlieb Buhle, *Über die Ächtheit der Metaphysik des Aristoteles* (1788).
6. For example, the article on "Metaphysical Imagination" in the *Dictionary of the History of Ideas* (1977) simply parses the term *metaphysics* as "fabricated from the Greek *ta meta ta physika*, i.e., the [books of Aristotle] after the *Physics*."
7. *Al-Farabi's Philosophy of Plato and Aristotle* (1962), 49–50.
8. Leo Strauss, *Persecution and the Art of Writing* (1952), esp. 18–19.
9. Heidegger, 17.
10. Ibid., 6.
11. Ibid., 11.
12. Ibid.
13. Ibid., 1.
14. Ibid. These moods share in common, to employ a formulation of Joseph Pieper's, the power to tear us out of our moorings in the "workaday world" where utility prevails and organizes all experience around its orientation and end. Cf. Joseph Pieper, *Leisure the Basis of Culture* (1963).
15. Heidegger, 6.
16. Ibid.
17. Ibid., 5.
18. Ibid., 8.
19. Ibid.
20. Ibid., 6.
21. Ibid., 6–7. Cf. *The Piety of Thinking: Essays by Martin Heidegger*, tr., notes, and comm. by J. G. Hart and J. C. Maraldo (1976), 5–21.
22. *Al-Farabi's Philosophy*, op. cit., 49–50. Emphasis added.
23. Cf. *Guide* 3: 12, where the view, erroneously held by both common and wise alike, that history attests to the preponderance of evil over good is criticized by Maimonides in the name of the provident design of the natural order.
24. Twersky's view—"love and fear are treated here as complementary, almost simultaneous, attitudes"—fails to see the subtlety in Maimonides' analysis. See Isadore Twersky, *Introduction to the Code of Maimonides (Mishneh Torah)*, (1980), 216, n. 63.
25. Cf. Joseph Albo, *Sefer ha-Ikkarim*, 3: 30.
26. Leo Strauss, "The Mutual Influence of Theology and Philosophy," in *The Independent Journal of Philosophy*, 111 (1980).
27. Heidegger, 7.
28. There is, of course, no question of being guided to the same end. However one interprets the "recoil" that Maimonides describes, and its relation to the contemplation of nature, it remains critically different from the "leap" of which Heidegger speaks.

BIBLIOGRAPHY

Hermann Cohen, *Religion of Reason out of the Sources of Judaism,* Simon Kaplan, tr. (1972).

Jacob Klein, *Plato's Trilogy* (1977).

Immanuel Levinas, *Totality and Infinity,* Alphonso Lingis, tr. (1969).

Franz Rosenzweig, "Vertauschte Fronten," in *Franz Rosenzweig: Der Mensch und sein Werk. Gesammelte Schriften,* 3 (1983).

Midrash

מִדְרָשׁ

David Stern

Midrash is the name for the activity of biblical interpretation as it was developed and practiced by the rabbis in Palestine during the first centuries of the Common Era. The word derives from the Hebrew root *d-r-sh,* "to inquire" or "to seek after," a root whose verbal form is often used in the Bible to refer to the act of seeking out God's will (Ex. 18:15; II Chron. 30:19). The locus for that search was eventually identified with the text of the Torah (cf. Ezra 7:14), and in postbiblical literature the word *midrash* came to designate the study of the Torah (as in *beit midrash,* the house of study) and thus the specific way the rabbis studied Scripture and interpreted its meaning for themselves. In addition to designating this activity of interpretation, the word *midrash* is applied to individual interpretive opinions—a specific midrash of a verse or word. Finally, the term is also used as the title for the literary compilations in which the separate interpretations, many of them originally oral, were eventually collected and preserved for us today—in, for example, the Midrash Rabbah, as the great collection of homiletical midrashim on the Pentateuch is called.

The origins of Midrash lie in the Bible and in its internal exegetical tendencies. The tradition of biblical interpretation is surely as ancient as the biblical text. Later biblical authors can be seen to have re-used earlier sacred traditions in the new contexts of their times, elaborated upon fixed ideas and words, harmonized conflicting texts, and transformed old imagery in order to respond to changing needs. In the centuries immediately before and after the Common Era, as the biblical canon was receiving its final shape, literary activity among Jews in Palestine shifted in general toward overt and explicit forms of scriptural interpretation. This tendency can be witnessed in such typically late antique literary genres as the translations of the Bible (the Aramaic *targumim* are appropriate examples), in books that retell the biblical narrative (Pseudo-Philo's *Biblical Antiquities*), and, most clearly of all, in the apocalyptic commentaries of the Dead Sea sects. The same tendency can be seen in another form in the Gospels of the New Testament, where the life of Jesus is itself portrayed as an exegetical noumenon. The precise generic connection between these works and midrash as it is found in later rabbinic literature is still a matter of scholarly (and, to some extent, theological) controversy, but it is clear that rabbinic midrash shares with the works just mentioned and others like them many common exegetical strategies and preoccupations. A good number of the *middot,* the hermeneutical principles that the rabbis utilize in midrash, such as the *kal ve-ḥomer* (the argument a fortiori) and the *gezerah shaveh* (verbal analogy), have parallels in Greco-Roman legal interpretation. Others, like *gematria* (arithmology) and *notarikon* (interpretations of acrostics), are, as Saul Lieberman has pointed out, typical of techniques of dream interpretation that circulated throughout the ancient world.

In the hands of the rabbis, however, scriptural exegesis, midrashic commentary, became a thoroughly original medium for the presentation of the oral Law *(Torah she-be-al peh),* as the rabbis called the accumulating body of extrabiblical traditions that they claimed had originated at Sinai in the same divine revelation in which God had given Israel the written text of the Torah. The oral Law encompasses all of rabbinic teaching, halakhah as well as aggadah, and though it would appear likely that midrashic energies were initially expended mainly upon the interpretation of the legal sections of the Torah (if only because of their practical urgency), the same characteristics inform midrash when it interprets aggadah as when it deals with halakhah. These characteristics can be described briefly as follows.

First, there is nothing systematic or programmatic about midrashic exegesis. Although various lists of the *middot,* the hermeneutical principles of rabbinic exegesis, were drawn up at different times, the motive behind their compilation appears to have been either polemical or apologetic, to justify and rationalize existing midrash against the competing claims of other schools of exegesis or religious groups, rather than to guide or encourage the creation of new midrash.

Second, midrash is largely concerned with the smaller units of Scripture—verses, phrases, single words—rather than with such larger components as its books, narratives, or recurring themes. The verse-centeredness of midrash, as James Kugel has aptly described this feature,[1] may reflect the way Scripture was actually taught by the rabbis, and it is exemplified in the midrashic habit of atomizing the biblical text, breaking up a verse into tinier units and mining its separate phrases and words for meanings that tend to emerge out of connections with phrases and words in other verses rather than from the first verse's original context. For example, the phrase "over there" *(ad koh)* in the statement, "The boy and I will go over there" (Gen. 22:5), that Abraham addresses to his servants as he leads his son Isaac to be sacrificed, is given the following interpretation by Rabbi Joshua ben Levi: "We will go and see what shall be the outcome of God's blessing to me that began 'So *(koh)* shall your offspring be' [Gen. 15:5]" (Gen. R. 56:2). The word *koh* is thus changed from a deliberately vague geographical pointer into a specific, even overspecified, textual site—the blessing in which God promised Abraham to multiply his seed, a promise whose fulfillment Abraham realizes is in serious jeopardy as he now proceeds to offer up to God his son. This tendency to fragmentize Scripture in order to draw unpredictable nexuses of meaning across Scripture is reflected, in turn, in the fragmented, discontinuous character of midrashic discourse itself.

Third, midrashic interpretations typically originate out of problems in Scripture. Lexical oddities, implicit or outright contradictions, unknown place names or unidentified personages, cases of awkward syntax—any of these irritants in the scriptural text can furnish the rabbis with an occasion for interpretation, and where no obvious problem is evident one is frequently invented to justify midrashic exegesis. This feature of midrash also accounts for its scholasticism, or schoolish cleverness, and its improvisatory style: many midrashim appear to have been invented to respond to immediate and ad hoc questions. Because midrash is so closely connected to problem solving—some would say to unriddling or decoding—it is common for the rabbis to give more than one solution to a problem. Moreover, since a single verse may pose several problems, and since solutions to different problems may result in conflicting opinions, contradictory interpretations of the same verse sometimes appear right next to each other, let alone in different midrashic collections.

Fourth, midrash is frankly and unabashedly ideological. Through midrash the rabbis were at once able to affirm the authority of their tradition in Scripture, and thus confirm its veracity against rival interpretations of Judaism that also claimed to be the true heritage of the biblical tradition, and to maintain the centrality of the biblical text in their lives by using midrash to extend the Bible's laws and beliefs to the issues of their contemporary existence. Unembarrassed ideological motives can be found throughout midrash; they can be seen in the many typological exegeses that use the biblical past as intimation and anticipation of the rabbinic present, and no less so in interpretations that apply the blandest scriptural phrases as references to the most specific realities of third-century Palestine, as in Leviticus Rabbah 1:1, where the phrase in Psalm 103:20, "mighty creatures who do His bidding," is taken to refer to Jews who obeyed the strictures of the Sabbatical year even when they had to pay the *annona,* a special land-tax the Romans required from the Jews. Such interpretations are saved from heavy-handedness, however, by the playfulness of midrashic exegesis and the rabbis' preternatural sensitivity to the subtlest nuances in Scripture—to the slightest bumps in the textual surface. For example, the presence of the first person plural in Jeremiah 9:17, "Send for the skilled women, let them come; let them quickly start a wailing for us, that our eyes may run with tears, our pupils flow with water," was cause enough for the rabbis to assert that God mourned over the destruction of the Temple—*his* Temple, after all—along with the nation of Israel (Lam. R., ed. S. Buber, 4). Similarly, the rabbis noted that the use of the future tense in the verse introducing the Song at the Sea, "Then sang *(az yashir)* Moses" (Ex. 15:1) was proof that the Torah testifies to the resurrection of the dead, at which time a song will be sung in its honor (Mekh. Shir. 1).

The various features of midrash just described characterize rabbinic exegesis from its earliest testimony to its latest. About the inner history of the development of midrash little is known except for what can be deduced from the midrashic texts themselves. Most midrash presumably originated within those institutions in which the rabbis taught and studied the Bible, the academy and the synagogue. The various midrashic compilations were most probably edited in order to provide teachers and preachers with collections of exemplary interpretations of Scripture. The tannaitic collections, called after the tannaim, the sages who lived between 70 C.E. and 220 C.E. and whose opinions are cited in them, are mainly anthologies of individual interpretations, listed simply by the scriptural verse they comment upon, verse after verse through an entire (or nearly entire) book in the Pentateuch.

These collections were probably edited in the late third and fourth centuries.

While the tannaitic midrashim tend to concentrate upon those sections of the Torah that have some legal import, the midrashic collections of the amoraim, the sages who lived between 220 C.E. and the end of the fifth century C.E., are more aggadic in content. The major amoraic collections, edited between the late fifth and eighth centuries, represent the classical period of rabbinic midrash. Much more sophisticated than their tannaitic models, these collections are characterized by uniquely midrashic literary forms that serve to organize scriptural exegesis into ever more complex rhetorical structures. Of these none is more typical than the *petiḥta* or proem, a form that may have begun, according to Joseph Heinemann, in a kind of mini-sermon that introduced the initial verse of the weekly Torah reading. Instead of beginning with that verse, however, the proem opens with another remote scriptural quotation that to all appearances is unrelated to the Torah verse; it then constructs a series of exegetical bridges that unexpectedly culminate in the latter verse. The following *petiḥta* on Leviticus 24:2—"Command the Israelite people to bring you clear oil of beaten olives for lighting, to maintain lights regularly"—provides a brief example of the form:

> Bar Kapparah recited a *petiḥta:* "It is You who light my lamp; the Lord, my God, lights up my darkness" (Ps. 18:29). The Holy One, blessed be He, said to man: Your lamp is in my hand, as it is said, "The lifebreath of man is the lamp of the Lord" (Prov. 20:27), and my lamp is in yours, "to maintain lights regularly." To which the Holy One, blessed be He, added: If you will light my lamp, I will light yours. That is the meaning of "Command the Israelite people . . ."
>
> (Lev. R. 31:4).

The separate interpretations of Psalm 18:29, Proverbs 20:27, and Leviticus 24:2 all have independent origins, but the *petiḥta* joins them through their common imagery in order to make its own rhetorical point. This point, the *petiḥta*'s theme, is the reciprocity of the deeds of God and man, and it also underlies the nascently allegorical interpretation of Leviticus 24:2 and of the sanctuary candelabrum as a symbol for the human soul—an interpretation that is discovered in the *petiḥta*'s conclusion.

The structure of the *petiḥta* is replicated elsewhere in midrash. In some amoraic collections, entire chapters appear to be organized as literary homilies that imitate the form of sermons that might once have been delivered in synagogues. Other amoraic midrashim, particularly of the Yelamdenu-Tanḥuma variety, begin with a halakhic question and reflect, it seems, still another type of sermon. Because of the difficulty in dating rabbinic literature, it is impossible to construct a genuine history of midrash, but it would appear that following the classical amoraic period midrashic collections tend to branch off and develop into other literary genres—into more continuous narratives, less encumbered and fragmented by exegesis, and into ethical or moral treatises. While encyclopedias of midrashic tradition were compiled throughout the Middle Ages, actual interpretive energies waned until the new forms of *peshat-* or plain-sense-oriented exegesis emerged in the eleventh century in Europe. Finally, in the twelfth and thirteenth centuries, the literary forms of classical midrash were taken up by the fledgling kabbalistic movement in such works as the *Sefer Bahir* and the *Zohar,* where they were infused with a new mystical content and thereby transformed into a medium for esoteric teachings. At this point, however, another literary tradition has begun.

From the preceding sketch, the overall course of midrash can be seen as a process through which an interpretive stance gradually developed its own literary language and modes of discourse. Within the tradition itself, however, midrash was rarely if ever seen this way. Midrash aggadah in particular was neglected in favor of halakhic literature, and even the classical commentators on midrash were mainly concerned with elucidating the "logic" behind midrashic exegesis. The most ambitious project of this kind was undertaken by Zeeb Wolf Einhorn (Maharzu) in his lengthy commentary upon Midrash Rabbah, published in 1856, in which he attempted to show how every midrashic opinion derives from one of the thirty-two hermeneutical principles attributed to Rabbi Eliezer. Not until the very end of the last century was the literary character of midrash fully acknowledged. The earliest statement of this kind was made in 1892 by Leopold Zunz in his monumental literary history of the Jewish sermon, while the first modern scholar to stand outside the midrashic tradition and to consider the inner dynamics of rabbinic exegesis was Isaak Heinemann, in his seminal work *Darkhei ha-Aggadah,* appearing in 1951. Heinemann, whose work was strongly influenced by late Romantic philosophy and hermeneutics, identified midrash as a type of "creative philology" and "creative historiography," terms Heinemann coined to capture both the mythopoeic aspect of midrash and what he saw as its authentic concern with questions of language and the past. Heinemann likened midrashic traditions to folk literature: its "philological" and "historiographic" creativity were for him an alternative approach to the discursive rationalism of modern philology and historiography. More recently, another version of this approach has been invoked by the deconstructionist philosopher Jacques Derrida and some of his disciples who have proposed midrashic interpretation as an alternative to the logocentric theory of meaning that has until now dominated Western thought. In contrast to the Greek and Christian metaphysics of presence, which seeks to get "behind" the text to recover its meaning, midrashic hermeneutics, in the deconstructionist view, sees meaning in the language of the text itself, especially in the intertextual reality it constructs and in the possibility of a plurality, even plethora, of meanings that overflow from the text and frustrate our efforts to fix upon a single, static presence behind it.

The question that must be addressed to such approaches defining midrash is whether these features—which admittedly do, in a sense, characterize rabbinic interpretation—derive from a genuinely unique hermeneutical stance or whether they follow from a specific view of the Torah that, though never spelled out explicitly, might be called a virtual ideology of rabbinic thought. According to this ideology, the Torah is not so much a text—it is certainly unlike every other text in human reality—as it is a trope for God, not in the later kabbalistic sense in which the very words of the Torah are said to constitute the names of God and to embody his attributes, but in a metonymic fashion, whereby the Torah's being is treated as a kind of figurative extension of God's: just as he is timeless, so the Torah is beyond all temporality; just as all his deeds are meaningful, so every word in the Torah is full of significance; and so on.

If the rabbis' Torah is indeed such a trope for God, then midrashic exegesis itself might be considered a working out of that trope. This activity need not necessarily be construed in an overtly theological sense, but it does help us to appreciate how midrash, the commentary par excellence, could become, in Gershom Scholem's phrase, a category of revelation. The singularity of midrash—its genius, as it were—lies in the way it occupies a unique literary space. This space is bounded by conventional literature on one side, and by standard exegesis on the other: where the former presents itself as autonomous and self-contained, the latter subordinates itself to the privilege of another text that it claims to serve. Without ever crossing over to either side, the rabbis staked out the gray area between the two as the space of midrash and therein gave expression to their creativity. In doing this, the rabbis also created a model for a uniquely Jewish way of studying the Torah, a mode of study—of reading, as it were—that turns into writing, into literature in its own right.

REFERENCES

1. James Kugel, "Two Introductions to Midrash," in *Prooftexts* 3 (1983), 146.

BIBLIOGRAPHY

Michael Fishbane, "Torah and Tradition," in Douglas A. Knight, ed., *Tradition and Theology in the Old Testament* (1977).

Isaak Heinemann, *Darkhei ha-Aggadah,* 3rd ed. (1970).

Joseph Heinemann, "The Proem in the Aggadic Midrashim: A Form-Critical Study," in *Scripta Hierosolymitana,* 22 (1971).

James Kugel, "Two Introductions to Midrash," in *Prooftexts,* 3 (1983).

Saul Lieberman, "Rabbinic Interpretation of Scripture," in *Hellenism in Jewish Palestine* (1950).

Miracle

נס

Allan Arkush

The Bible reports the wondrous ways in which God redeemed Israel from slavery, gave it a law and a land, and guided its subsequent life as a nation. It tells us, on occasion, how the Israelites reacted when God performed signs and wonders for their sake. Observing the Egyptians dead upon the seashore, for instance, "Israel saw the wondrous power which the Lord had wielded against the Egyptians, the people feared the Lord; they had faith in the Lord, and in His servant Moses" (Ex. 14:31).

The "wilderness generation" saw and believed. Later generations are expected to believe without having seen. It is true, of course, that "in every generation a man is obligated to see himself as if he had gone forth from Egypt,"[1] but that is an obligation he can shoulder only if he already has faith in the veracity of the biblical reports.

Many things stand in the way of such faith. There is, first of all, the idea of nature, unknown to biblical Hebrew but eventually introduced to the Jews by the Greeks. Acquaintance with this concept inevitably leads to the question of whether the wonders reported in the Bible are consonant with the known nature of things. Skeptics have good reason to argue that they are not. Defenders of the faith, in turn, have two basic ways of responding to the skeptics' charges. They can attempt to show that the biblical narrative, properly understood, does not report unnatural occurrences at all, but only highly unusual ones for which there are natural explanations, or they can acknowledge that the biblical wonders contravene nature, but maintain that it is within God's power to do so. These two responses are not mutually exclusive. Moses Maimonides, for example, sought to explain biblical wonders, as far as possible, in accordance with the natural order. But where naturalistic explanations seemed hopelessly irreconcilable with the biblical text, he was prepared to invoke the supernatural power of God.

Those who share Maimonides' belief in God's power to contravene nature have no difficulty in accepting the possibility of any of the miracles recorded in the Bible. Belief in the possibility of miracles is not, however, sufficient reason for accepting the historicity of those particular miracles. There may be a God who can suspend nature but who never did so for the benefit or edification of the Israelites. What proof do we have that he ever did?

We have no proof, says the Jewish philosophical tradition, but we do have the unimpeachable testimony of the Bible that multitudes of our forefathers witnessed the defeat of the Egyptians, the giving of the law, and the other miracles of central importance to our faith. This may be sufficient for those who believe that the biblical wonders were fully consonant with the natural order. It is also, in principle, an argument acceptable to those who believe that God has rendered the impossible possible. But to others, who do not share such beliefs, the biblical accounts of miraculous events threaten to undermine the authority of the Bible.

To Baruch Spinoza, it is evident that the ancient Hebrews conceived of and reported events in a manner very different from the way in which they actually occurred. In order to know the truth about these events, "it is necessary to know the opinions of those who first related them, and have recorded them for us in writing, and to distinguish such opinions from the actual impression made upon their senses." If we do not do this, we run the risk of confounding "actual events with symbolic and imaginary ones."[2]

Spinoza attempted to distinguish the opinions of the Hebrews from the plain facts they had observed. It was his belief that these opinions were nothing but the "prejudices of an ancient people."[3] The Hebrews ignorantly imagined the power of God over nature "to be like that of some royal potentate"[4] over his subjects. They believed that God loved them above all men, and was prepared to exercise that power for their sake. These prejudices distorted their perception of the events through which they lived, leading them to believe that they had witnessed impossible things.

Spinoza's attack on the credibility of the biblical Hebrews is entirely persuasive only to those who share his belief that natural law is inviolable. Believers in the possibility of miracles, on the other hand, will not follow Spinoza's rejection of the testimony of the ancient Israelites simply because they were so credulous as to believe they had witnessed miracles. Nevertheless, Spinoza's critique reminds even the orthodox that their confidence in the literal truth of the biblical narrative ultimately rests on faith alone.

This faith is not dead. However, it is, for the most part, absent from the hearts of the leading representatives of modern Jewish thought. They have followed not Maimonides but Spinoza, and have abandoned the idea of a God who has the power to contravene nature. As a result, they have also accepted the validity of Spinoza's attempt to distinguish between the opinions of the ancient Israelites and the events they actually observed. But that is where the similarity ends. They do not share Spinoza's scorn for the Israelites' unsophisticated response to their experiences. In general, they agree with Mordecai Kaplan that "the mere fact that we cannot accept as historical the record of miraculous events in the Bible and elsewhere does not imply that we regard the miracle stories as of no significance in our thinking about God and human life."[5] They differ, however, in their analysis of the religious significance of the miracle stories.

Kaplan believes that we need the tradition affirming miracles in order

to realize that we have come upon our present idea of God after considerable groping and searching for the truth. That tradition records the gropings and searchings which went on in the consciousness of our ancestors. Would we want to forget our own childish notions? Are they not essential to our experiencing our personal identity? Likewise, our tradition is indispensable as a means to our experiencing our continuity with our ancestry and our Jewish people. If we study that tradition carefully, we are bound to discover nuances and anticipations of attitudes toward life that are not only tenable but well worth cultivating.[6]

Here, condescension to the Israelites takes the place of Spinoza's contempt for them. Still, the miracle stories are said to have a positive significance. They remind us of who we are and attach our sympathies to books that can provide us with useful guidance.

Other modern thinkers, such as Martin Buber, have spoken not condescendingly but reverently of the Israelites' "experience of event as wonder."[7] Buber like Kaplan believes that the Israelites perceived things other than as they actually occurred. They were overwhelmed by "vast historical happenings," events so enormous that they could only perceive in them "deeds performed by heavenly powers."[8] The people responded to these events with "saga-creating ardor";[9] they mythicized history. The biblical narratives represent therefore "nothing other than the report by ardent enthusiasts of that which has befallen them."[10] Yet "it may very well be doubted whether in the last resort the report of an unenthusiastic chronicler could have come closer to the truth."[11] By "the truth" Buber does not, of course, mean a factually correct account of the actual events and their causes. He has in mind a deeper truth, that of the divine–human encounter that has taken place on a plane invisible to the "unenthusiastic chronicler." It is primarily as the record of this encounter that the Bible has meaning for us.

Franz Rosenzweig's most frequently quoted remark on the question of miracles is found in a letter to a number of his collaborators in the Frankfurt *Lehrhaus.* "All the days of the year," he wrote, "Balaam's talking ass may be a mere fairy tale, but not on the Sabbath wherein this portion is read in the synagogue, when it speaks to me out of the open Torah." What it is on that day he cannot say, but it is "certainly not a fairy tale, but that which is communicated to me provided I am able to fulfill the command of the hour, namely, to open my ears."[12] These words have often been taken as evidence that Rosenzweig was "unable simply to believe all Biblical miracles."[13] Yet Rosenzweig was also capable of saying that "Every miracle is possible, even the most absurd, even that an ax floats."[14] Whatever his final view on this matter may have been, however, it is unmistakably clear that for Rosenzweig as for Buber the truth of divine revelation did not hinge on the literal accuracy of the biblical narrative.

Even while pursuing, for the most part, the skeptical path Spinoza marked out, modern Jewish thought has circled around behind him to reconnect itself with the biblical miracles in new, nonliteralist ways. It affirms the religious significance of the miracle stories without accepting their factual accuracy. This is a momentous step, with broad theological implications.

REFERENCES

1. Passover Haggadah.
2. Baruch Spinoza, *Theological-Political Treatise,* R. H. Elwes, tr. (1955), 93.
3. Ibid., 82.

4. Ibid., 81.
5. Mordecai Kaplan, *Judaism Without Supernaturalism* (1958), 10.
6. Ibid., 112.
7. Martin Buber, *Moses* (1958), 16.
8. Ibid.
9. Ibid.
10. Ibid., 17.
11. Ibid.
12. Nahum Glatzer, ed., *Franz Rosenzweig* (1953), 246.
13. Leo Strauss, *Spinoza's Critique of Religion* (1962), 14.
14. Glatzer, *Franz Rosenzweig,* 290.

BIBLIOGRAPHY

Martin Buber, *Moses* (1958), 13–20.
Mordecai Kaplan, *Judaism Without Supernaturalism* (1958), Pt. 1.
Baruch Spinoza, *Theological-Political Treatise,* R. H. Elwes, tr. (1951), 81–98.
Leo Strauss, *Spinoza's Critique of Religion* (1962).

Mizveh

אַ מצווה

Moshe Waldoks

Max Weinreich, the preeminent historian of Yiddish, explained that a distinctive process of language "fusion provided Yiddish with a wealth of new synonyms that offer the opportunity of nuancing."[1] This is particularly true in the case of the close to five thousand identifiable Hebraisms in Yiddish. The appropriation of Hebrew was vital in upholding the traditional elements of Eastern European Jewish life, which was a transcending culture system that did not operate within a dichotomy of religion and the world. As the linguistic matrix of this culture, Yiddish reflects the Jewishness of its speakers in all aspects of their lives. This overarching character of Yiddish broadens the original meaning of Hebrew words of either biblical or mishnaic origin.

The Yiddish word *mizveh* (in Hebrew, *mizvah*) is a case in point. Whereas the Hebrew usage of the word primarily refers to the specific divine commandments and the procedures of their fulfillment, the Yiddish usage denotes a good deed. *Mizveh,* therefore, not only means the specific religious commands delineated in the Bible (and its commentaries), whose total number is 613 and whose authority is ultimately derived from the revealed word of God, but also encompasses moral deeds not explicitly enjoined by the religious teachings of Jewish tradition.

To ask someone to do a *mizveh* for another means that social interactions are equal in value to purely ritual actions that take place between man and his creator. This interpersonal dimension of Jewish life, reflected more vibrantly in Yiddish than in Hebrew, serves as a conduit for the divine into the mundane.

The Yiddish Hebraism *mizveh* also denotes a sense of community solidarity. By coming to the aid of his fellow Jew, the Jew imitates God's concern for the world. By using *mizveh* rather than *tovyeh* (another Yiddish Hebraism, derived from *tovah,* literally, good), which alludes to a more conventional type of favor, an individual Jew provides his prospective benefactor with the opportunity to exercise his innate spiritual generosity. This type of entreaty thus overcomes differences of class and status in the community and encourages social responsibility.

The expression *a mizveh oyf im* (literally, a *mizveh* upon him) can be utilized in both positive and negative ways. In its positive connotation the term expresses praise for a special good deed, or is a supplication for future opportunities for someone to perform additional *mizvehs* in the future. Negatively the term can be employed euphemistically to reflect a desire for ill to befall the recipient of the malediction. For example, "a pure and pristine atonement" is used as we would say, "Good riddance." This use of euphemism is a moderating factor in one of the most colorful of folk elements in Yiddish, the curse.

Mizveh is used not only in the context of interpersonal relations; one may urge someone to do a *mizveh* for himself. This intrapersonal, or intrapsychic, dimension also broadens the original Hebrew sense of *mizvah*. The fulfillment of the Hebrew commandment must be externally visible. It cannot be fulfilled through meditation or changes in consciousness (except in the case of the *mizvah* of *teshuvah* [repentance], although even here external actions would be necessary to corroborate internal achievements). The Yiddish use of *mizveh* on an intrapersonal level would accept the notion that psychic well-being is in and of itself an act of piety.

REFERENCES

1. Max Weinreich, *The History of the Yiddish Language,* J. Fishman, tr. (1980), 648.

Modern Jewish Philosophy

פילוסופיה יהודית בעת החדשה

Steven S. Schwarzschild

The very notion of Jewish philosophy (even leaving aside the notion of modernity) has been much debated. Isaac Husik, the standard historian of medieval Jewish philosophy, held that starting with the Renaissance there could no more be Jewish (or any other religionist) philosophy than there could be such a thing as Canadian mathematics. Julius Guttmann, the standard historian of the full sweep of Jewish philosophical history, in a way went Husik one better, although to different effect, by esteeming modern "philosophy of Judaism" quite as highly as its medieval predecessor, on the ground that the latter depended on Plato, Aristotle, the Kalam, and Al-Farabi no less than do the moderns on Hume, Kant, and Hegel. The view held here, on the other hand, is that philosophy is Jewish by virtue of a transhistorical primacy of ethics; non-Jewish thought will, of course, sometimes also arrive at such an ethical primacy by rational means to one degree or another, and Jewish philosophy, like Judaism at large, will then gratefully use or bend to its purpose its non-Jewish infusions.

Philosophy that is both Jewish and modern is by general consent dated as having begun with the eighteenth-century German Jew Moses Mendelssohn. The character of the birth of modern Jewish philosophy presages a number of important features of its life history. In the first place, modern Jewish philosophy remained, as it began, in bulk a German-Jewish enterprise until Nazism put an end to German Jewry as well as to German-Jewish philosophizing. During its career it increasingly branched out beyond German Jewry, and it received significant input from elsewhere. At the present time, it is carried on very much in the places where Jewish life is concentrated and under the impact of those cultures—first and foremost the United States and Israel, and then France, Britain, and elsewhere. Mendelssohn is, in the second place, rightly regarded as symbolically the first "modern" Jew—that is, thoroughly Jewish while reasonably integrated with modern European society and culture—but this is true in a historical, not in a philosophical, sense. Philosophically, he could really more accurately be described as the last Enlightenment rationalist and *Popularphilosoph* (ideologist). Well before Mendelssohn's death, Immanuel Kant had revolutionized the philosophical world, and, though always respectful of Mendelssohn both personally and intellectually, he thus also and in so many words made Mendelssohn's thought a matter of finished history. While the Jewish community leaders in the subsequent period continued to flock to Mendelssohn's banner, Jewish thinkers such as Marcus Herz, Solomon Maimon, and Lazarus Bendavid clustered around Kant and around his philosophical legacy.

The conventional histories of modern philosophy describe fairly enough how German absolute idealism and especially Hegel and Hegelianism used (or misused) especially Kant's *Critique of Judgment,* mostly in order to close the gap that, as they saw and still see it, Kant had opened up between experienced reality and theoretical, to them "metaphysical," truth—the latter heading encompassing matters that are usually regarded as the substance of religious philosophy, including Judaism. Somewhat simplistically one can say that the nineteenth and twentieth centuries attempted philosophically to close the gap between noumenon and phenomenon, rationality and actuality, God and the world, in one of two fashions (which sometimes come to the same thing): either reality was made to disappear into ideality, as in the thought of Hegel, or ideality was made to collapse into actuality, as in Marxism and positivism.

As soon as one sees things in this light it becomes clear that Jewish philosophers and thinkers were likely to want to stipulate some significant reservations about the thesis that the actual is the rational or that there is naught but the actual, for at least two reasons—one historical, the other conceptual: historically, Jews continued to live in a real world that they could scarcely regard from their perspective, at least, as ideal; and conceptually, the absolute transcendence of God and everything he is taken to stand for is firmly embedded in the very foundations of historic Jewish culture. As a consequence, the Jewish Hegelian or quasi-Hegelian thinkers of the first half of the nineteenth century all held, in one way or another, that Judaism differed from Christianity (and paganism) in that it preserved the discreteness of God from nature and, what amounts to the same thing, of the power of reason and moral freedom in the world. This was the principal effect of Solomon Formstecher's religious philosophy and of that of even the most Hegelian of these thinkers, Samuel Hirsch. Solomon Ludwig Steinheim performed a Jewish operation on Hegel in some ways similar to Kierkegaard's Christian operation by identifying reason with necessity and science while attributing truth to revelation, freedom, and "miracles." The Italian Jewish thinker Samuel D. Luzzatto, like his similarly minded German contemporary Samson Raphael Hirsch (both spokesmen for a sort of modern traditionalism), though rejecting Maimonidean rationalism in favor of Judah Halevi's quasi-neo-Platonism, nonetheless insisted, as Mendelssohn had done at the dawn of the Age of Emancipation, on the "liberal" virtues of moral citizenship as derived from "the reasons for the commandments" (taamei ha-mizvot). Nachman Krochmal, writing in Hebrew and in Russian Poland, tried to elevate Israel above the contingencies of history by subordinating it to the perpetuity of God alone (more or less what Hegel had significantly called Absolute Spirit and what Rosenzweig was to reformulate in the next century).

Historians have noticed that as the nineteenth century grew older the emancipationist thrust of German philosophy grew weaker and had virtually died by the middle of the century. It was, interestingly, usually Jews who, in philosophy as in politics, in the second half of the century sounded, in Otto Liebmann's famous phrase, the call to return to Kant. By general consent it is the greatest of the Jewish philosophers of the closing of the nineteenth and opening of the twentieth centuries, Hermann Cohen, who carried out the program of philosophically and in Jewish terms restoring the "infinite" gap between ideality and reality and of explicating in technical detail what the actionable consequences of that gap are for science, ethics, aesthetics, religion, and social policy. His disciples were typically Jews— Germans like Ernst Cassirer, eastern Europeans like Samuel Atlas, and, in a more complicated way, the contemporary Rabbi Joseph B. Soloveitchik— so that other schools of neo-Kantianism, which typically sought some sort

of compromise between Kantianism and Hegelianism, spoke of "the Marburg School" of Hermann Cohen as a Jewish distortion. For Cohen, Judaism was "religion of reason" par excellence, and the task of the Jewish
people was to carry its "ethical monotheism" to the ends of the earth.

By the time of World War I, a number of concrete problems of a general
philosophical character and of specifically Jewish importance took hold.
They all tend to revolve about the complaint that Cohen's, and rationalist,
"critical" thought in general, was too abstract, that is, that the gap between
reason and reality swallowed up received values of history, peoplehood, and
individuality. Here the philosopher other than Mendelssohn who, by means
of a different periodization, may be regarded as the beginning of Jewish
modernity, the seventeenth-century ex-Jew Spinoza, could be invoked, as
he had been invoked in the transition from Kant to Hegel: neither Hegel
himself nor the early Jewish Marxists such as Moses Hess made a secret of
their admiration for Spinoza, because the motto *deus sive natura* entailed
the thesis that truth is to be discerned in, not beyond, reality. Ex-Jews like
Henri Bergson, with his espousal of vitalism, and Edmund Husserl, with his
rallying cry of "Back to the things themselves!," exemplify this trend in
general philosophy. More specifically Jewish, Martin Buber's early Nietz-
scheanism asserted the decisive realities of mystical experience and of
"folkish" culture, and even in his later, "dialogic" thought, "actual man"
and "actual experience of God" are superordinated to what Cohen had
called pure cognition. Franz Rosenzweig started out under the impact of
his German, Hegelian teachers, became a favorite, though always
intellectually differentiated, disciple of Cohen's, and then became Buber's
closest associate. His magnum opus, *The Star of Redemption,* a thoroughly
neo-Hegelian enterprise, proclaims a "new thinking" of the "realities" of
man, God, and the world, and in his last essay he awards the prize to Martin
Heidegger over a "scholastic" Cohen essentially because Heidegger himself
had rebelled against (among other things) theoretical reason.

Cohen has remained a significant, though usually unacknowledged, philosophical influence for the rest of the century. This is clearly illustrated by
the role he plays in the work of such different thinkers as Cassirer and Rabbi
Soloveitchik and, among non-Jews, in present-day German "transcendental
philosophy" and, in the United States, in the thought of Cassirer's student
Suzanne Langer. Usually, however, it is a radically reinterpreted Cohen
(inspired by Rosenzweig's existential reading of him) who is alleged to have
broken out of critical idealism in his posthumously published philosophy of
Judaism. Emmanuel Levinas, at present perhaps the most creative specifically Jewish philosopher, affirms that Buber and Rosenzweig helped him

extricate himself from the Greek, ontologistic thicket of Husserl and Heidegger ("à partir de Husserl et Heidegger"). In pre-state Israel and later, Yehezkel Kaufmann and even Jakob Klatzkin, not to speak of Julius Guttmann and other philosophers like Samuel Hugo Bergmann, tried to combine a notion of Jewish "folkish" genius with ethical monotheism as formulated in the nineteenth century. Rabbi Abraham Isaac Kook's kabbalistic panentheism and A. D. Gordon's secular quasi-pantheism arrive at a similar conclusion, though obviously from different philosophical premises.

In the United States the philosophical foundations of even Mordecai Kaplan's Reconstructionism can be seen in at least two ways to be remote and divergent derivatives of the German-Jewish philosophical tradition: Kaplan devoted an entire book to an interpretation of and an argument against Cohen's *Religion of Reason,* and his philosophical teacher, John Dewey, came into American pragmatism from German idealism (as Charles S. Peirce and William James had done). Kaplan, though, makes the historical and social reality of the Jewish people, rather than "reason," constitutive of Jewish religious civilization.

Among the devout there is the temptation to assert an at least equal, if not superior, realm of the numinous beyond the realm of ethics. Thinkers like Judah Halevi in the past and Rabbi Soloveitchik in our time, with his conception of a "higher will," as well as Leo Baeck, with his duality of "mystery and commandment," illustrate such a natural religious pull. When this pull is powerfully exerted, thinking tends to abandon what can still be called philosophy and becomes theology or even mysticism. The degrees of identification of "the holy" with "the good," all the way from the biblical prophets down to modernist Judaism and contemporary philosophy (compare, for example, Abraham J. Heschel), may then be seen, in our perspective, as the measure of the power of the ultimate and dominant Jewish claim in its many different expressions.

If this reading of modern Jewish philosophy in terms of the struggle between Kantianism and Hegelianism (widely acknowledged in Continental philosophy as a fundamental structure) is accepted, the question arises whether, as would then seem to be the case, Jewish philosophy is only an accommodation to non-Jewish philosophical truth—a tail, so to speak, on the kite of secular philosophy. As we have seen, in itself this would, even if true, not necessarily be an objection; the entirety of Jewish philosophy has been, in a way, a Jewish variant of philosophy at large. Philosophically, furthermore, if reason be truth, and Judaism true, then all rational beings must be capable of the Jewish truth (cf. the halakhic concept of the Noachites). Still, historically, it should always be noted that in modern as in classical

Jewish philosophy the dualism of God and creation, freedom and nature, always tends to reassert itself in Jewish philosophy, in contrast to the Greek assertion of the primacy of metaphysics over ethics.

At the outset of modernity Mendelssohn discerned Jewish particularity in the law, itself an expression of essentially rational morality. We have seen how even the Jewish Hegelians of the nineteenth century and certainly Cohen and his disciples proclaimed Kant's "primacy of practical reason." The traditionalist Jewish thinkers like Rabbi Kook and Rabbi Soloveitchik must, of course, always uphold the centrality of halakhah. Buber's and Heschel's thought emphasize the ethical and social demands made by the reality of the human-divine encounter. And at the present time all of Levinas' work centers on the ultimacy of the ethical God "beyond essence." (The Hegelians Krochmal and Rosenzweig, in contrast, address themselves perhaps least to ethics.) The claim may thus be made that Jewish philosophy is not finally the tail on the kite but the string that leads it.

BIBLIOGRAPHY

Jacob B. Agus, *Modern Philosophies of Judaism* (1941).
Julius Guttmann, *Philosophies of Judaism* (1964).
Nathan Rotenstreich, *Jewish Philosophy in Modern Times* (1968).
Steven S. Schwarzschild, "An Agenda for Jewish Philosophy in the 1980's," in N. Samuelson, ed., *Studies in Jewish Philosophy I: Jewish Philosophy in the 1980's* (1981).

Music

מוסיקה

Moshe Idel

A Jewish theological conception of music truly crystallized only during the Middle Ages. In this period the arts were construed as intended to serve religious objectives, so it is not surprising that the finest artistic expressions of the epoch were essentially religious. This is particularly true with respect to music, to which medieval thinkers, whether Jewish, Christian, or Muslim, assigned various extra-aesthetic religious purposes. These purposes may be divided into several categories, of which we will mention but three: educational, therapeutic, and ecstatic.

Musical instruction became part of the general educational curriculum, and, along with physics, astronomy, and mathematics, was seen as a subject of study necessary for an understanding of the natural world. This curriculum was consonant with the view then current in philosophy that the study of natural phenomena was essential for obtaining an understanding of the Divinity. Thus, music was viewed more as a subject for investigation than as a medium of aesthetic expression and appreciation. In addition, various ancient traditions perceived music as containing unique therapeutic properties; accordingly, music was often employed in the treatment of the sick.

Here, of course, we are talking of musical performance, not the intellectual investigation of music. Yet here too the aesthetic element merely served the extra-aesthetic objective of restoring the ill to health and to God's grace. A clear expression of this sentiment may be found in the writings of philosophically oriented musical composers of the period.

The educational and therapeutic conceptions of music received much attention in medieval philosophical theology, which tended to emphasize the importance of intellectual perfection and spiritual integrity over and above the concrete expression of religious values in positive actions, or what in the Jewish context is called the performance of *miẓvot* or commandments.

In the medieval period music was also assigned a unique role in inducing mystical ecstasy. This theme had a particularly significant impact on the Jewish religious imagination. Already, in the early period of Jewish mystical literature (the first to the eighth centuries C.E.), namely in the writings of the *Heikhalot* or *Merkavah*, music was an essential part of the technical nomenclature of mysticism. Its purpose was the elevation of the soul, which ascended by virtue of music and incantation to the *Merkavah*, the realm of the divine chariot or throne. It was also incumbent upon one who beholds the *Merkavah* to sing particular hymns, and by means of song travel from one heavenly chamber to another until reaching the throne of glory.

In the thirteenth century, hundreds of years after the *Merkavah* literature had ceased to be the principal fulcrum of Jewish mystical theology, we find music returning as one of the central mystical techniques of the "prophetic kabbalah" of Abraham Abulafia. For him and many of his followers as well, music was an integral feature of the mystical technique devised to attain prophetic inspiration. This genre of kabbalah—whose paramount objective was the attainment of ecstasy or even the mystical union of the soul with the Divinity—created a distinctive musical form out of the vocalized permutations of the letters of the holy names found in the Hebrew Scriptures. Specifically, the music thus created sounded the vowels at different tones based on the visual cues of the vowel marks. Hence the vowel *ḥolam* (the "oh" sound) is intoned at the highest pitch, for it is placed above the letter, whereas the vowel *ḥerik* (a long "e"), which appears as a single diacritical point below the letter, receives a lower note. This mode of chanting, which is melodically very simple, embraced by virtue of various "mathematically" arranged permutations virtually all the letters and vowels of the Hebrew alphabet. It is clear that Abulafia and his disciples were primarily interested in developing this form of liturgical chanting as a technique to help focus the individual's consciousness on his primary goal, the attainment of ecstasy. Accordingly, the aesthetic dimension of music was subordinated to this overarching goal.

The use of music in the prophetic kabbalah clearly parallels in form similar practices found in Islamic Sufi mysticism as well as in Indian mysticism. It is, indeed, reasonable to assume that the Sufis influenced at least the later versions of Abulafia's mystical techniques, which like those of the Sufis incorporated instrumental music.

Abulafia's conception of music as an essential component of mystical technique found an echo among the kabbalists of sixteenth-century Safed, and perhaps also within the Ḥasidic use of music as an aid to the attainment of ecstasy. Whereas the theological concerns of Abulafia centered upon the methods of attaining the "prophetic state," that is, an altered state of consciousness with the use of music employed to this end, the main purpose of the most influential school of kabbalah, the theosophical kabbalah associated with the *Zohar*, was to effect a harmony among the divine attributes or forces—the *sefirot* (lit., spheres)—which through the sin of Adam were made unbalanced. Theosophical kabbalah, which endeavors to explain on the basis of the fate of the *sefirot* the entirety of the Jewish experience, viewed the performance of *mizvot* as an essential component in the work of bringing about divine harmony. Within this context, music was seen as serving the purpose of renewing the bond between the attributes or *sefirot* of *tiferet* (beauty, a masculine function) and *malkhut* (kingdom, a feminine function), or between the attributes *hokhmah* (wisdom, masculine) and *binah* (understanding, feminine). This theurgic dimension of music did not receive a great deal of attention, however, in the early writings of the theosophical kabbalah, nor did it enter into the ritual practice of the time.

It is only with the beginning of the latter half of the fifteenth century that we find an increasing number of writings that testify to the assumed theurgic power of music, particularly as a concomitant to ritual and prayer. The unique power of music was celebrated by the most important luminaries of the Palestinian kabbalistic center in Safed: Shlomo Alkabetz, author of the popular Sabbath hymn *"Lekha Dodi,"* Moses Cordovero, and Isaac Luria, known as the Ari, who composed special hymns for the Sabbath meals. One may assume that the many liturgical hymns that originated in this circle of kabbalists were composed in respect of the purported theurgic power of music.

It may be asked: What is the significance of the fact that music attained such mystical meaning precisely during the period of the Renaissance? Why did the fifteenth-century kabbalists give such credence to the theurgic power of music, even to the extent of incorporating music so conceived as a central component of normative Jewish ritual practice? A partial answer lies in the humanistic culture and sensibility that emerged during that period. We find among both Jewish and Christian writers of the time an elevation of the nonintellectual human faculties in general and the aesthetic in particular. It is possible that some of the Jewish mystical thinkers of the Renaissance period derived their esteem for music and its mystical properties from Christian thinkers of Florence.

In the writings of many kabbalists at the end of the thirteenth century, still another theological quality of music was given emphasis: Music is said to protect against the negative influences of the *sefirah* of *gevurah,* or stern judgment, by "sweetening" its unbridled and hence baleful impact. (The kabbalah regarded the independent activity of the *sefira* of stern judgment—unmodified by the quality of *hesed* or mercy—as the ultimate source of evil.) This view of music is associated with the growing importance that the question of evil attained in the kabbalistic thought of the period. This conception, in turn, brought immediately in its wake the appreciation of music as a magical prophylactic in general. Here we must distinguish two complementary conceptions of music. On the one hand, the thirteenth century renewed interest in the song of the Levites from the period of the temple cult—a long-dormant practice—as a "sweetener" of the power of "stern judgment," and, on the other hand, it advanced the view that music and song may be employed to neutralize the power of evil. The characterization of the music of the first type found expression in the words of an anonymous thirteenth-century kabbalist who wrote:

> And I behold David the son of Jesse, the Bethlehemite, who performs music in the presence of *gevurah,* that is, the All Powerful, the attribute of judgment. Indeed, hymn and song correspond to the *sefirah* of judgment—and genuine awe duly emanates therefrom. And thus the musical inventiveness of the Levite singers, derived from this ever-emanating awe, was for the sake of mollifying the anger of the oppressive *sefirah* of stern judgment. For this is David called "The pleasant singer of Israel, the powerful hero [*gibbor*]" [2 Sam. 23].
>
> (Paris Ms. [BN], 859, fol. 21b)

In the kabbalah the Levites symbolize the *sefirah* of judgment, or power (*gevurah*), which is found on the left side of the ten-branched sefirotic tree. The Levites' song is directed to the lessening of the influence of this *sefirah.* This relationship between music and *gevurah* is embodied in the person of King David, who according to the anonymous kabbalist just cited exemplifies the functions of the singer and the hero (*gibbor*).

A similar concept of the Levitic song is also to be found in one of the writings of Moses de Leon, the redactor of the *Zohar*. Because the *Zohar* became the single most influential work in the dissemination of kabbalistic ideas, this passage deserves to be cited extensively:

> If one would come close to a fire he would be burnt by its powerful heat. So, too, one should avoid the "left side" [of the godhead], the power of fire, and accordingly bring oneself closer to the "right side." Therefore, did King David say "because He is at my right hand I shall not be moved" (Ps. 16:8). The secret of this is the relation between the mundane attribute of judgment [*Din*] and the supernal attribute of judgment. . . . The feminine principle derives from the "left side" [of the godhead]. There she stands in judgment, with an ever-rising voice. Due to her generation from fire, the feminine principle rises to the extent that even her laughter is louder than masculine laughter. Thus, also the Levites: being characteristically oriented toward the "left side," they were appointed to the pulpit of the Holy Temple to sing and raise their voices in song. Deriving from the "left side," the Levites partake in the nature of fire. On the other hand, the *kohanim* (the priests), their qualities associated with the "right side," are unqualified to fulfill the Levitical functions, because the quality of the service required and their own attributes are incompatible. Thus it is the Levites who are appointed to all matters pertaining to judgment, although they are far removed from the priestly domain. Now we must understand that the secret of the quality of the Levite song was its ability to improve and gladden, to soften their own attribute in order to bind the "left" to the "right" through the pleasantness of song's sublime harmonization, and thereby to perform their service. Thus, with respect to all manner of song, it relieves despondency, cools anger and brings joy as a result of the bonding of the attribute of the "right side" to all else. For in the joy of this unification, the sorrowful influence of stern judgment [as an autonomous factor] is removed from the world. Therefore, the Levites, through the pleasant sweetness of their song and the coordination of its goodly influence . . . bring about a unification of stern judgment with the power of mercy so that all would be unified in equanimity.
>
> Thus precisely because this manner of song is ordained from on high, a Levite whose voice is too low, unseemly, or weak is disqualified from the Temple service. So, too, when a Levite reaches the age of fifty he is removed from his service because the quality of his voice at this age becomes flawed and he is no longer equal to his Levite companions. This is necessitated by [the function] of the Levites to emanate the effluence of gladness and joy upon the *sefirah* of stern judgment—the source of despondency and anger—thereby bringing it into harmony with the other *sefirot*. And certainly this is all for exalted purpose, for nothing is beyond the efficaciousness of the secret, purposeful wisdom.
>
> (Moses de Leon, "Munich Manuscript," 43:342b–43a)

Two motifs concern us here. First, the Levites, through their song, influence the divine realm, as was also strongly emphasized by the kabbalists in the generation of the Spanish Expulsion. However, we must bear in mind now that there is a fundamental difference between the theurgic use of music that became prevalent after the Expulsion and the conceptions of Moses de Leon and the *Zohar*. The Zoharic conception of Levitic song focuses primarily on the effect that this music has on "sweetening" the stern judgments that concern our world directly. In contrast, the theurgic explanation of music given by the generation of the Expulsion from Spain focuses on the effect that music has on the divine realm. The restoration of divine harmony was their main concern: The earthly effects of this were incidental results, not the central matter.

Second, in the writings of Moses de Leon and in the *Zohar,* emphasis is placed on the "lifting of the voice in pleasantness," by virtue not of its aesthetic function but of its magical function. The focus of attention of the Levitic song is not the human audience but the attribute of stern judgment. Therefore, when the power of the singer's voice is weakened by age he is disqualified, regardless of whether or not his voice remains melodious. Here again, we witness the imposition of theological categories on music, even at the possible expense of aesthetic considerations.

By the medieval period, the temple songs of the Levites had long ceased, and their melodies were no longer known. Yet there were kabbalists who attributed to the daily prayers a function similar to that of Levitic song with regard to their potency to neutralize demonic influences. This conception crystallized at the end of the thirteenth century. It appears that the first kabbalist who gave voice to it was Joseph Gikatilla, who in his book *Sha'arei Orah* (Gates of Light) writes that the musical cantillation of the Psalms in the daily prayers blazes a trail for the prayers to ascend heavenward, since by the power of the song the adversaries who prevent the upward flow of prayer are gathered up, and bad influence is "cut asunder" (*zemer*).

The etymological motif employed by Gikatilla, who plays on the Hebrew word *zemer,* which means "song" as well as "cut asunder," became part of the permanent heritage of the kabbalah and provided a new understanding for the use of the Psalms in the daily prayers. This understanding came to replace the earlier conception of the sweetening of the judgments resulting from the Levite song, which, up to that point, did not find an echo in the practice of the daily prayer.

In conclusion we may cite yet another text, in which the previously discussed kabbalistic conceptions of music are fused in a novel interpretation of the traditional burial rite. Yizḥak Ya'akov Alfiye, a mystical sage who was among the last generation of Jews living in the old city of Jerusalem before its capture by the Jordanians in 1948, writes in *Kuntres ha-Yechiel* (1938; fol. 62a–b):

> When the bier is being taken to the grave there are those who are enjoined to chant the Song of Songs with its musical cantillations in a tranquil and suitable mode. There are places where the singers are also enjoined to sing Ecclesiastes with the necessary cantillations. The singers do not rush through the scriptural passages, rather they chant them with the appropriate tranquility. There are also those who are appointed to sing praises and hymns to the Lord, and there are those who accompany the procession on musical instruments throughout the journey to the grave. And there may be poets and cantors who chant and sing in a pleasant manner.
>
> The reason for chanting the Song of Songs is due to its being the most sublime of all songs, for in the Scripture it represents the Holiest of the Holy. It arouses the love of lovers, the conjoining of the Congregation of Israel in the Divine Presence, making the Presence manifest. For there is no better way to intoxicate the impure powers [the *kelipot*] than through poetry and song, which removes the spirit of worry and the evil spirit in man, facilitating the indwelling of the influences of gladness and joy so that the Divine Spirit may sound its rhythm within man. . . . Thus the Song of Songs is chanted before the deceased throughout his journey to the grave, in order to cast away from him the prosecutors and the spirits that lead astray. . . . And like a groom that goes out to meet his bride so is the soul glad and filled with great joy. For just as the heart of the groom is vibrating with the anticipation of the added dimensions of the joy of his new station, so, too, in the humbleness of our opinion, is the soul of the righteous man gladdened by the illumination of the Divine Indwelling Presence that appears to the soul at the moment of death, and by the many angels who go out to greet the soul that departs life a groom meeting his bride when the many exalted and sublime dimensions of the supernal worlds come into his domain.
>
> To this end is the longing aroused; and the love and conjugation within the Gracious God whose Name is Blessed are accompanied by the Holy of Holies, who is aroused from below through the chanting of the Song of Songs, in order to emanate upon the soul tranquility in the higher worlds.

This passage represents a summation of the various kabbalistic conceptions of music, which cumulatively constitute the most sustained Jewish theology on the subject. For the kabbalists, as we have noted, the purpose of music clearly transcended any aesthetic consideration. Theological and theosophical concerns that are brought to bear in these writings on music virtually never relate to any specifically musical or aesthetic matters. This perspective holds true for all the art forms pertaining to the Jewish experience; aesthetics per se was of no relevance to Jewish theology. Hence, the music that developed under the inspiration of Jewish theological and mystical reflections did not particularly stress the aesthetic element, either in the form of ritual guidelines or in actual practice.

BIBLIOGRAPHY

Israel Adler, *Hebrew Writings Concerning Music in Manuscripts and Printed Books from Gaonic Times up to 1800* (1975).
Karl E. Grözinger, *Musik und Geseng in der Theologie der frühen jüdischen Literaturs* (1982).
Moshe Idel, "Ha-Perush ha-Magi ve-ha-Teurgi shel ha-Musikah ba-Tekstim Yehudiim me-Tekufat ha-Renasans ve-ad ha-Ḥasidut," in *Yuval* 4 (1982).
Moshe Idel, "Musikah ve-ha-kabbalah ha-Nevuit," in *Yuval* 4 (1982).

Mysticism

תורת־הסוד

Moshe Idel

Insight into the spiritual universe of the millennial Jewish mystical tradition may be obtained by a phenomenological explication of two fundamental yet contrasting attitudes found throughout the course of its development, which can be called the moderate and the intensive modes of mystical concern or experience. The difference between these attitudes has been manifest since the very beginnings of Jewish mysticism in the second century C.E. Moreover, each of these modes of mystical expression tended to flourish separately in its own distinctive milieu, although occasionally the two did link up with one another, as, for instance, in the late medieval and early modern periods.

The moderate mode of mystical experience can be described as theosophical speculations that guide the mystic to a position of influencing and contemplating the divine harmony. In contrast, the principal concern of the intensive mode of mystical experience has been the study of particular techniques conducive to the attainment of mystical experience. The significant difference between these two modes notwithstanding, the development of

Jewish mysticism has been characterized by an inner relationship between them.

The moderate mode of Jewish mystical experience may be illustrated through several citations from the classical rabbinic writings that point to a unique type of mysticism whose objective is attained by the study of Torah. Many of the most significant expressions of this type of mysticism focus on the person of Rabbi Akiva.

> Rabbi Tarfon says, "Akiva, concerning you the scriptures say [Job 28:7], 'From the issuing of tears he bound together streams and brought to light that which was hidden.'" Things that were previously hidden from the sight of man were brought to light by Rabbi Akiva.
>
> (ARN[1], ch. 6)

From the context of this quote we cannot infer the nature of those things "hidden from the sight of man." Some commentators interpret this expression as referring to the revelation of various points of law that were unknown before their explication by Rabbi Akiva.

There exists a passage parallel to the one quoted above, however, that allows another interpretation:

> "Who turned the rock into a pool of water" [Ps. 114:8]. This refers to Rabbi Akiva and Ben Azzai, who in the beginning of their careers were unproductive like rocky soil, and for whom, due to their toil and asceticism for the sake of the study of Torah the Holy One, Blessed be He, opened [new] paths into the Torah, so that the words of the Study Houses of Hillel and Shammai were not able to stand up to the words of those two. . . . And as for those Torah passages whose meanings were previously hidden to the world, Rabbi Akiva came and explicated them, so it is written [Job 28:7]. "From the issuing of tears he bound together streams and brought to light that which was hidden." This verse alludes to the fact that the eyes of Rabbi Akiva beheld the merkavah [divine chariot], in the manner in which it was beheld by the Prophet Ezekiel. Thus, one verse states [Ps. 114:8], "Who turned the rock into a pool of water."
>
> (Midrash Hallel, in I. O. Eisenstein, Ozar ha-Midrashim, 131)

In this midrashic passage we are thus told that, due to his austerity and painstakingness, that is, his sincere weeping and fasting, Rabbi Akiva merited not only the discovery of laws that were unknown to Hillel and Shammai, but also that he gazed at the merkavah and beheld it in the same manner as did the Prophet Ezekiel.

The question may be asked, What is the implication of the relationship between these two images—the transformation of a rock into a pool of water and the vision of the *merkavah?* The answer may be found in yet a third rabbinic text:

> Said Rabbi Meir: "Anyone who sincerely studies the Torah for its own sake merits many things. Not only this, but we may say the entire world is found deserving due to him! He is called 'beloved.' He loves the Divine Presence and loves all of creation . . . and to him is revealed the mysteries of the Torah. He is transformed into a spring that never runs dry and into a river whose course rushes with increasing power."
>
> (M. Avot 6:1)

This passage reveals that the study of Torah for its own sake is a means through which one acquires the knowledge of the mysteries of the Torah, by which one is transformed into an everlasting "spring" and a mighty "river." Here again we find the images used above to characterize Rabbi Akiva. Rabbi Meir, the source of the passage cited above, was a younger contemporary and student of Rabbi Akiva. We may therefore assume that he is uttering a characterization of his teacher or, at the very least, expressing a sentiment in the spirit of Rabbi Akiva, to wit, that the study of Torah is the proper means by which one may attain to the appreciation of the mysteries of the Torah.

There is, then, a clear parallel between the passage from the *Midrash Hallel,* where we read that Rabbi Akiva beheld the *merkavah,* and the words of Rabbi Meir regarding the revelation of the "mysteries of the Torah," for, as is stated in the Talmud, "the workings of the *merkavah* are the secrets of the Torah" (BT Hag. 11b–12a).

We thus have a tradition, associated with the person and manner of study of Rabbi Akiva, that teaches that through the dedicated study of Scripture and God's law one reveals the secrets of Torah and attains the vision of the *merkavah.* But how is this experience actually attained? The answer is essentially as follows: There exists a primordial Torah, "engraved upon the limbs of the Holy One, Blessed be He," which is the archetype of the Torah as it is revealed in this world. Through the dedicated study of Torah as it is revealed in this world, one reaches the level of the primordial Torah. The Torah's laws and the stories of the nation's ancestors are transformed into supernal secrets as a result of a mental concentration inducing ecstatic vision by virtue of which the text containing the laws and legends attains the metaphysical stature of the primordial text. In consequence, the literal statements of the law and the tales are accorded metaphysical interpretations.

Accordingly, we read in the *Midrash Tehillim* (105) that Rabbi Yose ben Halafta told his son, Rabbi Ishmael: "[So] you are seeking a vision of the Divine Presence in this world? Study Torah in the Land of Israel, for it is written 'Seek the Lord and His strength, entreat His countenance continually' [Ps. 105:4]." The study of Torah, in other words, is the means by which one beholds the divine Presence in this world. Rabbi Yose ben Halafta, incidentally, is counted among the principal disciples of Rabbi Akiva. Another well-known disciple of Rabbi Akiva, Rabbi Simeon Bar Yohai, is quoted as saying:

> There is no witness except Torah. This may be likened to a king who had a daughter. He built a palace for her and installed her dwelling within seven antechambers. He then let it be known that "anyone who enters for a visit with my daughter should regard himself as having come for a visit with me."
>
> (Midrash Tanh., Pekudei)

Here contemplation of the Torah is likened to the contemplation of the Divinity. In addition, there is here another motif, namely, that the Torah—like the Divinity himself in the *Heikhalot* (a fifth-century body of literature describing the techniques and visions of the adept's mystical ascent to the heavenly chambers)—is to be found in the innermost chamber of the "palace," surrounded by seven antechambers. The appearance of the *Heikhalot* motif in the above passage is noteworthy, for it indicates a clear relationship between the "Torah study" or moderate mysticism of Rabbi Akiva and his disciples and the intensive mysticism of the *Heikhalot,* of which, as we shall see, Rabbi Akiva is also a chief exponent.

The type of mystical revelation that occurs as a result of the study of the Torah is also discussed in the *Midrash Eliyahu Zuta* (ch. 1), as follows:

> After a person has studied the Torah, Prophets and Scriptures, and read the Midrash, Mishnah, Aggadah and Talmud, and engaged diligently in the subtle analysis of the Law, immediately the Holy Spirit descends upon him; for it is written "The Spirit of the Lord spoke within me, and His word was on my tongue."
>
> (II Sam. 23:2)

According to this passage, then, the appearance of the Holy Spirit is a consequence of diligent analysis of the law. The Hebrew word *lishmah*—diligent study for its own sake—echoes the words of Rabbi Meir quoted in connection with the revelation of the mysteries of the Torah. We may therefore assume that the passage quoted from the *Eliyahu Zuta* derives from the school of Rabbi Akiva.

However, by far the most interesting passage indicating the relation between the study of the Torah and the attainment of mystical experience is found in words attributed to Rabbi Ishmael, a contemporary and colleague of Rabbi Akiva. This passage from the *Midrash Mishle* (ch. 10) merits close analysis:

> Said Rabbi Ishmael: "Come and see how awesome will be the Day of Judgment, when in the future the Holy One, Blessed be He, will judge the entire world in the Valley of Jehoshaphat. When a scholar appears before Him, He will ask 'Did you toil in the study of Torah?' The scholar will answer 'yes.' The Holy One, Blessed be He, will continue: 'Since you say that you studied, tell Me something of what you learned and reviewed.' From this exchange the sages have issued a warning that everything that a person studies should be secure in his hands, and that which a person reviewed should be secure in his possession, so that he would not come to shame and disgrace on the Day of Judgment."

It is clear from this passage that on the Day of Judgment scholars are expected to undergo an examination on what they studied. The crucial challenge posed by this examination is how well the scholar's memory retains his earthly studies. The text continues:

> If before God appears a man who is secure in his knowledge of Scripture, but who does not possess knowledge of the Mishnah, the Holy One, Blessed be He, will turn aside His face and immediately the torture of hell will overpower him like hungry wolves, and will take him and cast him into Hell.

The fate of one who is proficient in Scripture alone is unenviable—he is cast to doom. Here, undoubtedly, we find a statement influenced by the rabbinic anti-Christian polemic, for the early Christians contented themselves with the study of Scripture and ignored the rabbinic, that is, mishnaic, tradition. The passage continues:

> If one appears before Him who is secure in his knowledge of [only] two or three orders of the law, the Holy One, Blessed be He, will ask 'My son, why did not you study all of the laws?' If He says afterwards, 'Let him be,' it is good. If not, his fate is the same as the first.

Apparently Rabbi Ishmael is commenting on those of his contemporaries who decided that it is enough to study and observe only part of the law, namely, the Jewish-Christians who even after their breach with Judaism continued to observe parts of the rabbinic tradition. Their fate is the same as those of the first category. We read further in the midrash:

> If one appears before Him who has in his possession the basic corpus of the law, He asks him, "My son, why did you not study the laws pertaining to the Priesthood?" If one appears before Him who is proficient in his knowledge of all the five books of Moses, the Holy One, Blessed be He, asks him, "Why did you not study the Aggadah, for when a sage sits and expounds, I forgive and absolve the Jews of their sins. Not only then, but also when one answers [in the congregational response of the kaddish], 'Amen, may the Great name be blessed forever . . . ' even if one's fate has already been signed and sealed I forgive him and absolve him of his sins." If one comes possessing knowledge of Aggadah, the Holy One, Blessed be He, tells him, "My son, why did you not study Talmud, for it is written [Eccles. 1:7], 'All of the rivers flow into the sea yet the sea is not full'; this refers to the study of the Talmud."

Hitherto it is clear that, according to the midrash, God examines the scholars to determine the extent of their study of the traditional Jewish literature: Scripture, Mishnah, Aggadah, and Talmud. We find here an itemized hierarchical list of works, with the Talmud occupying the highest level. But the passage now takes an interesting turn:

> If one appears, who possesses proficiency in the study of Talmud, the Holy One, Blessed be He, asks him, "My son, since you did occupy yourself with the study of the Talmud, did you gaze upon the *Merkavah*? For in my world there is no real pleasure except when sages are sitting occupied with the words of Torah and gaze and look, behold and meditate upon this: The Throne of Glory, where does it stand? What is the function of the first leg, what is the function of the second leg, and *hashmal* [silent speech], how does it function . . . . Greater than these [questions] is the deep deliberation on the Throne of Glory: How is it constructed? What is the distance between one gate and the next?—And when I pass through what gate should I use? . . . Greater still: What is the measure from the nails of My toes to the top of My skull? How do I stand? What is the measure of My arm, what are the dimensions of the toes of My feet? Greater still: My Throne of Glory, how is it constructed? What [winds, spirits] does it use? What [winds, spirits] does it use on the third day of the week—or on the fourth? What [wind, spirit] carries it? Is this not what constitutes My Beauty? This is My Greatness. This is the splendor of My Beauty, when the sons of man recognize My Distinction. . . ." From here, Rabbi Ishmael used to say, "Happy is the scholar who is secure in his studies, so that he has an open mouth to answer the Holy One, Blessed be He, on the Day of Judgment."

In this passage we do not find Rabbi Ishmael mentioning another literary level of study beyond that of the Talmud. The student of the Talmud is required to attain the mystical experience not through the study of a particular body of literature (such as the *Heikhalot,* which was written after the tannaitic era), but through contemplation of the *merkavah* and the divine Majesty. What is referred to is the mystical visionary experience of the divine realm, and it is assumed that this vision is secured through assiduous study of the Talmud. Upon the student-sage rests the obligation—in the course of his study of the Talmud—to "peer" into the divine mysteries.

In this text we have a parallel to the passages quoted earlier regarding the devoted study of Torah for its own sake, which brings in its wake the secrets of the Torah, and as was the case with Rabbi Akiva, the visionary experience of the *merkavah.* These statements bespeak the transformation of the exoteric text, as a result of in-depth study, into the spiritual vision of the Divine, the experience of which enables the sage to attain to the epitome of his religious culture.

Whoever is suited to the in-depth study of the law, which brings with it the mystical vision of the *merkavah,* also merits an additional benefit: "His studies remain with him," meaning that he overcomes the blight of "forgetfulness." For it is said that when one merits through his study of Torah a vision of the *merkavah* he attains a level where his mind expands to the extent that he is no longer subject to forgetfulness.

In this connection it is written with regard to Rabbi Ishmael, who said of his teacher Rabbi Neḥunya ben ha-Kanah:

> Upon being revealed the secrets of the Torah, immediately his heart was illuminated by the Eastern Gates and [his] eyes beheld the unfathomable depths, and all of the pathways of the Torah were open to [him]. Since then, nothing was ever lost from [his] memory. . . . Said Rabbi Ishmael, upon hearing the words of my great master the entire world changed for me and became purified. My heart felt as if I had entered into a new dimension, and each day my soul likens itself within me, to when I was standing before the Throne of Glory.
>
> (*Merkavah Shelemah* 4b)

The experience of the revelation of the secrets of the Torah brings about a mystical transformation that allows the sage to be constantly aware of his proximity to the Throne of Glory. This heightened awareness is, in turn, conducive to the further revelation of the secrets of the Torah.

On the basis of this understanding we may explain the talmudic passage

"A great issue—the account of the *Merkavah;* a small issue—the discussions of Abaye and Rava" (BT Suk. 28a). For the *merkavah* mystic, the process of halakhic decision making is secondary to the understanding of the account of the *merkavah,* and this process of understanding is perhaps secondary to the actual experience of gazing at the *merkavah.*

Thus far we have considered a unique form of Torah study, which brings the student to the mystical experience in the forms of reception of the secrets of the Torah, the infusion of the holy spirit, and the vision of the divine form. These experiences are brought about by the sage's deep concentration on the important normative works of the Jewish exoteric tradition—the Talmud and Midrash. Most of the texts quoted thus far are of the classical rabbinic corpus. Further, these texts assume that the practice of this mystical form of study is incumbent upon all those who dedicate themselves to the study of the Torah and that this mode of Torah study does not involve an esoteric technique reserved for an elite few.

In contrast to this exoteric religious orientation, in the Jewish literature of the late classical rabbinic period there are works of an opposite orientation, describing intense mystical experiences of a *merkavah*-visionary nature in terms suggesting that these experiences are fraught with danger and are reserved for select individuals who fit narrowly prescribed criteria designed to attract only those whose ethical behavior and spiritual temperament can safely withstand the power of the divine vision. This religious tendency finds its expression in the Talmud in the well-known story of the four who entered the *pardes,* the mystical heavenly grove containing all the secrets of the Torah (BT Hag. 14b; see also the *Heikhalot* literature of the late talmudic period). From this literature, it is evident that the adept undertakes his journey to mystical experience by engaging in particular meditations; Torah study as the means necessary for bringing the individual to this experience is nowhere mentioned.

The methods found in these texts include the recitation of magical-mystical hymns and secret names, whose purpose is to carry one through a system of heavens or antechambers the entrances of which are guarded by an angelic hierarchy who examine the spiritual credentials of the aspirants and slay those found unworthy.

It is therefore possible to distinguish two significantly different paths to the mystical vision of the *merkavah:* the exoteric path, not regarded as particularly perilous, open to all who employ the study of Torah, and especially the study of the Talmud, as the proper means of attaining the visionary experience; and the esoteric path, reserved for an elite few, who use as their means magical names and incantations designed to overcome the many dangerous impasses that lie in wait for the mystical aspirant.

These two mystical approaches contrast with each other in several significant ways: in the characterization of the nature of the Divinity, in the nature of the techniques employed for the attainment of mystical experience, and in the social status of these techniques. What is the proper historical framework wherein these two tendencies may be understood? Are we dealing here with two altogether different conceptions of the Divinity that bear no social-historical relationship to each other?

The primary techniques employed in the magical-mystical model of Jewish mysticism, as we have seen, involve the chanting of divine names and the recitation of sacred hymns, resulting in an acute mystical experience that is reserved for or available to a chosen elite. This description certainly calls to mind the priestly elite of the Second Temple period, for the pronunciation of the ineffable name was significant in one priestly nomenclature reserved in its employment for the high priest (upon entering the holy of holies on the Day of Atonement). The Temple service itself was accompanied by the recitation of sacred hymns.

We may likewise observe that the danger faced by the *merkavah* visionary in the *Heikhalot* literature corresponds to the foreboding associated with the experience confronting the high priest as he enters the holy of holies. The expression "he entered in peace and he exited in peace," used in the Talmud (BT Hag. 14b) to describe the unique success of Rabbi Akiva in the story of the four who entered the *pardes,* is also used to describe the success of the high priest in the performance of his functions on the Day of Atonement in the holy of holies.

By contrast, the Torah-study mode of Jewish mysticism is available to the populace at large and is less fraught with danger. In fact, this form of mystical experience is demanded of every Torah scholar when he seriously engages in studying the sacred texts, and does not threaten him with the possibility of mortal danger.

In the mystical literature of the medieval period, that is, the classical kabbalah, the two modes of mystical experience clearly diverge and are developed into two distinct types: the theosophic kabbalah and the prophetic or ecstatic kabbalah.

The theosophic kabbalah, whose central work is the *Zohar,* is founded on the idea that there are two essential aspects in which the divine Existence is expressed. There is the hidden aspect, called the *Ein-Sof* (the infinite), and the revealed aspect, expressed in anthropomorphic forms as the ten *sefirot* (attributes or divine powers). Within this revealed aspect of the Divinity works a dynamic that was brought about by the need to repair the disharmony that resulted from the sin of Adam, which caused a split within the attributes between the masculine and feminine functions or, in the language of the *sefirot,* between *tiferet* (beauty), the masculine function, and *malkhut* (kingdom), the feminine one. The purpose of human existence is to attempt to heal this split by creating the union anew. The means to this end is the performance of the *miẓvot* with mystical intention. Thus, at the center of this mysticism stands the halakhah, which assumes a theurgic function. It is not only the *miẓvot* that acquire theosophic meaning, however. The entire Torah literature also comes to be seen as a network of symbols that express the dynamic of the *sefirot,* and the *sefirot* themselves come to be seen as the "archetypal Torah."

This kabbalistic school was developed by a number of important medieval halakhic authorities: Rabbi Abraham ben David of Posquières (Rabad), Rabbi Moses ben Naḥman (Naḥmanides), Rabbi Solomon ben Abraham Adret (Rashba), and others. They established the halakhic study of Torah as a prerequisite for the study of kabbalah. The principal objective of this school, as previously noted, was the restoration of the divine harmony through performance of the *miẓvot.* The individuals engaged in this endeavor were required to be of high intelligence and possess unique spiritual capacities. It may be that this school ought not to be classified as mystical as such, since it is not the ecstatic experience of the kabbalist that is considered important, but his ability to reestablish the primal harmony of the divine *sefirot.*

Many aspects of the theosophic kabbalah hark back to the school of Rabbi Akiva, which stressed the study of Torah as the key to attaining mystical experience. Notwithstanding the apparent difference between, on the one hand, the vision of the divinity and, on the other, the interpretation of sacred symbols, there exists a fundamental similarity between these schools, for in mapping out the field of symbols the theosophic kabbalah transforms the Torah into an anthropomorphic picture of the Divinity.

Thirteenth-century kabbalistic literature is replete with many instances in which the Torah is perceived in human form, as in the following example:

Torah—it contains both open and closed sections. This indicates an architechtonic structure that suggests one form of man who is constructed in the holy and pure image of the Divinity. Just as in the human body the limbs are connected to each other, so too, in the Torah, this function is fulfilled by the closed sections. The Torah portions "And it came to pass when Pharaoh had let the people go. . . " (Ex. 13:17) and the Mystery of the Song "Thus sang Moses" (Ex. 15:1)

form the arm of God. The Torah portion "Give ear ye heavens" (Deut. 32:1) refers
to the Divine ears, and the portion "Then sang Israel . . ." (Num. 21:17) contains
the mystery of the signs of the covenant. Thus is the Torah called so [*Torah* meaning reference—etymologically related to the word *hora'ah*] for it indicates the
form of the Divinity.

(Rabbi Joseph of Hamdan,
Comm. [ms.] on the Kabbalistic Rationale of the Miẓvot,
Jerusalem 8° 3925 fol. 110b)

From the beginning, the kabbalah assigned a clearly theurgic function to
the performance of *miẓvot*. This type of interpretation is found extensively
in the many works expounding upon *"taamei ha-miẓvot,"* "the reasons for
the commandments," that were written at the end of the thirteenth century.
Their central theme is that the purpose of the performance of the *miẓvot* is
to achieve harmony within the Divinity. The *miẓvot* are *"ẓorekh gavoah,"*
"for the sake of the Supernal One," who derives his essential pleasure from
sacred human activity.

As we have seen, both the *merkavah* school of Rabbi Akiva and the adherents of theosophic kabbalah engaged in Torah study as a means to seek the
revelation of the divine Form. The theosophic tradition did not view the
decipherment of symbols as a dangerous enterprise, just as the Torah-study
mysticism of the school of Rabbi Akiva did not view its pursuits as inherently dangerous.

In contrast to the theosophic school there developed another kabbalistic
methodology, which called itself prophetic or ecstatic kabbalah. It flourished during the second half of the thirteenth century, with Abraham Abulafia as its main spokesman. Its primary aim was to bring the practitioner
to the "state of prophecy." The techniques used to achieve this ecstatic state
do not involve the study of Torah per se; rather, they involve the mystical
permutation of divine names and musical vocalizations, together with other
techniques such as body postures and controlled breathing. Here we find a
clear correspondence to the magical-mystical school reflected in the *Heikhalot* literature mentioned earlier.

In both instances the techniques employed are not within the boundaries
of halakhah and may sometimes even be considered antihalakhic, since
there is a clear rabbinic prohibition against pronouncing the name of God.
Even when the prophetic kabbalah does employ the Torah as a mystical
medium, it does so in a unique way. The theosophic kabbalah manifests a
traditionalist orientation to the text, since the words, structure, and syntax
of the Torah are preserved, albeit interpreted symbolically. The prophetic
kabbalah, in contrast, breaks up words into their constituent letters by mys-

tical permutation, and thereby also disregards the syntax of the text. Moreover, the purpose of the prophetic mystic is not necessarily to come to a deeper appreciation of the Divinity, but to achieve an intense mystical transformation. The process of this mystical transformation may entail various mortal dangers. Here, too, we find a correspondence to *Heikhalot* mysticism. In fact, in the writings of Abulafia and his school we find descriptions of mystical experiences that clearly reveal the influence of the *Heikhalot* literature, in particular the sections of the Hebrew Book of Enoch describing the mystical transformation of Enoch.

It is important to emphasize that in the theosophic kabbalah it is the Divinity who is the principal beneficiary of man's performance of *miẓvot,* whereas in the prophetic kabbalah the sole beneficiary is the mystic. This same distinction is found within the two schools of the *merkavah* period. On the one hand, we have the magical path, whose practitioners are not obliged to enter upon it but who, upon doing so, endanger themselves in order to attain a mystical experience, from which the Divinity, upon all accounts, derives no benefit.

To a certain extent, the dispute between the early generations of east European Ḥasidim and their opponents, the *mitnaggedim,* concerning the priority of prayer over study may reflect the differences between theosophical and prophetic kabbalah. Many of the *mitnaggedim,* including their leader, Elijah, the "Vilna Gaon," practiced a form of theosophical kabbalah and thus stressed the importance of Torah study. In contrast, the Baal Shem Tov, the founder of the Ḥasidic movement, emphasized prayer, which he associated with meditation on the divine Name.

The tension between the two modes of Jewish mystical experience may be highlighted by a look at Franz Kafka's parable *Vor dem Gesetz* ("Before the Law"). Whether the mystical experience entails persistent study, as in the moderate mode, or the courage to face attendant dangers, as in the intensive mode, the mystic nonetheless tenaciously pursues his quest. In striking contrast, the hero of Kafka's tale is, by virtue of his psychological constitution, unable to attain his objective of contemplating the law because he lacks the resolve to confront the watchman who seeks to block his way. In a previously cited passage from the *Midrash Tanhuma,* the Torah was portrayed as a being residing within seven antechambers. According to the *merkavah* literature, in order to approach this being the mystic must endanger himself and resolutely decide to embark upon his quest. This resolute daring is characteristic of magical mysticism. For Kafka's hero, however, such resolve is unthinkable. He finds himself in an utterly powerless state, a condition of paralysis that regards the taking of any initiative as utterly out of the question. The warning of the first watchman is sufficient to deter him from making any deliberate attempt to attain a fair verdict.

Kafka's parable presents a situation that is totally antithetical to the basic conception of Torah study, mystical and otherwise. The Torah was given in order to be investigated, and it is man's obligation to confront this challenge. Moses, in many of the midrashic renditions of the biblical story, ascended to heaven in order to receive the Torah, although he knew he would encounter great peril. In Kafka's story, however, the watchmen are there to pacify and effectively subdue the defendant.

The success of Moses in confronting the angels and emerging victorious and the success of the *merkavah* visionary in obtaining a vision of the divine glory stand in opposition to the powerless passivity of modern man, symbolized by Kafka's hapless defendant, who faces a meaningless, alienated world. For Kafka, the ability to obtain justice is the acid test of the heroic propensities of human nature. But modern man, having lost his living connection with the law—the Torah—has also lost his ability to re-create this connection. Thus, the cold, abstract laws from which one is irremediably estranged may be contrasted with the conception of the Torah found in Jewish mysticism.

BIBLIOGRAPHY

Moshe Idel, "Tefisat ha-Torah be-Sifrut ha-Heikhalot ha-Yehudit be-Yamei ha-Benayim," in *Jerusalem Studies in Jewish Thought,* 1 (1981).
Gershom Scholem, *Major Trends in Jewish Mysticism* (1967).
Gershom Scholem, *Les origines de la Kabbale* (1966).
Gershom Scholem, *Kabbalah* (1974).

Myth

מיתוס

Galit Hasan-Rokem

"**M**yth and Judaism" is deemed by many to be an impossible combination of words. Both Jewish and Christian scholars, regardless of whether their point of departure has been theological or secular, have been loath to attribute the concept of myth to Jewish religious literature. Accordingly, in this essay the specific literary character of the relevant texts will first have to be considered. It will be noted that these texts enable us to test—and reformulate—some prevailing conceptions of myth and its place in the Jewish religious imagination.

Myth may heuristically be defined as the genre that represents generically the modes of thought classified as mythic. It is further assumed that there is a phenomenological relationship between myth as a mode of thought and myth as a literary genre. It should be stressed that this relationship is far more complex than the simple equation according to which the existence of the mythic mode in culture engenders the genre of myth or than the fact that in a known culture there is a text that can be defined as a myth, from which the existence of a mythic mode of thought may be inferred. Furthermore, it should be understood that there exists a span of time, a temporal distance between the composition of a text (or what has been called the production of the text) and its reception, influence, and elaborations. This temporal span or distance, which may be termed the *hermeneutic span of the text,* should always be taken into account when interpretations of a text are attempted. Similarly, the dynamics between the reconstruction of the original form and context of the production of the text, based mainly on philological and historical premises, and the changing contexts of reception in its various forms (belief, exegesis, rejection, interpretation, elaboration, reference, citation, and so on) are necessary in the description of any literary myth and even more necessary to the understanding of it. It can also be argued that because of the transient, paradigmatic, and comprehensive nature of myth this dynamic relation between its literary reception and the context of its production is especially crucial.

The different theories of myth and their implications with regard to biblical literature have, of course, been reviewed by a number of authors.[1] As in discussions of myth in general, the theories of biblical myths fall into a more or less clear division between those scholars who adhere to a cognitive definition of myth, which is then seen as a category of experience of the world and of man in the world—such a definition makes a distinction between a mythical religious experience of God and an amythical one—and those who adhere to an operative approach, which again results in a formal and contextual definition of myth as a definite genre, referring specifically to such traits as mythical time *(Urzeit-Endzeit)* and mythical space (concentric and lateral space). This division has on the one hand produced definitions of myth by thinkers such as André Jolles and Ernst Cassirer along the lines of experiential categories and their expressions in language, and on the other hand, as in the work of Claude Lévi-Strauss, shown myth to represent the total cognitive structure of culture. Further, myth has been defined by Paul Ricoeur as a specific literary expression of the symbolical mode of thought in discourse that provides recourse to the experience of the sacred.

A number of new definitions regarding myth seem to emerge when myth in Judaism is discussed. Research has allowed for the identification of so-called mythological motifs in the biblical text. Those motifs have, according to scholarly views, been inserted into the text either with indifference to their ideological-theological background or in direct confrontation and negation of them. Thus mythical beasts, spirits, and beings may have become concrete adversaries of the omnipotent one God of the Israelite religion in order to be crushed and conquered by him. Myths may also be referred to in minimal and reduced forms, as in allusions or quotations, so that it may be assumed that the myths were to some extent known by the recipients of the biblical text, although not necessarily ideologically affirmed or acknowledged either by the biblical authors or by their audiences. A quite widely accepted definition of myth sees it as the kind of narrative that offers a total explanation of the origins of the world and its major components and inhabitants, chiefly man. Myth is also regarded as a story that provides a plausible background to everything that is known by man at a given time, as well as a narrative that establishes a meaningful link between being and nonbeing, between past, present, and future. Myth as a religious text carries a message not only about the epistemological status of creation but also about its moral nature. With such a cognitive, rather than theological, definition of myth in mind, one may readily discern myths even in the Bible (for example, the stories of Creation, the Flood, and the Tower of Babel).

Some literary definitions of myth ascribe limits to the temporal and spatial modes that distinguish myths from other genres of collective narratives, such as legends and folktales. The first ten and a half chapters of Genesis conform to these modal criteria, since they relate to events situated at the very beginning of time; moreover, the setting of these events is mostly cosmic rather than a geographically specified space. Most of the events related here are directly initiated and carried out by God himself in his capacity as creator rather than in the capacity of omnipotent ruler of an already existing universe. The events fall into a pattern by which both the physical conditions of the world and the human condition are being established.

Postbiblical rabbinic literature has often been characterized as unambiguously free of myth. Here, too, this judgment would seem a bit hasty. To be sure, tannaitic writing, being mainly concerned with halakhic matters—that is, rules of behavior—does not lend itself to myth. Yet there are narrative passages in tannaitic literature and even in its explanatory discourse dealing with halakhah that are clearly influenced by mythical thought. A change is to be discerned, however, in amoraic literature, which is inspired and informed by the major spiritual event of the era, namely, the failure of messianic expectations. This experience is correlated to specific historical events such as the destruction of the Second Temple and the suppression of the Bar Kokhba uprising and a number of minor Jewish rebellions in Palestine and elsewhere, as well as to the physical and religious oppression and atrocities of the Trajanic–Hadrianic era.

The nonmythical genres cultivated by the tannaim were not rejected by the amoraim; on the contrary, they served as the point of departure for the organic development of halakhic thought. But this period also generated a new genre of literature—the Midrash Aggadah—which in many respects is unparalleled in the whole history of Jewish literature. As no other text before or after it, the Midrash Aggadah reveals the paradigmatic potentiality of the Bible as a myth and discloses its symbolical value. We have here an example of myth as a dynamic phenomenon. On the one hand, mythic narration is actualized in and through a contemporary context, in a way that has been termed by Yizhak Heinemann "organic thinking" and "creative historiography."[2] On the other hand, the original biblical myth is therein also reaffirmed. The paradigmatization of the biblical text as it occurs in the Midrash Aggadah seems to be an alternative to the direct mythicization of the text, or to the reaffirmation of its mythical character. The well-known phenomenon of reaffirmation through ritual exists, parallel to historical-narrative reaffirmation, in Midrash. It also takes place in the ritual of the synagogue, where the original text, namely, the Bible, is continually read and explicated. Similarly, most of the holidays and celebrations of the Jewish liturgical year reenact primordial events, which the people are principally acquainted with from the Bible, that is, from its myths.

With respect to the myths of Judaism we should make a clear distinction between myths proper, that is, universal and strictly total myths, which bear absolute values, and national myths. Strictly speaking, the tales of a nation *in history* are not myths; from a theoretical-folkloristic point of view they should rather be regarded as legends, having defined parameters of time and place. On the other hand, already the prophets interpreted the history of the nation in universal terms, rendering it a paradigmatic history and therefore introducing the dimension of timelessness into this otherwise utterly temporal reality—history. This seems a fitting intellectual background for the rise of national messianism, in which universal and national categories of redemption blend and are sometimes interchangeable.

From a hermeneutical point of view, by which the response of a known historical audience becomes a central consideration in the processes of remythologizing versus demythologizing, it is possible to explain the recurrent fluctuations of presence and absence of myth in different cultures. Mythical texts in Jewish tradition are often taken up in later texts either to demythologize, as frequently happens in philosophical renderings or interpretations of the biblical narratives of creation, or to remythologize. Thus the kabbalistic renderings of the biblical myths, culminating first in the Zohar and later in the Lurianic kabbalah, forcefully endeavored to remythologize the Bible; in these efforts new mythological elements and personifications were especially read into the original tale of creation, for instance.

It is interesting to note that, whereas myth is usually understood to be a folkloristic genre, probably the boldest mythical formulation of kabbalah—in the Zohar—was created by an individual, Moses de Leon. In that version of myth the biblical text is interpreted as a series of anagrams and rendered paradigmatic, a procedure that allowed the creation of new mythic "heroes" through the personification of the Torah and the *Shekhinah,* the female aspect of the godhead, which in earlier literature was largely a non-mythical image. In modern discourse secular concepts and forms of thought have tended to displace and yet, paradoxically, often also revalorize traditional mythical ideas and idioms. Thus Zionism has employed the modern concepts of "national liberation" and "social justice" as primary vehicles for the realization of the "myth" of redemption. Not only Zionists, of course, sought to evoke traditional mythic messianic images. Liberal Jews, for instance, often spoke of the Jewish "mission" to the peoples of the world, consciously regarding it as a revitalized expression of Israel's prophetic responsibilities. What we witness here is the transformation of mythical—messianic—images and their removal from their original *"Urzeit-End-zeit"* (primal and ultimate time) axis into pragmatic, historical categories. As such, these categories cease to serve as a comprehensive explanation of the nature of the world, thereby perhaps depriving Jewish culture of the power of myth to provide a living contact with the absolute.

REFERENCES

1. For a comprehensive overview of German, French, British, and American scholarship, with, however, less attention to Jewish and especially Israeli scholarship, see J. W. Rogerson, "Myth in Old Testament Interpretation," in *Beiheft zur Zeitschrift für die altertestamentliche Wissenschaft,* 134 (1974).
2. Yiẓḥak Heinemann, *Darkhei ha-Aggadah* (1950).

BIBLIOGRAPHY

Theodor H. Gaster, *Myth, Legend and Custom in the Old Testament* (1969).
Robert Graves and Raphael Patai, *Hebrew Myths* (1964).
J. W. Rogerson, "Myth in Old Testament Interpretation," in *Beiheft zur Zeitschrift für die altertestamentliche Wissenschaft* 134 (1974).
Gershom G. Scholem, "Kabbalah and Myth," in Scholem, *On the Kabbalah and Its Symbolism* (1965).
Ephraim E. Urbach, *The Sages: Their Concepts and Beliefs,* 2nd ed. (1979), chs. 2–10.

Natural Law

חוק־הטבע

Jeffrey Macy

The term *natural law* has been used to describe various doctrines that, while differing in detail, present a relatively consistent outlook regarding the existence of some natural standard that is or should be the standard for law and human action. There are at least two common elements that can be found in the various doctrines of natural law: (1) the existence of a general or universal (that is, natural) standard—based on principles more binding and permanent than custom, convention, or human agreement—that can serve as the basis for human action and societal norms; (2) the acknowledgment that the natural standard can and should be used as a criterion by which particular laws or legal codes can be judged or grounded. Alternatively offering legitimization or criticism of existing legal codes, this natural standard can provide criteria for appeals to a higher standard of justice than that standard contained in a particular legal code and can serve as the basis for resolving legal questions when the existing code of laws does not make reference to a particular problem. Among the various doctrines of natural law, however, there exist differences in the definition of the standard that is called natural and is the basis of the natural-law theory.

There is no unequivocal answer to the question whether there exists a concept of natural law in Jewish thought. At the outset, it is worthwhile to note that there is no word for nature in the Bible; the Hebrew word *teva*—with the meaning "nature"—first appears only in medieval Jewish philosophic literature. It is therefore not surprising that there is no reference to a specific concept of natural law in the Bible. Despite the absence of a specific reference to natural law in biblical literature, there have been Jewish thinkers who have argued that there is a notion of natural law implicit in the Noachite commandments. This position is seemingly supported by reference to certain talmudic and other rabbinic passages, which suggest that in the case of all but two of the seven Noachite commandments, even "if they had not been written [in Scripture], they should by right have been written" (BT Yoma 67b). Indeed, according to traditional Jewish sources, the Noachite commandments are considered to be the sine qua non for civilized human life, as well as the minimum standard that must be met by a non-Jew who desires to live as a resident alien among Jews. Nevertheless, the equation of the Noachite laws with natural law is far from universally accepted by Jewish thinkers, either ancient or modern.

It would appear that the lack of reference to nature in the Bible is a necessary corollary of God's omnipotence—a position that the Bible assumed and emphatically developed. Thus, the absence of independent laws of nature and the emphasis on divine creation and control of everything that exists and occurs highlight the position that everything in our world is subject to the absolute authority of God and is responsive to his will.

In addition to having absolute power over the creation and continued existence of the physical objects which exist in the world God is also perceived to be the legislator who revealed the true and perfect law that he gave to his chosen people. Further, God is said to possess absolute power over the reward and punishment of men, and he is said to reward those who act in accordance with his divinely revealed law and to punish those who transgress that law. Any attempt by man to act in a way that contradicts the ways that are pleasing to the Lord therefore inevitably will meet with a suitable divine response. In such a context, there surely is no room for an independent category of human law that is superior to the divinely revealed law and that could be said to be based upon an independent natural principle; the only law that is true and perfect is the law the Lord has revealed. Thus, according to the scriptural account of the Jewish law, there is no place for an additional and independent category of law that would be called natural law, at least in the sense in which almost all philosophers discuss natural law. At most, one can observe that certain human actions appear, customarily, to lead to certain results—or one can repeat the dicta of Scripture that certain actions will inevitably lead to certain results (which may be construed as divine reward and punishment). An example of a scripturally supported inevitable result, which certainly could not be defined as natural law in any normal use of the term, is the divine pledge to the children of Israel recorded in Deuteronomy 11:13-21:

> If, then, you obey the commandments that I enjoin upon you this day, loving the Lord your God and serving Him with all your heart and soul, I will grant the rain for your land in season, the early rain and the late. You shall gather in your new grain and wine and oil—I will also provide grass in the fields for your cattle—and thus you shall eat your fill. Take care not to be lured away to serve other gods and bow to them. For the Lord's anger will flare up against you, and He will shut up the skies so that there will be no rain and the ground will not yield its produce; and you will soon perish from the good land that the Lord is giving you.

As has been mentioned, there is no explicit reference to nature or natural law in either biblical or rabbinic literature. Nevertheless, there is scholarly dispute regarding the possibility that at least some of the rabbinic sages accepted a doctrine of natural law. The dispute regarding the existence of a rabbinic concept of natural law is the result of disagreement as to the proper interpretation of certain passages in rabbinic literature; the issue is further complicated by the fact that the modern interpreters of these passages hold different positions regarding the definition of natural law. The scholars who hold that at least some of the rabbinic sages accepted a doctrine of natural law argue that there are several passages in rabbinic literature that may affirm the existence of standards of justice and morality that exist independently of the divinely revealed Jewish law; these standards are perceived to be the basis of a natural-law doctrine. The following reference to rabbinic material is limited to a brief mention of the passages that are cited most frequently and that are most central to the analysis of the rabbinic position on natural law.

In addition to the rabbinic discussion of the Noachite commandments, which is sometimes interpreted as demonstrating that the rabbis recognized the existence of natural standards of justice and morality (cf. BT Sanh. 56a–59b; Tosef. Av. Zar. 8:4), there are at least two other talmudic discussions that are analyzed by modern scholars in an attempt to prove or disprove the rabbis' acceptance of natural law. The first talmudic dictum is from BT Yoma 67b:

"You shall keep my statutes" [Lev. 18:4]. This refers to those commandments which, if they had not been written [in Scripture], they should by right have been written [din hu sheyikatevu]. These include [the prohibitions against] idolatry, adultery, bloodshed, robbery, and blasphemy.

The second talmudic passage is from BT Eruvin 100b:

Rabbi Yohanan stated: "If the Torah had not been given, we could have learned modesty from the cat, [aversion to] robbery from the ant, chastity from the dove, and good manners from the cock."

The above two passages, in addition to the rabbinic statements regarding the Noachite commandments, all point to the possibility that certain laws or moral actions might be ascertainable without reference to the content of the divinely revealed Jewish law. On the other hand, all of these laws are already contained in the Jewish law, and all of these laws may be the result of divine ordering of the world rather than an independent principle or standard of nature. Further, although this point is not necessarily decisive, it should be noted that no explicit reference is made to unaided human reason as the source of knowledge to discover these proper laws. Thus, as in fact is the case in the relevant scholarly literature, it is possible to interpret the above passages as either confirming or denying the existence of natural law, depending on the definition of natural law that is proposed. It would appear that these passages do not provide a clear proof that the rabbinic sages accepted a doctrine of natural law, although they do seem to suggest that there are standards for action that should be generally accepted by all human beings.

Two important versions of natural-law theory that should be noted in the context of Judaism's treatment of natural law are the doctrines of the Stoic philosophers and Thomas Aquinas. The Stoic doctrine of natural law contends that the whole universe is governed by laws that can be comprehended by perfected human reason—as these universal natural laws exhibit rationality. The Stoic sage understands these natural laws through his reason, and his actions will be based on the principles of the natural law. Since, at least in theory, living on the basis of reason is possible for any individual regardless of the locale or political community in which he lives, and since those who devote themselves to the life of reason are able to understand and act according to natural law, the Stoics speak of all wise men wherever they live as being members of the same *cosmopolis;* that is, *polis* (political community) of the *cosmos.* The attainment of wisdom is therefore the only criterion of citizenship in the best regime (which is based on the laws of nature), and no ultimate significance should be attached to membership in any imperfect regime.

The Stoic doctrine of natural law is developed in Roman law as *ius naturale*. This concept usually is considered to be a universal rational principle that in theory could be used as a criterion to establish law in cases where there is no existing law or where the existing law is inadequate. In certain periods *ius naturale* becomes recognized as the basis for those laws that are binding on non-Romans, although this category usually is classified as *ius gentium* (which also includes international law) and not *ius naturale*. This latter category may bear some relationship to the attempt by the rabbis to articulate the biblical Noachite laws as the minimal legal standard that should be binding on all non-Jews who live in areas under Jewish political control.

The theory of natural law as it is developed later by Thomas Aquinas is significantly different from the Stoic theory of natural law. Aquinas continues to accept the rational foundation of natural law as well as the positive injunction to follow those laws that reason reveals, yet he does not see the natural law as being complete in and of itself. According to Aquinas, natural law, like revealed law, has its origins in God and the eternal law, but natural law, which man knows on the basis of his reason, does not provide knowledge of those things that are part of the revealed law. Thus, knowledge of natural law by means of reason is not comprehensive enough to be the sole criterion for attaining human perfection or for attaining citizenship in the most perfect regime—acceptance of the revealed law by means of faith and divine grace is also necessary. On the other hand, natural law also is too general to be the only criterion for human action or for citizenship in the best possible regime. This point is emphasized by Aquinas' description of his fourth category of law, human law. According to Aquinas, human law must be based on the principles of natural law, but it is composed of the different positive laws that exist in various political regimes and that present the necessary development and specification of those principles within the context of a particular political regime. Thus, in contrast to the Stoics, Aquinas does not contend that the only true political regime is a universal one, nor does he contend that there is only one true political regime. While it is true that the principles of the eternal law that are contained in the revealed law and the natural law are open to individuals wherever they live (the one through the acceptance of Christianity, the other through the development of reason), it is legitimate and even necessary that there exist different political regimes in different locations and that these regimes develop the specifics of their human law in various ways.

Returning to the discussion of natural law in Jewish sources, there were several Hellenistic and medieval Jewish thinkers who consciously attempted to introduce into Judaism the idea of natural law (or a variant of this idea—rational law). The doctrines of natural law that were articulated and utilized by these Jewish thinkers are not based on a single theory of natural law; indeed, these various attempts to introduce the concept of natural law into Judaism often were based on significantly different theories of natural law that were developed by divergent groups of non-Jewish thinkers who flourished in the surrounding community in different historical periods.

Examples of natural law theories among Jewish thinkers include the following: Philo, who was strongly influenced by Stoic and other Hellenistic theories of natural law, speaks of the law that Moses brought as being based on the principles of nature. The Jewish law indicates that "the world and the Law are in mutual accord, and that a man who is law-abiding is thereby immediately constituted a world citizen [*cosmopolites*], guiding his actions correctly according to nature's intent, in conformity with which the entire universe is administered" (*On the Creation of the World,* 1, 3).

Saadiah Gaon, in his treatise *Sefer Emunot ve-Deot (Book of Beliefs and Opinions)*, presents a theory of rational law that borrows heavily from the Islamic *Mu^{C}tazilite* theologians. Saadiah contends that the Jewish law is composed of rational laws and revealed laws, and that "wisdom, which is identical with reason," has required the acceptance of the rational laws, which necessarily have been commanded by the omniscient deity. The rational laws fall into three categories: (1) submission to and worship of God, (2) proscriptions not to blaspheme God or swear falsely in his name, and (3) laws designed to enforce the practice of justice, proper social relations, and ethical actions among humans. According to Saadiah, the actions man is commanded to perform or to desist from performing on the basis of the above laws are actions decreed by reason. There are aspects of this theory of rational law that correspond to natural law, inasmuch as all of the rational laws are consistent with the transcendent principle of wisdom, which is knowable by human reason rightly used. Further, Saadiah states explicitly that the contents of the Jewish law will never conflict with true reason; this position leads him to contend that the opponents of Judaism will never be able to bring a rational proof that can succeed in disproving the truth of Jewish law and belief, even if the disputer of Judaism does not accept its divine authority. Nevertheless, Saadiah—on this point in agreement with Judah Halevi after him—denies the ability of human reason to arrive at all the details of the rational laws. According to Saadiah, unaided human reason can discern the general principles of the rational law, but regarding the specifics of these laws—whose details are contained in the divinely revealed Jewish law—reason is not a sufficient guide, inasmuch as "our views would differ and we would not agree on anything" (Sefer Emunot ve-Deot, tr. 3, ch. 3). For this reason, Saadiah argues, it was rationally necessary for God to transmit by means of prophecy all of the commandments of the Jewish law, including the rational laws.

Moses Maimonides, the preeminent medieval Jewish philosopher, rejects Saadiah's discussion of rational law; he contends that what Saadiah terms rational law is, in reality, conventional (or generally accepted) law, inasmuch as such law, strictly speaking, is not rational. In this context Maimonides comments that the classification of conventional law as rational law is a mistake that has been made by "some of our recent sages, who suffer from the sickness of the Islamic theologians [mutakallimūn]" (Comm. on the Mishnah, Shemonah Perakim, ch. 6). This statement is sometimes taken as proof that Maimonides did not accept the possible existence of rational law or natural law; such a conclusion, however, is not accurate. In at least one passage in his Guide of the Perplexed Maimonides makes reference to two laws of the Bible that are rational laws in the true sense. These two laws are "the existence of the Deity and His being one." Maimonides continues: "As for the other commandments, they belong to the class of generally accepted opinions [conventional law] and those adopted in virtue of tradition, not to the class of the intellecta" (Guide 2, 33). Thus, it is possible that Maimonides does accept a category of rational law, but it should be clear that his description of such law limits it to purely rational principles (which do not include a fully developed legal code per se)—a position different from those held by Philo and Saadiah. Maimonides' position on the existence of rational law, conventional (or generally accepted) law, and traditional law is similar to the threefold categorization of law made by the tenth-century Islamic philosopher al-Farabi.

In contrast to Maimonides and Saadiah Gaon, the fifteenth-century Spanish Jewish thinker Joseph Albo uses the term natural law—rather than rational law—in his discussion of the existence of different types of law in his Sefer ha-Ikkarim (The Book of Roots). According to Albo, who on this point may have been influenced to a limited extent by Aquinas' categorization of the law, there are three types of law: natural law, nomos (or conventional law), and divine law. Albo's natural law, like that of Aquinas, is known through human reason and contains the basic principles that promote justice and remove wrongdoing "among all peoples, at all times, and in all places" (*Sefer ha-Ikkarim*, bk. 1, ch. 7); thus natural law is necessary to permit and sustain political associations. However, in contrast to Aquinas' description of natural law as providing guidance for almost all virtuous human actions, Albo does not suggest that an individual who follows the natural law will thereby attain virtue in any significant sense. Further, in direct contrast to Maimonides (and in partial contrast to Saadiah), the subject matter of this law is not the attainment of intellectual or spiritual perfection, but rather is limited to moral and political principles that are necessary for the attainment of this worldly justice and peace. In this regard Albo's choice of the term *natural law* is more appropriate than *rational law* to describe this category, even though the principles of natural law can be arrived at through human reason. Albo's next category of law, *nomos*, or conventional law, bears some similarity to Aquinas' human law in that it contains the specification and application of general principles that are contained in the natural law—specification that may vary in different political associations "owing to differences of place, time and the nature of those who are to be governed by it" (*Sefer ha-Ikkarim*, bk. 1, ch. 7); yet, Albo's discussion of conventional law also differs from Aquinas' discussion of human law inasmuch as conventional law is considered by Albo to be a qualitative improvement on natural law. Albo's final category of law, the divine law, like Aquinas' revealed law, is made known to man through divine revelation rather than through human reason; according to Albo, the divine law contains the laws and teachings relating to divine worship and spiritual perfection that make possible man's attainment of true happiness and the perfection of his soul. Thus, the following hierarchy of dignity, which is quite different from Aquinas', is found in Albo's categorization of the law: (1) divine law (which is the only law that can guide man to ultimate happiness and perfection of his soul), (2) *nomos* or conventional law, and (3) natural law (the latter two categories being political or concerned with the welfare of man's body rather than his soul).

In contemporary Jewish scholarship there are at least two dominant approaches to the issue of the possible existence of natural law and, if it does exist, to the relationship between natural law and Jewish law. The first approach argues that natural law is not consistent with the basic premises of divine omnipotence and the relative weakness of unaided human reason; as a result, natural law does not and cannot exist—or, if it does exist, it is inferior to the divinely revealed Jewish law, and exists provisionally and, perhaps, only as a rough standard for non-Jews. This approach adheres to the position that God is not bound by humanly knowable standards; thus it is impossible for human reason to discover the perfect laws that should be man's standard and guide. The only true law is the law the Lord has revealed through his prophets, and this revealed law is known to be genuine because it has been transmitted from the prophets to our generation by means of an unbroken chain of reliable tradition.

A second approach to natural law that can be found in modern Jewish sources argues that natural law does exist and that it is a direct expression of divine wisdom. According to this approach, the divinely revealed Jewish law contains within it the principles of the divinely constructed natural law, and by accepting the tenets of the Jewish law one can come to know, and live by, the universal principles of natural law. This position attempts to demonstrate that even if it is true that the Jewish law contains more than the universal principles of natural law, the contents of Jewish law will not be in conflict with the natural law's universal standards of justice and morality. (These thinkers find support for their position in their interpretation of relevant rabbinic texts, which have been mentioned above.) Further, if it appears that elements of Jewish law conflict with natural law, this is a reflection of the insufficiency of unaided human reason to understand fully God's wisdom (and the *natural law* that he created) rather than a limitation or inconsistency in the divinely revealed Jewish law. Thus, while natural law is universally applicable, it is possible that unaided human reason is insufficient to discover or correctly identify it in its entirety. An additional point, which the proponents of this approach emphasize, is that the everlasting existence of universal standards of justice and morality is ensured when it is recognized that natural law is based on God's wisdom and will. To be certain, the transrational elements of this formulation of divinely authored natural law are quite different from that which is found in the traditional philosophic definitions of natural law, where no intrinsic limitations are placed on the ability of human reason to gain an accurate conception of natural law. Indeed, one of the implications of this religious formulation of natural law is that philosophic inquiry is inferior to the acceptance of divine revelation as a source of knowledge for the discovery and understanding of natural law.

BIBLIOGRAPHY

Marvin Fox, "Maimonides and Aquinas on Natural Law," in *Diné Israel* 3 (1972).

Marvin Fox, ed., *Modern Jewish Ethics* (1975). See, in particular, the following articles: Aharon Lichtenstein, "Does Jewish Tradition Recognize an Ethic Independent of Halakha?" and Marvin Fox, "On the Rational Commandments in Saadia's Philosophy: A Reexamination."

Ralph Lerner, "Natural Law in Albo's *Book of Roots*," in Joseph Cropsey, ed., *Ancients and Moderns* (1964).

David Novak, *The Image of the Non-Jew in Judaism: An Historical and Constructive Study of the Noahide Laws* (1983).

Leo Strauss, *Natural Right and History* (1953), especially "The Origin of the Idea of Natural Right," 81–119.

David Winston, "Philo's Ethical Theory," in *Aufstieg und Niedergang der römischen Welt* (1984), II, vol. 21.1, especially "Natural Law," 381–88.

Oral Law

תורה שבעל-פה

Jacob Neusner

The myth that when God gave the Torah to Moses at Mount Sinai he gave it in two parts, one in writing, the other not in writing but formulated for memorization and then handed on orally, comprises the theory of revelation represented by the oral Law, the Torah-that-is-memorized. The power of the myth lies in its capacity to account for those beliefs, and the books that contain them, which emerged long after the close of the biblical canon. The beliefs held authoritative yet not found in the Hebrew Scriptures derive, it is then explained, from that other, oral revelation. Books that present principles and beliefs handed on through the oral Law's processes of formulation and transmission enjoy the status of the written Torah. In this way, the conception of a canon of authoritative books that is forever able to receive new works serves to make room for the religious genius of Israel in all periods of the history of the nation. Indeed, viewed from one perspective, the effect of the conception of the oral Law is to state, in mythic terms, the position of Reform theologians concerning progressive or continuing revelation: that is to say, God speaks through the prophets and sages of each generation. Revelation is not exhaustively contained only in Scripture, or in Scripture and its rabbinic amplification, but goes on even now. While the conception of the oral Law would in principle accord with that theological position, in fact the contents of the oral Law attain canonical status only through the consensus of the sages. Revelation of Torah may prove continuous, but it is not promiscuous.

The documents accorded the status of oral Law in the formative age of the rabbinic canon begin with the Mishnah, dating from the beginning of the third century C.E. For its part, the Mishnah refers back to no source of truth other than the written Torah, and so apparently lays claim to constitute the second document after Scripture, thereby excluding every written form of God's message that Israel had produced from the close of the Pentateuch in the time of Ezra, around 450 B.C.E., to the Mishnah's own time—a veritable burned library of revelation. Nevertheless, the Mishnah contains no myth of its own origin, and its authors make no claim that in principle what they say comes from Sinai. They even ignore the morphology, syntax, and word choices of biblical Hebrew. They do not allege that what they say has reached them through angelic or other revelation. They do not introduce the names of authentic prophets, such as Jeremiah or Ezra, and they do not call their book a *torah*, or revelation. The established and conventional means by which earlier Israelites secured credence for their writings all prove useless.

The Mishnah's first apologetic, the tractate *Avot* (also known as *Pirkei Avot*, or Sayings of the Fathers), does say that Moses received Torah at Sinai and handed it on to Joshua and thence onward; this passage ends with the names of authorities of the Mishnah, such as Hillel and Shammai, and includes, on the one side, Hillel's family (in the Mishnah's day, allegedly continued in the figure of the patriarch, Judah), and, on the other, Hillel's disciples (in the Mishnah's day continuing on in the sages of the Mishnah itself). Accordingly, the connection of the Mishnah to Sinai, so far as the framers of the chains of tradition in *Avot* are concerned, lies through both the person of the sage and the family of the patriarch. But that claim does not also allege that the Mishnah in particular, either in actual formulation (which would have been incredible) or in principle, derives from Sinai. Nor do we commonly find any such allegation in Tosefta or in Avot, or other documents that constitute the Mishnah's sector of the canon of Judaism in its formative age. The myth of the two Torahs appears only rarely until we reach the two Talmuds, the one of the land of Israel, dating from 400 C.E., the other of Babylonia, dating from 600 C.E., and in the associated documents in the talmudic sector of the rabbinic canon.

In the Talmud of the land of Israel we find, nearly fully worked out, the myth of the two Torahs, though the last stages in the expression of the myth are scarcely reached before the Babylonian Talmud. But both Talmuds make clear that at Sinai there was a double revelation, one in writing, the other oral. While the Talmud of the land of Israel scarcely testifies to the actual language of Torah-in-writing and Torah-in-memory, the distinction between revelation in writing and revelation formulated and transmitted orally is well established there. Some of the collections of biblical exegesis (midrashim) associated with the talmudic sector of the rabbinic canon also reveal the same facts. We may say with certainty, therefore, that the myth of the two Torahs had come to full expression by approximately 400 C.E.

The polemical and political utility of the myth hardly requires much comment. Where, in the two Talmuds, we find the most vigorous assertions that there were two Torahs, we commonly deal with stories of controversy—for example, Hillel, Shammai, and the proselyte (BT Shab. 31a) and Johanan ben Zakkai and the Sadducees (BT Men. 65a). Christian apologists had concentrated their principal attack on Judaism in the claim that the Jews falsified Scripture and did not understand its true meaning. The credence claimed for the Mishnah and the writings that succeeded it in the rabbinical movement—then the effective bureaucracy and government of the Jewish people in both the land of Israel and Babylonia—offered a tempting target. When in the aftermath of the conversion of Constantine in the early part of the fourth century Christianity rose to the position first of the dominant and then of a state religion, and when in 361 C.E. the emperor Julian's promise to rebuild the Temple turned into a fiasco, with the consequence that Christianity returned to power in a militant and frightened mood, determined to wipe out paganism and humiliate Judaism, the urgent utility of the myth became apparent.

At that time Israel's leaders, the rabbis represented in the Talmud of the land of Israel and associated documents, had for the first time to confront the reality of Christianity and cease to delude themselves that they could place Christianity in the undifferentiated and unimportant backdrop covered by the word *paganism* (*avodah zarah* or foreign worship in general, and *minut* or heresy in particular). At that time we find two closely connected activities. First, the same authorities who produced the Jerusalem Talmud also engaged in a second work of exegesis, done along parallel lines. Just as, in the Talmud itself, they systematically worked out an exegesis of the Mishnah, so, in the earliest compilations of biblical exegeses beyond the tannaitic ones, they systematically worked out an exegesis of principal books of the Pentateuch. In Genesis Rabbah and Leviticus Rabbah they con-

structed discourse about Scripture along precisely the same logical principles that they followed in framing discourse about the Mishnah. The second
activity brings us to the present topic. The sages then expressed, in their
exegeses of both the Mishnah and Scripture, the conviction about the oral
Law that we have briefly outlined here. So the fully exposed myth of the
oral Law, that is, the conviction that at Sinai God had revealed to Moses a
dual Torah, one written down, one formulated and transmitted orally and
through memorization, served remarkably well to defend the Judaism
defined by the sages of the Mishnah and the Talmud, to account for its
origins, and to validate its message.

This was accomplished in the face of the first glimmerings of the challenge, first from Christianity, then from Islam as well, that Judaism would
have to confront for the remainder of its history in the West: to justify and
validate those teachings and the books that contained them that Jews alone
held, beyond Scripture, to constitute God's Torah to Moses at Sinai. Judaism
as we know it, that is, the distinctive Judaism of the doctrine of the two
Torahs, therefore was born in the encounter with triumphant Christianity,
just as, in its formative century, Christianity had come into being in the
encounter with an established Judaism of Temple, land, and self-governing
state.

It must be noted that this picture will puzzle the many faithful Jews who,
accepting at face value the allegations of the Talmuds, believe that the oral
Law comes from Sinai. It also stands at variance with the convictions of
Reform and secular scholars of an earlier period that the concept of the oral
Law characterized the pre-70 C.E. Pharisees in particular, who were supposedly the teachers of the dual Torah. If, however, we did not know in
advance that such a myth had circulated before 70 C.E., we should hardly
find an unequivocal statement of it in any of the passages that are adduced
in evidence. These speak only of traditions in addition to Scripture. For a
formulation of the claim that extrabiblical traditions—a commonplace
among a whole range of Jewish groups—constituted the oral Torah revealed
to Moses at Sinai, we have to wait until the appearance of the Talmuds, four
centuries later. If we take seriously the fact that only much later do we find
the doctrine fully exposed, we also realize that, when it first reached full
formulation, the myth had to explain a particular fact, namely, the authority
and standing of the Mishnah and associated writings. Then, as is clear, we
have also to formulate our explanation in response to the circumstance that
required the sages to account for their distinctive traditions, law and theology alike. The explanation derives, at first view, from the circumstance
that precipitated it: the triumph of Christianity and the disappointment,

after Emperor Julian's fiasco, of the Jewish people. But the explanation is also to be sought in the document in which it first occurs as a fully exposed and commonplace myth, namely, the Talmud of the land of Israel, coming, it is generally assumed, approximately forty years after 361. Once held authoritative, the myth of the oral Torah or, more precisely, of the dual Torah, would serve to defend that very corpus of revealed law and theology that defined and made Judaism distinctive, and further to explain and justify the inclusion, within that corpus, of the teachings of the authoritative sages of the Torah in every succeeding generation down to our own day.

BIBLIOGRAPHY

George Foot Moore, *Judaism in the First Centuries of the Christian Era: The Age of the Tannaim* (1927), 3–124, 235–80.

Jacob Neusner, *Judaism: The Evidence of the Mishnah* (1981).

Jacob Neusner, *Judaism: The Evidence of the Yerushalmi* (1983).

Ellis Rivkin, *A Hidden Revolution: The Pharisees' Search for the Kingdom Within* (1978).

Efraim E. Urbach, *The Sages: Their Concepts and Beliefs* (1975), 286–314.

Orthodox Judaism

יהדות אורתודוקסית

Emmanuel Rackman

Orthodox Judaism is the Judaism of those Jews who are committed to the doctrine that the Pentateuch, the written Law, is the word of God, which was given to Moses together with oral interpretations and a method of exegesis called the oral Law. Together, the written Law and the oral Law constitute the principal sources of the halakhah, by whose mandates Orthodox Jews feel bound. However, Orthodox Judaism is by no means monolithic; the diversity in faith and practice is legion. It has no ultimate authority or hierarchy of authorities, and has never been able to mobilize even one national or international organization in which all of its groupings would speak as one.

The diversity in halakhic rulings is typical of most legal systems. It may confound an observant Jew when he must act with respect to a particular problem. But the diversity in this area stems principally from reliance on different sources, all of which are deemed authoritative, or on methods of reasoning applied to the sources, which are also deemed normative by all halakhists. Philosophy or teleology plays no part in the decision-making process except for a few among the modern Orthodox.

The diversity, however, that evokes considerable acrimony revolves around three issues: the nature and scope of revelation; attitudes toward secular education and modern culture; and the propriety of cooperation with non-Orthodox communities. To systematic theology very little attention is given. The writings of the medieval Jewish philosophers are studied and expounded, but they appear to stimulate no new approaches. Orthodox Jews may be rationalists or mystics, naturalists or neo-Hegelians, or, at present, even existentialists. Indeed, one eminent contemporary Orthodox thinker who has incorporated aspects of the existentialist mode is Joseph B. Soloveitchik. Starting from the premise that all the law is God's revealed will, Soloveitchik holds that logically it must all have theological significance. Therefore, he sees the totality of the law as a realm of ideas in the Platonic sense, given by God for application to the realm of the real. Just as the mathematician creates an internally logical and coherent fabric of formulas with which he interprets and integrates the appearance of the visible world, so the Jew—the man of halakhah—has the Torah as the divine idea that vests all of human life with direction and sanctity. The halakhah, according to this view, is a multi-dimensional, ever-expanding continuum which cuts through all levels of human existence from the most primitive and intimate to the most complex relationships. And though the halakhah refers to the ideal, its creativity must be affected by the real. Man responds to the great halakhic challenge not only by blindly accepting the divine imperative but also by assimilating a transcendental content disclosed to him through an apocalyptic revelation and fashioning it to his peculiar needs.

For Soloveitchik the highest form of religious experience is not the loss of one's self in blissful contemplation of the infinite. It is rather the experiencing of life's irreconcilable antitheses—the simultaneous affirmation and abnegation of the self, the simultaneous awareness of the temporal and the eternal, the simultaneous clash of freedom and necessity, the simultaneous love and fear of God, his simultaneous transcendence and immanence. "From the deep" of antinomies, doubts, and spiritual travail, Soloveitchik calls to God.

As for conceptions of the hereafter and the resurrection of the dead, Soloveitchik holds with Franz Rosenzweig that no man can fathom or visualize precisely what they signify in fact, but the beliefs themselves can be deduced logically from the proposition that God is just and merciful. God's attributes of absolute justice and mercy require that we provide rewards and punishments and that he redeem himself by being merciful to those most in need of mercy, that is, to the dead. Soloveitchik holds with Naḥmanides that the immortality of the soul after death is to be distinguished from a this-worldly resurrection of the dead in a post-messianic period, itself only intended to establish international peace and order.

Essentially, such doctrines simply represent fulfillment of Judaism's commitment to an optimistic philosophy of human existence. However, theology and eschatology generally receive very little attention from Orthodox Jewish thinkers. This is not the case with revelation.

With regard to revelation, the range in views is enormous. There are those who hold that God literally dictated 'the Pentateuch to Moses, who wrote each word as dictated, and there are those who maintain that how God communicated with Moses, the Jewish people, the patriarchs, and the prophets will continue to be a matter of conjecture and interpretation, but that revelation is nonetheless historical. As creation is a fact for believers, although they cannot describe its process, so revelation is a fact, although its precise manner is elusive. This less fundamentalist approach would not deny a role to man's subjective response to the encounter with the divine, but all Orthodox Jews would agree that the doctrine of divine revelation represents direct supernatural communication of content from God to man.

While some believe in the literal inspiration of the Pentateuch, the Five Books of Moses, there are others, less rigid in this connection, who nonetheless regard the Pentateuch as the ultimate source for a Jewish philosophy of history rather than Jewish history itself. This accounts for the fact that at present some authorities insist that Orthodox Jews must hold the age of the earth to be something over five thousand years, while others have no difficulty in accepting the findings of modern geology and astronomy.

With regard to the legal portions of the Pentateuch, many insist that they are eternal and immutable. Others maintain, however, that the oral Law itself affords conclusive proof that there are laws that are neither eternal nor immutable. In the oral Law one also finds that some commandments were deemed by one authority or another to have been not mandatory but optional. Such were the commandments with regard to the blood-avenger and the appointment of a king. However, exponents of Orthodox Judaism generally affirm the eternity and immutability of halakhah, even as they engage in the development of halakhic discourse.

With regard to those parts of the Bible other than the Pentateuch, some Orthodox assert them to have been written under the influence of the Holy Spirit, while others are more critical and do not dogmatize with regard to their authorship, textual accuracy, dates of composition, or literal interpretation.

Further, there are some who extend the doctrine of the inviolability of the Pentateuch to all the sacred writings, including the Talmud and the Midrash, and do not even permit rejection of any of its most contradictory legends or maxims. Others are "reductionists" and restrict the notion of inviolability to the Pentateuch.

Many of the views we have described were expressed well before the modern period. They are found in the writings of Jewish philosophers of the Middle Ages, and some are clearly expressed in the Talmud and Midrash. It is the modern period, however, that gave birth to Orthodoxy's argument with secular education and modern culture and raised the issue of how much cooperation was permissible to Orthodox Jews in their dealings with non-Orthodox Jews.

There were Orthodox rabbis who bemoaned the emancipation and the dismantling of ghetto insulation because they well fathomed its impact upon the solidarity of the Jewish community and especially the future of its legal autonomy. Jewish law, previously applicable to the personal, social, economic, and political existence of Jews, would henceforth be relevant to only very limited areas in the life of the Jew. These rabbis opposed any form of acculturation with their non-Jewish neighbors. Others advocated acculturation in social and economic matters, but retained commitment to a Judaism totally unrelated to and unaffected by the ideas and values that dominated the non-Jewish scene. Others advocated the fullest symbiosis; among them are Abraham Isaac Hacohen Kook and Soloveitchik. Kook maintained a very positive attitude to all modern cultural and scientific developments; Soloveitchik described the believing Jew as one who is forever in dialectical tension between being a member of the covenanted community and his obligation to fulfill his socio-ethical responsibilities with and for all humanity in a rapidly changing world. Their disciples often find that their secular education and exposure to modern culture deepen their understanding and appreciation of their own heritage, even as it helps them to evaluate modernity with greater insight and a measure of transcendence.

The attitudes of Orthodox Jews to their non-Orthodox coreligionists also range from one end of the spectrum to the other—from hate presumably based on revered texts to toleration, total acceptance, and even love, similarly based on revered texts. Those indulging in hate are responsible for the physical violence occasionally practiced against any who deviate from the tradition. Theirs is a policy of noncooperation in any form whatever with any who disagree with them, and they not only pray for the destruction of the State of Israel but even take measures to achieve that end. Others simply want total separation from those who deviate from their customs and practices even in the matter of dress. A third group is reconciled to the fact of pluralism in Jewish life but has no affinity whatever for the non-Orthodox. A fourth group loves all Jews irrespective of how they behave, but does not accord even a modicum of tolerance to organizations that represent non-Orthodox rabbis and congregations. This group is more tolerant of secular groups—no matter how antireligious. Indeed, they welcome the clear demarcation: They are "religious" while the others are not. A fifth group is even willing to cooperate with non-Orthodox groups in all matters pertaining to relationships between Jews and non-Jews, at least in the United States. Even they are less open-minded with regard to the situation in Israel. Only a very small group goes all the way with the inescapable implications of the thought of Kook and Soloveitchik and welcomes the challenge of non-Orthodoxy, even as it views secular education and modern culture as positive factors in one's appreciation of the tradition.

It is also this last group that is most prone to project halakhic decisions that are based on the sources but not necessarily the weight of the authorities. Especially with respect to the inviolability of the persons of all human beings, including Jewish dissenters, they are zealots. Thus, they encourage dialogue with all Jews, solutions to the painful problems in Jewish family law, and more community sanctions against the unethical behavior of Jews in business, in the exaction of usury, in the evasion of taxes, and in the exploitation of the disadvantaged. They propose the use of more theology and teleology in the process of halakhic decision. Their principal difference with so-called right-wing conservative rabbis is that they do not want to "update" the halakhah to adjust it to the spirit of the time. Rather, within the frame and normative procedures of the halakhah—its sources and its method of reasoning—they want to express the implications of the halakhah for the modern Jew and his existential situation.

The enormous diversity among Orthodox Jews in both creed and practice has led to the characterization of Orthodox Judaism as reflecting ultra-Orthodox, Orthodox, and modern Orthodox sectors. Yet, in each of these groups there is substantial diversity, and the outlook in a free world and open society is for more rather than less diversity.

The diversity and factionalism in contemporary Orthodoxy is not its principal problem. What is more significant is its fear of modernism and scientific approaches to the study of its sacred sources. Orthodoxy must train scholars who can address themselves to the challenge of *Wissenschaft des Judentums* (Science of Judaism) and especially the so-called higher criticism of the Bible. It must also encourage its gifted adherents to participate in the political, social, economic, and cultural life of *Klal Yisrael* (the Jewish community) in Israel and all over the world. It has coped successfully with the challenge of natural science; it must have faith that it can do so with the challenge of the social sciences.

BIBLIOGRAPHY

Isidore Epstein, *The Faith of Judaism* (1954).
Norman Lamm and William S. Wurzburger, eds., *A Treasury of Tradition* (1967).
Emmanuel Rackman, *One Man's Judaism* (1970).
Joseph B. Soloveitchik, *Halakhic Man,* Lawrence Kaplan, tr. (1983).

Peace

שלום

Aviezer Ravitzky

The Hebrew word for peace, *shalom,* is derived from a root denoting wholeness or completeness, and its frame of reference throughout Jewish literature is bound up with the notion of *shelemut,* perfection. Its significance is thus not limited to the political domain—to the absence of war and enmity—or to the social—to the absence of quarrel and strife. It ranges over several spheres and can refer in different contexts to bounteous physical conditions, to a moral value, and, ultimately, to a cosmic principle and divine attribute.

In the Bible, the word *shalom* is most commonly used to refer to a *state of affairs,* one of well-being, tranquillity, prosperity, and security, circumstances unblemished by any sort of defect. *Shalom* is a blessing, a manifestation of divine grace. In inquiring about the peace of one's fellow, one inquires as to whether things fare well with him. (In a borrowed sense, we read: "*Va-yish'al David . . . li-shlom ha-milhamah*"; "David asked of him . . . how the war prospered" [II Sam. 11:7].) The usage of the term is thus not restricted to international, intergroup, or interpersonal relations. It signifies a state of prosperity, of blessed harmony, on several levels, physical and spiritual.

Of course, *shalom* also denotes the opposite of war, as in "a time for war, and a time for peace" (Eccles. 3:8), for the absence of war, too, suggests an orderly, prosperous, and tranquil state of affairs. In several scriptural passages the word *peace* refers to a value, and is used in the sense of equity, or loyalty (cf. Zech. 8:16; Mal. 2:6).

In the rabbinic texts, *shalom* primarily signifies a value, an *ethical category*—it denotes the overcoming of strife, quarrel, and social tension, the prevention of enmity and war. It is still, to be sure, depicted as a blessing, a manifestation of divine grace, but in a great many sayings it appears in a normative context: The pursuit of peace is the obligation of the individual and the goal of various social regulations and structures. The majority of passages on the subject of peace are concerned with family or communal life, that is, with internal peace among the people, and only a minority are concerned with external relations between Israel and other peoples, between nations and states. Nevertheless, the two realms are not always differentiated from one another, and at times they appear to be continuous; we read, for example: "He who establishes peace between man and his fellow, between husband and wife, between two cities, two nations, two families or two governments . . . no harm should come to him" (Mekh. Ba-ḥodesh 12). The series of regulations ordained by the Sages "in the interest of peace" *(mi-pene darkhei shalom)* were also meant to affect relations both among the Jews themselves and between the Jews and the Gentiles.

The Sages went to great lengths in their praise of peace, to the point of viewing it as a meta-value, the summit of all other values, with the possible exception of justice. Peace was the ultimate purpose of the whole Torah: "All that is written in the Torah was written for the sake of peace" (Tanḥ. Shofetim 18). It is the essence of the prophetic tiding—"The prophets have planted in the mouth of all people naught so much as peace" (Bamidbar R. Naso 11:7)—and of redemption, "God announceth to Jerusalem that they [Israel] will be redeemed only through peace" (Deut. R. 5:15). *Shalom* is the name of the Holy One, the name of Israel, and the name of the Messiah *(Derekh Erez Zuta, Perek ha-Shalom)*, yet the name of God may be blotted out in water for the sake of peace (Lev. R. 9:9). Other sayings in the same vein are numerous.

Nevertheless, alongside this sort of expression the Sages discuss the question of the relationship between peace and other competing values, of situations in which different norms might conflict with one another. For instance, peace was opposed to justice: Rabbi Joshua ben Korḥa taught that "where there is strict justice there is no peace, and where there is peace there is no strict justice," and he consequently instructed the judge to "act

as an arbiter," that is, to rule for compromise, which is justice tempered
with peace (see JT Sanh. 1:5; BT Sanh. 6b; the opposing view is "let justice
pierce the mountain," that is, justice at all costs). On another level, peace
was contrasted with truth: It was said in the name of Rabbi Eleazar ben
Simeon that "one may deviate from the truth for the sake of peace" (BT
Yev. 65b); in an even stronger formulation, it was said, "All falsehood is
forbidden, but it is permissible to utter a falsehood for the purpose of making peace between a man and his fellow" (*Derekh Erez Zuta,* loc. cit.). In
all of these instances, even where peace is given priority and tips the balance, it is viewed as an individual, partial value that must compete with
other values. In contrast with this dichotomous approach, however, we also
find another approach that attempts to harmonize the separate values and
make them complement one another: "By three things the world is preserved, by justice, by truth, and by peace, and these three are one: if justice
has been accomplished, so has truth, and so has peace" (JT Ta'an. 4:2).
Here, not only is peace made among men, but also the competing values
are reconciled.

Drawing upon a fine distinction between the terms used in several scriptural expressions, one rabbinic saying proposed an interesting differentiation between two types of obligation. The first type is that which arises from
a given situation, that is, man's obligation to respond in a particular way to
a given set of circumstances. The second type, on the other hand, demands
that one create situations and shape them in such a way as to bring the
obligation upon himself. The first group includes all of the commandments,
the second the pursuit of peace alone:

> Great is peace, for of all the commandments it is written: "*if* [emphases added]
> thou see," "*if* thou meet" (Ex. 23:4, 5), "*if* [there] chance" (Deut. 22:6); that is,
> if the occasion for this commandment should arise, you must do it, and if not,
> you need not do it. In relation to peace, however, [it is written]: "seek peace, and
> pursue it"—seek it in your own place, and pursue it even to another place as
> well.

> (Lev. R. 9:9)

It may be asked, to be sure, whether peace alone should be included in the
second group. Nevertheless, the distinction itself draws our attention, and
the need to clarify it conceptually and to determine its outlines is an open
invitation to the philosopher.

Finally, several sayings concerning the power of peace go beyond the
social-ethical realm to enter the domain of the cosmic: The Holy One makes

peace between the supernal and the lower worlds, among the denizens of the supernal world, between the sun and the moon, and so on (Lev. R., loc. cit.; Deut. R. 5:12; and see Job 25:2). Most of these passages in fact acclaim yet more ardently the pursuit of peace among men, in an a fortiori formulation: "And if the heavenly beings, who are free from envy, hatred and rivalry, are in need of peace, how much more are the lower beings, who are subject to hatred, rivalry, and envy" (Deut. R., loc. cit.).

The unique development of the Jewish sources in the Middle Ages is reflected in their portrayal of peace as an *ontological principle*. While the term—particularly in halakhic and ethical literature—retained its classical denotations, it was simultaneously elevated—particularly in the philosophical and mystical literature—to the level of the cosmic, the metaphysical, the divine.

Peace is the foundation of all being, the condition for the existence and preservation of reality. This is reflected both in the existence of each individual being and in the harmonious existence of reality as a whole.

First, each object, every individual substance, is composed of opposing elements; it embodies various conflicting forces attempting to overcome one another. This internal tension threatens to undermine and destroy every being; were it not for that principle which reconciles, balances, and "equalizes" its internal components, the substance would cease to exist. In the words of Joseph Albo:

> Each opposing element seeks to overcome and vanquish the other, and once it has overcome the other it will not rest until it has absolutely destroyed it and wiped it out of existence, and the composite [object] will thus cease to exist. . . . Conciliation between these two opposing elements is called peace, and on its account being is sustained, and the composite entity can continue to exist.
>
> (*Sefer ha-Ikkarim* 4:51)

On the physical level, then, peace is embodied in the dialectical tension between the diametrically opposed elements within the object, which in their mutual neutralization form a unified system. This taut harmony is ultimately the very essence of physical existence (we hear in this a distant echo of the ideas of Heraclitus). On the spiritual level, on the other hand, peace would be described as the utter absence of tension, the ultimate cessation of all conflict. This would no longer be a matter of the conciliation of opposites; it is an a priori harmony, which alone constitutes supreme, perfect peace.

Second, peace is not only the principle of the existence of the individual object; it is also the principle of reconciliation between the separate elements of reality as a whole. In the words of the fifteenth-century philosopher Isaac Arama: "Peace is the thread of grace issuing from Him, may He be exalted, and stringing together all beings, supernal, intermediate, and lower; it underlies and sustains the reality and unique existence of each" (*Akedat Yizhak*, ch. 74). Peace, like the "sympathy" of neo-Platonism, appears here as that system of mutual relationships by which all objects, all of the separate components of the universe, are joined to one another. It is ultimately the same as divine providence:

> And that is why God is called peace, because it is He who binds the world together and orders all beings according to their particular character and posture. For when things are in their proper order, peace will reign . . . as light is the opposite of darkness, so is peace the opposite of evil.
>
> (Isaac Abrabanel,
> Comm. to M. Avot 2:12;
> his words were directly derived from those of Arama)

The way is short from these ideas to a conception of peace as the embodiment of the divine immanence in the world. "Peace, *shalom,* is the essence of perfection, *shelemut,*" and there is no true perfection but the divine (*Netivot Olam, Netiv ha-Shalom,* sec. 1). Peace is the sum of the all, and only the divine comprehends all. Peace is the ultimate realization, the actualization and fulfillment of every potential essence; and God alone exists eternally in actuality, as pure, immaterial form. In the words of Rabbi Judah Loew of Prague, "God is the ultimate form of the world, and in this He comprehends all and joins and unifies all, and this is the very essence of peace" (ibid.). Loew goes on to declare the supremacy of *shalom* over all the other divine attributes (such as truth), for peace alone denotes comprehensiveness and totality, in contrast to the partiality of all other entities and values. Peace is thus none other than divine perfection. It transcends the planes of the physical, the social, and even the cosmic to enter the theological realm: "God alone constitutes the essence of peace" (ibid.).

In the kabbalistic texts, *peace* signifies a divine quality or emanation, the *sefirah* of *Yesod,* which links upper and lower, right and left in the world of the *sefirot*: "It makes peace between them and draws them to dwell together without separation or division in the world" (Gikatila, *Shaarei Ora,* ch. 2).

How do these portrayals of peace relate to earthly, historical peace? Does the identification of peace with ultimate perfection strengthen its power and buttress the concrete, immediate demand it presents to man in history? Or does it, perhaps, neutralize its normative validity and deprive that demand of its force? What is the power of the exalted status assigned to peace, and what potential dangers does it present in terms of both consciousness and reality? These questions will be discussed at the conclusion, after an analysis of the status in Jewish thought of political peace, of the cessation of war between nations, states, and faiths.

Jewish sources, from the Bible onward, acknowledge war as a given of human existence. War is viewed as a historical phenomenon—undesirable, but nevertheless tolerable within certain limits. It is a reflection of the real, yet fallen, human condition in history, as opposed to the metahistorical era of the End of Days.

There is thus no pacifist conception to be found here. Violence is permissible in certain circumstances, and the halakhic literature in fact defined and delimited the notions of an obligatory war and an optional war. It cannot be said, then, that any kind of peace is preferable to any kind of war. But neither is war considered a natural or necessary phenomenon, the essential fate of man by virtue of his very humanity, as it was by some thinkers of ancient times and of the Renaissance. War reflects the real situation of man, but not his destiny.

An inner tension may be discerned in the sources regarding the origin of war. On the one hand, war was described as a manifestation of direct divine intervention in the world, as a dramatic expression of God's power to do justice and bring salvation: "The Holy One said to them: it is I who made wars, as it is written [Ex. 15:3]: 'The Lord is a man of war'" (BT Av. Zar. 2b); "Mt. Horev: the mountain on which the sword [herev] was heard" (Tanh. Num. 7). Thus, war is not a natural consequence of the world order. It is a manifestation of the outstretched arm of God, ready to smite the wicked. The same is true of the days to come: "War is also the beginning of redemption" (BT Meg. 17b).

On the other hand, war is conceived as a manifestation of man's own wickedness and fall. Culture and history as they stand, suffused with war and bloodshed, are an expression of the corruption of man's nature, the fruit of sin. This motif is reflected, for instance, in those midrashim that speak of war and bloodshed as having their source in the figure of Cain and in the civilization founded by his heir, Tubal-cain, "the forger of every cutting instrument of brass and iron" (Gen. 4:22), or of war as stemming from the wickedness of the four kings who first waged it in the time of Abraham: "The wicked have drawn out the sword [Ps. 37:14]: those were the four kings, namely—Amraphel and his fellows [Gen. 14], for there had not yet been war in the world, and they came and drew out the sword, and thus they made [i.e., created] war" (Tanh. Lekh Lekha 7). This same motif is echoed in some statements of Philo regarding the deterioration of human society into warfare in the wake of its enjoyment of plenty and ease, as well as in the writings of several medieval thinkers (such as Isaac Abrabanel) and in the ideas of some modern thinkers (such as Abraham Isaac Kook).

Either way, war is viewed as the product not of nature but of sin: from the first point of view, war and its terrors are the punishment of the wicked, a strike from on high drawn down by sin (and salvation for the just). From the latter perspective, war itself is a manifestation of wickedness and corruption, the fruit of sin. Either way, freedom from sin also constitutes freedom from the sword.

Throughout Jewish history neither war nor peace really stood as concrete options for the Jewish people: The Jew, lacking political sovereignty, had no status in the international debate, and the question of war or peace in the here and now did not press him for an immediate response or decision. Only the wars of the Gentiles belonged to concrete historical reality, and that reality was the Jew's involuntary lot. On the other hand, the ancient wars of Israel were a matter more for theology than for politics. They took place in Scripture, either in the distant past or, at the approach of the messianic era, in the distant future. The Jew waged concrete war against the evil inclination more than he did against any historical foe. Peace, too, was discussed primarily from a utopian perspective, in light of the vision of the End of Days, and it too belonged mainly to the theological realm: The unity of the human race in the time to come was representative of the unity of God, the creator of all men (that is, of monotheistic truth), and peace for humanity would come about when all its members had accepted the kingdom of God.

The course of history set the Jewish scholars an exegetical challenge that was the opposite of that which faced their Christian counterparts. In the postbiblical Jewish sources we find a distinct trend toward the spiritualization of scriptural passages dealing with such things as war, might, and the sword. The "sword and bow" mentioned in the Bible (Gen. 48:22; Ps. 44:7) are in fact "prayer and beseeching" (Targum Onkelos to the verse in Genesis; Tanh. Beshallah, ch. 9). "The soldier and warrior" and "those who repel attacks at the gate" in the Book of Isaiah (3:2; 28:6) are not warriors in the literal sense, but "those who know how to dispute in the battle of the Torah" (BT Hag. 14a; BT Meg. 15b). The sword of the mighty is the Torah (Mid. Ps. 45:4). The generals of the Bible were transformed into scholars and heads of the Sanhedrin, and even "David's warriors" (II Sam. 23:8) were none other than manifestations of the might of his spirit "as he took part in the session [of scholars]" (BT MK 16b). This tendency to spiritualize scriptural verses dealing with might and war is prevalent throughout the aggadic (as opposed to the halakhic) homiletical literature, and it reappears in new and different guises in the philosophical and mystical literature of the Middle Ages; in the former these verses are interpreted as referring to the struggle between different faculties of the soul and in the latter as referring to divine attributes.

The tendency we have described has a most illuminating converse parallel in the Christian exegesis of New Testament passages dealing with war and the sword. Christianity set out with a pacifist message. This message was expressed in several passages in the New Testament, particularly in the Sermon on the Mount, and it was as pacifists that the early Christians were depicted in their own time. Later on, however, when Christianity had become the religion of the Roman Empire, it developed the doctrine of the "just war." Augustine, the chief spokesman for this doctrine, buttressed his arguments by citing sayings of the prophets in their literal, original senses; the pacifist verses in the New Testament had to be given a new, nonliteral interpretation, however. Here, too, this was done by way of spiritualization—not of texts that called to battle, but of those that rang with pacifism: The latter were interpreted as referring to man's inner state, to the depths of his spirit, and not to concrete historical reality. Such was the way of a faith that had recently entered the political arena and become a power, in contrast to that of a faith long absent from that same arena.

A third stage in the Christian theory of war developed in the Middle Ages—that of the holy war, as manifested in the Crusades. This, too, has a partial converse parallel in the development of Jewish tradition. (See M. Yad. 4:4 and MT Hil. Melakhim 5:4, which neutralize a holy commandment to wage war against the seven peoples [indigenous to the land of Israel] with respect to the present and future; see also JT Shev. 6:1 on the messages sent by Joshua to the land's inhabitants.) According to Maimonides, the notion of an "obligatory war" can refer only to a war waged "to deliver Israel from an enemy attacking them"; this may be comparable with the Christian concept of the "just war," but not with that of the "holy war."

The Jewish people's loss of political sovereignty and its remove from the realm of concrete decision-making with regard to war and peace did not preclude the theoretical study of these issues. It was only natural, however, for such discussion to be confined to a utopian plane, to a future time that transcended the immediate historical domain. This discussion took place at once in the shadow of the bloodshed that had been such a dominant characteristic of human history and in the light of the prophetic vision of eternal peace.

It is customary to distinguish between three possible approaches to understanding the phenomenon of war: they hold, respectively, that the root of war is to be found in the nature and upbringing of the individual, in the structure of international relationships, or in the order of society and the state. These approaches have their counterparts in three fundamental conceptions regarding the way to make an end to war and bring about a state of peace. According to the first, this can be done by reforming man qua man—that is, by changing the consciousness of the individual; according to the second, by reconstructing the international framework—that is, by creating a new world order; and according to the third, by an internal reformation of society—that is, by a change in the political order (see, for example, K. N. Waltz, *Man, the State and War,* 1954). The same three approaches are to be found in the models of peace put forward in medieval Jewish sources.

1. Peace and the Conciousness of the Individual: conception of peace as stemming from the consciousness of the individual focuses on the root of human existence, on the nature and consciousness of man. Putting an end to war involves subduing those internal impulses and motives that impel man to violence. Peace will come about as a consequence of the perfection—either intellectual or psychological—of humankind.

1a. Peace By Virtue of Knowledge: Maimonides viewed the prophetic vision of peace foretold by the prophets as a natural and necessary outgrowth of the dominion of the intellect over man's destructive impulses. According to him, violence and war, the inflicting of harm by people on one another, have their source in irrationality and ignorance. However, the apprehension of truth—"knowledge of God"—displaces man's awareness from his attachment to illusory goods and interests, and completely eliminates the irrational factors that arouse mutual conflict between individuals, groups, and nations:

Through cognition of the truth, enmity and hatred are removed and the inflicting of harm by people on one another is abolished. . . . The cause of the abolition of these enmities, these discords, and these tyrannies will be the knowledge that men will then have concerning the true reality of the deity [Guide 3, 11]. In that era there will be neither famine nor war, neither jealousy nor strife. The one preoccupation of the whole world will be to know the Lord [MT Hil. Melakhim 12:5]. "They shall not hurt or destroy in all My holy mountain, for the earth shall be full of the knowledge of the Lord" [Isa. 11:9]: The reason for their neither robbing nor injuring has been given in their knowledge of God. (*Treatise on Resurrection;* cf. Abraham ibn Ezra, Comm. on Isa. 11:9)

Intellectual perfection is the guarantor of peace. This follows not upon a change in man's nature, but rather upon the fulfillment and realization of his rational self, an overcoming, as it were, of original sin, which is interpreted by Maimonides as man's fall from the world of intellect and apprehension to the world of lust, conflict, and struggle between good and evil (*Guide* 1:2).

This portrayal of peace is clearly utopian. History is the realm of war. In one place Maimonides writes that the people of Israel were conquered and driven from their land because they had not learned the art of war (*Iggeret le-Ḥakhmei Marsilia*) and in another that they will return to their land and gain a firm hold upon it by means, among other things, of war (MT Hil. Melakhim 11). However, the ultimate, universal redemption, as distinguished from the national redemption, is destined to transcend history (if only from the point of view of the norm, the eternal task, it sets) to achieve perfect peace.

1*b*. Peace By Virtue of Love: Like Maimonides, Abraham bar Ḥiyya (in his book *Hegyon ha-Nefesh*) describes the peace foretold by the prophets as the consequence of a radical change in human consciousness. His catalogue of the causes of war—namely, man's destructive impulses—is also similar to that of Maimonides: "zealotry, hatred, and covetousness." However, it is in precisely this realm, that of interpersonal relations, that the transformation of consciousness in the messianic era is to take place. Man's destructive impulses are to be overcome not by intellect, but by the sense of intimacy and mutual identification that will grow among men once they have all chosen to adopt the same path, "the same way of life, one of faith and fear of God." The projected utopian peace will be expressed and embodied in the universal effectiveness of the commandment to "love thy neighbor as thyself"—spreading outward from the Jewish people to all the peoples of the world:

This commandment will be observed and upheld by all of the world's inhabitants in that great time. And if each and every one of them shall love his fellow as he loves himself, then zealotry, hatred, and covetousness must vanish from the world; and it is these that are the causes of war and slaughter in this world. That is why Scripture says of the messianic era (Isa. 2:4): "And they shall beat their swords into plowshares, and their spears into pruning-hooks; nation shall not lift up sword against nation."

(*Hegyon ha-Nefesh*, 4)

In this conception, unlike that of Maimonides, the overcoming of original sin depends upon direct, miraculous divine intervention: "He shall transform the impulse of man, which was evil from his youth, and make it good and upright from his youth" (cf. Naḥmanides, Comm. on Deut. 30:6, 28:42, and elsewhere). The anticipated universal brotherhood, the quelling of the bloodshed that had been a fundamental characteristic of human history, is in fact an individual instance of this new creation.

2. Peace and the World Order: According to this conception the world's peoples will be made to live in peace by being brought together under a single universal framework, which will be established either through law and justice or through domination and force. Descriptions of all mankind turning toward Zion or being ruled from Zion are often found together, in passages by the same author, with descriptions of the ultimate spiritual perfection to be attained by each individual person: On the path to the fulfillment of the utopian vision, the establishment of a universal political order is the prelude and steppingstone to the ultimate perfection of humanity.

2a. Peace By Virtue of Justice: The image of world peace described by several medieval commentators and thinkers took the form of a judicial arrangement between the rival nations, a kind of international court that would mediate their quarrels and conflicts. This vision speaks not of a human society that has risen above all striving and conflict or of a man whose intellect has completely overcome his destructive impulses; it speaks, rather, of a procedure for conflict resolution presided over by a supreme, utopian judge whose authority and righteousness are accepted by all. As justice takes the place of violence between man and his fellows, so will it do so between peoples and countries. The prophetic tiding "and he shall judge between the nations" (Isa. 2:4, Micah 4:3), which would seem in its original sense to refer to the kingship of God rather than to some particular person or institution, is interpreted as referring to the Sages of Jerusalem or the Messiah. The judicial institution is granted universal authority:

> The judge is the King Messiah . . . for if there should be a war or quarrel between two nations, they will come for adjudication before the King Messiah, the lord of all peoples, and he will judge between them, and say to the one found in the wrong: put right the offense against your opponent; and so there will be no more war between peoples, for they will settle their conflicts and have no more need of weapons.
>
> (David Kimhi, comm. to the above passages;
> cf. Abraham ibn Ezra on the same verses)

The quarrels and wars up to that time between the different groups of heathens had arisen on account of the faulty character of their laws, which did not accord with the nature of truth; and those whose causes were adjudicated under them therefore were not placated and could not accept them. Under the perfect justice administered by the King Messiah, however, they shall abandon war and strife.

(Arama, *Akedat Yizhak*, ch. 46;
cf. MT Hil. Teshuvah 9:2:
"All of the nations shall come to hear him")

2b. Peace By Virtue of World Regime: Other thinkers interpreted the envisioned international structure as a kind of Pax Judaica, a single, central government in Zion to which all peoples would be subject: "There would remain no nation that was not under the rule of Israel" (Saadiah Gaon, *Book of Doctrines and Beliefs*, 8:8). These portrayals of the destined universal dominion of the people of Israel or the king-messiah rest upon biblical or midrashic sources, but they also bear the mark of contemporary historical reality: living out the present in submission, subject to the gentile powers, the Jews anticipate a complete reverse, a time when all the world's peoples will be subject to the people of Israel and the king-messiah (Saadiah, op. cit., 8:6; cf. BT Eruv. 43b); the people that lost its inheritance will someday inherit the whole earth (see bar Ḥiyya, *Megillat ha-Megallei*, 76, in contrast to the ideas from his *Hegyon ha-Nefesh* quoted above; cf. Sif. Deut. 11). This hope that "the nation will ultimately rise to a splendid height," that there would arise "in Israel a king who will govern all the world" (Joseph Albo, *Sefer ha-Ikkarim* 4:42), clearly exerted a significant influence over the consciousness of a degraded, subjugated people. Not by chance did Maimonides voice his explicit objection to the inclination to set this hope at the center of religious consciousness and of the people's vision of redemption:

The sages and the prophets did not long for the days of the Messiah that Israel might exercise dominion over the world, or rule over the Gentiles, or be exalted by the nations, and not to eat and drink and rejoice, but that they be free to devote themselves to the Law and its wisdom, with no one to oppress or disturb them.

(MT Hil. Melakhim 12:4;
Ḥasdai Crescas was later to emphasize that
the messiah would "reign over Israel and Judah"—
that is, presumably, over them alone.
See *Or ha-Shem* 3:8:1)

In any event, portrayals of a universal government emanating from Zion appear in several different versions. Some hold that this government will be established permanently (as in the above examples), others that it is a transitional stage preparatory to the final redemption (Abrabanel, *Yeshu'ot*

Meshiḥo 57). The universal government was to be founded variously upon miracle, upon force, or upon its spiritual exaltation. Some thinkers formulated an intermediate position between this model and the previous one, as in the following passage by Maimonides himself:

> All nations will make peace with him, and all countries will serve him [the king-messiah] out of respect for his great righteousness and the wonders which occur through him. All those who rise against him will be destroyed and delivered into his hands by God . . . and [there will be an] end of wars. . . . "Nation shall not lift up sword against nation, neither shall they learn war any more" [Micah 4:31].
>
> (Comm. on the Mishnah, intro. to Perek Ḥelek)

3. Peace and the Socio-Political Order: this conception focuses on social patterns and on the political structure: Peace will come about as a result of the annulment or improvement of existing political structures. Despite the obvious fact that the exile of the Jew, his remove from an independent political life, did not encourage him toward concrete, detailed political thinking, it is nevertheless worthwhile to examine two interesting models manifested in the medieval literature, one of which is confined entirely to the utopian plane while the other addresses actual, historical reality.

3a. Peace and the Annulment of Political Order: In the teachings of Isaac Abrabanel, war and bloodshed are described as a consequence of man's historical and cultural fall, a fall that is embodied preeminently in man's technological civilization and political tradition.

To begin with, the construction of a technological culture and the establishment of an artificial human civilization alienate man from his natural state and from his natural satisfaction and fulfillment. The culture of the implement, of manufacturing, and of iron, and the continual effort to extract from nature more than it spontaneously proffers are founded upon lust and covetousness, upon man's urges to acquisitiveness, domination, and rivalry. Conversely, this material culture continually refuels man's lust and covetousness, inciting him toward strife, plunder, and war. It violates the natural, primal peace of humankind. Thus the most outstanding representative and product of this culture is the sword: "The sword is an artificial instrument, made in order to destroy natural things" (Abrabanel, Comm. on Gen. 3:22; 4:1, 17; 11:1).

Now, the capstone of this civilization is manifested in its sociopolitical order. The city, the state, the kingdom—the various forms of human government—are all described as vessels alien to man's nature, artificial structures that direct human awareness toward false goals (honor and power) and that are founded upon confrontation between earthly realms (rivalry and war). They all represent a situation wherein man has disowned his natural state, in which he is ruled solely by God, in favor of the perversions of material culture—and so also of war and the sword. The pattern of this transition is depicted in the Book of Genesis, beginning with man's expulsion from the Garden of Eden into the realm of the "flaming sword which turned every way," continuing through the first bloodshed committed by Cain and the advent of Tubal-Cain, "who sharpened instruments of brass and iron, sword and spear, for the sake of bloodshed," and on through the sin of the generation that built the Tower of Babel; and the whole unhappy chronicle was interpreted by Abrabanel in light of this model:

> They did not suffice with the generous natural gift of their Creator, but sought to put out their hands and set their minds to discovering the crafts required to build a city and to make of themselves polities . . . with all that this involves—fame and ordinations and governments, and imaginary honors, and the desire to multiply possessions, violence, thieving, and bloodshed.
>
> (Abrabanel, op. cit.)

Whatever the Jewish and Christian sources of this conception (and the biographical background from which it sprang) may have been, its implications were also borne out in Abrabanel's messianic vision, which foresaw a universal theocracy, the kingship of God on earth. Ultimate redemption would involve the disappearance of national and political boundaries and the abrogation of political structures through the unification of all humanity in the light of the monotheistic faith—that is to say, through the religious perfection of mankind. Redemption, moreover, is destined to bring about the demise of materialistic civilization and a return to the Garden of Eden, which is the garden of contemplation, the primordial condition of man.

Abrabanel explicitly objected to that conception which envisioned world peace as the product of a universal juridical framework. Such a conception left the separate states and nations as they were, though "Scripture says in the name of the peoples that all of them *together* [emphasis added] shall say, 'come ye, and let us go up to the mountain of the Lord'" (Comm. to Isa. 2:4; cf. Judah Loew of Prague, *Nezaḥ Israel,* sec. 163: "The world shall be one, with no more division or separation."). Abrabanel was also careful to distinguish the nature of the future Pax Judaica from that of the ancient Pax Romana: "Jerusalem and her king shall not rule the world by the sword and spear, as did the Romans and other great empires . . . but by the spirit of God, for all the peoples shall submit to her on account of the holiness and divinity of God" (Comm. to Micah 4). Looking closely at the causes of war in the Middle Ages, moreover, Abrabanel notes that the unification of all mankind into a single faith would demolish not only the political goads to war but also the religious ones:

> For most wars among the Gentiles are occasioned by their religious differences, as in the wars between Edom [the Christian nations] and Ishmael [the Moslem world], and so when all of them shall call upon the name of the Lord and submit to His Torah and His commandments, they shall dwell in safety, with no more thieving and violence.
>
> (*Mashmia Yeshu'a* 46b)

3b. Peace and the Reform of the Political Order: In the writings of Isaac Arama, peace and war are discussed in relation to the law of the state, the presently operative political and judicial order. Arama points to the social causes of war, the motives that stir individuals, groups, or peoples to take up the sword, and considers how these causes might be moderated and their motives diminished. Unlike the conceptions described above, in which peace was portrayed primarily from a utopian point of view in light of the messianic vision, Arama looks at this issue in light of actual, contemporary historical reality as well. While he does, of course, also discuss peace as a utopian and even a cosmic concept, he goes on to inquire into the possibilities for preventing or reducing the evils of war in the present day.

The basic reason for the phenomenon of strife and war is to be found in the perverted laws and defective ways of society. It is their sense of wrong and of the perversion of justice that drives individuals and nations to take up the sword:

> For if the social order and law [*nimmus*] are defective and distant from the natural truth . . . quarrel and strife cannot but break out amongst them, for their minds are not at ease, and they cannot consent to this; and such strife spreads to become the great wars that lay waste to civilization.
>
> (*Akedat Yizhak,* ch. 46)

Two optimistic assumptions regarding the human condition may be discerned in this conception: First, Arama implies that men have a natural, universal sense of justice, and the closer the laws and the political order come to satisfying that sense, the more peace will tend to overcome war. To be sure, the ultimate perfection of social justice is to come to light in the law of the Messiah, but this does not detract from the value of a partial, historical reform. Second, Arama argues that people are not partial to war for its own sake (cf. Aristotle, Nicomachean Ethics, I:7, 1177b, 5–11). Apart from a few murderous individuals, human motives and purposes in setting out to war go beyond a desire for violence. It is thus the task of the lawgiver to ordain a social order that will reduce and remove these motives, both on the part of the ruler and on the part of his subjects. Furthermore, the lawgiver should make ordinances for times of war that would lessen, as far as possible, the harm and the terrors of the sword:

> Since war involves so many evil matters and sins, it is impossible that any man would choose these for their own sake, for anyone who would do so would be called an oppressor or a murderer . . . and it is therefore fitting and incumbent upon an honest and thorough lawgiver to guide the king and people in these matters, so that all of these evils will be prevented . . . and to take care to distance those matters and activities that utterly deprive man of the [moral] order of good and evil, as happens in war.
>
> (ibid., ch. 81)

Arama makes full use, in this regard, of all the *midrashim* on the subject of peace. In his view, the obligation to pursue peace both in one's own place and in others as well applies not only to internal social relations but also to international political relations:

> One must pursue and seek [peace] . . . and one may not say: it is sufficient for me to try to mediate between [the contenders] and reconcile them if they should happen to come before me. And this is all the more true in the case of wars between peoples and kingdoms, for the greater and more numerous they are, so are the attendant evils and afflictions multiplied. . . . Even as one sets out to drive peoples away from oneself by war, he is obligated to seek peace and pursue it.
>
> (ibid., 105a)

Moreover, the Torah's commandment "When thou drawest nigh unto a city to fight against it, then proclaim peace unto it" (Deut. 20:10) is not fulfilled merely by a call to the enemy to surrender; it requires "entreaties and supplications offered in the most conciliatory possible way, in order to turn their hearts . . . for this follows necessarily from the human wisdom of peace, and the divine will consent" (ibid.; see Tanh. Zav, ch. 3; Deut. R. 5:13).

This essay has been devoted to a survey of the different usages of the term *peace* in Jewish literature and to the analysis of various models in the light of which the abolition of war and the establishment of peace were depicted in medieval Jewish literature. The relationship between the historical and conceptual survey outlined above and the present sociopolitical condition of the Jewish people is also worth examination.

One outstanding characteristic manifested in most of the sources and conceptions surveyed is the elevation of peace to utopian and even cosmic heights, transcending concrete historical reality. This is especially apparent in the sources of medieval Jewish thought. To be sure, the various understandings of the causes of war described above were not entirely cut off from the political circumstances of their time and place: They reflect different ways of comprehending historical events, different perspectives regarding the nature of man and society as they were, and not only regarding the nature of the redemption that was to come. However, discussions of peace and the abolition of war in these sources usually went beyond their historical setting to assume the logic of the end of time. Several phenomena contributed greatly to this development: (1) the linguistic identification of the word *shalom* with the concepts of *shalem* and *shelemut,* wholeness and perfection; (2) the reality of Jewish existence, in which the people lacked political sovereignty and so, consequently, the power to make immediate and concrete decisions regarding questions of peace and war; and (3) the gulf between the bloodshed that had always been a basic fact of human history and the prophetic vision of world peace.

What potential options and dangers does this demand for perfection present when faced with a historical reality that is not devoid of tensions, interests, and enmities, when it encounters a historical realization molded by the partial, the gradual, and the contingent? When peace is discussed in a utopian framework, in light of a perfect vision, does this increase its cogency, its real demands within the concrete political context—or may it, perhaps, neutralize peace as a normative value, annulling its real, immediate claim upon the present era? On the one hand, the exalted status assigned to peace embodies a positive ethical potential: It guides man to strive, in any kind of circumstances, for the ultimate perfection of man and society. As noted by Abrabanel in his commentary to Isaiah 2:5, "The prophet did not describe this destiny [of peace] for the end of days for its own sake . . . but in order to derive from it a lesson for his generation." On the other hand, this perfect image of peace demands a price, for it may take a dim view of anything that is not perfect, complete, and ultimate, that does not beat swords into plowshares and create an ideal state of harmony. Will the Jewish people, in its encounter with historical, earthly reality, in a time when the Messiah still tarries, be able to realize a concept of peace that is not taken from the realm of the absolute? And if it is able to do so, will this necessarily mean a relinquishing of the utopian horizon that has molded the people's consciousness since time immemorial, a betrayal of classical images and visions? The answers will not be found in any legal or philosophical sources; they are nowhere engraved upon the tablets.

BIBLIOGRAPHY

Morris N. Eisenstadth, "Sanctions for Peace: Judaism," in *World Religions and World Peace,* Homer A. Jack, ed. (1968).

Paul D. Hanson, "War and Peace in the Hebrew Bible," in *Interpretation: A Journal of Bible and Theology,* 38, 4 (1984).

Itzhak Rafael, ed., *Torah she-be-al Peh,* 21 (1980) (special volume on peace in the halakhah).

David S. Shapiro, "The Jewish Attitude Toward Peace and War," in his *Studies in Jewish Thought,* 1 (1975); reprinted in *Violence and the Value of Life in the Jewish Tradition,* Yehezkel Landau, ed. (1984).

M. Wald, *Jewish Teaching on Peace* (1944).

People of Israel

עַם יִשְׂרָאֵל

Alon Goshen-Gottstein

The patriarch Jacob, after his struggle with the angel, was the first to receive the name *Israel*. This name then became the name of a people known as the people of Israel (*am Yisrael*). The name *Israel* refers, however, not only to the historical people present upon earth, but also to a soul—to an ongoing spiritual work of the people that takes place on planes beyond the visible, mundane order. The work of Israel done here on earth is but an extension of the endeavors of the supernal, larger Israel.

The patriarch who was named Israel is the patriarch from whom the people of Israel, and they alone, are born. Unlike his fathers—Abraham and Isaac—Jacob's whole progeny is contained within the fold of the people of Israel. It is for this reason that they bear his name. We can learn something about the meaning of what Israel truly is by looking at the name of the patriarch, shared by his descendants: the one who struggled with God. In Genesis 32:25–32, we read:

> Jacob was left alone, and a man wrestled with him until the break of dawn. When he saw that he had not prevailed against him, he wrenched Jacob's hip at its socket, so that the socket of his hip was strained as he wrestled with him.

Then he said: "Let me go, for dawn is breaking." But he answered, "I will not let you go, unless you bless me." Said the other: "What is your name?" He replied: "Jacob." Said he: "Your name shall no longer be Jacob, but Israel, for you have striven with beings divine and human, and have prevailed." Jacob asked, "Pray tell me your name." But he said, "You must not ask my name!" And he took leave of him there. So Jacob named the place Peniel, meaning "I have seen a divine being face to face, yet my life has been preserved." The sun rose upon him, as he passed Peniel, limping on his hip.

The primary meaning of *Israel* is thus the one who struggled with God. Through Jacob's struggle is attained rebirth, an elevation to a new level of existence. Born Jacob—the crooked, possibly treacherous one (Gen. 27; 36)—his struggle is that of self-transformation of the former self. The crooked here becomes straight, as in the etymology of Israel *(yashar-el)*. The struggle also takes its toll—"limping on his hip." The impairment attendant on the struggle is of significance to all future generations. Yet this struggle yielded a blessing, expressed in the new name for the one who has fought with God, overcome, and come to a new life. From this new life proceeds the people of Israel.

From this original act of naming Israel we thus learn something important concerning what Israel truly is. *Israel,* not only the patriarch but the people that flows from him, embodies a struggle, a rebirth, and the collective emergence into a higher level of existence.

Within the context of humanity, we may again view Israel in the same process of struggling to attain this higher spiritual level of existence. The struggle of Israel is not isolated from the struggle of humanity. The very blessing by which the patriarch is given the name *Israel* by God is accompanied by the promise of many nations being born unto him (Gen. 35:9–11). There is an intrinsic relation between the struggles of Israel and the struggles of humanity as a whole.

The metaphor through which the relation between Israel and the nations can best be expressed is an organic metaphor, that of the body. As the body has various limbs, so the world has various nations. As the body must work as a whole, so the various nations must work in peace and harmony. As the evolution of the body proceeds to degrees of greater and higher refinement, to degrees of greater cultural and spiritual achievement, so humanity evolves to ever higher levels of ability to recognize God and to give expression to the spiritual aspirations of mankind.

Israel, as suggested, is a dynamic entity, one that relates to struggle and to a dynamic process of growth. In this respect the organic metaphor may be inappropriate, for the body is a defined, closed entity. Yet in the Jewish tradition there is an alternative image of the body that will allow us to incorporate the dynamic element we have related to the concept of Israel. This image, propounded by the kabbalists and upon which we will here elaborate, does not evoke that of the mere physical body.[1] The kabbalah speaks of a supernal body composed of energy centers, of spiritual centers, which are known as the *sefirot* (lit., "spheres").

The *sefirot* are formed in accordance with the structure of the body and they, as a whole, form one organic unity, which enables the divine manifestation through which God as well as all created beings operate. Humanity as a whole may also be viewed as such a body. Within this body are different spiritual centers. Each nation is related to a center or to an aspect of a specific spiritual center, a specific spiritual *sefirah*.

The process of humanity is one of higher and higher evolution, not only in its cultural achievements but also spiritually, through the formation of spiritual centers within humanity. As humanity evolves, it becomes possible for greater and greater aspects of divine perfection to be embodied within humanity. Within this process, we can discern the formation of diverse spiritual centers. A spiritual center that is formed necessitates a specific vehicle or a vessel. The dynamic element that is embodied in the people of Israel is thus the process of the formation of a distinctive spiritual center within humanity, the people of Israel serving as its vessel.

In an altogether different context, we find the structure of the body as a most prominent concept in kabbalistic teaching. The reference is to the supernal divine body of God. Some kabbalistic teachers regard the supernal Israel, as opposed to the manifest historical Israel, as the heart center within the body of God. In one tradition, we even find Israel as the supernal crown (*keter*)—the highest rung in the sefirotic order:

> The supernal crown which is called "primordial Israel." . . .
> The primordial Israel which is the secret of the supernal crown.
> (*Sefer Maraot ha-Ẓoveot* 82:31; 210:5)

Our presentation of Israel's position within the body of humanity shall proceed from this understanding. Israel is the *keter* within the body of humanity. However, this position is not to be regarded as a source of pride and hubris, for one of the foremost qualities of the *sefirah keter* is its humility. Indeed, one of *keter*'s many names is "nothingness." The rabbis describe God as saying to Israel, "You are the smallest of peoples" (Deut. 7:7), and, as the rabbis say, "Even when I bestow greatness upon you, you humble yourselves before me" (BT Hul. 89a). It is this quality of humility that characterizes the work of *keter*.

As the first emanation in the sefirotic order, *keter* is that which takes the divine light and transfers it onto others. The quality of *keter* is the quality of the will of God—the will of God being the first divine emanation. When we refer to Israel as *keter,* it is, then, an anchor point allowing the will of God to emanate. Through Israel, God's will emanates to humanity.

In kabbalistic teaching the various *sefirot* are divided according to the qualities of openness, constriction, and a quality of mitigation, or balancing of these polar spiritual forces. *Keter* is, however, beyond such a division: It is all good, without any constriction, without any limitation. No evil enters *keter,* the quality of which is absolute compassion. In light of all this, therefore, the designation of Israel as *keter* denotes not only an entity but also a purpose; it is a designation of responsibility, of a mission.

In light of our understanding of Israel's position within humanity and the process of the formation of a spiritual center within the body of humanity, we may appreciate the importance of the story of Israel's formation as told in the Bible. The center point of the biblical story of Genesis is the formation of the nation—the formation of a spiritual center. The trials and tribulations of the patriarchs and the story of Israel's Exile in Egypt are all aspects of the process of the formation of the nation. God promises Abraham to form a new nation from him, according to our understanding—a nation that is to bring a new spiritual quality to the world. God's promise to Abraham appertains to humanity as a whole (Gen. 12:3). Later, a covenant is made between God and Abraham which defines the special relationship between God and Abraham's seed (Gen. 17). God is to be their God, and Abraham's seed is to keep God's covenant. On this occasion, a founding moment of the future Jewish people, the land of Israel is promised to Abraham's seed. It is also noteworthy that on this occasion Abram is renamed Abraham, signifying he is to become the father of many nations. Thus, the founding covenant of the Jewish people is firmly linked with the future of humanity. The covenant made with Abraham focuses on God's promises to Abraham and to the future people of Israel. Israel's commitments to God are also expressed through a covenant, made between God and Israel at Mount Sinai. We may view this covenant—following the Exile in Egypt—as fulfilling the process of the formation of the nation of Israel. Israel's birth takes place between these two covenants. In the latter covenant the specific way of life required of Israel is revealed. Through the path revealed in this covenant Israel is to grow and to fulfill its mission. This mission is clearly stated as a preparation to the revelation at Sinai:

Now then, if you will obey me faithfully and keep My covenant, you shall be My treasured possession among the peoples. Indeed, all the earth is Mine, but you shall be to Me a kingdom of priests and a holy nation.

(Ex. 19:5–6).

The two related aspects depicted in the covenant with Abraham are again to be found here. Israel is to be both—vis-à-vis itself and God—and a "kingdom of priests." One will note that a priest is someone who serves on behalf of others; thus, Israel is to be a nation of priests serving on behalf of all humanity.

Israel's very creation, then, as *keter* is one that endows it with an immense responsibility to be a nation that lives by the will of God, that brings to the world the will of God, and that emanates the will of God. The process by which Israel is to achieve this is through the various covenants it makes with God.

It is noteworthy that, in the covenant made with Abraham, we find the promise for the land of Israel going hand in hand with the promise of the formation of the people of Israel, though both are as yet unknown by these names. Here we touch upon the deeper reason for the common name shared by the land and the people. It is not merely because the land is given to the people of Israel, or vice versa, that those who inhabit the land are called the people of Israel; the connection between land and people is deeper—Israel as a nation represents a spiritual center within the body of humanity. As pointed out, the sefirotic organization, by spiritual energy centers and patterns, is one that is not unique to humanity, but is the organizational pattern determining all that is. Therefore, earth—the land itself—is organized along similar lines. The land of Israel is the center of the earth, representing that which Israel is to represent among people. The connection of Israel the people and Israel the land is therefore vital. It is by dwelling in a place possessing certain qualities and properties that the people of Israel is to partake in these attributes, to fulfill them, and to emanate them. There is an interchange, an interflow between the land of Israel and the people of Israel. The clearest indication of this fact is in Israel's history. When Israel fails to live up to what is expected of it, the land "spews" the people of Israel out (Lev. 20:22). Israel is no longer fit to remain in the land.

The Exile from the land of Israel, following Israel's failure to live in accordance with the standards required by the land, brings us to reflect upon one of the most crucial elements in Israel's history—suffering. Jacob became Israel through a struggle with—and toward—God. Though victorious, Jacob was wounded in battle. Jacob prefigures his descendants, who rise and fall in their struggle with and on behalf of God. Their forefather, limping at sunrise, is the source of their strength in the struggle, as well as of their vulnerability to the blows, the falls, and the failures that are their lot until the day of ultimate victory. The history of Israel is the story of Israel's struggle, of its alternating successes and failures to rise to what had been given it as its task. Thus it is that Israel's formation is brought about through suffering, which is a byproduct of the struggle itself. Accordingly, the suffering of the Exile in Egypt is a constitutive element in the formation of the Jewish people, for only in Egypt is Israel truly formed into a nation. On the other hand, failure to live up to the covenant with God, made so evident in the archetypal story of the Golden Calf, is what brings upon Israel a series of great calamities. This suffering is not merely punishment for Israel's transgressions. It is a means through which Israel is to assume its destiny. As its original formation was brought about by suffering, so its purification from its wrongdoing takes place in the process of suffering. In suffering, the force of *keter* is realized. Through this purification Israel is enabled to maintain its position as a holy nation, to realize its being, and to fulfill its mission.

Essentially, Israel's task is to emanate a spiritual force that has not yet been embodied on earth by a nation. It is the force through which sin is to be eliminated. Historically, Israel has yet to succeed fully in its task. Indeed, one may say it has succumbed to sin. The point is so far-reaching that, on account of Israel's failure in history, other peoples have recurrently come to regard themselves as the true Israel. From the perspective of Judaism such claims are patently false, for Israel is a divine creation. Israel is an entity entrusted with a mission. Just as a foot does not become a head, so someone cannot become someone else. Certainly, when a foot can no longer perform its preordained task the hand may have to take over and assist. When an organ is weak and ailing, other parts of the body may have to put in an extra measure of work to compensate, but in a healthy, functioning body each organ and limb is allotted its own responsibility and position. So it is in the case of Israel. Sin and wrongdoing have played a very important part in the process of Israel's rising to become what God ordained it to be. In light of the prefigurative example of Jacob one may even wonder whether being bruised in the process of the struggle—succumbing and faltering in battle—is an unavoidable, indeed necessary aspect of the battle—a battle against evil and for—and toward—God.

Israel's fulfillment of its ultimate being is thus intrinsically bound up with struggle, suffering, and purification. In all this, however, Israel has never forfeited its true essential being. It has merely failed to reach the height it is destined to reach, and to actualize and realize its ultimate essence within the historical order.

Reflecting upon the process of suffering, cleansing, and purification brings us to the consideration of Israel as a "soul." In speaking of the organization of humanity in the form of a body, we were referring to the manifest earthly reality of humanity. However, this humanity is merely a visible aspect of a much greater entity. Judaism affirms that our life here on earth is merely a preparation for the life on the various higher planes of existence. Our earthly life is merely a school, an arena for education: "This world is like an antechamber before the world to come; prepare yourself in the antechamber so that you may enter the banquet hall" (M. Avot 4:16). The true life, so to speak, is the life that takes place on planes beyond our own mundane existence. It is, therefore, impossible for us to judge fully what Israel is, what Israel's position is, what Israel's responsibility is, and, conversely, how far-reaching its wrongdoing is and how necessary its purification is. The work of Israel is a work that takes place not only on this plane but also on the planes beyond. When we talk of Israel, the people, we must therefore remember that we are addressing not only their earthly reality but also the people as they belong to a much greater whole.

A statement by Rabbi Akiva may be regarded as an epigraphic summary of the spiritual significance of the people of Israel:

> Beloved is man, for he was created in the image of God. . . . Beloved are the people of Israel, for they are called children of God. . . . Beloved are the people of Israel, for a precious tool was given to them, with which the world was created.
>
> (M. Avot 3:14)

In this mishnah we can recognize three distinct stages, the first discussing man, the next two discussing Israel specifically. As we shall later suggest, a continuum exists between the various stages depicted in Rabbi Akiva's words. We should note the expression of God's emotion found in these statements All three levels are examples of God's love—for mankind and for Israel, manifest in each of the three levels mentioned by Rabbi Akiva.

On the first level, God's love is of man created in his image. Regarding the meaning of the divine image, a further statement made by Rabbi Akiva and his colleagues is instructive. Rabbi Akiva taught: "He who sheds blood is regarded as though he has diminished the *demut* [the divine image]. What is the proof? 'Whosoever sheds the blood of man, By man shall his blood be shed.' What is the reason? 'For in His image did God make man'" [Gen.

9:6]. Rabbi Eleazar Ben Azaria taught: "He who refrains from procreation diminishes the *demut*." Ben Azzai taught: "He who refrains from procreation is as though he sheds blood and diminishes the *demut*" (Gen. R. 34:14).

This passage can possibly shed light on the meaning of the previous statement by Rabbi Akiva describing man's belovedness by virtue of being created in the image of God. What is this *demut* that the second passage mentions? The term *demut* obviously derives from Genesis 1:26: "Let us make man in our image [*zelem*], after our likeness [*demut*]." The use of *demut* here, however, is clearly more far-reaching than the basic notion that man is created in the image of God. The statement teaches us that there is a larger whole to which each individual life belongs. Moreover, each life constitutes an expansion of that whole, and thus the prevention of birth is tantamount to bloodshed as far as it concerns the *demut*. We must note that the biblical verse explicated by the various sages appears as part of the Noachite commandments. Its relevance is, therefore, universal, and the meaning of *demut* derived from it should likewise maintain universal significance.

From the foregoing it can thus be concluded that the concept of *demut* implies that mankind as a whole was created in the image of God. One may then view all of humanity as constituting one organic whole, actually structured in a form said to be that of God. This form or body may be viewed as the body through which God is manifested. Thus the idea of God creating man in his image may be rendered as God manifesting himself through the totality of humanity, presented in a form or image—a *demut*.

From such an understanding several points emerge: It is humanity as a whole that is said to be an embodiment of the divine. This fact is grounded in the order of creation, wherein man—mankind—is so fashioned as to resemble and embody the divine. Mankind is, therefore, to be viewed as a totality, as an organic whole. It is within the context of this organic, divine whole that the position and significance of Israel is to be considered. When we state with Rabbi Akiva, "Beloved is man, for he was created in the image of God," we are hence referring to the totality of the body of humanity.

Within the body of humanity, Israel occupies a special position, which is the progression within the words of Rabbi Akiva from the first to the second statement. The second statement discusses the special position of Israel. Here the people of Israel are called children unto God. It seems, especially in contradistinction with the third statement of Rabbi Akiva, that the idea underlying Israel's being called children is that God's love for them is enduring and everlasting. Even when the son ceases to behave as he ought to and ceases to fulfill his filial obligations, his sonship endures: a son always remains a son. Similarly, Israel's position within humanity is one that will not, or has not, changed in accordance with Israel's behavior. Israel may have failed to fulfill its task fully. Nevertheless, its position as son has not changed. The idea of sonship, then, expresses the immanent value of Israel as a creation, as a being within the body of God.

Israel's sonship underscores God's unconditional love. At this point we should recall, however, that Israel was not only called "children unto God" but was also called God's "firstborn son" (Ex. 4:22). The designation of firstborn can be used to describe the relationship between the first son and the other children. It is obviously the responsibility of the firstborn to aid his parents and assist them in rearing his younger brethren. The position of firstborn describes a relation between the older son and his younger brethren as well as a relationship between the firstborn son and his parents.

The people of Israel are firstborn to *keter*. They are the ones who have to take up that energy and disseminate it into the world. Their position and responsibility is that of the older brother in relation to his brethren. In one way, we may say that everyone is firstborn to his own unique quality and capacity. A more specific approach may view *keter,* the first emanation, as firstborn par excellence, for it is the firstborn within the sefirotic order.

Israel is also called the beginning, the first (Lev. R. 35:4, quoting Jer. 2:3). If we return to what we have said concerning the will of God being that which Israel must emanate to the world, we can understand Israel's being first in the following manner. The will of God really is the first: the first stage in the process of creation, the first in the institution of a divine plan. It is from the will that everything else proceeds. Israel, then, as first or firstborn, has the responsibility to emanate this power of the will of God. In this capacity it is firstborn to *keter.*

It is precisely because Israel's position as children is not only one of unconditional love but also one of responsibility that Rabbi Akiva's words proceed to describe the love of Israel as an outcome of the fact that a precious tool has been given to them, with which the world was created. What is this tool? The common understanding views this tool as the Torah, which was instrumental in the process of God's creation of the world: "God looked into the Torah—and created the world" (Gen. R. 1:1). We may say that the Torah is the way of life—the covenantal statutes—entrusted unto Israel.

The covenant with God ensures his dwelling within Israel. God's dwelling is enabled by means of the presence of a divine force, called the *Shekhinah,* God's dwelling or presence. The presence of this force is a precondition for certain aspects of spiritual life, as well as for life itself. It is the

creative force, used in the creative process. It is the power through which
direct knowledge of God is rendered possible and through which the presence and reality of God can be known. This force can be said to be the
backbone of life itself. All of life's endeavors reach their fuller realization
when this power is employed. It is a powerful force—for it is the force of
life itself. The immense power associated with this force necessitates strict
measures guarding it against abuse. The consequence of misuse of the *Shekhinah* may be detrimental and may bring about destruction—both seen
and unseen—affecting a range of existence far greater than one's immediate
visible environment. The presence of this force is a special gift of God, to
be employed in a manner fitting the divine design. This force has been given
by God to Israel. Through its presence Israel's mission is to be fulfilled. This
power of God is necessary for the full opening of the spiritual centers, and
is thus vital for the full realization of what "Israel" is—for the formation
and the opening of *keter* within humanity.

The *Shekhinah*'s presence within Israel is, however, dependent upon
Israel's behavior. It is the *Shekhinah* that is given to Israel under the circumstance of the covenant, and it is the *Shekhinah* that is removed from Israel
as a result of its sins. As Israel has been in exile, so God's *Shekhinah* has
been in exile. Israel's redemption is the process of the return of the *Shekhinah* from its exile.

The catastrophe of Israel's exile is thus not merely a catastrophe for Israel
alone. It is a catastrophe for the entire world. One may even say it is a
catastrophe for the divine. For, as we have suggested above, Israel exists not
merely on the earthly plane but on planes above. God and the divine plan
for earth and for humanity are, therefore, affected by and dependent upon
Israel's fulfillment of its responsibilities.

Without the return of the *Shekhinah* to Israel, it would be impossible for
Israel to become what it must and to emanate to the world what it must.
To be sure, a certain measure of Israel's true identity had been maintained
in exile. For the last two thousand years, growth in thought and understanding has taken place, alongside a multifaceted contribution in many areas of
life. Nevertheless, Israel has not yet risen to its destined height.

This precious tool entrusted to Israel, we may further suggest, is God's
Shekhinah, the power of God's dwelling. For it is through the *Shekhinah* that
the world was created. This is the basis for the portrayal of Israel—or of
certain individuals—as partners to God in the creative process. Not merely
through the study of Torah as an intellectual exercise, but through the power
of the divine present amidst them, Israel can become the partner of God in
the creative process. It is thus Israel's position within the body of humanity,

emanating the force of *keter* by virtue of the presence of the *Shekhinah*, that finally brings humanity as a whole to perfection.

The three stages described in Rabbi Akiva's statement form a self-contained circle. The first stage is not subservient to the third; rather, we have here a total circle. When Israel assumes its responsibility in full, then the image of God upon earth, manifested through humanity, can reach fulfillment.

We opened our discussion with the struggle and the blessing. The struggle is the struggle of Israel to prevail in its endeavor to be *keter*, to wipe out evil, to emanate the force of the will of God to the world. The growth and rebirth are not for Israel alone; its growth and rebirth are within humanity and for humanity. The blessing bestowed upon Israel is not a blessing for it alone; it is a blessing appropriated for humanity and on behalf of humanity. The dwelling of God, the presence of the *Shekhinah* within Israel, is not of significance for Israel alone, but for mankind as a whole. For "this people I formed Myself, that they shall declare my praise" (Isa. 43:21).

REFERENCES

1. The organic metaphor has long been employed in Jewish thought, specifically to denote Israel's relation to other peoples, where it, significantly, is used to assign Israel a place of esteem in the body of mankind, and indeed often one of supremacy. Thus Judah Halevi in the *Kuzari* (2:36) likens Israel to the heart within the body. The heart for Halevi, to be sure, is the most vital and significant organ of the body (2:26). One must, however, clearly note that Halevi was cognizant that this was but a metaphor. He employed the imagery of the heart only to underscore what he believed to be Israel's position within humanity. He did not wish to suggest that humanity was actually structured as a body.

BIBLIOGRAPHY

Moses Cordovero, *The Palm Tree of Deborah*, Louis Jacobs, tr. (1974), esp. 70ff.
Judah Halevi, *The Kuzari*, Hartwig Hirschfeld, tr. (1946).
David ben Yehuda he-Ḥasid, *Sefer Marot ha-Ẓoveot*, D. C. Matt, ed. (1982).
Abraham Isaac Kook, *The Lights of Penitence: The Moral Principles, Lights of Holiness, Essays, Letters and Poems* (1978), s.v. "Israel."
Abraham Isaac Kook, "Orot Yisrael," in *Orot* (1923).
Israel ben Gedaliah Lipschutz, *Tiferet Israel (Boaz)*, ad loc. M. Avot 3:14.

Political Theory

תורת־המדינה

Ella Belfer and Ilan Greilsammer

pproaches to the concept of politics have evolved considerably. For certain authors the narrow definition, inherited from Greek antiquity, remains the only useful one: Politics (from the Greek *polis* + *techne*) includes only that which concerns the state and its institutions, excluding all other forms of social organization. This perspective, which views the state as fundamentally distinct because it is endowed with sovereignty, has been gradually displaced in modern thought by a broader and more nuanced conception of politics. For many political scientists today, politics entails everything concerning the phenomenon of power: that is, authority, government, and leadership, and these not just in national politics, but in all forms of human society.

In discussing Judaism and politics, however, one is obliged to adopt an even broader definition of politics. Our question is thus not simply, "What does Judaism have to say about the phenomenon of power?" but rather, "What does Judaism have to say about the phenomenon of life within an institutionalized society?" At that point, even if one does not accept an exclusively political conception of Judaism as viewed from the perspective of ostensible Zionist normalization, one is led to examine the message or messages of Judaism in such diverse areas as economics, social organization, political regimen, and societal institutions, including their authority and their regulations.

For certain schools of thought the question posed here merits a simple answer: Judaism is not and should not be concerned with politics. This position is represented, in extreme form, by Josephus Flavius, for whom Judaism is merely a religious collective that should thus resist any "temptation" of political power, lest the latter destroy it. In contrast to this position one might cite Spinoza, who systematically denies the religious significance of the ancient biblical theocracy, and in consequence developed a totally political definition of Jewish existence. Religion, in Spinoza's view, leads to a perspective upon Jewish existence that is *only* political.

The first notion, that Judaism is alien to politics and, therefore, has nothing to say about the subject, was adopted by such well-known twentieth-century historians of Judaism as Simon Dubnow and Salo W. Baron, who were inspired by the desire of the newly emancipated German Jewry for an exclusively spiritual definition of Judaism. According to some followers of this school, Judaism virtually never had any political pretensions. According to others, the Jews have somehow "given up" politics. In any event, according to this school of thought, in order to fulfill itself, the Jewish people neither requires a state of its own nor needs to pursue politics in general.

This view, however, has never been universally accepted. Among the many authors who have searched within Judaism for its relation to institutionalized society, and who regard Judaism as having a political dimension, we should make a careful distinction between those who hold two quite different positions. Some writers, such as Daniel J. Elazar, Eliezer Schweid, and Harold Fisch, hold that Judaism contains a basic political doctrine, that is, that it possesses a certain number of fundamental principles to guide the Jew in his interpretation of social facts and in his social conduct. Judaism accordingly contains systematic political attitudes, indeed, a general political theory based on several key ideas. One such key idea would be, for example, the central position of the land of Israel; another would be the idea of the covenant. Some explicitly speak of a "Jewish political tradition."

Other writers claim that, although it does not convey a true political doctrine or a political tradition based on a central idea, Judaism does contain a certain number of political ideas (the distinction between a doctrine and ideas being critical). But here, too, one finds two divergent approaches. Some argue that within Judaism there are a number of central political themes that appear as early as the emergence of Torah and persist throughout the centuries of Jewish thought until the present day. Those themes must thus be analyzed as fundamental to Jewish thought, without specific relation to a given period in Jewish history, or to a given form of expression (rational, mystical, or legal). For others, Jewish thought has included extremely varied political ideas, not necessarily connected with each other, and varying from period to period. Those ideas can be understood in a purely historical context, arising and disappearing in response to events, and as a function of the political and social systems within which the Jews found themselves. According to this approach, an analysis of Jewish political thought should be limited to the political ideas espoused by Jews within a particular period and by the different groups composing Jewish society of that period.

We must note here that there is nothing astonishing about finding such contradictory views concerning the existence or nonexistence of a Jewish political tradition or of a primary political thematic. After all, Jewish historical memory and consciousness are nuanced and complex. It may be observed that the adoption of one of the aforementioned positions often corresponds to the thinker's approach to Judaism. Those historians who claim that Judaism has no political message, or that the Jews have "given up" all sovereignty, are precisely those individuals who had the greatest misgivings about modern Zionism or who were frankly opposed to it. Conversely, Zionist historians such as Gedaliya Allon are apt to argue most strongly that Judaism has a political content, even a doctrine of the state. Martin Buber's idea of dialogue as a central reality in Jewish thought had very specific consequences on the nature of his own political commitment to Jewish statehood.

A parallel must thus be drawn between the notion of a continuum in the meaning of Jewish history and Judaism and a continuous adherence to a small number of central themes that recur throughout Jewish literature, whether it be in the Torah, the prophets, the Talmud, rabbinical literature, responsa literature, the kabbalah, or modern Jewish thought. There are certainly many themes other than those we shall mention here, which are the most fundamental ones. They are not, moreover, strictly political themes, but merely political aspects of the essential meaning of Jewish identity. Before presenting these, we must emphasize that they are not intellectual hypostases, separate from each other, but rather pairs of ideas in a state of tension. A priori they appear to contradict each other, but is that really the case?

The first question to be asked—insofar as the conception of the land of Israel (*erez Yisrael*) is doubtless the most fundamental and permanent political theme in Jewish history—is the following one: What is the land of Israel? The answer offered by the traditional texts is twofold. On the one hand, it is certainly a limited geographical territory, with borders, a climate, and a topography—in brief, concrete reality. But just as the "earthly" Jerusalem has its meta-reality in a "heavenly" Jerusalem, so the "mundane" land of Israel also has a spiritual dimension: The land of Israel is thus said to sustain Jewish spiritual, moral, and social being. Thus the first tension, which has a character and consequences that are eminently political, is that between territory and spiritual-moral signification.

A second question constantly posed in the traditional texts concerns the normal, natural mode of existence for a Jew. Is that natural structure the *medinah,* the sovereign state or the political-national community that gives expression to Jewish existence as a people? Or is it the religious community, the *kehillah?* Here as well two answers, although apparently antagonistic, are equally persistent.

The third question is that of the relations between the Jewish people and other peoples. Clearly, one finds within Jewish tradition both a particularistic, even ethnocentric perspective—"There is a people that dwells apart, not reckoned among the nations" (Num. 23:9)—and a universalistic perspective according to which the Jewish people, as a chosen people, are a "blessing for all the families of the earth" and must be open toward the world in order to be "a light to the nations."

In addition to the relations between the Jewish people and the other nations, there is the question of the relations between the individual and the social group as well as human relations in general. In dealing with this problem, the Jewish tradition takes up a question that is clearly of a political order: Must there be a dominant, elite group, or does Judaism aspire to social equality? Here we find the tension between egalitarianism ("All Israel are friends") versus elitism ("The judgment of the authorities is legally binding").

Another problem that appears constantly is that of the pursuit of Jewish virtues and interests: Must one lean toward extremism, or rather the absolute accomplishment of one's task, tending toward fanatical perfectionism? Or should one seek moderation, tolerance, and what some might call an attitude of compromise? The cleavage between zealotry and moderation is symbolized by the two rabbinic schools of the Mishnah, that of Shammai and that of Hillel.

Finally, there is the question of the method, the *derekh,* for achieving collective goals. The decisive choice here seems to be between the path of total revolution, including the aspiration to apocalypse, and the path of maintaining order, norms, and traditions as directed toward "the restoration of the world," which leads to a certain conservatism. No less in this context one finds both aspirations and methods within Judaism, although a priori they are mutually contradictory.

These six polarities—territory versus moral value; national community versus religious community; particularism versus universalism; egalitarianism versus elitism; zealotry versus tolerance; revolution versus tradition— are in constant tension due to their contradictory nature. Why is there such a polarity? Here, too, there are many reasons, of which the following three are basic.

One explanation for the polarity is to be found in the unique history of the Jews. Two illustrative examples may elucidate this fact. Life in the Diaspora is full of ambiguity because it is the life of a people without a land. The Jewish people cannot exist at a distance from its land while still living only for its land, unless it is willing to interiorize and integrate that tension. Another example is the rebirth of the sovereign Jewish state. The concept of state implies a framework of order, authority, and laws. How can morality and the fluctuating claims of justice accommodate themselves to such an all-powerful framework? In trying, therefore, to live as both a national community and a religious community, divided between particularism and universalism, one lives in permanent tension.

Another ambiguity is that Judaism rests upon a double centrality: the centrality of God and the centrality of man. Is the Bible not simultaneously the basis of a religion and an ethnic primer as well as a book of history? Most of the political tensions to which we have alluded derive from that double centrality, contradictory and insoluble. One example, among others, is the problem of the insoluble conflict between the king, who wishes to establish a human kingdom, and the prophet, who speaks not for the present but for the future, who has a vision, and who is privy to the divine plan.

Finally, Jewish identity itself is a source of tension. It all starts with Abraham, who breaks the idols and sets forth from his native city. Abraham's identity is clearly one of rupture with the past, a revolutionary identity. Abraham revolts against the world around him: the Jew's mission is to change the course of history. But simultaneously, the Jewish people is affected by history, and Jews adapt themselves to the political systems in which they live and learn to play the game of politics according to the rules of those systems. The issue, then, is how one can both remain within history and transform it.

The fundamental problem still remains: Can these tensions be resolved? Does Judaism offer clear-cut solutions? Does it render a judgment, saying, in some way, that the halakhah has such and such political consequences? Can one say, as certain people do, that Judaism opts for revolution, for democracy, for liberalism, or even for socialism? Or, as others claim, that it is a theocratic or, at least, conservative political ethic?

One way of answering might in fact be to view the poles of these tensions as absolutely dichotomous; there would be no hope of reconciliation between them and the only way out would be in crisis, or rather in successive crises, following which, depending on the age, one or another of the poles would prevail. Is that not the common presupposition of Josephus Flavius and Spinoza, that in the end either the purely religious or the purely political elements of Judaism will prevail?

But it would seem that the thrust of Judaism is opposed to such an exclusive, definitive solution. Any choice, any victory of one pole over another, is at bottom the renunciation of a part of the Jewish heritage. These poles, which are a priori antagonistic, are in fact tied together by a dynamic or a dialectic that does not allow for an absolute choice. It is the tension of the polar opposites, not their resolution, that is ontologically decisive.

For the political scientist, such a tension is expressed in the concept of the New Nation in a constant state of revolution (a theory espoused in the American sociologist Seymour Martin Lipset's analysis of American history). The revolutionary state is a society that both constructs itself as a political society, with all that that implies of order, authority, and control, and at the same time aspires to moral perfection, never believing that it has reached its goal. The revolutionary state is thus, at the same time, both within politics and outside it. Or else it is a never-ending revolution that is continuously dissatisfied with itself.

What must be distinguished are two different realities: the historical present, with its short-term programs and perspectives, and the visionary era, the ultimate goal, the essential direction. Within history, it is the radical opposition between poles of tensions such as we have described that prevails: There now exists the State of Israel, where all problems and antagonisms bear upon current events, in contrast to periods when the Jewish people did not enjoy political sovereignty. Israel is then not only a definition of a new historical reality, but also an illumination of the future. In the time of *ḥazon,* of vision, the antagonisms will fuse in a dynamic dialectic and the message will at last appear to be coherent.

BIBLIOGRAPHY

Gerald Blidstein, *Ikkronot Medinl'im be-Mishnat Ha-Rambam* (1983).

William D. Davies, *The Territorial Dimension of Judaism* (1982).

Daniel J. Elazar, ed., *Kinship and Consent: The Jewish Political Tradition and Its Contemporary Use* (1981).

Julius Guttmann, *Philosophies of Judaism* (1964).

Efraim E. Urbach, *The Sages: Their Concepts and Beliefs* (1973).

Stuart A. Cohen, "The Concept of the Three Ketarim. Its Place in Jewish Political Thought and its Implication for a Study of Jewish Constitutional History." in *A.J.S. Review, Vol. ix* 1, Spring 1984.

Prayer

תפילה

Michael Fishbane

Prayer is at the heart of Judaism and its spiritual life, tied intimately as it is to its daily rituals and to its modes and possibilities of contact with God. "Prayer is greater than good deeds," according to an early rabbinic saying; another saying calls it "more precious than sacrifices" (BT Ber. 32a). With the assurance of mystical insight, Rabbi Baḥya ben Asher, in a comment on Deuteronomy 11:12, stated that the sphere to which true prayer ascends is higher even than the supernal source of prophecy. And so it was that rabbinical Judaism considered the practice and cultivation of prayer as "the core and mature fruit of one's time" (*Kuzari*, 5:5), and from the earliest periods gave the prescription of its times and formularies distinct preeminence: the first tractate of the Talmud, *Berakhot,* deals with prayer, and so, accordingly, do the first sections of the great medieval legal codes produced by Moses Maimonides and Joseph Caro. In its life of active service to the divine Presence, then, Judaism does not consider prayer to be either a casual or superfluous adjunct, but rather the nurturant wellspring of its entire active life and an inherent component of it as well. The duty of prayer at fixed times and seasons is thus one commandment among the many positive (rabbinical) commandments of Judaism; indeed, many of these commandments have a traditional formulary whose precise recitation is essential for their proper performance. God-directed speech and God-directed deeds are thus closely related in Jewish religious praxis—even as each also has its own separate realm.

As in Judaism generally, the scope and details of prayer life give expression to the essential realization that no area of human existence is irrelevant before God and no earthly pain or productivity is separable from divine reality. The cultivation of a personal consciousness focused upon the quotidian—the food that is eaten or needed; the distress that is present or relieved; the search that is spiritual or disturbed—as well as a diffused transpersonal realization of one's origin and end in eternity are, then, the dialectical poles and goals of Jewish prayer. In the daily and festival services, the person concentrates upon all the yearnings and joys and even the many resentments and responsibilities of human existence and gives them verbal expression before God; and more than this, too, since in Jewish prayer the Jewish person evokes the memories and hopes of past and present Jewish communities as part of a living prayer quorum. The set order of the services is thus a historical—and so transtemporal—order linking the mortal generations to immortal divinity. The occasional eruption of a personal voice in this set communal service is, therefore, noticeably minimalized or regulated. Distinctively, for example, such personal expressions occur in the morning liturgy recited before one enters the social milieu of the common prayer hall, or as a meditative adjunct to *Shemoneh Esreh*—the "Eighteen Benedictions," that great collection of divine acknowledgment, praise, and petition offered at the apex of each service. Spontaneous individual prayer, on the other hand, has no fixed time or season, and no fixed language or place; it can be the voiced or voiceless longing of the heart, the cry for God's Presence of the mystic or the diffuse groan of the hungry, the scrawled note of the unlettered or the crafted work of the God-intoxicated artist—it is the language of the solitary self before God. The forms and formulas of Jewish communal prayer, on the other hand, give the individual a mortal solidarity and an ageless voice before the terrors of historical existence. "Because the mind is unstable," suggested Baḥya ibn Paquda, "our sages . . . composed the Order of Prayers" (*The Duties of the Heart,* ed. M. Hyamson, 4, 72).

Looked at more typologically, the traditional and spontaneous prayers of Judaism, as of other world religions generally, fall into four categories: petition, intercession, praise, and contemplation. Each of these has, moreover, its particular subtypes, and emphasizes distinctive dynamics of the self's relationship to God. Concisely, the category of petition is a request, by the individual or group, for something needed by the individual or group now or in the future, and is therefore distinguishable from prayers of intercession that are requests on behalf of another—be that another person or a collectivity. Hereby, love of self is expanded to love of neighbor, and the desire for self-acknowledgment and fulfillment give way to the sensibilities of compassion and empathy. Along this continuum, the third category of prayer, here called praise, is the outpouring of individual or public thankfulness, directed to a personal God, for the earthly bounties received (and so "blessed," and their divine source acknowledged). To receive these benefits without any expression of thankfulness is, says a repeated rabbinic dictum, to be like a thief (cf. Tanh. Ve-zot ha-Berakhah 7): for the earth and its fullness are the Lord's, and this realization is the root of that self-transcendence that leads beyond love of neighbor to love of God, who sustains all things. But praise of the transcendent One is still marked by self-regard and regard for God's beneficence to his creatures, until divine acknowledgment and praise rise to adoration of divine Selfhood—God as he is, and not with respect to ourselves. In turn, this level of spiritual adoration rises to contemplative prayer, which in Judaism may focus (as a strategy of mystical consciousness) on the inner life of the godhead in all its dynamic Selfhood, or even beyond the divine Self to the annihilation of personal self-awareness in the transpersonal divine Ground. Less theosophically put, the movement from petition to contemplation is a movement in one's prayer life from a self-centered desire for God to provide mundane benefits to a self-directed (even Being-directed) acknowledgment of God as he is, as the One who floods being with his eternal Presence.

The preceding remark is as paradoxical as it is crucial for the life of prayer. For as we have suggested, the principle feature of petitionary prayer and even intercessory prayer is the self's awareness of lack and need and the articulation of this awareness to a God who is present through the intention of the one who prays but who is also decidedly—even painfully—absent in the concrete world of desires and satisfactions. From this point of view, the spiritual concern of one who praises God for benefits received is not altogether removed from that of one who requests these benefits. To be sure, there is in prayers of praise a focused or overwhelming awareness of the divine Presence in the concrete world; but these, like petitionary prayers, are pitched on the polarity of a self-directed sense of emptiness and fulfillment. It is only where praise is realized as adoration for the divine in itself, as the source and foundation of all being—a realization that folds into contemplative states of mind—that God as Presence is the dominating religious awareness of prayer, quite irrespective of what the praying person has or does not have in terms of material benefits. Seen thus, what the developed life of prayer wants is God's Presence, and that alone, so that permanent consciousness of this Presence is the one thing needful. "I run to the Source of true life," said Judah Halevi, "and therefore hate the life of lies and emptiness" ("Likrat Mekor Ḥayyei Emet"). Of course, even the petitioner for concrete benefits wants God and acknowledges him; but as the human self's desire is transcended through a shifting of religious consciousness from a self-centered focus on needs to an awareness of being the recipient of divine existence as such, which pervades and sustains all being, there dawns the realization that God is always present—in his truth. The modalities of consciousness of divine presence or absence may, then, be correlated with the foci of one's physical or spiritual concern, or—more hierarchically viewed—with the levels of one's spiritual development.

The life of Jewish prayer may thus be seen as the cultivation of mindfulness of God and his initiatives in different degrees. At the level of solitary selfhood, this mindfulness is the awareness of God as the sponsoring source of breath, food, and knowledge; of colors and sense; of imagination and creativity; in short, of the self and the vast domain of nonself that supports and impinges upon it at all times. These realities are acknowledged and desired, and their absence or frustration or removal are also acknowledged and desired. From the anthropological level of which we speak, the praying person trusts that God will be a "hearing ear" and "seeing eye," in some sense, and that his mundane desires (whether for peace of self or others) will not fail to register a responsive chord in divinity, however that reverberates in human existence—that we be neither ashamed nor abashed forever. As noted earlier, such petitions may be intercessions for other persons, and it is just here that mindfulness of God and his initiatives achieves the realization that divinity works through other persons and the community—in the present and in the past. And so Jewish prayer memorializes acts of divine historical grace for his people and recites hopes for a collective redemption; and so, too, Jewish prayer acknowledges the communal setting of existence and sanctity by its collective voice and confession.

As a communal quorum, moreover, which in mystical terms represents the symbolic world of divine unity, the mindfulness of God in prayer rises to a higher awareness of the self within a global and cosmic community or setting. This mindfulness deemphasizes the individual self and puts into a larger perspective the "life of lies and emptiness," of personal gratifications, pains, and desires. Put differently, the wandering or selfish mind, the mind assaulted by "strange thoughts" in prayer, raises these thoughts toward God as the source of all life—being mindful of God as cosmic life and not as personal helper—and strives to transcend the disunity felt in the self's world by unifying or strengthening the life of all beings. This involves a willingness to move from the "I am" of sentient self-regard to the "I am" of Sinai who initiated the covenant community of Israel, to the eternal "I am" who in his truth "shall be as he shall be." The necessary humility of the mortal self with all its needs is hereby transfigured or transcended, through a rising prayer consciousness, to a social self whose needs must be related to others, and from there to a profound humility when one knows oneself to be the recipient of the life of God's eternity. "May I be worthy that my heart be the dwelling of your glory. . . . And everywhere I come, wherever I dwell or travel by your will, may I be worthy to find there your divinity, truthfully" (Rabbi Naḥman of Bratzlav, in *Likkutei Tefillot*).

"If it were possible to worship without words," said Rabbi Menaḥ Lonzano (in his *Derekh Ḥayyim*), "if the heart could be offered alone: this would be sufficient to fulfill the commandment [of prayer]." And why? Because "our object in prayer is but the consummation of the soul's longing for God" (Baḥya ibn Paquda)—for an unmediated tasting and seeing of the goodness of the holy, blessed One. But alas, because of our exile, said Maimonides (and we may gloss here)—because of our deep spiritual dislocation from divinity, the mediating form of linguistic prayer was established by our sages. Language, then—and in the life of the spirit the language of prayer is emblematic—is a sign and fact of human absence from divine Reality, and so of the need to fill the space between persons and God with "God-intending" words. "The language of the heart is central; [whereas] the spoken word serves merely as an interpreter between the heart and the listener" (Abraham ibn Ezra, ad loc. Ps. 4:5).

"The Merciful One wants the heart" (BT Sanh. 106b), goes an ancient rabbinical dictum on prayer. Just what does this mean? For one thing, and most basically, it means the proper focus of the self in prayer before God—whether for petition or for praise. For this reason, "the early pietists," as we learn from an early Mishnah, set aside one hour for contemplation before morning prayer that their "heart be directed to their Father in Heaven" (M. Ber. 5:1). Naturally, from these early times to the complex meditative pyrotechnics of late medieval kabbalah, a profound dialectic arose between the proper spiritual focus of the mind and heart and the proper enunciation of the words of prayer. At times the one was a preparation for the other, so that mental-spiritual centeredness could yield focused prayer, and the reverse. At other times the two were complexly intertwined, so that the theurgical dimension of prayer—whether it used the words of prayer as concrete magical formulas or as esoteric codes of enormous theosophical power—was strengthened. Both dimensions, stripped of their theosophical garb, are of immense spiritual significance for the modern person. Indeed, one may even observe a partial stripping of the theosophical layers in early Ḥasidism, at the onset of modernity. Two aspects may be singled out. The first pertains to the concord between mind or heart and language—which mediates its desires—that is considered the ideal or goal of prayer. As repeatedly stated in the first generations of Ḥasidism, the person in prayer should try to unify these dimensions as a symbol of the deepest unity, which may obtain in all realms of being: one must "enter the word" and extract its hidden light. In short, so seen, prayer is a specialized case of all directed communication and the human capacity to unify will and desire in harmonious action: it is a realm of contemplation and devotion that is no less a preparation for life. The wandering mind in prayer, which Ḥasidism and earlier moral literature refer to as "strange thoughts"—these being the fantasies of desire—is thus a sign to the person of a lack of spiritual or psychological integration. Consciousness of these eruptions within the silent space of prayer is thus the heart's teacher, revealing the deep work of *heshbon ha-nefesh,* or self-scrutiny, which prayer life sponsors.

A second aspect of the relationship between word and heart (or thought) to which we may draw attention is this: The words of prayer, human language, if not themselves distillations of the mystery of being, are at least signs and symbols of the deeply dialogical character of reality, of the eternal projection and introjection of communication in patterns of unity or disunity. The language of prayer, as God-directed speech, is the deep mythos of this truth, which we ever again actualize in concrete human intercourse. Accordingly, the words of prayer in all their new combinations and figurations symbolize the capacities of language to bind and unbind life and achieve unity at different levels. At its highest ascent, the song of prayer may thus transcend its concrete verbal articulations, the *shirei zimrah,* and express the ineffable surplus of the heart, the *shayarei zimrah,* so loved by God (following Rabbi Wolf of Zhitomer). In this moment of profound meditative communication between the self and divine eternity, language returns to its source in God, the One, and the multiplicity of words and the frustrations of disunified and disunifying communication are stilled. The anguished self, the lonely ego, finds "rest from its labors." For God is wholly present here—and what more can one ask of eternity but that it be present? Now the exiled heart is brought into the holy shrine, and hears its high priest confirm: "You are because I am."

BIBLIOGRAPHY

Gabriel Cohen, ed., *Prayer in Judaism: Continuity and Change* (1978).
Nahum Glatzer, ed., *Language of Faith* (1975).
Joseph Heinemann, *Prayer in the Talmud* (1977).
Louis Jacobs, *Hasidic Prayer* (1973).

Prophecy

נבואה

Peter S. Zaas

J ewish theology cannot be said to share the preoccupation of contemporary biblical criticism with the Hebrew prophets. Nonetheless, a consideration of the prophetic phenomenon, of its message, and, indeed, of its decline from primary consideration in Jewish thought, can provide a useful perspective from which to view Jewish theology, especially in the connections it makes between morals and ethics, revelation and history.

As far as Judaism is concerned, prophecy is a phenomenon with a distinct beginning and a distinct end. The prophets appear concurrently with the Sinai theophany as exemplars of the religious man seized by direct revelation of the divine word, and their disappearance is noted at the beginning of the Hasmonaean age in 164 B.C.E.: Moses is the first and greatest of the prophets, and the line comes to an abrupt end in the sixth century B.C.E. with the postexilic figures of Zechariah and Malachi. With the single exception of the predicted return of Elijah as the messianic herald, prophecy in Judaism is a phenomenon of the distant past. In this respect, Jewish theology is sharply to be distinguished from its Christian and Moslem relatives, both of which depend heavily on prophetic revelations posterior to Hebrew prophecy, and both of which, at least in some manifestations, require that prophecy be a continuing process. For Judaism, prophecy's decline is as significant as its rise.

Biblical criticism emphasizes the diversity of the Hebrew prophets. It yields no unified morphology of prophecy, no unified prophetic message or prophetic role. But Judaism has always tended to view the biblical prophets monolithically. Furthermore, each group of Jewish interpreters has viewed them as supporting its own enterprises. Thus the rabbis emphasized that the prophets were paragons of halakhic Judaism, laying no new revelation alongside the eternal law. They saw Moses as the "lord of the prophets" and the prophets as belonging to the direct line of tradition between the "elders" and the "men of the Great Synagogue" (M. Avot 1:1), neither adding nor subtracting anything from the law (BT Meg. 14a). By contrast, contemporary liberal Jewish theology sees the prophets in its own mirror, as champions of freedom from the domination of the priesthood.

Historically, prophecy ceased in Judaism at the same moment that the oral Law gained ascendancy, during the Hasmonaean revolution (I Macc. 4:46). Jewish leadership after 70 C.E., regrouping to face the bleak prospect of a world without the Temple cultus, found little room for the charismatic figures who were now dearer to Christian than to Jewish life. The rabbinic antipathy toward a continuing prophetic institution must have been in part defensive. Religiously, this narrowing of the vector of revelation led to Judaism's characteristic preoccupation with the halakhic text, a text that, by legal dictum, itself subsumed the old prophetic roles. But the rabbis were antipathetic only to new prophets, not to the old ones, whose poetic imagination supplied much of the substance of their liturgy.

Jewish theologians of the pre-Enlightenment era were more interested in meta-prophetic questions than in the message of the Hebrew prophets. Their concerns focused on describing the mechanism of the prophetic revelation, on the qualifications of the men chosen for the prophetic role, and on the obvious conclusions to be drawn about the superiority of Israel from the phenomenon of prophecy itself. For Judah Halevi, for example, the very fact that the Scripture contains revealed prophecy demonstrates its divine origin, and does so irrespective of the precise content of that revelation. Modern Jewish theologians, far from emphasizing the commonality of the prophetic experience, emphasize the phenomenon's otherness. Thus for Abraham Joshua Heschel, the most sublime modern interpreter of Hebrew prophecy, it is the direct prophetic experience of the "divine pathos" that is preeminent; the prophets embody the relationship between God and

Israel in a specialized way. Martin Buber similarly emphasizes the quality of immediacy in the prophetic faith.

Recent biblical criticism has noted the extent to which the prophets are faithful supporters of the halakhah: they were in no way opposed to the law. Nonetheless, theology must continue to emphasize the prophetic contribution in the ethical sphere. It can be argued that ethics per se begins with the Hebrew prophets, whose insistence that a moral imperative follows directly from the sacred covenant commences a long and rich tradition within Judaism of defining morality differently from law. Through their statement of the relationship between the moral and the religious, the Hebrew prophets implicitly provide Judaism with an ethical principle that transcends the law. Thus, Hosea, on God's instruction, violates the law by remarrying Gomer: God's love for Israel extends beyond the terms of the covenant. His moral will exceeds the law. Indeed, to trust that the *mizvot* are sufficient as well as necessary for inclusion in the righteous remnant may be, for the Hebrew prophets, the most vicious of all vices.

There are several names for this characteristic vice: religiosity, self-righteousness, ritualism. The Hebrew prophets, beginning with Amos, condemn religious ritual if it stands in the way of righteousness. Pride in the intensity of one's observance of the law is a vice in itself, as is religious observance pursued for reward. Amos connects Israel's unrighteous conduct with its national religious expectations; despite the people's apparently rigid adherence to the priestly cult, the Day of the Lord will be its destruction, bringing darkness, not light (Amos 5:18). Amos is thus the first Jewish thinker to add an ethical dimension to eschatology—the first moral theologian of history.

In this respect the Hebrew prophets are to be contrasted with the moral theologians who succeeded them, the anonymous writers of Jewish apocalyptic literature. Although the prophets fight for the purity of the cult, and thus for the centralization of religious authority, they fight as well for the authority of the individual to make religious and moral decisions, and for individual as opposed to group responsibility. This tendency stands in sharp contrast to the apocalypticists who claim to inherit the prophetic mantle. Their emphasis on predestination precludes any individual's change in moral status before God. This radical ethic is far removed from the prophetic emphasis on repentance and forgiveness, and firmly separates authentic prophecy from the apocalyptic vision. The prophetic goal is to free men from the sourness of their fathers' grapes, the apocalyptic goal to remind men of the immutability of God's decree. Prophecy, not apocalypse, retains a hallowed place in the Jewish theological tradition.

Although the Hebrew prophets never lost their position of high esteem in

Judaism, prophecy as a living institution did not survive the Jewish Commonwealth. No treatment of the subject can ignore the fact that for Judaism, God's revelation is through his Torah, and though, in ancient days, he spoke directly through his servants, the prophets, he does so no longer. This vector of revelation is closed. Modern Judaism cannot look to contemporary prophets for consolation or moral guidance; it can only look to the Torah and to the (ancient) prophetic imperative that legal observance be just.

The biblical prophets announced the coming of an age of universal justice should the nation heed their call to justice in the present age. Jewish theology embodies this prediction by assigning a prophet to herald the messianic kingdom. This is the only future role of a prophet in the Jewish mythos, and it is a fitting one: the prophet, the earliest exponent of a Jewish theology of history, announces history's prophetic denouement.

BIBLIOGRAPHY

Martin Buber, *The Prophetic Faith,* C. Witton-Davies, tr (1949).
Abraham Joshua Heschel, *The Prophets* (1962).
Lou Silberman, "Prophets and Philosophers: The Scandal of Prophecy," in Arthur A. Cohen, ed., *Arguments and Doctrines* (1970).

Providence

השגחה

Hillel Levine

The term *providence* derives from the Greek root meaning "to perceive beforehand." While it first appears in the fifth century B.C.E., only in the later books of biblical literature, under Hellenistic influences, does the term leave any traces. In medieval Jewish thought, under combined Greek and Islamic influences, providence was designated by terms such as *hanhagah* (governance), *hashgahah* (attentive care), and *shemirah* (guarding).

The history of the term, however, is an imprecise demonstration of the influence of the concept. Notions of providence are integral to biblical ontology and ethical orientation. The "rain in due season" is endowed not as God's caprice or as a fixed result of natural cycles but as a reward for faith in God and for pious acts.

Providence as a concept must be located in interaction with a series of philosophical and theological concepts such as grace, predestination, fate, reward and punishment, salvation, certitude, freedom, and meaning in history. The resulting discourse has produced some of the variations in concepts of providence: the sources of providence in a personal or nonpersonal divinity, the mediators of providence as the immutable laws of nature or the subjective experience of faith and hope, and finally, the objects of providence, including even the smallest detail or merely a general order, each individual and his destiny or a chosen people.

These variations attained elaboration as well as historical significance in the movements by which they were embraced; they became the basis of political as well as intellectual controversy. Concepts of providence, not always pressed rigorously to their logical conclusions, were pivotal in the sectarian controversies during the Second Temple and shortly thereafter. Radical notions of predestination among the Dead Sea sects were compatible with their ascetic otherworldliness and pietism. Their notion of providence may have made it not only undesirable but rather useless for members to oppose foreign political and cultural incursion. The Sadducees, on the other hand, seemingly appropriated Greek notions of an impersonal fate.

The rabbis, in their paradoxical aphorisms on providence, tried to reconcile such extreme ideas as the affirmation of God's active concern in mundane affairs with notions of human choice. Thus, they distinguished between God's foreknowledge, as expressed in the dictum, "Everything is foreseen but free will is granted" (M. Avot 3:15) and God's actual control, for example, in making each and every blade of grass grow or decreeing even the most minor mishap that may befall an individual. Nevertheless, the moral and spiritual freedom of the individual were vouchsafed, as expressed in the saying, "Everything is in the hands of heaven except for the fear of heaven" (BT. Ber. 33b).

In the Middle Ages, conflicting concepts of providence emerge as important issues. Rabbinic assertions about God's attentiveness to the smallest of creatures notwithstanding, Moses Maimonides limits providence in the subhuman world to entire species. In regard to humans as well, Maimonides limits God's providence by his claim that it is mediated through man's intellectual attainment. In developing his God-given understanding and analytical abilities, man avoids danger. Maimonides' naturalistic approach to providence blunts the biblical and rabbinic emphases upon God's active intervention in the course of nature and upon man's ethical merit. Maimonides' opponents were quick to sense this peril to traditional notions of miracles and reward and punishment, and this stoked the controversy that surrounded him.

In the Sephardi orbit in particular, astrology as an intellectual pursuit and occasional outbursts of messianism bolstered the sagging belief in providence. In Ashkenazi countries, particularly in the wake of the persecution of the Crusades, martyrdom dramatized the concern to sustain the plausibility of God's providence. While motivated by faith and the conviction that they would attain rewards in other worlds, martyrs, by devaluing the world of everyday life as a reflection of ultimate truths—to the point of the surrender of life itself—protected belief in God's providence from the disconfirmation of history.

In spite of the recurrent persecutions in both western and eastern Europe, there was little effort to establish the nature of the political, economic, and social conditions that contributed to the attacks. But some of the chronicles of the sixteenth and seventeenth centuries and even an occasional communal ordinance of the Council of Four Lands do point to adversities and dangers not prompted by sin. The attribution of natural causes was impeded by faith in providence. In this regard, the development of Jewish mysticism, and the popularization of Lurianic kabbalah in particular, may have had unanticipated consequences. While these spiritual currents strengthened conceptions of providential cosmic order, their influence in shifting the burden of redemption onto individuals led to a new activism. This activism was altogether otherworldly, although through complex sets of historical circumstances the world of everyday life could provide for some Jews a new arena for that activism.

Jewish conceptions of providence came under assault from many opposing quarters in the early modern period. The profound and pervasive disappointment that followed the failure of the Sabbatean movement in the seventeenth century left in the souls of many Jews more than a residue of doubt regarding providence. Manipulating kabbalistic constructs, Shabbetai Ẓevi himself is alleged to have concluded that the "Cause of Causes does not influence nor does it oversee the lower worlds."[1]

An eighteenth-century disciple of Shabbetai Ẓevi, Jacob Frank, similarly challenged God's providence when commenting on incidents of suffering. Nevertheless, his ritual inventiveness and political intrigues reveal his own efforts to conjure God's providence.

Although his influence on the thinking of his Jewish contemporaries was slight, Baruch Spinoza's challenge to God's election of and providence over Israel had long-term effects. Jewish survival, in which both Jews and Christians saw a sign of divine providence, was explained by Spinoza in terms of the material law of things. According to Spinoza, gentile enmity and Jewish suffering, the providential history about which Jews and Christians agreed, had sociological functions in preserving the Jews, rather than theological purposes of expiation, as Jews would claim, or a punishment for deicide and a prod to the Jews' acceptance of Christian verities, as Christians would claim. While Spinoza extended a modicum of hope in regard to the circumstances under which Jews would reestablish themselves as a nation, these happy circumstances would be brought about by worldly political activity rather than by spiritual merit leading to God's intervention in history. Spinoza's influence on the English Deists and, through them, the French *philosophes,* contributed to the negative terms in which the Jews were depicted during the late eighteenth-century discourses on the position of Jews in a transformed European society. The rejection of Jews based upon their alleged personal and social deficiencies rather than upon theological grounds was at the root of the political anti-Semitism that developed in the late nineteenth century, with increased virulence and tragic consequences in the twentieth century.

Political absolutism and scientific empiricism generated a double attack on Jewish concepts of providence in the late eighteenth century. The prospects of attaining political rights and integration as individuals within the nation-state created pressures upon the Jews not only to cast their fate with the larger society but also to envisage their futures in accord with the utopian imagination of their fellow citizens rather than with Jewish providential notions of the End of Days. The diffusion of empirical science, with its claims of accurately describing celestial as well as terrestrial space, undermined the ontological plausibility of a special sphere defined by Jewish truth claims, including providence.

Both the political and cognitive socialization of the Jews into the modern world, therefore, impinged upon traditional notions of God's providence over Israel. At the same time, the nation-state and scientific empiricism generated new and compelling notions of determinism and even providence. Nineteenth-century movements as diverse as Saint-Simonism, Marxism, historicism, and psychoanalysis, in which Jews played a prominent role and were often statistically overrepresented, fostered secular notions of providence. At the same time new notions and new applications of providential concepts began to develop among Jews. Their ultimate role as a separate group within European society could be justified by recourse to their alleged service as "a light unto the nations." While Jewish nationalism was iconoclastic, it restored notions of providence by shifting the emphasis from the welfare of the individual Jew, as in the earlier emancipation movements, to the collective fate of the Jewish people. Zionism in particular, though worldly in its orientation—from draining the swamps and building the cities of the land of Israel to restoring the Jews to the arena of international politics and global diplomacy—nevertheless has generated notions of providence. In contemporary Israel, ironic expressions of the intractability of Jewish fate have been sounded, particularly at moments of danger and frustration in attaining the support and understanding of non-Jews. These expressions tend to undermine political efforts and the ultimate efficacy of worldly action.

While secularization and modernization as global forces have demonstrated their transformative capacities, religious attitudes also have demonstrated an unanticipated persistence. Belief in providence compensates for the effects of those modern conditions that foster meaninglessness and loneliness. After the Holocaust, it would seem that belief in providence, for Jews in particular, would be difficult to sustain. And yet, for many this is apparently not impossible.

REFERENCES

1. Gershom Scholem, *Shabbetai Zevi* (1973), 184.

BIBLIOGRAPHY

Yitzhak Fritz Baer, *Galut* (1947).
Mircea Eliade, *The Myth of the Eternal Return* (1954).
Julius Guttmann, *Philosophies of Judaism* (1964).
Yosef Yerushalmi, *Zakhor* (1983).

Rabbi and Teacher

רב ומורה

David B. Ruderman

The title *rabbi* (lit., my master) first appeared in ancient Palestine around the first century of the Common Era to designate an individual of exceptional learning and expertise in Jewish law. The term *rav* (lit., master) emerged several centuries later in Babylonia to distinguish a learned sage consecrated by his mastery of the Torah. The professional rabbinate, however, became visible only in medieval times, although the precise origin and development of this new and distinctive communal institution remain somewhat obscure.

Simḥah Assaf's definition of the traditional rabbi, presented in his early study of the subject, represents, more or less, a conventional characterization of this religious leader: "A scholar with authority *over* the Jewish community to adjudicate, to teach and to direct its religious life."[1]

Such a definition, however, obscures a critical ambiguity regarding the source of rabbinic authority. Did the rabbi hold power over the Jewish community by virtue of his sanctified status as scholar or did he derive his authority from the community itself? Stated differently, was the rabbinic function a concept of leadership emerging primarily within the context of

Jewish communal institutions or a concept of learning and scholarship unrelated to public service? Without exception, rabbis viewed their roles and standing among other Jews neither as deriving from nor depending upon the Jewish community. Nevertheless, because of the growing professionalization of the rabbinate and the gradual subordination of the rabbi to the communal will since the late Middle Ages, a degree of uncertainty remained regarding the rabbi's status and function. In more recent times, the contemporary rabbi often finds himself in an even more difficult and paradoxical position than his medieval ancestor. He strives to maintain his autonomy and integrity when employed by people he seeks to lead.

The rabbi of late antiquity, however, unambiguously functioned as a holy man whose devotion to the study of Torah in both its written and oral forms distinguished him as the dominant religious leader of his community. Earning his livelihood from sources unrelated to his religious role, the rabbi assumed a relatively independent status within the community. As a religious judge and a kind of divine magician, he was seen to possess a special knowledge of Torah that enabled him to perform supernatural acts and eventually to effectuate the redemption of Israel.

Sometime in the twelfth century a new rabbinic office emerged, embedded directly in the novel forms of Jewish self-government evolving in medieval Europe. In Muslim countries, the primary function of the rabbi remained judicial; he was essentially a scholar of Jewish law who strove to interpret the norms of Judaism in the context of the changing conditions of Jewish life in the Diaspora. In Christian countries, the rabbi functioned in a similar capacity, although his sacerdotal responsibilities as chief officiary of the Jewish community were more pronounced. Assuming duties more closely analogous to those of a Christian priest, the rabbi became more directly associated with a specific synagogue or congregation. Moreover, the rabbis themselves assumed greater ecclesiastical prerogatives; in some instances, they even demanded the honorific distinction of being called to the reading of Torah prior to those claiming priestly ancestry, whose normative privilege this would be.

The growing professionalization of the rabbinate in Christian Europe reached a further stage of development sometime in the fourteenth and fifteenth centuries. By that time, most rabbis received various tax exemptions and salaries from the communities they served. They supplemented their regular income by revenue from weddings, divorces, civil litigations, and other such private services.

In the same period, a fixed formula of ordination distinguished by the title *Moreinu ha-rav* ("our teacher, the rabbi," equivalent to the Christian titles *Meister* and *Magister*), together with the stipulation of well-defined rabbinic qualifications and privileges, was instituted among Ashkenazi Jewish communities in Christian Europe. Rabbis previously had been ordained in ancient Palestine, receiving maximal judicial privileges operative within the framework of a Jewish court system. When this earlier institution was abolished, rabbis personally authorized their most worthy students to function as rabbis. The Ashkenazi institutionalization of this practice was considered a necessity for safeguarding the academic standards of the rabbinate at a time when social and cultural upheaval threatened the continuity of traditional Jewish life. However, as soon as the granting of rabbinic diplomas was routinized, standards for entering the rabbinate gradually were lowered. This practice was severely criticized by Sephardic rabbis such as Isaac Abrabanel in the fifteenth century, who cynically noticed the parallel between the rabbinic certificate and a university degree: "I have no idea how this [Ashkenazi] practice originated except for the fact that they were jealous of the ways of the non-Jews who award doctorates and thus they did the same."[2]

By the late Middle Ages, the rabbinate had become a more complex and multi-faceted office. As communal functionary, the rabbi still acted as judge and chief expert on Jewish law, but he also served as occasional preacher who sought increasing opportunities to exhort his congregation to observe the law. He supervised the ritual life of the community, directed the educational program of its youth, and, in some cases, also served as cantor. Despite the growing responsibilities of his position, the rabbi's actual hegemony within the Jewish community was increasingly attenuated. Most rabbis were appointed only for limited terms; government officials and powerful communal leaders often interfered with their decisions, and rabbinic posts sometimes went to the highest bidder.

Nevertheless, the institution of the rabbinate was still associated with the tradition of sanctity and transcendent scholarship originating in ancient times. Notwithstanding the stark realities of economic and political power upon which every Jewish community was based, individual rabbis continued to occupy the central religious and cultural role among their constituencies. By virtue of their prodigious learning, their personal piety, and their own spiritual vocation to shape the Jewish community in the image of God, they refused to accept the mere status of communal appointees. They continued to speak in the name of a hallowed tradition that transcended all powerful special interests within the community.

By the late eighteenth century, first in western Europe and later elsewhere, the rabbi suffered an even greater crisis of authority, brought about by the cataclysmic forces of Enlightenment and political and social emancipation. Writing at the beginning of the seventeenth century, the illustrious Italian rabbi Leone Modena still described the rabbinic leader in traditional terms:

> These men, that is to say, the Cacham [ḥakham], Rab, or Morenu, decide all controversies concerning the things that are either Lawful or Prohibited, and all other differences; they Marry, and give Bills of Divorce; they Preach also, if they can; and are the Chief men in the academies before mentioned; they have the uppermost seats in their Synagogues, and in all Assemblies; and there is generally great Respect shewed unto them in all things.[3]

Of course, Modena's idealized portrait already did not reflect the reality he knew so well. Most Italian rabbis of his day, including Modena himself, had limited judicial authority and meager economic resources, and were not always shown "great respect in all things."

Some two centuries later in Germany, Zechariah Frankel clearly had a strikingly dissimilar concept in mind in discussing what he considered to be the ideal contemporary rabbi. For Frankel, "To be intimately familiar with the Talmud is not enough; the muses must also not be strange to him. . . . Would our age in fact take instruction from a man trained otherwise?"[4] Even more divergent was the startling characterization of the American rabbi attributed to Solomon Schechter, who lived only one generation after Frankel: "From now on, no one can be a rabbi in America who does not know how to play baseball as well as study Talmud."[5]

Common to Frankel's and Schechter's perceptions of the modern rabbi was their view of his transformed function and status: His professional duties were now tailored to the new social context in which he operated. The modern rabbi, unlike his medieval counterpart, was primarily a synagogue pulpit rabbi, secularly educated, oratorically gifted, and adept at pastoral guidance. He functioned in a community where his power and prestige were highly circumscribed, which allowed him no coercive power, and where the constituency he served was becoming increasingly secular and increasingly illiterate in Jewish affairs. Like the Protestant minister, the modern rabbi served as preacher, pastor, administrator, priest, and social ambassador. Yet unlike his Christian colleague, he worked in a community suffering a more acute sense of loss of confidence and commitment to its inherited values of the past.

No doubt the leap from Modena's to Schecter's concepts of the rabbinic office authentically reflects the major disruptions in Jewish life that mark the last three centuries. The American milieu especially has produced a singular expression of the rabbi who serves a community whose interest and involvement in Jewish beliefs and practices are decreasing. Quite often, the American rabbi is given an unwritten proxy by his congregation to excel in those Jewish qualities and deeds to which every member aspires but usually fails to realize. He becomes an exemplary Jew who commands no special authority except by virtue of the quality of his personality, sincerity, and devotion to the values he espouses. He performs his duties as a leader of prayer; as a spokesman for Judaism, albeit neither as scholarly in Jewish matters as some of his traditional predecessors nor as informed in secular matters as some of his congregants; as a custodian of Jewish knowledge and observance; as a hired hand, subjected sometimes painfully to the whims and passions of congregational leaders, and on precious occasions, as a figure whose personal piety and human concern touch the lives of some of his congregants. The recent dramatic entrance of women into a profession that had previously excluded them has yet to have any perceptible impact on the function and style of this sort of American rabbi.

Such blatant discontinuities with the past, however, need not obscure the vital and substantial bonds that premodern and contemporary rabbis have continued to share. The sharp dichotomy often portrayed between the secure authority of the traditional rabbi, in contrast with his modern counterpart, is usually exaggerated and misplaced. Rabbinic authority, even in most traditional settings, could be limited, as we have seen, by lay leadership. Rabbis in the past were also economically dependent on the communities they served. Like the modern rabbi, they also assumed a multiplicity of roles, including sacerdotal and pastoral functions. And also like the modern rabbi, their rabbinic function encouraged them, indeed required them to immerse themselves in both Jewish and non-Jewish spheres of knowledge. To know only Jewish texts was never enough. On the contrary, an overwhelming number of rabbis living in both western and eastern Europe regularly fostered cultural liaisons with the outside world. Many were versed in literature, philosophy, and science. They saw their function not as adversaries to general learning but as cultural intermediaries between the Jewish and non-Jewish worlds—primary interpreters of non-Jewish cultural modes within the context of traditional Jewish values and mores. Above all, the medieval and modern rabbi continue to share a common psychological condition. They remain communal role models whose personal authenticity is measured by their ability to know and live the law. Despite the changed circumstances of modern Jewish life, rabbis are still perceived to have a "calling"; they are still differentiated from the Jews they serve by another "realm of being," by an aura of saintliness associated with the traditional responsibility of knowing and living the Torah.

What might one speculate about the future of the rabbi, especially the American rabbi, in the light of the apparent mutability and erosion of the community he or she will continue to serve? However bright or lugubrious the future of Jewish life in America may be, there is little doubt about the pivotal importance of rabbinic leadership to that future. Jews, whether diminished in numbers by the declining birth rate or deflated by intermarriage and assimilation, still require teachers and practitioners of Judaism. They seek a sympathetic human being, a holy man or woman, a role model who offers them the cultural treasures and warm human links binding them to their ancestral tradition. Some Jews have attempted to subvert the rabbinic role by making the rabbi a surrogate Jew through whom other Jews live vicariously. Too often the rabbi is tempted to fill the void of Jewish observance by obliging a congregation and acting Jewish for everyone else. No doubt there is a fine line between surrogate and role model, but only the latter role offers any promise that the rabbi might achieve minimal success.

Undeniably the rabbi has suffered some loss of political power to lay groups within the Jewish community; the rabbi also sees his or her exclusive claim to expertise in Jewish matters somewhat eclipsed by the new breed of Judaic scholars in university and seminary settings. Yet lack of political power was a constant in the history of the rabbinate and to the committed rabbi and teacher it never remained an impediment to effective communal leadership and communication of values. The new Jewish academics are neither hostile nor unsympathetic to the rabbinic calling; many of them are rabbis themselves. Not all rabbis in the past were great scholars; like contemporary rabbis, many had little opportunity for uninterrupted study. Nevertheless, they were aware and appreciative of scholarly distinction, and they were able to utilize and disseminate the erudition of great rabbinic teachers to educate their own congregations. They performed the unique function of mediating between esoteric scholarship and the needs of the lay community. Little has changed in this respect. The modern rabbi need not be a great scholar in Jewish or in secular matters, though some are. Yet the rabbi has the capacity of being conversant and stimulated by academic issues and provides the unique bridge between pure book learning and pragmatic human concerns. In short, he or she performs a function the academic scholar can never perform: to learn in order to teach and in order to do. By studying, applying, and living the Torah, the rabbi remains, in the language of Salo W. Baron, "the chief protagonist in the drama of Jewish communal survival."[6]

REFERENCES

1. Simḥah Assaf, *Be-Ohalei Ya'akov* (1943), 27 (emphasis added).
2. Isaac Abrabanel, *Naḥalat Avot,* ad loc. M. Avot 6:2.
3. Leone Modena, *History of the Rites, Customs and Manners of Life of the Present Jews Throughout the World,* Edmund Chilmead , tr. (1650), 69–70.
4. Quoted in Ismar Schorsh, "Emancipation and the Crisis of Religious Authority," in Werner E. Mosse, Arnold Paucker, and Reinhard Rürup, eds., *Revolution and Evolution: 1848 in German-Jewish History* (1981), 217.
5. Quoted in Editor's note, "The American Rabbinate: A Centennial View," in *American Jewish Archives,* 35 (1983), 90.
6. Salo W. Baron, *The Jewish Community,* 2 (1942), 77.

BIBLIOGRAPHY

Salo W. Baron, *The Jewish Community,* 2 (1942), 66–94.
Reuven Bonfil, *Ha-Rabbanut be-Italya be-Tekufat ha-Renasans* (1979).
Mordecai Breuer, *Rabbanut Ashkenaz be-Yamei ha-Beinayim* (1976).
Jacob Neusner, *American Judaism: Adventure in Modernity* (1972), 35–60.
Ismar Schorsch, "Emancipation and the Crisis of Religious Authority: The Emergence of the Modern Rabbinate," in Werner E. Mosse, Arnold Paucker, and Reinhard Rürup, eds., *Revolution and Evolution: 1848 in German-Jewish History* (1981).

Reason

תבונה

Eugene Borowitz

For Greek philosophers, reason itself authoritatively explained reality and mandated action. In that sovereign role (one that much of Western civilization accepted) reason has been both a problem and an opportunity for believing, thoughtful Jews. The biblical authors knew God had spoken to them and to their people. Having that certain source of knowledge, they acknowledged no other beside it. Perhaps biblical wisdom literature reflects a common-sense ethics and piety that one might reach without revelation; indeed, precisely its independent notion of wisdom has led scholars to suggest it manifests a Hellenic influence. The rabbis, who know something of Greek culture and philosophy, wipe out any trace of ambiguity in this matter. They insist on the ultimacy of Torah and the subordinate status of general wisdom. To be sure, rabbinic literature manifests the explicit use of reason much more than does the Bible, but it operates in terms laid down by Torah. The "logic" of *derash* (homiletical interpretation) and of halakhic reasoning derives from the oral Torah, not from autonomous speculation. For classic Judaism, reason serves as a handmaiden to revelation.

Jewish tradition took note of reason as a source of truth equivalent to or, in fact, superior to revelation only when Jews found philosophical claims so compelling they could not easily be ignored. The work of Philo of Alexandria (unknown to Jewish tradition until recent centuries) illustrates the problem so intriguingly that opinion remains divided concerning it. Does Philo's allegorization of Scripture merely reflect his intuition that Hellenistic thought and the Torah must contain the same truth? Or by vigorously employing an idealizing hermeneutic does he mean to replace biblical historical concreteness with Greek intellectual abstractions?

Reason acquired an honored place in Judaism through the writings of the medieval Jewish philosophers. For about six centuries, a small elite, which occasionally gained a sizable following, acknowledged reason's claims upon them and therefore sought to situate it within Judaism. This shift of attitude partially arose from the success of Moslem philosophy in separating Greek philosophy from its idolatrous context and in arguing that it yielded the purest form of monotheism. Medieval Jewish philosophy may therefore be read as a series of variations on the dialectic between reason and revelation. Maimonides and Gersonides, who give reason preeminence, find their counterpoise in Judah Halevi and Ḥasdai Crescas, who exhibit equal cognitive competence but use it only to demonstrate the validity of revelation.

Emancipation confronted Jews with an understanding of reason radically more secular than that of the Middle Ages. Nonetheless, most Jews found its claims irresistible. Moses Mendelssohn foreshadows much of the later problematic of Jewish thought in his pioneering effort to come to terms with modernity. The pre-Kantian rationality of his day established a truth precious to Mendelssohn: every rational person had the capacity to participate in society as an equal—and thus so did Jews. The universality of reason supplied the intellectual justification for emancipating the Jews; hence, to deny the authority of reason implied validating discrimination. But if truth were universally available, why remain Jewish and, as Mendelssohn did, be disciplined by its mandates? Mendelssohn forthrightly answered that, as Christians surely admitted, history as well as reason yields religious truth. Esteeming reason, Judaism had a sublime openness to ideas and taste, but God had once given it a law (the written and oral Torahs as one) that remained forever binding upon it. A Jew could be fully modern in thought and style but live as God's revelation required.

This *compartmentalization* of the self, as contemporary observers of Orthodoxy have termed a similar phenomenon, proved unacceptable to most of Mendelssohn's contemporaries. They sought greater integration of self than his philosophy supplied, and thus identified the issue that has remained at the center of modern Jewish thought: What integration of modern reason and Jewish tradition, if any, does justice to them both?

In time, the overwhelming majority of modern Jews found additional grounds for making reason the arbiter of their Judaism. Science explained so much more and so much better than did revelation that it discredited the latter. Practicality also played a major role. Modernizing Jews knew that the ghetto-shaped way of life they had inherited clashed with the ethical truths and aesthetic goods reason liberatingly indicated. Besides, nineteenth-century German idealism clarified what remained everlastingly valid in Judaism and what might be changed. It taught that every worthwhile human movement contained an eternal truth that it expressed, necessarily, in transient historical form. The essence of Judaism was ethical monotheism. It and all the ceremony that cultivated it should never be surrendered by any rational being. All other Jewish rites and customs might be maintained as long as they did not violate modern Judaism's increasing understanding of ethical monotheism.

In addition to explaining this radical departure from classic Jewish faith, reason validated it. Instead of asserting a unique revelation to Jews, Judaism, like religions in general, would now be thought of in terms of human spiritual search and development, and thus understood in the same terms one applied to any human phenomenon. This perspective not only overcame Judaism as a schizoid existence; it proved Judaism's superiority to Christianity, to which many Jews had been drawn. If reason mandated a pure ethics and monotheism, Judaism was the more rational faith. This nineteenth-century point of view gradually became the standard ideology of liberal, or non-Orthodox, Jews. Many Jews still find that it provides the language with which they can most easily explain their religion.

Though some efforts to create a modern Jewish philosophy predate Hermann Cohen, the sophistication of his work established it as the academic ideal to which all succeeding Jewish thought would aspire. Cohen, a creative philosopher, originated the form of reason he used to describe Judaism, namely, Marburg neo-Kantianism. This philosophy and the broader sense of rationality of which it was a part lost philosophic appeal after World War I, but lingered on in the Jewish community for some decades as the background for most modern Jewish thought.

Succeeding generations saw other conceptions of reason come and go. What seemed so obvious once was superseded some years later. The concept of reason itself lost constancy, and redefining it and espousing the virtues of one's mode of rationality became a major philosophic activity. Jewish rationalism naturally sought to follow the new philosophic currents.

But as reason became less self-evident truth and more the utilization of premises one found useful, skepticism grew about making a given version of it the foundation of one's existence.

Jews had additional reasons for doubting the adequacy of a rationalism as rigorous as Cohen's. For one thing, piety rather than ratiocination had characterized most Jewish lives in the past. This led Leo Baeck to modify Cohen's rationalism by proposing religious consciousness (after the fashion of Rudolf Otto) as an equivalent, other source of Judaism. To avoid the excesses of romanticism, he further insisted that ethics remain the criterion of religious duty. This mitigated rationalism still kept the truth of Judaism on the universal level and reduced Jewish particularity to a means for its expression. Mordecai Kaplan, to make a stronger case for Jewish ethnicity and utilize what he considered a better rationalism, developed a philosophy of Judaism based on American naturalism. Taking sociology as his scientific guide, he argued for the central creative role of ethnic groups in human life. Since all such groups needed a fully articulated culture, including religion, he could make a rational case for "Judaism as a civilization."

With naturalism and other rationalisms languishing in recent years, Jewish rationalism has suffered a serious decline. Thus, some thinkers have called attention to the virtues of working with Whiteheadian process theology, perhaps the dominant mode of argument in contemporary Protestant philosophical theology. However, no substantial Jewish process theology has yet appeared. This decline may also explain the neglect of the French Jewish rationalist Emmanuel Levinas. Moving beyond Edmund Husserl's phenomenology, he has created a metaphysics that seems to him to have Jewish application. But Levinas' lack of followers may be due to the difficulties many thinkers find with this uncommon form of rationality.

A Jewish version of existentialism arose as part of the Western turn from pure reason. Franz Rosenzweig pointed to death as proving that existence took priority over essence and then went on to live rather than systematically think as a Jew. Martin Buber more fully elaborated a nonrational system. He described two dynamic modes of relating to reality, the I-It, which corresponds roughly to dispassionate reason, and the I-Thou, which utterly transcends the I-It in quality but depends upon it for continuity and structure. Neither Rosenzweig nor Buber attacked reason in the fashion of Søren Kierkegaard, and both made a considerable if secondary place for it in their thought.

Abraham Heschel called his major statements *philosophy,* but he used the term in quite uncommon fashion. For Heschel, reason had no independent status. All thought had to begin with the realization of God's overwhelming greatness and this, he argued in traditional Jewish fashion, will lead one to accept God's revelation. Essentially, he assigned reason a self-critical role, utilizing it to move people from a humanocentric to a theocentric understanding of life.

The line between Heschel's thought and modern Orthodoxy remains unclear, since both make God's reality and revelation the base for all reasoning about Judaism. Modern Orthodox thinkers display various relationships to reason. For some, Jewish Orthodoxy is an existential choice requiring no further validation, and reason may then operate freely within the limits it sets. For Joseph Baer Soloveitchik, a halakhic approach to existence makes possible a rationality as exalted as any known by secular philosophy. For Michael Wyschogrod, the ontology of Martin Heidegger, when utilized in terms of God's reality, provides a suitable hermeneutic for educing Judaism's basic faith.

Two further issues with regard to reason's role in Judaism must be noted. The older of these is the Holocaust and the extent to which it can adequately be dealt with in rational categories. Elie Wiesel, in his essays and novels, and Emil Fackenheim, in a major philosophic statement, have argued that the Holocaust's uniqueness shatters prior notions of rationality and Judaism. Its brute reality must be the basis on which life must now be built and any structure of thought erected. Most Jewish thinkers, however, while determined not to reduce the awesomeness of the Holocaust, consider it another case, if the most difficult one, of the generally intractable problem of theodicy.

The more recent challenge to the role of reason in Judaism has come from the rebirth of Jewish mysticism. While the movement remains too inchoate for description, its initial literature shows more interest in experience than in theosophy, in image than in structure. Of particular interest will be the clarification by the non-Orthodox mystics of the grounds upon which they reject the fully commanding power of Jewish law.

In sum, what reason might mean or do in contemporary Jewish theology depends on the interrelated answers to a number of metarational questions: To what extent should we seek to integrate rather than compartmentalize our existence? Does reason proceed from its own premises or from certain human or theological givens? If the latter, what are these givens? Which variety of reason in our culture commends itself for our use in its own terms and in terms of Judaism? Why do thinkers of other schools not find that judgment reasonable?

These vexing issues characterize contemporary Jewish theology, distinguishing it from the heady rationalist confidence of the late nineteenth century as well as engendering much of its liveliness and vitality.

BIBLIOGRAPHY

Eugene B. Borowitz, *Choices in Modern Jewish Thought* (1983).
Emil Fackenheim, *To Mend the World* (1982).
Julius Guttmann, *Philosophies of Judaism* (1964).
Joseph B. Soloveitchik, *Halakhic Man* (1983).
Michael Wyschogrod, *The Body of Faith* (1983).

Reconstructionism

יהדות מחודשת

Harold Schulweis

Reconstructionism is the only Jewish spiritual, sectarian movement indigenous to the American environment. Its ideology remains the creation of its founder and theoretician, Mordecai Menahem Kaplan (1881–1983). His major work, *Judaism as a Civilization,* first published in 1934, laid the architectural basis of Reconstructionist thinking. In 1959 Rabbi Ira Eisenstein assumed the leadership of the Reconstructionist Foundation, and when the Reconstructionist Rabbinic College was founded in Philadelphia in 1968, Reconstructionism emerged from its role as a school of thought into the fourth religious movement in America, alongside Orthodox, Reform, and Conservative Judaism.

Kaplan may best be understood as a philosopher-statesman. His sociological analysis of the Jewish condition and his proposed theological reconstruction were motivated by an overriding concern: to preserve the identity, unity, and creativity of a Jewish people threatened by the ambivalent forces of modern nationalism and naturalism. Kaplan viewed modern Jewry as an old-new people whose present sociopolitical and religious state of affairs are unprecedented in its history. No analogy with other Jewish communities in the premodern past properly applies to present-day Jews who are citizens of democratic societies. The forces of emancipation and Enlightenment shattered the unity of Judaism and the Jewish people so that this unity could no longer be assured by a uniform theology and ritual practice.

Kaplan addressed a new American Jewish audience—secularly educated, unwilling to accept the premises of supernaturalism or the authority of otherworldly tradition, and unconvinced that public and private life should be regulated by revealed law. Reconstructionism was designed to effect a creative adjustment to modern life in order to salvage and strengthen the communal will to live. Kaplan argued for the values of living simultaneously in two civilizations. He proposed new categories to deal with the radically different conditions of world Jewry: he called for a reevaluation of the meaning of individual and collective salvation, for a restructuring of Jewish institutions, and for the formulation of new programs to redefine the modern status of world Jewry.

Kaplan's social strategy was not simply that of a statesman's accommodation to the undeniable reality of modernism. For him, naturalism, humanism, and democracy were not inimical forces to be fought against; they contributed insights and values indispensable for the revitalization of Judaism. With equal force, Kaplan warned against the perversion of those values into reductionist scientism, chauvinism, and privatism. Nothing less than an axiological synthesis of tradition and modernity could secure the continuity and creativity of Judaism.

Basic to such a grand plan for reconstructing Judaism was Kaplan's characterization of Judaism as a religious civilization. On theoretic and pragmatic grounds, Kaplan held that the post-Enlightenment categories that view Judaism as either a religion or a nationality distorted the complex, varied, and growing expressions of a living organism, the Jewish people. Judaism as a civilization refers to the collective articulation of a people's wants, needs, yearnings, and discoveries of sanctity and meaning. Jewish civilization is the human product of a particular people whose transactions with its environment yield laws, mores, language, history, art, attachment of a people to a land, and religion. The religious character of civilization is the expression of a people's spiritual personality—its self-awareness as a community striving for the salvation or realization of all who belong to it. Kaplan's holistic perception of Judaism as a religious civilization enlarged the domain of Jewish interests and talents, incorporated the diversity of Jewish religious and cultural expression, and focused attention on the organic interdependence of culture, religion, and peoplehood.

Judaism is existentially rooted in a living organism with an instinctual will-to-live. The matrix of the Jewish civilization is the Jewish people. Belonging, the need to feel part of a people whose salvation is linked with individual self-fulfillment, takes precedence over believing. The superstructure of Judaism must be responsive to the needs of the people, and must be responsible for the spiritual actualization of the people. Judaism as an evolving religious civilization is "*existentially* Jewish peoplehood, *essentially* Jewish religion and *functionally* the Jewish way of life."[1] The priority of Jewish existence over Jewish essence lies at the heart of Kaplan's self-declared "Copernican revolution." The Jewish heritage exists for the sake of the Jewish people, not the Jewish people for the sake of the Jewish heritage. Kaplan's social existentialism means that the existential reality of the Jewish people is prior to and transcends any doctrinaire set of beliefs and practices. In the past, the process of adjusting tradition to the needs of the day was largely unconscious, devoid of historic perspective. Revitalizing the spiritual values of the tradition and making the transition from traditional Judaism to a Judaism capable of surviving into the future involves an awareness of the chasm between the traditional and modern worldview and the courage to risk meaningful change.

Kaplan is his own best illustration. Together with such thinkers as Milton Steinberg, Eugene Kohn, and Ira Eisenstein, he applied Reconstructionist theory to Jewish liturgy. After publishing a widely criticized new Haggadah in 1941, he published the pioneering Reconstructionist Sabbath Prayer Book four years later. Kaplan observed Jews who, unable to accept portions of the traditional worship text, abandoned prayer itself. Kaplan himself shared many of their objections to those sections of the prayer book whose theology and morality ran counter to his own beliefs. The Reconstructionist solution was neither to pray without believing nor not to pray at all, but to reinterpret the liturgy in a new key. The contemporary theological and moral sensibilities of Jews were to be respected. Prayers discriminating against women, slaves, and Gentiles were omitted and replaced by positive formulations. Petitions for the restoration of animal sacrifice in a rebuilt Temple in Jerusalem were deleted, along with those affirming belief in physical resurrection and in God's rewarding and punishing of Israel by granting or withholding rainfall.

While the Reconstructionist prayer book reinterprets many of the traditional liturgical texts, it explicitly rejects those extolling God's exclusive election of the Jewish people and his revelation of Torah as the only doctrine expressing God's will. Reconstructionism is the sole Jewish religious ideology to reject the idea of God's chosen people and the rationale other Jewish movements offered in its favor. For Kaplan, the idea of divine chosenness introduces invidious distinctions between Jews and Gentiles, implies the superiority of the chosen over the rejected, and raises sibling rivalries among religions and peoples each claiming the exclusive approval of the father, thus placing obstacles in the way of peace and harmony. Kaplan preferred, instead, to speak of vocation: the Jewish people, seeking to become a people in the image of God, chooses its vocation, which implies no claim to superiority. Nothing in the doctrine of vocation precludes other peoples or religions from becoming just as holy and dedicated to serving God by embodying the universal values that their historic experiences have revealed to them.

Kaplan's liturgical and ritual innovations, which included the total acceptance of women in the religious life of the synagogue—for example, counting women in the minyan (quorum)—were not meant for every Jew or every synagogue. They were addressed to a major Jewish constituency that felt so great a dissonance between its intellectual and moral belief systems and the worldview of the prayer book that they had turned away from the religious community. The pragmatics of Kaplan's Reconstructionism was designed to leave no excuse for apostasy.

Kaplan placed considerable emphasis upon the stabilizing force of *sancta* to provide the element of continuity and sameness that makes possible the ongoing reevaluation of traditional concepts and practices where it is called for. *Sancta* refers to the constellation of historic realities—heroes, events, places, folkways, myths, writings—that serve as the common sacred referents of a people. The *sancta* shared by the widest variety of Jews help preserve the unity in the diversity that characterizes the condition of Jewish life.

The major adjective qualifying civilization is *religious*. Jewish religion is the natural, social product of a people's life, the soul of its civilization. Without the Jewish religion, Judaism is devoid of the self-consciousness that a civilization attains when it becomes aware of its purpose, or what Kaplan calls its salvation. But religion is not synonymous with or isolated from the whole of Judaism: "To have religion a people must have other things in common besides religion."[2] Paradoxically, the religious regeneration of a people demands that religion cease to be its sole preoccupation.

Correlation is a key Kaplanian concept linking divinity with peoplehood and the idea of God with the idea of salvation. *God* is a correlative term that relates to a people in the same manner that other functional nouns relate, for example, parent to child, teacher to pupil, shepherd to flock. *God* denotes a relationship of supreme importance to a people or to mankind. The functional idea of God is derived not from metaphysical speculation or supernatural revelation but naturalistically from the process of discovering the meaning of human self-fulfillment or salvation. Whatever constitutes salvation for a religious community determines its idea of God. A people's historic transaction with its environment in its quest for maximum life leads it to identify those aspects of the cosmos that support its goal. That which brings order out of chaos and fosters world responsibility, love, and creativity manifests divinity and shapes the idea of God. The conscious quest for self-fulfillment presupposes that reality is patterned so as to contain the means of satisfying its ideal intent. The inference from the yearning and striving for salvation to the existence of conditions favoring salvation is a "willed faith" that derives not from logic but from the conscious quest to live with a maximum fullness. Such faith is neither passive nor arbitrary but calls for wisdom to explore the real and potential good and for the will to activate that good. The uniqueness of the Jewish idea of God reflects the historic uniqueness of the Jewish people's career in its search for purpose and meaning. For the individual Jew the Jewish people is the chief source of his salvation.

REFERENCES

1. Mordecai M. Kaplan *The Purpose and Meaning of Jewish Existence* (1964), 300.
2. Ira Eisenstein and Eugene Kohn, eds., *Mordecai M. Kaplan: An Evaluation* (1952), 18 (original emphasis).

BIBLIOGRAPHY

Ira Eisenstein and Eugene Kohn, eds., *Mordecai M. Kaplan: An Evaluation* (1952).
Mordecai M. Kaplan, *Judaism as a Civilization* (1957).
Mordecai M. Kaplan, *Questions Jews Ask* (1956)

Redemption

גאולה

Arthur A. Cohen

A characteristic signature of the classical rabbinic style is its interweaving of various theological motifs and preoccupations, its refusal to separate out high argument from examples drawn from the most mundane events of life, its continuous care for using simple fidelities and loyalty to the halakhah as occasions for promising large redemptions. It is consequently extremely difficult to set forth a doctrine of redemption in the classical tradition that does not entail consideration of every other teaching, since redemption is contingent upon performance of the commandments, overcoming of the evil *yezer* or impulse, devotion to the community, right intention and purity of heart, the exhibition of all the virtues, just behavior in treating the stranger and the poor, and a whole galaxy of similar and dissimilar moral and spiritual undertakings. The consequence of this is that the conception of redemption that obtains in the classical tradition becomes almost a catchphrase for a kind of concrete perfection, the integral saint being he who is redeemed, redemption coming to mean God's generosity to the fully faithful and exigent Jew. At the same time that redemption is offered to reward a whole variety of ancient virtues and performances, it tends—by the very tensility and encompassing character of its usage—to lose some of its force, to become a term by which to hold out the promise of divine justification and reward to the believing practitioner of rabbinic Judaism.

Another characteristic as outstanding and unique is the paucity and spareness of the rabbinic description of redemption. Redemption is, after all, an encompassing divine resolution that includes as many aspects of the divine justification of human obedience as can be imagined. It is *the* eschatological concept, and precisely because it is preeminent its power tends, on first examination, to be muted by such overwhelming notions as the End of Days, the advent of the Messiah, the restoration of the Jewish people to their land, the unification of all mankind in service of the one true God, and the resurrection of the dead. Are not all of these dimensions of redemption?

It may, however, be asked at the outset: What calls forth the need and beseechment for redemption? What does man seek in the promise of redemption? The predicament of human beings is that they conduct a difficult life in this world. Even if they be rich and comfortable, the days of man are numbed with unfulfillment, wavering concentration, the demands of the body, weariness of spirit, frustration of will, the trials of self-contempt and humiliation, diminishment of pride, falsehood, and evildoing. Even those then who are beyond privation conduct their lives in deprivation. How much more so with those who gain their livelihood in trial and precariousness, who suffer illness and anguish, who live unsatisfying and unsatisfiable lives? Whatever the situation of human beings, their days are marked with finitude and limit, constrained by the boundary markings that infect their days with temporality, loss, uncontrol, anxiety, and despair. These "limit situations," as Karl Jaspers called them, are categoric conditions of the human. No person evades them, not even the *zaddik,* the righteous man, since even he—or he above all human beings—is aware of the discrepancy between the human and the divine life, between the situation of Jewish faithfulness and the demands of God. In one sense, then, God is always dissatisfied with human performance. It may be metaphysical churlishness on God's part, since he made his creatures in his image, but the ambit of expectation in which God moves seems narrower than the demand for human perfection. God does not expect human perfection, but he does expect as a portion of the reciprocity entailed by the covenant with Abraham and Moses that the Jewish people exert themselves to service and obedience. The ambiguous moral freedom of the Jew constrains the self to limit its extension, to keep rein upon those passions that debase the creature, and to observe a structure of laws whose justification is not rational but simply reflects the obdurate and impenetrable will of God.

Against such a background, what emerges as the substantial relevance of a doctrine of redemption is limited and secondary. Redemption is no goal, nor is redemption the bestowal of a clear and individuated justification. Redemption is an aura-concept, since in a religion of study, attention, continuity, and covenantal unity reward is coeval with acts of performance and service, and punishment that is experienced in the self-alienation of sinfulness and dereliction is coeval with the loss of integration and community. Redemption is finally only a bestowal in ratification of what has already transpired. Redemption confirms and seals what is already accomplished.

To speak of redemption as an aura-concept is to raise the suspicion that the idea of redemption is somehow devalued to mere spectacle, to the status of an ornamental figuration of deeper and less accessible notions. This is truly the case in the sense that redemption is a concept without fixed content, unlike, let us say, the phenomena of covenant, or specific *miẓvot,* or acts of mercy and justice. The latter have settled definitions and significance and cannot be molded and shaped to meet the requirements of shifting communal sentiment, whereas redemption—precisely because it lacks fixed content—can include all the eschatological notions of the tradition, subsuming them to its unique promise. On the other hand, redemption is uniquely suited to being and maintaining itself as an aura-concept precisely because its content should never be settled and fixed for all time. Redemption can be maintained to be everything from ransoming the holy land to justifying the enterprise of the human race to do good and seek mercy— that is, all the way from the most narrow definitions of religious nationalism to the most universal assertion of divine care for the species. Precisely because it is formally constituted to receive every variety of human hope, the concept of redemption is both limited to parochial preoccupation and sufficiently expandable to encompass the hopes of the race.

The great consolation prophecies of Isaiah and Jeremiah provide the classical source for the imaging of redemption. A people in despair, broken and in exile, elicits from its God the mercy and promise that bespeak redemption. Not forever, God promises; not for eternity shall the people be tormented; but in the right time, God will ransom them from their brokenness and heal their disconsolation. Redemption—were it narrowly filled with specific and precisely defined content—could not serve the demands of hope. Were redemption only God's fulfilling his commitment to reward and raise up his serving people, to return them to promised lands, to succor them with bounty and plenteousness, the concept would lose the considerable power that indefiniteness affords it. Over the centuries of dispersion, when the Jewish people were encumbered with servitude and powerlessness, had redemption been overspecified the concept would not have served to inspirit hope. God's promises can never be too precise or unambiguous where precise, lest in fulfilling (or failing to fulfill) their detail God be deemed deceiver. Rather let the eschatological promise maintain its effulgence as aura-concept, as notion that signifies hope without narrowing it, as conception that maintains sufficient breadth that every religious imagination can find comfort within its promise.

The question remains, nonetheless: What does redemption redeem? Does it redeem specific persons? Does it justify concrete behavior? It does not seem likely that a concept without formal content can be focused with such precision. Redemption addresses human hope in a different manner than through reward and punishment, providence, and an answer to theodicy. Surely redemption is the most extraordinary granting of reward and the most encompassing rebuke to the triumph of evil in a thoughtful universe, but it is still not clear for all this what it is that redemption redeems.

The metaphysical question remains that redemption is not the justification of mind and thinking, nor is it the reward of fulfillments and enactments, nor is it justification of individual accomplishment. Redemption is not wasted upon the domain of contingency and fortune. Only the unreflective believer could imagine that God devises redemption to gratify personal particularity. And yet redemption is never general and vague. It must always be specific without falling into particularity, must always redeem something concrete.

Let us suppose that the way in which an aura-concept receives the abundance of human hope and returns it as love, consolation, and compassion is that redemption is not only (or solely) existential, but rather ontological. The beseeching person knows only of existential suffering and despair, but God knows being and the situation of being, the nature of the limit and the privation of finitude. What is for the human race the search for redemption out of trial and despair is for God the repositioning of himself in the direction of being; repentance and turning is in God's ordering of things a revaluation of the human condition of being in the world. When man asks the question of his being in the guise of his beseechment for redemption, God answers with justification that repositions his own being in new alignment with the finite and constrained being of his creatures. Redemption is seen here as an ontological re-formation, a re-presentation of the transitive and future-turned Divinity "who will be there when he will be there" (Exodus

3:14), who is always ahead of his creatures, whose ontological presence is always in advance of existence and therefore always ready and able to redeem the being of his creatures.

If redemption were only a historical ransoming and justification, the reality of the unredeemed and unransomed (as the various depredations and disasters of the historic Jewish people make abundantly clear) would effectively cancel the promise of redemption and the relevance of its divine sponsor. But it is argued here that the relation between the creature and God is never historical, that the relation of man to God is existential, but that the relation of God to man is ontological in the most profound sense. God's care for his creatures is concrete in that the turning of being toward God (the re-formation that is at the core of repentance) is ontological and redemption is thus the ontological bestowal of a Divinity grateful that his creatures turn toward him and seek his promise.

BIBLIOGRAPHY

Max Kadushin, *Organic Thinking: A Study in Rabbinic Thought* (1938).
Jacob Neusner, *A Life of Rabban Yohanan ben Zakkai* (1962).
Solomon Schechter, *Some Aspects of Rabbinic Theology* (1909).

Reform Judaism

יהדות, מתקדמת

Michael A. Meyer

R eform Judaism is both an organized branch of religious
Judaism, which today numbers some 1.2 million adherents,
mainly in North America, and a religious philosophy that
attempts to harmonize Jewish tradition with modern culture. It began as a
movement for religious change within central European Jewish communities, especially in Germany, at the end of the eighteenth and in the first half
of the nineteenth centuries, spreading thereafter to the United States, to
other Jewish communities in the West, and, most recently, to the State of
Israel. Its theology and ideology have remained fluid, allowing for both gradual and radical change and permitting a diversity of contemporaneous
interpretations.

Reform Judaism emerged out of the confrontation between traditional
ghetto Judaism and the intellectual and aesthetic environment of the eighteenth-century Enlightenment. A conflict of values soon became apparent,
and made the Jewish heritage appear inappropriate in the new context. At
the same time, an intensifying process of social and political integration cast
doubt upon the continuing relevance of exclusivist elements enshrined in

Jewish thought and liturgy. The early Reformers sought both to create a Jewish theology that could withstand hostile currents of contemporary Christian and philosophical thought and to reshape the institutions of Judaism in such a way as to appeal to the transformed religious and aesthetic sensibilities of an acculturating Jewry.

While Moses Mendelssohn is usually considered in cultural terms to be the first modern Jew, his significance for the Reform movement is limited to his advocacy of reform on one issue: the traditional early burial of the dead. In practice Mendelssohn remained a fully observant Jew, convinced that the law divinely given at Sinai was not subject to human amendment regardless of changes in the political, social, or intellectual situation of the Jews. At the same time, his conviction that the basic beliefs of Judaism were equivalent to those of natural religion, attainable by unaided human reason, relegated the uniqueness of Judaism to its law, in effect eliminating a specifically Jewish theology. For the Reform movement, which transferred the emphasis in Jewish religious expression from law to belief, Mendelssohn left no basis upon which to build an identifiable faith. As early as 1792, Saul Ascher recognized this problem and suggested—contra Mendelssohn—that Judaism did possess articles of belief that differentiated it both from Christianity and from natural religion. Ascher was also among the first to argue that Jewish observance was to be regarded not as an end in itself, but rather as a means to religious devotion. Means that were effective in one political, social, and intellectual context might be ineffective or even counterproductive in another. Hence the need to select, as Ascher himself did, from among the customs and ceremonies of Judaism those that seemed still to be viable.

The conception of Jewish ceremonial law as means was linked to a fundamental religious reorientation. Traditionally, the spiritual disposition of the person who performed ritual commandments was either secondary or of no account. However, in the latter part of the eighteenth century, especially under the influence of Immanuel Kant, the notion of a God who requires worship through symbolic deeds fell into disrepute. Religion became subjectivized, and Jews too began to ask whether their prayers in the synagogue or their performance of ritual acts outside of it left them with a sense of religious edification or deepened moral commitment. These criteria were increasingly applied to the religious service, resulting in a program of practical reforms.

First in Amsterdam (1797), then in Westphalia (1808), Berlin (1815), and Hamburg (1818), efforts were made to create a synagogue service that would elevate the spirits of worshipers for whom prevalent practice had become meaningless, distasteful, or even repugnant. The most common, and least controversial, innovations were those relating to order and decorum: the synagogue was redefined as a sanctuary that required an atmosphere of reverence. Sermons delivered in the language of the country and intended to edify rather than expound the law were likewise introduced, and soon spread even to traditional synagogues. More controversial were the introduction of the organ to accompany the choir, the use of German hymns, and the shortening of the service by the elimination of redundant or peripheral elements such as the medieval poetry called *piyyut*. The greatest opposition was aroused by the elimination, especially in Hamburg, of certain liturgical elements on ideological rather than aesthetic grounds. The Hamburg prayer book omitted or altered passages that referred to the hope of return to Zion and the reestablishment of the sacrificial service. In part these alterations were made with an eye to the political situation of the Jews, but more basically they reflected the internalization of new values and attitudes: Europe no longer seemed like exile, the prayer for physical redemption expressed an unfelt longing, and animal sacrifice seemed a primitive mode of worship that God could scarcely desire in the future.

Opposition to the Reform movement on the part of reactionary governments and more traditional Jews slowed its organizational progress in the twenties and thirties of the nineteenth century, but did not prevent an intellectual ferment that expressed itself in the formulation of characteristic doctrines. Against the prevalent currents in Western theology and philosophy, Reform thinkers were constrained to assert that Judaism was not consigned to the past as the mere relic of an earlier stage in the development of religion. They argued that, on the contrary, Judaism possessed its own inherent dynamism and that it not only kept pace with the advance of the human spirit but made possible its progress. The Jewish people was understood as the recipient of a divine revelation not exhausted by the biblical text. Its rejection of the identification of God with world was seen to set Judaism apart both from the Christian idea of the incarnation and from pantheism in both its ancient pagan manifestations and its modern ones in contemporary philosophy. With its lack of emphasis on halakhah, Reform theology came to stress Judaism's moral distinctiveness through its insistence on free human response to the imperatives of a transcendent God.

Theological ferment was accompanied by the establishment of a close link between religious reform and *Wissenschaft des Judentums* (the scientific study of Judaism). The Reformers early recognized that their liturgical innovations would remain arbitrary unless they could be justified by reference to Jewish history. Thus leading figures like Abraham Geiger devoted themselves to historical studies, attempting to show that Judaism had undergone multiple stages of development, that it had interacted with its environment, and that therefore the contemporary norms of orthodoxy had to be understood as relative rather than absolute. Although some Reformers hesitated to engage in biblical criticism, eventually the movement—in contrast to the more traditional branches of Judaism—brought even the Pentateuch within the purview of its historical criticism.

In the 1840s the Reform movement in Germany awoke to new organizational activity. A generation of university-educated rabbis, who had already created scholarly and popular journals and newspapers, sought to achieve collective authority by coming together in a series of rabbinical assemblies held in Germany from 1844 to 1846. These assemblies tried to reach compromise positions on such matters as the use of Hebrew in the service, celebration of the Sabbath and holidays, and the position of women in Judaism. It was from these assemblies that German Reform Judaism (soon more frequently called Liberal Judaism) emerged as a more clearly defined denomination, which soon became dominant within the local unified communities. It separated itself both from the more conservative "positive historical" trend on the one hand, and from a more radical, militantly anti-traditional lay movement that was institutionalized in the small and separatist Reform congregation of Berlin.

By the middle of the nineteenth century, the Reform movement had spread to the Hapsburg Empire and to England. Shortly thereafter it began to flourish in the highly conducive atmosphere of America, where multiple denominations populated the religious landscape, progress had become a demigod, and the constraint of maintaining united communities under government control was lacking. A division between more radical Reformers, especially on the East Coast, and more conservative ones in the Midwest and South did not prevent the creation of national institutions, notably the Union of American Hebrew Congregations in 1873, the Hebrew Union College in 1875, and the Central Conference of American Rabbis in 1889.

In America, Reform Judaism soon became considerably more radical in practice than its European counterpart. Its worship was briefer, included more of the vernacular, and was in a number of instances held on Sundays. Both in Europe and America the movement dissociated itself from Zionism, which was widely believed to contradict the prevalent idea of the mission of Israel: God's providential dispersion of the Jews to bring higher religious and moral truths to the Western nations. Although neither anti-Zionism nor the idea of the Jewish mission was unique to Reform Judaism, they assumed an intensity within it that diminished only gradually in the twentieth century as the movement became fully Zionist.

The religious development of Reform Judaism in the United States can be seen clearly by comparing the three platforms adopted by Reform rabbis in Pittsburgh (1885), Columbus, Ohio (1937), and San Francisco (1976). The Pittsburgh Platform is suffused with universalism, rationalism, and the belief in spiritual progress. It prefers to speak of a Jewish "God-idea" that originates in Scripture but has been developed and spiritualized by later generations. It defines the Jews as "no longer a nation but a religious community," and as bound only by the moral, not the ceremonial, laws of Judaism. In contrast to the Reform movement in Europe, it stresses a religiously motivated social activism aimed at overcoming the inequities between rich and poor. By contrast, the Columbus Platform, reflecting in part the new influence of eastern European Jews in the movement, is far more traditional and particularist. It affirms a providential God, a progressively revealed Torah consisting of both the written and oral Law, and an Israel that is a people, not merely a religious community. While it reiterates the mission of Israel, it also speaks of building a Jewish homeland and a spiritual center in Palestine. A full third of the document is devoted to religious practice, not only in the synagogue but also in the home and school. The most recent platform continues this trend except that it reflects wider divergence in theology. Against the background of the Holocaust and the fact of full cultural integration in America, it admits that "the trials of our own time and the challenges of modern culture have made steady belief and clear understanding difficult for some." To this it can add, however: "Nonetheless, we ground our lives, personally and communally, on God's reality and remain open to new experiences and conceptions of the Divine." Although there has developed within American Reform Judaism after World War II a traditionalist theological trend that has stressed the ongoing force of the covenant between God and Israel, the movement has embraced as well a large number of rationalists and a small humanistic trend.

The 1976 platform both reflects and conceals unities and divergences that currently characterize Reform Judaism. Most Reform congregations today are more traditional and ethnic in orientation than were their counterparts a generation ago, yet some remain loyal to the earlier form, today usually called Classical Reform. The current Reform prayer book, *Gates of Prayer,* published in 1975, in its variety of options attests to a very broad spectrum of belief and practice. While on the one hand organized Reform Judaism has become much more conscious of halakhah and has issued collections of Reform responsa and guides for Jewish observance, it continues to insist as well that religious decisions rest ultimately with the individual. While it has in some respects moved closer to traditional Judaism, its greater openness to the realities of Jewish life in the West has tended to set it farther apart. Thus the recognition of patrilineal—not just matrilineal—descent in determining Jewishness and the willingness to tolerate a large minority of Reform rabbis who perform mixed marriages (generally with the provision that the children be raised as Jews) has provoked loud criticism outside the movement. Yet even these untraditional positions have been inspired by concern for Jewish "survival," a term that is lacking in the earlier Reform platforms but dominates the statement of 1976.

For most Reform Jews today, their particular expression of Judaism represents less a revolt against tradition than it does the denominational framework for a wide variety of religious and ethnic commitments, separated equally from a purely secular Jewish nationalism and from more traditional positions that to a greater degree restrict their conception of a creative confrontation with modernity.

BIBLIOGRAPHY

Bernard Martin, ed., *Contemporary Reform Jewish Thought* (1968).
Jakob J. Petuchowski, *Prayerbook Reform in Europe* (1968).
David Philipson, *The Reform Movement in Judaism,* rev. ed. (1967).
W. Gunther Plaut, *The Growth of Reform Judaism* (1965).
W. Gunther Plaut, ed., *The Rise of Reform Judaism* (1963).

Religion and State

דת ומדינה

Aharon Lichtenstein

The problematic character of the relation between religion and state is no historical accident. It is rather a natural result of the coexistence of two distinct orders within any given society—indeed, within the structure of human life generally. A polity that acknowledges the existence and significance of religion at all must inevitably come to grips, theoretically and practically, with the formulation of the role of religion vis-à-vis the civil and political spheres. Hence, the problem of religion and state is not a specifically Jewish issue but a universal question that Jewry confronts from its own perspective. Nonetheless, several factors have served, philosophically and historically, to give the issue a particular Jewish cast, sharpening it in one sense and attenuating it in another.

Starting at a general level, it seems fairly clear that the basic approaches possible are quite limited in number. A priori, one can postulate three primary positions. Civil and religious authority may virtually coincide, power being concentrated in the hands of a king-priest or curia, as in numerous primitive societies or in some instances in contemporary Islam. At the other extreme, the two may be theoretically totally separated, as in the United States. Intermediately, there may be some blend of difference and association, this being the prevalent pattern in most modern European countries. The choice of approach may depend upon either pragmatic or ideological considerations—for example, upon an evaluation of which system best preserves social harmony while protecting religious interests, or upon a determination of which best reflects the optimal balance between temporal and supernal values. It may also be affected by tortuous historical processes.

With respect to this cardinal issue, there can be little doubt about the classical Jewish position. Traditional Judaism has thoroughly rejected the fusion of secular and religious authority. Confrontation between prophets and monarchs was a hallmark of the First Commonwealth. Even as regards the relatively more mundane institution of priesthood, Naḥmanides states that its members are halakhically enjoined from assuming the throne, and he goes so far as to suggest that the Hasmonaean dynasty was divinely punished to the point of extinction because its scions, as priests, "should not have ruled but only labored in the service of God" (Comm. on Gen. 49:10). On the other hand, radical severance has been equally out of the question. A people defined as "a kingdom of priests and a holy nation" (Ex. 19:6) is hardly prone to divorce its political from its religious institutions.

Judaism has consequently opted for the median position—not as a compromise but as an expression of its perspective upon the whole of human life and upon the relation, both metaphysical and functional, between its sacred and secular components. Judaism has consistently regarded the sacral and the mundane as distinct but not disjunct. Pervasive halakhic norms relate to all areas of personal and communal existence, even as objective categories demarcate the sacred and the profane. The goal is harmonious integration, but by no means an obliterative leveling. Kiddush and havdalah, sanctification and differentiation, are both miẓvot; indeed, with regard to the Sabbath, possibly two facets of the same miẓvah.

The ideal polity, then, is one within which religion and state interact. From a halakhic perspective, this assertion holds true for all communities. All the more so, however, with respect to knesset Yisrael (the congregation of Israel), whose very existence as a national entity is defined, primarily, in spiritual rather than geopolitical terms; whose gestation and birth were the result of religious aspiration rather than contiguity or consanguinity; and which exists as a people, as Saadiah Gaon stressed, "solely by dint of its torot" [normative revelations] (Sefer Emunot ve-Deot, 3, 7).

The halakhic state is thus ruled jointly. Within it, a civil sovereign—initially, a chief judge or monarch but conceivably an oligarchic or democratic entity as well—coexists with the Sanhedrin (the term is of Greek origin but the institution biblical), a supreme ecclesiastical assembly invested with both legislative and judicial powers. The latter serves in a dual role. On the one hand, it constitutes the contemporary repository of Torah learning. As Moses Maimonides put it: "The [members of the] supreme *bet din* [religious court] which is in Jerusalem are the mainstay of the Oral Law, and from them law and statutes issue to all of Israel . . . and whoever believes in Moses our teacher [*rabbenu*] and his Torah is obligated to base religious action upon them and to rely upon them" (MT *Mamrim* 1:1). On the other hand, this ecclesiastical body enjoys a measure of governmental authority parallel to that of the civil sovereign. "Then the Lord said to Moses: 'Gather for Me seventy of Israel's elders of whom you have experience as elders and officers of the people, . . . [and] they shall share the burden of the people with you, and you shall not bear it alone'" (Num. 11:16–17). The respective civil and ecclesiastical authorities operate on the basis of radically different mandates and from very different perspectives, but each can make demands and impose limitations, and each can enforce them. Hence, while some areas may be clearly delineated as relating to the service of God or as the province of Caesar, respectively, others are clearly the domain of both religious and secular law. Given the broad latitude of halakhah, this means that large tracts of personal and communal life—virtually the whole social and economic sphere, for instance—are, in effect, independently ruled by two powers whose wills may but need not conflict. In other areas, however—notably that of foreign policy—checks and balances prevail. While foreign relations are generally regarded as the province of the secular order, some initiatives—the declaration of war, for instance—require the consent of the Sanhedrin.

The precise nature of the relationship is nowhere delineated in primary sources. The Talmud specifies that where civil law conflicts with halakhah, the latter takes precedence (BT Sanh. 49a). However, it does not spell out the degree of independence to be accorded secular law. The medieval author of the fourteenth-century *Derashot ha-Ran* allowed for the existence of a wholly separate codex, with its own rules of evidence, torts, and so on. Maimonides seems to have taken a more moderate position, as the only civil punishment he specifically sanctions is the right to inflict capital punishment upon a murderer, inasmuch as public safety is endangered (MT *Roẓeaḥ* 2:4). Others, appalled by the prospect of nonhalakhic justice, have explicitly rejected any but theocratic law and have largely confined the civil order to executive and administrative functions. Whatever the theoretical formulations, however, the potential for conflict is clear. Within an integrated polity, organized religion may control the state or be controlled—perhaps only supported—by it. As medieval history richly attests, the very existence of coordinate civil and ecclesiastical authorities invites incessant conflict. No theoretical construct can preclude such a possibility, and the halakhic model, within which power is partly divided and partly shared, is no exception. Nevertheless, Judaism's commitment to integration of the civil and the religious realms clearly points to some mode of interaction.

The structure of government and the allocation of power between the respective orders and their plenipotentiaries unquestionably constitutes an important facet of the problem of religion and state, and from the classical period through the Renaissance it generally loomed as the most dominant. In the modern era, however—surely, in the modern State of Israel—other aspects have come to the fore. The primary issue is no longer the mutual relation of civil and religious rulers, but the relation of both—particularly of the latter—to the citizen. The growing secularization of Western culture and the concomitant libertarian individualism have brought into question the right of any power—especially of a religious order—to impose its will in spiritual matters. Even those who, during this century, have championed the massive interference of the state within the socioeconomic sphere have generally defined the religious realm as the domain of personal conscience. Diaspora Jews, in particular, motivated by both principle and self-interest, have sought to sever the religious from the mundane, and they have championed the private character of the former so as to neutralize sociopolitical forces that had often persecuted or undermined them and whose discrimination has hampered their progress in post-Enlightenment Western society.

The emergence of the problem of religion and state as one of the most persistent cruxes of Israeli sociopolitical life needs to be seen against this background. With respect to the specific libertarian issue, Jewish tradition has nurtured differing and possibly conflicting tendencies. On the one hand, it has staunchly championed the significance of the individual as a creative spiritual being. It has defined him as created in the "image of God" (ẓelem Elohim)—"the human face divine," in Milton's phrase—invested with cosmic uniqueness; and it has proclaimed that "whoever saves a single soul is regarded as having preserved an entire world" (BT Sanh. 37a). Moreover, it has posited freedom—unadulterated Pelagian freedom—as the basis of the spiritual life. On the other hand, tradition has conceived of society in general, and of knesset Yisrael in particular, in organic terms, and consequently has emphasized both collective responsibility and historical destiny. Hence, while obviously striving to educate to encourage freely willed religious commitment, it has not flinched from a measure of coercive enforcement—in part out of a need to maintain a modicum of national identity and character, and in part out of a sense that, at some deeper level, those who are coerced identify with the values in whose name action is taken against them and recognize the ultimate justice of that action.

Within the predominantly religious society of classical and medieval Jewry, such recognition was quite pervasive. In the modern State of Israel, however, it often manifestly does not exist. Hence, the imposition of religious law has become far more problematic, both practically and morally. Within the political arena, the issue has generated heated controversy, pitting those who regard some religious legislation as both necessary and justified in order to ensure the country's basic Jewish character against a coalition of secularists who do not want the country to be too religiously Jewish and libertarians who, while possibly acknowledging the importance of Jewish identity, contend that it should not be attained at the expense of civil rights.

In many cases, the very existence of this opposition has led philosophical advocates of religious legislation to question its wisdom. Some have concluded that, given the scope and intensity of possible backlash, with respect to some laws coercive legislation is both inadvisable and undesirable. They have contended that, in the long-range interest of religion proper, even when the opportunity for passing new laws presents itself both prudence and moral sensitivity may dictate restraint. Others have rejected this counsel, however, and, since the mid-1970s, as the overall cultural struggle has intensified, attitudes toward the role of government in religion have polarized. While zealous activists at one end of the spectrum have sought to expand that role, radical separatists at the other have challenged not only the corpus of religious laws but also state support for religious institutions. Hence, a broadly based readiness to muddle through, even at the clear expense of consistency, has been somewhat attenuated; and as many have adopted a more rigorous ideological stance the tenuous status quo maintained since the inception of the state has become increasingly fragile.

From the outset, the debate has been exacerbated by two factors. First, unlike the halakhic model, which envisioned an independent religious component sharing in the governmental process by relating to the people directly, the current situation entails the use of secular institutions and their sanctions in order to impose religious norms. This both antagonizes secularists and perturbs halakhists who fear that the integrity of Judaism is sometimes compromised by the Erastian interference of civil authorities in religious matters. The second aggravating factor stems from the fact that, to an extent, the flow of events caught the halakhic world unawares. In the absence of a Jewish state for close to two millennia, the process of gradual adaptation—the grappling with new problems and the groping for legitimate halakhic solutions—that marked the development of halakhah in other locales barely took place with respect to the governmental sphere. Modes of thought and intuition, models of response and initiative, patterns of judgment and action—a whole tradition of political theory and practice as related to the continuous historical scene—was, as the State of Israel was coming into being, relatively inchoate. And while a whole generation has passed since the establishment of the state, much remains to be articulated and done before such a tradition will be firmly established. On the secular side, likewise, the leading spokesmen are often the voices of crude and strident anticlericalism; here, too, much work remains to be done. Such developments would not necessarily solve the problems at hand, but they would at least clear the air and clarify the issues, thus raising the quality of discourse.

BIBLIOGRAPHY

Christopher Dawson, *Religion and the Modern State* (1936).

Simeon L. Gutterman, "Separation of Church and State: The Historical Perspective," in Norman Lamm and Walter S. Wurzburger, eds., *A Treasury of Tradition* (1967).

Aharon Lichtenstein, "Religion and State: The Case for Interaction," in Arthur A. Cohen, ed., *Arguments and Doctrines* (1970).

Remnant of Israel

שארית ישראל

Nahum N. Glatzer

The remnant of Israel (she'erit Yisrael) denotes the concept, especially cultivated by the biblical prophets, that a defeat of Israel will never be total and irreversible; a remnant will remain and allow a new epoch to unfold. This concept mediated between the prophecies of doom and the promises of redemption. The clearest expression of the idea of the remnant is to be found in Isaiah's call to prophecy in 740 B.C.E., the year of King Uzziah's death. The ground "lies waste and desolate . . . and deserted sites are many in the midst of the land. But while a tenth yet remains in it, it shall repent. It shall be ravaged like the terebinth and the oak, of which stumps are left even when they are felled; its stump shall be a holy seed" (Isa. 6:11–13). "[A] remnant shall return, . . . a remnant of Jacob to Mighty God" (Isa. 10:21). "[T]here shall be a highway out of Assyria for the remnant which is left of His people" (Isa. 11:16). And in the report on the attempt of the Assyrian king Sennacherib to conquer Jerusalem it is written: "The surviving remnant of the House of Judah shall again take root downward and bear fruit upward; for out of Jerusalem shall go forth a remnant and out of Mount Zion a band of survivors"

(II Kings 19:30–31). To give his idea symbolic strength, Isaiah calls a son of his "a remnant shall return," a name that denotes both defeat and hope. He appears before the king in the company of his son to impress upon the king that defeat will be followed by an era of hope.

Isaiah's contemporary Micah announced that the Lord will "bring together the remnant of Israel" (Micah 2:12), but this passage is considered to be a later addition. Jeremiah, who lived in the last period of Judah and witnessed the destruction of the Jerusalem Temple in 586 B.C.E., speaks of the gathering of "the remnant of My flock from all the lands to which I have banished them" (Jer. 23:3). Ezekiel, the prophet mainly of the Babylonian Exile, which lasted from 586 to 516 B.C.E., is afraid the Lord might "annihilate all that remains of Israel" (Ezek. 9:8; cf. Ezek. 11:13). The prophet Joel, whose dates are undetermined, describes a severe plague of locusts, the "day of darkness and gloom" (Joel 2:2), the "most terrible day of the Lord" (Joel 2:11), followed by the call for repentance and the rescue of the remnant, the outpouring of the spirit. "There shall be a remnant on Mount Zion and in Jerusalem, as the Lord promised. Anyone who invokes the Lord will be among the survivors" (Joel 3:5).

Among the Jewish sectarians of the second and first centuries C.E. the term *remnant of Israel* was—naturally—known and used, mostly with reference to Israel's past. For example, we find in the writings of the Zadokites, as the Qumran community called itself, the following: "When he remembered the covenant of the forefathers, he caused a remnant to remain of Israel" (*The Zadokite Documents* 1:4). "He raised for Himself men called by name, in order to leave a remnant for the land" (*ibid.,* 2:11). In their present situation the sectarians referred to themselves by such titles as "sons of light," "sons of righteousness," "sons of truth," and "men of holy perfection."

Related to the concept of the remnant is the membership of the pious in *olam ha-Ba,* the World to Come, the realm of the just (Apoc. Abr. 17:29; I Bar. 14:13, 48:50, 51:38). In a number of texts the just are referred to as the "chosen ones" (I Enoch 1:1), the "humble ones" (I Enoch 5:7ff.), the "chosen of the Lord" (Wisd. 3:9). The reference is not to Israel as such, but to the pious ones in Israel and, at times, to the pious from among the Gentiles (I Enoch 48:4; Sibyl. 3, 195). What matters is not belonging to Israel but justice before God; this alone will bring about divine mercy (Tob. 13:3–6). It became necessary to include the righteous of the past and those who died as martyrs among the returning remnant, "that they may return and stay themselves on the day of the elect one" (I Enoch 61:5).

The names of the elect, of the remnant, are written down in the "scroll of remembrance . . . of those who revere the Lord and esteem His name" (Mal. 3:16). While the biblical concept of the "remnant" refers to the future and to the land of Israel, the category of the "elect" encompasses both the past and the future, the latter mainly a future that necessitates resurrection. For it appeared unjust to have a glorious era reestablished without the heroes of the past participating in it. Indeed, figures such as the patriarchs, Moses, Elijah, David, and Hezekiah were seen as the natural leaders of this new community. So too were Enoch, who was "taken" to heaven and would return to earth, and Daniel, who was told "to go on to the end; you shall rest, and arise to your destiny at the end of days" (Dan. 12:12). Also included was Baruch, the companion of Jeremiah who shall come back to bear testimony at the judgment of the nations (II Bar. 13:3). Especially significant is the promise of the resurrection of Adam. According to legend, the promise of his resurrection depended on his readiness to give up all evil; then he will be offered to taste from the Tree of Life and live forever, according to the *Life of Adam and Eve* (28:41), a pseudepigraphon preserved in Greek from a Jewish first-century-C.E. archetype. Thus history that started with Adam the sinner comes to a conclusion with Adam the resurrected to eternal life, which he had lost at the beginning. Equally interesting is the conclusion of the Greek version of the Book of Job, which speaks of Job who is to rise from the dead. The man who, in his debates with his friends, both feared death and wished for death is finally redeemed from this curse of man and, as the representative of mankind, will be granted a new life— the eternal life.

All the recently departed pious persons shall also join the pious of the past. Here, martyrs are the first that come to mind. As pioneers of faith and witnesses of faith they deserve to partake in the highest reward: return to life. Indeed, the martyrs hope and expect to be called back to life. The seven brothers mentioned in the Second Book of Maccabees became examples of heroism of faith. One of them addressed the king: "You, you fiend, are making us depart from our present life, but the King of the universe will resurrect us, who die for the sake of His laws, to a new eternal life" (II Mac. 7:9). Another brother stretched forth his hands, saying, "I received these from Heaven. . . . From Him I hope to receive them back" (II Mac. 17:11). The next brother died expressing his hopeful expectation that the martyrs will again be raised up by God, while there will be no resurrection for the king (II Mac. 7:14–42). Another sufferer invoked the Lord of life and spirit to restore his body to him (II Mac. 14:46). Judah the Maccabee brought an offering to Jerusalem, "a deed altogether fitting and proper, for he had their resurrection in mind. Indeed, if he did not expect the fallen to be resurrected, it would have been superfluous and foolish to pray for the dead" (II Mac. 12:43–44).

The Psalms of Solomon stress the happy lot of the righteous: "The destruction of the sinner is for ever . . . but they that fear the Lord shall rise to life eternal" (3:11ff.). That is, there is a strict difference between the just and the wicked: The latter go under and do not return. Whether *the just* refers only to the just in Israel is not clear in the texts.

Biblical and talmudic-midrashic views on the remnant were sufficiently strong and numerous to provide faith and hope for centuries. One expression of this faith occurs in the daily liturgy, where the term *remnant of Israel* appears in the petitionary prayer: "Guardian of Israel, guard the remnant of Israel, and suffer not Israel to perish, those who say 'Hear O Israel.'" In the twentieth century a startlingly different interpretation of the remnant is proposed by the philosopher Hermann Cohen in his *Religion of Reason out of the Sources of Judaism*. Cohen sees a profound relationship between the remnant and the suffering servant of Deutero-Isaiah; both are fulfilled in messianism. In the sufferings of the Jewish people through the ages as depicted in Isaiah, Israel, the messianic people, suffers as the representative of universal suffering. The remnant has the historical task of translating monotheism to its realization in messianism. Israel suffers for the deficiencies that to this day hinder the realization of messianism.

These sufferings are not confined to the actual historical representative of messianism. The people of Israel, in its role as servant of God, as remnant, accepted into its fold the "pious from among the peoples of the world"; these assume a full share, with Israel, in the messianic suffering.[1] This extension of ethics is the true meaning of messianism. External national and denominational limits are to be removed; then the suffering servant, the remnant, will be more than a symbol.[2]

Cohen's disciple, Franz Rosenzweig, is closer to the Hebrew sources in his discussion of the remnant. In his *Star of Redemption,* Rosenzweig points to the idea of the remnant as a concept that has been governing Israel's inner history ever since the time of the prophets. The remnant is the group of those who have remained faithful, the true people within the people. The idea of the remnant unites both the acceptance of the "yoke of the commandments" and "the yoke of the Kingdom of God," to use talmudic terminology.

Jewish history, Rosenzweig continues, is the history of this remnant. "If the Messiah came today, the remnant would be ready to receive him. In contradistinction to temporal history that deals with expansion, Judaism, and only Judaism, maintains itself by subtraction, by the formation of ever new remnants. Such a remnant adjusts to the outside world so that again and again it may withdraw into its own inner world."[3]

After World War II and the horror of the concentration camps, the "surviving remnant," DP's, or displaced persons, as they were called, gave the idea of the remnant a renewed meaning. The Jewish DP came to see Jewishness as an all-pervading fact of existence, the foundation of his consciousness. Using the term *she'erit ha-pleitah* (lit., the surviving remnant), the survivors of the camps and underground fighting groups felt a great obligation to the dead. The remnant's mission took the form of a defiant affirmation of life and national rebirth. Judaism is to emerge from the great catastrophe healthier and morally purified. This stress on Judaism and rebuilding of the land of Israel in no way restricts universalism, in which Jews have had a decisive part. The Jews' recent tragedy must become the starting point of a new humanism, a wider moral development. The ideal of Judaic civilization—the perfecting, on this earth, of every individual human being—coincides with the ideal of Western European culture at many points. And so the surviving remnant accepts a neo-humanism as its cultural ideal.

REFERENCES

1. Hermann Cohen, *Religion of Reason out of the Sources of Judaism* (1919), 311ff.
2. Ibid., 313.
3. Franz Rosenzweig, *Star of Redemption* (1964), 404.

BIBLIOGRAPHY

Nahum N. Glatzer, ed., *The Dynamics of Emancipation: The Jew in the Modern Age* (1965), 127 37.

Samuel Gringauz, "On the Tasks of the Jewish Remnant in Europe," in *Jüdische Rundschau* 6 (1946).

Repentance

תשובה

Ehud Luz

The Hebrew word for repentance, *teshuvah*, has two distinct meanings. The first derives from the verb "to return"; when used in this sense, it signifies going back to one's point of origin, returning to the straight path, coming back home after a period of absence. The second derives from the verb "to reply," and denotes response to a question or call that has come from without. The Jewish idea of *teshuvah* embraces both these meanings: It is a movement of return to one's source, to the original paradigm of human—or national—life, and also, simultaneously, a response to a divine call. The act of returning to one's original self is thus in and of itself a return to God and his teaching; and this is true on both the individual and the national levels.

Teshuvah is a central concept in Jewish religious literature, and may be said to express the essence of the religious and ethical ideal of Judaism. Though this idea occurs, in different forms, in most religions, it has been extensively developed only by those monotheistic faiths that see the relationship between God and man as primarily ethical in nature and view God's ethical claim upon the individual as absolute. In Judaism, this relationship is conceived as a covenant between two partners, each of whom has a role to play in bringing the world to perfection. When man sins, he violates this covenant and ruptures normal relations between himself and God. *Teshuvah* is the process by which this break is mended and the covenant renewed. Since Judaism views man's devotion to God's teaching and commandments as the means by which the covenant is to be realized, returning to God means a return to his teaching. There is a dialectic tension evident here, since *teshuvah* is at once both restorative and utopian in character; it is an effort to return to an ancient model, an ideal state that is imagined to have existed in the past (before man sinned in the Garden of Eden), but also, simultaneously, an endeavor to reach a perfect future, radically different from any reality that now exists or has existed in the past (the messianic era). Every movement for religious renewal that has appeared within Judaism, from the very beginning of its history, may thus be defined as a movement of *teshuvah*.

Although the term *teshuvah* was coined by the sages, the idea has its origins in the Bible, especially in its prophetic passages. These formulated a historiosophic model, which dominated Jewish religious thought for many generations and was founded upon the cycle of sin, violence, repentance, and return to God. Moreover, they emphasized the essential importance of spiritual and ethical purity as a necessary condition for the atonement and forgiveness of sin. The sages took up this attitude in their religious thought. However, while the prophets had devoted their thinking first and foremost to the whole people, which had violated the covenant and must return, the sages were more concerned with the psychological and practical aspects of the *teshuvah* of an individual. The community of Israel as a whole, *keneset Yisrael*, could not sin; it was individuals who sinned by distancing themselves from the community. To cleave to the *keneset Yisrael*, to feel a sense of solidarity with the people as a whole and share in its distress—these, in the sages' view, were necessary conditions of *teshuvah*. Medieval Jewish philosophy and the later *musar* literature continued to develop these rabbinic ideas but had no qualitative innovations of their own to add to them.

The development of the idea of *teshuvah* took a significant turn on the eve of the modern period. The Lurianic kabbalah, and subsequently Ḥasidic thought, endowed *teshuvah* with a metaphysical, cosmic dimension by correlating it with the idea of *tikkun* (the restoration and perfection of the world) and with that of the ingathering of the divine sparks that had been scattered throughout the universe. They also delved more profoundly into the psychological aspects of sin and repentance, and thereby arrived at a positive evaluation of the evil forces at work in man's soul, or, more precisely, of their importance to the psychological process of *teshuvah*. This heightened psychological awareness was pursued further by the Lithuanian Musar movement and by twentieth-century Jewish thought.

Contemporary Jewish thought has sought to endow the idea of *teshuvah* with new significance, in light of two processes that have deeply affected modern Jewish life: secularization and assimilation. Previously viewed as the alternative to a life of sin against God, in our time *teshuvah* also offers the Jew an alternative to secular life and to total absorption into his gentile surroundings. However, the basic meaning of the idea of *teshuvah,* that of a spiritual transformation by which the Jew returns to his source and to an authentic way of life, remains valid today. This meaning is especially prominent in two important schools of modern philosophical thought: existential philosophy, whose point of departure is the problem of the authenticity of human existence in view of the temporary and ephemeral character of human life, and dialogic philosophy, which argues that the true character of humanity is fulfilled first and foremost by a life of dialogue between man and his fellow and between man and God.

There are two main reasons for the modern Jew to seek a return to his sources. First, he lives in a world in which nationality has become a universally accepted mark of identity, and hence his desire for membership in the historical Jewish people. Second, he may feel a sense of disappointment with secularism as an ideal and so search for an authentic Jewish way of life. Those thinkers who have, from this point of view, made the most signal contributions to illuminating the philosophical and psychological aspects of the idea of *teshuvah* are Hermann Cohen, Franz Rosenzweig, Martin Buber, Abraham Isaac Kook, Joseph B. Soloveitchik, and A. D. Gordon. *Teshuvah* is central to the thought of all six—a fact readily understandable considering their efforts to confront the processes of secularization and assimilation. Almost all of them see the Jew's potential for *teshuvah* as resting upon his ability to reinterpret the religious significance of the tradition to make it applicable to a secular world. *Teshuvah* depends upon a new apprehension, dialectical and comprehensive, of modern reality (Kook), upon a spiritual reorientation that will be bold enough to make secular values part of a religious worldview (Rosenzweig), or upon transforming the self in such a way as to lead man away from an inauthentic way of life lacking in independent creative force and toward that authenticity that will be characterized by continual creativity and renewal (Buber, Soloveitchik, Gordon).

According to an idea originating primarily in Ḥasidic literature, there always remains in the inner soul of the sinner a single point of purity, a divine spark that is never extinguished. As Kook put it, God remains close to man even when man has become distant from God. *Teshuvah* is, thus a "natural" process. Hermann Cohen called this divine element in man the "holy spirit." It forms a link between God and man, and this is but a conceptual and philosophical expression of the idea of the covenant. The spirit—the divine image in man—is everlasting, and it serves to guarantee man's abiding capacity for ethical renewal. The idea of *teshuvah* assumes that sin, far from being the product of a congenitally corrupt human nature, has the character of a mistake, a momentary deviation. Judaism thus has no room for the idea of original sin in any ontological, substantive sense; it conceives, rather, of a perpetual struggle between good and evil in the heart of man. Man is always developing, and that is why his concrete acts in the world (his performance of the commandments) are given such emphasis. The process of *teshuvah,* centered as it is upon the action of man, is never finished. God helps man only after man himself has taken the first step.

First noted by the sages, the dialogic nature of *teshuvah* has received renewed emphasis in the modern philosophies of Cohen, Rosenzweig, and Buber. *Teshuvah* is man's response to a divine call. God, out of his love for man, calls out to him, "Where art thou?"—meaning, where are you in the world? What is your place? Stirred by these questions, man begins to reorient himself in the world, to move toward an authentic mode of existence, that is, a dialogic way of life. The principal problem of religion is that of man's reconciliation with God, which is also a condition of his own self-reconciliation. Religion is thus grounded upon man's recognition of his own sin.

Man's sense of sin involves a combination of aesthetic, intellectual, and moral elements. Sin taints him; it produces alienation between himself and God and arouses in him a feeling of self-loathing. It gives rise to a sense of guilt, and it is through this that man arrives at an awareness of his true self; for he discovers thereby his responsibility for himself. Certain secular theories attempt to liberate man from this inner sense of guilt by attributing its causes to various psychological or socioeconomic factors over which the individual has no control. Deterministic theories of this kind can have the effect of driving man to despair, of causing him to throw off or ignore his own responsibility and cast the blame for his misdeeds upon his surroundings (his parents, society, or country). The idea of *teshuvah,* on the other hand, is based upon the individual's recognition of his own guilt, which he may not attribute to his parents or to the society in which he lives. Moreover, this recognition stems not from the transgression of some socioethical taboo, but from the individual's very consciousness of the gap between the ideal or absolute demand that is directed toward him and the extent to which he has actually been able to realize it. Buber has shown that various manifestations of the sense of guilt are explainable only on the basis of the individual's recognition that sin represents the violation of some supernal order. Guilt is thus fundamentally an existential rather than a psychological concept, referring to man's dread of his essential self. It is only on the basis of this existential guilt that the phenomenon of psychological guilt can be understood.

Deep within himself, man is torn. His sense of sin and guilt are symptomatic of the split within his soul. The sinner's self is fragmented, and his soul—as the kabbalists would say—is in exile. Kook held that sin evolves from the division that man brings about in the primal unity of existence; it is by apprehending this unity that he can begin to repent. Every man bears within him a longing for what William James called "the unity of the self," or, in Jungian terms, an inner urge to integrate all the forces of his soul. The self must resolve its internal contradictions and impose an inner unity. This aim may be achieved gradually, or it may come about all at once. Psychology cannot help us to explain how this is accomplished. Ever since Plato, philosophy—and psychology in its wake—has claimed that man has the ability to harmonize the powers of his soul by subjecting them to his reason. Religion, however, argues that such integration can be achieved only with the help of God. The self experiences the integration of its powers as a miracle, a wonder unexplainable on the basis of its own intrinsic capacity; it senses the intervention of a supernal power in bringing this about. It is God who shows man how to resolve the contradictions within his soul. The success of a person's *teshuvah* thus depends upon a reciprocity between himself and God. Were he not certain that God loves him and, therefore, atones and forgives his sin, he would be unable to begin to repent. There is a dialectic between despair and faith at work in *teshuvah:* man's very despair of himself becomes a source of faith in his capacity to work an inner transformation. From his hour of trial and distress he draws his faith in a supernal power that acts to help him.

This same dialectic underlies the close connection between *teshuvah* and prayer. Prayer expresses man's struggle with himself and his despair and, simultaneously, his search for illumination and a way to unify his heart—as Hermann Cohen put it, a path to reconciliation with God and with himself. Prayer and repentance force man's guilt out from behind the mask that ordinarily conceals it and into the light of consciousness. The person becomes aware of his guilt and willing to admit to it verbally, through confession. His confession is tangible proof that his pride has been humbled and broken, a necessary condition for his opening up to the divine and human "thou" as well as for the "unification of his heart." In a profound sense, the inner struggle involved in this confession is his "atonement" or "sin-offering."

Objective time, the stage on which transpersonal reality is played out, is irreversible. It is always oriented from the present to the future. *Teshuvah,* however, assumes the possibility of reversing the past. Past, present, and future come together in the unity of human consciousness. Despite reality's flow, within this unity the future may transform the meaning of the past. The sages long ago stated that *teshuvah* existed before the creation of the world, that is, that it is not subject to the usual order of time; or, as Rabbi Naḥman of Bratslav had it, since time does not exist for God, "*teshuvah* is essentially above time." By returning to God, man rises above time and so becomes able to correct the wrongs of the past and see himself as though he were newly born. When this happens, even his former days are transformed for the positive. To use Soloveitchik's expression, the most essential aspect of *teshuvah* is that "the future has overcome the past." Man's regret over his past behavior breaks the consequential chain of wicked deeds that brought him to despair; it allows him to conquer that despair and make a fresh start. The healing power of repentance lies in the surgery it performs on his soul, an operation that has both experiential-emotional and conscious-intellectual aspects. It cuts away the damage and disease caused the soul by sin and guilt, and demonstrates the power of choice that lies in our hands: If we but wanted, we could be otherwise. There is thus both suffering and joy to all true repentance: suffering over the flaws of the past, and joy over the more perfect future in prospect. The person's suffering and struggle presage his approaching salvation.

Man's ability to change the past by casting it upon the future is also reflected in the way he deals with the evil forces within himself. Drawing upon Ḥasidic thought, thinkers like Kook and Soloveitchik distinguished between repenting out of fear, that is, for fear of punishment and retribution, and repenting out of love, which is motivated by a new way of viewing reality. Repenting out of fear will enable one to eradicate the evil in his soul. But *teshuvah* that springs from love has the power to transform evil itself into a positive, constructive force, one that will aid in the process of repentance; it becomes, as the Ḥasidim say, a "descent for the purpose of ascent." The dialectic at work in sin raises man to heights he could never have reached had he not sinned; and so evil lays the foundation for good. It is this that the sages had in mind when they said that "even the utterly righteous cannot reach the place occupied by those who have repented" (BT Ber. 34b).

Through *teshuvah*, man creates himself. A new personality emerges out of his struggle and distress—and this is a work of creation to parallel that of the cosmos. If God in his goodness "daily renews the work of creation," so also does man. This vision of the essential regeneration of man is the most profound dimension of man's yearning for redemption. The redemption cannot come about without *teshuvah*. *Teshuvah* represents the full realization of human freedom, the transformation of blind fate into a chosen destiny. It is not a one-time deed, but a process enveloping all of man's life, an unending quest for the ideal upon which, though it can never be reached, the realization of the true nature of humanity depends.

Kook spoke of three kinds of *teshuvah*: that of the individual, that of *keneset Yisrael*, the Jewish community as a whole, and that of the whole world returning to its divine source. Taking up the mystical idea of *tikkun*, he saw *teshuvah* as a cosmic force acting upon the world to improve and perfect it. The process of *teshuvah* has its source in the eternal dissatisfaction of existence itself, which ever yearns for the primal divine unity. Mankind as a whole, and *keneset Yisrael* in particular, play an important role in the dynamic of this development. Man's *teshuvah* is sustained by an optimistic view of reality as a whole. In light of these assumptions Kook took the bold view that the heresy of modern times is a creative force, acting in concert with the cosmic process of *teshuvah* to purify faith of its defects. This utopian vision was significantly influenced by the messianic sentiments stirred by the appearance of Zionism.

Classical rabbinic thought was concerned with the *teshuvah* of the individual, not that of *keneset Yisrael*. Religious Zionism added a new, communal-collective dimension to the idea of *teshuvah*. It was Judah Alkalay who in the nineteenth century first made a clear distinction between *teshuvah* on the individual and on the communal levels. While the sages had spoken of the *teshuvah* of the individual, the single man's return to his God, the *teshuvah* of the whole community, the people's return to the land of Israel, ought to take precedence over this. Religious Zionist thought brought public attention back to the manifest relationship between the people's return to God and its return to Zion (Deut. 30). The revolutionary, historic power of the idea of *teshuvah* thus showed itself anew: "natural" redemption from the Exile must necessarily precede the "miraculous" redemption envisioned by the prophets. Though the movement advocating the return to Zion was primarily secular in character, the religious Zionist thinkers believed that secular nationalism would be but a transitional stage, a way for the people to move away from the assimilationist philosophy of the

Enlightenment toward a full return to the teachings of God. Heresy could never take root permanently among the people of Israel. Kook developed this idea even more profoundly, representing secular Zionism as a necessary stage in the process of the people of Israel's return to its land and its God.

An original, almost secular interpretation of the idea of *teshuvah* was offered by A. D. Gordon. The term *teshuvah* has but one meaning in Gordon's writings: man's return to nature. For him, the Exile of the people of Israel reflected not only the rift between the Jew and his homeland, but also that between mankind and the cosmos. He attributed this to the dominance gained by an extreme rationalism over the soul of man in the past few centuries, which had led to the distortion of man's true nature and the loss of its original, creative character. For Gordon, the Jews' return to their land symbolized man's return to nature and the renewal of the relationship (or covenant) between man and the cosmos, which was a necessary precondition for the regeneration of mankind as a whole, and the Jew in particular.

Two different types of "returning" current in our times demonstrate the tension between the restorative and utopian elements of *teshuvah*. Orthodoxy, seeking to ward off the dangers of modernization, tends to emphasize the restorative aspect of *teshuvah*, viewing it as a return to the bosom of the Orthodox approach to Judaism's traditional teachings and to its age-old way of life—that is, to the ways of Jewry in prenineteenth-century Europe. A person who makes this kind of "return" often will not only totally abandon his former community, but also relinquish to a large extent the customs and values of the secular world. He will, at the same time, accept uncritically the authority of the Orthodox community's leaders and its beliefs and way of life (such as its frequently negative attitude toward Zionism). In contrast to this approach, which involves a total transformation of the person's former way of life, Franz Rosenzweig offered a form of "returning" that would be compatible with modernity. Returning to Judaism as he presented it would not require an utter desertion of the values of European humanism, but rather an indefatigable effort to integrate these values with those of the Jewish faith. *Teshuvah* for Rosenzweig thus had a markedly utopian, dynamic character: The modern Jew who returned to the Torah would be ever on the way, never finally at home. Rosenzweig's image serves as a model for many modern, educated Jews seeking a way to return to their religious tradition without abandoning all that seems positive in European humanism.

BIBLIOGRAPHY

Janet Aviad, *Return to Judaism: Religious Renewal in Israel* (1983).
Hermann Cohen: *Religion of Reason, out of the Sources of Judiasm*, tr. Simon Kaplan (1972).
Abraham Isaac Kook, *Philosophy of Repentance*, tr. Alter B. Mezger (1968).
Franz Rosenzweig, *On Jewish Learning*, ed. N. N. Glatzer (1955).

Rest

שבת

Arthur Waskow

In the biblical traditions of the people Israel, there seem to be two strands of thought regarding *shabbat*—rest from work—in the sense not only of the seventh day, but also of social repose and renewal in the seventh month and the seventh year. One of these strands sees *shabbat* as a reflection and expression of cosmic rhythms of time embedded in creation. The other sees *shabbat* as an affirmation of human freedom, justice, and equality. The biblical tradition regards these strands not as contradictory but as intertwined; indeed, the second is probably a midrash on the first, which arose in a period of Israelite history when social conflict between the rich and poor was intense and the desire to see *shabbat* as an affirmation of social justice was strong.

The first strand, that of cosmos and creation, dominates the books of Genesis and Exodus. Perhaps its focus on birth, creation, and nourishing emerges from the birth experience of the Jewish people. The second is more characteristic of the books of Deuteronomy and the prophets Jeremiah, Ezekiel, and Second Isaiah, which are probably connected with a period of internal social conflict; and the two are most effectively intertwined and come closest to fusion in Leviticus 25, which is possibly from the same period of social upheaval.

The cosmic strand begins with the biblical story of the creation. God ceases, pauses, or rests (shavat) on the seventh day from the work of creating, blesses the seventh day, and calls it holy (Gen. 2:1–4). This "calling" speaks to the depths of reality, but not yet to human ears. Even the explicit tales of contacts and covenants between God and the world—through Adam and Eve, Noah, the generation of Babel, Abraham and Sarah—do not describe any explicit communication of the holiness of shabbat. Not until the generation of the Exodus do human beings learn that shabbat is necessary. Perhaps this silence should be heard as evidence that early biblical Israel had no knowledge of observance of shabbat as a day of rest or of any focus on it among the surrounding peoples, or for that matter in its own earliest history.

The first communication of shabbat to human beings is placed by the Torah in the midst of one of the tales of the rebellious generation in the wilderness (Ex. 16). God sent manna to feed the Israelites. On the sixth day, twice as much manna as usual appeared, and unlike the manna that the Israelites had earlier tried to hoard overnight, this twofold portion did not rot on the seventh day. Even so, some Israelites went out on the seventh day to look for more manna—but none had fallen. Not until then did Moses explain these unusual happenings as the consequence of God's giving the people a shabbat. "Let no one leave his place on the seventh day," says Moses; so the people learned to "rest," or "pause," or "remain inactive" (Ex. 16:29–30). The shabbat portrayed here follows directly from God's creation of reality—from, one might say, the nourishing breast of reality, which feeds and pauses, gives and withholds. Only afterward is this reality put in explicit words of command.

It is only after the direct experience of the shabbat reality that the people learn of shabbat as a central and crucial element in their lives, as one of the ten formal proclamations that come from God at Sinai. Of the ten commandments, the shabbat is the longest and most detailed. "Remember" the day of shabbat, says the version preserved in Exodus 20. It proclaims six days of work and prescribes rest on the seventh day for adults, children, slaves, cattle, and strangers "within your gates"—all this because God had rested after working to create the world.

Thus Exodus sees the seventh-day shabbat as a cosmic event, placed by God within the rhythms of the universe, allowed to emerge from within those rhythms themselves in order to impinge upon the human consciousness, and then to be carried out as a symbol and an enactment of that cosmic and creative rhythm.

The cosmic strand of *shabbat* connects it closely with the sanctuary that represents a microcosm, a miniature version of the universe in which God dwells. When Moses ascends Mount Sinai he hears from God a detailed description of how to build a portable shrine, a *mishkan* (bearer of the Presence) that the people are to carry through the wilderness. This description is completed with a repetition of the command to keep *shabbat* on pain of death (Ex. 31:12–17). For *shabbat* is to be for the Israelites a symbol of their covenant with God—the God who made heaven and earth in six days, and then on the seventh day *"shavat va-yinafash,"* "paused and caught a breath," or "rested to become spiritually refreshed." The text itself seems to be strongly suggesting that just as God made *shabbat* after constructing the world—and perhaps could complete and fully hallow the building only by an act of "not building"—so the people Israel, constructing the micro-world of the *mishkan,* must hallow the process of building by pausing for *shabbat.*

In transmitting to the people the command to build the *mishkan,* Moses begins with an admonition to observe the *shabbat* and adds a specific prohibition respecting work: "You shall kindle no fire throughout your settlements on the day of *shabbat"* (Ex. 35:2–3). This prohibition becomes the basis for a description in Numbers 15:32–36 of how the *shabbat* is enforced. During the wilderness trek, the passage reports, the Israelites discovered someone gathering firewood on *shabbat.* He was brought for judgment before Moses, Aaron, and the community as a whole. God ordered Moses to put him to death by stoning; and it was done. (Note that this punishment for gathering firewood required an expansion of the command not to kindle a fire.)

Although the cosmic vision of *shabbat* dominates the Book of Exodus, there is also a hint there of *shabbat* as an act of social justice, liberation, and equality. For Exodus 23:12 commands rest from work on every seventh day "so that your ox and your ass may rest and that your bondman and the stranger may catch their breath." This command is closely connected with the command to make every seventh year a year of *shemittah,* when the land shall be free of cultivation and the poor shall have free access to its freely growing produce (Ex. 23:10). And perhaps a penumbral power of *shabbat* appears in the requirement that those who have had to sell themselves into indentured servitude must be freed in the seventh year of their service (Ex. 21:2).

The cosmic connection between *shabbat* and the sanctuary is repeated in Leviticus 19:30 and 26:2: "You shall keep my sabbaths [*shabbatot*] and venerate my sanctuary: I [am] YHWH your God." It is also Leviticus that connects the concept of *shabbat* with the longer rhythms of natural time. It is here that the seventh month and the seventh year, as well as the seventh day, are made *shabbat*. The first, tenth, fifteenth, and twenty-second days of the seventh month (corresponding to the festivals we now know as Rosh Hashanah, Yom Kippur, Sukkot, and Shemini Azeret) are each to be observed as *shabbaton,* and of these Yom Kippur is described even more intensely as "shabbat shabbaton" (Lev. 23:23, 32, 39).

As for the seventh year, Leviticus 25 caps this expanding spiral of rhythmic time by providing that in every seventh year the land itself shall observe a *shabbat*. It shall have a *shemittah* (rest, release, or liberation) so as to be free of cultivation or organized harvesting. And in the fiftieth or jubilee year, after a *shabbat* of sabbatical years, or in other words after seven sabbatical years, the land is to rest yet again and each piece of it is to be returned to its original owner. For "the land is Mine," says God (Lev. 25:23).

These Levitical provisions reinforce the sense that *shabbat* is embedded by the creator in the cosmic rhythms of time and must be honored by the people in order to recognize and keep the covenant with the creator. For just as the earth in its daily rotation around the sun marks *shabbat* at the seventh turning, so the moon marks *shabbat* in its seventh renewing, and the earth again in its seventh annual revolution around the sun.

Two provisions of Leviticus 25 weave into this cosmic rhythm of *shabbat* the liberating and justice-making aspect of *shabbat*. One of these is the provision for restoration of equality in landholding, to be accomplished every fifty years by restoring to those who have become poor their family's equal share in the land—and conversely, by withdrawing from those who have become wealthy the surplus land that was not originally in their family's possession. The other is the provision for the freeing of all slaves in the jubilee year.

The liberating aspect of *shabbat* becomes its central element in the Deuteronomic version of the Sinaitic decalogue, which grounds *shabbat* not in the creation but in the liberation from slavery in Egypt, and gives as its rationale the release of slaves as well as masters from their work (Deut. 5:12–15). Perhaps it is no accident that the Deuteronomic version begins not with a command to "remember" *shabbat* but with the more activist and prophetic injunction to "observe" it. Deuteronomy also strengthens this political-historical aspect of *shabbat* by providing that in the seventh year, the year of freeing the land from cultivation, all debts shall be annulled (Deut. 15:1). Thus those whom improvidence, bad luck, laziness, or generosity has reduced to borrowing from their neighbors are restored to their equal station. And Deuteronomy strengthens the provision for the seventh-year release of individual servants by providing that their liberation shall include severance pay in the form of grain, oil, and animals of the flock (Deut. 15:13–14).

In the crisis that befalls the people of Israel beginning just before the destruction of the First Temple and extending through the Babylonian Exile and the Return, this sense of *shabbat* as redemptive social force is powerfully expressed by Jeremiah, Ezekiel, Second Isaiah, and Nehemiah.

Jeremiah calls for merchants to pause from their carrying of commercial burdens through the gates of Jerusalem[1]—and promises that if they do, the Davidic kings will be carried freely, in triumph, through those same gates (Jer. 17:21–25): if the people can free themselves from the burden of the burden carriers, they will be freed from the burden of the fear of foreign domination. As a consequence of their creating *shabbat* on the seventh day, a greater *shabbat* will be created for them.

Conversely, Jeremiah invokes the jubilee tradition of the *dror,* or liberation, of all slaves—and calls for it to be done. When the masters first agree and then revoke their *dror,* Jeremiah proclaims a *dror* to war and famine (Jer. 34:13–22). As II Chronicles 36:21 reports, Jeremiah's prophecy was fulfilled: for the times the people did not let the land keep *shabbat,* "the land paid back its *shabbat;* as long as it lay desolate it kept *shabbat,* till seventy years were completed."

Ezekiel connects desecration of *shabbat* with child sacrifice, bribery that resulted in the death of the innocent, the taking of interest, the oppression of the poor (Ezek. 20:12–24; 22; 23; 28)—or possibly sees each of these betrayals as an aspect of the desecration of *shabbat.* In either case, these betrayals, and especially the betrayal of *shabbat,* brought on the Exile. And for Ezekiel, a most powerful image of redemption is that a renewed priesthood will hallow *shabbat* in a new way by bringing for it a new sacrifice that vividly symbolizes the rhythm of workdays and rest: six lambs and a ram.

For Second Isaiah, making *shabbat* a delight is intimately intertwined with feeding the poor and freeing the prisoner (Isa. 58). How is *shabbat* to be made delightful? By halting the pursuit of normal business so as to honor precisely the God who loves the poor. This passage, later assigned by the rabbis to be read on Yom Kippur—itself the *shabbat shabbaton*—may originally have been spoken by Second Isaiah on a Yom Kippur ("What is the fast I demand from you?" [58:5]). Since each jubilee was to begin on Yom

Kippur, it may even have been a call to make this *shabbat shabbaton* into a still greater and more delightful *shabbat* by enacting the jubilee. Indeed, elsewhere Isaiah specifically calls for "the year of the Lord's favor" (Isa. 61:2)—a year when the oppressed shall hear good tidings and the captives shall be freed, probably a jubilee.

Nehemiah recites as a moment of spiritual triumph and devotion his decision to stop the rich and powerful merchants of Jerusalem from bringing grain, wine, grapes, figs, and fish into the city to sell on the day of *shabbat* (Neh. 13:15–22). He warns them that precisely such a commercial desecration has been the cause of the Exile.

Deuteronomy, Leviticus, and the prophets felt no contradiction between this theme of liberation and justice and the theme of cosmos and creation. Cosmic creation and social re-creation were seen as analogous, even in a sense isomorphic. Rest, or *shabbat,* was seen as the action (or inaction) that expressed both. And *shabbat* was closely related to the concepts of *shemittah* and *dror,* release and liberation.

What are we moderns to make of so tight a connection between the cosmic-natural and the historical-political, two areas of life we usually hold separate? What moderns call social justice is, in this biblical outlook, treated as one form of rest—as social repose or social renewal. Institutional structures of domination and control are themselves seen as a kind of work, not only because of the economic work they do, but also because of the "work" they are—simply by existing, simply by dominating and controlling. The structures themselves, not only the economic work they do, must be periodically dissolved for *shabbat;* the social-political and the cosmic fuse.

To rest means to return to a state of nature, which is seen as loving, not "red in tooth and claw." For nature is where the earth grows peacefully as it wishes, without economic coercion, and the human community grows peacefully in natural clans and families, without institutional coercion. In this state of repose, the land and the community are directly in touch with each other: the land freely feeds the people without intervention by owners, masters, employers, or creditors, and the people freely "feed" the land without sowers, dressers, cultivators, or harvesters.

This is *shabbat.* It re-creates the *shabbat* of the beginning, the *shabbat* that seals the creation, because at that *shabbat* all was free, loving, and in the state of plenitude, sharing, and repose. For human beings and the earth to act in this way is most fully to honor and imitate the creator. And indeed for the creator to act again in this way—as in the liberation from Egypt and from every slavery—is most fully to repeat the act of creation.

Shabbat emerges from its cosmic place to dwell among the people Israel as the first step in the redemption of the human race from the curse of endless toil that ends the delight of Eden: "In the sweat of your brow shall you eat bread," says God to Adam; between Adam and *adamah* (lit., ground), between human and humus, "all the days of your life" there shall be agony and conflict (Gen. 3:17–19). But in the moment of liberation from slavery there rises up from its hidden cosmic place one day that will not be toil and agony: one day of rest, of Eden. To begin with, only one day—and only for one people. But it is because *shabbat* echoes the fullness of Eden that it also beckons us toward the messianic days when all days will be fully *shabbat* for all peoples.

From this perspective it is no accident that just as in Eden the war between humans and the earth is precipitated by an act of eating, so in the wilderness the advent of *shabbat* comes with an act of eating. For eating—in strife or in peace—is the crucial nexus between humans and the earth.

In the next great crisis of the people Israel, in the period of cultural and military conquest by Hellenism and dispersal from the land of Israel across the whole Mediterranean and Near East, there occurred yet another redefinition of *shabbat*. The agrarian *shabbat* of the *shemittah* and jubilee years was diminished in force; the seventh-day *shabbat* was made more "portable"—less rooted in the land—and the prohibitions of work made detailed and urban.

By the time of the codification of the Mishnah, around 200 C.E., abstentions from work and the definition of rest had been greatly broadened. The Mishnah's discussions of the boundaries of permissible work suggest some interesting underlying ideas. For one thing, the Mishnah tractate *Shabbat* opens with a seemingly odd discussion—and then assertion—that an act that would be work if one person did it, and therefore prohibited on *shabbat*, is not work if it is begun by one person and completed by another. The underlying thought may be that work is the full accomplishment of a willed act by a single willing soul. Perhaps an act that is only initiated or only concluded by a single person is what today would be called play, and this is permissible on *shabbat*. One might even detect in this seemingly dry halakhic discussion—especially because it begins the whole examination of *shabbat*—a hint that, in the beginning, God's making of the world in the first six days was a fully accomplished act—a piece of work—that could not be continued on *shabbat*.

For six chapters, the Mishnah examines and in a workmanlike way settles such issues as whether cloth may be dyed before *shabbat* if the colors will continue setting into the *shabbat*, and how the oil may be placed in the *shabbat* lamp. Only after this examination is under way does the Mishnah turn in the seventh chapter to take up certain broader questions of general principle—as if the Mishnah itself were moving from work to *shabbat*. Among these principles is the enunciation of the labors that are forbidden on *shabbat*, cast in a near-poetic or liturgical form in that the Mishnah says not a prosaic "thirty-nine" but:

> Main labors: forty minus one.
> Sowing, ploughing, reaping, binding;
> Threshing, winnowing, combing, grinding;
> . . . .
> Here they are—
> Main labors: forty minus one.

The Talmud, redacted by about 500 C.E. from sayings heard and learned over the previous centuries, acknowledges that these "forty minus one" main labors are known from the Torah (BT Shab. 49b). But the Talmud is at first not certain why this is so. Do the thirty-nine labors correspond to thirty-nine mentions of the word *labor* in the Torah? The Talmud concludes that they actually correspond to the forms of labor necessary to build the traveling shrine or *mishkan* in the wilderness. Presumably, the rabbis make this theological leap because the broad commands for resting on *shabbat* come from God to Moses and from Moses to the people in the context of the command to build the *mishkan* (Ex. 35). For in building the *mishkan*, says the Talmud, "they sowed; hence you must not sow; they reaped, hence you must not reap; they lifted up the boards from the ground to the cart, hence you must not carry in from a public to a private domain."

Although many additional forms of prohibited work are deduced from these "forty minus one" basic forms, in principle from at latest the time of Talmud on, the rest undertaken by the Jewish people on *shabbat* consists of abstinence from the work that built the shrine of God's presence on earth. God rested from making the cosmos, hence the people rest from making the microcosm (the *mishkan*); they rested from making the microcosm, hence we rest from remaking the cosmos. The holiest act of work— even, indeed, especially the holiest act—is fulfilled only by stopping, by recognizing and celebrating its completeness.

The "forty minus one" main forms of work, and their directly deducible lesser forms that the Talmud concludes are prohibited by the Torah itself, are extended by the rabbis' own prohibition of still other activities. These rabbinic prohibitions are called *shevut* (rest, from the same root as *shabbat*) and include such acts as blowing the shofar or throwing an object from one private domain to another. The rabbis enjoin the people to avoid situations that would make *shabbat* violations more likely—handling tools, for example—out of fear that if the tools are close to hand someone·may forget it is *shabbat* and use them.

Besides elucidating special forms of rest, we must note, the rabbis also give *shabbat* a special air of celebration by prescribing special meals, the lighting of candles and the drinking of wine at the beginning and end of the day, the wearing of festive clothes, walking slowly rather than hurrying. Among all Jewish communities, it was understood that the whole community was responsible for ensuring that all families had the food, wine, shelter, and companionship to celebrate *shabbat* with joy rather than pain. Through this practice, *shabbat* became a time to affirm and act out—for only a moment, and therefore imperfectly—the social equality of all Jews.

This direct experience of *shabbat* as a moment of utter release from the burdens of work, commerce, and poverty, and into the realm of song, joy, sharing, prayer, and Torah study—this direct experience lay beneath the rabbis' comments that *shabbat* was a foretaste of the messianic age, and that if all Israel kept *shabbat* properly just one time (or, said some, twice in a row—possibly to prove it was no accident), the messianic age would begin. The connection between *shabbat* and the days of the Messiah—days that would be *"yom shekulo shabbat,"* fully *shabbat*—is an index to the seriousness with which Jewish tradition has taken *shabbat* as a theological category. *Shabbat,* and only *shabbat,* connected the three supernal moments of history: the creation of the world, the revelation of the Torah at Sinai, and the messianic redemption. The entrance of *shabbat* into human experience, which is the first step in curing the post-Edenic wound of painful toil and enmity between human beings and the earth, will be fulfilled when the world can fully celebrate *shabbat.*

At the same time that the rabbis were expanding and encoding the practice of the *shabbat* of the seventh day, they were restricting the practice of *shemittah* and *dror* in the seventh and fiftieth years. As they lost control over the economy of the land of Israel to the growing power of Hellenists and Romans—and then as the Jewish population was scattered across the world—it became less and less tenable to celebrate or enforce the year-long "rest" of the economy. Debts were no longer annulled, the practice of fallowing the land was not carried into the Diaspora, and the jubilee was explained away as inoperative when the Jewish people was even partly in exile. So while the seventh-day repose was developed in ways that made it much more portable, the other *shabbat* rhythms mostly lapsed.

We have sketched three moments of crisis in Jewish history in which there appeared a change in the formulation of *shabbat:* the moment in which the people was first formed in its own self-understanding, when *shabbat* was seen as a cosmic reality embedded in the rhythms of the created world, to be reenacted by human beings; the crisis of internal social conflict, the Babylonian threat, and the Exile, when *shabbat* was turned into an instrument of social justice and liberation, and the crisis of Hellenism, before and after the destruction of the Second Temple, when the rabbis encoded the repose of the day and gave it a much stronger messianic significance. We now seem to be in another such crisis moment, living as we do in a time of struggle to reformulate Judaism in the wake of the disintegration of the rabbinic version of it under the pressure of modernity.

In these circumstances, such postmodern thinkers as Erich Fromm and Abraham Joshua Heschel have again reformulated *shabbat*. In an era of technological triumph, writing in the immediate aftermath of the Holocaust and the first use of nuclear weapons, they see *shabbat* as an affirmation of values beyond technology. Says Fromm, *"Work is any interference by man, be it constructive or destructive, with the physical world. "Rest" is a state of peace between man and nature."*[2] Fromm interprets in this light the seemingly obsessive prohibitions of Jewish tradition upon accomplishing on *shabbat* even the lightest, least effortful changes of the ownership or place of objects in the world. So *shabbat* becomes for him an actual (though brief) transformation of the human path into a real experience of messianic harmony and peace. For Heschel, *shabbat* is an affirmation that holiness is borne more by the flow and rhythm of time than by objects in space, and he too sees *shabbat* as a challenge to a "technical civilization" obsessed with the conquest of space and the improvement of objects:

> To set apart one day a week for freedom, a day on which we would not use the instruments which have been so easily turned into weapons of destruction, a day of detachment from the vulgar, of independence of external obligations, a day on which we stop worshipping the idols of technical civilization, a day on which we use no money, a day of armistice in the economic struggle with our fellow men and the forces of nature—is there any institution that holds out a greater hope for man's progress than the Sabbath?[3]

It is notable that both Fromm and Heschel suggest that the practice of *shabbat,* in some form, may be of profound importance to the whole human race—and not to the Jewish people alone—in redeeming the world from the threat of untrammeled technology.

The current crisis of modernity and technology may be profoundly connected with another crisis, the remaking of relationships between women and men. And the connection may extend into the world of *shabbat*. It is becoming clear that the traditional forms of practice of *shabbat,* as well as its theology, face new questions in the wake of the advent of full participation by women in all aspects of Jewish life. The traditional practice of *shabbat* neither required nor encouraged women who were doing the work of nurturing a family and raising children to rest from that work. Rather, traditional Judaism saw precisely such nurturance and communion as rest rather than work—and while *shabbat* freed men to do this resting, it did not free women from the worklike aspects of it.

In a world where men were assigned to acting and women to nurturing, once action became unbridled technology the involvement of women in public life may have been in part an attempt to redress the balance in a new way by bringing nurturance out of the ghetto of the family into the public sphere. Under the new conditions of new forms of relationship between women and men, the full celebration of *shabbat* may require that, on that day, there be an even fuller sharing of nurturance and community, an even more conscious shattering of separate roles of women and men, than on the six workdays. And this new understanding of *shabbat* may also have theological implications. For if *shabbat* entered the conscious practice of the people Israel as a first step in reversing the post-Edenic curse upon Adam that he must toil in the sweat of his brow to wrest bread from the hostile earth, then it may also become a first step in reversing the post-Edenic curse upon Eve: that she must be ruled over by her husband and must suffer child-rearing as painful labor.

From these complementary postmodern perspectives, there might emerge a reexamination not only of the *shabbat* of the seventh day, but of the *shabbat* of the seventh year and fiftieth year. For the human race as a whole, can "the land" be seen as "the earth"? What would be the implications of pausing every seventh year from technological research and development, to reevaluate its meaning and direction? What would it mean to proclaim a *shabbat* upon the development of new weapons?

The advent of such questions within the Jewish community may signal another moment in the reformulation of *shabbat.* If the Deuteronomic period saw the theme of social justice and liberation as an unfolding of the cosmic theme of *shabbat,* we may see ourselves as taking the process of unfolding another spiral turn: for we are moving from concerns over human justice and liberation toward reaffirming the creation and pausing from production in order to preserve the creation itself (and with it, human freedom and justice). At the end of an epoch in which the human race has gained enormous knowledge and great mastery, *shabbat* remains the emblem and practice of mystery. If we do not know what to do next, instead of trying to conquer our ignorance we may more fruitfully—and truthfully—celebrate *shabbat* as our way of acknowledging that we do not know: that there is in the world not merely ignorance, but mystery.

REFERENCES

1. It should be noted that Jeremiah's criticism was probably directed at commercial transactions on *shabbat,* not at riding a horse or donkey on *shabbat,* since in II Kings 4:23 we have evidence that in Elisha's day some two hundred and fifty years before, it was normal to ride a donkey on *shabbat* in order to visit a "man of God," or a seer.
2. Erich Fromm, *You Shall Be as Gods,* 154 (italics in original). See also Erich Fromm, *The Forgotten Language,* 241 ff.
3. Abraham Joshua Heschel, *The Sabbath* (1962), 28.

BIBLIOGRAPHY

Abraham Joshua Heschel, *The Sabbath* (1962).
Arthur Waskow, *Godwrestling* (1978), 110–27.
Arthur Waskow, *These Holy Sparks* (1983), 78–79.

Resurrection of the Dead

תחיית המתים

Arthur A. Cohen

B elief in the resurrection of the dead *(teḥiyyat ha-metim)* is an explicit dogma of classical Judaism, reaffirmed and elaborated by Moses Maimonides, treated by Ḥasdai Crescas as a "true belief" (rather than as a fundamental principle of Judaism), retracted to a more debatable level of deduction by Joseph Albo, and all but lost as a central teaching ever since the close of the medieval discourse. Nonetheless, despite its fall from the dogmatic eminence in which it, among other beliefs, was regarded as a sine qua non of rabbinic eschatological teaching, resurrection continues to be affirmed in the traditional liturgy. Introduced as the second blessing of the Eighteen Benedictions (the *Shemoneh Esreh*) recited during the *Amidah* (lit., standing prayer), it asserts that God keeps faith with those who lie in the dust and will, according to his mercy, raise the dead, restore them bodily, and grant them eternal life.

Bodily resurrection, that is, resurrection of the flesh, the reunification of soul to corporeal individuality, became a cardinal doctrine of rabbinic Judaism, making its appearance in "proto-pharisaic theology" in the fourth century B.C.E.[1] Despite the aristocratic hostility of Ben Sira (Ecclus. 10:11;

17:27; 41:3), it was further refined by the Book of Daniel (Dan. 12:1–4) and collateral apocalyptic literature and ultimately consolidated as pharisaic doctrine. Even earlier than these apocalyptic formulations of resurrection as an assertive teaching of Jewish eschatology is the famous passage in Isaiah, shown by Yehezkel Kaufmann to be of eighth century B.C.E. Isaianic authorship: "Oh, let Your dead revive!/Let corpses arise!/Awake and shout for joy/You who dwell in the dust!—/For Your dew is like the dew on fresh growth/You make the land of the shades come to life" (Isa. 26:19).[2]

Among the characteristic popular sentiments of those who live in the twentieth century is the oft-heard wish that life not be prolonged unduly, that beyond strength and lucidity there is no value to life. Coupled with this rejection of the ability of medical science to prolong length of days without comparably guaranteeing the quality of life lived is the collateral, albeit ironically expressed, hope that there be no life after death, no ongoing immortal soul, and surely no reunified flesh and spirit as offered in the promise of resurrection. It is enough, one thinks, to have survived this century's warfare and genocide and the pressures of an increasingly inhumane society and to have come in fullness of years beyond even the "three score ten and if by reason of strength four score" (Ps. 90:10) augured by Scripture. What is it then to believe that even beyond these generous years God offers to the just the eternal life of reconstituted and ensouled flesh at the End of Days? How is one to take this promise, and to what end is it believed to be offered?

The underlying presupposition behind the doctrine of the resurrection is that eternal life in the presence of God is indeed an immense and unmerited generosity. Resurrection, as described by the tradition—whether in its popular and anthropomorphic mythology as an almost Oriental banquet or in its more austere promulgation as eternal study in the supernal yeshivah whose director, guide, and spiritual master is none other than God himself—is a meaningful gift only to those who in this life have thirsted for God and whose thirst has not been satisfied. We have no longer a communal consensus that stakes the value and reward of life upon the certainty of the living God. Indeed, millions may be obedient to Torah, believers according to their lights, but nonetheless lack that obsessional attentiveness that made God-talk no less commonplace in the markets of medieval Europe than discussion of the price of bread. Not everyone in the Middle Ages was devout or, for that matter, aware of the provocative disputes that arose in Spain, Provence, and France about the writings of Maimonides (notably his views on resurrection), but many were—despite their lack of scholarship—constantly aware of God's weight and pressure in their lives.

The resurrection of the dead strikes us in its formulation as a portion of Jewish eschatological teaching as unpersuasive in the invariable way in which an alogical, antirationalist assertion inevitably fails: Its poetry is too coarse. It cannot be demonstrated except in the respect that theology may ratify, and thereby assert to be self-evident, any doctrine that has the warrant of scriptural revelation. But even if one accepts the Maimonidean principle that one (or two) citations in Scripture are quite sufficient to confirm a teaching based on Scripture, it does not help; even assuming a fundamentalist theological method, Scripture denies a vitality beyond death with no less clarity than it affirms it. Indeed, Scripture is hardly the place to go when one wishes to form a consensus on the more vague issues of Jewish belief, especially those that relate to its eschatology. It offers too many views, and despite exegetic methods of distinction and analogical reasoning, the contradictions within Scripture are sufficiently bold and asseverative to militate against reconciliation. Moreover, even if one were to secure complete scriptural clarity, the miracle of resurrection would be obliged to ground itself upon yet another miracle, divine revelation. Whatever it might commend to faith, it could not commend to reason. Indeed, if immortality of the soul ceases to be a major doctrine in the Jewish philosophic agenda after Kant's demolition of the argument in its favor in Moses Mendelssohn's *Phaedon,* how much more so the resurrection of the dead, which relies less upon Greek philosophic modes than it does upon parallel notions of the afterlife common in ancient Egypt and Persia?

The observation that the poetry of doctrinal resurrection is coarse grained does not apply to the second blessing of the *Amidah,* which is, if anything, exquisite, drawing as it does upon the extraordinary metaphor of Isaiah, in which the light dew that vivifies the parched earth of summer is construed to be the dew that restores the dead to life. Rather, what appears to be coarse is the intellectual hedging that begins with Saadiah Gaon's almost mechanistic account of resurrection[3] and is succeeded later by Maimonides' novel but unenthusiastic tergiversations on resurrection, culminating in his *Treatise on Resurrection,* in which *tehiyyat ha-metim* becomes an adjunct of the terrestrial reign of the Messiah, followed by a second death and subsequent spiritual immortality in the World to Come (*Olam ha-Ba*). Few indeed among the philosophers rise to the enthusiasm of that nascent kabbalist the thirteenth-century poet mystic Meshullam ben Solomon da Piera, also known as En Vidas de Gerona, who boldly asserts: "I believe in resurrection when the body and soul will arise and the bones will come to life again."[4] For the most part, the Jewish medieval philosophic tradition squirms to uphold resurrection, since it is rabbinic dogma. At the same time, contradicting as it does the whole care of Jewish philosophy that its doctrine be made pure, intellectually coherent, and nonmythological, the resurrection of the dead—whatever its values to the popular imagination as both carrot and stick with which to reward and punish—remains a doctrinal embarrassment.

What remains profoundly unclear is why thinkers as eminent as Maimonides among the Jews and Avicenna among the Muslims struggled so mightily to veil their theological disdain of bodily resurrection, apparently constrained to do so not only by an overriding consensus of the faithful, but also by those who guarded orthodoxy against heretical opinion.[5] What is there about the doctrine at once so appealing to general sentiment and so disquieting to reason?

Indeed, the more one thinks about the matter of the resurrection of the dead, the more one is obliged to wonder at its theological persistence and its mythologic power. Why does it endure? Few indeed are those who continue to imagine the earth is flat, or that God created heavens and earth less than six thousand years ago, or that the sun stood still at Jericho. Despite even the willingness of the most profoundly committed believers to interpret the odd science of ancient Scripture, there is no concerted effort to expunge the explicitly literal formulations of Jewish liturgy with regard to resurrection. The blessing stands and is spoken thrice daily. It may be claimed that although it is spoken, it is nonetheless disbelieved, but this may be doubted. Any formula of faith spoken persistently and over millennia may be questioned, but the willingness of the faithful to speak it even with an attitude of skepticism indicates that it strikes a chord so deep and acoustically inaccessible that its resonance remains deeply personal and inarticulate. It is, therefore, to the teaching of resurrection as a profound structure of the religious consciousness that we now turn.

Our undertaking is not to supply a different doctrine to replace the eschatological drama of bodily resurrection, but—quite the contrary—to set the matter of resurrection into the situation of modern man and the modern world. To do this, we must recognize the agonized longing of man to evade death without integrating it into life, thereby avoiding the passion that illumines all the great modern partisans of resurrection in the flesh such as Søren Kierkegaard, Miguel de Unamuno, Franz Rosenzweig, and Lev Shestov. Viewing death as an unnatural, however commonplace and pervasive, conclusion to the ongoing striving of self to create, endure, and transform has caused the hope of resurrection to become an extension into eternity of the conviction that anything as miraculous as the existence of each single creation cannot be allowed to perish by an economic, unprofligate, and ceaselessly imaginative God. Otherwise put, God has better uses for life than to create it and then to condemn it to an unransomed death.

The principal difficulties that the idea of resurrection presents to a theological tradition of reasonableness is that it wrests from God a promise that distorts the accepted characterization of his nature and behavior. The pressure in the Jewish philosophic tradition is to make God's ways compassable to reason, his behavior orderly, and his care for the world persuasive to the good and the holy, rather than eccentric, irrational, or capricious. A capricious God harks to paganism; a reasonable God is one who makes his Torah the model of conduct, whose just and merciful nature commends morality for its own sake without need for the baited hook of resurrection. Of course, it could be argued that all of the promises of eschatology are baited hooks—the coming of the Messiah, the kingdom of God, the World to Come—no less than resurrection. Each element of the eschatological skein of hope is grounded upon a miraculous bringing to pass. And if these are miracles that can stand in faith, why not resurrection, which is not a promise of a communal restoration or a transformation of the order of human society, but a guarantee of God's mercy upon flesh and spirit? Resurrection in the flesh is a miracle that God works for the individual, and its consequence—given its emplacement within the messianic era or, for some, within the kingdom of God—is both a supernatural judgment upon the life completed and an assertion of God's immense and unpredictable love. What fails within nature and dies is restored in the kingdom, transformed, strained of the agitations of flesh, and purified by miraculous grace.

"On that day the Lord shall be One and His name One." This promise of the messianic reintegration, part of the *Aleinu* (lit., it is upon us) recited at the conclusion of prayer services, bears striking resemblance to the Christian assertion of apocatastasis, expressed in I Corinthians 15:26–28, where Paul—the mystic who had never seen his redeemer in the flesh—asserts: "The last enemy that shall be destroyed is death. . . . And when all things shall be subdued unto him . . . that God may be all in all." The Christian analogue of resurrection is brought forth here not as proof of our own, but rather to suggest a currency of argument that extends beyond the theological into a domain where metaphysics alludes to the greatest of mysteries. The presumption of the *Aleinu* is that until the very end, the finale of the universe before its transformation under God, the consciousness of God is rent, his person still distinguishable from the seal of his name. However, in the very last, when God ends the created order and supplants it with a perfection it has not known, the finality of death, the end of terrestrial consciousness among creatures, is overcome by the same overcoming that ends division within God. God is reunited, his name rejoined to his person, his being now one and indivisible; for us, creatures in an imperfect universe where with all striving of consciousness to assert life, to press the claims of its eternity in the vivacity and intensity of life's enactment, death is now conquered and God bestows upon the dead a unity analogous to that which he has won for himself—a unity of illuminated consciousness and perfected flesh.

Resurrection remains a mystery, scandalous to reason, obnoxious to those with a deficient sense of the deep mythos of consciousness, embarrassing to thinkers who believe divinity reasonable and sufficient. For this thinker, the task of faith is so immense and unsatisfied, the pain of consciousness so extreme, the presence of death so constant that the conviction of resurrection—even if it must be kept a private belief shared only with God in prayer—is so overwhelmingly gratifying, so true to what one still loves about God (his unpredictable generosity no less than his unpredictable disengagement) that it is held by us as a doctrine in trust, neither pressed upon others nor denied by ourselves. Samuel Hugo Bergmann, the philosopher, captured this appeal of the doctrine in summarizing his beliefs on his eightieth birthday, in 1963: "I believe in the Holy One, Blessed be He, creator of the heavens and the universe. Secondly, we know from this that the world is not subject to blindness. . . . Thirdly, I do not accept the reality or actuality of death. Our lives are possessed of a significance entirely different from that which we usually ascribe to them. . . . I am saying here that people will live after death and will have to account for themselves. . . . Everything we do here on earth has an eternal, cosmic meaning."[6]

REFERENCES

1. Louis Finkelstein, *The Pharisees,* 3rd ed., 2 (1962), 747.
2. See Yehezkel Kaufmann, *Toledot ha-Emunah ha-Yisraelit,* 3 (1), 186ff.
3. Saadiah Gaon, *Book of Beliefs and Opinions,* Samuel Rosenblatt, tr. (7), 264–89.
4. Daniel Jeremy Silver, *Maimonidean Criticism and the Maimonidean Controversy, 1118–1240* (1965), 189.
5. Joshua Finkel, "Maimonides' Treatise on Resurrection: A Comparative Study," in Salo W. Baron, ed., *Essays on Maimonides* (1941), 119.
6. Eli Shai, "Samuel Hugo Bergmann: A Partial Portrait," in *Ariel* 57 (1984).

BIBLIOGRAPHY

Joshua Finkel, "Maimonides' Treatise on Resurrection: A Comparative Study," in *Essays on Maimonides,* Salo W. Baron, ed. (1941).

Louis Finkelstein, *The Pharisees,* 3rd ed. (1962), 145–59, 742–53.

Daniel Jeremy Silver, *Maimonidean Criticism and the Maimonidean Controversy, 1118–1240* (1965).

Miguel de Unamuno, *The Tragic Sense of Life in Men and Nations,* Anthony Kerrigan, tr. (1972), 236–81.

Gerardus Van der Leeuw, "Immortality," in *Man and Transformation (Eranos 5)* (1964).

Revelation

התגלות

Shalom Rosenberg

The term *revelation* has a twofold meaning in English as well as in other languages—like, for example, *Offenbarung* in German. The first meaning denotes the hidden God's revelation of himself; the second denotes the God who reveals not himself but rather "the Torah from heaven" *(Torah min ha-shamayim)*—the God who communicates information or commands. Revelation in this second sense is expressed in the realm of language, whereas revelation in the first sense goes beyond the linguistic sphere to indicate a fact—the encounter between God and man. This distinction between the two meanings of the term parallels the distinction between propositional and nonpropositional conceptions of revelation in modern theology. However, this parallel is applicable only with certain restrictions. Any discussion of revelation in the framework of Judaism requires us to concern ourselves not only with revelation whose content is the Torah, that is, with the revelation of some information about God, man, or the world, but also with revelation whose content is religious commandments, namely, a system of norms and laws. If we understand *proposition* in this broader sense, which includes commands, then the parallel is valid.

The study of the history of this distinction in the framework of Jewish thought leads us to the work of Salomon Ludwig Steinheim, who lucidly described both meanings in his book on revelation according to the teachings of Judaism.[1] Nathan Rotenstreich summed up his position as follows: "According to Steinheim, revelation is theory. That is, it belongs in the realm of propositions for inquiry and cognition and not in the realm of concrete reality and its various levels."[2] Steinheim also expressed, symbolically, the distinction between the two concepts by comparing them to the differing functions of the eye and ear in revelation. This distinction was later to become more accepted in the form expressed by Heinrich Graetz in one of his early works:

> This fundamental difference in the conception of the divine can be developed still further. To the pagan, the divine appears within nature as something observable to the eye. He becomes conscious of it as something seen. In contrast, to the Jew who knows that the divine exists beyond, outside of, and prior to nature, God reveals Himself through a demonstration of His will, through the medium of the ear. The human subject becomes conscious of the divine through hearing and obeying. Paganism sees its god, Judaism hears Him; that is, it hears the commandments of His will.[3]

Over against the Christian incarnation, Judaism places "the divinely given Torah." The incarnation is unquestionably foreign to Jewish thought, but it is certainly possible to extend the concept of the revelation of various entities from hypostases of divine attributes to angels and supernatural messengers. The concept of revelation can be broadened to encompass a very great variety indeed of mystical phenomena, from the revealing of the *Shekhinah* (the divine Presence) to the revealing of the prophet Elijah. Yet broadening this concept, however necessary, creates a new problem— where to draw the boundaries between the meanings. For example, one might well ask which kind of revelation the intuition of ideas constitutes.

Broadening the second meaning of revelation makes continuity between the two meanings possible, but then we are faced once again with the necessity of drawing the precise boundaries between revelation as an event belonging to the real, concrete world and revelation in the realm of language.

However, we should be very cautious in our use of this formulation. A study of the writings in the various branches of classical Jewish thought does not permit any limitation of the medium of revelation to the sphere of language in the ordinary sense of the term. We must also allow for revelation via things and events that are by no means linguistic creations but are nonetheless revealed as symbols of another reality. Such a view is based upon the approach to prophecy found in the main currents of medieval Jewish philosophy. In a vision, some form of reality is revealed to the prophet, although that reality is nothing but the result of the joint action of rational and imaginative faculties. Accordingly, in the words of Ḥasdai Crescas, the vision is simply a transformation of "a spiritual and cognitive overflow from God to man, either directly or. . ."[4]

This passage shows how problematical was the early attempt to define the difference between the meanings of revelation. Of course, this observation cannot obscure the fundamental distinction between the meanings; it can only make us aware of the doubts that arise in many cases, and not necessarily borderline cases at that. Hence we perceive a need to broaden the concept of the language revelation employs and to establish clear boundaries between concrete and symbolic revelation.

The distinction between concrete and symbolic revelation is blurred when we come to the teachings of the kabbalah. In the kabbalistic framework, both the Torah and all of concrete reality are symbols of a higher reality. The symbolic essence of the Torah is expressed in the statement that the Torah is nothing but a tissue of the names of God. The words of the Torah are not only linguistic creations consisting of information about God and the world, but also concrete objects—"names." This identity of symbols and reality leads to an understanding of the sacredness of the Torah as well as to consciousness of its divine status. An extreme instance of this view is found in the teachings of Ḥayyim ben Isaac of Volozhin, who considered the Torah itself to be a part of the worlds of the Infinite (the kabbalistic conception of God before his self-revelation through finite creation).[5]

In consonance with the symbolic conception of revelation, Steinheim considered revelation as Torah.[6] In this sense, Steinheim considered himself close to Moses Mendelssohn. The difference between them parallels the possible changes in the understanding of Torah. According to Mendelssohn, the content of revelation is commandments. According to Steinheim, its content is theology, that is, truths that mankind could not have acquired on its own.

In the twentieth century, Franz Rosenzweig subjected the concept of revelation to a new systematic discussion in which he placed the concept in the framework of a conceptual triangle consisting of creation, revelation, and redemption. This framework is fruitful and important, particularly because of its insistence upon a fundamental pluralism in reality in which the various entities cannot be juxtaposed. Relying on Rosenzweig, Buber shows that it is Christianity "which fused the essentials of revelation and the essentials of redemption in Christ."[7] The conflation of the two, Buber underscores, is indicative of the concrete conception of revelation.

The work of modern thinkers on this issue raises such fundamental questions as: Does the concept of concrete revelation exist in classical Jewish philosophy? Can we find in the latter any characteristic features of the former, such as the separation between creation and redemption?

We shall demonstrate the difficulty of giving unequivocal answers to these questions by quoting a number of passages from kabbalistic and philosophical literature, without regard for chronological or systematic order. The first example is taken from Moses Ḥayyim Luzzatto's commentary on the Lurianic kabbalah, *Kelaḥ Pitḥei Ḥokhmah* (ch. 4):

> The *Ein Sof* [the Infinite], blessed be He, wanted to bestow the perfect good, and thus deemed to reveal manifestly his full unity. Accordingly, he set down this governance, the Torah, by which he governs and by virtue of which evil will be restored to good.

In this passage, Luzzatto interweaves two motifs. According to the first, the creation itself represents an act of revelation: "God's purpose in creating the world is to bestow goodness in accordance with his passionate love of the ultimate good" (ibid., ch. 3). According to the second, redemption is revelation, "the revealed unity." The first motif is the classical one, although innumerable changes in the basic scheme are conceivable. Thus, for example, in Ḥayyim Vital's *Eẓ Ḥayyim*[8] the creation is explained as God's compulsion, so to speak, to expend

> his activities and powers by means of actions and products [because otherwise] He could not, so to speak, be called *Shalem* [whole] . . . because He is [also] called the Lord, and the meaning of lordship is having servants over whom one is the lord, and if He did not have creations, He could not be called the Lord.[9]

In these different versions there is an element of revelation or even of self-revelation in the very act of the creation.

The second motif, which appears in the passage from Luzzatto cited above—namely, the revealing that is linked to redemption—also contains the possibility of nuances that would be suited to the changing content of the concept of redemption. In *Kelaḥ Pitḥei Ḥokhmah*, revelation is cosmic. An instance of individual revelation is that of the *Shekhinah* to the righteous (*ha-ẓaddikim*) during their lifetimes or after their deaths.

So far we have seen the concept of revelation as a fundamental component of creation and redemption. However, between creation and redemption there extends the sequence of time on the stage of history. According to Buber, the fact that the elements of creation, revelation, and redemption exist without being identical creates a place for "the essence of time, which was closely allied to the essence of our spirit . . . time which distinguishes between past, present, and future." However, Buber adds, we must qualify the temporal distinction: "From the point of view of the Bible, revelation is, as it were, focused in the middle, creation in the beginning, redemption in the end."[10]

What does "revelation . . . in the middle" mean? Can it be translated in the terms of classical Jewish thought into a concept in its own right whose systematic function parallels such a use of revelation?

To judge from the context, this concept is surprisingly close to that of providence (hashgaḥah). Of course, providence should not be identified with any dogmatic teaching about reward and punishment. Providence is expressed in God's attitude to man, his "interest" in the activities of flesh and blood. The category of divine knowledge also expresses this attitude, but from the standpoint of God. Providence is a reflection of this attitude from the perspective of man, and accordingly it is the revelation of divine knowledge to man and the world.

I have underscored this aspect of the issue in order to stress that the classical parallel of the concept of revelation in the sense of uncovering does not exist in the concept of "the divinely given Torah," but rather sometimes in the doctrine of providence, which represents, to a certain extent, a philosophical transformation of "the revealing of the Shekhinah." An instance of the linkage between the concept of revelation in modern thought and the classical doctrine of providence may be found in Moses Maimonides' writings on God's revelation to Moses in the cleaving of the rock (Ex. 33:12-23). In his commentary on these verses, Maimonides suggests several fundamental principles that determine the framework for the classical Jewish understanding of the revealed Torah:

> Know that the master of those who know, Moses our Master, peace be on him, made two requests and received an answer to both of them. One request consisted in his asking Him, may He be exalted, to let him know His essence and true reality. The second request, which he put first, was that He should let him know His attributes. The answer to the two requests that He, may He be exalted, gave him consisted in His promising him to let him know all His attributes, making it known to him that they are His actions, and teaching him that His essence cannot be grasped as it really is.
>
> (Guide, 1:54)

Although Maimonides is referring to the doctrine of attributes, his ideas may be translated into the concepts of the doctrine of revelation. The "essence and true reality" of God go beyond his watching over man, beyond his self-revelation. Only God's attributes are within human comprehension—but what are these attributes?

> His request regarding the knowledge of God's attributes is conveyed in his saying: "Show me now Thy ways, that I may know Thee, and so on" [Ex. 33:13]. Consider the wondrous notions contained in this dictum. For his saying, "Show me now Thy ways, that I may know Thee," indicates that God, may He be exalted, is known through His attributive qualifications; for when he would know the *ways,* he would know Him.
>
> (ibid.)

The knowledge of God is simply the knowledge of his ways. God's self-revelation is the revealing of his ways. And in fact the doctrine of revelation is no more than the doctrine of providence.

The parallel between revelation and providence is more than a purely formal one. Medieval Jewish thinkers were greatly exercised by the dilemma of personal versus general providence. These two possibilities actually delimit what may be called in the realm of revelation nature and history. Revelation is universal by its very nature, whereas historical revelation possesses a particular essence like that of the personal providence of classical Jewish philosophy. If we do not simplistically identify providence with the doctrine of reward and punishment, then this concept comes closer to the search for a metahistorical layer, for a God beyond nature, for a reality that behaves according to its wont—in short, the search for the hidden God.

The concept of the divinely given Torah, which is unquestionably a close parallel of the propositional meaning of revelation, became ever more central in the late Middle Ages. This phenomenon seems absurd in view of the centrality of the Torah to every Jewish philosophy. Nonetheless, a change did come about that was more than merely semantic. Earlier this concept had constituted a branch of the prophetic doctrine, which also determined the method by which it was derived. As a branch of the prophetic doctrine, the differentiation of the concept assumes the existence of a philosophical, theoretical system on the basis of whose assumptions the possibility of revelation may be proved. This system is the Torah that God gave Moses. But inasmuch as this was a historical, not a metaphysical, affair, it must be studied by means of an essentially historical method. This reservation notwithstanding, we shall attempt to explain the doctrine of revelation within the framework of the given theological method.

An example of the renewed discussion of revelation is to be found in the teaching of Hasdai Crescas, whose innovative approach influenced the formulation of the principles of faith. According to Crescas, the classical discussion of the doctrine of the principles of faith, precisely because it is anchored in various philosophical systems, is unsystematic. The new systematic method that Crescas employs is a transcendental deduction based upon the existence of the Torah. This starting point may be phrased as a question, "How can the Torah exist?" The answer is to be found in the Jewish system of principles. Crescas calls these transcendental principles "Toraic fundaments," in order to distinguish them from the true beliefs originating in revelation.

> Concerning the fundaments [*pinnot*] of the Torah, that is, the foundations and pillars upon which the house of the Lord shall be established [cf. Isa. 2:2] and by virtue of their existence the existence of the Torah, as given by God, becomes conceivable. And if one of these fundaments were missing, the Torah in its entirety would fall, God forbid.
>
> (*Or Adonai* 2, preface)

The belief in the existence of God is the root that lies even beyond the transcendental principles. The fundaments are "one, God's knowledge of existing things; two, His providence over them; three, His power; four, prophecy; five, [man's power of] choice; six, the purpose of the Torah" [ibid.]. Although we may disagree on the contents of this list of principles, it nonetheless provides us with a stratification, since it is the "divinely given Torah" that is the main principle. Before it comes the first root, which is "the beginning of all the beliefs in the Torah and is the belief in the existence of God, blessed be He," and the "fundaments," which elucidate the concept of revelation and make possible the existence of the Torah and the religious commandments.

The term *divinely given Torah* and its parallels enable us to understand the sharp distinction between the different meanings of the concept of revelation. This distinction applies also to classical Jewish thought, although we should note one exception that unified the different concepts through the use of a single term. I am referring to Judah Halevi's concept of the "divine cause," which is prophecy (*The Kuzari* 1:43, 95) connected with concrete evidence "which will bring down to them the cause of God so that they may see it and receive it as they received the pillar of smoke and the pillar of fire in the Exodus from Egypt" (1:97) or that "His light seen through them [the Jews] is the same as that seen in heaven" (2:50). The term *divine cause* certainly gives the reader the impression of an impersonal entity, as if it were a power that performs purely mechanical actions. The term is borrowed from Islamic philosophy, but Halevi identifies it with the *Shekhinah*: "because you will experience, with [the help of] My *Shekhinah*, the best of your land" (1:109). The adherence to the divine cause is identified with the revealing of the *Shekhinah*. Thus we have come full circle.

In the teaching of Judah Halevi, the commandments are a preparation for receiving the divine cause (1:84), and man cannot reach the divine cause except by the word of the Lord, that is, "according to God's commands" (1:98). So the goal of observing the Torah, the ultimate reward, is the sight of the supernal world, the hearing of the speech of the Lord (1:103), "the closeness of the Lord" (1:109, 115). This is the accepted interpretation of Halevi's view of the purpose of the commandments. However, this interpretation is incomplete. For the purpose of the commandments is not merely to prepare man for receiving the divine cause. Rather they represent, at least in part, a portion of the bond to the divine: "We still hold a connection with the Divine Influence through the laws which He has placed as a link, a covenant *(brit)* between us and Him. This is the circumcision . . . and the Sabbath" (2:34). The covenant is simply revelation, which is an encounter, and the commandments of the covenant are our steps toward this encounter.

Halevi's view requires us to examine another instance of a possible transition between the different meanings of revelation. Indeed, modern thought has pursued this line, producing a reduction that converts the revealed into a byproduct of the encounter. Revelation is conceived of as an "encounter," and the Bible, formerly a means or an organ of revelation, now becomes human testimony to the occurrence of revelation. The essence of the liberal interpretation is that it shifts the nature of revelation from its content, that is, "divinely given Torah," to the formal meaning. This interpretation is a function of the decline or even the total negation of the place of halakhah (religious law) in Jewish thought. When this approach does devote any attention to halakhah, it takes the form of a reinterpretation of the meaning of religious law as a human response to the experience of the encounter with the divine.

We find this linkage in Buber's attempt to remove the law from the revelatory encounter. Encounter is not in itself a process, but sets off, as it were, a process that is completed in the law. This process is nothing but the revelation of man to himself. The Torah exists within man, to be awakened where there is a call.[11]

Is this reduction of the concept of revelation legitimate? Any answer to this question must perforce involve one's personal theological commitments, so in fact no purely objective answer is possible. I should nonetheless like to examine one issue that will be encountered in any attempt at answering this question. Maimonides considered the binding of Isaac as evidence of prophecy, and as revelation, noting that like Abraham

> the prophets consider as true that which comes to them from God in a prophetic revelation. For it should not be thought that what they hear or what appears to them in a parable is not certain or is commingled with illusion just because it comes about *in a dream and in a vision*. Accordingly [Scripture] wished to make it known to us that all that is seen by a prophet in *a vision of prophecy* is, in the opinion of the prophet, a certain truth, that the prophet has no doubts in any way concerning anything in it, and that in his opinion its status is the same as that of all existent things that are apprehended through the senses or through the intellect.
>
> (*Guide* 3:24)

This approach to the binding of Isaac may be understood in the framework of Maimonides' interpretation, which views every test as a kind of drama. Though the protagonists are unaware that they are merely actors, this is a type of play in which the various events, that is, the commands, facts, and actions, are not directed at the personalities directly involved, but rather at the audience that hears or reads:

> The purpose of the test of a person performing a certain act is not the act itself but rather the purpose is that it should be an example to learn and follow.
>
> (ibid.)

If we draw the proper conclusions from Maimonides' position, then the binding of Isaac expresses two assumptions that lie at the heart of biblical prophecy. The first is explicit in Maimonides' interpretation. Although the prophetic vision is a phenomenon that may be termed subjective, it is no illusion. The binding of Isaac proves that prophecy must contain the criterion for its own verification, namely, the element of self-evidence. The second assumption, which Maimonides does not formulate explicitly but which is implicit in his interpretation, underscores the principle that prophetic revelation is the divine revealing of a "content" and not merely a call for a human response. The test of the binding is meaningless unless the command given to Abraham was a divine one. Thus, if revelation is only an encounter and the commandment merely man's response to it, then the binding is blasphemy and sacrilege. To my mind, the tragedy of the binding is that it points up two conflicts in the human condition. The first is that which usually exists between personal interest, inclinations, natural urges, and religious commandments. The second is the conflict between the various commandments that sometimes confront man in a concrete human situation.

However, conflict is created in the wake of the revelation, and the test is meaningless unless the revelation explicitly includes the implication of "divinely given Torah." Any teaching that views revelation as an encounter, and what is revealed as a response, will interpret the binding of Isaac as a mere illustration of the difficulties of ethical monotheism in educating man.[12] But it will be blind to the tormenting struggle between the religious and the moral, which testify to the existence of the Ineffable who bursts in upon us "from the Heavens" to reveal the Torah.

REFERENCES

1. *Die Offenbarung nach dem Lehrbegriffe der Synagoge,* 4 vols. (1835–1865).
2. Nathan Rotenstreich, *Modern Jewish Thought* (1950), 169ff.
3. Heinrich Graetz, *The Structure of Jewish History,* Ismar Schorch, tr. and ed. (1975), 68.
4. *Or Adonai,* Vienna ed., bk. 2, pt. 4, 41a.
5. See Nachum Lamm, *Torah le-Shmah* (1972), 77–83.
6. Rotenstreich, 167. For a discussion of the concept of revelation in the teaching of Steinheim see ibid., 180.
7. Martin Buber, "The Man of Today and the Jewish Bible," in Buber, *On the Bible: Eighteen Studies,* N. N. Glatzer, ed. (1968), 7.
8. Ḥayyim Vital, *Heikhal Adam Kadmon,* ch. 1, para. 1.
9. According to Vital, this passage is based upon the *Zohar,* "The Portion of Pinchas" (257b): "Before He created the world He was called by all these titles because of the creatures that were to be created."
10. Buber, "The Man of Today and the Jewish Bible," 7–8.
11. Martin Buber, *Israel and the World* (1948), 114. See also the exhaustive bibliography in Benny Kraut, "The Approach to Jewish Law of Martin Buber and Franz Rosenzweig," in *Tradition,* 12:3–4 (1972), 49–71, and Emil Fackenheim, "Martin Buber's Concept of Revelation," in *The Philosophy of Martin Buber,* P. A. Schilpp and M. Friedman, eds. (1967), 288–90.
12. Cf., for example, J. H. Gumbiner, "Existentialism and Father Abraham," in *Commentary* (1948).

BIBLIOGRAPHY

Joshua Haberman, "Salomon Ludwig Steinheim's Doctrine of Revelation," in *Judaism*, 17 (1968).

Shlomo Pines, "Spinoza's Tractatus Theologico-Politicus, Maimonides, and Kant," in *Scripta Hierosolymitana*, 20 (1968).

Shalom Rosenberg, "Hitgalut Mitmedet," in Moshe Halamish and Moshe Schwartz, eds., *Hitgalut, Emunah ve-Daat* (1980).

Reward and Punishment

שכר ועונש

Ephraim Rottenberg

Belief in retribution is an essential doctrine of every religion. It serves as an incentive to the worship and service of God. In Judaism, a religion of laws, instructions, and commandments given by an all-powerful, all-knowing, and all-good God, this doctrine assumes even greater importance. The word of God, vouchsafed in Torah and reiterated through his prophetic messengers, cannot be contradicted. Moses Maimonides elevated belief in divine retribution to an article of faith, and rightly so, since the denial of this principle is tantamount to the denial of the principle of the divine origin and immutability of the Torah as well as the message of Moses and the prophets regarding reward and punishment. Hence, retribution—reward for personal virtue and obedience to the Torah and punishment for evil and disobedience whether by an individual, a congregation (Num. 14:16), a nation, or mankind (as evidenced by the biblical Flood)—is a basic principle of Jewish religion.

The reason for making retribution an inducement to choose the way of Torah and observance of the commandments is given by Maimonides in his *Commentary to the Mishnah* (Intro. to Sanh. 10:1) and in the *Mishneh Torah*

(MT Hil. Teshuvah, 9:1; 10:5). Man, Maimonides argues, is accustomed to strive in life either to gain benefit or to avoid harm, but never with indifference to the realization of some moral objective. Maimonides compares the mass of Jews to children who need to be persuaded to study and observe by the promise of rewards; however, in their maturity, Jews are to be chided to aspire to something greater—to achieve a position of honor in society as scholars or professionals. Such persons may at last realize that their purpose in studying should be to know the truth, to know God, rather than to pursue narrow self-interest. Similarly, the mass of Jews should be encouraged to worship and live according to the Torah in the hope of recompense. Sincere devotion to God and to a life of piety even in the expectation of a reward may ultimately direct one to the disinterested worship of God, that is, to do his will purely out of love for him. Although one who worships God for the sake of receiving a reward is not transgressing and will be rewarded for it, it is nonetheless considered worship of a lower order. The true servant of God is he who cleanses himself of such ulterior motives and is animated solely by his love for God who commanded him to a complete and total love (Deut. 6:5). The exhortation of the early-second-century-B.C.E. rabbinic sage Antigonus of Sokho that a Jew should not "be like servants who minister to their masters upon the condition of receiving a reward, but be like servants who minister to their masters upon condition of not receiving a reward, and let the fear of heaven be upon you" (M. Avot 1:3) has become the critical focus of the Jewish doctrine of retribution.

Throughout the Talmud and the Midrash, in the writings of the medieval thinkers and moralists, particularly Baḥya ibn Paquda, and the sixteenth-century safed kabbalists Elijah ben Moses de Vidas (*Reshith Ḥokhmah,* 1578) and Eleazar ben Moses Azikri (*Sefer Ḥaredim,* 1601) to the Ḥasidic masters, *ahavat ha-Shem* (love of God) and *yirat ha-Shem* (fear of God) are the primary motives to worship. Fear of God should not be fear of punishment, but rather awe and reverence before the creator of the universe.

But what is the nature of this retribution? What reward is offered for obedience to the word of God and what punishment is provided for rebellion? Scriptural retribution clearly belongs to this world: Those who keep the commandments will prosper and be blessed, the nation of Israel will enjoy peace and be victorious over her enemies, and God will make the Jewish people fruitful and cause it to live a good life, happy in the sureness of God's presence in its midst. Those, however, who break the covenant of God will suffer sickness, famine, and pestilence. If the entire nation of Israel commits a breach of the covenant, it will in addition be visited by war and desolation, bereavement, and, finally, exile from its land; the appalling maledictions of the *Tokhaḥot* (Lev. 26; Deut. 28) will be realized.

Nothing is said in Scripture about retribution after death, although the sages have found intimations and allusions to such a doctrine. The verse "that you may fare well and have a long life" (Deut. 22:7) is interpreted by the rabbis to mean that it may be well with you in the world that is entirely good and that your days may be prolonged in the world that is all-enduring (literally, "all-long") (BT Kid. 39b; BT Ḥul. 142a). Another verse stating that "that person shall be cut off—he bears his guilt" (Num. 15:31), is interpreted to mean cut off from this world as well as from the next. This reading of the text is found in the Talmud, which interprets the double use of the Hebrew word for "cutting off" (hekaret tikaret) in the biblical passage as not simply a homiletic truth, but as an oral tradition going back to Moses (BT Sanh. 64b). On this basis Maimonides categorically declares that retribution—reward or punishment—entails not only this world, but also the World to Come. Maimonides believes that the great good that is preserved for the righteous is life in the World to Come, that is, life that does not end in death, a good that knows no evil, an everlasting bliss in the awareness of God's being that could not be attained in the flesh (MT Hil. Teshuvah 8:1–5). By contrast, the greatest possible punishment for the wicked is "the cutting off" (karet)—the complete annihilation and extinction of the soul. By living a life of evil, sinners forfeit their claim to the estate of eternal life (MT Hil. Teshuvah 8:5).

Why, then, is emphasis laid in the Torah and in the prophets upon earthly reward, while heavenly retribution is merely alluded to? Maimonides deals with this objection by indicating that eternal life must be earned by keeping the commandments and by learning to love God through contemplation of the wisdom implicit in creation (MT Hil. Yesodei Torah 2:2). God gives man the blessing of health and ease in order that he may have the leisure to pursue a life of love and fear of heaven, and he protects him from war and famine lest he be hindered in his keeping the commandments (MT Hil. Teshuvah 9:1, Commentary to Mishnah, Sanh. 10). This is a reasonable explanation for the emphasis given in the Torah on thisworldly retribution. But the question may still be asked, Why are reward and punishment in the hereafter never explicitly mentioned? We must bear in mind, however, that in the opinion of Maimonides, an oral tradition conveyed to the people by Moses disclosed the implications of eternal life in Numbers 15:31 and Deuteronomy 22:7. The people were thus made aware of heavenly retribution insofar as obedience was conducive to life everlasting and a life of transgression to total perdition.

There is yet another reward, that of resurrection (tehiyyat ha-metim), the rising again to life ordained for the righteous. To what order of reward does resurrection belong? According to Maimonides, life for the resurrected will be a natural terrestrial existence. After an extremely long and happy life resembling existence envisaged for the messianic age, the resurrected will die again (because natural life must inevitably come to an end), and the soul will return to its original home, the *Olam ha-Ba,* the World to Come (Commentary to Mishnah, Sand. 10:1; Treatise on Resurrection, ch. 4). To summarize, Maimonides holds that souls will enter the World to Come following their terrestrial existence. At the time of the resurrection, the soul will be united with its earthly body, and finally, upon dying again, the soul will return to the World to Come, where it had sojourned before rejoining its body at the resurrection.

Naḥmanides differs with Maimonides both on the nature of life following resurrection and on the place where souls reside after death. The soul departing from the body goes to the Garden of Eden, which is literally construed as a garden of trees (including the Tree of Life and the Tree of Knowledge), but bearing fruit unlike any other fruit. This garden is a replica, a mirror image reflecting all the supernal worlds. It is like an architect's plan from which may be learned the foundation, the origin of all creation—physical, spiritual, and angelic—and all else that a creature is able to conceive about the creator. Adam, the handiwork of God, the perfect creature of consummate intelligence, was placed in the garden for his bodily good as well as to experience everything that is humanly appropriate about his creator. When the soul enters the Garden of Eden after death, it is rewarded with the spiritual endowments of Eden: attaining attachment to and union with the supernal worlds.

What, then, is the World to Come? The term literally implies, Naḥmanides claims, a world that does not yet exist; God will create that world after the days of the Messiah and the resurrection. It will entail a complete revival of body and soul; however, unlike the body of this world, the body then will have no need of sustenance. Rather, its nourishment will come from the radiance of the divine Presence, the *Shekhinah.* The resurrected will be sustained like Moses during the forty days he spent on Mount Sinai, and like him will experience an awareness of God and an intimacy with him that is unattainable in this life.[1]

Maimonides and Naḥmanides were the only thinkers to treat the subject of retribution extensively and systematically. Despite their disagreement on some particulars, they arrived at essentially the same conclusions. They, like the prophets, psalmists, the author of the Book of Job in particular, and the sages of the Talmud, were aware of the problems that belief in divine reward and punishment raised, no less than nonbelieving philosophic prophets have been. David Hume, for example, observed that the skeptical questions posed in the third century B.C.E. by Epicurus still remain unanswered.[2] Hume apparently accepted Epicurus' demurral, but to believers in a good and powerful divinity, the denial of God remains the answer of "the fool" or "the vile person" (Ps. 14:1). Already the biblical prophets anticipated the skeptics' objections, as when, for example, Jeremiah pleads for understanding, believing profoundly in divine justice (Jer. 12:1–3), and Habakkuk reproachfully complains that God has not answered his cries for justice—no wonder, therefore, that the Torah is neglected and the right perverted (Hab. 1:1–4, 13). The psalmist admits that he in fact almost strayed from the right path and asks in virtually Epicurean terms: "How could God know? Is there knowledge with the Most High?" (Ps. 73:2, 11). A beneficent God, aware of the affairs of the world, would not allow evil to prevail. Moreover, the whole colloquy in the Book of Job revolves around precisely this question. The author of the book rejects the simplistic belief of Job's three friends who naively equate the good with reward and the evil with punishment. Despite all the unresolved questions that the author of Job raises, he concludes by affirming God's goodness, attributing man's lack of understanding to the limitations of reason. In conclusion, all the prophets and inspired thinkers and poets of the Bible profess belief in God's justice and virtue; that he does not cause suffering to no purpose and that man's reason is insufficient to comprehend God's mysterious ways: retribution though sometimes slow will surely come at the appointed time. If the wicked prosper, as Maimonides later observed, it is because of God's acknowledgment of some good accomplished, and if the righteous man dies it is because of an unknown sin. Only God can be the judge of a man's merits and transgressions—a man's worth is beyond the reach of human comprehension (Guide 3: 17; MT Hil. Teshuvah 3:2; 6:1).

Peoples, even as individuals, stand under divine judgment. The Bible often depicts nations sent—or permitted—to rebuke Israel as themselves motivated by a wickedness that God in his providential design will later punish. Human beings, either individually or collectively, cannot elude divine retribution.

In our day, the traditional teaching notwithstanding, a believing Jew is faced with a terrible dilemma. For centuries Jews have acquiesced in the assertion of the prophets that "on account of our sins we have been exiled from our land" (Amidah for the Holiday Additional Prayers). Religious Jews could reasonably accept that exile and persecution come as punishment for sin. But after Auschwitz, while still believing with their hearts, reason asks with exasperation why it is that with all power, love, and mercy numbered among his immense attributes, God did not prevent the Holocaust. This question is perpetual in the mind of every Jew of the Holocaust generation; indeed, it is a question that cannot be hidden from God, for, as the Talmud instructs us, God does not want to be lied to, that is, we should not seek to suppress or disguise our questions (BT Yoma 69b). We attempt neither to justify nor to vindicate. Nor are we engaged in the formulation of a theodicy of disaster. Clearly, however, post-Holocaust Jewish existence can have meaning only in the belief that Jewish history is sacred history, that Jewish existence is of cosmic importance. Affirming this belief, like Habbakuk we must forbear and wait for the divine enlightenment which is sure to come (Hab. 2:1). Only this belief can sustain the believing Jew in face of the painful enigma of seemingly inexplicable suffering.

REFERENCES

1. "Sha'ar ha-Gmul," in *Kitvei Ramban* 2 (1964), 302.
2. David Hume, *Dialogues Concerning Natural Religion,* Norman Kemp Smith, ed. (1947), 198.

BIBLIOGRAPHY

Moses Maimonides, *Guide of the Perplexed,* Shlomo Pines, tr. (1963).
Moses Maimonides, *Mishneh Torah,* Moses Hyamson, tr. (1981).

Righteousness

צדיקות

Joshua O. Haberman

The meaning of righteousness is best expressed by the Hebrew word *zedek* which, in time, absorbed the connotations of *mishpat* (justice), *hesed* (fidelity to covenant), and *emet* (truth), as well as the adjectives *yashar* (straight, of integrity) and *tamim* (whole, without blemish). Righteousness, as illustrated in biblical and rabbinic usage, is morality in its totality or the moral ideal in all spheres—private, social, and religious. At the same time, righteousness is of the very essence of God, the one attribute that, through revelation in Torah, may be open to human comprehension: "I will make all My goodness pass before you" (Ex. 33:19).

Ethical abstractions are alien to the spirit of Judaism. Characteristically, the editor of the Mishnah, Judah ha-Nasi, asks, "Which is that right way which a man should choose?" (M. Avot 2:1). The inquiry is not about the *summum bonum,* the highest good—a question that intrigued classical philosophy and its interpreters throughout the centuries—but about specific rules for life. As in Judah ha-Nasi's answer, so in all of biblical and rabbinic Judaism, the "right way" is defined in terms of Torah commandments.

Righteousness is the pattern of conduct that is stipulated by the covenant relation between God and man and its implications for relations between man and his fellow. God's holiness and human righteousness are inseparably linked in the covenant. The key sentence "You shall be holy, for I, the Lord your God, am holy" (Lev. 19:2) provides the foundation of Jewish ethics as an *imitatio Dei,* that is, man, made in the image of God, emulating his Maker.

The Talmudic sage Simlai suggested that all of the 613 commandments of the Torah may be compressed in any one of several single sentences from the Prophets or Writings that accentuate righteousness as the summation of God's demands, for example: "Observe what is right and do what is just" (Isa. 56:1), or "the righteous man is rewarded with life for his fidelity" (Hab. 2:4). Psalms 15 and 24 confirm the often repeated point of prophetic preaching that no one is nearer to God than the righteous—a theme richly developed in rabbinic literature. Rabbi Aibu taught that the sinfulness of man, beginning with Adam, caused the *Shekhinah* (divine Presence) to withdraw from the earth until Abraham and the most righteous of his descendants reversed the process: "For the wicked caused the *Shekhinah* to depart while the righteous cause it to dwell on the earth" (Num. R. 13:2).

The Jewish concept of righteousness must be sharply distinguished from what is commonly called virtue. Virtues are various kinds of competence, such as the diligence of a student, the bravery of a soldier, or the loyalty of an employee, developed as character traits and endorsed by the community. However laudable these traits may be, they are not always or necessarily devoted to good ends. Righteousness, on the other hand, is inspired by divinely ordained law, which may radically differ from the prevailing community practice, as is indicated in many cases of prophetic protest against the commonly accepted standards of society (for example, Amos 5:10).

One cannot fail to note a striking difference between the righteousness of man and of God. The Bible shows an amazing consistency and certainty in specifying the meaning of righteousness with reference to human conduct. But the righteousness of God is often problematic. Abraham is appalled by the possibility that God's retribution may "sweep away the innocent along with the guilty" (Gen. 18:23); the psalms include many anguished outcries of innocent sufferers (for example, Ps. 44 and 74); Jeremiah rages against the unbearable burdens God imposed upon him and curses the day he was born (Jer. 20); Ecclesiastes flatly contradicts the notion of God's justice (Eccles. 9:2). And the most profound discussion of innocent suffering, the Book of Job, leaves the question about God's fairness in limbo. Despite such wavering, God's righteousness is overwhelmingly affirmed. If not evident in the present moment, his righteousness is the redemptive power of the future: "Zion shall be saved by justice, her repentant ones by righteousness" (Isa. 1:27). Ultimately, in the messianic future, God "will instruct us in His ways. . . . And they shall beat their swords into plowshares" (Isa. 2:3–4). The vindication of God's justice in life hereafter, already envisaged in a late biblical source (Dan. 12:2), became a dominant theme in Pharisaic and rabbinic Judaism.

Nowhere is there a greater gap between Jewish and Christian thought than on the redeeming power of righteousness. To the Jew, the commandments of Torah are both sacrament and salvation. They are vehicles of divine grace insofar as in their joyful performance the Jew is brought into the closest possible relation with God. New Testament distinctions made by Paul between a righteousness of faith and of works (Rom. 4) appear to the Jewish mind as irrelevant. But, if such a distinction had to be made, rabbinic sages would affirm the efficacy of righteous works even in the absence of true faith. In this spirit, Joshua made his famous comment: "The righteous of all nations have a share in the world to come" (Tos. Sanh. 13). Rather daring is the statement found in *Pesikta de-Rav Kahana* 15, which cites Ḥiyya bar Abba, who said: "It is written, 'your fathers . . . deserted Me and did not keep My Torah' [Jer. 16:11]. If only they had kept studying My Torah! Indeed, if they forsook even Me, all would turn out well, provided they kept studying My Torah."

Paul's characterization of the law of Torah as temptation to sin—"If it had not been for the Law, I should not have known sin. . . . I was once alive apart from the Law, but when the Commandment came, sin revived and I died" (Rom. 7:7, 9)—is quite incomprehensible to the Jew. The Torah is the only means by which evil can be overcome. The righteous draws his strength from the commandments: "God who created the *Yeẓer ha-Ra* (evil urge) has created the Law, as an antidote against it" (BT BB 16a).

In Ḥasidism, the fusion of holiness and righteousness is complete. Sweeping over Europe in the eighteenth century as the most powerful Jewish revival movement of the millennium, Ḥasidism added a charismatic dimension to the meaning of righteousness. The spiritual leader of the Ḥasidic community, called *ẓaddik* (the righteous one), is seen as mediator between God and man. Purified by his righteousness, the *ẓaddik* is, so to speak, a conductor of divine grace and power, which can be channeled by him toward those in need of healing or help.

The talmudic statement that common sense or human needs would dictate fundamental laws of righteousness if they had not already been revealed in the Torah (BT Yoma 67b) encouraged Jewish philosophers through the centuries to corroborate revealed laws of righteousness by independent rational inquiry. Thus, medieval thinkers such as Baḥya ibn Paquda and Moses Maimonides validated righteousness grounded in Torah with terms and concepts borrowed from Platonic and Aristotelian thought, respectively.

Two modern Jewish philosophers stand out by their radically different approach. Hermann Cohen applied the principle of correlation, through which the being of the world is related to the becoming of God, to the realm of morality. God and man are linked through the holy spirit. This link makes possible a correspondence or mutual involvement of God in man and man in God: "You might imagine that God is called the Holy One because He is hidden in unfathomable obscurity. Against this delusion of mysticism Isaiah . . . coined the sentence 'the Lord of Hosts is exalted in righteousness' [Isa. 5:16]"[1] Cohen interprets this to mean that the Lord becomes the holy God only through the act of sanctification; this holiness is brought about "through action which man has to accomplish."[2] Thus, the ultimate object of all man's righteous acts is to sanctify God.

Martin Buber, the only major Jewish thinker to insist on absolute moral autonomy, rejects the binding character of Torah or any other codification of righteousness. In his most explicit discussion on the subject, "The Question to the Single One," Buber argues that moral decisions must be reached in genuine response to personal encounters with God. Therefore, he cannot submit the relation of faith to a "book of rules" in which to look up "to discover what is to be done now, in this very hour."[3] He must leave himself open "to experience what God desires of me for this hour . . . not earlier than *in* the hour."[4] This highly individualistic approach does not rule out concern for the community, yet "no program, no tactical resolution, no command can tell me how I, as I decide, have to do justice to my group before the Face of God." For example, he may feel impelled to oppose community standards if "aware that God's love ordains otherwise."[5] Of what value, then, is the moral tradition of his people in the Torah? Buber would not deny his community's influence on personal moral decision making. The group's moral consensus provides a certain orientation, but this "must not be substituted for the decision."[6] Merely to follow a group judgment is, for Buber, an escape from responsibility. Despite all the risks of misunderstanding or self-delusion, he must make his "decisions properly only from that ground of his being at which he is aware of the event as divine speech to him."[7]

Nothing occurred during the Holocaust that invalidates Judaism's moral imperatives. On the contrary, every violation of human rights, every denial or miscarriage of justice, every atrocity helped destabilize European society and led to the moral paralysis that made possible the horrors of World War I and World War II and culminated in the Holocaust. Thus, history confirmed the age-old Jewish association of righteousness with prosperity, security, and peace and the opposite equation of evil with disaster. Totalitarian regimes that, in defiance of the prophetic word "not by might, nor by power, but by My spirit" (Zech. 4:6), put naked power in the place of law and order have brought calamity not only upon their victims but also upon themselves.

Speaking collectively for all mankind, one can still make a strong case for a law of moral causality in history, such as Isaiah alluded to: "The work of righteousness shall be peace and the effect of righteousness, calm and confidence forever" (Isa. 32:17). The cause of righteousness is upheld by a system of retribution that is rooted in the moral sensitivities of man and generally operative in human affairs.

The specific theological concept most compromised by the Holocaust is the doctrine of individual retribution. As stated most emphatically in Ezekiel 18, each individual should expect rewards or penalties in accordance with his own merit. Such a doctrine would necessitate, in countless individual cases, God's redemptive intercession on behalf of the righteous and punitive visitations upon the wicked. The Holocaust has dealt shattering blows to this expectation.

Post-Holocaust generations, however, need not go to the other extreme of cynicism and conclude that God is entirely indifferent to human righteousness or to the perpetration of evil. Man's freedom of will is fundamental in biblical and postbiblical Judaism. It includes the freedom to do evil. However, the rabbis of the Mishnah found a way of reaffirming man's moral freedom while crediting God with creating incentives that encourage the righteous to continue in the pursuit of righteousness even while the wicked are allowed to descend the road to perdition. In response to those who cry out, Where was God during the Holocaust? Why did God not stop the evildoers?, rabbinic theology would point to the tension and interaction of human responsibility and divine guidance, but tip the scale in favor of human responsibility. Often quoted is the rabbinic saying: "As for those who would draw near unto God, God also brings them closer to Himself,"[8] that is, God matches the initiative of those who uphold his ways. The opposite is also true. Said Rabbi Meir: "If you neglect the Torah, many causes for neglecting it will present themselves to you" (M. Avot 4:12), that is, defectors from God's Torah will become increasingly alienated from him as temptations multiply.

Ultimately, Judaism must rest its case upon biblical theology. In the theological blueprint underlying the Bible, the central theme is what the sages call *tikkun ha-olam,* the repair of the world. It is God's response to evil, or, to put it positively, God's struggle to make the world safe for righteousness. It is a struggle first waged by God alone and then continued in covenant and partnership with Israel. Divine revelation delivers Torah to Israel (and through Israel to mankind) as the most potent weapon against evil. This theme is developed ever more explicitly in chapters 3, 4, 6, 11, and 12 of Genesis, and brought to culmination in Exodus 19 and Isaiah 2:2–4.

The biblical narrative illustrates in a series of crises how vulnerable man is to corruption. The first reference to a corrupting agent in the world God created is the serpent in Paradise (Gen. 3). It is not an explanation of evil, but merely a statement of an evil impulse seeking to undermine God's plan. The next crisis is Cain's fratricide (Gen. 4:1–8). Here the power for evil is more clearly identified. It is "sin" *(hatat),* referred to as a separate ontological entity, ever ready to infect man, yet manageable: "Sin crouches at the door; . . . yet, you can be its master" (Gen. 4:7). Unanswered remain all questions as to the origin of sin. If God did not create sin, who did?

As the first human family multiplies, so does evil. Now the crisis is worldwide; the world is filled "with lawlessness" (Gen. 6:11). The Hebrew word *hamas* translated as "lawlessness" has the connotation of violence. Widespread evil provokes God to purge the world by means of the Flood. Only Noah's family is preserved as the nucleus of a new mankind. In this chapter, the Bible introduces for the first time the word *covenant* or *brit* (Gen. 6:18). Noah and his sons are bound to God in a covenant whose terms are spelled out in Genesis 9:1–15. Rabbinic theology elaborates Noah's covenant in the doctrine of the seven Noachide laws, which are binding upon all mankind.

The next crisis, the arrogance of power of the generation of the Tower of Babel (Gen. 11), proves that the covenant with Noah is not an adequate defense against evil. A more fully expanded intervention is required of God in the form of specific guidance of mankind through revelation. The first act in the renewed struggle against the evil is God's call to Abraham to create a nation in whose descendants "all the families of the earth shall bless themselves" (Gen. 12:3).

Subsequent chapters narrate the growth of the patriarchal family into tribes, gradually welded together as a nation. Israel's redemption from Egyptian bondage and the Exodus underscore the view that the nation entirely owes its existence and survival to God, and therefore properly belongs to him and should be bound to him in the covenant at Sinai as a "kingdom of priests and a holy nation" (Ex. 19:6). Given the Torah with its numerous commandments and prohibitions, Israel is afforded adequate resources with which to resist the corruption of evil.

In the light of this theological scenario, the chief purpose for the revelation of Torah is to arm mankind against sin. The Holocaust has not invalidated this view. One may still hold to the belief that a Torah-true Israel would be best equipped to resist the power of evil. But what about the gentile world? The Holocaust experience reinforces the realization that Israel cannot stand alone in its devotion to Torah. The innocent cannot survive in a world of wickedness. Righteousness must be universalized. The world can be safe for Israel only if the nations of the world are saved from corruption and lawlessness. Enlightenment in the way of Torah and the end of violence go hand in hand. Swords will be turned into plowshares, in Isaiah's vision, when, in the End of Days, all nations shall be instructed in God's ways and "walk in His paths" (Isa. 2:2–4). How all the nations of the world are to be united in the Torah way of life, whether by Israel's teaching mission or by another divine intervention, remains, however, part of the messianic mystery.

REFERENCES

1. Hermann Cohen, *Religion of Reason Out of the Sources of Judaism,* Simon Kaplan, tr. (1972), 110.
2. Ibid.
3. "The Question to the Single One" in *Between Man and Man,* Ronald Gregor Smith, tr. (1957), 68.
4. Ibid.
5. Ibid.
6. Ibid., 69.
7. Ibid.
8. Sif. Num. *Beha'aloteha, Sifre debe Rab,* M. Friedmann, ed. (1864), sec. 78, 20b.

BIBLIOGRAPHY

Martin Buber, "The Question to the Single One," in *Between Man and Man,* Ronald Gregor Smith, tr. (1957).
Hermann Cohen, *Religion of Reason Out of the Sources of Judaism,* Simon Kaplan, tr. (1972).

Sacred Text and Canon

כתבי קודש

David Stern

The Jewish concept of a sacred text derives directly from the Bible's description of the origins of its own laws. In the famous passages in Exodus 19 and 24 narrating the Sinaitic revelation, the sacrality of the laws revealed there is set forth as a function of both their divine origins and their authority for all time. Repeated in the book of Deuteronomy (cf. 31:9–13), these functions were eventually extended to every book in the Hebrew Bible in its three parts, the Pentateuch (*Torah*), the Prophets (*Neviim*), and the Writings (*Ketuvim*), all of which were believed to be divinely inspired and hence authoritative as guides for religious practice and belief. These canonical texts were treated as definitively fixed (Eccles. 3:14; cf. Deut. 4:2; 13:1) and as objects of special study (cf. Deut. 31:10–13); one can assume that from an early period, the notion of a canonical text carried with it the idea that such a text required interpretation, both for its intrinsic importance and because it had to be constantly reinterpreted in order to maintain its relevance.

Modern scholars have been wary of accepting the biblical account of its origins at face value. While many passages in the later books of the Bible echo earlier traditions, there are few unequivocal testimonies that would prove the canonization of specific texts as literary documents of sacred status; even in the passages in Exodus and Deuteronomy cited above, it is not clear precisely what revelation is being described. Most scholars today believe that the canonization of the Bible and its formation into the present text we possess took place at a date much later than the Bible claims; according to current scholarly consensus, the first book in the Bible to reach canonical status was Deuteronomy, during the time of the Josianic reform in 622 B.C.E. (cf. II Kings 22:8; 23:1–3). The remainder of the Pentateuch, in its several sacred traditions, was joined to Deuteronomy in the late fifth and early fourth centuries B.C.E., following the return from the Babylonian Exile under the leadership of Ezra and Nehemiah (cf. Neh. 8:2–3). The Prophets, as a collection, was closed in the third century B.C.E., following the period of Persian hegemony in Palestine, while the Writings, the final section of the Bible, was not completed until perhaps the late first or early second centuries C.E., following the destruction of the Second Temple in 70 C.E., at a rabbinic synod supposedly held at Jabneh. In the case of both the Prophets and the Writings, however, it is clear that individual books in the collections were considered sacred and had been canonized long before the collections in their entirety.

Precisely how these final canonical decisions were made is not known. The Bible itself does not describe the process of canonization (except, perhaps, in the passages in II Kings and Nehemiah), and the extrabiblical evidence is at best equivocal. The library at Qumran suggests that the sectarians who lived there possessed a biblical canon slightly larger than that of the rabbis and subsequent Judaism, and by examining books like Ben Sira and Jubilees that were not included in the rabbinic canon, modern scholars have speculated, not very successfully, upon the criteria the rabbis may have used in fixing their final canon. In a recent study, however, S. Z. Leiman has reviewed all the supposed evidence in rabbinic literature and concluded that there is no proof that the rabbis ever decided the canon. The synod at Jabneh was not about canonization of Scripture, and the meaning of the terms that the rabbis use to describe supposedly canonical books—terms like "books that defile the hands" (M. Kelim 15:6; M. Yad. 3:5)—is unclear. As Leiman points out, the rabbis never propose as a candidate for Scripture any book that was known to them to have been authored after the third century B.C.E., the time at which they believed classical prophecy ceased, or any book that was published after the second century B.C.E. Accordingly, Leiman concludes that the rabbis, in fact, inherited a canon of Scripture that had been fixed no later than the second century B.C.E.; at most, they made some minor changes in it—establishing, for example, the sacred status of some books, like Ecclesiastes and the Song of Songs, whose divine authorship had been a matter of controversy. Leiman also reviews the evidence for the canonization of the earlier sections of the Bible, the Pentateuch and the Prophets, and suggests that these books, too, reached their final form at dates much earlier than modern scholars have proposed, and much closer to the ones the rabbis claimed for them, largely on the Bible's own testimony.

The importance of Leiman's study lies less in the specific matter of chronology than it does in the distinction Leiman draws between sacred texts and canonical books. The latter group, he argues, including books like Ben Sira (and according to some rabbis, Ecclesiastes and the Song of Songs), could be accepted as authoritative for behavior and doctrine even though the specific text was not considered to be divinely inspired. As Leiman points out, divine authorship necessarily implies authoritativeness, but the opposite is not the case. Nor is there any evidence that the rabbis decreed a work to be divinely inspired that was not already considered authoritative. The entire notion of canon and its significance for the Hebrew Scriptures therefore needs to be reconsidered. We might also add that the words for canon that the rabbis used—*middah* in Hebrew, *mekhilta* in Aramaic— mean, like the Greek *kanon,* a measure, hence a collection of exemplary objects, not a closed and finite list; the latter use of the word is first attested in the fourth century C.E. when the Bishop Athanasius used the word *kanon* in reference to the list of books the Church authorized as divinely inspired and hence as canonical; in fact, the earliest use of the word *canon* in regard to the secular literature of the ancient world occurred in the eighteenth century in David Ruhuken's edition of *Rutilius Lupus.* It should also be noted that if Leiman is correct in ascribing the canonization of the Bible to the second century B.C.E., this kind of literary activity was being pursued elsewhere in the ancient world at that time: during the same period, the Alexandrian lexicographers were compiling the *pinakes,* the lists of exemplary poets known as *classici,* or writers of the first class—the canon, as it were, of ancient literature.

The distinction between sacred texts as represented by the Hebrew Scriptures—the only literary texts in Judaism believed to be divinely inspired— and canonical, that is, authoritative, books becomes even more important in the postbiblical period. The most decisive source in the history of Judaism, it can be argued, has been not the canon of Scripture itself but the canon of scriptural interpretation, specifically the oral Law (*torah she-be-al peh),* as the rabbis called the entire corpus of their traditions, halakhic and aggadic, which they claimed God had revealed at Sinai along with the written text of the Torah. As its name suggests, the oral Law is not a specific text but an open-ended, ever-unfolding process of interpretation, "even that," says an oft-quoted Talmudic passage, "which a distinguished disciple is destined to teach before his master" (JT Peah 17a). Despite this paradoxical formulation of its development, the claim for its sacred origins establishes the oral Law as the basis for the very identity of rabbinic Judaism, a fact the rabbis hinted at when they stated that God gave the oral Law to the Israelites "to distinguish them from other nations" (Num. R. 14:10), making possession of the oral Law the mark of Israel's singularity. The canon, as it were, constitutes the nation. It is therefore not surprising that virtually every great schism in the history of rabbinic Judaism, beginning with the Sadducees (cf. Josephus, *Antiquities* 13:10; *War,* 2:8) and later the Karaites, has arisen over the question of the canonicity of the oral Law and its interpretation of the Bible.

Yet while the tradition of the oral Law is sacred and canonical in rabbinic Judaism, the status of the texts that eventually come to represent the literary documentation of the oral Law is another matter. About the canonization of these works—the Mishnah of Rabbi Judah, the Jerusalem and Babylonian Talmuds, and later works—virtually nothing is known. For example, Rabbi Judah's Mishnah was only the last of several attempts to organize and (perhaps) codify the teachings of the rabbis. Yet our only explanation for how his Mishnah became authoritative (and effectively stopped the composition of more codes or collections that might have supplanted its authority) is the statement of Sherirah ben Hanina Gaon in the late tenth century C.E.:

> When everyone saw the beauty of the structure of the Mishnah, its true reasoning and exact expression, they forsook all the other *mishnayot* they were studying. These laws spread throughout the land of Israel, while the other laws became like *beraita* [outside]. Consulting them was like consulting a commentary or expansive version. But the authority for Israel was these laws [of Rabbi Judah]. Israel accepted them as soon as they saw them, faithfully, and there is no one who would contest them.
>
> (Sherirah ben Hanina Gaon, Iggeret, B. M. Lewin, ed. 1921, 30)

Although this passage describes the superiority of Rabbi Judah's Mishnah, it tells us little about the actual process of its canonization. Furthermore, as David Weiss-Halivni has shown, the actual reception the Mishnah received from Rabbi Judah's successors, even from some of his contemporaries, was not as unanimously positive as Sherirah makes it out to be. While everyone paid lip service to the unquestioned authority of Rabbi Judah, whose personal prestige as patriarch was unsurpassed, later rabbis often ignored his halakhic rulings in the Mishnah or emended his statements in order to overturn his decisions.

Although Rabbi Judah's ambitions for the Mishnah to become the final halakhic authority may not have been fully realized, it is the case nonetheless that the Mishnah and other rabbinic traditions in the Tosefta and in uncollected *beraitot* (external teachings of the tannaim not in the Mishnah) are treated in the Talmud in much the same way as the words of Scripture are treated in the oral Law—that is, as a sacred text whose statements are all internally consistent, harmonious, and significant. This has nothing to do with belief in divine authorship; as Sherirah notes, the Mishnah's stylistic perfection is self-evident. Rather, this tendency suggests how, in the history of rabbinic Judaism, a text could be absorbed into the tradition of canonical interpretations by being subjected to the modes of canonical interpretation (like those established in midrash), and by proving itself capable of sustaining such interpretive scrutiny. The same hermeneutical procedure is repeated upon the corpus of the Jerusalem and Babylonian Talmuds by their subsequent commentators, and, generation after generation, upon subsequent interpreters of the tradition. In this way, the canonical tradition may be said to have maintained its canonicity.

There is, of course, no guaranteed canonicity. The history of medieval Jewish literature is studded with examples of works that did not attain canonical authority. This is particularly evident in the discipline of halakhah, the most famous case of such a failure undoubtedly being that of the *Mishneh Torah* of Maimonides, who aspired for his code to become second to the Bible in authority, which did not occur, perhaps partly because Maimonides himself attempted to sidestep the authority of earlier canonical tradition, indeed to supplant it. On the other hand, Joseph Caro's *Shulḥan Arukh* (The Prepared Table), written in the sixteenth century, did become the canonical halakhic code, although only after the accretion of commentaries that elaborated, extended, and modified its halakhic rulings.

In the field of nonhalakhic literature, the question of canon is even more complicated, as one can see particularly in the history of mystical works and their reception in Jewish tradition. On the one hand, there is a work like the *Shi'ur Komah*, an authentically early Jewish commentary on the Song of Songs, dating from the second or third century, whose very authenticity as a Jewish work was dismissed by Maimonides because he found its blatant anthropomorphizing repugnant to his philosophical rationalism. On the other hand, the *Zohar,* written in the thirteenth century, was attributed by its real author, Moses de Leon, to the second-century tanna Rabbi Simeon bar Yohai, who was said to have composed the mystical work through divine inspiration; in later kabbalistic tradition the *Zohar* was treated virtually as a sacred text. The writings of different Hasidic masters, like the *Tanya* of Shneour Zalman of Ladi (1747–1812) or the tales of Nahman of Bratslav in the nineteenth century, have also been accepted by these masters' followers as texts of figurative, if not literal, canonical status. Non-Hasidic Jews, however, and even Hasidim who are not followers of these particular masters, would not accord to these texts the same authoritative status.

As such examples illustrate, the Jewish canon is no longer monolithic or uniformly accepted, and it can differ from one movement or subtradition in Judaism to another. As the concept of a sacred text has become increasingly elastic, and as universal norms of Jewish practice and belief have steadily collapsed, the notion of a Jewish canon has become more problematic. It has also become more ideologically significant, for canonical decisions now directly figure in debates over what constitutes the definition of Judaism. This can be seen especially in the way these controversies have arisen in modern Jewish historiography. The famous debate between the rationalist historians of the *Wissenschaft des Judentums* and Gershom Scholem over the place of kabbalah in Jewish history should be understood within the context of canon formation. Yet even if one were to accept Scholem's historiographical and theological anarchism, it surely does not follow that every Jewish book claiming to be canonical would find a place within the Jewish canon. And what of Scholem's own work, and of modern Jewish historiography in general? Inasmuch as the postbiblical Jewish canon has been a tradition of interpretation, modern Jewish historiography largely remains within that tradition. Furthermore, few other forms of Jewish literature in this century have been received by the Jewish public with greater authority, or have been more decisive in shaping Jewish thought. Yet what are the criteria for converting history into theology, for canonizing literary works that are decidedly secular in character and purpose?

A definitive answer to these questions may not exist, but it is possible to suggest some preliminary considerations to be followed in constructing a Jewish canon. First, the notion of a sacred text itself needs to be renovated so that its authority is seen not so much or solely as an inherent feature in the text but also as a function of a relationship, a covenant, between the text and its audience. A sacred text, as Harold Fisch has written, is a text that commands, and this covenantal authority distinguishes a sacred text from a classic. Yet in constructing a contemporary Jewish canon, it may be necessary to create a hierarchy of texts rather than a simple dichotomy of sacred (canonical) and profane (noncanonical) books. Just as the Hebrew Bible is canonized in three sections, so, too, in a contemporary canon it may be necessary to differentiate between the uniquely sacred category of Torah, a second category of canonical Jewish interpretations of the Torah (all falling within the tradition, albeit variously), and a third collection of works that have been decisive and authoritative in determining Jewish belief and practice although they are clearly not sacred. A canon of this sort will undoubtedly be controversial; yet I can imagine no task more compelling for a contemporary theology of Judaism. Besides, as anthropologists have recently shown, the formation of canons is an essential activity in every culture. As such, it is a challenge that modern Judaism cannot avoid or evade.

BIBLIOGRAPHY

Harold Fisch, "The Sanctification of Literature," in *Commentary*, 63 (June 1977).

Shelomo Z. Havlin, "Al 'ha-Ḥatimah ha-Sifrutit' ke-Yesod le-ha-Ḥilukah le-Tekufot be-Halakhah," in *Meḥkarim ba-Sifrut ha-Talmudit* (1983).

Sid Z. Leiman, ed., *The Canon and Masorah of the Hebrew Bible: An Introductory Reader* (1974).

Sid Z. Leiman, *The Canonization of Hebrew Scripture: The Talmudic and Midrash Evidence* (1976).

David Weiss-Halivni, "The Reception Accorded to Rabbi Judah's Mishnah," in E. P. Sanders, ed., *Jewish and Christian Self-Definition,* 2 (1981).

Sanctification of the Name

קידוש השם

Hyam Maccoby

In popular parlance, *kiddush ha-Shem* (sanctification of the Name) has come to mean mainly one thing: martyrdom for Judaism. The antonymic phrase, *hillul ha-Shem* (profanation of the Name) has also come to mean mainly one thing: behavior that brings discredit on Judaism in the eyes of non-Jews. This narrowing of the meaning of the two terms has taken place for good historical reasons, but it has impoverished the theological content of them both and has obscured the antithesis between them. An inquiry into the full theological meaning of the terms will not only bring out the scope of the antithesis in the classical sources, but also put into perspective the place of martyrdom in Judaism.

The original simple meaning of *kiddush ha-Shem* is to show respect for God by one's behavior toward his sanctuary and his priesthood (Lev. 21–22). The Temple area, foodstuffs, and personnel that were dedicated to God's service were to be treated as special, that is, holy. To treat them as merely ordinary (*hol*) constituted disrespect, that is, *hillul ha-Shem*, which thus means "profanation" rather than positive contempt. The priests themselves were especially enjoined to practice *kiddush ha-Shem* in this sense, since their constant presence in the holy area made them especially liable to infringements of respect. Thus, for example, they were enjoined to take particular care over ritual uncleanness; ordinary Israelites, who entered the Temple area infrequently, did not receive such a severe injunction. All the laws of ritual purity are concerned primarily with the duty of *kiddush ha-Shem*. It is thus not a sin to be ritually unclean except in circumstances that constitute *ḥillul ha-Shem*.

So far, then, *kiddush ha-Shem* appears as a system of etiquette applicable to God's house, comparable to the protocol applied in the palaces of earthly kings. Even from this perspective, however, a moral dimension is present, for boorishness and slovenliness are value terms indicating moral faults, namely lack of self-respect and respect for others. Also, a religious dimension, that is, a sense of personal relationship with God, is undoubtedly present, for in all the rules of protocol and etiquette there is an awe and consciousness of the nearness of God. This explains why the rules of ritual purity have relevance not only to the Temple but to mystical experience, as evidenced in the rabbinic *heikhalot* literature. To enter the heavenly palaces, the mystic had to be in an even purer state than is required to enter the earthly Temple.

Nevertheless, it is not easy at first to see how the transition took place from this basic meaning of *kiddush ha-Shem* to the meaning with which the term became especially identified later, martyrdom in the cause of Judaism. It appears that the transition took place through the increasing application of the concept of *kiddush ha-Shem* to the moral sphere. To behave well toward one's fellowman was now regarded as a sanctification of God's Name; to behave badly, as a profanation. Examples are Jeremiah's stigmatization of inhumanity to slaves as *ḥillul ha-Shem* (Jer. 34:16) and Amos's condemnation of oppression and sexual immorality (Amos 2:7).

How did this transition take place? There are several possible explanations, which are not mutually exclusive. (1) Since the moral commandments were given by God, to disobey them is lèse majesté, disrespect to God. (2) Since the Jews are the chosen or priestly people of God, any bad behavior on their part brings discredit on God himself and impedes the progress of ethical monotheism in the world, as well as acting as a bad example to fellow Jews and a discouragement to them in their task of acting as God's priests. (3) Every moral deed carries with it a dimension of *kiddush ha-Shem*, since Judaism is not merely a humanistic ethical system. Of these three explanations, the third is the most important, but some comments are required for each.

The first explanation is of strictly limited validity, since Judaism, contrary to Kant's view, is not a heteronomous religion. A moral commandment is regarded not as an arbitrary fiat of God, but as an expression of the goodness of God, who himself exemplifies the moral qualities (for example, mercifulness, justice) that he requires of his creatures. This explains why the rabbinic writings entertain the possibility that God himself, on occasion, might be in danger of perpetrating moral *hillul ha-Shem*, quite apart from the simpler concept that God might perpetrate *hillul ha-Shem* by failing to advertise himself sufficiently in the world (see, for example, Ezek. 20:9, 14). Abraham, for example, is represented as pointing out to God that it would be *hillul ha-Shem* to destroy Sodom and Gomorrah, since God's moral record would be blemished by his failing to distinguish between the guilty and the innocent (Gen. R. 49:9).

The second explanation is of much wider validity than the previous one, though still not fully adequate. The concept of noblesse oblige has certainly been a spur to good conduct among Jews as among other groups. Its negative version of "not letting the side down" is perhaps even more potent for good, since it introduces the concept of loyalty to one's people and traditions. In all this loyal behavior, however, the idea of sanctification of God is liable to be lost. Instead the concern tends to be merely to avoid bringing discredit on the group to which one happens to belong. Moreover, there are moral dangers in the concept that "We, of all people, should not behave like that"; for even though, in the case of the Jews, the sense of being special has nothing to do with caste or aristocratic birth (by which elitist morality or sense of "honor" is supported in other cultures), but refers only to having been chosen by God as a priest-nation, there is still some danger of confusing the honor of God with one's own. The term *hillul ha-Shem* has never degenerated into meaning merely "an act bringing discredit on the Jewish people," for there is always in it a reference to the Jewish religion, and the task of the Jews to present it creditably to the world in such a way as to advance the recognition of God by all nations. Yet there is a regrettable loss of meaning in the term *hillul ha-Shem* if it is confined to the area of Jewish–Gentile relations, since every immoral act, on a true understanding of the classical sources, carries with it an aspect of *hillul ha-Shem*.

Nevertheless, there remains high moral value in the aspect of *kiddush ha-Shem* evinced in stories such as that of Simeon ben Shetah returning to its owner (a non-Jew) the precious gem found in the fur of an animal he had bought (JT BM 2:5; Deut. R. 3:3). That the Jews stand in a position of special responsibility that they must not betray by behavior questionable even from a supererogatory standpoint is an important principle of great historical force. That behavior constituting *hillul ha-Shem* retards the progress of monotheism and renders meaningless the election and mission of the Jews explains Rabbi Akiva's dictum that *hillul ha-Shem* is the unforgivable sin (ARN 39).

The deepest meaning of *kiddush ha-Shem*, however, is to be found in the third explanation, namely that all right action constitutes worship of God. This concept must be distinguished sharply from heteronomy, a moral system in which an action is right only because it has been decreed by God. On the contrary, while heteronomy reduces all virtues to one, obedience, the concept of *kiddush ha-Shem* raises the value of moral actions to cosmic proportions and enhances the status of man by identifying love of one's fellowman with love of God.

In normal circumstances, right action receives various kinds of societal support and is reinforced by considerations of prudence and approval of one's peers. In certain extreme circumstances, however, all these supports fall away, and the only remaining spur and support to right action other than the rightness of the action itself is the love of God. These are the supreme instances of *kiddush ha-Shem*, since in them *kiddush ha-Shem* has become the central motive, rather than one motive among many.

The most extreme of such situations is that in which the right action can be performed only at the cost of one's life. In such a situation, all the self-seeking motivations that are ordinarily mixed with even the most altruistic act are absent, and only the motive of *kiddush ha-Shem*, the honoring of God, remains. It is this most extreme situation that represents the prime example of *kiddush ha-Shem*.

Yet the rabbinical sources do not support the narrowing of the designation to this situation alone. Thus the case of Joseph's resistance to sexual temptation is regarded as a paradigm of *kiddush ha-Shem*, though this did not involve the sacrifice of his life (BT Sot. 36b). The reason is that this case too was an instance of pure moral choice, where the only influence was the love of God. Joseph was at the extreme of temptation in a strange and unsupportive environment.

It should also be noted that *kiddush ha-Shem* does not necessarily involve any public demonstration of loyalty to God. Joseph's struggle with temptation was intensely private. In the case of martyrdom, the element of public demonstration does enter the picture, but not in the manner associated with the popular meaning of *hillul ha-Shem*, that is, not as a matter of maintaining the credit of Judaism in the eyes of non-Jews. Thus, under certain circumstances, martyrdom is called for in public but not in private; but the definition of "in public" given in this connection is not "in the presence of an audience of non-Jews," but "in the presence of ten Jews." An act such as, for example, the desecration of the Sabbath or the eating of forbidden food, that one is forced to perform in private on pain of death is merely a case of individual sadism or other self-gratification on the part of the persecutor; but if this same act is required to be performed in the presence of a congregation (edah) of ten Jews, it is being given a representative, official character that makes it into an act of apostasy from Judaism. Thus in the first case martyrdom is not required, since in a straight choice between the duty of preserving one's life and the duty of observing the Sabbath or the laws of permitted foods that of preserving life is paramount; but in the second case martyrdom is required, as the alternative is apostasy.

Along with the prohibition against apostasy, two other prohibitions are regarded as more important than the injunction to preserve one's own life, and therefore as providing occasions for martyrdom: that against taking the life of another, and that against sexual depravity (incest or adultery) (BT Sanh. 74a). It is important to note, then, that the concept of martyrdom carries no special mystique in Judaism; it has no sacrificial connotation, and consequently no import of vicarious atonement. It is merely a question of the conflict of duties: on rare occasions, the duty of preserving one's own life may be outweighed by even greater duties. Martyrdom is never to be sought; he who embraces it by failing to seek safety in flight is a sinner, being partly responsible for his own death. Since martyrdom was thus regarded as an occasionally unavoidable necessity rather than as a duty or a sacrament, some rabbis opposed the institution of a special blessing (berakhah) to be pronounced before undergoing martyrdom.

Nevertheless, under the pressure of extreme persecution during the Crusades certain Jewish communities in Germany did invest martyrdom with a mystique, relating it invalidly to the Akedah (binding) of Isaac. This was an understandable if pathetic aberration, which occurred also in certain Hasidic communities during the Nazi persecution. The basic life-affirming meaning of kiddush ha-Shem, however, was reasserted in the halakhic ruling that during the Nazi era the truest kiddush ha-Shem was to preserve one's life if possible, since the Nazi aim was not only to destroy the Jewish religion but the Jews themselves.

Thus the term kiddush ha-Shem, which has been applied especially to martyrdom, does not really belong to it in any unique sense, but is rather a concept that pervades the whole life of a Jew, though in martyrdom it is present in a particularly pure form. It signifies the way in which a Jew, in the performance of all duties and commandments, dedicates this performance to the one God.

BIBLIOGRAPHY

H. G. Friedman, "Kiddush ha-Shem," in *Hebrew Union College Annual* (1924).
Max Kadushin, *Organic Thinking: A Study in Rabbinic Thought* (1938).
Jacob Katz, *Exclusiveness and Tolerance* (1961).
R. J. Zwi Werblowsky, *Joseph Karo: Lawyer and Mystic* (1962).

Science

מדע

Hillel Levine

B eyond providing techniques for coping with life, science
also constitutes a means of conceiving of life. As such, it can
be part and parcel of the efforts of the religious man to make
the cosmos meaningful in human terms. Until the modern period, in
method and in substance science was not wholly differentiated from other
modes of knowing and explaining such as philosophy, mysticism, and
astrology. It has been argued that in the late Middle Ages in Western Christendom theological as well as institutional changes within the church
spurred the growth of empirical science. In the modern period, as the belief
becomes more pervasive that science can solve a growing number of vexing
problems and as new technologies actually begin to change the contours of
day-to-day life, science, its constructs, its admissible facts, its canons of
evidence, and its plausible hypotheses attain a privileged position. The "cult
of useful knowledge" is fostered by, as it instructs, those who seek to shape
society.

What is the role of science as a mode of religious knowledge and a genre
of literature within Judaism? Insofar as Jews lived contiguous to the centers

of scientific exploration in the early modern period, why was their contribution to the beginnings of modern science negligible?

It has often been noted that elements of biblical religion such as the belief in a universal, all-powerful, but transcendental God who created and governs the cosmos but is not identical with nature might have made of the ancient Hebrews, as much as any of their neighbors in the Near East or even in the Greek world, primary candidates to conduct scientific exploration. The intellectualism of rabbinic Judaism might have led to the development of science as one of the Jewish literary genres along with biblical commentary, liturgy, halakhah, and aggadah.

Against these predictions, it must be pointed out that while biblical Judaism downgrades magic and calls for the elimination of potencies separate from God, it does not find the existence of these potencies totally implausible. Strong traditions of folk religion, Gnosticism, and mysticism influenced mainstream Judaism to a varying degree from period to period, thereby mitigating the rigors of monotheism and transcendentalism and tempering the implications of the God of Isaiah who is the author of everything, including evil. These cosmologies made the search for fixed patterns less promising and less rewarding than would be the analysis of a cosmos more strictly governed by conceptions of God's immutable laws or even God's will. Moreover, within the biblical tradition a strong tendency developed to shift the focus of divine concern from nature to history, from space to time. This can be seen in a particularly striking manner in the reconstitution of holy days in the Jewish calendar out of their antecedents in pagan traditions more rooted in pastoral environments.

A growing otherworldliness, resulting particularly from the traumas of the destruction of the First and Second Temples and the loss of political sovereignty, made it difficult for Jews to affirm links between the real and the ideal, between the state of nature as it is and as it should be. Sitting "by the waters of Babylon," memories of Zion rather than insight into the nature of being abounded. External reality and mundane arrangements no longer provided the symbolic molds for spiritual aspirations. This otherworldliness contrasted with the world rejection of Christian monks, for example, who were associated with the majority and dominant societies and for whom monasticism was a choice.

While the study of God's word as represented in Torah took on an expanding significance in rabbinic Judaism, there is no reason to believe, as Max Weber so glibly asserts in *Ancient Judaism* (1917–1919) and *The Sociology of Religion* (1921–1922), that this growing Jewish intellectualism and rationalism were deflected into casuistry or siphoned off by Jewish needs to keep resentment against Gentiles under control, and, therefore, Jewish rationalism did not contribute to the growth of market capitalism, as Weber suggests—or, for that matter, of empirical science.

There are reasons to believe, however, that the need to explain Jewish dispersion and vulnerability and to reconcile the vicissitudes of Jewish history with the beliefs in divine providence and chosenness reduced the curiosity that Jews felt toward nature and, consequently, their involvement in scientific exploration. While the heavens might still declare God's glory, meditation upon nature was to lead not to aesthetic pleasure, conceptual elaboration of its immutable laws, or plausible theodicies based on natural causation, but rather to piety.

Jews demonstrated perspicacity precisely in those areas of scientific investigation such as calendric calculation that had implications for the fulfillment of the precepts. Because of their dispersion and the movement between different Jewish communities, Jews were prominent in mediating scientific knowledge between civilizations from the classical world and the Renaissances of Islam and Christianity. The opportunities for Jews may have been particularly great in medicine because of the personal risks attached to the role of the healer in premodern societies. However, within the large corpus of Jewish literature, the number of original tracts on science, in any sense of the word, is rather small, although a few of those works, such as Isaac Israeli's medical writings and ibn Ezra's astronomical works, were indisputably influential.

Yet Jewish aphorisms register the fact that scientific speculation was taking place. To cite but a few examples, talmudic dicta sentence the best of doctors to hell and praise King Hezekiah for repressing the "Book of Medicine," yet forbid a scholar from living in a city lacking medical personnel. Similarly, categorical admonitions against investigating "what is above and what is below" abide in the rabbinic literature together with the interpretation that Rabbi Jonathan attaches to the verse in Deuteronomy 4:6, "For this is your wisdom and your understanding in the sight of the peoples," according to which the study of astronomy is a matter of national pride as well as an educational imperative. Such divergent positions could be selectively evoked with a full measure of authority in later generations to bolster or to undermine the preoccupation with science.

Rabbi Jonathan's statement points to a particular problem posed by natural science. Beyond those areas of scientific inquiry in which the rabbis justifiably felt that Jews were accomplished, it was clear that even greater strides had been made among the Greeks and other nations. Jewish savants often claimed that science had its origins in Judaism; insofar as scientific knowledge had been forgotten by Jews, it was because of the tribulations of exile. But in later generations, particularly in the early modern period, when the acknowledged gap between Jewish and non-Jewish involvement in science was even broader, it was difficult to support this claim. Consequently, in addition to the debate held among medieval Christian as well as Jewish philosophers on the primacy and authority of different modes of knowledge—faith, tradition, and reason—Jewish scholars had to reconcile truth claims of science with scriptural and rabbinic statements, and assess the valence of "Greek wisdom" while defending Jewish national pride. From Alexandrine syncretism to the efforts of medieval Jewish rationalists to accept Aristotle's physics without his position on creation *ex nihilo*, the study of science called for justification and evoked apologetics among Jewish savants. Various epistemological solutions were developed.

Moses Maimonides, for example, seemingly resolves issues of national pride, epistemology, and metaphysics in one formulation. He argues that Gentiles had some authority in those areas of physics dealing with the sublunary regions. The rabbis, after all, had based their claims in these matters upon calculation rather than revelation, and thus they could be contravened. But in the study of metaphysics, which includes knowledge of superlunary regions, all assertions are nothing but speculation. This distinction averts a clash between rabbinic authority and gentile science. It provides for the possibility of further scientific investigation by claiming uncertainty and insulating the truth claims of faith from science. The domains of physics and metaphysics and their relative authority remained fluid but essentially intact as long as the distinction between sub- and superlunary regions remained ontologically convincing.

Rabbi Judah Loew of Prague defends the study of astronomy but treats it as subordinate to the study of Torah. While echoing the distinction suggested by Maimonides between knowledge of the sublunary spheres and metaphysics, Rabbi Loew proceeds to challenge the authority of gentile scholars even in matters of natural science, thus diminishing the importance of their accomplishments. Nevertheless, and again, in contrast to the position of Maimonides, Rabbi Loew argues that natural science based upon empirical observation is a more reliable mode of knowledge and a stronger basis of piety than metaphysical speculation. In his homilies he describes nature as the messenger of God; this is repeated aphoristically by later writers. The dangers of encroachment of gentile knowledge—particularly cosmology and ontology—upon the meaning of Jewish history are underscored in his reflections upon the Jew in exile, *galut*. The state of exile is the quintessence of the unnatural, sustained by and itself an attestation of God's providence and on-going miracles; therefore, a concept of nature that is so determined as to exclude the intervention of God undermines the conceptual basis of Jewish endurance.

Another epistemological device by which medieval Jewish scholars legitimated the study of science is the famous aphorism whose originator is believed to be Bernard of Chartres, "dwarfs on the shoulders of giants." It is first cited in Jewish sources in the middle of the thirteenth century by Zedekiah ben Abraham Anav in the name of Isaiah ben Mali di Trani. There the aphorism is used to bolster the legal authority of latter-day rabbis against the rulings of their predecessors. From this use it was transposed to the argument in support of the validity of empirical science.

By the end of the sixteenth and beginning of the seventeenth century— the point at which modern science allegedly emerged—Jewish savants such as Rabbi Loew, Azariah de Rossi, and Joseph Solomon Delmedigo had laid the epistemological groundwork for empirical scientific exploration within rabbinic Judaism. It is all the more intriguing, therefore, to speculate as to why Jews seemed not to participate in the development of modern science. Persecution turned the Jews inward; institutional restrictions on study at universities or on participation in the emerging academies of science certainly inhibited Jewish involvement. Jews who were able to overcome these disabilities, such as medical students at the University of Padua or the early-eighteenth-century English Sephardim who were admitted to the Royal Academy of Science, reflect an interest and level of attainment among Jews in science.

Another explanation for the declining interest among Jews in rationalism and empirical science from the end of the sixteenth century relates to the growing influence of the notions of Lurianic kabbalah. This spiritual movement contributed to the resacralization of Jewish Europe just at the moment when those areas of Christian Europe in which science had its most important development, under the influence of the Protestant Reformation, were becoming increasingly desacralized. As kabbalistic beliefs and practices shifted the existential emphasis away from empirical reality, nature was viewed by Jews not so much as an attestation of God's glories but rather as that which separates God and Israel. The constructs of kabbalah explained more than science of what curious Jews wanted to know, and in a more convincing manner. The fear of anthropomorphism (hagshamah) in the wake of the Sabbatean debacle put a damper on mystical investigation. It may have led to reticence in regard to scientific speculation as well.

By the second half of the eighteenth century, the secular absolutist rulers, using state power, promulgated scientific truth claims as self-evidently true.

The distinction between Enlightenment-inspired reform and the more familiar *gezerah*, decree, would be lost upon beleaguered Jews who had to defend both their communal rights and their faith. Consequently, they did not necessarily experience science as universally valid but simply as the source of religious persecution in a new key. The modes by which Jews resisted alien religions could now be used against science.

Nevertheless, at least some Jews, in thinking about the God of Israel in relation to the nature that Gentiles were busily learning to describe and even control, were perplexed. Some traditional Jews sought to continue the work of their medieval predecessors in reconciling science and Judaism. Some sought to compile new encyclopedic presentations of science to obviate the need for Jews to resort to non-Jewish texts. This integrative work was pursued with a greater or lesser degree of conceptual naïveté and scientific simplicity. Still others sought to compartmentalize between the truth claims of science and those of Judaism, assigning a greater scope and degree of importance either to the first, as in the case of Naftali Herz Wessely, whose notion of the law of man included science and ethics while the law of God was limited to religious law and ritual; or to the second, as in the case of Moses Sofer, who downgraded science and emphasized that Judaism deals primarily with questions of law.

By the beginning of the nineteenth century, the division between modernizers and traditionalists was such that the efforts to provide religious legitimations for the study of science and to reconcile the two sets of truth claims became somewhat moribund. In the publicistic literature that developed in the second half of the century, recent technological innovations were glorified more to broaden the vistas of backward brethren than to stimulate new religious thinking. As a basis for the study of science, one finds little of the romantic reaction to Enlightenment and modernization until the rise of political Zionism at the end of the nineteenth century and the beginning of the twentieth; the "natural supernaturalism" of William Wordsworth finds its echoes in A. D. Gordon.

In the modern period, when Jews have had access to training and research institutes, their contribution to science has been disproportionately large, as measured by numbers of Jewish scientists and Nobel Prize laureates. While strictly avoiding the perverse Nazi attributions of a "Jewish science" or some of the banal reductionistic notions of spurious ties, for example, between Judaism and modern psychology, it would still provide an interesting research agenda to consider the elements of the Jewish heritage—cognitive, social, ethical, or existential—that spurred or inhibited this contribution and that may account for certain propensities.

BIBLIOGRAPHY

Salo W. Baron, *A Social and Religious History of the Jews*, 2d ed., 8 (1958).

Julius Guttmann, *Philosophies of Judaism* (1964).

Julius Guttmann, *Dat u-Madah* (1955).

Hillel Levine, "Paradise Not Surrendered: Jewish Reactions to Copernicus and the Growth of Modern Science," in *Epistemology, Methodology and the Social Sciences*, R. S. Cohen and M. W. Wartofsky, eds. (1983).

Moritz Steinschneider, *Jewish Literature from the Eighth to Eighteenth Century*, 2d ed. (1967).

Secularism

חילוניות

Ben Halpern

*S*ecularism, an ambiguous term, may be defined as the tendency to divest religious authority of its control of political, economic, social, and cultural activity.

In modern Jewish history, the idea of secularism is a recent one, discontinuous with the past. Traditional vocabulary does not have terms distinguishing *secular* specifically from *sacral*. The terms *kodesh* (the holy) and *hol* (the profane) refer to a dichotomy both of whose parts are immediately subject to religious law. The only areas of Jewish life in principle outside the exclusive religious jurisdiction of Judaism were those upon which a controlling gentile influence impinged: for example, philosophy and science, characteristically referred to as "foreign" or "external wisdom" (*hokhmah hizonit*). And, indeed, the history of Jewish secularism (unlike secularism in Occidental Christendom, which is a native growth maturing over the whole extent of European history) is the application to Jewish matters of standards carried over from the outside. As a conscious ideology, it is an innovation imported into Jewish history well after the onset of the modern era, conventionally dated in the eighteenth century.

Israel, where a Jewish state has been created, most clearly exhibits expressions of Jewish secularism, but secularism has also existed in Diaspora Jewry, where it first arose. The political and civil emancipation of the Jews in the eighteenth and nineteenth centuries created objective pressures that required renunciation of control over many "profane" activities traditionally subject to Jewish religious law. Judaism, understood as a "religion" in the Western (and Christian) sense, was expected to confine itself to the "holy" matters of belief and ritual, expressed publicly in the synagogue and privately in the home by observers.

Of course, the proclaimed definition of anything as complex as Judaism is never precisely congruent with reality. During the years of rabbinical domination of Jewish culture and institutions, there was always a division of authority between lay and clerical leaders; and while the rabbis by interpretation might bring some "foreign" sources of law under the aegis of Torah, it was primarily lay influence that channeled essentially secular standards into Jewish life. The same might be said, mutatis mutandis, about the Judaism of postemancipation Jewries. While Judaism was conceived as a "religion" confined to roughly the same functions as the contemporary Church in Western Christendom (relinquishing everything "secular" to the nation-state), each Jewish community in fact exercised plainly secular functions, uniting it in every country with other Jewish communities beyond the borders of the state to which it belonged. This was true, in different ways, for both the Reform Judaism that discarded much of tradition and the Western Neo-Orthodoxy that tried to preserve it intact. It was even more pointedly true of those Jews who dropped any connection with the synagogue and yet remained Jews—in their own eyes, as well as others'.

In terms of religious affiliation, postemancipation Jewries exhibited a fourfold division. There were Reform Jews, free to discard traditional rabbinic law; Orthodox Jews, who claimed to preserve it intact: sometimes also "positive-historical" or Conservative Jews, who tried to maintain an intermediate position, and, finally, "unsynagogued" Jews, who neglected or rejected any religious affiliation or practice. Since Orthodox Jews—and for a considerable time, most of the others—strongly rejected intermarriage across religious lines, Jewish ethnic bonds could have been severed (and might still be) if extreme consequences had been drawn from the religious division that took place. Against this outcome there stood the strong force of the common hardships all suffered together by virtue of their Jewishness: a condition that occasioned more or less the same anti-Jewish prejudice and oppression for all, regardless of their religious differences.

This fate shared in common functioned not merely as a barrier against ethnic division in the wake of religious differences. It also served as a secular bond, detached from the strictly religious lines of coherence, which united the Jewish community in positive actions and institutions: in local agencies of social welfare and political intercession and in programs of international action, like those of the Alliance Israelite Universelle or the Jewish Agency for Palestine.

Although such associations and activities were objectively secular, Western postemancipation Jewries preferred to see them as works of charity appropriate for a religious community when undertaken on behalf of its coreligionists. In eastern Europe, however, there arose out of despair of fulfilling the hope of emancipation in a foreseeable time a positive, conscious Jewish secularism, a concept of a secular Jewishness detached from, or in uneasy relations with, traditional Judaism.

The generally anticlerical leaders of the Bund, the Jewish socialist party, eventually found in the culture of Yiddishism (in contrast to Hebrew, which they rejected as both sacral and bourgeois) a national ideology—specifically opposed to "nationalist," that is, Zionist ideology—to ground a secular Jewish identity. Zionism was from the start an unstable combination of religious *(dati)* and secular *(hiloni*—a term invented by modern Hebraists) Jewishness. On the part of the religious Zionists, that is, the Orthodox, cooperation was based on a recognition, usually tacit and provisional, of the legitimacy of claims for a secular Jewish identity. The secular Zionists varied in their attitude to traditional Judaism (whose legitimacy as Jewishness was undeniable, but sometimes regretted) and other types of religious Jewishness. Thinkers like Ahad Ha-An, Judah Magnes, or Solomon Schechter sought to ground their Zionism in humanist or theist values perceived as the quintessence of the evolving Judaic tradition. Others, like Micha Josef Berdyczewski or Joseph Hayyim Brenner, rebelled against the trammels of tradition; their Zionism was a call for the existential freedom of oppressed and desperate Jews, that is, it was radically secular and antisacral.

For all that the State of Israel was founded as a secular polity, it arose subject to certain conditions that diverge from the norms of its historical models. Israeli law has an Ottoman as well as a British base of precedent. It has followed the Ottoman concept of *millets*, combining ethnic with religious division in integrated corporate units recognized in public law. In terms of their personal status—in marriage, divorce, and similar matters— all Muslims (Arabs) come under Islamic law, and all Jews come under Orthodox rabbinic law, while other recognized gentile ethno-religious communities control personal status among their members. It is true that this status is conferred on the sacral establishment by action of the secular parliament and is subject to the overriding jurisdiction of the secular High Court. But when the Orthodox rabbinate controls cardinal questions of personal identity and tends to extend its sway further, the scope of an alternative secular Jewish identity becomes constricted. Moreover, the foundations of a Jewish secular nationalism in the Diaspora have been sapped not only by the destruction of European Jewry, where a secular Jewish culture throve, but by the rise of Israel.

The brief history of the State of Israel has also illuminated another aspect of the limits of Jewish secularism. The prospect of becoming "like all the nations," and the prediction that Israel's peculiar plague, anti-Semitism, would dissipate when the homeless Jews became rooted in their ancestral soil, failed to materialize, and so the chosenness of the Jews was once more freshly perceived. There were also positive, inwardly motivated forces that worked to the same effect.

Secularism in the history of the European nation-state, the model for the Jewish national awakening, was largely a process of gaining control of spheres once under sacral authority. The nation expropriated from the church political legitimacy, historical significance, the arts, language, and literature, and it gave to all these the specific perspective of its national location, replacing the soft, diffused focus of the *ecumene*. Two spheres nevertheless remained beyond nationality: humanistic science, a secular domain common to Western civilization at large; and the domain of ethics, in principle the universal rule for all rational men, but mediated for all Christian nations by the symbolism of the (Occidental or Eastern) church. Thus the nation-states of Europe, liberated through secularism, did not become isolated in their independence, but were a community bound together by shared, institutional values. This is a model that Israel could not replicate completely.

The restoration of Jewish political independence and the revival of Hebrew speech and culture fulfilled some of the model's requirements. The secular humanities and sciences and the technology of Western civilization were fully acquired. But Israel must express universal ethical norms in its own symbolism, rivaling those of the world religions by which other nations are bound together in mythic-moral transnational communities. Israel alone remains isolated in its chosenness.

BIBLIOGRAPHY

Jonathan Frankel, *Prophecy and Politics: Socialism, Nationalism, and the Russian Jews, 1862–1917* (1981).

Ben Halpern, *The American Jew: A Zionist Analysis* (1983).

Henry J. Tobias, *The Jewish Bund in Russia: From Its Origins to 1905* (1972).

Sermon

דרשה

Marc Saperstein

The written records of Jewish preaching in the Middle Ages and early modern period provide important and insufficiently utilized source material for the study of Jewish theology. While it is unlikely that truly original theological ideas are often articulated in sermons, their value is of a different nature. Unlike the more technical, original, and profound books of theological content, which were read by a small segment of the population, the sermon is by its nature intended for the Jewish community as a whole. Sermons therefore reflect not only the beliefs of the preacher, but the preacher's assessment of his congregation's theological sophistication, receptivity, and needs. When ideas from the philosophical or kabbalistic literature begin to appear in sermons, often in a simplified, popular form, linked in a new way with passages from the Bible or rabbinic literature, such ideas can be seen to be spreading to broad circles of the Jewish population.

The theological issues discussed in sermons of a particular period reveal the beliefs that were especially important and problematic at that time. An example is the doctrine of divine providence, including God's knowledge of particular occurrences on earth. This was a standard problem of philosophical theology, pitting a pure Aristotelian theology against the biblical and rabbinic tradition. When preachers spoke to Jewish congregations in the wake of historical upheavals, the problem was much more immediate: Jews wanted to know whether God was responsible for, or even aware of, what had happened. The frequent recurrence of sermons insisting on God's knowledge of particulars and providential concern for the Jews shows a persistent psychological need to affirm God's intimate connection with Jewish suffering.

Occasionally, we find the theological system with which a preacher is working in tension with the emotional needs of the hour. A particularly poignant example is a sermon by Rabbi Israel of Belzec, delivered immediately after the Chmielnicki massacres of 1648. The preacher develops an ingenious explanation of what happened, based on rabbinic statements about Greece, that is, the Greek Orthodox Ukrainian Cossacks, and a simplified form of the Lurianic kabbalah just beginning to have an impact in Poland at this time. This is a mechanistic model: the behavior of Jews causes certain effects in the supernal realm, which in turn affects events on earth. But the preacher begins and ends with emotional appeals to God to rise up and avenge the blood of the martyrs, drawn from biblical rhetoric and a theology quite different from that which informs the body of the sermon.

Unlike their Christian neighbors, Jews had little formal institutional structure to regulate the orthodoxy of doctrines preached. Consequently, the cases in which preachers got into trouble for something they said test the limits of toleration for theological diversity in the community as a whole. Complaints about allegorical interpretations that turned biblical and rabbinic passages into esoteric statements of philosophical doctrines were a central theme in the conflict over the study of philosophy in 1302–1305. In the fifteenth century, traditionalists charged that sermons were filled with syllogistic arguments and quotes from Greek philosophers, while the Torah itself was all but overlooked.

Even the use of philosophical arguments in sermons to support the pillars of Jewish belief met with resistance. According to a contemporary report, a Spanish preacher discussing the unity of God was interrupted by a deeply religious Jew who said, "They seized all of my property in the massacres of Seville [in 1391]; they beat me . . . until they left me for dead. All this I endured through my faith in 'Hear O Israel . . . the Lord is One.' Now you come upon the tradition of our ancestors with your philosophical investigation, saying, 'If He is not One, such and such must follow' [leading to a *reductio ad absurdum*]. I believe more in the tradition of our ancestors, and I have no desire to hear this sermon." With this, the speaker walked out of the synagogue, and most of the congregation followed.[1]

Specific philosophical doctrines also aroused controversy when preached, and leading rabbinic authorities were often consulted. Leone Modena, asked about someone who preached in Amsterdam the Maimonidean doctrine that the world would last forever, concurred that such subjects, about which endless arguments can be given on both sides, are not appropriate for public discussion before a general congregation. When Hakham David Nieto of London was reported to have said in a sermon that "Nature and God are the same," a storm erupted that lasted for two years, finally subsiding after a decision in Nieto's favor by Hakham Zevi Ashkenazi of Altona.

Kabbalistic material became controversial in a later period. Modena, an implacable foe of kabbalah, warned against incorporating kabbalistic doctrines into sermons because of the confusion it might engender in the masses and the possibility of misuse by Christians for polemical purposes. There was an on-going debate about the transmigration of souls. Rabbi Levi ben Habib, an important sixteenth-century rabbinic authority, tried to prohibit public preaching about transmigration. Near the end of the seventeenth century, the popular but learned preacher Elijah ben Solomon Abraham ha-Kohen of Smyrna devoted most of a long sermon to this theme, including the reincarnation of human souls into animals. Justifying himself by appeal to other authorities, he concluded that "it is a mitzvah to make this known to all, to implant it in the minds of the people, for this doctrine helps solve many enormous problems that cause people to turn away from God, such as the problem of the righteous who suffer."[2]

Much of the propaganda for the Sabbatean movement and its theology was carried on by itinerant preachers. The theological radicalism of eighteenth-century Polish preachers has recently been documented in a masterful and provocative study.[3]

For the most part, medieval Jewish preachers would have considered the claim that they were speaking God's word or that God was speaking through them to be overly audacious. Occasionally, to be sure, we find reference to preaching in an ecstatic mode. Rabbi Solomon ben Abraham Adret reports that he heard from reliable sources of a German Jew who astounded the greatest scholars with the sermons he delivered by means of a mystical "Name, called the Preaching Name (*Shem ha-Doresh*)."[4] He also claims to have seen a certain Abraham of Cologne—apparently not a rabbi—who came to Spain and preached in the synagogue of Adret's father, "and all the rabbis present testified that no rabbi in the land could have preached such a sermon."[5]

However, such divine inspiration was generally associated with Christian preaching theory. Isaac Abrabanel suggested that Zechariah 13:2, in which God promises to "make the prophets and the unclean spirit vanish from the land," refers to "certain groups of preachers among the Christians, who claim that the Holy Spirit descends upon them while they are delivering their sermon."[6] Even the appeal for God's help, which became a formal part of the medieval Christian sermon (the *protheme*), was not ordinarily used by Jewish preachers, who spoke rather *be-reshut*, that is, "with the permission" of God, the Torah, the scholars and dignitaries present, and the congregation as a whole.

Where the primary function of the sermon was educational—interpreting biblical verses or rabbinic *aggadot*, showing unexpected connections between different parts of the sacred literature, informing the people about the laws they were expected to observe—there was no need to involve God directly in the theory of preaching. There already existed the model of the rabbi expounding sacred text, and the rabbis had repudiated the claim to direct divine inspiration in this process. Even when the function of the sermon was to provide solace and encouragement for a congregation that had experienced tragedy, the preacher could articulate God's providential concern for the people without claiming to be the mouthpiece for God's own message.

It was the sermon of rebuke and ethical criticism that led in the eighteenth century to new theories making God a more active participant in the preaching event. The literature reveals keen awareness of a painful dilemma. The rebuke of the congregation for their ethical and religious failings was an obligation imposed on the preacher by the Torah and sanctioned by tradition. Yet it was clear that calls to repentance were rarely efficacious, resulting more often in hostility than in a transformation of behavior. And, paradoxically, if unsuccessful in changing conduct, the preaching of rebuke would actually harm the congregation, for once the people had been made fully aware of their sins, they became willful rebels in their transgressions.

In a *Seliḥot* (penitential) sermon of 1757, Rabbi Ezekiel Landau tried to find a way out of this paradox. The preacher is not a prophet; he cannot know in advance whether he will be effective or not, and he must therefore try his best. "When he stands up to deliver his rebuke, the preacher himself does not know how he will marshal his words, with regard either to the content or to the manner of speech. All depends upon the divine inspiration that comes to him, not upon his own merit."[7] If the congregation is ready to respond to his words, God will inspire him with rhetorical power and eloquence so that his message will have an optimal impact. But if the congregation is not prepared to repent, then even if the preacher himself is worthy, God will give no help at all, preferring that the sermon be bumbling and inarticulate so that the punishment for not accepting the rebuke will be less.

Landau's theory posits a dynamic interplay in which the preacher's own merit and abilities are far less important than the degree of divine inspiration, which is determined by the congregation's readiness to accept the message and repent. Eloquence is a sign from God that the congregation will respond, while an ineffective, truncated, stammering sermon is a sign from God that the congregation would not have responded to anything. Psychologically, it seems like an explanation of failure by shifting the blame for bad preaching to the congregation; theologically, it transforms the sermon into an immediate expression of God's will.

Even more radical are theories that emerge from the circle of disciples of the Maggid of Mezhirech. Here the theological stance of quietism, emphasizing the total passivity of the human being, whose individuality all but disappears as he becomes little more than a vessel of God, is fused with a social reality in which the preacher of rebuke is expected to denounce the shortcomings of powerful and ruthless opponents. The accentuation of God's role turns human passivity into a channel for social activism, enabling the preacher (at least theoretically) to criticize the conduct of the most powerful without fearing for his own popularity or well-being. The idea is succinctly expressed in the following quotation:

> One who preaches rebuke with pure motivation must think that the sermon is not his at all . . . but that whatever he says comes from God. If so, there is no reason why he should hold back on his instruction, or fear anyone. He is just like a shofar: something comes in one end and goes out the other. So God places in his heart the words of ethical instruction that he will speak, and each word burns fiercely within, impelling him to utter them. If, on the other hand, he thought that he spoke his own mind, giving of his own knowledge and wisdom, he would refrain from speaking critically when he was afraid of someone.[8]

The image of the shofar is taken from Isaiah 58:1, a verse used in discussions of Jewish preaching at least from the mid-fifteenth century. The fact that this verse was so frequently taken as paradigmatic of the preacher's role shows that at least one aspect of continuity between the prophet and the preacher was assumed. But here the important point is the motif of passivity expressed through the musical instrument. While used in classical Jewish texts with regard to the role of the prophet, this represents a strikingly new conception of the nature of Jewish preaching, in which God is held responsible not only for the manner but for the content of the message, while the preacher is enabled to criticize without fear the imperfections of the society he sees.

The emancipation, the *Haskalah* (Enlightenment), and the Reform movement brought fundamental changes to Jewish preaching in the nineteenth century. Different in aesthetic mode and theological content from the traditional sermons surveyed in this article, and openly influenced by Christian homiletical models, the "modern Jewish sermon" remains a valuable source of evidence for the diffusion of new ideas through western European Jewry.[9] The systematic study of twentieth-century American sermons for their theological content is a task that has hardly even begun.

REFERENCES

1. Ḥayim ibn Musa, "Letter," published by David Kaufmann, *Beit ha-Talmud* 2 (1882), 118. This and other sources discussed below are included in the forthcoming *Jewish Preaching 1200–1800*, by Marc Saperstein (Yale Judaica Series).
2. *Midrash Eliyahu*, Sermon 3 (1860), 17d.
3. Mendel Piekarz, *Be-Yamei Ẓemiḥat ha-Ḥasidut* (1978), especially 175–302, 383.
4. Solomon ben Abraham Adret, *Responsa* 1 (1958), 548.
5. Ibid.
6. Isaac Abrabanel, *Commentary on Prophets and Writings* (1960), 241b.
7. Ezekiel Landau, *Ahavat Ẓiyon* (1966), 2a.
8. Benjamin ben Aaron of Zalozce, *Torei Zahav*, 56d, quoted in Rivka Shatz-Ufenheimer, *Ha-Ḥasidut ke-Mistikah* (1980), 117–18.
9. See Alexander Altmann, "The New Style of Preaching in Nineteenth-Century German Jewry," in *Studies in Nineteenth-Century Jewish Intellectual History* (1964), 65–116.

BIBLIOGRAPHY

Israel Bettan, *Studies in Jewish Preaching* (1939).
Joseph Dan, *Sifrut ha-Musar ve-ha-Derush* (1975).
Louis Jacobs, *Theology in the Responsa* (1975), Index, s.v. "Preaching."
Marc Saperstein, *Jewish Preaching, 1200–1800* (forthcoming).

Silence

דומיה

André Neher

Silence forms an integral part of the Jewish theology of the covenant. Indeed, in the dialogue between God and man established by the covenant, silence is more than simply a pause, a hiatus without significance or content. It is as essential to the understanding of the revealed message as is a musical pause to the understanding of a piece of music. Silence is not an interruption of the word: it is its reverse, its alternative, its other face, or, once again to use the biblical metaphor, it represents the "hidden" face of God as against the "visible" face represented by the word.

The silence of God in the Bible can be understood first of all as a sign of reproof or anger. God, when consulted, is silent because the person who consults him is in a state of sin or error. This is the interpretation given by the priestly oracle of the *Urim ve-tummim* (the device for obtaining oracles that is attached to the breastpiece of the priest's garment), when the priest, instead of answering the consultant positively or negatively, is silent and refuses to reply. This ritual aspect also extended to the consultation of the prophets. The man in a state of sin who comes to consult a prophet receives confirmation of his sin from the prophet's refusal to reply to him. In I Samuel 28:6 this principle is applied to King Saul. Saul's excruciating solitude and morbid sense of guilt were exacerbated by the fact that he failed to receive an answer through any of the channels usually provided by God: "And Saul inquired of the Lord, but the Lord did not answer him, either by dreams or by Urim or by the prophets." In chapter 20 of the Book of Ezekiel we find this principle extended to the entire people of Israel: a group of elders, representing the people before the prophet, are informed that because of their many sins enumerated in that chapter they will not receive an answer to their questions: "I will not respond to your inquiry." And this is also the interpretation that must be given to the prophet's declaration in the first two chapters of the Book of Amos. The peoples of the Middle East—Damascus, Tyre, Ammon, Moab, Edom, Israel, and Judah—come, through the intermediacy of the prophet, to inquire of God concerning the Assyrian menace, but the prophet answers: "Because of three transgressions and because of four, lo ashivenu—I will not revoke it!" This leitmotif of a refusal to answer represents an answer in itself: God wraps himself in silence because the peoples, owing to their sins, are unworthy of hearing God. It is precisely this silence that is the sign of their deep guilt.

The psychological projection of this aspect of silence is the state of panic described in a number of psalms (for example, 30:8 and 143:7) before the reality or simply the possibility of God hiding his face—a metaphor for his silence. If God hides his face and refuses to speak, it means that man is unworthy to live and must return to nothing. This nothingness or void is described by the term duma (stillness), which is synonymous with sheol (the nether regions, Hades), but with a root that denotes the silence of night and death.

While assimilating this negative aspect of silence, the major prophets—Isaiah, Jeremiah, Ezekiel—endowed it with a positive function by placing it within the biblical dialectic of catastrophe and salvation. The metaphor of the hidden face and silence of God thus became a distinctive feature of the prophetic theology of history. God's declaration in Isaiah 54:7: "For a little while I forsook you, But with vast love I will bring you back," interprets the idea of silence qua anger and the word qua compassion in terms of an eternity of compassion in which silence lasts but a moment. One has here a polarity of word and silence in which the fearfulness of the anger embodied by the silence is eliminated, insofar as the silence is only a form of stress whose resolution is virtually assured.

Silence may also be a vehicle of divine revelation. In this respect it is even more important than the word, for it acts as a paradoxical criterion of the truth of prophecy. The problem of distinguishing between true prophecy and false is not only a theoretical and hypothetical one in the Bible (see Deut. 18:21–22): some prophets experience it existentially, and in a rather touching manner. They ask themselves whether they are not victims of an illusion, a fantasy. Faced with other prophets who, like themselves, claim to be sent by the God of Israel and who prophesy a message opposite to their own, they seek a criterion that will enable them "to divide the straw from the wheat" (Jer. 23:28), and they find that criterion in silence. The false prophets are loquacious: they always find something to say. If necessary they "steal" the word like thieves. For the true prophets, on the other hand, prophecy is a divine endowment, a rare gift that is sometimes given, sometimes withheld. It is a burden the prophet assumes against his will. The noncommunication between God and the prophet expressed in the periods of silence provides the prophet with the proof of the genuineness of his prophecy. This principle was expounded at length in Jeremiah and experienced by him when the people consulted him after the murder of Gedaliah (Jer. 42). Despite the urgency of the situation, which would have prompted a false prophet to think up an answer on the spot, Jeremiah was constrained by God to remain silent for the long period of ten days, a delay that showed the authenticity of his message (Jer. 42:7).

God's silence is also a test of man's faith. Hence, man is occasionally subjected by God to a test as a metal is subjected to fire in order to see if it is able to withstand it and, at the same time, to come out strengthened from the process. Every test has a specific duration: it has a purpose and it has an end. Between the beginning and the end there is a period of suspense in which one necessarily finds the silence of God. This silence perforce fills the vacuum that has been created by divine will.

The classic example of God's silence as a test is the story of the sacrifice of Isaac, the *Akedah* in Genesis 22: for three long days filled with the heavy silence of God, Abraham and Isaac journeyed toward Mount Moriah, the site where the sacrifice was to take place. There are many other stories in the Bible that illustrate this theme, even if the term *test (nisayon)* does not specifically appear. In the long dramatic story of Joseph there is a period of twenty-two years of divine silence (Gen. 37:1–46:2) from the moment when Joseph leaves his father until their reunion in Egypt—a period as trying for the father as it is for the son. The Book of Esther is another example: not only is God silent throughout the story, he is not even mentioned. The very name of Esther (from the Hebrew root *hester*, hidden) draws attention to the fact that this whole episode, in which the fate of the Jewish people hangs in the balance, takes place before the hidden face of God and surrounded with his silence.

Although in general the test concludes with a "happy ending," in the

Book of Job it is different. Here the suspense resulting from God's silence is the most long-drawn-out (stretching from chapters 3 to 37), the most troubling, and the most problematic. The prologue is a kind of trial held in camera, and although the epilogue partly restores Job to his previous condition, it does not give him back his children who were taken away from him at the beginning. Unlike Abraham in the *Akedah* and the patriarch Jacob, Job, although blessed with new offspring, does not regain the children he has lost. The structure of the test in the Bible is not necessarily that of the tale of the Sleeping Beauty. The test can go wrong. The silence of God can have tragic implications, especially, as we see in the case of Job, where this tragic silence involves a man who is essentially innocent.

The case of Job does not represent something exceptional and unique in the Bible. On the contrary, it is a reflection of the normal situation of every human being before the creator within the framework of the covenant. God's silence encompasses every man, and man's sense of wonder before the creation reaches its climax in the feeling of wonder he expresses before silence. What particularly strikes the psalmist in the symphony of the heavens that "relate" the glory of God is that this tribute of the creation to the creator is a silent tribute: "There is no utterance, there are no words, whose sound goes unheard" (Ps. 19:4). This silent tribute of the cosmos finds its counterpart in the silent tribute of man. Himself a part of the creation, man too cannot conceive the absolute of praise to the creator otherwise than in terms of silence: "To Thee, silence is praise" (Ps. 65:2).

The silence of nature, which evokes feelings of admiration in the psalmist, is experienced problematically by Job (Job 37:1–42:7). It is in these verses that God finally breaks his long silence, but only in order to replace the ethical silence with a meta-ethical silence. When God decides to speak, it is through his creation. He speaks out of a whirlwind (Job 38:1), which has the effect of making his word unintelligible and incapable of answering Job's cries and questions, so that, faced with the heavy silence of the "hidden God" of the creation, Job too can respond only with silence (40:3–4; 42:6).

A similar lesson follows from the story of the prophet Elijah in chapters 18 and 19 of the first book of Kings, which constitutes a kind of diptych with contrasting panels. In chapter 18—the scene on Mount Carmel—Elijah used the word as a test in order to demonstrate the validity of the true God: "The God that answer, let him be God" (I Kings 18:24). The success of this test, however, was only presumed, for in historical fact the scene on Carmel was a failure. Jezebel's convictions remained unaffected by it, as Elijah himself learned a few days later, and in the contrasting scene on

Mount Horeb he discovered that as much as or even more than in the word and in the fire, the authentic revelatory voice of the true God is to be found in *kol demamah dakkah,* the "thin voice of silence" (I Kings 19:2). In this diptych silence changed its direction: "The living God," cried the people in chorus in the scene on Carmel, "is the God of the word and the response," but in the scene upon Horeb the prophet Elijah learned in his solitude that the living God was the God of silence.

The prophet Isaiah was also acquainted with this living God of silence. In a verse remarkable for its doctrinal and philosophic formulation Isaiah declared: "You are indeed a God who concealed Himself" (Isa. 45:15). This formula of the hidden God was later to develop a universal application, nearly always cosmic and mystical, in all the religious philosophies that grew out of the Bible or were inspired by it, but in the Bible itself the phrase had an ethical and historical meaning. In the actuality of a particular moment of his history and that of his people, Isaiah faced the hidden God and laid a wager on the unknown and on its silence, drawing from this experience an ethical lesson of hope: "So I will wait for the Lord, who is hiding His face from the House of Jacob, and I will trust in Him" (Isa. 8:17). Isaiah here expressed the usual attitude of biblical man to the silence of God: he felt it as a challenge to his faith. Between hope and the absurd— abandoning his faith—he chose hope. By that choice he responded to silence, which he thus accepted as the supreme form of the word—the word of a God who, through his silence, sought to bring man to assume his responsibilities, that is, his capacity of responding, within the dialogue of the covenant.

In postbiblical Jewish literature, we find the theme of silence applied to the tragic theme of martyrdom, or *kiddush ha-Shem.* It became its necessary ethical precondition: it is only when God is completely hidden in silence that martyrdom becomes truly a sanctification of his name. The Midrash (Shir ha-Shirim R. 7:8) traces this idea to the Bible. According to this mid-rash, Daniel's three companions, Hananiah, Michael, and Azariyah, were the men who came to consult the prophet Ezekiel in chapter 20 of the Book of Ezekiel. God's refusal to reply to them, transmitted through the prophet, was intended to create an area of silence in which the three men could show whether they were ready to experience martyrdom. They gave proof of this readiness by the two crucial words *hen-lo* (even if not), which they flung at their persecutor Nebuchadnezzar when cast into the fiery furnace: "But even if He does not [deliver us], be it known to you, O king, that we will not serve your god or worship that statue of gold that you have set up!" (Dan. 3:18). The English rabbinic scholar Israel Abrahams claimed that these two words, *hen-lo*, represent one of the permanent values in Jewish thought: they are the source of the theme of "nevertheless," which remains characteristic of Jewish thinking and Jewish attitudes through the present day.

In the twentieth century, the trauma of the Holocaust has led to a systematization of the Jewish theology of silence. The analysis of silence has generally centered around the *Akedah* and the Book of Job. As Stefan Zweig pointed out, the Holocaust has reawakened the "eternal question of Job" in the Jewish consciousness.[1] The Jewish fate has been associated with the trial of Job, which took place within the isolation of God's silence; Margarete Susman has suggested that the character of Satan in that book embodies the mysterious presence of evil in history.[2] The modern reinterpretation of the biblical metaphor of the hidden face reveals a new probing of silence, and Martin Buber invented a new and audacious expression to describe it: the "eclipse of God."[3]

The rabbinic and medieval treatment of silence has also been reworked and enriched by various twentieth-century poets and writers. In the work of Itzhak Katznelson, Nelly Sachs, Elie Wiesel, Shin Shalom, and Shmuel Yosef Agnon there are many variations on the theme of the martyrs of the Holocaust, whom the poet Uri Zvi Greenberg called succinctly "*kedoshei dumiah*—the martyrs of silence."[4] An ambivalence between an attitude of revolt and of submission that was inherent in the medieval treatment of the theme of martyrdom persists in the approach of these modern writers to the silence of God, but in general a sense of indignation prevails over an attitude of submission. Those who adopt an attitude of rebellion often refer back to Rabbi Menahem Mendel of Kotsk. As for the submissive approach, when it is not purely religious it relates to the atmosphere of hopeless entanglement that characterizes the stories and characters of Franz Kafka, and then it is no longer a matter of submission but of an existential situation within the ontological silence of man.

Thus, all the Jewish approaches to silence from the Bible onward recur in the Jewish interpretations of the silence of the Holocaust, but these interpretations generally appear scattered in various texts in a fragmentary and unrelated manner. This writer, however, has attempted a systematic, comprehensive treatment of the subject in *The Exile of the Word*, which examines the implications of the silence of the Holocaust from a Jewish standpoint. The work locates the heart of the theological problem of silence in the Holocaust in the fact that in the Holocaust both God and man, the two partners bound together in a spoken dialogue through the covenant, withdrew into silence simultaneously. In their mutual silence there appeared a void into which a third force, evil, introduced itself. This radical evil, symbolized in the Book of Job by Satan, found its historical incarnation in the Holocaust. It constitutes a challenge to the word of man, and the response to that challenge can only take the form of a wager. Just as Job wavered and ultimately had to choose between despair and hope, so man, faced with the silence of the Holocaust, is obliged to decide between these two polar responses to divine silence. This choice is a wager between the historical actuality of silence and the metahistorical potential of the word. Indeed, the Jewish attitude to silence is characterized by recurring attempts to create the word anew by means of a wager upon life. The creation of the State of Israel soon after the Holocaust is an expression of this phenomenon in the form of a wager upon the renewal of the life of the Jewish people in the biblical land of the word. The termination of the historical exile through *shivat Zion* (the return to Zion) means the end of the exile of the word and the metaphysical return from the actuality of silence toward the potentiality of the word.

REFERENCES

1. Stefan Zweig, *Die Welt von Gestern* (1955), 389.
2. Margarete Susman, *Das Buch Hiob und das Schicksal des jüdischen Volkes* (1968).
3. Martin Buber, *Eclipse of God: Studies in the Relation Between Religion and Philosophy* (1957).
4. Uri Zvi Greenberg, "Kedoshei Dumia," in *Reḥovot Ha-Nahar.* (1951), 216.

BIBLIOGRAPHY

Martin Buber, *Eclipse of God* (1952).
André Neher, *The Exile of the Word: From the Silence of the Bible to the Silence of Auschwitz* (French edition, 1970; American edition, 1981).
George Steiner, *Language and Silence*, 2d ed. (1970).
Elie Wiesel, *The Gates of the Forest* (1966).

Sin

חטא

Adin Steinsalz

The Hebrew language, in both biblical and postbiblical literature, has numerous names for the concept of sin, each with its own unique sense and shade of meaning. Moreover, from the books of the Bible—especially the prophets—to the latter-day homiletic writings, Jewish literature is filled with reproachful discourses inveighing against all manner of sins.

Nevertheless, the concept of sin in and of itself is never fully developed or clarified in Judaism. Despite the existence of so many definitions of an endless variety of sin, and despite the stern reproof voiced against sin and sinners, concern with sin itself occupies an insignificant place in Jewish thought. The problem of sin (and even, to a large extent, the problem of evil) is, in effect, treated as a secondary issue. Sin is viewed as a correlate of *mizvah*; it is treated not as a separate, independent entity but rather as a shadow-essence or even, at times, a reverse image of *mizvah*. The concept of sin and the attitude taken toward it thus stem directly from how *mizvah* is understood. For example, Judaism divides the world of religious activity into two groups of commandments, positive and negative. Since sin is defined, from both a halakhic and a theological point of view, as the negation of *miẓvah,* where positive commandments are concerned it consists of abstention and where negative commandments are concerned it consists of action. In every case, that is to say, it is conceived as the negation of something else, and not as an independent entity in its own right.

The several theological understandings of sin to be found in Judaism are not concepts in their own right, and several of them appear in the extensive religious literature only by way of allusion. We arrive at them by first understanding the definition of *miẓvah* and then drawing conclusions with regard to the meaning of sin. But the various concepts of the nature of the *miẓvot* are only rarely to be found in distinct and defined form, and far more frequently (even in the case of fairly systematic thinkers) several of them come into play at once. The concept of sin, too, thus often has several ideational components coexisting alongside one another.

One conception of *miẓvah* sees its principal significance in the divine command. The performance of a *miẓvah* is essentially an act of obedience, through which man approaches God by accepting the yoke of heaven, the supernal discipline. Sin, from this point of view, is thus primarily an act (by deed or default) of rebellion. The sinner is one who will not obey, one who, on account of external or internal factors, refuses to accept the "sovereignty of heaven" and prefers a different kind of rule, whether it be that of other men, other gods, or his own appetites. This conception in a sense gives equal value to all of the *miẓvot,* in that all of them alike express man's acceptance of the sovereignty of God. All sins, similarly, can be reduced to a single one—that of disobedience.

Another understanding of *miẓvah* conceives of it as the right way, the straight and good path. The commandments, for example, as an expression that has its source in the *Zohar* would have it, are viewed as God's good counsel for man, his revelation of the true path that it is natural and right for man to follow as he makes his way through life. Sin, then, is conceived as a straying or deviation from this natural path. If it is committed unwittingly, it is the consequence of a mistake, of lack of knowledge or understanding. If, on the other hand, it is committed intentionally, it is essentially an act of perversity, an intentional distortion of nature. This conception, too, does not make a qualitative distinction between sins of different kinds. In a psychological sense, however, it does differentiate between obvious, easily recognizable distortions and those that can be known only to one who has already learned the true path.

Another conception views the *miẓvah* essentially as an act of rectification or completion. The world is not a fully perfect entity, and the task of the *miẓvah* is to bring about the perfection that is lacking. Sin, then, is essentially the want of something, a defect in reality; if a sin is one of default, it consists of a failure to rectify some aspect of the world or of man, while if it is one of deed the sinner has added to the imperfection of reality. Man, possessing free will, is the active force in the world, and he is therefore its guardian and keeper. When he does not fulfill this function he blemishes reality or allows it to deteriorate. In this view man is not the exclusive subject of *miẓvah* or of transgression but rather an instrument, an implement in the service of reality as a whole, in which he exists both as an active agent of influence and change and as a passive part.

These conceptions appear in most ethical and theological discussions in various combinations. The same thinker will at times emphasize one aspect of the problem while in other contexts viewing *miẓvah* and sin from a different perspective. Nevertheless, a deeper look will show that all these approaches have a common denominator: They do not see evil as a concrete subject or entity existing in and of itself. Even in those descriptions that view the history of the world or the inner spiritual life of man as a battle between good and evil, evil is not grasped as an essence to be defined independently. It is but the "other side" (*sitra aḥra,* in the terminology of the kabbalah) of reality, which is good, and it has no existence or essential definition of its own.

This view of evil as something purely negative is found in a great many Jewish sources, despite the differences among them. The evil deed is viewed as an empty activity, an exercise in futility, a meaningless labor that must come to nothing. Evil is merely "chaos" or "vanity," not an entity in its own right.

Another common aspect of the different attitudes toward *miẓvah* (and so also toward sin) is their view of individual actions within the framework of a comprehensive whole. Despite each man's individual responsibility and obligations, he functions as an integral part of the world as a whole. Moreover, this is not only a matter of the societal influences he exercises upon his surroundings. Even a sin committed privately and in secret is part of this comprehensive fabric, just as the *miẓvah* incumbent upon each individual is part of the comprehensive network of relations between the creator and the world. Sin, however it is conceived, not only blemishes the connection between a particular person and his creator, but also corrupts the general quality of the relations between God and man. That is why there is a need for extensive individual involvement in the conduct of society, why each individual has an obligation to concern himself with the *miẓvot* and sins of his fellow, and why society as a whole has an obligation and responsibility toward its individual members. The influence of the defect caused by a single sin, by its very commission, extends to the people as a whole and even to the world as a whole.

Nevertheless, sin and the sinner, as we have said, are but shadows of the network of divine–human relations, and they are not a subject for study in and of themselves. Even scholars who have studied and held forth upon the good qualities for which man should strive have not concerned themselves with defining bad qualities in their own right. Bad qualities can be defined only within the context of the world of *mizvot,* and not beyond it. We might say, in fact, that the qualities of the soul are objective entities that can be evaluated as good or bad only in terms of how they relate to the sacred domain. Certain of these qualities, to be sure, are generally considered worthy of reproach: jealousy, lust, striving for personal honor, pride, laziness. Even these reprehensible qualities, however, are not evaluated in terms of their intrinsic nature, but only in relation to their specific context or in light of the manner in which they are manifested. We see in the Bible that even qualities or deeds that would normally have a negative connotation can at times, in different contexts, express positive motivations (cf. the varying expressions of "jealousy" in Numbers 5:14 and 25:11, 13).

Even traditional Jewish works on the problems of ethics concern themselves primarily with describing the right way and scarcely treat the problem of sin and the sinner. Rather, these works focus almost exclusively on exhorting their readers or explaining to them how they are to do good or attain to a higher level of righteousness or piety. We likewise find very few inquiries into the psychology of the sinner or the question of what causes man to sin. To be sure, the disregard of this subject is to be explained in part by the pessimistic view generally taken of man's nature. The presumption that "the devisings of man's mind are evil from his youth" (Gen. 8:21) appears already in the Scriptures, and this evaluation has not changed much with the passage of time. Precisely because evil is not grasped as an independent entity, however, man's attraction to it is seen as stemming not from a specific pull toward perversity but rather from other factors that have primarily to do with his weaknesses and not with some particular wicked quality. The conflict between body and soul often cited as an explanation for man's inner struggle is not really a conflict between good and evil; it occurs, rather, on account of man's preference for a partial, immediate view of things over a more comprehensive understanding, for the good of the moment over that which is everlasting, or, sometimes, on account of an incongruence between the merely pleasant and the truly desirable. Sin is also at times defined as forgetfulness, as a situation in which man temporarily fails to recall his obligations and his true needs and concerns himself with other things instead. Following another classical explanation, according to which "man sins only when a spirit of foolishness has entered him" (BT Sot. 3a), sin may also be seen as an act of foolishness or self-delusion. Knowing transgression and even conscious rebellion stem only from error, whether it lies in a failure to see things in their proper proportion or in a generally misguided understanding.

The approaches we have outlined do not necessarily lead to sin and the sinner's being seen in a forgiving light, but they do make a difference as to how the significance of punishment is understood, both where the punishment is meted out by heaven and where it is meted out by society. Punishment from heaven is viewed not as revenge but rather as the natural consequence of distortion or error. Just as deviation from or rebellion against the laws of nature really harms only the person who is at fault, so too in the case of deviation from the *miẓvot*. The principal purpose of punishment by society is also seen as rectification, either of the world as a whole (which has been blemished and perverted by the sinner or by his action) or of the individual sinner. Improving one's ethical conduct, moreover, lies not in exercising greater strength in the act of choice but in activating or raising one's consciousness. The higher mankind's level of consciousness, the less possibility there is for sin. The bearer of reproach, from the very earliest image of the prophet, has always been described as the man of clear vision; his function is to awaken others, to teach them to see and to guide them to a more perfect understanding.

BIBLIOGRAPHY

David Daube, *Sin, Ignorance and Forgiveness* (1960).
Adin Steinsalz, *The Essential Talmud* (1976), 85ff.
Adin Steinsalz, *The Thirteen Petaled Rose* (1981).
Ephraim E. Urbach, *The Sages: Their Concepts and Beliefs* (1975), 420–523.

Soul

נפש

Rachel Elior

The development of the Jewish conception of the soul has been determined by two basic, contradictory attitudes regarding the soul's nature and its relationship to the world. The one views man as a psychophysical unity, while the other claims a separate metaphysical existence for the soul. The former conception, founded on the biblical worldview, has little religious significance; it considers the soul subordinate to time and nature, existing within the confines of physical reality alone. The latter view, which developed under the influence of Greek ideas regarding the metaphysical, immortal nature of the soul, radiates deep religious significance.

The decisive Jewish conception of the soul is thus founded to a large extent upon the assumption that man does not, fundamentally speaking, belong to the natural world; his essential being is not corporeal, for its source is divine; and the temporal and spatial distinctions governing nature do not apply to it; that is to say, the soul's existence does not depend upon its physical expression, for it existed before the body and will remain after it. The definition of man is therefore fundamentally metaphysical, belonging to the supernatural order, and the laws governing the soul are therefore neither physical nor rational, but metaphysical. It is from this point of departure that Judaism's attitude toward the nature and function of the soul and its role in religious thought are determined.

The severance of the soul from existential experience and its bursting of the bounds of physical reality are expressed in the development of the doctrine of preexistence, in the theurgical orientation of the kabbalah, in the development of ideas of reincarnation and postexistence, and in eschatological conceptions of the soul's ultimate destiny. The pivotal role played by the metaphysical view of the soul in shaping classical Jewish religious thought is explained by the fact that apart from its divine source, as expressed by the idea that man was created "in the image of God," the soul partakes of the divine in that it represents orders of existence that transcend time and nature. An interesting consequence of this orientation is that the Jewish conception of the soul is without anthropocentric interest. Its interest is entirely theocentric, for it is concerned with the soul only in its metaphysical manifestations. It dwells upon the mutual influences reciprocated by the human soul and its divine source. Its point of departure is God, not man. A further dimension of this theocentric interest is reflected by the fact that the Jewish conception of the soul is not primarily concerned with man's life in the present, but with what preceded it and what will follow after it; such an outlook perforce focuses its attention upon metahistory and eschatology rather than upon history. Even where it does concern itself with the present, its interest is in the ability of the soul to burst out of the confines of physical existence and unite with the divine.

According to the prevalent anthropocentric view, it is man's existence that expresses the relationship between God and his world, and it is in relation to man that God's kingship and providence are effective. The doctrine of the soul, however, takes an opposite, theocentric view, for it sees man's existence as having meaning only in relation to God. As he actualizes his potential metaphysical essence, man simultaneously distances himself further and further from his physical, material substance. The guarantee of his capacity to attain the realm of the spirit is to be found in the internal structure of his soul, which ascends level by level from the material to the spiritual. If man is created in the divine image and so has a fundamental relationship to God and an innate ability to serve him, it is by virtue of the structure and elements of his soul, which reflect the divine reality and endow him with the capacity to conceive of God.

The idea that man's essence is directed toward the spiritual dimension of existence, by which the divine aspect of his soul is drawn from the realm of the potential to that of the real, is bound up with the concept of the perfection (shlemut) of man. Man does not belong to the natural order, which is complete in itself. Rather, he is viewed *ab initio* as being destined for perfection in a realm transcending that order. This notion of perfection, which shapes the purpose of man, thus relates to him as a supernatural rather than a natural being. It is by means of the Torah and its commandments, in the various ways in which these are understood in relation to the soul, that man's supernatural purpose can be realized. The Torah and the commandments are viewed as a force acting upon man to make his hidden metaphysical dimension a reality, that is, to expose the divinity of his soul and reunite it with its source. They are the points of contact between man and his metaphysical aspect, for it is by virtue of them that he can make his spiritual breakthrough from the confines of his physical existence, both during the course of his life and—since it is the Torah and the commandments that determine his spiritual fate—in time to come.

The Jewish doctrine of the soul, in its passage from its biblical beginnings to the later versions wrought by philosophy, the kabbalah, and Ḥasidic thought, has undergone a far-reaching transformation. In the Bible, body and soul are viewed as one, and existence and meaning are attributed to the soul on the physical, human, and historical plane. With the passing of time, however, the soul came to be viewed as a metaphysical entity that belonged to, affected, and was affected by the realm of the divine, transcending the confines of history and nature. The biblical conception, as noted, views the soul as part of the psychophysical unity of man, who, by his very nature, is composed of a body and a soul. As such, the Bible is dominated by a monistic view that ascribes no metaphysical significance to human existence, for it sees in man only his tangible body and views the soul simply as that element that imparts to the body its vitality. The soul is, indeed, considered the site of the emotions, but not of a spiritual life separate from that of the body, or of a mental or emotional life in conflict with that of the body; it is, rather, the seat of all of man's feelings and desires, physical as well as spiritual.[1] Such a conception views the entire entity of man as a "living soul," or, to put it in our terms, a psychophysical organism created in the image of God, whose existence has religious significance within the reality of time and place alone. Nevertheless, the fact that man is defined as having been created in the image of God allowed for the expansive development of postbiblical thought.

The talmudic conception of man has its roots in the biblical worldview, but it was also influenced by developments in religious thought and by ideas current in the postbiblical world, especially within Hellenism, which embraces the possibility of the soul's simultaneous existence on both a physical and a spiritual level.[2] Although in rabbinic texts we find the heritage of the biblical conception regarding the psychophysical unity of the soul, under Greek influence there begins to develop alongside it a moderately dualistic anthropology suggesting a different status for body and soul.[3]

Once belief in the immortality of the soul, the revival of the dead, and the World to Come had become part of postbiblical Judaism, its religious view of man in relation to the world underwent a change. The religious significance of the world was no longer limited by concrete reality or by its psychophysical expression in a human entity, which consisted of a united body and soul existing within historical time. Alongside that reality was another, different one, which looked beyond the historical present and future. Thus, Judaism began to adopt a transcendental view of history and the meaning of human existence, and at the same time to view the soul as existing on a spiritual plane. It began, too, to speak of the soul remaining beyond the demise of the body, and of a spiritual life beginning prior to material existence.[4]

The rabbinic view of the soul as an entity having a spiritual character and as a fixed, defined metaphysical element almost certainly developed under the influence of Orphic and Platonic Greek thought. We may assume, too, that the Greek view of the soul as belonging to the realm of the divine, infinite, and eternal, and the body to the realm of the material, finite, and mortal, also left its mark upon Jewish thought. Plato's idea of the preexistence and eternity of the soul, derived from his dualistic outlook, which set matter and spirit at odds with one another, was also influential. We must bear in mind, however, that for all that the dualistic anthropology expressed in the rabbinic texts had in common with the Platonic and Stoic attitudes current in the Hellenistic world, the rabbinic sages' conception of this dualism and of the conflict between flesh and spirit was far less radical than that of the Greeks, who viewed body and soul as an absolute dichotomy.[5]

The dualistic conception of man in which body and soul are diametrically opposed bears within it, in addition to its metaphysical significance, the first stirrings of a religious striving toward the ideal of liberating the soul from the bonds of the physical, thereby enhancing its spiritual purity. This kind of outlook was entirely foreign to biblical Judaism, but became highly developed in medieval thought and especially in the kabbalah.

Having accepted the idea of the divine essence of the soul, Judaism now had to elaborate the nondivine, more vital and functional aspects of the human soul. This need to elaborate, as well as the influence of Greek thought, led to the development of the distinctions between the soul's material and spiritual elements, between its intellectual, vital, and vegetable natures, and between the divine soul and the animal soul. These divisions gradually yielded symbols of spirit and matter, of nonbeing (*ayin*) and being (*yesh*).

In later stages of development, the Jewish conception of the soul was influenced by Greek philosophical views, as these were reformulated and interpreted by the Moslem and Christian theologians of the Middle Ages. For the first time, Judaism viewed the doctrine of the soul as belonging to the realm of philosophy, and medieval Jewish thought made a unique attempt to adapt these philosophical views to the Torah and to make them a means for interpreting concepts relating to ethics, religious piety, prophecy, and the knowledge of God. Medieval Jewish thought focused its attention on the one hand on the immortality of the soul and the relationship between body and soul, or between matter and spirit, and on the other on the hierarchy of the upper worlds and the theory of knowledge. The answers that were proposed for these problems were clearly influenced by the medieval interpretations of Stoicism, Neo-Platonism, and Aristotelianism.

In consonance with these influences, the medieval Jewish doctrine of the soul was often associated with the idea of perfection. Personal perfection could be achieved by means of the soul's communion with or, as the Hebrew had it, cleaving to (*devekut*) the spiritual element surrounding it, that is, the "universal soul," the "active intelligence," or God himself. Looked at from a different perspective, the emphasis on communion meant that man's relationship to God was established through intellectual effort, philosophical contemplation, or mystical devotion.

The Jewish doctrine of the soul, however, did not remain within the confines of the Greek schools of thought and their view of the soul as being essentially a philosophical problem. The philosophical concepts it had acquired regarding the spiritual hierarchy of the universe and questions bound up with the conception of the soul underwent a mythical-Gnostic transformation in the twelfth century, when they encountered the early kabbalah and the *Sefer ha-Bahir*.[6]

In the *Sefer ha-Bahir*, the creation and the molding and sustenance of souls is bound up with an erotic myth that speaks of sexual union between cosmic entities in the world of the *sefirot* (divine emanations) and of the process of creation in general. The text alludes, in highly symbolic language, to a system that was further developed in the *Zohar* and other kabbalistic literature. Three stages of development are discerned in the formation of souls: the ideal, the ontological, and the actual. These stages parallel both the processes of intercourse, pregnancy, and birth, by which the physical body comes into being,[7] and the relationships between the *sefirot* in the supernal world. The erotic symbolism by which the dynamic relationship between the various aspects of the divine is described in the kabbalistic system relates to the idea that the creation of souls takes place in connection with an act of cosmic union. In addition, it reflects deep religious implications regarding the exalted nature of the soul that were attached to human sexual union on account of its archetypal parallel in the supernal worlds.[8]

The kabbalistic doctrine of the soul is based upon three fundamental assumptions regarding the nature of man: (1) the divine origin of the human soul; (2) the idea that man is structured in the image of the *sefirot*, and that his soul reflects the hierarchy of the supernatural worlds, and (3) the idea that man can influence the world of the divine.[9]

The kabbalah borrowed the philosophical division of the soul into parts and superimposed a mystical quality upon it, holding that each part was expressive of different *sefirot*. The transition from the philosophical version of the tripartite division of the soul to that of the kabbalah took place toward the end of the thirteenth century. Man, by virtue of the origin of the elements of his soul and their relationship to strata within the hierarchy of the transcendent worlds, enjoyed therefore a fundamental connection with the hierarchy as a whole and with each of its separate manifestations. His spiritual structure made him capable of affecting and being affected by all of reality, on every level. Each element of his soul was able to affect the higher level from which it had sprung. All of the realms and all of the souls exerted a continuous influence upon one another. The tendency of the kabbalists to build their spiritual structures upon the principle of the infinite mutual reflection of their foundations left its mark upon the mystical significance of the doctrine of the soul. Since the structure of the soul parallels that of the hierarchy of the *sefirot*, it would seem that man may decipher the secret of the divine by contemplating these qualities that exist in his soul: "For anyone who knows the secret of the wisdom of the soul knows the secret of divine unity."[10]

The anthropology of the kabbalah took shape on the basis of these assumptions. It taught that the essential quality of humanity was to be found not by determining man's relationship with the other creatures of the earth, but rather by defining the bidirectional links connecting him with the *sefirot*. On the basis of its assumption of the divine nature of the human soul and of the intimate relations binding it to the godhead, the kabbalah arrived at a most important conclusion: man's relationship with God could not be reduced to his one-sided need for heavenly mercy; it was characterized, rather, by reciprocal influence and mutual assistance. The kabbalah's conception of the soul was shaped by a theurgical orientation. Man was sustained by the downward flow from the world of the *sefirot*, but he also exerted an upward influence of his own. By means of special *kavvanot* (pl. of *kavvanah*, lit., directed intention) and *yihudim* (pl. of *yihud*, lit., unification) recited in conjunction with his religious activities, he was able to endow the divine *sefirot* with vitality and assist their harmonization. In the view of the kabbalah, moreover, the harmonious interplay of the spheres of divine life depends upon the actions of man. The worship of God thus took on a magical, theurgical dimension. This conception of the soul as a spiritual power that brought man into communion with God and exerted its own influence upon the divine was of crucial importance in shaping the kabbalistic interpretation of the worship of God, according to which the purpose of all the commandments is to enable the soul to unite with God and to bring about a union of the elements of the divine.

A further link between the kabbalah's interpretation of the commandments and its doctrine of the soul is to be found in the doctrine of reincarnation, which came to Judaism from Platonic thought. There is evidence of its presence in Jewish circles, where it aroused a good deal of controversy, from the eighth century onward. It occurs in *Sefer ha-Bahir*, and the kabbalah therefore accepted it as sacred doctrine.

Reincarnation means that the soul exists within different bodies at different times; in other words, the life of the soul is independent of the confines of the physical existence of the individual. The doctrine of reincarnation thus represents an attempt to endow human life with broader dimensions, both in terms of time and in terms of its spiritual and religious dimensions.[11]

Because of its halakhic implications (with respect to levirate marriage and the rules of ritual slaughtering), the kabbalah cloaked the basically irrational concept of reincarnation with a good many surface coverings of rationality. Moreover, the concept received an added dimension of significance in connection with the concepts of exile and redemption. It came to symbolize the situation of the unredeemed world, the discord that had entered the primeval order on account of the sin of the first man. The external, physical exile of Israel on the historical level is paralleled, on a metaphysical level, by the inner exile of the soul. Reincarnation and exile become the main symbols of the "shattered" reality. The world was in need of restoration and redemption on both a physical and a spiritual level; with the end of the historical exile, the bodies of men would be redeemed and the exile of the souls—the cycle of reincarnation—would cease.[12]

The doctrine of the soul became more and more central to Judaism with the growing influence of mystical trends, which removed religion from the realm of history and the physical world, emphasizing instead the life of the godhead, metahistory, and redemption.

In the latter stages of kabbalistic thought, the Platonic ontology upon which the above interpretation of man's creation in the image of God had been founded was no longer dominant. The monistic theology that had described a unidirectional hierarchy of emanation that was reflected in the divine soul of man gave way to a dialectic conception of the universe that viewed the divine essence and its human counterpart as being characterized by an ontological split.

From the Lurianic kabbalah onward, kabbalistic thought was founded upon a recognition of the basic polarization of all existence and upon the idea that the divine life is played out through two simultaneous processes, that of emanation and that of *zimzum* (contraction); that of creation and actualization and that of annihilation. Moreover, this ontological duality within the divine essence was assumed to have its counterpart within the soul of man.[13] The dialectical polarization characterizing all of reality is reflected in the idea that man has two souls, a divine soul and an animal one. These represent two opposing but interdependent systems, which manifest themselves throughout the universe in concealment and exposure, the hidden and the revealed, being and nonbeing, flow and contraction, covering and uncovering, unity and separation.

These two poles have their counterparts, as noted, in the two conflicting spiritual elements within man's soul—his divine soul and his animal soul. The divine soul represents the principles of flow, spirituality, uncovering, and infinity, while the animal soul represents limitations, physicality, covering, restriction, and finitude. The animal soul cannot exist without the divine soul, which gives it life, but the divine soul, too, can have no individual existence without the animal soul, which restricts and clothes it; the two are thus dependent upon one another. The divine soul represents the yearning of the spirit to return to its source and its awareness of the truth of the world of unity, from the divine perspective. The animal soul, in contrast, represents material being, differentiated reality, a way of being that does not see itself as part of the divine unity, and man's thirst for the physical aspects of life. The relationship between the divine and the animal souls parallels that between the spiritual and the material, the infinite and the finite, throughout existence. This relationship is not static, for the divine soul continually yearns to transform the animal soul and bring it within the sphere of the divine, while the animal soul yearns to transform the essence of the divine soul and bring it down into the world of being. Man's existence is thus paradoxical, for his animal soul provides the constitutional element necessary to conceal the revealed divine essence and bring it into the world of being, while his divine soul yearns with all its might to do away with this concealing element so that it can reach the sublime, unconcealed divine essence.

In the kabbalah and Ḥasidic thought we find a dualistic ontological structure in which positive and negative spiritual systems parallel one another, united by their common origin despite their very different manifestations. These systems are called by different names, depending upon the epistemological plane on which they are being discussed. On the one side we find nothingness, holiness, unity, and substance, which are expressed through the divine soul; on the other we find Being, the *sitra aḥra* (lit., the other side, that is, the realm of evil), separation, and concealment, which are represented by the animal soul. The dialectic between being and nothingness is the same as that between the animal soul and the divine soul, and that between impurity and holiness; a metamorphosis that takes place on any one of these levels thus has implications for all the rest. This dualistic ontology gradually underwent a mythic-Gnostic transformation. The conflict between the divine and the animal soul came to be viewed as a struggle between good and evil, between the *Shekhinah*, the divine Presence, and Satan, or between holiness and the impure *kelippot* (shells). This struggle began with the sin of the first man, and would end only with the ultimate redemption, the defeat of the *sitra aḥra* and the victory of the holy.[14]

The reason for the centrality of the doctrine of the soul for Jewish mysticism is thus clear: the soul had become the arena in which the cosmic struggle between the holy and the *kelippot* was played out, with the two sides to the dialectic represented respectively by the divine soul and the animal soul. They were aided in their struggle by, on the one hand, the performance of the commandments and the recitation of the various *yiḥudim*, *kavvanot*, and *tikkunim* (pl. of *tikkun*, lit., restoration) that accompany this performance, and, on the other, acts of sin and transgression and extraneous evil thoughts. The relationship between the divine and animal souls was a reflection both of the changing metaphysical situation within the divine being and of the active influence exerted by the human soul upon the cosmic struggle between good and evil.

REFERENCES

1. Cf. I. Licht, "Soul," in *Encyclopedia Mikrait* (1968); A. Murtonen, *The Living Soul* (1958).
2. Efraim E. Urbach, *The Sages: Their Concepts and Beliefs*, 2d ed., 1 (1979), ch. 10.

3. Cf. W. Hirsch, *Rabbinic Psychology* (1974).
4. See Julius Gutmann, *The Philosophy of Judaism* (1964), ch. 1.
5. Cf. Efraim Urbach, *op. cit.*, ch. 10.
6. See Gershom Scholem, *Reshit ha-Kabbalah* (1948), ch. 1.
7. See *Sefer ha-Bahir*, secs. 22, 57, and 119; Isaiah Tishby, ed., *Mishnat ha-Zohar* 2 (1961), 28–29.
8. Cf. Naḥmanides, *Iggeret ha-Kodesh* in *Kitvei ha-Ramban* 2, 324, 327, 333.
9. Cf. Isaiah Tishby, *op. cit.* 2, 3–93.
10. Eliezer of Worms, *Ḥokhmat ha-Nefesh*.
11. Cf. Moses Cordovero, *Pardes Rimonim*, sec. 31; M. Recanati, *Perush al ha-Torah*, ad loc. Ex. 6:8; 9:13–16.
12. See *Sefer ha-Temunah* 24, 37–41; *Galia Raza*, Rachel Elior, ed. (1981), 56–57, 68–73, 140–45; Ḥayyim Vital, *Shaar ha-Gilgulim*.
13. See Isaiah Tishby, *Torat ha-Ra ve-ha-Kelippah be-Kabbalah ha-Ari* (1966), secs. 3–4.
14. See *Galia Raza*, 140–47; *Tanya*, chs. 1–7.

BIBLIOGRAPHY

Rachel Elior, *Torat ha-Elohut ba-Dor ha-Sheni Shel Ḥasidut Ḥabad* (1982), ch. 5.
Saul Horovitz, *Die Psychologie bei den jüdischen Religions-Philosophen des Mittelalters von Saadia bis Miamuni* (1898–1912).
Isaiah Tishby, ed., *Mishnat ha-Zohar*, vol. 2 (1961), 1–180.
Gershom Scholem, *On the Kabbalah and Its Symbolism* (1965).
Efraim E. Urbach, *The Sages: Their Concepts and Beliefs*, 2d ed. (1979).

Soul Searching

חשבון נפש

Adin Steinsaltz

Although the term *soul searching (ḥeshbon nefesh)* is relatively new in the lexicon of Jewish thought—its use dates only from the Middle Ages—the concept of a spiritual reckoning is as old as Jewish culture itself. The forms of this reckoning and the issues it encompasses may have changed from generation to generation, but it has remained a principal element in the Jewish life and thought of all periods. The rabbinic sages have called soul searching "world reckoning" *(ḥeshbon shel olam)*, in accordance with the concept that it is really a reckoning of broad generalities and of major principles, an audit encompassing a whole world (BT BB 78). Of course, there are those accounts that focus on small sums or are even squandered on pennies, but true soul searching is basically all-embracing, penetrating every aspect of one's world. Even when it begins or ends with small things, it always arises out of a feeling of the importance of those small things. Where this feeling of importance, of significance, is absent we do not have a true searching of the soul, even where the objects of review are very great. True soul searching must always be subjective, substantive, thorough, and fundamental.

Obviously, no soul searching or world reckoning can be carried out without some basic assumptions regarding its viability. In the absence of basic criteria that define its parameters, there is no substance to evaluation and reckoning. The criteria need not necessarily be religious or moral in the usual sense of the words, but they must be acceptable to the seeker as a yardstick against which he can measure his spiritual state. In fact, every reckoning, of whatever kind, can be carried out only on the basis of established criteria. Where these are absent, there is no reckoning. For this reason, soul searching can be undertaken only against a specific cultural background that recognizes certain given values and rules as fundamental. Their absence or relativization denies a society, and the individuals making up that society, the basis from which such a reckoning might be made. More than this, in order for introspection to be a true exploration of the soul, a reckoning in which the individual or the community judges and weighs deeds, acts, and thoughts, that culture must possess a tradition of introspection. That is, the criteria in question must be consciously integrated and not remain merely external.

Jewish culture, which is basically a culture of values grounded in the belief in good and evil, clearly provides the normative perspective in light of which effective soul searching may take place. What is more, the Jewish worldview, with its absolute standards and qualities, actually requires this accounting, both of the community, including the world community and the community of Israel, and of the individual within that community. In the Bible as a whole, and in particular in the Torah, soul searching is primarily on a communal scale, whether it appertains to one nation or to the whole world. Perhaps it is not surprising therefore that the first example of true soul searching in the Scriptures is one made on a universal scale and apparently by God himself: "The Lord saw how great was man's wickedness on earth, and how every plan devised by his mind was nothing but evil all the time. And the Lord regretted that He had made man on earth, and His heart was saddened. The Lord said, 'I will blot out from the earth the men whom I created . . . , for I regret that I made them'" (Gen. 6:5–7).

In spite of the theological problems inherent in this passage, it is still a classic example of soul searching, a general reckoning in which deeds are assessed. Like any significant accounting, soul searching must draw some conclusion, whether negative or positive. That this particular reckoning is being made by the Almighty does not detract from its fundamental significance; in fact, it can also serve as a model, as an example, calling on men to do likewise. This great principle of *imitatio Dei*, the imitation of God, is an explicit motif throughout the Bible: "You shall be holy, for I, the Lord

your God, am holy" (Lev. 19:2). Thus, this first instance of soul searching—
and its aftermath, the Flood—contains all the elements essential to the process: review, recognition of offense, regret, repentance, and remedy. Elsewhere in the Scriptures we find other examples no less powerful, as in the
stern admonitions of Leviticus 26:3 and Deuteronomy 28:30. In all these
exhortations, one element stands out: whenever man errs and sins, whenever the prevalent notions appear impervious to reproof and new ideas,
there is nothing like calamity and disaster to bring the nation to its senses,
to encourage soul searching. This is something that is emphasized again and
again by all the prophets, both in the historical books of the Bible and later,
in explicit calls to repentance. "Let us search and try our ways and turn
back to the Lord" (Lam. 3:40) is the call; everything else is but an elaboration upon this prophetic exhortation.

In postbiblical literature, spiritual introspection also has a prominent
place, whether this is manifested in general admonitions or in an emphasis
on and encouragement to soul searching. "Come, let us reckon the world's
account," or "Come let us make our reckoning with the world," figure
prominently, whether tacitly or overtly, in homilies and exegeses. However,
there is a marked difference between the biblical calls to introspection and
those found in the Talmud and later literature. While the approach in the
Bible is public and national, the accounting later acquires a more individual,
personal character.

In the Bible, the kings of Israel and Judea are exhorted to repent not
because of their importance as individuals but because their behavior
(including their most private actions) has a significance that affects the
whole nation. It is possible to discern an occasional duality of attitude in
that the prophets regarded private sin, even a grave one, with less severity
than they did a minor public transgression. There are many examples of
this distinction, notably in relation to the sins of Saul and David. Saul's sin,
his disobedience to the prophet Samuel, was punished by the cessation of
his dynastic line (I Sam. 13:13–14). David's sin in the episode of Uriah and
Bathsheba (II Sam. 11) was forgiven even though at the personal level he
was severely punished. The sages comment that this striking difference lies
in the very essence of those sins. Saul's transgressions, great and small, were
in the national sphere. He sinned as a king and as a leader. David's sin was
private and personal, so that his punishment, as it were, fitted the crime
and did not imply a total rejection of his line. Thus we see that the prophetic
admonitions are directed mainly toward the nation, the community of
Israel, in which individuals are only part of the whole. In the Talmud, on
the other hand, the admonition, the call to repentance and to soul search-

ing, is more likely to be addressed to the individual. It appears that this difference is not only of principle but is rather a matter of social outlook, and has two distinct aspects: the nation as a spiritual entity and the nation as a political organization.

The prophets did not address themselves to specific individuals but to the nation as a whole because individuals tend to act not only of their own volition but also in accordance with and in response to the general consensus. The prophets themselves were not representative of their generation but were outsiders to it, struggling against the tide and against the conventions of their society. The need for revision that they preached did not therefore relate to the individual level; it was a call for national change and was aimed at those very sectors of society that had the power to bring about such changes and to introduce innovations: "Hear this, priests, attend, O House of Israel, and give ear, O royal house; for right conduct is your responsibility" (Hos. 5:1). In other words, "you" have the power to change things.

From the time of the Second Temple, however, matters changed considerably. This was not because people suddenly became paragons of virtue, but because the general worldview altered. The national consensus had changed, inspired as it was by the leadership of the day—the scholars and the rabbis. Individuals and whole groups, including the leadership itself, might sin—willfully or in error—but a general consensus existed as to what in fact constituted transgression or sin, and certain norms and rules were common to the Jewish people as a whole. From this point in history, soul searching, world reckoning, was no longer a call for drastic change, for a different perspective on the world, or for renewed national awareness. Rather, it became a detailed examination of the exceptional—of correction at the individual level.

Soul searching was now to become an essential aspect of Jewish religious practice. For generations both the *maggidim* (preachers) in the cities and the itinerant preachers who visited the outlying hamlets and villages preached repentance and soul searching. Several days of the year were set aside for this purpose, such as the entire period from the beginning of the month of Elul (August/September) until the Day of Atonement itself, a day of fasting devoted to intense introspection. What is more, for centuries it was the accepted custom among all the communities of Israel to set aside the eve of every new month as a day of repentance and fasting known as a "minor Day of Atonement." On these days, the central theme of sermons and study was the soul searching incumbent on the individual vis-à-vis the creator and the reckoning that same individual must make with himself. Many people dedicated several hours daily to studying Musar literature, which dealt with ways of improving and correcting the soul. This kind of introspection was intended not for outstanding scholars and for the pious, but for the ordinary Jew—the Jew who throughout the year was absorbed with the problems of livelihood and business and all the other cares of daily life. Needless to say, soul searching was more refined and developed (and even became the central issue) in those circles and groups that devoted themselves to an intense spiritual life—for instance, the kabbalists among Sephardic Jewry and the Ḥasidim among the Ashkenazi Jews. For such people, soul searching was a matter of profound, daily significance, and whether they were Torah scholars or not, they set aside some time for reviewing the deeds, words, and thoughts of each day. The long version of the Shema recited on retiring at night, containing as it does a passage of repentance and regret, was considered by many to be particularly appropriate to this purpose.

Soul searching is a long and complex process, and requires a certain amount of preparation or at least a tacit assumption of doubt, insecurity, the need for review and revision, and the need to reassess one's life. This awareness of the need for review is an essential condition of soul searching. Even within the normal routine of daily life, most people do make some kind of accounting which, as often as not, contains a basic defect that reveals itself only under the most scrupulous examination. Soul searching carried out in the rough and tumble of active life, without pausing or leaving room for reciprocity, may be fundamentally incorrect. The summing up may be accurate, the calculations precise, but what is considered as credit is actually debit, and what the arithmetic books define as profit proves in reality to be loss; that which seems clear and straightforward is revealed as a futile dream. Errors of this sort, which are, of course, more than mere errors of arithmetic, are not revealed by a routine accounting process. In other words, as long as the matter in question is assessed on the basis of the same fundamental assumptions with which one started out, the errors in the account will remain standing until some disaster occurs to reveal the defect. As noted, people do not make mistakes over "petty cash," the adding up of the pennies of the daily round. Here, a reasonable degree of accuracy is maintained. What is more, the very fact of routine, of the methods and systems used in this kind of accounting, makes it possible for it to function regardless of the existence of some fundamental error. Small mistakes are quickly discovered, and as quickly rectified; the fundamental error, in contrast, produces a whole complex interdependent structure, which in its own confined sphere becomes a law unto itself. The fundamental error thus contains its own feedback mechanism, which serves to reinforce and verify it. Soul searching, on the other hand, obliges one to look afresh at those things that seem to be whole, good, and beautiful. A certain Ḥasidic Rebbe Velvel is reported to have said: "When I think of repentance I don't review those deeds I know to have been sins, but rather those *miẓvot* and good deeds that I have performed."

Soul searching is therefore much more than a profit-and-loss accounting. Regardless of the kind of problem it deals with, moral, economic, or political, it is an overall reckoning, one that includes in it a presupposition of the possibility of error, of a great and fundamental mistake.

There is a well-known fable of the animals who decide to repent because their sins have brought disaster on them: The tiger and the wolf confess that they prey on other creatures, and are vindicated. After all, it is in their nature as predators to hunt and kill. So all the animals in turn confess their sins and, for one reason or another, are all exonerated. Finally, the sheep admits that she once ate the straw lining from her master's boots, and here at last is obviously the true cause of the animals' misfortune. All fall on the evil sheep and slaughter it—and everything is in order again.

This fable is usually taken to illustrate the hypocrisy of the animals, who ignore the sins of the strong and attack those of the weak. However, the basic issue is something rather more profound: What we have here is an example of the kind of soul searching that merely confirms the status quo and the obvious. The wolf may hunt and the tiger may prey on others because it is in their nature to do so. As long as soul searching does not address itself to such basic and fundamental issues, as long as it does not question even the most obvious assumptions, then the sin singled out for correction will be trivial and no overall change will be forthcoming.

True soul searching is based on quite a different premise, one that assumes that those matters we take for granted, the status quo, the general consensus, are the very things that require review and revision. In the Bible this is expressed in Leviticus 26:40, "And you shall confess your sins and those of your fathers," an exhortation that finds its echo in the confession in the biblical passage recited in the daily prayers, "But we and our fathers have sinned" (Jer. 3:25). This inclusion of the fathers in the confession is not accidental. Rather, it is an attempt not only to examine oneself at the level of present being, but also to penetrate to the very roots of one's existence.

BIBLIOGRAPHY

Bahya ben Joseph ibn Paquda, *Duties of the Heart,* Moses Hyamson, tr. (1945), sec. 8.
Schneur Zalman of Liadi, *Liqqutei Amarim (Tanya),* Nissan Mindel, tr. (1962), pt. 1.

Spirituality

רוחניות

Arthur Green

Spirituality as an essential value of the Jewish tradition is a striving for the presence of God and the fashioning of a life of holiness appropriate to such striving. As such, the spiritual life that stands at the center of Judaism is the shared goal of biblical priest and prophet, of Pharisee and Essene sectarian, of Hellenistic contemplative and law-centered rabbi, of philosopher, halakhist, kabbalist, and ḥasid. Among these there are vast differences of opinion as to precisely how life in the presence of God is to be defined and achieved, but all would assent to the importance of this value. Postbiblical Judaism has striven to cultivate in ordinary human affairs the quality of holiness that was originally associated with sacred space and time, the temple precincts, and the holy days. The notion of the entire people of Israel as a "kingdom of priests" (Ex. 19:6) is essential to the Pharisaic transformation of biblical religion and stands at the center of any Jewish religious self-definition.

The definition of spirituality proposed here does not coincide with *ruḥaniyyut*, the Hebrew equivalent of the term *spirituality*. This Hebrew term, not found in the Bible or in early rabbinic speech, is an artifice of the medieval translators, first created to express philosophical and scientific concepts that were Hellenic in origin and taken over only afterward by kabbalists and pietists to describe a religious ideal that by then was a thorough amalgam of the spiritual legacies of Israel and Greece. Spirituality in the Western sense, inevitably opposed in some degree to "corporeality" or "worldliness" (all apologetics to the contrary notwithstanding), is unknown to the religious worldview of ancient Israel and is a latecomer, though an important one, among the elements that comprise the religious legacy of medieval and later Jewry.

The appreciation and cultivation of those ways of living, including inward states, in which the divine presence is most to be felt takes many forms in the history of Judaism. The rabbinic admonition that *ruah ha-kodesh* (the holy spirit) is the culmination of a long series of moral and religious virtues becomes standard fare in the Jewish moral curriculum. Such influential later moralistic works as Ḥayyim Vital's *Sha'arei Kedushah* (Gates of Holiness) or Moses Ḥayyim Luzzatto's *Mesillat Yesharim* (Path of the Upright) begin their instruction with such "outer" virtues as patience, modesty, discipline, and the conquest of anger, only afterward moving toward those more esoteric aspects of training that lead to the evocation of God's presence. Many a Jewish moralist has deprecated the search for "religious experience" altogether, claiming that such a quest is in itself only a subtle form of pride, inappropriate to the true goals of holy living. While both spiritual and material blessings are frequently promised as a reward for faithfulness, the higher path has always been seen as that which "serves not in order to receive reward" (M. Avot 1:3). For some authors, even the reward of "gaz[ing] upon the beauty of the Lord" (Ps. 27:4) itself is seen as a reproachful goal.

The style of Jewish spiritual life has always found its common expression in the deed, meaning specifically the commandments of the Torah as amplified by the classical halakhah. The formulations of mystical or pietistic spirituality often grow out of the halakhic institutions themselves, as in the relationship between sanctifying the act of eating and the dietary laws of *kashrut* or "building a palace in time" (cf. Abraham J. Heschel, *The Sabbath*) and the institution of the Sabbath. In these cases the halakhah is the soil in which the spiritual expressions take root. In modern times, all attempts to build a spiritual life on the foundations of Judaism have had to contend with the issue of halakhah. A certain unfortunate polarization may be seen in such attempts, in which those committed to halakhah lose their spiritual focus in the great struggle to preserve the forms of traditional Jewish piety while the nonhalakhic (the primary example here is the kibbutz movement) drift toward secularism. The possibility of a heterodox or nonhalakhic Jewish spirituality, such as is powerfully evoked by the writings of Martin Buber, is only in our generation beginning to move toward realization.

While all of the commandments are capable of spiritual interpretation, it is especially around the act of prayer that Jewish spiritual teachings have tended to cluster. Some teachings offer interpretations of the prescribed liturgy or instructions for prayer as contemplation, turning the essentially public and communal act of group worship into a meditative exercise in which the individual, even in the midst of a congregation, is alone with God. Others have added the practice of *hitbodedut,* solitary concentration on the presence of God, as a separate discipline. Spiritual masters of various ages, including kabbalists such as Abraham Abulafia and Ḥayyim Vital, and such Ḥasidic masters as Naḥman of Bratslav and the leaders of the *Ḥabad* school, have each offered their own instructions for the meditative art. It should be noted, however, that rationalist as well as kabbalist versions of Judaism contain a commitment to the spiritual life. Maimonides' description of the love of God as "a great and exceeding love, so strong that one's soul shall be knit up with the love of God and one should be continually enraptured by it, like a love-sick individual, whose mind is at no time free from his passion" (MT Teshuvah 10:3), as well as the beatific vision with which he concludes his *Guide of the Perplexed,* bear ample witness to the fact that Jewish philosophy bears within it a contemplative ideal fully as intense as that of the kabbalists.

The love and fear of God, as well as the proper balance between the two, comprise the emotional groundwork of Jewish spiritual strivings. Each of these has several aspects, as articulated by Jewish moralists, and the subtle gradations within them fill many a treatise on the spiritual life. Love of God may range from a lowly love of divine reward for doing good to a lofty and pure basking in God's presence or to an utterly unselfish sense of fulfillment in following his will. A sense of deep longing for utter absorption within divinity, including an annihilation of the separate self, is also frequently to be found in the teachings of Jewish mystics. The fear of God includes both fear of wrath and punishment, at the lowest end of the spectrum (said by some to be an entirely improper motivation for religious behavior), and a trembling and awestruck sense of divine grandeur, the emotion most associated with the thunderous presence of God at Sinai, surely the greatest single paradigm in the tradition for later religious experience. The psalmist's "rejoice with trembling" (Ps. 2:11) might be said to be especially characteristic of Jewish piety; the awesome and overwhelming presence of God is occasion for exaltation rather than terror. Awe and intimacy tend to go hand in hand in the life of Jewish piety: the object of worship may indeed be the king of kings, majestic emperor of the universe, but the worshiper is that king's beloved child or faithful servant, one whose plea the king will never spurn. A sense of being "at home" in the king's palace, including an ability at times to argue with him and challenge what seems to be divine injustice, is an ancient part of Israel's spiritual legacy.

Acceptance of the love of God bears with it a willingness to suffer for the sake of that love. *Kabbalat yissurim be-ahavah,* the acceptance of suffering in love, is a long-standing virtue in the world of Jewish spirituality. The challenge to divine justice is usually taken up for the sake of others; for one's own life, a joyous resignation to God's will is seen as the proper attitude. This was especially the case in those ages when suffering and martyrdom for God's sake were a common experience among Jews, but is applied in all ages to the universally known pains of illness, death, and loss. Israel serves as God's witness in the world; its testimony is significant only because it has known suffering as well as goodness at his hand. The witness of those who have known such pain is tortured, and in modern times even ambivalent, but the affirmation that emerges from it is profound and not easily contradicted.

The love of God also calls forth a love of God's creation, and specifically a love of all humans, who are created in his image. There is also a special sense of love and mutual responsibility among Jews, *ahavat yisra'el.* At its best this specific love, like that within an extended family, is expansive rather than exclusive. The love of God's creatures calls for a sense of responsibility in the realm of human affairs, compassion for the oppressed and the poor, and a willingness to serve as peacemaker within the human community. Judaism's commitment to the reality of this world, rooted in the demands of Israel's ancient prophets, does not allow for a spirituality of an entirely otherworldly character. The only true test of one's love of God is one's ability to share in the love of God's creatures. Only in human community are the virtues learned in spiritual training made real. The careful balancing of worldliness—including the commitment to halakhic responsibility—and inwardness is perhaps the most clearly distinguishing mark of Jewish spirituality. The fact that Jewry has no special class of "religious" to devote themselves wholly to spiritual pursuits, but rather demands both the life of holiness and the responsibilities of family and worldly sustenance from all its folk, lends reality to this sense of balance. The ultimate spiritual and parental models here are Abraham and Sarah, showing the love of God to others and bringing them "under the wings of the *Shekhinah*" (divine Presence) and thereby enriching their own lives with God as well.

BIBLIOGRAPHY

Arthur Green, ed., *Jewish Spirituality,* 3 vols. (1985).
Abraham Joshua Heschel, *God in Search of Man* (1956).
Lawrence Kushner, *The River of Light* (1981).

State of Israel

מדינת ישראל

Michael Rosenak

A consideration of the State of Israel in theological terms may, to historians of Zionism and observers of contemporary Israel, appear contrived, or at least paradoxical. Israel was envisioned, molded, and established by the Zionist movement, and although this movement could point to pious precursors and adherents, it was in many respects a rebellion against religious tradition. Most of its enthusiasts were modern in consciousness and predominantly secular in orientation. They tended to see in Zionism an alternative to classical Judaism and its theological assumptions rather than a continuation or vindication of a holy tradition.

The opposition, however, of some rabbis and theologians does not determine the ultimate place of Zionism and the State of Israel in Jewish religious faith, for Zionist ideals of Jewish responsibility, creativity, return to the land, and national rehabilitation may be regarded as having religious significance. To be sure, the value of collective self-defense, of the Jews' responsibility for their physical survival, was for some the consequence of the erosion of faith in the divine guardian of Israel; but others, with equal right or rigor, defended this value as a religious imperative in an age of Holocaust and return to the land. Zionism may be explained as mystic, as liberal and rational, or as redemptive. Indeed, there is a vast polemical literature in which it is debated whether the Zionist movement and the State of Israel point toward the successful secularization of the Jews or toward a divine redemption, which sweeps even secular Jews into its overpowering orbit while providing them with an ideological disguise. For some writers, Israel and Zionism represent a new development in Jewish religion; for others a new nonreligious phase of Jewish spiritual history; and for still others a merciful liberation from a unique historical status and significance. One may venture the thought that this literature has itself become a kind of theological genre, since it deals with what, for most modern Jews who reflect upon Judaism, is the central positive event in two millennia of Jewish history: the emergence of the State of Israel.

The literature dealing with the religious-theological significance of Israel centers upon four main issues: (1) messianism and interpretations of redemptive signs and events that may be seen as signifying the end of *galut* (exile); (2) *ereẓ Yisrael* (land of Israel) and its place within the faith-system of Judaism; (3) the Jewish people and its nature and task, as these touch on the Jews' relationship to God and their relationship to the other peoples of the world; and (4) the demands and parameters of Torah, and how to relate to those who reject its authority or perceive its demands and scope differently. Needless to say, the hierarchical manner in which these various categories are ordered determines to a large degree how each of them is interpreted; moreover, the way contemporary circumstances (and modernity in general) are evaluated influences one's understanding of these theological issues.

Once the relevant theological terms are located and the conflicts that arise in the modern situation are identified, the disagreements become more intelligible and can be placed in appropriate contexts. For example, the radical difference between the ultratraditional Neturei Karta (Aramaic, lit., Guardians of the City) sect of Jerusalem and the religious-Zionist Gush Emunim (lit., Bloc of the Faithful) movement is not due to the fact that one is more messianic, more pacifistic, or less devoted to traditional Jewish law than the other. Both groups, the violently anti-Zionist votaries of Neturei Karta and the Zionist zealots of Gush Emunim, eagerly await the Messiah, share the assumption that God has promised to restore his people to the land of Israel in its biblical borders, and agree that the Torah, as interpreted by Orthodox sages, is the raison d'être and cosmic task of the Jewish people. No one in either group regards *galut* as anything but a curse and a punishment. Both anticipate the ultimate acceptance of God's kingdom by all men, and both consider contemporary humanity, by and large, idolatrous and spiritually benighted. They differ with regard to the State of Israel: whether its establishment is a redemptive or a demonic event, whether it is the result of providence or sin, and, thus, whether the State of Israel enhances or defames the sanctity of *erez Yisrael*. Their dispute over the application of the Torah to the Jewish state flows naturally from their disagreement regarding the true or false messianic nature of Zionism.

The bitter controversy between these particular groups illustrates the rule that serious theological disagreement is always predicated on at least some common terms of reference, which are then diversely interpreted. These terms, parenthetically, are grounded in theological assumptions that, until the advent of the modern age, all Jews shared. These assumptions were that the Jews are God's people, that they are in exile, that the Torah is binding but cannot be fully carried out in *galut,* and that God will eventually restore Israel to its land and usher in a new age through his Messiah. The Messiah, as Maimonides describes him (MT Hil. Melakhim 11), will conquer the land, rebuild the Temple, and reconstitute a Jewish society in *erez Yisrael* established according to the norms of the Torah. At that time, God will grant glory to Israel, all peoples will acknowledge his dominion, and there will be universal peace. It is within the historical context of these assumptions and in the reactions of modern Jews to them and to previous understandings of them that our approaches to the theological significance of Israel may be located.

Four basic conceptions of theological significance with regard to the State of Israel may be discerned: (1) theologies of negation: the State of Israel is an act of rebellion against God or is historically regressive. It is, therefore, to be regarded as militating against the authenticity or relevance of Judaism; (2) theologies of symbiosis: Israel is significant as a vital feature of Jewish civilization, but it has no normative meaning in isolation from other constitutive elements of Judaism; (3) theologies of Torah and *erez Yisrael:* Israel, as a Jewish society in the land of covenant, is of central halakhic and moral significance in the sacred system of Judaism; and (4) theologies of historical redemption: Israel is the embodiment of God's saving acts, which mark the fulfillment of his promise and the end of *galut.*

Theologies of negation can be found in a thoroughgoing religious opposition to the State of Israel in the ultra-Orthodox communities of Israel and the Diaspora on the one hand, and in the radical Reform movement and its offshoots in non-Orthodox Diaspora Judaism on the other.

The opposition of the ultra-Orthodox is based on the belief that the anticipated redemption can be effected only by God and his anointed one, who will implement that prophetic (and midrashic) promise of redemption in full. Until that divinely appointed hour, when God will end *galut* and restore Israel to his land, human attempts to hasten the redemption are forbidden; the Zionists who brazenly take the redemption into their own hands are merely heretics who espouse a false messiah. According to the thinking of Neturei Karta and the Satmar Ḥasidic sect, Zionism is the most pernicious movement in Jewish history, for it has flouted the oath imposed upon Israel not to "scale the walls," that is, not to attempt to conquer *erez Yisrael,* and not to rebel against gentile domination (BT Ket. 111a). In rebelling against the nations, Zionists have, in fact, rebelled against God and are thereby delaying the true redemption. The historical successes of Israel, especially those that appear miraculous (such as the victory in the Six-Day War), are interpreted demonically, as a temptation to the righteous remnant who must withstand the lure of the alleged salvation.[1]

Milder forms of this theological orientation are found within the right wing of the Orthodox Agudat Yisrael movement, guided by various Ḥasidic leaders and rabbinic authorities who head the prominent talmudic academies (*yeshivot*) in Israel and the Diaspora. In these circles, Israel Independence Day is thus generally ignored. Relations with the general, that is, non-religious and Zionist, public in Israel are conducted in accordance with the needs of the community of the faithful and its public interests. Agudat Yisrael's accommodation to the Zionist state is pragmatic and, in principle, no different from a politics pursued with gentile authorities. Yet this accommodation is marked by a curious ambivalence, for Israel is, after all, in *erez Yisrael,* and its leaders are Jews who may yet return to true Judaism.[2]

Negation of Israel on religious grounds in radical Reform Judaism is now confined almost exclusively to the American Council for Judaism, but it once constituted a significant anti-Zionist position, which held that since their dispersion, the Jews have not been a nation and must be seen rather as constituting only a religious faith community. Indeed, the dispersion of Israel was providential, making possible a realization of the biblical prophecy that Israel be "a light unto the nations." Zionism is thus a regressive conception, and the State of Israel seeks to narrow Jewish identity by creating a secular version of what was but an early stage in Israelite religion.[3]

Though the Reform movement no longer subscribes to this position, milder expressions of it are sometimes found among liberal Jewish educators and leaders who maintain that a secular state noted primarily for its military prowess is irrelevant to the spiritual meaning and on-going life of Judaism.

The second theological approach, the theologies of symbiosis, assigns religious significance to the State of Israel for having restored a constituent element to the structure of full and balanced Jewish life, namely a Jewish society in *erez Yisrael*.

Israelis who espouse this position tend to consider the "restorative" thrust of the State of Israel in a political-Zionist and thus nontheological fashion: the Jewish commonwealth makes it possible for Jews to leave the "abnormal" condition of life among the gentile nations. According to this view, in the natural habitat of the Jewish people fundamental religious issues can be clarified and religious faith may be purified, for here religion is not distorted by the "survival" functions placed upon it in the *galut*. However, the state has no religious meaning in and of itself; it is an instrument, liberating the Jews from the burden of life in a gentile civilization that is not conducive to a fully Jewish and halakhic existence.[4] Similarly, it has been argued that the separation between religion and state that should be consistently respected in Israel, as behooves a modern liberal state, may allow a modern Jewish national culture to absorb freely Judaism's religious spirit.

Diaspora exponents of this theological approach are, like their Israeli fellows, wary of ascribing too much theological meaning to the State of Israel, though their primary concern is to maintain the integrity of Jewish spirituality and life outside the land. While the Israeli thinkers of this school generally negate the value of Diaspora life, their colleagues in the *Golah* (Diaspora) consider the Diaspora a legitimate and enduring feature of Jewish civilization. Yet they see the State of Israel as an exhilarating development and a vital component of a complete Jewish existence, for it brings to Jewish life and culture its comprehensive social, political, and particularistic aspects. These aspects, however, are—and must be—complemented by the Diaspora element of Jewish life. The latter, it is alleged, is characterized by greater interaction with world culture; it is better placed to emphasize the universal features of Judaism, and presents the unique religious challenge to maintain the Jewish faith and people in the midst of the nations. In this view, the model for a normative dichotomy in Jewish life is the Jerusalem-Babylon relationship, each pole making its singular social, literary, and religious contribution.[5]

The third theological orientation, the theologies of Torah and *erez Yisrael*, draws primarily on normative conceptions of Torah as the instrument of covenant and explores prescribed relationships between Torah and *erez Yisrael*, the land of covenant.

In its traditional formulations, in which Torah is viewed through a predominantly halakhic prism, this orientation emphasizes that *erez Yisrael* is the normative locus of the Torah and that the land has a defined and central halakhic status with regard to the divine commandments. Not only are certain laws of the Torah applicable only in *erez Yisrael* (such as the sabbatical year and tithes), but the entire Torah is the covenantal law designed for the people of Israel in the land that is "the Lord's portion." Thus, the renowned medieval exegete and rabbinic authority Naḥmanides notes that the commandments were given for *erez Yisrael* and the obligation to carry them out in exile is so that "they will not appear as new [i.e., unfamiliar] when we return to the land" (Commentary on Lev. 18:25). Naḥmanides is also cited for his halakhic ruling that the conquest of *erez Yisrael,* circumstances permitting, is a requirement of the Torah. For those who hold this theological position, *galut* is seen as a diminution of the Torah, an aspect of divine punishment or a voluntary renunciation of Judaism. As one thinker expresses it, anyone who believes that Judaism can be fully realized under conditions of freedom anywhere may be affirming the value of emancipation, but is also implying a radical revision of Judaism.[6]

Liberal-humanistic theologies in this group also stress the place of *erez Yisrael* in the life of covenant; the latter, however, is not usually defined halakhically but is understood as the moral demands addressed to the Jewish people, demands that take on their specific content in the situation in which they are experienced. These moral demands are best "heard by" and addressed to a society in a concrete historical situation and in a natural framework of comprehensive community. For the Jewish people, the concrete historical and natural situation that rescues spirituality from the danger of disembodied ethereality and irrelevance is grounded in the holy land; here Israel is charged with the task of constructing a society that will be truly a kingdom of God.[7]

If theologies in the previous category emphasize the normative aspect of Torah, however understood, and its inadequate "functioning" without the land of the Torah, those of the fourth category, the theologies of historical redemption, are focused on the messianic pole of Jewish faith. Here, the emphasis is not on God's demands and man's deed but on God's mighty acts as they are perceived by man, and how man should respond to such miraculous interventions.

According to theologians who hold this view, the events of our time mean that God is leading his people back to their land, as he did after the Exodus from Egypt. Even the Holocaust must be seen in the context of the end of *galut*. The biblical and midrashic passages that describe the desolation of the land during Israel's exile as an intimation of the divine promise of return and of the land's "loyalty" to Israel are understood to reflect the actual situation (of "the desolate land") that writers as recent as Mark Twain described upon visiting the holy land. Conversely, the blossoming of the arid hills, foreseen in ancient visions of the coming redemption, and the influx of Jews from all corners of the earth are evoked as evidence that we are now in a new biblical epoch, in which God is again taking his people out of the "house of bondage" and, with fire and cloud, leading them to the promised land. Needless to say, the Israeli victories in the War of Independence and the Six-Day War are evoked in support of this approach; these victories were perceived as moments of salvation, inviting a biblical sense of wonder. Even the world's obsessive preoccupation with events in Israel is said to testify to Israel's theological significance, for believers in a competing faith (that is, Christianity) must denounce as a scandal that which, from within the allegedly atavistic Jewish faith, is clearly "seen" as miraculous.[8]

In its more cautious and humanistic formulations, this theology emphasizes the tentative character of divine redemption and its dependence for fulfillment on the positive response of Israel to the divine call through *aliyah* (immigration to the land), through the building of a just Jewish society, and through dedication to the moral destiny of Israel. Some also point out that the end of *galut* and the beginning of a new Israel-centered epoch in Jewish history require new understandings of the Jewish religious tradition that will incorporate modern insights and learn, from God's present redemptive acts, what the demands of Israel are today.[9]

Radical formulations of this theological approach tend to a more unequivocal messianism and, thus, to a more deterministic view: the tumultuous events of our century, and the Holocaust particularly, are to be recognized by "real believers" as the very "birth pangs of the Messiah" described in trepidation as well as anticipation by the talmudic rabbis. Understandably, those who take the more radical theological view of Israel's historical-messianic significance tend to a more uncompromising position regarding the possible return to non-Jewish dominion of parts of *erez Yisrael,* even in exchange for peace. Their argument is that relinquishing these territories after God has returned them to Israel obliges him, as it were, to bring upon Israel and its neighbors further conflict so that he can carry out his redemptive purpose. Paradoxically, therefore, compromise for the sake of peace is seen as delaying the complete redemption that will usher in universal peace.

A modified version of this historical-redemptive theology posits that, after the Holocaust, the State of Israel alone maintains the viability of Judaism as a faith in God's historical presence. The State of Israel is seen as giving Judaism a new lease on life; it is the embodiment of Judaism as a historical reality, mysteriously endowed with more than mere historical meaning.[10]

In conclusion it may be noted that there are grounds to suspect that many Jews never think about the State of Israel in theological terms of any kind. For those who believe that Israel points to the moral and religious richness of Jewish life, now again made possible by faithful Providence, this inability or refusal to deal with Israel as a basic religious datum of contemporary Jewish life more than anything else reveals the crisis of present-day Judaism—both in Israel and in the Diaspora.

REFERENCES

1. Norman Lamm, "The Ideology of the Neturei Karta," in *Tradition* 12, 2 (Fall 1971).
2. Shneur Zalman Abramov, *The Perpetual Dilemma: Jewish Religion in the Jewish State* (1976).
3. Michael Selzer, ed., *Zionism Reconsidered* (1970).
4. Yeshayahu Leibowitz, *Yahadut, Am Yehudi u-Medinat Yisrael* (1975).
5. Simon Rawidowicz, "Jerusalem and Babylon," in *Judaism* 18 (1969).
6. Eliezer Berkovits, "The Galut of Judaism," in *Judaism* 4 (1955).
7. Martin Buber, *Israel and the World* (1963).
8. Menachem M. Kasher, *Ha-Tekufah ha-Gedolah* (1968); Uriel Tal, "The Land and the State of Israel in Israeli Religious Life," in *The Rabbinical Assembly Proceedings* 38 (1976).
9. Yitzhak Greenberg, "The Interaction of Israel and American Jewry After the Holocaust," in Moshe Davis, ed., *World Jewry and the State of Israel* (1977).
10. Emil L. Fackenheim, *God's Presence in History* (1978).

BIBLIOGRAPHY

Martin Buber, *On Zion:The History of an Idea* (1973).
Harold Fisch, *The Zionist Revolution: A New Perspective* (1978).
Arthur Herzberg, *The Zionist Idea* (1959).
Uriel Tal, "Jewish Self-Understanding and the Land and State of Israel," in *Union Seminary Quarterly Review* 26 (1971).

Stranger

גר תושב, גוי

Joseph Levi

From biblical times to the present, the concept of the *ger toshav,* the resident alien, in its various senses, has served to shape the attitudes of Jewish thought and legislation in relation to the non-Jew who has to a certain extent drawn close to the basic principles of Judaism. His relationship to and observance of several fundamental universal principles of Judaism entitled the *ger toshav,* by definition, to the protection of Jewish society, an obligation that was imposed both on its individual members and on the society as a whole, through its representatives. Opinions differed for generations regarding the ethical norms to which Jewish society was bound and those basic principles of Judaism by whose means the outlines of a "society of universal culture" composed of both Jewish and non-Jewish members, each subject to the same rules of ethical conduct, might be delimited. The debates on this issue were influenced by their historical and political contexts and by the civilizations within which the Jewish thinkers, legal experts, and *poskim* (halakhic arbiters) who took part in them were and continue to be active.

Following the transformations that have taken place in the concept of the *ger toshav* will help us to understand the degree to which Judaism has been willing to include the non-Jew within the framework of a Jewish society governed by universally applicable rules of ethical conduct, and so also to understand Judaism's own concept of itself as a universal religion.

The idiomatic phrase *ger toshav* is used in the Bible to refer both to members of the Jewish-Israelite people and to others who accompanied or attached themselves to it. In relation to God, who is God of the land, the Israelites are called *gerim ve-toshavim*—strangers and settlers: "But the land must not be sold beyond reclaim, for the land is Mine; you are but strangers resident with Me" (Lev. 25:23). In a different sense, the term is used in biblical legislation to designate the status of a minority group originating either in those remnants of the land's former population that had not been wiped out by the Israelite conquest or in strangers from outside the homeland who had come and attached themselves to the tribes. These minority groups had a permanent relationship with the society of the Israelite tribes and lived on its margins. The Bible distinguishes between the *ger toshav* and, on the one hand, the *ezrahim*—the "homeborn," who had full rights and obligations—and, on the other, the *nokhrim*—"foreigners," who had no permanent relationship with the majority society and to whom the particularistic morality of that group therefore did not apply (Deut. 15:3, 23:21). The groups of resident aliens had no land and no right to own land, and served as hired laborers. The law of the Torah nevertheless took care to grant them special protection and to equalize their legal status with that of the Jewish majority (Lev. 19:33–34). Their status was set on a par with that of another group that lacked economic rights—orphans and widows. They were thus equal in status to the poor with regard to the rights of *leket* and *shikhehah,* by which the indigent were entitled to gather gleanings and forgotten sheaves left in the fields after reaping (Lev. 23:22; Deut. 24:19). The Torah makes sure that they be paid their just wages (Deut. 24:14), that they not be oppressed (Ex. 22:20), that they be given a share of the tithes (Deut. 14:29), that they be enabled to share in the festival rejoicing (Deut. 16:11, 14), and that justice not be perverted where they are concerned (Deut. 24:17, 27:19). In certain ritual matters this assurance of their rights is accompanied by some ritual requirement or precondition. Thus, for example, their participation in the Passover sacrifice is conditional upon circumcision (Ex. 12:47–48).

The legal protection granted the *ger toshav* by the Torah is founded in the Bible upon the special protection and love of the God of Israel for the stranger, which becomes imbued with an ethical and historical pathos, through God's command to his people: "You too must befriend the stranger, for you were strangers in the land of Egypt" (Deut. 10:19).

The renewed Exile of the Jews and their presence as strangers in a foreign land after the destruction of the First Temple created the conditions for the growth of a universalistic approach within Judaism and for the abandonment of the idea that relations between members of the group and those who had attached themselves to it from without were to be founded upon relations of overlordship and ownership. As Yehezkel Kaufmann has so lucidly argued,[1] the concept of *giur*—the process of becoming a *ger toshav*—grew progressively farther away from its former ethnic and economic basis and came to signify a covenant that was solely religious in nature. More and more, it meant the adoption of a universal religious consciousness based upon rejection of the world of idolatry. At the same time, Judaism's own conception of itself as a religion with a universal mission in the Hellenistic world also prepared the ground for a precise determination of the process by which others might attach themselves to it, by converting from their faith to become *gerei ẓedek* (proselytes; lit., righteous Gentiles). The gates of Judaism were now open to all the gentile peoples, not only to those who came from the areas where the tribes had settled, and once the rules for conversion had been determined, the *gerim* were no longer seen as a distinctive class, as they had been in biblical society.

Once the concept of *ger ẓedek* had been established, the *ger*, with respect to almost all of his ritual and social rights, acquired the status of the homeborn in the full sense of the word. The rabbinic exegetical literature thus tended increasingly to neutralize the original meaning of the scriptural verses that relate to the *ger toshav* and to interpret all those biblical texts that refer to the *ger* as though they referred to the *ger ẓedek*. The covenant made by the Israelites on the plain of Moab, in which they undertook to observe the commandments, was seen as also including all those *gerim* who would someday convert to the faith (BT Shevu. 39a).

The idea of the absolute equality of obligations between the *ger* and the native-born Jew appears in the *Midrash ha-Gadol* to Leviticus 19:34:

> "The stranger who resides with you shall be to you as one of your citizens; you shall love him as yourself, for you were strangers in the land of Egypt"—as the citizen who has undertaken to observe all of the duties in the Torah, so is the *ger* who has undertaken to observe all the duties in the Torah. The Sages have therefore said: A *ger* who has undertaken to observe all the duties in the Torah but one is not to be accepted; Rabbi Yose ben Judah says: "Even if [what he does not undertake is] some small duty ordained by the scribes.

To be sure, the opening of the way to the spread of Judaism among the peoples of the classical world through acceptance of the *ger zedek* did not entirely eliminate the older concept of the *ger toshav*. In its spread throughout the Hellenistic world during Second Temple times, Judaism attracted numbers of *gerim toshavim*, Gentiles and partial converts who had drawn close to it in varying degrees. Opinions differed during that period as to the degree of proximity to Judaism necessary for a person to be considered to belong to a universal Jewish society that would be governed by the biblical rules of ethical conduct. According to one view it was sufficient for this purpose to embrace monotheism; according to another, one had also to adopt the natural ethical laws governing man's relationship to society and to live according to right rules of social conduct and a humanistic conception of man and the living world; yet a third view conditioned enjoyment of the benefits of Judaism's societal ethics on an almost total embrace of the Torah and its commandments.

> Who is considered a *ger toshav*? Anyone who commits himself before three of his fellows to renounce idol worship; this is the opinion of Rabbi Meir. But the Sages say: Anyone who commits himself to the seven commandments undertaken by the sons of Noah. Others say: Who is considered a *ger toshav*? A *ger* who eats the meat of animals that have not been ritually slaughtered, but has committed himself to observing all the commandments specified by the Torah apart from the prohibition of such meat.
>
> (Ger. 1:1; BT Av. Zar. 64b)

The biblical term *ger toshav* appears to have been replaced by such expressions as "fearers of God" and "righteous Gentiles," which reflected an attachment to Jewish society that was based not on economic and territorial bonds but upon a religious or ideological affinity.

Given the political and ideological context within which the people of Israel lived and the interreligious rivalry that characterized the ancient world, these conversionary trends, in which members of different peoples within the land of Israel or outside it attached themselves in varying degrees to Judaism, on occasion gave rise to ambivalent attitudes on the part of both Jews and non-Jews. The political demise of the Hasmonaean kingdom and the subsequent elevation of Christianity, from the point of view both of numbers and of its legal status within the Roman Empire, shaped some of the difficulties that must have faced the framers of several statements reflecting a negative attitude toward the acceptance of converts: "Evil will befall those who accept converts" (BT Yev. 109b); or casting doubt upon their loyalty: "Do not trust a convert until twenty-four generations have passed" (Yalkut Shimoni, Ruth, sec. 601).

Christianity's domination of the Roman Empire in both Europe and Byzantium and the rise and spread of Islam presented Judaism with a new historical and ideological reality. Hopes for turning Judaism into the universal religion of the cultured world faded, and the struggle to maintain the majority status of the Jewish society in the land of Israel was lost. The Jewish communities constituted minority societies in all the lands of their dispersion, and they became increasingly dependent upon their surroundings. A new society founded upon a monotheistic faith had risen upon the ruins of the ancient world, and the struggle against paganism was thus no longer a primary concern. Moses Maimonides saw the Muslims not as idolators but as fellow believers in the monotheistic idea. He advocated the universalistic trends that had developed in Jewish thought in ancient times: "Moses bestowed the Torah and the commandments upon Israel . . . and upon any of the Gentiles who wishes to convert" (MT Hil. Melakhim 5:10). His attitude toward the concept of the *ger toshav* follows that expressed in a saying by Rabbi Simeon ben Eleazar: "The commandments concerning the *ger toshav* are practiced only in a time when the Jubilee year is in effect" (MT Hil. Issurei biah 14:18), that is, only in the messianic era, at a time when the Temple stands; the practice of these laws thus depends upon a global political transformation in the circumstances of the Jewish people. Maimonides did, however, take up the midrashic distinction between the *ger toshav,* a concept that he regarded as identical with that of the "righteous Gentile," and the gentile sage:

> Anyone who undertakes to keep the seven [Noachite] commandments and observes them strictly is considered a righteous Gentile, and he has a part in the World to Come; but only if he undertakes to do them because they are commanded by God . . . but if it is an intellectual conclusion that has led him to do them, he is not considered a *ger toshav* or a righteous Gentile, [but] a gentile sage.
>
> (MT Hil. Melakhim 8:11)

Unlike Judah Halevi, who expressed an opposing view in the *Kuzari* (ch. 1, sec. 27), Maimonides was not led by the political demise of Judaism to adopt a chauvinistic, ethnocentric attitude; from the very depths of Israel's humiliation and Exile he was able to construct a philosophical interpretation, in the intellectual spirit of his time, of Judaism's universal message.

Of great significance is the position taken by Maimonides' great follower

Menaḥem Ha-Meiri, who lived in southern France at the end of the thirteenth century. Ha-Meiri made a basic distinction between the cultural world of ancient times and that of the Middle Ages, differentiating, from a halakhic and theological point of view, between the peoples of the ancient world, who "were not bound by proper customs"—that is to say, who did not belong to a monotheistic society with right and orderly institutions—and the peoples of his own time, who "are bound by proper customs." In his view, those talmudic sources that discriminated between Gentile and Jew in terms of society's legal and ethical attitude toward them were referring to the idolatrous peoples of long ago, who were unworthy of anything better. By contrast, "Anyone who belongs to those peoples that are bound by proper customs and serve God in some way, even if their faith is distant from ours . . . are to be considered in exactly the same way as Jews with regard to these things . . . with no differentiation at all" (*Bet ha-Beḥirah,* Kalman Schlesinger, ed., 1940, BK, 320). Similarly, Ha-Meiri determined that the commandment to return a lost object applies to things that belong to "your brother, and that means anyone who is bound by proper customs" (*Bet ha-Beḥirah,* BM, 100). As Jacob Katz has stressed, Ha-Meiri belonged to a rationalistic school of thought that, taking Maimonides as its guide, saw man's ultimate purpose, in the religious realm as well as elsewhere, as the achievement of intellectual awareness: "to put aside falsehood and attain the truth, and this is the ultimate perfection."[2]

The concept of "bound by proper customs," which establishes a universal ethical standard to which Christianity, too, is a party, essentially parallels the idea of the seven Noachite commandments and takes the place of the concept of the *ger toshav* as it was used in talmudic times. The open relations it allowed between Jews and Gentiles were limited, to be sure, to specific areas, and the rule in no way displaced the validity of those Jewish laws that were meant to keep the Jews separate from the Gentiles. Nevertheless, the relative tolerance expressed in this concept was later to influence the controversy over this issue, which began to stir enlightened Jewish society in the eighteenth century and went on to permeate halakhic thought in the twentieth century.

The medieval exegesis of those verses in the Torah concerning the *ger* and the *ger toshav* was, of course, still dominated by the talmudic view, which interpreted the *ger* mentioned in the biblical laws that were directed at achieving equality among the members of the society as a *ger ẓedek,* a convert. Following the transformation that had taken place in talmudic thought, medieval scholars regarded the biblical ethic as applying to those who had converted to Judaism, rather than to those who had attached themselves to the Jews solely on a social and economic basis. They did, however, express special sympathy for the situation of the convert, reflecting the reality of the Middle Ages, in which there had not yet been an end to the passage between faiths or to the struggle to establish the status of the recent proselyte within his new society. Only thus can Rashi's reiteration of the midrashic interpretation of Leviticus 19:34 be properly understood: "For you were strangers in the land of Egypt—do not denigrate your fellow [the convert] for a defect which you bear as well, 'for I am the Lord your [pl.] God'—I am your God and his" (Rashi ad loc. BT BM 59b).

The exegetes of the period of the emancipation unhesitatingly read into the biblical laws concerning the *ger toshav* the complexities they faced with regard to their own political and religious identity. They gave the Torah's laws on the *ger* a humanistic and apologetic interpretation intended to demonstrate, both to their fellow Jews and to the gentile world, how far the Bible went in equalizing the status of foreign guests sojourning in the host country with that of the native residents of that country. Both traditional commentators, such as Samuel David Luzzatto and Elijah Benamozegh in Italy and Samson R. Hirsch in Germany, and those of a more philosophical bent, such as Hermann Cohen, Martin Buber, and Leo Baeck, discerned a similar message of civil egalitarianism in the attitude of the laws of the Torah regarding the *ger*. At times they even expressed a startlingly new understanding of the concept of the *ger toshav* itself:

> The Torah not only accepted the presence of the pagan stranger in the land, but, with paternalistic concern, required of Israel that he be given sustenance and support. . . . The Israelite had to relate to the stranger either as a *ger*—or simply, as a *toshav*—a stranger—that is, a pagan who had the right to dwell in the Land of Israel, on the sole condition that he refrained from worshiping idols. "If your brother, being in straits, comes under your authority, and you hold him as though a resident alien, let him live by your side" (Lev. 25:35). The foreigner is called "your brother," who is even closer than one's fellow.[3]

Benamozegh's famous opponent Samuel David Luzzatto, one of the founders of the academic discipline of *Wissenschaft des Judentums*, went so far as to name his son Philxene, "lover of the stranger." Regarding the expression "you shall love him as yourself" (Lev. 19:34), which appears in connection with the prohibition against dealing fraudulently with the stranger, he commented:

> The Gentiles of ancient times loved exclusively those who belonged to their own people, and had no distaste for dealing fraudulently with the stranger; that is why

it is said here, "love him as yourself"—behave toward him as you would wish others to behave toward you if you were a *ger,* the sense being similar to that of the previous writ, "love your neighbor as yourself."[4]

Moreover, even the commandment to "love your neighbor as yourself," which the talmudic literature had interpreted restrictively as applying only to members of one's group, was widened here to transcend its former particularistic significance: "Complete egalitarianism with regard to the *ger* and the attitude taken toward him, [expressed] not only in the law, but also in sentiments and deeds of love, to the extent that it is commanded to 'love him as yourself,' the sense of which is similar to 'love your neighbor as yourself.'"[5]

The same sentiment was expressed even more strongly by the emancipation's philosophical thinkers and exponents. In his interpretation of Leviticus 25:25–26, Hermann Cohen saw the *ger* as a brother, and like Luzzatto and Hirsch contrasted the ethics of the other ancient peoples with those of the Torah:

> "There shall be one law for the citizen and the stranger who dwells among you" (Ex. 12:49). Thus the distinction from the citizen is invalidated in favor of the stranger. The law has to be uniform for all who live in the country and do not merely pass through it. And the stranger does not need a patron in order to conduct a case in court, as he did in Greece and in Rome, for "the judgment is God's" (Deut. 1:17). Law does not have its origin in human statutes but comes from God. Therefore God gives also to the stranger his share in the law of the land, although he does not profess the one God. This is a great step, with which humanitarianism begins, namely, in the law and in the state.[6]

The parallel here with the controversy over the civil status of German Jewry is clear. It is no longer theological principles that are central, but rather social and legal principles, such as equality before the law, which are drawn from humanistic philosophy and whose precursors are now seen in the ancient laws of the Bible.

According to Jacob Katz,[7] the foundations of this egalitarian ethical conception are already to be found in the halakhic thought of the seventeenth century, where it had an essentially pragmatic character and was applied mainly to internal relations. The enlightened Jewry of the nineteenth century, had, however, internalized the demands of rational ethics and believed that its roots were to be found in the Bible itself. It acknowledged the framework of the secular state as fulfilling in some sense the minimal requirements of those ethics and in effect accepted the idea that Christianity fulfilled the universal basic principles of Judaism. These perceptions were grounded on the idea of natural law and the humanistic rationalism that lay at the bottom of the religious tolerance that had been preached by Mendelssohn and was later reformulated in Leo Baeck's study of the foundations of biblical ethics.[8]

Study of the egalitarian ethos and of the problematics of universalism was confined in the nineteenth century to the realms of enlightened philosophy and exegesis and made no significant inroads into the halakhic domain of Eastern Europe. With the advent of political Zionism and the Balfour Declaration (expressing Britain's sympathy with Zionist aspirations), however, this halakhic culture was faced with a new challenge: It now had to suggest a halakhic model for relations between Jews and non-Jews in the framework of a Jewish state, either an ideal one or the concrete one that was steadily becoming a reality. The creation precisely in the land of Israel of a Jewish majority with a non-Jewish minority in its midst brought back to the surface the buried strata of controversies that had raged in biblical, talmudic, and medieval Jewish thought regarding relations between Jews and non-Jews in the land of Israel, under Jewish sovereignty.

A brief survey will show that both in ultra-Orthodox rabbinic circles, which reject modernity and base their outlook primarily upon medieval exegesis, and in more moderate rabbinic circles, which accept modernity and seek to reconcile it with the world of halakhah, some significant changes in attitude have ensued in the wake of three signal events: the issuance of the Balfour Declaration in 1917, the establishment of the State of Israel in 1948, and the Six-Day War of 1967 and its consequences. As early as 1904, Abraham Isaac Kook, the first Chief Rabbi of Palestine, declared in a letter that halakhic decisions in this area ought to be based upon the opinion of Ha-Meiri, according to which those peoples in his own day who were "bound by proper customs and laws" were to be considered observers of the Noachite laws and treated accordingly.[9]

Even more outspoken was Isaac Herzog, who succeeded Kook as chief rabbi and held office at the time of the founding of the state. Drawing upon the views of Kook, he ruled that there was no prohibition against even the sale of land in Israel to members of a people observant of proper laws and customs, and they were to be accorded the status of the *ger toshav* even in the present day, when the law of the Jubilee year is not operative (and the land does not revert back to its original Jewish owners at the end of the fifty-year period, as it would have in biblical or messianic times). Rejecting the view of Maimonides, he held that it was not necessary for members of such a people to undertake in a Jewish court of law to abstain from idol worship in order for them to have the right to reside in the land of Israel. Following the lead of moderate legal scholars from the beginning of the modern era, Herzog determined that the Noachite laws did not include a prohibition against *shittuf* (polytheism), so that Christians, too, could be considered to have the status of "peoples bound by proper laws and customs" who enjoyed the rights of the *ger toshav,* for "in our time even Catholics are not idol worshippers in the original sense, but their hearts are turned to heaven." This, then, was Herzog's opinion from a normative point of view. From a practical point of view, moreover, he recognized that the circumstances of current political reality made it impossible for the Jewish state to be established without the consent of the other peoples of the world, "and until the Messiah comes, we will have need of their protection against a sea of foes . . . and there is also no doubt that they will not grant us a Jewish state unless we ordain the rights of minorities under the law and in the judicial system."[10] Moreover, there was another, pretalmudic precedent, for in the new state the Jews had, as it were, to make a covenant with the non-Jews, like the covenant that the returning exiles from Babylon in Second Temple times had made with the peoples they found in the land.[11] From this analogy Herzog derived some new normative principles, according to which Muslims and Christians were not included among the peoples subject to the talmudic proscription and the law applicable to them was, rather, that of the *ger toshav.*

Chief rabbis Ben-Zion Meir Ḥai Ouziel and Isser Yehudah Unterman followed Herzog in his approach. Ouziel permitted cases involving both Jews and non-Jews to be heard in Jewish courts and allowed the creation within the country's judicial system of a single, unified judiciary. He also based his opinion on the ruling of Ha-Meiri, making alternate use, like his predecessor, of normative arguments ("bounded by proper customs and laws") and pragmatic arguments (*dina de-malkhuta dina*—"the law of the state is law for the Jews"—and the imperative to avoid desecration of the name of God).[12] Unterman broadened the framework for relations between Jews and non-Jews ordained by the Sages of the Talmud "for the sake of peace." While that framework had originally had a pragmatic significance and had been interpreted accordingly, he gave it an ethical, idealistic interpretation, holding that its ideological basis lay in the understanding that all the Torah's "ways are ways of pleasantness, and all her paths peace."[13] "For their desire to encourage the growth of feelings of peace and friendship among people led the Sages to find it necessary to enact preventive measures."[14]

From the Balfour Declaration up to the Six-Day War of 1967, the mod-

erate rabbinic leadership had the wisdom to give the sources a new interpretation that was not without foundation in traditions emanating from
medieval halakhic thought. It was able, moreover, to incorporate into the
halakhic discussion and its conclusions modern trends of thought and ideas
of social and political ethics, the same ones as were accepted among the
peoples of Western Europe. The model that served the rabbis of the pre-
state period was the same one that served the Israeli legal system as a whole,
namely the British legal system.

The ultra-Orthodox rabbis who opposed Zionism, however, took a very
different view. Unencumbered by collective responsibility for the political
reality that was taking shape in Palestine and then the State of Israel, they
clung to the letter of the medieval halakhah. Thus, against Herzog's opinion
that the prohibition against allowing non-Jews to purchase property in the
land of Israel did not apply to the Christians and Muslims who lived there,
Isaiah Karlitz, known as the Ḥazon Ish, held that the prohibition against
selling land to non-Jews remained in effect, even where such a sale might
benefit the Jews.[15] Rabbi Zolti, following Maimonides, held that as long as
the Jubilee year is not in effect there can be no recognition of the status of
ger toshav. Rejecting the opinions of Kook and Herzog, Zolti believed that
contemporary Arabs do not enjoy the rights accorded the ger toshav by biblical law because they have not undertaken before a Jewish court to observe
the Noachite laws.[16] Such trends within the halakhah lead to a radical discrepancy between the utopian Jewish legal system—whose full realization
is relegated to the messianic realm—and the legal reality taking shape
within the State of Israel with respect to relations between the Jews and
Arab citizens of the state. Any "rights" of the land's Arab population are
founded, from the point of view of the ultra-Orthodox, upon a single sweeping prohibition that the Jews undertook to observe after the destruction of
the Second Temple—the prohibition against changing the historical reality
in which Jewish society found itself, or to which it was subject. Changing
that reality was a task for the messianic era.

The third turning point in our survey is Israel's victory in the Six-Day
War, which altered perspectives and upset the pragmatic and ideological
trends that had characterized the moderate religious sector on the one hand
and the ultra-Orthodox on the other. The halakhic views of the ultra-Orthodox were increasingly influenced by considerations relating to the real
world, which compelled them to deal in a nonutopian way with the political
and social questions facing the State of Israel and its Jewish society. As a
result, they now took the very stance that religious Zionism had taken at

the beginning of the century. Religious Zionism, on the other hand, borne upon the crest of new messianic enthusiasm following the Six-Day War, now retreated from the universalistic outlook that had developed yet more strongly within it in the period following the establishment of the state. It drew back into a particularistic outlook, seeking a new exegesis of the sources that was fundamentally different from that which it had adopted heretofore. That exegesis was, in fact, utopian, ahistorical, and restorative in character. Taking a historically anachronistic pose, it sought to apply the laws concerning relations between Jews and non-Jews that had been in effect in the last centuries of the Second Temple period and the first centuries of the Common Era to the historical and political reality of modern Israel. In so doing, it sought to reestablish the particularistic ethic of the talmudic period, supporting it with medieval philosophical distinctions that sound to the modern ear like pure and simple racism.

Thus, in a collection published by Alon Shevut (a yeshivah associated with religious Zionism) dealing with relations between Jews and Arabs and taking the form of a bibliographic study by an "academic staff of Torah scholars"—most of whom were educated in modern *yeshivot* patterned on the model of the famous talmudic academy founded by Abraham Isaac Kook, *Merkaz ha-Rav*—the editors have the following comment to make on one of the articles they include: "This article is published within the framework of our study that sets out to survey halakhic disquisitions on the subject [of Jewish–Arab relations] and is included herein because the author acknowledges the *fact* that Judaism views the Gentile as an inferior creature, and that this [is] the basis of the attitude of the halakhah toward him." As we have seen, a historical analysis furnishes no ground for such a statement. Further on, in elucidating their understanding of the significance of religious tolerance, the editors explain: "The way . . . to clarify this matter is to set the Gentiles, believers in other religions, on an entirely different plane from that on which the Jews stand . . . , a distinction that was formulated by Rabbi Judah Halevi in his book *Ha-Kuzari*."[17]

From a normative standpoint, the members of this camp, in opposition to long-standing halakhic tradition, incline to class both Muslims and Christians as idolators and to hold that there is thus certainly no need, from a halakhic point of view, to include them in the category of the *ger toshav*. Shneur Zuta Reis, for instance, states that the Arabs of our time—unlike those of the Middle Ages—must be considered outright idolators.[18] Yehudah Gershuni, who before 1967 had declared, on the basis of Ha-Meiri's famous ruling, that the modern-day Gentiles, the Muslims and the Christians, were "bound by proper custom and the rule of laws, and we are [therefore] required to violate the Sabbath for their sake [that is, in an emergency],"[19] later stated (in an article published in 1981) that "the Muslims, who are not idolators, are held to be as the *ger toshav* with respect . . . to their residence in the land, but not with respect to the question of whether to save their lives [in violation of the Sabbath]."[20] With regard to Christians, he justifies the use of ethical standards in accordance with the talmudic principle demanding such conduct "for the sake of peace" by the pragmatic explanation that "we have not the strength on our own, and we still require the aid of the peoples of the world." In contrast to the view of Chief Rabbi Unterman, who had written before 1967 that these laws are to be understood as having an ideological and ethical basis, Gershuni finds it preferable to explain and interpret them from a pragmatic point of view.

In contrast to these processes, by which the "moderate" camp has removed itself from the historical into the utopian realm, ultra-Orthodox rulings from the post-1967 period display a retreat from talmudic-medieval utopianism toward a halakhic posture that relates to the political reality within which the halakhah must operate. Thus, the leading Sephardi rabbi of the contemporary generation, Ovadiah Yosef, a graduate of the anti-Zionist Lithuanian academies, rules that "it is in no way a sacred duty to make war and risk lives in order to defend our retention of territories we have conquered in opposition to the view of the Gentiles . . . and therefore if it is possible for us to give back territories and so avoid the danger of war with our enemies, we must do so on account of the commandment to save life." This ruling is based on political-halakhic considerations influenced by the nature of political reality, "for the generals of the Israel Defense Forces also . . . are of the opinion that no danger to the Jews dwelling in the land will ensue from the return of territories, and there is thus no reason for apprehension about returning territories in order to forestall the immediate danger of war."[21]

The struggle to equalize the status of the Palestinian Arabs can thus serve the interests of both the particularist/fundamentalist and the egalitarian/universalist streams, depending upon the speaker and the arguments he uses and upon the historical and political reality he seeks to establish. The concept of the *ger toshav,* with its several scriptural, talmudic, medieval, modern, and postmodern layers of meaning, will thus remain an issue in Jewish religious thought and in the conflict within the world of the halakhah between modernist and egalitarian trends, on the one hand, and anachronistic, antiegalitarian trends, on the other. No end is yet in sight to the contest between particularism and universalism.

REFERENCES

1. Yehezkel Kaufmann, *Golah ve-Nekhar,* Pt. 4 (1964), 209–56.
2. See Jacob Katz, *Exclusiveness and Tolerance* (1962), 114–30.
3. Elijah Benamozegh, *Be-Shevilei Musar,* S. Marcus, tr. (1952), 118–24.
4. *Perush Shadal al Hameshah Humshei ha-Torah,* 2nd ed. (1966), 420. Cf. the commentary of Samson R. Hirsch on Ex. 22:20, *Der Pentateuch,* 4th ed., 2 (1903), 288.
5. Samson R. Hirsch, ad loc. Lev. 19:34, *Der Pentateuch* 3: 432.
6. Hermann Cohen, *Religion of Reason out of the Sources of Judaism,* Simon Kaplan, tr. (1972), 121.
7. See Katz, op. cit., 164–68.
8. See Leo Baeck, *The Essence of Judaism* (1961), 190ff.
9. *Igrot ha-Rav Avraham Yizhak Ha-Kohen* [Kook] (1961), 99.
10. Jacob Herzog, "Zekhuyot Miyutim le-fi ha-Halakhah," in *Tehumin,* 2 (1981), 169–79.
11. Ibid., 170.
12. Ben-Zion Meir Hai Ouziel, "Ovdei ha-Kokhavim ve-ha-Nokhri be-Dinei Yisrael," in *Ha-Torah ve-ha-Medinah* (1952), 4–6.
13. Isser Yehudah Unterman, "Darkhei Shalom ve-Hagdaratam," in *Or ha-Mizrah* 4 (1965), 227–31. Cf. Prov. 3:17.
14. Ibid., 220.
15. See Unterman, op. cit.
16. Abraham Mordecai Hirshberg, "Be-Inyan Mekhirat Karka le-Ovdei ha-Kokhavim be-Shevuit," in *Ha-Pardes,* 26 (1952), 7–13.
17. Uri Desberg and Asaf Cohen, eds., *Yahasei Yehudim ve-Aravim; Skirah Bibliografit* (1985), 1 (emphasis added).
18. Shneur Zevta Reis, "Iy Yesh le-Umot ha-Olam ha-Zekhut Ladum al Baalut Yerushalayim ve-Erez Yisrael?" in *Ha-Meir* (1967), cited in Desberg and Cohen, op. cit., 9.
19. Yehudah Gershuni, "Nozrim u-Muslemim le-Or ha-Halakhah," in *Or le-Mirzah* (1967), 32–37.
20. Gershuni, "Ha-Miyutim ve-Zekhuyotehem be-Medinat Yisrael le-Or ha-Halakhah," in *Tehumin,* 2 (1981), 180–82.
21. Ovadiah Yosef, "Hahzarat Shetahim mi-Erez Yisrael Bimkom Pikuah Nefesh," in *Oz ve-Shalom,* 3 (1982), 5–10.

BIBLIOGRAPHY

Moritz Gutmann, *Das Judentum und seine Umwelt* (1927).
Jacob Katz, *Exclusiveness and Tolerance* (1961).
Saul Lieberman, "Gentiles and Semi-Proselytes," in Lieberman, *The Greek in Jewish Palestine* (1942).
Gershon Tschernovitz, *Ha-Yahas bein Yisrael le-Goyim lefi ha-Rambam* (1940).

Study

תלמוד תורה

Aharon Lichtenstein

In Jewish thought and experience, few values are as cherished as *talmud Torah,* the study of Torah; and few cultures, if any, have assigned to learning of any kind—let alone the mastery of scriptural and legal texts—the status it enjoys within Judaism. That priority is not the result of much-vaunted Jewish intellectualism. Quite the contrary; it is, if anything, the latter's cause rather than its effect. Its true source is the specifically religious role that Jewish law and tradition have accorded talmud Torah.

This religious role is multifaceted. The study of Torah constitutes, at one level, a halakhic act, entailing the realization of a divine commandment—and one of the preeminent commandments at that. As such, it has a dual basis. On the one hand, it is a distinct normative category, positing specific goals and prescribing, like other *miẓvot,* clearly defined conduct enjoined by a particular mandate. The *miẓvah* of talmud Torah charges the Jew to acquire knowledge of Torah, insofar as he is able; but it addresses itself primarily to the process rather than the result. Its minimal demand, some daily study of Torah, is formulated in verses included in the first portion of the Shema: "Take to heart these instructions with which I charge you this day. Impress them upon your children. Recite them when you stay at home and when you are away, when you lie down and when you get up" (Deut. 6:6–7). On the other hand, it is included in the far more general charge enjoining the Jew "to love the Lord your God, and to serve Him with all your heart and soul" (Deut. 11:13)—that service requiring, as the midrash postulates, the study of Torah apart from ritual and prayer (Sif. Deut. 5).

At a second level, talmud Torah is viewed axiologically—both as an independent value and as a means of ensuring and enriching spiritual existence, both personal and collective. Engagement with Torah for its own sake, *lishmah,* is a prime goal. Its raison d'être need not be sought by reference to other categories, moral or religious. Can study that "only" entails live contact with the revealed and expounded divine Word be less than invaluable? Obviously, that contact can ordinarily have instrumental value as well—in two respects. First, study provides knowledge requisite to halakhic living even as it deepens halakhic commitment. Second, since talmud Torah enables a person, within limits, to cleave unto God, it has moral, passional, and pietistic repercussions.

These elements exist on the collective plane as well. Beyond them, however, one may note a more strictly public aspect. As Torah itself is the basis of Israel's covenant with God, so is its study a means both of cementing that bond and of providing communal uplift. In one sense, this applies to the oral Law in particular, as the intimacy of the covenantal relationship is experienced within it uniquely. "Rabbi Johanan stated: 'The Holy One, blessed be He, entered into a covenant with Israel only because of oral matters, as it is written [Ex. 34:27]: "For after the tenor of these words I have made a covenant with thee, and with Israel" '" (BT Git. 60B). The principle, however, applies to Torah in its entirety, with its full conceptual and experiential import.

At a third level, the role of talmud Torah is conceived in cosmological and mystical terms, bordering, in some formulations, on the magical. From this perspective, it attains continuous cosmic significance as a metaphysical factor affecting the fabric of reality—indeed, as that which supports and sustains the very existence of the universe. The Talmud cites this concept in the name of Rabbi Eleazar, who, interpreting a biblical verse in this vein, saw it as attesting to the significance of Torah: "Rabbi Eleazar said: 'Great is Torah for, were it not for it, heaven and earth would not exist, as it is stated [Jer. 33:25], "If my covenant be not day and night, I have not appointed the ordinances of heaven and earth" '" (BT Ned. 32a); and elsewhere the Talmud explains the gravity of *bittul Torah*—literally, "the negation of Torah," that is, the failure to study it adequately—on a similar basis (BT Shab. 33a). Rabbi Ḥayyim Isaac Volozhiner, founder in 1802 of the archetypal Lithuanian yeshivah and the most vigorous modern proponent of this view, went so far as to arrange for some measure of Torah study at his yeshivah at all times in order to ensure cosmic existence. To many, this may surely seem naively bizarre anthropocentrism. Be that as it may, the underlying attitude, shorn of its literalist application, is deeply rooted in rabbinic tradition.

The object of study can of course be any and every part of Torah. The Midrash, commenting upon the verse "Give ear, my people, to my teaching" (Ps. 78:1), notes: "Let no one tell you that the psalms are not Torah, for they are indeed Torah, and the prophets are also Torah . . . as are the riddles and the parables" (Mid. Ps. ad loc. Ps. 78:1). And from a purely normative standpoint, the *miẓvah* is fulfilled, regardless of which area of Torah is being studied. Historically, however, the major emphasis—particularly, but not exclusively, at more advanced levels of scholarship—has been upon the *Torah she-be-al peh,* the corpus of law and tradition, homily and exegesis, primarily formulated and preserved in the Talmud. Jews often recited *tehillim* (psalms) as a pietistic exercise, but learning was more likely to deal with the Mishnah, the Gemara, or the collection of talmudic aggadot, *Ein Ya'akov.* The Talmud itself postulates that periods of study should be apportioned, "one third to Scripture, one third to midrash, and one third to Talmud [that is, Gemara]" (BT Kid. 30a). However, one classical medieval authority, Rabbenu Tam, held that the study of the Babylonian Talmud sufficed, since all three elements were blended within it, while another, Moses Maimonides, stated that this counsel applied only in the early stages of intellectual development, during which the raw material of Torah was being absorbed and digested, but that once the infrastructure existed a person should devote himself to the subtle analysis of the Gemara. Whatever the rationale, the primacy of Torah is fairly clear.

This primacy derives, in part, from concern about potentially heterodox tendencies springing from direct and independent study of Scripture. Primarily, however, it is grounded in the centrality of law and rabbinic tradition within Jewish consciousness and experience. The encounter with God as commander lies at the heart of Jewish existence; to the extent that it is realized through talmud Torah, the legal corpus, as developed within the oral tradition, is a prime vehicle for this encounter. To an outsider, much of traditional talmud Torah no doubt borders on the absurd. From a purely rational or pragmatic perspective, the prospect of a group of laymen studying the minutiae of complex and often "irrelevant" halakhot may indeed be bizarre. In light of Jewish commitment and experience, however, it is thoroughly intelligible.

That commitment is the key to the traditional conception of the nature of talmud Torah. Study is of course an intellectual and largely critical activity, but in this case it is significantly molded by its religious character. The effect is both enriching and constricting. On the one hand, Torah study, regarded as an encounter with the *Shekhinah* (the divine Presence), is enhanced by an experiential dimension. Hence the importance that the rabbis assigned to the confluence of prayer and study: They urged that one should preferably engage in both at the same place, even if in most views this entails praying in private rather than in public. In this vein, talmud Torah can assume an almost visceral quality, and aggadic texts abound with similes comparing Torah study to sensuous and even sensual activity, elemental and exotic alike. Commenting upon the verse "A lovely hind and a graceful doe, let her breasts satisfy thee at all times" (Prov. 5:19), Rabbi Samuel ben Naḥman expounds: "Why were the words of the Torah compared to a hind? To tell you that as the hind has a narrow womb and is relished by its cohabitant at each and every moment as at the first hour, so it is with words of Torah. They are relished by their students at each and every moment as at the first hour. . . . Why were Torah words compared to a nipple? As with a nipple, however often an infant fondles it he finds milk in it, so it is with Torah words. As often as a man ponders them, he finds relish in them" (BT Er. 54b).

Conceived in such terms, talmud Torah is invested with a dual nature. In part, it is oriented to accomplishment, with the acquisition of knowledge and skills being obvious goals. Teleological considerations aside, however, the process, as has been noted, is no less important than its resolution; and even if one has retained nothing, the experience itself—live contact with the epiphanous divine will manifested through Torah, and encounter with the divine Presence, which hovers over its student—is immeasurably important. Talmud Torah is not just informative or illuminating; it is ennobling and purgative. He who studies Torah, says the Mishnah, "is called friend, beloved, lover of God, and lover of men. He rejoices God and men. The Torah invests him with modesty and reverence, and enables him to be virtuous, pious, upright, and faithful. It distances him from sin and draws him near to virtue" (M. Avot 6:1). It is this emphasis upon process and its purgative character that renders abstruse study both possible and meaningful. From a pragmatic standpoint, much talmud Torah is futile or irrelevant, or both. Religiously regarded, however, it is eminently sensible. The bather is refreshed, regardless of where he dips into the ocean. Does he refrain from going to the water merely because he cannot reach the other shore?

But if the religious conception of talmud Torah extends its horizons in one sense, it constricts them severely in another. The religious view implies, in effect, that study that is not grounded in commitment is, at best, of limited value, and that has indeed been the traditional position. With reference to more extreme cases—presumably those involving patently negative attitudes—the rabbis stated that while Torah is life-giving to those who approach it rightly, "to the sinister, in relation to it, it is a poisonous herb" (BT Shab. 88b). However, even purely dispassionate study, the very ideal of much of the academic world, has been regarded with great reservation. This attitude has not been grounded in a mystical view of Torah as a gnosis to be reserved for the initiate; it has sprung, rather, from the perception that talmud Torah cannot be realized by approaching sacral material from a secular perspective.

While the sacral character of talmud Torah has generally been universally assumed by Jewish tradition, its scope has been very much in dispute. Of course, relatively few have doubted that much learning is a desirable thing; but opinions have differed over how much could be normatively demanded or ordinarily expected. Some have held that while the *miẓvah* of talmud Torah clearly required a modicum of daily study, anything beyond the barest minimum was more a matter of lofty aspiration than of halakhic duty. Others, however, have insisted that while minimal daily study could be singled out as an inescapable and irreducible charge, maximal commitment— flexibly perceived—constituted an obligation rather than a meritorious desideratum. As Rabbenu Nissim, one of the last of the great medieval authorities, put it in the fourteenth century: "Every person is obligated to study constantly, day and night, in accordance with his ability" (Comm. on BT Ned. 8a).

The key phrase is, of course, "in accordance with his ability" (*kefi koho*), but its practical substantive import remains wholly amorphous so long as one has not come to grips with the critical question of the relation of talmud Torah to other areas of human endeavor, secular or religious. In one sense, this is simply a variant of the broader problem of the definition of priorities and the apportionment of energies, resources, and commitment between the mundane and the spiritual realms, respectively. This specific point was debated in the twelfth century by Rabbenu Tam and his grand-nephew, Elhanan ben Isaac of Dampierre, who, in interpreting the aphorism "Excellent is talmud Torah together with a worldly occupation" (M. Avot 2:2), disagreed as to which component was primary. Presumably, they dealt with practical rather than axiological primacy; nevertheless, their controversy is clearly significant. At a second level, however, the problem concerns the relation between different elements of the spiritual life proper—between the outreach of charity and *gemilut ḥasidim* as opposed to self-centered spirituality; or between talmud Torah and prayer as aspects of the contemplative life.

Surveying much of the current yeshivah scene and its recent east European, and particularly Lithuanian, background, one often gets the impression that, as a spiritual value, talmud Torah is not only central but exclusive. From a broader perspective, however, the picture is more balanced—especially with reference to the talmudic sages. Statements to the effect that "talmud Torah is equal to them [that is, a list of key *miẓvot*] all" (Pe'ah 1:1), or the famous counsel "Turn it over and turn it over [that is, the Torah] for all is in it" (M. Avot 5:25), are complemented by sharp asseverations that single-minded talmud Torah is not only incomplete but distorted. "Whoever says that he has nothing but Torah," expounds the Talmud in the tractate *Yevamot,* "does not even have Torah. Why? Rav Papa said, 'Scripture states, "Study them and observe them faithfully" [Deut. 5:1]. Whosoever relates to observance relates to study, whosoever does not relate to observance does not relate to study'" (BT Yev. 109b). Elsewhere, we encounter an even more radical statement. "He who engages solely in Torah [study]," declares Rav Huna, "is as one who has no God. For it is written [II Chron. 15:3], 'Now for long seasons Israel was without the true God.' What is meant by 'without the true God'? It means that he who engages solely in Torah [study] is as one who has no God" (BT Av. Zar. 17b).

Unquestionably, emphases differ among both the talmudic sages and subsequent generations. The Talmud relates that when Rav Huna saw Rabbi Hamnuna prolonging his prayer at the expense of talmud Torah, he commented: "They forsake eternal life and engage in temporal life"; and it goes on to explain that Rabbi Hamnuna evidently held that there should be "a time for prayer apart, and a time for Torah apart" (BT Shab. 10a). Analogously, the practice of the Palestinian *amora* Rabbi Joshua ben Levi, who "would not go to a house of mourning save to that of one who had been childless, for it is written, 'Weep sore for him that goeth away, for he shall return no more nor see his native country' [Jer. 22:10]" (BT MK 27b), presumably so as not to divert time and energy from talmud Torah, reflects this singular emphasis. But one principle is beyond question, namely, that Torah exists within a larger axiological complex. It both complements other values and is complemented by them, and even if it reigns supreme, it surely does not rule alone.

Clearly, then, the assertion of Rabbenu Nissim that one is obligated to engage in talmud Torah "day and night, to the extent of one's ability [*kefi koḥo*]," remains, in practical terms, ill defined. Only after one has determined the scope of other legitimate concerns and has allocated to them their respective time and effort does *kefi koho* become clear. Nevertheless, the formulation—with its implicit assumption that there is a basic total commitment to talmud Torah, from which one then subtracts—is highly significant in its own right. It clearly reflects the singular importance that, whatever the continuing dialectic between intellection and implementation, Judaism has uniquely assigned to the study of Torah, even at the popular level. One might note that the concern with talmud Torah attains further significance as a source of the heightened time-consciousness that is so integral a part of Jewish sensibility and experience.

Finally, as to the scope of talmud Torah, it is very broad in one sense and extremely limited in another. As a value, its range is well nigh universal. It relates to Gentiles and Jews alike, to both men and women, to children as well as adults. "Rabbi Meir stated, 'Whence that even a Gentile who engages in [the study of] Torah is as a high priest? For it is stated [Lev. 18:5], "Which if a person do [i.e., the *mizvot*], he shall live by them." It does not say, "Kohanim, Levites, and Israelites," but "a person" '" (BT Sanh. 59a). As a normative *mizvah*, however, it devolves only upon Jewish men. For others, it is regarded in part as an admirable aspiration and in part as a means for acquiring the knowledge requisite for the fulfillment of other *mizvot*, but not as a duty to pursue knowledge for its own sake. Moreover, concern lest half-baked knowledge be abused has, at times, actually led to discouraging such voluntary study. This fear of dilettantism has, historically, been a prime reason for the relatively limited level of Torah study by women. Given the changes in women's overall social and educational status and the nature of their total cultural experience within the modern world, many have felt that this benign neglect is no longer warranted; and, indeed, since the turn of the century, much has been done to redress the imbalance in the talmud Torah of men and women. How far this process will develop and whether it has built-in halakhic limits remains to be seen. Be that as it may, the axiological and historical centrality of talmud Torah remains a cardinal fact of Jewish spiritual existence.

BIBLIOGRAPHY

Louis Ginzberg, "The Rabbinical Student," in *Students, Scholars and Saints,* 2nd ed. (1958).

Aharon Lichtenstein, "Does Jewish Tradition Recognize an Ethic Independent of Halakha?" in Marvin Fox, ed., *Modern Jewish Ethics: Theory and Practice* (1975).

Joseph B. Soloveitchik, *Halakhic Man* (1983).

Suffering

סבל

David Hartman

A Jew loyal to the covenant perceives every aspect of reality as expressive of the personal will of God. Schematically speaking, we may say that the covenantal community experiences God as an active personal will in its consciousness of its physical existence, its sociopolitical existence, and its normative daily life. First, the creation of the physical world and the human species is not perceived as merely a single act of the divine will in the distant past. Rather, as the first benediction of the Shema ("Hear, O Israel . . ."; the proclamation of God's unity) puts it, Jews see God as he who "in his goodness renews every day the work of creation." At every present moment, the will of God decides whether the physical existence of the human being shall continue or cease. Second, the Jews' sense of history and social consciousness takes its beginning from the story of the Exodus, in which a stupefied mass of slaves was transformed into a living social reality through God's decision to lead them out of the social chaos of Egypt. Just as nature is not to be explained without the God of creation, so the community owes its social and historical existence to the Lord of history through whose intervention it was born. Neither the physical nor the communal existence of halakhic Jews is intelligible without reference to a transcendent personal will. Third, the Torah functions as a permanent mediator of God's personal relationship to the community. The *mizvot* are not abstract demands implied by a Platonic form or a Kantian categorical imperative; they are demands made by a personal will and presuppose a personal relationship to God.

Given, therefore, that everything in the universe is related to a personal God, how did the rabbinic tradition educate Jews to sustain commitment to God in spite of the serious gap that often develops between expectation based on the biblical covenantal promise and the reality of human suffering? When suffering and tragedy strike without any explanation once, twice, and repeatedly, individuals in the community no longer know what kind of world they are living in. Like Job, they may ask, "Why do you hide your face and treat me like an enemy?" (Job 13:24).

It would be a mistake to think that the negative consequences of suffering were not a serious religious problem for the rabbinic tradition because the relational immediacy of the living God of revelation had been neutralized by the talmudic emphasis upon study of Torah and upon questions of legal authority and practice. The enormous concern with exegesis and fine legal distinctions should not be thought to have diminished the vitality of the covenantal passion for God. Rabbinic teachers brought the religious intensity of the living God present at the revelatory moment of Sinai even into their daily experience of the study of Torah.

Jews loyal to the covenant, therefore, cannot judge their own self-worth independently of what they believe to be God's responses to their actions. A covenantal religious consciousness is always vulnerable to self-doubt and to feelings of rejection and guilt. Prolonged drought, for example, not only brings economic hardship but also awakens feelings of rejection. The response, accordingly, is to "place limits on business transactions, on building and planting, on betrothals and marriages, and on mutual greetings, as befits persons under divine displeasure" (M. Ta'an. 1:7).

In examining how the rabbis sought to handle this problem, we may say that their approach belongs more to what we would now call religious anthropology than to philosophical theology. This distinction is of basic importance. To the philosopher or theologian concerned with the problem of theodicy, the existence of morally indifferent causes of suffering appears to be incompatible with the existence of an all-powerful and benevolent God. Such an individual is faced with the problem of reconciling what seems to be this incompatibility of facts and beliefs. How is it logically possible to claim that God is the just Lord of history in view of the senseless evil manifest in the world? The problem of suffering appears in a different light, however, when the focus is more on its anthropological than its theological implications. The questions then become: How do we respond to events that can call into question our whole identity as God's covenantal community? Can we allow ourselves to embrace a personal God knowing that chaos can at any moment invade our reality and arbitrarily nullify all our efforts and expectations? Do we have the strength to open ourselves to a personal God in a world filled with unpredictable suffering? When her child dies, the question a mother faces is less how to explain the logic of God's omnipotence than whether she has the strength and emotional energy to love again.

From the anthropological perspective on the problem of suffering, therefore, the prime concern is not so much to defend the notions of divine justice and power. It is, rather, as in other personal relationships, to determine what measure of continuity, stability, and predictability can enable the relationship with God to survive all shocks.

How the rabbis confronted the problem can be shown by examining some texts, of which the first contains a discussion by the sages of two conflicting descriptions of divine providence.

> He who performs one *mizvah,* good is done to him, his days are prolonged, and he inherits the land. But he who does not perform one *mizvah,* good is not done to him, his days are not prolonged, and he does not inherit the land.
>
> (M. Kid. 1:10)

Although some authorities take "he inherits the land" to mean "he has a part in the World to Come," the emphasis in this statement is decidedly thisworldly. Indeed, this statement from the Mishnah is hardly different in spirit from the Bible, with its perspective that is earthbound. The Mishnah typically invites one to expect prosperity in this world if one is loyal to God's *mizvot,* to anticipate rain in due season, abundant crops, many children, security from adversity, a long and good life.

The *baraita* (the external teaching of a tanna not included in the Mishnah) to the above mishnah, however, claims that when people strive to be righteous in this world, God's response is to inflict upon them suffering that will expiate their sins, so that they can enjoy complete bliss in the World to Come. But people who prefer iniquity to righteousness are allowed to prosper in this world, because they have already ensured themselves punishment in the World to Come.

The mishnah and the *baraita* embody different kinds of expectations that individuals may permit themselves in their living relationship with God, different risks that they are prepared to take in the light of that felt relationship. Since the aim of the talmudic discussion is to find a viable way of life, not a metaphysical truth, the Talmud does not give exclusive preference to any of the ways offered. Some Jews may find one outlook more consonant with their sensibilities and personal experience than another; others may feel more at ease with the other. Both ways are authentic, because both seek to preserve commitment to the *miẓvot*.

In the talmudic discussion, Rava points out that the *baraita* accords with Rabbi Jacob, who taught that there was no reward for *miẓvot* in this world and that wherever the Torah promises a reward for a *miẓvah* the reward is to be expected only in the next world. To illustrate his teaching, Rabbi Jacob told a story of a child who died immediately after fulfilling two *miẓvot:* the child obeyed his father, who had told him to take birds from the loft, and he obeyed the biblical requirement of letting the mother bird go free before taking the young ones. Yet although the Bible promises long life to those who fulfill either of these *miẓvot,* on descending from the loft the boy fell and was killed (BT Kid. 39b).

Rabbi Jacob refused to expose people to the risk of expecting that their obedience to the *miẓvot* would ensure them material prosperity and a long life. For when people hold such expectations, the sudden death of a child who has just performed *miẓvot* that promised long life may create a total value disorientation. If things happen that suggest that the promises of God cannot be relied upon, trust in him and readiness to perform his *miẓvot* may collapse. The solution chosen by Rabbi Jacob was simple and drastic. Eliminate every expectation of reward in this world for the performance of *miẓvot*. Remember that the covenantal relationship with a personal God does not end with death. Look forward to the promised resurrection of the dead. Never forget that God loves you and that this is why he gave you the Torah and the *miẓvot,* which will guarantee you reward in the World to Come.

The authors of the statement in the mishnah, on the other hand, preferred to educate Jews to believe that everyday reality can also contain joy. To give up anticipation of reward in this world for *miẓvot* could destroy the vitality of the sense of personal relationship with God that animates covenantal religious life. The distant promise of the resurrection of the dead is too weak a peg to bear on its own the entire weight of human expectations. The living God of the Bible must be seen to be active also in present reality if Jews are not to grow weary of God's covenant and despair of his love. If we are taught to expect reward for *miẓvot* also in this world, then sometimes we may be disappointed, but we will also attach greater significance to the joyful moments in our lives by seeing them as signs of divine approval. When the impetus to live that joyful moments provide is thus reinforced, we will also be able to take the disappointments in our stride.

The rabbis of the mishnah and Rabbi Jacob did not disagree regarding belief in a personal God. Both also shared the same objective reality: a world of painful tragedy and undeserved suffering, of people snatched away in the midst of performing noble deeds.

Nonetheless, they are able to have different expectations of a personal God and different styles of living the covenantal life. The choice between the different views is left to the sensibilities of the individual reader. All that the Talmud demands of its readers is that they find some approach that will enable them to maintain their commitment to the *mizvot* in the world as they experience it. There is even nothing to prevent the same person from alternating between different approaches at different moments in his or her life.

That the very same person could in different circumstances interpret the workings of Providence in completely different ways is exemplified in rabbinic literature by Rabbi Akiva. We find rabbinic traditions reporting that Akiva sometimes interpreted joy and suffering with a thisworldly reference, but also rabbinic statements that he sometimes saw them as pointing to the next world. Neither view is more evidently the authentic Akiva than the other.

When Rabbi Akiva was about to be executed for teaching the Torah in defiance of an edict of the Roman authorities, his explanation for his suffering had nothing to do with reward and punishment.

> Once when Rabbi Akiva was being tried before the wicked Tineius Rufus, the time arrived for reading the Shema and he began to recite it joyfully. Said [Rufus]: "Old man, old man, either you are a magician or you bear pain with contumacy." Rabbi Akiva answered him: "Woe to that man! I am neither a magician nor do I bear pain with contumacy; but all my life I have read this verse: 'And you shall love the Lord your God with all your heart and with all your soul and with all your might' [Deut. 6:5—the second verse of the Shema]. I loved Him with all my wealth [that is, might], but I was never called upon to face the ordeal of 'with all my soul' [that is, at the cost of my life]. Now that I experience 'with all my soul' and the time for reading the Shema has arrived, and I have not thrust it aside, therefore I am reciting the Shema with joy."

> (JT Sot. 5:5)

Rather than focus on repentance and on suffering in this world in order to receive reward in the next, Akiva interpreted his own suffering as an occasion to realize his great religious dream to love God unconditionally with a passion that transcended the normal human instinct of self-preservation. Akiva did not focus on reward and punishment at the moment of his death, not because he rejected this view of Providence, but because, as a lover of God, it would have been beside the point for him to seek to draw comfort from the fact that his suffering was a down payment for future reward.

In general, the rabbis sought to transform suffering into a means of deepening their understanding of the Torah and the *mizvot*. When tragedy occurred, their characteristic question was, "What can we learn from this?" Typically, they taught that repentance (*teshuvah*) was always a proper response to suffering.

> If a man sees that painful sufferings visit him, let him examine his conduct. For it is said: "Let us search and probe our ways, and return to the Lord" [Lam. 3:40]. If he examines and finds nothing, let him attribute it to the neglect of the study of the Torah. For it is said: "Happy is the man whom Thou chastenest, O Lord, and teachest out of Thy Torah" [Ps. 94:12]. If he did attribute it [to that], and still did not find [anything amiss], let him be sure that these are chastenings of love. For it is said: "For whom the Lord loves, he corrects [Prov. 3:12]."
>
> (BT Ber. 5a)

By utilizing tragedy and suffering as a catalyst for active moral renewal, the Judaic tradition prevents political powerlessness from creating feelings of personal impotence and loss of self-esteem. If events in the larger world are unpredictable, if the nation is subject to the violence and whims of foreign rulers, the rabbinic mind does not fall victim to despair, disillusionment, and escapism, but rather focuses on the personal and the communal as the framework to contain its activist dignity. The call to repentance—"If a man sees that painful sufferings visit him, let him examine his conduct"— should not, therefore, be seen as a metaphysical justification of evil. Rather, it is advice that encourages the Jew to sustain and give meaning to the covenantal relationship despite the mystery of suffering.

From the viewpoint of religious anthropology, the emphasis on repentance as a response to suffering helps sustain the significance of *mizvah* action by its focus on what one can do, what one is called upon to achieve. It deflects attention from absorption with irrational forces to areas of human adequacy. It encourages questions such as: In what sense is my own world capable of receiving some normative order? To what degree can I build into that normative order sufficient dignity to countervail the forces dominant in the larger arenas of history, which are beyond my control?

The rabbis thus devised many ways of responding to the disorientation that may arise from disappointed expectations of God. But how long can one sustain *any* attempt to cope with the gap between expectation and reality? How long is it before an individual decides that the covenantal relationship no longer exists or that it is not worth having?

To this question there is no single universal answer applicable equally to all human beings. The situation is like that of one's relationship to other persons. When there is a deep commitment to a relationship, but the relational partner begins to behave in ways that are problematic, the normal reaction is to seek ways of interpreting that behavior that will enable the individual to feel that the partner's love and commitment to the relationship continue to exist. One does not readily believe that a beloved parent, spouse, or friend has rejected him. If the problems continue, however, a person may reach a breaking point at which no attempts to cope have any attraction anymore. Whether, when, and how a breaking point is reached depends very much on the individual concerned. It is hardly possible to predict how long a given individual can continue to interpret suffering as an expression of God's love or as a call to repentance and spiritual growth. As in relationships between human beings, it depends upon whether the particular experiences and memories of that specific individual have the power to carry him or her through difficult moments that cast doubt upon the quality of love in the relationship. Human relationships and relationships with God are so individual, so closely tied to the unique sensibility of a particular person, that it is hard to be sure why some people are sustained for years by memories of joy, whereas others have a low threshold for tolerating pain. Some abandon the covenant after the death of a single loved one, but others retain belief in God's love for and commitment to themselves despite having lost whole families in the Holocaust. One human being leaves Auschwitz as an atheist and another as a person whose belief has grown stronger. For some, suffering is bearable if it results from the limitations of finite human beings, but it becomes terrifying and demonic if it is seen as part of the scheme of their all-powerful creator. Others would find life unbearably chaotic if they could *not* believe that suffering, tragedy, and death were part of God's plan for the world. Feeling that there is meaning and order in the world and that God in his wisdom decided to terminate the life of a loved one makes their tragedy bearable.

Rabbinic teachers did not offer one single model of how to respond to suffering and how to anticipate the divine response to observance of the *mizvot*. The context, the situation, all that has occurred in a person's life, will influence the type of perception that the person will bring to God in a particular situation. The consciousness of a living personal God that grows out of the biblical story of God the creator and sustainer of life, God the redeemer of Israel from slavery, and God the source of the commandments at Sinai does not permit a consistent one-dimensional theology. Rabbinic Judaism forswore systematic theology, not because the rabbis could not think in a coherent philosophical way, but because systematic theology could not do justice to the vitality and complexity of experience.

The rabbis responded to suffering by telling stories of how individual people built their relationship with the God of the covenant. In not laying down as authoritative a line on theology as they did with regard to practice, they refrained from constricting the multiple possibilities that one may develop in making sense of the covenantal relationship with God. One can claim, I believe, in the spirit of the rabbinic tradition, that so long as the centrality of *mizvot* and the eternity of the covenant are not undermined, there is enormous room for building multiple images of God and of his relationship to the community, nature, and history, a multiplicity that enables the covenant to remain a live option. Maimonides followed in the spirit of the rabbinic tradition and suggested multiple theological models for understanding divine providence. He did not, however, embrace all that the rabbinic teaching tradition permitted, as he personally rejected the view of chastenings of love.

Judaism is not only concerned with obedience to the authority of the halakhah. It above all strives to make the halakhah expressive of the covenantal relationship with God. As long as the relationship with God is held before Jews as the telos of halakhic practice, they will continue in the spirit of the rabbinic tradition to tell different stories of how they make sense of suffering in living with the God of the covenant.

BIBLIOGRAPHY

Adolf Buchler, *Studies in Sin and Atonement in the Rabbinic Literature of the First Century* (1962), 119–211.
David Hartman, *Judaism: A Living Covenant* (1985), chs. 8 and 9.
Efraim E. Urbach, *The Sages: Their Concepts and Beliefs* (1975), 420–523.

Survival

השרדות

Yossi Klein Halevi

A lone among peoples, the Jews have justified their national existence by a universalist goal, however distant or deferred: the gathering of the nations in worship on Mount Zion, a divine redemption not confined to the spiritually gifted but amplified publicly, embracing all humanity.

To effect this universalist vision, the Jewish people was, paradoxically, set apart—as a testing ground for the possibility of redemptive interaction between humanity and God. For, as a people, the Jews are a random cross-section of humanity. And if this people could be transformed into an instrument for divine intimacy, then the hope of a realized transcendence could be extended, eventually, to all peoples.

The Jewish nation was inducted into its task in a mass exodus and revelation, history's first experiment in egalitarian redemption. A handmaiden at the Red Sea, says the midrash, received greater revelation than Ezekiel in his vision of the chariot (Mekh. 110). The Jewish calendar reinforced this message by celebrating miracles experienced by the collective, and, in order to impress upon Jews the redemptive capacity of the world they were given *miẓvot,* commandments, which manifest the potential holiness in everything material.

The Nazi assault on Jewry was, in essence, an attempt to defeat its egalitarian messianic vision. For Adolf Hitler, that vision threatened to enervate brute man's struggle for mastery by imposing upon him a responsibility for his weaker fellow. In seeking to free the world of Jewish messianism and replace it with a radical social Darwinism, Nazism defined its own role as messianic. Hitler envisioned an apocalyptic end-war between evenly matched protagonists: "The mightiest counterpart to the Aryan is represented by the Jew."[1] And the outcome of their struggle would determine the fate of humanity: "If . . . the Jew is victorious over the other peoples of the world, his crown will be the funeral wreath of humanity, and this planet will, as it did thousands of years ago, move through the ether devoid of men."[2]

To defeat the Jewish messianic threat required the discrediting of history as sacred process. The Jews had had the profound audacity to offer their own tortured history as proof of this world's promise, a challenge the Nazis accepted. If Jewish history could be aborted, then Marxists, liberal democrats, and all other adherents of "Judaic ideological derivatives," whom Hitler so despised, would not again dare to imagine a just culmination to history.

Parodying God, the Nazis chose the Jewish people as their testing ground to prove the absence of a historical plan. "Where is your God now?" SS officers taunted Jews before the mass graves. The rhetorical question was directed not only to Orthodox believers but to all of European Jewry. No Jewry at any time had devised so many varied and practical strategies for hastening redemption as the Jewish communities of Europe. Jewish Marxists, Zionists, and Reform rabbis all agreed on one point: Theirs was the time of messianic fulfillment. Hitler feared the Jews of Europe and their messianic restlessness, attributing to them the most awesome conspiracies for world domination—a fear that was justifiable in the sense that Europe's Jews were actively conspiring to remake the world in their image. By revealing the impotence of Israel's God, the Nazis were really striking at the Redeemer of history in all his modern guises.

Antithetical to the religion of redemption, Nazism often deliberately timed its attacks for Jewish holidays, celebrations of sacred history. The final destruction of the Warsaw Ghetto began on the first night of Passover, 1943. On *Purim,* 1942, ten Jews were hanged in Zdunska-Wola to avenge the hanging of Haman's ten sons, a retroactive undoing of the Purim miracle. The following year in Zdunska-Wola, another ten Jews were hanged on Shavuot, festival of Sinai, in revenge for the Ten Commandments.

Unconsciously, perhaps, but no less precisely, the Nazis subverted the traditional prophetic imagery of redemption. The prophets had envisioned an ingathering of scattered exiles, and the Nazis ingathered from Tunisia to the Ukraine. The prophets had promised that the Gentiles would acknowledge Jewish chosenness and centrality in history, and Nazi ideology obliged. The prophets had imagined a rational heaven on earth, and the Nazis created death camps that were a perfectly rationalized hell. Having actualized, in reverse, the myth of redemption, the Nazis achieved their greatest success, poisoning the very motive for Jewish survival.

The Jews in the Diaspora did not merely await redemption, but repeatedly rebelled against exile, through ecstatic movements initiated by false messiahs and, more subtly, through apocalyptic speculation. Yet after every failure to conjure redemption, the Jewish people resumed its historic pattern of cautious persistence, transplanting from one exile to another and rebuilding the ruins. For however great the disappointment or the disaster, Jewish survival and the messianic vision on which its legitimacy depended remained unquestioned.

After the Holocaust, however, most survivors instinctively realized that if they accepted history's slow progression toward redemption Jewry would not long endure. If the Jews failed now to emulate the Nazis and impose *their* vision on history, if they failed to summon a divine revelation as awesome as Auschwitz, they would concede redemption, the justification for Jewish existence, to the demonic. Most Jews, already removed from tradition, would then find the notion of redemptive history and, consequently, of a positive Jewish identity an unbearable irony. Surely some Jews would maintain the faith. But their impetus would no longer be vision but spite, or inertia; and only by exiling Judaism into otherworldliness could they uphold a religion whose antagonist had been far more successful, however perversely, at implementing the messianic vision.

When, in 1945, after decades of divisiveness and ambivalence, a majority of Jewry finally embraced the idea of return to Zion, it determined that group survival now depended on a leap into metahistory. While most Jews, perhaps, would have denied their Zionism to be anything more than a political strategy for survival, they were nevertheless conceding that survival was now possible only through the realization of the central event in Judaism's eschatology: the return of the exiles to *erez Yisrael* (the land of Israel), metaphor as well as catalyst for the return of an exiled world to its source.

By ingathering the exiles into *ereẓ Yisrael* and restoring the redemptive direction of history, Zionism reappropriated messianic imagery and could therefore challenge, if not negate, the Nazi counterredemption. Those religious Jews who remained unmoved by Zionism even after the Holocaust became proponents of an untenable paradox, a Judaism that deferred redemption into oblivion. Europe's shattered yeshivah and Ḥasidic worlds heroically rebuilt their ruins, but by retaining their prewar hostility to Zionism isolated themselves from the Jewish consensus that demanded a post-Holocaust departure from mere reconstruction. In rejecting Zionism, fundamentalist Orthodoxy denied the dialectic upon which post-Holocaust Jewry was founded: that modernity, having created literal hell, had now become the arena of myth fulfillment, thereby making redemption, too, possible for the first time.

Auschwitz is the rationale for the nuclear age. If man at his most civilized can now effect the global final solution, his motive for self-annihilation was acquired in the planned, dispassionate genocide of the Holocaust. For the Nazis appropriated rationalism, the foundation of civilization, as the functional basis for mass murder. Turned against itself, civilization flirts with suicide.

Gradually, the nuclear world awakens to the same choice that faced the Jews in 1945: transcend or perish. Old patterns of survival have become untenable. If the nations continue to stagger from conflict to conflict, they must one day blunder into nuclear war. World survival now depends on the nations transcending their differences, humbled by the vision of extinction.

The nuclear world needs the State of Israel not only because its mere existence is proof that modernity can yield redemption, but because Israel, whose society has ingathered the most concentrated microcosm of the nations, is the incubator for a new world consciousness. Israel is the world's only truly modern society, its people having tasted modernity's potential for both annihilation and redemption; it is in those polar experiences that the illusion of human separateness dissolves. When, in moments of extremity, Israeli society has laid aside its multiple differences, humanity has glimpsed the possibility of its own survival through transcendence.

Describing the Jews assembled before Sinai, the Torah says, "And there Israel camped" (Ex. 19:2). The singular form, notes Rashi in his commentary on this verse, describes the unity of the tribes "as one man, as one heart." Only when they had merged their separate selves into a monotheism of peoplehood could the Jews connect with the One. Thirty-five hundred years later, in the Six-Day War of June 1967, the Jewish people reenacted that unity, perhaps not since Sinai so focused on a single event and emotion—culminating in the revelation of return to Jerusalem.

Christianity and Islam, as each came into being, proclaimed the Jewish vision of human solidarity and then turned against the Jews for persisting in their separateness. Yet the Jews refused to relinquish either their premessianic exclusivity or their universalist vision, deferring a resolution of the paradox to a distant future.

With the onset of the Enlightenment, however, the ability to sustain that paradox collapsed, and the Jewish people divided into rival camps of particularists and universalists. Artificially severed from one another, means and end became distorted. Particularists saw in redemption a private Jewish affair, and universalists denied the requirements for self-preservation.

But with the creation of Israel in the nuclear era, both camps must know they are working toward the same goal, because Jewish cohesion is now a universalist imperative. The Jewish people will become a model for world harmony when its particularists concede that Jewish survival is ultimately for the sake of all humanity and when its universalists perceive in unity among Jews the most hopeful first step toward world reconciliation. When Jewish cohesion is no longer a passing response to crisis but the basis of national existence, the Jews will be positioned for a revelation of oneness, toward which all spiritual striving aspires. The prophets linked the return to Zion with world redemption, and only now is a possible connection between the two discernible. "For My House shall be called a house of prayer for all peoples. Thus declares the Lord God who gathers the dispersed of Israel"(Isa. 56:7–8).

REFERENCES

1. Adolf Hitler, *Mein Kampf* (1971), 300.
2. Ibid., 65.

BIBLIOGRAPHY

Eliezer Berkovits, *With God in Hell* (1979).
Emil L. Fackenheim, *God's Presence in History* (1972).
Abraham Isaac Kook, *Orot ha-Kodesh* (1985).
Abraham Isaac Kook, *Lights of Holiness, Lights of Penitence: The Moral Principles, Essays, Letters, Poems,* Ben Zion Bokser, tr. (1978).

Talmud

תלמוד

Adin Steinsalz

The Talmud is the main (though not the only) work of the oral Torah (*Torah she-be-al peh*). It is second only to the written Torah, that is, the Bible, in its sanctity, and its impact upon the life of the Jewish people throughout the centuries has been no less than that of the Bible—if not greater.

The Talmud, in the broad sense of the word, incorporates two different works: the Mishnah and the Talmud (or Gemara, lit., completion) proper. The Mishnah is a comprehensive collection of laws and regulations touching upon nearly every area of Jewish life. Its final redaction was performed about 200 C.E., in the Galilee region of Palestine, by Rabbi Judah ha-Nasi. Even though its final editing took place at this time, it includes a great deal of earlier material, part of which was already set in its literary form during the last few centuries B.C.E. The Mishnah is the fullest crystallization of the oral Torah up to the date of its editing. Its language is the Hebrew of that generation, which differs somewhat in syntax, grammar, and vocabulary from biblical Hebrew.

The Mishnah is divided into six main divisions or *sedarim* (lit., orders), each of which deals with a specific group of subjects, and these in turn are divided into a total of sixty-three tractates (*masekhtot*) of different sizes, each of which treats one central subject. Each tractate is further divided into a number of chapters, and each chapter into individual sections (*mishnayot*).

Generally speaking, the Mishnah is arranged as a code of law, each *mishnah* constituting an individual point of law, expressed either in an abstract manner or, more typically, as an instruction on how to behave under given circumstances. Frequently, a number of different opinions are cited regarding the halakhah, without any clear conclusion; likewise, various opinions may be cited in the name of specific sages. Less frequently, there is also discussion of the different opinions cited, albeit in abbreviated form. While most of the material found in the Mishnah consists of normative statements of law, there are also occasional historical descriptions as well as ethical exhortations (such as the tractate *Avot,* which deals entirely with the field of ethics). The language of the Mishnah is one of very exact, but concise, legal terminology, which generally gives neither sources nor reasons for its decisions.

The Talmud, in the narrow sense of the word, is the corpus of commentaries, discussions, and theoretical analyses of the teachings of the Mishnaic sages, but it goes far beyond the exegetical realm, both in the development of the legal system itself and in its penetrating analysis of the foundations and principles of that system.

The Talmud itself consists of two different works: the Jerusalem Talmud, composed primarily of the teachings of the Palestinian sages and edited by a number of scholars in Tiberias and Caesarea around 400 C.E.; and the more important and influential Babylonian Talmud, which contains the teachings of the sages of Babylonia (that is, Mesopotamia), compiled by Rav Ashi and his disciples in Sura around the year 500 C.E. Even though the Talmud is arranged as a commentary to the Mishnah, it does not encompass all tractates of the Mishnah; for some tractates no Talmud was ever compiled, while for others the Talmud has been lost. The language of the Talmud is an Aramaic jargon, reflecting the dialects spoken by the Jews of Palestine and Babylonia over the course of many generations, mixed with many words and idioms taken from Hebrew, as well as a considerable number of Hebrew quotations from the teaching of the sages of the Mishnah.

At first glance the Talmud appears to be an expanded commentary to the Mishnah; the sages of the Talmud are referred to as *amoraim,* a term literally meaning "translators." Indeed, a considerable portion of the Talmud does consist of textual and other exegeses of the Mishnah. However, in reality the Talmud is as old as the Mishnah itself, constituting the theoretical framework underlying the final rulings formulated in the Mishnah. Moreover, unlike the Mishnah, which is primarily a code of law whose primary purpose is to instruct the individual or the Jewish community how to act, the talmudic discussions are essentially theoretical and are directed toward clarifying the basic principles of the law and the different schools of thought therein; practical inferences are considered essentially derivative, secondary conclusions drawn, for the most part, from the abstract discussion.

Discussion in the Talmud generally begins with the text of the *mishnah* and follows one of several fixed forms: elucidation of the origins of the Mishnaic law in the biblical text; examination of the relationship of the *mishnah,* which generally appears anonymously, to the system of a given sage; or the resolution of contradictions between the *mishnah* under discussion and another *mishnah* or other legal source from the Mishnaic period. The talmudic interpretation of the Mishnah may also include textual criticism, both linguistic and comparative, as well as harmonization of various different approaches.

Talmudic discussion only infrequently has recourse to abstract terms; instead, it constructs various hypothetical situations, from the analysis of which the inherent abstract principle comes to the fore. Since these situations do not necessarily stem from real life, these cases may deal with unrealistic or nearly impossible problems; as we have already observed, however, the main function of the Talmud is to serve not as a compendium of practical law but as a vehicle of theoretical explication. The theoretical character of the Talmud also influenced the method of discussion and of proof. Even though the axiomatic framework of the discussion is not explicit in the Talmud itself, such a framework, which bears considerable similarity to that used in mathematics, nevertheless does exist. The statements of the Mishnaic sages are discussed as though they were geometrical theorems, both in terms of the precision and compactness of their expression and in the search for convincing arguments by which they may be proven or disproven. At times, the law may be decided in practice on the basis of inadequate or incomplete proofs, but this is never the case in the theoretical discussion. Even though there was a need to rule in practice among different options within the halakhah, on the theoretical plane (which constitutes the bulk of the Talmud) the halakhah is best understood by comparison to a complex equation with a number of possible solutions. From this follows the talmudic saying, "Both of these are the words of the living God, and the halakhah follows so-and-so" (BT. Er. 13b). Each solution is deserving of full clarification in its own right. The fact that a given approach is not accepted for purposes of halakhic decision making does not deny its truth value or its importance in principle. The determination of the halakhah is understood primarily as the application of one of the true solutions to a given actual situation, and not as an absolute statement concerning the truth of the argument per se or the validity of an approach that has not been accepted in practice.

Most of the material in the Talmud is structured as a kind of précis of the discussions held in the study house (beit midrash) among different individuals. The problems discussed there were similar, despite the geographic and historical distance between different schools and different generations. While each school approached issues somewhat differently, in keeping with the outlook and personalities of the sages involved, the essential elements were transmitted from one place to another (sometimes via special emissaries) and from one generation to another. Despite the historical layering and the variations between different places and approaches, the essential discussion, from many times and places, was thus known everywhere. For this reason, the Babylonian Talmud not only reflects the school of Rav Ashi, but serves as an ahistoric platform for discussion in which the sages of all the generations participate.

Although the arrangement of the Talmud follows the sequence of the Mishnah, it glides into many other subjects related to one another in an associative manner—sometimes through similarity of subject matter, sometimes through stylistic or linguistic similarity, and sometimes through authorship by a particular sage. Subjects mentioned in passing may become a central subject, which in turn may lead on to other, more remote subjects. The associative flexibility of the interconnections notwithstanding, the work is precisely arranged in terms of its stylistic details. There are exact and fixed formulas and meanings in the internal order of each discussion and in the usage of words within the discussions.

A certain portion of the Talmud (which is not fixed, and is greater in the Babylonian than in the Jerusalem Talmud) deals not with halakhah, that is, problems of law and legal norms, but with the area known as aggadah (lit., sayings). The aggadah of the Talmud is not all of a piece; it includes biblical homiletics and exegesis, discussions of theology and ethics, stories and parables, historical descriptions, and practical advice dealing with all aspects of life. Although there was always a certain distinction between the realms of halakhah and of aggadah, and there were sages who dealt primarily with one or the other area, there is no clear dividing line between the two, and they are intertwined with one another without any clear demarcation. Sometimes there are practical conclusions drawn from the aggadah, while on other occasions a halakhic discussion may bear theological or other nonlegal implications. Speaking generally, aggadic discussions are less precise and more poetic in their form of expression. Moreover, much of the aggadah is symbolic, though there are no clear, uniform keys to the understanding of its symbolism, leaving room, both at the time they were composed and in later generations, for many different schools of interpretation. To an even greater degree than in the halakhic realm, we find a multitude of parallel schools of interpretation without any felt need to reach an unequivocal consensus.

The impact of the Talmud upon the Jewish people has been immeasurable. Throughout the generations, Jewish education demanded considerable knowledge of the Talmud, which functioned as the basic text of study for all. Indeed, much of posttalmudic Jewish literature consists of commentaries, reworkings, and new presentations of the Talmud. Even those areas that were not directly related to the Talmud drew upon it and were sustained by it, and there is hardly a work in any area of Judaism that does not relate to it.

Of even greater significance than this was the methodological influence of the study of the Talmud. In the opinion of virtually every modern scholar, "the Talmud was never closed"—not only in the historical-factual sense, but also with regard to the manner of its understanding and study. The method of Talmud study was an extension of the Talmud itself; its interpretation and analysis required the student continually to involve himself in the discussion, to evaluate its questions and argumentation. As a result, abstract reasoning and the dialectic method became an integral part of the Jewish culture.

The open-ended character of talmudic discussion did not detract from the reverence felt toward the Talmud as a text with religious sanctity. The methods of study, like the conclusions of the work itself, became the undisputed basis for religious legislation in all subsequent generations. Both medieval Jewish philosophy and Jewish mysticism, despite an ambivalent attitude toward the exclusive study of Talmud, treated the Talmud with great respect, and later kabbalistic literature even found in it concealed allusions to mystical truths. In the final analysis, the Talmud was understood as, and in fact created, the unique phenomenon of "sacred intellectualism."

BIBLIOGRAPHY

Jacob Neusner, *Judaism: The Evidence of the Mishnah* (1981).
Adin Steinsalz, *The Essential Talmud* (1976).
Ephraim E. Urbach, *The Sages, Their Concepts and Beliefs,* Israel Abrahams, tr.,2 vols., (1979).

Theodicy

צידוק־הדין

Byron L. Sherwin

Theodicy is a term generally attributed to the philosopher Gottfried Wilhelm Leibniz. In his treatise *Theodicy: Essays on the Goodness of God, the Freedom of Man and the Origin of Evil* (1710), Leibniz attempts to reconcile his well-known claim that ours is "the best of all possible worlds" with the observation that evil is a feature of human experience. Leibniz derives the term *theodicy* from the Greek *theos* (God) and *dike* (justice). Theodicy deals, then, with the defense of God's justice and righteousness in the face of the fact of evil.

In Western philosophy and theology, discussion of theodicy, the problem of evil, often entails the attempt to reconcile three premises: (1) God is good and benevolent; (2) God is omnipotent and (3) evil is real. These premises assume that if evil is real, a benevolent God would not want evil to occur, and, being omnipotent, could prevent evil from happening. David Hume, the eighteenth-century British philosopher, put it this way: "Epicurus' old questions are yet unanswered. Is he [that is, God] willing to prevent evil, but unable? then is he impotent. Is he able, but not willing? then is he malevolent. Is he both able and willing? whence then is evil?"[1]

David Hume is correct in saying that these questions remain unanswered, for as Naḥmanides observes, the problem of evil is "the most difficult matter which is at the root both of faith and of apostasy, with which scholars of all ages, peoples and tongues have struggled."[2]

Theological and philosophical attempts to solve the problem of theodicy often concentrate upon modifying, redefining, or denying one or more of the aforementioned premises: God is good; God is omnipotent; evil is real.

The first premise, that God is good, raises the question both of the origin and of the continued existence of evil. If God is good, why is there evil? Whence is there evil? Jewish theological speculation has offered a variety of responses to these questions. Three examples follow.

The first view begins with the assumption that God, being good, by nature and by definition, cannot be associated with evil. Therefore, since God could not be the author of evil, the source of evil must be other than God.

The second view, while acknowledging that it is God's nature to be totally good, asserts that for the good to be recognizable and identifiable in the world, evil is required as contrast and relief. Thus the created world cannot be totally good. To choose the good freely, for example, logically and morally demands the availability of its opposite; free choice of the good would be meaningless in a world without evils.

The third view reasons that if creation requires both good and evil to be complete, then a wholly complete God must contain elements of evil as well as good. *Shlemut,* the Hebrew word for perfection, also means wholeness or completeness. Thus, for God to be perfect in this sense he must be complete, embracing qualities both of good and of evil.

The first position—that God, being good, could not be the source of evil—takes on a variety of forms in Jewish theological literature. One view maintains that "nothing evil dwells with God" (Mid. Ps. 5:7, ed. S. Buber, 1891, 54), that "evil does not descend from Above" (Gen. R. 51:3; see also BT Ber. 60b; Gen. R. 3:6). This claim leads some to conclude that because God is good and the creation is "very good" (Gen. 1:31), and because "everything God does is for the good" (BT Ber. 60b), the agent through whom evil enters existence must be a being other than God, an individual capable of moral choice and of doing evil, that is, man. In this view, evil enters reality and is perpetuated through human misuse of freedom, through the human introduction of the evil of sin into the world. Through the identification of evil with human sin, through the explanation of evil as punishment for sin, human deeds rather than God's actions become the catalyst for the presence of evil in the world. God's goodness seems thereby to be preserved.

By linking both natural and moral evil in the world to human sin (see, for example, Lev. 26:14–17, 20; Deut. 11:13–17, 28), Scripture attempts to explain human suffering and natural catastrophe as necessary correlatives of divine justice. The need for theodicy appears to be alleviated by interpreting evil as a byproduct of human deeds and as a proper expression of divine justice. For Scripture, God's benevolence is inseparable from his justice. For God to reward evil and to punish righteousness would be a violation of his nature, of his justice, and of his goodness. For Scripture, divine benevolence requires divine justice, but it also entails divine mercy in mitigating the severity of punishment (see, for example, Ex. 32:11–14, 34:6–10; and God's "prayer" in BT Ber. 7a).

This theory of divine retribution, which maintains that sin requires punishment and that righteousness demands reward, is the most representative and the most prevalent response throughout the history of Jewish theological speculation to the problem of evil and human suffering. Individual affliction, natural catastrophe, and national disaster were pervasively interpreted as punishment for sin. Introduced and reiterated in numerous scriptural texts, this approach was reaffirmed throughout postbiblical Jewish literature. The representative rabbinic position is that of Rabbi Ammi, "There is no death without sin, no suffering without transgression" (BT Shab. 55a).

The inclusion in traditional Jewish liturgical texts of divine retribution as the predominant explanation for evil and suffering, particularly for national Jewish tragedies, reflects the status of divine retribution as a virtually codified Jewish theodicy. The *musaf* liturgy for festivals, for instance, considers the exiled status of the Jewish people as punishment for sin: "Because of our sins, we were exiled from our country and removed far away from our land." Throughout the liturgical lamentations (*kinot*) recited on Tishah be-Av, ancient and medieval national catastrophes are related to divine retribution. In a *kinah* by Abraham ibn Ezra, for example, the author bluntly states, "The Sanctuary was destroyed because of our sins, and because of our iniquity our Temple was burnt down" (*Kinot*, ed. A. Rosenfeld, 1965, 38). In the "Elegy on the Martyrs of York," written in the twelfth century by Joseph of Chartres, the attempt of the victims of York to preserve divine justice by means of their own martyrdom is depicted: "The judgment of their Creator they accepted, but they did not break off his yoke; they justified the righteousness of the Rock, whose work is perfect" (*Kinot*, 168).

In situations where the sins of the afflicted were clearly not consistent with the degree of suffering visited upon them, the doctrine of divine retribution was broadened in an attempt to accommodate experience to theology. This conceptual expansion takes three major forms: horizontal, vertical, and eschatological.

Horizontal divine retribution holds that a given individual or group may be afflicted for the sins of another individual or group. The corporate personality of the Jewish people, which assumed the moral responsibility of the group for each individual member and of each individual member for each other, led to the view that the group may suffer for the sins of an individual member of the group. A scriptural example is the episode of Achan (Josh. 7), a talmudic example the story of how Jerusalem was destroyed because of one man's mistreatment of another (BT. Git. 55b–56a).

Deutero-Isaiah's portrayal of the "suffering servant" illustrates most clearly the notion of horizontal retribution. Identified both by medieval and modern scholars with the people of Israel, the suffering servant takes on suffering for the iniquities of all the rest of the peoples of the world in order to allow them access to God and to eventual redemption.[3] Other rabbinic and medieval sources maintain that righteous individuals may suffer for the sins of others.[4]

Vertical divine retribution holds that individuals may be punished for the sins of their forebears. Lamentations 5:7 puts it best: "Our fathers sinned and are no more, and we must bear their iniquities."[5] Not only punishment for sin but also reward for the righteousness of previous generations was an essential feature of the notion of vertical divine retribution.[6] A final feature of this notion is that not only may descendants be rewarded or punished for the deeds of their ancestors, but that forebears may also be punished for the deeds of their progeny, at least until a child reaches the age of majority (see, for example, Gen. R. 63:10, which is the basis of the traditional blessing releasing a father from responsibility for the deeds of his son at the occasion of the son's bar miẓvah).

Jewish eschatology embraces three ideas: messianic redemption, resurrection of the body, and the World to Come. All three are related to the notion of delayed, yet assured, divine retribution. The observed clash between theological assumptions regarding God's justice and observations of the prosperity of the wicked (Jer. 12:1–2; Job 21) and of the suffering of the righteous led to a merging of the idea of divine retribution with eschatological expectations. Justice denied in this world, it was claimed, would be assured in the future, that is, the messianic future, the time of bodily resurrection and of the World to Come. As a midrash puts it: "In this world the righteous are smitten, but in the World to Come they will have firm footing and strength" (Mid. Ps. 1:20, 11b).[7]

In the succinct words of the Jewish philosopher Saadiah Gaon, "The prophets, peace be upon them, were all agreed upon this: that the reward for a man's behavior is not meted out in this world but is only given in that which comes after it." For Saadiah, divine retribution in the afterlife is not only a doctrine of scriptural origin but is also one of "logical necessity" (*The Book of Beliefs and Opinions*, 9:2, tr. S. Rosenblatt, 1948, 327–30). Furthermore, the idea of transmigration of souls, introduced into Judaism by the medieval Jewish mystics, suggested that justice denied in one lifetime would be dispensed in the next. The kabbalists employed this notion, along with that of reincarnation, in their multifaceted attempts at formulating a variety of theodicies.[8] Finally, with regard to the Messiah and divine retribution, it should be noted that in late rabbinic and medieval Jewish literature the biblical figure of the suffering servant was transmuted into the figure of the suffering Messiah, who takes on suffering for the sins of others.[9]

Although the doctrine of divine retribution achieved almost dogmatic status, it was unable to satisfy the quest of many for a satisfactory theodicy. Too much suffering by the righteous remained unexplained. Too much reward of the wicked remained unjustified (see, for example, Jer. 12:1–2; Job 9:24). Were the tradition assured that divine retribution operated effectively and consistently, were it adequately convinced of the validity of the doctrine of divine retribution, it would not have sought nor would it have posited alternative explanations to human suffering. Furthermore, the forthright rabbinic claim that "there *is* death without sin and suffering without transgression" undermines the fundamental assumption upon which the doctrine of divine retribution rests (compare Rabbi Simeon ben Eleazar's statement of this claim in BT Shab. 55b with Rabbi Ammi's statement in BT Shab. 55a, and note the affirmation of Rabbi Simeon ben Eleazar's refutation of Rabbi Ammi at the conclusion of the passage).

In the wake of the European Holocaust, the doctrine of divine retribution as an acceptable response to catastrophe has come under severe criticism. Jewish theologians now almost unanimously reject divine retribution as a viable post-Holocaust theodicy. What sin, they ask with regard to the Holocaust, could justify such massive, devastating punishment? And even if such a sin could be identified, what kind of sadistic, cruel God emerges, capable of inflicting such horrible punishment? Theologians such as Eliezer Berkovits and Emil Fackenheim find it unacceptable, even "obscene," to apply the doctrine of divine retribution to the Holocaust in an attempt to interpret theologically the deaths of more than a million Jewish children.[10]

Divine retribution may serve as a viable theodicy to explain some evil and some suffering, but it is clearly inadequate to explain satisfactorily all evil and all suffering. By assigning the origin and the perpetuation of evil to human beings, it attempts to dissociate God from evil. Even if it is correct to claim that human beings engender evil, the doctrine of divine retribution is not correct in its desire to separate God from evil and suffering. It cannot escape the assertion that while God may not actually have created evil, he nevertheless must have created the potential for evil; otherwise evil could not have come to be. Furthermore, the doctrine of divine retribution, if assumed to be valid and properly operative, may adequately defend the claim that God is just, but it does not seem sufficient to defend an affirmation of a single divine being who is exclusively good and removed from all evil. To distance God from evil and suffering is to distance him from his creation, from his creatures. Maimonides' claim that God's self-sufficiency and his perfection exclude the possibility of his relationship with things of time and space, that is, with his creation and with his creatures (*Guide* 1, 52), may be philosophically compelling, but it is a theological absurdity when applied to a living faith.

As has been discussed above, the theory of divine retribution rests on the assumption that human beings, and not God, are responsible for introducing and for perpetuating the existence of evil in the world. Despite this attempt to preserve God's pristine goodness, it is clear that in a monotheistic faith the one God must be the source of all, including evil. For some, evil does not represent the human perversion of a world perfectly created by God. Rather, evil is viewed as having been created by God. Evil is considered an element endemic to creation:

> Is it not at the word of the Most High
> That good and evil befall?

> (Lam. 3:38)

> I form light and darkness
> I make good and evil—
> I the Lord do all these things.

> (Is. 45:7; see Job 2:10; Eccl. 7:14)

These texts form the foundation of a theodicy that maintains that evil exists because it serves the good, that to expect God to produce the good without the evil upon which it depends is to demand a logical and an ontological impossibility. Without evil, good would be unrecognizable and unattainable. Free moral choice between good and evil would become unrealizable.

This view maintains that a polarity of opposites characterizes everything in creation. Only God remains beyond all dichotomies. Everything else, particularly good and evil, exists as a member of a pair of opposites. The existence of one necessarily implies the existence of the other. The *Sefer Yezirah,* for example, states: "God has set each thing to correspond with another; the good against the evil, and the evil against the good" (*Sefer Yezirah* 6:2, 1968, 59b; see also *Midrash Temurah* in A. Jellinek, ed., *Beit ha-Midrash,* 2d ed., 1, 1967, 106–114). From this perspective, the existence of evil flows not from the essential nature of God, but from the nature of creation and from the nature of the creative process. In the sixteenth century, the Lurianic kabbalists further developed this approach. Some modern theologians refer to the evil element, the random and irrational factor built into the fabric of creation, as the "dysteleological surd."

Lurianic kabbalah describes destruction, evil, and imperfection as necessary aspects of the process of creation.[11] In this view, God cannot create without destroying, not because he is essentially imperfect, but because it is an essential feature of the creative process to include destruction and because creation, by its very nature, must be imperfect; creation, in other words, must embody dichotomies such as good and evil. Further, that creation embodies evil as well as good also derives from the empirical observation that evil is a component of created existence. In the Lurianic view, though God *(Ein Sof)* is perfect in essence, God must nevertheless will to relinquish absolute perfection in order to act as creator.

The Lurianic conception of *zimzum* (divine contraction) has God withdraw into himself, thereby corrupting his essential perfection, as the initial step in the process of creation. Furthermore, the Lurianic concept of "the breaking of the vessels" teaches that there is an initial flaw in creation and that this cosmic flaw reaches back to the creative process itself. Through the process of *tikkun* (restoration), the human creature can repair the flaw that forms part of the initial fabric of creation.[12]

A corollary of this view is that human actions can either amplify through sin or reduce through righteousness the flaw that God has built into the creation. From here a conceptual jump can be made from the affirmation of a perfect God who compromises his perfection in order to become a creative God to the claim that the elements of good and evil embedded in creation reflect parallel components in the nature of the creator.

While the Lurianic mystics envisaged the continuous purging of the implicitly evil element in the godhead as a central scene in the divine drama, the earlier kabbalistic text *Sefer ha-Bahir,* dating from the twelfth century, explicitly states, "There is in God an attribute that is called evil" (*Sefer ha-Bahir,* ed. R. Margaliot, no. 162, 1951, 71).

Scripture, rather than the *Sefer ha-Bahir,* may be the earliest source of the claim that in a monotheistic faith evil as well as good must ultimately be referred back to God. Reflecting upon such biblical episodes as God's unfathomable and unexplained attack on Moses (Ex. 4:24), some modern biblical scholars maintain that biblical theology holds that the single God must embrace a duality in his nature of good and evil, of the benevolent and the demonic, of the merciful and the sinister.[13]

Affirmation that the divine nature includes capacities for good and evil, for creativity and destruction, when translated into ethical-theological terms would mean that God performs both acts of virtue and sinful deeds. In a talmudic text God is described as having made a flawed creation, as having unjustifiably punished one of his creatures—the moon—and as having "sinned." Even more remarkable is this text's assertion that human beings may act to atone for God's "sin" (BT Hul. 60b).

According to this view, evil is an ontologically necessary component of existence, and perhaps even a theologically necessary feature of the divine. Rather than concluding that the necessary existence of evil leads inescapably to nihilism and despair, and rather than perceiving the human condition as one of random victimization, this position asserts to the contrary that the human person may become an active protagonist in the ongoing battle to contain and to control the evil element within the self and within the world. This approach aims at reducing the power of evil in the self, in the world, and even within God, by means of redemptive acts. It perceives evil to be a fact of life, a feature of existence to be reckoned with, rather than a problem to be solved. Bordering on the pragmatic, this position affirms concrete redemptive human action rather than abstract theological speculation as the most effective attempt at a theodicy.

In the preceding discussion of the first assumption that leads to an attempt at a theodicy, namely, the assumption that God is good, a number of ways in which some Jewish theological sources relate to the assumption of divine omnipotence already have been presented. Nevertheless, a number of further observations regarding the relationship of divine omnipotence to the problem of evil bear mention.

While most of the medieval Jewish philosophers stressed divine omnipotence as a crucial feature of a self-sufficient perfect God, the notion of divine omnipotence seems either unknown or irrelevant to biblical and to rabbinic theology. Certainly, biblical and rabbinic sources discussed the "power" of God, but omnipotence, as it was understood by many of the

Jewish philosophers, does not seem to have been a characteristic of Jewish thought until the Middle Ages, when it was probably introduced through Islamic philosophical influence.

The understanding of the divine nature reflected throughout Scripture, particularly in the classical prophetic writings, and amplified in rabbinic literature, particularly in texts where God is called *Shekhinah* (divine Presence), emphasizes divine pathos and not divine omnipotence.[14] In this view, God is a participant in human suffering and a victim of moral evil.[15]

From the assumption that God is not omnipotent, that God is affected by evil human deeds, flows the claim that God's power in the world is contingent upon the nature and the quality of human acts. Thus, "anthropodicy" replaces theodicy as the issue at hand. Rather than trying to justify God's deeds and evil human deeds that God might prevent, the problem becomes the justification of human deeds vis-à-vis other people and vis-à-vis God.

A number of rabbinic and kabbalistic texts are oblivious to the problem of how to reconcile divine omnipotence with the existence of evil. Instead, they assume that God, not being omnipotent, relies upon human efforts to increase what power he does have. Human deeds can serve either to enhance or to reduce divine power in the world. Evil in the world becomes a reality for human beings to ameliorate by means of sacred deeds, rather than a concept to be made consistent with the doctrine of divine omnipotence. Those midrashic and kabbalistic sources that describe the divine reliance upon human beings took seriously the statement in Psalms 68:35 "Give strength to God." For example, a midrash reads: "Hence Moses's plea: 'And now, I pray thee, let the strength of the Lord be enhanced' [Num. 14:17]. . . . When men do not do His will, then, if one dare say such a thing, 'The Rock that begot thee, thou dost weaken' [Deut. 32:18]. . . . Whenever Israel do the Holy One's will, they enhance the power of the Almighty" (Midrash Pesikta De Rab Kahana, 25:1, ed. B. Mandelbaum, 1962, 380; tr. Braude and Kapstein, 1975, 386–87). In the words of the *Zohar* (Vilna ed., 2, 65b), "The Holy One, as it were, said: When Israel is worthy below My power prevails in the universe; but when Israel is found to be unworthy she weakens My power above."

Regarding the third assumption upon which the problem of theodicy historically rests, namely, that evil is real, a variety of views are found throughout Jewish theological literature. These views come in three major forms: denial, redefinition, and confrontation.

For those who, like Maimonides, affirm God's goodness and his omnipotence, the most promising path to an intellectually viable theodicy is to deny the claim that evil is real. For Maimonides, "all evils are privations," that is, evil is nonexistent, nonbeing, a privation of good, a state in which the good is absent (Guide, 3, 10). What are perceived as evils by human beings, according to Maimonides, are sufferings that come upon them because of human actions that represent privations of knowledge or privations of virtue. Furthermore, Maimonides understands human suffering as a correlative of human free choice. "It is because of our own deficiencies that we lament and call for aid. We suffer because of evils that we have produced ourselves of our free will; but we attribute them to God" (Guide, 3, 12).

Maimonides attempts to reconcile divine omniscience and omnipotence with free will by claiming that divine foreknowledge of human deeds cannot be construed as a cause of human deeds. More recent theological speculation has maintained that free will is a precarious gift God must give human beings to allow them to be truly human, that is, free moral agents. In this view, God chooses to limit his power so that humans may exercise their freedom. Evil then becomes the price that humans must pay and that God must tolerate.[16] This approach may be useful with regard to some manifestations of evil, but with regard to catastrophic events such as the Holocaust it fails. If God is assumed omnipotent and if miracles are assumed possible, then God's lack of intervention to prevent massive catastrophes remains unexplained.

A second approach deals with evil by maintaining that what may appear to be evil is really not evil but good, when seen from an alternate perspective. Here evil and suffering are virtually redefined as being good. One example of this approach found in rabbinic literature and in the medieval literature of Jewish martyrology is that "suffering is precious" (BT Sanh. 101a), that "one should be happier with suffering than with good" (Sif. Deut., 32, ed. Finkelstein, 1940, 56), that what seems evil "is also for the good" (BT Taan. 21a).

The assumption upon which this seemingly masochistic view is based is that suffering atones for sins committed in this world so as to free one from punishment for sin in the next world. Rooted in the doctrine of divine retribution, this view fails to reconcile the necessity of severe human suffering with the alleged goodness and mercy of the Divine.

A further example of the approach that attempts to neutralize the reality of evil appeals to the finiteness of the human being when compared to the infinity of God (see, for example, Job 38–39). Seen from God's panoramic view, what appears to us as evil may not be so. Further, since it is beyond the ken of human ability to understand the ways of God, what we experience as evil may actually be a fulfillment of God's purpose and must therefore be good. While an appeal to divine knowledge and to divine mystery may intellectually satisfy some, it cannot serve to explain suffering to the afflicted. A final example of this approach sees suffering as educative rather than punitive, and, therefore, as ultimately good (for example, Ps. 73; 119:67; Prov. 3:12).

The third approach, that of confrontation, posits the existence of evil, affirms the presence of undeserved suffering, and calls God to account regarding it. This approach provides no theodicy, but it offers a scream of frustrated protest toward a God who appears apathetic, who seems to be acting contrary to his covenantal commitment and in contradiction to his qualities of justice and mercy. Abraham's cry "Shall not the Judge of all the earth deal justly?" (Gen. 18:25) echoes down through the ages (also see Hab. 1:1–3; Jer. 12:1–2; Job 21:7; Ps. 22:2). Aware that "the earth is handed over to the wicked one" (Job 9:24), advocates of this view challenge God to reconcile their observation with his claim that the world is "very good" (Gen. 1:31). Believing in God in spite of God, they cajole God to emerge from his silence (for example, see Mekh. 142).

One must finally conclude that the many attempts at a theodicy betray the impossibility of formulating a conceptually acceptable solution to the problem of evil, a solution that would also prove acceptable to the afflicted and suffering. Certainly the Holocaust demonstrates that there can be no "final solution" to the problems engendered by that event—certainly not a theological one.

The Talmud quotes Moses as asking God, "Lord of the Universe, why is it that some righteous men prosper and others are in adversity; some wicked men prosper and others are in adversity?" (BT Ber. 7a). The only acceptable answer is that theology can provide responses to evil but not solutions, for in the final analysis "it is not in our power to understand either the suffering of the righteous or the prosperity of the wicked" (M. Avot 4:5).

REFERENCES

1. David Hume, *Dialogues Concerning Natural Religion* (1966), 66.
2. Nahmanides, *Perush le-Sefer Kohelet* in *Kitvei Rabbenu Moshe ben Nahman*, ed. (C. Chavel, 1 (1963), 193.
3. See Isa. 53–54; add Rashi's commentary to Isa. 53; Joseph Klausner, *The Messianic Idea in Israel* (1955), 161–63; H. W. Robinson, *Corporate Personality in Ancient Israel* (1964), 16–20.
4. See, for example, *Midrash Pesikta de-Rav Kahana* 26:11, ed. B. Mandelbaum, vol. 2 (1962), 399.
5. See also Mid. Yalkut Shimoni, "Ruth," no. 600 (1944), 1040; BT Shab. 32b.

6. For example, Ex. 20:5; 24:7. See also Solomon Schechter, *Aspects of Rabbinic Theology* (1909), 170–99.
7. See also BT Rosh ha-Shanah 16b–17a; BT Hag. 15a; BT Kid. 40b; Gen. R. 9:8, 33:1; Mid. Ps. 1:22, 12b.
8. See, for example, Naḥmanides' commentary to Job 33:3 in op. cit., 101 and n. 30.
9. For example, *Midrash Pesikta Rabbati* 37, ed. Friedman, 2d ed. (1963), 162b.
10. See, for example, Eliezer Berkovits, *Faith After the Holocaust* (1973), 89.
11. For rabbinic precedents of this view see especially Gen. R. 9:2 and the sources noted in Abraham Heschel, *Torah Min ha-Shamayim* 1 (1962), 90–92.
12. See Louis Jacobs, *Seeker of Unity* (1966), 49–64 and sources noted therein.
13. See, for example, Helmer Ringrenn, *The Religion of Israel* (1966), 73.
14. See Abraham Heschel, *The Prophets* (1962) and *Torah Min ha-Shamayim* 1 (1962), 65–92.
15. See, for example, BT Meg. 29a; BT Hag. 15b; Mekh., ed. Horovitz-Rabin, 2d ed. (1960), 52.
16. See, for example, Eliezer Berkovits, *God, Man and History* (1959), 79.

BIBLIOGRAPHY

Eliezer Berkovits, *Faith After the Holocaust* (1973).
Arthur A. Cohen, *The Tremendum* (1981).
John Hick, *Evil and the God of Love* (1966).
Solomon Schechter, "The Doctrine of Divine Retribution in Rabbinical Literature," in *Studies in Judaism,* 1st series (1958).
Byron L. Sherwin, "Portrait of God as a Young Artist, "in *Judaism* 33 (Fall 1984).
Isaiah Tishbi, *Torat ha-Ra ve-ha-Kelipah be-Kabalat Ha-Ari* (1963).

Theology

תיאולוגיה

Arthur A. Cohen

Theology in Judaism is an intellectual discipline with a continuous history but a discontinuous tradition. Despite the unbroken production of works either partly or wholly concerned with the asking of theological questions, the issues they have raised have not always been considered central or even germane to the conduct of Jewish religious life.

The classical rabbinic literature is clearly marked by the consideration of theological questions—the nature, person, and manifestation of God, the relation between God and history, evil and freedom, redemption and eschatology—but answers to such questions were not regarded by the tradition as either decisive to the acceptance of God's dominion or useful in the clarification and interpretation of Jewish law and practice. We can reconstruct the assumptions and worldview of the rabbis and thereby devise for them a virtual theology, but we have little reason to believe that we accomplish more by such an exercise than the exposition of their theology as we construe it. The classical tradition either regarded theology as secondary to the elaboration of the halakhah—its assumption and presupposition, so to speak—or else distinguished its own mode of speculation so radically from the Greek and Hellenistic tradition of which it was aware as to have pass as theology what the Western (Christian) intellectual tradition, more cognizant of its Greek than of its Hebrew roots, might not consider theology at all. Rabbinic theology may well be a unique genre that depends upon a different canon of evidence, even an original logic, surely a different arrangement of speculative priorities than was common among the Greeks and their Christian legatees. It remains an ongoing predicament of historical interpretation whether to regard aggadah as the literary form par excellence of classical Jewish theology. Clearly, the aggadah is the authentic mode of Jewish theologizing, but whether it yields an internally coherent theology is debatable.

It may well be the case that the rabbis undertook to deal with theological questions in a manner so inapposite to the discourse made familiar by Christian inquiry that Jewish thinkers are obliged to construe the discipline of theology differently. Clearly, the halakhah is grounded upon assumptions about the nature of the created universe so distinct from Christian parsings of the formulas of dogma that, ab initio, whatever may be termed theology in Judaism must be differentiated from its more familiar Christian manifestation. It may then follow that the Jewish understanding of theology is skewed by a prudent unwillingness to have its method confused with that of Christians, who have, over the centuries, preempted theology. Jews cannot, for that reason, assert—as is so often done with an almost cavalier unsophistication—that theology is not a proper mode of Jewish inquiry. Theology is, after all, a scrutiny of the language and interpretation of the ultimate reality that is God.

Heuristic considerations aside, the rabbinic tradition surely concerned itself with the formulation of normative beliefs insofar as these reinforced the obligatory demands of halakhah. Insofar as belief in Providence, reward and punishment, the coming of the Messiah, and resurrection of the dead constellate a rabbinic system of hope that confirms and solidifies normative practices and supplies an ultimate justification for obedience and performance of the *mizvot,* one may speak of a virtual rabbinic theology. Moreover, it is correct to regard the halakhah as itself the embodiment and expression of theological conviction. The formulation of Jewish beliefs independently of halakhah is in some respects appropriate to their formal nature, namely beliefs that entail no correlative acts (as in those of eschatology), while in other respects, as for instance in the ordinances governing prayer, theological conviction is collateral to and complementary with the performance of halakhic obligation.

At the very outset, what may be recognized as a consistent characteristic of Jewish religion (and presumably then of any Jewish theology that would elaborate it) is that the relation between the Jew and God is manifested in a complex and interconnected structure of acts, beliefs, gestures, and words. The rabbinic Jew scarcely questioned the provenience, presence, and providence of God; they were the presuppositions out of which classical Judaism lived. It is correct then to argue that for the rabbinic Jew—insofar as the rabbinic Jew conducts life within the settled delineations of Torah— the theological care for clarification and definition of first principles of belief hardly exists. The rabbinic Jew does and hears as the tradition affirms that God authorized acts and instructions. It matters less that such a Jew understands the God who lies behind the law; rather more important is that the logic and implication of the law be explicit and clear.

The discipline of theology emerges to the forefront only in the historical situation in which the bond of practice and obedience and the assumed persuasiveness of divine justification have to whatever degree eroded. The erosion—whether acknowledged or not—begins with the challenging assault mounted by the formulation of Christian belief during the patristic age. It matters not at all that few if any talmudic sages afford us evidence of their discomfiture in the face of Christian challenge. What is known is that many Jews of the Roman and Hellenistic Diaspora did succumb to Christian suasion, proof at least that the fortress of halakhic faith was not impervious. Christianity, unlike rabbinic Judaism, could not, however, help but be theological, since its message is not contained within a structure of acts and instructions but is rather a series of assertions about a bizarre drama of salvation that require belief and the acquiescence of the intellect.

Theological reflection among rabbinic Jews is thus always posterior to acts; for Christians, however, it is always prior. All Christian sacramental acts incarnate prior beliefs, manifesting them as mysteries. All Jewish beliefs interpret and elaborate the mystery of acts themselves, determining finally that many, even those regarded as critical, derive their justification from no rationalization, no human logic, but merely because they are the will and ordinance of God.

The Christian assault upon Judaism during the apostolic and patristic era, accompanied by the diffusion of gnostic permutations of the substance of Greek philosophic inquiry, left its mark upon rabbinic Judaism principally in respect of the latter's increasing reluctance to engage in theological confrontation and debate. In the few theological encounters that did occur (recorded only by their Christian protagonists, as in the celebrated dialogue of Justin Martyr with the Jew Trypho), the Christian imputes to his Jewish interlocutor an interest in organizing his confession of faith in both logical and systematic order, always grounding assertion, however, upon scriptural warrant. Even more so in the case of those encounters between pagan and Jew recorded in the Midrash, the effort of theological crystallization and the offering of summations of Jewish belief and intention derive their power and authority from biblical texts.

The Bible has always been the foundation upon which any Jewish theology grounds itself. It is the first document of divine generosity toward mankind and, although not the last (since any enterprise of the human hearing of God may be counted an instance of ongoing grace), to the extent that human hearing wishes to stand within the continuum of such audition, it makes first appeal to the warrant of its most ancient revelation. Such a tradition of hearing beginning in ancient times was pursued, virtually unbroken, through the Middle Ages. It was one thing, for example, for Saadiah Gaon to undertake an interpretation of the foundations of knowledge and understanding, but quite another when such philosophic curiosity collided with explicit scriptural announcement. The philosophic undertaking can proceed independently of theological noesis only so long as piety does not require its contradictory contention to return to Scripture for correction. Where contradiction occurs, as in the discussion of the eternity of the world or its creation ex nihilo by divine will, or in matters relating to the abstract and negative character of man's knowledge of God's attributes when contrasted with the vivid anthropomorphism of many biblical texts, the task of philosophic theology is to develop a language of distinction that preserves scriptural integrity while at the same time proposing to reason a theory that accords well with the most exquisite and delicate of divine gifts—man's ability to think coherently.

Jewish theological language during the Middle Ages, although employed in the creation of many of that era's most intense pietistic and mystic works (in which terminology shifts from epistemological groping to ontological postulation), survived and remained influential principally in its nonmystical formulation. Whatever the reason for the suppression of the contrarational current of medieval Jewish thought, it appears that the major thinkers who continued to be read as sources of instruction to postmedieval Jewish thought (including our own) were preoccupied principally with establishing coherence and complementarity between substantive Jewish beliefs and the skilled employment of reason rather than with the transmission of a normative mythos of the divine–human transaction.

Clearly, whatever we shall first begin now to learn for theology from Gershom Scholem's interpretation of the mystic tradition in Judaism will require a double rinsing of our mythological tradition; first, to ensure that the relation of the biblical mythos and theology is clear, and, having accomplished that, to devise a language that enables the mythos to be made public, namely to radiate discourse, to enhance lucidity, to check its list to obscurity, and to insist that its findings be compassed—even if they cannot be absorbed—by both reason and Scripture. Since Jewish mysticism was not a doctrine of solitary contemplation but an esoteric excursus upon the fundamental problems of the universe and Jewish existence within it, such mysticism can never become more than a curiosity unless it can be rendered public, its internal logic and interior drama translated analogically, and its findings properly subsumed and ordered to prior and more conventional realities of Jewish thought. The temptation of the inexperienced to make Judaism esoteric before they have mastered its exoteric concreteness is one against which we need to guard.

The theological language that was strained through the meeting and response of Jewish thought to the early challenge of the Enlightenment (Haskalah) can be summarized thus: God remained the absolute and unsurpassable reality, whose creation had established the human community and inaugurated the historical antecedents that gather and swell into the Jewish people, congregated in Egypt and led forth to covenant and revelation; revelation supplied that people with a law that defined its civil independence as well as autonomous ritual crystallized in the Temple cultus and subsequently destroyed by historical misfortune. In the dispersion to which the Jews came, the practice of the law and the ongoing deliberation of its implication became the normative praxis of Jewish existence. Theological speculation slumbered, the annotation of Jewish history remained episodic or was elevated into a transhistorical mythos, and a complementary mystic tradition emerged to supply a wholly original narrative metaphysics to Jewish existence.

For the enlightened among the Jews, emancipation and free access to European culture augured the imminent end of classical Judaism, the only task remaining being that of documenting its course in order to provide the archives with an accurate summary of its achievement before its demise; on the other hand, those without conscious interest in Jewish religion began the work of national rescue and regeneration based no less patently upon the assimilation of secular ideologies of social liberation to the tasks of Jewish revitalization. For the one, Jewish theology was merely the history of Jewish ideas whose sway and significance had ended; for the other, Jewish theology consisted of a body of notions about the universe that were either obscurantist and benighted or else available for transformation into the secular language of Zionist politics and social vision. Only two sectors of Jewish life continued to deal with the reality of God: the committed orthodox of Eastern Europe, for whom the panoply of Enlightenment—Bible criticism, modern science, Jewish historiography—implied a radical assault upon the halakhah and its observance, and the new Jewish thinkers—Salomon Ludwig Steinheim, Naḥman Krochmal, Solomon Formstecher, Hermann Cohen, Leo Baeck, Martin Buber, Franz Rosenzweig, et al.—who attached themselves to one or another aspect of the theological problem and undertook its renovation.

In broad strokes, the issues of historical theology that carry us up to World War II can be set forth: Hermann Cohen argues the case for construing Judaism as the moral religion of reason that Kant had sought and had denied Judaism exemplified; Martin Buber imposes upon Judaism a metaphor of dialogue by which to describe the ontological grounding of revelation whose authoritative content he nonetheless rejects; Franz Rosenzweig extends the terrain of phenomenological ingathering to describe a Jewish metaphysics that successfully interprets classical texts in such a way as to harvest a conceptual framework of creation, revelation, and redemption that all but strips the Jew of historical reality. In the same era in which these major theologians are at work effectively severing the connection of the Jew to history by making of history either a temptation or a myth, the great Jewish historians—Simon Dubnow, Salo Baron, Yehezkel Kaufmann, Yitzhak F. Baer, and others—are defining a Jewish historiography of event and causality in which theological ideas are exhumed but appear hardly decisive. The alienation of theology and history is virtually complete at the time of the advent of Hitler and the destruction of European Jewry.

It cannot be speculated what Cohen, Buber, and Rosenzweig might have thought had they survived the Hitler era and been agile enough to entertain its grotesque implications. Cohen was long since dead, Rosenzweig had died young, and Buber, vaguely undertaking to deal with the Holocaust, proposed a refurbishing of such millennial notions as the *deus absconditus* and "the divine eclipse." Among younger postwar theologians, either the Holocaust is represented as such a great mystery that nothing theological can be said that is relevant, or else the Holocaust is treated as an historical *novum* from which we may derive moral imperatives and messianic hopes but hardly theological clarity.

It is contended, moreover, that there can be no Jewish theology in this most terrible of centuries unless it is prepared to ask: What do we know *now* about the creator God in whose universe such horror is permitted? It may well be the case that the appropriate reply of classical traditionalists is that nothing can be asked about God's nature, that he keeps the mystery to himself, that we are obliged only to persevere in serving him. To this the reply has been made: Why continue then to serve such a God? If the traditional God is he who cares and is merciful, so much for the value of his scriptural promises. If it is said that all who perished—stressing the children, as Emil Fackenheim has done—were sinners, so much for the divine understanding of sin. And if, as is also done by some religious Zionists who enjoy hearing the rustle of the messianic wind in the establishment of a Jewish state, the birth of Israel is to be credited to divine redemption, must not the Holocaust be ascribed as well to God—and, it might be added, is even that excellent, but beleaguered, state worth six million Jewish lives?

All of the foregoing perplexities are intended to illustrate the difficulty of standing with the classical agenda of Jewish theology: a God of absolute authority and perfect understanding, all-powerful and cognizant, creator, revealer, redeemer according to his own will and council, lawgiver and instructor to a nation of imperfect creatures, offering free will but reserving the privilege of intervention, using history to correct and instruct by both action and passivity. This theological description remained possible so long as the predicament of man remained one that philosophers and theologians could address in personal, existential terms, where loss of trust and erosion of faith were predominant, where Jews could still think of leaving Judaism for Christianity as an issue of personal decision, indeed where the task of theology was construed as the instruction of private conscience, the clarification of religious understanding, the turning of personal knowledge from egoistic preoccupation to the divine object of contemplation.

If, however, such a God no longer exists or, as is suggested, never did exist, the task of theology is not optional and secondary to Jewish tradition, but unavoidably primary. Without addressing He Who Spoke and Created the Universe as though he were new to us, as though everything that had been thought about him was now demonstrably implausible or morally inadequate, the Jewish religious enterprise (and no less that of all theist religions) must be abandoned. It is not enough for believers to believe, although there will always be those who continue to keep faith long after it has ceased to be true, and any faith, all faiths may be sustained with uncritical tenacity; one suspects, however, that as faith becomes increasingly fanatic, as politics replaces belief with an ideology that tests the truth of God only with successes won by power, it is hardly likely that such a faith will long survive (indeed, it may be questioned whether civilization will long survive).

It has always been the starting point of my own method of theological inquiry to acknowledge in faith that God has told us *that* he is (this is the starting point of theology in faith); God has disclosed his name in order that he may be addressed and worshiped, itself the starting point of prayer and blessing; God has revealed his Torah that he may be served according to his will, itself the starting point of obedience; God has revealed the promise of futurity and redemption—that he will be with us when he chooses to be with us, this theophany asserting the mystery of his historical presence. He has left to us, however, always and most particularly, the ascertainment of his nature. We possess the who of God's person and the how of his intimacy, but we know little of his nature. To that question he turned his back to Moses at Sinai and symbolically refused to us any guarantee that the compliments paid his nature by traditional theology are justified. All that needs to be believed in order for us to allow our God to survive the Holocaust (along with a remnant of his people) is that his infinitesimal uncontrol be acknowledged to be as much a treasure of uncertainty to God as it is a kingdom of unknowing to man, that God can do almost everything, but not everything, that man's freedom is not simply a gift, but an indispensable surd of the divine nature, and that man's very existence reflects upon and corroborates God's limit. The primordial nature of God is inexhaustible, but the consequent, effectual nature of God—the God of acts—has dire consequences for historical life. Both natures must be explored again as if starting over.

Put as an assertion of faith from which theology must begin its reflections, the classical conception of God was a working out of the entente between Scripture and philosophy. As long as the universe held that sustained both faith and reason, it was possible to abide with the definitions the classical tradition devised. The modern understanding of God was a working out of the entente between philosophy and history; as long as the universe held that permitted the dialectic of their enraveled dominions, it was possible to abide with the tension produced by their definitions. Both universes—the classical and the modern—are irretrievably gone, plundered by cruelty, still threatened by annihilation.

The God of Israel is worth the undertaking, and the time is now to build again upon the wreckage of previous understandings. The God who will endure—who has endured, who still seeks us—may well prove to be less imperious and authoritarian, but may gain in credibility and truth what he has lost in unconditional absoluteness.

BIBLIOGRAPHY

Arthur A. Cohen, *The Natural and the Supernatural Jew: An Historical and Theological Introduction* (1963).

Arthur A. Cohen, *The Tremendum: A Theological Interpretation of the Holocaust* (1981).

Julius Guttmann, *Philosophies of Judaism: The History of Jewish Philosophy from Biblical Times to Franz Rosenzweig,* David W. Silverman, tr. (1964).

Franz Rosenzweig, *The Star of Redemption,* William Hallo, tr. (1971).

Gershom Scholem, "Reflections on Jewish Theology," in *On Jews and Judaism in Crisis* (1976), 261–97.

Time

זמן

William E. Kaufman

Judaism is a religion of time, a religion of history. "It was the glory of Greece to have discovered the idea of cosmos, the world of space; it was the achievement of Israel to have experienced history, the world of time."[1] More precisely, whereas the emphasis in ancient Greek thought was on the discovery and elaboration of the idea of the cosmos, it was ancient Israel that discerned an ultimate or transcendent meaning to history. This was in large measure due to the emancipation of biblical Hebraic thought from a cyclical to a linear conception of historical time, although one must beware of rigidly oversimplifying the distinctions between ancient Greek and Hebraic thinking. Nevertheless, the Hebraic transformation of agricultural festivals into commemorations of historical events aptly illustrates that to biblical Israel the unique events of historic time were spiritually more significant than were the repetitive processes in the cycle of nature. This was in marked contrast to the Greek emphasis on the eternal recurrences of nature. Furthermore, to the Greek Eleatic philosophers, the immutable held a higher interest and value than the historical world of change and becoming. In this intellectual climate, dominated by the belief in the rationality of the cosmos, there was little room for the universal significance of a unique, incomparable historic event.

In contrast, the will of Israel's biblical God was revealed primarily in the unique events of history. To be sure, the Hebrew Bible speaks of the revelation of God in nature. But the foundation of biblical religion lies in the unique events of Exodus and Sinai. It was because of a profound sense of time that biblical man believed that he had witnessed at Sinai an event without parallel in human history. The uniqueness of this event to the biblical mind is underscored by the Deuteronomist: "You have but to inquire about bygone ages that came before you . . . has anything as grand as this ever happened or has its like ever been known? Has any people ever heard the voice of a god speaking out of a fire, as you have, and survived?" (Deut. 4:32, 33). It follows that the Hebrew Bible is more concerned with time and history than with space and nature. The world is viewed by the biblical authors primarily through the dimensions of temporality and historicity.

The centrality of time in biblical Hebraic thinking is in marked contrast to the treatment of time by the medieval Jewish philosopher Moses Maimonides, who held to the Aristotelian concept of time. Aristotle defined time as "the number of motion according to before and after" (*Physics* 4:11, 219b). In his *Guide of the Perplexed,* Maimonides stated: "For time is undoubtedly an accident, and, according to our opinion, one of the created accidents, like blackness and whiteness; it is not a quality, but an accident connected with motion . . . which in itself is an accident of a moving object" (*Guide* 2, 13). The reasoning leading to this view of time is as follows. Aristotle held that all reality falls into two classes: substance and accident. A substance is something that exists in itself, an accident something that exists in something else. Since time is something fleeting, consisting of past and future, neither of which has any actual existence, time is therefore an accident. Since we have no perception of time unless we have a perception of motion, time is an accident of motion. Motion itself is an accident of body or corporeal substances. Time, therefore, is an accident of an accident, possessing only a quasi-reality.

Hasdai Crescas, in contrast to Maimonides, rejected Aristotle's definition of time. Attempting to free time from dependence on motion, Crescas maintained that time is the duration or continuance of a thinking mind. As duration, time exists independently of motion. Unlike motion, duration does not depend for its existence upon external objects and does not arise in our mind out of the motion of external things. Rather, it is the continuity and flow of the activity of the thinking mind, which may be the mind of

God, the universal soul, or even our own mind. This concept of time as duration, advanced by Crescas, can be traced back to Plotinus. According to H. A. Wolfson, "Students of Bergson, too, may perhaps find in it some suggestion of his distinction between pure duration and mixed time."[2]

It was Henri Bergson, a thinker on the extreme periphery of Judaism, who developed the concept of real time as duration into a full-fledged philosophy of time. Bergson distinguished between clock time and duration or "lived" time. Clock time is based on the spatialization of time; measurement implies the juxtaposition of equal units: time is homogeneous. In contrast, experience reveals that moments of time are not alike; each moment has its own distinctive qualitative tone. Time as duration is not a homogeneous medium like space but instead a heterogeneous stream, ever flowing, never repetitive. Bergson's analysis of time as duration made possible a new philosophy of process. This process philosophy entailed a rejection of scientific materialism. If scientific materialism were correct, all change would be reducible to the predictable motions of material particles, and freedom of the will would be an illusion. But the experience of duration, Bergson pointed out, revealed change to be a far more dynamic, organic, and highly interrelated process than the mere motions of mass particles. To Bergson, each moment of duration involves the emergence of new qualities. Thus the future is truly open and novelty is real. Scientific materialism, accordingly, must be replaced by an organic philosophy of nature, which Bergson elaborated in his *L'évolution créatrice* (*Creative Evolution*, 1907). The force that drives the evolutionary process Bergson called the *élan vital* or vital impetus, which can be comprehended only by intuition.

Samuel Alexander, the first Jew to be elected a fellow of an Oxford or Cambridge college (he obtained a fellowship at Lincoln College in 1882), presented a sustained metaphysics of process in his Gifford Lectures, published as *Space, Time and Deity* in 1920. In this work, Alexander cites Bergson as "the first philosopher to take time seriously."[3] By "taking time seriously" Alexander meant the construction of a view of nature as a process that is essentially historical—that is, there is an irreversible direction defined by "Time's Arrow." Time, for Alexander, represents the creative advance into novelty: the whole universe is an on-going nisus bringing forth new emergent qualities. The highest emergent quality greater than mind, toward which the universe is tending, Alexander calls deity. God, in Alexander's metaphysics, thus represents the whole universe as moving toward deity.

The philosophies of Bergson and Alexander, with their rehabilitation of the notion of time, represent a metaphysical conceptual framework for the centrality of time in contemporary Jewish thought. Time is crucial, for example, in the theology of Abraham J. Heschel. "Judaism," Heschel writes, "is a *religion of time* aiming at the *sanctification of time* [emphases added]. Unlike the space-minded man to whom time is unvaried, iterative, homogeneous, to whom all hours are alike, qualityless, empty shells, the Bible senses the diversified character of time. There are no two hours alike."[4] Heschel's concept of holiness in time and his emphasis on sacred moments find metaphysical support in Bergson's analysis of the qualitative uniqueness of "lived" time or duration.

Mordecai M. Kaplan's conception of Judaism as an evolving religious civilization and his notion of God as the power or process that makes for salvation represent another example of temporal, dynamic, and evolutionary categories replacing the static concepts of medieval philosophy. Kaplan quotes approvingly Samuel Alexander's view that "the mind of man is the prelude to Godhood."[5] The process philosophies of Bergson and Alexander, taken together with the theological implications of this type of thinking as exemplified in the thought of Heschel and Kaplan, constitute the basis of a Jewish process philosophy to be both compared and contrasted with contemporary Christian process philosophy based on the thought of Alfred North Whitehead. The implications of this trend in modern and contemporary Jewish thought have yet to be worked out systematically.

Time is also crucial in the theology of Franz Rosenzweig. His "new thinking, like the age old thinking of common sense, knows that it cannot have cognition independent of time."[6] Temporality is thus essential to human experience. But, for Rosenzweig, the Jew has his own sense of time. "The Jewish sense of time is revealed time; it is time already anticipating redemption."[7] Rosenzweig's view of eschatological time had the problematic consequence of undermining the relevance of history for the Jew.

The metahistorical character of Rosenzweig's theology is criticized by Emil Fackenheim. Rosenzweig died in 1929, prior to the Holocaust and the birth of the State of Israel. These epoch-making events render Rosenzweig's vision "distant."[8] It is Fackenheim's contention that Jewish philosophical and religious thought cannot be indifferent and immune to history, for the events to which Jewish thought is required to make itself vulnerable— the Holocaust and the rise of the State of Israel—are unique and unprecedented.

Just as biblical Hebraic thought emphasized the epoch-making events of Exodus and Sinai, so too must contemporary Jewish thought orient itself to the unique and unprecedented character of the Holocaust and the State of Israel as historic events.

Fackenheim's emphasis on the uniqueness of contemporary historic events to the Jewish consciousness underscores the continuity of present Jewish thought with the historical and time-oriented character of biblical thinking.

Contemporary Jewish thought thus discloses an ever-expanding realization of the significance of time and the uniqueness of historical events to the Jewish consciousness.

REFERENCES

1. Abraham J. Heschel, *God in Search of Man* (1956), 206.
2. Harry A. Wolfson, *Crescas' Critique of Aristotle* (1929), 97.
3. Samuel Alexander, *Space, Time and Deity* 1(1920), 44.
4. Abraham J. Heschel, *The Sabbath* (1951), 8. Emphasis added.
5. Mordecai M. Kaplan, *The Religion of Ethical Nationhood* (1970), 111.
6. Nahum Glatzer, *Franz Rosenzweig: His Life and Thought* (1953), 196–97.
7. Arthur A. Cohen, *The Natural and the Supernatural Jew* (1962), 142.
8. Emil Fackenheim, *The Jewish Return Into History* (1978), 189.

BIBLIOGRAPHY

Samuel Alexander, *Space, Time and Deity*, 2 vols. (1920).
Arthur A. Cohen, *The Natural and the Supernatural Jew* (1962).
Abraham J. Heschel, *The Sabbath* (1951).
Abraham J. Heschel, *God in Search of Man* (1956).
Harry A. Wolfson, *Crescas' Critique of Aristotle* (1929).

Tolerance

סובלנות

Alan Udoff

The concept of tolerance, when sounded as a theme in Jewish thought, is gravely resonant. It recalls the civil and religious disabilities that virtually every Jewish community has endured in the course of the Diaspora, that is, it brings first to mind Jewish suffering. Historically, the association is understandable: Arguments in favor of tolerance originate in the conviction of the need for tolerance, a conviction that arises out of the experience of its want. These arguments are, however, not simply the product of suffering; rather, they are evidence of a certain attitude toward suffering, an implicit recognition of its injustice, and also of human invention. This attitude stands, therefore, in direct opposition to the view of suffering that has predominated in Jewish theology, namely, the belief that sin occasions suffering in the exact measure of its offense (what rabbinic thought typologizes as *midah ke-neged midah*). This theology of history does not, to be sure, simply reduce to resignation, to what Sartre termed the "masochism of inauthentic Jews."[1] Even the ascetic teaching of Baḥya ibn Paquda distinguishes between the forbearance that humility imposes on oneself as the victim of injustice and the obligation to redress the victimization of others (*The Book of Directions to the Duties of the Heart*, 1973, ch. 6, F:9, 318). These qualifications notwithstanding, there is a sense in which the active concern with tolerance on the part of earlier Jewish thinkers at points reflects—at points presages—what in time will manifest itself fully as a fundamental shift in the nature of Jewish awareness. Where that awareness is concentrated most forcefully, that is, with the rise of political Zionism, the nature of that shift is articulated with greatest clarity and theoretical rigor:

> The peculiarity of Zionism as a modern movement comes out most clearly in the strictly political Zionism presented first by Leon Pinsker in his *Autoemancipation* and then by Theodor Herzl in his *The Jewish State*. Pinsker and Herzl started from the failure of the liberal solution, but continued to see the problem to be solved as it had begun to be seen by liberalism, i.e. as a merely human problem. The terrible fate of the Jews was in no sense to be understood any longer as connected with divine punishment for the sins of our fathers or with the providential mission of the chosen people and hence to be borne with the meek fortitude of martyrs. It was to be understood in merely human terms, as constituting a purely political problem which as such cannot be solved by appealing to the justice or generosity of other nations, to say nothing of a league of all nations.[2]

In the work in question Leo Strauss does not consider further, certainly not directly, Zionism's attempt to supersede liberalism. That is to say, he passes over in silence the question of whether or not Zionism, in its transition from theory to statecraft, or, more importantly, the evolution of Jewish self-understanding (which includes Zionism as but one of its expressions), has demonstrated a justice or wisdom superior to other attempts that have failed. Since traditional Jewish teaching (in this instance at one with the founding traditions of Western moral philosophy) holds that it is better to suffer than to commit injustice, the question Strauss leaves open—when sounded as a theme in Jewish or philosophical thought—is most gravely resonant, for it calls to mind not the disabilities that Jews have suffered at the hands of others, but the disabilities that they themselves have imposed—at times on the stranger, more often on their brother. It was not without reason, then, that John Knox, seeking precedent and justification for his own discriminatory ends, turned to Israelite history:

> While the posterity of Abraham were *few in number*, and while they sojourned in *different countries*, they were merely required to avoid all participation in the idolatrous rites of the heathen; but *as soon as they prospered into a kingdom*, and had obtained *possession of Canaan*, they were strictly charged to suppress idolatry, and to destroy all the monuments and incentives. The same duty was *now* incumbent on the professors of the true religion in Scotland.[3]

Nor may the citation of Israel's example by Knox, the circumstances of whose argument required that it carry the force of immediate conviction and that it be received as stating a commonly acknowledged belief, simply be dismissed. Rather, it accords fully with authoritative formulations of Jewish law, such as are found in the works of Moses Maimonides, where the reach of retribution extends to the Jewish subject with even greater stringency (MT Hil. Av. Zar.10:1). These laws, moreover, proscribe not only the practice of idolatry, but all intermediate stages of association—including, if not especially, the reading of idolatrous works (MT Hil. Av. Zar. 2:2). With the interdiction of texts, a familiar pattern of suppression completes itself, one that lends substance to the charges of authoritarianism[4] and intolerance[5] that continue to be leveled against Judaism, for which *Pharisee* has become a byword. In fact, the extent to which the evidence of censorship substantiates these charges is considerable; the mitigating circumstances that, one might argue, obtain in the case of idolatry (an issue on which the whole of the Torah is at stake: MT Hil. Av. Zar. 2:4), or atheism (an issue on which Locke himself, in his classic *Letter on Toleration,* refuses to grant the clemency of tolerance), were not relevant in determining the culpability of many books eventually banned. Instead, the reasons actually adduced often reveal ideological biases wholly out of proportion to the provocations at hand, at times excluding works from the narrow circle of legitimacy by reason of their genre, or even the language of their composition.[6]

It is not necessary, then, to go beyond the case of censorship, the possibility and effectiveness of which presupposes an entire network of institutional and ideational alliances functioning in concert, reinforcing one another, for the question of Jewish intolerance to emerge as a source of concern. The concern, of course, takes many forms, as varied as the contexts in which the retrograde effects of intolerance score their indelible marks. What remains at question, however, is the way in which this concern enters the domain of the theologian, or if it enters that domain at all. The question may be formulated precisely, although somewhat circuitously, by reflecting on a text of C. S. Lewis in which he discovers the essence of friendship in the equivalency of love and a common concern for the truth:

> In this kind of love, as Emerson said, *Do you love me?* means *Do you see the same truth?* Or at least, "Do you *care about* the same truth?" The man who agrees with us that some question, little regarded by others, is of great importance can be our Friend. He need not agree with us about the answer.[7]

It is clear that Lewis intends the idea of friendship to convey the special sense in which an Augustine and Nebridius loved each other, or in which the followers of Plato could be called Friends of the Forms, that is, friendship as a virtue or excellence that exists in the "marriage of true minds." Tolerance, too, is a form of befriending. As such it consists in a virtue or excellence that can be spoken of only in relation to a truth. In tolerance, however, that relation exists only insofar as the other does "not agree with us about the answer" to the question of that truth. Tolerance, then, is a virtue, or perfection, that commits one to the truth and at the same time to its denial by another—not the denial of its importance, but the denial of the content through which it expresses itself. It is under these conditions that the theologian must address the issue of tolerance: In what sense, if any, does befriending the other, the other in whom the limit of our truth is proclaimed, constitute a virtue, and thus a good actively to be sought?

In raising the question of tolerance as a virtue, that is, as a state whose presence or want in some measure defines the excellence of man, it is necessary to bear in mind that the notion of this virtue—as well as the conditions of its coming into being—are subject to the radical distinction between virtue as philosophically or theologically conceived, that is, the distinction between Athens and Jerusalem, between "the source of conscience" as "the dictate of . . . one's own cultured mind" and "the source of conscience" as "the will of God."[8]

The briefs that argue on behalf of philosophical tolerance, or what passes for philosophical tolerance, must be carefully prepared. Evidence to the contrary, particularly in the case of Judaism,[9] is abundant, and its lineage is as ancient as the origins of philosophy itself.[10] Nevertheless, there is a soil, so to speak, a cultivated ground, from out of which tolerance as a befriending of the other in the name of the pursuit of the truth emerges. Friedrich Nietzsche described the form of this befriending with characteristic penetration:

> A philosophical frame of mind. Generally we strive to acquire one emotional stance, one viewpoint for all life situations and events: we usually call that being of a philosophical frame of mind. But rather than making oneself uniform, we may find greater value for the enrichment of knowledge by listening to the soft voice of different life situations; each brings its own views with it. Thus we acknowledge and share the life and nature of many by not treating ourselves like rigid, invariable, single individuals.[11]

The philosophical experience, or frame of mind, is thus literally circumscribed by the presence of others. This classical experience differs, then, from its modern equivalent, the rationalism that is premised on the deduction of reality from the inner content of the solitary mind, and its ancient

counterpart, the singular Other of revelation. In contrast, the classical philosophical experience is constituted by its engagement of a plurality of
minds—for example, the city in Plato; the history of philosophy in Aristotle.
This engagement is not properly conceived as the surplus of a rhetorical
energy, or the way in which the plenitude of *logos*—in its gathering together
of all things—perforce materializes itself. Rather, it is in the need for other,
the *logos* of the other, that philosophy evokes the *word*. The source of this
need is simply the limitation of human understanding itself. To know the
world humanly is to be situated at the vertex of an acute angle of vision.
The extent to which this angle may broaden depends on others and the
vantage of their own seeing. But no insight of wisdom or experience, no
matter how far the lines of vision extend in breadth or time, can escape the
angularity that shapes the human way of knowing. In these circumstances,
the need for tolerance, for "listening to the soft voice of different life situations" and "views," is an imperative of prudence and a declaration of
wisdom.

No similar values obtain, however, for the difference or dissent of the
other when belief has been constituted by revelation, that is, where absolute
truth and certitude inform the consciousness of the believing witness. This
assertion is doubtless contradicted by experience. Orthodoxy and pluralism
have often allied themselves in the practice of a democratic ideal. However,
the mere fact of this practice, the sociological datum, is insufficient

> to determine the principle on which we can base a tolerance which is really a
> counter-intolerance, but which is not, at the same time, the expression or mark
> of a complete skepticism, but rather the living incarnation of a faith.[12]

Whatever form that principle is to take, whatever reason or authority it
is to invoke, it must prove compelling to

> someone who has absolute faith and for whom the possibility of being mistaken
> does not arise. The real question is that of determining whether the supposedly
> complete certainty such a person has of possessing the truth precludes the pos-
> sibility of manifesting a genuine tolerance for those who think differently.[13]

For Gabriel Marcel, then, tolerance is to be understood neither as an indifference to the truth or specific truth claims in question nor as a skepticism
with regard to one's own claim to the truth. In either case, the possibility
of befriending—conceived along the lines drawn above in reference to C.
S. Lewis—would have lost its final cause. Similarly, tolerance is not to be
identified with the expediency that is the lot of those who have no choice:

for "there is only tolerance of what can be prevented."[14] (Here, indeed, is the true test of tolerance, that is, when purpose and power combine in one who nevertheless defers, on principle, to the right of the other, refusing to exercise the rule for which circumstance—so often interpreted as God's will manifesting itself historically—has provided opportunity.) Rather, its proper understanding requires that the positive elements that constitute its nature be identified. For Marcel, this means showing in what way tolerance is an expression of love's mediation of the "blinded consciousness" of unbelief and God's salvific end:

> Here we are dealing with a triadic relation. . . . To serve this divine will means in this context to act as a mediator between it and the other consciousness whom I assume is blinded. . . . It is evident that it is only by showing love to this person . . . that I am really mediator between him and an unknown will which refrains from revealing itself as a material power; and this love must go out to the soul as it is, with the belief which nourishes it and which must also be included in my embrace; my love must be strong enough to allow this soul to be transformed . . . in such a way that . . . its belief . . . is transfigured and throws off the elements of heterodoxy, the fate which threatens to strangle it.
>
> It is also evident that I am an instrument in the entire situation, that I am absolutely not a cause, that nothing issues from me, that I preserve a state of absolute humility relative to God's will which safeguards the latter's transcendence.
>
> On the other hand, we must recognize that from the moment the divine will is served in a way which fully protects its transcendence, we have gone far beyond the tolerance mentioned earlier; here nothing is conceivable without charity, without grace; and I tend to think that conversely, whenever I act towards my fellow creature in this way, whatever the actual contents of my mind may be, God's transcendence is really embodied in my action.[15]

Marcel's analysis succeeds, far in advance of similar efforts, in charting a course into the understanding of tolerance as a theological virtue. As a result, the principal question raised here—in what sense, discounting social utility, does tolerance belong to the domain of theological virtue?—has been given a provisional answer. It must be noted, however, that in securing a place for tolerance among the virtues that are reckoned as theological, Marcel commits himself to certain positions that remain problematical: for example, whether a form of mediation that is defined in terms of the agency and action of human love can be accommodated to a concept of self that has been reduced to an instrumentality under the radical supervention of grace, that is, whether a metaphysics of presence does not already underlie the analysis such that the blinded consciousness of unbelief and God's transcendent will are hypostasized as present to each other (although spatially apart), awaiting a mediation that connects but does not create. These questions bear on the discussion at hand in a particular way, for they set off in relief the strategically primary question of whether, in situating tolerance within the order of theological virtues at the point faith occupies (that is, controls), the essential understanding of tolerance has not been decided in advance of any further inquiry. Preliminary to all other considerations, then, it is necessary to raise anew the question of the place tolerance is to hold within the matrix of theological reflection. This placement itself must be determined by the defining characteristics of tolerance.

Tolerance is, in essence, a mode of reception. In this reception, the other is received as (potentially) en route to the point that has already been attained by the one who receives. The nature of this reception cannot be elucidated properly, however, unless it is brought within the circumspection of a temporal analysis—what Franz Rosenzweig perceived as the "secret" (Geheimnis) of the wisdom of the "new thinking."[16] He who is received is not to be brought into the fullness of faith's present. The present of faith, insofar as it has actualized itself—materialized itself—is already entrenched in the world, is already resolved, outfitted, as it were, for battle. In this battle, the power of faith is revealed as twofold: the power that faith exercises (here the metonymy of faith's "knights" stands in place of a vast complex of power), and the power that exercises faith, even to the endpoint of martyrdom. The virtue of tolerance, theologically conceived, religiously enacted, cannot occupy this present. The powerlessness that true tolerance requires already suggests this: tolerance serves, it serves the other.

In serving what is unactualized, what may never come to pass, the fullness and power of faith's present is temporally taken up into the time of the other—the enroutedness that belongs to the future, and which only the other possesses. To receive the other, then, means to enter his time, which is to say, his unfulfillment. In crossing the threshold of that entry point, faith has no choice but to yield to hope—the present that confirms must acknowledge the supersession of the future that consummates. Tolerance, then, as a waiting for the other, unfolds itself in time. That waiting is, of course, not the passive waiting of the disinterested (pseudotolerant) observer but, rather, the active waiting of one for whom the neutrality of time has been replaced by the purposiveness of history, the telos of salvation. Tolerance, in sum, belongs to the freedom and projectedness (in the most serious sense of the word—the play) of hope.

With the preliminary identification of hope as the temporal region within which tolerance is to be located, the way is secured for its further analysis as a theological virtue. Such an analysis is beyond the intended scope of the present reflections. Rather, their end has been to indicate, in part, what is at issue and at stake in re-sounding the theme of tolerance for Jewish thought, and why the resonances that first attended the opening of this discussion now seem rightfully attenuated at its close.

REFERENCES

1. Jean-Paul Sartre, *Anti-Semite and Jew* (1977), 109.
2. Leo Strauss, *Spinoza's Critique of Religion* (1965), 4.
3. Isaac D'Israeli, "On Toleration," in *Curiosities of Literature* (1871), 146–47. Emphases in original.
4. For example, Immanuel Kant, *Religion Within the Limits of Reason Alone* (1960), 116ff.
5. For example, Georg Wilhelm Friedrich Hegel, *Early Theological Writings* (1971), 188.
6. Cf. Moshe Carmilly-Weinberg, *Censorship and Freedom in Jewish History* (1977).
7. C. S. Lewis, *The Four Loves* (1960), 97. Emphases in original.
8. Karl Löwith, "Can There Be a Christian Gentleman?" in *Nature, History and Existentialism* (1966), 207.
9. Cf. Nathan Rotenstreich, *The Recurring Pattern* (1963).
10. Cf. Heraclitus, Frag. 42, in Kathleen Freeman, ed., *Ancilla to the Pre-Socratic Philosophers* (1966), 27.
11. Friedrich Nietzsche, *Human, All-Too-Human* (1984), 256–57. Emphases in original.
12. Gabriel Marcel, "The Phenomenology and Dialectic of Tolerance," in *Creative Fidelity* (1970), 216.
13. Ibid., 217.
14. Ibid., 211.
15. Ibid., 218–20.
16. Franz Rosenzweig, "Das Neue Denken," in *Der Mensch und Sein Werk*, Rheinhold and Annemarie Mayer, eds. (1984), 149.

BIBLIOGRAPHY

Jacob Katz, *Exclusiveness and Tolerance* (1961).
Gustav Mensching, *Tolerance and Truth in Religion* (1971).
Samuel Morell, "The Halachic Status of Non-Halachic Jews," in *Judaism* 18 (1969).
Benedict Spinoza, *A Theological-Political Treatise,* in *The Chief Works of Benedict Spinoza,* R. H. M. Elwes, ed., vol. 1 (1951).
Max Wiener, "Jewish Piety and Religious Dogma," in Alfred Jospe, ed., *Studies in Jewish Thought: An Anthology of German Jewish Scholarship* (1981).

Torah

תורה

James L. Kugel

If one were to seek a single term that might summon up the very essence of Judaism it would certainly be *torah,* a concept whose centrality has endured from the biblical period to the present day. As such, it is an idea that defies easy summary. Indeed, the very word *torah* underwent a complicated evolution from its earliest attested usages in the Bible until its definitive formulation in classical rabbinic texts, and this evolution in itself provides an interesting *pars pro toto* for the emergence and development of rabbinic Judaism.

The earliest beginnings of *torah* are obscure and, even today, the cause of disagreement among Hebrew philologists. The verbal stem from which it might appear to be derived, *horah,* is believed by some to be a linguistic back-formation from the nominal form *torah* (rather than vice versa), in which several scholars propose to see the possible influence of Akkadian *tèrtu* (oracle). This derivation, however, is far from being universally accepted. Within Hebrew, the root *yarah* (cast) as in the casting of lots or arrows to predict the future (both of which practices are attested in the Bible and in other ancient Near Eastern texts) has been proposed as another possible ancestor for *torah,* and may in any case be suggestive as to the word's development and semantic spread, as are the place names Elon Moreh in Genesis 12:6 and Elonei Moreh in Deuteronomy 11:30 (whose apparent linking of this root with the oracular is strengthened by the name Elon Me'onenim, or Soothsayers' Terebinth, in Judges 9:37). All of this remains highly speculative, however, and it is impossible to know whether the earliest uses of this word belong to the domain of the oracular, the instructional, the legal, or yet some other sphere of activity.

When one considers how *torah* is used within the biblical corpus itself, some broad patterns and distinctions do emerge. The word is found in early texts, often in the plural, *torot,* in frequent apposition to words for *law, statute,* or *commandment.* Apparently its linguistic range in these texts is no greater than that of its apposites and is similar in meaning. It is used in Leviticus and Numbers in the singular to designate specific priestly cultic instructions—e.g., "This is the *torah* of the burnt offering . . ." (Lev. 6:2), "the *torah* of the nazirite . . ." (Num. 6:13)—a usage paralleled in Ezekiel, as well as in the plural as an apposite of *laws.* A similar connection of the term to specifically priestly instruction is found later on as well, in the prophetic writings of Haggai and Malachi. But apparently this usage overlapped with a broader and more inclusive sense. Thus Hosea (4:6) employs "the *torah* of your God" in a broad sense, perhaps meaning the totality of cultic legislations, or again in apposition to "my covenant" (8:1); Amos exhibits a similarly broad usage (2:4), as does his younger contemporary Isaiah (e.g., 1:10, 2:3). Another general usage, and one closely connected to the word's later development, is found in the Deuteronomic corpus: Here one encounters almost without exception the word as an overall and inclusive designation, usually in the singular, defined, state ("the *torah*" or "this *torah*"), which, in context, seems clearly to designate an entire corpus of statutes or, still more broadly, the book of Deuteronomy as a whole. Thus the term *torah* was apparently used in both a restrictive and an inclusive sense, the former frequently designating cultic ordinances and the teaching of priests, the latter referring to a totality of (sometimes specifically divinely given) laws or instructions.

Wisdom literature, and especially the Book of Proverbs, presents a rather different usage for our word. Here the sense of *torah* seems to have been expanded or displaced: It is used in apposition to words associated with wisdom teaching, such as *good counsel* and *discipline; torah* may apparently refer to an individual's store of learning, the *"torah* of the wise man" (13:4), or of a parent (1:8). The fact that this literature treats its *torah*-as-wisdom in much the same way as Deuteronomy treats its notion of *torah* is reflected in the common store of words and expressions found in each. Just as Deuteronomy insists that Israel "keep," "heed," and "guard" the divine covenant, whose contents are "your very life" and should therefore never be "forgotten" or "abandoned," so these same terms and expressions are applied to the (sometimes very down to earth) wisdom presented in these wisdom books. Is this fact a reflection, as some have suggested, of the wisdom milieu in which the Deuteronomic corpus might have originated? Or does it represent a conscious attempt to present the pursuit of wisdom in language of specifically Israelite resonance (torah), indeed to fuse two domains that might once have been regarded as quite separate (cf. Deut. 4:6)? Much later, one finds Ben Sira's striking definition of wisdom as torah in Ecclesiasticus 24; indeed, wisdom there is "the covenant book of supernal God, the Torah which Moses commanded us" (Ecclus. 24:23, but cf. Ezra 7:25).

Finally, it is to be noted that the expressions "the torah of Moses," "the book of Moses," or "the torah of the Lord" and "the torah of God," as they appear in the latest stratum of biblical narrative, have been understood by some critics as designating specifically the Pentateuch. This is a particularly difficult question to resolve since, as seen above, torah and various combinations thereof are used in earlier texts to designate, for example, divine teaching generally or, perhaps, the Book of Deuteronomy. Such an understanding of some of the foregoing phrases would certainly be appropriate for their use in the historical books of Joshua, Judges, Samuel, and Kings, and might well have carried over into post-Exilic historical writings. On the other hand, the evidence from some of these later historical books is of a society in possession of a written, authoritative text, "the book of the Torah of Moses" (Neh. 8:1 ff.), and it seems entirely plausible that this and similar references do designate specifically the Pentateuch more or less as we know it today.

If the relatively later biblical evidence argues for a broader, and more varied, use of the term torah, postbiblical usage, and in particular classical rabbinic texts, may be seen merely to have continued this trend. Indeed, rabbinic texts use "Torah" (and here it is fitting to capitalize the term) in various characteristic senses: as a designation specifically of the Pentateuch (as above); as a synonym for Scripture as a whole, clearly identifying verses from the prophets or the writings as proofs "from the Torah"; as a term for the study of sacred texts and their interpretation, and as a term encompassing all the unwritten statutes and interpretations that eventually came to comprise the torah she be'al peh, the "oral Torah." It is to be noted that these various usages have in common the understanding of Torah as a designation of authority, that is, authoritative teaching, although, of course, the applicability and gradation of that authority were not therefore uniform.

The issue of the authoritativeness of this expanded Torah is nuanced, but it is clear that the divine origin or authorship that had at first been attributed only to certain parts of what was to become the Bible was gradually extended to include all of Scripture, indeed, soon all of Torah in its broadest sense. This gradual spread in different communities is witnessed in the earliest commentaries, refractions, and expansions upon Scripture that we possess, whether in the so-called apocrypha and pseudepigrapha of the Hebrew Bible, community writings such as those found at Qumran and elsewhere (the "Dead Sea Scrolls"), the New Testament, or early biblical commentaries, including even those of the Pentateuch-centered Philo of Alexandria. Although the primacy of the Pentateuch is still in evidence—not only in the specialized linguistic usage of Torah-as-Pentateuch seen above, but, still later, in the Pentateuch's exclusive role in such varied domains as rabbinic halakhah, Samaritan practice, and so forth—nevertheless the inclusion of prophetic, historical, wisdom and other ancient texts under this authoritative rubric must correspond to an attribution of authority that had begun at an early date. Like the laws given to Moses on Mount Sinai, these texts too were in some sense of divine provenance.

This theme has been presented in various formulations. Striking is the one attributed to Rabbi Isaac, commenting upon Exodus 20:1, "And God spoke all these words, saying . . . ," i.e., both upon the apparently emphatic "*all* these words," and perhaps as well on the word *saying,* which was sometimes interpreted as "to say later on"):

> That which the prophets were later to prophesy in every subsequent age, they received here at Mount Sinai. For thus did Moses report to Israel [Deut. 29:13–14], "Not with you alone do I make this covenant, . . . but with both those who are standing here among us today, and with those who are not here among us today." Now "not *standing* among us today" is not written [in the last clause], but only "not among us today"; for these are the souls that were yet to be created, who have no substance, and of whom "standing" could not be said. For though they did not exist at the time, every one of these received his portion. . . . And not only did all the prophets receive their prophecies from Sinai, but also the sages who were to arise in every generation—each one of them received his [teaching] from Sinai, as it is written [Deut. 5:19], "These words the Lord spoke to all your assembly on the mountain amid the fire, the cloud, and the darkness, with a great noise, *and did not cease.*"
>
> (Ex. R. 28:6; cf. Mid. Tan. Yitro 11)

Here, not only were all the prophets present in spirit with Moses at the time of the Sinai revelation—indeed, it was then that they received their prophecies, for in essence Sinai was the *only* divine revelation to man—but the rabbinical sages as well received their teachings and interpretations at the same occasion.

This idea is to be connected to that much-discussed rabbinic theme of the coexistence and equal importance of the two Torahs, the oral and the written. Well known is the case of a proselyte who asked the sage Shammai, "Rabbi, how many Torahs do you have?," to whom Shammai is said to have replied, "Two, one that is written and one that is oral" (ARN[1] 15). The account further relates that the proselyte, doubting the authority of the oral Torah, approached Shammai's contemporary Hillel with the same question. By way of reply, Hillel wrote out for the proselyte letters from the alphabet and, pointing at the first, asked:

> "What is this?" "Aleph." "That is not aleph but beth! And what is this?" "Beth." "No, it is not beth but gimel!" Then he added: "Whence do you know that this is aleph and this beth and this gimel, save that our ancestors have handed down by tradition that this is aleph and this beth and this gimel? Just as you have firmly accepted this [teaching], so accept that [of the oral Torah] as well.
>
> (ARN[1] 15)

That the proselyte in the story should even have approached these sages with his peculiar question must certainly reflect the fact that the rabbinic "oral Torah" was not unopposed—it was in fact derided—in other circles. Perhaps especially because they well understood the crucial point embodied in Hillel's above-cited response did the rabbis sometimes insist on this radical definition of Torah: The oral Torah was the written Torah's completion, and its "interpretations" in effect become another text, utterly the written Torah's equal in authority:

> It is further taught [in a *baraita*]: The verse "For he has had contempt for the word of the Lord" [Num. 15:31, where the text refers to the willful violator of a divine statute, whose violation therefore also contains an element of blasphemy] applies to anyone who says that the Torah is not from Heaven [i.e., of divine origin], and even to someone who says that the whole Torah in its entirety is from Heaven save for this one verse that was spoken not by God but by Moses on his own initiative—to such a person applies "For he has had contempt for the word of the Lord." And even one who says that the whole Torah in its entirety is from Heaven save for this one traditional interpretive point, for this one commonly

accepted a fortiori inference, for this one usual understanding based on textual comparison—to such a person applies "For he has had contempt for the word of the Lord."

(BT Sanh. 99a)

As with the above-cited passage from Exodus Rabba, so here the traditional interpretations of the sages are held to be an inseparable part of Torah, and any doubts cast upon their authority are comparable to an attack upon the authority of the text itself.

It is clear that this broad Torah, bifurcated into "oral" and "written," emerged only gradually as a theme in rabbinic writings, and some scholars have stressed the apparent early autonomy of the "words of the scribes" and "words of the elders" from Torah-as-Scripture. Yet eventually Torah emerged as the exclusive mantle of authority, and its authority was, as seen above, that of divine revelation. For still later ages, all Torah came "from Sinai," and that one primal divine revelation came to infuse all of Jewish belief and practice: Torah is the entire fabric of Judaism.

The foregoing account, while hardly exhaustive, should provide an overview of the composite origins of this central concept of later Judaism, its evolved character, and especially the breadth and flexibility that characterized its use in late biblical and rabbinic texts. If one should seek to find a single English phrase as an equivalent for Torah in its most characteristic rabbinic sense, one would ultimately have to turn to "sacred learning," "divinely given (or sanctioned) instruction," or some similar combination embodying (1) the idea that Torah always has at its heart the movement from God to man, and from a primal moment of revelation ("Sinai") to a later moment of transmission and understanding; and (2) the basically instructional character of Torah, which is, moreover, conceived not merely as a revelation given to one particular age or group or set of circumstances, but as an eternally valid corpus of precepts and a textual reservoir of ethical models and moral instructions for daily life. But having said this, we would still not have accounted for the dynamic relationship between the biblical and postbiblical uses of the word, a relationship that is both in itself paradigmatic and, what is more significant, informative about Torah's inner life.

As the dialect known as Mishnaic Hebrew (now itself subdivided into different periods and stages) is to the older biblical Hebrew in its various forms and phases, so is the religion of the rabbis to the various beliefs and practices that preceded it in the biblical period—from the earliest reconstructable aspects of patriarchal faith and worship through the time of the Exodus and Israel's earliest memories of settled life in Canaan, to the kingdom of David and Solomon and on to the divided monarchies, the shock of conquest and exile, then restoration and reconstruction, and all the vicissitudes of Jewish history in the closing centuries before the Common Era, when the immediately antecedent institutions of rabbinic Judaism began to be formed. This linguistic analogy is worth pausing over, for the origins of Mishnaic Hebrew are various, and although there are many elements that connect Mishnaic Hebrew to late biblical Hebrew, the relationship ought not to be viewed (and is not by scholars) as a simple straight-line continuation. Rather, Mishnaic Hebrew and the antecedent biblical language would more properly be described as two separate dialects or even languages—fundamentally distinct idioms, as different as Czech is from Polish, for example. Yet—and here is a striking uniqueness—it is the particular pleasure of writers of Mishnaic Hebrew generally to overlook their idiom's divergence from the language of the Bible and to act, despite considerable evidence to the contrary, as if Hebrew were all one language. Indeed, one of the most characteristic traits of rabbinic exegesis is the willful distortion of a biblical text by treating its verbal forms as if they corresponded to Mishnaic Hebrew's tenses, its difficult or rare words as if they were the biblical equivalent of some similar sounding but quite different word in Mishnaic Hebrew (or sometimes even Greek or Latin), and so forth.

As with the speech, so is it with the religion of the rabbis, a complex structure whose intellectual origins remain obscure and which, despite a certain obvious communality with elements of early post-Exilic Judaism, is distinct even from this phase of biblical religion—and strikingly different from pre-Exilic belief and practice—in such fundamentals as its concept of God; the relation conceived to exist between God and Israel, God and the nations, and God and the individual; forms of worship; and, as we have seen, its understanding of Torah. Yet it is also the well-known characteristic of classical rabbinic texts to act as if this were not so, indeed, to read the rabbinic view of things into biblical texts whose plain sense is sometimes utterly removed from the doctrines being attributed to it; to assert not only that rabbinic standards of (divinely dictated) behavior are being urged in biblical texts where they may well not be, but also to assume that these same norms had been practiced from the Sinai revelation on. Indeed, the rabbinic religion is alleged to have been observed by Israel's ancestors even before Sinai: the patriarchs kept the Torah's precepts and even studied Torah in a prototype of the rabbinical academy. In fact, the Torah and all its precepts had existed since the beginning of time, and Moses, through whom it was finally communicated to the people of Israel, is typically presented as "Moses our Rabbi," the prototype of all later rabbinic teachers.

In keeping with this tendency, the religion of the rabbis does not conceive or present itself at all as such, but as the religion of Moses: The authority that its principal figures claim for themselves is almost exclusively that of faithful transmitters and interpreters. It was Moses who had given the "Torah" (both in the relatively narrow, and in the broad sense seen earlier) to Israel; indeed, it was the one revelation at Sinai that provided Israel with all its divine teaching—not only the Pentateuch but, as we have seen, the prophets and all of Scripture, the oral Torah and all of scriptural interpretation. So in this sense not only did this rabbinic concept of Torah go well beyond the substance of any *torah* in Scripture, but, having expanded its meaning to include all that we have seen, it further insisted that all this *was* little more than Torah in the narrow sense, that interpretation was merely text read aright, that, in other words, the Pentateuch did contain explicitly or implicitly the whole of Torah, not only the teachings of later prophets . . .

> Said R. Joshua b. Levi . . . Moses spoke all the words of the [later] prophets as well as his own [prophecy], so that anyone who [later] prophesied was a mere reflection of Moses' prophecy.
>
> (Ex. R. 42:8)

. . . but indeed the entire rabbinic path.

One might well ask here: Why did the rabbis maintain this position, in which Torah is construed as little more than Torah in the narrowest sense, while elsewhere they seemed to pull in just the opposite direction, asserting, as we have seen, the existence of a separate entity known as the oral Torah? That is, why was not Shammai's answer to the proselyte, "We have but one Torah, a written one, in whose words are to be found all the teachings later expounded in different form by our prophets and sages"? The answer is that these two positions reflect a tension at the heart of the rabbinic idea of Torah. Torah is often presented in its narrowest sense, Torah as Pentateuch, to which the rest of Scripture is but a subservient and wholly concordant appendix and of which the oral Torah is nought but the interpretation, an interpretation that flows naturally and unavoidably from the written word. Yet lest that interpretation be questioned, and the text thus thrown open to new arbitration, the interpretive tradition is also asserted to possess an authority and standing no less than that of the Pentateuch itself. Indeed, it becomes an independent entity, the oral Torah, which is the written Torah's correspondent and equal.

It is not within the scope of the present essay to discourse on the vicissitudes that the concept of Torah has undergone since the time of the sages, or to do more than simply evoke its rich and variegated history in the evolution of medieval Jewish philosophy, in the whole span of Jewish mysticism from late antiquity to the rise of Spanish kabbalah and through still later periods of Jewish thought on to the present day. But perhaps, in alluding to these developments, one final aspect of our linguistic analogy will be relevant. For it is a fact that Mishnaic Hebrew provided the basic framework for almost all subsequent Hebrew writing from late antiquity to modern times. (There were, of course, some not inconsiderable exceptions to the fact that its grammar and vocabulary have provided the scaffolding for Hebrew in later ages. How appropriate, even metaphorical, is the fact that it was primarily in the domain of morphology that biblical Hebrew came back to reconquer Mishnaic Hebrew's spoils, ultimately eliminating nearly every trace of the latter not only in medieval and later Hebrew compositions, but even in rabbinic texts themselves, which came largely to be respelled—and pointed—in accordance with biblical Hebrew norms.) Even when the linguistic sophistication of medieval grammarians forced a broadened understanding of Rabbi Yohanan's passing observation that "the language of Scripture is one thing and the language of the sages another" (BT Av. Zar. 58b; BT Hul. 137b), this observation did not lead to any wholesale abandonment of the rabbinic idiom nor, perhaps just as significantly, to any utterly successful rooting out of Mishnaic Hebrew influences in the scattered attempts that were made to revive a "pure" biblical idiom. Similarly, it is the central, and global, notion of Torah presented by the rabbis that has become the "idiom" of all subsequent stages of Judaism, surviving—one might even say prominently—in the Karaite schism, and underlying all postrabbinic struggles with and modifications of the meaning of Torah.

It is of interest to consider in conclusion the role of this tenacious rabbinic notion of Torah in the modern setting, particularly in regard to what is termed the "crisis of biblical authority" engendered by the rise of modern biblical scholarship. This crisis, which is certainly not Judaism's alone, or even principally, is nonetheless one of great consequence for the career of Torah, the potential for upheaval being certainly no smaller than those developments that have challenged Torah's traditional place in centuries past; the rationalist disenchantment with elements of rabbinic exegesis; the Karaite challenge; the rise of linguistic study of biblical Hebrew in medieval

Spain; the flowering of philosophical speculation in the same community; and so on. In the light of the foregoing discussion, perhaps two observations impose themselves. The first is that the principle of the oral Torah's own and equal authority has now become more than a defense of that body of teaching. It is likewise a bulwark, a protective fence, around the written Torah that saves it from the fate of the Dismembered Bible worried over elsewhere—the text that has disintegrated into its own composite origins, original literary genres and historical context, and redactional accretions. For just as the oral Torah has been granted to be an authoritative reading of particulars, so are its most basic assumptions about the written Torah an authoritative defining of that text's most significant traits. Here we might reverse the order of things as presented in the above-cited *baraita* (BT Sanh. 99a) and say that as rabbinic authority is decisive with regard to a single interpretive point or to one commonly accepted a fortiori inference, so is it decisive with regard to Scripture's integrity and harmony and the validity of its teaching. This reading (in the largest sense) of the Bible is that of the rabbis, and on the strength of their Torah does it rest. To put things thus is certainly a shift in emphasis (one that, as we have seen, runs counter to the rabbis' own view of things), but perhaps it is appropriate to an age like the present, in which a would-be proselyte might indeed conceivably be more ready to accept the relatively coherent body of doctrine imparted by a chain of Palestinian and Babylonian rabbinical authorities than the authority of a text increasingly argued to be an assemblage of independent, often contradictory, fragments of occasionally dubious merit.

The second observation follows from this. For just as such an approach to the questions of scriptural unity and authority is strikingly narrow—it addresses these issues only from within the rabbinic perspective—so ought the problems to which it is addressed be identified as arising out of an equally narrow framework, namely, the approach to Scripture championed by various Protestant churches beginning in the sixteenth century. The principle of *sola scriptura,* predicated on the flush encounter between interpreter and text unmediated by tradition, has always contained within it this fundamental contradiction, that it was tradition and not the words of the texts themselves that created Scripture in the first place: Stripped of that tradition, Scripture ceases to be the unitary word of God, that is, it ceases to be Scripture and becomes the various and historically conditioned words of men. If the rise of modern biblical scholarship has served to underline afresh the dependence of Scripture on tradition for its very existence, it has likewise undermined some of the supposed communality among the "biblical religions." For whatever might be a Protestant response to the current crisis (which was, as noted, generated by the very unmediated stance upon which Protestantism itself was predicated), it will certainly lie outside of the domain of that which has been delineated above, the complex and subtle concept of Torah handed down and developed in rabbinic Judaism.

BIBLIOGRAPHY

Henri Cazelles, "Torah et Loi," in Gerard Nahon and Charles Tovati, eds., *Hommages à Georges Vajda* (1980).

Max Kadushin, *Organic Thinking* (1938), 16–94.

J. LeMaire, *Les écoles et la formation de la Bible* (1981), esp. 77–78.

Efraim E. Urbach, "Halakhah and Prophecy," in *Tarbiz*, 18 (1946–47).

Tradition

מסורת

Nathan Rotenstreich

Tradition is essentially a mode of generational relation, whose structure and meaning are inherently historical (history understood here as a succession of events that affect and relate people living at different times). Tradition implies, therefore, a reality transmitted from past to present that demands of each succeeding generation that its formulated past be accepted by the generation that inherits it.

Indeed, many of the most fundamental spheres of human activity depend upon the continuity of generations, most notably the reality of language and its employment. Language is neither created by those who use it nor generated by a single generation of those who first employ it. Language is rather a resource treasure transmitted from generation to generation, shaped and altered as each individual utilizes it. Clearly, however, communication as such presupposes common assumptions and historical community prepared in advance of the actual use of language. Linguistic tradition, in the most literal sense, is something passed from generation to generation. It may lack the physical immediacy of monuments of plastic art, which are, after all, directly before one's eyes, insuring their endurance by their sheer physicality. This is not the case with language, which lacks physical presentness but whose continuity is nonetheless evident in that there is a palpable process of transmission and a clear substance transmitted.

The issue of language is obviously critical to our concerns here, since the Hebrew word for tradition, *masorah* or *masoret,* means explicitly the process of transmitting texts from one generation to another. The nineteenth-century philosopher Franz Molitor observed that *masorah* is implicit in the biblical text because of the nature of the Hebrew language: it is written only in consonants. To read Hebrew texts aloud requires a combination of vowels and consonants and involves in this very fact the establishment of textual vocalization, which facilitates the transmission of an oral rendition of the written text.

This characteristic of the biblical text suggests at most the visible aspect of its writing. Combined with it, however, is the reality of a special authority that imposes upon it a binding obligation, since the text is believed to be the word of God and to reveal God's commandments. The prophetic writings go beyond the Pentateuch in that not only do their texts reveal the word of God, but also the prophet himself—as messenger of God—transmits the words of the divine Other rather than expressing his own invention. The *masorah* is thus oriented toward the past insofar as it connects the generations, but it is also dependent upon a source that is above and outside the historical continuity of generations.

The relevance of Gershom Scholem's observation regarding the historical and suprahistorical aspects of revelation and tradition[1] is evident in the approach of this discussion. Clearly, the dialectical relationship between historical and suprahistorical dimensions of revelation and tradition does not result in an ontological harmony between them.

It has been observed that traditions are beliefs with a particular social structure: they are a consensus through time. In contrast to such a view, traditional Judaism has proposed that any scholarly innovation was already implicit in God's communications with Moses on Sinai. This claim clearly is a major principle of any approach to text grounded upon revelation and transmitted in *masorah.* It is one of the means by which innovation is legitimized, by making it both immanently rooted in the past and derived from a suprahistorical source revealed in the past. The relevance of consensus is somewhat compromised because in this case the meaning of the past is not settled by a transmitted agreement, but by the acceptance of the authority of that which is transmitted. It is less a matter of the thematic core transmitted from generation to generation than of acknowledgment of the suprahuman authority underlying the process.

The observation of Hans-Georg Gadamer that the most genuine and solid tradition does not naturally persist in consequence of an inertial transmission, but rather needs to be affirmed, embraced, and cultivated, is surely relevant. No receiving generation is ever totally immersed in past generations whose heritage is transmitted, because generation is to be understood as a historical reality, not as a biological transmission. The process of acceptance undertaken by the receiving generation implies an activity whereby it consents to subdue itself in order to authenticate the authority of the transmitted. In our case that authority enjoys a twofold character: it entails historical precedence and is suprahuman in origin. The preference given to the past in the very process of tradition is not due to the inferiority of the present vis-à-vis the past but rather because the revelation took place in the past. It is for this reason that the past of revelation is more prominent than the present.

The special position of the past results from the fact that the deposit of the word of God initiates the process of tradition and confirms its authority. Such a point of view is confirmed by the activity of the rabbinic sages in erecting fences around the Torah. Since the text of the Torah is not self-explicating and hence not automatically preserved, it requires interpretation in order to emphasize and highlight its implications. The act of preserving the text by fencing it with interpretation is a human activity, indeed, a paradigmatic activity insofar as it defines the function of human beings as that of protecting the deposit of faith, articulating guiding principles of human behavior, and clarifying the human position in the universe. The notion of tradition consequently combines an attitude of acquiescence with acceptance of the authoritative text as both revealed text and interpreted text.

The interpretation of the inaugural text of any tradition is not an invention, but by its very nature becomes open again in a kind of hermeneutic circle to yet other interpretations. This chain of interpretation, exemplified in the relation that existed between the rabbinic sages and the revelation to Moses on Sinai, leads to further observations on the nature of interpretation as we have defined it.

Despite the fact that every interpretation that strives to be correct and faithful to the word constitutes itself as an actual experience of the word of God, there nonetheless remains a difference that is both temporal and textual between the text and the interpretation. The difference is underscored by the fact that the text is ontologically situated on a level that radically distinguishes its position as divine from the human and historical position of interpretation. The understanding of the interpreter is always human understanding, whereas the text is always surrounded with its divine aura.

An additional aspect of interpretation is that of enlarging and applying the simple declarativeness of the text. If the text presents a commandment—for instance, the observance of the Sabbath—the commandment per se does not contain all the details of human behavior requisite to its proper observance. The specification of those relevant details requires an extension of the text, which does not explicitly contain them, while at the same time interpreting the existential ground to which, as a principle of obligation, the commandment refers. Such a procedure by explication and extension effects concretizations that are implicit, but which, without interpretation, would remain buried. Moreover, in addition to the abstract relationship between interpretation and text, the historical dimension enters both de jure and de facto: since the historical components of human existence are by definition impermanent, facts that were not available to the earliest interpreters of the laws of Sabbath must nevertheless be taken into account—for example, in the late nineteenth century, the phenomenon of electricity. The practical application of the commandment is obliged to take into account changing and novel elements of human existence to which the general commandment remains the guiding principle. Moreover, it is precisely the continuous will to preserve the mandatory aspect of the commandment that elicits interpretations as a means of extending its application.

Even within the phenomenon of interpretation just described we can identify a difference between the structure of interpretation and the historical spheres to which it refers. Even when we must deal with novel occurrences for which the law must account, the tradition strives to preserve the continuity of interpretation. A distinction is acknowledged between the recognition of such occurrences and the continuity of our attitude toward the authoritative text: acknowledging the former, we recognize change; while bowing to the latter, we undertake to maintain a continuity that absorbs changes and does not recognize ruptures or breaks within the process of transmitting the deposit of faith from generation to generation. In deference to this reality the dilemma implicit in the two possible interpretations of history is underscored: the one regards history as a process, the other as the transmission of a specific content.

It is precisely because tradition—understood in its religious sense—obliges reference to revelation that it faces a paradoxical complexity. On the one hand the authority of tradition derives from and depends upon its transcendent origin, while on the other hand its human dimension is evident in its intergenerational transmission and in the phenomenon of human interpretation, which, at the same time as it acknowledges that its ultimate validity is beyond and above the human, must nonetheless accommodate the human aspect of the process of interpretation.

This paradoxical character of tradition is evident in all discussion of the reasons for the commandments issued by God to the Jewish people. Obviously, all assertion of reasons reflects the perspective of the human being receiving the commandments. The question abides, however, whether human beings can devise reasons for the promulgations of revelation, that is, for the assertions of divine reason. Does divine reason in any way conform with human reason and human reasoning? This question is at issue in Saadiah Gaon's distinction between commandments that are rational and those that he calls commandments of listening and hearing, whose reasonableness does not follow from their accord with human reason. In the latter case validity follows not from their reasonableness but from the fact that they are commanded by God, that is, revealed. The opposite is true with respect to those commandments Saadiah considers rational, since in their case human beings acquiesce to their rationality and comprehend their justification. Human beings always examine the commandments from a human point of view and seek to establish the conformance between what is promulgated by divinity and what is congenial within the human sphere.

Recognizing the Saadiahan distinction is central to the understanding of tradition, since it not only brings into focus the fact that divine authority is always mediated by human interpretation but also legitimates the possibility of a variety of human interpretations conformable to reason. This is borne out in the argument advanced by Moses Mendelssohn regarding the commandments, which in part follows the distinction advanced centuries earlier by Saadiah Gaon. Mendelssohn took the commandments as articulations of what he called divine legislation that essentially refers only to the Jews. What was of rational character he regarded as a portion of the Enlightenment, which advanced metaphysical and ethical propositions considered universally valid. However, only the Jews received such divine legislation. Saadiah's commandment of hearing and listening became for Mendelssohn the characteristic feature of the divine commandments addressed exclusively to Jews. The metaphysical (or rational) character of revelation has been replaced by an immanent metaphysical system, and what cannot be incorporated into such an interpretation is not intended to conform to rational interpretation. Saadiah Gaon's classification, which placed two categories of commandments on the same level, is now replaced by a separation of the two in terms of both their essence and their universal application. This attempt to transform even the commandments of hearing and listening into rational commandments is evidenced, for instance, in the English terminology used for the laws of *kashrut*. To speak of dietary laws implies that a certain latent or hidden reason is implicit in the commandments, fitting some physiological need of human beings, and transforming a structure of divine imperatives formulated in Scripture, indifferently to their rational significance, into a system wherein their rationality is equated with their human physiological or psychological function.

Adherence to tradition also entails a choice either in the direction of accumulation or in the direction of selection. Clearly, the accumulative option does not require discrimination of the components that make up the tradition, whereas any selection involves a more explicit principle of choice and therefore calls for a principle of justification in order to legitimate both the concrete selection and the process of selection in itself. The principle of selection is justified most often by reference to the general historical climate in which it is exercised. Notable examples of this phenomenon are the emergence of messianic universalism in modern times, which is henceforth construed by some as the essence of Judaism, and, at the same time, the shift to the ethical interpretation of Judaism, which follows upon the penchant of modern philosophy to interpret religion in ethical rather than metaphysical terms. A selective conception of tradition is no less authenticated by the need to preserve the national entity of the Jewish people through renewed emphasis upon language and land in the tradition. Along with the historical aspects grounded in the situation of each generation, a second issue has become prominent, namely, that of trying to identify the basic, essential, or constant features in the accumulated profile of Judaism.

The position of philosophic understanding and interpretation with respect to religious tradition is dialectically complex and must be scrutinized. The philosophic encounter with tradition occurs upon the meeting ground of culture, but obviously such philosophic understanding, founded as it is upon the rational activity of human beings, is rendered ambiguous when it must interpret such a notion as the fashioning of man in the image of God. To what extent, it may be asked, is the concept of man as one ordained in the image of God endowed with semi-independence or autonomy, and to what extent is it dependent upon God as eternal and ineffaceable paradigm? It is well recognized that the interpretations of this notion will vary in relation to prevailing philosophical attitudes: Plato, who was not informed by the biblical tradition, nonetheless speaks about something divine in man, and thinkers such as Philo and the sixteenth-century Italian Jewish philosopher Leone Ebreo both proposed that biblical notions preceded the philosophical not only in principle but chronologically, and, hence, philosophy was influenced by biblical ideas. From such an approach, the philosophical interpretation is not considered at variance with the biblical or revelational source, but rather both constitute a common undertaking to discern an original meaning underlying both approaches to interpretation.

Religious traditions can also accommodate philosophical currents by doing as Maimonides did when he applied Aristotelian concepts to the interpretation of biblical texts in order both to debunk their anthropomorphic narratives and to introduce philosophical concepts such as form, the first mover, the cause of causes, and creation out of nothing into the interpretation of biblical formulations. Moreover, Maimonides was well aware that the mode of philosophical exegesis and that of normative biblical interpretation need not be in conformance (notably in the conflict between the putative eternity of world and its created existence). It was for this reason that Maimonides formulated the principle that "the gates of interpretation [i.e., of commentary] are not closed" (Guide, 2, 25). Maimonides' position in this context reflects his recognition that wherever there is conflict between two interpretive approaches, interpretation must be amplified in order to accommodate the breadth of philosophic inquiry. The horizon before interpretation is to be opened not only to the passage of time but also to conceptual variety. Of course, the very fact of conceptual variety raises a specter to the accumulative essence of tradition. Tradition generally absorbs various possibilities of interpretation even when, literally speaking, one interpretation has prevailed over another (as in the case of the school of Hillel, which prevailed in the vast majority of cases over the school of Shammai). That which has not been accepted has still been retained, identified, and cited.

A characteristic feature of Judaism and the Jewish people in modern times is the shift that has occurred from the accumulated interpretation of tradition toward a more selective interpretation. Such a deliberate selection has been accompanied by a consciousness that from the spectrum of components and vectors some were to be selected and regarded as binding even upon those engaged in the process of selection. Despite such obvious circularity, the significant currents in modern Jewish life all evidence this characteristic: Orthodox Judaism, in which the distinction between the realm of Torah and the ways of the mundane world (derekh erez) leaves open a considerable domain to selectivity; Reform Judaism, with its emphasis upon the ethical dimension of Judaism in distinction and frequent separation from both metaphysics and mizvot; Zionism, grounded as it is upon land and language, both of which are construed as being attributes of national existence. These examples, significant though they are from the point of view of their impact upon the existence of the Jews in modern times, must be seen within the broader context of the continuity of tradition as well as the changes wrought within or despite that continuity. This must be underscored: The accumulative approach presupposes continuity, but the approach of selectivity does not necessarily negate continuity. Selectivity operates against the background of continuity by choosing certain attitudes, principles, or tendencies to be binding because they are rational, because historical circumstance (for example, the separation of religion and state in the modern world and the removal of Christianity from a position of political dominance) has facilitated the selection, or because the social mobility of the modern economic system or the shift from personal philosophy to the more anonymous and universal modes of scientific inquiry validate it. Since tradition is understood as a sum total of principles intended to guide the day-to-day existence of human beings, changes that occur in the modes of that existence make it mandatory that the principles of the tradition be restated. Clearly, the acknowledgment of selection as a valid principle is in profound conflict with adherence to tradition as a totality. This conflict has resulted in a new and considerable dispute within modern Judaism.

It must be noted that the selective approach is to a very large extent correlated with the approach of scholarship. It is no wonder that the science of Judaism *(Wissenschaft des Judentums)* emerged in modern times, and, along with it, the various partial interpretations of the continuous and all-embracing tradition. The scientific approach is intended to be objective and uninfluenced by any interpretation transferred whole from one generation to the next; moreover, its inquiry seeks to identify historical contexts and particular textual meanings, despite the fact that both are most probably absorbed by the accumulative process into one broad and indistinguishable texture. Modern interpretation identifies its sources and grounds them historically—it does not eternalize them and, consequently, does not accept without scrutiny their binding authority.

REFERENCES

1. Gershom Scholem, "Revelation and Tradition as Religious Categories in Judaism," in *The Messianic Idea in Judaism* (1971).

BIBLIOGRAPHY

Hans-Georg Gadamer, *Truth and Method* (1982).

Franz Joseph Molitor, *Philosophie der Geschichte oder Über die Tradition* (1851).

Nathan Rotenstreich, *Tradition and Reality* (1972).

Gershom Scholem, "Revelation and Tradition as Religious Categories in Judaism," in *The Messianic Idea in Judaism* (1971).

Efraim E. Urbach, *The Sages: Their Concepts and Beliefs*, 2 vols. (1975), especially 286ff.

Truth

אמת

Peter Ochs

In Hebrew Scripture, in rabbinic literature, and for most Jewish thinkers, truth is a characteristic of personal relationships. Truth is fidelity to one's word, keeping promises, saying with the lips what one says in one's heart, bearing witness to what one has seen. Truth is the bond of trust between persons and between God and humanity. In the Western philosophical tradition, truth is a characteristic of the claims people make about the world they experience: the correspondence between a statement and the object it describes, or the coherence of a statement with what we already know about the world.

As if divided by their dual allegiance to the traditions of Jerusalem and of Athens, Jewish philosophers often believe themselves forced to choose between the two meanings of truth, producing what we may call objectivist and personalist trends in Jewish thought.

Before the time of Descartes, the objectivists tend to be Aristotelians. They identify the created world of Scripture with the finite cosmos of Hellenistic philosophy, and the spoken words of creation with the natural laws of the cosmos (*logoi*). They argue that the laws of personal relationship, revealed in the Torah, are particular instances of natural law and that, therefore, the religious conception of truth as fidelity is derivative of the philosophic conception of truth as correspondence to the natural world. Saadiah Gaon exemplifies this approach, arguing that prophecy was necessary only to specify how Israel would enact the rational laws of the Torah, while Maimonides so emphasizes the dichotomy between moral and natural laws that he prefigures some of the argumentation of the modern or post-Cartesian objectivists. In his *Guide of the Perplexed,* Maimonides claims that Adam's original intellect gave him the power to distinguish truth and falsehood, that is, scientific knowledge, which degenerated through his corporeal inclinations into the power to distinguish good and evil, which is to say merely moral knowledge. This suggests that the revealed laws of personal relationship may serve conventional, moral functions that the philosopher considers secondary to the task of uncovering cosmic truths. Pushing this dichotomy one crucial step further, Spinoza introduces modernity into Jewish thought by identifying the Torah with religion and thereby separating the conventional functions of Torah from the pursuit of scientific knowledge of the natural world. Modernity imposes on modern Jewish thinkers the burden of proving that Judaism, as a distinct faith, offers something more than a collection of particular, conventional rules of behavior.

Personalists tend to defend the faith of Israel against what they consider the corrosive effects of philosophical criticism. Their arguments are often political as well as philosophical in that they are grounded in the observation that philosophers may condemn Jewish particularity in favor of a professed universalism that actually serves the political or economic interests of competing social groups. They argue that truth is correspondence not between a statement and the world, but between a statement and the intentions of the person who uttered it. Judah Halevi, for example, argues that the truths of philosophical reasoning are merely hypothetical, or relative to the conditions of knowing that give rise to them. They are reliable only when the philosopher controls those conditions—for example, in mathematics. In natural science and for moral knowledge, however, certainty is acquired only through experience, the experience of the senses and, ultimately, direct experience of God, in mystical life and prophecy. These experiences appear only within the particularity of Jewish history and are recorded only within Jewish tradition.

In appearance a traditionalist, the personalist draws on neo-Platonic sources that eventually exert a radicalizing influence. From Al-Ghazali (1058–1111) to Giordano Bruno (*ca.* 1548–1600) and Descartes, the neo-Platonic tradition exhibits increasing distrust of mediated knowledge and a preoccupation with cognition and epistemology, as opposed to tradition and hermeneutics. For Western and Jewish philosophers, the effect is to unite personalists and objectivists in the vain search for nontraditional foundations that has characterized modern thought until the twentieth century.

For students of Ludwig Wittgenstein, "foundationalism" is the attempt to discover rational foundations for rational inquiry. In practice, that definition is too restrictive. Since humans always seek reliable premises for action, foundationalism may be defined more broadly as the human response to a loss of trust in traditional systems of behavior. The Athenian philosophers mistrusted mythological traditions, but soon replaced them with traditions of rational inquiry grounded in the moral universe of the Athenian polis. On certain issues, the Jewish Aristotelians and neo-Platonists replaced trust in rabbinic authority with trust in the Athenian traditions. However, the technological revolutions of the Renaissance and Enlightenment and the sociopolitical revolutions of the Reformation and the new industrial age encouraged mistrust of all finite systems of knowledge and behavior, Athenian as well as rabbinic or scriptural. If most Jews were insulated from that mistrust until the emancipation, Jewish philosophers knew it even before Spinoza. Ḥasdai Crescas' personalism and Isaac Luria's mysticism may be seen as attempts to protect Israel's faith against the corrosions of European skepticism.

In the context of modernity, neither personalism nor objectivism offers lasting protection against skepticism. Each contributes to an untenable dichotomy between world and personhood and, thus, a confusion of the object and ground of truth.

Truth is not an everyday concern. We go about our daily business trusting that whatever the past has taught us about the world will continue to work in the future. If curiosity stimulates us to investigate things in the world we have not yet seen, it is not because we seek to "know the truth." We simply want to discover more instances of what we already know, reconfirming and deepening our convictions. The pursuit of truth is a signal that something has gone wrong, that the world is not behaving according to our expectations. We find ourselves unable to conduct daily affairs and, at least momentarily, have lost faith in our ability to act in the world. The pursuit of truth is an effort to recover that faith. The simple object of this pursuit, the object of truth, is the world. We want to recover knowledge of an environment that suddenly seems beyond our control. Certainty about the world, however, is always grounded in a prior trust of the persons who have taught us what the world is and how to act in it. We want first, therefore, to recover the ground of truth, which is trust in persons and in the knowledge they provide us. The pursuit of truth is the effort to recover ground and unite it with object.

Personalists and objectivists err by devoting exclusive attention to either ground or object. Objectivists declare that truth lies in the world, that is, that we may solve our problems by examining our environments. The world is mute, however, until interpreted by a system of knowledge, and we have no interest in such systems until we gain trust in the persons who teach it. Personalists declare that truth lies in fidelity to such persons and trust in what they teach. We would not care about truth, however, if we did not have reason to doubt our teachers; knowledge is meaningless independent of its application to experience.

Since the nineteenth century, Jewish thinkers have looked to the critical philosophy of Immanuel Kant as a way out of the dialectic of personalism and objectivism. Kant is aware that the dialectic is ill-founded and devotes his work to overcoming the separation of the ground and object of truth. Unfortunately, his efforts remain within the framework of a neo-Platonic personalism. No matter how earnestly his disciples desire contact with the objective world, they understand that world only as a modality of human personality: the world is an object of intention and desire, instead of a source of new experience. Hermann Cohen, for example, declares that "truth is the accord of theoretical causality (cognition) with ethical teleology (ethics)."[1] Both cognition and ethics, however, belong to the activity of the human mind, which means that Cohen identifies ground with object rather than seeking their resolution by way of human interaction with an external world. Cohen's truth belongs neither to the world nor to traditional knowledge, but only to the cogito. Buber seeks to bring the Kantian tradition into the world; Rosenzweig seeks to reconnect it as well to traditional knowledge. Neither succeeds fully, because Kant's restrictive premises betray their efforts.

Generated out of an appreciative critique of Kant, Charles Peirce's pragmatism offers Jewish thinkers a theory of truth most faithful to Jewish practice, that is, to the methods of problem-solving most emphasized in rabbinic tradition. For the pragmatist, the pursuit of truth is a three-stage process of inquiry, stimulated by the experience of behavioral failure and completed only through the successful correction of that failure.

The first stage of inquiry is the attempt to recover the ground of truth. This means that the inquirer seeks to recover lost trust in some tradition of knowledge and in the persons who represent that tradition. For Emmanuel Levinas, this stage finds its paradigm in the Israelites' relation to God at Mt.

Sinai. According to one midrash, the Israelites were forced into accepting a Torah whose benefits they could not yet appreciate (BT Shab. 88a–b). Like the angels who declare "We will do and we will hear" (Ex. 24:7), the Israelites had to enact the commandments before comprehending them, trusting God before trusting themselves.[2]

In Scripture, the first stage of inquiry is indicated by two uses of the term *truth (emet)*: (1) truth as trust, as in "the laws of truth" (Neh. 9.13), which means laws in which the people Israel could trust (following ibn Ezra's comment on Genesis 24:49 that truth used in this way displays its derivation from the term *faith (emunah)*; (2) truth as fidelity to one's word, as in "these are in the things you shall do: speak truth, each man to his neighbor" (Zech. 7.9), which means, as David Kimḥi (known as Radak) observes, to say what one means and, thereby, to inspire confidence.[3] But confidence requires testing against experience.

The second stage is the attempt to recover the object of truth. This means that the inquirer examines his problematic experience, to make as much sense as he can of it within the limits of his present knowledge. Philosophers call this examination descriptive science; for rabbinic tradition it is *mada* (lit., science), an aspect of "knowledge of the ways of the world" *(derekh ereẓ)*. Since the Enlightenment, objectivists and personalists have vied for control of this activity: the former argues that rabbinical authorities have no business interfering with the procedures of science, while the latter asserts that natural science threatens the autonomy and sanctity of Jewish life. Again, the argument rests on a confusion of ground and object of truth.

By definition, the object of truth lies beyond the ken of traditional knowledge; inquiry is seeded in the failures of extant knowledge to anticipate this object. Descriptive science is therefore a tool of discovery, a means of presenting the inquirer with data—patterns of sense perceptions—that he has not previously encountered. For traditional Judaism, recognition that the Lord is God signals the inquirer's conviction that no knowledge is complete in itself and that, therefore, new discovery is always possible. Problematic experience is the inquirer's encounter with the finitude of creaturely knowledge and, therefore, with the majesty of the Lord God. Behavioral failure is the means through which God shows his creatures that they do not fully understand his word. At the same time, descriptive science cannot in itself provide knowledge of the problematic object of truth. Knowledge of the object means knowledge of how to interact with the object, or how to act in the world. The data offered by science are mere generalities, which delimit the ways in which the inquirer may interact with the object, but cannot themselves legislate specific choices of action. Such choices are defined by principles available only in the inquirer's tradition of knowledge.

In Scripture, the second state of inquiry is indicated by references to truth as correspondence to object, as in, "You shall investigate and inquire and interrogate thoroughly. If it is true, the fact established . . ." (Deut. 13:15). In testifying to the truth of a matter, witnesses offer data whose significance is disclosed through authoritative interpretation: "If the charge proves true, that the girl was found not to have been a virgin, then . . ." (Deut. 22:20; cf. Rashi ad loc.). The consequences of this evidence are disclosed only in a third stage of inquiry.

The third stage is the attempt to reapply object to ground. This means that the inquirer at once defines the problematic experience in the language of traditional knowledge and modifies that tradition to accommodate the new object. Contemporary philosophers call this stage hermeneutics or interpretation; in rabbinic tradition, it is midrash. Midrash is a mediating activity that perfects tradition by putting it to the test of experience, reuniting object and ground as matter and form.

Midrash is what objectivists like Saadiah call rational verification of traditional faith, except that reason is practical, not abstract, and the meaning of faith is not disclosed prior to the activity of verification. Midrash reveals the truth that traditional knowledge receives from its original source but which is not clear until the completion of particular acts of inquiry. Truth is the response traditional knowledge offers to particular crises of knowledge. Immanent in the tradition, it does not make itself known until behavioral failures signal the need for previously revealed truths to be modified.

In Scripture, the third stage of inquiry is indicated by references to truth as the final result of inquiry: "'The Lord, The Lord, a God merciful and gracious, slow to anger and abundant in mercy and truth'" (Ex. 34:6). "In truth" means "faithfully rewarding those who perform His will" (Rashi, ad loc. Ex. 34:6), "in truth" fulfilling his word (Abraham ibn Ezra, ad loc. Ex. 34:6). "The Lord is a true God, a living God and king of the world" (Jer. 10:10). The true God can fulfill his word, comments Rashi, because he lives, while humans die, and because, as David Kimḥi notes (Commentary on Jer. 10:10), he fulfills promises, while the stars remain mute.

Truth, say the rabbis, is the seal of God. But to declare that God is truth is not yet to have received God's truth, which comes, ultimately, in the end of time, or piecemeal, at the end of each act of inquiry. It is, rather, to declare one's conviction that the failures we suffer are God's means of correcting our incomplete knowledge of his word and that by repairing our failures we come to know his word more deeply.

REFERENCES

1. Hermann Cohen, *Religion of Reason out of the Sources of Judaism* (1971), 410.
2. Emmanuel Levinas, *Quatre lectures talmudiques* (1968), 69ff.
3. See Rashi, ad loc. Ex. 18:21 (commenting on "men of truth").

BIBLIOGRAPHY

Arthur A. Cohen, "The Philosopher and the Jew," in Arthur A. Cohen, ed., *Arguments and Doctrines* (1970).

Arthur A. Cohen, *The Tremendum* (1981).

Emmanuel Levinas, *Quatre lectures talmudiques* (1968).

Charles Sanders Peirce, *The Collected Papers,* Charles Hartshorne and Paul Weiss, ed. 6 vols. (1934–1935).

John F. Smith, *Purpose and Thought: The Meaning of Pragmatism* (1978).

Unity

אחדות

Charles Elliott Vernoff

Unity is an essential concept within Judaism and a principle that grounds the entire structure of the Judaic worldview. An understanding of Judaic unity may be approached through consideration of the context of its emergence, its systematic structure, and its development within historical Judaism.

Recognition of Judaic unity may originally have emerged some four millennia ago. Around the era usually assigned to Abraham, Mesopotamians had begun to conceptualize justice as an autonomous principle and had started to insist upon it by right rather than divine whim. The textual evidence for this demand intimates the birth of yearning for rectification of the entire world system of ancient Sumer. In this yearning, very probably, lay the germ of incipient breakthrough to the Judaic principle of unity. The contours of Hebraic faith may in any case be anticipated through systematic negation of the Sumerian religious perspective. First, justice could be assured in principle only if the gods open to caring personal relationship with humans were not minor, as in Sumer, but indeed the very One who wields decisive power in administering the cosmos. Second, justice effectively means that each element of reality is emplaced in appropriate relation to others within an overall integral order, and thus requires a view of the cosmos as embodying a potentially unified, essentially harmonious design. Sumer, in contrast, presupposed endemic cosmic conflict. Third, each element of nature is a substance whose functions are necessarily determined by its fixed characteristics and thus must apparently clash with elements having conflicting characteristics. The power to conceive and actualize a unified cosmic design, that is, to effect comprehensive justice, therefore cannot even arise at this level of substantive reality with its necessary inherent conflicts, whose forces the gods of Sumer personified. A power capable of ordaining ultimate harmony among the elements of physical and human nature could only be superordinate to them, a God uniquely transcending the gods personifying natural forces. Fourth, the essential character of this power would have to reside in a capacity to override the inherent necessities that seem to impel natural forces into conflict. But any substance, of whatever subtle composition, behaves according to the necessity of its nature. The power that unifies, in its essential contrast with necessity, could not then be "substance" at all in this sense. Rather, that power would have to consist in what may be called spirit, contrasting with substance; its character, as overriding necessity, is definable as freedom. As transcendent absolute freedom, it would differ radically from all powers subject to its governance.

These four points anticipate four cardinal aspects of the Judaic principle of unity as subsequently ascribed paradigmatically to the God of Israel, namely, God is singular (*ehad*), unified (*meuhad*), unique (*yehida'i*), and one (*ahduti*). The equation of the divine personal name (*Adonai*) with the divine office of administering the cosmic powers (*Elohim*) asserts that it is a single god (*ehad*) who cares personally for humans and who governs the great impersonal forces of nature. Because God is essentially unified (*meuhad*) within himself, he has the capacity to draw subsidiary elements into a unified and integral (*mitahed*) order. This capacity for exerting the power of unification (*yehud*) implies that God is unique (*yehida'i*) in alone transcending the elements he governs, creating and integrating them. God's transcendent power to determine all conditioned entities implies the absolute oneness (*ahdut*) of his nature as completely without restrictions and conditions, determining itself in pure freedom. Only a deity of this description could meet the deepest spiritual needs likely engendered in late Sumer for a god of justice, freedom, and harmony, essentially nullifying the slave status of Mesopotamian humanity with its intrinsic proclivity to injustice while altering the political scene—a wearisomely futile, violent, and enslaving cycle for Sumer—in the direction of meaningful progress toward global harmony and peace.

Appearance of such a deity would furthermore signify the decisive breakthrough to the elevation of personal over impersonal being as the ultimate principle of reality. Ancient India's contrasting spiritual crisis began with the compromise of distinctions among the various impersonal forces of nature, as the identities of their divine personifications blurred. That crisis accordingly yielded to an answer that dissolved all discrete entities, gods included, into an ultimate substantive ground of impersonal being. Because Mesopotamia's crisis developed precisely within an entrenched sociocultural commitment to maintain witness to the distinct characteristics of natural forces despite their attendant conflicts, this crisis could resolve itself not through uncovering a radically immanent substratum, as in India, but only through discovery of a radically transcendent freedom that could reconcile contradictions while respecting and upholding discrete integrities. To the extent that human beings recognize themselves as persons in contrast with nonpersonal entities, they understand self-directing freedom as a primary distinguishing attribute of personal existence, even though humans also experience themselves as partly determined. A power conceived of as absolutely self-determining could eventually, therefore, be identified only as the absolute person, unique in the pure and unconditioned oneness of its fully actualized freedom.

A basic paradigm for the Judaic principle of unity appears in the biblical account of creation. By virtue of his unique transcendence, itself an aspect of unity, God becomes known only through his actions toward the world, beginning with the acts of creation. The Genesis account proceeds by a series of distinct actions, each of which distinguishes further realms within the original formless primordial mass that God's action had initially brought into being. These distinctions are not random or indefinitely extended, however. Rather, each contributes to a unified cosmic whole, an orderly design pronounced "very good" with its completion on the sixth day. On the seventh day, God ceases creating (*shavat*) and sets this unified cosmos apart to contemplate, as it were, the divine work (*vayikadesh*, "and he hallowed," from a root meaning "separated" or "set apart").

A unified cosmic design bespeaks the unity of the designing intelligence. This axiom implies a portrait of the one God in terms of the modality of action: God's *kedushah* or "holiness" constitutes God's essential separateness from the creative process of introducing separateness (*vayavdel*, "and he distinguished"), which allows God to monitor the process toward achieving a teleological unity of design that reflects God's own absolute unity. This portrait thus incorporates three structural elements that mutually define one another to produce a coherent image: (1) the "horizontal" separating of the creative process (havdalah), whose action produces and sustains the discrete elements of the world; (2) the "vertical" separateness of transcendence (kedushah) that defines the uniqueness of the divine source of the process and protects it from being, as it were, drawn into divisiveness such that the process itself loses unified reference, and (3) the "nonseparability" of the source itself, whose inviolable oneness (aḥdut) guarantees fulfillment of an ultimate cosmic unity of design despite any apparent "excessive separations" manifesting along the way to fully actualized cosmic unification.

The Judaic principle of unity first emerges, therefore, in a characterization of the divine person performing the acts of creation. To grasp this principle more fully requires situating it within a general and universally accessible account of human reality. The Bible itself provides warrant for doing this by specifying that human personhood is created in the image of the divine person. To locate a universal aspect of human personhood corresponding to the biblically derived portrait of the divine person would then situate Judaic unity within the compass of general human understanding. Phenomenological introspection in fact discloses a homology between the biblical portrait and the structure of personal identity, that is, the sense of distinctive individuality characterizing an empirical consciousness shaped by its unique personal history. Corresponding elements in the structure of personal identity are: (1) the unique series of distinct events, that is, actions performed by or upon a person, that cumulatively build a unique personal experience retained in conscious and unconscious memory; (2) the self's awareness of both being shaped by these events and yet somehow standing transcendentally above them, cognizant of their continuity through the shifting identities of child, adult, and elder, able to shape them by determining their future course to greater or lesser extent and even reshape them through insight, which resolves conflicts among past memories; (3) the empirical ego or "I," which makes possible such transcendence of experience by functioning as the unifying point that coordinates all experiences within a given personal history simply by referring them to itself. These three elements are mutually determining. For example, unless the "I" can maintain its transcendence, it may weaken and collapse into a succession of distinct experiences, which would thereby lose their integration as a single coherent personal experience. Conversely, the inherent telos of personal identity is maximum integration of the empirical consciousness—its achievement of fullest individuality through harmonizing all component elements into a truly unique "one."

The structure of personal identity, as the ordered wholeness of experiences constituting a concrete personal life, reveals the general structure of relations among unified wholes and their parts in the concrete world. It discloses, in other words, the logic of any ordered whole or cosmos—cosmological structure itself. From this standpoint, the Judaic principle of unity is the key to the elemental structure of empirical reality or, in Judaic terms, the creation. Creation consists of nested orders of cosmic structure, that is, integral wholes composed of distinct parts, ranging from atomic microcosm to galactic macrocosm in the inorganic sphere, from cell to body in the organic sphere, and from individual through family to community, nation, and—potentially—the community of nations in the social sphere. The goal or telos envisioned by Judaism is, quite simply, the completion of creation through the perfection of cosmos at every level. For humans, the task of cooperating in this completion lies chiefly in the social sphere.

As revelation of cosmic structure, the Judaic principle of unity includes the following points. First, any whole is more than the sum of its parts; that is, while the whole is composed of its parts, the quintessence of the whole as their principle of unitive interrelation necessarily transcends the individual parts. It stands higher than the parts in some way, although immanently structuring them. The ground of unitive interrelation for the cosmos in its entirety, creation as such, is the transcendent oneness of God. Second, a whole cannot be itself or function as it should unless each part is fully itself in its unique identity and properly situated in its functional environment within the whole. Thus the whole depends upon its parts, each of which contributes a unique and indispensable function to the whole. The part, in turn, can realize its unique identity and fulfill its functional potential only within the whole of which it is a part and outside of which it is devoid of meaning. Therefore each part depends upon the whole to define itself and become actualized as uniquely meaningful and valuable. The uniqueness of the part and the completeness of the whole are reciprocal values that can be actualized only in and through their inherent mutuality. Thus, for example, unique personal individuality and total corporate solidarity—both Judaic emphases—are not contradictory, but complementary aspects of unity. Third, to the extent that the parts of an entity become integrated into a true whole through the process of unification (yiḥud), that entity becomes a true individual (yaḥid) with a unique identity (yeḥidi) irreducible to any other; because the constellation of parts is unlike any other, although various parts may be similar to those in other constellations, the principle of unitive interrelation among the given parts—its individuality (meyuḥadut)—once manifested is unlike any other. And only through actualizing this individual uniqueness (yehidiut) may the fully unified (mitahed) being fulfill its unique function in some higher-order whole of which it is potentially a part. In achieving full individuation, a person, for example, becomes authentically one and many at the same time: one because unified within himself or herself, one of the many because for the first time truly unique, no longer a mere configuration of associated elements but an individual unlike any other, and thus able to assume a unique role as one of many uniquely valuable parts in the unified functioning of a wider reality. Only unification (yihud) produces the individual (yahid), which may then in turn contribute to unification at higher levels. Fourth, a person who has not achieved considerable actualized unification is enslaved to whatever component of his being exerts the most power at any given moment. He exists under the "principle of Sumer," as it were. Only as the process of unification resolves conflicts among components does an individual capable of making a true unitary choice through the individuated wholeness (yehidiyah) of his or her being emerge. Only such capacity for univocal self-determination by the wholeness of a being, unconditioned by the pressure of some disintegral part, constitutes freedom. Because God is essentially unified, he is perfectly free. The perfect oneness (ahdut) of the divine personal identity therefore furnishes the asymptotic model for all human efforts toward unification (yihud) and freedom. Conversely, the more an individual attains unification, the more he will intuit the reality of the divine One to whom he has achieved a significant likeness.

The Judaic principle of unity constitutes the deepest organizing pattern for historical Judaism. Examples of other fundamental terms in Judaic theology embodying aspects of the principle include: ẓedek (justice)—emplacement of parts in appropriate relation to others within a whole; tik-kun (reparation)—active repair of a whole by restoring its parts to their proper conditions and places; shalom (peace)—harmony that obtains when the completeness (shleimut) of a whole has been achieved; bittahon (faith)—conviction that God, because one, can and does unify all circumstances, however discordant, toward redemption; geulah (redemption)—the ultimate goal of unifying the entire creation into a coherent whole.

Judaism has developed historically through application, appropriation, and internalization of the Judaic principle of unity. In biblical times, from Hebrew origins through Babylonian exile, this principle gradually became accepted as the shaping and binding force in Israel's life. The Bible applies it both to space, as cosmic structure, and to time, as the linear temporality of history, envisioning time as a unified whole in which each distinct event uniquely contributes to an unfolding design. Much of the biblical narrative

treats the quest for unifying harmony within the patriarchal family, among
the tribes executing and consolidating their conquest of Canaan and—
inwardly—in the long struggle for the hearts of the people, whom suffering
alone weans from worship of the diverse forces of nature to an unequivocal
devotion toward the one transcendent creator.

It remained for Judaic unity to become thoroughly appropriated within
the spheres of action, thought, and feeling: outward behavior, intellectual
rationale, and inward identity. During the epoch of classical Judaic development, these tasks were accomplished respectively and consecutively by
rabbinic interpretation, medieval philosophy, and mystical theosophy. The
rabbis assumed each discrete element of the revealed text to have a unique
function that contributed an indispensable component to the wholeness of
Torah, whose commanded actions shape personal wholeness. Maimonides
found that reason could contemplate the discrete purposes inherent in the
workings of creation and thereby come to a lofty appreciation of both
nature's teleological unity of design and the unity of its divine designer. The
Zohar uncovers a paradigm, applied subsequently to the human person as
well, that shows the divine personal identity itself to consist of a diversity
of functions animated, integrated, and transcended by a purely unitive quintessence. Unification (*yihud*) in Judaic mysticism came to signify the
theurgic reintegrating of aspects of the divine identity that were strained or
even shattered through the tension of relating to finitude.

Kabbalah and Hasidism also introduced immanent interpretations of
divine unity (*ahdut*) that moved far toward pantheist dissolution of the
world into God, although the distinction was never entirely eradicated as in
India. The notion of unity as union (*ihud*), that is, identification or identity
of apparently distinct essences, provides a ruling ideal for several religions
and does play an auxiliary role in Judaism. Concepts—well-rooted in rabbinic tradition—that Israel and Torah are one, in that Torah embodies the
essential form of Israel's corporate life, and that Torah and God are one, in
that Torah expresses the essential intentionality of the divine mind, con-
verge in the kabbalistic dictum asserting that Israel, Torah, and God are one
(*ehad*). Kabbalistic theosophy of the tenth *sefirah* (number) further identifies
Israel (*knesset Yisrael*) as vehicle of the divine Presence (*Shekhinah*) that
maintains God's direct sovereignty (*malkhut*) within the world. But even
Judaic mysticism does not relax a fundamental Judaic valuing of discrete
identity that precludes any ontic fusion of divine and human persons. This
notion of union, in fact, discloses another basic aspect of the Judaic principle of unity: the functional uniting of discrete substantive elements with
the corporate form of unification that places them in integral mutual rela-

tion. It is precisely in this sense that Torah is essentially united with people as the ideal and integral form of Israel's corporate life.

BIBLIOGRAPHY

Martin Buber, *The Way of Man* (1966).

Thorkild Jacobsen, "Mesopotamia," in Henri Frankfort, ed., *The Intellectual Adventure of Ancient Man* (1946).

Ellis Rivkin, "The Unity Concept," in Michael A. Meyer, ed., *Ideas of Jewish History* (1974).

Utopia

אוטופיה

Lionel Kochan

In the strict meaning of the term—*no place*—the concept of utopia has no application in Judaism. The characteristic feature of the customary utopia is its remoteness in time and space. It will be inaccessible or perhaps exist in no recognizable area of the world. It may even be located on the moon. It is also frequently set at some future date, or is perhaps a purely intellectual construction. In this sense no Jewish utopian schemes seem to exist. Even those that come closest to it—the Zionist utopias discussed below—are unambiguously located in the land of Israel. If, however, utopia is taken to signify the impulse toward some sort of ideal society, then of course it does have its Jewish counterpart, if not precise equivalent, in the concept of the messianic age. What belongs to the utopian genre in the gentile world belongs to the messianic in the Jewish. There is certainly no identity but a considerable overlap. It is this that helps to account for the Jewish contribution, in the form of a secularized messianism, to radical and liberal movements of varied outlook. But the dominant strain within the Jewish context is to emphasize the indispensability of the physical, territorial dimension, although there are occasional tendencies in later kabbalism and Hasidism to spiritualize the messianic ideal and even to spiritualize the land. The ideal society can exist only within the land of Israel (although this, of course, may well be variously defined) and would itself have universal applicability. A second distinctive characteristic of the Jewish utopia is the absence of precise description. It seems that the utopian future is to be visualized in terms of a society that embodies a broad framework of values, with their precise implementation in the mechanism of daily life being left an open question. A third feature is the catastrophic nature of the redemption that eschews evolution in favor of upheaval. Thus the prototype of the salvation process is the first Exodus (Jer. 16:14–15). The values to be realized in this indeterminate way are, however, comprehensive in that the Jewish state will be theocratic and subject to the direct rule of the divine. In the terrestrial era it is the priests who bless Israel; in the future era, "God himself will bless Israel" (Ps. 29:11). Located in Zion, having its capital in a restored Jerusalem, and ruled by the scions of the ideal house of David, the state will be the incorporation of righteousness. Men themselves will possess only good inclinations (BT Suk. 52a). They will be infused with the spirit of the Lord and the spirit of learning, in contrast to the ignorance and partiality of the present. In social terms, the messianic era will be one of abundance and fertility (Joel 4:18), marked also by health, human longevity, and the absence of disease. Man will enjoy the fruit of his own labor: "They shall not plant and another eat" (Isa. 65:22). "In that day—declares the Lord of Hosts—you will be inviting each other to the shade of vines and fig trees" (Zech. 3:10). Toward this desirable state of affairs Israel will lead the way, through its cleaving to the Torah. Indeed, the messianic-utopian age can be regarded as the fulfillment of the very aim of the Torah. "All the prophets only prophesied for the days of the Messiah" (BT Sanh. 99a). Indeed, the last days will be incomparably richer than the first, so as to represent a different and altogether unprecedentedly higher order of reality in that "the land shall be filled with knowledge of the Lord as water covers the sea" (Isa. 11:9).

But this is not relevant to Israel alone, for the restored and rebuilt holy land will serve as a focus, model, and source of inspiration for the improved life of mankind in general, so that all nations shall share in the blessings of peace, the rule of righteousness, and the overthrow of the wicked and perverted.

Rabban Shimeon ben Gamliel said: in the [messianic] future all the nations and all the kingdoms will be gathered in the midst of Jerusalem. For it is said [Jer. 3:17] "all the nations will be collected thither for the name of God"; elsewhere

[Gen. 1:9] it is said, "Let the waters under the heavens be collected"; as "collection" in the latter verse means that all the waters of creation should be collected in one place, so "collection" in the former verse means that all the nations and kingdoms will be assembled in one place, Jerusalem.

(ARN, ch. 35)

In the same way as the utopian state has a place, it also has a time—historical time. It does not seem that there is unanimous expectation of an entirely new order of reality. The Messiah, being mortal, will die, and so, too, will his sons (Maimonides, *Commentary on the Mishnah* , Sanh. 10). The messianic era leaves history as open-ended as ever. The historical and the utopian lie along the same continuum. This sobriety is a particular characteristic of Maimonidean thinking, which is careful to caution against the illusion that the world in the days of the Messiah will depart from its accustomed course "or that there will be a change in the order of creation" (MT Hil. Melakhim 12:1). If there are prophetic utterances that do suggest such a change, for example, that the wolf will lie down with the lamb and the leopard graze with the goat, then their purport is not literal but figurative and symbolic: to signify, in this particular case, that "Israel will dwell in peace with the wicked men of idolatry who are likened to wolves and leopards" (MT Hil. Melakhim 12:1). In accordance with his consistent attempt to introduce a cautionary and sobering note into the world of utopian and messianic hope, Maimonides quotes the third-century Amora of Babylon, Samuel, to the effect that "the only difference between this world and the days of the Messiah is the subjection of Israel to the nations" (BT Sanh. 91b). Similarly, Maimonides warned against any attempt to divine the messianic process by astrology or any other means (cf. Maimonides, *Epistle to Yemen*). In fact, when it would happen, how it would happen, and what would happen were all concealed; the sages had no clear traditions and, in any case, no article of faith was involved. The whole subject was to be avoided as a fruitless exercise (MT Hil. Melakhim 12:1). On the other hand, Maimonides, in the *Epistle to Yemen,* did reveal a tradition in his family to the effect that the Messiah would come in 4976, or 1216 C.E.

The attempt to combat messianic hopes and discredit their exponents was perennial, all the more so when messianism was coupled with antinomianism. It began perhaps with Rabbi Torta's attack on Rabbi Akiva for his support of Bar Kokhba in 132 C.E. and the anathema pronounced on all "who calculate the end"; it is represented in the Gaonic period by Natronai Gaon, continues with Rabbi Azariah dei Rossi's attack in 1573 on the predictions and astrological calculations of Rabbi Abraham bar Ḥiyya in the twelfth century and Don Isaac Abrabanel in the late fifteenth century, and reaches its climax in the onslaught directed by Rabbi Jacob Sasportas on Shabbetai Ẓevi, Nathan of Gaza, and the Sabbatean movement in general, which flourished from 1666 to 1676. In the nineteenth and early twentieth centuries the same tradition is maintained in the attacks made on the Zionist movement by Rabbi Joseph Rozin, the Rogachover Rebbe. It is indeed symptomatic of the new movement's secular and antinomian tendencies that it should produce the closest Jewish counterparts to the conventional utopian fancies of the gentile world—Herzl's *Altneuland (Old-New Land)* (1902) and Elhanan Leib Lewinski's Hebrew tract *Journey to the Land of Israel in the Year 5800* [C.E. 2040] (1892). But even in these works the territorial dimension is of course unmistakable. The new state of Herzl's *Altneuland* is located in Palestine, lying east and west of the Jordan with indeterminate boundaries to the south and north that do, however, stretch into Syria. It is based on a form of anarcho-syndicalist ideals and lacks means of coercion. Land is publicly owned. A form of public ownership governs the operations of banks, industries, newspapers, and retail stores. Agriculture flourishes, fertilized by vast irrigation works, which also bring life to the desert areas. The swamps have been drained. Transport is electrified, the energy being drawn from water power, particularly from a canal created by the excavation of a vast tunnel joining the Mediterranean and the Dead Sea. The latter's chemical resources in bromium and potassium have made the country a world production center. The towns are spacious and well-planned, enjoying the benefits of a noiseless mass transit system. Men work a seven-hour day; women have the vote. Cooperation is the keynote of political, agricultural, and social life, eliminating the exploitation of man by man. Criminals are not punished but reeducated. Education up to university level is free. The old city of Jerusalem is surrounded by modern suburbs, parks, institutes of learning, markets, and architectural triumphs. In cultural respects, *Altneuland* is marked by tolerance for all faiths, religion being relegated to the status of a private concern, although the Sabbath remains the general Jewish festival. The reestablished Temple takes the form of a modern synagogue. But society does not concern itself with whether men worship the Eternal "in synagogue, church, mosque, in the art gallery or the philharmonic concert."[1] There is no official language, although German predominates. Among the favored pursuits of the population of *Altneuland* are attendance at German opera and French drama and participation in English outdoor sports. There are institutes for the study of culture and philosophy and a Jewish academy of forty members modeled on the *Académie française*. Moreover, the establishment of *Altneuland* has eliminated anti-Semitism through reducing the impact of Jewish competition elsewhere.

In a similar vein, though with a more marked Jewish emphasis and less attention to detail, Elhanan Leib Lewinski imagined a society in which health—individual, social, and communal—is the norm. Physical well-being is fostered by the climate, form of diet (kashrut), agricultural way of life, purity of family life, and the ready availability of medical services. There is no longer a profusion of little shopkeepers—"once almost our second nature because of our history,"[2] they have returned to the land to lead a natural life. The social health of the community is manifest in its prevailing equality. There is no labor question and no capitalist question, "for there are no workers and all are masters."[3] Drunkenness and crime are absent—there is no hardship and therefore no crime. "There is nothing but peace and nothing but tranquility in the house of Israel."[4] Intellectual health is shown in the profusion of learned lectures, to which no entrance fee is demanded, as in Europe, and in the multitude of serious publications. The countryside blossoms as never before. The Dead Sea has been transformed into a thriving community. "How great are thy deeds, O man!"[5] exclaims Lewinski.

It is also possible to conceive of a utopian future not in terms of a polity embodying certain values but rather in terms of its legal arrangements. This is the achievement of the rabbis of the Mishnah, who created a system of laws, supposedly derived from that prevailing at the time of the First Temple and intended for the restored Third Temple. Thus, "The rabbis of the Mishnah intended to describe Israel's institutions from the point of view of messianic historicism, projecting an ideal future on the model of an ideal past."[6]

Similarly, the system of civil laws and government elaborated by the sages of the Mishnah has been understood as an attempt to devise an ideal polity formed partly from the materials of a distant past and partly from "their own vivid hopes of how things must be done at some point in an undifferentiated future."[7] In general, the paucity of utopian speculation in Jewish thinking is the counterpart to an abiding preoccupation with the here and now. The utopian hope is indeed present, but it is subsumed within a concern for the means rather than the end.

REFERENCES

1. Theodor Herzl, *Altneuland* (1902), 286.
2. E. L. Lewinski, *Masa le-Erez Yisrael be-Shanat Tat* (5800) (1892), 40.
3. Ibid., 44.
4. Ibid., 50.

5. Ibid., 51.
6. Benzion Wacholder, *Messianism and Mishnah* (1970), 391.
7. Jacob Neusner, "The Description of Formative Judaism," in *Association of Jewish Studies Review* 5 (1980).

BIBLIOGRAPHY

Miriam Eliav-Feldon, "If You Will It, It Is No Fairy Tale: The First Jewish Utopias," *Jewish Journal of Sociology* (1983).
Theodor Herzl, *Old-New Land,* tr. Lotta Levensohn (1941).
Michael Higger, *The Jewish Utopia* (1932).
Elhanan Leib Lewinski, "Masa le-Ereẓ Yisrael be-Shanat Tat (5800)," in *Pardes* 1 (1892).

Women and Judaism

אישה

Blu Greenberg

At the risk of frustrating reader and writer alike, I should like to explore the subject at hand exclusively through questions, the first of which is: Why questions? One answer is, quite simply, that the questions present themselves, almost endlessly. At every turn, paradoxes and inner contradictions virtually leap off the hallowed page. These very contradictions highlight a central fact: no single definition of the role or status of women in Judaism can be extrapolated from the sources. Instead we find both equality and hierarchy, respect and condescension, deference and disability, compassion and callousness. Indeed, examining the tradition through the veil of new values for women is a far more complex enterprise than we had imagined at the outset.

A second answer to "Why questions?" is that questions have a remarkable quality, a flexible resonance that allows them to be heard in many different ways. A question for one becomes an answer for another, rhetoric for a third, dilemma for a fourth. Thus, each individual reader can find the proper resting spot for the questions, as befits a work of essays on theology.

Let us begin at the beginning, with creation of humankind. The Book of

Genesis offers two different accounts: both male and female created in the image of God, symbolizing equality (ch. 1); and male created first, with female fashioned from his rib, suggesting hierarchy (ch. 2).

How else do the accounts differ? The first pericope is divine oriented, replete with overtones of sacredness, perfection, majesty, and mysterium. This is life as it exists in its ideal form. The second story is earthy, physical: Human life is born of dust and ashes and returns thereto. It is a poignant tale, recording human vulnerability and existential loneliness. Yet a theme of romance dominates, with the phrase "bone of my bones, flesh of my flesh" (Gen. 2:23) heightening the sense of human sexuality. Nevertheless, the second creation account is also derivative: man loves and needs woman, but woman is derived from man, and he has the power of naming her.

What is the relationship between the two stories? Is the first a description of male and female as they exist (as equals) in the eyes of God, while the second is one of male and female in their (unequal) human relationships? If so, why is the human-relational version framed in a creation story? If, on the other hand, this too is primarily the tale of God's creation, does it imply that a difference in status between male and female was divinely conferred—that it is God's will that male and female be ranked, with the significant sex alone rendering vows null (Num. 30), constructing and severing marriages (Gen. 24:51, Deut. 24:1), and sufficing as the whole count of the people Israel (Num. 1)? Did God create male and female with the intention that they relate to each other within the confines of a hierarchy? Does being ranked in relation to each other mean also to be ranked in the eyes of God? In other words, is one sex preferred, more special, more chosen by God?

Or should we instead understand the rib pericope, as some have, to be an indication of women's superiority: woman, created last, is highest on the phylogenetic scale; and unlike man, she is not dependent upon the full complement of *mizvot* to keep her good and honorable.[1]

Or is the whole purpose of this creation story to serve as a backdrop to the single most romantic verse in the Bible: "Hence a man leaves his mother and father and clings to his wife, so that they become one flesh" (Gen. 2:24)? In this passage we find elements of privacy, intimacy, sexuality, procreation, and a long-standing commitment—essentials of a good marriage. How, then, shall we read this story?

In another relational pericope, in the Fall from the Garden of Eden, woman emerges as temptress and the source of evil. Never mind the snake. Never mind that Eve learned of the prohibition secondhand (she had not yet been created when God instructed Adam regarding the tree). The fact is, Eve sinned, brought down Adam with her, and begs punishment for it. Her punishment is bound up with her function as wife and mother: "I will make most severe your pangs in childbearing; in pain shall you bear children. Yet your urge shall be for your husband, and he shall rule over you" (Gen. 3:16).

How does a contemporary woman relate to the verse "and he shall rule over you"? Is it intended as paradigm for all male–female relationships, or is it punishment for Adam and Eve alone? If a paradigm, was this the verse that resonated when Maimonides ruled that a woman who refused to wash her husband's feet could be chastised with a rod (MT Hil. Ishut 21:7–10), and that a woman could not leave home to visit her parents without securing her husband's permission?[2] If so, why did this same halakhist—and, indeed, the majority of scholars—ignore this clearcut message of male dominance when they legislated punishment for the grave offense of wife beating?[3] Can we read with our right eye the scriptural verse "and he shall rule over you" and with our left the talmudic statement that enjoins a man to consult with his wife in all matters (BT BM 59a)?

Perhaps we should understand this verse not as paradigm but rather as a curse to be set aside as we strive toward perfection. And yet if we interpret God's words here, "and he shall rule over you," as nonparadigmatic, must we also similarly interpret the adjacent phrase, "yet your urge shall be for your husband"? Surely the acknowledgment in Jewish tradition of women's sexual passions was far more progressive than the attitude of most other religions. Judaism alone has a law of *onah*—the formal obligation of a husband to sexually satisfy his wife (Ex. 21:10).

Does the proximity of the two phrases in Genesis 3:16 imply that a man must recognize and satisfy his wife's sexual needs, yet simultaneously maintain the dominant edge? Is the first hint of sexual politics to be found in this verse of the Torah? Does later rabbinic legislation of the optimal sexual posture—the man on top—echo, even remotely, these original verses in Genesis (Sh. Ar. OH 240:5)?

What predisposed one rabbi to deduce from this verse a notion of female sexual modesty, to wit: "A man initiates with words, a woman with her heart . . . and this is a fine quality in women" (BT Eruv. 100b), while another rabbi deduced from it female passion, that is, that a woman longs for her husband when he goes out on the road and therefore it is his obligation to remember this and satisfy her before he takes his leave of her (BT Yev. 62b)?

Or is the entire pericope not primarily about men and women but about the power, omniscience, and compassion of God—a God who takes pity on these two poor souls, Adam and Eve, sews them a garment of leather, and dresses them as a great, loving, nurturing, caring God must do?

Another mystery: woman is blessed with the greatest of all blessings—to bear new life. Not surprisingly, the punishment of woman takes the form of a diminution of this great gift: menses, pregnancy, and childbirth will henceforth be attended by pain.

Given the fact of female biology, it seems highly incongruous that the rabbis interpreted the *mizvah* of *peru u-revu*—"Be fertile and increase, fill the earth and master it" (Gen. 1:28)—as applying to men only. Even though the talmudic discussion openly acknowledges that God was addressing Adam and Eve, the ruling remains that procreation is not a woman's *mizvah*. And why? Because the commandment applies to those whose nature it is to "master." Further confirmation lies in the spelling of the word *kivshuha* ("and master it"): Though its reading is plural in form, its spelling is truncated, as if to signify the omission of women from this commandment (BT Yev. 65b).

But one must probe the sources more deeply to understand the law's intent. Elsewhere, we find these rationales: Since it is a woman's natural tendency to procreate, she needs no mandate; and inasmuch as pain and danger accompany childbirth, a woman cannot be commanded to do that which would bring harm to her person.[4] These are not merely rhetorical flourishes but are in fact the theological bases for female contraception and abortion.[5]

Nevertheless, *mizvah* is not only obligation, it is also reward. We count our actions and the passage of our lives in terms of *mizvot*. And a staple of Jewish philosophy is that the heavenly court counts as well. Surely a rabbinic concept such as *pikuah nefesh*—where lifesaving takes precedence over performance of a *mizvah*[6]—would adequately have covered those situations in which conception or birth would endanger a woman's life. In sum, then, while magnanimity and logic are apparent in these halakhic deliberations, they are not of adequate measure, for the question remains: Why were women not included in the *mizvah* of *peru u-revu?*

Jews are members of a covenantal community, as the word *brit* (covenant) implies: Circumcision *(brit mila)* is the ritual that celebrates the fact that this community stands in special relationship to God. A *brit* affirms that this newborn is the child not only of a particular biological family but also of all of the Jewish people: a child who enlarges the community by one.

Circumcision is one sign of the covenant, Shabbat another, Torah another. Women, of course, were obligated to observe the *mizvah* of Shabbat. Women experienced the revelation at Sinai; the Torah is theirs too. The question then becomes: Are women members of the covenantal community? If so, how did they achieve that special status—simply through birth, without attendant celebration, ritual, and fanfare? Is it higher to be automatically included than to require a ritual to enter the covenant? Or do we celebrate communally the addition of males to the covenant because males are inherently more precious, more valuable to the community? Or more vulnerable, as we experienced in the Holocaust?

Is a covenantal ceremony of circumcision suitable for males only because their reproductive organ is external to the body while female circumcision—still practiced in primitive cultures—would diminish sexual pleasure in women? If the emphasis is covenantal and not surgical, why has no covenantal ceremony for women developed over the course of four thousand years? And did the silent, unritualized accession of women to the covenant have a domino effect on other areas of women and community, on self-perception, and on the celebration of other rites of passage for women as Jews? Was women's passivity at the onset of Jewish maturity (bat mizvah) or their silence in the marriage ceremony (another covenantal relationship) merely a replay of their passive entry at birth into the covenantal community? Is there any connection between women's covenantal status and their loss of community healing in the experience of reciting kaddish (the mourner's prayer)?

Let us trace one instance of this domino effect upon the notion of community. The grace after meals (birkat ha-mazon) is convened by a quorum of three males. Why men only? Because embedded in the grace is the verse, "We thank You . . . for the covenant which you have signed in our flesh."[7] Is inclusion of that verse sufficient for excluding women from the quorum (community) that convenes the grace—women who have likely prepared and served the meal for which all now give thanks, yet who instantly become nonpersons because of the phrase "in our flesh"?

And yet it is also true that while males may be partners in the covenant, women are the pivotal figures in the earliest formation of the covenantal community. Isaac carries the blessing not because of circumcision but because he marries a woman of the covenantal family, while his brother Ishmael marries the daughters of Enar and Eshkol. Jacob takes the blessing not because he buys it from Esau but because he, too, marries two sisters who carry in their blood the covenantal line. Rabbinic law defined a Jew as one born to a Jewish mother. Is there some perfect symmetry here: Men perform the covenantal roles while women carry the covenantal genes? Or was matrilinear descent simply a function of the fact that maternity could always be ascertained, while paternity could not? What, then, is the relationship of women to covenant—half in, half out?

With regard to the issue of property, scriptural and rabbinic law teach that a wife may not inherit her husband's property (BT BB 109b, 111b; BT BK 42b; BT Ket. 83b). Considering the emphasis placed on the family as a unit, this law seems anomalous. Could its function be to teach community responsibility and compassion for—and at the expense of—widows? Or did the law serve to ensure, as did the laws of Jubilee, an equitable distribution of land among the twelve tribes so that no one household, through bonds of marriage, could amass great landholdings while others became impoverished? If this latter function were served on native land in the days of the First and Second Commonwealth, why did the law persist into rabbinic times when there was no longer a tribal confederation to be equitably preserved? And how do we reconcile this law of noninheritance by wives with other legal structures by means of which wives most assuredly did inherit their husbands' property? For example, the *ketubah* (marriage contract) contained provisions for continued maintenance or for lump sum settlements for a surviving wife; whole parts of an estate could be bequeathed to a wife in the form of a gift, if not an inheritance.[8]

Daughters and property were a slightly different matter, thanks to the plea of Zelophehad's daughters. Zelophehad died, leaving five daughters and no sons. As the law required, his property reverted to his brother's family. The five daughters protested (the first feminist protest regarding property). So complex an issue was it that Moses saw fit to consult the Ultimate Arbiter. God ruled in favor of the daughters of Zelophehad: When there are no male heirs, females inherit (Num. 27).

The story is remarkable not so much in its outcome as in its telling. Why, one wonders, is the story told in the first place? Were every law in the Torah to be accompanied by historical development or anecdotal background, we would need fifty Books of Moses, not five. Is the story told with real-life characters—five vulnerable orphaned daughters—so as to make it more palatable to a patriarchal folk? Or is the Torah's purpose to show that justice and truth can reside in a female plea?

The Talmud gives more detail on matters of property. When a man died, his sons were to inherit his estate. However, from this estate the sons were required to maintain and support their sisters (BT BB 139b). Thus at the same moment that a man acquired capital on which to build his own small or large fortune, his sister became daughterlike to him. And yet how can we categorically describe this system as inequitable when the mishnah teaches us that if an estate was small, that is, insufficient to support both sons and daughters, then the daughters were given the entire estate and the sons had to go begging (M. BB 9:1)?

In matters of torts and damages, Israelite women enjoyed great equity. In contrast to other civilizations, including our own, where the value of a person is more often based on earning power than on his or her essential being, Jewish law compensated men and women equally.

Although the cry of "chattel" has recently been raised by feminists regarding women in ancient Israel, the law tells a different story. A woman could not be sold into slavery, as could a man, to pay off her father's debts. If she was "sold," it was to become the master's wife or his son's wife, and she was treated accordingly. If the husband no longer desired her, she was to be set free, unencumbered by debt, and could not be passed on to another (Ex. 21:7–11). But then how do we account for a law such as this: If two men fight and a pregnant woman nearby is struck, resulting in miscarriage, the culprit pays the fine for the loss of the fetus to the father (Ex. 21:22)? Does this suggest that any of the wife's products—whether wrought through work or through pregnancy—are the property of her husband?[9] Or shall we view this law more benignly—that damage to a woman's person, and even to her fetus, may not go without some sort of retribution?

With regard to marriage, the Torah states that a man "takes" or "gives" a woman in marriage (Deut. 24:1–5). What do these terms mean? Not acquisition, the rabbis explained, but *kiddushin* (BT Kid. 2a ff.). A woman is sanctified, set aside, for this man only. The transfer of an item of value or a deed may look like a purchase, but it merely symbolizes her changed status to wifehood. Why was there no similar setting aside of a man solely for his wife? Because polygyny was permitted, but polyandry was not, an answer that begets another question to which we will shortly return: Why polygyny?

Rabbinic law states that a woman may not be married without her consent. The rabbis based this on the scriptural account of Rebecca, who was asked by her brother, Laban, if she wished to go with the servant of Abraham to be Isaac's wife (Gen. 24). One cannot help but wonder: Close readers of the text that the rabbis were, how could they have read the passage the way they did? Rebecca was asked if she wished to go only after the marital agreement had been negotiated and the bridal price transferred from Eliezer to Laban. This manner of marriage is confirmed in the story of Rachel and Leah, whose father determined who married whom, and when. What possessed the rabbis to misread the text? Was it to ensure women's autonomy in the choice of marital partner—for the sake of romantic love?

If tradition valued romance and love and not merely procreation, how can we begin to understand polygyny? Did it have more to do with demographics and wars than with a differential value attached to men or women? Was it to ensure Jewish survival through more births? Or was it, in fact, a protection for women, so that no woman would remain single for life, no woman forever be deprived of having a child?

If the reproductive urge in women was more powerful a force than the humiliation of sharing a husband or the existential loneliness of remaining single and childless, how do we translate this into contemporary life, with a demographic imbalance of several hundred thousand more females than males? How do the options of divorce and serial marriage, or having children without the bonds of marriage, compare with that of polygyny, as we consider the new status of women? And yet if polygyny had any redeeming features at all for human relationships, why did it taper off in biblical times? Or, of greater sociohalakhic curiosity, why did Jewish law as it evolved in close contact with other religions continue to legitimate polygyny in Oriental and Islamic societies but forbid it in Christian ones, where even monogamous sexuality was barely countenanced?

A Jewish marriage is terminated by either death or the giving of a *get,* the writ of divorce. "And he shall write her a writ of divorce and give it to her in her hand" (Deut. 24:1). Until the *get* is tendered, a Jewish man and woman are considered married, regardless of whether they may have parted through formal or informal procedures, by accident or by design.[10] Rabbinic tradition formalized the *get* proceedings, the essence of which is the husband's declaration, "I release you and you are now free to become the wife of any other man."

Not some remote theoretical or historical issue, traditional Jewish divorce law is today a matter of immediate and pressing concern. The problem grows not so much out of the transfer of the divorce writ—which may even lend a needed point of psychological closure to divorce proceedings—but rather with its unilateral initiative: Only a husband has the power to serve the *get.* This can relegate the woman to the limbo status of *agunah* (anchored wife), anchored to a husband who is either unable (for reasons of disappearance, insanity, or illness) or unwilling (for reasons of spite or blackmail) to deliver the *get* and release his wife from the marriage.

It behooves us to ask whether the unilateral initiative was the essence of biblical law or whether the *get* was the essence, and whether who gives the *get* to whom was merely a matter of form. Further, why did rabbinic tradition interpret loosely the biblical phrases "he shall write," "he shall give," and "in her hand,"[11] yet remain unswerving in interpreting male initiative—and this despite the rabbis' great compassion for *agunot?*[12] If the answer lies in the rationale that since man created the marriage bond he must also be the one to sever it (BT Kid. 9b), how can we resolve the problem of recalcitrant husbands without also disturbing the ancient and binding laws and customs of Jewish marriage?

And most painful of all, how are we to view those currently in positions of authority who can say, in the face of thousands of tragic *agunot* today, that their hands are tied? Are these religious authorities models of faithfulness and piety, or ineffectual and misguided leaders?

We move now to the even more difficult subject of women and rape. In all societies, since time immemorial, laws concerning rape have been insufficient. They convey a lack of understanding of the total traumatization of the victim, and consequently fail adequately to punish the perpetrator.

Biblical law distinguishes between the rapist of a married woman and the rapist of a virgin. The former is put to death; the latter pays a fine and is required to marry his victim—that is, if she is willing to have him (Deut. 22:23–29). Was this law a protection for a woman who, having lost her virginity, would no longer be desirable or marriageable? Did the laws have more to do with issues of property and spoiled merchandise, as payment of fines to the virgin's father would indicate? Does the meager punishment hint at complicity, that most heinous of accusations of the violated?

And yet what legal system can be compared to the rabbinic tradition, which explains and expounds the Torah: A woman's subjective judgment is accepted as the sole criterion of whether or not she was raped; concepts of indignity and psychological pain are introduced; suspicion and the taint of complicity are virtually eliminated (JT Sot. 4:4). And how can we not marvel at a system that forbade marital rape two thousand years before the concept was even debated in Western societies (BT Eruv. 100b)? Still, why is the rapist of a virgin punished by a monetary fine in Jewish law, and why is it paid to her father?

With regard to other legal matters, with very few exceptions, rabbinic law explicitly disqualifies women from giving testimony in a Jewish court of law (JT Sanh. 3:9). This ruling is based on the scriptural verse "A case can be valid only on the testimony of two witnesses [masc. pl.] or more" (Deut. 19:15). Setting aside for a moment the fact that elsewhere—in many other places—the masculine plural noun is interpreted generically and exclusively, we must still probe the question, Why is women's testimony disqualified?

Shall we understand it, as some do, that women were protected in the private sector and thus could not be summoned forth into the public courts, in much the same way that they could not be required to perform certain public *mizvot?*[13] Does it mean anything at all that the disqualification of slaves as witnesses derives from the law concerning women as witnesses, and that other unsavory and unreliable types such as usurers and pigeon racers were also disqualified (BT BK 88a)? Or is the disqualification merely a technical one, the proof being that credible statements, in contrast to witnessed testimony, are sufficient in ritual matters and are accepted as equally valid and reliable from woman or man?[14]

Is it possible that women were disabled because they were thought to be given to imprecision?[15] Did the seemingly innocuous description elsewhere of women as lightminded leave its impact on rabbinic consciousness, only to be exercised when the question arose in the house of study as to who may or may not testify?[16] (BT Shab. 33b–Kid 80b). Or is it possible, as some scholars believe, that women at one time in our history were empowered to witness, but that this power receded in subsequent generations?[17] Or could the whole matter be reduced to very practical factors: that women were excluded from ownership of property, and therefore must necessarily be excluded from the judicial processes related to such matters?[18]

What does the law say today about women's evaluative powers? Do we have a record, anywhere, of women of previous generations feeling a sense of injustice? Can we use the precedent of Deborah, who served as a judge, to say a fortiori that if a woman could serve as a judge certainly she could act as a witness? But why did the rabbis who asked themselves this perplexing question answer it by saying that Deborah was not a judge but rather served to guide the people and instruct the judges in the law?[19] Was *judge* merely a term equivalent to *political leader*? Could a woman be a political leader and not make civil or religious judgments? What was the process whereby Deborah became a judge or leader in a patriarchal society?

Confronting the issue of women and ritual leads us down yet another path. Who would have imagined, some two thousand years ago, that issues of devotion in a particularist community would be raised in the twentieth century under the rubric of broad notions of equality for women? Yet facts that lay quietly for centuries now demand analysis. The study of Torah, communal prayer, the performance of time-bound positive commandments—women's exemption from obligation in these areas is difficult to fathom with our new awareness of women's potential.

The scriptural peg for releasing women from the study of Torah comes from the Torah's central affirmation of faith, the Shema. "And you shall teach them [the words of the Torah] to your sons" (Deut. 11:19). Why did the rabbis exclude women from this commandment, when they so often understood *vanekha* as "children" and not only as "sons"? Was it because

Jewish society was so constructed in their time, or was it nuanced from Sinai to mean "sons" and not "daughters" (BT Kid. 29b)? And why did the opinion of Rabbi Eliezer condemning women's study of Torah prevail over the opposite view of his colleague, ben Azzai (M. Sot. 3:4)?

Were women truly perceived to be lightheaded when it came to sustained study of Torah and Talmud? Or was it that Talmud Torah, the study of Torah, was the route to leadership and authority, and therefore the interpretive keys were withheld from women? Is it less than just, honorable, and dignified to throw sacred study out of the realm of the holy and into the ring of politics? Or was the giant *mizvah* of Talmud Torah given to men as compensation for being deprived of the great blessing and sacred task of childbirth?

Rabbinic literature offers no reason for female exemption from time-bound positive commandments; thus, we can only conjecture. Does the exemption suggest that a woman's time is not her own, and that time spent in study or religious obligations would be time stolen from primary tasks as wife, mother, homemaker, and enabler?[20] Or was the exemption from formal structured communal prayer a halakhic response to women's choice of opting out of this formidable obligation in favor of a lesser, personal, private, individualized prayer mode?[21] Or is the domino effect operating here—were women, not being full-fledged members of the covenantal community, by extension denied equal access to the spiritual congregation? Or does this exemption have nothing at all to do with time, but rather with place—a man's place in the public sector of synagogue, courts, and house of study, and a woman's place in home and family?[22]

If, in fact, women's role is secondarily sacramental and primarily pro-creational and nurturant, why was this not openly celebrated in the tradition? In truth, the three *mizvot* associated with women—*niddah* (laws of family purity), *hallah* (baking Sabbath bread), and *nerot* (lighting candles)—represent the powerful role that women played in family, religion, and society: *Niddah* governs sexual relations and procreation; *hallah* suggests observance of *kashrut* (the dietary laws) in the home, and *nerot* is a symbol of the Sabbath and the holidays—three significant areas of a Jew's life entrusted to women's care and attention[23]—three areas as important as prayer and Talmud Torah, yet never acknowledged in the sacred sources for what they are and what they remain.

On the other hand, women of all the generations before ours were encouraged and enabled to fulfill themselves in these roles—and felt fulfilled by them as well. Perhaps the new questions for today are: How can we reverse the diminished value placed on woman as childbearer-nurturer?

How will we counterbalance social forces that incline women to deny or sublimate this biological orientation? Does not the tradition have much of value to teach us regarding distinctive roles of male and female?

The questions about women's role in traditional Judaism seem endless, but a sufficient number has been raised to allow us to draw certain conclusions. Nevertheless, we must still ask the most basic question of all: How can a faithful, loving daughter of the tradition raise any questions at all? And yet, how can she not?

We have been challenged by a new and prevailing set of values for women. We are impelled to address the questions and we must do this with truthfulness. I would have liked nothing better than to cite only the positive statements of the tradition, which, happily, outweigh the negative ones. Regarding the latter, I feel great temptation to cover, apologize, protect, defend, rationalize. But I cannot do so with integrity. Moreover, I have come to understand that a faithful daughter of the tradition can engage both a critical eye and a loving heart at one and the same moment. Raising questions is not tantamount to challenging the word of God. On the contrary, I have to believe that Torah and tradition are stronger than any human critique and that they will, in fact, emerge even stronger from any examination. Let us, then, draw several conclusions from all this questioning.

The tradition is exceedingly vast—a rich, thick vein to mine and then to mine again. "Delve into the Torah again and again, for everything can be found there" (M. Avot 5:22).

The tradition regarding women runs somewhat like a crazy quilt. It is magnanimous, fair, and biased—sometimes all three on the same sacred page.

The status and role of women in Jewish tradition are not static. Ethical, social, and cultural considerations have all left their impact on Jewish law.

There seems to be at times a certain arbitrariness and at other times a brilliant consistency in rabbinic codification of women's roles. What is in or out, incumbent upon women or not, is not always predictable. Moreover, seemingly illogical explanations may contain a profound rationality and sensitivity, while that which appears to be perfectly logical is not necessarily congruent with reality—for example, the exemption of women from recitation of the Shema but their inclusion in the obligation to recite the *Megillah* (scroll of Esther), or the differential application of the laws pertaining to rape.

The traditional sources clearly do not show the fine hand or voice of women. Interpretation of the law is made about the class of women, or about individual women, but not by women. Had the reverse been true, Jewish divorce law would have developed differently. Had women had a say in the process, they certainly would not have written themselves out of the *mizvah* of procreation.

Considering this very lack of input by women and the concomitant powers of interpretation vested exclusively in male authorities, there is a considerable balance, benevolence, and deference to women throughout the sources. This fact should not be taken lightly, and should affect the tone with which we approach the sources.

Finally, everything points to the impossibility of rewriting history. We should study the sources well, with an open heart and with good will; and we should not dissipate energy railing at past inequities, become enmeshed in a storm of rhetoric, or expend vast amounts of time in trying to reconcile the paradoxes and inconsistencies regarding women and Judaism. Our central focus should be on finding solutions to the real problems that remain.

Thus, we should begin with the proposition that the lot of Jewish women was in the tradition quite good; that there are sufficient precedents of equality upon which to build a sturdy structure for the future, consistent with rabbinic Judaism; that tradition and patriarchal Judaism need some midcourse correction but have much to teach us—men and women alike— about being human; and that we are fortunate to live in a time when equality for women and commitment to Jewish tradition are not mutually exclusive alternatives but rather can enhance each other—and ourselves—in the process of joining together.

REFERENCES

1. See, for example, S. R. Hirsch, *The Pentateuch,* vol. 1: *Genesis* (1971), 33.
2. This is derived from the *baraita* in BT Kid. 30b. See also Maimonides' Commentary to the Mishnah, ad loc. Kid. 1:7.
3. Maimonides, MT Hil. Hovel u-Mazzik 4:16–18. Some believe Maimonides derives this from BT BK 8a or BT Ket. 55b. Cf. Hagahos Maimunios and Kesef Mishneh on Maimonides, ad loc.
4. For a succinct discussion of the issues, see David M. Feldman, *Birth Control in Jewish Law* (1968), 53–56. See also BT Yev. 65b–66a for rulings in real situations where women wanted the full *ketubah* and release in order to remarry a man who is able to give them children.
5. Abortion is legitimated in the tradition only in the event of danger to a woman's life (M. Oho. 7:6).
6. With the exception of three commandments that require martyrdom rather than transgression: murder, incest, and idol worship.
7. The reasoning takes a somewhat circuitous route. Because women did not undergo *brit* or inherit "the good land which You gave to our fathers," theirs is a lesser obligation in reciting the *birkat ha-mazon*. Consequently, they cannot

call others to fulfill the obligation. See Tosafot and also Rashi, ad loc. BT Ber. 20b.

8. See Moshe Meiselman, *Jewish Women in Jewish Law* (1978), ch. 15. See also Zev Falk, *Jewish Matrimonial Law* (1973). Falk traces the development of salutary inheritance laws through medieval times.

9. There are sources that would indicate such, particularly M. Ket. 6:1.

10. Civil divorce, separation, disappearance, and even the suspected but unverified death of a spouse during dangerous travels—none of these constitutes a Jewish divorce.

11. A scribe or others, including the woman herself, may do the writing; an agent may deliver and receive it (M. Git. 2:5, 3:2, 3:3–4, 6:1); in her hand—in her workbasket or thrown onto the parapet where she stands (BT Git. 77a–79a, M. Git. 8:3, 8:1).

12. See especially BT BB 168a, where the rabbis legislate that a woman may pay the scribe in order not to delay her release. See also BT Git. 3a, where the laws of testimony are altered in order to prevent her *aginut;* and BT Yev. 106a, on the principle of *kofin oto,* "we force him until he says I want to [divorce her]."

13. See BT Shev. 30a and BT Git. 40a. The scriptural peg cited in the Talmud in instances of release or exemption of women from certain obligations is, "The honor of the king's daughter is within (her home)" Songs 45:14.

14. See Meiselman, *Jewish Women in Jewish Law,* ch. 13.

15. See, for example, Yal. 1:82 on Gen. 18:16, "Then Sarah denied," which comments that the reason women were invalidated as witnesses is because Sarah did not tell the truth. Even as contemporary and well-intentioned a scholar as Getsel Ellinson compares women's and men's testimony along the lines of imagination versus precision. See Getsel Ellinson, *Women and the Mizvot* (1974), 185.

16. BT Shab. 33b; contrast this with the opposite theme, that women have an extra measure of understanding, BT Nid. 45b.

17. Boaz Cohen, *Jewish and Roman Law* (1966), 128f.

18. See Ellinson, op. cit., 184–88, including the contemporary suggestions that the law be amended to admit women's testimony in pecuniary matters.

19. See, for example, Tosafot on BT Nid. 50a, "Kol hakasher ladun."

20. See *Sefer Abudraham Hashalem* (1959). Weekday prayers, morning blessings. See also Judith Hauptman, "Images of Women in the Talmud," in Rosemary Radford Ruether, ed., *Religion and Sexism* (1974), 197–200.

21. On this theme see Meiselman, *Jewish Women in Jewish Law,* chs. 20–24.

22. Saul Berman, "The Status of Women in Halachic Judaism," in Elizabeth Koltun, ed., *The Jewish Woman* (1976).

23. The Lubavitcher Rebbe has often sounded this theme of a broad interpretation of women's *mizvot.*

BIBLIOGRAPHY

Rachel Biale, *Women and Jewish Law* (1984).
Getsel Ellinson, *Women and the Mizvot* (1974).

David M. Feldman, *Birth Control in Jewish Law* (1968).

Blu Greenberg, *On Women and Judaism* (1981).

Judith Hauptman, "Images of Women in the Talmud," in Rosemary Ruether Radford, ed., *Religion and Sexism* (1974).

Susannah Heschel, *On Being a Jewish Feminist* (1983).

Elizabeth Koltun, ed., *The Jewish Woman* (1976).

Moshe Meiselman, *Jewish Women in Jewish Law* (1978).

Work

עבודה

Avraham Shapira

The biblical expressions referring to labor (*avodah* and *melakhah*) imply a power to make and create, be it divine or human. God is depicted in the creation story in Genesis as a creative artisan. The identification of God's role as shaper (*yozer*) with his role as creator (*boré*) of all appears a number of other times in the Bible: " . . . whom I have created [*berativ*], formed [*yezartiv*], and made for My glory" (Isa. 43:7); " . . . the Lord who created you [*borekha*], O Jacob, who formed you [*veyozrekha*], O Israel" (Isa. 43:1). This idea is also echoed in such verses as: "When I behold Your heavens, the work of Your fingers, the moon and stars that You set in place" (Ps. 8:4); "For it is He who formed [*yozer*] all things . . . Lord of Hosts is His name" (Jer. 10:16). It should be pointed out in this context that the verb *y-z-r* is also used in the Bible to describe human labor, particularly that of building and of fashioning material objects.

Labor is understood in the Bible as man's destiny; there is a close connection between man (*adam*) and soil (*adamah*) that is rooted in man's (Adam's) having been created "from the dust of the earth [*adamah*]" (Gen.

2:7), and this connection is concretized, in the main, through labor. Because of man, God curses the soil, and it is man's actions, his sins, that determine the soil's fate. A way of life based on creative work must be accompanied by responsibility for settling the planet and putting it in order. The first task imposed upon man after he is created and placed in the garden of Eden is "to work it [le'ovdah] and keep it [leshomrah]" (Gen. 2:15). The talmudic sages see this as an expression of the great importance of labor. The reference, they maintain, is to manual work pure and simple: "Rabbi Eliezer says: Great is work, for even Adam did not eat a bite until he had worked, as it is said, 'And [God] placed him in the garden of Eden, to work it and keep it'" (ARN², ch. 21).

The description of the creation of the world as the handiwork of God is, as we have suggested, one of the roots of the sanctity attributed to labor. Man, created in God's image (Gen. 1:26), is called upon to be, like him, a creative artisan. As God created the world in six days and rested on the seventh, so is man, the "crown of creation," commanded to do: "Six days you shall labor and do all your work [melakhtekha], but the seventh day is a sabbath of the Lord your God: you shall not do any work [melakhah]" (Ex. 20:10–11). It is also on the basis of this verse that the sages determine that "even as the Torah was given as a covenant, so was work [melakhah] given as a covenant" (ARN¹, ch. 11).

The life situation of the early halakhah was the life of peasants in Palestine, whose worldview included confidence in divine Providence, a sense of the inviolability of interpersonal relations, and a practical devotion to the common good. Their economy was tied to the rhythms of nature. The pious features of their emerging utopianism came from a heartfelt faith.

At first no distinction was made, in this idyllic society, between the sage and the peasant: "If a man had in his house untithed figs and [he remembered them] while he was in the house of study or in the field . . ." (M. Demai 7:5). It was a society based upon the tilling of the soil.

The sages saw the peasant's life of labor as both a matter of destiny and an ideal:

Said Rabbi Levi: Once, when Abraham was still going about his business in Aram Naharayim and Aram-Nahor, he saw [the local people] eating and drinking and reveling. He said: May my lot not be in this land. But when he reached the Ladder of Tyre and saw [the inhabitants] weeding at weeding time and hoeing at hoeing time, he said: May my lot be in this land.

(Gen. R. 39:8)

"Those who cultivate the world (meyashvei olam)" are seen by the talmudic sages as being the opposite of "those who destroy the world (mevalei olam)" (BT Sot. 22a)—a dichotomy not far removed from that between the "wheat" and the "thorns":

> Said Rabbi Ḥanina ben Pazi: "These thorns are not sown nor can they be weeded out; they spring up of their own accord. But as for this wheat, see how much anguish and effort must be expended before it begins to sprout."
>
> (Gen. R. 45:4)

Here manual labor is identified with man's power to create and give form, which implies that it is also a channel for exercising his ability to choose. In rabbinic anthropology, evil arises from weakness, indecisiveness, and submission, while good is a product of creative human responsibility.

The profound esteem accorded physical labor was characteristic of the entire rabbinic period. To be sure, there were times when, because of historical circumstances, its status diminished, but these episodes do not figure prominently in tannaitic or amoraic literature.

The sages view man's constructive, cultivative activity as a moral good. There were even individuals and sects among them for whom it had a religious sanctity. This view receives full expression in a text attributed to "the Sages of Yavneh," where the tillers of the soil play a role equal to that of the scholars, "those who dwell in the Tent of Torah":

> I am God's creature, and my fellow [the nonstudent] is God's creature. My work is in town, and his work is in the country. I rise early for my work, and he rises early for his work. Just as he does not presume to do my work, so I do not presume to do his work. Will you say I do much and he does little? We have learned [BT Men. 110a], "One may do much or one may do little; it is all one, provided he directs his heart to heaven."
>
> (BT Ber. 17a)

But the sages not only expressed their ideas beautifully; they also had a beautiful way of putting them into practice. Quite a few of them did physical work, either as day laborers or as independent artisans. Conditions made it impossible to live exclusively on the study and teaching of Torah, and there were also those who refused on principle to live off public funds, preferring to support themselves by their own labor. It has been argued that rabbinic sermons in praise of work were intended, among other things, to shore up the social status of those rabbis who were workers or artisans.

To sum up, one may speak of the rabbinic approach to the commandment of labor as having three bases:

(1) The spiritual/moral basis: labor elevates man and provides an outlet for his creativity. The development of his good side gives man deep satisfaction and keeps him from succumbing to his evil impulses and degenerating. "You shall enjoy the fruit of your labors; you shall be happy and you shall prosper" (Ps. 128:2).

(2) The social basis: labor settles the planet and builds human society.

(3) The religious basis: labor is man's assigned task in the world. Through it, he fulfills the divine command and is thus privileged to walk in God's ways and draw closer to him.

Rabbinic expressions of the value of labor are rooted in analogous expressions in biblical culture. While in many areas rabbinic interpretations of and expansions upon scriptural ideas change them radically, such is not the case with the idea of labor as human destiny.

It would be reasonable to assume that during the period of exile, when the people of Israel did not dwell in its own land or bear full responsibility for its own path in history, the value of labor was diminished in Jewish eyes. But up until the twelfth or thirteenth century, Jewish spiritual leaders continue to proclaim as an ideal the mingling of sacred law and learning, on the one hand, with deeds and work on the other. Maimonides writes:

> Anyone who resolves to engage in Torah and live off charity rather than work has committed sacrilege, brought scorn upon the Torah, and dimmed the light of religion, to his own detriment; he has removed himself from the world. For it is forbidden in this world to derive [material] benefit from the words of the Torah. The Sages say: "Anyone who benefits from the words of the Torah brings about his own destruction" [M. Avot, 4:17]. They further charge us: "Do not make of them a crown for your own self-aggrandizement or a spade with which to dig" [ibid, 4:7]. And they command us: "Love labor and hate mastery" [ibid, 1:10]. "All [study of] Torah that is not combined with work is futile and brings sin in its wake" [ibid, 2:2], and [one who would only study] will end up robbing his fellow human beings.

> (MT Hil. Talmud Torah 3:10)

The same spirit is evident in Maimonides' *Commentary on the Mishnah,* in his references to M. Avot 4:5 and other passages.

A similar trend of thought is prevalent at the time of the Tosafists in the twelfth and thirteenth centuries. Thereafter there is a growing tendency toward study without practical activity and work. In most Diaspora countries Jews engaged less and less in crafts and agriculture, and in recent centuries occupied themselves principally in various forms of trade and in services and intellectual occupations. In the process, physical work was less regarded as a thing of value and became marginal. Those Jews who engaged in it did not enjoy high status among their own people.

The Zionist idea, in its various forms, had a revolutionary effect on the course of Jewish history. Although the spirit of Judaism had shown a capacity for renewal and development through all the vicissitudes of the past, it now seemed to many to be frozen in the grip of the ultra-Orthodox "guardians of the walls," who stood opposed to history, preferring eternal to temporal life and contenting themselves with the passive expectation of the End of Days. To the Zionists, the faithful could no longer be seen as the legitimate spiritual leadership of the Jewish people. Rather, it was in the Zionist enterprise—as its advocates saw it—that the creative Jewish spirit would experience a renaissance.

The movement for a return to Zion was born out of a negation of ritual, which seemed to many to have lost its grounding in faith. It was a rebellion against the pathologies of exile: overspiritualization and detachment from responsibility for one's own history. "[There] came young men with new tidings," Abraham J. Heschel writes. "They no longer wanted to live on miracles; they wanted freedom, a natural way of life. They did not want to live spiritually off the past; they refused to live on bequests; they wanted to begin anew."[1] After many generations of nurturing an abstract homeland in their own midst, these Jews, the Zionists, undertook to bring the "heavenly land of Israel" down to earth.

Zionist thinking had to be tied to realization, Zionist *midrash* (teaching) to *ma'aseh* (action). Thus labor Zionism became the moving force in the revival of the Jewish people. The founding fathers of the Jewish labor movement in Palestine saw Zionism as the return of the Jews to the kind of history that is rooted in the land. What this meant in practice was "intense efforts to found a Jewish society that would have a productive life of its own," writes Gershom Scholem, describing the Third Aliyah (wave of immigration from 1919 to 1923) in his volume of memoirs.[2] Young Jews who felt a sense of Jewish responsibility hoped to see their highest aspirations realized in labor on the land and for the land.

The Hebrew worker translated longing for the return to Zion into devotion to labor. He saw himself as taking responsibility for creating a country and rehabilitating a people. In the terminology of the pioneering movement labor is understood in terms of building: the workers spoke of "building the country" and "building a new society" as well as creating a "new man." They saw themselves as the "builders of the people."

The founding fathers' vision of labor drew upon the literature of Israel's past, particularly the Bible and rabbinic works. Alongside these sources there was a feeling of familiarity with the Ḥasidic worldview, in which *avodah begashmiut* (service to God in the material world) is a concrete value-concept.

The ideas of man being created in the image of God and playing a central role in the world; his consequent responsibility; his power of decision, freedom of choice, and creative ability—notions that are fundamental to Judaism's view of man—provided a basis for the efforts of the Second Aliyah (1904–1914).

The Zionist vision of labor was initially expressed by isolated individuals. They were scattered and few when they started their "conquest of labor." But by the strength and stubbornness of their vision they brought Jewish history to a turning point. One of these *haluẓim* (pioneers), as they were called, describes the feelings and the dreams that characterized the early days of the labor movement in Palestine:

> In their heart of hearts they reassured themselves with a mystical hope, opposed to all logic and experience, that after them would come great encampments, people in the thousands, and receive from them the new Torah of the conquest of the land through labor; that the latter would share their thoughts about the redemption of the people and the redemption of the land. And the multitudes, the thousands, could change the face of the people and the land, turning an impoverished people, a people of middlemen and brokers, into a people conquering its own land and creating it anew.[3]

In the reality of their lives there was a transition from the conquest of labor to its sanctification; the joy of shared labor provided the underpinnings of a working way of life and the network of workers' settlements, the kibbutzim and moshavim, which in turn served as the "cornerstone" (Zech. 4:7) of the upbuilding of Palestine. Without labor, then, Zionism would have remained a dream and never become a historical reality.

Labor was seen as the Zionist destiny and the essence of the Zionist vision. The attitude of the worker-pioneers toward labor was characterized by dedication and even extreme devotion. It played a role in their lives analogous to the role of prayer in the lives of the Ḥasidim, something in which one invests the whole force of his personality and all his longings. The same spiritual energies that had informed the traditional Jew's service of God (*avodat ha-shem*) were now put to the service of the creative enterprise of worker-settlers.

How much of self-sacrifice, of love for the people, of Sanctification of the Holy Name are found in the modern Jews, in their will to suffer in order to help! The zeal of the pious Jews was transferred to their emancipated sons and grandsons. The fervor and yearning of the Ḥasidim, the ascetic obstinacy of the Kabbalists, the inexorable logic of the Talmudists, were reincarnated in the supporters of modern Jewish movements. Their belief in new ideals was infused with age-old piety.[4]

While himself helping to put into practice the values of the Second Aliyah, Aharon David Gordon also gave original intellectual expression to them, drawing upon the age-old Jewish spiritual heritage. His writing, which enjoys a unique place in modern Jewish thought, includes comprehensive discussions of the creative value of labor. In the act of creation, he says, all the powers of the mind and the body are joined in an inner unity, which then becomes an expression of the fullness of man's world: "In creating, he gives his all and receives his all." Creation requires special inner concentration, rooted and focused in "the sudden illumination of the soul, the brilliant flash of perception, a kind of sublime abundance suddenly poured forth without man knowing whence it comes or how . . . the same power once known as the holy spirit, inspiration, and the like, and referred to today as intuition."[5] This illumination, described in what amounts to kabbalistic terminology, is an outgrowth of the fact that "human feelings are more and more attuned to existence itself and all that existence reveals to everything alive and everything that is. This is the origin of religious, moral, and poetic feelings, of all higher human sentiments."[6] Or in another version, also kabbalistic in its language: "Man's creativity" is the fruit "of an awakening from above, of heavenly bounty."[7]

In Gordon's teaching, the essence of the act of creation lies in man's deliberate arousal of himself against the unthinking routines of his present life, an aspiration that begins with the desire of the individual to be faithful to his true self in the way he constructs his life. Gordon distinguishes between "creation through contraction" (yeẓirah she-be-ẓimẓum) and "creation through expansion" (yeẓirah she-be-hitpashtut). The two are distinguished from each other "not so much by the act of creation itself as by the relationship of the soul to life, to the world around it, and to the content of the creative act, and by the source within the soul from which the creativity derives."[8]

In "creation through expansion," man breaks out of his own constrictedness and achieves oneness with the thing he creates. His creative activity is in relation to spheres external to him, the worlds of nature and man. "It is like a cosmic revelation that takes place in a momentary private vision, a revelation out of nowhere, unanticipated, as if one's life were suddenly merged with the totality of creation and as if all of creation were suddenly merged with oneself."[9] By virtue of this connection the creative person is made privy to revelation, to a spiritual rebirth. This illuminating discovery Gordon refers to elsewhere as "a moment of eternity." The reciprocal tie with the universe, radiated outward through a divine presence, entails not only a spiritual relationship but also a practical one, in which "man is a real comrade to nature in producing life and a real partner to it in creation.[10]

"Creation through contraction" is a form of self-expression in which the creating individual is walled up within himself and "grows with his shell." A bifurcation thus arises between man's creative side and his humanness; his greatness as a creator does not necessarily mean human greatness. Creation through contraction is also termed *mechanical activity (maaseh mekhani)* or simply *doing (asiyah)*.

The transition "from the world of creation [through expansion] to the world of [mere] doing is the transition from living labor rooted in the devotion of the heart and soul to mechanical work that consists of little more than cogitation and busywork [*maaseh*]."[11] "Mere doing" is characterized by the alienation of the worker from his work. It is activity with a superficial, utilitarian purpose, whose worth is measured in terms of monetary compensation, prestige, and so on. The difference between creating and doing is like that between *homo creator* and *homo faber*.

Man's efforts can be made creative wherever there is the possibility of "renewal, ceaseless coming-into-being. . . . The light of human life derives not from what he takes ready made or even from what he gives others ready made, but rather in what he creates."[12]

The creative life does not readily brook a distinction between manual and intellectual work. "What we seek in labor," Gordon wrote, "is life, matter as well as spirit; and if we are true lovers of life we must not discriminate between types of devotees—physical work in the name of socialism and intellectual work in the name of the nation."[13] For him, Zionism is "a living creation," not to be cut in two "any more than one cuts living creatures in two, saying, 'This is the spirit and this is the flesh.'" Creation encompasses all of life: "The whole spirit that is alive within us, all the powers of our bodies and souls, are in need of correction, so that they find expression in the fullness of our lives. In the creation of our lives from beginning to end, in every kind of work, in every form of labor, in every act, just as in the things of the heart and mind."[14]

Like Gordon, most of the other leading figures of the Second Aliyah saw creativity as a motive force. The demands they made upon themselves were nourished by an inner moral imperative. Labor for them was a destiny and a heartfelt obligation, not merely an apodictic law or doctrine, set forth by society, a party, or a movement and confronting man from without. They saw creative activity as the product of an inner drive toward elevation and meaning. One can sense in their approach, too, the life-affirming spirit that is fundamental to Judaism. The creative life was, for them, a mode of self-discovery, an expression of man's inner superiority. They also saw as creative the contact between souls, the clinging of one spirit to another. Individuation and collaboration seemed to them different aspects of a single creative process. There is an echo of this idea in Tzvi Schatz's essay of 1915 "On the Commune":

> We shall not always know how to bring to life that which is hidden within our souls. But there are times when a mere touch of a magic wand can awaken the modest hidden spring. . . . To touch secretly and bring what is precious out into the light of day before it withers, before it is beyond reach. . . .
> The life of the commune is of necessity filled with such moments. They teach us that most exalted of arts, that religion of art, to which the soul has long aspired. . . . Certain privileged individuals are able then, with their brushes, their pens, or their violin bows, to create life, while we, to the extent that that creative power still burns and bubbles within us, can pour it out in a glance. A single, shining, wordless glance, heart to heart, mediated and unintended, . . . ties one heart to another with strings of purity and mutual understanding[15].

And if we grasp the nature of the organism in which personal relationships and responsibilities, communal labor, and the idea of perfecting and redeeming the world as a whole were brought together, we can discern the outlines of ḥaluẓic utopianism.

One could not become a worker without undergoing a personal transformation. The latter was fed and fertilized by inner spiritual resources and promptings, among them a longing for social change and national redemption. In fact, this vision did not limit itself to the organic interaction of this one people with its sons. Those who conceived and propagated the vision saw the unification of wisdom and action—a legacy of rabbinic Judaism—as a precondition for human betterment in general: "Without combining the man of the spirit and the man of deeds in a single, new human type," Berl Katznelson maintained, "it is doubtful whether the enlightened society for which mankind longs can ever come into being."[16] What is being expressed here, clearly, is a desire for the redemption of humanity as a whole.

Down through the ages, Jewish culture had given rise to a series of ideal human types: the halakhic man, the *talmid ḥakham* (scholar), the *ẓaddik* (saint), the *ḥasid* (pious one). Now the labor-Zionist movement had posited a new ideal type, unprecedented in Jewish spiritual history: the *ḥaluẓ* (pioneer). The ḥaluẓic way of life is based upon the idea of "the day of small beginnings" (Zech. 4:10), a devotion to the seemingly petty, gray details of daily activity; a life given over to steady, plodding, anonymous effort as opposed to daring but isolated acts of heroism.

Unless the productive person identifies completely with his activity, such a way of life is impossible. "Each drop of brow's sweat paved/The way of the Lord," Bialik says, in his poem "The Blessing of a People," which became the anthem of the labor movement in Palestine. As the generation comes to an end these creative giants are described as

> Gnarled trunks, powerfully thick,
> Growing in warm soil,
> Stubbornly, patiently,
> The stuff which carbon
> Unwittingly uses
> To form its diamond sparks.[17]

"The day of small beginnings" means spadework, done in the conviction that without "peace of soul" there can be no saving the world. The worker-pioneers saw self-realization as being of fateful significance for Jewish historical continuity. A single small act of redemption in the long-suffering land of Israel was weightier in their eyes than all of the Diaspora's revolutionary rhetoric. For them, *avodah be-gashmiut* (serving [God] in the concrete, material world) meant applying themselves to a microcosm. The cardinal principle of devotion to "small beginnings" was that neither the nation nor the world could be healed until the individual was healed. And the healing of the individual began, as Rabbi Naḥman of Bratslav taught, with "the healing of the heart" (*tikkun ha-lev*).[18] This philosophy of life is rooted in early Jewish mysticism. The *Sefer Yeẓirah (Book of Creation)*, which according to Gershom Scholem was written between the third and the sixth centuries C.E., already speaks about man as a microcosm.

The idea of beginning with the fundamentals, with inwardness, appears in an expression coined by Katznelson as emblematic of the path chosen by the Hebrew labor movement: *mi-bifnim* (from within). It was to "healing the heart" and "peace of the soul" as points of departure that Gordon had referred when he wrote:

The principal distinguishing feature of what we are creating lies in the fact that each of us must begin by recreating himself. And this is the main thing. Every one of us must look deep into himself. . . . He is bound to recognize that it is in our own torn souls that the national rupture took place. And so let each one come and make himself whole, bringing peace to his own spirit. . . . Thus, each in his own way, shall we arrive at a pure national self.[19]

Such a path, based on long-range inner commitment, is sustained by redemptive impulses. It is a practical utopianism that constantly reaches out to the timeless, to the unseen horizon; its aim is the fashioning of a model society and the perfection of the world.

Each ḥaluẓ pursues his unique individual path in the common undertaking. The ḥaluẓ movement, Katznelson said in 1918, is perhaps the only modern movement centered not on a particular leadership cadre or program but on the life and work of the rank and file. "The comrade is [our] purpose. His life, efforts, failures, victories, weaknesses and strengths— these are what make up the movement."[20] The labor Zionist movement believed that in taking the fate of the Jewish people on its shoulders and assuming responsibility for its future it was contributing to the perfection of the family of man as a whole. "Zionism could not have arisen, and will not arise, in a world that denies justice and liberty to anyone created in God's image. Nor shall [this movement ever] deny these human values, for in doing so it would pronounce sentence on itself,"[21] declared Katznelson. It was he who had found the roots of labor Zionism's "messianic-humanistic" program in historic Judaism: "Our forefathers in Sura and Pumbedita, in the dark, walled ghettos, in the cellars of the Inquisition era, everywhere persecuted and ostracized, saw the redemption of Israel as a universal event, of significance to all mankind, one that would lead to the perfection of the world under the kingship of the Almighty."[22]

The spirit of the classical sources of Jewish culture echoes throughout the writings of the labor movement, even when the role of these sources qua sources is not acknowledged.

The great teachers of labor Zionism understood the secret of linking past and future. "It is not a new seed," said Gordon,

but a tree with many roots and branches that is about to be planted in the soil prepared for it, there to live and grow once again. If we are to be renewed, we must accept labor as a new value in our lives, as the foundation of all the spiritual wealth we shall acquire in the future, but we must not abandon the spiritual wealth that is already ours.[23]

In his view, the ḥaluẓic renewal had to be conscious of its sources and turn to them for nourishment.

> To educate, to revive the Jew, we will have to start with the fundamentals, with man. The Jew cannot be a complete human being without being a complete Jew. The assimilationist is mistaken in thinking that he becomes more of a human being by becoming less of a Jew. Just the opposite: he is less of a human being, and thus also less of a Jew. . . . To the extent that the Jew destroys the natural Jewish core of his soul, he puts in its place an unnatural national core, becoming, that is, an unnatural Russian, an unnatural German, etc.[24]

Since the second decade of the State of Israel, and particularly since the changes brought about by the Six-Day War of June 1967, there has been a decline in the values that shaped prestate Palestinian Jewish society. The values of the labor movement have increasingly been cast aside (the flight from manual labor being only one expression of this development). No longer are the worker and the pioneer held up as ideal types. The labor movement itself has become impoverished, failing to produce a new generation of guiding spirits, and has lost its preeminent position in Israeli society and in the Jewish world at large. The result could be disastrous for the quality of life in Israel and perhaps even for the future of Zionism. Israeli society cannot meaningfully survive, cannot fulfill its true destiny, merely as a "kingdom of priests and a holy nation" (Ex. 19:6), relying upon others to do its work and be its "hewers of wood and drawers of water" (Josh. 9:21). The longing to return to Zion was a longing for a just and moral society in the land of Israel. Only such a society can create a Jewish culture that is rooted in the heritage of the past even as it comes to grips with the existential circumstances of our own day.

REFERENCES

1. Abraham J. Heschel, *The Earth Is the Lord's* (1966), 103.
2. Gershom Scholem, *From Berlin to Jerusalem* (1980), 166.
3. Shlomo Lavi, *Aliyato shel Shalom Layish* (1964), 55.
4. Heschel, op. cit., 103–104.
5. "Ha-Adam ve-ha-Teva," in *Kitvei A. D. Gordon* (1952), 2, 149ff.
6. "Le-Birur ha-Hevdel bein ha-Yahadut ve-ha-Noẓrut," op. cit., 2, 278.
7. Ibid., 295.
8. "Ha-Adam v-ha-Teva," op. cit., 2, 151.
9. Ibid., 152.
10. Ibid.

11. "Le-Birur Emdatenu," op. cit., 1, 330.
12. "Ha-Adam ve-ha-Teva," op. cit., 2, 151.
13. "Le-Birur Emdatenu," op. cit., 1, 225.
14. "Me-Kozer Ruaḥ," op. cit., 1, 142.
15. Tzvi Schatz, *Al Gevul ha-Demamah* (1929), 94ff.
16. Berl Katznelson, "Adamah le-Am ve-Ruaḥ ha-Am," in *Ktavim* (1950), 12, 50.
17. Abraham Balaban, "Niẓuẓot," in *Devar,* Sept. 14, 1980.
18. *Likkutei Moharan Kama* 60:6.
19. *Kitvei A. D. Gordon* (1952), 1, 543.
20. *Sefer Aliyat ha-Noar* (1941), 324–26.
21. Ibid.
22. Ibid.
23. "Universitah Ivrit," in *Kitvei A. D. Gordon* (1952), 1, 170.
24. Ibid., 265ff.

BIBLIOGRAPHY

M. Ayali, *Labor and Work in the Talmud and Midrash* (1984).
A. D. Gordon, *Selected Essays,* F. Burnce, tr. (1938).
Max Kadushin, *The Rabbinic Mind* (1965).
Anita Shapira, *Berl: The Biography of a Socialist Zionist,* Haya Galai, tr. (1984).

Zionism

צִיּוֹנוּת

Ben Halpern

Zionism is a nationalist movement differing from others because it reflects the history of a people uniquely identified with a world religion. Its purpose was to restore the dispersed, stateless Jews to sovereign independence in the land from which tradition taught they had been exiled by God's will as a punishment for their sins. Hence, Zionism was challenged to define itself either as a rebellion against the divine decree of exile, or a fulfillment of the divine promise of redemption.

Zionism arose at a time when the traditional status of the Jews in Christian states had been called into question by the Enlightenment and, in some countries, radically altered by emancipation. Before then, where tolerated, Jews had lived as a corporate body, subject to the conditions of a contract with their overlord and governing their internal affairs autonomously, with rabbinic law as a guide. This autonomy, widely abridged under the pressure of enlightened absolute monarchs, was abandoned in Western countries, together with corporate status, for the sake of emancipation.

But the new nation-states had two options, not one, for dealing with the

Jews. They could make the Jews citizens of the state and members of the nation individually—but only if they did not regard Jews as aliens. The other option, used as a defensible rationale by opponents of emancipation who contended that the Jews were an alien nation, was to segregate Jews in a province or country of their own. In response, many Jews declared that they were not aliens in their birthplace or domicile; this entailed defining positions ideologically opposed to Zionism before Zionism arose. They denied that Jews were a nation, or could properly organize politically in partisan self-interest, and they renounced the traditional hope of restoration in Zion or interpreted it as merely symbolic—applicable, perhaps, to the French Revolution.

In eastern Europe, there was no emancipation in the nineteenth century, and when many concluded that there was no hope for basic rights in their time, conditions suitable for the rise of Jewish nationalism had appeared. Traditional autonomous institutions of the community in Russia had no legal power, and those elders and notables whose power rested on their collaboration with oppressive government policies sacrificed their authority. In Rumania, the newly independent nation-state simply declared the Jews an alien people and denied them vital civil rights as well as citizenship. But in these areas rabbinical authority, both Mitnaggedic and Hasidic, remained effective, even though without government support or in defiance of the constituted authorities. The traditionalist community that the rabbis led had its own inhibitions against anything like Zionism. The Sabbatean and Frankist apostasies had confirmed their view that the restoration to Zion must be left strictly to God's providence, while Jews awaited the appointed time in pious quietism. Active intervention in history, implied in nationalism, spelled pseudo-messianism.

Yet both modern Western Jews and Eastern traditionalists were active in Palestine in ways that anticipated later Zionist projects. The *Yishuv,* the Jewish settlement in the four holy cities of Palestine—Jerusalem, Hebron, Safed, and Tiberias—increased in the nineteenth century at a rate that brought congestion, disease, and the other ills of poverty to a point that continually strained the resources of the charity upon which most of the community, including virtually all the Ashkenazi European immigrants, depended. Western Jewish philanthropists, seeking to bring the benefits of their own emancipated, enlightened condition to the benighted East, provided medical care and vocational and general (secular) schooling as the indicated remedies that would help convert the dependent *Yishuv* into a self-supporting community. They pursued methods of private lobbying and diplomatic intercession in aid of these goals, and bought land on which to build housing, hospitals, schools, and even farms. The traditionalist leaders of the *Yishuv* also lent their hand to those efforts that could improve the living conditions and solvency of their followers, but the Ashkenazi rabbinate in Jerusalem and elsewhere offered a stern resistance to the introduction of secular studies, which were likely to divert men from the holy studies and pious devotions that should absorb them totally in the holy land. There were other rabbis, however, who saw in the return of Jews to a secular life in the holy land a way to renew the observance of certain sacred laws applicable only there, and this they saw as a prerequisite stage, a preliminary part, of the messianic era.

Thus, when Zionism arose in the 1880s, there were already in effect the kinds of efforts it intended to pursue: retraining rootless Jews (in Yiddish *luftmentshen,* lit., men of air) in "productive" trades; acquiring and resettling land in Palestine, and seeking through discreet political pressure and persuasion to gain Turkish assent to these activities. But the supporters of such efforts, both emancipated and traditionalist, acted on assumptions implicitly opposed to the ideology Zionism would announce; the rise of Zionism challenged these assumptions and forced decisions. Opposition in principle, not necessary to stress earlier, now emerged in sharp anti-Zionist statements from both modernist and traditionalist quarters. Their commitment in practice to proto-Zionist projects in Palestine required them either to redefine their intentions in clear contrast to the Zionist programs or to seek a basis of cooperation with a redefined, moderate version of Zionism.

Historic Zionism arose through the conversion to secular nationalism of Russian Jewish intellectuals who had grown detached from the rigorous tradition and, instead, committed their hopes to the promise of an (evolving or revolutionary) enlightened Russia of the future. The 1881–1882 pogroms were a trauma that shook the faith of that radical generation, especially after some revolutionaries hailed the pogroms as harbingers of popular uprisings against the regime. Those most severely shaken now returned as penitents to their ethnic community, but not, in most cases, in religious contrition. They came with a new sense of themselves as "national" Jews, possessing a secular Jewish identity. In this way a radically new self-consciousness was injected into the stream of Jewish history.

The secular nationalists had at first no clearly defined ideology, but only a clear emotional response to their recent experience and hence to the Jewish condition. What they felt most sharply was acute revulsion against Jewish helplessness and their dependency on gentile toleration and good will. In traditional terms readily available to them, this meant a revived sense of the Exile. But they now experienced this concept as an immediate, and shameful, reality—a perception decisively opposed to that of the tradition-alists, for whom Exile was a mythic idea consecrated in rituals of sublimated guilt, or of the modernists, who either denied Exile outright or transformed its meaning into a holy mission to enlighten the Gentiles. Against the quietism of the one and the optimistic accommodation of the other vis-à-vis the subjugated Jewish condition, the secular Zionists placed their new doctrine of "auto-emancipation"—a secular, activist version of the tradi-tional idea of redemption, requiring Jews to liberate themselves and not simply await divine intervention or the progress of gentile enlightenment.

How a self-emancipated Jewish nation might be constructed remained initially indefinite. The Zionists harbored many romantic and utopian notions of its structure, reflecting by contrast what was concretely real to them in their particular situations—the various features of the condition of Exile that oppressed them. They were ready to approve whatever inherently opposed their known ills and to try any method that seemed to lead to the goal.

Such indefinite intentions made possible cooperation, or even a merger, between the secular nationalists and others concerned with the Jewish set-tlement in Palestine. In eastern Europe, the philo-Zionist movement that arose, *Ḥibbat Ẓion* (Love of Zion), was a combination of traditionalists, long committed to support the growing *Yishuv,* and newly recruited secular nationalists. Eastern European immigrants to Western countries brought Zionism with them, among other Old Country values, and were joined by leaders drawn from Western circles. The movement labored under frustrat-ing handicaps in the 1880s and 1890s, making the compromises essential to this cooperation seem unavoidable. But these compromises nevertheless restricted the appeal of Zionism to potential supporters in each of the coop-erating parties.

The initial impulse to cooperate in *Ḥibbat Ẓion* was sustained by the pen-itent mood of secular Zionists, which led some traditionalists to hope they might be won back to piety. These hopes soon turned into demands, par-ticularly upon those who wished to settle as farmers in Palestine and depended on *Ḥibbat Ẓion* for material aid, and the pressures were soon resented, on grounds of conscience and also of practicality, by secularists. Both sides, moreover, were under attack by critics of their own persuasion in matters of belief who condemned their partnership as a betrayal. A many-sided Zionist debate developed on the relation between Jewish nationalism and Jewish religion.

A central figure in the debate was Asher Ginzberg, who wrote under the modest pen name "One of the People," Aḥad Ha-Am. He was acutely conscious of the defects Zionists typically condemned in others: the "slavery within freedom" of Western assimilationist Jews and the inert submission of Eastern Jews—both to an oppressive Exile and to their own "petrified" tradition, no longer able to bind the whole people together, let alone guide them in freely choosing their future. He gave primacy, therefore, to restoring an active national consensus, based on the revival of Hebrew, for a free, secular culture; his biting criticism of the contemporary Zionist settlement in Palestine rested on the argument that in its dependency on a single, paternalist philanthropist, Baron Edmond de Rothschild, the new *Yishuv* betrayed its authentic purpose, which was to become the nuclear center of a living, Hebraic, Jewish culture. He was not by any means a militant anti-clerical agitator, but his critique and the projects he and his adherents launched in Palestine and the Diaspora, especially the modern nationalist Hebrew schools, aroused fierce opposition among traditionalists, including those who were Zionists.

Aḥad Ha-Am came under attack from another side as well. With ruthless logic, he drew extreme conclusions from a situation all Zionists had to acknowledge. The pogroms that initially set off the Zionist awakening also precipitated a spurt of emigration from Russia, which continued in mounting volume thereafter. The Zionists originally conceived of themselves as an integral part of that demographic movement and hoped to direct it to its proper destination, Palestine, where alone a concentrated Jewish settlement could achieve the national goal. But, of course, the migration went in other directions, and the Palestine settlement bore no relation to the need for new homes for the Russian outflow. Aḥad Ha-Am bluntly rejected the whole issue, saying that Zionism was meant to solve the "problem of Judaism," not the "problems of Jews." This, so directly put, was not an approach that could satisfy the ardor of Zionists stirred by their immediate experience of Jewish suffering; nor could the program it entailed, one of slow and cautious preparatory labors, quench their activist thirst.

Young radical Zionists irked by Aḥad Ha-Am's cautious, skeptical gradualism were also likely to be those who rebelled against his line of cultural policy, made starkly clear in his editorial conduct of *Hashilo'ah,* the journal he made the prime organ of the Hebrew national revival. Aḥad Ha-Am, seeking common values in the tradition of Jewish culture that could cement a new consensus in a secular time, declared a commitment to absolutely impartial justice to be the quintessential element, unchanging in all the variations of Jewish history. He opposed this ethos, following in the footsteps of many predecessors, to Hellenic aestheticism and to Christian altruism or, as he called it, "inverted egoism." The consequences for editorial policy were that he was inclined to reject mere "art for art's sake" belles lettres and favored heavily essays of substance and weight conducive to national improvement. By this attitude he provoked the opposition of the *Zeirim* (lit., youths), a group of writers who took a strikingly different position.

The hero of this set of litterateurs was Friedrich Nietzsche, a popular figure in the German avant-garde of the student years of these intellectuals. Imbued with Zionist pessimism, they were particularly receptive to Nietzsche's observations on Jewish "slave morality" and his countercultural "revaluation of values." Micha Josef Berdyczewski, a leader among them, subverted the whole purpose of Aḥad Ha-Am's search for the quintessence of Jewish culture with his own far more extensive researches in the tradition. All the *Zeirim* disavowed the search for quintessential common Jewish values and demanded full freedom to render in Hebrew the whole modern experience and the entire treasury of human culture, whatever its source. Berdyczewski went further and ransacked the Jewish biblical and midrashic literature, finding traces and reconstructing portraits of the countercultural heroes disavowed or virtually suppressed in the normative tradition. With this circle, there began the fascination not merely with Ḥasidism but also with the antinomian Shabbetai Zevi and the Frankists that flowered in the work of Gershom Scholem, as well as the appreciation of the Bible as a kind of Homeric epic out of which, together with the midrashim, a heritage of pagan-style legendary heroes could be recovered.

Theodor Herzl came to such people as a long-looked-for answer to the impasse of Zionism. He restored the movement's élan through his campaign to gain by political action a legal base for the transfer and settlement en masse of Jews in Palestine, setting aside the small-scale "infiltration" that had previously occupied Zionist societies, until the charter he sought could be obtained. The excitement he generated in this way was sustained by the annual congresses the Zionists held under his direction. In this framework, the ideological factions among the older Zionists—and some new trends such as the socialist Zionism that arose out of the revolutionary mood in Russia and revulsion (mixed with cold Marxist analysis) against the Jewish socio-economic plight—hardened into organized political parties. Thus, old issues about the relation of religion and Zionism were transferred to the new arena, where they were much more subject to calculations of immediate political advantage.

Herzl at first welcomed the accession of traditionalists to his Congress. He had a romantic appreciation (like his taste for the aristocratic style) for the symbolic value of the clergy to a movement like Zionism, and after the German rabbis had protested against the convening of the first Zionist Congress, he needed the attendance of Eastern rabbis at the second as a legit-imation. But he soon found the quarrels between the Orthodox, who wanted to control all Zionist cultural work or rule it out altogether, and the secular Zionists of Aḥad Ha-Am's persuasion, who wanted the Congress at large to control it, to be a gratuitous annoyance, and sharply limited the debate. By virtually yielding to the Orthodox minimum demand to exclude Jewish cul-ture from the scope of Zionist activity, Herzl won the loyalty of some tra-ditionalists (though others joined the ranks of the anti-Zionist opposition after the second Congress). They could join him in activities to meet the material needs of Jews so long as he avoided issues of their spiritual welfare. After Herzl's death, however, his policy on religious matters was gradually superseded, and the Congress eventually approved a program of cultural activity. This again led some of the traditionalists to leave the Zionist move-ment, while others developed a new basis for remaining—one that has per-sisted into the politics of Israel today. They demanded that the Zionist movement respect religious customs in its public functions and run parallel cultural programs for secularists and traditionalists, the latter independently controlled by them; and they made clear their intention to work within the Zionist framework to make rabbinic law prevail for all and rule the future Jewish state.

Herzl's other achievement was to convert Zionism into a more universal Jewish movement, bringing a larger involvement of Western Jews. Their motivation, like his own, reflected the offended pride of emancipated men who found, having experienced the rise of political anti-Semitism, that they were not accepted as equals in the nation-state, and concluded that the Jewish problem was their own and not simply the eastern Europeans'. Few, however, took so simple and direct a view as Herzl, who acted unequivo-cally as a Jewish statesman, a national Jew. Others, like Herzl, held a Jewish state in Palestine (or elsewhere, according to some) to be the solution of the Jewish problem, and the proper response to modern anti-Semitism, but they stressed that eastern Europeans must go there to escape pogroms while they themselves lived in favored circumstances—in spite of anti-Semitic insults—and could not be expected to emigrate. They were loyal citizens of the nation-state, participants in the national culture of their home—whether or not fully accepted in the ruling nation.

A different attitude arose among a part of the Western Zionists, who sought a closer cultural bond with the eastern Europeans. This was con-nected, in many cases, with religious objections to the extent of the depar-ture from traditional Jewish practice in their community. Such circles in Germany and America were attracted to the writings of Aḥad Ha-Am; Mar-

Buber, in Germany, and Judah L. Magnes and Mordecai Kaplan, among others, in America, converted his secularist nationalism into an ethnicist (or *völkisch*) religiosity.

The creation of the State of Israel in 1948 converted Zionism from the dynamic myth of a dedicated minority to a convention generally shared among Jews. The defense and support of Israel amid the threats and hardships it still confronts have become institutional activities of the whole community, forming a major element in its social coherence in the Diaspora. Also, the Israeli community is both a symbol of ethnic Jewishness and a resource sustaining Jewish identity in an increasingly divided and diversely acculturated world Jewry.

But this very function is one of the factors inherently challenging Israel to a further test, conceived by some as explicitly transcendent, and in any case inescapable for a people rendered distinct from all others by its uniquely-possessed religious tradition: the test of converting a political victory over a condition of exile into a cultural and social redemption. Both critics and defenders necessarily judge Zionism by standards that guarantee its dynamic continuance under pressure, as often irritating as it is inspiriting.

BIBLIOGRAPHY

Arnold M. Eisen, *The Chosen People in America* (1983).
Ben Halpern, *The Idea of the Jewish State* (1961).
Arthur Hertzberg, ed., *The Zionist Idea* (1959).
Nathan Rotenstreich, *Tradition and Reality* (1972).
David Vital, *The Origins of Zionism* (1975).

Glossary

abbr.	abbreviation	Gr.	Greek
Aram.	Aramaic	Heb.	Hebrew
B.C.E.	Before the Common Era	lit.	literally
c.	circa	pl.	plural
C.E.	Common Era	sg.	singular
d.	died		

Abrabanel, Isaac (1437–1508) Portuguese, and later Italian, statesman, philosopher, and biblical exegete. His commentaries and other writings reveal a coherent philosophical system that treats issues of prophecy, history, politics, and eschatology. Among his works are expositions and refutations of Maimonides' *Guide of the Perplexed.*

Abrabanel, Judah (Leone Ebreo, also called **Leo Hebraeus**; c. 1460–after 1523) Portuguese, and later Italian, philosopher, Hebrew poet, and physician. His *Dialoghi di Amore* was one of the foremost metaphysical works of the Renaissance. Its central theme is love as the motivating force of the universe, seeking the union of all creatures with the sublime beauty and goodness—and the sublime intellect—of God.

Abraham ben David of Posquières (acronym **Rabad**; c. 1125–1198)   Provençal rabbinical authority. His many contributions to the various types of halakhic literature show precision in the conceptual method of talmudic study. He wrote critical scholia on Maimonides' *Mishneh Torah,* which are printed together with that work.

Abulafia, Abraham (1240–after 1291)   Spanish kabbalist. He studied Maimonidean philosophy, which he interpreted in terms of the kabbalah. He believed himself the recipient of prophetic inspiration and propagated a doctrine of mystical meditation and ecstasy.

Adon Olam ("Lord of the Universe")   Rhymed *piyyut* proclaiming the eternity and unity of God and his providence over man.

Adret, Solomon ben Abraham (acronym **Rashba**; c. 1235–c. 1310)   Spanish rabbi and scholar. His 11,000 responsa were a source of guidance for Jewish communities the world over, clarifying problems of biblical interpretation, religious philosophy, and the fundamentals of belief.

Aggadah (or **haggadah**; pl. **aggadot**; lit., "narrative")   Narrative part of rabbinic literature, or individual teaching thereof. The aggadah amplifies the narrative, historical, and ethical portions of the Bible. Aggadah and halakhah together comprise the oral Law.

Agnon, Shmuel Yosef (acronym **Shai**; 1888–1970)   Galician, and later Israeli, Hebrew writer; Nobel Laureate in Literature. One of the central figures in modern Hebrew fiction, his stories about pious Jews deal with contemporary spiritual concerns, such as the disintegration of traditional ways of life and the consequent loss of faith and identity.

Aḥad Ha-Am (pseudonym of **Asher Hirsch Ginsberg**; 1856–1927)   Russian Hebrew essayist, thinker, and leader of the Ḥibbat Zion movement. The founder of cultural Zionism, he defined Judaism in terms of its national identity and abiding religious values.

Akedah (lit., "binding")   Narrative in Genesis 22:1–19 in which, upon God's command, Abraham "bound" Isaac to the altar as a sacrifice. The *Akedah* became in Jewish tradition the supreme symbol of obedience to God's will.

Akiva (c. 50–135 C.E.)   *Tanna.* Probably the foremost scholar of his age, he exercised a decisive influence on the development of the halakhah. He was martyred by the Romans for his support of the Bar Kokhba revolt.

Albo, Joseph (15th century)   Spanish philosopher and preacher. He authored *Sefer ha-Ikkarim* ("Book of Principles"), a famous treatise on the articles of Jewish faith, attempting to show that the basic doctrines of the Jewish faith—the existence of God, divine revelation, and reward and punishment—bore the essential character of "divine law."

Almosnino, Moses (c. 151ᵊ c. 1580)   Salonikan rabbi, scholar, and preacher. His numerous publish ⸲ works include responsa, commentaries, sermons, and a popular ethical treatise.

Amichai, Yehuda (1924–   )   Israeli poet and novelist. His work marked the emergence of a new school of Hebrew poetry. It replaced the biblical model of poetic language with elements from the modern vernacular, and the classical sacred themes with the realia of Israeli society.

Amidah (lit., "standing")   Main prayer of the three daily services, recited while standing. The *Amidah* is known among Ashkenazim as *Shemoneh-Esreh* ("Eighteen") because of its eighteen original benedictions, and in talmudic sources is called *Ha-Tefillah* ("The Prayer" par excellence).

Amora (pl. **amoraim**; lit., "expounder" or "interpreter," i.e., of the Mishnah)   Designation of scholars from the completion of the Mishnah (c. 200 C.E.) until the completion of the Jerusalem and Babylonian Talmuds (end of the fourth and fifth centuries, respectively). The discussions of the *amoraim* form the bulk of both Talmuds and the various aggadic Midrashim.

Ani Ma'amin ("I believe")   Short, anonymous creed based on the thirteen articles of faith enumerated in Maimonides' Commentary on *Helek* (M. Sanh. 10:1). The article on belief in the Messiah was chanted by those taken to their death in the extermination camps during the Nazi Holocaust.

Arama, Isaac (c. 1420–1494)   Spanish rabbi, philosopher, and preacher. His influential work, *Akedat Yizhak* ("The Binding of Isaac"), seeks to demonstrate the superiority of revelation to reason through philosophical homilies on the Bible.

Arukh ha-Shulhan ("The Preparation of the 'Table'," i.e., of the *Shulhan Arukh*)   Halakhic work of novellae and rulings on the *Shulhan Arukh* by Jehiel Michal Epstein (1829–1908) of Belorussia. The author definitively updated the codification of the halakhah in his time.

Ashkenazi (pl. **Ashkenazim**)   Designation of original northwestern European Jewry and its descendants, or of their common cultural heritage.

Atlas, Samuel (1899–1977)   Lithuanian, and later American, philosopher and talmudist. He followed Hermann Cohen's critical idealism in his works on Jewish legal and philosophical thought.

Baeck, Leo (1873–1956)   German rabbi, religious thinker, and leader of Progressive Judaism. He held that ethical relations between men constitute true piety; at the same time, he preserved the importance of the Jewish religion by stressing its faith in God as the basis of ethics and its concern with improving the world.

Bahir, Sefer ha- ("Book of Brightness")   Earliest work of kabbalistic literature. It is a midrashic anthology containing mystical interpretations of biblical verses and of the ten *sefirot*. It appeared in southern France at the close of the twelfth century, although it may contain earlier elements.

Bahya ben Asher (13th century)   Spanish biblical exegete, preacher, and kabbalist. His popular commentary on the Torah, *Kad ha-Kemah* ("Jar of Flour"), draws from many genres of theological literature.

Balfour Declaration   British declaration of sympathy with Zionist aspirations, signed by Foreign Secretary Arthur James Balfour on Nov. 2, 1917, and greeted with enthusiasm by the Jewish community. Great Britain's War Cabinet was motivated by an interest in removing Palestine from the control of Turkey, which had sided with the Central Powers, and by a desire to enlist the support of American and Russian Jews for the Allied cause.

Baraita (pl. **baraitot**; Aram.; lit., "external")   Tannaitic tradition not included in Judah ha-Nasi's Mishnah. *Baraitot* are preserved in the collection known as the Tosefta (lit., "addition") and in the Talmud.

Bar Kokhba (d. 135 C.E.)   Leader of the ill-fated Judean revolt against Rome in 132–135 C.E. He was an imperious ruler who inspired messianic longings among the people and probably harbored messianic aspirations.

Bashevis Singer, Isaac (1904–   )   Polish, and later American, Yiddish novelist, critic, and journalist; Nobel Laureate in Literature. A skilled storyteller, he draws on Old-World Jewish tradition and secular Yiddish culture to capture the conflicting forces within the human psyche: the fantastic and the realistic, the demonic and the sacred, the sexual and the social.

Benjamin, Walter (1892–1940)   German philosopher and literary critic. His extremely independent thought at first took a metaphysical direction, following Kant, and then turned toward Marxism.

Berdyczewski (later **Bin-Gorion**), **Micha Josef** (1865–1921)   Russian, and later German, Hebrew writer and thinker. Opposing the Haskalah, he called for a Nietzschean "transvaluation" of Judaism and Jewish history, and for the expansion of the canons of Hebrew literary style.

Bergman, Samuel Hugo (1883–1975)   Czech, and later Israeli, philosopher. In his works on religion and faith he stressed a direct, "dialogic," experience of God, reflecting the attitudes of Rudolf Steiner, Buber, and Rosenzweig, as well as Christian thinkers and Indian philosophers, such as Aurobindo.

Bergson, Henri Louis (1859–1941)   French philosopher and Nobel Laureate in Literature. His *L'Evolution créatrice* was a prominent effort to develop a metaphysical system based on the concept of "duration" as the change which takes place within time. This change results from an inner energy, the *élan vital,* and is conceived by intuition.

Berkovits, Eliezer (1900–   )   Transylvanian, and later American, rabbi and theologian. As both a modern Orthodox theologian and a Zionist, he was deeply concerned with the tensions between Jewish religious tradition and secular Jewish nationalism.

Betar (Bethar)   Bar Kokhba's headquarters and last stronghold in his war against Rome. The ruins of the fortress and traces of the besieging troops' rampart and camps are still visible seven miles southwest of Jerusalem.

Bet Din (pl. **battei din**; lit., "house of judgment")   Jewish court of law. From the Second Temple period to modern times central and local *battei din* have held judicial, legislative, and sometimes administrative powers in the Jewish community. They dealt with religious matters affecting family life and ceremonial law, and when permitted by the ruling authorities they arbitrated civil and criminal cases between Jews.

Bet (ha-) Midrash (pl. **battei (ha-)midrash**; "house of study")   Center of instruction in the law. Since early in the Second Temple period the *bet ha-midrash* has been a primary means of disseminating the teachings of Judaism among the common people.

Bialik, Ḥayyim Naḥman (1873–1934)   Russian Hebrew poet, essayist, storywriter, translator, and editor. His Hebrew poetry, the greatest of modern times, forged a new idiom that was superior both stylistically and aesthetically. In his literary work Bialik followed Aḥad Ha-Am in attempting to reconcile traditional Judaism with modern secularism, in the context of a new national Jewish culture.

Brenner, Joseph Ḥayyim (1881–1921)   Russian, and later Palestinian, Hebrew writer. He was a major representative of the "psychology" approach in modern Hebrew literature. Brenner held that redemption was to be sought in overcoming the idleness of Diaspora existence through new social and economic patterns.

Buber, Martin (1878–1965)   Austrian, and later Israeli, philosopher, theologian, and Zionist thinker. His "Hebrew Humanism" conceives of the "holy way" of Zionism as the creation in Palestine of *Gemeinschaften*, communities based on direct personal relationships. In his philosophy of "dialogue" such "I-thou" relations lead to knowledge of the "Eternal Thou." This idea of revelation is deeply influenced by Buber's study of Ḥasidism.

Bund (abbr. of **Algemeyner Yidisher Arbeter Bund in Lite, Poyln un Rusland** [General Jewish Workers' Union in Lithuania, Poland and Russia])   Jewish socialist party founded in Russia in 1897. It came to be associated with devotion to Yiddish, autonomism, and secular Jewish nationalism.

Caro, Joseph (1488–1575)   Turkish, and later Palestinian, halakhist and kabbalist. In addition to his *Shulḥan Arukh*, he authored a commentary on Maimonides' *Mishneh Torah*, responsa, and a mystical diary inspired by revelations from a heavenly mentor.

Celan, Paul (pseudonym of **Paul Antschel**; 1920–1970)   Rumanian, and later French, poet and translator. His visionary poems, among the works in German by many other Jewish victims of the Holocaust, helped establish the Nazi-era plight of the Jews as a symbol of man's inhumanity to man in postwar German literature.

Cohen, Hermann (1842–1918)   German philosopher. He initiated the Marburg School of neo-Kantianism, in which religion was seen as a mere historical presupposition for ethics. After his attempts to fight anti-Semitism, Cohen reaffirmed his commitment to Judaism in a religious philosophy based on the "correlation" of God's "being" and man's "becoming," leading toward the messianic unity of mankind.

Cordovero, Moses (1522–1570)   Palestinian kabbalist. An outstanding mystical thinker, in his two large systematic works and commentary on the Zohar he tried to unify the transcendent and immanent concepts of the Deity through his elaborate doctrine of the dialectical emanation of the *sefirot*.

Crescas, Ḥasdai (d. 1412?)   Spanish philosopher, theologian, and statesman. Along with his polemical works against Christianity, his anti-Aristotelian and anti-Maimonidean classic *Or Adonai* ("The Light of the Lord") was motivated by a desire to save Judaism in Spain, where Jewish intellectuals had used Aristotelianism to justify desertion of their faith.

Dead Sea Scrolls   Collections of manuscript material found since 1947, mostly in the Qumrān region west of the Dead Sea. The scrolls date primarily from the first centuries B.C.E. and C.E. They include fragments of ancient biblical versions and commentaries, apocryphal and pseudepigraphal texts, and documents describing the beliefs and practices of a fundamentalist Jewish apocalyptic sect.

Derashot ha-Ran ("The Sermons of the Ran," i.e., of Rabbi Nissim)   Collection of twelve homiletical works. The traditional attribution to Nissim ben Reuben Gerondi is probably correct. The author uses philosophical questions for drawing moralistic conclusions from verses of the Torah, in an attempt to prove the superiority of prophecy over philosophy, and thereby to strengthen the people's faith during times of severe persecution and polemical pressures.

Dubnow, Simon (1860–1941)   Russian historian and political ideologist. His life-work was the study of Jewish history and its sociological interpretation. Dubnow believed that the autonomous existence of medieval Jewry within a larger society could constitute a prototype for the self-rule of the Jews and other peoples living in modern European countries.

Ein Ya'akov ("The Fountain of Jacob")   Collection of talmudic *aggadot* with commentary by the Spanish scholar Jacob ibn Ḥabib (1445?–1515/16). The author stressed the plain meaning of the text in an effort to inculcate uncritical faith, eschewing philosophical interpretations.

Eleazar of Worms (c. 1165–c. 1230)   German halakhist, theologian, and exegete. He was the last major scholar of the *Ḥasidei Ashkenaz*, the "pietists" of Germany. He authored a popular legal code with an introduction on ethics, commentaries on the Torah and the liturgy, many *piyyutim*, and a large work on esoteric theology.

Elijah ben Solomon Zalman (known as **Ha-Gra**, from the acronym of *Ha-Gaon Rabbi Eliyahu* ["Excellency Rabbi Elijah"], or as **Elijah Gaon** or the **Vilna Gaon**; 1720–1797)   Lithuanian spiritual and intellectual leader of Jewry. His works on halakhah, aggadah, and kabbalah regard the Torah as eternal and the slightest undermining of a single detail of Jewish observance as a blow to the foundation of the Torah as a whole. Thus he vehemently opposed philosophy, Haskalah, and Ḥasidism.

Epicurus (342–270 B.C.E.)   Greek philosopher and founder of Epicureanism. His views on religion led to the association of his philosophy with religious deviance in the ancient Jewish and Christian literatures. However, these literatures also adopted some of Epicurus' ethical teachings.

Frank, Jacob (1726–1791)   Podolian, and later Polish, false messiah and founder of the Frankist movement. His antinomian sect, the last development of Sabbateanism, was hostile to Judaism, condemning the Talmud and claiming the truth of the blood libel. He and some of his followers converted to Christianity but continued their sectarian existence secretly or openly.

Frankel, Zacharias (1801–1875)   Czech, and later German, rabbi and scholar. His "positivist-historical," "Breslau" school advocated moderate reform in the ritual and influenced the modern Conservative movement.

Galya Raza ("Revelation of the Secret")   Kabbalistic book. This enormous, original work was written in the mid-sixteenth century in the Near East. Suffused with the atmosphere of the school of Safed in Palestine, it explains the lives of biblical heroes in terms of metempsychosis.

Gehinnom ("Valley of [the Son(s) of] Hinnom"; Gr. Geenna; "Gehenna")   Valley south of Jerusalem; metaphorically, place of torment of wicked after death. During the biblical monarchy it was the site of a cult which involved the burning of children.

Geiger, Abraham (1810–1874)   German rabbi, leader of the Reform movement, and scholar of *Wissenschaft des Judentums*. He aspired to make Judaism an integral part of German culture through social assimilation, the elimination of the Jewish national character, and the emphasis of Judaism's universalistic religious mission.

Gemara (lit., "completion" or "tradition," i.e., of the Mishnah)   The Talmud, consisting of amoraic discussions and elaborations of the Mishnah.

Gematria (from Gr. *geōmetria* ["geometry"]; lit., "manipulation" or "calculation")

Aggadic hermeneutical rule for interpreting the Torah. It consists of explaining a Hebrew word, or group of words, by calculating the sum of the numerical values of its letters—actual or substituted—according to one of several methods.

Genesis Rabbah   Aggadic Midrash on Genesis. The earliest, largest, and most important amoraic exegetical Midrash extant, it was redacted in Palestine around the early fifth century.

Gordon, Aharon David (1856–1922)   Russian, and later Palestinian, Hebrew writer and spiritual mentor of the Zionist labor movement. He believed that self-realization of the Jewish people required the formation of a productive society through settlement on the land and a life of labor, which would inspire a renewed sense of cosmic unity and holiness.

Greenberg, Uri Zevi (pseudonym **Tur Malka**; 1894–1981)   Galician, and later Israeli, Hebrew poet. He used his poetic genius for ideological rhetoric, asserting a mystical, ultranationalistic view of Zionism that was shaped by his witnessing of anti-Jewish massacres in Poland and Palestine. Finally, the Nazi Holocaust, which he had foreseen in verse, filled Greenberg with both a tragic cynicism and an anticipation of the messianic redemption.

Guide of the Perplexed (Arabic *Dalālat al-Ḥā'irīn,* Heb. *Moreh Nevukhim*)   Moses Maimonides' major work on the philosophic interpretation of Scripture. Written for the religious Jew who was also a student of philosophy, the *Guide* showed that the anthropomorphic and anthropopathic expressions in the Bible have spiritual meaning that applies to God. Maimonides' Aristotelian system profoundly influenced subsequent Jewish thought and Christian scholasticism.

Halakhah (pl. **halakhot;** lit., "practice" or "rule")   Legal system of Judaism, or individual teaching thereof. As distinct from *aggadah,* halakhah in the rabbinic literature embraces personal and social relationships, as well as all Jewish religious observances. Because of its practical importance and difficult subject matter, the study of halakhah became the supreme religious duty.

Haskalah ("Enlightenment")   Enlightenment movement and ideology within European Jewish society in the late eighteenth and nineteenth centuries. Adherents of the Haskalah (*maskilim*) advocated secular education, assimilation, and work productivization as preconditions for Jewish emancipation in the modern state.

Havdalah (lit., "distinction")   Blessing recited at the termination of Sabbath and festivals to emphasize the distinction between the departing sacred day and the coming ordinary weekday. One of the most ancient blessings, it is preceded by a number of scriptural verses and three blessings—over wine, spices, and light—all comprising the *Havdalah* ceremony.

Heikhalot and Merkabah, Literature of the   Earliest literature of Jewish mysticism, originating in the talmudic period in Palestine. The texts describe the theurgical techniques of ecstatic ascent through the seven "palaces" (*heikhalot*) of the highest firmament and their angelic hosts, to the celestial "Chariot" (*merkabah*) and the ultimate contemplation of the Throne above it portrayed in Ezekiel's *ma'aseh merkabah* vision.

Heine, Heinrich (1797–1856)   German poet and essayist. He was one of Germany's greatest lyric poets and its outstanding Jewish writer. His career was marked by conflict and paradox: he underwent baptism but ridiculed it, and was drawn to "enlightened" Judaism intellectually but to its Orthodox counterpart emotionally.

Ḥelek, Commentary on   Section of Maimonides' *Commentary on the Mishnah* on the tenth chapter of the tractate *Sanhedrin,* which begins with the words "All Israel has a portion (*ḥelek*) in the world to come." Here Maimonides enumerates thirteen principles of belief incumbent upon all Jews, dealing with the Creator, prophecy, the Torah, providence, and eschatology.

Heschel, Abraham Joshua (1907–1972)   German, and later American, scholar and philosopher. He wrote works on medieval Jewish philosophy, kabbalah, and Ḥasidism. Heschel's influential philosophy sought to illumine the living relationship between God and man through the objective, yet sympathetic, understanding of Jewish religious literature and traditional piety.

Hess, Moses (1812–1875)   German socialist and precursor of modern Zionism. He believed that past history was characterized by racial oppression, which would in the future give way to the harmonious regeneration of independent nations, including that of the Jews in Palestine.

Ḥibbat Zion ("Love of Zion")   Zionist movement in Europe and the United States in the late nineteenth century. Although its adherents were in favor of political activity, conditions confined their efforts primarily to settlement in Palestine and philanthropy, especially in the wake of pogroms in Russia.

Hillel (the Elder; 1st century B.C.E.–1st century C.E.)   Sage and head of the Jewish community in Palestine. He was president of the Sanhedrin and exercised strong spiritual authority in religion, ethics, civil law, and economic matters, and established a dynasty of scholars that was to rule Jewish life for over four hundred years.

Ḥinnukh, Sefer ha- ("Book of Instruction")   Systematic work on the 613 *miẓvot* of the Torah. Based largely on the writings of Maimonides and Naḥmanides, it was composed in Spain around the turn of the fourteenth century. *Sefer ha-Ḥinnukh* describes each commandment in terms of its general character; biblical source and rabbinic interpretation; rationale, whether textual, conceptual, ethical, or societal; and rules of application.

Hirsch, Samson (ben) Raphael (1808–1888)   German rabbi, writer, and leader of Orthodox Jewry. Although sympathetic to the desire of many Jews for participation in modern German culture, he rejected all but slight reform in the religious norms of Judaism. For Hirsch the halakhah was the divinely ordained content of the Sinaitic revelation, not a historically evolving system of human speculation.

Ibn Ezra, Abraham (1089–1164)   Spanish Hebrew poet and grammarian, biblical exegete, philosopher, astronomer, and physician. He traveled widely, introducing the fruits of Spanish-Jewish intellectual life—originally recorded in the Arabic language—to the Jews of Europe through his Hebrew treatises. Ibn Ezra was best known for his biblical commentaries, which incorporated critical acumen and deep insight with a neo-Platonic world view.

Ibn Gabirol, Solomon (Lat. **Avicebron;** c. 1020–c. 1057)   Spanish Hebrew poet and philosopher. His *piyyutim,* or liturgical poems, were the apogee of the tradition, and fused virtuosity in biblical Hebrew with the style of Arabic verse, astronomical expertise with neo-Platonic images, and the wealth of rabbinic literature with a potent mystical symbolism. His philosophical opus, preserved as *Fons Vitae,* had considerable impact in Franciscan circles.

Ibn Paquda, Bahya (late 11th century) Spanish moral philosopher. His famous Arabic treatise *Kitāb al-Hidāya ilā Farāʾiḍ al-Qulūb* (*Ḥovot ha-Levavot* ["Duties of the Hearts"]) divides religious obligations into "duties of the limbs"—the ritual and ethical commandments—and the duties of man's inner life. The latter include beliefs, such as the existence and unity of God, and attitudes, such as love and fear of God.

Israel ben Eliezer (**Ba'al Shem Tov** ["Master of the Great Name"], acronym **Besht**; c. 1700–1760) Podolian charismatic healer and first leader of eastern European Hasidism. He disseminated widely the edifying message vouchsafed to him in visions; individual redemption through joyous "adhesion" (*devekut*) to God and the efforts of one's "saint" (*ẓaddik*). His emphasis on mystical prayer rather than intellectual study ensured success among the simple people and aroused his learned opponents.

Jabneh (Yavneh) City that served as seat of the Sanhedrin (Great Assembly) between 70 and 132 C.E., located on the coastal plain south of Jaffa. Under the influence of Johanan ben Zakkai, Jabneh temporarily replaced the destroyed Jerusalem as the religious center of Palestinian and even Diaspora Jewry.

Jacob ben Asher (known from the title of his major work as **Tur**; 1270?–1340) German, and later Spanish, halakhist. His *Arba'ah Turim* ("The Four Rows") subsumes the entire halakhah under sections on liturgy and holy days, ritual law, women and marriage, and civil law and personal relations. The code followed the rulings of Jacob's father Asher ben Jehiel (acronym *Rosh*) and Maimonides, and became authoritative.

Johanan ben Zakkai (1st century C.E.) *Tanna.* He was the leading sage of his period, and established Jabneh as the religious and national center to preserve Judaism after the destruction of the Second Temple.

Judah Halevi (before 1075–1141) Spanish Hebrew poet and philosopher. His *Sefer ha-Kuzari* claimed the superiority of religious faith over philosophical knowledge. Halevi's attempt to reach the Land of Israel was first anticipated and then recounted in his unique "poems of Zion."

Judah ha-Nasi ("Judah the Patriarch"; late 2nd–early 3rd century C.E.) Political head of the Jewish community in Judea and redactor of the Mishnah. He spread knowledge of the Torah and the observance of its *miẓvot,* and maintained the unity of the nation under Roman rule. Known simply as "Rabbi," Judah established the legal canon for Judaism.

Judah Loew ben Bezalel (acronym **Maharal of Prague**; c.1525–1609) Moravian and Bohemian rabbi, talmudist, moralist, and mathematician. He was revered for his knowledge and piety, and was a prolific writer. Maharal's original interpretation of the aggadah is the foundation of his works, which treat the relationship between God and Israel, the Torah as mediator between them, and exile and redemption.

Kabbalah (lit., "reception" or "tradition") Major form of Jewish mysticism, originating in the late twelfth century. It combines gnostic and neo-Platonic tendencies in a powerful doctrine that views mundane existence as symbolic of a corresponding dynamism within the divine *sefirot.* Beginning with *Sefer ha-Bahir,* its

its chief historical stages include the Zohar, the circle of Isaac Luria, the Sabbatean movement, and Ḥasidism.

Kafka, Franz (1883–1924)   German writer of Czech origin. In his masterful stories the hero searches unremittingly for identity, but is thwarted by grotesque obstacles. Kafka's longing to escape existential bewilderment and achieve a genuine, "pure" life paralleled his desire to overcome religious alienation through a deepening appreciation of Judaism.

Kant, Immanuel (1724–1804)   German philosopher. He held that true religion was ethical religion, to which belonged Christianity with its teaching of pure love, but not Judaism with its national-political and legalistic essence. Yet Kant's thought attracted liberal Jewish intellectuals, since they saw in Judaism a rational, universalistic system of ethics.

Kaplan, Mordecai Menahem (1881–1983)   American rabbi and founder of the Reconstructionist movement. According to Kaplan, the religious aspect of Judaism undergoes an evolution of values with individual quests for meaning, rather than adhering to a static revelational criterion. As a civilization, too, it changes in contact with secular culture, instead of clinging rigidly to outdated forms.

Kashrut (lit., "fitness" or "propriety")   Jewish dietary laws. *Kashrut* is concerned with the types of animals, birds, and fish permitted; the method of slaughter; examination for defects that would prohibit consumption; preparation of the meat, which involves removing nonveinal blood by salting or roasting; and separation of meat and milk.

Kavvanah (pl. **kavvanot**; lit., "direction" or "intention")   State of mental concentration and spiritual devotion during prayer and the performance of *miẓvot,* or individual thought attending this state. The kabbalah, especially that of Isaac Luria, produced written guides to *kavvanot* of a mystical nature.

Kelippah (pl. **kelippot**; lit., "shell" or "husk")   Symbol of that element of the kabbalistic vessels of emanation that becomes evil toward the end of the cosmogonic process, forming the *sitra ahra*. The *kelippot* contain a "kernel" of holiness, which is to be freed through man's piety so that it may return to and perfect its divine source.

Keneset Yisrael ("The Community of Israel")   Rabbinic term for the totality of the Jewish community. It is used as the personification of the Jewish community in its dialogue with the Almighty. This title was adopted officially by the Jewish community in Palestine in 1927.

Kiddush (lit., "sanctification")   Prayer over a cup of wine in the home and synagogue to consecrate the Sabbath or a festival. It formally fulfills the biblical commandment in Exodus 20:8, "Remember the Sabbath day, to keep it holy."

Kierkegaard, Søren (**Aabye**; 1813–1855)   Danish philosopher and founder of existentialism. He criticized the rationalism of Hegel's system, which left no room for religious faith. In his treatment of the *Akedah,* he characterized Abraham as the "knight of faith," whose existential commitment to divine command took precedence over the moral order of the "man of ethics."

Kimḥi, David (acronym **Redak**; also called **Maistre Petit**; 1160?–1235?)   Provençal Hebrew grammarian and biblical exegete. His linguistic treatise evinces interests in the continued development of postbiblical Hebrew and the establishment of the correct text of Scripture. Kimḥi's commentaries stress philological analysis as opposed to homiletical digression, and incorporate his philosophical and polemical ideas.

Kook (Kuk), Abraham Isaac (1865–1935)   Latvian, and later Palestinian, rabbinical authority, thinker, and first Ashkenazi chief rabbi of modern Palestine. He held that practical activities were inseparable from spiritual aspirations, seeing religious meaning in both mysticism and social concern, ultimate universalism in the evolution of national life, and divine redemption in the return to the Land of Israel.

Krochmal, Nachman (1785–1840)   Galician philosopher, historian, and leading exponent of *Wissenschaft des Judentums* and the Haskalah movement. His life-work, *Moreh Nevukhei ha-Zeman* ("Guide of the Perplexed of the Time"), is indebted to the idealist philosophers and the kabbalah in describing creation *ex nihilo* as the infinite self-confinement of the Absolute Reality.

Kuzari, Sefer ha- ("Book of the Kuzari"; frequent designation of the Hebrew translation of the Arabic *Kitāb al-Ḥujja wa-al-Dalīl fī Naṣr al-Dīn al-Dhalīl* ["Book of Argument and Proof in Defense of the Despised Faith"])   Polemical work by Judah Halevi. Its popular name is after the king of the Turkic Khazar nation, who provides the book's framework by engaging in a dialogue with an unidentified rabbi. The king accepts Judaism—historically, circa 740 C.E.—finding that Aristotelian philosophy cannot claim direct experience of God, while Christianity and Islam are poor adaptations of the Jewish prophetic heritage.

Lazarus, Moritz (1824–1903)   German philosopher and psychologist. He wrote many works on the psychology of nations. In his *Ethik des Judentums* Lazarus propounded an empirical, positivistic approach that derives the ethical system of Judaism from its classical sources, rather than from a philosophic formalism.

Leviticus Rabbah   Midrash on Leviticus. It was probably composed in fifth-century Palestine and is one of the oldest Midrashim extant. Leviticus Rabbah consists of separate homilies, each based on the beginning of a weekly lection and drawn from a number of synagogue sermons.

Locke, John (1632–1704)   English philosopher. He initiated the age of enlightenment and reason in England and France. He favored the separation of church and state, arguing in his *Letter Concerning Toleration* that civil rights for the Jews would not make them more abominable than they already were.

Luria, Isaac (known as **Ha-Ari** ["The Lion"] from the acronym of *Ha-Elohi Rabbi Yiẓḥak* ["The Divine Rabbi Isaac"]; 1534–1572)   Safed kabbalist. He attracted many disciples, whom he taught orally halakhah and his original system of theoretical kabbalah. His doctrines of *ẓimẓum, shevirat ha-kelim* ("the breaking of the vessels," i.e., the vessels of divine emanation), and *tikkun* accord the entire Jewish people the messianic mission of cosmic restitution.

Luzzatto, Moses Ḥayyim (acronym **Ramḥal**; 1707–1747)   Italian kabbalist, moralist, and Hebrew poet. The members of his study circle entertained messianic aspirations, inspired by Luzzatto's spiritual mentor, the kabbalah of Isaac Luria, and some affinity for the Sabbatean movement. Luzzatto's chief ethical work, *Mesillat Yesharim* ("The Path of the Upright") became a classic, and his verse dramas inaugurated a new era in Hebrew literature.

Luzzatto, Samuel David (acronym **Shadal**; 1800–1865)   Italian scholar, philosopher, biblical exegete, and translator. He decried the rationalistic scrutiny of

Jewish sources by those who would distinguish morality from religion, and objected to the utilitarian motives of the proponents of emancipation. Luzzatto's theology upholds the Sinaitic revelation, Jewish tradition, and the election of Israel as embodying Judaism's own unique humanitarianism and universalism.

Ma'aseh Bereshit (lit., "the work of creation")   First chapter of Genesis describing the creation of the world. Its interpretation in talmudic literature included esoteric traditions as well as refutations of gnostic and other heretical views. Speculation on *ma'aseh bereshit* in the kabbalah is concerned with the *sefirot*, while medieval Jewish philosophy identified it with the study of physics.

Ma'aseh Merkavah (lit., "the work of Chariot")   First chapter of Ezekiel describing the world of the divine Throne and its Chariot. Its mysteries are detailed in the Heikhalot and Merkabah literature. In the Middle Ages the term *ma'aseh merkabah* was used by kabbalists to designate their theosophical doctrines and by philosophers to designate metaphysics.

Magnes Judah Leon (1877–1948)   American, and later Palestinian, rabbi and communal leader. He was the moving spirit of the Jewish community in New York City and later became the first president of the Hebrew University of Jerusalem. A leading Zionist and disciple of Aḥad Ha-Am, he dreamt of bringing Jews and Arabs together in a binational state in Palestine.

Maimonides, Moses (Moses ben Maimon; acronym **Rambam**; 1135–1204)   Spanish, and later Egyptian, rabbinic authority, philosopher, and physician. He was the greatest posttalmudic spiritual leader of the Jewish people, exerting incalculable influence to the present day. Maimonides' *Commentary on the Mishnah, Sefer ha-Miẓvot, Mishneh Torah,* and *Guide of the Perplexed* are each unequaled in its field, and together represent a consummate intellectual and practical program of Judaism.

Marrano (probably derived from the Spanish for "swine," perhaps coalescing with the late Arabic *barrān* ["outside"])   Derogatory term for the Conversos or "New Christians" of fifteenth-century Spain and Portugal, regarded by later Jewry as a badge of honor. The Marranos were baptized due to mob violence, royal decree, and sometimes missionary preaching. They lived outwardly as Christians, but generally tried to maintain Jewish faith and observance secretly. They and their descendants suffered from popular animosity and the official Inquisition.

Marx, Karl Heinrich (1818–1883)   German social philosopher and founder of Marxism. Converted as a child, he became deeply attached to Christianity and German culture. Although Marx favored political emancipation of the Jews, Judaism for him was synonymous with the hated bourgeois capitalism and he used violent anti-Semitic language in his works.

Masada (*Meẓadah*)   Herod's royal citadel and last Zealot outpost during the Jewish war against Rome in 66–70/73 C.E. Adjacent to the Dead Sea Valley, it contains the earliest known synagogue. The mass suicide of the defenders—960 men, women, and children—defying submission to the oppressor, has made Masada a unique symbol of Jewish courage and independence.

Meir Loeb ben Jehiel Michael (acronym **Malbim**; (1809–1879)   Volhynian, and later Rumanian, rabbi, preacher, and biblical exegete. His commentary was intended to strengthen the position of Orthodox Jewry in knowledge of Hebrew, exegetical method, and exposition of the literal meaning—all areas in which

Reform scholars, whom Malbim opposed vehemently, had achieved proficiency.

Memorbuch   Jewish community prayer book in central Europe. It consisted of prayers read from the synagogue *bimah* or "platform," and memorial necrologies and martyrologies. *Memorbücher* originated after the massacres of Rhenish Jewry during the First Crusade (1095–1096) and grew longer with each successive catastrophe, including the Black Death persecutions (1348–1349) and Chmielnicki pogroms (1648).

Mendelssohn, Moses (1729–1786)   German Enlightenment philosopher and spiritual leader of German Jewry. His philosophy followed the classical doctrine of the universal religion of reason, but he defended the independent validity of Judaism as a "revealed law." He also envisioned the loyal participation of Jews in the civic life of the modern state without their giving up Jewish religious belief and practices.

Menorah ("candelabrum")   Seven-branched candelabrum in the biblical Tabernacle and the Jerusalem Temples; emblem of the Jewish people and the State of Israel. It has been used widely as a religious symbol, particularly in synagogue art. The eight-branched Hanukkah *menorah* (*hanukkiyyah*) commemorates the eight days during which the oil burned miraculously following the Hasmoneans' liberation of the Temple from the Syrians in 164 B.C.E.

Mezuzah (lit., "doorpost")   Encased parchment scroll affixed to the doorpost of rooms in the Jewish home. It is inscribed with the passages of the *Shema* in Deuteronomy 6:4–9 and 11:13–21. In modern times the *mezuzah* is sometimes worn around the neck.

Mishnah (pl. **mishnayot**; lit., "repetition" or "study," i.e., of the oral Law)   Collection of halakhic traditions of the *tannaim,* or individual teachings thereof. The Mishnah that became the primary postbiblical source of Jewish law as developed in the Talmud was that of Judah ha-Nasi, redacted around 200 C.E. It is divided into six orders on: agriculture and daily liturgy, Sabbath and festivals, marital relations, jurisprudence, Temple sacrifices and dietary practices, and ritual purity.

Mishneh Torah ("The Repetition of the Law"; also referred to as *Ha-Yad ha-Ḥazakah* ["The Strong Hand"])   Moses Maimonides' code of Jewish law. It was unprecedented both in its systematic classification of the entire halakhic literature by subject matter and in its philosophical introduction. The *Mishneh Torah* was severely criticized for its failure to cite previous authorities, but this very fact was the reason for its prominence in the later study of the halakhah.

Miẓvah (pl. **miẓvot**; "commandment")   Precept of Jewish law or, generally, any meritorious deed. Following the statement of the *amora* Simlai, there are traditionally 613 commandments in the Torah: 248 positive mandates and 365 prohibitions. With the increased ritual obligations imposed by the rabbis, the *miẓvot* were also classified as "biblical" and "rabbinic." The medieval Jewish philosophers further divided them into "rational" and "revealed."

Miẓvot, Sefer ha- (Heb. translation of the Arabic *Kitāb al-Fara'id* ["Book of Commandments"])   Moses Maimonides' work enumerating the 613 *miẓvot* of the Torah. Maimonides introduces his work with a lengthy treatise on the fourteen principles that guide his logical classification of the commandments, which formed the basis for subsequent literature on the subject.

Molcho, Solomon (originally Diego Pires; c. 1500–1532)   Portuguese kabbalist and pseudo-messiah. Born of Marrano parents, he reverted to Judaism and fled the Inquisition. He associated himself with the adventurer David Reuveni and undertook missions to European rulers. Molcho's preaching and prophecies gained him many followers—Jews, Marranos, and Christians—who remained faithful after his death at the stake, and influenced the Sabbatean movement.

Musar Movement   Movement for strict ethical behavior in the spirit of halakhah, founded by Israel Lipkin (Salanter; 1810–1883) among the yeshivot of Lithuania. Lipkin's program aimed to preserve the moral quality of Jewish communal life through the reading and contemplation of traditional ethical works to evoke an emotional response and instill an alertness of moral habit.

Naḥmanides (Moses ben Naḥman, acronym Ramban; 1194–1270)   Spanish rabbinic authority, philosopher, kabbalist, biblical exegete, Hebrew poet, and physician. His novellae on the Talmud and halakhic monographs fused the traditions of the Spanish, Provençal, and northern French schools. His commentary on the Torah interprets the sequence of the narrative as foreshadowing Jewish history and probes the deeper theological meaning of the text.

Naḥman of Bratslav (1772–1811)   Podolian and Ukrainian Ḥasidic ẓaddik ("saint") and spiritual leader of Bratslav Ḥasidism. His radical doctrine is influenced by the Sabbatean and Frankist heresies in its claim that the only true ẓaddik, who is of messianic nature, is Naḥman himself. As such, Naḥman restores sinful souls as the object of faith, pilgrimage, and confession, and as the intermediary of prayer.

Neo-Orthodoxy   Modernistic faction of German Orthodoxy in the second half of the nineteenth century. Its goal was the symbiosis of traditional Orthodoxy and modern German culture as envisioned by Moses Mendelssohn and Samson Raphael Hirsch.

Nietzsche, Friedrich Wilhelm (1844–1900)   German philosopher. His nihilistic critique of liberalism, democracy, and modern culture contributed to the rise of irrational political movements, including Nazism. While Nietzsche's works do contain many remarks against Judaism, his main reproach was that it had given birth to the despised Christianity. He also accorded praise to Jews and Judaism and became an inveterate foe of anti-Semitism.

Nissim ben Reuben Gerondi (known as Rabbenu Nissim ["Our Rabbi Nissim"], acronym Ran; 1310?–1375?)   Spanish talmudist. His renown rests chiefly on his halakhic works, which are among the most important produced in Spain. He wrote a commentary on the Torah and probably was the author of the *Derashot ha-Ran*.

Pardes   Mnemonic for the four hermeneutical devices used in biblical exegesis. It is an acronym of *peshat* ("simple"), *remez* ("allegory"), *derash* ("homily"), and *sod* ("mystery"). Moses de Leon, author of the Zohar, coined this expression, which is conveniently identical with the mystically charged term for garden—*pardes*, not unlike "paradise." According to a talmudic tradition (BT Hag. 14b), of the four who entered *pardes*, only Akiva emerged unscathed.

Pharisees (Perushim, lit., "separatists")   Major Jewish religious and political party or sect during the Second Temple period. They tried to imbue the people with a spirit of holiness based on study and observance of the Torah and oral law, and to remove religious control from the aristocratic Sadducees by transferring worship from the Temple to the synagogue and home. Their doctrines of providence and free will, and resurrection and redemption, expressed the hopes of the oppressed masses and became the theological foundations of Judaism.

Philo Judaeus (Philo of Alexandria; c. 20 B.C.E.–50 C.E.) Egyptian biblical exegete and philosopher. His many Greek writings on the Pentateuch—legal expositions, philosophical interpretations, and literal and allegorical exegeses—attempt to present Judaism as a philosophical system. He also wrote treatises on purely philosophical topics, combining Stoic, Platonic, and neo-Pythagorean elements, as well as two books on contemporary history.

Pirkei Avot ("Chapters of the Fathers"; frequent designation of *Avot* ["The Fathers"], popularly referred to in English as "Ethics of the Fathers") Treatise of the Mishnah containing aggadic statements of the fundamental principles of Judaism. It traces the transmission of the oral Law among the sages from the Sinaitic revelation through the destruction of the Second Temple. *Pirkei Avot* has been a popular text for synagogue recital since at least the early Middle Ages.

Piyyut (pl. **piyyutim**; from Gr. *poiētēs* ["poet"]; "hymn" or liturgical "poem") Lyrical composition intended to embellish a prayer or religious ceremony. The *piyyut* literature began in Palestine in the first centuries C.E. while the obligatory prayers were being canonized. Later centers of creativity in Italy, Germany, and especially Spain, produced superb works that were absorbed into the established liturgy.

Rashi (acronym of **Solomon ben Isaac**; 1040–1105) French commentator on the Bible and Talmud. His concise biblical commentary consists of informed philological explanations and midrashic quotations, the latter having been altered to achieve lucidity and uniform style. His talmudic commentary is unique in discussing reasons for the halakhot, difficulties in structure and terminology, and the psychological and realistic background of talmudic times; the Talmud would be unintelligible without it.

Responsa (Heb. *She'eilot ve-teshuvot* ["queries and replies"]) Exchange of letters in which one party consults another on a halakhic matter, e.g., to explain a difficult point or resolve a dispute. Responsa literature first emerged as an important literary and historical phenomenon in the sixth to eleventh centuries, when it played a key role in disseminating the oral Law and establishing the Babylonian Talmud as the sole authority in the life of the Jewish people.

Rosenzweig, Franz (1886–1929) German theologian. The main thesis of his *Der Stern der Erlösung* ("The Star of Redemption") is that revelation is God's identifying himself to man in love. Man responds in kind, living the permanent reality of redemption through the Jewish religious calendar and liturgy and through relations with his neighbor—through "commandments" *(Gebot)*, not "laws" *(Gesetz)*. Together with a number of influential Jewish intellectuals, he organized the Freies Jüdisches Lehrhaus ("Free Jewish House of Learning"), where both teachers and students sought to move from the periphery of European culture toward the center of authentic Jewish sources.

Rosh Ha-Shanah ("Beginning of the Year") Festival of the Jewish New Year, celebrated on the first and second days of the month of Tishri. The liturgy stresses the themes of God's kingship and judgment. With the sounding of the *shofar* ("horn," usually of the ram) in the synagogue, God is solemnly entreated to show mercy to his creatures.

Rossi, Azariah dei (c. 1511–1578) Italian scholar of Hebrew letters. He wrote a work on earthquakes, occasioned by the disaster in Ferrara in 1571, and a study of ancient Jewish history. He was attacked for using his unusual knowledge of Latin and Italian literature and the new critical-historical method of the Renaissance in weighing the validity of Jewish sources according to non-Jewish sources.

Saadiah (ben Joseph) Gaon (882–942)   Egyptian, and later Babylonian, rabbinic authority, philosopher, biblical exegete and translator, and Hebrew grammarian and poet. As *gaon* ("excellency") or head of the talmudic academy of Sura, his powerful personal influence and systematic literary efforts dominated world Judaism. Saadiah's Arabic *Kitāb al-Amānāt wa-al-l'tiqādāt* (*Sefer ha-Emunot ve-ha-De'ot;* "Book of Beliefs and Opinions") set the precedent for the enterprise of medieval Jewish philosophy—rational proof for the oral and written Law.

Shabbetai Ẓevi (1626–1676)   Turkish pseudo-messiah and central figure of the Sabbatean movement. His bizzare manic rituals that countered Jewish law were seen kabbalistically as the messiah's fight against evil on its own ground, necessary to redeem the last captive "scintilla" of holiness. His conversion to Islam was so interpreted, justifying the experience of his former Marrano followers, as was his death. Sabbatean groups continued secretly for centuries, some copying Shabbetai Ẓevi's "holy" transgressions and apostasy.

Sadducees (*Ẓedukim,* probably derived from Zadok, the high priest in the time of David and Solomon)   Jewish sect of the latter half of the Second Temple period. They were wealthy and Hellenized priests, merchants, and aristocrats, who controlled the Temple rites. They held conservative religious attitudes, refusing to accept the oral traditions with which the Pharisees supplemented the written Law.

Sages (*ḥakhamim,* sg. *ḥakham*)   Spiritual and religious leaders of Jewry who shaped the oral Law from the beginning of Second Temple times to the Arabian conquest of the East. The term encompasses the men of the Sanhedrin or Great Assembly, scribes, Pharisees, members of the Sanhedrin, *ḥasidim* ("pietists"), mystics, *ḥaverim* ("members," i.e., of a group that meticulously observed the laws of tithing and purity), *tannaim,* and *amoraim.*

Samuel ben Meir (acronym **Rashbam**; c. 1080–1085–c. 1174)   French commentator on the Bible and Talmud. Although deeply indebted to his grandfather Rashi, Samuel rarely employed halakhic and midrashic interpretations of Scripture, preferring strict adherence to the literal meaning. His early, prolific *tosafot* ("additions," or glosses on the Talmud) propound and resolve textual difficulties, and propose and weigh alternative explanations.

Sanhedrin (from Gr. *synedrion* ["assembly"])   Supreme political, religious, and judicial body in Palestine during the Roman period.

Schechter, Solomon (1847–1915)   Rumanian, and later American, rabbinic scholar and founder of Conservative Judaism. He combined scholarliness with piety, and piety with flexibility in doctrine and practice, admitting change in response to the religious needs of the age. As president of the Jewish Theological Seminary of America, he made it a major center of Jewish learning and Jewish intellectual and national revival.

Sefirot (sg. **Sefirah**)   Kabbalistic term for the ten stages of emanation from *Ein Sof* (the "Infinite" *deus absconditus*), forming the realm of manifestation of the divine attributes. The rhythm of the unfolding *sefirot* is also that of all creation and is discernible in each of its levels.

Sephardi (pl. Sephardim) Designation of original Spanish and Portuguese Jewry and its descendants, or of their common cultural heritage.

Shammai (the Elder; c. 50 B.C.E.–c. 30 C.E.) Sage and vice-president of the Sanhedrin during the presidency of his colleague Hillel. Shammai's disciples generally favored a stringent position on halakhah as compared with the school of Hillel.

Shekhinah (lit., "dwelling" or "resting") Rabbinic term for the divine Presence. It refers to the numinous immanence of God in a particular place, object, individual, or whole people, but at the same time the "radiance" of the *Shekhinah* is everywhere. Most medieval Jewish philosophers, concerned about possible anthropomorphic interpretations, considered the *Shekhinah* a created entity. In kabbalah, it is the tenth *sefirah*.

Shema ("Hear") Declaration of God's unity recited twice daily, named after Deuteronomy 6:4: "Hear, O Israel, the Lord is our God, the Lord is one." By the second century C.E. it consisted of Deuteronomy 6:4–9 and 11:13–21 and Numbers 15:37–41—including the obligations to love and serve God and to observe his *mizvot*—together with opening and closing benedictions.

Shneur Zalman of Lyady (1745–1813) Belorussian halakhist and founder of Ḥabad Ḥasidism. "Ḥabad" is an acronym of the kabbalistic expression *hokhmah, binah, da'at* ("germinal, developmental, and conclusive" knowledge). Yet Shneur Zalman's *Likkutei Amarim* ("Collected Sayings"), which was accepted as the "written law" of the "Ḥabad" movement, complemented the intellectual emphasis with stress on spiritual meditation and practical observance. He also asserted the average Jew's independence from the *zaddik*, or Ḥasidic saint, in achieving contact with the immanent Deity.

Shulḥan Arukh ("The Prepared Table") Joseph Caro's halakhic code. It is a synopsis of Caro's *Beit Yosef*, his commentary on Jacob ben Asher's *Arba'ah Turim*. With the additions of Moses Isserles, which clarified the customs of Ashkenazi Jewry, and other commentators, it still serves as the ultimate authority in Jewish law.

Siddur (Seder) Tefillah (lit., "order of prayer") Prayer book. The *siddur* developed in the posttalmudic period, prior to which the writing of prayers was forbidden. The text differs slightly between the Sephardi and Ashkenazi rites, the latter having been edited according to Isaac Luria's *kavvanot* and adopted by the Ḥasidim. The Conservative, Reconstructionist, and, especially, Reform movements have made changes in the *siddur*.

Sifrei ([Aram.] "Books") Halakhic Midrash on Numbers and Deuteronomy. It really consists of two separate works, both originating no earlier than the end of the fourth century C.E. in Palestine, but from different tannaitic schools.

Sitra Aḥra (Aram., lit., "the other side") Kabbalistic term for the domain of cosmic evil and the *kelippot*. It is understood neo-Platonically as the darkness caused by estrangement from the divine source in the last links of the chain of emanation, or gnostically as a separate substantiation of the divine power of judgment with its own ten "sinistral" *sefirot*.

Sofer, Moses (known from the title of his collected responsa as Ḥatam Sofer; 1762–1839) German, and later Hungarian, rabbinic authority and leader of Orthodox Jewry. He founded the largest yeshivah since the great academies of Babylonia and made it the center of the struggle against the Reform movement and

the Haskalah. He also wielded great influence on Jewish life through his voluminous halakhic writings.

Soloveitchik, Joseph Dov (1903–   )   Belorussian, and later American, talmudic scholar and religious philosopher. He is the leader of modern Orthodoxy
in North America, known popularly as "the rabbi." His main published work,
Ish ha-Halakhah ("Halakhic Man"), argues that man actively sanctifies his life
through halakhah, ceasing to be a mere creature of habit.

Spain, Expulsion from   Forced exodus of all Jews who refused baptism, about
100,000 in number, from Spanish soil by edict of Ferdinand and Isabella in
1492. It was due largely to continued secret practice of Judaism by Marranos
despite the intensified Inquisition. Most of the exiles reached Portugal, from
which the Jews were expelled in 1496–97, founding the thriving Sephardi Diaspora throughout the Old and New worlds.

Spinoza, Baruch (Benedict) De (1632–1677)   Dutch philosopher. He developed
a rationalistic critique of Judaism and revealed religion. In Spinoza's metaphysics
the world is a necessary aspect of the only possible substance—God, or Nature,
the logical cosmic order. His concept of the freedom of rational understanding
from emotion is basic to the ideology of secularism.

Sukkot ("Tabernacles")   Festival commemorating the *sukkot* (sg. *sukkah*) in
which the Israelites dwelt in the wilderness after the Exodus, beginning on the
fifteenth of the month of Tishri and lasting seven days. Special observances
include dwelling in a *sukkah,* as weather permits, and holding the *arba'ah minim*
("four species") of citron, myrtle, palm, and willow. *Sukkot* is followed by *Simḥat
Torah,* on which the annual reading from the Torah scroll is concluded, and a
new cycle is begun, following which the Torah scrolls are carried in procession
in the synagogue.

Talmid Ḥakham (pl. **talmidei ḥakhamim;** "disciple of the wise")   Rabbinic
appellation given to a scholar who fulfilled the ideal standard in learning and
conduct. The main qualifications were comprehensive knowledge of the written
and oral Law, extreme piety, attendance upon one's teacher, and proper personal deportment and etiquette. The *talmidei ḥakhamim,* made up an aristocracy
of learning and enjoyed considerable social privileges.

Talmud (lit., "study" or "learning")   Body of teaching comprising the commentary and discussions of the *amoraim* on the Mishnah, or the teachings of an individual scholar. There are both the Jerusalem and Babylonian Talmuds, completed around 400 and 500 C.E., respectively. These documents formulated
every facet of Jewish life—halakhah and aggadah, custom and belief, science and
superstition—but it was the Babylonian Talmud that overwhelmingly shaped
Judaism.

Tam, Jacob ben Meir (known as **Rabbenu Tam** ["Our Rabbi Tam"]; c. 1100–
1171)   Tosafist, i.e., author of *tosafot* ("additions" or "glosses" on the Talmud). He was the greatest halakhic authority of his generation. The *tosafot*
printed in the Babylonian Talmud are based on his explanations and decisions,
and he introduced major ordinances which were followed by Ashkenazi Jewry
for nearly a millennium.

Tanna (pl. **tannaim;** Aram., lit. "teacher," from *teni,* "to hand down orally")
Designation of scholars from the period of Hillel (c. 20 C.E.) to the completion

of the Mishnah (c. 200 C. E.). The discussions of the *tannaim* make up the bulk of the Mishnah and extant *baraitot,* and of the halakhic midrashim. Their efforts preserved Judaism through the crippling defeats of both wars against Roman rule (c. 72/73 and 135 C.E.).

Tefillin (sg. **tefillah**; possibly from the root *p-l-h,* "to separate" or "to distinguish," i.e., the Jew from the non-Jew; usually translated inaccurately as "phylacteries") Two black leather boxes containing four biblical verses and bound by black leather strips on the left hand and on the head for morning services, except on Sabbaths and festivals. The four passages— in Exodus 13:1–10 and 11–16 and, from the *Shema,* in Deuteronomy 6:4–9 and 11:13–21— require the Jew to place the words of the law as "a sign upon thy hand and a frontlet (or "memorial") between thine eyes."

Temunah, Sefer ha- ("Book of the Image") Kabbalistic work. It interprets the "image" of God according to the shapes of the Hebrew letters, viewed as expressions of the manifestation of God in his *sefirot.* The importance of this work lies in its enigmatic theory of *shemittot* ("remissions") or cosmic cycles of creation. *Sefer ha-Temunah* was written in the mid-thirteenth century in Spain or Provence.

Tetragrammaton Name of God, written in the Bible as *YHVH.* It is probably a causative form of the root *h-v-h* ("to be"), meaning "He brings into existence." By at least as early as the third century B.C.E., pronunciation of the sacred Tetragrammaton was avoided by substituting *Adonai* ("my Lord"), which was further replaced with *ha-Shem* ("the Name).

Tikkun (pl. **tikkunim**; lit., "restoration") Lurianic doctrine of the restoration of the flawed universe to its original design, or specific act which helps to effect this process. Renewed divine emanations and human religious and contemplative efforts are to eventually end the cosmic exile of the *Shekhinah* and the historic exile of the Jewish people.

Tishah be-Av ("The Ninth of [the month of] Av") Day of mourning for the destruction of the Temples in Jerusalem. The First Temple was destroyed by the Babylonians in 586 B.C.E.; the Second, by the Romans in 70 C.E. The day marks the occurrence of other calamities as well, including the defeat of the Bar Kokhba revolt and the Spanish Expulsion.

Vital, Ḥayyim (1542–1620) Palestinian kabbalist. He was the principle disciple of Isaac Luria, whose teachings he elaborated and arranged in written form. Vital thus became the chief formulator of Lurianic kabbalah as it was understood in later generations.

Volozhiner, Ḥayyim ben Isaac (1749–1821) Lithuanian rabbi and educator. He was the acknowledged spiritual leader of Lithuanian Jewry in his day and his yeshivah was the prototype for the great talmudic academies of eastern Europe, Israel, and the English-speaking countries. In reaction to the ecstatic subjectivism of the Ḥasidim, he emphasized the cognitive teleology of Torah study.

Wessely, Naphtali Herz (1725–1805) German Hebrew poet and linguist, biblical exegete, and exponent of the Haskalah. He pioneered in the revival of biblical Hebrew. His *Shirei Tiferet* ("Poems of Glory"), a didactic epic on the life of Moses and the Exodus, is suffused with the rationalist spirit of the age and may be considered the major literary work of the German Haskalah.

Wiesel, Elie (1928–   )   Rumanian, and later American, novelist and journalist. Most of his books reflect his experience of the horrors of the Nazi concentration camps—a haunting religious mystery perceived through the prism of Talmud, kabbalah, and Ḥasidism. Wiesel challenges the world to address the nightmarish reality of its recent past as it approaches its present and future.

Yeshivah (pl. **yeshivot**; lit., "sitting")   Academy of talmudic learning. The yeshivot of antiquity produced the Mishnah and the Jerusalem and Babylonian Talmuds, and were the central authoritative religious bodies for world Jewry. The local yeshivah provides advanced study of the halakhah, including rabbinical training, and religious leadership for the community.

Yeẓirah, Sefer ("Book of Formation")   Cosmological book. It describes the creation of the world by means of God's 32 secret paths of wisdom: the ten *sefirot* (here, apparently "numerical" metaphysical principles) and the 22 letters of the Hebrew alphabet. Probably written in Palestine between the third and sixth centuries C.E., the work spawned a large literature of philosophical and kabbalistic commentary.

Yigdal ("May He be Magnified")   *Piyyut* based on the thirteen principles of Jewish faith enumerated in Moses Maimonides' Commentary on Ḥelek. Composed in fourteenth-century Italy, it was incorporated into the liturgy.

Yiḥud (pl. **yiḥudim**; lit., "unification")   Meditative exercise in Lurianic kabbalah, entailing mental concentration on combinations of divine names. In the *yiḥudim, kavvanah* became an independent instrument for attaining divine inspiration.

Yom Kippur (also **Yom ha-Kippurim**; "Day of Atonement")   Holiest day in the liturgical year, occurring on the tenth of the month of Tishri. It is the climax of the "Ten Days of Penitence" which begin on Roṣh ha-Shanah, and is devoted to prayers asking God's forgiveness for past transgressions and his blessing for the future. Fasting and other forms of abstinence are the rule, and as on the Sabbath all manner of work is forbidden.

Ẓimẓum (lit., "contraction")   Lurianic doctrine of the withdrawal of God into himself to make room for creation. The resulting primordial space is filled with emanations from the *Ein Sof,* which imposes order and structure on the universe.

Ẓiẓit (pl. **ẓiẓiyyot**; lit., "fringe")   Tassel attached to each of the four corners of the *tallit* ("covering" or prayer shawl) or *tallit katan* ("small *tallit*" worn with daily dress), fulfilling the commandment in Numbers 15:37–41 and Deuteronomy 22:12. It serves as a reminder to observe the *miẓvot,* a function similar to that of the *mezuzah* and *tefillin.*

Zohar ("Splendor"; frequent designation of *Sefer ha-Zohar* ["Book of Splendor"])   Central work of Jewish mysticism, written mainly by the Spanish kabbalist Moses de Leon (c. 1240–1305). This mystical midrash on the Torah contains pseudepigraphic narratives of the second-century *tanna* Simeon bar Yoḥai, and its language is an anachronistic Aramaic. With its highly developed theology and symbolism, the Zohar constitutes the peak of the kabbalah in Spain and the foundation of all later kabbalistic thought.

List of Abbreviations

Abr.	Philo. De Abrahamo.
Acts	Acts of the Apostles (New Testament).
Ant.	Josephus, Jewish Antiquities (Loeb Classics ed.).
Apion	Josephus, Against Apion (Loeb Classics ed.).
Apoc.Abr.	Apocrypha of Abraham.
ARN1	Avot de-Rabbi Nathan, version (1) ed. Schecter. 1887.
ARN2	Avot de-Rabbi Nathan, version (2) ed. Schecter, 1945
Av. Zar.	Avodah Zarah (talmudic tractate).
BB	Bava Batra (talmudic tractate).
IBar.	I Baruch (Apocrypha).
IIBar.	II Baruch (Apocrypha).
B.C.E.	Before Common Era (= B.C.)
Bek.	Bekhorot (talmudic tractate).
Ben Sira	See Ecclus.
Ber	Berakhot.
BK	Bava Kamma (talmudic tractate).
BM	Bava Mizia (talmudic tractate).
BT	Babylonian Talmud.
Cher.	Philo, De Cherubim.
I (or II) Chron.	Chronicles, books I & II (Bible).

I (or II) Cor.	Epistles to the Corinthians (New Testament).
Dan.	Daniel (Bible).
Dem.	Demai (talmudic tractate).
Deus	Philo, Quod Deus immutabilis sit.
Deut.	Deuteronomy (Bible).
Deut. R.	Deuteronomy Rabbah.
E	according to the documentary theory, the Elohist document (i.e., using Elohim as the name of God) of the first five (or six) books of the Bible
Eccles.	Ecclesiastes (Bible).
Eccles. R.	Ecclesiastes Rabbah (Midrash).
Ecclus.	Ecclesiasticus
Er.	Eruvin (talmudic tractate).
II Esd.	II Esdras (Apocrypha)
Ex.	Exodus (Bible).
Ezek.	Ezekiel (Bible).
Ezra	Ezra (Bible).
Gal.	Galatians (New Testament).
Gen.	Genesis (Bible).
Gen. R.	Genesis Rabbah.
Ger.	Gerim (post-talmudic tractate).
Git.	Gittin (talmudic tractate).
Guide	Maimonides, Guide of the Perplexed.
Hab.	Habakkuk (Bible).
Hag.	Haigah (talmudic tractate).
Haggai	Haggai (Bible).
Heb.	Epistle to the Hebrews (New Testament).
Hil.	Hilkhot (e.g. Hilkhot Shabbat).
Hos.	Hosea (Bible).
Hul.	Hullin (talmudic tractate).
Isa.	Isaiah (Bible)
J	according to the commentary theory, the Jahwist document (i.e., using YHWH as the name of God) of the first five (or six) books of the Bible
Jer.	Jeremiah (Bible).
Jos. Wars	Josephus, The Jewish Wars
Josh.	Joshua (Bible).
Judg.	Judges (Bible).
J.T.	Jerusalem Talmud.
Ket.	Ketubbot (talmudic tractate).
Kid.	Kiddushin (talmudic tractate).
Lam.	Lamentations (Bible).
Lam. R.	Lamentations Rabbah (Midrash).
Lev.	Leviticus (Bible).
Lev. R.	Leviticus Rabbah (Midrash).
I, II, III, & IV Macc.	Maccabees, I, II, III (Apocrypha), IV (Pseudepigrapha).
Mal.	Malachi (Bible).

Matt.	Gospel according to Matthew (New Testament).
Meg.	Megillah (talmudic tractate).
Mekh.	Mekhilta de-Rabbi Ishmael (Midrash).
Men.	Menahot (talmudic tractate).
MGWJ	Monatsschrift fuer Geschichte und Weissenschaft des Judentums (1851–1939).
Mid.Ag.	Midrash Aggadah
Mid.Hag.	Midrash ha-Gadol.
Mid.Job.	Midrash Job
Mid.Jonah	Midrash Jonah
Mid.Ps.	Midrash Tehillim (Eng. tr. The Midrash on Psalms (JPS, 1959)).
Mid.Yal.	Midrash Yalkut.
MK	Mo'ed Katan (talmudic tractate).
MT	Maimonides, Mishneh Torah.
Ned.	Nedarim (talmudic tractate).
Neh.	Nehemiah (Bible).
Nid.	Niddah (talmudic tractate).
Num.	Numbers (Bible).
Num.R.	Numbers Rabbah (Midrash).
OH	Orah Hayyim.
Oho	Oholot (mishnaic tractate).
PdRE	Pirkei de-Rabbi Eliezer
PdRK	Pesikta de-Rav Kahana.
Pes.	Pesahim (talmudic tractate).
Prov.	Proverbs (Bible).
Ps.	Psalms (Bible).
1QH	Thanksgiving Psalms or Hodayot from Qumran.
1QS	Manual of Discipline or Serekh ha-Yahad.
R.	Rabbi; Rav.
Rom.	Epistle to the Romans (New Testament).
Sam.	Samuel, books I & II (Bible).
Sanh.	Sanhedrin (talmudic tractate).
Shab.	Shabbat (talmudic tractate).
Sh.Ar.	Shulhan Arukh.
Shev.	Shevi'it (talmudic tractate).
Shevu	Shevu'ot (talmudic tractate).
Sibl.	Sibyline
Sif.Deut.	Sifrei Deuteronomy.
Sif.Num.	Sifrei Numbers.
Sof.	Soferim (post-talmudic tractate).
Song	Song of Songs (Bible).
Sot.	Sotah (talmudic tractate).
Suk.	Sukkah (talmudic tractate).
Ta'an.	Ta'anit (talmudic tractate).
Tanh.	Tanhuma.
Tob.	Tobit (Apocrypha).

Tos.	Tosafot.
Tosef.	Tosefta.
Wars	Josephus, The Jewish Wars.
Wisd.	Wisdom of Solomon (Apocrypha).
Yad.	Yadayim (mishnaic tractate).
Yal.	Yalkut Shimoni.
YD	Yoreh De'ah.
Yev.	Yevamot (talmudic tractate).
Yoma	Yoma (talmudic tractate).
Zech.	Zechariah (Bible).

List of Contributors

HENRY HANOCH ABRAMOVITCH is a psychologist and anthropologist who teaches at the Tel Aviv University Medical School. He is the author of the forthcoming *Abraham: Psychology of a Spiritual Revolutionary and His Hebrew Chroniclers*. He has pursued fieldwork research on mortuary customs both in Jerusalem and in Madagascar. **DEATH**

JACOB B. AGUS (1911-1986) was ordained by Yeshiva University in 1935 and received his advanced degrees from Harvard University. Among his many books are *Modern Philosophies of Judaism* (1941), *The Evolution of Jewish Thought* (1959), *Jewish Identity in an Age of Ideologies* (1978). In addition to serving a congregation, Rabbi Agus has taught at Temple University and Dropsie College and for more than a decade served as editorial consultant on Judaism and Jewish history to the *Encyclopaedia Brittanica*. **MEDIEVAL JEWISH PHILOSOPHY**

ALLAN ARKUSH has taught Jewish Studies at Colgate University and Cornell University. He is the translator of Moses Mendelssohn's *Jerusalem* (1983). He is currently Assistant Professor of Jewish Studies at the State University of New York at Binghamton. **IMMORTALITY; MIRACLE**

JACOB A. ARLOW, a graduate of the New York Psychoanalytic Institute, and former president of the American Psychoanalytic Association as well as editor-in-chief of the psychoanalytic journal, *Quarterly,* is a member of the Board of Jewish Education (New York City), emeritus Professor of Clinical Psychiatry at Albert Einstein College and Professor of Clinical Psychiatry at the College of Medicine of New York University. GUILT

HENRI ATLAN is Professor of Medical Biophysics at Hadassah Medical School-Hebrew University. In addition to a considerable body of original scientific work, Atlan has published numerous essays on general and Jewish philosophy, a portion of which appeared in *Entre le Cristal et la Fumee* (Paris, 1979) and *Mystiques et Sciences* (Paris, 1984). CHOSEN PEOPLE

JANET AVIAD, a sociologist, teaches at the school of Education and the Melton Center for Jewish Education at The Hebrew University. Among her publications is *Return to Judaism: Religious Renewal in Jerusalem* (1983). EDUCATION

ELLA BELFER is Senior Lecturer at the Department of Political Science of Bar-Ilan University, has published essays on Marxism, secular and religious messianism, and is the editor of *Spiritual Leadership in Israel* (Hebrew, 1982). POLITICAL THEORY

DAVID BIALE, associate professor of History and Judaic Studies at the State University of New York (Binghamton) is the author of *Gershom Scholem: Kabbalah and Counter-History* and is presently engaged in an extended study of Jewish attitudes toward love, marriage, and the family. EROS: SEX AND BODY; FAMILY

DAVID R. BLUMENTHAL, Jay and Leslie Cohen Professor of Judaic Studies at Emory University (Atlanta, Georgia), is editor of the series, *Etudes sur le judaisme medieval,* and author, among other works, of *The Commentary of hoter ben Shelomo to the Thirteen Principles of Maimonides, Understanding Jewish Mysticism,* and editor of a series in medieval Jewish thought, *Approaches to the Study of Judaism in Medieval Times.* MERCY

EUGENE B. BOROWITZ, rabbi and Professor of Education and Jewish Religious Thought at the New York School of Hebrew Union College-Jewish Institute of Religion since 1962, is the founder and editor of *Sh'ma, a Journal of Jewish Responsibility.* He is the author of numerous theological and general works including *Liberal Judaism* and *The Masks Jews Wear.* FREEDOM; REASON

ARTHUR A. COHEN (1928-1986) was the author of *Martin Buber* (1959), *The Natural and the Supernatural Jew: An Historical and Theological Introduction* (1962), *The Myth of the Judeo-Christian Tradition* (1970), *The Tremendum: A Theological Interpretation of the Holocaust* (1981). He also edited the theological writings of Milton Steinberg, *The Anatomy of Faith* as well as *Arguments and Doctrines* (1970) and *The Jew: Essays from Martin Buber's Journal, Der Jude, 1916–1928* (1980). He was also a novelist; his *Artists and Enemies* was published posthumously. ESCHATOLOGY; REDEMPTION; RESURRECTION OF THE DEAD; THEOLOGY

GERSON COHEN, presently Chancellor of The Jewish Theological Seminary of America and its Jacob H. Schiff Professor of History, is the author of the critical edition of Abraham ibn Daud's *Book of Tradition* and a contributor to *Great Ages and Ideas of the Jewish People* (1956). Professor Cohen has recently announced that he will resign as Chancellor of the Seminary during 1986.   **CONSERVATIVE JUDAISM**

HAIM H. COHEN retired in 1981 from the Supreme Court of Israel where he served for more than twenty years as Associate Justice and later as Deputy President. Prior to his appointment to its Supreme Court, he had served as Israel's Attorney-General and for a time as Minister of Justice. In addition to his mastery of secular law, Justice Cohen had pursued rabbinical studies at Yeshivat Merkaz HaRav (Jerusalem). Among his many works are *Jewish Law in Ancient and Modern Israel* (1971), *The Trial and Death of Jesus* (1968, 1971), and *Human Rights in Jewish Law* (1984).   **JUSTICE**

JOSEPH DAN, Gershom Scholem Professor of Kabbalah in the Department of Jewish thought at The Hebrew University, has written extensively on the history of Jewish mysticism, his works including numerous Hebrew studies, including *The Esoteric Theology of Ashkenazi Hasidism, The Hebrew Story in the Middle Ages, Studies in Ashkenazi Hasidic Literature,* as well as such English language volumes as *The Teachings of Hasidism, Jewish Mysticism and Jewish Ethics, Gershom Scholem: The Mystical Dimension of Jewish History,* and *Three Types of Ancient Jewish Mysticism*.   **IMAGO DEI**

ARNOLD EISEN, until 1984 Assistant Professor in the Department of Religion at Columbia University, is presently lecturer in the Department of Jewish Philosophy at Tel Aviv University. The author of numerous essays and critical studies, he has published *The Chosen People in America: A Study in Jewish Religious Ideology* (1983) and *Galut: Jewish Reflections on Homelessness and Homecoming* (1986).   **COVENANT; EXILE**

RACHEL ELIOR, Senior Lecturer in Kabbalah and Hasidism at The Hebrew University of Jerusalem, is the author, among other works, of *The Theory of Divinity in Hasidut Habad* (Hebrew, Jerusalem, 1982) as well as critical editions in Hebrew of *Galia Raza* (Jerusalem, 1982) and *Hekhalot Zutarti* (Jerusalem, 1982).   **SOUL**

DAVID ELLENSON, Assistant Professor of Jewish Religious Thought at Hebrew Union College-Jewish Institute of Religion in Los Angeles, is the author of numerous studies that have appeared in the *American Academy of Religion, The Hebrew Union College Annual, Modern Judaism,* and *Semeia*.   **ETERNITY AND TIME**

EMIL L. FACKENHEIM taught at the University of Toronto where he was Professor of Philosophy for over thirty years. In 1983 he immigrated to Israel where he is now a Fellow of the Institute of Contemporary Jewry at the Hebrew University at Jerusalem. Among his numerous publications are: *The Religious in Hegel's Thought* (1967) and *To Mend The World* (1982).   **HOLOCAUST**

ZE'EV FALK has been since 1970 Berman Professor of Family and Succession Law at The Hebrew University of Jerusalem, as well as serving as visiting professor at several American universities. He is the author of several works among which are *Hebrew Law in Biblical Times: An Introduction* (1964), *Introduction to the Jewish Law* *of the Second Commonwealth* (1977–78), and *Law and Religion. The Jewish Experience* (1981). **JURISPRUDENCE**

MICHAEL FISHBANE, Samuel Lane Professor in Jewish Religious History and Social Ethics at Brandeis University, is the author of numerous studies, including *Text and Texture. Close Readings of Selected Biblical Texts* (1979) and *Biblical Interpretation in Ancient Israel* (1985). **HERMENEUTICS; PRAYER**

DAVID FLUSSER is the Gail Levin de Nur Professor of Comparative Religion at the Hebrew University of Jerusalem. His publications and research activities include: Judaism of the Second Temple Period; the New Testament and its Jewish background; the Dead Sea Sect; and early Church history. He is the author of RABBINIC PARABLES AND PARABLES OF JESUS (Vol 1, 1981), THE LAST DAYS OF JESUS IN JERUSALEM (1982), PSALMS, HYMNS AND PRAYERS IN JEWISH WRITINGS OF THE SECOND PERIOD (1984). He is the recipient of the Israel Prize for Jewish Thought (1980), and a member of the Israel Academy of Sciences and Humanities. **CHRISTIANITY**

ERICH L. FRIEDLAND was educated at Boston University, the Hebrew Teachers College of Boston, and Brandeis University. Since 1968, he has been the Harriet Sanders Professor of Judaic Studies at three colleges and a United Methodist seminary in Dayton (Ohio). **LITURGY**

ALBERT H. FRIEDLANDER, Dean and Senior Lecturer at the Leo Baeck College (London) and rabbi of the Westminster Synagogue in London, was educated at the University of Chicago and the Hebrew Union College (Cincinnati). He is the author of *Leo Baeck: Teacher of Theresienstadt* (1968) and editor of *Out of the Whirlwind* (1969). **DESTINY AND FATE**

MAURICE FRIEDMAN is Professor of Religious Studies, Philosophy, and Comparative Literature at San Diego University. He is the author of many books including the three volume biography of *Martin Buber* and the translation of many volumes of Buber material including *Pointing the Way: Collected Essays.* **I AND THOU**

EVERETT GENDLER, rabbi at Temple Emmanuel in Lowell (Massachusetts), serves as Jewish Chaplain and instructor in philosophy and religious studies at the Phillips Academy in Andover (Massachusetts). He is the author of numerous innovative essays on Jewish liturgical practice. **COMMUNITY**

NAHUM N. GLATZER taught for many years at Brandeis University and is presently a University Professor and Professor of Religion at Boston University. Among his numerous publications are *Geschichte der Talmudischen Zeit* (1937), *Franz Rosenzweig: His Life and Thought* (1953), *The Dimensions of Job* (1969), *Franz Kafka: The Complete Stories* (1971), and *Essays in Jewish Thought* (1978). **APOCALYPSE; REMNANT OF ISRAEL**

LEWIS H. GLINERT, Lecturer in Hebrew Language and Literature in the School of Oriental and African Studies at the London University since 1979, is the author of

A Reference Grammar of Israeli Hebrew and other works on Hebrew linguistics and literature. **HEBREW**

ALON GOSHEN-GOTTSTEIN, a graduate of Yeshivat Ha-Kotel and Yeshivat Har Etzion, is currently instructor in Rabbinic Thought at The Hebrew University of Jerusalem. **CREATION; PEOPLE OF ISRAEL**

ARTHUR GREEN, Dean of the Reconstructionist Rabbinical College, is the author of *Tormented Master: A Life of Rabbi Nahman of Bratzlav* and the editor of *Jewish Spirituality from the Bible through the Middle Ages.* **HASIDISM; SPIRITUALITY**

BLU GREENBERG is an author, a lecturer, and a community artist. Her two recent books were: *On Women and Judaism: A View from Tradition* and *How to Run a Traditional Jewish Household.* **WOMEN AND JUDAISM**

MOSHE GREENBERG, Professor of Bible at The Hebrew University, received his doctorate in Oriental Studies from the University of Pennsylvania and was ordained a rabbi from the Jewish Theological Seminary of America. A member of the translation committee of the Jewish Publication Society of America responsible for *Ketuvim (The Writings)*, he is the author of *Understanding Exodus* (1969), *Ezekiel 1–20* in the Anchor Bible (1983), *Biblical Prose Prayer* (1983), and translator and editor of the abridgement of Yehezkel Kaufmann's *The Religion of Israel* (1960). **EXEGESIS**

ILAN GREILSAMMER, was educated in Paris, and is an associate professor at the Department of Political Science of Bar-Ilan University. He has published a number of books including *Les Communistes Israeliens* (1969), *The Jewish Community of France* (Hebrew, 1981), *Israel et l'Europe* (1982). **POLITICAL THEORY**

ZE'EV GRIES, lecturer in Ethical and Mystical Literature in the Department of Jewish Thought, The Hebrew University of Jerusalem, is the author of two forthcoming Hebrew works, *The History of Hasidic 'Regimen Vitae'* and *The Early Hasidic Generations from the Baal Shem Tov to the Kotzker.* **HERESY**

ALLEN GROSSMAN, Paul E. Proswimmer Professor of Poetry and General Education at Brandeis University, is a poet whose most recent volumes include *The Woman on the Bridge over the Chicago River* (1969) and *Of the Great House* (1981). He is the author as well of *Poetic Knowledge in the Early Yeats* (1969) and with Mark Halliday, *Against Our Vanishing Conversations on Poetry and Poetics* (1981). **HOLINESS**

JOSHUA O. HABERMAN is Senior Rabbi of the Washington Hebrew Congregation (Washington, D.C.) and received his doctorate from the Hebrew Union College. He is co-chairman of the North American Board of the World Union for Progressive Judaism and president of The Foundation for Jewish Studies. He has published critical studies on Steinheim, Rosenzweig, Buber and other figures of the German-Jewish theological renaissance. **RIGHTEOUSNESS**

YOSSI KLEIN HALEVI is a contributing editor of *Moment* magazine and of the *Village Voice*. A recent resident of Jerusalem, Yossi Klein Halevi is completing a book on the West Bank city of Hebron.   SURVIVAL

BEN HALPERN, Richard Koret Professor Emeritus of Near Eastern Studies at Brandeis University, is the author of *The American Jews: A Zionist Analysis, The Idea of the Jewish State, Jews and Blacks: America's Classic Minorities*. For many years, Professor Halpern served as editor of *The Jewish Frontier*.   SECULARISM; ZIONISM

DAVID HARTMAN, a student of Rabbi J. B. Soloveitchik, received his rabbinic ordination in 1953 and his doctorate in philosophy from McGill University. Following his aliyah in 1971, he founded in Jerusalem the Shalom Hartman Institute of which he is director. He is Associate Professor of Jewish Philosophy at The Hebrew University. His books include *Maimonides: Torah and Philosophic Quest* (1977), *Joy and Responsibility: Israel, Modernity and the Renewal of Judaism* (1978), and *A Living Covenant* (1985).   CHARITY; HALAKHAH; SUFFERING

GEOFFREY HARTMAN, Karl Young Professor of English and Comparative Literature at Yale University, is the author of numerous books, among which are *Beyond Formalism: Selected Essays* (1970), *The Fate of Reading: Literary Essays 1970–1975* (1975), *Saving the Text: Literature/Derrida/Philosophy* (1981), *Easy Pieces: Literary Essays and Reviews* (1985).   IMAGINATION

STEVEN HARVEY received his undergraduate degree from St. John's University in Annapolis and his doctorate in Medieval Philosophy and Jewish Intellectual History from Harvard University. He is presently teaching Jewish Philosophy at the Baltimore Hebrew College.   LOVE

WARREN ZEV HARVEY teaches Medieval Jewish Philosophy at Hebrew University in Jerusalem. At the present he is working on a monograph of Hasdai Crescas. He has written extensively on Maimonides, on Crescas, and on many medieval and modern Jewish philosophers. He is particularly interested in Jewish political thought from the biblical to the modern period.   GRACE OR LOVING–KINDNESS; KINGDOM OF GOD

GALIT HASAN-ROKEM teaches Jewish folklore and Midrash at The Hebrew University of Jerusalem where she also serves as the chairperson of the Jewish Folklore Program. She is co-editor of *Jerusalem Studies of Jewish Folklore* (Hebrew, bi-annual) and associate editor of *Proverbium. Yearbook of International Proverb Scholarship*. Among her varied publications are *Proverbs in Israeli Folktales: A Structural-Semantic Analysis of Folklore* (Helsinki, 1982) and *The Wandering Jew: Interpretations of a Christian Legend* (co-edited with Alan Dundes, Bloomington, 1985).   MYTH

SUSANNAH HESCHEL is a doctoral candidate in the Department of Religious Studies at the University of Pennsylvania. Her book, *On Being a Jewish Feminist: A Reader* was published by Schocken Books (1983).   FEMINISM

PAULA E. HYMAN is the Lucy Moses Professor of Modern Jewish History at Yale University. She is the author of FROM DREYFUS TO VICHY, THE REMAKING OF FRENCH JEWRY (1979), and the co-editor of THE JEWISH WOMEN IN AMERICA (1976). Most recently she co-edited THE JEWISH FAMILY. MYTHS AND REALITY (1986). She is currently working on a book entitled EMANCIPATION AND SOCIAL CHANGE. EMANCIPATION

MOSHE IDEL teaches Jewish mysticism and Kabbalah at The Hebrew University of Jerusalem. Among his numerous publications are *The Mystical Experience of Abraham Abulafia* (SUNY, 1986) and a forthcoming work, *Kabbalah. New Perspectives.* MUSIC; MYSTICISM

LOUIS JACOBS, rabbi of the New London Synagogue (London), is professor of Talmud and Theology at the Leo Baeck College (London) and visiting professor at the Harvard Divinity School. Among his books are: *Principles of the Jewish Faith* (1964), *Theology in the Responsa* (1975) and *Jewish Mystical Testimonies* (1977). FAITH; GOD

WILLIAM E. KAUFMAN was ordained at the Jewish Theological Seminary of America in 1964 and received his doctorate in philosophy from Boston University in 1971. He is the author of two books, *Contemporary Jewish Philosophies* and *Journeys: An Introductory Guide to Jewish Mysticism* as well as numerous essays on Jewish philosophy, mysticism, and theology. He is rabbi of Temple Beth El in Fall River, Massachusetts. TIME

MENACHEM KELLNER, a Senior Lecturer in the Department of Jewish Thought at University of Haifa, received his doctorate from Washington University (St. Louis). Dr. Kellner's publications include the anthology, *Contemporary Jewish Ethics,* an annotated translation of Isaac Abravanel's *Rosh Amanah (Principles of Faith),* and *Dogma in Medieval Jewish Thought* (1985). DOGMA

LIONEL KOCHAN, the first incumbent of the Bearsted Readership in Jewish History at the University of Warwick in 1969, was educated at Cambridge University and the London School of Economics. The author of *The Jew and His History* (1977), he is presently engaged on a study of Jewish messianic thought and activity. UTOPIA

JAMES L. KUGEL, Starr Professor of Hebrew Literature at Harvard University since 1982, is a co-founder and an editor of *Prooftexts* as well as a member of the Advisory Board of Crossroad Biblical Studies. He is the author of *The Techniques of Strangeness* (1971), *The Idea of Biblical Poetry* (1981) and a forthcoming examination of Biblical exegesis, *The Dismembered Bible and the Mind of Midrash.* TORAH

YESHAYAHU LEIBOWITZ received his doctorate from the University of Berlin in 1924 and his medical degree from the University of Basle in 1934. Since 1935, he has taught organic and biological chemistry at The Hebrew University of Jerusalem. Although retired in 1970, Professor Leibowitz is still active in research and public life. In addition to his numerous scientific papers, Professor Leibowitz has published extensively in Jewish religious philosophy and contemporary Israeli affairs. Among his many books in Hebrew are *Faith, History and Values* (Jerusalem, 1983), *Judaism, the Jewish People and the Jewish State* (Tel Aviv, 1976), and *The Faith of Maimonides* (Tel Aviv, 1980). COMMANDMENTS; HEROISM; IDOLATRY

JOSEPH LEVI. A scion of an old Italian Jewish family, Dr. Joseph Levi was born in Jerusalem in 1946. He studied at various *yeshivot* and later earned a B.A. at The Hebrew University of Jerusalem, and a Diplome d'Etudes Approfondies from the Ecole des Hautes Etudes, Paris. His Ph.D. in philosophy and psychology was awarded by the University of Copenhagen. From 1976–80 he was a fellow at Jean Piaget's Center for Genetic Epistemology in Geneva. He presently works as a psychologist in Jerusalem and is writing a major study on the Italian physician Joseph Solomon Delmedigo, a 17th century kabbalist and a disciple of Galileo. STRANGER

HILLEL LEVINE, Professor of Sociology and Religion at Boston University, is Director of its Center for Judaic Studies. His published works include studies in social theory, comparative historical sociology, and the social epistemology of Judaism. The Israel Academy of Science and Humanities has recently published his book, *The 'Kronika': On Jacob Frank and the Frankist Movement*. PROVIDENCE; SCIENCE

AHARON LICHTENSTEIN, formerly professor of Talmud at Yeshiva University in New York City, is presently Rosh Yeshiva of the rabbinical academy Har Etzion near Jerusalem. Among his considerable writings are *Henry Moore. The Rational Theology of a Cambridge Platonist* (1962). RELIGION AND STATE; STUDY

EHUD LUZ is presently teaching modern Jewish thought at Haifa University and Oranim (the school of education of the Kibbutz movement). His book *Parallels Meet*, on the conflict of religion and nationalism in the Zionist movement, appeared recently in Hebrew and is soon to appear in English. REPENTANCE

HYAM MACCOBY was educated at Balliol College, Oxford, where he received his Master's Degree in 1951. He is presently lecturer and librarian at the Leo Baeck College (London). Among his publications are *Revolution in Judaea* (1973), *Judaism on Trial: Jewish-Christian Disputations in the Middle Ages* (1982), and *The Sacred Executioner* (1982). ANTI-JUDAISM, ANTI-SEMITISM; SANCTIFICATION OF THE NAME

JEFFREY MACY, lecturer in classical and medieval Islamic and Jewish political thought and history in the Department of Political Science at The Hebrew University of Jerusalem, is shortly to publish a book on Maimonides's political philosophy. NATURAL LAW

TZVI MARX, ordained at Yeshiva University (1969), is presently Educational Director of the Shalom Hartman Institute for Advanced Judaic Studies in Jerusalem. CHARITY

PAUL MENDES-FLOHR teaches modern Jewish thought and intellectual history at The Hebrew University of Jerusalem. Among his numerous publications are: *Von der Mystik zum Dialog: Martin Buber's geistige Entwicklung bis hin 'Ich und Du'* (1976);

with Jehuda Reinharz, *The Jew in the Modern World: A Documentary History* (1980); *A Land of Two Peoples: Martin Buber on Jews and Arabs* (1983), a volume which has also appeared in French, German, Hebrew, Italian and Spanish. He is currently working on a cultural biography of Franz Rosenzweig, which is being supported by a fellowship from the John Simon Guggenheim Memorial Foundation.   CULTURE; HISTORY

MICHAEL A. MEYER, who teaches at the Hebrew Union College-Jewish Institute of Religion, is presently engaged in preparing a comprehensive history of the Reform movement in modern Jewry.   REFORM JUDAISM

ALAN MINTZ, Associate Professor on the Robert H. Smith Chair of Hebrew Literature, serves as well as Director of the Meyerhoff Center for Jewish Studies at the University of Maryland. He is the author of *George Eliot and the Novel of Persuasion* and *Hurban. Responses to Catastrophe in Hebrew Literature*. He is co-founder and an editor of *Prooftexts: A Journal of Jewish Literary History*.   CATASTROPHE

ANDRE NEHER settled in Jerusalem in 1968 after many years as a professor at the University of Strasbourg. He is the author of a score of works among which are *Moses and the Vocation of the Jewish People, The Prophetic Existence, The Exile of the Word, The Dialectical Theology of the Maharal of Prague*.   SILENCE

JACOB NEUSNER, University Professor and Ungerleider Distinguished Scholar of Judaic Studies at Brown University, is the author of numerous works, among the most well-known of which are *A Life of Yohanan ben Zakkai* (1962), *A History of the Jews in Babylonia* (1965–1970), *A History of the Mishnaic Law of Purities* (1974–1977), *Judaism: The Evidence of the Yerushalmi* (1983), and the recently launched *The Talmud of the Land of Israel*, a multi-volume series of translation and interpretation.   ORAL LAW

PETER OCHS, Assistant Professor of Religion and Philosophy at Colgate University, with degrees in rabbinics (Jewish Theological Seminary of America) and philosophy (Yale University), has written on pragmatic philosophy, Jewish thought and educational theory in several periodicals. He is presently working on a study of Peirce's pragmatic traditionalism and, as editor, is preparing works on his teacher, Max Kadushin, and the French philosopher, Emmanuel Levinas.   INDIVIDUAL; TRUTH

EMMANUEL RACKMAN is chancellor and the former president of Bar-Ilan University in Ramat Gan. A rabbi and lawyer by training, Dr. Rackman taught at Yeshiva University and the City University of New York as well as serving as president of the Rabbinical Council of America before coming to Israel. He is the author of *Israel's Emerging Constitution* and has contributed articles to many American Jewish and Israeli periodicals.   ORTHODOX JUDAISM

AVIEZER RAVITZKY is a senior lecturer in the Department of Jewish Thought at The Hebrew University of Jerusalem. He has published numerous essays on the philosophy of Hasdai Crescas, the esoteric interpretation of Maimonides's philosophy, messianism and Zionism.   PEACE

NISSIM REJWAN, historian and journalist specializing in Middle East and Israeli politics and culture, is the author of *Nasserist Ideology: Its Exponents and Critics* (1964), *The Jews of Iraq: History, Society, Heritage* (1985), and *Arabs Face the Modern World: A Century of Intellectual Endeavor* which is forthcoming. Mr. Rejwan lives in Jerusalem. ISLAM

MICHAEL ROSENAK is on the faculty of the School of Education at The Hebrew University and the Melton Center for Jewish Education in the diaspora. He is presently working on theological aspects of Jewish educational philosophy. STATE OF ISRAEL

SHALOM ROSENBERG is currently the Chairperson of the Department of Jewish Thought at The Hebrew University of Jerusalem. He has published extensively in medieval and modern Jewish thought and on the philosophy of religion. ETHICS; REVELATION

DAVID G. ROSKIES, Associate Professor in Jewish Literature at the Jewish theological Seminary of America, is co-founder and an editor of *Prooftexts: A Journal of Jewish Literary History*. He is the author of *Against the Apocalypse: Responses to Catastrophe in Modern Jewish History* (1984). MEMORY

NATAN ROTENSTREICH, Emeritus Ahad Ha'am Professor of Philosophy at The Hebrew University, immigrated to Palestine from Poland in 1932 and received his advanced education at The Hebrew University where he has served as dean of the Faculty of Humanities and rector of the University. The author of many works on philosophy and history of ideas in Hebrew, German, and English, he is the translator (with S. H. Bergmann) of the three critiques of Immanuel Kant into Hebrew. Among his best known works are: *Between Past and Present* (1958), *The Recurring Pattern, Studies in Anti-Judaism in Modern Thought* (1963), *Jewish Philosophy in Modern Times: From Mendelssohn to Rosenzweig* (1968); *Jews and German Philosophy* (1984). Professor Rotenstreich is the recipient of the Israel Prize for the Humanities (1963) and is Vice-President of the Israel Academy of Arts and Sciences. TRADITION

EPHRAIM ASHER ROTTENBERG is heir to a Hasidic lineage of Jewish learning and piety. Rabbi Rottenberg attended the yeshivah of Rabbi Shimon Grunfeld in B'szent Mihaly, Hungary, and was ordained in 1932 by his uncle, Rav Yisrael Zvi Rottenberg, the last Hasidic master of Mezokaszony to whom he is discipled. Arriving in Los Angeles in 1938 (a year after his father who became the first Hasidic rabbi to settle in that city), Rabbi Rottenberg has been a leader of West Coast Orthodoxy in the United States. REWARD AND PUNISHMENT

RICHARD L. RUBENSTEIN, Robert D. Lawton Distinguished Professor of Religion at Florida State University and presently Visiting Professor of Modern Jewish Thought at the University of Virginia, is President of the Washington Institute for Values in Public Policy in Washington, D.C. He is the author among other works of *After Auschwitz: Radical Theology* and *Contemporary Judaism* (1966), *The Religious Imagination* (1967), *My Brother Paul* (1972), *Power Struggle: An Autobiographical*

Confession (1974) and, most recently, *The Age of Triage: Fear and Hope in an Over-crowded World* (1983).   **EVIL; EXISTENCE**

DAVID B. RUDERMAN, Professor of Religious Studies and Chairman of the Judaic Studies Program at Yale University, received his doctorate at The Hebrew University. He is the author of *The World of a Renaissance Jew: The Life and Thought of Abraham ben Mordecai Farissol*.   **RABBI AND TEACHER**

MARC SAPERSTEIN, associate professor of Jewish Studies at the Harvard Divinity School, received his doctorate in the Department of Near Eastern Languages and Civilizations at Harvard University. He is the author of *Decoding the Rabbis* (1980) and is completing a major study of the history of the sermon in Jewish tradition, provisionally titled, *Jewish Preaching, 1200-1800: An Introduction with Examples*. **SERMON**

DAVID SATRAN was educated at Amherst College and received his doctorate at The Hebrew University where he is presently a lecturer in its Department of Comparative Religion.   **HELLENISM**

GERSHOM SCHOLEM, until his death in 1982, was the world-famous expositer of the history and doctrine of Jewish mysticism. After serving for many years as the first librarian of The Hebrew University, he established its department of studies in the Jewish mystical tradition and served as Professor of Jewish Mysticism from 1933-1965. From 1968 to 1974 he was president of the Israel Academy of Sciences and Humanities. Among his most important works were *Major Trends in Jewish Mysticism, The Messianic Idea in Judaism, On the Kabbalah and Its Symbolism, Sabbatai Zevi: The Mystical Messiah, On Jews and Judaism in Crisis*. The essay on Judaism published here is based upon a transcript of his conversations with members of the Center for the Study of Democratic Institutions (Santa Barbara) and is published here with its permission.   **JUDAISM**

HAROLD M. SCHULWEIS, rabbi of Valley Beth Shalom in Encino (California), is adjunct professor of the University of Judaism in Los Angeles and author of *Evil and the Morality of God*.   **RECONSTRUCTIONISM**

DANIEL R. SCHWARTZ earned his doctorate at The Hebrew University where he has served as Lecturer in Jewish History since 1980. His research focuses on Jewish religion, history and historiography of the late Second Temple period. He is currently completing a work on King Agrippa I.   **KINGDOM OF PRIESTS**

STEVEN S. SCHWARZSCHILD, professor of philosophy and Judaic studies at Washington University (St. Louis) is the author of numerous critical studies on Jewish philosophy and religious thought, including most recently "A Critique of Martin Buber's Social Philosophy—A Loving Reappraisal," *Leo Baeck Institute Year Book XXXI* (1986), "An Introduction to the Thought of R. Isaac Hutner," *Modern Judaism* (1985), and "On the Jewish Eschatology" in *The Human Condition in the Jewish and Christian Tradition*, ed. by F. Greenspahn (1985).   **AESTHETICS; CONSCIENCE; MODERN JEWISH PHILOSOPHY**

ELIEZER SCHWEID received his doctorate in Jewish Philosophy at The Hebrew University in 1961 and has been a professor at that institution since 1982. He is the author of many works dealing with issues of Jewish culture and nationalism, most recently *Democracy and Halakhah* (Hebrew, 1979), *Judaism and Secular Culture* (Hebrew, 1981), and *Homeland or Land of Destiny* (English, 1985). LAND OF ISRAEL

ROBERT M. SELTZER, associate professor at Hunter College and the Graduate School, the City University of New York, is the author of *Jewish People, Jewish Thought* + *the Jewish Experience in History.* ENLIGHTENMENT

ABRAHAM SHAPIRA, a member of Kibbutz Yizrael and teacher in the Department of Jewish Philosophy at the University of Tel Aviv, is the author of the forthcoming work, *Dualistic Structures in the Thought of Martin Buber,* as well as having edited the seminal work, *The Seventh Day* (1970). He is currently the editor-in-chief of the collected Hebrew edition of the works of Gershom Scholem. WORK

BYRON L. SHERWIN, Vice President for Academic Affairs and Vernon Professor of Jewish Philosophy and Mysticism at Spertus College of Judaica in Chicago, is the author of seven works including *Mystical Theology and Social Dissent: The Life and Works of Judah Loew of Prague, The Golem Legend: Origins and Implications,* and *Abraham Joshua Heschel.* FEAR OF GOD; THEODICY

ERNST AKIVA SIMON is professor Emeritus of Education at The Hebrew University and the author of many works on philosophical, educational, and historical subjects, including *Ranke and Hegel* (German, 1928), *Pestalozzi and Korczak* (Hebrew, 1949), *Are We Still Jews? Essays* (Hebrew, 1982). With Edith Rosenzweig-Scheinmann, he edited *The Letters of Franz Rosenzweig* (German, 1935). HUMANISM

AARON SINGER received his Doctor of Hebrew Letters from the Jewish Theological Seminary of America (New York City) in 1979 and has taught at The Hebrew University, University of Toronto, and the Catholic Union (Chicago). Presently, he is the Dean of Overseas Students at The Hebrew University. He is the author of many studies, including "The Rabbinic Fable" in *Jerusalem Studies in Jewish Folklore 4* (1983). HOLY SPIRIT

JACK SPIRO, Rabbi of Congregation Beth Ahabah (Richmond, Virginia), is director of Judaic studies and affiliate professor of religious studies at Virginia Commonwealth University. Dr. Spiro is a contributing editor of *Currents and Trends in Contemporary Jewish Thought* and is the author and editor of a number of other works including *To Learn and to Teach,* a philosophy of Jewish education. MEANING

BERNARD STEINBERG taught Jewish Philosophy at the School for Overseas Students of The Hebrew University and at the Pardes Institute of Jewish Studies in Jerusalem, as well as directing the Wesleyan University Israel Program. Since 1984–1985 he has been a Visiting Professor Jewish Thought at the Cleveland College of Jewish Studies. HUMILITY

ADIN STEINSALZ is the head of The Israel Institute for Talmudic Publications, the Yeshivah Makor Hayim, and the Shefa Institute of Advanced Studies in Judaism. Among his numerous publications is a commentary and translation into modern Hebrew of the Babylonian Talmud of which seventeen volumes have thus far appeared. Rabbi Steinsalz is the author in English of *The Essential Talmud* (1976), *The Thirteen Petaled Rose* (1981), and *Biblical Images* (1984).   Sɪɴ; Soᴜʟ–Sᴇᴀʀᴄʜɪɴɢ; Tᴀʟᴍᴜᴅ

DAVID STERN, assistant professor of medieval Hebrew literature at the University of Pennsylvania, has written essays on midrash, literature, and literary criticism. A member of the editorial board of *Prooftexts*, Professor Stern is currently completing a study on parables in midrash and (with Mark Mirsky) an anthology of original translations of narratives from medieval Hebrew literature.   Aɢɢᴀᴅᴀʜ; Mɪᴅʀᴀꜱʜ; Sᴀᴄʀᴇᴅ Tᴇxᴛ ᴀɴᴅ Cᴀɴᴏɴ

JOSEF STERN, an assistant professor of Philosophy at the University of Chicago, works primarily in the philosophy of language and linguistics and in medieval Jewish philosophy.   Gᴇꜱᴛᴜʀᴇ ᴀɴᴅ Sʏᴍʙᴏʟ; Lᴀɴɢᴜᴀɢᴇ

GEDALIAHU G. STROUMSA received his B.A. at The Hebrew University and his doctorate from Harvard in 1978. A Senior Lecturer in the Department of Comparative Religion at The Hebrew University, he is the author of *Another Seed: Studies in Gnostic Mythology* (1984).   Gɴᴏꜱɪꜱ

SHEMARYAHU TALMON, J. L. Magnes Professor in the Department of Bible Studies at The Hebrew University since 1955, has served as visiting professor at numerous universities in the United States and Europe. He is the author of a vast corpus of scholarly essays and reviews as well as having edited with F. M. Cross, *Qumran and the History of the Biblical Text* (1975) and with G. Siefer, *Religion und Politik* (1978).   Jᴇʀᴜꜱᴀʟᴇᴍ

ALAN UDOFF, Assistant Professor of Philosophy at the Baltimore Hebrew College, is the author of *Franz Kafka and the Contemporary Critical Performance: Centenary Readings* (1986) and the forthcoming *The Play-Ground of Textuality: Modern Jewish Intellectualism and the Horizons of Interpretation*. He has written extensively on Franz Rosenzweig, Leo Strauss, Walter Benjamin, and other contemporary figures of the Jewish religious renaissance.   Mᴇᴛᴀᴘʜʏꜱɪᴄꜱ; Tᴏʟᴇʀᴀɴᴄᴇ

CHARLES ELLIOTT VERNOFF received his advanced training at the University of Chicago, Harvard University, The Hebrew University, and the University of California (Santa Barbara) who awarded him his doctorate. Since 1978 he has been chairman of the Department of Religion at Cornell College (Iowa). The author of many essays on theory and method in the study of the history of religion, his articles have been published in the *Journal of the American Academy of Religion* and other journals.   Hᴏᴘᴇ; Uɴɪᴛʏ

STEPHEN WALD is a Fellow of the Shalom Hartman Institute of Advanced Jewish Studies in Jerusalem.   Aᴜᴛʜᴏʀɪᴛʏ

MOSHE WALDOKS, Assistant Professor of Jewish Studies at Clark University (Worcester, Massachusetts), has recently completed his doctoral dissertation on Hillel Zeitlin for Brandeis University. **MENTSH; MIZVEH**

ARTHUR WASKOW, a member of the faculty of the Reconstructionist Rabbinical College and executive director of The Shalom Center, is the author of *Godwrestling, Seasons of Our Joy, These Holy Sparks,* and *Rainbow Sign.* **REST**

GERSHON WEILER teaches philosophy at the University of Tel Aviv. He is the author of *Mauthner's Critique of Language* (1970) and *Jewish Theocracy* (Hebrew, 1976). **ATHEISM**

MOSHE WEINFELD, Professor of Bible at The Hebrew University, is editor of the *Annual for Biblical and Ancient Near Eastern Studies* and member of the editorial board of *Vetus Testamentum.* He is the author of several books among which are *Deuteronomy and the Deuteronomic School* (1972), *Commentary to the Book of Genesis* (Hebrew, 1975), *Justice and Righteousness in Israel* (Hebrew, 1984). **BIBLE CRITICISM**

R. J. ZWI WERBLOWSKY, Martin Buber Professor of Comparative Religion at The Hebrew University, received his Docteur des Lettres from the University of Geneva (1951) and taught in England until he joined The Hebrew University in 1956. Since 1975 he has served as Secretary General of the International Association for the History of Religion; he is also currently the editor of the Association's journal, *Numen.* Among his many works are *Joseph Karo: Lawyer and Mystic* (2nd ed., 1977), *Beyond Tradition and Modernity: Changing Religions in a Changing World,* and "Messianism in Jewish History" in Ben-Sasson and Ettinger's volume, *Jewish Society through the Ages* (1969). A colleague of the late Gershom Scholem, Professor Werblowsky was responsible for the English translation of the later's *Sabbatai Zevi* and most recently has edited Scholem's *Origins of the Kabbalah* (1987). **MESSIANISM**

GEOFFREY WIGODER is presently at the Institute of Contemporary Jewry, Hebrew University, Jerusalem. He is also editor-in-chief of the Encyclopedia of Zionism and he has held this position for the Encyclopædia Judaica. He is Vice-Chairman of the Israel Interfaith Organization and is Israel's representative to the International Jewish Committee for Interreligious Consultations. **ECUMENISM**

JOCHANAN H. A. WIJNHOVEN was a Benedictine monk until 1960 and received his education at The Hebrew University and Brandeis University. He is presently Professor of Religion and Biblical Literature at Smith College and is the author of *Sefer ha-Mishkal: Text and Study* as well as numerous articles in *Judaism, Jewish Social Studies, The Journal of Religion* and other periodicals. **CONVERT AND CONVERSION**

DAVID WINSTON is Professor of Hellenistic and Judaic Studies at the Graduate Theological Union, director of its Center for Judaic Studies, and Visiting Professor in the Department of Near Eastern Studies at the University of California (Berkeley). He is the author, among many scholarly works, of a new translation and commentary on *The Wisdom of Solomon* (1979), *Philo of Alexandria* (1981), and with John

Dillon, *Two Treatises of Philo of Alexandria: A Commentary on De Gigantibus and Quod Deus Sit Immutabilis.*   **FREE WILL**

PETER ZAAS, assistant professor of Religious Studies at Siena College (Loudonville, New York), was educated at Oberlin College and the University of Chicago where he received his doctorate from the Department of New Testament and Early Christian Literature (1982). A specialist on the Pauline literature, he is working on a full-length study of Pauline sexual ethics.   **PROPHECY**

Index

Aaron, 393
Aaron ha-Levi of Barcelona, 249
Aaronites
 priests, 527, 530, 533
Aaron of Starosielce, 319
abortion, 1042
Abrabanel, Isaac, 144, 145, 1077
 on exile, 221
 on love, 562
 on messianism, 1036
 on peace, 701
 and preaching, 870
 on rabbis, 743
 on war, 697, 698–699
Abrabanel, Judah (Leone Ebreo, Leo
 Hebraeus), 1077
 philosophy and tradition, 1012–
 1013
Abraham
 God's silence, 875

grace or loving–kindness, 300–302
Hegel on, 455
hope, 418
idolatry, 424
individuality, 484
Islam, 489
Jerusalem, 496
Jewish identity, 719
midrash, 615
people of Israel, 706
Abraham bar Ḥiyya
 on messianism, 1035–1036
 on peace, 694
Abraham ben David of Posquières, 1078
 on God, 293
 Kabbalah, 653
Abraham ibn Ezra, 1084
 on divine retribution, 961
 on priests, 533
Abrahams, Israel, 877–878

absence, sign of, 393, 394
abstention, 882
Abulafia, Abraham, 1078
  on music, 636–637
  on prayer, 905
  on prophetic kabbalah, 653
Adam
  covenant, 111
  death and sin, 131
  eros, 181
  fire, 277–278
  individuality, 484
  language, 544, 546
  punishment, 205
  remnant of Israel, 781
Adam and Eve
  exile, 220
  Gnosticism, 287
  women and Judaism, 1040–1042
  See also Eve
Adonai (my Lord), 1095
Adon Olam (Lord of the Universe), 1078
Adret, Solomon ben Abraham (Rashba),
    1078
  heresy, 345
  kabbalah, 653
  on sermons, 896–870
AESTHETICS, 1
  group memory, 585
  humanism, 425
  imagination, 453
  moral values, 196
  music, 635, 641
  Zionism, 1073–1074
afflictions from love, 44
afikoman
  symbolization, 277
afterlife, 132
  divine retribution, 963
  eschatology, 184
  and meaning of life, 569–570
  See also Immortality; Resurrection of the
    Dead; World to Come
AGGADAH (aggadot), 7, 1078
  Ein Ya'akov, 1082
  gematria, 1083
  hermeneutics, 354, 357, 358, 359
  Holy Spirit, 410
  Islam, 489, 490
  Judah Loew ben Bezalel, 1085
  Judaism, 508
  jurisprudence, 509, 511

  midrash, 614
  Sabbath, 468–469
  sermons, 870
  study, 941
  study of and mysticism, 646, 648
  study of Torah, 942
  Talmud, 956–957
  theology, 972
aggregation (proselutueo), 105
Agnon, Shmuel Yosef, 1078
  on Holocaust martyrs, 878
  and imagination, 461, 462
agnosticism, 296–297
  and atheism, 24–25
Agudat Yisrael movement, 912
agunah (anchored wife), 1046–1047
Aḥad Ha-Am (Asher Hirsch Ginsberg),
    1028, 1080
  on exile, 224
  mission concept, 169
  on Zionism, 865, 1072–1074, 1075
Aibu, Rabbi, 834
Akedah (binding) 1078
  and holiness, 394
Akiva (Joseph Tanna), 1078
  free will, 271–272
  imago Dei, 474
  kingdom of God, 523
  on language, 328, 549
  memorialization, 583
  messianism, 1035
  mysticism, 644–647, 653
  people of Israel, 709–711, 713
  on suffering, 935–936
Albo, Joseph, 144, 577, 1078
  on fear of God, 249
  on God, 292
  on love, 562
  and meaning of life, 569
  natural law, 669–670
  on Noachite commandments, 103
  on peace, 688
Alenu, 523, 811
Alexander, Samuel, 983, 984
Alfiye, Yizḥak Ya'akov, 640
Algemeyner Yidisher Arbeter Bund in Lite,
    Polyn un Rusland. See Bund
alien, resident (ger toshav). See Stranger
aliyah (immigration to the land), 915, 1059,
    1060
Alkabetz, Shlomo, 637
Alkalay, Judah, 791

allegory
  and imagination, 455
  Scripture, 356
Alliance Israelite Universelle, 865
Allon, Gedaliya, 717
Almosnino, Moses, 1078
  on love, 562
Alon Shevut, 928
am. See people
American Council for Judaism, 912
Amichai, Yehuda, 1078
Amidah (or *Shemoneh Esreh* or Eighteen
    Benedictions), 724, 1078–1079
  gesture, 278–279
  liturgy, 554
  resurrection, 807, 809
Ammi, Rabbi, 961, 963
amora; amoraim, 1079
  and heresy, 340
  midrash, 617–618
  myth, 659–660
  Talmud, 954
Amos, 733
Amsterdam
  Reform Judaism, 768
Am yisrael. See People of Israel
Anan ben David, 214
angels
  and imagination, 453–454
anger
  and silence, 874
aninut ("mourning"), 133–134
Ani Ma'amin (I believe), 1079
anthropodicy, 967
anthropology
  ethics, 197–200
  soul, 890
  suffering, 932–933, 936
anthropomorphism
  aggadah, 10
  God, 292–293
  and imagination, 453–455
  imago Dei, 474–478
  kabbalah, 653–654
  language, 549–550
Antigonus of Sokho
  on fear of heaven, 247
  on reward, 828
**ANTI-JUDAISM AND ANTI-SEMITISM,
  13**
  and Conservative Judaism, 92
  ecumenism, 149–152

Gnosticism, 289
  nationalism, 1075
  and providence, 738
  State of Israel, 866
antinomianism
  and messianism, 1035
Antschel, Paul. *See* Celan, Paul
anxiety
  fear of God, 246
apikores
  Torah, 26
APOCALYPSE, 19
  eschatology, 184
  Gnostic mythology, 287
  messianism and history, 377
  prophecy, 733
  response and memory, 584
  resurrection, 808
apocryphal literature
  Gnostic mythology, 287
apostasy
  and martyrdom, 853
Aquinas, Thomas
  atheism, 25
  natural law, 667–670
Arabia
  Jews, 488
Arabs
  land of Israel, 540–541
  as strangers, 927–929
  See also Islam
Arama, Isaac, 144, 577–578, 1079
  on peace and war, 689, 699
Aramaic
  Jewish forms, 329
  Talmud, 954
Ardon, Mordecai, 4
Aristobulus, 333
Aristotle
  on humility, 430–431
  on love, 562
  metaphysics, 603
  on time, 982
Armenians
  genocide, 400
art. *See* Aesthetics
artifacts
  as art, 2
Arukh ha-Shulḥan (The Preparation), 1079
  See also Shulḥan Arukh
ascent. *See* descent and ascent
Ascher, Saul, 768

Asher ben Yeḥiel, Rabbi, 280
Ashi, Rav, 954, 956
Ashkenazi; Ashkenazim, 1079
    catastrophe, 43–44
    ecumenism, 152
    immigrants, 1070–1071
    providence, 736–737
    rabbis, 743
Ashkenazi, Ḥakham Ẓevi, 869
Assaf, Simḥah, 741
assembly
    community, 81
Assi, Rabbi, 48
astronomy
    Hellenism, 335
    study of, 857–858
Astruc, Jean, 35
Athanasius, Bishop, 843
ATHEISM, 23
    and belief of God, 298
    faith, 234–235
Atlas, Samuel, 1079
atonement
    and repentance, 790
    See also Yom Kippur
attributes, doctrine of, 820
Augustine
    "just war," 692
Auschwitz. See Holocaust
Austin, John, 510
AUTHORITY, 29
    secularism, 863
auto-emancipation, 1072
autonomy
    and freedom, 263, 265–266
avodah (labor). See Work
Avodah (prayer), 282
awe of God. See Fear of God
ayin. See nothingness
Azzai, ben
    mysticism, 644
    on procreation, 710
    on women's study of Torah, 1049

Ba'al Shem Tov. See Israel ben Eliezer
baal teshuvah (Jewish convert), 111
Babylonian Talmud, 674–675, 954, 956, 1094
    amora, 1079
    canonization, 844–845
    study, 941
    tosafot, 1095

Baeck, Leo, 633, 976, 1079
    on covenant, 110
    on destiny, 140
    on rationalism, 752
    on strangers, 923
Baer, Yitzhak F., 976
Baghdad
    Jews, 491
Bahir, Sefer ha- (Book of Brightness),
    1079
    Gnosticism, 289
    Good and evil, 965–966
    imago Dei, 475–478
    soul, 891–892, 893
Baḥya ben Asher, 1079
    on fear of God, 250
    on love of God, 560–561
    on prayer, 723
Baḥya Ibn Paquda, 141, 575, 1085
    love of and fear of God, 248, 828
    on prayer, 724, 727
    on righteousness, 836
    on tolerance, 987
Baillie, John, 440
Bajja, Ibn (Avenpace), 198
Balfour Declaration, 925, 1079
ban (ḥerem)
    and heretics, 341–342
baraita; baraitot, 1079
    suffering, 933–934
Bar Kokhba, 1079
Baron, Salo W.
    historiography, 976
    political theory, 716
Barth, Karl, 440
beauty (tiferet), 652
    music, 637
befriending
    and tolerance, 990
behavior
    conscience, 87
    heroism, 363
    and immortality, 480
    redemption, 761
    sanctification of the Name, 851–852
being (yesh), 319
    See also Existence
belief, 141
    charity and, 47, 53–54
    in miracles, 622–623
    Reform Judaism, 768

belief in God, 291, 973
  eschatology, 187–188
  faith, 233
  idolatry, 446
  Islam, 490
  and meaning of life, 567
Benamozegh, Elijah
  Noachite covenant, 104
  on strangers, 923
benediction (berakhah), 553–554
  See also Amidah
benevolence
  theodicy, 961
Benjamin, Walter, 1080
  allegory, 462
  and the future, 374
  on history, 383–384
  on hope, 456
Benjamin of Tudela, 491
Bentham, Jeremy, 510
  See also Amidah
Berdyaev, Nicholas, 440
Berdyczewski, Micha Josef, 1080
  on tradition, 461
  Zionism, 865, 1074
Berger, Peter, 123–24
Berhman, Samuel Hugo, 633, 1080
  on resurrection, 812
Bergson, Henri Louis, 632, 1080
  on time, 983, 984
Berkovits, Eliezer, 1080
  on divine retribution, 963
  ecumenism, 149–150
  Holocaust, 209
Bernard of Chartres, 859
Bernstein, Eduard, 79
Betar; Bethar, 1080
bet din; battei din (house of judgment), 1080
Bethar. See Betar
bet (ha-) midrash; battei (ha-) midrash (house
    of study), 157, 1080
  Talmud, 956
Bialik, Ḥayyim Naḥman, 1080
  aggadah, 11
  on philology, 461
  on Sabbath, 468
Bibago, Abraham, 144, 145
Bible
  canonization, 841–843
  catastrophe, 41–42
  descriptions of God, 292

exegesis, 211–217
and existence, 228–229
and freedom, 261
Hebrew, 326
historical narratives, 373
and imagination, 459–460
law and stories, 462
meaning of life, 566
midrash, 613
miracles, 621–622
myth, 658–661
profanation, 462–463
and revelation, 822
and righteousness, 838
soul, 889
soul searching, 898–899
Talmud, 953
theology, 974
time, 982
Torah, 996–998, 999–1003
and unity, 1030–1031
  See also Scripture
BIBLE CRITICISM, 35
  Conservative Judaism, 92–93
  exegesis, 211
  on God, 295–296
  prophecy, 732
  Reform Judaism, 770
biblical prophecy
  apocalypse, 19
  Holy Spirit, 410, 411
Bin-Gorion. See Berdyczewski, Micha Josef
  Havdalah, 1083
Bloc of the Faithful (Gush Emunim)
  and heresy, 349–350
  Zionism, 910–911
body. See Eros: Sex and Body
body and soul. See Soul
bondage
  and freedom, 262
Borowitz, Eugene, 110
Brenner, Joseph Ḥayyim, 1080
  Zionism 349, 865
Breslau school, 1082
Breuer, Issac, 347
"Brightness, Book Of." See Bahir, Sefer ha-
    brit. See Covenant
Brunner, Emil, 440
Buber, Martin, 632, 634, 976, 1081
  on covenant, 110, 111
  on destiny and fate, 137, 139

Buber, Martin (*continued*)

on ecumenism, 148
ethnicist religiosity, 1075–1076
Ḥasidism, 320
on humility, 430, 433
I and Thou, 435
on Jewish culture, 124–125, 127
kingdom of God, 524
on language, 544–545
and meaning of life, 567
on miracles, 623–624
on morality, 202
political theory, 717
on prophecy, 733
on reason, 752
Reform Judaism, 347
on religion, 425
on repentance, 787, 788, 789
on revelation, 817–818, 819, 822
on righteousness, 836
on silence, 878
on strangers, 923
and truth, 1020
Buhle, Johann Bottlieb, 604
Bund (Algemeyner Yidisher Arbeter Bund in
    Lite, Polyn un Rusland), 1081
    secularism, 865
burial, 132–133
    Reform Judaism, 768
    and song, 640–641
burning bush, 392–393
bushah (self-esteem)
    orphans and marriage, 50
bittaḥon. See trust

Cain
    exile, 220
    and war, 690
calendar
    history, 372
calligraphic art, 4
Camus, Albert
    and meaning of life, 567
Canaan
    conquest of, 367, 368
Canada
    Conservative Judaism, 91
canon. *See* Sacred Text and Canon
capital punishment
    and dignity, 427

Caro, Joseph, 578, 1081
    and canon, 845
    on eros, 179
    on prayer, 723
    Shulḥan Arukh, 1093
Casper, Bernhard, 439
Cassirer, Renst, 658
CATASTROPHE, 41
    exile, 712
    theodicy, 961
Catholic church
    and Judaism, 148–149, 150, 151
catholic Israel (*Kelal Yisrael*), 95
Celan, Paul (Paul Antschel), 1081
    profanation, 463
Central Conference of American Rabbis,
    770
chanting, 636
"Chapters of the Fathers" (*Pirkei Avot*),
    1091
CHARITY, 47
"chastisement of love"
    and evil, 208
childbirth
    and women, 1042
children of God
    people of Israel, 710–711
Chmielnicki massacres, 868
CHOSEN PEOPLE, 55, 505
    Christianity, 61
    emancipation, 169
    and guilt, 307
    Reconstructionism, 757–758
    remnant of Israel, 781
CHRISTIANITY, 61
    anti-Semitism, 15–18
    chosen people, 57–58
    and Conservative Judaism, 92
    ecumenism, 147
    Gnosticism, 286, 288, 289
    God's rejection of Jews, 105
    Holocaust, 401
    post-Holocaust theology, 404–405
    humility, 429
    idolatry, 447
    and imagination, 465
    and Islam, 492
    Jewish survival, 951
    modern Jewish philosophy, 631
    preaching, 870
    priesthood, 532

providence, 737–738
and rabbis, 742
redemption, 69
revelation, 818
and science, 858
strangers, 920–921, 922, 924–925, 926, 928–929
study of Scripture, 647–648
and Talmud, 675
theology, 972, 973–974
war and peace, 692
chronology
history, 372
circumcision (brit milah)
Conservative Judaism, 98
covenant, 1042, 1043
and family, 241
Priestly Source, 36–37
symbolization, 276
citizenship
emancipation, 167
"civic amelioration" of the Jews, 166
civil authority. See Religion and State
civilization, religious
Reconstructionism, 756–757, 758
Clark, C. H. D., 566
Classical Reform Judaism, 771
See also Reform Judaism
Clearchus
on Jews, 332
cleanliness
Islam, 489–490
See also purity
clock time, 983
cognition
and truth, 1020
Cohen, Arthur A., 209
Cohen, Hermann, 631–632, 634, 976, 1081
on aesthetics, 4–5
on ecumenism, 148
on ethics, 89
on freedom, 264
on history, 375–376
on humility, 430, 433
I and Thou, 436
on immortality, 481
on reason, 751–752
remnant of Israel, 782
on repentance, 787, 788, 789
on righteousness, 836
Sinai covenant, 110

on strangers, 923, 924
on truth, 1020
Cohen, Morris Raphael, 414–415
collective memory. See Memory
COMMANDMENTS, 67
commemoration
gesture, 281–282
commentary
Bible, 462
Jewish writing, 460
Committee on Jewish Law and Standards (Rabbinical Assembly), 96–98
communication
Hebrew, 329
language, 544–545
prayer, 728
Scripture, 356–357, 358, 359
COMMUNITY, 81
charity, 50, 52
covenant, 111
ecumenism, 150
education, 155–156, 157, 160
emancipation, 167
and evil, 207–209
feminism, 256
halakhah, 310, 312–315
individuality, 484–485
Keneset Yisrael, 81, 1086
kingdom of God, 521–522, 523
mizveh, 628
moral values, 305, 206
natural law, 666
Orthodox Judaism, 682
prayer, 724, 726–727
rabbis, 741–742, 743, 744–745, 746
Reconstructionism, 756
redemption, 761
Reform Judaism, 771
repentance, 791
rest, 800, 803
righteousness, 836
secularism, 864, 865
sermons, 867
sin, 786
soul searching, 898, 899
spirituality, 906
women, 1042–1044
commutative justice, 516
completeness (shleimut)
and unity, 1030

confession
  and repentance, 789–790
confrontation
  and suffering, 969
CONSCIENCE, 87
  guilt, 306
  idolatry, 72
consciousness
  and peace, 693, 694
  and prayer, 724, 725, 726, 727
  and rationalism, 752
  and repentance, 789–790
  and sin, 885
  and suffering, 931, 932, 937–938
CONSERVATIVE JUDAISM, 91, 145
  emancipation, 168
  liturgy, 555
  secularism, 864
contemplation
  metaphysics, 606–608
  prayer, 724–726
contraception, 1042
contraction, See zimzum
conversion. See Convert and Conversion
Conversos, 1088
CONVERT AND CONVERSION, 101
  Conservative Judaism, 98
  strangers, 920–921, 922–923
conventional law, 669, 670
Coptic Gnostic texts, 285
Cordovero, Moses, 1081
  Hebrew, 329
  messianism, 601
  music, 637
cosmic fantasy, 455–456
cosmology
  and science, 856
  study of Torah, 940
cosmos
  existence, 228
  peace, 687–688
  rest, 795–798, 800, 805
  unity, 1025–1026, 1027–1028, 1029
COVENANT, 107
  catastrophe, 41–43
  chosen people, 55–56
  community, 83
  duty, 266–267
  evil, 205–209
  halakhah, 310, 311, 314
  hope, 417–418, 419

kingdom of priests, 527–529
  and meaning of life, 567–568, 570
  and memory, 581
  mercy, 590–594
  Noachism, 103–104
  people of Israel, 706–708
  political theory, 716
  repentance, 786, 788–790
  rest, 797
  retribution, 828
  righteousness, 834
  silence, 873
  State of Israel, 914
  and strangers, 191
  study of Torah, 940
  suffering, 931, 932, 935, 936, 937, 938
  women, 1042–1044
covenantal community, 111
CREATION, 113
  and destiny, 137
  and existence, 228, 231
  and evil, 205, 964–965
  God's will, 931
  good and evil, 960
  I and Thou, 440–441
  language, 543–544, 545
  and repentance, 791
  and rest, 795–796, 800
  and revelation, 817–819
  and silence, 876
  time, 190
  and unity, 1027–1028, 1029
  women, 1040
  and work, 1055–1056, 1061–1062,
    1063
creativity
  fire, 277
creature-consciousness, 432–433
Crescas, Ḥasdai, 144, 577, 1081
  on free will, 273
  on love of God, 563
  personalism, 1019
  on reason, 750
  on revelation, 817, 821
  on time, 982–983
criticism
  sermons, 870
  See also Bible Criticism
crown (keter)
  and people of Israel, 705–706, 707, 711,
    712, 713

Crusades
  massacres, 43–45
  and war, 692
CULTURE, 119
  education, 157, 160, 162–163
  emancipation, 165, 166
  soul searching, 898
  technology and war, 697
  Zionism, 1074–1075
cyclical time
  and history, 376

da'at. See knowledge
Da Costa, Uriel, 342
Daniel, Book of, 20, 808
D'Arcy, M. C., 440
Daud, Abraham Ibn, 248, 249
daughters
  and property, 1044–1045
David
  conquest of Jerusalem, 367, 368
  I and Thou, 435
  Jerusalem, 497, 499
  remnant of Israel, 781
Davidic succession, 42
Day of Atonement. *See* Yom Kippur
Day of Judgment
  and scholars, 647
"day of the Lord"
  eschatology, 183
Dead Sea Scrolls, 1081
  Gnosticism, 287
Dead Sea sects
  and providence, 736
DEATH, 131
  eschatology, 187
  heroism, 364–365
  kaddish, 395
  and meaning of life, 569
  and moral principles, 202
  as punishment, 205
  retribution after, 829
death of God, 297, 320–321
De Beauvoir, Simone, 256–257
debts
  and rest, 799, 803
Declaration on the Relation of the Church to
    Non-Christian Religions, (*Nostra
    Aetate*), 148
defeat
  remnant of Israel, 779

deism
  and atheism, 26
Delmedigo, Joseph Solomon, 859
democracy
  Reconstructionism, 756
demonology, 455
demut (divine image)
  people of Israel, 709–710
deontological theory of ethics, 195–196,
    198, 200
Derashot ha-Ran (The Sermons of the Ran),
    1081
derekh erez (way of the earth), 511
Derrida, Jacques, 619
Descartes, Rēsnais
  and freedom, 263
descent and ascent (*yeridah zorekh aliyah*)
  Hasidism, 321–322
despair
  and repentence, 789, 790
DESTINY AND FATE, 137
  covenant of destiny, 110–111
determinism
  and free will, 263, 270–271
Deutero-Isaich
  and evil, 204, 207
Deuteronomy
  canonization, 842
  criticism, 37–38
  and rest, 795, 798–799, 800
  Torah, 996–997
De Wette, W. M. L., 37–38
Dewey, Joh, 633
dialogue
  ecumenism, 149–153
  humor, 464
  I and Thou, 436–437, 438, 439, 441
  repentance, 787
Diaspora
  community, 83
  education, 162
  faith and hope, 419
  land of Israel, 537, 538, 541
  mission concept, 168
  political theory, 719
  rabbi, 742
  redemption, 949
  religion and state, 776
  rest, 803
  secularism, 864, 866
  State of Israel, 911, 912, 913, 916

Diaspora (*continued*)

    tolerance, 987
    work, 1058
"Diaspora meekness," 369
dietary laws. *See kashrut*
dignity
    and humanism, 427
disenchantment of the world
    existence, 229–230
disobedience
    and evil, 205, 207–208
    sin, 882
displaced persons
    remnant of Israel, 783
divine
    representations of, 2–3
divine cause
    revelation, 821–822
divine ground of being
    existence, 227–228
divine-human communality, 82–83
divine image (*demut*)
    people of Israel, 709–710
divine intervention
    and free will, 269
divine message
    legal terms, 509
divine rule
    kingdom of God, 522
divine sparks (*nizozot*), 321–323
    Gnosticism, 280
    repentance, 786, 787–788
divorce
    Conservative Judaism, 98
    women, 1046–1047
DOGMA, 141
    eschatology, 184
Dov Baer of Mezhirech, 318–319
dror (liberation of slaves), 799, 800,
    803
dualism
    creation, 114–116
    Gnosticism, 285–286
dual Torah, 673–677
Dubnow, Simon, 716, 976, 1081–1082
Duran, Simeon ben Zemah, 144
duration
    and time, 982–983

Ebner, Ferdinand, 437
Eco, Umberto, 125

ecstasy
    music, 636–637
ecstatic kabbalah, 651, 653
ECUMENISM, 147
EDUCATION , 155
    and culture, 121
    Enlightenment, 171–173
    and heresy, 343–345
    music, 635
    Talmud, 957
egalitarianism
    strangers, 924, 929
egoism, philosophical, 200
Egyptian servitude
    and holiness, 392–393
Ehrlich, Eugen, 510
Eichhorn, Johann Gottfried, 35
Einhorn, Zeeb Wolf (Mahar), 618
Ein Sof (the infinite; nothingness), 293–294,
    295, 651
    and existence, 227
Ein Ya'kov (The Fountain of Jacob), 1082
Eisenstein, Ira, 755
Elazar, Daniel J., 716
Eleazar, Rabbi
    imitatio Dei, 201
    study of Torah, 940–941
Eleazar ben Azaria, Rabbi
    on procreation, 710
Eleazar ben Moses Azirki
    on love of and fear of God, 828
Eleazar ben Simeon, Rabbi
    humanism, 427–428
    on truth and peace, 687
Eleazar ben Zabok, Rabbi
    on evil, 208
Eleazar of Worms, 1082
    fear of God, 250
election
    conversion, 101
    See also Chosen People
elegies (*kinot*)
    liturgy, 555
Elhanan ben Isaac of Dampierre, 943
Eliade, Mircea
    on history, 376
    holidays, 469
Eliezer, Rabbi
    women's study of Torah, 1049
Elijah
    God's silence, 876–877
    remnant of Israel, 781

Elijah ben Moses de Vidas
   on love of and fear of God, 251–252, 820
Elijah ben Solomon Abraham ha-Kohen of
   Smyrna, 869
Elijah ben Solomon Zalman (Ha-Gra, Elijah
   Gaon, Vilna Gaon,), 1082
   theosophical kabbalah, 654
Elisha ben Avuyah, 288
Elohim (God), 36
   and justice, 516
Elohist, 36, 38
EMANCIPATION, 165
   Enlightenment, 171
   and freedom, 262–263
   land of Israel, 539–540
   and memory, 584
   Orthodox Judaism, 682
   preaching, 872
   and reason, 750
   Reconstructionism, 756
   strangers, 923–924
   Zionism, 1069–1070
emotive theories
   ethics, 196–197
emunah. See Faith
encounter
   and revelation, 822–824
End of Days
   apocalypse, 20
   eschatology, 184
   immortality, 479
   messianism, 599
   redemption, 762
   resurrection, 808
engaged love (rahamim)
   and mercy, 590, 591, 594
ENLIGHTENMENT (Haskalah), 171,
   1083
   education, 158–159
   preaching, 872
   Reconstructionism, 756
   Reform Judaism, 767
   theology, 975–976
   world cultures, 120
Enoch
   remnant of Israel, 781
Enoch, Book of
   apocalypse, 22
En Vidas de Gerona
   resurrection, 809
Epicurus, 1082
   on retribution, 831

epikorsut
   heresy, 339–341
epistemology
   scientific exploration, 850
equality
   and justice, 517
   and rest, 795, 797, 798
   women, 255, 256, 258, 1040, 1045
EROS; SEX AND BODY, 177
   See also sexuality
eroticism, 177, 180–181
ESCHATOLOGY, 183
   divine retribution, 962
   imagination, 465
   messianism, 598
   redemption, 762, 763, 764
   resurrection, 807–808, 809
   soul, 888
   and theology, 972
   time, 984
eschaton (ultimate fulfillment at the End of
   Days), 599
essentialist concept of language, 544–547,
   551
eternal life
   eschatology, 183
ETERNITY AND TIME, 189
   history, 372, 376
   imagination, 467–469
   See also Time
ETHICS, 195
   aesthetics, 5
   conscience, 88–89
   freedom, 264–265
   grace or loving–kindness, 302
   holiness, 390, 391
   humility, 429
   jurisprudence, 511
   Mishnah, 954
   mizvot, 74–75
   peace, 685
   prophecy, 733
   reason, 751, 752
   repentance, 785–786
   righteousness, 834
   secularism, 866
   sin, 884, 885
   strangers, 917
   truth, 1020
Ethics of the Fathers. See Pirkei Avot
ethnicity
   and rationalism, 752

etiquette
  sanctification of the Name, 850
Euhemerus of Messene, 424
Europe
  Jewish culture, 121–123, 124
  Jewish nationalism, 1070
  Jewish society, 157–158
Eve, 1040–1041
  See also Adam; Adam and Eve
EVIL (*ra*), **203**
  anti-Semitism 14–15, 18
  atheism, 24
  and belief in God, 296
  and faith, 236
  fear of God, 251
  and freedom, 273
  and history, 373
  Holocaust, 413, 879
  and repentance, 790
  and righteousness, 837–839
  and sin, 883, 884
  Sitra Aḥra, 1093
  theodicy, 959
  and women, 1040
EXEGESIS, 211
  aggadah, 8
  catastrophe, 43
  Conservative Judaism, 96
  and gesture, 276
  Gnosticism, 287–288
  God's will and suffering, 932
  Hellenism, 333, 335
  hermeneutics, 355
  kingdom of God, 522–523
  midrash, 613
  oral law, 675–676
  pardes, 1090
  Scriptural language, 547–548
  Talmud, 954–955
  war, 691–692
exemplification
  gesture, 276, 277–279
EXILE (*galut*), **219**
  betrayal of Shabbat, 799, 800
  covenant, 109
  education, 156
  emancipation, 166, 167–168
  and history, 377, 378–379
  and Holocaust, 405–407
  and imagination, 456, 457
  and knowledge, 858–859
  land of Israel, 537–538, 539–540

people of Israel, 707–708, 712
  as punishment, 831
  soul, 893
  State of Israel, 910–911, 913, 914–915
  strangers, 919
  survival, 949–950
  and work, 1058
  Zionism, 1069, 1071–1072
EXISTENCE, 227
  God and, 291
  meaning of, 565
  soul, 887
existentialism
  faith, 235
  on God, 295
  Ḥasidism, 320
  Orthodox Judaism, 680
  reason, 752, 753
  Reconstructionism, 757
  redemption, 764, 765
  repentance, 787
Exodus
  kingdom of priests, 527
  messianism, 599
  rest, 795, 796–797
expiation
  death of martyrs, 63
explicatio
  hermeneutics, 353–354
expression
  gesture, 276, 278–279
Eybeschuetz, Rabbi Jonathan, 342
Ezekiel
  Ma'aseh Merkavah, 1088
  remnant of Israel, 780
  rest, 795, 799
Ezra Apocalypse, 21
ezraḥim (homeborn)
  and strangers, 918

Fackenheim, Emil L.
  on covenant, 110
  on divine retribution, 963
  on eternity and time, 192, 984
  on Holocaust, 209, 977
  on reason, 753
FAITH (*emunah*), **233**
  commandments, 67
  and culture, 127–128
  dogma, 142
  eschatology, 186–187
  fear of God, 251

God's silence, 875
and hope, 417–421
and idolatry, 446–447, 448
Islam, 487
law, 511
miracles, 621–622, 623
and Reconstructionism, 759
remnant of Israel, 781, 782
and repentance, 789
and theology, 977–978
and tolerance, 993
and truth, 1019
and unity, 1030
falsehood
and history, 373
FAMILY (mispaḥa), 239
community, 81
moral values, 305–306
Farabi, al-
law, 669
metaphysics, 604, 606
morality, 198–199
Farmer, Herbert H., 440
fasting
soul searching, 900
fate. See Destiny and Fate
father's house (bet av), 81
fear
and repentance, 790
FEAR OF GOD (yirat shamayim), 245
Christianity, 62
converts, 103
humility, 431–432
metaphysics, 607–608
punishment, 828
spirituality, 905
Zohar, 32–33
fear of harm
and fear of God, 248, 250
fear of heaven, 247
See also Fear of God
fear of sin (yira ḥeit), 247, 248, 249, 250, 251
FEMINISM, 255
"chattel," 1045
property, 1044
Shekhinah, 456–457
See also Women and Judaism
fertility
and family, 241
Feuerbach, Ludwig, 435–436
Final Solution. See Holocaust

fidelity
and truth, 1017–1018, 1020, 1021
Findlay, John, 24
fire
symbolization, 277–278
First Commandment
Zohar, 32–33
Fisch, Harold, 716, 846
Fison, J. E., 440
folklore
aggadah, 7
and imagination, 453, 454
myths, 659
foolishness
sin, 885
foreigners (nokhrim)
strangers, 918
foreign policy
Sanhedrin, 775
foreign wisdom, 331–337
forgetfulness
sin, 884–885
forgiveness
death, 133–134
and mercy, 592, 593
Formation, Book of. See Yeẓirah, Sefer
Formstecher, Solomon, 631, 976
ecumenism, 147
foundationalism
and truth, 1019
Fountain of Jacob (Ein Ya'akov), 1082
fragmentation
creation, 114
Frank, Jacob, 1082
on providence, 737
Frankel, Zacharias, 1082
on rabbis, 744
Frankfurt School
aesthetics, 5
Frankist movement, 1082
Zionism, 1070, 1074
FREEDOM, 261
and destiny and fate, 137–138, 139–140
and evil, 960
faith and hope, 419–420
humanism, 423, 426
miẓvot, 74–75
religion and state, 776–777
and repentance, 791
and rest, 795
and unity, 1026, 1027, 1030
See also Free Will

FREE WILL, 269
and evil, 968
faith and hope, 419
and freedom, 262, 263
See also Freedom
Freies Juedisches Lehrhaus, (Free Jewish
House of Learning), 161
friendship
I and Thou, 435
Fromm, Erich
on rest, 804
fruit of the soil
symbolization, 277
fundamentalism
and ecumenism, 149
Jewish people, 61–62
funeral service, 132–133
future
and history, 373–374, 375, 377

Gabirol, Solomon Ibn (Avicebron), 1085
imagination, 453
and Muhammad, 488
Gadamer, Hans-Georg, 1009
Galicia
Enlightenment, 173
galut. See Exile
Galut Judaism, 405–407
Galya Raza (Revelation of the Secret),
1082
Gans, Eduard, 122–123
Gaon of Sura, 214
Garden of Eden
and souls, 830
Gaster, Theodor, 469
Gates of Prayer, 771
Gatherer, The (Ha-Meassaf), 172–173
Geertz, Clifford, 125
Gehinnom (Valley of Hinnom), 1082
Geiger, Abraham, 1082–1083
on culture, 126
kingdom of priests, 528
mission concept, 169
Reform Judaism, 347, 769–770
Gemara, 1083
study, 941
See also Talmud
Gematria, 1083
gemilut ḥasadim., *See* Grace or Loving-
kindness
General Jewish Workers' Union in
Lithuania, Poland and Russia. *See* Bund

generativity
and God, 392–393
Genesis
criticism, 36–37
exile, 220
family, 239–240
holiness, 392–393
Ma'aseh bereshit, 1088
rest, 795
and sexuality, 178
women, 1040–1041
Genesis Rabbah, 1083
genocide
Holocaust, 402
genre
Bible, 459
Gentiles
Israeli priests, 533
secularism, 863
strangers, 928–929
Gentile, pious (*Ger shaar*), 103, 105
Gentiles, righteous (*gerei ẓedek*)
ger ("stranger" or "sojourner"), 102–103, 105
See also Stranger
gerei ẓedek. See Gentiles, righteous
ger emet (true proselyte). *See ger ẓedek*
German
Jewish forms, 329
German-Jewish philosophy, 630, 633
Germany
Enlightment, 173
Holocaust, 399
Reform Judaism, 767, 768–769, 770
ger shaar (pious Gentile), 103, 105
Gershuni, Yehuda, 928–929
Gersonides. *See* Levi ben Gershom
ger toshav (loyal resident alien), 103, 104,
See also Stranger
ger ẓedek (true proselyte), 103, 104
GESTURE AND SYMBOL, 275
get (divorce writ). *See* divorce
geulah. See Redemption
gevurah. See Power
Gideon, 521–522
Gikatilla, Joseph, 640
glorification of God
and meaning of life, 566
GNOSIS, 285
Gnosticism, 285–290
anti-Semitism, 14, 15–16
goals
miẓvot, 70, 78–80

GOD, 291
  and conscience, 306
  covenant, 107
  eternity and time, 190–191
  and evil, 204
  existence, 227–228, 574, 575
  existence of and atheism, 23–26
  existence of and faith, 233, 234–235
  holiness, 389
  imagined, 466–467
  imago Dei, 473
  individuality, 483–484
  justice, 515
  lordship, 373
  and meaning of life, 567
  mercy, 589
  messianism, 597–598
  and nature, 664
  pathos, 411
  peace, 689
  Reconstructionism, 758–759
  and righteousness, 834–835
  silence, 873
  theodicy, 959
  unity, 1026–1027
  See also belief in God
God's love
  people of Israel, 709, 710–711
God's presence. *See Shekhinah*
Gogarten, Friedrich, 440
Goitein, S. D., 489, 491
golah (dispension), 221–222
Goldenberg, Naomi, 257
golden calf, 448
Gooch, George Peabody, 377
good
  and history, 373
  See also Evil
goodness
  creation, 115
  and holiness, 392, 393
Gordon, Aharon David, 633,
    1083
  on repentance, 787, 792
  on work, 1061–1062, 1064–1066
Gottlieb, Lynn, 258
government
  kingdom of God, 521, 524
  and peace, 696–698
  religion and state, 776
GRACE OR LOVING-KINDNESS, 299
  See also Love

Graetz, Heinrich
  on Judaism and Gnosticism, 286
  on revelation, 816
grammar
  Hebrew, 329
Greece
  See Hellenism
Greenberg, Uri Zevi (Tur Malka), 1083
Gronemann, Sammy, 348
Gross, Rita, 257
Guardini, Romano, 440
GUILT, 305
  and repentance, 788–789
  and silence, 874
Gush Emunim (Bloc of the Faithful)
  and heresy, 349–350
  Zionism, 910–911
Guttman, Julius, 629, 633

Ḥabad Ḥasidism, 319–320
  on God, 294–295
  prayer, 905
  Shneur Zalman, 1093
Haim Hillel ben Sasson, 223–224
HALAKHAH (pl., halakhot), **309**, 509, 1083
  aggadah, 7, 11–12, 1078
  Arukh ha-Shulḥan, 1079
  canon, 845
  charity, 49–50, 51
  Conservative Judaiam, 95, 96–98
  covenant, 109, 111
  deontological theory of ethics, 196
  eros, 177
  ethics, 72, 202
  and faith, 342
  Hebrew, 327–328
  and heresy, 346
  hermeneutics, 354, 357, 358, 359
  Hirsch, S. R., on, 1084
  and history, 379–380
  human existence, 366–367
  humility, 438
  Jacob ben Asher, 1085
  Judaism, 506–507, 508
  jurisprudence, 510–511
  justice, 519
  land of Israel, 539
  messianism, 599–600
  midrash, 614
  Mishnah, 954, 955–956
  Mishneh Torah, 1089
  miẓvot, 68–69, 70, 74, 77

HALAKHAH (continued)

mysticism, 652, 653, 654
myth, 659–660
oral law, 679, 680, 681, 683
oral tradition, 489
prophecy and prophets, 732, 733
Reform Judaism, 92, 168, 769, 771–772
religion and state, 774, 775, 776, 777–778
responsa, 1091
revelation, 822
Sabbath, 468–469
Soloveitchik, J. D., on, 1094
spirituality, 904–905
strangers, 925–929
study of Torah, 939–940, 941–942
suffering, 938
and theology, 971–972, 976
ḥallah (baking Sabbath bread), 1049
Hallel
    Ḥanukkah, 367
    lulav, 280
ḥaluẓ (pioneer), 1064–1066
Hama bar Hanina, Rabbi, 300–301
Hamburg
    Reform Judaism, 768–769
Ha-Meassef (The Gatherer), 172–173
Hamnuna, Rabbi, 944
Hanhagah (governance). See Providence
Ḥanina ben Ḥama, Rabbi, 271
Ḥanina ben Pazi, 1057
Ḥanukkah
    Hallel, 367
    menorah, 1089
Harlap, Rabbi Yaakov Moshe, 79–80
harmony
    mysticism, 643–644
    peace, 688
ḥaroset
    symbolization, 276
Harrison, Jane, 463
ha-Shem (the Name), 1095
Hashgaḥah (attentive care). See Providence
ḥasid
    humility, 432–433
hasidei umot olam (pious Gentiles). See ger
    shaar
HASIDISM, 317
    canon, 846
    chosen people, 56–57
    ethics, 199

fear of punishment, 252
on God, 294–295
Hebrew, 329
Israel ben Eliezer, 1085
liturgy, 554–555
music, 637
mysticism, 654
Passover, 371–372
prayer, 728
repentance, 786, 787, 790
righteousness, 835
soul, 895
soul searching, 901
and unity, 1031
Zionism, 1074
Haskalah. See Enlightenment
Hasmonaean revolt, 333–334
Ha-Tefilla (The Prayer). See Amidah
Havdalah, 1083
    gesture, 277–278
ḥavurah movement, 84
ḥayyim, sefer ha- (book of life)
    liturgy, 555
Ḥayyim ben Isaac of Volozhin
    on education, 189
    revelation, 817
Hazaz, Ḥayyim, 381
HEBREW, 325, 546–547
    Conservative Judaism, 95, 98
    Enlightenment, 172
    European culture, 124
    literature, 1080
    Mishnah, 953
    modern idiom, 462
    Reform Judaism, 92
    Talmud, 954
    tradition, 1008
    Yiddish, 627
    See also Mishnaic Hebrew
Hebrew Union College, 770
Hebron
    Zionism, 1070
Hecateus of Abdera, 332
Hegel, Georg Wilhelm Friedrich, and
        Hegelianism
    on European culture, 120
    and freedom, 264
    Hebrew God, 454–455
    modern Jewish philosophy, 630–632,
        633, 634
Heidegger, Martin, 632, 633
    eternity and time, 192

metaphysics, 605–606, 609
on reason, 753
Heimarmenē
    free will, 270, 272
Heine, Heinrich, 1084
Heinemann, Isaak, 618–619
Heikhalot, 646, 649, 653, 654
    Gnosticism, 288–289
Heikhalot and Merkabah, Literature of the,
    1083–1084
    ma'aseh merkavah, 1088
Heim, Karl, 440
HELLENISM, 331
    cosmos, 981
    history, 374, 375
    humanism, 425
    imagination, 453, 454–455
    Jerusalem, 368
    priesthood, 531–532
    reason, 749–750
    soul, 889–891
    spirituality, 904
    theology, 972
helplessness
    and mercy, 592, 593, 594
Herberg, Will, 442
Herder, Johann Gottfried, 120
herem (ban)
    and heretics, 341–342
HERESY, 339
    culture, 123
    dogma, 144, 145
    Gnosticism, 288
    and repentance, 791, 792
HERMENEUTICS, 353
    Gematria, 1083
    and imagination, 465
    myth, 658, 660
    midrash, 618–619
    pardes, 1090
    and truth, 1022
HEROISM (*geburah*), **363**
    and memory, 582
    remnant of Israel, 781
Herzl, Theodor
    on exile, 224
    utopia, 1036
    Zionism, 988, 1074–1075
Herzog, Isaac, 925–926, 927
Heschel, Abraham Joshua, 634, 1084
    ecumenism, 150
    eternity and time, 190, 191

fear of God, 252–253
    on free will, 273
    Ḥasidism, 320
    on humility, 430
    I and Thou, 441
    on justice and mercy, 516
    prophecy, 732
    on reason, 752–753
    on rest, 804
    on time, 984
    on Zionism, 1059
ḥesed, 590
    humility, 432
    See also Grace or Loving–Kindness
Hess, Moses, 169, 1084
Ḥevra Kadisha. See Jewish Burial Society
Hezekiah, 781
Ḥibbat Ẓion (Love of Zion), 1072, 1084
    Enlightenment, 174
hidden face of God
    silence, 873, 874, 875, 877
hierarchy
    women, 1040
hierocracy
    kingdom of God, 521
High Court in the Temple in Jerusalem
    religious authority, 29
High Holyday liturgy
    fear of God, 253
Hillel (the Elder), 1084
    charity, 51
    oral law, 674, 675
    on paschal sacrifice, 212
    political theory, 718
    on Torah, 999
ḥillul ha-Shem. See profanation of the Name
Ḥinnukh, Sefer ha- (Book of Instruction),
    1084
Hirsch, Samson (ben) Raphael, 631, 1084
    on culture, 126
    and heresy, 347
    mission concept, 169
    on strangers, 983
Hirsch, Samuel, 631
    on Christianity, 147
historiography, 377–378
    and canon, 846
HISTORY, 371
    community, 485
    Conservative Judaism, 93, 94, 95
    eschatology, 184
    eternity and time, 190, 191–192

HISTORY (*continued*)

and faith, 236
faith and hope, 420–421
God's will, 931–933
halakhah, 310–311
and holiness, 393
Holocaust, 401–402
memory, 581
and miracles, 624
myth, 660
Nazi discrediting of, 948
Orthodox Judaism, 681
people of Israel, 707–708
and political theory, 719, 720
prophecy, 734
revelation, 820
righteousness, 837
and science, 856
soul, 890
and State of Israel, 915–916
theology, 975–976
time, 981
and tradition, 1007
and utopia, 1035
war and peace, 694
hitbodedut (solitary concentration on the
    presence of God), 905
Hitler, Adolf
messianism, 948
Ḥiyya bar Abba, Rabbi
charity, 50
on righteousness, 835
ḥokhmah (divine wisdom)
Gnosticism, 286
Ḥasidism, 318–319, 320
music, 637
See also Wisdom
holidays
eternity and time, 191
HOLINESS, 389
Hebrew, 326, 327, 329
and idolatry, 447–449
kingdom of priests, 529–531, 534
miẓvot, 77–78
righteousness, 834, 835, 836
spirituality, 903
in time, 984
and unity, 1027
holistic theology
holy spirit, 414

HOLOCAUST, 399
Ani Ma'amin (I believe), 1079
and belief in God, 236
divine retribution, 831–832
faith and hope, 421
and God's mercy, 593
Greenberg, U. Z., on 1083
and group and memory, 585
as history, 984
as punishment, 209, 831
reason, 753
righteousness, 837
and silence, 878
survival, 948–950
and theology, 976–977
holy nation
and kingdom of priests, 528
Holy One of Israel (*yhvh kedosh Yisrael*),
    391–392
HOLY SPIRIT (*ruaḥ ha-kodesh*),
    409
mysticism, 646
Orthodox Judaism, 681
repentance, 788
and righteousness, 836
spirituality, 904
holy tongue, 327, 328
holy war, 692
home
and exile, 221
homeborn (ezraḥim)
and strangers, 918
homecoming
and exile, 223–224
homelessness
Holocaust, 407
See also Exile
homilies
aggadah, 7
HOPE (*tikvah*), **417**
and history, 375
and redemption, 763–764
and tolerance, 993
horror vacui, 424
Horwitz, Rivka, 439
Talmud, 956
ḥozer bi-teshuvah (one who returns in
    repentance), 350
HUMANISM, 423
and Reconstructionism, 756
return to Judaism, 792

humanistic studies
Jewish education, 158
human law
and natural law, 667–668, 670
Hume, David
atheism, 24
on evil, 959–969
on reward and punishment, 830–831
HUMILITY, 429
keter, 705
humor
aesthetics, 4
imagination, 464
mentsh, 584
Huna, Rav, 944
Hupfeld, Hermann, 35–36
Husik, Isaac, 629
on free will, 272
on God, 296
Husserl, Edmund, 632, 633
hymns
mysticism, 650–651
piyyut, 269, 1091

I AND THOU, 435
dialogue, 464
reason, 752
iconicity
and idolatry, 453
iconography
group memory, 585
idealism
modern Jewish philosophy, 630–631,
633
and reason, 751
identity, Jewish
political theory, 719
IDOLATRY, 445
Abraham, 424
and art, 2
decorative arts, 453
Imago Dei, 424
mizvot, 73, 77
strangers, 919, 920, 921, 925–926, 928–
929
and worship of God, 295
Iggeret Ha-Kodesh (Letter of Holiness), 180
IMAGINATION, 451
myth, 657
IMAGO DEI, 473, 2
ethics, 202

and humanism, 423–424, 427
soul, 889
imitatio Dei
ethics, 201–202
grace or loving–kindness, 300–301
humility, 431
and marriage, 241
righteousness, 834
soul searching, 898–899
study, 156
IMMORTALITY, 479
and meaning of life, 569
Orthodox Judaism, 681–682
Saadiah on, 574
soul, 890, 891
See also afterlife; Resurrection of the Dead
impulse (*yezer*)
redemption, 761
indentured servitude
and rest, 797, 799
India
and unity, 1027
INDIVIDUALITY, 483
inheritances
women, 1044
inspiration, divine
sermons, 871
intellectualism
science, 856–857
study of Torah, 939
intercession
prayer, 724
intermarriage, 864
community, 84
interpretatio
hermeneutics, 353–354, 357–358,
359
interpretation
canon, 843–844
hermeneutics, 353
Maimonides on, 548–550
and tradition, 1009–1010, 1011, 1012,
1013, 1014
Isaac
exile, 220
Isaac, Rav
eros, 179
Isaac ben Jacob ha-Kohen
divine realm, 476
Isaiah
hidden God, 877

Isaiah (*continued*)

  remnant of Israel, 779–780
  on resurrection, 808
Isaiah, Book Of
  catastrophe, 42
  "sheep to the slaughter", 369
Isaiah ben Mali di Trani, 859
Ishmael, Rabbi
  language, 549–550
  mysticism, 646, 647–649
ISLAM, 487
  chosen people, 57–58
  and dogma, 142
  ecumenism, 151
  and Hellenism, 335–336
  and heresy, 344
  imagination, 453
  Jewish survival, 951
  and Judaism, 62
  strangers, 921
Israel
  catastrophe, 43
  chosen people, 55
  Christianity, 62
  converts, 102–103
  covenant, 108–112, 205–210
  destiny and fate, 138, 139–140
  freedom, 261–262
  Jerusalem, 495
  oral law, 844
  retribution, 828
  spirituality, 906
  Torah, 838–839
  and unity, 1031
  See also Land of Israel; People of Israel;
    Remnant of Israel; State of Israel
Israel ben Eliezer (Ba'al Shem Tov, Besht),
    1085
  Ḥasidism, 318
  imago Dei, 477
  mysticism, 654
Israel of Belzec, Rabbi, 868
Isserles, Moses, 249
Istanbul
  Jewish community, 492
I-Thou relationship. *See* I and Thou

Jabès, Edmond, 461, 463
Jabneh, 1085
Jacob
  people of Israel, 703–704, 707–708

Jacob, Rabbi
  on reward, 934–935
Jacob ben Asher (Tur), 1085
  charity, 47–48
  fear of God, 249
Jacob ben Meir. *See* Tam, Jacob ben Meir
Jacob ibn Ḥabib, 1082
Jacob Joseph of Polonnoye, 252
Jacobs, Louis, 253
Jahwist, 36, 38
James, William, 633
  divine Thou, 436
  unity of the self, 789
Jebusites, 499
Jeremiah
  on Jerusalem, 501
  messianism, 600
  remnant of Israel, 780
  rest, 795, 799
  silence and prophecy, 875
Jeroboam, 529
JERUSALEM, 495
  conquest of, 367, 368
  land of Israel, 536, 538, 539
  remnant of Israel, 779, 780
  and rest, 799, 800
  utopia, 1034, 1035, 1036
  Zionism, 1070
Jerusalem Talmud, 954, 956,
    1094
  amora, 1079
  canonization, 844, 845
Jerusalem Temple, 42
Jesus Christ
  Catholic church, 148–149
  faith, 64
  message of love, 65
  and redemption, 62–64, 152
  revelation, 818
  See also Christianity
Jewish Agency for Palestine, 865
Jewish Burial Society, 132, 133–134
Jewish Theological Seminary of America
  Conservative Judaism, 91–95, 96
Job
  remnant of Israel, 781
Job, Book of
  and evil, 208
  God's silence, 876
  reward and punishment, 831
Joel
  remnant of Israel, 780

Johanan ben Zakkai, 1085
  commandments, 72
  grace or loving-kindness, 301–302
  as hero, 308
  oral law, 675
Jolles, André, 658
Jonah
  converson, 101
Jonathan, Rabbi
  on science, 857
Joseph
  divine silence, 875
  exile, 220
Joseph, Morris, 252
Joseph Ibn Kaspi, 35
Joseph of Chartres, 961
Joseph Tanna. See Akiva
Josephus Flavius, 716
Joshua
  conquest of Canaan, 367, 368
  on righteousness, 835
Joshua, Rabbi, 301–302
Joshua ben Korḥa, Rabbi, 686–687
Joshua ben Levi, Rabbi, 944
Jubilee
  land and strangers, 925, 927
  and rest, 799–800, 803
Judah, Rabbi, 844–845
Judah, tribe of
  Jerusalem, 499–500
Judah bar Nahamani, 302
Judah ben Samuel he-Ḥasid, 250
Judah Halevi, 1085
  divine cause, 821–822
  dogma, 141
  on exile, 222
  on free will, 272
  on Gentiles, 928
  on God, 292
  Hebrew, 327, 328
  on idolatry, 448
  Kuzari, Sefer ha-, 1087
  land of Israel, 538, 539
  on language, 546–547
  people of Israel, 713
  philosophy, 576–577, 633
  on prophecy, 732
  and rational law, 668–669
  on reason, 750
  Song of Songs, 453
  on strangers, 921
  on truth, 1018

Judah ha-Nasi, (the Prince), 1085
  Hebrew, 326
  Mishnah, 953
  on righteousness, 833
Judah Loew ben Bezalel of Prague, 1085
  on language, 326
  love of God, 251
  on peace, 689
  on scientific study, 858, 859
Judah the Maccabee
  remnant of Israel, 781–782
JUDAISM, 505
  and atheism, 25
  and Christianity, 61, 152
  dogma, 141
  and Gnosticism, 285–290
  and Islam, 487
  modern philosophy, 629
  monotheism, 58
  religious authority, 29
  Spinoza on, 510
judges
  women as, 1048
judgment (mishpat)
  ethics, 201
  and music, 638
Judgment Day
  scholars, 647
judiciary
  rabbis, 742, 743
JURISPRUDENCE, 509
JUSTICE, 515
  concept of history, 375–376
  covenant, 590
  and mercy, 591–592, 593
  and peace, 686–687, 695, 699–700
  and rest, 795, 797, 798, 800
  and righteousness, 834–835
  theodicy, 959
  and unity, 1025–1026, 1030
"just war," 692

kabbalah, 651–652, 1085–1086
  Abulafia, Abraham, 1078
  Bahir, Sefer ha-, 1079
  canon, 846
  on creativity, 1061
  divine sparks, 321, 323
  eros, 180–181
  family, 242
  Galya Raza, 1082
  Gnosticism, 289

kabbalah (continued)

on God, 293–294, 295
good and evil, 965–966, 967
grace or loving–kindness, 302
Ḥasidism, 318–319
and heresy, 345–346
hermeneutics, 356
on history, 379, 380
idolatry, 447
and imagination, 455–458
imago Dei, 475–478
kavvanah, 1086
kelippah, 1086
land of Israel, 539
languages, 329, 545
liturgy, 554
medieval philosophy, 578
messianism, 599, 601
midrash, 618
music, 636–642
myth, 660–661
peace, 689
prophecy, 651, 653
revelation, 817
sefirot, 1093
sermons, 869
Sitra Aḥra, 1093
soul, 890, 891–895
soul searching, 901
theodicy, 963
and unity, 1031
yiḥud, 1096
Zohar, 1096
See also Lurianic kabbalah
kaddish, 133, 134
and holiness, 393–394, 395
Kadushin, Max, 11
Kafka, Franz, 1086
and imagination, 462
and mysticism, 654–655
Kant, Immanuel, 1086
on aesthetics, 4–5
on ethics, 89
and freedom, 263
on God, 295
on immortality, 481
modern Jewish philosophy, 630, 631–
632, 633, 634
Reform Judaism, 768
on Sinai covenant, 110
on truth, 1020

Kaplan, Mordecai Menahem, 1086
Conservative Judaism, 94, 95–96
on culture, 125–126
ethicist religiosity, 1076
on God, 297
halakhah, 511
on miracles, 623
process philosophy, 984
and rationalism, 752
Reconstructionism, 633, 755
Karaism
dogma, 142
exegesis, 214, 215
Karlitz, Isaiah, 927
kashrut (dietary laws), 1086
Conservative Judaism, 98
Islam, 490
Katz, Jacob, 922, 924
Katznelson, Berl, 1063, 1064, 1065
Katznelson, Itzhak, 584–585, 878
Kaufmann, Yehezkel, 633
on exile, 224
Jewish historiography, 976
on resurrection, 808
on strangers, 919
kavvanah; kavvanot, 1086
halakhah, 313, 314
Islam, 490
meditations, 554
soul, 983
yiḥud, 1096
Kedoshim, 72
kedusha, 393–394, 395
kefirah ha-ikkar, 339, 340–341
kehillah (religous community), 718
Kehillah Kedoshah (holy congregation), 584
Kelal Yisrael (catholic Israel), 95
kelippah; kelippot (shell or husk), 1086
Sitra Aḥra, 1093
Kermode, Frank, 466
keter (crown)
and people of Israel, 705–706, 707, 711,
712, 713
ketubah (marriage contract), 240
kibbutz
kingdom of God, 524
and labor, 1060
kiddush (sanctification), 393, 1086
kiddush ha-Shem. See Sanctification of the
Name
Kierkegaard, Søren, 1086
on faith, 235

I and Thou, 436
  on reason, 752
  on resurrection, 810
Kimḥi, David (Radak), 1086–1087
  on truth, 1021, 1022
kingdom (malkhut), 652
  Ḥasidism, 318, 319, 320
  music, 637
KINGDOM OF GOD, 521
  peach, 691
KINGDOM OF PRIESTS, 527, 707
  and politics, 774
  spirituality, 903
kinot (elegies)
  liturgy, 555
Klatzkin, Jakob, 633
knowledge (da'at)
  gnosis, 285
  Ḥasidism, 319
  and science, 855–856
  and truth, 1020–1022
Knox, John
  on idolatry, 988
kodesh. See Holiness
kofer (he who denies), 25–26
Koheleth, 565, 566
Kohn Eugene, 757
komah shelemah, 477
Kook, Abraham Isaac, 633, 634, 1087
  eternity and time, 190–191
  on exile, 224
  on heresy, 349
  on idolatry, 448
  Orthodox Judaism, 682
  on perfection, 79
  on repentance, 787, 789, 790, 791, 792
  on strangers, 925
Korah
  idolatry, 448
  priests, 529, 530
Koran
  Islam, 487, 488–489
Kraus, Karl, 463
Krochmal, Nachman, 631, 634, 1087
  Enlightenment, 173
  and heresy, 349
  historicism, 383
  on humility, 430, 433
  theology, 976
Kurzweil, Baruch, 124
Kuzari, Sefer ha- (Book of the Kuzari),
  1087

labor (avodah). See Work
Lamentations, Book of
  catastrophe, 42, 43
  and memory, 581
land
  and rest, 798, 800
Landau, Ezekial, 870–871
LAND OF ISRAEL, 535
  and exile, 222–225
  individuality, 485
  medieval philosophy, 577
  people of Israel, 706, 707–708
  political theory, 716, 717–718
  providence, 738
  remnant of Israel, 781
  repentance, 791–792
  and rest, 803
  and State of Israel, 910–915
  strangers, 918, 921, 925–926, 927
  survival, 949–950
  Talmud, 674–675, 677
  utopia, 1033, 1034, 1035
LANGUAGE, 543
  and imagination, 461
  Mishnaic Hebrew, 1000–1001, 1003
  prayer, 727–728
  revelation, 815, 816, 817
  theology, 974–975
  and tradition, 1007–1008
  Yiddish, 627
  See also Hebrew
language, religious
  Ḥasidism, 320–321
language of holiness. See Hebrew
law
  bet din (house of judgment), 1080
  bet (ha-) midrash (house of study), 1080
  conscience, 88, 89
  divine law, 669, 670
  exegesis and, 212, 215
  female testimony, 1047–1048
  holy spirit, 411, 414
  jurisprudence, 509
  Mishnah, 953–954
  mizvot, 72, 76
  priesthood, 531–532
  rabbis, 741, 743
  Shulḥan Arukh, 1093
  and strangers, 924–928
  theology, 973
  See also halakhah; Justice
"Laws of Idolatry" (Shulḥan Arukh), 3

Lazarus, Moritz, 1087
learning
    metaphysics, 603
    rabbi and teacher, 741
    See also Education
legends
    aggadah, 7
    and myth, 659, 660
Leibniz, Gottfried Wilhelm
    theodicy, 959
Leibowitz, Yeshayahu, 350
Leiman, S. Z., 842–843
Leiner, Mordecai Joseph, of Izbica, 273
Lessing, Gotthold Ephraim
    on pure truth, 79
    on toleration, 426
Letter of Holiness (*Iggeret Ha-Kodesh*), 180
Levi, Rabbi
    on work, 1056
Levi ben Gershom (Gersonides)
    on God, 296
    on reason, 751
Levi ben Ḥabib, Rabbi, 869
Levi Isaac ben Meir of Berdichev, 252
Levinas, Emmanuel, 632–633
    on rationalism, 756
Levinsohn, Isaac Baer, 173
Lévi-Strauss, Claude
    on history, 382
    on myth, 658
Levites
    song, 638–640
Leviticus
    rest, 796–798, 800
Leviticus Rabbah, 1087
Lewinski, Elhanan Leib, 1036
liberal Judaism, 770
    reason, 751
liberation
    and rest, 797, 798, 799, 800, 803
libertarian individualism
    religion and state, 776, 777
life
    and resurrection, 808
lifnim mi-shurat ha-din (law that is beyond
        the line of legal requirement), 312
Lipkin, Israel, 1090
literacy
    European culture, 124
literature
    aggadah, 7
    canon, 845–846

enlightenment, 172, 173
Gnosticism, 286–287
and imagination, 461–462
as Jewish art, 2, 4
midrash, 613
myth, 657
responsa, 1091
and science, 855–856, 857, 860
Talmud, 957
See also rabbinic literature; wisdom
        literature
Lithuania
    Enlightenment, 173
Litman, Jane, 257
LITURGY, 553
    eternity and time, 191
    memory, 583
    Reconstructionism, 757
    Reform Judaism, 769
    resurrection, 807
    retribution, 961
loans
    and charity, 53
Locke, John, 1087
    atheism, 25
Lonzano, Menah, 727
LOVE, 557
    eros, 179
    and mercy, 590
    and repentance, 790
    and tolerance, 992
    See also Grace or Loving–Kindness
love of God, 560–563
    and fear of God, 247–248, 249, 250–251
    humility, 431–432
    law, 512
    metaphysics, 607–608
    prayer, 725
    sanctification of the Name, 852
    spirituality, 905–906
    worship, 828
loving–kindness
    ethics, 201
    holy spirit, 412
    See also Grace or Loving–Kindness
lulav (palm frond) ritual, 280–281
Luria, Isaac, 1087
    on exile, 223
    Gnosticism, 289
    on God, 294
    liturgy, 555
    messianic activism, 380

music, 637
mysticism, 1019
Lurianic kabbalah, 1087
  creation and evil, 965
  imago Dei, 477
  messianism, 601
  myth, 660
  providence, 737
  repentance, 786–787
Luzzato, Moses Ḥayyim, 1087
  fear of God, 251
  revelation, 818
  on spirituality, 904
Luzzato, Samuel David, 631, 1087–1088
  exegesis, 216
  on strangers, 923–924

ma'aseh bereshit (work of creation), 1088
ma'aseh Merkavah (work of Chariot), 1088
Maccabees, 367–368
MacMurray, John, 440
Maggid of Mezhirech, 871
magical mysticism, 650–651, 654
Magnes, Judah Leon, 1088
  ethnicist religiosity, 1076
  Zionism, 865
Maharal of Prague. *See* Judah Loew ben
  Bezalel
Maimonides, Moses, 1088
  Abrabanel on, 1077
  Abraham ben David on, 1078
  Abulafia on, 1078
  on afterlife, 132
  on aggadah, 9–10
  on *Ani Ma'amin* (I believe), 1079
  on atheism, 25–26
  on biblical terms, 356
  on canon, 845
  on catastrophe, 43
  on charity, 47–48, 49
  on chosen people, 56, 57
  Commentary on Ḥelek, 1084
  Conservative Judaism, 95
  and contemplation, 905
  on divine attributes, 43
  on divine providence, 938
  dogma, 141, 142–145
  on eternity and time, 190
  on evil, 203–205, 966–967
  on exile, 222
  on existence, 231
  on faith, 237

  on fear of God, 248–249
  on foreign wisdom, 336, 337
  on free will, 272–273
  on God, 291, 293
  on God's perfection, 964
  on grace or loving-kindness, 299, 301,
    302
  Guide of the Perplexed, 1083
  halakhah, 311, 314–315
  on Hebrew, 327, 329
  on heresy, 340–341, 343–345
  on holiness, 391, 396
  on humility, 430–433
  on idolatry, 445–446
  on imagination, 452, 455
  on immortality, 479–480, 482
  on justice, 518
  on land of Israel, 539
  on language, 547–551
  on love of God, 561, 563
  on love of neighbor, 558–559
  on the Messiah, 911
  on messianism and unity, 1035
  metaphysics, 606–609
  on miracles, 622
  Mishneh Torah, 1089
  on *miẓvot*, 78, 79, 569
  Miẓvot, Shefer ha-, 1089–1090
  on moral conduct, 196–197, 198, 199–
    200
  philosophy, 575–576
  philosophy and tradition, 1013
  on prayer, 723, 727
  on proselytes, 103
  on providence, 736
  on rational and natural law, 669
  on reason, 751
  on religion and state, 775
  on religious authority, 29–32
  on resurrection, 808, 810
  on retribution, 827–828, 829–830, 989
  on revelation, 819–820, 823
  on righteousness, 836
  and science, 858
  on sex, 180
  on strangers, 921
  study of Torah, 941
  on time, 982
  on truth, 1018
  on unity, 1030
  on war and peace, 692, 693–694, 696,
    697

Maimonides, Moses (continued)

on women, 1041
on work, 1058
Malbim. See Meir Loeb ben Jehiel Michael
maleness
and feminism, 258
malkhut (kingdom), 652
Hasidism, 318, 319, 320
music, 637
Malkhuyyot, 523
Manichaeism
and Gnosticism, 286
manual labor, 1056, 1062
Maqdisi, al-, 491
Marburg neo-Kantianism, 751
Marcel, Gabriel
I and Thou, 440
on tolerance, 991–992
Marrano, 144, 145, 1088
marriage
Conservative Judaism, 98
faith, 239–240, 241, 242–243
intermarriage, 864
justice, 519
mixed, 772
orphans, 49–50
sexuality, 177–178, 179
women, 1045–1046
See also divorce
marriage broker (shadkhan), 242
marriage contract (ketubah), women's rights,
240
martyrdom, 132
catastrophe, 44
Christianity, 63
and exile, 405
holiness, 391
and Holocaust, 406, 407
providence, 737
remnant of Israel, 780, 781
sanctification of the Name, 849, 852–854
and silence, 877–888
Marx, Karl Heinrich, and Marxism, 1088
anti-Semitism, 14, 15
Masada, 1088
and heroism, 308
mashal (story simile), 458
maskilim, 169, 171–172, 173, 174, 1083
masochism
and guilt, 307
masturbation, 178

Maybaum, Ignaz, 209
MEANING, 565
meassifim, 172–173
Mecca, 488
mediation
and tolerance, 992
medicine, 857
MEDIEVAL JEWISH PHILOSOPHY, 573
natural law, 664
providence, 735, 736
reason, 750
repentance, 786
resurrection, 809–810
revelation, 817
soul, 891
Talmud, 957
Medina, 488
medinah (sovereign state), 718
meditations. See kavvanah; kavvanot
mefursamot (moral values)
ethics, 196–197
Me'iri of Perpignan, 51, 52
Meir Loeb ben Jehiel Michael, 1088–1089
on execution, 427
mysticism, 645, 646–647
on strangers, 920
study of Torah, 945
Torah neglect, 837–838
Meir Simhah ha-Kohen of Dvinsk
on holiness, 449
Melchizedek
Jerusalem, 496, 497
priesthood, 529
Memorbuch, 1089
MEMORY, 581
individuality, 484
See also History
Mendel, Menahem, of Kotsk
and silence, 878
Mendelssohn, Moses, 630, 631, 634, 1089
on commandments, 1011
and education, 159
on emancipation, 166
Enlightenment, 172–173
on exile, 223
on immortality, 480–481, 482
on reason, 750
on Reform Judaism, 768
on revelation, 817
Menelaus
priesthood, 530
menorah (candelabrum), 1089

MENTSH, 587
mentshheyt (humankind), 588
mentshlichkeyt (humanity), 588
MERCY, 589
  and concept of history, 375
  and justice, 516–517
  and punishment, 961
  See also Grace or Loving–Kindness
Merkavah (Divine Chariot), 1088
  Gnosticism, 288
  music, 636
  mysticism, 644–645, 648–650, 654
Meshullam ben Solomon da Pira. *See* En
    Vidas de Gerona
Mesopotamia
  and unity, 1026–1027
Messiah
  eschatology, 186
  and the future, 373–374
MESSIANISM, 597
  destiny, 139
  divine retribution, 962, 963
  eros, 181
  eschatology, 184
  and the future, 377
  Gush Emunim, 350
  heresy, 345–346
  history, 380–381, 384
  imagination, 465–466
  immortality, 481
  Maimonides on, 576
  myth, 660, 661
  Nazism, 948, 949
  providence, 736
  redemption, 762
  remnant of Israel, 782
  resurrection, 811
  rest, 803
  State of Israel, 910, 911, 914–915
  utopia, 1033–1035
  and Zionism, 1071
metaphor
  and imagination, 455
  gestures, 278–279
METAPHYSICS, 603
  Bergson, H. L., 1080
  ethics, 200
  reason, 752
  redemption, 764
  resurrection, 811
  and science, 858
  soul, 887–888

Spinoza, 1094
  study of Torah, 940
  time, 983–984
  tradition, 1011
Metatron, 288
Mezhirech school
  Ḥasidism, 318–319, 320–321
mezuzah (doorpost), 1089
Micah, 780
Michel, Ernst, 440
middot, 614
  ethics, 511
MIDRASH, 613
  aggadah, 9–10
  amoraim, 1079
  catastrophe, 41, 44
  charity, 48
  creation, 114
  divine power, 967
  exegesis, 213, 215
  Genesis Rabbah, 1083
  halakhah, 315
  Hebrew, 326, 328
  humor, 464
  Leviticus Rabbah, 1087
  love of God, 560–561
  Orthodox Judaism, 682
  sexuality, 178
  Sifrei, 1093
  and silence, 877
  study of Torah, 941
  and tradition, 461
  and truth, 1022
  war, 690
Midrash Eliyahu Zuta, 646–647
Midrash Haggadah
  myth, 660
Midrash Hallel, 645
Midrash Mishle, 647
Midrash Rabbah, 613
Midrash Tehillim, 646
military heroism, 364–365, 369, 370
Mill, John Stuart
  on God, 296
minim (heresies)
  Gnosticism, 288
minut
  heresy, 339, 340–341
minyan
  women, 97
MIRACLE, 621
  and God, 295

mishkan (bearer of the Presence)
and rest, 797, 802
Mishnah; Mishnayot, 953–955, 956,
1089
canonization, 844–845
exile, 222
Gemara, 1083
Hebrew, 327
Judah ha-Nasi, 1089
mysticism, 646, 647, 648
oral law, 674, 675, 676
Pirkei Avot, 1091
and rest, 801
study, 941, 942
suffering, 933–935
Talmud, 1094
tannaim, 1095
utopia, 1037
Mishnaic Hebrew
Torah, 1000–1002, 1003
Mishneh Torah (The Repetition of the Law),
1089
as canon, 845
mispaha (clan or family), 81, 239
moral values, 305–306
mishpat (judgment)
ethics, 201
mission theory, 168–169
mitnaggedim
Torah study, 654
mizvah; mizvot, 67–80, 1089
charity, 48
dogma, 142
eternity and time, 191
fear of God, 249
halakhah, 310, 313, 314
Hebrew, 328
Hinnukh, Sefer ha- (Book of Instruction),
1084
holiness, 390, 392
kavvanah, 1086
and meaning of life, 568–570
music, 636, 637
mysticism, 652–653
personal will, 932
prayer, 724
prophets, 733
redemption, 761
revelation, 815, 822
and sin, 881
study of Torah, 939, 941, 943, 945
suffering, 933–935, 936, 937–938

tradition, 1010, 1011–1012
women, 1040, 1042, 1049
See also Commandments; Torah
MIZVEH (Yiddish *mizvah*), **627**
Mizvot, Sefer ha- (Book of Commandments),
1089–1090
mizvot ma'asiot
and heresy, 342
Modena, Leone
on rabbis, 744
on sermons, 869
modernism (art), 3–4, 6
modernity
Enlightenment, 171
and providence, 738–739
and reason, 751
Reconstructionism, 755
and Reform Judaism, 767
repentance, 792
and rest, 804
strangers, 925
survival, 950
and truth, 1018, 1019
MODERN JEWISH PHILOSOPHY, 629
repentance, 787
modesty
and humility, 430, 431
Molcho, Solomon (Diego Pires), 1090
Molitor, Frank, 1008
monism
and Hasidism, 318
monotheism
chosen people, 57–58
Christianity, 61
emancipation, 169
free will, 269
God and evil, 964
idolatry, 447
imago Dei, 474
Islam, 487
Judaism, 506
justice and God, 515
Protestant thought, 92
reason, 750, 751
repentance, 785
Moore, George Foot, 93
Morais, Sabato, 91
morality
conscience, 87
ethics, 195, 197
fear of God, 246
grace or loving–kindness, 300

guilt, 305
  prophets, 733
  righteousness, 833, 836–837
mortality
  death, 131
Moses
  biographies, 466
  on death, 132
  prophecy, 731, 732
  religious authority, 29–30
  remnant of Israel, 781
  and rest, 797
  Torah, 997, 998, 999, 1002
Moses de Leon
  myth, 661
  on music, 639
  pardes, 1090
  Zohar, 578, 846
Moses of Tachav, 292
moshavim
  and labor, 1060
Moslem philosophy
  reason, 750
motion
  and time, 982
Mount Moriah
  Jerusalem, 496
Mount of Olives, 134
Mount Sinai
  and Mount Zion, 498, 499
Mount Zion
  Jerusalem, 498, 499, 500
  remnant of Israel, 779, 780
mourning (aninut), 133, 134
Muhammad
  Islam, 487
Musaf (Additional Service for the New Year),
  523
  retribution, 961
Musar literature
  repentance, 786
  soul searching, 900–901
Musar movement, 1090
  ethics, 199
  fear of punishment, 252
  repentance, 787
Muselmann, 403, 406
MUSIC, 635
  aesthetics, 2, 4
  Reform Judaism, 769
Muslims
  strangers, 928–929

Mutazilite school, 573–574
mysterium tremendum, 108
mystical philosophy, 578
MYSTICISM, 643
  eroticism, 180
  existence, 228, 231
  Gnosticism, 288
  Hasidism, 317
  Heikhalot and Merkabah, 1083–1084
  heresy, 345–346
  idolatry, 447
  kabbalah, 1085–1086
  man as microcosm, 1064
  messianism, 600–601
  music, 636–638
  providence, 737
  reason, 753
  soul, 893–894
  Talmud, 957
  theology, 974–975
  unification, 1031
  Zohar, 1096
MYTH, 657
  aggadah, 7
  Gnosticism, 286–287
  imagination, 454
  oral law, 673
  pagans, 454, 463
  theology, 975

Nag-Hammadi texts, 287
Nahman Bar Yizhak, 431
Nahmanides (Moses ben Nahman), 1090
  on Adamic language, 544
  on evil, 960
  halakhah, 312
  Jewish law, 511
  kabbalah, 653
  on land of Israel, 914
  on love of God, 561
  on love of neighbor, 558
  Orthodox Judaism, 680–681
  philosophy, 578
  on priests, 533, 774
  on religious authority, 32
  on retribution, 830
  on sexuality, 180
Nahman of Bratslav, 1090
  on Aramaic, 320
  canon, 846
  dialogue, 464
  liturgy, 555

Naḥman of Bratslav (*continued*)

on prayer, 905
on repentance, 790
nakedness
and family, 240–241
Nathan of Gaza, 289, 1036
nation
people of Israel, 706–708
soul searching, 900
See also Land of Israel; State of Israel
national deliverance
Reform Judaism, 92
national freedom, 266
nationalism
providence, 738
and Reconstructionism, 755
Zionism, 1069
Natronai Gaon, 1035
naturalism
and belief in God, 297–298
Ḥasidism, 321
and rationalism, 752
and Reconstructionism, 755, 756
naturalization
emancipation, 166
NATURAL LAW, 663
ethics, 196, 197, 200
Noachism, 103–104
and truth, 1018
natural phenomena
evil, 204
natural science, 857, 858
and love of God, 561
nature
imagery, 453–454
man's return to, 792
miracles, 621–622, 623
and rest, 800
and science, 856, 857, 876
and unity, 1026–1027
Nazism
anti-Semitism, 14, 15
and memory, 584
and sanctification of the Name, 853
survival, 948–949, 950
See also Holocaust
negation
State of Israel, 911
negativum
aesthetics, 2–3
Nehemiah, 800

Neḥunya ben ha-Kana, 649
neighbor, love of, 557–558, 562, 694
and prayer, 725
strangers, 924
Neo-Orthodoxy, 1090
emancipation, 168
heresy, 347
secularism 864
nerot (lighting candles), 1049
Neturei Karta (Guardians of the City), 910–911, 912
"New Christians," 1088
New Nation, 720
New Testament
and ecumenism, 152
niddah (laws of family purity), 1049
Niebuhr, H. Richard, 440
Niebuhr, Reinhold, 440
Nietzsche, Friedrich Wilhelm, 632, 1090
on befriending, 990
on history, 374–375
on humility, 429
Zionism, 1074
Nissenbaum, Isaac, 407
Nissim ben Reuben Gerondi, 1090
Derashot ha-Ran, 1081
study of Torah, 943, 944
niẓhiyut ha-nefesh (eternality of the soul), 480
niẓoẓot (divine sparks), 321–323
Gnosticism, 289
repentance, 786, 787–788
Noachism
and Christianity, 62
conversion, 103–104, 105
Noachite commandments
natural law, 664, 666, 667
righteous Gentiles, 921
Noah
conversion, 101–102
Nobel Nehemiah, 161
nokhrim (foreigners), 918
"Notes on the Correct Way to Present the Jews and Judaism in Preaching and Catechesis in the Roman Catholic Church," 148
nothingness (*ayin*)
Ḥasidism, 318–319
nothingness (*duma*, stillness)
silence, 874
nothingness (Ein Sof), 227, 293–294, 295, 651

nuclear war
  and survival, 950
nurturance
  and rest, 805

Obadiah ben Jacob Sforno, 533
obedience
  God's law, 512
  redemption, 762
objectivism
  and truth, 1017, 1019, 1020, 1021
obligation
  peace, 687
"obligatory war," 692
olam emet (World of Truth)
  death, 132
Oldham, J. H., 440
Old Testament
  and ecumenism, 152
omnipotence, divine
  theodicy, 966–968
ontology
  redemption, 764, 765
  soul,. 984–895
optimism
  and history, 374–375
ORAL LAW, 673
  aggadah, 1078
  canon, 843–845
  Islam and Judaism, 489
  midrashic commentary, 614
  Orthodox Judaism, 679
  responsa, 1091
  retribution, 829
  study of Torah, 940
  Talmud, 953
  Torah, 999–1000, 1002–1003, 1004
Orḥot Ẓaddikim, 250
orphans (yatom)
  marital needs, 49–50, 51
Orthodox churches
  ecumenism, 149–150
ORTHODOX JUDAISM, 506, 679
  afterlife, 132
  dogma, 145
  education, 159
  freedom, 265
  heresy, 347–348, 350
  liturgy, 555
  reason, 753
  repentance, 792
  secularism, 864

State of Israel, 911–912
strangers, 925, 927
tradition, 1013
Zionism, 540, 950, 1075
See also Neo-Orthodoxy
Other
  women, 256–257, 258
other side, the (sitra aḥra), 1093–1094
  soul, 895
Ottomans
  and Jews, 492
  law influence, 865
Ouziel, Ben-Zion Meir Ḥai, 926
oysmenths, 588
Ozick, Cynthia, 256

pacifism, 365–66
  New Testament, 692
paganism
  deities, 454
  imago Dei, 423–424
  repetition, 463
pain
  and women, 1042
painting
  aesthetics, 4
Palestine
  Balfour Declaration, 1079
  Conservative Judaism, 95
  and Islam, 492
  Keneset Yisrael, 1086
  Magnes, Judah Leon, 1088
  Reform Judaism, 771
  utopia, 1036
  work, 1056, 1059–1060, 1064
  Zionism, 1070, 1071, 1072, 1073, 1074
Palestinian Arabs
  strangers, 929
Pallière, Aimé, 104
panentheism, 294
  Ḥasidism, 319, 321
  idolatry, 447
  modern Jewish philosophy, 633
Papa, Rav, 944
pardes, 1090
parity treaties
  as covenants, 108, 111
particularism
  emancipation, 169–170
  survival, 951
paschal sacrifice, 212
passion, 557

Passover
    and history, 371–372
Passover Haggadah, 555
pathos, divine
    catastrophe, 43
    and evil, 967
patriarchs
    remnant of Israel, 781
patriarchy
    feminism, 255
Paul
    on righteousness, 835
Paul VI, Pope, 25
Pauline Christianity
    anti-Semitism, 15–18
Pax Judaica, 696, 698
PEACE (*shalom*), **685**
    Jerusalem, 495–496
    land of Israel, 915
    and unity, 1030
peasant
    and work, 1056
Peirce, Charles S., 633
    on truth, 1020
pele (marvel), 295
penitential prayers (*selihot*), 555
Pentateuch
    and belief, 236
    canonization, 841, 842
    criticism, 35, 37–38, 39
    education, 157
    Orthodox Judaism, 679
    Torah, 997, 1002
    See also Septuagint
people (*am*)
    community, 81
PEOPLE OF ISRAEL (*am Yisrael*), **703**
    Reform Judaism, 771
    remnant of Israel, 782
    and repentance, 792
    rest, 799, 800–801, 805
People of the Book, 490, 491
perfection (*shelemut*)
    creation, 116, 117–118, 965
    destiny, 139
    ethics, 198, 200
    good and evil, 960, 965
    mizvot, 78–79
    and peace, 685, 689, 694, 695, 701
    redemption, 761, 762
    and repentance, 786
    soul, 889, 891

personal identity
    and unity, 1028–1030
personalism
    and truth, 1018–1019, 1020,
        1021
petihta (proem), 617
petition
    prayer, 724–726
Pharisees, 1090–1091
    priests, 530–531
Philo Judaeus, 1091
    on free will, 272
    Gnosticism, 286–287
    Hellenism, 333, 334
    imagination, 453
    imitatio Dei, 201
    Moses, 466
    natural law, 668
    philosophy and tradition, 1012–1013
    priesthood, 531–532, 533
    reason, 750
philology
    exegesis, 215
philosophy
    ethics, 195
    metaphysics, 603
    Orthodox Judaism, 679
    sermons, 868–869
    study and heresy, 345
    and tradition, 1012
    truth, 1017
    See also Medieval Jewish Philosophy;
        Modern Jewish Philosophy; Theology
physics
    study of, 858
pictorial representation
    gesture, 276
pietism, 575–576
piety
    fear of God, 249
    spirituality, 905–906
Pines, Shlomo, 272–273
Pinsker, Leon, 988
pioneer. *See haluz*
pious
    remnant of Israel, 780, 781
Pires, Diego. *See* Molcho, Solomon
piyyut; piyyutim, (hymn), 269,
        1091
plain (historical) sense
    exegesis, 213
Plaskow, Judith, 257

Plato
  atheism, 25
  metaphysics, 604
Plotinus, 286
Plumb, J. H., 382
pluralism
  creation, 116
  Jewish culture, 123–124
pneuma. See Spirit
Polish Frankists, 181
political community
  kingdom of God, 521–522
political integration
  emancipation, 166, 167
political power
  rabbis, 746
POLITICAL THEORY, 715
  providence, 738
polyandry, 1045
polygyny, 1045–1046
Portugal
  expulsion of Jews, 1094
  Marranos, 1088
Positive-Historical School, 168, 1082
poverty
  charity, 48–49, 51–53
power (*gevurah*)
  and music, 638
  politics, 715–716
  religion and state, 776
pragmatism
  history, 373
  and truth, 1020–1021
praise
  prayer, 724–726
PRAYER, 723
  Alenu, 523, 811
  Amidah, 1078–1079
  daily, 98
  halakkah, 314
  Hebrew, 328
  and holiness, 394–395
  Islam, 490
  Kaddish, 133, 134
  kavvanah, 1086
  Kiddush, 1086
  and language, 551
  liturgy, 553
  Memorbuch, 1089
  and mercy, 594
  mysticism, 654
  piyyutim, 1091

Reconstructionism, 757
repentance, 789
siddur tefillah, 1093
and song, 640
and study, 156–157
spiritual teaching, 905
study of Torah, 942–944
women, 1049
preacher
  rabbi, 743
  soul searching, 900
  See also Sermon
precedence
  Holocaust, 399–400
predestination
  and free will, 270–271
preexistence
  soul, 888
present, the
  messianism, 598, 599
preventive charity, 48
Priestly Source, 36, 38
priests
  and rule, 774
prior right
  holiness, 392
process philosophy
  and time, 983, 984
procreation
  eros, 177
  faith, 239–242
  women, 1042
proem (*petihta*), 617
profanation
  and imagination, 462–463
profanation of the Name, 849, 851–852
profane history, 376
Progressive Judaism, 1079
promissory grant
  as covenant, 108
property
  women, 1044–1045
PROPHECY, 731
  exegesis, 212, 213, 215
  holy spirit, 409
  and imagination, 452
  Jerusalem, 500
  land of Israel, 538
  medieval philosophy, 575–576
  and memory, 581
  Muhammad, 487–488
  redemption, 763

PROPHECY (*continued*)

repentance, 786
revelation, 817, 823
and rest, 800
retribution, 831
sermons, 871–872
silence, 873–875
soul searching, 899–900
Torah, 998–999
truth, 1018
See also Apocalypse; biblical prophecy
prophetic kabbalah, 651, 653
Prophets (*Neviim*)
canonization, 841, 842, 843
proselutueo (aggregation), 105
proselytism, 102, 104
proselytoi (associate Jews), 103
prostration
symbolization, 282
Protestantism
ecumenism, 149, 151
and Judaism, 92, 150
kingdom of priests, 533
Protestant Neo-Orthodoxy
I and Thou, 440
PROVIDENCE, 735
and revelation, 819, 820
sermons, 867–868
and suffering, 933, 935–936, 938
Przywara, Erich, 440
Psalms of Solomon
apocalypse, 21
remnant of Israel, 782
psalmists
reward and punishment, 831
psalmodic literature
Jerusalem, 498
pseudepigraphy
Gnostic mythology, 287
and imagination, 460–461
pseudo-messianism
nationalism, 1070
public school, 162
punishment
eschatology, 185, 186
evils, 204–205, 207–209
fear of God, 247, 248, 249, 250, 251
and free will, 273
and mercy, 591–592
sin, 885

theodicy, 961
See also Catastrophe; Reward and
    Punishment
purification
death, 134
purity (*taharot*), 69
sanctification of the Name, 850
women, 357, 1049

Qumran (Dead Sea) Scrolls, 1081
free will, 270
Qumran Community
proto-Gnosticism, 287
Zadokites, 780

Rabbenu Tam. *See* Tam, Jacob ben Meir
RABBI AND TEACHER, 741
canon, 842–843
and providence, 736
talmid ḥakham, 1094
and unity, 1031
women, 97
Rabbinical Assembly, 96–98
rabbinic Judaism
aggadah, 8, 10–12
canon, 844, 845
catastrophe, 42–43
holy spirit, 411–413
and intellectualism, 856
suffering, 932
Torah, 997, 1000–1002, 1003, 1004–1005
rabbinic law
women, 1043, 1045, 1047–1048
rabbinic literature
aggadah, 8, 9, 10, 1078
fear of God, 246
halakhah, 1083
kingdom of God, 521–522, 523
midrash, 613
myth, 659
natural law, 665–666
reason, 749
righteousness, 834
sanctification of the Name, 850
theology, 971
truth, 1017
Radak. *See* Kimḥi, David
raḥamim (engaged love)
and mercy, 590, 591, 594
rainfall and rainwater
land of Israel, 537

ransoming of the Jews, 184
rape, 1047
Rashi (Solomon ben Isaac), 1091
    charity, 48
    and education, 157, 159
    and heresy, 340
    on priests, 533
    on strangers, 923
rationalism
    destiny, 139
    education, 158
    foreign wisdom, 336–337
    medieval philosophy, 574, 575, 578–579
    and reason, 751–752
    Reform Judaism, 771
    and science, 856–857, 859
rational law
    and natural law, 668–669, 670
rational virtues
    ethics, 200
Rava
    on humility, 431
    on reward and suffering, 934
rea. See neighbor
reality
    peace, 688–689
    revelation, 817
REASON, 749
    and faith, 234–235
"reasons for the *mizvot*" (*taamei ha-mizvot*),
    74
rebellion
    State of Israel, 911–912
rebuke
    sermons, 870–871
reckoning
    soul searching, 897
RECONSTRUCTIONISM, 755, 95–96
    dogma, 145
    liturgy, 555
    modern Jewish philosophy, 633
Reconstructionist Foundation, 755
Reconstructionist Rabbinic College, 755
REDEMPTION (*geulah*), **761**
    divine retribution, 062
    and the future, 373–374
    and history, 376–377
    hope, 418, 149
    I and Thou, 440–442
    and imagination, 457
    messianism, 600, 601

    and peace, 698
    and revelation, 817–819
    State of Israel, 910, 911–912, 914–915
    and survival, 947, 948, 949, 950, 951
    and unity, 1030
    utopia, 1034
    Zionism, 1069, 1072
Red Sea crossing
    and Passover, 371, 372
reenactment
    gesture, 281–282
REFORM JUDAISM, 767
    and Conservative Judaism, 92
    dogma, 145
    emancipation, 168, 169
    heresy, 347–348
    liturgy, 555
    preaching, 872
    secularism, 864
    State of Israel, 911, 912
    tradition, 1013
Reik, Theodor, 469
reincarnation
    soul, 893
Reis, Shneur Zuta, 928
RELIGION AND STATE, 773
religious authority. *See* Authority
REMNANT OF ISRAEL (*she-erit Yisrael*),
    779
repair of the world (*tikkun ha-olam*)
    and righteousness, 838
reparation. *See tikkun*
REPENTANCE (*teshuvah*), **785**
    conversion, 101
    and redemption, 764, 765
    sermons, 870–871
    soul searching, 899–900
    and suffering, 936
repetition
    writing, 463
representation
    of the divine, 2
    gesture, 276–277
resident alien (*ger toshov*). *See* Stranger
responsa, 1091
    and history, 378
REST (*shabbat*), **795**
RESURRECTION OF THE DEAD, 807
    apocalyptic vision, 20–21
    divine retribution, 962
    eschatology, 184

RESURRECTION OF THE DEAD (*continued*)

and immortality, 479
Orthodox Judaism, 680–681
remnant of Israel, 781
redemption, 762
as reward, 829–830
retaliation
justice, 516
reticence
and imagination, 465, 466–467
retribution
theodicy, 961–964
See also Reward and Punishment
"returning"
and repentance, 792
revealed law
and natural law, 667, 668, 669, 670, 671
REVELATION, 815
Buber on, 1081
creation, 113
eternity and time, 191–202
holy spirit, 412
I and Thou, 440–442
law, 511
oral law, 673–675
Orthodox Judaism, 680–681
prophecy, 732, 734
reason, 749, 753
resurrection, 809
silence, 874–875
tolerance, 991
tradition, 355, 1008, 1010, 1011
See also Apocalypse
revolution, 719, 720
REWARD AND PUNISHMENT, 827
eschatology, 184–185
fear of God, 247
free will, 273
providence, 735
redemption, 762
righteousness, 837
spirituality, 904
suffering, 935–936
Ricoeur, Paul
on history, 382
on myth, 658
on time consciousness, 376
right and wrong, 195–196
righteous judgment
covenant, 590

RIGHTEOUSNESS (*zedakah*), **833**
charity, 48, 49
ethics, 201
holy spirit, 410
Islam, 490
prophets, 733
theodicy, 959
utopia, 1034
ritual
gesture, 275
Rogachover Rebbe. *See* Rozin, Joseph
romantic thought
Judah Halevi on, 576–577
Rosenthal, Erwin, 489
Rosenzweig, Franz, 347, 1091
on culture, 119, 127
on ecumenism, 148
on education, 160–162
on eternity and time, 191–192
on exile, 224
on existence, 231
on foreign wisdom, 337
on Hebrew, 329–330
on historical memory, 372
historical scholarship, 384
on history, 430, 433
I and Thou, 436–347, 439, 440–442
and imagination, 468
language, 544–545
on miracles, 624
philosophy, 468, 632, 634
Orthodox Judaism, 680
on reason, 752
on remnant of Israel, 782–783
on repentance, 787, 788, 792
on resurrection, 810
on revelation, 817
speech thought, 467
theology, 976
on time, 984
and truth, 1020
Rosh Ha-Shanah (Beginning of the Year),
1091–1092
Rossi, Azariah de, 1092
on messianism, 1035
on science, 859
Rotenstreich, Nathan, 816
Rothschild, Baron Edmond de
Zionism, 1073
Royal Academy of Science
Jews, 859

Rozin, Joseph, 1036
ruaḥ ha-kodesh. *See* Holy Spirit
ruḥaniyyut. *See* Spirituality
Rumania
  Jewish nationalism, 1070
Russia
  Enlightenment, 173
  Jewish nationalism, 1070

Saadiah (ben Joseph) Gaon, 1092
  on commandments, 1011
  Conservative Judaism, 95
  on culture, 125, 126
  on divine retribution, 963
  dogma, 141, 142
  ethics, 196
  exegesis, 214
  on exile, 379
  on free will, 272
  imago Dei, 477
  Knesset Yisrael, 774
  on knowledge, 974
  on natural law, 668–669
  philosophy, 573–574
  prophecy and truth, 1018
  on resurrection, 809
  Gnosis, 289
  on messianism, 1036
  on providence, 737
  and Zionism, 1074
Sabbatenism, 1092
  and Ḥasidism, 321–322
  and heresy, 342, 345–346
  imago Dei, 477
  and messianism, 1036
  preachers, 869
  Shabbetai Ẓevi, 1092
  and Zionism, 1070
Sabbath
  Conservative Judaism, 97, 98
  Hebrew, 329
  and holiness, 392, 393
  and imagination, 468–469
  land of Israel, 583
  liturgy, 91
  miẓvot, 73
  Priestly Source, 36–37
Sabbath Prayer Book, 757
Sachs, Nelly, 878
sacred intellectualism
  Talmud, 957

sacred history, 376
**SACRED TEXT AND CANON,
  841**
  exegesis, 211
  oral law, 673
  sermons, 870
sacrifice
  heroism, 364–365
Sadducees, 1092
  oral law, 675
  providence, 736
Safed
  music, 637
  Zionism, 1070
sages (*hakhamim*), 1092
  Gentiles, 921
  and heresy, 341, 342, 343, 344
  holy spirit, 412–413, 414
  individuality, 483
  on peace, 686
  on repentance, 786, 788
  on strangers, 919, 9120
  study of Torah, 944
  Talmud, 954–955, 956
  and tradition, 1009
  on work, 1056–1057
  See also amora, amoraim; tanna, tannaim
salvation
  eschatology, 186
  Reconstructionism, 758–759
Salonika
  Jewish community, 492
Samuel ben Meir, 1092
Samuel ben Naḥman, 942
sancta, 758
sanctification
  holiness, 390–391
  kaddish, 395
  of life, 407
  righteousness, 836
sanctification of God
  and meaning of life, 566
SANCTIFICATION OF THE NAME
  (*kiddush ha-Shem*), **849**
  heroism, 364
  martyrdom, 877
  and memory, 583, 584
sanctity
  chosen people, 56
sanctuary
  and rest, 798

Sanhedrin, 1092
  Commentary on Ḥelek, 1084
  Jabneh, 1085
  religion and state, 775
  sages, 1092
  Shammai, 1093
Sasportas, Jacob, 1036
Satmar Ḥasidic sect, 912
Saul
  guilt and silence, 874
Schatz, Tzvi, 1063
Schechter, Solomon, 1092–1093
  fear of God, 247
  Jewish Theological Seminary, 92, 93, 94,
    95
  on rabbis, 744
  Zionism, 865
Schneidau, Herbert N. 128
Schoenberg, Arnold, 4
Scholem, Gershom
  on apocalyptic messianism, 377
  on exile, 223
  and history, 380, 381, 383
  kabbalah, 321, 846
  on labor, 1059
  midrash, 619
  normative Jewish thought, 465
  Shiur Komah, 476–477
  theology, 974–975
  on tradition, 1008
  and Zionism, 1074
Schopenhauer, Arthur, 565–566
Schweid, Eliezer, 716
SCIENCE, 855
  education, 158
  and reason, 751
  secularism, 866
  and truth, 1018, 1021
Science of Judaism (Wissenschaft des
    Judentums)
  Conservative Judaism, 93
  historical scholarship, 382–383
  kabbalah, 846
  Orthodox Judaism, 683
  Reform Judaism, 769–770
  and tradition, 1014
scientific empiricism
  and providence, 738
scientific materialism
  and time, 983
Scripture
  atheism, 25

fear of God, 245–246
free will, 269–270
hermeneutics, 354–360
historical memory, 582
justice, 517
language, 545–546, 547–548
Muhammad, 488
truth, 1017–1018, 1021–1022
  See also Bible
sculpture
  aesthetics, 4
Second Commandment
  and art, 2–3
  and imagination, 452–453
Second Ezdras. See Ezra Apocalypse
Second Isaiah, Book of
  rest, 795, 799–800
Second Maccabees, Book of
  Hellenism, 334
SECULARISM, 863
  repentance, 787
  spirituality, 904–905
  State of Israel, 508, 910, 912
  Zionism, 1071
secular learning, 158–159, 160,
    163
secular time
  and history, 376
seder
  symbolization, 277
sefirot; sefirah (emanations), 293–294, 295,
    652, 1093
  and family, 242
  Ḥasidism, 318–319
  land of Israel, 539
  music, 637, 638
  sexuality, 180–181
  Shekhinah, 1093
  soul, 891–893
self
  eschatology, 187–188
  and prayer, 725–726, 727
  reason, 750–751
  repentance, 788
self-esteem
  orphans and marriage, 50
self-help
  charity, 53
self-knowledge
  and humility, 431–432
self-realization
  ethics, 198, 199, 200

self-transcendence
  charity, 47
selihot (penitential prayers)
  liturgy, 555
Sephardi; Sephardim, 1093
  catastrophe, 44
  chosen people, 56–57
  ecumenism, 152
  providence, 736
  rabbis, 743
  scientific study, 859
Septuagint, 333, 334
SERMON, 867
  Reform Judaism, 769
  soul searching, 900
sexuality
  eros, 177
  Genesis, 240
  women, 1040, 1041
shabbat. See Rest
Shabbetai Zevi, 1092
shadkhan (marriage broker),
  242
Shalmon
  Jerusalem, 495
shalom. See Peace
Shalom, Shin, 878
Shammai (the Elder), 1093
  oral law, 674, 675
  political theory, 718
  on Torah, 999
shankbone (*zeroa*)
  symbolization, 279
Shavuot
  gesture, 281
she'erit Yisrael. See Remnant of Israel
Shekhinah (Divine Presence), 1093
  and family, 242
  Hasidism, 318–319
  imagination, 456–457
  medieval philosophy, 574, 575
  people of Israel, 711–713
  revelation, 818, 819, 822
  righteousness, 834
  study of Torah, 942
Shema, 1093
  divine will, 931
  God's kingship, 522
  liturgy, 554
  and imagination, 454–455
  mezuzah, 1089
  paragraph order, 30

soul searching, 901
  study of Torah, 940
shemittah
  and rest, 797, 798, 800, 801
Shemoneh Esreh (Eighteen Benedictions). *See*
  Amidah
Sherirah ben Hanina Gaon, 844, 845
Shestov, Lev, 810
shevut
  and rest, 802–803
Shimeon ben Gamliel, 1034
shirat ha-yam, 372–373
Shiur Komah, 474, 477, 478
shivah, 134
shleimut (completeness)
  and unity, 1030
Shneur Zalman of Lyady, 1093
  canon, 846
  on God, 294
  Habad Hasidism, 319–320
Shoah (total destruction), 399
shofar
  image in sermons, 871–872
  Rosh Ha-Shanah, 1092
  symbolization, 276–277
shtetl
  community, 83
Shulhan Arukh (The Prepared Table), 460,
  1093
  aesthetics, 3
  Arukh ha-Shulhan, 1079
  as canon, 845
  "commandments of men," 76
  and faith, 447
  halakhah, 309
  heroism, 363
  and imagination, 454
Sibyline Books, 22
Shulmanu
  Jerusalem, 495
sick
  music as treatment, 635–636
siddur tefillah, 1093
  contents, 459
  liturgy, 553
  "sheep to the slaughter," 369
Sifrei, 1093
SILENCE, 873
  and prayer, 551
Simeon Bar Yohai
  mysticism, 646
  Zohar, 846

Simeon ben Eleazar
  divine retribution, 963
  fear of God, 247
Simḥat Torah, 1094
Simlai, Rabbi
  grace or loving–kindness, 299–300
  righteousness, 834
Simon, Ernst, 439
SIN, 881
  creation, 115
  death as punishment, 131
  divine retribution, 961–962
  evil, 960–961
  fear of God, 247, 248, 249, 252
  people of Israel, 708
  repentance, 786
  and silence, 873–874
  soul searching, 899, 902
Singer, Isaac Bashevis, 1079–1080
  and imagination, 462
sin-offering, 790
Sira, Ben
  and free will, 270
  resurrection, 807
  wisdom as torah, 997
sisters
  as property, 1044
sitra aḥra (the other side), 1093–1094
  soul, 895
Six Day War, 915, 925, 950–951,
    1066
skepticism
  and truth, 1019
slavery
  freedom, 261–262, 799, 800, 803
  and humanism, 426
  Maimonides on, 311
  and rest, 798, 799
  women, 1045
"small beginnings," 1064
social justice, 800
society
  education, 157, 158
  emancipation, 165–166
  ethics, 197
  perfection, 198
  and providence, 738
  political theory, 717, 718, 719
  politics, 715–716
  religion and state, 776–777
  and sin, 883–884
  soul searching, 898

strangers, 917
  and war, 699–700
Society of the Friends of the Hebrew
    Language, 172
sociology
  and rationalism, 752
Sofer, Moses, 1094
  Hebrew, 328
  on science, 860
soil
  and work, 1055–1056
soldiers
  heroism, 364–365, 639
solipsism, 200
Solomon
  Jerusalem, 497
Soloveitchik, Joseph, 1094
  on covenant, 110–111
  on ecumenism, 150
  on faith, 127–128
  halakkah, 313, 315
  Orthodox Judaism, 680–681, 682
  philosophy, 631, 632, 633, 634
  on rationality, 265
  on reason, 753
  on repentance, 787, 790
song
  mysticism, 636, 638–640
Song of Songs
  burial rite, 641
  eroticism, 177–178
  I and Thou, 435
  and imagination, 453
  imago Dei, 474–475
sonship
  people of Israel, 710–711
SOUL, 887
  death, 131–132, 133–134
  immortality, 479
  metaphysics, 608
  people of Israel, 709
  perfection of, 198
  resurrection, 807
  retribution, 829, 830
  Saadiah Gaon on, 574
  survival, 480
  wrong action, 199
SOUL SEARCHING, 897
Soviet Jews
  and group memory, 585
space
  destiny, 138

land of Israel, 538
myth, 659
Spain
Crescas, 1081
Jewish dogma, 144
Jews expulsion, 1094
Marranos, 1088
Sperber, Manès, 400
Spinoza, Baruch (Benedict) De, 1094
on atheism, 25, 26
on ban, 342
exegesis, 215, 216
on exile, 223
on freedom, 74
on God, 294
on human behavior, 87–88
on jurisprudence, 510
on justice, 518
philosophy, 632
political theory, 716
on providence, 737
Torah and science, 1018
spirit (pneuma)
Gnosticism, 286
representations of, 3
SPIRITUALITY (ruhaniyyut), 903
Scripture, 691–692
State of Israel, 914
Sprechdenken (speech thought), 467
state
political theory, 719
STATE OF ISRAEL, 909
community, 85
Conservative Judaism, 98
ecumenism, 150–151
education, 162
eschatology, 148
and group memory, 585
halakhah, 511
heresy, 350–351
as history, 984
Judaism, 508
kingdom of God, 524, 525
labor movement, 1066
messianism, 601–602
national freedom, 266, 267
Orthodox Judaism, 682, 683
political theory, 720
post-Holocaust Judaism, 407
Reform Judaism, 767
religion and state, 776, 777–778
secularism, 864, 865–866

and strangers, 925–928
survival, 950, 951
war and heroism, 368–370
Zionism, 1076
Steinberg, Milton, 757
Steinbüchel, Theodore, 440
Steinheim, Salomon Ludwig, 631
on revelation, 816, 817
theology, 976
Steinschneider, Moritz, 383
stillness (duma), 874
Stoics
free will, 270, 272
natural law, 666–667
STRANGER, 917
love of, 559–560
Strauss, Leo
on philosophy and theology, 609
Zionism, 988
Streicher, Julius, 401
STUDY, 939
education, 156, 161
and holiness, 394
women, 1048–1049
and work, 1058
study house (bet midrash), 157,
1080
Talmud, 956
"subjugation to the nations," 262
SUFFERING, 931
divine retribution, 962, 963
and evil, 964, 968–969
people of Israel, 707–708
and spirituality, 906
theodicy, 961
and tolerance, 987–988
See also catastrophe
Sufi mysticism, 637
suicide, 132
Sukkot; Sukkah, 1094
gestures, 280
Sulamith, 121
Sumer
justice and unity, 1025–1027
superiority
chosen people, 56
supplications (tehinnot), 555
SURVIVAL, 947
soul, 480
surviving remnant, 783
Susman, Margarete, 878
Sutzkever, Abraham, 585

suzerainty treaty
  as covenant, 107–108, 109, 111
symbiosis
  State of Israel, 911, 913
symbol. *See* Gesture and Symbol
sympathy
  charity, 49
synagogue
  Reform Judaism, 768
  secularism, 864
  worship, 168

taharot (purity laws), 69
  Islam, 489–490
  sanctification of the Name, 850
  women, 257, 1049
Tal, Uriel, 148
talmid hakham; talmidei hakhamim (learned
      scholar), 1094
  aggadah, 7
TALMUD, 953, 1094
  anti-Judaism, 17
  charity, 47, 50, 53
  education, 159
  exegesis, 214
  Gemara, 1083
  Hebrew, 328
  and imagination, 459–460
  immortality, 474
  labors, 802
  love of God, 561
  love of neighbor, 558
  Nahmanides on, 1090
  natural law, 665–666
  Noachite covenant, 103
  oral law, 674–675
  Orthodox Judaism, 682
  prayer, 723
  property, 1044
  Rashi, 1091
  religion and state, 775
  sexuality, 178
  soul searching, 899–900
  strangers, 922, 926
  study, 941
  study of and mysticism, 646, 648, 650
  suffering, 934, 1935
  women's study of, 1049
talmudic-midrashic literature
  apocalypse, 22
  exegesis, 217

Tam, Jacob ben Meir, 1094–1095
  fear of God, 250–251
  study, 941
Tamar the Canaanite, 500
tanna; tannaim, 1095
  and heresy, 340
  and memory, 582
  midrash, 616–617
  mishnah, 1089
  myth, 659–660
Tanya, 846
targumim
  aggadah, 8
tax
  Islam, 490
teachings
  dogma, 141
technology
  and rest, 804
tefillin; tefillah (phylacteries), 73, 1095
  gesture, 278
  liturgy, 554
tehinnot (supplications), 555
teleology
  ethics, 197, 198
  Orthodox Judaism, 679
Temple, William, 295
Temple Mount, 368
temptation
  heroism, 363
Temunah Sefer–ha–(Book of The Image),
      1082
Ten Commandments
  authority, 30, 31
  halakhah, 310
  idolatry, 445
Tenth Commandment
  ethics, 199
teshuvah. See Repentance
Tetragrammaton, 1095
Teubal, Savina, 257
texts
  hermeneutics, 353, 354
  and imagination, 460
theocracy
  kingdom of God, 521
THEODICY, 959
  suffering, 932
THEOLOGY, 971
  covenant, 111–112
  and metaphysics, 606, 609

and music, 641–642
prophecy, 731
and rationalism, 752
reason, 753–754
sermons, 867
suffering, 938
theology of the slashed nose, 3–4
Theophrastus
on Jews, 332
theosophic kabbalah, 651–653, 654
Third World
and Judaism 150–151
Thirteen Principles, 143–144, 145
afterlife, 132
faith, 237
Throne of Glory, 648, 649
Thucydides, 425
Tiberias, 1070
tiferet (beauty), 652
music, 637
tikkun; tikkunim (reparation), 1095
repentance, 786, 791
and unity, 1030
tikkun ha-olam (repair of the world)
and righteousness, 83
tikvah. See Hope
Tillich, Paul
I and Thou, 440, 442
Judeo-Christian tradition, 152
TIME, 981
destiny, 138–139
Land of Israel, 538
messianism, 598
myth, 659
repentance, 790
rest, 798
revelation, 819
unity, 1030
See also Eternity and Time
time consciousness
and history, 376
timelessness, 190, 191
Tishah be-Av, 1095
liturgy, 556
TOLERANCE, 984
humanism, 426
Tolstoy, Leo
and meaning of life, 569
TORAH, 995
aggadah, 8–9
atheism, 26

Baḥya ben Asher on, 1079
as canon, 847
commandments, 67
Conservative Judaism, 94, 95, 98
covenant, 109
Derashot ha-Ran, 1081
education, 156, 157
Elijah ben Solomon Zalman on, 1082
exile, 219
faith, 234, 235
faith and hope, 420–421
fear of God, 245, 249
freedom, 261–262, 263, 265
gematria, 1083
grace or loving–kindness, 299–300
Hebrew, 325, 327–328, 329
heresy, 350
hermeneutics, 355–356, 357–361
history, 372–373
holy spirit, 410
idolatry, 445
imagination, 456, 457–458
land of Israel, 535–536, 537, 539
language, 543, 545, 549–550
love, 557
love of God, 560–561, 562–563
Maimonides on, 142–143
and meaning of life, 568
medieval philosophy, 574, 575, 577, 578
messianism, 600
midrash, 613
mysticism, 644–650, 652–655
Naḥmanides on, 1090
Orthodox Judaism, 680
Pauline Christianity 16, 17–18
peace, 686
people of Israel, 711
personal will, 932
prophecy, 734
rabbis, 742, 746
reason, 749
Reform Judaism, 771
religion and state, 775
and rest, 802
retribution, 827–828, 829
revelation, 815, 817, 819, 820, 821, 822, 824
reward and suffering, 934, 936
righteousness, 834, 835–836, 837–838
sacrifice, 368
soul, 889
soul searching, 898

TORAH (*continued*)

spirituality, 904
State of Israel, 910–911, 913–914
study, 394, 939
Sukkot, 1094
strangers, 918–920, 922–924, 926
Talmud, 953
tradition, 1009
truth, 1018
unity, 1031–1032
utopia, 1034
women, 255–256
women's study of, 1048–1049
See also mizvot
Torta, Rabbi, 1035
tosafot, 1094–1095
Tosefta, 1079
Tower of Babel
language, 546, 547
TRADITION, 1007
Enlightenment, 171–175
and history, 378
and imagination, 461–462
reason, 750
Reform Judaism, 767
revelation, 355
and truth, 1018–1019, 1020, 1022
and women, 1050–1051
Zionism, 1070–1076
transmigration
sermons, 869
souls and divine justice, 963
treaties
as covenants, 107–108
Trinity
Holy Spirit, 409
Troeltsch, Ernst, 383
trust (*bittahon*)
covenant, 417–418, 420
and truth, 1019–1020
See also Faith
TRUTH, 1017
and history, 373
and peace, 687–693
and reason, 750
search for, 79
Spinoza on, 216
and tolerance, 990

tumah (uncleanness)
death, 134
Turkey
Balfour Declaration, 1079
genocide, 400
Zionism, 1071

Unamuno, Miguel de, 810
uncleanness (*tumah*)
death, 134
unification. *See yihud, yihudim*
Union of American Hebrew Congregrations, 770
uniqueness
Holocaust, 399–400
and unity, 1026, 1037, 1028, 1029–1030, 1031
United States
Conservative Judaism, 91–92
modern Jewish philosophy, 633
rabbis, 744, 745, 746
Reconstructionism, 755
Reform Judaism, 767, 770–772
UNITY, 1025
creation, 114, 115–116, 117
Shema, 1093
universalism
chosen people, 57, 58
emancipation, 169
Reform Judaism, 771
stranger, 925, 929
survival, 951
Unterman, Isser Yehudah, 926, 929
UTOPIA, 1033
and work, 1056, 1063, 1065

"Valley of Hinnom" (Gehinnom), 1082
value-concepts
aggadah, 11
values
education, 157–158
heroism, 463
and humanism, 424
Maimonides on, 197
peace, 686–687
Velvel, Rabbi, 902
veneration of the dead, 132
Verein für Cultur und Wissenschaft der Juden (Society for the Culture and Science of the Jews), 121–122
via negativa, 606–7

violence
   and heroism, 370
virginity
   and rape, 1047
virtues
   righteousness, 834
   tolerance, 990, 992, 993
visions
   apocalypse, 19
Vital, Ḥayyim, 1095
   on prayer, 905
   revelation, 818
   on spirituality, 904
vocation
   Reconstructionism, 758
Volozhiner, Ḥayyim ben Isaac, 1095
   study of Torah, 941

war, 690–700
   heroism, 364–365, 370
   and peace, 685, 691–692
   views on, 365–369
war of holiness, 391
Waskow, Arthur, 258
way of the earth (derekh erez), 511
Weber, Max
   on Jewish intellectualism, 856–857
   on messianic hope, 380
Weil, Simone, 289
Weiner, Max, 347–348
Weinrich, Max, 627
welfare
   and charity, 52
Werblowsky, R. J. Zwi, 125–126, 378
Wessley, Naphtali, Herz, 1095
   on education, 158
   and science, 860
Westphalia
   Reform Judaism, 768
widows
   property, 1044
Wiesel, Elie, 1095–1096
   on Holocaust martyrs, 878
   I and Thou, 440, 441
   profanation, 463
   on reason, 753
wisdom
   fear of God, 250
   foreign influences, 331–332
   Hellenism, 331

metaphysics, 604
   reason, 749
wisdom literature
   aggadah, 7–8
   Gnostic mythology, 286
   Torah, 996–997
Wissenschaft des Judentums. See Science of
      Judaism
Wittgenstein, Ludwig
   and meaning of life, 567
   and truth, 1019
Wolf, Immanuel, 121–122
WOMEN AND JUDAISM, 1039
   community, 84
   Conservative Judaism, 97
   eros, 178, 179
   faith, 240
   and freedom, 265
   rabbis, 745
   Reconstructionism, 758
   and rest, 805
   study of Torah, 945
   See also Feminism
WORK, 1055
   and rest, 796, 797, 800, 801–802
World Council of Churches
   and Judaism, 150
World of Truth (olam emet)
   death, 132
world order
   and peace, 695–696
World to Come (olam haba)
   death, 132
   divine retribution, 962
   eschatology, 185
   and evil, 208
   fear of punishment, 251
   and heresy, 341
   Maimonides on, 143–144
   remnant of Israel, 780
   resurrection, 809
   and retribution, 829–830
   righteous Gentiles, 921
   and suffering, 933–934
   Torah, 234
worship
   and retribution, 828
   liturgy, 553
writing
   imagination, 459–463

Writings (*Ketuvim*)
   canonization, 841, 842, 843
Wyschogrod, Michael, 753

yatom; *yetomah* (orphans)
   marital needs, 49–50, 51
Yehudah, Eliezer ben, 126
yeshivah; yeshivot, 159, 1096
   Sofer, Moses, on, 1094
yezer (impulse)
   imagination, 451
   redemption, 761
Yezirah, Sefer (Book of Formation), 1096
   good and evil, 965
yhvh kedosh Yisrael (Holy One of Israel),
   391–392
YHWH (God), 36
   and mercy, 516
   monotheism, 269
Yiddish
   mentsh, 587
   mizveh, 627
   secularism, 865
Yigdal (May He be Magnified), 1096
yihud; *yihudim* (unification), 1096
   soul, 893
   See also Unity
yirat shamayim. *See* Fear of God
Yishuv, 1070, 1072
Yitzhak, Levi, of Berdichev, 440, 441
Yohanan, Rabbi, 1003
Yom Kippur (Day of Atonement), 1096
   humanism, 425–426
   mizvot, 69–70, 79
   mysticism, 651
   and rest, 798, 799–800
   soul searching, 900
Yose ben Halafta, 646
Yose ben Judah, 919
Yosef, Ovadiah, 929
Yose the Galileean, 524
Yossi ben Haninah, 281

zaddik (righteous one), 201
   and Jewish law, 512
   righteousness, 835
Zadokites
   remnant of Israel, 780
zealots
   Masada, 1088
   Orthodox Judaism, 683

Zedekiah ben Abraham Anav, 859
Zera, Rabbi, 374–375
zeroa (shankbone)
   symbolization, 279
Zhitlowsky, Chaim, 126
zimzumim (contractions), 294, 463, 1096
   and creation, 965
   Hasidism, 320
   soul, 894
Zion
   apocalypse, 21, 22
   See also Jerusalem
ZIONISM, 1069
   Ahad Ha-Am 1078
   Balfour Declaration, 1079
   Gordon, A. D., on, 1083
   Greenberg, U. Z., on, 1083
   and guilt, 307, 308
   haluz movement, 1064–1066
   heresy, 349
   on history, 381
   homecoming, 223–225
   Judaism, 506–507
   kingdom of God, 524
   land of Israel, 539–541
   love of Zion, 1084
   messianism, 602
   myth of redemption, 661
   national freedom, 266
   political theory, 717
   providence, 738
   Reform Judaism, 770
   repentance, 791–792
   secularism, 865
   State of Israel, 909
   strangers, 925, 927–928
   survival, 950–951
   tolerance, 988
   tradition, 1013–1014
   utopia, 1033, 1036
   wisdom, 337
   work, 1059–1060, 1062, 1064–1066
zizi, ziziyyot (fringe), 1096
Zohar, 651, 1096
   as canon, 846
   Cordovero, Moses, on, 1081
   divine power, 967
   fear of God, 251
   Hebrew, 327, 328
   and imagination, 460–461
   imago Dei, 476–477

medieval philosophy, 578
music, 637
myth, 660–661
religious authority, 32–33
on song, 639–640
soul, 891
unity, 1031

Zohar, Sefer ha- (Book of Splendor). See Zohar
Zolti, Rabbi, 927
Zunz, Leopold
   on exile and history, 377
   on history, 382–383
   midrash, 618
Zweig, Stefan, 878